INTERNATIONAL ACCOUNTING SUMMARIES

A GUIDE FOR INTERPRETATION AND COMPARISON

SECOND EDITION

COOPERS & LYBRAND (INTERNATIONAL)

JOHN WILEY & SONS, INC.

New York · Chichester · Brisbane · Toronto · Singapore

This text is printed on acid-free paper.

Coopers & Lybrand is one of the world's leading professional services organizations. Through our Member Firms we deploy over 67,000 people providing accounting and auditing, tax and consulting services on a globally integrated basis in more than 120 countries.

Our strategic intent is to create value for our clients and to bring competitive advantage to their activities. We meet their needs by combining our international capabilities and local market knowledge with our extensive range of skills and industry expertise.

The accounting summaries in this volume are designed to provide a general understanding of the accounting principles adopted in the countries concerned. Information contained in them should be used for guidance only. The summaries are not intended to be comprehensive, and no specific action should be taken on the basis of information contained in them without consultation.

This publication is designed to provide accurate and authoritative information in regard to the subject matter covered. It is sold with the understanding that the publisher is not engaged in rendering legal, accounting, or other professional service. If legal advice or other expert assistance is required, the services of a competent professional person should be sought.

ISBN 0-471-59246-3

Printed in the United States of America

10 9 8 7 6 5 4 3 2 1

FOREWORD

Recent years have seen the emergence and growth of a global economy—corporations, financiers and investors managing operations, seeking out opportunities or spreading their risks in many countries. To a large extent this has been made possible by advances in communications technology, providing access to financial and other information without regard to time or distance. However, financial information, usually prepared in accordance with national standards and customs, must be interpreted if it is to be understood and used as a basis of measurement or comparison. The barriers of language and currency are obvious difficulties to overcome; more subtle challenges are presented by the differing accounting principles used. The effect of such different accounting standards is often dramatic and should be thoroughly understood if business is to proceed with confidence. Consequently, the need for readily comparable accounting standards or, preferably, a single set of international accounting standards has never been greater, and I support the current initiatives being taken by international bodies to develop accounting standards that would obtain worldwide acceptance.

This survey of accounting standards in many countries not only provides a valuable service to business by assisting the interpretation of financial information, but vividly demonstrates the need for, and provides further impetus in the drive towards, increased harmonisation and comparability.

As chairman of a large multinational corporation facing these issues on a daily basis, I commend the initiative of Coopers & Lybrand (International) and its professionals around the world for compiling these concise but comprehensive summaries of accounting principles.

Sir Patrick Sheehy
Chairman
BAT Industries Plc

This publication was developed under the direction of the International Professional Standards Committee of Coopers & Lybrand (International):

Donald F. Moran, Chairman	United States
Justin T. Fryer	Canada
John Kelly	South Africa
Bernd Klotzbach	Germany
Matthew L. Patient	United Kingdom
Bernard Rabier	France
Kevin M. Stevenson	Australia

With the assistance of:

Paul G. Cherry	Canada
Mark D. Softy	United States
Steven P. Todd	New Zealand

PREFACE

This Preface discusses important trends and events affecting the large differences in accounting among nations in an increasingly global capital market. As we reported in the 1991 edition, the efforts of the International Accounting Standards Committee (IASC) to improve accounting standards at an international level are of particular interest. In this second edition we discuss the current status of the IASC's efforts and certain significant developments involving national standard-setting bodies.

There is a growing awareness of the different financial reporting practices followed around the world and continued pressure to search for common accounting standards. For example, the negotiation of the North American Free Trade Agreement between Canada, Mexico and the United States has prompted a study of financial reporting practices in those three countries. Similarly, a recent study of 25 airlines around the world concluded that the accounting differences among them not only complicate analyses but may lead to incorrect interpretations and conclusions. The initial enthusiasm for "harmonization" has, however, been tempered somewhat by a realization that accounting standards should continue to differ to the extent that those differences reflect diverse business and economic circumstances in different countries. Such differences in events or transactions should not be ignored merely for the sake of achieving uniformity of financial reporting.

The XIV World Congress of Accountants, held in Washington in 1992, examined the accountant's role in a global economy. A major topic of the Congress was the growing significance of International Accounting Standards (IASs). Following the Congress, representatives of national standard-setting bodies from around the world and the IASC met to discuss the accounting standard-setting environment, key accounting issues in individual countries, cooperative efforts to improve accounting standards and future efforts toward internationalization. They agreed to meet again in November 1993.

It now seems almost certain the IASC Improvements Project will be substantially complete by the end of 1993. A summary of the output of this project is contained in the chapter on International Accounting Standards. This important milestone will substantially reduce the number of optional accounting treatments permitted for the same transactions and events. Representatives of the International Organization of Securities Commissions (IOSCO) have been actively involved in the project. It remains to be seen, however, whether the member bodies of IOSCO will endorse the newly revised and improved IASs as an acceptable body of accounting standards. The IASC itself cannot require any enterprise to comply with its standards, and an endorsement from the member bodies of IOSCO would be seen as filling this void. Many also see an IOSCO endorsement as crucial in establishing the IASC's credibility in the world leadership role it seeks to play.

At its 17th Annual Conference last year, IOSCO did endorse the International Standards on Auditing, issued by the International Federation of Accountants, for certain international offerings. IOSCO members were encouraged to adopt measures in their respective home jurisdictions to accept audits conducted in accordance with the International Standards on Auditing as an alternative to compliance with the domestic auditing standards of each jurisdiction. The IOSCO endorsement of the International Standards on Auditing is a major accomplishment and may enhance the prospects of a similar endorsement of the International Accounting Standards.

There are, however, some clouds on the horizon. It has been pointed out that the Improvements Project includes two other objectives:

☐ ensuring that the IASs are "sufficiently detailed and complete"; and
☐ ensuring that the IASs contain adequate disclosure requirements.

This raises the question of the degree to which the IASs must achieve these two objectives before they can be considered acceptable for international reporting purposes. Various national standards differ significantly in terms of the breadth and depth of topics covered. Furthermore, the significance of specialized industries such as life insurance, oil and gas, and transportation varies greatly from country to country. It is unrealistic to expect that every major item or industry dealt with in a national standard must also be dealt with (and to the same extent) in an international standard. In exceptional cases, such as industries that operate extensively or are connected internationally (e.g., financial institutions), specialized international standards may be appropriate. However, it would take many years to complete all of the worthwhile projects and other improvements that have been suggested to date, and the list of items and their relative priorities will change as circumstances change in the future. There is a concern that the burgeoning list of add-ons will serve to forestall international agreement.

The recent agreement between Daimler-Benz and the US Securities and Exchange Commission under which Germany's largest industrial company will soon become the first German company listed on the New York Stock Exchange has attracted considerable attention. It may signal a readiness on the part of other European companies to modify their accounting standards for purposes of registration on US stock exchanges. On the other hand, it appears that the SEC is not entirely comfortable with anything that falls short of substantial compliance with US-style financial reporting.

A number of other significant initiatives could have a major impact on the evolution of national and international standards of financial reporting. In the past, various national standard-setting bodies have considered many of the same issues and yet often reached quite different conclusions. Now there is evidence of increasing cooperation and collaboration among standard-setting bodies. For example:

☐ The IASC and Canada are working together on the project on financial instruments.
☐ The UK, the US, Australia and Canada are jointly developing a discussion paper on accounting for future events, which will be discussed at the 1993 conference of standard-setters mentioned previously.
☐ The IASC, the US and Australia are considering joint work on earnings per share.

□ The IASC, Australia, Canada, France, Japan, the UK and the US are working on financial instruments.

□ Japan, New Zealand and the UK have recently completed work on segment information, while the IASC, Canada and the US have initiated projects on this topic. Canada and the US have a joint project with a stated objective of developing, if possible, a common standard.

□ Canada, the European Community Advisory Forum and the IASC each has a project on foreign currency translation.

□ Australia, Sweden, the UK and the US each has a project on consolidated financial statements.

These developments are encouraging. They demonstrate that standard-setting bodies are attempting to respond to the needs of users and preparers in a global marketplace.

This growing cooperation between standard-setters should lead to greater conformity of accounting standards worldwide. While this is unlikely to lead to a single set of standards in common use around the world, it should make it easier for the world's financial market regulators to accept a set of standards to be used in securities listings worldwide.

Until such time as that becomes a reality, there will continue to be a need for this publication, which provides information on the accounting principles of 37 countries as well as the IASC and the European Community. It reflects the combined knowledge and experience of Coopers & Lybrand professionals from around the world, who will continue to monitor international accounting developments to bring you up-to-date information in revised editions of this book.

We hope the book will both help people understand financial statements from around the world and, in its own way, contribute toward efforts to achieve the objectives of internationalization.

Coopers & Lybrand commitment to International Accounting Standards Committee

A number of partners of Coopers & Lybrand serve the IASC in various capacities, including:

Paul G. Cherry	*Canada*	*Member of IASC Board and Chairman of Improvements Steering Committee*
Sigvard Heurlin	*Sweden*	*Member of IASC Board*
Ronald J. Murray	*United States*	*Member of IASC Board and Chairman of Financial Instruments Steering Committee*
Michael J. Sharpe	*Australia*	*Vice Chairman, Chairman-Designate and Member of IASC Board*

ACKNOWLEDGMENTS

This book reflects the efforts of many individuals in countries around the world. We would like to acknowledge the contributions made by the following individuals of Member Firms of Coopers & Lybrand (International):

Argentina
Alberto Boruchowicz
Corina I. Pando
Australia
Kevin M. Stevenson
Brigid T. Curran
John Dyke
Belgium
Eddy Dams
Brazil
Samuel de Paula Matos
Paulo Manuchakian
Roberto Wagner Promenzio
Canada
Morley P. Carscallen
Paul G. Cherry
Colin A. M. Fleming
Central and Eastern Europe
Simon Mackay
Helena Cadanova
Ed D. de Bruin
Catherine Drayton
Jeremy Foster
Tim J. B. Heaton
Charles Mozley
J. Stanley Root
Channel Islands
Huw M. Bolle-Jones
Nicholas J. W. Pearson
People's Republic of China
Marina Y. P. Wong

Cyprus
Dinos N. Papadopoulos
Denmark
Jens Røder
European Community
Peter A. Holgate
Finland
Lars Blomquist
Sirpa Poski-parta-Kiiski
France
Pierre Riou
Germany
Peter H. Combrink
Hong Kong
Colin Y. N. Chau
India
Thomas Mathew
Syamal K. Mitra
Indonesia
Ross L. Gavin
Larry L. Luckey
International Standards
Paul G. Cherry
Republic of Ireland
William P. Cunningham
Italy
Raffaele Lorusso
Japan
Yasuhiro Inoue
Brian J. Dziengiel

Republic of Korea
 Tack-Kon Moon
 Hyuk-Jai Kwon
Luxembourg
 Dominique Robyns
 Didier L. Mouget
Mexico
 Felipe Pérez-Cervantes
 Raúl González-Lima
Netherlands
 Frans B. M. Deckers
 Peter de Wolff
New Zealand
 Michael J. Hill
 Sandra A. Moulder
Nigeria
 C. Oyeniyi O. Oyediran
 Anthony U. Enunwa
Norway
 Trond Tømta
 Fredrik Melle

Singapore
 David G. Compton
 Kelvin Lee
Republic of South Africa
 James Schnellen
Spain
 Ian M. Angus
 Harry Plunkett
 Encarnacion Rico
Sweden
 Erling Peterssohn
Switzerland
 Malcolm B. Cheetham
United Kingdom
 Barry Johnson
 Jyoti Ghosh
United States
 Stephen J. Lis

We would also like to acknowledge the following individuals from a Correspondent Firm:

Israel
 Israel Rabin
 Dov Sapir
 Assaf Shemer

We would also like to express our appreciation for the efforts of the editorial group associated with this book:

□ Steven P. Todd (New Zealand) and Mark D. Softy (US), who critically reviewed every chapter with an eye toward technical content and clarity of presentation; and
□ Myra D. Cleary (US), who served as editor and project coordinator.

To all those individuals, and any who were inadvertently omitted, go not only our thanks, but also the usual absolution from blame for errors and omissions.

Donald F. Moran, Chairman,
International Professional Standards Committee
of Coopers & Lybrand (International)

CONTENTS

INTRODUCTION

International Accounting Summaries, Second Edition, provides detailed summaries of accounting standards in 37 countries, plus the International Accounting Standards and European Community Directives. The information has been provided by Member Firms of Coopers & Lybrand (International). This edition of *International Accounting Summaries* reflects accounting standards in effect as of January 1, 1993, unless otherwise indicated.

Among those countries are four (the Czech and Slovak Republics, Hungary, Poland and Russia) included in a chapter on Central and Eastern Europe. The chapter includes an overview of economic and accounting reforms in the region, as well as accounting and financial reporting practices in the four countries.

For each country, an overview of generally accepted accounting principles applicable to the majority of business entities is presented. Specialized industry accounting practices, such as those of banks, insurance companies and governments, are not addressed.

To enable a particular topic to be found quickly, information about each country (with the exception of those in the chapter on Central and Eastern Europe) is in a separate chapter, and each chapter has been set out in a standard format, as follows:

GENERAL INFORMATION

1. Source of Generally Accepted Accounting Principles
2. Audit and Public Company Requirements

GENERAL ACCOUNTING

3. Financial Statements
4. Business Combinations
5. Joint Ventures
6. Foreign Currency Translation
7. Changing Prices/Inflation Accounting
8. Accounting Changes
9. Prior Period Adjustments
10. Post Balance Sheet Events
11. Related Party Transactions
12. Segmental Information

ACCOUNTING PRINCIPLES FOR SPECIFIC ITEMS—BALANCE SHEET

13. Property, Plant and Equipment
14. Intangible Assets
15. Leases
16. Investments
17. Accounts Receivable
18. Inventories and Work in Progress
19. Current Liabilities
20. Long-Term Debt
21. Contingencies
22. Capital and Reserves

ACCOUNTING PRINCIPLES FOR SPECIFIC ITEMS—INCOME STATEMENT

Generally, where a country's official language is other than English, significant accounting terms in the national language have been included, in parentheses following the English terms. This will assist the reader in identifying the main constituents of financial statements not prepared in English.

Each chapter (except that on Central and Eastern Europe) includes an Appendix presenting a macro-level comparison of standards or prevalent practice in the country with International Accounting Standards (IASs). This material, which is new to this edition, is intended to provide a fast means of determining whether a particular country's practices are substantially in compliance with the IASs. Because they are necessarily in summary form, these appendices should be used with caution and more detailed information should be sought from the chapters themselves.

To enable comparisons to be made between the accounting standards of different countries, quick reference matrices have been provided. In contrast to the individual chapters, which have been compiled by country, these matrices have been prepared by accounting topic. A quicker means of direct comparison is therefore available, subject to the proviso that information in these matrices should be used with care because it is, of necessity, at a broad level. Reference should be made to the chapters themselves for more detail.

This edition of the book includes two other new features. The first is a comprehensive checklist covering the IASs in effect at September 30, 1993. The checklist provides a means of ascertaining and recording whether a set of financial statements is in conformity with the IASs. The second new feature is a set of illustrative financial statements, based on a fictitious company, prepared in conformity with the IASs. These financial statements show typical disclosures and formats that might be used by an entity preparing consolidated financial statements in conformity with the IASs.

In preparing individual chapters, standard accounting terms were used without repeating their meanings in each chapter. A glossary of accounting terms is included at the end of the book. Terms included in the glossary appear in bold type the first time they are used in each chapter.

The choice of countries to include was not an easy one. The objective of presenting information most commonly sought by international businesspeople, analysts and investors is considered to be met through the 37 countries covered in this book. However, there are other countries that have a rightful claim to be included which will be considered for future editions.

For an international publication there is always the dilemma of choosing a form of spelling and usage that will be acceptable in different areas of the world. It is hoped that the conventions chosen will be acceptable to all and offend none.

For further information concerning the accounting principles noted in this publication, please contact the individuals at the offices of the Member Firms of Coopers & Lybrand (International) set out inside the front cover.

INTERNATIONAL ACCOUNTING STANDARDS

GENERAL INFORMATION

1. Source of Accounting Standards

General. **Accounting principles** have largely been developed on a national basis, often with significant differences from country to country. The need for uniform accounting principles for international financial reporting has been recognized for many years. A major step toward realizing this objective was taken with the creation of the International Accounting Standards Committee (IASC) in 1973, now widely recognized as the authoritative accounting standard-setting body to achieve harmonization of financial reporting.

International Accounting Standards (IASs) issued by the IASC are not mandatory unless and until they are adopted by a particular country. Many countries that do not have their own standard-setting body adopt the IASs as their national standards, often with the national standards preceded by a foreword dealing with local issues or limiting their applicability. Examples are Malawi, Malaysia and Pakistan. Other countries, such as Kenya and India, use the IASs as a basis for their own national standards; Hong Kong has recently announced that it will begin doing so in the future. On occasion, IASs are used by multinational enterprises to assist users from different countries in understanding their financial statements. For example, several large Swiss-based multinational companies have recently adopted the IASs. In addition, it now seems likely that the IASs will be adopted by many Central and Eastern European countries (a region that has a population in excess of 400 million). Indeed, a number of these countries have already translated the IASs into their national languages.

Until now, the IASs do not seem to have influenced standards in the leading industrial countries. There is evidence that this may now be changing:

☐ In the United States, the Financial Accounting Standards Board (FASB) has approved an international plan for a more focused, active and supportive role in the search for international standards. The FASB plans to focus more intensely on the IASs in its standard-setting efforts. Its intention is to consider adopting IASs that are judged superior to the US counterparts, or to try to persuade the IASC to conform to US standards that it considers to be superior.

□ The United Kingdom's standard-setting body, the Accounting Standards Board, proposes to state in its Foreword to Accounting Standards that: "FRSs [Financial Reporting Standards] are formulated with due regard to international developments. The Board supports the International Accounting Standards Committee in its aim to harmonise international financial reporting."

The inherent difficulty in obtaining agreement on uniform international **accounting standards** has resulted in many IASs permitting a choice of alternative treatments, thus diminishing the effectiveness of the IASs as a means of achieving worldwide harmonization. The IASC recognizes this and has recently implemented a program to eliminate alternative treatments. A comprehensive Statement of Intent, "Comparability of Financial Statements," has been adopted, which will all but eliminate the choice of treatments presently allowed by the IASs. The Statement of Intent will in due course lead to significant changes in certain IASs and is expected to affect some countries' national standards. Exposure drafts have now been issued for all IASs affected by the Statement of Intent, except for IAS 25 relating to the treatment of investments, including investment properties, and IAS 17 relating to leveraged leases. The IASC expects that final revised standards will be approved by the end of 1993. IAS 25 will be revised when the IASC's project on financial instruments is complete. The principal impacts of the Statement of Intent are summarized in the Appendix to this chapter.

Before implementing the Statement of Intent, the IASC will make other improvements to ensure that the IASs are sufficiently detailed and complete and contain adequate disclosure requirements to meet the needs of capital markets and the international business community. The revisions to existing IASs will not take effect until the IASC has approved and issued the revised standards.

The IASC is related to the International Federation of Accountants (IFAC) through common membership, common sponsorship and an agreement of Mutual Commitments. Nevertheless, the IASC has full and complete autonomy in the setting of IASs. The work of the IASC is controlled by a board consisting of representatives from accountancy bodies in 13 countries and from up to four other organizations with an interest in financial reporting.

2. Audit and Public Company Requirements

The requirements for audit and **public company** registration and reporting are established nationally. The IFAC deals with matters relating to the conduct of audits.

GENERAL ACCOUNTING

3. Financial Statements

Basic Accounting Concepts. The Framework for the Preparation and Presentation of Financial Statements (the Framework) sets out the basic underlying assumptions and qualitative characteristics of financial statements. The two underlying assumptions of financial statements are use of the **accrual** basis and the **going concern concept**. In addition, financial statements should have the four qualitative characteristics of understandability, relevance (including **materiality**), reliability (faithful representation, **substance over form**, neutrality, **prudence** and completeness) and comparability. Financial statements should convey a true and fair view of, or present fairly, the information they contain. The IASs deal with the general purpose **consolidated financial statements** of an enterprise. In rare instances, matters pertinent to parent company (unconsolidated) accounts are discussed, but additional information concerning the parent company is not required to be disclosed.

The Framework recognizes the **historical cost**, current cost, realizable (settlement) value and present value measurement bases, but does not favor any one over the others.

Contents of Financial Statements. Financial statements include a balance sheet, an income statement, notes, other statements and explanatory material, and a statement summarizing the funds (cash and cash equivalents) available to finance the activities of the enterprise and the uses to which such resources have been put. Both the **direct** and **indirect methods** of presenting cash flows are permitted, although the former is encouraged. Financial statements should show corresponding figures for the preceding period.

Format of Financial Statements. Details of information to be disclosed in financial statements are contained in the IASs. The IASs do not, however, propose a particular format for financial statements, and enterprises should choose the most appropriate format for their circumstances. Separate disclosure is required of individual categories of long-term and **current assets** and liabilities and shareholders' equity. Each enterprise should determine whether or not to present current assets and liabilities as separate classifications. Current assets and **current liabilities** should not be offset unless a legal right of offset exists or they relate to progress payments and advances on construction work in progress.

Disclosure of Accounting Policies. If a fundamental accounting assumption (going concern or accrual) is not followed, that fact should be disclosed, together with the reasons. The significant **accounting policies** used should be disclosed, as well as any change that has a material effect in the current period or may have a material effect in subsequent periods, together with the effect and the reasons.

Reference. Framework, IAS 1, IAS 5 and IAS 7.

4. Business Combinations[1]

Principles of Consolidation. A **parent company** should issue consolidated financial statements unless it is itself a virtually wholly owned **subsidiary**. The consolidated financial statements should include the results of all subsidiaries, except those acquired and held exclusively for disposal in the near future or those over whose assets and operations control is impaired by severe long-term restrictions on the transfer of funds. The reasons for consolidating a company in which less than half the voting power is owned, or of not consolidating a company in which more than half the voting power is

---

[1]See Appendix for principal impacts of Statement of Intent.

owned, should be disclosed. Consolidated financial statements should be prepared, where practicable, using uniform accounting policies. The difference between reporting dates of the parent and its consolidated subsidiaries should not exceed three months.

Accounting for Business Combinations. **Business combinations** should be accounted for under the **purchase method**, unless:

☐ The transaction is principally an exchange of voting common shares of the enterprises involved.

☐ Effectively all the net assets and operations of the combining enterprises are combined in one entity.

In those instances, the **pooling of interests method** may be used.

Control. Control is the power to govern the financial and operating policies so as to obtain benefits from an enterprise's activities.

Goodwill. Positive **goodwill** is recognized as an asset and amortized to income on a systematic basis over its estimated useful life, or adjusted immediately to shareholders' equity. **Negative goodwill** is either treated as deferred income and amortized to income on a systematic basis or allocated to depreciable nonmonetary net assets acquired in proportion to their fair values. Although no maximum time period for the amortization of goodwill is specified, goodwill should be charged immediately to income if it is found to be no longer supported by future income.

Equity Accounting. The **equity method** of accounting should be used for investments in **associated companies**, except when they are acquired and held exclusively for disposal in the near future.

Minority Interests. **Minority interests** are recorded in a business combination at either the acquisition values (fair values) of the net identifiable assets involved or the preacquisition carrying amounts of the net assets of the subsidiary (i.e., restatement of net assets to fair value is limited to the proportion attributable to the investing company).

Disclosure. Consolidation: Descriptions, dates and the accounting method of combinations should be disclosed. For the purchase method, the percentage of voting shares acquired, the acquisition cost, details of the purchase consideration, and the amount and treatment of goodwill should be disclosed. For the pooling of interests method, details of the shares issued, assets and liabilities contributed and results of operations of the enterprises prior to combination should be disclosed. On an ongoing basis, detailed disclosure should be made of the composition of the group (name, country of incorporation or residence, proportion of ownership and, if different, proportion of voting power held).

Equity accounting: Descriptions of significant associates, the proportion of ownership and, if different, the proportion of voting power held should be disclosed. Investments accounted for by the equity method should be classified as long-term assets in the consolidated balance sheet, and the investor's share of profits (losses) shown as a separate item in the consolidated income statement. The investor's share of unusual items, identified in accordance with the investor's accounting policies, should also be shown separately.

Reference.   IAS 5, IAS 22, IAS 27 and IAS 28.

5.   Joint Ventures

Accounting for Investments in Joint Ventures.   Jointly controlled operations: A venturer records the assets that it controls, the liabilities that it incurs, the expenses that it incurs and its share of the income of the **joint venture**.

Jointly controlled assets: A venturer records its *share* of the **jointly controlled** assets, any liabilities that it has incurred directly, its *share* of any liabilities incurred jointly by the joint venture, its *share* of income and expenses of the joint venture and any expenses that it has incurred directly.

Jointly controlled entities: **Proportionate consolidation** is the **benchmark accounting treatment**, although the equity method is an **allowed alternative accounting treatment**.

Transactions Between Venturers and the Joint Venture.   If the significant risks and rewards of ownership have been transferred to the joint venture, the venturer recognizes a gain or loss on the sale or contribution of assets to a joint venture. Only the portion of a gain attributable to the interests of the other venturers is recognized while the assets are retained by the joint venture. However, a loss should be recognized in its entirety unless it reflects a temporary decline in the value of the asset transferred.

Disclosure.   Where interests in jointly controlled entities are reported using the equity method, or the line-by-line reporting format for proportionate consolidation, the aggregate amount of each current asset, long-term asset, current liability, long-term liability, income and expense related to the interest in joint ventures is disclosed.

In addition, the following contingent liabilities are disclosed, unless the probability of loss is remote, separately from other **contingencies**:

☐   Contingencies incurred by the venturer concerning the joint venture and its share in each contingency incurred jointly with other venturers;

☐   Its share of the contingencies of the joint ventures for which it is contingently liable; and

☐   Those contingencies that arise because the venturer is contingently liable for the liabilities of the other venturers of a joint venture.

The aggregate amount of the following commitments with respect to an interest in joint ventures is also disclosed separately from other commitments:

☐   Capital commitments of the venturer in relation to its interest in joint ventures and its share of capital commitments that have been incurred jointly with other venturers; and

☐   The venturer's share of the capital commitments of the joint ventures themselves.

Accounting by Joint Ventures.   This topic is not dealt with in the IASs. There are no special rules regarding accounting by joint ventures.

Reference. IAS 5, IAS 10 and IAS 31.

6. Foreign Currency Translation[1]

Foreign Currency Transactions. **Foreign currency transactions** should be accounted for by applying the exchange rate in effect at the date of the transaction or a rate that approximates the actual rate. Outstanding foreign currency monetary items at each balance sheet date should be translated at the closing rate at that date, unless they are covered by forward contracts (in which case the closing, spot or forward rate is used).

Exchange differences on settlement of **monetary items** should generally be recognized in income for the period. Exchange differences on long-term monetary items may, however, be deferred and recognized on a systematic basis over the life of the items, provided that recurring exchange losses are not expected on those items.

Exchange differences arising on an intercompany monetary item that is part of the net investment in a foreign entity should be included in shareholders' equity in the consolidated financial statements. (Special rules, not detailed here, apply to severe devaluation or depreciation of currencies after recent acquisitions when there is no practical means of **hedging** available.)

Foreign Operations. For **self-sustaining foreign operations**, assets and liabilities are translated using the closing rates, and income statement items are translated either at the actual rates or average rate for the period; differences arising on translation are taken either to income or directly to shareholders' equity.

Integrated foreign operations should follow the same accounting rules as the parent would apply in similar circumstances.

Hedges. The difference between the forward rate and the spot rate at inception of a forward exchange contract hedge should be amortized to income over the life of the contract. If foreign currency loans and transactions are designated as, and are effective as, a hedge against a net investment in a foreign entity, the related exchange differences should be included in shareholders' equity to the extent that they are covered by exchange differences arising on translation of the net investment.

Disclosure. Disclosure should be made of the translation methods used, the net exchange differences taken to income and shareholders' equity, and whether closing or average rates were used for translating the income statement of foreign entities. In addition, disclosure should be made of any deferred exchange differences.

Reference. IAS 21.

7. Changing Prices/Inflation Accounting

General. In 1989, the IASC reduced the status of its standard on this topic (IAS 15) to nonmandatory because international consensus had (and still has) not been reached. Nonetheless, the Board of the IASC continues to encourage enterprises to conform with the standard. Both general purchasing power and **current cost** approaches to reflecting

---

[1]See Appendix for principal impacts of Statement of Intent.

changing prices are recognized as appropriate bases of accounting. Enterprises whose levels of revenues, profits, assets or employment are significant in the economic environment in which they operate are encouraged to disclose additional items using an accounting method reflecting the effects of changing prices. For enterprises reporting in the currency of hyperinflationary economies, the requirements are governed by a separate standard, the principal contents of which are also described below.

Additional Disclosures to Reflect Changing Prices.   The following items may be disclosed, either on a supplementary basis or as part of the primary financial statements, to reflect changing prices:

(a) The adjustment to (or the adjusted amount of) depreciation of property, plant and equipment.

(b) The adjustment to (or the adjusted amount of) cost of sales.

(c) Any adjustments relating to monetary items, the effect of borrowing or equity interests taken into account when determining income.

(d) The overall effect of (a)–(c) and any other adjustments made to reflect changing prices.

(e) Where a current cost method has been used, the current cost of property, plant and equipment and of inventories.

In addition, the method chosen and any indices used to compute the above are disclosed.

Reporting in Hyperinflationary Economies.   For enterprises reporting in the currency of a hyperinflationary economy, the financial statements are stated in terms of the measuring unit current at the balance sheet date. The gain or loss on the net financial position is included in net income and disclosed separately. A number of other specific disclosures are also made.

Reference.   IAS 15 and IAS 29.

8.   Accounting Changes[1]

Accounting Treatment of Changes in Accounting Principles.   Accounting policies: Changes in accounting policies are appropriate only if they are required by statute or an accounting standard-setting body, or if the change results in a more appropriate presentation. The resulting adjustment, if any, should be either:

☐ Reported by adjusting the opening retained earnings for the current period and amending comparative information for prior periods; or

☐ Separately disclosed in the current period income statement as part of net income.

Accounting estimates: Changes in accounting estimates should be treated as part of income from ordinary activities in the period of change if the change affects the period only, or in the period of change and future periods if the change affects both. Where the

---

[1]See Appendix for principal impacts of Statement of Intent.

change relates to an item previously treated as unusual, the change itself should be reported as unusual.

Disclosure. Disclosure of changes in accounting policies should be adequate to facilitate comparison of the figures for the periods presented. If a change in accounting policy has a material effect on the current period, or may have a material effect on subsequent periods, the effect of the change should be disclosed and quantified, together with the reason for the change.

If a change in an accounting estimate has a material effect on the current period, or may have a material effect on subsequent periods, the effect of the change should be disclosed and quantified.

Reference. IAS 8.

9. Prior Period Adjustments[1]

Definition of Adjusting Items. **Prior period** items are **adjustments** that arise in the current period as a result of errors or omissions in the preparation of the financial statements of one or more prior periods.

Accounting Treatment. Prior period items should be either:

☐ Reported by adjusting the opening retained earnings for the current period and amending comparative information for prior periods; or

☐ Separately disclosed in the current period's income statement as part of net income.

Disclosure. Disclosure should be made of the amount and nature of the prior period item and should be adequate to facilitate comparison of the figures for the periods presented.

Reference. IAS 8.

10. Post Balance Sheet Events

Definition. Post balance sheet events are events, both favorable and unfavorable, that occur between the balance sheet date and the date the financial statements are authorized for issue. Two types are identified:

(a) Events providing further evidence of conditions that existed at the balance sheet date.

(b) Events that are indicative of conditions that arose subsequent to the balance sheet date.

Accounting Treatment. Assets and liabilities should be adjusted for type (a) post balance sheet events. If the post balance sheet event is the proposal or declaration of dividends for the period covered by the financial statements, either an adjustment should be made to the financial statements or disclosure should be made.

---

[1]See Appendix for principal impacts of Statement of Intent.

Disclosure.   Disclosure, but no adjustment, should be made for those type (b) post balance sheet events that are of such importance that nondisclosure would affect the ability of users of the financial statements to make proper evaluations and decisions. Where disclosure is required, it should include the nature of the event, and an estimate of the financial effect or a statement that such an estimate cannot be made.

Reference.   IAS 10.

11.   Related Party Transactions

Definition.   Parties are considered to be related if one party has the ability to control or exercise significant influence over the other in making financial or operating decisions. A related party transaction occurs when there is a transfer of resources or obligations, regardless of whether a price is charged, between related parties.

Accounting Treatment.   Transactions with related parties are normally accounted for on the basis of the price established between the parties. However, because related parties may have a degree of flexibility in the price-setting process, the disclosures set out below are required.

Disclosure.   Related party relationships, where control exists, should be disclosed irrespective of whether there have been transactions during the period. If there have been related party transactions, the nature of the relationship, the type of transaction and the elements of the transaction necessary for an understanding of the financial statements should be disclosed. Similar items may be disclosed in the aggregate, unless separate disclosure is necessary for an understanding of the financial statements.

Certain related parties (e.g., trade unions, providers of financing, a single supplier) are excluded from the disclosure requirements. Similarly, disclosure of transactions between members of a group is unnecessary in consolidated financial statements (though transactions with associated companies should be disclosed).

Reference.   IAS 24.

12.   Segmental Information

General.   Enterprises, including subsidiaries, whose securities are publicly traded and other enterprises where levels of revenues, profits, assets or employment are significant in the economic environment in which they operate should report segmental information for all significant industrial and geographical segments (distinguishable components) of the enterprise. For subsidiaries whose securities are not publicly traded, the disclosure requirements apply only if national standards require similar disclosure for domestic entities.

Disclosure.   The activities of each reported industry segment and the composition of each geographical segment should be disclosed. In addition, the following should be disclosed for each segment:

☐   Sales or other operating revenues, distinguishing between those derived from customers and those derived from other segments.

□   Segment results.

□   Segment assets (either as money amounts or a percentage of consolidated totals).

□   The basis of intersegment pricing.

The segment totals should be reconciled to the consolidated information. Any material changes in identification of segments or accounting practices in reporting segment information should be reported, with an explanation and the effect of the change.

Reference.   IAS 14.

ACCOUNTING PRINCIPLES FOR SPECIFIC ITEMS— BALANCE SHEET

13.   Property, Plant and Equipment[1]

Classification of Capital and Revenue Expenditure.   Property, plant and equipment are tangible assets that are held for use in the production or supply of goods or services, for rental to others or for administrative purposes; they may include items held for the maintenance or repair of such assets. They should be intended for use on a continuing basis and not for sale in the ordinary course of business. Subsequent expenditures related to a capitalized item should be added to the carrying amount only if they increase the future economic benefit beyond the item's previously assessed performance.

Property, plant and equipment should be eliminated from the financial statements on disposal or when no further benefit is expected from their use and disposal. Gains or losses arising on elimination should be recognized in the income statement.

Basis of Valuation.   Property, plant and equipment may be carried at either depreciated historical cost or an amount established by valuation. Historical cost consists of the purchase price and any directly attributable costs to bring the asset to working condition for its intended use. Revaluations should be applied to an entire class of assets; alternatively, the selection of assets for revaluation should be made on a systematic basis.

An upward revaluation of assets should be credited directly to shareholders' equity as revaluation surplus, except to the extent that it relates to a previously recorded decrease that has been charged to income, in which case the increase may be credited to income. A downward revaluation should be charged to income unless there is a balance in the revaluation surplus arising from a previous upward revaluation of the same asset (or class of assets, where applicable).

On disposal of a previously revalued item, the difference between the net proceeds and the net carrying amount should be charged or credited to income. The amount in the revaluation surplus relating to an eliminated asset may be transferred to **retained earnings**.

Depreciation.   The depreciable amount of a depreciable asset should be allocated on a systematic basis to each accounting period during its useful life. The **depreciation** method chosen should be applied consistently unless circumstances (which should be reviewed periodically) alter and justify a change.

---

[1]See Appendix for principal impacts of Statement of Intent.

Disclosure. For each class of asset, disclosure should be made of the bases used for determining the gross carrying amount, including, where applicable, the method of revaluation adopted, indices used, whether an external valuer was involved and the frequency of revaluations.

In addition, disclosure should be made, for each class of asset, of depreciation methods used, useful lives (or depreciation rates used), total depreciation for the period and the gross amount of depreciable assets and related accumulated depreciation.

The effect of a significant change in the estimated useful lives of major depreciable assets (or classes) should be disclosed.

Reference. Framework, IAS 4, IAS 5 and IAS 16.

14. Intangible Assets

Accounting Treatment. **Intangible assets** are recognized in the balance sheet if they are expected to have future economic benefits, are controlled by the enterprise and have a cost or value that may be measured reliably. Goodwill on acquisition, and research and development costs are dealt with in Sections 4 and 25, respectively.

Valuation. No specific method of determining the valuation of intangibles is prescribed. Therefore, general rules for valuing assets are followed. Any reliable basis, including historical cost, current cost, realizable value and present value, may be used. The method adopted should be applied consistently.

Amortization. **Amortization** would generally be considered necessary only to the extent that there is an impairment in the recoverability of the asset.

Disclosure. Separate disclosure should be made of long-term intangible assets, including, if applicable, the method and period of amortization and any unusual write-offs in the current period.

Reference. Framework and IAS 5.

15. Leases

Classification. The treatment of leases depends on whether they are classified as **finance leases** or **operating leases**. The classification depends on the substance of the transaction rather than the form of the contract. A lease is classified as a finance lease if substantially all the risks and rewards incident to ownership are transferred to the lessee; all other leases are classified as operating leases.

Accounting Treatment in the Financial Statements of Lessees. Finance lease: An asset and a corresponding liability should be recognized at the lower of the fair value (net of grants and tax credits receivable by the lessor) or the present value of the minimum lease payments. Rentals should be apportioned between the finance charge and the outstanding liability so as to produce a constant periodic rate of interest on the remaining liability. The asset should be depreciated in a manner consistent with other similar assets (see Section 13).

Operating lease: Rental expense should be charged to income on a systematic basis that corresponds to the time pattern of the user's benefit.

Disclosure: Disclosure should be made of the amount of assets held under finance leases, related liabilities (differentiating between current and long-term portions), commitments for minimum lease payments under finance leases and under noncancellable operating leases with a term of more than one year (giving the amounts and periods in which the payments will be due), and significant financing restrictions, renewal or purchase options, contingent rentals and other contingencies arising from leases.

Accounting Treatment in the Financial Statements of Lessors.   Finance lease: The net outstanding investment in a finance lease should be recorded as a receivable. Finance income should be recognized in a pattern reflecting a constant periodic rate of return on either the lessor's net investment outstanding or the net cash investment outstanding in the lease. The method used should be applied consistently to similar leases. Manufacturer or dealer lessors should include selling profit or loss in income in accordance with the policy normally followed by the enterprise for outright sales. Initial direct costs should be charged to income at the inception of the lease.

Operating lease: Assets held for operating leases should be recorded as depreciable assets in a manner consistent with the lessor's normal policy for property, plant and equipment (see Section 13). Rental income should be recognized on a straight-line basis over the lease term, unless another systematic basis better corresponds to the time pattern of earnings.

Disclosure: Disclosure should be made of the gross investment in finance leases, the related unearned finance income and unguaranteed residual value of leased assets. The basis or bases used for allocating income should also be disclosed (net investment outstanding or net cash investment outstanding in the lease). Where a significant part of the lessor's business consists of operating leases, the amount of assets by each major class of asset and the related accumulated depreciation should be disclosed.

Leveraged Leases.   No specific accounting treatment is prescribed by International Accounting Standards for **leveraged leases**.

Reference.   IAS 17.

16.   Investments[1]

Valuation.   Valuation depends on whether investments are current or long term, regardless of whether the enterprise presents a classified balance sheet. Investment properties (land or buildings that are not occupied substantially for use by, or in the operations of, the investor) are treated either as property, plant and equipment and depreciated accordingly or as long-term investments. Special rules apply to the valuation of investments transferred from current to long term or vice versa.

Current investments should be valued at either market value or the lower of cost or market value. When the latter is used, the carrying amount should be determined either on an aggregate **portfolio basis**, in total or by category of investment, or on an individual investment basis.

Long-term investments may be carried at cost, revalued amounts or, for marketable

---

[1]See Appendix for principal impacts of Statement of Intent.

equity securities, the lower of cost or market value determined on a portfolio basis. When revalued amounts are used, entire categories of investments should be revalued at the same time. The carrying value of individual investments should be reduced to recognize declines in value that are other than temporary.

Treatment of Valuation Reserves.   Increases resulting from revaluations of long-term investments should be credited to revaluation surplus in shareholders' equity. For current investments, revaluations may be recorded either directly in income or in a revaluation surplus; the policy adopted should be followed consistently. To the extent possible, decreases should be offset against previous increases in the revaluation surplus for the same investment. Other decreases should be charged to income. To the extent that an increase corresponds to previous decreases that were charged to income, the increase should be credited to income.

Gains/Losses.   Gains or losses on sale of investments should be recognized in income. If a realized gain relates to an amount previously recognized in the revaluation surplus, that amount may be transferred to retained earnings or recognized in income in the current period. For gains or losses relating to current investments previously carried on a portfolio basis valued at the lower of cost or market, the gain or loss on sale should be based on cost.

Disclosure.   Disclosure is required of the accounting policies adopted for valuation, revaluation and treatment of gains and losses. In addition, detailed disclosure of investments should be made, including amounts included in income; market values of marketable investments; restrictions on realizability of investments or their income; dates, frequency and basis of revaluations; and changes in the revaluation reserve.

Reference.   IAS 25.

17. Accounts Receivable

Accounting Treatment.   Recognition: The recognition of **revenue**, and hence the related receivable, is described in Section 23.

Discounts: Trade discounts and volume rebates given should be deducted in determining revenue and the related receivable.

Allowances: The IASs make no specific mention of the need for allowances for possible bad debts. However, the Framework states that prudence should be exercised when preparing financial statements. While not justifying the creation of secret or hidden reserves, this would mean that reasonable provision should be made for doubtful receivables.

Factored Receivables.   The treatment of factored receivables is not addressed in the IASs.

Disclosure.   When a classified balance sheet is presented, trade and other receivables due within one year should be disclosed separately. Trade receivables may be included in their entirety as current assets, so long as the amount due after one year is shown.

Reference.   Framework, IAS 13 and IAS 18.

18. Inventories and Work in Progress[1]

General Accounting Treatment. **Inventories** should be valued at the lower of historical cost or **net realizable value**. Historical cost should include a systematic allocation of production overheads that relate to putting the inventories in their current location and condition. Other overheads may be included only to the extent that they clearly relate to that objective. Exceptional wastage or idle capacity costs should not be included in inventory.

Historical cost may be determined using the **FIFO**, weighted-**average cost, specific identification, LIFO** or **base-stock** formula.

Net realizable value estimates should be based on the most reliable evidence available, which may include firm contracted prices, if any, or general market prices. Estimates should not be based on temporary price or cost fluctuations. Inventories should be written down to net realizable value on either an item by item basis or by groups of similar items; the method chosen should be applied consistently. Materials and supplies held at normal levels for future production should not be written down if the related finished products are expected to realize amounts above historical cost.

Long-Term Contracts. For construction contracts, either the **percentage of completion** method or the **completed contract method** is used. The percentage of completion method may be used only if the outcome of the contract can be reliably estimated based on clear identification and knowledge of the costs attributable to the contract and the related income. The method chosen should be used consistently for all contracts meeting similar criteria. All foreseeable losses should be provided for in the financial statements.

Disclosure. Inventories: Inventories should be classified (in the balance sheet or notes) in a manner appropriate to the business and the amounts for each classification should be shown. The accounting policies adopted, including the cost formula used, should be disclosed. Where the LIFO or base-stock method is used, the impact on closing inventory compared with using either FIFO or weighted-average cost should also be disclosed.

Construction contracts: The following details should be disclosed:

☐ Amount of construction work in progress.
☐ Cash received and receivable as progress payments, advances and retentions.
☐ The amount receivable under cost plus contracts not included in construction work in progress.

If both the percentage of completion and completed contract methods have been used, the amounts of construction work in progress accounted for under each method should be analyzed separately.

Reference. IAS 2 and IAS 11.

19. Current Liabilities

General Accounting Treatment. Generally, a liability is recognized in the balance sheet when it is probable that an outflow of resources will result from the settlement of

[1]See Appendix for principal impacts of Statement of Intent.

a present obligation and the amount at which such settlement will take place can be measured reliably. An obligation may be excluded from current liabilities if the enterprise intends to refinance it on a long-term basis and there is reasonable assurance that the enterprise will be able to do so. However, the separate disclosure of current and non-current liabilities is optional.

Creation of General and Specific Provisions. Although prudence should be exercised in making the estimates required under conditions of uncertainty, this does not permit the creation of hidden reserves or excessive provisions or the deliberate overstatement of liabilities. Similarly, accruals for general or unspecified business risks are not appropriate. However, specific provisions in recognition of identified liabilities or contingencies (see Section 21), such as foreseeable losses on construction contracts, should be made. A distinction should be made between present obligations, for which a liability should be recognized, and future commitments.

Disclosure. Separate disclosure should be made for bank loans and overdrafts, current portions of long-term liabilities, payables (e.g., **accounts** and notes **payable**, payables to directors, intercompany and **associated company** payables) and significant items included in other liabilities, provisions and accruals (e.g., deferred taxes, deferred income and provisions for pensions). If the current portion of a long-term liability has been classified as long term, the amount of the liability and terms of the refinancing should be disclosed.

Reference. Framework, IAS 5 and IAS 13.

20. Long-Term Debt

General Accounting Treatment. International Accounting Standards do not specify the accounting treatment for long-term debt. Such debt should, however, be separately disclosed in the balance sheet.

Debt Restructuring. There is no specific accounting treatment prescribed for debt restructuring.

Debt Extinguishment. There is no specific accounting treatment prescribed for debt extinguishment.

Disclosure. Secured loans, unsecured loans, intercompany loans and loans from associated parties should be disclosed separately, excluding the portion repayable within one year. A summary of the interest rates, repayment terms, covenants, subordinations, conversion features and amounts of amortized premium or discount should be shown.

Reference. Framework and IAS 5.

21. Contingencies

Contingent Losses. Contingent losses should be accrued if it is probable that future events will confirm that, after taking into account any related probable recovery, an asset has been impaired or a liability incurred at the balance sheet date, and a reasonable estimate of the amount of the resulting loss can be made.

Contingent Gains.   Contingent gains should not be accrued.

Disclosure.   Contingent losses should be disclosed if the conditions stated above for accrual are not met, unless the possibility of loss is remote. Contingent gains should be disclosed if it is probable that they will be realized.

Reference.   IAS 10.

22.   Capital and Reserves

General.   Equity should be classified in the balance sheet between funds contributed by shareholders and other **surplus**. Recognition should be given to any reserves required by statute or national tax laws; transfers to such reserves should be treated as appropriations of retained earnings rather than expenses.

Disclosure.   Disclosure should be sufficient to make the financial statements clear and understandable. This entails separate disclosure of each class of **share capital** and certain information about each class (such as shares authorized, capital not yet paid, **par** or legal **value** per share, changes during the period and rights, preferences and restrictions on distributions of income or capital repayments). Separate disclosure should be made of other equity classifications (such as **share premium**, revaluation surplus, reserves and retained earnings), indicating changes during the period and any restrictions on distribution.

Reference.   Framework and IAS 5.

ACCOUNTING PRINCIPLES FOR SPECIFIC ITEMS— INCOME STATEMENT

23.   Revenue Recognition[1]

General Principles.   The general rule governing revenue recognition is that revenue should be recognized in the income statement when future economic benefits related to an increase in an asset or a decrease in a liability have arisen that can be measured reliably. Sales or service transactions should be recognized at the time of performance, provided that collection can reasonably be expected. For the sale of goods, performance is when:

□   The significant risks and rewards of ownership are transferred to the buyer.
□   No significant uncertainty exists regarding the consideration from the sale, the associated costs of producing or purchasing the goods or the extent to which goods may be returned.

For service transactions, performance should be measured under either the completed contract method or the percentage of completion method, whichever relates the revenue

---

[1]See Appendix for principal impacts of Statement of Intent.

to the work accomplished, provided that there is no uncertainty as to the consideration to be derived and the associated costs of rendering the service.

Long-Term Contracts. With the exception of construction contracts (see Section 18), International Accounting Standards do not require any special treatment for long-term contracts. They should therefore be accounted for under the general principles identified above.

Instalment Sales. When the consideration is receivable in instalments, revenue attributable to the sales price, exclusive of interest, should be recognized at the date of sale. The interest element should be recognized as revenue proportionately to the unpaid balance due to the seller. If collection is not reasonably assured, revenue should be recognized as cash instalments are received.

Rights of Return. Revenue recognition depends on the substance of the agreement. For normal retail sales, it may be appropriate to recognize the sale, with a suitable provision for returns based on past experience. In other cases, the agreement may amount to a sale on consignment, in which case revenue should not be recognized until a sale has been made to a third party.

Product Financing. For a transaction that is in substance a financing arrangement, the resulting cash inflow is not revenue and should not be recognized as such. These arrangements are normally accounted for as borrowings.

Disclosure. The accounting policies followed for revenue recognition should be disclosed. Sales or other operating revenue should be disclosed separately in the income statement. An enterprise should also disclose circumstances in which revenue recognition has been postponed pending the resolution of significant uncertainties.

Reference. Framework, IAS 11 and IAS 18.

24. Government Grants and Assistance

Accounting Treatment. Government grants (including nonmonetary grants at fair value) should be recognized on a systematic basis in the income statement, over the periods necessary to match them to the costs they are intended to compensate. However, they may be recognized only when there is reasonable assurance that the enterprise will comply with their conditions and that the grants will be received.

Grants relating to assets should be recognized in the balance sheet either as deferred income or as a deduction from the carrying value of the related asset. A grant receivable as compensation for past expenses or losses or for immediate financial support should be recognized currently in the income statement, as an unusual item if appropriate (see Section 28). A grant that becomes repayable should be accounted for as a revision to an accounting estimate (see Section 8).

Disclosure. The following should be disclosed:

□ The accounting policy adopted for government grants.
□ The nature and extent of government grants recognized in the financial statements

and an indication of other forms of government assistance from which the enterprise has benefited.

□ Unfulfilled conditions and other contingencies relating to government assistance that has been recognized.

Reference. IAS 8 and IAS 20.

25. Research and Development[1]

Definitions. Research is defined as original and planned investigation undertaken with the hope of gaining new scientific knowledge and understanding.

Development is defined as the translation of research findings or other knowledge into a plan or design for the production of new or substantially improved materials, devices, products, processes, systems or services prior to the commencement of commercial production.

Accounting Treatment. All research and development costs should be expensed as incurred, with the exception of development costs that meet the following criteria:

□ The product or process is clearly defined and attributable costs can be clearly identified.

□ The technical feasibility of the product or process has been demonstrated.

□ Management has indicated its intention to produce and market, or use, the product or process.

□ There is a clear indication of the future market for the product or process or, if it is to be used internally, its usefulness can be demonstrated.

□ Adequate resources exist, or are reasonably expected to be available, to complete the project and market the product or process.

Development costs meeting these criteria may be deferred to the extent of their expected recovery from future revenues when considered in conjunction with future development, production, marketing and administration costs. If a policy of deferral is chosen, it should be applied consistently to all development costs meeting the above criteria. Deferred amounts no longer meeting those criteria should be expensed immediately.

Deferred costs should be amortized on a systematic basis by reference to either the future sale or use of the product or process or the time period over which it will be sold or used.

Disclosure. The amount of research and development costs (including amortization of deferred amounts) expensed should be disclosed. The balance and changes in unamortized deferred costs should be disclosed, with the proposed or adopted basis of amortization.

Reference. IAS 9.

---

[1]See Appendix for principal impacts of Statement of Intent.

26. Capitalized Interest Costs[1]

Accounting Treatment. Capitalization allowed: Enterprises may capitalize borrowing costs as part of the cost of an asset by applying a capitalization rate to expenditures for the acquisition, construction or production of assets that require a substantial amount of time to get them ready for their use or sale. Alternatively, a policy of not capitalizing interest costs may be adopted. The policy chosen should be applied consistently.

Capitalization rate: The capitalization rate should be determined by relating the borrowing costs incurred during a period to the borrowings outstanding during that period. When a new borrowing is associated with a specific asset, the capitalization rate may be determined on the basis of the actual borrowing cost incurred. Total borrowing costs capitalized in a period must not exceed the borrowing costs incurred in that period (in consolidated financial statements, the consolidated amount of borrowing costs should not be exceeded).

Period of capitalization: Capitalization of borrowing costs should commence when:

☐ Expenditures for the asset and borrowing costs are being incurred.

☐ Activities necessary to prepare the asset for its intended use or sale are in progress (or, in the case of investments, when the investee has in progress activities necessary to commence its planned principal operations).

Capitalization ceases when the asset is ready for its intended use or sale (or, for investments, when the investee starts its principal activities). If active development is interrupted, capitalization should be suspended. Where construction occurs piecemeal and use of each part is possible as construction continues, capitalization for each part should cease on completion of that part.

Disclosure. The amount of borrowing costs capitalized in the period should be disclosed.

Reference. IAS 23.

27. Imputed Interest

General. **Imputed interest** is recognized under International Accounting Standards only with respect to finance leases.

Accounting Treatment. The discount factor used in computing the present value of the minimum lease payments is the interest rate implicit in the lease or, if it is not practicable to determine this rate, the lessee's incremental borrowing rate.

Disclosure. The disclosure requirements are outlined in Section 15.

Reference. IAS 17.

---

[1]See Appendix for principal impacts of Statement of Intent.

28. Extraordinary or Unusual Items

Unusual Items.   Unusual items are gains or losses that derive from events or transactions that are distinct from ordinary activities and therefore not expected to recur frequently or regularly. No separate category of extraordinary items is recognized in International Accounting Standards.

Disclosure.   Unusual items should be included in net income or loss, with the nature and amount of each unusual item disclosed separately.

Reference.   IAS 8.

29. Income Taxes

Accounting Treatment.   The tax expense for the period should be determined using tax-effect accounting, under either the **deferral method** or the **liability method**. All timing differences should normally be taken into account. However, if there is reasonable evidence that timing differences will not reverse for at least three years and no indication that they will subsequently reverse, they may be excluded. Timing differences that result in a debit to the deferred tax balance should not be carried forward as an asset unless there is a reasonable expectation of realization.

Taxes payable on distribution to the parent company of undistributed profits of subsidiaries should be accrued unless it is reasonable to assume that there will be no distribution or no tax liability on such a distribution. In the case of associated companies, accrual should be made when the investor recognizes the undistributed profits, unless it is reasonable to assume that there will be no distribution or no tax liability on such a distribution.

Tax losses: Taxes recovered from prior periods as a result of carrying back a tax loss should be included in net income in the period of the loss. The potential tax saving in future periods from carrying forward a tax loss should generally not be included in net income until it is realized. However, such a tax saving should be included in net income for the period of the loss to the extent of the net credits in the deferred tax balance that will reverse or can be reversed during the period within which the tax loss can be claimed as a benefit, and may be so included to the extent that there is assurance beyond a reasonable doubt that future taxable income will be sufficient for the loss to be realized.

Disclosure.   The **tax-effect method** used and an explanation of the relationship between accounting income and tax expense, if not explained by the tax rates in effect, should be disclosed.

The deferred tax balance should be shown in the balance sheet separately from shareholders' equity. The amount of timing differences, both current and cumulative, not accounted for should be disclosed.

Separate disclosure should be made of tax expenses related to ordinary income, unusual items, prior period items and changes in accounting policy. In addition, the tax effect, if any, of asset revaluations should be shown.

In respect of tax losses, disclosure should be made of the amounts included in net income either from other periods or the current period, and the amount and future availability of tax losses.

Reference.   IAS 12.

30.   Postretirement Benefits[1]

Accounting Treatment.   The accounting treatment for pensions depends on whether they are **defined benefit** or **defined contribution plans**.

Defined Benefit Plans.   The cost of retirement benefit plans should be determined consistently, using appropriate and compatible assumptions, under either the accrued benefit valuation method or the projected benefit valuation method. Current service costs should be expensed systematically over expected remaining working lives of participating employees. Past service costs, experience adjustments and the effect of changes in actuarial assumptions on retirement benefit costs may be credited or charged to income either when they arise or systematically over a period not exceeding the expected remaining working lives of participating employees. Changes in actuarial methods should be accounted for as changes in accounting policies (see Section 8).

Defined Contribution Plans.   The employer's contribution applicable to a particular period should be expensed in that period. If past service costs are included, they may be charged to income either when they arise or systematically over a period not exceeding the expected remaining working lives of participating employees.

Other General Accounting Treatments.   When a plan is amended and additional benefits are provided for retired employees, the associated costs may be charged to income either when they arise or systematically over a period not exceeding the expected remaining working lives of participating employees. When supplemental benefits that constitute a continuing commitment are promised to retired employees, the cost should be expensed at the time the promise is made.

On termination, or probable termination, of a plan, the unfulfilled obligations should be accrued and expensed immediately unless they are transferred to another plan.

Pension Fund Surpluses.   Refund of a pension plan's surplus will be governed by the fund's own trust deed and/or local legislation. The subject is not specifically addressed by International Accounting Standards, but presumably would be dealt with according to the underlying circumstances that gave rise to the surplus (e.g., experience adjustment or change in actuarial assumptions).

Disclosure.   Sufficient disclosure is required to provide an understanding of the significance of pension costs to an enterprise. This includes accounting policies adopted, matters affecting comparability with prior periods and differences between amounts funded and those charged to income. In addition, for defined benefit pension plans, any shortfall

---

[1]See Appendix for principal impacts of Statement of Intent.

of fund assets from the actuarially determined value of vested benefits, the funding approach adopted and the date of the latest valuation should be disclosed.

Reference.   IAS 19.

31. Discontinued Operations

General.   No accounting treatment for discontinued operations is prescribed in International Accounting Standards.

Disclosure.   Sufficient disclosure should be made so that the financial statements are clear and understandable. The effect of the disposal of subsidiaries on the financial position and results of operations (including the effect on comparative figures presented) should also be disclosed.

Reference.   IAS 5 and IAS 27.

32. Earnings per Share

General.   Currently, International Accounting Standards do not require disclosure of any information on earnings per share. The IASC is, however, preparing an exposure draft on this subject.

Appendix
SUMMARY OF THE PRINCIPAL IMPACTS OF THE STATEMENT OF INTENT

Section	Issues	Required or Benchmark Treatment	Allowed Alternative Treatment	Treatment Eliminated
4.	Accounting for business combinations	Purchase method for acquisitions		Pooling of interests method for acquisitions
		Pooling of interests method for uniting of interests		Purchase method for uniting of interests
4.	Positive goodwill	Recognize as an asset and amortize to income on a systematic basis over its useful life. The amortization period should not exceed five years, unless a longer period can be justified; in any case, the period should not exceed 20 years.		Adjust immediately to shareholders' equity
4.	Negative goodwill	Allocate over individual nonmonetary assets; amortize any remaining negative goodwill in same manner as positive goodwill	Treat as deferred income and amortize in same manner as positive goodwill	Adjust immediately to shareholders' equity
4.	Measurement of minority interests arising on a business combination	Measure at pre-acquisition carrying amounts	Measure at post-acquisition fair values	
6.	Recognition of foreign exchange gains and losses on long-term monetary items	Recognize in income of the current period unless hedged		Defer and recognize in income of current and future periods
6.	Recognition of foreign exchange losses on the acquisition of an asset that result from a severe devaluation against which there is no practical means of hedging	Recognize in income of the current period	Recognize as part of the cost of the asset	
6.	Exchange rate for use in translating income statement items of foreign entities	Exchange rates at the dates of the transactions (or average rate)		Closing exchange rates

Appendix—*Continued*

Section	Issues	Required or Benchmark Treatment	Allowed Alternative Treatment	Treatment Eliminated
6.	Treatment of differences on income statement items translated at other than the closing rate	Recognize in shareholders' equity		Recognize in income of the current period
6.	Exchange differences on foreign operations integral to those of the parent	Recognize in income of the period unless hedged	Recognize as part of the cost of an asset when they result from a severe devaluation against which there is no practical means of hedging	Defer and recognize in income of current and future periods
6.	Subsidiaries operating in hyperinflationary economies	Restate financial statements in accordance with IAS 29, *Financial Reporting in Hyperinflationary Economies*, before translation		Translate financial statements without prior restatement
8. & 9.	Correction of fundamental errors and omissions, and adjustments resulting from accounting policy changes	Adjust opening retained earnings (subject to certain exceptions)	Include in income of the current period	
		Amend comparative information	Present amended pro forma comparative information	
13.	Measurement of property, plant and equipment	Measure at cost	Measure at revalued amounts	
13.	Measurement of property, plant and equipment acquired in exchange for another asset	Measure at fair value for dissimilar assets acquired		Measure at net carrying amount of asset given up for dissimilar assets acquired
		Measure at net carrying amount of asset given up for similar assets acquired		Measure at fair value for similar assets acquired
13.	Recognition of a revaluation increase relating to a revaluation decrease previously charged to income	Recognize in income of the current period		Recognize in shareholders' equity

Appendix—*Continued*

Section	Issues	Required or Benchmark Treatment	Allowed Alternative Treatment	Treatment Eliminated
16.	Measurement of investment properties	Measure at cost with depreciation	Measure at revalued amounts	Measure at cost without depreciation
16.	Recognition of a realized gain previously recognized in revaluation surplus	Transfer to retained earnings		Recognize in income of the current period
18.	Assignment of cost to inventories	FIFO and weighted-average cost formulas	LIFO	Base-stock formula
18.	Recognition of revenue and net income on construction contracts	Percentage of completion method When the conditions for profit recognition are not met, recognize revenue to the extent of costs incurred that are recoverable		Completed contract method
23.	Recognition of revenue on transactions involving the rendering of services	Percentage of completion method When the outcome of the contract cannot be reliably estimated, recognize revenue to the extent of costs incurred that are recoverable		Completed contract method
25.	Development costs	Recognize as assets when they meet specified criteria and as expenses when they do not meet criteria		Recognize development costs that meet specified criteria as expenses
26.	Borrowing costs	Recognize as expense when incurred	Recognize as part of the cost of an asset that requires a substantial period of time to get ready for its intended use or sale; recognize as expense in other circumstances	
30.	Determining the cost of retirement benefits	Accrued benefit valuation methods	Projected benefit valuation methods	
30.	Use of projected salaries in determining the cost of retirement benefits	Incorporate an assumption about projected salaries		Do not incorporate an assumption about projected salaries

Appendix (*Continued*)

Section	Issues	Required or Benchmark Treatment	Allowed Alternative Treatment	Treatment Eliminated
30.	Recognition of past service costs, experience adjustments and the effects of changes in actuarial assumptions	Recognize systematically over a period approximating the average expected remaining working lives of participating employees (subject to certain exceptions)		Recognize in income of the current period as they arise

EUROPEAN COMMUNITY

GENERAL INFORMATION

1. Source of EC Accounting Regulations

General. This chapter focuses on the Directives and other proposals of the European Community (EC) on the subject of accounting.

The present Member States of the EC are Belgium, Denmark, France, Germany, Greece, the Republic of Ireland, Italy, Luxembourg, the Netherlands, Portugal, Spain and the United Kingdom. However, several other European countries, because of aspirations to join the EC or for other reasons, are implementing laws based on the Directives.

Directives on Company Law. Since its foundation, the EC has been making efforts to reduce the differences in accounting and auditing law in Member States. The main mechanism used to achieve this is the issuance of Directives, which are drafted by the Commission, adopted by the European Council of Ministers and implemented by the parliaments of the Member States.

The Directives are not directly applicable in the Member States, but take the form of binding instructions from the European Council of Ministers to individual Member States' governments to enact laws in accordance with their provisions. The intention of the Directives is to harmonize (although not make identical) the laws in Member States concerning corporations, how they conduct business, how they account for their actions, and so on. In many cases, the Directives define only minimum legal requirements or, in other cases, provide options. If they desire, Member States may, and often do, add more restrictive requirements or legislate more specific treatments for their own countries. Therefore, reference should be made to the chapters of individual Member States for information on applicable accounting practices.

Certain Directives (including the Fourth and the Seventh) have already been implemented by all EC Member States, as shown on the following page.

| | Date Implemented | |
	Fourth	Seventh
Denmark	1981	1990
UK	1981	1989
France	1983	1985
Netherlands	1983	1988
Luxembourg	1984	1988
Belgium	1985	1990
Germany	1985	1985
Ireland	1986	1992
Greece	1986	1987
Spain	1986	1989
Portugal	1989	1991
Italy	1991	1991

There are also several draft Directives whose proposals have met with varying degrees of controversy. An example is the Ninth Directive on links between undertakings, for which the various drafts and proposals may not have an effect until some time in the future, if ever.

The table below shows the current status of the major Company Law Directives. There are also Directives particularly relating to accounting by banks and insurance companies.

Directive on Company Law	Draft Dates	Date Adopted	Purpose
First	1964	1968	Ultra vires rules
Second	1970, 1972	1976	Separation of public companies, minimum capital, distributions
Third	1970, 1973, 1975	1978	Mergers
Fourth	1971, 1974	1978	Formats and rules of accounting
Fifth	1972, 1983	—	Structure and audit of public companies
Sixth	1975, 1978	1982	De-mergers
Seventh	1976, 1978	1983	Consolidated accounting
Eighth	1978, 1979	1984	Qualifications and work of auditors
Ninth	—	—	Links between public company groups
Tenth	1985	—	International mergers of public companies
Eleventh	1986	1989	Disclosures relating to branches
Twelfth	1988	1989	Single member companies
Thirteenth	1989	—	Takeovers
Vredeling	1980, 1983	—	Employee information and consultation

Fourth and Seventh Directives.   As explained above, the EC uses Directives to initiate regulations over the Community's corporate affairs. The rules relating to accounting practices are largely contained in the Fourth and Seventh Directives on Company Law.

The Fourth Directive sets down accounting provisions intended to give a true and fair view of the financial position and results of operations of **public** and private **companies**, and indicates that financial statements should be prepared in conformity with those provisions.

The Seventh Directive concerns consolidated financial statements, and seeks to harmonize practice throughout the EC regarding their preparation, audit and publication. Like the Fourth Directive, it includes many detailed requirements, but also many options, together with an overriding requirement that accounts should give a true and fair view. Whereas the Fourth Directive was based largely on German law, the Seventh was based substantially on British practice.

These two Directives do not apply to the accounts of banks and insurance companies, which are covered by separate Directives.

For the status of implementation of the Directives in the EC Member States, refer to the individual country chapters.

Other Relevant Community Initiatives.   In addition to the Directives that aim, broadly, to harmonize local country laws, there exist certain Regulations or Statutes that come into effect throughout the EC without the need for member state laws. An example is the creation, by a Regulation adopted in 1985, of the legal form of the "European Economic Interest Grouping," which is designed for multinational joint ventures. Another project of the Commission is the European Company Statute, whose ultimate objective is to provide a legal framework, independent of any nation state, in which a truly "European" company could operate and be regulated. It should be stressed, however, that the statute is as yet only in draft.

2. Audit and Public Company Requirements

Audits.   The annual financial statements of companies must be audited by a duly authorized auditor, who must also verify that the annual report is consistent with the accounts. The content of the audit report is not specified, but should include the auditor's opinion and appropriate comment in the event that the annual report is not consistent with the accounts. Audits are required for all large and medium-sized companies. The Fourth Directive allows Member States to exempt small companies from the audit requirement.

The Eighth Directive requires Member States to ensure that all auditors are suitably qualified and independent and that statutory audits are carried out with due professional care. The names and addresses of auditors must be published by the appropriate regulatory body in each Member State.

Publication.   All companies are required to publish their annual report, annual financial statements and auditor's report. Member States may, however, permit the annual report merely to be made available for public inspection at the company's registered office.

Exemptions for Small Companies.   Exemptions can be made with respect to filing and reporting requirements for small and medium-sized companies. To qualify, a company must meet two out of three criteria for two successive years. Member States may not set the criteria above the following (as amended in 1990):

	Medium-sized companies	Small companies
Maximum balance sheet total	ECU 6.2 million	ECU 1.55 million
Maximum net turnover	ECU 12.8 million	ECU 3.2 million
Average number of employees	Fewer than 250	Fewer than 50

Public, Private and Listed Companies.   The requirements of the Fourth and Seventh Directives apply in general to all limited liability companies. Most of these are either public limited companies or private limited companies. This distinction between legal forms exists in all EC Member States, although it does not exist in certain other countries, such as the United States. Only public limited companies (e.g., PLCs in the UK, AGs in Germany or SAs in France) are allowed to have a market in their securities; however, in most EC countries, most public limited companies do not have a market in their securities. Exemptions from audit or publication apply to private limited companies that are small or medium-sized, according to the size thresholds. The distinction between public limited and private limited companies is otherwise of little relevance for accounting purposes, but is relevant for other purposes. For example, the Second Directive, in setting out rules on what a company may distribute, imposes more restrictions on public limited companies. The Fourth and Seventh Directives contain no provisions that relate specifically to listed companies, although there are separate EC initiatives concerned with harmonizing listing requirements; these are outside the scope of this chapter. In the other chapters of this book, "public company" is used in its North American sense of there actually being a market in the company's securities (see the Glossary).

GENERAL ACCOUNTING

3. Financial Statements

Basic Accounting Concepts.   The Fourth Directive specifies that annual accounts are to be prepared according to five principles:

- ☐   The presumption that the company is a **going concern**.
- ☐   Consistent application of the valuation methods used.
- ☐   The **accruals concept**.
- ☐   Valuation on a prudent basis.
- ☐   Separate valuation of individual asset or liability items.

Departures from these principles are permitted in exceptional cases, although the reasons for and the effect of any departures must be disclosed.

The basic principle of the Fourth Directive is that financial statements should be prepared using the **historical cost** convention. However, the Directive does allow Member States to permit the revaluation of tangible fixed assets, financial fixed assets (e.g., noncurrent investments) and inventories and also allows a full system of inflation accounting.

The annual financial statements are to give a true and fair view of the company's financial position and profit or loss. Where a true and fair view is not otherwise obtained, additional information is to be given. In exceptional circumstances, a company should depart from the specific requirements if that is necessary in order to show a true and fair view.

Contents of Financial Statements.   The Fourth Directive provides that annual financial statements comprise a balance sheet, a profit and loss account, and notes to the accounts. There is no provision for a cash flow statement or a statement of source and application of funds.

Companies should also issue an annual report that contains a fair review of the development of the company's business and its position. The annual report should also contain information on any important events that have occurred since the year-end, research and development activities, acquisition by a company of its own shares and the company's likely future development.

Format of Financial Statements.   The Fourth Directive also details the information to be disclosed and the format and grouping of the balance sheet and profit and loss account.

Two balance sheet formats are provided, although a company may change from one format to the other only in exceptional circumstances. The formats are divided into major headings as follows:

Format 1

ASSETS
- Subscribed capital unpaid
- Formation expenses
- Fixed assets
- Current assets
- Prepayments and accrued income
- Loss for the financial year

LIABILITIES
- Capital and reserves
- Provisions for liabilities and charges
- Creditors
- Accruals and deferred income
- Profit for the financial year

Format 2

- Subscribed capital unpaid
- Formation expenses
- Fixed assets
    - Current assets
    - Prepayments and accrued income
    - Creditors: amounts becoming due and payable within one year

- Net current assets/liabilities
- Total assets less current liabilities
- Creditors: amounts becoming due and payable after more than one year
- Provisions for liabilities and charges
- Accruals and deferred income
- Capital and reserves

These are the main headings. The formats contain more detailed subheadings under many items, such as fixed assets.

Each Member State is responsible for prescribing one or both of the formats. Where both are prescribed, companies may choose between them. Comparative figures must be shown for the preceding financial year for each balance sheet item. Asset and liability items may not be netted.

Two fundamentally different profit and loss account formats are provided: One analyzes costs by type of expense (e.g., purchases of goods, wages and salaries, social security costs); the other analyzes costs by the purpose of the expenditure (e.g., cost of sales, distribution costs, administration expenses). In each case, a vertical and a two-sided version are allowed, making four formats in all. As with the balance sheet formats, each Member State is responsible for prescribing one or more of the formats. Where more than one is prescribed, companies may choose between them. Comparative figures must be shown for the preceding financial year for each item.

Disclosure of Accounting Policies.   The notes to the accounts should contain details of accounting policies used, where not indicated in the accounts themselves.

Reference.   Articles 2–27 of Fourth Directive.

4.   Business Combinations

Principles of Consolidation.   Under the Seventh Directive, consolidated accounts have to be prepared by all **parent** undertakings registered in the EC. The accounts should include all **subsidiary** undertakings on a worldwide basis. The term "subsidiary undertakings" is broader than just companies, and includes, for example, partnerships. Member States can exempt parent undertakings that are not companies. In addition, there are other exemptions, as set out below.

Consolidated financial statements are to be presented clearly and are to give a true and fair view of the group's financial position and results. They comprise the group consolidated balance sheet, the group consolidated profit and loss account and the notes to the accounts. The provisions of the Fourth Directive should be applied to the consolidated accounts, where relevant.

Undertakings to be Consolidated.   The Directive includes six definitions of the parent–subsidiary relationship in order to define a group for accounting purposes. Four of these are mandatory and two are optional. Thus, the definition of a group is likely to vary between Member States according to which definitions they adopt. An undertaking qualifies as a subsidiary undertaking, and therefore should be included in the consolidation, if the parent:

☐   Holds a majority of the voting rights of the undertaking;

☐ Is a shareholder (**member**) of the undertaking and has the right to appoint or remove a majority of the members of the administrative, management or supervisory body (the Board) of the undertaking;

☐ Is a member of the undertaking and controls alone or through an agreement with other members of the undertaking a majority of the voting rights; or

☐ Has the right to exercise dominant influence over the undertaking through a contract entered into with the undertaking or a provision in its memorandum or articles of association (the nature of the contract is not defined).

In addition, the following are the two optional definitions of a subsidiary undertaking:

☐ An undertaking in which the parent holds a participating interest and either (a) actually exercises dominant influence over it or (b) the two are managed on a unified basis. (A long-term holding of the capital of another company designed for the benefit of the holder that exceeds 20 percent is presumed to be a participating interest.)

☐ An undertaking in which the parent, through its being a member of another undertaking and exercising its voting rights, has appointed a majority of the members of the board who have held office during the preceding and current financial years and up to the time the consolidated accounts are prepared.

Certain exemptions from consolidation are permitted or required, notably:

(a) Parent financial holding companies may be exempted by Member States from the obligation to prepare consolidated financial statements where the financial holding company has not intervened in the past year in the management of the subsidiary, or exercised voting rights to appoint a member of the subsidiary's board in the past five years, and has made loans only to undertakings in which it owns a participating interest.

(b) Member States may exempt a group that is within the medium-sized or small company thresholds (see Section 2) from preparing consolidated financial statements. This exemption does not apply where one of the undertakings to be consolidated is quoted on a Member State's stock exchange.

(c) Subsidiaries whose activities are so different from those of the rest of the group that consolidation would impair a true and fair view must be excluded from consolidation.

(d) Subsidiaries may be exempted from consolidation if:
—they operate under severe long-term restrictions;
—the necessary information cannot be obtained without undue expense or delay;
—they are held exclusively with a view to subsequent resale.

(e) A company wholly owned by another EC-based undertaking, which prepares consolidated financial statements for the whole group, is exempted from sub-consolidation of the financial statements of its subsidiary undertakings. Member States need not exempt listed companies.

(f) A company at least 90 percent owned by a parent company is exempted from preparing sub-consolidated financial statements provided that the minority shareholders have approved the exemption. In cases where there is less than a 90 percent holding, Member States may allow exemptions, given specified protections for minority shareholders.

(g) If the ultimate parent company is established outside the EC, Member States may exempt an intermediate holding company from the need to prepare an EC sub-consolidation if the worldwide consolidated financial statements are prepared in a manner equivalent to the Seventh Directive and are audited by an authorized person according to the law governing the company that prepared them. The term "equivalent" has not been defined by the EC and is therefore open to interpretation. Exemptions of this sort are not permitted to exceed those adopted in (e) and (f) above.

Equity Accounting.   The Seventh Directive requires that associated undertakings be accounted for by the **equity method** in group accounts. Equity accounting is also used where a subsidiary undertaking is excluded from consolidation because of dissimilar activities.

Acquisitions and Mergers.   The Seventh Directive generally requires acquisition accounting. However, the Directive also allows Member States to permit or require merger accounting in certain defined circumstances. These are basically when a 90 percent holding of shares has been reached by means of an arrangement for the issue of shares, provided that the arrangement does not include a cash payment exceeding 10 percent of the nominal value of the shares issued.

Goodwill.   The Seventh Directive prohibits carrying consolidation **goodwill** as a permanent asset (i.e., as a fixed asset without **amortization**) and requires that it be eliminated in one of the following ways:

☐   Amortized through the profit and loss account over five years.
☐   Amortized through the profit and loss account over its useful economic life.
☐   Written off immediately to reserves.

Disclosure.   The notes to the financial statements should give details on certain matters designed to disclose the structure of the group, the identity of the group companies and the relationships between group companies. In addition, the notes should separately identify any financial commitments to affiliated companies that are not shown in the balance sheet.

Reference.   Fourth and Seventh Directives.

5. Joint Ventures

Accounting for Investments in Joint Ventures.   The Seventh Directive allows a Member State to either require or permit the use of **proportionate consolidation** for **joint ventures**. If proportionate consolidation is not used, then equity accounting must be, assuming that the holding in the joint venture falls within the definition of an associate.

Jointly Controlled Entities.   The Seventh Directive includes requirements relating to joint ventures, which are defined in the English version of the Directive as those managed jointly with one or more other undertakings. In some other languages, the Directive appears to say "**jointly controlled.**"

Jointly Controlled Operations. The Seventh Directive refers to "undertakings" rather than "companies," so the above rules for jointly controlled entities generally apply to jointly controlled operations as well.

Jointly Controlled Assets. The Seventh Directive does not refer to jointly controlled assets.

Transactions Between Venturers and the Joint Venture. The Seventh Directive requires that all its other rules on consolidation apply to proportionate consolidation, where appropriate. This suggests the elimination of certain transactions between the venturers and the venture. Similarly, if the equity method is used, appropriate eliminations are required.

Disclosure.

☐ Equity accounting: the names, registered offices and proportion of capital held should be disclosed.
☐ Proportionate consolidation: the above disclosures should be made, as well as the factors on which joint management (control) is based. Also, separate disclosure of the average number of employees during the year is required.

Accounting by Joint Ventures. The Directives apply to limited companies, so they would apply to joint ventures only if the latter were so organized.

Reference. Articles 32, 33 and 34 of Seventh Directive.

6. Foreign Currency Translation

Accounting Treatment. EC Directives do not specify any required accounting treatment.

Disclosure. The methods chosen must be disclosed in the notes.

Reference. Article 43 of Fourth Directive.

7. Changing Prices/Inflation Accounting

General. Although the Fourth Directive generally provides that the historical cost convention be used in the preparation of annual financial statements, it permits Member States to allow companies to revalue certain assets. Therefore, in certain countries, assets such as property, plant and equipment are revalued. At an extreme, these rules allow a full system of inflation accounting, but its adoption is rare.

Disclosure. Where financial statements are prepared under an inflation accounting basis, historical cost data for property, plant and equipment must still be provided to ensure reasonable comparability of financial statements.

Reference. Article 33 of Fourth Directive.

8. Accounting Changes

Accounting Treatment. EC Directives do not specify any required accounting treatment.

9. Prior Period Adjustments

Accounting Treatment. EC Directives do not specify any required accounting treatment.

10. Post Balance Sheet Events

Accounting Treatment. EC Directives do not specify any required accounting treatment.

Disclosure. The annual report must contain information on any important events that occurred since year-end.

Reference. Article 46 of Fourth Directive.

11. Related Party Transactions

Definition. Related parties are not defined in the EC Directives.

Disclosure. Disclosure in the notes should be made of the salaries, benefits, loans and credits provided to top management (the board of directors). Disclosure requirements with respect to affiliated undertakings are outlined in Section 4.

Reference. Article 43 of Fourth Directive.

12. Segmental Information

Disclosure. The notes should provide an analysis of net sales, geographically and by line of business.

Reference. Article 43 of Fourth Directive.

ACCOUNTING PRINCIPLES FOR SPECIFIC ITEMS— BALANCE SHEET

13. Property, Plant and Equipment

Basis of Valuation. **Fixed assets** should be stated at historical purchase price or production cost. Member States are, however, allowed to permit departures from historical cost for tangible fixed assets. Where such a departure is made, either the **replacement value** method or other methods based on current values may be used.

The value of fixed assets should be reduced where there is a permanent reduction in their value.

Depreciation.   **Depreciation** should be allocated to all fixed assets with limited useful lives so as to write off the asset over its life.

Disclosure.   Disclosure should be made of any amounts written off and the valuation methods used.

Reference.   Articles 33 and 35 of Fourth Directive.

14.   Intangible Assets

Formation Expenses.   Accounting treatment: Formation expenses may be included in the balance sheet as an asset and written off to the profit and loss account over a period that must not exceed five years.

Intangible Fixed Assets.   Definition: **Intangible** fixed **assets** may include the following items:

☐ Costs of research and development (see Section 25).
☐ Concessions, patents, licenses, trademarks and similar rights and assets if they either were acquired for valuable consideration and are distinguishable from goodwill, or were created by the undertaking itself.
☐ Goodwill to the extent that it was acquired for valuable consideration (see Section 4).
☐ Payments on account.

Amortization: Intangible fixed assets must be valued at their purchase price, which must be systematically reduced if they have limited useful economic lives.

Disclosure.   Disclosure should be made of any amounts written off.

Reference.   Articles 9, 10, 34, 35 and 37 of Fourth Directive.

15.   Leases

Accounting Treatment.   EC Directives do not specify any required accounting treatment.

Disclosure.   Commitments should be disclosed.

Reference.   Article 43 of Fourth Directive.

16.   Investments

Valuation.   The valuation of investments depends on whether they are regarded as fixed assets or **current assets**. The Fourth Directive indicates that fixed assets comprise assets that are intended for use on a continuing basis for the purposes of the undertaking's activities.

Fixed assets: Financial fixed assets should be stated at their purchase price. Member

States, however, are allowed to permit revaluations. The carrying value *must* be written down where there is a permanent reduction in the value of the investment. The carrying value *may* be written down where there is a temporary decrease in value.

Current assets: An investment classified as a current asset should be carried at the lower of cost or market value.

Gains/Losses. Where the purchase and sale of investments are not part of the company's ordinary activities, all gains and losses should be accounted for as extraordinary items (see Section 28).

Disclosure. If not shown elsewhere in the financial statements, the notes should provide details of amounts written off and the valuation methods used.

Reference. Articles 29, 32, 33, 35, 39 and 43 of Fourth Directive.

17. Accounts Receivable

Accounting Treatment. EC Directives do not specify any required accounting treatment.

Disclosure. According to the balance sheet formats, amounts receivable over more than one year should be separately disclosed.

Reference. Articles 9 and 10 of Fourth Directive.

18. Inventories and Work in Progress

Valuation. **Inventories** should be carried at the lower of cost or market value. In determining the purchase price or production cost, the weighted-**average**, **FIFO**, **LIFO** or other similar methods may be used. Inventories may be revalued at replacement value.

Long-Term Contracts. EC Directives do not specify any required accounting treatment for long-term contracts.

Disclosure. The notes should provide details of amounts written off, where not shown in the financial statements, and the valuation method used.

Reference. Articles 33, 39, 40 and 43 of Fourth Directive.

19. Current Liabilities

Accounting Treatment. EC Directives do not specify any required accounting treatment.

20. Long-Term Debt

Accounting Treatment. EC Directives do not specify any required accounting treatment.

Disclosure. Disclosure is required of all amounts payable more than five years from the balance sheet date.

Reference. Article 43 of Fourth Directive.

21. Contingencies

Accounting Treatment. EC Directives do not specify any required accounting treatment, although disclosure of ''financial commitments'' is required in the notes.

Reference. Article 43 of Fourth Directive.

22. Capital and Reserves

Accounting Treatment. EC Directives do not specify any required accounting treatment, except for restrictions on the use of the ''revaluation reserve,'' which arises when assets are revalued.

Disclosure. Separate disclosure of each reserve is required by the balance sheet formats. The amount of subscribed capital unpaid should be disclosed separately in the balance sheet.

Reference. Articles 33 and 43 of Fourth Directive.

ACCOUNTING PRINCIPLES FOR SPECIFIC ITEMS— INCOME STATEMENT

23. Revenue Recognition

General Principles. The general principles for recognition of **revenue** under the EC Directives are governed by the accounting principles described in Section 3. No specific guidance is provided in the Directives.

24. Government Grants and Assistance

Accounting Treatment. EC Directives do not specify any required accounting treatment.

25. Research and Development

Accounting Treatment. Research and development expenditure may be treated in the following ways:

- ☐ Capitalized and written off through the profit and loss account over five years.
- ☐ Capitalized and written off through the profit and loss account over its useful economic life.
- ☐ Written off immediately against earnings.

Disclosure.   Information concerning research and development activities should be shown in the annual report. The valuation method used should be disclosed in the notes to the financial statements.

Reference.   Articles 37 and 43 of Fourth Directive.

26. Capitalized Interest Costs

Accounting Treatment.   EC Directives do not specify any required accounting treatment.

27. Imputed Interest

Accounting Treatment.   EC Directives do not specify any required accounting treatment.

28. Extraordinary or Unusual Items

Accounting Treatment and Disclosure.   Profits and losses not relating to the ordinary activities of the company are to be shown separately in the profit and loss account as extraordinary items.

Reference.   Article 29 of Fourth Directive.

29. Income Tax

Accounting Treatment.   EC Directives do not specify any required accounting treatment.

30. Postretirement Benefits

Accounting Treatment.   EC Directives do not specify any required accounting treatment.

Disclosure.   Financial commitments concerning postretirement benefits that are not shown in the balance sheet should be disclosed separately.

Reference.   Article 43 of Fourth Directive.

31. Discontinued Operations

Accounting Treatment.   EC Directives do not specify any required accounting treatment.

32. Earnings per Share

Accounting Treatment.   EC Directives contain no requirements for the calculation or disclosure of earnings per share.

CENTRAL AND EASTERN EUROPE
(Including the Czech and Slovak Republics, Hungary, Poland and Russia)

INTRODUCTION

This chapter provides an overview of economic reforms, in the context of the political situation, in Central and Eastern Europe, designed to enable readers to view accounting developments from the perspective of the wider reforms adopted to create market economies in the region. The chapter summarizes the steps recently taken to develop accounting and reporting standards appropriate for a business and investing community in four countries of the region. Three of these countries—the Czech and Slovak Republics, Hungary and Poland—have been chosen because they have made the most progress. Russia has been included because of the significant level of foreign investment already made in that country and continuing interest in the West in investing further.

POLITICAL CONTEXT OF ECONOMIC REFORM

The introduction of *Glasnost* (openness) and *Perestroika* (restructuring) in the former Soviet Union began a chain of events that has transformed the geopolitical situation in Eastern Europe, as one by one the countries of the region broke with communism and embarked on the path of political and economic reform. First Lithuania, then the three Baltic States declared their independence from the Soviet Union, a lead quickly followed by the other republics. However, the pace of political and economic change has been variable, reflecting the diversity of cultural, political and economic conditions in different countries. The countries can be categorized into three groups:

☐ The *Central European* group of countries—the Czech and Slovak Republics (formerly Czechoslovakia), Hungary and Poland—have proceeded furthest toward market reform and the establishment of stable democratic systems. Political stability, reasonably well-developed infrastructures and large amounts of foreign direct investment have all contributed to the progress achieved.

☐ In the *Balkans*, the experience has been far less encouraging. In Bulgaria and Romania, severe economic problems and the resilience of former communists in society have held back reform. The disintegration of the former Yugoslavia and the violence in Bosnia–Herzegovina and parts of Croatia have overshadowed any consideration of reform.

□   The countries that have emerged from the *former Soviet Union* are even more disparate. As in Yugoslavia, some former republics—Armenia, Azerbaijan, Georgia, Moldova and Tajikistan—have experienced violent ethnic and political conflict; others, such as the Central Asian republics of Uzbekistan, Kirghizia and Turkmenia, are conservative and largely still following communism; in contrast, the western republics (Ukraine and Belarus) and the Baltic States (Lithuania, Latvia and Estonia) have turned decisively westward and are seeking to accelerate the pace of reform. The situation in Russia is extremely uncertain as macroeconomic stability continues to be elusive and the reformers are opposed by conservative nationalists.

The world is undergoing the first stages of what will be a prolonged period of adjustment to the new geopolitical situation following the disintegration of the Soviet Union. Some countries, such as the former Czechoslovakia, Hungary and Poland, the Baltic States and western former republics of the Soviet Union, are building new liberal-democratic societies and market economies; in other countries, such as most of former Yugoslavia, Transcaucasia and parts of Central Asia, previously latent ethnic conflicts are impeding progress toward reform.

ECONOMIC REFORM

In response to the consistent failure of centrally planned economies to provide a reasonable and improving material standard for the majority of their populace, the countries of Central and Eastern Europe have embarked upon ambitious programs to transform their societies through the creation of market economies.

Under the guidance of international institutions such as the International Monetary Fund (IMF) and the World Bank, a broadly similar set of interlinked policies has emerged at the heart of the reforms. The two key elements have been macroeconomic stabilization and structural reform: The former has focused on measures to stabilize the economy through the operation of restrictive monetary, fiscal and wage policies to prevent price and financial liberalization from leading to hyperinflation; the latter has the objectives of establishing the institutions of a market economy and improving supply-side performance.

Although there has been considerable debate about the correct sequencing of reform measures, the need is so great, and the measures so interlinked, that most countries are trying to make progress on all fronts simultaneously. The key measures adopted have been:

□   **Macroeconomic stabilization:**
> —*Monetary policy:* tight control over monetary expansion, particularly the growth of bank credit, to contain inflation.
> —*Fiscal policy:* reduction of government expenditure as a proportion of GDP and the restructuring of government finances.
> —*Wage policy:* restraint of wage growth below inflation to absorb excess demand (or monetary overhang).

□   **Market reforms:**
> —*Price liberalization:* elimination of price control and subsidies so that prices reflect the true opportunity cost of goods and services.
> —*Demonopolization of production and distribution:* introduction of competition by the breakup of state monopolies, privatization of enterprises and encouragement of investment from abroad.

—*Trade liberalization:* opening up of the economy to international trade through deregulation and the reduction of other barriers to trade.

☐ **Privatization and enterprise restructuring:**
—*Privatization:* the transfer of state assets into private ownership through property restitution and the sale of shares in privatized enterprises to domestic and foreign investors.
—*Inward investment:* encouragement of investment from abroad through the creation of a stable, supportive investment environment, including the provision of investment opportunities and an appropriate legal, regulatory and institutional framework.
—*Enterprise restructuring:* to be triggered by other reforms, e.g., privatization, market liberalization, demonopolization and foreign involvement in the economy.

☐ **Institutional reform:**
—*Legal, regulatory and institutional reform:* comprehensive reform of the framework for private economic activity.
—*Financial sector restructuring:* creation of a two-tier banking system and promotion of efficient capital markets.
—*Social welfare reform:* provision of an adequate safety net for those suffering the frictional effects of restructuring.

In all countries one of the highest priorities of reform is the encouragement of foreign participation in the economy since without a massive infusion of external capital, technical advice and management skills, economic regeneration will be extremely slow. The provision of a comprehensive, clearly defined legal, regulatory and institutional framework within which business can be conducted, and the efficient operation and consistent application of this framework, is an important prerequisite for substantial foreign investment. Reform of accounting and financial reporting requirements is seen as an important part of this process.

EVOLUTION OF ACCOUNTING IN THE REGION

Prior to World War II, accounting practices in Czechoslovakia, Hungary and Poland were part of a Central European commercial tradition that was strongly influenced by Germanic legislation. Prerevolutionary Russia had a rather different accounting tradition, which also influenced the Russian-occupied areas of Poland. Following the introduction of state-directed economic planning in the early 1950s, all countries of the Eastern Bloc became heavily influenced by practices developed and applied in the Soviet Union. Accounting and financial reporting were subordinated to the requirements of the planning system and reflected the diminished scope of financial management in centrally planned economies. The principal function of accounting became the provision of factual data to assess plan fulfillment and to generate statistics for other planning-related purposes. Accounting generally required adherence to a prescribed chart of accounts and did not involve taking a view on the financial position of an enterprise, since it was not answerable for its financial performance.

As discussed above, accounting practices in the Central and Eastern European countries are being reformed in the context of the wider reforms adopted to create the institutions of market economies. In the past three years Czechoslovakia, Hungary and Poland have made considerable progress toward the creation of Western European-style financial reporting regimes. In common with other areas of institutional reform, governments in the region are seeking, as far as possible, to ensure that their new laws are consistent with those of the European Community (EC) so as to facilitate eventual transition to full membership. With this in mind, new legislation has been strongly influenced by EC accounting practices, particularly the Fourth and Seventh Directives on Company Law, as well as by the International Accounting Standards (IASs). In general, financial reporting is becoming less rigid and, at least in principle, incorporates areas in which professional judgment must be exercised, thus providing a degree of flexibility necessary in a market economy. However, a body of case law to which auditors can turn for guidance on the interpretation of the law has yet to be developed.

CZECH AND SLOVAK REPUBLICS

Introduction

The dissolution of the Czech–Slovak Federation on December 31, 1992, and the successful completion of the first wave of "voucher" privatization, were the most significant political and economic events in Czechoslovakia during 1992.

The first of the projected five rounds of the first wave of Czechoslovakia's mass (or "voucher") privatization program began in July 1991. By December 1992, the five rounds had been completed and 93 percent of the shares entered into the first wave, accounting for almost 99 percent of investment points held by the population, had been allocated. Of 2,000 companies in the first wave of privatization, only 35 (as at the beginning of December 1992) had entered into joint ventures with foreign partners. The second, and final, privatization wave commenced in June 1992. At the time of this writing, approximately 70 percent of state-owned enterprises in the Czech and Slovak Republics have completed or are undergoing privatization.

Source of Generally Accepted Accounting Principles

The majority of **accounting principles** in the Czech and Slovak Republics are contained in the Czech and Slovak Federal Republic Accounting Act (Accounting Act No. 563/ 1991) approved in December 1991 by the Federal Assembly. A chart of accounts and accounting regulations were issued by the Federal Ministry of Finance in July 1992.

The majority of accounting principles contained in the Accounting Act became effective for accounting periods beginning on or after January 1, 1992. The effective date for certain provisions of the Accounting Act and the aforementioned chart of accounts and enabling regulations was delayed until January 1, 1993. This delay was related to delays in the tax reform, which also became effective on January 1, 1993.

The principal provisions of the Accounting Act that became effective in 1992 are:

- [ ] A requirement for consolidation accounting (to reflect the substance of the EC Seventh Directive). No enabling regulations have yet been published.
- [ ] A requirement for notes to financial statements, including a description of **accounting policies** and changes thereto. No enabling regulations have yet been published.
- [ ] The extension of the prescribed accounting period from one calendar month to one calendar year.
- [ ] New audit and filing requirements.

The major provisions taking effect in 1993 introduce the following **accounting concepts**:

- □ **Going concern**.
- □ Faithful representation of financial position and performance.
- □ Consistency and comparability.
- □ **Prudence**.

Those provisions are:

- □ The introduction of asset valuation policies, particularly the requirement to value **inventory** at the lower of cost or **net realizable value**.
- □ Increased discretion with respect to the creation of net realizable value provisions (e.g., for **accounts receivable** and inventory).
- □ Complete discretion with respect to the adoption of **depreciation** rates for accounting purposes (which parallels the introduction of separate prescribed depreciation rates for tax purposes) and the introduction of deferred tax (compulsory for companies in a group structure).

In essence, the new legislation seeks to introduce accounting principles that substantially mirror International Accounting Standards and the provisions of the Fourth, Seventh and Eighth EC Directives. The legislation changes the primary purpose of the financial statements from serving as a tax statement to the means by which owners and management measure the financial position and performance of the business.

Obligation to Prepare Financial Statements
All business entities have a December 31 year-end. The accounting regulations stipulate a standard format for financial statements. In addition, the structure of the general ledger is prescribed; the structure was revised effective January 1, 1993.

Audit Requirements
Beginning in 1992, the Accounting Act extended previous audit requirements. Annual audits are required for joint stock companies and any other business where either:

- □ **Revenues** for the preceding year exceeded 40 million koruna,
- □ Net assets at the end of the preceding year exceeded 20 million koruna, or
- □ **Consolidated financial statements** are prepared.

Consolidated financial statements are required when an enterprise either has at least a 20 percent interest in another enterprise or, irrespective of the interest held, is authorized to manage another company on the basis of a contract or the company statutes.

A new law relating to audit requirements was promulgated in 1992 and addresses a wide range of issues, including the scope of audits and qualifications of auditors. Unlike the Accounting Act, the audit legislation was not enacted at the federal level, but is at the discretion of the two Republics.

Auditors are required to pass an examination and to be registered with the Chambers of Auditors of the Czech and Slovak Republics, respectively. Audits may be performed by either registered individuals or enterprises.

With respect to the Czech Republic, beginning in 1994, in the case of registered enterprises, Czech auditors who are also Czech nationals are required to hold either a minimum of 60 percent of the enterprise's shares or 60 percent of the voting rights.

With respect to the Slovak Republic, beginning April 1, 1993, in the case of registered enterprises, auditors who have passed the examinations by March 31, 1993, or who will subsequently pass them, are required to hold either a majority of the voting rights or constitute 75 percent of the enterprise's executive.

Although it is clearly stated that the audit report shall contain an expression of opinion as to whether the financial statements are a true and fair representation of the financial position and result of operations, regulations relating to the scope of the audit, as well as to the content and form of the audit report, have not yet been published. Detailed audit regulations will be the responsibility of the newly established Chamber of Auditors, in both the Czech and Slovak Republics, and are expected to be published by the end of 1993.

Financial Statements

Basic Accounting Concepts.   Financial statements in the Czech and Slovak Republics are generally prepared under the **historical cost** convention on the basis of the following concepts:

- ☐ Transactions are recorded on the **accrual** basis. Small enterprises may, however, use the cash basis of accounting.
- ☐ Accounting policies should be applied consistently from one period to the next and should normally be specified in the company's internal accounting regulations. Where a change in accounting policy does take place, the full effect of the change should be disclosed.

Although the going concern concept is not specifically mentioned in the accounting regulations, commentators have made it clear that it is an underlying assumption.

Business Combinations

The requirement for consolidated financial statements is discussed above. Detailed regulations are expected to be published by the end of 1993. It is not clear whether the legislatures intend to introduce **equity accounting**.

Foreign Currency Translation

The Czech National Bank and the Slovak National Bank establish exchange rates for the Czech and Slovak korunas, respectively. Transactions are recorded at the official rate on the date of occurrence. Rates are specified for monetary assets and liabilities for balance sheet purposes.

Inflation Accounting

There are currently no regulations covering the use of inflation accounting or methods of accounting for price-level changes.

Fixed Assets

Tangible **fixed assets** are valued at purchase price or production cost. Depreciation is calculated according to a plan chosen by the enterprise based on the conditions of use of the related assets.

Devaluations may be made in the event of a permanent diminution in the value of fixed assets.

Intangible assets, such as software, costs of research and development, lump-sum licenses and the costs of incorporation, are written off within five years of acquisition date or the date of their incurrence, as applicable.

Inventories

Until 1993, inventories were not required to be valued at the lower of cost or net realizable value. Inventory values may be based on either:

☐ **Standard costs.**

☐ Weighted-**average costs** using **first-in first-out (FIFO).**

Beginning in 1993, the legislation requires enterprises to establish necessary net realizable value provisions, and standard costs, which were permitted in the past, will continue to be allowable for the valuation of only work in progress and finished goods.

Accounts Receivable

Beginning in 1993, the regulations require enterprises to establish necessary net realizable value provisions for both foreign and domestic accounts receivable. In the past such provisions were normally created for foreign accounts receivable, but were rare for domestic receivables.

In the past, the regulations reflected the State's desire to maximize tax collections, and as a consequence there was relatively little discretion to create accruals and provisions, particularly with respect to foreseeable losses, that had not yet materialized. Beginning in 1993, reasonably foreseeable liabilities are required to be reflected in the financial statements.

HUNGARY

Introduction

Hungary's early initiative toward market reform has made it the most popular country with foreign investors in Central and Eastern Europe. According to the latest statistics, the country has received almost half (US$ 3.4 billion) of the total foreign direct investment in the region over the past three years. The country provides a stable environment in which it is relatively easy to conduct business.

The Hungarian Stock Exchange was officially launched by its 42 founding members in June 1990. At the end of 1992, the shares of 26 enterprises were trading.

Source of Generally Accepted Accounting Principles

Generally accepted accounting principles and practices are derived principally from the Law on Accounting (Law XVIII of 1991; the Law). The Law defines the format of financial statements and includes rules for determining and recording assets, liabilities and equity.

The Law has been influenced by the EC Fourth and Seventh Directives and International Accounting Standards. It places emphasis on an entity's annual report and requires its publication in many cases. The Law generally became effective January 1, 1992; however, there are transitional arrangements for certain areas.

Because the Law has been in effect for only a short while at the time of this writing, the extent to which issues of interpretation of its provisions may arise is still uncertain. The Law does not include detailed explanations regarding compliance with it, and it is also not yet supported by any professional accounting literature.

Audit and Public Company Requirements

Every entity that is required to publish its annual report must appoint an auditor. Publication of the annual report should be in a national daily newspaper and is obligatory for:

☐ A Részvénytársarág or Rt (equivalent of a **public** limited **company**).

☐ A Korlátolt felelössegü társaság or Kft (equivalent of a limited liability company) with an original capital in excess of 50 million Hungarian forints (Ft).

☐ A single member Kft.

☐ An issuer of bonds.

Certain entities are permitted to prepare simplified annual reports and are not required to publish them. An Rt may not prepare a simplified annual report, even if it falls within the definition of a small company.

The auditor, who must be registered with an organization recognized by the Minister of Finance, is required to report whether the annual report has been prepared in accordance with the provisions of the Law.

Foreign Currencies

The annual report must be written in Hungarian, with amounts expressed in thousands of forints, except that companies operating in customs-free zones must use the convertible currency set out in their articles of association.

There are special regulations with respect to foreign currencies, attributable for the most part to the fact that the forint is not convertible.

Financial Statements

Basic Accounting Concepts.   Financial statements are prepared using the **historical cost** convention. The Law sets out a number of mandatory bookkeeping and reporting principles, namely, **going concern**, **matching**, **realization**, **prudence**, consistency, **individual evaluation** and clarity. The Law specifies the main layout (in classes) of the chart of accounts to be used by entities.

Content of Financial Statements.   The Law requires that most organizations prepare an annual report. Distinction is made between an annual report, a simplified annual report, a consolidated annual report and a simplified balance sheet.

A simplified annual report may be prepared by certain small companies. A small company is defined by the Law as one that meets at least two of the following conditions:

☐ Total assets less than Ft150 million.

☐ Net annual sales **revenues** of less than Ft300 million.

☐ Average number of employees less than 100.

All financial reports are required to have a December 31 balance sheet date.

The annual report comprises a balance sheet, an income statement, notes to the financial statements and a directors' report. There is no requirement for either a cash flow statement or a statement of changes in financial position.

The annual report must provide a "realistic" picture of the net assets and financial position of the business and of any changes therein. It must reflect the level of assets, capital, provisions and liabilities as well as the profit for the period, and must include all information and explanatory notes necessary to provide a "true" picture of the financial position, income and expenditure of the business.

Format of Financial Statements.   The form of the annual report is stipulated by the Law, and, as a result of using German interpretations of EC directives, closely follows the German model. Comparative information must be provided for both the balance sheet and the income statement.

The directors' report consists of a retrospective view of the financial results and financial position of the entity for the year and a prospective view of the expected developments of the business for the coming year. Any important subsequent events or important trends after the balance sheet date, information on the acquisition of the company's own shares (if any) and research and development activities should be stated in this report.

The **accounting policies** applied by the entity are disclosed in the notes to the financial statements. Where there has been a change in accounting policies, the notes to the financial statements should explain the economic conditions that caused the change and its impact on the results for the year and the financial position as at the end of the year.

There is currently no requirement for an entity to prepare consolidated financial statements; the law requiring consolidated financial statements will become effective in 1995.

There is no requirement to provide information on the effects of changing prices in financial statements.

Accounting Principles for Specific Items

Fixed Assets.   **Fixed assets** that individually cost more than Ft20,000 must be capitalized. Fixed assets costing less than this amount may be written off immediately.

Fixed assets are capitalized at either their acquisition cost or their cost of production. Furthermore, the Law requires that all expenses in connection with either the improvement or renovation of an existing asset should be capitalized.

Acquisition cost includes all costs that can individually be attributed to the asset. Interest on loans and credits directly related to the purchase or production of a fixed asset is regarded as part of the acquisition cost of the asset and should be capitalized.

Fixed assets are stated at historical cost. Revaluations are not permitted.

Depreciation is applied to write off the cost of an asset over its expected economic life. Additional depreciation should be charged where there is a permanent impairment in the value of the asset. Permitted methods of depreciation are **declining balance**, **straight line**, **sum-of-the-years'-digits** and **units-of-production**. Depreciation commences when the asset is placed in operation. Depreciation of land, forests and works of art is not permitted.

Intangible Assets.   The Law recognizes a number of types of **intangible assets**, including rights representing the future generation of money (such as leasing rights, trademarks and concessions), **goodwill**, intellectual property rights, the capitalized value of research and development expenditure, and the cost of foundation (incorporation costs) or restructuring.

Intangible assets are capitalized at historical cost in the balance sheet and should be amortized over their expected economic life. **Amortization** periods for certain assets are specified in the Law.

Leases.   All leases are treated as **operating leases**, and therefore no leased assets are capitalized. However, a new regulation on accounting for leases is being drafted.

Investments.   Long-term investments are stated at the lower of cost or market value. Until the requirement for consolidated financial statements comes into effect, majority-owned investments and investments in which the entity has a significant interest (defined as between 25% and 50%) will be included in long-term investments.

Short-term investments are stated at the lower of cost or market value and are presented as assets, including any shares or share quotas the company owns of itself.

Upward revaluation of investments is not permitted.

Receivables.   Revenues, and hence **accounts receivable**, are recognized when performance is complete and reasonable assurance exists regarding measurement and collectibility of the consideration.

Receivables are shown at their face value. Any allowance for doubtful debts is shown among liabilities.

Accounts receivable denominated in foreign currencies must be stated at the official buying rate on the invoice date; however, if the official buying rate has decreased when the financial statements are prepared, the closing rate should be used. If the amount has been paid by the time the financial statements are prepared, the accounts receivable must be shown at the official buying rate on the settlement date.

Inventories.   **Inventories** are stated at the lower of cost or **net realizable value**. Methods for assessing cost are actual cost on a **first-in first-out (FIFO)** basis or weighted-**average cost** for purchased inventories, and actual production cost or **standard** direct **cost** for manufactured goods and work in progress. It is not clear whether **last-in first-out (LIFO)** is an acceptable method for assessing the cost of inventory.

Provisions for slow-moving or obsolete inventory are reported among liabilities.

Liabilities.   **Accounts payable** denominated in foreign currency should be stated at the higher of the official selling rate on the date the payment was due or the closing rate. If the balance has been repaid before the financial statements are prepared, the official selling rate on the payment date should be used. If the amount repayable is higher than the amount received, the amount repayable must be shown in "other liabilities" or "overdraft debts" and disclosed in the notes to the financial statements. The difference must be shown in "prepaid expenses."

Capital.   **Share capital** and reserves are disclosed together on the balance sheet under the heading "equity."

Capital reserves may consist of the difference between the amount paid for shares and their **par value** (the **share premium**), any amount permanently transferred to capital reserves and the difference between the value of cash contribution in convertible currency by the foreign party in a **joint venture** company and its value calculated at the exchange rate valid upon its utilization.

Revenue.   Revenue is recognized when performance is complete and reasonable assurance regarding measurement and collectibility of the consideration exists.

There is no specified method for allocating profits on long-term contracts.

Extraordinary Items.   Extraordinary revenues and expenditures should be separately disclosed in the income statement.

Taxation.   Taxation is provided on the taxes-payable method; deferred taxation is not addressed by the legislation.

Pensions.   The pensions system was developed under the centralized planning system. Contributions are determined centrally and are based on gross wages and salaries. Contributions are expensed as incurred.

Contingent Liabilities.   Contingent liabilities must be disclosed in the notes to the financial statements.

Related Party Transactions.   Information on related party transactions is not generally required to be disclosed. However, certain specific transactions and balances must be disclosed. These include fees payable to members of the board of directors, the management and the supervisory board for their activities during the year, and the combined total for each group. The amount of advance payments made and loans granted to members of the board of directors, the management and the supervisory board, and the combined totals for each group, must also be disclosed. The information should include the interest rate and other important terms of repayment, the sums repaid during the year and any guarantee obligations.

POLAND

Introduction
The pace of recovery and reform has increased in Poland with the achievement of a stable government in July 1992. Economic prospects for the near term include a GDP growth of 3 percent and the private sector exceeding 50 percent of the economy by the end of 1993.

Source of Generally Accepted Accounting Principles
Generally accepted accounting principles in Poland are derived from the following sources:

☐   A decree of the Ministry of Finance dated January 15, 1991 on the principles of accounting. These apply to all corporations and to state enterprises. Sole traders and natural persons civil partnerships with **turnover** below a specified amount are exempt. Enterprises with no business activity and that do not receive government grants are also exempt. Banks and enterprises providing insurance services are still under the control of the National Bank and use the previous regulations.

□ The Polish Chamber of Chartered Accountants, which recently published a translation of the International Accounting Standards (IASs). However, the IASs have no legal status and may not supersede local regulations.

□ Commercial Law.

□ Fixed Asset Law.

Audit and Public Company Requirements

Audits. The audit laws of October 1991 require all types of enterprises to appoint an independent, qualified auditor to report on the truth and fairness of the accounting information produced on an annual basis.

There are two types of corporations in Poland: limited liability companies (spólka z ograniczona odpowiedzialnościa—"Sp. z o.o.") and joint stock companies (spólka akcyjna—"S.A.").

The following enterprises must be audited:

□ Joint stock companies.

□ Limited liability companies with more than 50 percent state ownership.

□ Banks (other than cooperative banks).

□ Enterprises providing insurance services.

The regulations contain exemptions for other enterprises based on a size test covering the average number of employees, the balance sheet gross asset value and net sales. To be subject to statutory audit for the year ended December 31, 1992, two of the three following conditions had to be met for the year ended December 31, 1991:

□ Average annual employees in excess of 50.

□ Gross assets in excess of ECU 1,000,000.

□ Net sales in excess of ECU 2,000,000.

A foreign-owned limited liability company must submit a certificate from its auditor to the Local Treasury Chamber before permission will be granted to repatriate dividends outside Poland.

All qualified auditors must register with the Polish Chamber of Chartered Accountants (Krajowa Izba Bieglych Rewidentów), an independent auditing body created by the audit laws. Only Polish qualified auditors (Biegly Rewident) may conduct Polish statutory audits. European Community, US or Canadian qualified accountants may apply for membership, provided they meet certain criteria.

The Polish State Auditing Board sets out the duties and responsibilities of auditors. These relate principally to reporting to the shareholders regarding the truth and fairness of the accounts and the company's compliance with the Ministry of Finance regulations.

Reference. Law Journal 111, 1991.

Public Companies. There are currently 16 quoted companies on the Polish Stock Exchange. Permission to be quoted on the exchange has to be obtained from the Securities Exchange Commission and the Stock Exchange.

Two weeks after the approval of the balance sheet at the shareholders' meeting, management should present to the registry court and the Ministry of Industry and Trade a balance sheet and income statement, report of activities and a copy of the resolution of the shareholders' meeting.

Reference. Commercial Code and Law Journal 21, 1992.

Financial Statements

Basic Accounting Concepts. Financial statements in Poland are prepared using the **historical cost** convention. However, **fixed assets** are periodically revalued by state decree (this is compulsory for state enterprises; private entities may also follow the decree).

- ☐ Transactions are recorded on the **accrual** basis.
- ☐ The commercial substance of a transaction should be followed where it conflicts with the legal form.
- ☐ In general, assets and liabilities should not be netted.
- ☐ In general, **material** items should be separately disclosed and not aggregated.
- ☐ The **going concern concept** is assumed.
- ☐ **Accounting policies** should be applied consistently from one period to the next. Where a change in accounting policy does take place, the full effect of the change should be disclosed.

Contents of Financial Statements. Financial statements normally include a balance sheet, income statement and notes to the financial statements. There is no requirement for a cash flow statement.

Accounting records must be maintained in Polish zloty (pzl), in the Polish language and physically in Poland.

Business Combinations

There is no requirement to prepare **consolidated financial statements** for **subsidiaries** and **associates** inside Poland.

The purchase price of a company (no matter what percentage is acquired) is shown at cost in the balance sheet as a long-term investment. Only profits from the date of acquisition may be distributed as dividends. Losses of the acquired company from the date of acquisition may not be offset against profits of the acquiring company. There is no consolidation of results, assets or liabilities.

Goodwill arising on acquisition of a business (not applicable to the acquisition of shares) is the difference between the consideration paid and the net book values of the assets and liabilities acquired. Goodwill is capitalized and is written off on a **straight-line** basis over a maximum of 10 years.

Disclosure. The method of calculating goodwill on acquisition of a business should be disclosed.

Reference.   Law Journal 10, 1991.

Foreign Currency Translation

The Polish State Central Bank establishes exchange rates for the Polish zloty.

Polish accounting regulations require translation of **foreign currency transactions** at State Bank rates; assets held or denominated in foreign currency must be revalued according to these rates. Exchange rate translation differences are included in the current year's income and expense, except for unrealized exchange gains, which are accounted for as deferred income.

Reference.   Law Journal 10, 1991, and Law Journal 21, 1992.

Changing Prices/Inflation Accounting

There is no Polish accounting standard relating to inflation accounting.

Accounting Changes

Changes in **accounting principles** may be made only in agreement with **accounting standards**. Enterprises may not change their accounting principles during an accounting year or retroactively.

Changes in accounting principles are disclosed in the notes.

Reference.   Law Journal 10, 1991.

Prior Period Adjustments

There is no specified accounting treatment for **prior period adjustments** in Poland. Any adjustments relating to prior periods are reflected in the income statement of the period in which they are discovered.

Post Balance Sheet Events

Adjustments to the accounts should be made or the existence of the event should be disclosed in the notes if the related information becomes available between the year-end and the signing of the accounts. The charge is extraordinary.

Reference.   Law Journal 10, 1991, and Law Journal 21, 1992.

Accounting Principles for Specific Items

Property, Plant and Equipment

General.   An expenditure is classified as a **fixed asset** if the asset will be used for more than one year and the expenditure is greater than 10 million pzl.

Expenditures less than 10 million pzl may be treated as **capital expenditures** provided that the item is not specifically exempted.

Basis of Valuation.   Tangible fixed assets are valued at purchase price or production cost.

Periodic decrees are made to revalue fixed assets according to specified indices. These are not mandatory for nonstate corporations. There is no requirement to write down the value of fixed assets due to a permanent decline in their value.

Depreciation. **Depreciation** is calculated according to a plan chosen by the enterprise based on conditions of use of the related assets.

Higher rates of depreciation may be used for equipment, machinery and motor vehicles (but not company motor cars) that, because of environmental or other factors, have a shorter life span than is normal. For buildings, other special conditions must apply in order to use accelerated depreciation.

Reference. Law Journal 30, 1992.

Intangible Assets

Definition. **Intangible** fixed **assets** may include the following items: patents, licenses, trademarks and similar rights, and goodwill.

Costs of **share capital** formation and computer software are also considered intangible assets.

All intangible assets should be amortized. Costs of share capital formation must be written off over five years, other intangible assets over 10 years. Rates of **amortization** cannot be changed.

Reference. Law Journal 30, 1992.

Leases

All leases are treated as **operating leases**. The lessee treats the rental payments as an expense, and the lessor treats the receipts as income. Only the lessor may capitalize and depreciate the asset.

Reference. Decree by Council of Ministers March 27, 1992.

Investments

Investments held as fixed assets, including subsidiaries and associates, are stated at the lower of cost or market value (if quoted) or directors' valuation (if not quoted) and are accounted for as either long-term or short-term investments in the balance sheet. Polish enterprises need not disclose their subsidiaries or associates in Poland. There are no equity accounting or consolidation accounting regulations.

Reference. Law Journal 10, 1991.

Accounts Receivable

Trade discounts are normally recorded as a reduction of sales **revenue**. Cash discounts are treated as an expense when taken by the customer. A provision for bad debts may be recorded only when the debtor goes into liquidation.

Reference. Law Journal 10, 1991, and Law Journal 21, 1992.

Inventories and Work in Progress

Inventories must be stated at the lower of cost or **net realizable value**. Inventory values may be based on **standard costs, average cost, first-in first-out (FIFO)** and **last-in first-out (LIFO)**. Associated costs of inventory must be included in cost.

There are no specific standards in Poland on accounting for long-term contracts. The excess of the amount of work in progress on long-term contracts over the related progress billings is shown as an asset in the balance sheet. There is no provision for immediate recognition of foreseeable contract losses.

Reference.   Law Journal 10, 1991.

Current Liabilities

General Accounting Treatment.   **Current liabilities** are segregated into the following categories: **creditors**, special funds and accruals.

Creditors include trade creditors, taxation, payroll and intercompany creditors. Most expenses are recorded during an accounting period when they are incurred. Expenses incurred for which payment is not yet due are recorded as accrued liabilities.

Amounts received or due from customers or clients with respect to goods to be delivered or services to be performed should be recorded as deferred income.

Creation of General or Specific Provisions.   It is not acceptable to create general provisions for future losses. Specific provision should be made for liabilities that are known, but whose amount must be estimated.

Disclosure.   Commitments for all significant off balance sheet items such as loan guarantees and discounted bills of exchange must be disclosed separately.

Reference.   Law Journal 10, 1991.

Long-Term Debt

Long-term debt includes long-term bank loans, debenture loans, promissory notes, bank overdrafts and overdue loans.

There is no official Polish standard addressing the accounting for **troubled debt restructuring** or debt extinguishment.

Contingencies

Contingencies are disclosed on the balance sheet in a supplementary note.

Capital and Reserves

Shareholders' equity is generally divided into share capital, reserves and **retained earnings**.

Share Capital.   For limited liability companies, the Commercial Code requires a minimum share capital of 40 million pzl divided into shares each of a minimum nominal value of 500 thousand pzl, which must be fully paid up before registration. For joint stock companies, the minimum share capital is 1 billion pzl, without any minimum nominal value.

Shares in joint stock companies may be issued in excess of nominal value, the premium being allocated to the legal reserve, and must be fully paid up before the company's registration. However, only 25 percent of the nominal share capital need be paid up before registration.

If shares are issued for noncash consideration, the total value must be received before registration. A company's shares may consist of different classes, each of which may have different voting and dividend rights. Generally a company is not allowed to buy its own shares, except to satisfy a claim against creditors who have no other assets and to acquire redeemable shares. Share capital cannot be reduced below the minimal value.

Legal Reserves.   To cover possible losses of a joint stock company, the following are transferred to legal reserves:

☐   8 percent of the net annual profit after tax until the reserve reaches at least one third of the share capital.
☐   **Share premium**.
☐   Any additional amounts paid in by shareholders in consideration of preferences granted by the company.

Other Reserves.   The company's articles may provide for other capital reserves for covering special losses or costs. State enterprises and cooperatives have other types of reserves.

Social and Housing Funds (Reserves).   State enterprises are obligated to provide social and housing funds. This obligation is not necessary for private enterprises.

Accounting Treatment.   Transfers to reserves are made by charges to the profit and loss account for state enterprises. The amount of the charge depends on the average wages for the previous year. State-owned enterprises may also transfer retained profits to these reserves.

Disclosure.   Reserves are shown separately in the balance sheet. Transfers between reserves are disclosed separately.

Distribution Restrictions.   Dividends may be paid only from accumulated retained earnings.

Reference.   Commercial Code.

Revenue

General Principles.   **Revenue** is recognized based on date of the sales invoice.
   Revenue on long-term contracts may be recognized proportionately to the stage of production based on physical completion or according to the **completed contract method**.
   Companies are required to disclose the components and the total amount of turnover in the income statement.

Reference.   Law Journal 10, 1991.

Government Grants
Government subsidies that reduce the cost of products must be recorded in the accounts. The amount of the subsidy and the number of products subsidized should be disclosed.

Reference. Law Journals 43, 76, 75, 31, 58, 61.

Research and Development
Certain research and development expenditures may be capitalized.

Reference. Law Journal 21, 1992.

Extraordinary or Unusual Items

Definition. Extraordinary items are gains or losses that derive from events or transactions that are distinct from ordinary activities and are therefore not expected to recur frequently or regularly. Examples are:

- [ ] Inventory write-offs.
- [ ] Cash or asset losses.
- [ ] Bad debt write-offs and recoveries.
- [ ] Penalty interest received or payable and other penalties or fines.
- [ ] Fixed asset write-offs.
- [ ] Charitable gifts.

Disclosure. Separate disclosure of material extraordinary items is required.

Reference. Law Journal 10, 1991.

Income Taxes
There is no regulation regarding the provision of deferred tax.

In the past, provision for income taxes was calculated on the basis of the accounting income for the period. Beginning in 1992, if a company has adopted an accounting treatment at variance with the Income Tax Department's normally accepted method, adjustments are required to the accounting income to arrive at the taxable income.

The future tax benefit of tax losses carried forward is not accounted for.

Both turnover taxes and income taxes are disclosed separately in the income statement. **Value added tax** (VAT) was introduced in July 1993 and replaced turnover tax.

RUSSIA

The process of reform has been slower in Russia than in other Eastern European countries, and the debate about the course and pace of reform divides politicians throughout the country. This lack of consensus has resulted in slow and often contradictory development of financial legislation.

Some progress has been made in constructing financial legislation that is more in line with Western practices, but many anomalies remain. Furthermore, the existing law is often imprecise, and there is a lack of experience and resources to spell out in detail what is broadly indicated in basic laws. This leaves many businesses unable to gain clarification of where they actually stand under the law. To help rectify this situation, the International Advisory Board for Accounting and Auditing has been set up with funding from the European Community to provide direct technical assistance to the Russian government.

As well as political instability, economic instability undermines the attempt to develop meaningful financial reporting in Russia. Since prices were freed on January 1, 1992, and rose between 10 and 20 times overnight, inflation has continued at an alarming pace. There is no agreement as how to account for the financial statement distortions caused by such inflation.

Source of Generally Accepted Accounting Principles

There has been some progress toward harmonization of Russian accounting law with that of the West. A series of laws and instructions has been issued after several years of consultation with international agencies such as the United Nations. The Chart of Accounts (Order No. 56, dated November 1, 1991) lays down a list of account numbers that all enterprises should use in their accounting systems and defines in some detail the different types of transactions that may appear in each account. **Generally accepted accounting principles** and practices are derived from the Law on Accounting (Order No. 10, dated March 20, 1992), which covers the general principles of financial statement preparation, and is in many ways close to internationally accepted principles, including, for instance, the notion of **matching** revenues and expenses in the period to which they relate. Both of the above apply from January 1, 1992.

The form and content of financial statements were defined by Order No. 38, dated June 9, 1992. This prescribes three statements: balance sheet (form 1), profit and loss account (form 2) and notes to the financial statements (form 5).

The fourth key accounting instruction is Order No. 552, dated August 5, 1992. This detailed instruction defines what costs can be included as costs of production and hence can be deducted from profit before tax. The distinction between tax allowable costs and nonallowable costs is one of the main sources of accounting adjustments between Western and Russian accounts.

Russian financial statements are primarily tax computations that are used by local and national governments for the purpose of assessing taxes due. Providing other parties, such as shareholders, with meaningful information is still not a primary purpose of Russian financial statements. There is accordingly no requirement to publish financial statements and not much legislation in the area of financial disclosure.

There is no concept of **consolidated financial statements** under Russian law.

The law defines the main **accounting concepts** to be applied, including:

☐   Consistency: all policies should be in accordance with the law, and any change in policy should be noted in the financial statements.

☐   **Accrual** basis.

There is no concept of **prudence** under Russian law because prudence implies an exercise of judgment, and Russian law does not recognize the need for judgment in preparing financial statements. Accounting is a matter of clear legal classification of transactions based on documentation.

There is no concept of **going concern** in Russian accounting since it is irrelevant to taxing authorities.

Audit and Public Company Requirements

All enterprises must use the calendar year as their accounting period. The accounts should be audited by an independent auditing company before the end of the following year. This requirement is stated very briefly in the tax law dated December 1991. All enterprises with foreign investments have to submit their financial statements to the local tax inspector by March 15 of the following year.

There is no licensing of auditors, and no qualifications, generally accepted auditing guidelines or standard audit report have been established. There is no law on auditing, although a draft has been under discussion for some time. Progress has been impeded by debate between those who see auditing as a means of state control and those who wish to see a strong independent auditing profession. In these circumstances, the law is open to interpretation by the local tax inspectors.

According to the tax law referred to above, the audit report should confirm two things: that the reported profit is fairly stated, and that the financial statements have been prepared in accordance with the law.

Accounting Principles for Specific Items

Fixed Assets.   **Fixed assets** are stated at historical cost, which is defined as the total material and labor costs expended in their construction. There is no direct reference in the law to the treatment of interest on loans used to acquire assets. However, paragraph 50 of the law states that cost of **inventory** can include interest paid on loans from suppliers. By inference, interest can be capitalized.

Revaluations are generally not permitted. However, in an attempt to bring asset values in line after a period of rapid inflation, Order No. 595, dated August 14, 1992, required all Russian enterprises to revalue their assets according to a table of coefficients set by the government. This increased the costs of assets, and the related accumulated **depreciation**, by up to 25 times.

Depreciation is a tax allowable expense. Therefore, depreciation rates are determined by government norms; only the **straight-line method** is used. Management has no discretion over the estimated useful life of its assets. This is another area that leads to differences between Russian and Western financial statements and renders Russian financial statements less meaningful.

One effect of rapid inflation is to lock in the cost of fixed assets originally bought for hard currency, and hence the rouble amount of depreciation charged each year. Very soon, this rouble depreciation bears little resemblance to the actual, hard currency cost of using the asset.

Intangible Assets.   The new chart of accounts introduced the concept of **intangible assets** into Russian accounts. Thus, license fees, trademarks and other rights are valued on the balance sheet. These assets should be amortized over their expected useful life.

Leased Assets.   The lessor accounts for leased assets as fixed assets at cost. The lessee treats all leases as **operating leases**. Guidelines on accounting for leases are given in Order No. 21, dated April 11, 1990. However, this Order was designed for the process of workers' collectives leasing their enterprise's assets from the State, and not to cover the many types of leasing common in the West.

Investments. Long-term and short-term investments are accounted for at acquisition cost. There is no concept of equity accounting.

Inventories. **Inventories** are stated at actual cost. Methods of determining cost include **FIFO** and weighted-**average cost**. Work in process may be valued at cost of raw materials in production or at planned cost. Finished goods are not normally valued on a line-by-line basis, but in the aggregate in the finished goods control account. The amount is arrived at after considering costs of production and estimated costs of goods sold.

Provisions for obsolescence and slow moving inventory can be made, and the costs written off to the profit and loss account in the period in which they are identified.

Receivables. The law allows sales to be recorded when shipped or at the date of receipt of cash from the customer. The cash basis has been traditional in Russia.

Bad debt provisions can be made based on a line-by-line assessment of the likelihood of collectibility. A provision is set up on the liabilities side of the balance sheet. Provided there is sufficient evidence supporting individual provisions, they will be allowable for tax purposes. General provisions are not allowable for tax purposes.

Amounts due in foreign currencies should be revalued at period-end, using the rate of exchange set by the Central Bank of Russia, which is close to a market rate. An exchange gain arising from the devaluation of the rouble should be recognized in income, and will be taxable even though unrealized. This is an anomaly in the tax law that has yet to be rectified.

Liabilities. Liabilities due in foreign currencies should be revalued at period-end, as outlined above. An exchange loss arising is taken to the profit and loss account and can be used to reduce tax due.

Capital. The statutory fund represents contributions to the enterprise's capital made by its owners in accordance with the foundation documents. The difference between the nominal value of shares issued and money actually paid for them should be recorded in an after-tax reserve account. This implies that **share premium** is not taxable, but clear guidance has not yet been issued by the tax authorities.

Another reserve fund is provided for in the law. Any transfer to this fund until it reaches 25 percent of the value of the statutory fund is eligible for tax relief.

Revenue. One of the most significant pieces of legislation affecting **revenue** is the law on the sale of hard currency revenues (Order No. 7, dated June 29, 1992). This requires all enterprises to sell 50 percent of their hard currency earnings through an authorized commercial bank for roubles at the market rate. This is expected to remain in effect as long as the Central Bank requires dollars to support a weak rouble.

All **foreign currency transactions** have to be recorded at the rate of exchange applicable on the day of the transaction.

The law permits either the cash basis of recording revenue or the accrual basis. This is seen as a transitional arrangement between the old cash basis and the accrual basis of International Accounting Standards. There is no clear guidance on how to account for profit on long-term contracts if the accrual method is adopted.

Expenses. Only a restricted number of expenses can be included in costs of production and hence reduce taxable profit. For instance, there are state norms for travel expenses

(Order No. 61, dated July 27, 1992). Any other business expenditures should be written off directly from post-tax reserves. Many such expenses are charged to reserves, and an analysis of such expenses is a main part of any reconciliation between Russian and Western financial statements.

Extraordinary Items.   There is no concept of extraordinary items in Russian accounting law.

Contingent Liabilities.   There is no concept of contingent liabilities in Russian accounting, and thus no disclosure requirement.

ARGENTINA

GENERAL NATIONAL INFORMATION

1. Source of Generally Accepted Accounting Principles

Generally Accepted Accounting Principles (GAAP). These are derived from authoritative pronouncements of the Argentine Federation of Professional Councils of Economic Sciences (Federación Argentina de Consejos Profesionales de Ciencias Económicas—FACPCE) called Technical Resolutions, as well as from accounting literature. Authority for issuing professional standards is vested in the Professional Councils that function in the various jurisdictions of the country. The Argentine Company Law also contains disclosure rules, and further regulations on the subject have been issued by the regulatory authorities.

2. Audit and Public Company Requirements

Audits. The Corporation Control Authority (Inspección General de Justicia—IGJ) requires the financial statements of all corporations (Sociedades Anónimas or SAs) to be certified by independent auditors. Only in exceptional cases are other types of business entities (such as limited liability partnerships and other partnerships) obligated to be audited.

Generally accepted auditing standards are embodied in Technical Resolution No. 7, which contains suggested procedures for carrying out different kinds of reviews, including audits.

Syndics (statutory auditors) and alternate syndics, who may be either public accountants (contadores públicos) or lawyers, are appointed by the shareholders of a corporation at the annual general meeting. Independent auditors are usually appointed by the board of directors or at the shareholders' meeting. Audit committees are not usual in Argentina.

In the case of companies whose shares are quoted on the Buenos Aires Stock Exchange, the appointment of auditors and approval of their fees occur at the shareholders' meeting. In the case of banks and other financial entities, the auditors are appointed by the board of directors, which must inform the regulatory authority, which is the Central Bank (Banco Central), of the appointment. The reappointment of auditors must also be reported to the Central Bank.

Reference.   Company Law, IGJ Resolutions and Stock Exchange Regulations.

Public Companies.   The Argentine Securities Commission (Comisión de Valores) approves applications for registration on the stock exchanges. Applicants must meet certain basic requirements, such as:

☐   Have a subscribed and paid-up capital above a certain limit, with a par value for all shares that is a multiple of the currency unit.

☐   Have financial and management arrangements satisfactory to the commission.

☐   Have statutes (such as charters or bylaws) conforming to the requirements of the commission, which include the following:
—No series or class of ordinary shares may be deprived of voting rights.
—Election to the post of director may not be restricted to a certain class of stock.
—Total remuneration paid to directors can be no more than 25 percent of total income for the fiscal year.
—Shareholders must have preemptive rights to subscribe for subsequent issues.

Publicly **listed companies** with an annual trading volume of more than 60,000,000 pesos (approximately US $60 million) for their shares, or with more than 1000 shareholders, are required to submit quarterly and annual financial statements that have been duly certified by a public accountant and in the form prescribed by the regulations set by the Argentine Securities Commission and the stock exchanges. Other publicly listed companies are required to follow similar procedures, but only for their annual financial statements. An "informative review," which must be approved by the board of directors, must be included in each filing. The Argentine Securities Commission has issued rules covering accounting valuation and disclosures for companies whose shares are listed on the stock exchanges.

Reference.   Argentine Securities Commission Resolutions No. 195 and 211, and Stock Exchange Regulations.

GENERAL ACCOUNTING

3. Financial Statements

Basic Accounting Concepts.   Inflation accounting has been adopted as a basic accounting concept, as explained in Section 7. The following four fundamental accounting concepts, which stem from common practice, underlie financial statements:

☐   The **going concern concept**.
☐   The **prudence concept.**
☐   The **matching concept.**
☐   The consistency concept. Accounting for similar items within an accounting period and from one period to the next should be consistent.

The following two considerations affect the application of accounting concepts in particular circumstances:

□ **Substance over form**.
□ **Materiality**. Financial statements should disclose all items that are material enough to affect users' evaluations or decisions.

Contents of Financial Statements. The Company Law specifies the general reporting requirements for company financial statements. The Corporation Control Authority has issued detailed regulations governing presentation, as well as the standard format for the basic financial statements and certain mandatory supplementary schedules providing additional data.

Format of Financial Statements/Disclosure. As required by Company Law, the basic financial statements, which must be prepared in constant currency (closing purchasing power) and released annually within specified time limits, comprise a balance sheet (balance general), a statement of income (estado de resultados) and a statement of changes in shareholders' equity (or net worth) (estado de evolución del patrimonio neto).

The Corporation Control Authority distinguishes between two types of corporations: those whose capital stock was more than 2,100,000 pesos on December 31, 1991 and those whose capital was under that amount (Company Law, art. 299).

For the first type, as well as for publicly listed companies, it is mandatory to file a statement of source and application of funds (estado de origen y aplicación de fondos) or a statement of changes in working capital (estado de variaciones del capital corriente). These corporations are also required to present financial statements in comparative format (showing the current year and the previous year).

Certain schedules, which must also be included in the financial package, contain detailed information on the breakdown of certain captions, the activity in certain accounts for the reporting period or a breakdown of expenses by major classifications. Certain significant minimum footnote disclosures are required by the regulations.

Reference. Company Law, IGJ Resolutions and Argentine Securities Commission Resolution No. 195.

4. Business Combinations

Principles of Consolidation. GAAP call for the presentation of **consolidated financial statements** of a controlling entity and its **subsidiaries** when the controlling entity holds sufficient voting rights to make policy decisions at the level of the subsidiaries (more than 50 percent of possible voting rights). These consolidated financial statements constitute additional or supplementary data with respect to the controlling entity's financial statements.

When a subsidiary's activity differs substantially from that of the group as a whole (e.g., banks or insurance companies), GAAP require the use of the **equity method**, including footnote disclosure of the circumstances.

When an investor ceases to control an investee, consolidation is no longer required; this fact must be mentioned in a footnote. Footnote disclosure is also necessary when a new entity is included in the consolidation.

In special circumstances, when effective control is lost or impaired, consolidation, with appropriate footnote disclosure of the facts, is still required.

The financial statements of the entities to be consolidated should be prepared or adjusted to apply consistent accounting criteria for valuing assets and liabilities, measuring results, recognizing inflationary accounting, foreign currency translations and financial statement classification. Intercompany transactions and results should be eliminated, except for any portion attributable to **minority interests** that is considered realized.

Goodwill (Llave de Negocio). Any difference between the price paid for a business acquisition and the net worth of the investee should be allocated to the related asset or liability values when it arises from accounting errors or differences between their book and current value. Any excess should be reflected as **goodwill** or as a current loss, depending on the underlying circumstances, while any shortfall is reflected in a deferred income account (as **negative goodwill**) or as current income, also depending on the underlying reasons for it.

No special rules exist regarding how goodwill should be amortized, but its book value may not exceed its recoverable value.

Equity Accounting (Método del Valor Patrimonial Proporcional). The use of the equity method of accounting for investments in controlled and related companies is obligatory in the investor's financial statements when the investor exercises control over the investee. Control is deemed to exist when the investor holds, either directly or indirectly, more than 50 percent of the voting rights.

When the investor exercises significant influence (although not outright control), the equity method of accounting is also used.

The following circumstances are indicative of exercising significant influence:

☐ Holding sufficient votes to influence the approval of financial statements and the distribution of profits.

☐ Representation on the board of directors or top governing body of the entity, or interchange of executives between the companies.

☐ Participation in policy making.

☐ Existence of significant transactions between the investor and investee (e.g., major supplier or customer) or a situation where the latter is technically dependent on the former.

Minority Interests (Intereses Minoritarios). Minority interests must be disclosed in a separate section of the balance sheet between liabilities and shareholders' equity, unless dividends are anticipated (in which case part of the minority interest is classified as a current liability). The minority interest in the net income or loss should be shown after net operating income and before extraordinary items in the statement of income.

Disclosure. The required disclosure includes: group companies' addresses, shares and percentage of votes held; changes in the entity's composition or activities; intercompany transactions; procedures followed for translation of financial statements originally prepared in a foreign currency; companies accounted for using the equity method and companies fully consolidated; and whether any investee's year-end date differs from the **holding company's** (no more than three months' difference is accepted).

Reference.   Technical Resolutions No. 4, 5, 8, 9 and 10.

5. Joint Ventures

There are no special rules regarding how **joint ventures** should be accounted for by the venturers. However, specific regulatory requirements apply to the recording of the joint ventures' transactions in their own official legal books, and it is becoming a current practice to disclose the transactions from the venturers' standpoint, based on **proportionate consolidation** accounting, not on the equity method.

6. Foreign Currency Translation

There are no specific accounting principles or regulations in Argentina governing the translation of foreign currency financial statements into Argentine currency.

GAAP with respect to consolidations require, among other things, that the financial statements of all the components of the entity be prepared applying similar procedures for restating the figures at closing purchasing power. A common practice is to restate the financial statements at closing purchasing power using a general price-level index of the country where the subsidiary operates, and then to translate the resulting financial statements into Argentine currency using closing exchange rates.

7. Changing Prices/Inflation Accounting

General.   The price-level adjustments required under Argentine GAAP and Company Law are oriented toward restating all the financial statement captions (including the prior periods presented) in terms of currency with the purchasing power prevailing at the end of the reporting period. The general wholesale price index is used for this purpose. For periods beginning on or after January 1, 1993, a new resolution (Resolution 10) applies, which places more emphasis on the utilization of current/**replacement costs** than acquisition costs adjusted for inflation.

Accounting Treatment.   The accounts are classified into **monetary** and nonmonetary **items**.

Monetary items do not require adjustment. Moreover, maintaining them over a period of time produces a loss due to inflation in the case of assets (as their real value diminishes) or a gain due to inflation in the case of liabilities (as the amount diminishes in real terms).

Nonmonetary items are required, however, to be adjusted for inflation. Because they generally fluctuate with inflation, their maintenance leads to neither a gain nor a loss on account of inflation. Nonmonetary captions comprise index-linked accounts receivable and payable, investments, inventories, fixed assets and net worth accounts.

For some captions, the preferred method is to use current/replacement costs. These are explained in Sections 13–20.

The gain or loss on exposure to inflation in the current period is included as a special caption in the statement of income. Income statement items are also restated in constant currency. Income and expenditure items are adjusted from the dates they were generated or incurred, except in the case of assets consumed (e.g., inventories and depreciation of fixed assets), which are recognized as charges to income at amounts based on the inflation-adjusted values of the underlying assets.

In highly inflationary economies, there are other inflationary effects that should be adjusted for. Purchasing and selling prices often include implicit interest designed to cover expected future inflation plus interest up to the payment/collection date. In view of this, implicit interest should be excluded from purchases and sales and the related accounts payable and receivable at the inception date, and accrued as interest expense or income over the life of the related account payable/receivable (see Section 23).

In addition, GAAP provide that the financial income (or expenditure) and exchange gains (or losses) generated by assets and liabilities must be presented in real terms, i.e., net of the inflationary content included in the corresponding interest rates, or the devaluation of the local currency in foreign currency terms.

Reference.   Technical Resolutions No. 6 and 10.

8. Accounting Changes

Accounting Treatment.   A change in **accounting policy** should both be justified and be disclosed by restating comparative amounts and the opening balance of retained earnings.

Disclosure.   A description of the former policy, the new policy and the justification for the change should be provided.

The previous year's figures should be restated and cross-referenced to the note disclosing the change. The effect on equity should be shown as an adjustment of the previous year's figures.

Reference.   Technical Resolutions No. 8 and 10.

9. Prior Period Adjustments (Ajustes de Períodos Anteriores)

Definition.   **Prior period adjustments** arise either from changes in accounting policies (see Section 8) or from the correction of errors.

Accounting Treatment.   Prior period adjustments are accounted for by restating the comparative amounts and the opening balance of **retained earnings**.

Disclosure.   The previous year's figures are restated and cross-referenced to the note disclosing the adjustment.

The effect on equity is shown as an adjustment of the previous year's figures.

The effect of the adjustment on minority interests is also disclosed. When an entity accounts for deferred tax, it should also disclose the tax effect of prior period adjustments.

Reference.   Technical Resolutions No. 8 and 10.

10.   Post Balance Sheet Events

Definition.   Post balance sheet events are events that occur between the balance sheet date and the date on which the financial statements are authorized for issue. Two types are identified: those that provide additional evidence of conditions that existed at the balance sheet date, and those that are indicative of conditions that have arisen subsequent to the balance sheet date.

Accounting Treatment. Conditions that existed at the balance sheet date: Financial statements are adjusted for events occurring after the balance sheet date that provide additional evidence of conditions existing at the balance sheet date, or that make it possible to improve upon estimates contained in the financial statements.

Conditions that have arisen subsequent to the balance sheet date: Financial statements are not adjusted for events occurring after the balance sheet date that do not affect the condition of assets and liabilities at that date.

Disclosure. Significant events, including commitments undertaken by the entity, occurring after the balance sheet date that do not affect the condition of assets or liabilities at the balance sheet date should be disclosed.

Reference. Technical Resolutions No. 8 and 10.

11. Related Party Transactions

Definition. Company Law classifies companies having a degree of common ownership as

☐ Controlling companies (one company has the necessary votes to exercise significant influence over the decisions of another company).
☐ Controlled companies (those in which another company holds control, as above).
☐ Related companies (one company holds more than 10 percent of the capital of another).

Disclosure. Related parties should be disclosed irrespective of whether there have been transactions during the period. If there have been related party transactions, the nature of the relationship, the type of transaction, elements of the transaction necessary for an understanding of the financial statements and the balances should all be disclosed.

Reference. Company Law, art. 33, Technical Resolutions No. 8 and 9.

12. Segmental Information

When an entity has different activities, it is a "recommended" practice (but not compulsory) to disclose the revenues and expenses for each activity in the financial statements or as supplementary information.

When various entities form an economic group that operates in different business segments, segmental information must be provided.

Reference. Technical Resolution No. 9.

ACCOUNTING PRINCIPLES FOR SPECIFIC ITEMS— BALANCE SHEET

13. Property, Plant and Equipment (Bienes de Uso)

General. Property, plant and equipment comprise tangible assets used for business purposes that have an estimated useful life in excess of one year and are not earmarked for sale. The caption also includes items that are under construction and advances to suppliers for **fixed asset** purchases.

Classification of Capital and Revenue Expenditure. Expenditures that represent improvements to fixed assets should be capitalized, whereas repair costs are chargeable to current period expense.

Basis of Valuation. Property, plant and equipment are valued at their original cost plus financing charges (see Section 26), restated in closing purchasing power, net of related accumulated **depreciation** through the end of the current **financial period**. As an alternative, they can be valued on the basis of **current cost**, which considers:

☐ Replacement cost.

☐ Specific indexes used for remeasurement or technical valuations (this option cannot be used by public companies).

Any increase in value resulting from the alternative criteria described above, as compared with the net carrying value stated in closing purchasing power, is accounted for as a capital **surplus**.

The value of the assets in subsequent periods will be that resulting from the restatement of the current cost figures in the closing purchasing power of the corresponding period. The index-adjusted asset values thus determined may not be in excess of their recoverable value, for each group of similar assets. If they are found to be overstated, an allowance should be set up for the difference.

The allowances may be adjusted in subsequent periods to the extent that the situation reverses.

The gain or loss on the sale of a fixed asset is recognized in income and is determined as the difference between the net carrying value of the asset (adjusted cost net of accumulated depreciation) and the selling price.

Depreciation. The most widely used methods of determining depreciation are the **unit-of-production method** and **straight-line** depreciation over the useful life of the asset.

Disclosure. Fixed assets are noncurrent assets; prepayments for fixed asset purchases are also included in this caption.

As supplementary information it is necessary to disclose:

☐ The valuation criteria employed for fixed assets.

☐ The opening balances, changes and closing balances for individual groups of assets, showing original values and accumulated depreciation separately, and classifying the changes according to their nature (additions, deletions, revaluations and current depreciation).

☐ Any restrictions regarding the ability to dispose of such assets.

☐ Any assets pledged as security for a debt, the amount of the debt that they secure, the liability caption in which the debt is included and the nature of the encumbrance.

Reference.   Technical Resolutions No. 6, 9 and 10.

14.   Intangible Assets (Activos Intangibles)

Accounting Treatment.   **Intangible assets** comprise franchises, privileges, patents, copyrights, preoperating and organization costs or similar items, including advances for the purchase thereof, that are neither tangible assets nor claims against other parties, and whose value depends on their potential for producing income.

Valuation.   Intangible assets that are salable (i.e., trademarks, franchises and patents) are valued on the basis of current cost or, if this is not possible, at their restated original cost less accumulated amortization through the end of the current financial period. Other intangibles are valued at their restated original cost less accumulated **amortization**.

Amortization.   Amortization of intangibles depends on the maximum legal or contractual useful life of the asset, as well as other factors, such as the possibility of replacing it or the probable effect of obsolescence on it. It is necessary to write down intangible assets where the asset's ability to produce future benefits has diminished or disappeared.

Disclosure.   Intangible assets and any prepayments relating to them are accounted for as noncurrent assets.

It is necessary to provide supplementary information on the nature of intangible assets; the valuation method used; opening balances, changes and closing balances of the items comprising this caption, showing the original values separately from accumulated amortization; and any restrictions with regard to the ability to dispose of these assets.

Reference.   Technical Resolutions No. 9 and 10.

15.   Leases (Locaciones)

Classification.   There are no specific accounting standards dealing with leases. Both **financial** (capital) **leases** (locación financiera) and **operating leases** are entered into. A financial lease is distinguished by the ability of the lessee to acquire the asset at the end of the lease by making an additional payment.

Accounting Treatment.   It is common practice to treat a financial lease like a purchase that is paid for in instalments.

This involves:

☐   Recognizing the asset (property, plant and equipment or investments, as applicable) at the amount that would have been paid in the event of its cash purchase.

☐   Recording the financial liability at the sum of the instalments to be paid (including the final payment for the purchase option).

☐   Considering the difference between the above-mentioned amounts as deferred interest.

16.   Investments (Inversiones)

Valuation.   Investments may be current or noncurrent, depending on the intended holding period.

Short-term investments: Short-term investments are stated on the basis of their face value, adding or deducting any applicable accrued or unearned income.

Marketable securities: Marketable securities are valued at market quotations at the closing date, less estimated selling expenses. The values so determined are used provided they are representative of the estimated net realizable amounts and do not result merely from temporary market fluctuations.

Gains/Losses: Holding gains or losses on investments, net of their implicit financial components, are recorded as financial income or expense. Sales of investments must be recognized in the financial period in which their ownership is transferred.

Equity in other companies: When the investor has a controlling interest or exercises significant influence, the investment is stated at equity value. If the significant influence condition does not apply, the methods used, in order of preference, are:

☐ Market quotations.
☐ Equity.
☐ Original cost, restated in closing purchasing power.

Disclosure. The following supplementary information is required to be disclosed:

☐ Valuation criteria employed, including the methods used for depreciating real estate properties and movable assets and the methods used for valuing withdrawals of commodities (government securities and others).
☐ An analysis of investments in other companies.
☐ Changes in and an analysis of investments in assets similar in nature to fixed assets, indicating their characteristics, original values, net carrying values and depreciation.
☐ Restrictions on the entity's ability to dispose of assets.
☐ Foreign currency assets, stating their amounts, currency in which they are denominated and closing rate of exchange.
☐ Legal form of rights and obligations.
☐ Interest rates and guidelines for updating the value of the principal loan investments.

Reference. Technical Resolutions No. 9 and 10.

17. Accounts Receivable (Cuentas por Cobrar)

Accounting Treatment. The recognition of **revenues** and related receivables is described in Section 23.

The implicit financial components of such balances should be segregated if significant and if they can be reasonably estimated (see Section 27).

Discounts: Cash discounts granted to customers for prompt payment are treated as financial expenses.

Allowances: No specific method for determining bad debt allowances is prescribed. In practice they are calculated on the basis of an analysis of individual customer balances. Bad debt allowances are shown as deductions from the corresponding receivable account.

Noncurrent receivables are valued at the estimated present value of future cash inflows.

Disclosure. Trade receivables, relating to sales of the goods and services in which the entity normally trades, must be segregated from other types of receivables. Receivables are classified as current or noncurrent, depending on whether they are expected to be converted into cash or cash equivalents within one year. The intention of the entity's governing body is also taken into account.

Supplementary information to be provided includes the valuation criteria; balances denominated in foreign currencies; how the receivables are legally documented; transactions and balances with affiliated, controlled or controlling entities; and changes in the bad debt allowance.

Reference. Technical Resolutions No. 9 and 10.

18. Inventories and Work in Progress (Bienes de Cambio)

General Accounting Treatment. **Inventories** include advances to suppliers with respect to the purchase of assets intended for sale.

Inventories are valued at their replacement or reproduction cost at year end, determined under normal purchase or production terms for that entity, as the case may be, but not in excess of their recoverable value, or, as an exception, at their original cost, restated in closing purchasing power. Recoverable value is the greater of **net realizable value** or the value based on their usefulness to the entity. If this comparison indicates that the adjusted cost is greater than the recoverable value, an allowance must be established.

Readily marketable commodities requiring no significant sales effort are valued based on the closing quotations for them on the market on which they are normally traded (net of normal selling expenses). The values thus determined are recognized provided they are representative of the estimated net realizable value, and not due to temporary fluctuations.

Long-Term Contracts. See Section 23.

Disclosure. Inventories (including advances for their purchase) that are expected to be converted into cash or cash equivalents within one year of the financial statement date are classified as current.

Supplies used for marketing and administration purposes (e.g., samples and office supplies) are shown separately from inventories under "other assets."

Certain supplementary information must be disclosed, including the inventory valuation criteria; the breakdown of the inventories at the financial statement date; restrictions on the entity's ability to dispose of inventories, such as those arising from certain loan contracts; inventories pledged (indicating the caption under which they are classified, their accounting valuation, the amount of the debt for which they have been pledged, the liability caption in which it is included and the nature of the pledge); the breakdown of production costs or the cost of acquiring inventories or services, based on the nature of their components; and the determination of cost of sales.

Reference. Technical Resolutions No. 9 and 10 and Argentine Securities Commission Resolutions.

19. Current Liabilities (Pasivo Corriente)

General Accounting Treatment. Liabilities are commitments that are certain and determined or determinable. They include those due at the end of the financial period, those that will become due or payable within 12 months of the date of the financial statements and accruals set up for meeting contingent obligations that may become certain and payable obligations within the aforementioned 12-month period.

Accounting standards require that the valuation of liabilities should, in general, include the related accrued financial gains or losses up to the end of the period (exchange differences, index adjustments, interest or other applicable items), but not any implicit financial components; any foreign currency liabilities should be translated to Argentine currency at the closing rate of exchange applicable to the settlement of the transaction, bearing in mind the economic facts and other than temporary fluctuations. Liabilities to be settled other than in cash should be stated at the greater of the inflation-adjusted consideration received or the value assigned to the asset that must be delivered in settlement or the goods or services necessary for meeting the liability, if they do not form part of the entity's assets, but are readily obtainable.

Disclosure. The following supplementary information must be provided:

- [ ] Valuation criteria employed.
- [ ] Amounts owed in foreign currency.
- [ ] The legal form of commitments.
- [ ] Balances due to affiliated, controlled or controlling companies.
- [ ] If there are liabilities covered by real[1] guarantees, it is necessary to disclose the assets pledged or mortgaged, the asset caption in which they are included and their book value, the amount of the debt they are securing, the liability caption in which it is included and the nature of the guarantee.
- [ ] Significant commitments undertaken by the entity that are not firm liabilities at the date of the financial statements.

Reference. Technical Resolutions No. 8, 9 and 10.

20. Long-Term Debt (Deuda a Largo Plazo)

General Accounting Treatment. Noncurrent liabilities (those not maturing or payable until after one year from the financial statement date) may be of the same types as **current liabilities** and are valued at the estimated present value of future cash outflows.

Disclosure. The disclosures required for short-term debt also apply to long-term debt.

Reference. Technical Resolutions No. 8, 9 and 10.

21. Contingencies (Contingencias)

General Accounting Treatment. **Contingencies** are classified based on the degree of probability that those circumstances will occur. From this viewpoint, contingencies are classified as either probable, reasonably possible or remote.

---

[1]Real guarantees are defined as all guarantees except personal guarantees.

Contingencies that are classified as probable based on the information available up to the date of issue of the financial statements and that can be reasonably quantified should be given accounting recognition and expensed currently.

Probable contingencies that are not readily quantifiable and contingencies classified as reasonably possible or remote are not given accounting recognition.

Gain contingencies require more careful evaluation. The rules provide that gain contingencies should be accounted for when there is a *high* probability that the event leading to the gain will materialize and, even then, only when its effects may be suitably quantified. Furthermore, the rules call for a detailed explanation in the notes to the financial statements concerning the basis underlying the recognition of the contingencies involved.

Disclosure. The nature and estimated amount of loss contingencies should be disclosed.

When a contingency has been given accounting recognition, the aforementioned elements of it should be disclosed in a note. Footnote disclosure should also be given of the nature of probable and reasonably possible contingencies, indicating that they cannot be readily quantified. When it is possible to estimate the amount of a reasonably possible contingency, this information should be provided.

Reference. Technical Resolutions No. 8, 9 and 10.

22. Capital and Reserves (Patrimonio Neto)

General. The caption comprises capital, reserves and **retained earnings**.

Share Capital. All shares must have the same face value. The share certificates may cover one or more shares.

Both ordinary and **preferred shares** are permitted. The former may be entitled to privileges involving up to five votes per share, provided they do not at the same time enjoy preferential rights. Multiple vote shares may not be issued once the company has been authorized to offer its shares to the public. Preferred shares may enjoy preferential rights with regard to dividends or upon liquidation of the company, but they may not have voting rights (except in certain cases specifically covered or envisioned in the terms of issue).

The corporate capital must be fully subscribed and at least 25 percent must be paid up at the time of incorporation; any stockholders' subscriptions consisting of nonmonetary assets must be fully contributed before the regulatory authority's approval of the incorporation is requested.

Companies are allowed to repurchase their own stock only to retire it following a decision to reduce the entity's capital, in exceptional instances to avoid serious harm to the company, or in connection with a merger. Such stock repurchases may only be made using liquid and realized profits or free reserves. If based on a decision of the board of directors, the board must report its action to the next annual general meeting and justify it.

The corporate capital may be reduced upon the decision of an extraordinary meeting of stockholders, which must be supported by a special report from the syndic, and entails the fulfillment of certain formalities designed to safeguard creditors' rights, unless it is accomplished using profits or free reserves to repurchase fully paid company shares. A reduction of the corporate capital is compulsory when the accumulated loss has eroded all free reserves and 50 percent of the corporate capital.

Reserves. These include:

□ Capital reserves, such as premiums on issue of shares. (Shares may not be issued below par.) The reserve may not be distributed except in the event of a reduction in the corporate capital.

□ Profit reserves, which may be mandatory reserves called for by law, by the company's bylaws or as a result of contractual arrangements.

□ Discretionary reserves, which are set up at the decision of the entity's governing body and should be restated in closing purchasing power terms.

□ Technical revaluation reserves.

Distribution Restrictions. Companies must allocate 5 percent of the liquid and realized profits of each financial year toward a legal reserve until the latter equals 20 percent of the **share capital**. The rest of the entity's profits may be distributed in the form of dividends, either in cash, in kind or in shares.

The terms of issue of some preferred shares may ensure the right to a fixed dividend percentage from the profits of each financial year; this may or may not be cumulative. When such a right is cumulative, no profits may be distributed to the holders of common shares unless the preferred shares have first received their dividend for the period, as well as the outstanding balance of any dividend corresponding to previous years not yet paid.

Disclosure. The net worth caption must be segregated into the following information:

□ Contributions by owners: This comprises the subscribed capital and irrevocable contributions made by the owners (whether capitalized or not and whether made in cash, in the form of assets or in the form of rights) and profits reinvested. The face value of the capital should be shown separately from its inflation adjustment. Premiums on shares issued are shown at their restated value.

□ Reserves and retained earnings: These include profits reserved (whose breakdown must be disclosed), unallocated profits or losses and technical revaluations (the counterpart of the increased value of fixed assets arising from the application of accounting methods that differ from wholesale price indexation).

Reference. Company Law, Technical Resolutions No. 8, 9 and 10.

ACCOUNTING TREATMENT FOR SPECIFIC ITEMS— INCOME STATEMENT

23. Revenue Recognition (Contabilización de Ingresos)

General Principles. For **revenue** to be recognized in a given financial period, the fact or event that substantially generates it must have taken place in that period, the revenue must be measurable as objectively as possible and the risks inherent in the transaction must have been prudently assessed.

The substantial events required for accounting recognition of a sale are, for the sale of goods, the transfer of ownership to the buyer, and, for a service rendered, performance of the service.

Returns. The accounting recognition of sales returns should be reflected in the same period in which the underlying sales occurred. This means that at the end of each financial period it is necessary to estimate the goods that will be returned after the end of that period corresponding to sales made during that period.

Rights of Return. In some exceptional cases, sales of certain goods (such as newspapers and periodicals) are made granting the buyer the discretionary right to return the goods acquired. When the delivery return cycle is short, this type of sale is fairly straightforward from an accounting point of view. When it is longer, a problem arises as to defining the period to which sales revenue should be allocated. The alternatives vary depending on the date of sale or the date on which the right of return expires. Some guidelines that are observed for classifying such transactions are as follows: If the seller grants the buyer the right of return, sales revenue should be recognized on the date of sale only if all the following conditions are met:

- ☐ The selling price is substantially fixed or determinable at the date of sale.
- ☐ The buyer has paid (or is committed to pay) the seller and the commitment is not dependent on the resale of the product.
- ☐ The buyer's obligation to the seller will not change in the event of the theft, physical destruction or damage of the product.
- ☐ The economic substance of the buyer acquiring the product for resale is separate from that of the seller.
- ☐ The seller has no major obligation to take any future action for achieving the resale of the product by the buyer.
- ☐ The amount of the future returns can be reasonably estimated.

Sales and cost of sales that are not recognized at the time of sale because all the aforementioned conditions are not fulfilled should be accounted for when they are fulfilled or when the buyer's right of return has expired, whichever takes place first.

Discounts. Discounts are accounted for under the general criterion that they should be allocated to the financial period in which the underlying sales took place.

Cash Discounts. The discounts offered by sellers to buyers for prompt payment in cash should be deducted from the prices billed in order to arrive at the true costs and selling prices.

Construction Contracts. Some entities' revenue arises entirely or partially from activities involving the construction of assets, for which the earnings process spans more than one financial period. In such cases, the length of the earnings process generates a significant accounting problem of allocating the results of this process to the different accounting periods. These problems are discussed further below.

Typical construction contracts can generally be classified in one of the following groups:

☐ Fixed price contracts (in Argentina, normally denominated in foreign currencies because of its history of inflation).

☐ Fixed price contracts subject to index-linking in order to recognize the effects of inflation on outstanding instalments.

☐ Contracts based on aggregating the actual costs incurred (as defined in the contract) and a profit percentage or fixed fee.

Accounting Treatment. There are various methods for recognizing long-term construction project revenue. The main ones are the **completed contract method** and the **percentage of completion method**. Under the completed contract method, income is recognized only when the project has been substantially finished. Consequently, the costs of contracts in progress and related billings are accumulated in asset and liability accounts over the construction period, and no allocations are made to profit and loss accounts except for possible allowances or reserves for an ultimate loss that is foreseen.

When the percentage of completion method is employed, revenue is recognized as the contract progresses. The percentage of completion is established, unless a better method exists, by relating the costs incurred at the balance sheet date to the total anticipated costs (costs incurred to date plus estimated future costs required to complete the contract based on the most recent available information). Accordingly, the portion of revenue connected with jobs under construction may be recognized as an asset, regardless of whether it has been billed or not. If the estimate of the total cost indicates a loss will arise, an allowance or reserve should be set up for the total loss that will result from the contract.

Regardless of which method is followed, the cost recognized should include an allowance or reserve for disbursements to be incurred after the delivery of the asset under construction for the cost of repairing any defects in construction that may arise.

24. Government Grants and Assistance

Government assistance to private-sector companies is primarily through a reduction in or exemption from income and other taxes for companies operating in specific areas, as well as tax reimbursement on exports.

Any tax reimbursements or abatements directly connected with sales are accounted for as part of sales revenue. When the reimbursements or abatements are connected with both sales revenue and the cost of sales, they must be allocated accordingly. If it is not possible to determine the allocation, the net gain arising from them is added to the net sales profit (gross sales revenue less cost of sales) to arrive at the gross profit.

Reference. Technical Resolution No. 9.

25. Research and Development (Gastos de Investigación y Desarrollo)

There is no specific standard regarding research and development. The following practices are commonly applied:

□ Matching income and related expenses, thereby also determining the accumulated research and development costs to be deferred because they will benefit future financial periods.

□ Ensuring that each such deferred asset account is stated at the lower of its acquisition cost or net recoverable amount, and expensing it if there are significant doubts as to the final feasibility of the project.

26. Capitalized Interest Costs (Intereses Activados)

Accounting Treatment. Expenses generated by the use of third party borrowings to finance construction, production or completion of an asset that extends over a period of time, up to the point when it is ready for marketing, can be used for producing other assets or is started up, as applicable, are deemed part of the cost of the asset.

In this connection, the amount to be recognized is the net result of offsetting all the financing costs and income connected with the project (explicit and implicit interest, inflation adjustments, exchange differences, hedging insurance, gains on the exposure of the related liabilities to inflation, inflationary overpricing, discounts and so forth).

When the entity has elected to capitalize such net financial costs, they must be restated in closing purchasing power in the same way as other costs.

Interest on owners' capital may also be determined, but its disclosure should be considered as additional information and it is not required to be given accounting recognition.

Reference. Technical Resolution No. 10.

27. Imputed Interest

The computation of sales and purchases is straightforward when the price has been fixed in currency values as of the date of the transaction.

However, if the price includes inflationary overbillings and implicit interest, the problem arises as to whether the revenue has in fact been measured in currency values prevailing at the date it was accounted for, or in the purchasing power of the date when it is expected to be collected. In this case, it becomes necessary to segregate the implicit financial charges and recognize an inflation adjustment on the revised figure, as follows:

□ The receivable or payable is recognized net of the implicit interest and inflationary overpricing allocable to future periods, and the related revenue or asset is also accounted for at its net value.

□ The financial charges corresponding to each period are accrued over the life of the **accounts receivable** or **payable**.

Reference. Technical Resolution No. 10.

28. Extraordinary or Unusual Items (Partidas Extraordinarias o Inusuales)

Extraordinary income and expenditure items are items that have occurred during the period and are exceptional and atypical; in addition, they must have occurred infrequently in the past and be expected to occur infrequently in the future.

Disclosure.   Extraordinary items are included in the income statement after ordinary income or loss, net of minority interests and income tax effects (if the deferred income tax method is used).

Individually significant extraordinary items should be separately disclosed either in the income statement or in the notes, with appropriate explanations of their origin.

Reference.   Technical Resolution No. 9.

29.   Income Taxes (Impuesto a las Ganacias)

Accounting Treatment.   Under Argentine GAAP three acceptable methods coexist:

- □   The tax payable method.
- □   The **liability method**.
- □   The **deferral method**.

The balances are classified as current or noncurrent based on the expected reversal date of the underlying timing difference.

Loss Carryforwards (Quebrantos Impositivos Compensables).   Under Argentine law, losses determined for income tax purposes may be carried forward only for offsetting against future years' taxable income arising within the next five fiscal years. There is no carryback of losses. The possibility of giving accounting recognition to loss carryforwards that will reduce income tax amounts payable in future years must be evaluated.

Tax loss carryforwards should be disclosed in a note to the financial statements, mentioning the amount of the loss available for offsetting and how long it will be available.

The tax effect of the offsetting of a loss carryforward is commonly characterized as an extraordinary item.

Recommendation No. 7 limits the establishment of deferred tax assets to the extent that realization is assured beyond any reasonable doubt.

Reference.   Recommendation No. 7 of the Technical Institute of Public Accountants and Technical Resolution No. 10.

30.   Postretirement Benefits (Planes Previsionales)

General.   Company-sponsored pension and other postretirement benefit plans are not common in Argentina, and no formal pronouncements exist on accounting for such plans. However, there is a government pension plan that establishes a mandatory system covering pension benefits. The government pension plan is funded through employer and employee contributions; the employer's obligation is limited to payment of monthly contributions, calculated as a percentage of salaries paid.

31.   Discontinued Operations (Actividades Discontinuadas)

Accounting Treatment.   Supplementary information should disclose details of the discontinued operations and quantify their effect on the components of the basic financial statements (net worth, current income and expenditures, changes in working capital or funds) and on the shareholders' equity or current working capital at the beginning and end of the previous period, as applicable. The supplementary information describing the effect of discontinued operations should refer to the captions subject to change within the basic financial statements.

Reference.   Technical Resolution No. 8.

32.   Earnings per Share (Utilidad por Acción)
There is no requirement to disclose earnings per share in Argentina.

Appendix
DO ARGENTINEAN STANDARDS OR PREVALENT PRACTICE SUBSTANTIALLY COMPLY WITH INTERNATIONAL ACCOUNTING STANDARDS?

Section	Topic	Substantially complies with IAS?	Comments
3.	Basic accounting concepts and conventions	Yes	Except that in some instances gains and losses are recognized earlier than under IAS 15
	Contents of financial statements	Yes	Except that a statement of changes in financial position and comparative figures for the previous period are required only by large or public companies
4.	Business combinations*	Yes	Except that there are no specific rules regarding the amortization of goodwill
5.	Joint ventures	Yes	Not covered by Argentine standards, but prevalent practice complies
6.	Foreign currency translation*	Yes	Not covered by Argentine standards, but prevalent practice complies, except that all exchange differences are charged to the profit and loss account
8.	Accounting changes*	Yes	
9.	Prior period adjustments*	Yes	
10.	Post balance sheet events	Yes	
11.	Related party transactions	No	Those parties deemed to be related are fewer than under IAS 24
12.	Segmental information	No	
13.	Property, plant and equipment*	Yes	
15.	Leases	Yes	Not covered by Argentine standards, but prevalent practice complies
16.	Investments	Yes	Except that the equity method may be used to

Appendix (*Continued*)

Section	Topic	Substantially complies with IAS?	Comments
			account for investments in companies over which significant control is not exercised
17.	Accounts receivable	Yes	Except that a finance charge may be imputed as part of the receivable
18.	Inventories and work in progress*	Yes	
19.	Current liabilities	Yes	
20.	Long-term debt	Yes	
21.	Contingencies	Yes	Except that contingent gains may be accrued if realization is highly probable
22.	Capital and reserves	Yes	
23.	Revenue recognition*	Yes	
24.	Government grants and assistance	NCE	The only government assistance provided is through tax incentives
25.	Research and development*	No	
26.	Capitalization of interest costs*	No	Argentine standards allow the capitalization of interest on owners' capital on long-term construction projects
28.	Extraordinary or unusual items*	Yes	
29.	Income tax**	No	
30.	Postretirement benefits*	NCE	

*These topics are subject to change as a result of the IASC Improvements Project—see the appendix to the International Accounting Standards chapter.

**The IAS on accounting for taxes on income is currently being revised, and an exposure draft has been issued.

NCE—Not commonly encountered in Argentina.

Comparison in this table is made to International Accounting Standards in force at January 1, 1993. For further details, see the International Accounting Standards chapter.

AUSTRALIA

GENERAL NATIONAL INFORMATION

1. Source of Generally Accepted Accounting Principles

Generally accepted accounting principles in Australia are derived from the following sources:

☐ Australian Companies Legislation (known as the Corporations Law and Regulations). This legislation provides for the regulation of companies in Australia and sets out in Schedule 5 of the Regulations (Schedule 5) various disclosure requirements for corporate entities.

☐ Annual Reporting Acts, or their equivalents. These set down the general accounting requirements for public-sector reporting entities.

☐ Statements of Accounting Concepts (SACs). These are issued by the Australian Accounting Research Foundation (AARF) on behalf of the two Australian accounting bodies, The Institute of Chartered Accountants in Australia and the Australian Society of Certified Practising Accountants, and compliance with them is required of directors and auditors who are members of these professional bodies. SACs are discussed further in Section 3.

☐ Australian Accounting Standards (AASs). Issued by the AARF, these cover public-sector reporting entities and noncorporate reporting entities in the private sector.

☐ **Accounting standards** issued by the Australian Accounting Standards Board (AASBs). Companies are required to comply with these accounting standards by virtue of provisions in the Corporations Law. The AARF provides technical support for the Board.

☐ Accounting Guidance Releases (AAGs). Issued by the AARF to assist in the interpretation of particular standards and to give early guidance on emerging issues. They do not establish new **accounting concepts** or standards and do not amend existing concepts or standards.

☐ Undocumented **accounting principles** or practices that are commonly accepted.

2. Audit and Public Company Requirements

Audits.   The Corporations Law requires that all companies be audited by registered company auditors. The only possible exception relates to exempt **proprietary companies**, which may elect, if all the members agree, not to appoint an auditor.

Registered company auditors must be members of one of the two professional accounting bodies in Australia or have a degree from a recognized tertiary institution that includes appropriate studies of accounting and company law; and have at least three years practical experience (including specific experience in auditing). They cannot be officers of the company, or partners, employers or employees of an officer. They also cannot be indebted to the company for more than $5000.

Auditors are initially appointed by the directors and remain in office until the first annual general meeting after appointment, at which time a general resolution of the shareholders is required for reappointment. Once appointed, the auditors continue in office until the shareholders decide to appoint new auditors. This action requires the approval of the Australian Securities Commission (a federal body that administers the Corporations Law) before it becomes effective.

The Corporations Law sets out the basic duties and responsibilities of auditors, which relate principally to reporting to the shareholders on the truth and fairness of the financial statements and on the company's compliance with the requirements of the Corporations Law. It also prescribes the basic format for the auditors' report. These basic obligations are amplified by the professional accounting bodies, which issue Statements of Auditing Standards (AUS), Statements of Auditing Practice (AUP) and Auditing Guidance Releases (AuGR). AUS 1 sets out the basic principles under which audits are conducted (covering such issues as independence, confidentiality and required level of skill), while the AUPs and AuGRs provide authoritative guidance on the auditing procedures to be followed to ensure that the auditing standards are correctly applied.

Compliance with the requirements of professional statements is mandatory for members of the professional bodies.

Reference. Corporations Law s.324–334, 1278–1280; AUS 1; AUP 1-33; and AuGR 1-10.

Public Companies. **Public companies** seeking to trade their shares in Australia must apply for listing on the Australian Stock Exchange Limited (ASX), the controlling body for the stock exchanges located in the capital city of each state. The ASX establishes and enforces reporting requirements and a code of behavior for **listed companies**. These requirements are in addition to the normal statutory requirements imposed on companies, and the ASX has the power to enforce compliance with its rules by delisting companies that do not meet its requirements.

Admission requirements: The requirements for obtaining a listing on the ASX vary depending on whether the company is an industrial, mining or trust management company, and on whether it is an Australian or foreign-owned entity. The main requirements for an industrial company are:

□ A minimum of 500 shareholders each owning shares having a value of at least $2000.

□ Net tangible assets of at least $2 million, or an aggregate operating profit before tax over the past three years of $1 million, with at least $400,000 earned in the 12 months immediately preceding listing.

Continuing reporting requirements: Once admitted, a company has to comply with ASX listing rules, which include requirements to notify its local exchange of certain actions such as changes in business activities, the acquisition or disposal of major assets and changes in key personnel.

There are also requirements to produce half-yearly and annual financial information. The annual information includes the company's financial statements as prepared under the Corporations Law.

Listed companies must file their financial statements with their local stock exchange annually, within four months of the end of the **financial period**, and must provide details of their results every six months, within 75 days of the close of each half-yearly period.

In addition, companies that borrow money from the public (borrowing corporations) must submit audited financial statements to the Australian Securities Commission every six months.

Annual financial statements, once prepared, must be approved at a directors' meeting, signed by the directors, have an audit report attached and be presented to and adopted by the company's annual general meeting within five months of the year-end. They must then be filed with the Australian Securities Commission as part of the company's annual return.

Reference.   ASX Official Listing Rules Sections 1 and 3, and Corporations Law s.245,316.

GENERAL ACCOUNTING

3.   Financial Statements

Basic Accounting Concepts.   The basic concepts underlying the selection of **accounting policies** and the preparation and presentation of financial information are contained in Statements of Accounting Concepts issued by the AARF.

SAC 1, *Definition of the Reporting Entity*, defines and explains the concept of a reporting entity and establishes a benchmark for the minimum required quality of financial reporting for such an entity. SAC 1 specifies that reporting entities are to prepare general purpose financial reports that comply with Statements of Accounting Concepts and accounting standards.

SAC 2, *Objective of General Purpose Financial Reporting*, states that the purpose of financial reporting is to provide information to users that will help them make decisions about the allocation of scarce resources.

SAC 3, *Qualitative Characteristics of Financial Information*, explains in more detail the qualitative characteristics that such financial information must have to achieve this end and that therefore must be taken into consideration when accounting policies and disclosures are considered.

These qualitative characteristics are classified between those related to the selection of financial information for inclusion in financial reports—relevance and reliability—and those related to the presentation of those reports—comparability and understandability.

SAC 3 also considers the role of **materiality** as a test of admission of information into an entity's statements and the constraints on an entity's ability to provide relevant and reliable information, that is, the time requirements and the relativity of the costs and benefits involved.

SAC 4, *Definition and Recognition of the Elements of Financial Statements*, establishes definitions of the elements of financial statements and specifies criteria for their recognition. It also provides guidance regarding the application of accounting concepts to particular accounting issues.

SAC 4 applies to reporting entities in the private and public sectors for the first reporting period ending on or after June 30, 1995. However, its existence is expected to significantly influence financial reporting practices, and even the contents of specific accounting standards, before then.

In addition to the broad general guidelines contained in the Statements of Accounting Concepts, specific accounting standards give additional guidance on selecting accounting policies appropriate for the preparation of financial information.

These standards presume that financial statements will be prepared in accordance with **historical cost accounting** and the **going concern concept**. In the case of private-sector financial statements, the **accrual concept** is also presumed. However, the adoption of these bases is not mandatory. Departures from historical cost accounting are permitted for noncurrent assets (which can be carried at valuation); departures from the accrual and going concern concepts occur only in unusual circumstances and require explanation.

Contents of Financial Statements. Companies are required under the Corporations Law and accounting standards to prepare financial statements comprising a profit and loss account, balance sheet, statement of cash flows and related notes.

The financial statements must be prepared so as to give a true and fair view of the company's profit or loss and state of affairs (financial position) and must be accompanied by a directors' statement (signed by two directors) and an audit report commenting on the truth and fairness of the information. If the company is a **holding company**, similar consolidated information must also be presented.

Financial statements of reporting entities other than companies usually contain similar information to that described above.

Format of Financial Statements. The financial statements should be prepared in accordance with applicable accounting standards and, in the case of companies, with the requirements of Schedule 5. Schedule 5 prescribes a variety of information that must be disclosed and, in particular, requires a specified format for the presentation of this information in the profit and loss account and balance sheet, including specified headings. Departures from this fixed format are permitted only if it can be demonstrated that adopting the fixed format would impair the true and fair view given by the financial statements and if supporting reasons are given by the directors.

Statements of cash flows, reported using the **direct method**, are required by accounting standards. Cash flows are to be presented so as to provide users with relevant information about the operating and other activities, appropriately classified, of the entity. The view adopted in the standards is that profit-seeking entities normally would need to distinguish between cash flows from operating, investing and financing activities.

Disclosure of Accounting Policies. A reporting entity must describe in its financial statements all material **accounting policies** that have been adopted in their preparation. However, the going concern concept and, for private-sector financial statements, the accrual concept need be mentioned only if they are not used and the effect is material. For public-sector reporting entities, the summary of accounting policies needs to identify the statutory reporting requirements, ministerial directives or other government authority that has determined accounting policies. The summary of accounting policies should be located in the initial section of the notes to the financial statements.

Reference. Corporations Law s.292–310; Schedule 5; AASB 1001/AAS 6; AASB 1018/AAS 1; AASB 1026/AAS 28; and SACs 1–4.

4. Business Combinations

Principles of Consolidation. The Corporations Law and accounting standards require the **parent** entity in an economic entity to prepare consolidated information. The notion of control rather than ownership is the criterion for identifying the existence of a parent entity/controlled entity (**subsidiary**) relationship and the requirement to prepare **consolidated financial statements**.

Accounting Treatment of Business Combinations. Only the **purchase method** is permitted. Cost is determined by reference to the fair value of shares or assets exchanged in the acquisition.

Control. Control is defined as the capacity of an entity to dominate decision making, directly or indirectly, in relation to the financial and operating policies of another entity so as to enable that other entity to operate with it in pursuing the objectives of the controlling entity. The requirement to prepare one set of consolidated financial statements applies even if:

☐ Control is temporary.
☐ Dissimilar activities are conducted by member entities.
☐ The parent entity holds only a minority ownership interest in the subsidiary.

Goodwill. A distinction is drawn between purchased **goodwill** (which includes consolidated goodwill) and internally generated goodwill. Internally generated goodwill should not be recorded. Purchased goodwill is defined as the difference between the fair value of the consideration given and the fair value of the identifiable net assets acquired. It can arise through the acquisition of a business entity or part thereof, the assets therein or some or all of the shares in another entity. Purchased goodwill should be:

☐ Measured as the excess of the fair value of assets given up over the fair value of the identifiable net assets acquired.
☐ Recognized as an asset at acquisition and included in the financial statements as an intangible noncurrent asset.
☐ Amortized by systematic charges to income over the period the company is expected to benefit from it, which in any event should not exceed 20 years.

To the extent that the excess of the fair value of assets given up over the fair value of the net assets acquired does not represent goodwill, the amount should be written off to the profit and loss account immediately.

Negative goodwill should be accounted for by reducing proportionately the fair values of the nonmonetary assets acquired until the negative goodwill is eliminated.

Equity Accounting.   Disclosure is required in the notes to the financial statements of certain information in relation to **associated companies**. This information is determined in accordance with the principles of the **equity method** of accounting. The use of the equity method in the accounting records of a company or group of companies is not permitted. Consequently associates must be accounted for using the cost method, with only dividend income recognized in the profit and loss account.

If an investor holds 20 percent or more of the voting power in an investee, this leads, in the absence of evidence to the contrary, to a presumption that the investor has significant influence over the investee. Significant influence means the capacity of an investor to affect substantially either, or both, the financial and operating policies of an investee. Representation on the board of directors is indicative of such capacity, but is neither conclusive evidence of it nor the only method by which the investor may be capable of exercising significant influence.

Minority Interests.   The outside equity interest in operating profit and extraordinary items is shown as a separate line item deducted on the face of the profit and loss account in arriving at operating profit attributable to members of the holding company. The outside equity interest in subsidiaries is disclosed in the shareholders' equity section of the balance sheet, identifying separately the capital, **retained earnings** or accumulated losses and reserves components of that amount.

Reference.   Schedule 5; AASB 1016; AASB 1018/AAS 1; and AASB 1024/AAS 24.

Disclosure.   Consolidation: Detailed disclosures are required in the consolidated financial statements relating to parent entities and subsidiaries, including their identities, countries of incorporation, ownership interests, acquisitions and disposals, contributions to the consolidated profit or loss, and gains and losses on new issues of shares by subsidiaries. The accounting policy adopted for goodwill and details of amortization are required to be disclosed.

Equity accounting: In addition to the equity accounting information required in the notes (including share of retained profit and other reserves, and dividends), detailed information about associated companies should be disclosed, including activities, balance sheet date, post balance sheet events and dissimilar accounting policies, together with details of the investors' ownership interest.

Reference.   Corporations Law s.46; Schedule 5; AASB 1007/AAS 12; AASB 1015/AAS 21; AASB 1016; AASB 1024/AAS 24; and ASX Official Listing Rule 3C.

5.   Joint Ventures

Accounting for Interests in Joint Ventures.   Standards covering accounting for and disclosure of information about interests in **joint ventures** are set out in AASB 1006/AAS 19, *Accounting for Interests in Joint Ventures*. It should be noted that the definition of joint venture set out in AASB 1006/AAS 19 differs from the definition in International

Accounting Standard (IAS) 31, *Financial Reporting of Interests in Joint Ventures*, which is the definition in the Glossary at the end of this book.

AASB 1006/AAS 19 defines a joint venture as an unincorporated contractual association, other than a partnership or a trust, between two or more parties to undertake a specific business project in which the venturers meet the costs of the project and receive a share of any resulting output. The concept of **joint control**, as referred to in IAS 31 and the Glossary, is not referred to in AASB 1006/AAS 19. The other major difference between the definitions is that in Australia a joint venture must be an unincorporated contractual association other than a partnership or a trust.

Interests in joint ventures are accounted for by including in the financial statements, in their respective classification categories:

□ The venturer's share in each of the individual assets employed in joint ventures.

□ Any liabilities incurred by the venturer in relation to joint ventures.

□ The venturer's share of any costs incurred by the joint venturers.

Jointly Controlled Entities.   Jointly controlled entities are not covered by AASB 1006/AAS 19. Interests in such entities are accounted for as investments (see Section 16). Where a jointly controlled entity is a company, it will usually satisfy the definition of an associated company, in which case the disclosures discussed in Section 4 apply.

Transactions Between Venturers and the Joint Venture.   The accounting treatment by venturers of contributions to and other transactions with a joint venture is as described in IAS 31.

Accounting by Joint Ventures.   Generally accepted accounting principles apply to all assets and liabilities and operations of joint ventures. A joint venture is permitted to change its basis of accounting, but would need to keep sufficient records to satisfy the accounting needs of all venturers.

Disclosure.   For interests in joint ventures as defined in the Australian standards, the following disclosures are required:

□ The share of assets employed in all joint ventures, categorized as current or non-current and shown by class of assets.

□ Contingent liabilities and capital expenditure commitments with respect to all joint ventures.

□ For each interest in a joint venture, identification of the joint venture, a description of its principal activities and the venturer's percentage interest in its output.

Corporations listed on the ASX, borrowing corporations and companies whose gross assets exceed $10 million or whose gross revenues exceed $20 million must disclose additional detailed information about interests in corporations that are individually material and interests in material business undertakings that are carried on other than as corporations. The additional disclosures are summarized in Section 16.

Reference.   Schedule 5; AASB 1006/AAS 19; and AASB 1016.

6.   Foreign Currency Translation

Foreign Currency Denominated Transactions.   Each asset, liability, **revenue** or expense arising from entering into a **foreign currency transaction** should initially be measured and recorded in the domestic currency using the exchange rate in effect at the date of the transaction. Foreign currency **monetary items** outstanding at the balance sheet date should be translated at the spot rate then current.

Exchange differences relating to monetary balances should generally be recorded in the profit and loss account in the period in which the exchange rates change. The only exception to this rule relates to monetary items that are related to the acquisition of the service potential of assets being constructed by or for the company. These assets are known as qualifying assets and until such time as they are ready for use by the company, exchange differences on any related monetary item can be included in their acquisition cost.

Exchange differences relating to foreign currency monetary items forming part of the net investment in a **self-sustaining foreign operation** should be accounted for in the same way as other monetary items; on consolidation, they should be transferred to a reserve designated as a foreign currency translation reserve.

Foreign Operations.   The financial statements of a self-sustaining foreign operation should be translated at the reporting date using the **current (exchange) rate method**. Any exchange difference should be charged or credited directly to the foreign currency translation reserve.

The financial statements of an **integrated foreign operation** should be translated using the **temporal method**. Resulting exchange differences from translating monetary items should be recorded in the profit and loss account in the period in which the exchange rates change.

Average or standard exchange rates may be used provided that the effect of their application is not materially different from that of actual rates.

Hedges.   A transaction should be classified as a **hedge** of a specific foreign currency exposure only if it is expected to continue to be effective as a hedge. Exchange differences on transactions undertaken to hedge foreign currency exposure should, except as noted below, be recorded in the profit and loss account in the period in which the exchange rates change. Any losses (costs) or gains arising at the time of entering into hedge transactions should, if material, be accounted for separately from the exchange differences on the hedge transactions and be recorded in the profit and loss account over the lives of the hedge transactions.

For transactions intended to hedge the purchase or sale of goods or services, exchange differences (to the extent that they occur up to the date of purchase or sale) and losses (costs) or gains arising at the time of entering into the transactions should be deferred and included in the measurement of the purchase or sale.

Disclosure.   The financial statements should disclose details of the treatment and amount of exchange differences, changes in the foreign currency translation reserve and foreign currency exposure at the reporting date.

Reference. AASB 1012/AAS 20.

7. Changing Prices/Inflation Accounting

General. The accounting bodies have issued a Statement of Accounting Practice (SAP) entitled *Current Cost Accounting* (CCA), which deals with methods of calculating and reporting the effects of changing prices. Application of the statement is recommended but not mandatory.

CCA supplementary financial statements should include a profit and loss statement, a balance sheet, a statement of change in shareholders' equity and explanatory notes.

Reference. SAP 1.

8. Accounting Changes

Accounting Policies. When a reporting entity changes an accounting policy to comply with a statutory requirement, an accounting standard or an accounting concept that specifically requires an accounting entry to give retroactive effect to the changed method of accounting, the resulting gain or loss should be adjusted directly against retained profits or accumulated losses at the beginning of the period in which the change is made.

Disclosure. Adequate disclosure of a change in accounting policy should be made in the financial statements, including the nature of the change, reason and financial effect, if material or expected to become material.

Reference. AASB 1001/AAS 6 and AASB 1018/AAS 1.

9. Prior Period Adjustments

General Principles. Retrospective adjustments to prior period reported figures are not permitted other than those arising from reclassifications necessary to ensure consistency of presentation in comparative balance sheets.

Accounting Treatment. Adjustments applicable to prior years should be included in operating profit for the current period and, if material, separately disclosed as either abnormal or extraordinary items, depending on the circumstances. The only exception is when a business entity changes an accounting policy for the reasons described in Section 8.

Reference. AASB 1018/AAS 1.

10. Post Balance Sheet Events

Accounting Treatment. Financial statements should be prepared on the basis of conditions existing at the reporting date. The financial effect of an event occurring after the reporting date should be recognized in the financial statements if:

□   The event assists, by further elucidating conditions that existed at the reporting date, in determining an amount that was uncertain at the reporting date; or

□   The event leads to a different assessment of an amount properly attributable to an item at the reporting date, by revealing for the first time a condition that existed at that date.

A post balance sheet event that does not satisfy either of the above criteria should not be recognized in the financial statements. However, such an event (e.g., a major acquisition or disposal) should be disclosed in a note, if material.

Disclosure.   For material post balance sheet events not recognized in the financial statements, disclosure in a note must include a description and an indication, where possible, of the financial effect of the event, and a statement that the event occurred after the reporting date and that its financial effect has not been recognized in the financial statements.

In addition, the directors' report accompanying the financial statements must include details of any matters that have arisen since the end of the financial year that have affected or may significantly affect the company's or the group's operations, results and state of affairs in any ensuing financial period.

Reference.   Corporations Law s.304(10), 305(10); and AASB 1002/AAS 8.

11.   Related Party Transactions

Definition.   Parties are considered related if one has control or significant influence over the other. Related parties include directors, spouses of directors, relatives of directors and entities under the control or significant influence of directors, spouses of directors or their relatives.

Accounting Treatment.   Related party transactions commonly occur as part of the activities of many reporting entities. Frequently such transactions are conducted as part of normal operations and are accounted for on a normal commercial basis. In other circumstances, the amounts ascribed to related party transactions may be more or less than their fair values or such transactions may not be recorded at all.

Disclosure.   Accounting standards require disclosure of material related party transactions with specified classes of related parties, including, in most cases, the nature of the terms and conditions of each different type of transaction and aggregate amounts for each combination of type of transaction and nature of terms and conditions. Numerous specific disclosures are required, including information on **directors' emoluments** and other director-related disclosures such as loans and pensions. Director-related disclosures are deemed material regardless of the amounts involved.

Reference.   Schedule 5 and AASB 1017/AAS 22.

12.   Segmental Information

General.   All companies should disclose segmental information, on the basis of both industry and geographical location. Only material segments are required to be disclosed.

A segment is material if its revenue, profits or assets represent more than 10 percent of the total revenue, profits or assets of the company or group of companies. Sufficient individual segments must be identified to ensure that the reportable segments constitute at least 75 percent of the total revenue, expenses and assets. One segment is acceptable only if it constitutes over 90 percent of revenue, profits and assets. The determination of material segments should also take into account interperiod comparability.

Generally, interest income and interest expense are not included in segment disclosures but constitute a reconciling item between the individual segment disclosures and the total figures reported in the financial statements. Similarly, extraordinary items and income taxes are normally not considered to be part of segment disclosures.

Disclosure.   For each individual segment identified (both geographical and industrial), a general description and details of revenue, profits, asset values and the basis of inter-segment pricing should be disclosed.

Reference.   AASB 1005/AAS 16.

ACCOUNTING PRINCIPLES FOR SPECIFIC ITEMS— BALANCE SHEET

13.   Property, Plant and Equipment

Classification of Capital and Revenue Expenditure.   Expenditures other than **capital expenditures** are expensed as incurred.

Basis of Valuation.   **Fixed assets**, which include property, plant and equipment, are generally carried at depreciated historical cost or at a revalued amount, provided that the net book value of an individual asset does not exceed its recoverable amount. For this purpose recoverable amount means the amount expected to be recoverable from the total cash inflows less relevant cash outflows from its continued use or through its sale.

If a company chooses to revalue its fixed assets upward, the entire class of assets must be revalued on a consistent basis to an amount that is not in excess of the recoverable amount. Any accumulated **depreciation** relating to that class at the date of revaluation must be deducted from the asset account and the net amount revalued. Depreciation should then be provided on the basis of the revalued amount. A downward revaluation is permitted only if the carrying amount is greater than the recoverable amount; the asset should be revalued to its recoverable amount.

Both purchased and self-constructed assets are permitted to be capitalized at a cost that fairly reflects expenditures necessarily incurred to bring the assets to their present location and a condition ready for use. Interest and overhead on self-constructed assets may be capitalized provided that it can be demonstrated clearly that these are costs of making the asset ready for use.

If fixed assets are disposed of, the proceeds should be compared with their net book value (based on depreciated original cost or revalued amount) and the resulting gain or loss (unless it qualifies as an extraordinary item) should be reflected in operating profit before income tax and disclosed separately, if material. Provision should be made for any capital gains tax payable.

Depreciation. The method of depreciation selected should be appropriate to the type of asset and reflect the using up of the asset's service potential. The two most common methods are the **straight-line method** and the **diminishing balance method**. Depreciation rates and the underlying assessment of useful life should be reviewed annually.

Disclosure. The accounting policies adopted in relation to valuation and depreciation of fixed assets must be disclosed. In addition, details of cost, depreciation and valuations of each class of fixed asset must be shown.

If an interest in land and buildings is not included in the accounts at current value, corporations listed on the ASX, borrowing corporations and companies whose gross assets exceed $10 million or whose gross revenues exceed $20 million must disclose the current value in a note. Current value means the most recent valuation made within three years of the current year-end.

Reference. Corporations Law s.294(4); Schedule 5; AASB 1001/AAS 6; AASB 1010/ AAS 10; and AASB 1021/AAS 4.

14. Intangible Assets

Accounting Treatment. The most common **intangible assets** recognized in the balance sheet are technology-based (patents, trademarks, licenses), media-based (newspaper and magazine mastheads and TV and radio licenses), brand names and distribution rights.

In determining whether it is appropriate to identify and capitalize an intangible asset, the following factors are normally considered:

☐   Does it convey a right capable of enforcement?
☐   Is it capable of producing revenue in its own right?
☐   Is it capable of being sold separately without disposing of the business as a whole?

Valuation. Intangible assets are valued essentially the same way as other noncurrent assets. Intangible assets are accounted for at their purchase price or production cost. They are carried forward on the balance sheet as long as they provide a measurable future economic benefit controlled by the entity.

Intangible assets may be revalued in the same way as other **capital assets**. However, the directors are required to ascertain whether any noncurrent asset is recorded at an amount that exceeds what it would have been reasonable to expend to acquire that asset at the end of the financial year. Similarly, a noncurrent asset should not be carried at an amount in excess of the recoverable amount.

Amortization. If intangible assets have a finite useful life, or it can be demonstrated that an asset's recoverable amount is declining, it is usual practice to amortize the recorded amount over the useful life of the asset to the net amount expected to be recovered on its sale.

However, it is sometimes argued that intangible assets have an infinite economic life, or that their residual value can be maintained at its current level by expenditures designed to lengthen their life, and that therefore the amount of **amortization** required is minimal (if any).

Disclosure.   Separate disclosure of intangible assets is required on the face of the balance sheet. In addition, amounts of goodwill and patents, trademarks and licenses included in intangibles; the total amount of amortization charged; and the relevant accounting policies adopted must be shown.

Reference.   Corporations Law s.294(4); Schedule 5; AASB 1001/AAS 6; AASB 1010/AAS 10; AASB 1013/AAS 18; AASB 1021/AAS 4; and AAG 5.

15. Leases

Classification.   A **finance lease** is one whereby the lessor effectively transfers to the lessee substantially all the risks and benefits incident to ownership without actually transferring legal ownership. An **operating lease** is one in which the lessor effectively retains these risks and benefits.
   The following are indications that a lease transfers the risks and benefits of ownership:

- ☐ The lease is not cancellable, *and*
- ☐ Ownership is transferred at the end of the lease term; or
- ☐ The lease contains a bargain purchase option; or
- ☐ The lease term is for 75 percent or more of the useful life of the lease property; or
- ☐ The present value of minimum lease payments is equal to or greater than 90 percent of the fair value of the leased property.

A lessor must classify finance leases as sales-type or direct finance leases. A sales-type lease is one in which the lessor also acts as manufacturer or merchant rather than solely as financier. All other finance leases are direct finance leases.

Accounting Treatment.   Finance leases (lessee): A lessee is required to separately capitalize as a noncurrent asset each finance lease at its fair value at the inception of the lease, along with a corresponding lease liability. For each period, lease payments should be allocated between interest expense and the principal lease liability component according to the implicit rate of interest in the lease. The leased asset should be amortized over its useful life in the same way as other noncurrent assets.
   Sales-type leases (lessor): The lessor must recognize immediately as profit the difference between the fair value and cost of the leased property, net of any initial costs of establishing the lease. Thereafter the lease is accounted for as any other finance lease.
   Direct finance leases (lessor): The lessor's accounting for direct finance leases is the mirror image of that used by lessees.
   Operating leases (lessee and lessor): The lessee charges operating lease payments to the profit and loss account in the periods in which they are incurred. The lessor credits income as it is earned.

Leveraged Leases.   The leasing component of a **leveraged lease** should be accounted for in the same way as other leases, and the debt component should be accounted for as a liability (see Sections 19 and 20).

Disclosure. Lessees are required to disclose detailed information about material finance leases, including amounts capitalized, amortization, finance charges and lease commitments. For operating leases, lessees must disclose rental expense and lease commitments. If leases are material, accounting policies should also be disclosed.

Lessors are required to disclose the total value of any finance lease receivables, and to identify separately the unguaranteed residual values included therein. If lessors have a significant number of operating leases, they must disclose in the aggregate and by class of asset the value of leased assets and any related depreciation.

Reference. Schedule 5; AASB 1008/AAS 17; and AAG 3.

16. Investments

Valuation. General: The valuation of investments depends on their classification as noncurrent assets (i.e., those held for the medium or long term) or **current assets** (i.e., those representing a temporary investment of surplus funds).

Current investments: Current investments should be stated at the lower of cost or **net realizable value**. Net realizable value normally is market value net of transaction costs. The comparison should be made on an individual investment basis and a provision made for each investment whose net realizable value is below cost. The resulting write-down should be recognized in the profit and loss account and separately disclosed as an abnormal item (see Section 28), if material. Revaluations of current investments to reflect increases in market value above cost are not permitted except in certain special circumstances, for example, insurance companies and pension funds.

Noncurrent investments: Noncurrent investments are stated at cost, adjusted as necessary for any provision for permanent diminution in value. Any write-down of noncurrent investments arising from a line-by-line assessment of the investments' recoverable amount should be recognized in the profit and loss account except when it reverses a previous revaluation increment that was credited to an asset revaluation reserve. In these circumstances, the write-down should be charged to the reserve. Write-downs that are charged to profit should be recognized in the determination of operating profit and separately disclosed as an abnormal item, if material.

Noncurrent investments may be revalued to reflect increases in market value above cost, provided that the revalued amount does not exceed the recoverable amount. Revaluation increments must be credited directly to an asset revaluation reserve except when they reverse a related write-down previously charged to the profit and loss account; in that case, the increment should be credited to the profit and loss account for the current year.

Reversal of write-downs: If an investment has been written down in prior years either to reflect a permanent diminution in value of a noncurrent investment or to net realizable value for a current asset, the investment should be restored, either in whole or in part, to its original cost or to a revalued amount if the reasons for making the write-down have ceased to apply.

Capital gains tax: Capital gains on disposals of assets acquired after September 19, 1985 are subject to a capital gains tax. The impact of the tax should be taken into account if there has been a decision to sell a revalued asset. If an asset has been revalued and it is likely that its primary benefit to the entity will be through a sale, the potential capital gains tax liability should be disclosed in a note.

Treatment of Valuation Reserves.   Reserves arising from the revaluation of noncurrent investments are treated as revenue reserves and are included directly as part of shareholders' equity. For additional information on the treatment and disclosure of revenue reserves, refer to Section 22.

Gains/Losses.   When investments are sold, the profit or loss to be recognized is measured as the difference between the net proceeds received for the investment and its carrying amount at the time of the sale. This gain or loss should generally be included in the operating profit and disclosed as an abnormal item, if material. In calculating the profit or loss on disposal of part of a holding, the **average cost** method is used.

Disclosure.   Detailed disclosure is required of each different type of investment held, including cost, valuations and amounts written off, and accounting policies adopted. Further disclosure is required for quoted investments and capital gains tax effects on valuations.

Material gains and losses arising from the sale of noncurrent investments are required to be disclosed, together with the amounts charged to the profit and loss account arising from any diminution in value of investments. Such gains and losses would generally be disclosed as abnormal or extraordinary items (see Section 28).

Corporations listed on the ASX, borrowing corporations and companies whose gross assets exceed $10 million or whose gross revenues exceed $20 million must also disclose additional detailed information about interests in corporations that are individually material and interests in material business undertakings that are carried on otherwise than as corporations. Depending on the circumstances, the additional information required may include the name of the corporation or undertaking, its principal activities, the amount and percentage interest held, the contribution to the investor's profit or loss and the value of products and services directly received from the undertaking.

Reference.   Corporations Law s.294(4); Schedule 5; AASB 1001/AAS 6; AASB 1010/ AAS 10; AASB 1018/AAS 1; AAG 8; and AAG 9.

17.   Accounts Receivable

Accounting Treatment.   Recognition: The recognition of revenues, and hence the related receivables, is described in Section 23.

Discounts: Sales and **accounts receivable** are normally recorded net of trade and quantity discounts. Since the recognition of cash discounts occurs at the time of payment, it is usually not necessary to consider potential cash discounts in determining the amounts of accounts receivable.

Allowances: There are two methods of computing a provision for doubtful accounts: specific assessment or by reference to a formula based on previous experience. If a formula is used, its continuing appropriateness should be kept under review.

Factored Receivables.   Where **factoring of receivables** has occurred for cash consideration, the accounts receivable should be excluded from the balance sheet. Discounts given should normally be accounted for in the same way as cash discounts. If the purchaser has recourse to the seller for bad debts, disclosure of the **contingency** and provision for probable losses should be made. There may be cases where the continuing risk to the seller is so great or so uncertain that the transaction may need to be accounted for as a loan rather than as a factoring of receivables.

Disclosure.   Receivables are segregated into various classes, such as trade debtors (accounts receivable), bills receivable, prepayments, deposits and other debtors, with the balances of any provisions for doubtful accounts shown as deductions from each class. Disclosure is required of current and noncurrent receivables (i.e., those amounts due within one year and after one year) for each class.

Separate disclosure is also required showing the amounts charged to the profit and loss account for bad and doubtful accounts (by class), and the amount of any unearned revenue.

Reference.   Schedule 5.

18.   Inventories and Work in Progress

General Accounting Treatment.   **Inventories** should be measured at the lower of cost or net realizable value. In determining the carrying amount of inventories, each item should be dealt with separately or, where this is impracticable, similar items should be dealt with as a group.

In determining cost, the following methods are considered appropriate:

☐   **Specific identification method**.
☐   **Average cost**.
☐   **FIFO**.
☐   **Standard cost**.

The method selected to assign cost to particular items of inventory should be appropriate to the circumstances and applied consistently from period to period.

LIFO, latest purchase price and **base stock** are not considered acceptable. **Replacement value** is not acceptable in historical cost accounting unless it approximates net realizable value (when it is lower than cost).

For manufactured inventories, cost should be determined using **absorption costing** techniques (based on an entity's normal operating capacity). Standard costing is acceptable provided that the standards are realistically attainable, reviewed regularly and revised as necessary in the light of current conditions.

Net realizable value is the estimated proceeds of sale less all further costs to completion and marketing, selling and distribution costs. Costs of a general nature, for example, general administrative and general marketing costs, that cannot be clearly attributed to specific items or groups of items of inventory normally should not be deducted in arriving at net realizable value.

Long-Term Contracts.   The gross amount of construction work in progress and, as a deduction therefrom, the related aggregate progress billings should be disclosed. The gross amount of construction work in progress includes all costs that can reasonably be allocated to the contract plus any profits recorded in accordance with the **percentage of completion method**, less any foreseeable losses. Further guidance on recognizing revenue for long-term construction contracts is contained in Section 23.

Disclosure. Inventories: All significant accounting policies relating to inventories need to be disclosed. More specifically, the general bases and methods adopted in inventory valuation, including methods of assigning costs, should be disclosed. The notes should disclose inventories in the following classifications:

- ☐ Raw materials and stores.
- ☐ Work in progress.
- ☐ Finished goods.
- ☐ Land held for resale.

No guidance is given on the criteria for inclusion in a specific classification; this is a matter of judgment in the particular circumstances of each business. Separate disclosure is required of any inventory valued otherwise than at cost.

Construction work in progress: In addition to the requirement to disclose separately gross construction work in progress and the progress billings, set out above, the aggregate of cash received and receivable as progress billings (including retention allowances) and advances on account of construction work in progress should be disclosed.

Reference. Schedule 5; AASB 1001/AAS 6; and AASB 1019/AAS 2.

19. Current Liabilities

General Accounting Treatment. Generally accepted accounting principles for recognizing liabilities are set out in SAC 4, *Definition and Recognition of the Elements of Financial Statements*.

The concept of liabilities adopted in SAC 4 encompasses financial obligations imposed by considerations of equity or fairness, and by custom or usual business practices, as well as those imposed by legal obligations. Obligations under noncancellable unconditional purchase commitments would normally satisfy the criteria for recognition as liabilities.

Creation of General and Specific Provisions. The term provision is used in Australia to describe liabilities whose measurement involves a degree of subjective judgment.

General provisions are not permitted. To satisfy the definition of a liability, provisions must relate to a specific existing obligation. Similarly, provisions for future expenses or losses are not permitted unless the circumstances giving rise to the expense have occurred.

Disclosure. Schedule 5 requires that **current liabilities** be disclosed on the face of the balance sheet under one of three subheadings: **creditors** and borrowings, provisions and other. Specific components of these balances, regardless of materiality, must be disclosed. Within creditors and borrowings, the balances of bank loans, bank overdrafts, debentures, bills of exchange and promissory notes, trade creditors (**accounts payable**) and lease liabilities must be disclosed. Within provisions, the amounts relating to dividends, taxes and employee benefits must be disclosed. Material balances of other current liabilities must be separately disclosed.

If liabilities are secured by a registered or unregistered charge over assets, Schedule 5 also requires disclosure of the amount and nature of the security.

Reference. Schedule 5 and SAC 4.

20. Long-Term Debt

General Accounting Treatment. The most common forms of long-term debt in Australia are debentures, convertible notes, mortgages and other long-term bank loans. The general accounting treatment applied to these items is basically the same as for current liabilities, that is, they are included in the balance sheet at their face value as long as they continue to represent a present obligation of the entity.

AAG 10, *Measurement of Monetary Assets and Liabilities,* sets out the general principle underlying the measurement of interest-bearing assets and liabilities: They are to be measured at an amount representing the discounted value of the cash flows associated with their service and eventual payment. That amount is determined by discounting the cash flows at the rate of interest implicit in the original contract or other arrangements.

Interest accrued on long-term debt is calculated on a time basis and separately disclosed.

Debt Restructuring. There are two types of debt restructuring: where the existing debt is settled by repayment or replacement, and where the terms of existing debt are substantively modified. In both situations, the existing debt is accounted for as extinguished, and any gain or loss is recognized in the profit and loss account in the period in which the restructuring occurs.

Debt Extinguishment. A debt is accounted for as having been extinguished only when it has been:

- ☐ Settled by repayment or replacement with another liability;
- ☐ Subject to a legal **defeasance**; or
- ☐ Subject to an in-substance defeasance.

The standards do not permit debt to be accounted for as if either the principal or interest element has been separately defeased. However, they do permit instantaneous defeasances, whereby a company assumes a liability and at the same time enters into an agreement to defease it. Such transactions are treated in the same way as normal in-substance defeasances, if they meet the criteria.

All gains and losses on a defeasance transaction must be recorded in the period in which the defeasance transaction is entered into, usually as part of operating profit.

Disclosure. General: Long-term debt is shown in the balance sheet under the subheading "creditors and borrowings." The notes separately disclose bank loans, debentures, bills of exchange and promissory notes. If any liabilities are secured, disclosure of the nature, terms and amount of the collateral is also required.

Convertible notes are treated as liabilities if redemption of the securities is the probable outcome. They are treated as part of shareholders' equity, however, if they are more likely to be converted to shares than redeemed. Additional disclosures are required if the latter treatment is followed.

Debt restructuring: There are no specific disclosure requirements; however, the disclosure of any material accounting policies adopted would be required.

Debt extinguishment: The notes should disclose details of the amounts involved and their treatment, if the information is material.

Reference. Schedule 5; AASB 1001/AAS 6; AASB 1014/AAS 23; AAG 10; AAG 11; and SAC 4.

21. Contingencies

Contingent Losses. Material contingent losses should be recognized if at the reporting date it is probable that a loss will arise as a result of a past transaction or other event, and that loss can be reliably measured.

If the above criteria are not satisfied, information relating to material contingent losses must be disclosed in the notes, unless the possibility of loss is remote.

Contingent Gains. Material contingent gains should be recognized if at the reporting date it is probable that a benefit will arise as a result of a past transaction or other event, and that benefit can be reliably measured. Contingent gains that do not meet these recognition criteria should be disclosed in the notes, if material. The nature of the contingency must be clearly disclosed to ensure that a misleading impression is not given as to the likelihood that the gain will be realized.

Disclosure. Schedule 5 requires that details of contingent losses should be disclosed in a note.

Reference. Schedule 5; AASB 1002/AAS 8; and SAC 4.

22. Capital and Reserves

General. Shareholders' equity is generally divided between **share capital** and reserves. Reserves are usually classified as either capital reserves or revenue reserves.

Share Capital. The Corporations Law requires that a company state in its memorandum the amount of its authorized capital and the division of this into shares with a specified **par value**. The authorized capital sets the maximum limit on the shares that can be issued to shareholders.

Shares need not be issued at par, but any excess of the share issue price over its par value must be credited to a **share premium** reserve. The issue of shares at a discount from par is generally not permitted. Shares are not necessarily required to be paid for in full on issue, but if the balance is called by the directors it must be met by the shareholders or the shares forfeited. After issue, a company generally may not reduce its share capital except with the special permission of the court. The Corporations Law permits companies to buy back their own shares in certain circumstances.

A company's share capital may be divided into different classes, each characterized by its voting, dividend and capital repayment rights. The main classes of shares are ordinary and **preference shares**. The exact rights of each type are included in the company's memorandum and articles.

Other Reserves. Capital reserves can be utilized only for certain purposes and are generally distributable to shareholders only on liquidation of the company. Revenue reserves, subject to any special limitations contained in the company's memorandum and articles, can be utilized in any manner the directors choose.

Capital reserves include:

□ Share premium: The share premium reserve is required to be created when the issue price of shares exceeds their par value; the difference is credited to this reserve. The reserve can be used to issue additional shares to existing shareholders for no consideration (bonus shares), write off company formation expenses or provide for the premium payable on redemption of preference shares.

□ Capital redemption: The capital redemption reserve is required to be created when a company issues redeemable preference shares that it intends to redeem other than by a new share issue. The company must transfer from its retained earnings to the reserve an amount equivalent to the nominal value of the shares to be redeemed. Once created, this reserve becomes part of the company's share capital and in general cannot be utilized until liquidation. The company may create the reserve in full when the shares are either issued or redeemed. However, it is more common for companies to create the reserve by appropriations from profit over the life of the shares.

Revenue reserves include:

□ Foreign currency translation: This reserve arises as a result of translating the financial statements of a self-sustaining foreign operation (see Section 6).

□ General: This reserve is usually an appropriation of profits made from retained earnings by the directors at their discretion.

Disclosure. Share capital: Companies must disclose details of their authorized and issued capital, including any uncalled amounts and calls in arrears. Details of any shares issued during the period, including both number and class of shares, and the purpose of the issue must also be disclosed. If options have been granted requiring the issue of shares at a later date, relevant details must be disclosed, as must the terms and conditions of any preference shares, for example, dividend rate, date and conditions of redemption.

Reserves: Companies must disclose the name and amount of each material reserve and details of any material transfers to or from those reserves.

Reference. Corporations Law s.187–195; Schedule 5; AASB 1012/AAS 20; AASB 1018/AAS 1; and SAC 4.

ACCOUNTING PRINCIPLES FOR SPECIFIC ITEMS— INCOME STATEMENT

23. Revenue Recognition

General Principles. Generally accepted accounting principles for the recognition of revenue are set out in SAC 4, *Definition and Recognition of the Elements of Financial Statements.*

Revenue from a transaction involving the sale of goods is usually recognized when the seller has transferred to the buyer the significant risks and rewards of ownership of the asset sold. This requires an analysis of the substance of the transaction. In most cases, transfer of the legal title either results in or coincides with the passing of possession (e.g., most retail sales) or transfer of the risks and rewards of ownership to the buyer (e.g., the dispatch of goods without condition), and therefore revenue is usually recognized at this point. However, the seller may retain significant risks of ownership (e.g., liability for unsatisfactory performance in excess of the normal warranty), and revenue should not be recognized until those risks have been reduced or eliminated.

Revenue from service transactions is usually recognized as the service is performed.

Revenue should be recognized only when no significant uncertainty as to its collectibility or measurement exists. If uncertainty arises subsequent to the time of sale or the rendering of the service, recording a separate doubtful accounts provision is the appropriate treatment, rather than adjusting the original revenue recorded.

Long-Term Contracts.   The percentage of completion method should be used in recognizing revenue from long-term construction contracts when the outcome of a contract can be reliably estimated. This requires that reliable estimates of revenue, cost to date, stage of completion and cost to complete can be made. This may mean that, in certain circumstances, no profit is recognized until the contract is complete.

If it is expected that there will be a loss on a contract as a whole, a provision should be made for the entire amount of the loss as soon as it is identified. This has the effect of reducing the cost attributable to the work done to date to its net realizable value. Where unprofitable contracts are of such magnitude that they can be expected to absorb a considerable part of the company's capacity for a substantial period, indirect costs (e.g., general administrative and selling costs) to be incurred during the period to completion of those contracts should also be included in the calculation of the provision for losses.

Instalment Sales.   The general principles of revenue recognition apply to **instalment sales**. Thus, if the significant risks and benefits of ownership pass to the buyer at inception of the transaction, the fact that the purchase price is to be received in instalments will not prevent the seller from recognizing the transaction in full at that time and creating a receivable for the deferred payment. The only impact that delayed payment would have in this instance is in relation to the interest component of the instalment sale, which should be recognized in the period in which the payment is received.

Rights of Return.   The fact that a buyer can return goods is usually not an ownership risk of significant magnitude to prevent a seller from recognizing a sale at the time possession initially passes to the buyer. However, if the right of return did constitute a significant ownership risk, revenue recognition would be deferred until the risk was eliminated or sufficiently reduced. The holding by the seller of a reservation of title clause designed to protect the collectibility of the amount due is also unlikely to represent a significant risk of ownership such that revenue recognition should be deferred, although this would depend on the transaction involved. If the seller thinks that the clause may need to be relied on, the more appropriate course of action is to record a provision for a doubtful receivable rather than deferring recognition of the revenue.

If a put option allows return of goods, the likelihood of the put option being exercised would need to be assessed before revenue could be recognized. If the option is expected to be exercised, recognition of the sale would be inappropriate. The existence of put options, where material, is normally disclosed.

Product Financing. The broad general principles relating to the transfer of risks and benefits of ownership apply in determining the appropriate accounting treatment for **product financing arrangements**. Under most of these agreements substantially all the risks and benefits of ownership do not pass to the buyer, and therefore recognition of revenue would not be appropriate and the transaction should be treated as a financing transaction.

Disclosure. Companies are required to disclose total operating revenue and, where material, its separate components of sales revenue and other revenue (by components). Sales revenue includes revenue from the sale of goods or provision of services and usually represents revenue derived from the company's main trading activities. Other revenue includes the gross proceeds from the sale of any noncurrent assets.

The gross amount of construction work in progress and, as a deduction therefrom, the related aggregate progress billings should be disclosed separately. If progress billings exceed the gross amount of construction work in progress, the net amount should be shown as a current liability. The gross amount of construction work in progress is defined as all costs incurred plus any profits recorded less any losses, including foreseeable losses.

The basis used to recognize profit on construction contracts should be disclosed in the notes.

Reference. SAC 4; AASB 1001/AAS 6; AASB 1004/AAS 15; AASB 1009/AAS 11; and AAG 10.

24. Government Grants and Assistance

General. Generally accepted accounting principles for the recognition of government grants and assistance are set out in SAC 4, *Definition and Recognition of the Elements of Financial Statements*. Accounting requirements relating specifically to government grants and assistance provided to local governments are set out in AAS 27, *Financial Reporting by Local Governments*.

Accounting Treatment. In general, nonreciprocal government grants and assistance are recognized as revenues unless they are contributions by owners, in which case they should be classified as equity.

Contributions made by governments to profit-seeking, public-sector entities are sometimes analogous to contributions made by company shareholders in that they are provided with the expectation of receiving from the entity a specified or desired rate of return, and the government has rights relating to distributions by the entity that are analogous to those attaching to company shares. In such cases, the grants should be recognized as equity. Most other government grants and assistance received by public-sector entities are treated as revenues, as are government grants and assistance received by private-sector entities.

Disclosure. Except in the case of local governments, there are no specific disclosure requirements relating to government grants and assistance, although the accounting policy adopted for material amounts received should be disclosed. Local governments are required to disclose revenues from government grants, classified by function, together with specified information regarding conditions on grants.

Reference.   AASB 1001/AAS 6; AAS 27; and SAC 4.

25. Research and Development

Definition.   Research and development is defined as "systematic investigation or experimentation that involves innovation or technical risk, and is carried on for the purpose of acquiring new knowledge, developing a new product or bringing about a significant improvement in an existing product."

Accounting Treatment.   The general rule is that research and development costs must be expensed as incurred unless they satisfy the criterion for deferral. This criterion is that costs can be deferred only to the extent that they, along with any existing unamortized deferred costs, are considered beyond any reasonable doubt to be recoverable. Generally only development activities undertaken with a specific commercial objective meet this criterion.

Once capitalized, research and development costs must be amortized so that they are matched with related benefits, commencing with commercial production. Further, deferred research and development costs should be reviewed at each reporting date and, if the capitalized expenditure exceeds the recoverable amount, the excess should be written off immediately. Research and development expenditures that have been written off should not be reinstated, even if the uncertainties that led to their being written off no longer apply.

Disclosure.   The notes should disclose the amount of research and development costs charged to the profit and loss account, the amount (for the period and cumulative) deferred, amount of amortization (for the period and cumulative) and the basis of amortization.

Reference.   AASB 1011/AAS 13 and SAC 4.

26. Capitalized Interest Costs

Accounting Treatment.   There is no specific prescribed accounting standard dealing with capitalization of interest. It is, however, accepted practice to capitalize interest as part of the cost of an asset if the interest is incurred in bringing the asset to the condition and location of its intended use. This includes assets being constructed for continuing use in the entity and construction contracts being carried out for others.

Disclosure.   Disclosure is required of the amount of interest capitalized by class of assets and, where interest capitalized is material, the accounting policy adopted.

Reference.   Schedule 5; AASB 1001/AAS 6; and AASB 1009/AAS 11.

27. Imputed Interest

Accounting Treatment.   AAG 10, *Measurement of Monetary Assets and Liabilities*, provides guidance about the need to determine the interest and principal components of cash flows that are spread over time. For leases, defeasance arrangements, deferred purchase or sale agreements, zero coupon bonds and other such transactions, it calls for determining outstanding balances of assets or liabilities by discounting future cash flows at the interest rates implicit in the transactions.

Disclosure.   Disclosure of the accounting policies used is required where transactions are material.

Reference.   AASB 1001/AAS 6 and AAG 10.

28. Extraordinary or Unusual Items

Extraordinary Items.   Extraordinary items are defined as items of revenue and expense attributable to transactions or other events of a type that is outside the ordinary operations of the reporting entity and not of a recurring nature. They do not include abnormal items that, though exceptional on grounds of size and effect (and which therefore require separate disclosure), derive from the ordinary activities of the business. They also do not include prior year items merely because they relate to a prior year.

Disclosure.   Extraordinary items should be disclosed separately on the face of the profit and loss account, showing the total extraordinary items and related tax. Separate disclosure of the details of each extraordinary item is required in the notes.

Reference.   Schedule 5 and AASB 1018/AAS 1.

29. Income Taxes

Accounting Treatment.   Accounting standards require the use of the **liability method** of income **tax allocation**.

Where possible, future income tax benefits attributable to a tax loss may be offset against the deferred income tax provision to the extent that the provision relates to timing differences that will reverse in the period during which the tax loss benefit is available. Otherwise, a future income tax benefit may be carried forward as an asset only if the benefit can be regarded as assured beyond any reasonable doubt.

Disclosure.   Details of income taxes attributable to the profit or loss account, deferred income tax liability/future income tax benefit, income tax payable and the extent and treatment of tax losses should be disclosed. A reconciliation of income tax attributable to operating profit and extraordinary items with the prima facie tax payable on the operating profit and extraordinary items is required where these two amounts differ by more than 15 percent.

Reference.   Schedule 5; AASB 1020/AAS 3; and AAG 2.

30. Postretirement Benefits

General.   An exposure draft of proposed accounting standard ED 53, *Accounting for Employee Entitlements*, was issued in August 1991 by the AARF. The exposure draft sets out proposed standards for accounting for and disclosure of information about employee entitlements, including postretirement benefits.

Defined Benefit Pension Plans.   ED 53 proposes that the liability (or asset) in respect of **defined benefit pensions** should be measured as the difference between the present value of employees' accrued benefits at the reporting date and the net market value of the pension plan's assets at that date. The liability for accrued benefits represents the value of the present obligation to pay benefits to members and other beneficiaries and is determined as the present value of expected future payments that arise from membership of the plan to the reporting date. The present value is measured by reference to expected future wage and salary levels and by application of a market-determined, risk-adjusted discount rate and appropriate actuarial assumptions.

Pension expense for the financial period would represent contributions made, plus or minus any increase or decrease in the pension plan liability during the period.

Defined Contribution Pension Plans.   Pension expense in respect of defined contribution pensions is the employer's required contribution for the period. The liability is measured as the amount of the employer's contribution that remains payable to the plan or has accrued at the reporting date.

Pension Fund Surpluses.   Pension fund surpluses can arise only in relation to defined benefit pension plans and occur when the net market value of the pension plan's assets exceeds the present value of employees' accrued benefits.

The rules regarding the distribution of surpluses are determined by the fund's own trust deed. However, as a general rule, pension fund surpluses cannot be distributed until the pension fund is liquidated. The usual way in which overfunding is controlled is by the actuaries recommending that the sponsoring company reduce, or cease to make, contributions until the surplus is eroded.

Other Postretirement Benefits.   Other postretirement benefits may take various forms, including postretirement medical benefit plans and retirement, termination, retrenchment or redundancy payments other than pensions.

ED 53 proposes that postretirement benefit plans be categorized as defined benefit or defined contribution plans and accounted for in the same way as pension plans.

The timing of the recognition of liabilities relating to retirement, termination, retrenchment or redundancy of employees depends on the existence of a present obligation of the employer (see Section 19). Where a present obligation exists, the liability should be measured as the present value of the future payments expected to be made by the employer in respect of services provided by employees to the reporting date. The present value is measured by application of a market-determined, risk-adjusted discount rate.

Disclosure.   Schedule 5 requires certain disclosures by corporations listed on the ASX, borrowing corporations and companies whose gross assets exceed $10 million or gross revenues exceed $20 million. These companies are required to disclose details of their pension plans, the latest actuarial valuation and the company's commitment to the plans.

All companies are required to disclose pension contributions made in connection with the retirement of directors and principal executive officers.

ED 53 proposes additional disclosure requirements, including aggregate pension expenses and liabilities (or assets), the basis of measurement of liabilities for each type of employee entitlement (including the average inflation and discount rates applied), the effect of material changes in pension plans and, in respect of defined benefit plans, the date of the most recent actuarial report and details of the major classes of pension plan assets.

Reference.   Schedule 5 and ED 53.

31. Discontinued Operations

Accounting Treatment.   There is no prescribed method of accounting for discontinued operations in Australia. The following comments are based on preferred practice for accounting for related costs arising from the discontinuation or reorganization of a business segment.

Reorganization and business closure costs are recognized when there is a firm commitment to reorganize or discontinue operations. All costs relating to a particular reorganization or closure should, as far as possible, be recognized at the same time. Thus it is usual to include, in the aggregate reorganization costs, such items as employee termination payments, write-downs of current assets, adjustments to fixed asset values and the costs of settling claims from customers or suppliers. Uncertainties may arise, however, in the treatment of revenue, expenses or operating losses incurred from the date the reorganization is recognized to the completion date. It is appropriate to include in reorganization costs short-term costs that are related to the completion of work in process or that are incurred to obtain the best realization of assets. General overhead expenses that are likely to continue after the reorganization or closure has been completed should not be included.

Disclosure.   Material reorganization costs should be disclosed separately in the notes. It is normally desirable for the accounting policies to explain the treatment of reorganization costs.

Reference.   AASB 1001/AAS 6.

32. Earnings per Share

General.   Standards for the calculation and disclosure of information on earnings per share (EPS) are set out in AASB 1027, *Earnings per Share*. The standard applies to listed companies for the first reporting period ending on or after June 30, 1993.

Definitions.   EPS represents the portion of earnings for a financial period attributable to an ordinary share of issued capital of an enterprise.

Methods of Calculation.   AASB 1027 requires the calculation of EPS on two bases. The first calculation is based principally on the weighted average number of ordinary shares outstanding during the financial period and is known as basic EPS. The second calculation takes into account any reduction in EPS that will probably arise from the payment of outstanding calls on ordinary shares or the exercise of options, convertible notes or other similar securities. This is referred to as diluted EPS.

Earnings figures used in the calculations are operating profits after income tax adjusted for specific items relevant to basic and diluted EPS.

Disclosure.   AASB 1027 requires disclosure of basic and diluted EPS together with related disclosures, including the weighted average number of ordinary shares used in the calculation of basic EPS and the number and nature of any potential ordinary shares that are not dilutive and are not used in the calculation of diluted EPS.

Reference.   AASB 1027.

Appendix
DO AUSTRALIAN STANDARDS OR PREVALENT PRACTICE SUBSTANTIALLY COMPLY WITH INTERNATIONAL ACCOUNTING STANDARDS?

Section	Topic	Substantially complies with IAS?	Comments
3.	Basic accounting concepts and conventions	Yes	
	Contents of financial statements	Yes	
4.	Business combinations*	Yes	Except that equity accounting for associated companies is by way of a note to the financial statements only; the pooling of interests method is not permitted
5.	Joint ventures	Yes	Except that for incorporated joint ventures proportionate consolidation is not common
6.	Foreign currency translation*	Yes	
8.	Accounting changes*	Yes	
9.	Prior period adjustments*	Yes	
10.	Post balance sheet events	Yes	
11.	Related party transactions	Yes	
12.	Segmental information	Yes	
13.	Property, plant and equipment*	Yes	
15.	Leases	Yes	
16.	Investments	Yes	
17.	Accounts receivable	Yes	
18.	Inventories and work in progress*	Yes	
19.	Current liabilities	Yes	
20.	Long-term debt	Yes	
21.	Contingencies	Yes	
22.	Capital and reserves	Yes	
23.	Revenue recognition*	Yes	

Appendix (*Continued*)

Section	Topic	Substantially complies with IAS?	Comments
24.	Government grants and assistance	No	Government grants and assistance are recognized immediately as revenues, unless they are contributions by owners
25.	Research and development*	Yes	
26.	Capitalization of interest costs*	Yes	
28.	Extraordinary or unusual items*	Yes	
29.	Income tax**	Yes	
30.	Postretirement benefits*	Yes	

*These topics are subject to change as a result of the IASC Improvements Project—see the appendix to the International Accounting Standards chapter.

**The IAS on accounting for taxes on income is currently being revised, and an exposure draft has been issued.

Comparison in this table is made to International Accounting Standards in force at January 1, 1993. For further details, see the International Accounting Standards chapter.

BELGIUM

GENERAL NATIONAL INFORMATION

1. Source of Generally Accepted Accounting Principles

Generally accepted accounting principles are essentially established by law and implemented by Royal Decree.

The basic accounting law of July 17, 1975 was primarily a consequence of the European Community's (EC's) Fourth Directive, which sought to harmonize accounting practices in EC member countries. The Basic Law (BL) is supplemented by a number of Royal Decrees (RD), the most important of which are the RD of October 8, 1976, which contains the detailed format for financial statements; the RD of September 12, 1983 on the content and presentation of a minimum standard chart of accounts; and the RD of March 6, 1990 on the **consolidated financial statements** of enterprises. Despite the changes that have been brought about by the accounting law and related Royal Decrees, decisions on accounting matters are still substantially influenced by tax considerations as the statutory accounts of a company form the basis on which taxes are determined.

In addition, the Belgian Coordinated Company Law (CCL) (Lois coordonées sur les sociétés commerciales [F], Gecoordineerde wetten op de handels-vennootschappen [D])* contains provisions regarding profit appropriations, preparation and publication of financial statements and the appointment of auditors.

An Accounting Standards Commission (ASC) (Commission des Normes Comptables [F], Commissie voor Boekhoudkundige Normen [D]) has been established to advise the Belgian government on interpretation of the accounting law and on changes that may be considered necessary to the law. Regular Bulletins are published by the Commission clarifying accounting issues.

2. Audit and Public Company Requirements

Audits.   An audit is required for all enterprises deemed to be large.

Large enterprises are defined as those that meet any two of the following criteria:

☐   Annual sales of at least BEF 170 million.

---

*Terms presented in French and Dutch are indicated by [F] and [D], respectively, following the term.

□ Total assets of at least BEF 85 million.

□ Average number of employees of at least 50.

Any enterprise whose number of employees exceeds 100 is deemed to be large. If a group (national or international) meets the above criteria, the individual companies in the group have to comply with the legislation relating to large enterprises.

Large enterprises are required, among other things, to prepare financial statements in conformity with the complete legal requirements and to publish the statements by submitting them for filing with the National Bank of Belgium, where they can be referred to by the public. The requirements for small enterprises are considerably less onerous.

Appointment and Qualification of Auditors. Only members of the Belgian Auditors Institute are authorized to perform audits. An appropriate university degree or its equivalent in economic and financial studies is required for membership in the Institute. A candidate must, in addition, pass the Institute's entrance examination as well as serve a three-year training period with a qualified statutory auditor, during which the candidate has to continue studies and pass the Institute's examinations.

Auditors are elected by the shareholders at the annual general meeting for a period of three years. Where there is a workers council, it must approve the nomination. If the nomination is not endorsed, auditors are appointed by the Commercial Court.

A workers council consists of representatives of employees and management. Financial and commercial information as well as explanations concerning the evolution of the enterprise are supplied to the council by management on a regular basis throughout the year to facilitate cooperation between management and employees, especially in areas affecting employment policies and practices.

Statutory auditors should be independent, competent and individuals of professional integrity. Under the CCL, the responsibilities of auditors are to give an opinion on the financial information presented by an enterprise, including whether the financial statements present a true and fair view of the financial position and results of operations, and on the enterprise's compliance with the CCL.

Auditors are also required to report on the detailed annual information provided to the workers council by management, in accordance with the RD of November 27, 1973.

Auditing standards are issued by the Belgian Auditors Institute. They follow closely the International Standards on Auditing.

The Superior Council of the Belgian Auditors Institute is a consultative institution, attached to the Ministry of Economic Affairs and composed of individuals nominated by the King. It oversees directives concerning auditors to ensure that audits are performed in the public interest.

Public Companies. Public ownership of most **listed companies** is concentrated in a relatively small number of shareholders and, as a result, few shares are available for trading on the stock exchanges.

A prospectus for a public subscription should include details of the company and its history, the report of the directors giving the reason for the subscription and the terms of the offer.

There are four stock exchanges in Belgium, the principal one located in Brussels. These stock exchanges consist of a market for securities that have an official quotation.

The stock exchanges are controlled by the Stock Exchange Commission, which is ultimately responsible for official quotation prices. To obtain a listing, approval must be sought from the Quotation Committee, and an affirmative ruling from the Banking and Financing Commission is required. There must be a market sufficient to justify the listing.

All public companies must publish audited financial statements in compliance with their constitutions and in accordance with the CCL. They are required to file their annual financial statements with the stock exchange, as well as six-month interim summary financial statements with the Banking and Financing Commission.

GENERAL ACCOUNTING

3. Financial Statements (Comptes Annuels [F], Jaarrekening [D])

Basic Accounting Concepts. Four accounting concepts are fundamental to the preparation of financial statements in Belgium. These are the concepts of **prudence**, **going concern**, consistency and **accruals**. Financial statements are prepared using the **historical cost** basis, although revaluation of fixed assets is allowed if it can be justified (see Section 13).

No offset between assets and liabilities, between entitlements and commitments or between income and expenses is allowed except where specified in legislation. Examples mentioned in legislation are fixed assets and accumulated depreciation, accounts receivable and bad debts provision and inventory and inventory provisions.

Reference. RD October 8, 1976.

Contents of Financial Statements. The annual financial statements include a balance sheet, income statement and notes. The auditors' report must be included in the published financial statements. A statement of changes in financial position or of cash flows is not required.

A directors' report, commenting on important developments during the year and other specified matters, must either be published with the financial statements or be available on request at the company's registered office.

Financial statements must be clear and the figures must come directly from the company's accounting records, on an account-by-account basis; the records must be maintained in conformity with the minimum legal standard chart of accounts. They must give a true and fair view of the financial position of the enterprise at the end of the period and of its operating results for the period on a consistent basis.

The financial statements must clearly set out:

☐ The amount and description of the company's assets, its debts, obligations and commitments and its equity at the balance sheet date.

☐ The amount and description of the company's income and expenses for the period ending on the balance sheet date.

The financial statements must reflect the proposed profit appropriation for the year.

Extensive notes to the financial statements have to be furnished covering such matters as commitments and guarantees entered into, investments in affiliated companies, overdue amounts payable to the tax and social security authorities and amounts due from and guarantees given on behalf of directors.

Format of Financial Statements.   The financial statements must be prepared in accordance with the format prescribed by law.

Since the simplest manner of preparing financial statements for filing is on the forms established by the National Bank, it is often convenient to use financial statements prepared on these forms at general meetings as well as for publication.

Only in special circumstances will the Minister of Economic Affairs, acting on the advice of the ASC, authorize exemptions from the prescribed format.

Smaller enterprises are permitted to use an abbreviated format and to provide more limited disclosures.

Disclosure of Accounting Policies.   All assets and liabilities of the enterprise must be individually valued and recorded for accounting purposes. The **accounting policies** used to make the valuations have to be defined, recorded and included in the valuation rules approved by the board of directors. A summary of the valuation rules must be included as part of the financial statements.

The policies adopted should be appropriate for the particular characteristics of the business. Specifically, the policies used in accounting for depreciation, writing off assets, making revaluations and determining provisions required should be identified.

In exceptional cases, where application of accounting policies set out in the law would result in the financial statements not being fairly presented, these policies may be departed from. The details and justification of any such departures must be explained in the notes, and the difference resulting from the departure must be indicated.

Reference.   BL and RD October 8, 1976.

4. Business Combinations

Methods of Accounting for Business Combinations.   **Business combinations** are accounted for using the **purchase method**.

Principles of Consolidation (Principes de Consolidation [F], Consolidatieprincipes [D]).   The RD of March 6, 1990, which is based on the Seventh Directive of the EC, sets forth the requirements for the preparation of consolidated financial statements. Holding companies recognized under the RD of November 10, 1967 are required to prepare consolidated accounts in accordance with the RD of November 25, 1991.

All **parent companies** must prepare, in addition to their own financial statements, consolidated financial statements consisting of a balance sheet, income statement and notes. A parent company is an enterprise that controls, alone or jointly with one or more enterprises, one or more **subsidiaries**.

A parent company is exempt from preparing consolidated financial statements if:

□   It is a subsidiary of a company that prepares and publishes audited consolidated financial statements; or

□   On a consolidated basis, it does not exceed one of the following limits:
Turnover: BEF 1700 million

Total assets: BEF 850 million

Average number of employees: 500

These exemptions do not apply if all or part of the shares of any of the enterprises in the group are listed on a stock exchange in the EC, or if an enterprise is required to prepare consolidated financial statements for the information of employees or for an administrative or judicial authority.

In general, all subsidiaries should be consolidated. However, in certain circumstances, as set out below, a subsidiary can be accounted for using the **equity method**.

A subsidiary need not be included in the consolidated financial statements if:

- ☐ It is not material to the consolidated position (two or more subsidiaries satisfying this requirement are considered in the aggregate);
- ☐ Serious long-term restrictions substantially hinder the effective control over the subsidiary or the use of its assets;
- ☐ The information necessary for inclusion of the subsidiary in the consolidated financial statements cannot be obtained without disproportionate expense or undue delay; or
- ☐ The shares are held exclusively with a view to their subsequent resale.

Justification must be given in the notes if a subsidiary is excluded from consolidation for any of the above reasons.

Control. Control signifies the power to exercise, de jure or de facto, decisive influence on the appointment of the majority of the board of directors or general management or on changes in operating policies of another entity. **Joint control** exists when control is exercised jointly by a limited number of shareholders and when it is agreed that decisions with respect to an enterprise's operating policies cannot be made without the mutual consent of those shareholders.

A consortium exists where one or more unaffiliated enterprises are under central management such as, for example, where management comprises, for the most part, the same persons or where centralized management results from agreements among the enterprises. Consolidated financial statements must be prepared for a consortium. Capital and reserves included in the consolidated financial statements should be the aggregate amounts attributable to each of the enterprises forming the consortium.

Goodwill (Ecarts de Consolidation [F], Consolidatieverschillen [D]). Goodwill, positive or **negative**, based on the difference between the value of consideration given and the book value of net assets acquired at the acquisition date, should be allocated, as far as possible, to assets and liabilities with market values above or below their carrying values. Any remaining difference is included in the consolidated balance sheet under the heading ''Consolidation differences'' as an asset if positive or as a liability if negative.

A positive consolidation difference must be written off in the consolidated income statement over its estimated useful life. If the estimated useful life is more than five years, this must be justified in the notes. The consolidation difference is subject to supplementary amortization or exceptional write-off if, due to changes in economic or technological circumstances, maintaining the value in the consolidated balance sheet cannot be economically justified.

Negative consolidation differences are normally not included in the consolidated income statement. However, if a negative consolidation difference arises from the expectation of unfavorable future results of a subsidiary or from charges that the subsidiary may incur in the future, the difference is included in the consolidated income statement when the future events materialize.

Equity Accounting (Mise en Equivalence [F], Vermogensmutatiemethode [D]). Investments in associated enterprises are accounted for using the equity method. An **associated enterprise** is any enterprise, other than a subsidiary or joint venture, in which the investment is of a permanent nature and the investor exercises significant influence over operating policies. In the absence of evidence to the contrary, significant influence is presumed to exist if 20 percent or more of the total voting rights is owned.

Subsidiaries are accounted for by the equity method if:

- ☐ Inclusion in the consolidation would result in consolidated financial statements not giving a true and fair view of the assets, liabilities, financial position and operating results of the group;
- ☐ Activities are so different that inclusion would distort the true and fair view of the group's financial statements; or
- ☐ Subsidiaries are in liquidation, have ceased activities or can no longer be considered as carrying on their business as going concerns.

If the financial statements of the above subsidiaries are not published in Belgium, copies must be attached to the consolidated financial statements or made available to the public at the registered office of the parent company.

Minority Interests. The consolidated balance sheet should show **minority interests** separately. The portion of net income or loss of fully consolidated subsidiaries attributable to shares held by parties other than the enterprises included in the consolidation is included in the consolidated income statement under the heading ''Share of minority interests in the results.''

Disclosure. The consolidation policy, including the criteria on which it is based, must be disclosed.

The names and registered offices and, for enterprises governed by Belgian law, the VAT (**value added tax**) national identification numbers and the proportion of the capital held must be disclosed for subsidiaries, joint subsidiaries, associated enterprises and enterprises where at least 10 percent of the capital is held by the group.

If subsidiaries or joint subsidiaries are not consolidated, the reasons for their exclusion must be given.

The elements underlying the existence of joint subsidiaries must be disclosed.

Changes in consolidation differences and differences resulting from the application of the equity method must be included in the notes. Positive and negative differences are shown separately.

A statement is also required describing relationships with affiliated enterprises not included in the consolidation. The amount of the investment, shares owned and other pertinent information should be disclosed.

Reference. RD March 6, 1990.

5. Joint Ventures (Filiales Communes [F], Gemeenschappetijke Dochterondernemingen [D])

Accounting for Investments in Joint Ventures. Belgian accounting standards do not address the different forms of **joint ventures** detailed in International Accounting Standard (IAS) 31, *Financial Reporting of Interests in Joint Ventures*.

Jointly Controlled Operations. The accounting treatment in IAS 31 would be appropriate in Belgium.

Jointly Controlled Assets. The accounting treatment in IAS 31 would be appropriate in Belgium.

Jointly Controlled Entities. The RD on consolidated accounts recommends use of the **proportionate consolidation method**, especially when a substantial part of the activities of the company is exercised through joint ventures. If the activities of the joint venture are less integrated with the venturer's main activities, the equity method may be used. In the single entity statutory (unconsolidated) financial statements, the investment in a joint venture is shown at cost.

Transactions Between Venturers and the Joint Venture. The transactions between the venturer and the joint venture are shown in the unconsolidated financial statements at their transaction values without any profit or loss adjustment. With respect to contributions of net assets to a joint venture, an adjustment is made upon consolidation to eliminate unrealized gains and losses up to the proportion of the venture held.

Disclosure. The disclosures for joint ventures follow the same rules as for other investments. The accounting method used (proportionate consolidation or equity method) has to be disclosed.

Accounting by Joint Ventures. There are no specific accounting standards for joint ventures, which follow accounting standards applicable to other companies.

Reference. RD March 6, 1990.

6. Foreign Currency Translation

Foreign Currency Denominated Transactions. Transactions in foreign currencies should be recorded at the exchange rate prevailing at the transaction date. Foreign currency **monetary items** outstanding at the balance sheet date should be translated at the spot rate in effect at the balance sheet date.

If foreign currency borrowing is used to finance nonmonetary assets, any unrealized losses on exchange may be allocated over the period in which the assets will generate income.

If an unfavorable change in exchange rate affects sales orders received or purchase orders issued, resulting in a loss, a provision for loss on exchange should be recorded.

The ASC recommends that unrealized exchange gains should be deferred, and unrealized losses should be expensed. Unrealized losses or gains should be calculated on the net asset or liability position per currency. However, enterprises may also use the **closing rate method** to convert assets and liabilities into Belgian francs.

Foreign Operations. The financial statements of foreign subsidiaries included in consolidated financial statements must be translated into Belgian francs using either the **current/noncurrent method** or the **current rate method**.

If the current/noncurrent method is used, translation differences must be recorded in the income statement. Unrealized exchange differences may, however, be treated using the methods applied by the consolidating enterprise.

If the current rate method is applied, exchange differences must be recorded in the liabilities section of the balance sheet under the heading "Translation differences."

In special circumstances, such as the consolidation of subsidiaries located in a country with very high inflation, enterprises may apply different rules for translation differences, provided that the method satisfies the requirement of the true and fair view and of objective criteria consistently applied.

Hedges. Monetary assets or liabilities denominated in foreign currencies and hedged through a foreign currency forward contract are translated into Belgian francs at the hedging rate.

Disclosure. The methods used to translate foreign currency items and financial statements of foreign subsidiaries and associated enterprises into Belgian francs must be disclosed. The treatment of differences arising on translation should also be disclosed.

Forward contracts for goods purchased, goods sold, currencies purchased and currencies sold must be disclosed in the notes.

Reference. RD March 6, 1990 and ASC Bulletin No. 20.

7. Changing Prices/Inflation Accounting

Belgian enterprises are not required to disclose information relating to changing prices, and such disclosures are rare.

8. Accounting Changes

Accounting Treatment. The accounting policies of each enterprise are disclosed in its valuation rules. The effects of changes in valuation rules are normally accounted for prospectively.

Disclosure. Any change in the valuation rules must be disclosed and justified in the notes. An evaluation of its effect on the financial statements must also be given in the period in which the change occurs.

Reference. RD October 8, 1976.

9. Prior Period Adjustments

All items that relate to prior periods are included in the income statement of the current year. However, the notes should disclose if income or expenses of the current year are significantly affected by those relating to a previous period.

Reference. RD October 8, 1976.

10. Post Balance Sheet Events

Accounting Treatment. All foreseeable liabilities, contingent losses and diminutions in value arising during the current period or in prior periods should be accounted for to the extent that they become known prior to the final approval of the financial statements by the responsible body of the enterprise (e.g., the shareholders at the annual general meeting).

Disclosure. If due to the absence of objective appraisal standards, valuation of foreseeable liabilities, contingent losses and diminutions in value is uncertain, this must be disclosed in the notes. Important events subsequent to year-end have to be mentioned in the directors' report.

Reference. RD October 8, 1976 and CCL.

11. Related Party Transactions

Definition. Related parties are subsidiary and affiliated enterprises, enterprises in which the company owns or controls at least a 10 percent participating interest, and directors.

Accounting Treatment. No specific rules govern the accounting treatment of related party transactions, and normal accounting principles and practices are followed. Belgian tax legislation requires that related party transactions be recorded on an arm's-length basis.

Disclosure. The following disclosures are required for affiliated enterprises and enterprises linked by participating interests:

☐ Amount of financial fixed assets (noncurrent investments), distinguishing between investments, subordinated amounts receivable and other amounts receivable.
☐ Amounts receivable due after one year and within one year.
☐ Current investments, distinguishing between shares and amounts receivable.
☐ Amounts payable after one year and within one year.
☐ The amount of personal and real guarantees given or promised by the enterprise as security for debts or commitments of affiliated enterprises, as well as the amount of personal and real guarantees given or promised by affiliated enterprises as security for debts or commitments of the enterprise.
☐ Other significant financial commitments.
☐ Income from financial fixed assets, income from current assets, other financial income, interest and other debt charges and other financial expenses.
☐ Gains and losses on disposal of fixed assets.

Disclosure is required of amounts receivable from directors, and guarantees and other significant commitments given on their behalf, together with the main conditions relating to each of these amounts. This information must also be disclosed for individuals or legal entities that control the enterprise directly or indirectly.

Directors' salaries and pensions included in the income statement should be disclosed.

Reference.   RD October 8, 1976.

12.   Segmental Information

Disclosure.   An analysis of **turnover** by activity and geographical markets must be disclosed, where significant.

Reference.   RD October 8, 1976.

ACCOUNTING PRINCIPLES FOR SPECIFIC ITEMS— BALANCE SHEET

13.   Property, Plant and Equipment (Actifs Immobilisés Corporels [F], Materiele Vaste Aktiva [D])

Classification of Capital and Revenue Expenditure.   Expenditures that have a lasting benefit are considered **fixed assets**. They are grouped into the following classifications: formation expenses, intangible fixed assets and tangible fixed assets. Immaterial amounts may be expensed if the threshold for capitalization is disclosed in the notes.

Expenditures to maintain operations should be expensed as incurred.

Basis of Valuation.   Property, plant and equipment are generally stated at acquisition cost less **depreciation**. Acquisition cost includes installation expenses. Fixed assets may be revalued if their estimated useful value clearly and permanently exceeds their book value. The surplus arising from the revaluation is recorded and maintained as a revaluation surplus reserve until the assets are disposed of. This surplus may, however, be transferred to distributable reserves to the extent that depreciation is charged on the surplus amount. The reserve may be incorporated into capital; it has to be reduced to the extent that there is a permanent diminution in value.

Depreciation.   Fixed assets with limited useful lives must be depreciated following an established plan. Only recorded depreciation is accepted as a deductible expense by the tax authorities. Acceptable depreciation methods for tax purposes include the straight-line method and the double declining method. In accordance with existing tax regulations, accelerated depreciation methods may also be used. If use of such an accelerated method leads to more rapid depreciation than can be economically justified, the excess expense for the year and on an accumulated basis must be disclosed.

Fixed assets with limited useful lives are subject to supplementary or exceptional depreciation when their book value exceeds their value to the enterprise; for example, because of changes in economic or technological circumstances.

Tangible and intangible fixed assets with unlimited useful lives must not be written down except for a permanent impairment or diminution in value.

Tangible fixed assets no longer in use may be subject to exceptional depreciation to ensure that their book values reflect estimated realizable values.

Disclosure. The valuation and depreciation accounting policies adopted must be disclosed in the notes. Details of the depreciation methods and the rates of depreciation must also be presented.

A summary by each main category of fixed assets is required, showing changes during the year in cost, valuation and depreciation and the net book values at the end of the year. If fixed assets were revalued during the year, the details of the revaluation must be disclosed in the notes.

Reference. RD October 8, 1976.

14. Intangible Assets (Immobilisations Incorporelles [F], Immateriele Vaste Aktiva [D])

Accounting Treatment. The law requires the following items to be included in **intangible assets**:

☐ Research and development expenses.
☐ Concessions, patents, licenses, trademarks and other similar rights.
☐ Acquired goodwill.

Formation expenses, which include costs relating to capital increases, loan issues and reimbursement premiums as well as capitalized reorganization costs, are disclosed under a separate heading.

Valuation. Intangible fixed assets are recorded at cost, provided that cost does not exceed the value of their estimated usefulness or future contribution to the enterprise.

Amortization. Intangible assets are amortized over their useful lives. The rules that apply to the depreciation of fixed assets (see Section 13) also apply to the **amortization** of intangible assets, except that research and development costs, goodwill and formation expenses should normally be amortized over a period of five years, and premiums on loan issues should be amortized over the period of the loan. In exceptional circumstances, amortization of these assets is spread over a longer period; the reasons for the use of an extended amortization period should be given in the notes.

Disclosure. Changes in cost and amortization during the year and the closing net book values at the end of the year have to be shown in the notes.

The valuation rules must indicate the basis of valuation and the amortization policies.

Reference. RD October 8, 1976.

15. Leases

Classification. Leases that effectively transfer the risks and rewards of ownership are treated as **finance leases**. The following conditions must be met for a lease to be classified as a finance lease:

☐ The instalments foreseen in the contract are at least equal to the purchase cost of the asset.

□ It must be a noncancellable lease.

□ Title to the property will be transferred at the end of the contract, or the contract includes a purchase option clause.

Accounting Treatment. Lessee: Fixed assets held under a finance lease or similar arrangement are recorded at the amount defined in the lease agreement. The corresponding commitment is recorded as a liability, representing the instalments to be paid in the future less interest. Instalments due beyond one year from the balance sheet date are reported as long-term debt. The asset is depreciated following the policies used for similar fixed assets. The part of the instalment representing interest is recorded as a finance charge.

Instalment payments for leases that do not meet the criteria for finance leases are expensed when due.

Lessor: A finance lease transaction is treated as a sale; interest is recorded as income over the period of the lease contract.

Leveraged Leases. There are no special rules or reporting requirements for **leveraged leases** in Belgium; however, netting the investment in financial leases and the related debt for financial statement presentation purposes is not permitted.

Disclosure. The lessee must disclose as a separate item in the balance sheet, assets held under leasing and similar rights; changes in these assets during the year are shown in the notes. The valuation rules must include details of the depreciation policy.

The lessor includes the total amount receivable with other amounts receivable on the balance sheet, divided between short-term and long-term portions.

Reference. RD October 8, 1976.

16. Investments (Participations [F], Deelnemingen [D])

General. Investments are classified as fixed (noncurrent) or **current assets**.

Valuation. Fixed investments, referred to as financial fixed assets (immobilisations financières [F], financiele vaste aktiva [D]), are recorded at cost. If the value of an investment clearly and permanently exceeds its book value, the investment may be revalued. If there is a permanent decrease in value, the asset must be written down to its value to the enterprise. Current investments are recorded at acquisition cost and must be written down if at year-end their market value is less than their cost. The comparison of cost and market value should be made on an individual investment basis.

Financial fixed assets include investments in shares of affiliated enterprises, investments in other enterprises linked by participating interests and investments in enterprises where a permanent relationship is sought. Long-term amounts receivable from these enterprises are similarly classified.

Current investments (placements de trésorerie [F], geldbeleggingen [D]) include **treasury shares** purchased and other short-term investments and deposits.

An enterprise in Belgium may acquire its own shares provided that this is authorized by its statutes. Only fully paid shares may be acquired and the acquisition must not discriminate between shareholders. Information regarding treasury shares, together with the related accounting policies, should be disclosed in the notes. The shares that can be acquired cannot exceed an amount equivalent to profits available for distribution, and a corresponding undistributable equity reserve of equal value must be created. The investment in treasury shares cannot exceed 10 percent of the total issued **share capital**, and the shares can remain uncancelled for up to two years.

Other short-term investments and deposits include investments in stocks and bonds that the enterprise intends to dispose of within the following 12 months. Term deposits with financial institutions maturing more than one month after year-end are included in current investments.

Gains/Losses. Gains and losses from sales of investments represent the difference between the net proceeds and the carrying value of the investment sold. Gains on investments are included in the income statement with financial income, and losses with financial expenses.

Disclosure. The notes to the financial statements must list all affiliates and companies of which at least 10 percent is held directly or indirectly. The name and registered office of each company and the number and percentage of shares or rights held directly and indirectly by category should be disclosed. The equity and net income for the most recent period for which financial statements are available are also shown. The same information needs to be given for conversion and subscription rights held directly or indirectly. Details of any revaluation of investments made during the year must be disclosed in the notes.

For current investments, the notes must disclose shares held, including any uncalled amounts (on partly paid-up shares); fixed income securities, indicating those issued by credit institutions; and term accounts with credit institutions, indicating whether their residual term or their notice of withdrawal is less than or equal to one month, between one month and one year or over one year.

Reference. CCL and RD October 8, 1976.

17. Accounts Receivable

Accounting Treatment. Recognition: Receivables are recorded when there is a contractual basis for invoicing.

Discounts: Trade receivables are recorded net of trade discounts. Cash discounts are recorded as financial charges when payment is received within the stipulated period.

Allowances: Provisions must be established for doubtful accounts. The provisions may be based on specific doubtful accounts, on an overall assessment of collectibility or on a combination of the two methods. The tax authorities have established parameters for allowable deductions for tax purposes relating to general provisions for receivables. Long-term receivables on which interest is not charged, or is charged at a rate below commercial rates, should be discounted to present value.

Factored Receivables. When trade receivables are factored, they are excluded from the balance sheet. A distinction has to be made between **factoring** with and without recourse. If receivables have been factored with recourse to the vendor, the amount of the receivables sold has to be disclosed in the notes and a provision made for possible losses.

Disclosure.　A summary of the valuation rules relating to the provisions for doubtful accounts and the rules relating to the translation of receivables expressed in foreign currencies has to be included in the notes. The amount of trade receivables written off and of subsequent collections of previously written off receivables is also shown.

Receivables are separated into amounts receivable within and after one year. Trade receivables have to be separately disclosed in the balance sheet.

An analysis of deferred charges and accrued income has to be given if the amounts involved are significant.

Reference.　RD October 8, 1976.

18.　Inventories and Work in Progress (Stocks [F], Voorraden [D])

General Accounting Treatment.　In general, **inventories** are valued at the lower of acquisition cost or market value at the balance sheet date. Accepted methods for the valuation of inventories are specific cost, weighted **average**, **FIFO** and **LIFO**.

Finished manufactured goods and work in progress should include the cost of material and labor and a reasonable allocation of overhead costs. Enterprises may, however, elect not to include all or part of the overhead costs. Interest costs may be included in inventories only when production takes more than one year.

Long-Term Contracts.　No differentiation is made between short-term and long-term contracts in Belgian accounting law. A distinction is made between work in progress relating to the normal production of finished goods and specific contracts in progress. Although both are valued at production cost, the value of contracts in progress may include a portion of the profit to be earned on the contract, based on the state of completion, provided that the profit is reasonably assured. Alternatively, an enterprise may record contracts in progress or specific types of such contracts at production cost until completion and sale.

Work in progress and contracts in progress should be written down when production cost, increased by the estimated expenses still to be incurred, exceeds either the expected net selling price at the balance sheet date or the contract price.

Disclosure.　Inventories are classified in the balance sheet as contracts in progress, raw materials and consumables, work in progress, finished goods, goods purchased for resale, immovable property acquired or constructed for resale, or advance payments for inventories.

The valuation rules should disclose the basis on which inventories are valued.

Disclosure of the following items is required in a note:

- ☐ If the LIFO method of valuation is used and the book value of inventories differs materially from the market value at the balance sheet date, the amount of the difference must be disclosed.
- ☐ Any write-offs, or write-backs of stocks previously written off, that were recorded during the year.
- ☐ Interest included in inventory valuation.
- ☐ For manufactured finished goods and work in progress, the basis on which overheads are included, or a statement that the enterprise has opted to exclude all or part of

indirect costs in its inventory valuation. The amount of excluded indirect costs has to be disclosed.

☐ The methods and criteria applied to value contracts in progress.

Reference. RD October 8, 1976.

19. Current Liabilities

General Accounting Treatment. Current liabilities are classified into the following categories:

☐ Current portion of long-term debt.
☐ Amounts due to credit institutions, distinguishing between loans and other amounts.
☐ Trade payables and trade bills payable.
☐ Advances received from customers on contracts in progress.
☐ Taxes, salaries and social security.
☐ Accrued charges and deferred income.

Creation of Specific and General Provisions. Provisions are recorded only for specific expenses or losses that, at the balance sheet date, are either likely to be incurred or certain to be incurred but uncertain as to amount. Such provisions must satisfy the criteria of prudence, substance and good faith and be recorded in accordance with the valuation rules of the enterprise.

Disclosure. Details have to be given of the tax liability, showing taxes due, taxes not yet due and estimated tax liabilities.

Details of accrued charges and deferred income have to be given if the amounts involved are significant.

Reference. RD October 8, 1976.

20. Long-Term Debt

General Accounting Treatment. Long-term debt consists of debts or portions of debts due more than one year from the balance sheet date. These debts are included in the balance sheet at their nominal value. Where no interest is charged on the debt or the rate of interest is below normal commercial rates, long-term debt is discounted to present value. The discount is shown as an asset under deferred charges and is written off over the period of the loan.

Amounts payable due after one year are separated into financial debts, trade debts, advances received on contracts in progress and other amounts payable. Financial debts are further separated into subordinated loans, unsubordinated debentures, leasing and other similar obligations, amounts owed to credit institutions and other loans. Trade debts and bills of exchange payable are separately disclosed.

Debt Restructuring and Debt Extinguishment. There are no published pronouncements on accounting for debt restructuring or extinguishment in Belgium. However, normally any gains or losses resulting from these transactions are included in net income.

Disclosure.   Liabilities and expenses that are probable or are certain but for which the amount has to be estimated are disclosed in the balance sheet under the heading "Provision for liabilities and charges." These liabilities have to be separately presented for pensions and similar obligations, tax claims resulting from adjustments made to taxable income by the tax authorities, major repairs and maintenance obligations, and other liabilities. Other liabilities include provisions for contingent losses or expenses resulting from guarantees given to secure debts or commitments of third parties, commitments to purchase or dispose of fixed assets, the completion of orders placed or received, foreign currency positions or forward commodity transactions, technical warranties relating to sales made or services already rendered and for litigation in progress.

Information has to be provided in the notes, giving:

☐   An analysis following the long-term liability balance sheet classifications, showing current portion, portion due between one and five years and portion due in over five years.

☐   Details of secured liabilities, debts guaranteed by affiliates and real guarantees given on any asset.

☐   Amounts payable (for both long- and short-term liabilities) guaranteed by Belgian public authorities and secured by the enterprise's assets.

Reference.   RD October 8, 1976.

21.   Contingencies

General.   The accounting law defines the various types of **contingencies** whose amounts have to be disclosed in the notes.

Contingent Losses.   If the amount of a loss can be estimated, an appropriate accrual should be made. If the amount cannot be estimated, the loss should be disclosed in a note.

Contingent Gains.   Belgian accounting regulations do not specifically address contingent gains. Such gains would not be accrued but, if significant, would be mentioned in the notes.

Disclosure.   Disclosure is required of all significant rights and commitments not reflected in the balance sheet, such as guarantees given, assets pledged, mortgages granted, significant commitments and contingencies, litigation and pension commitments (including a brief description of the plan).

Reference.   RD October 8, 1976.

22.   Capital and Reserves (Capitaux Propres [F], Eigen Vermogen [D])

General.   Capital and reserves on the balance sheet are separated into capital, **share premium**, revaluation surplus reserves, accumulated profits/losses and investment grants.

Capital represents the funds provided by third parties for which these parties receive in return voting powers based on their shareholdings.

Reserves are generally created through retention of profits. Certain reserves cannot be distributed to shareholders in the normal course of business.

No dividend distribution is permitted if it would result in the net assets of the enterprise being reduced below the amount of **share capital**.

Share Capital.   The authorized capital has to be detailed in the constitution of an enterprise and does not have to be completely issued. For a public company at least 25 percent of the issued capital must be paid up; a minimum paid-up share capital of BEF 1,250,000 is mandatory. When the contributions are in kind, the total contribution must be made within five years.

The total issued capital subscribed to by the shareholders, whether called or uncalled, has to be disclosed; the uncalled capital is shown as a deduction from the issued capital.

Shares can be either bearer or nominal shares (i.e., registered in the name of a specific individual or company). Shares may be issued without a par value and can be subdivided into different classes with different voting and dividend rights.

Capital may be paid in cash or in kind. Contributions in kind must be capable of being economically appraised and can include know-how and goodwill. The auditors must report on contributions in kind, indicating whether, in their opinion, a fair value was received for the shares issued.

Shares may be issued at a premium.

Reductions of share capital are not uncommon in Belgium. There are, however, legal requirements protecting the creditor and third party rights.

Reserves.   The following reserves have to be separately disclosed:

□   Share premium account.

□   Revaluation surplus—The unrealized **surplus** from the revaluation of fixed assets (see Sections 13 and 16).

□   Legal reserve—At least 5 percent of the profit available for appropriation has to be transferred to the legal reserve until the reserve equals 10 percent of the share capital. Distribution of the legal reserve is restricted.

□   Reserves not available for distribution—Amounts transferred from **retained earnings** by the enterprise to acquire its own shares and other reserves that cannot be distributed by decision of a simple majority of shareholders.

□   Untaxed reserves—Fiscal legislation allows the exclusion from taxable profits of certain specified gains, provided that they are transferred to a special reserve and are not available for distribution as dividends in the normal course of business.

□   Reserves available for distribution—Reserves that can be distributed by decision of a simple majority of shareholders.

□   Accumulated profits or losses.

□   Investment grants—Grants from public authorities that are transferred to income as the related fixed asset acquired is depreciated.

Disclosure.   The notes to the financial statements must disclose:

□   The number of shares issued by category, the amount of issued capital for each category and changes during the period.

☐ Capital segregated into registered and bearer shares.

☐ The amount of uncalled capital.

☐ The number of treasury shares held by the company and its subsidiaries and the corresponding amounts for the previous year.

☐ Commitments to issue shares, indicating the amount of outstanding convertible loans, the number of outstanding subscription rights, the maximum number of shares to be issued and the corresponding amount of capital to be subscribed.

☐ The amount of authorized capital not issued.

Reference. CCL and RD October 8, 1976.

ACCOUNTING PRINCIPLES FOR SPECIFIC ITEMS— INCOME STATEMENT

23. Revenue Recognition

General Principles. There is no accounting pronouncement specifically addressing revenue recognition in Belgium. The accounting law indicates that income must be accounted for irrespective of the date received, unless collection is uncertain.

In general, **revenue** from the sale of goods is recognized when the risks and rewards of ownership are transferred. Revenue from services is recognized when the service is performed.

Long-Term Contracts. Long-term contract revenue may be recognized using both the **percentage of completion method** and the **completed contract method**. Contract profit must be reasonably assured if the percentage of completion method is used. If the contract is expected to result in a loss, a provision should be recorded immediately.

Instalment Sales. Sales revenue is generally recognized when ownership has passed. Interest on **instalment sales** is included in income over the period of the sales contract.

Rights of Return. There are no specific rules in Belgium on sales transactions where the right of return exists. Revenue is generally recognized upon delivery to the customer even though performance warranties may exist.

Product Financing. **Product financing** is not common in Belgium, and hence there are no specific accounting rules in this area. Such arrangements would normally be treated as financing transactions if the risks and benefits of ownership have not passed to the buyer.

Disclosure. Total operating revenue is disclosed, together with the details of turnover.

Other operating revenue includes amounts received from public authorities to compensate for reduction in income as a result of tariff policies, as well as operating income that does not result from the sale of goods or services in the normal course of business and that does not have the characteristics of financial or extraordinary income.

Reference. RD October 8, 1976.

24. Government Grants and Assistance

Accounting Treatment. Investment grants (Subsides en capital [F], Kapitaalsubsidies [D]) for the acquisition of tangible fixed assets are accounted for net of deferred taxes in a special reserve account (see Section 22). The reserve is systematically amortized to revenue at the rate that depreciation is charged on the related fixed assets.

Other government assistance is recorded on receipt as other revenue. This assistance is generally intended to cover interest charges on loans used to finance the acquisition of tangible fixed assets.

Disclosure. The amount of operating subsidies and compensatory amounts received from public authorities must be disclosed in the notes.

Reference. RD October 8, 1976.

25. Research and Development

Definitions. Research and development costs are not defined in the accounting law but they are generally understood to include the cost of developing prototypes and research and experimentation that will benefit the enterprise through new knowledge, developing new products and improving the production process.

Accounting Treatment. Research and development costs may be capitalized as intangible fixed assets only to the extent that they do not exceed a prudent estimate of their useful value or their future profit contribution to the enterprise.

Capitalized research and development costs must normally be depreciated over five years following an established plan.

If research and development costs are subsidized by government authorities, the subsidy is either included as other operating revenue or deducted from the capitalized costs.

Disclosure. The valuation rules adopted to capitalize research and development costs have to be disclosed. Depreciation spread over more than five years must be justified.

Reference. RD October 8, 1976.

26. Capitalized Interest Costs

Accounting Treatment. The acquisition cost of tangible and intangible fixed assets may include interest, for the period preceding their being ready for their intended use, on capital borrowed to finance their acquisition. The cost of inventory and contracts in progress may also include interest, if the normal production or completion period exceeds one year. Interest expense in the income statement is shown net of capitalized interest.

Disclosure. Interest included in the cost of tangible or intangible fixed assets and in production costs of inventory or contracts in progress must be disclosed in the valuation rules. The amount of interest capitalized must be disclosed separately in the notes.

Reference. RD October 8, 1976.

27. Imputed Interest

General. The imputation of interest in specific circumstances is required by Belgian accounting law. Unless otherwise specified, interest should be calculated at the market rate prevailing for similar transactions when the transaction is recorded.

Accounting Treatment. If amounts receivable or payable are stated at their nominal value, the following must be recorded as deferred income and credited to income as earned:

☐ Any interest included by agreement between the parties relating to the nominal value of the amounts receivable or payable.

☐ Any difference between the purchase price and the nominal value of the amounts receivable or payable.

☐ Any discount on amounts receivable or payable that are noninterest bearing or bear an exceptionally low interest rate, provided that these amounts are receivable or payable after one year and relate either to transactions recorded as income or expense in the income statement or to the purchase price of fixed assets or of a business segment.

Disclosure. There are no specific disclosure requirements.

Reference. RD October 8, 1976.

28. Extraordinary or Unusual Items (Produits/Charges Exceptionnels [F], Uitzonderlijke Opbrengsten/Kosten [D])

Extraordinary Items. Extraordinary items are defined as all income or expenses that do not result from the normal activities of the enterprise. Extraordinary items must be separately disclosed in the income statement.
    The following specific items are considered extraordinary:

☐ Adjustments to provisions for extraordinary liabilities and expenses recorded in prior years.

☐ Gains or losses on disposals of fixed assets, if significant and unusual.

☐ The write-back of amounts previously written off for intangible and tangible fixed assets.

☐ Exceptional depreciation and the exceptional write-off of formation expenses, intangible and tangible fixed assets.

☐ Financial fixed asset write-offs and adjustments to financial fixed assets written off in previous years.

☐ Supplementary or exceptional depreciation due to technological changes or changes in the economic environment to ensure that book values do not exceed the value of the assets to the enterprise.

Disclosure. Extraordinary income and expenses, without adjusting for taxes, are shown in the income statement prior to income before taxes. If the amounts are material, they should be explained in the notes. Their effect on the tax charge for the year should be separately disclosed.

Reference. RD October 8, 1976.

29. Income Taxes (Impôts sur le Résultat [F], Belastingen op het Resultaat [D])

Accounting Treatment. Income tax expense is based on taxable net income. There is presently no requirement to record deferred taxes on timing differences, except for deferred taxes on investment grants and on certain untaxed reserves. However, information on deferred taxes and accumulated tax losses deductible from future net income should be disclosed in the notes.

Disclosure. The income statement should separately present adjustments on the settlement of previous years' tax liabilities. The notes should disclose tax expense for the current year and supplementary charges from previous years.

Reference. RD October 8, 1976.

30. Postretirement Benefits

General. Belgian companies often have supplementary group insurance pension plans for their staff, funded by the payment of premiums to an outside insurance institution.

Internally funded pension plans were common in Belgium before 1986. However, since January 1, 1986, liabilities resulting from staff pension plans must be assumed by independently established pension funds organized as noncommercial legal entities, with representatives of both the staff and the enterprise on the governing boards. These entities have to comply with the Belgian legislation relating to insurance institutions.

Accounting Treatment. The methods used by Belgian insurance companies to calculate the annual pension premiums do not generally provide pension costs that approximate a level percentage of the current and expected future pensionable payroll.

The outstanding liability for early retirement plans for personnel is recorded when the decision is made to grant early retirement.

Postretirement benefits other than pensions have to be provided for in full in accordance with the general matching principle, although no specific standards exist. Such benefits are, however, exceptional in Belgian companies since the state-owned social security system provides benefits to retirees.

Disclosure. The increase or decrease in the provision for pension and similar obligations has to be disclosed in the notes, as well as a brief description of any supplementary retirement or survivors' pension plan for personnel or executives. How the entity funds these liabilities should also be disclosed.

Reference. RD October 8, 1976.

31. Discontinued Operations

Belgian accounting legislation does not specifically address discontinued operations. Some guidance is given on accounting for reorganization costs.

If part of a company's operations are discontinued, the relevant costs should be recognized when the decision to discontinue is made. These costs may be capitalized when they are clearly defined and relate to a substantial change in the structure or organization of the enterprise, provided that the change is intended to have a lasting and favorable effect on the profitability of the enterprise. A statement of compliance with these conditions must be given in the notes. These capitalized costs generally include employee termination, write-downs of current assets, extraordinary depreciation of fixed assets, provision for liabilities and charges resulting from claims.

Capitalized amounts must be included with formation expenses and should be depreciated following the valuation rules of the enterprise.

Disclosure.   Formation expenses should be disclosed in the notes, including changes in cost, depreciation and net book value. Details on the amount of reorganization costs recorded should also be disclosed.

Reference.   RD October 8, 1976.

32. Earnings per Share

There is no requirement to disclose earnings per share in Belgium. However, certain large quoted companies mention earnings per share in their annual reports. The figure is calculated by dividing net profit by the number of outstanding shares.

Appendix
DO BELGIAN STANDARDS OR PREVALENT PRACTICE SUBSTANTIALLY COMPLY WITH INTERNATIONAL ACCOUNTING STANDARDS?

Section	Topic	Substantially complies with IAS?	Comments
3.	Basic accounting concepts and conventions	Yes	
	Contents of financial statements	No	No cash flow statement or statement of changes in financial position is required
4.	Business combinations*	Yes	
5.	Joint ventures	Yes	
6.	Foreign currency translation*	Yes	
8.	Accounting changes*	Yes	
9.	Prior period adjustments*	Yes	
10.	Post balance sheet events	Yes	
11.	Related party transactions	No	Disclosures are limited to certain transactions and balances with directors and group companies
12.	Segmental information	No	Disclosure is limited to an analysis of net turnover
13.	Property, plant and equipment*	Yes	
15.	Leases	Yes	
16.	Investments	Yes	
17.	Accounts receivable	Yes	
18.	Inventories and work in progress*	Yes	Except that valuation at direct cost (no overhead allocation) is permitted
19.	Current liabilities	Yes	
20.	Long-term debt	Yes	
21.	Contingencies	Yes	
22.	Capital and reserves	Yes	
23.	Revenue recognition*	Yes	
24.	Government grants and assistance	Yes	
25.	Research and development*	Yes	
26.	Capitalization of interest costs*	Yes	

Appendix (*Continued*)

Section	Topic	Substantially complies with IAS?	Comments
28.	Extraordinary or unusual items*	Yes	
29.	Income tax**	No	Tax effect accounting is required only in consolidated financial statements
30.	Postretirement benefits*	No	

*These topics are subject to change as a result of the IASC Improvements Project—see the appendix to the International Accounting Standards chapter.

**The IAS on accounting for taxes on income is currently being revised, and an exposure draft has been issued.

Comparison in this table is made to International Accounting Standards in force at January 1, 1993. For further details, see the International Accounting Standards chapter.

BRAZIL

GENERAL NATIONAL INFORMATION

1. Source of Generally Accepted Accounting Principles

Generally Accepted Accounting Principles (Princípios Fundamentais de Contabilidade). **Generally accepted accounting principles** are derived from authoritative pronouncements, accounting literature and well-established practice.

Accounting Standards. Brazilian Corporate Law (Lei das Sociedades por Acões—Lei no. 6,404, de 15.12.1976) contains the basic requirements for financial statement preparation and disclosure and is applicable to all companies organized to do business as a "Sociedada Anônima" (SA), which is a corporate form and is the required form for all **public companies**.

Accounting standards for public companies in Brazil are the responsibility of the Securities Exchange Commission (Comissão de Valores Mobiliários [CVM]).

The Federal Accounting Council (Conselho Federal de Contabilidade [CFC]), the Brazilian Accountants' Institute (Instituto Brasileiro de Contadores [IBRACON]), issues and codifies accounting standards that form the body of generally accepted accounting principles in Brazil. If such pronouncements are approved by the CVM, they become obligatory for public companies. When there is no codified accounting standard issued by the CFC, CVM or IBRACON, general acceptability is based on principles and methods that have been established through practice as acceptable. The basis for this judgment may in certain instances, however, be a perception of well-established practices.

The great majority of Brazilian companies, including many subsidiaries of multinational corporations operating in Brazil, are structured as "Limitadas." Unlike SAs, these companies are not required to publish their financial statements. Unless they are subject to independent audit, they tend generally to adopt **accounting procedures** acceptable to the tax authorities, which may not be fully in accordance with generally accepted accounting principles.

2. Audit and Public Company Requirements

Audits. Public companies are required to file and publish audited comparative financial statements. Audits are performed by independent auditors registered with the CVM.

Auditors are chosen by the company's administrative council (Conselho de Administração), which is its governing board and is elected by the shareholders.

Companies organized to do business as SAs are governed by Corporate Law 6,404. Nonpublic SAs are required to publish comparative financial statements, which do not have to be audited.

Financial statements are published in the official state register and in one other paper with large circulation where the company is headquartered. The financial statements must be published within certain time periods preceding the general annual shareholders' meeting, as specified in the Corporate Law.

A public company auditor must comply with specified independence requirements and must be a member of the professional accounting body in Brazil. Membership requires a degree and practical experience.

The CFC has ultimate responsibility for auditing standards. CVM and IBRACON also issue certain auditing standards. In general, the majority of auditing standards have been codified.

Public Companies.   Admission requirements: Companies desiring to issue securities to the public in Brazil must apply for a listing with the CVM. The application requires filing of various corporate documents, financial statements (the latest year audited) and a specific form detailing information about the company.

Continuing reporting requirements: A registered company has to comply with periodic information requirements such as financial information, corporate bylaws and shareholder meeting notices and minutes.

Financial information is submitted to the CVM on a quarterly basis 45 days after the end of each quarter (except for the last quarter) or at the time such information is released to the shareholders or the public, if earlier. Quarterly information is reviewed by the auditors. Annual audited financial statements are submitted one month prior to the date of the general annual shareholders' meeting or when published, if earlier.

GENERAL ACCOUNTING

3.   Financial Statements

Basic Accounting Concepts.   **Historical cost** is the primary basis of measurement. Transactions and events are recognized in financial statements at the amount of cash or cash equivalents paid or received or the fair value ascribed to them when they took place. Since Brazil has had chronic high inflation, the historical cost basis is modified to express the original cost in the equivalent number of units of current purchasing power as of the financial statement date. This is done by adjusting, or indexing, certain nonmonetary assets classified as permanent assets (ativo permanente), such as fixed assets and related accumulated depreciation, investments and deferred costs, and shareholders' equity accounts. Inventories are not considered nonmonetary items. The index used to adjust permanent assets is defined in legislation as the index recognized by the federal government for measuring the devaluation of the local currency by adjusting the short-term federal government debt (treasury bills). The entry to adjust these accounts is recorded in income for the year in the monetary correction adjustment account (correçso monetária de balanço).

Corporate Law permits appraisal write-ups of assets to market value. Although Corporate Law indicates the possibility of appraising all assets, in practice appraisals are performed only for fixed assets. Market value for fixed assets is defined as current replacement cost less a provision for technical and physical depreciation. Corporate Law establishes the basic procedures for appraisals, and IBRACON Pronouncement XVII defines specific procedures required for such appraisals to be in accordance with generally accepted accounting principles. Required procedures include:

☐ The appraisal write-up is recorded as an increase to the asset and a corresponding credit to a special equity account called appraisal reserve (reserva de reavaliação). For appraisal write-ups recorded on or after January 1, 1993, the credit made to the appraisal reserve must be reduced by income taxes, resulting in a deferred tax liability.

☐ The amount of the appraisal write-up is determined on an asset-by-asset basis.

☐ The appraisal write-up, related asset and special equity account are adjusted for the effects of inflation. The asset, including appraisal write-up, is amortized or depreciated or incorporated into cost of production over the remaining useful life indicated in the appraiser's valuation report. Such amortization or depreciation is not tax-deductible.

☐ The appraisal reserve equity account is allocated to each accounting period in the same proportion as the underlying assets. The amount of the appraisal reserve equity account allocated to the period, net of related tax effects, is reclassified to retained earnings. The related portion of the deferred tax liability is reclassified to the current accrual for income taxes.

☐ The effect on income each year from the depreciation, amortization or other allocation of the appraisal write-up is to be disclosed in the notes to the financial statements. If the appraisal write-up equity account is used to increase the company's capital or offset accumulated losses, treatments that are accepted but not recommended in Pronouncement XVII, the amounts must be disclosed in the notes; the remaining appraisal write-up, net of accumulated depreciation or amortization, in the asset accounts must also be disclosed until the company's net worth is no longer affected.

Financial statements are prepared on the assumption that the entity is a **going concern**.

Items are recognized in the financial statements on the **accrual** basis of accounting (**matching concept**).

Transactions and events should be accounted for and presented in a manner that conveys their substance rather than their legal or other form.

The qualitative characteristics important in the preparation of financial information are objectivity, **conservatism**, **materiality** and consistency.

Reference. CFC Pronouncement, *Brazilian Accounting Standards*, IBRACON Pronouncement, *Basic Conceptual Structure of Accounting* (*Estrutura Conceitual Basica da Contabilidade*); Corporate Law 6,404, articles 8, 182, 183 and 185; and CVM Deliberation No. 27.

Contents of Financial Statements (Demonstracões Financeiras). Financial statements include a balance sheet, income statement, statement of changes in shareholders' equity and statement of changes in financial position. Notes to financial statements are an integral part of the statements. Financial statements should be comparative. They are accompanied by a report of the administrative council commenting on the business and financial statements.

Reference. Corporate Law 6,404, article 176.

Format of Financial Statements. Corporate Law specifies the basic format to be used for financial statements. Assets and liabilities are segregated between current and non-current in the balance sheet. Classification is based on the longer of the operating cycle or one year.

The basic format for the income statement includes operating and nonoperating items, the adjustment for the balance sheet effects of inflation and participations and contributions, such as **minority interests**.

Reference. Corporate Law 6,404, article 187.

Disclosure of Accounting Policies. An entity should describe **accounting policies** significant to its operations, especially if judgment has been exercised, and **accounting principles** and methods peculiar to the industry in which it operates. These disclosures are normally presented in the first note to the financial statements.

Reference. Corporate Law 6,404, article 176.

4. Business Combinations

Principles of Consolidation (Consolidacão). Corporate Law requires **consolidated financial statements** to be prepared for public companies more than 30 percent of whose net worth is represented by investments in **subsidiaries**. The 30 percent test is based on the balances of all investments (equity basis) plus related **goodwill** and write-down provisions, if applicable.

With certain exceptions, public companies are required to consolidate controlled subsidiaries (see "Control" below). Examples of acceptable exceptions, which must be approved by the CVM, to the consolidation rules are when:

- ☐ Control by the **parent company** is temporary—The alternative is to use the net realizable value or carrying value as determined by the **equity method**.
- ☐ The subsidiary is under judicial receivership (concordata), is bankrupt or insolvent (falência) or is undergoing a complete reorganization—The alternative is to use the lower of estimated **net realizable value** or carrying value as determined by the equity method.
- ☐ Financial statement components of a subsidiary are so dissimilar to those of other companies in the group that their inclusion in the consolidated financial statements would not provide an informative presentation (e.g., consolidation of a banking subsidiary by an industrial conglomerate)—The alternative is to use the equity method.

The consolidated financial statements are prepared and are published together with those of the parent company.

Reference. Corporate Law 6,404, articles 249 and 275, paragraph 3; CVM Instruction No. 15, articles 21 and 24; CVM Deliberation No. 28; and IBRACON Pronouncement XII.

Accounting for Business Combinations. **Business combinations** are transactions in which one company obtains control of another company or of a group of assets that constitutes a business entity. Transactions between companies under common control are not business combinations. Business combinations are accounted for by the **purchase method**, except in those rare instances where an acquirer cannot be identified; in such cases, the **pooling of interests method** is used.

Goodwill. The cost of the acquiring company's interest in identifiable assets and liabilities should be based on their fair values at the acquisition date. The difference between the purchase price and the acquiring company's interest in the identifiable net assets should be accounted for as **goodwill** (ágio) or **negative goodwill** (deságio) on the balance sheet. Goodwill is accounted for and amortized in separate components based on origin, as follows:

- [ ] The difference between book value and market value of assets—Amortized over the remaining useful lives of the assets.
- [ ] Differences in expected future profitability—Amortized over the period used in the projections, unless impairment of value is noted prior to the termination of the period.
- [ ] Intangibles, customer lists and similar items—Amortized over the estimated period of use, unless impairment of value is noted prior to expiration of the period.

Reference. CVM Instruction No. 1.

Control. A subsidiary, referred to as a controlled subsidiary (controlada), is a company in which the parent has predominance in decision making and the power to elect a majority of the administrative council. Normally, these conditions are met when the parent owns, directly or indirectly, more than 50 percent of the voting shares of the subsidiary.

Reference. Corporate Law 6,404, article 243.

Equity Accounting (Equivalência Patrimonial). Companies are affiliated (coligada) if one company owns at least 10 percent of the capital (either **common** or **preferred shares**) of the other. Ownership must be direct to meet the 10 percent test; indirect ownership is not mentioned in the law. Corporate Law mandates equity accounting for investments in affiliates that are relevant (as defined below) and whose administrative council can be influenced by the investor or in which the investor owns 20 percent or more of the capital, and for controlled subsidiaries of companies that do not have publicly traded securities.

For affiliates in which a company owns between 10 percent and 20 percent of the capital, Corporate Law requires equity accounting if the investor has influence over the administration of the affiliate.

Corporate Law defines a relevant investment as an investment in an affiliate or subsidiary for which the book value is equal to or greater than 10 percent of the net worth of the investor or, when considered together, the book value of all investments in affiliates and subsidiaries is equal to or greater than 15 percent of the net worth of the investor.

Reference.   Corporate Law 6,404, articles 247 and 248.

Minority Interests (Participacão Minoritária).   SAs presenting consolidated financial statements show minority interests in a subsidiary's assets and liabilities at the carrying values recorded by the subsidiary. Minority interests are presented on the balance sheet between liabilities and shareholders' equity. Minority interests in the results of operations for the year are shown separately in the income statement as the last item prior to consolidated net income.

Disclosure.   The accounting policies note should describe the consolidation principles used. There should be a statement that all material intercompany transactions and the related tax effects, including unrealized profits, have been eliminated. Entities included in the consolidation are also listed in this note. If a subsidiary meeting all requirements for consolidation is excluded from consolidation, the reason(s) for the exclusion should be disclosed.

The notes should include information on all significant business combinations, including the accounting method used. The following details should be included: the name and description of the business acquired (combined), the date of the acquisition (combination) and the period for which the results of operations of the acquired (combined) business are included in the income statement.

The notes also should include the following information for each subsidiary and affiliate:

- [ ] Name, capital and net worth.
- [ ] Number, kind and class of shares held and, if applicable, the corresponding market value of the shares.
- [ ] Net income for the period.
- [ ] Intercompany receivable and payable balances, indicating terms, conditions and guarantees, if any.
- [ ] The amount of equity in net income (loss) of unconsolidated subsidiaries (affiliates) included in net income of the investor for the period (the total of all investments is reflected separately in net income split between operating and nonoperating results).
- [ ] Method of recognizing and amortizing goodwill.
- [ ] Conditions existing in any agreements between shareholders regarding administration and/or distribution of profits.
- [ ] Subsequent events that could have a relevant effect on future consolidated results of operations or financial position.

Reference.   Corporate Law 6,404, articles 176 and 244; CVM Instruction Nos. 1 and 15; and Orientation Opinion No. 4.

5. Joint Ventures

Forms of Joint Ventures. Brazilian Corporate Law does not clearly define the different forms of **joint ventures**. In practice, two forms of joint ventures have been utilized: **jointly controlled** entities and jointly controlled operations and/or assets (consortium).

Accounting for Investments in Joint Ventures. The following methods should be adopted by the venturers:

☐ Jointly controlled entities—A venturer should report its interest in its financial statements using the equity method.

☐ Jointly controlled operations and/or assets—A venturer should recognize its interest through **proportionate consolidation**, as follows:

—its share of jointly controlled assets, classified according to the nature of the assets;

—any liabilities that it has incurred;

—its share of any liabilities incurred jointly with the other venturers in relation to the joint venture;

—any income from the sale or use of its share of the output of the joint venture, together with its share of any expenses incurred by the joint venture; and

—any expenses that it has incurred with respect to its interest in the joint venture.

Disclosure. Disclosures under equity accounting are similar to those described in Section 4. Where proportionate consolidation is used, the following should be disclosed:

☐ A general description of the objective of the joint venture, its activity, duration and other relevant terms of the contractual arrangement.

☐ The share of the venturer of the output, income, expenses, results and assets and liabilities of the joint venture.

☐ Any contingencies that the venturer has incurred in relation to its interest in the joint venture and its share in each of the **contingencies** incurred jointly with other venturers.

☐ The venturer's share of the contingencies of the joint venture for which it is contingently liable.

☐ Those contingencies that arise because the venturer is contingently liable for the liabilities of the other venturers in a joint venture.

Reference. Corporate Law 6,404, articles 247, 248, 249, 250, 278 and 279.

6. Foreign Currency Translation

Bases of Translation. Domestic operations: **Foreign currency** denominated **transactions** and balances (**monetary items**) are translated at current exchange rates. Exchange gains and losses are included in income.

Foreign operations: For subsidiaries or affiliates operating in countries with hard and stable currencies (not specifically defined), or countries without hard currencies but with systems that adequately adjust for the effects of inflation on the financial statements, balance sheet items are translated into the Brazilian currency using the **current exchange rate** at the balance sheet date. For subsidiaries or affiliates operating in countries with high inflation, soft currencies and no system to adequately adjust for the effects of inflation, the Brazilian inflation accounting methodology of adjusted historical cost is used for nonmonetary items in the balance sheet, excluding inventories. An acceptable alternative for high inflation countries is to first adopt a hard currency as the functional currency and translate the financial statements into it, and then convert nonmonetary items into the Brazilian currency using the current rate.

Exchange gains or losses resulting from the translation of the financial statements of foreign operations are included in the results of operations of the period.

Hedges. If a **hedge** is a monetary item, it is translated at the current rate, and any gain or loss will automatically offset the loss or gain on the transaction or balance hedged. If the hedge is a nonmonetary item, there will be no current exchange gain or loss. Any gain or loss from the translation of the hedged item will be currently recognized in the income statement.

Disclosure. In addition to the normal disclosures required for subsidiaries and affiliates (see Section 4), the accounting policies note should describe how the financial statements were prepared and the methods used to translate amounts originally recorded in a foreign currency.

Any change in the translation or conversion method used is considered a change in accounting principle.

Reference. IBRACON Pronouncement XXV, *Investments in Foreign Operations and Criteria for Conversion of Financial Statements in Other Currencies to Local Currency*, and CVM Deliberation No. 28.

7. Changing Prices/Inflation Accounting

General. As stated in Section 3, Brazilian companies adjust the balance sheet for the effects of inflation. In addition to the preparation and publication of the financial statements required by Corporate Law 6,404, companies listed with the CVM must also prepare and publish a complete set of comparative financial statements in constant currency (correção integral). The government index (see Section 3) must be used to adjust the financial statements into the functional currency. All transactions during the year are remeasured into the functional currency. At year-end, units of constant purchasing power are converted into units of nominal local currency using the published value of the index of that date. Prior year financial statements are also converted from the units of constant purchasing power to nominal units of local currency at the latest year-end date.

In addition to remeasurement, the instructions for constant currency financial statements require that:

☐ Inventory be considered a nonmonetary item and remeasured using the functional currency. (As stated in Section 3, inventory is a monetary item in financial statements prepared in accordance with Corporate Law.)

☐ Noninterest-bearing monetary items be discounted to their present value. Discounting reflects the inflationary gains and losses on monetary items in the proper reporting period on an accrual basis. The discounts reduce appropriate line items in the income statement. For example, a discount of trade accounts receivable is accounted for as a reduction of sales. A discount of accounts payable is accounted for as a reduction of the related balance sheet or income statement account.

☐ The adjustment of the balance sheet for inflation (described in Section 3) is reclassified to the appropriate line items in the income statement. For example, the portion of the adjustment resulting from holding accounts receivable is reclassified as a reduction of sales. This adjustment is comparable to a gain or loss on the translation of financial statements of operations in high inflation countries.

Disclosure. The accounting policies note should contain a summary of the methodology used to prepare the constant currency financial statements. The disclosure should include the functional currency used, classifications of discounts to present value and reclassification of gains or losses from holding monetary items.

Reference. CVM Instruction Nos. 64, 67, 108 and 138.

8. Accounting Changes

Changes in Accounting Principles (Mudanças nos Princípios Contábeis). Changes in principles, policies and methods are permitted; a new principle need not be preferable to the one it replaced, provided that the new principle is an acceptable alternative accounting principle. The net cumulative effect of the change is accounted for by adjusting opening **retained earnings**.

Accounting Estimates (Estimativas). A change in an estimate arises from new information or developments. The effect of a change in an accounting estimate should be accounted for prospectively.

Disclosure. Footnote disclosure is required for all material changes in principles, policies and methods. The effects of the change on the beginning balance sheet and on net income of the previous year are disclosed. The adjustment to opening retained earnings is shown separately in the statement of changes in shareholders' equity.

Reference. Corporate Law 6,404, article 177.

9. Prior Period Adjustments (Ajustes dos Exercícios Anteriores)

Definition of Adjusting Items. **Prior period adjustments** relate to changes in accounting principles, policies or methods or the correction of a known error that cannot be attributed to subsequent or current events.

Accounting Treatment. Prior period adjustments are recorded as an adjustment to opening retained earnings.

Disclosure. The nature of the error and its effects on the financial statements of the prior year are disclosed in the notes. The adjustment to opening retained earnings is shown separately in the statement of changes in shareholders' equity.

Reference. Corporate Law 6,404, articles 176 and 186.

10. Post Balance Sheet Events (Eventos Subseqüentes)

Definition. Two different types of post balance sheet events are identified in the accounting standards:

☐ Those that provide further evidence of conditions that existed at the financial statement date.

☐ Those that are indicative of conditions that arose subsequent to the financial statement date.

Accounting Treatment. The financial statements should be adjusted for events occurring between the financial statement date and their release date that provide additional information relating to conditions existing at the financial statement date.

Disclosure. Disclosure should be made in a note of material events relating to conditions arising after the financial statement date. The note should indicate both the nature of the event and, when practical, the estimated financial statement effect. No disclosure is required for events relating to conditions existing at the financial statement date.

Reference. Corporate Law 6,404, article 176, paragraph 5i, and CVM Orientation Opinion No. 4.

11. Related Party Transactions (Transações Entre Partes Relacionadas)

Definition. A related party is an entity, corporate or individual, with which a company could conduct transactions that might not be at arm's length. For example, one entity or its controlling shareholders might have an ownership interest in another entity, giving the first entity the ability to influence the decision-making process of the second entity. The definition also includes the following economic relationships:

☐ Companies directly or indirectly controlled by the same company.

☐ Companies with common administrative council members who could influence and/or benefit from decisions of the companies.

☐ Shareholders, administrative council members or family members of shareholders or council members.

☐ Directly or indirectly controlled subsidiaries and affiliates or shareholders or council members of such subsidiaries or affiliates.

☐ Suppliers, customers or creditors with which the company has a relationship of economic or financial dependency, or any other relationship that could permit non-arm's-length transactions.

Accounting Treatment. Related party transactions are recorded in accordance with normal accounting practices and principles.

Disclosure. Disclosure of the nature and extent of related party transactions is required to assist users of financial statements in understanding the impact of transactions between parties that, because of their relationship, are not dealing at arm's length.

The following information should be disclosed:

☐ A description of the nature and extent of related party transactions, including whether the transactions were made under general market conditions.

☐ A description of the relationship of the entities involved.

☐ Amounts due to or from related parties and the volume and amounts of transactions during the period, segregated between transactions conducted in the normal course of business and those not, and usually including "no charge" transactions.

☐ A description of any circumstances in which the entity is economically dependent on a major customer, supplier or lender.

Reference. CVM Deliberation No. 26 and IBRACON Pronouncement XXIII.

12. Segmental Information

General. There are no formal requirements for accounting for or reporting results from various segments of an entity or business. In some circumstances, disclosures for subsidiaries and affiliates may provide information relevant to business segments. Also, Corporate Law requires the administrative council to publish, together with the financial statements, a report detailing lines of business and principal administrative actions during the period.

In addition to this information, the CVM has published guidance on the preparation of the administrative council's report for public companies. Among the suggested disclosures is a description of businesses, products and services and the volume and amount of sales during the past two years. Some companies present line of business or segment information if it is important to an understanding and evaluation of the business.

Reference. Corporate Law 6,404, article 133, and CVM Orientation Opinion Nos. 15 and 17.

ACCOUNTING PRINCIPLES FOR SPECIFIC ITEMS— BALANCE SHEET

13. Property, Plant and Equipment (Ativo Imobilizado)

Classification of Capital and Revenue Expenditure. Expenditures that significantly increase the useful life and capacity of an asset are capitalized as part of its cost. Expenditures to maintain normal operating efficiency are expensed as incurred.

Basis of Valuation. Property, plant and equipment are accounted for on the basis of historical cost, adjusted as described in Section 3. Regardless of the carrying value, the net book value should not exceed the amount expected to be recovered through normal operations or sale. Gains and losses arising on the disposal of property, plant and equipment are included in income for the period. Both purchased and self-constructed assets are permitted to be capitalized at a cost that fairly reflects expenditures necessary to bring them to their present location and in a condition ready for use. Thus, for self-constructed assets, indirect and overhead costs are also capitalized. There is no provision in Brazilian GAAP for capitalizing interest during construction.

Depreciation. Various **depreciation** methods are used. The **straight-line method** is the most common in practice; however, any consistently applied method that produces a reasonable and systematic allocation over the asset's useful life is acceptable. If an asset was appraised, subsequent depreciation charges should be based on the new value and the new or reconfirmed useful life cited in the appraisal report.

Disclosure. Disclosure requirements for property, plant and equipment are as follows:

- [ ] Principal classes and type of **fixed assets** must be disclosed on the face of the balance sheet or in the notes.
- [ ] Adjusted acquisition cost and accumulated depreciation are separately disclosed.
- [ ] Basis of valuation; if appraisals were performed, the date, amount and type of appraisal are disclosed.
- [ ] Depreciation method(s) and rates.
- [ ] Assets mortgaged, pledged or subject to liens.
- [ ] Changes in methods or in criteria for accounting for fixed assets are changes in accounting principles and require the disclosures noted in Section 8.
- [ ] Assets that are not used or that are totally depreciated should be disclosed separately, if material.
- [ ] Insurance coverage.

Reference. Corporate Law 6,404, article 176, paragraph 5.

14. Intangible Assets (Ativo Intangível)

Accounting Treatment. **Intangible assets** acquired from a third party are recognized in the balance sheet.

Valuation. Valuation is the same as for purchased tangible assets.

Amortization. Intangible assets without fixed or determinable lives should be amortized over the expected period of benefit.

Disclosure. The following should be disclosed:

- [ ] Method and period of **amortization**.
- [ ] General description of origin of the asset.

Reference. Corporate Law 6,404, articles 179, 183 and 185.

15. Leases (Arrendamento Mercantil)

Classification. For lessees, all leases, regardless of their economic substance, are treated as **operating leases**. For lessors, only public companies and regulated financial institutions in the leasing business are required to account for the substance of lease transactions as opposed to their form. In general for these lessors, classification is either as a capital lease or an operating lease.

Accounting Treatment. Operating leases: The rental payments are expensed by the lessee and recorded as revenue by the lessor in the periods to which they relate.

Capital leases: Public company or regulated financial institution lessors account for a capital lease as a sale or financing transaction.

Disclosure. Lessors: The accounting method used should be disclosed.

Lessees: For public company lessees, if capital leases have been accounted for as operating leases, disclosure is required in the notes, showing the amount of the asset and liability as if the transaction had been accounted for as a capital lease. Other lessees may but are not required to provide this information.

Reference. CVM Instruction No. 58, article 4.

16. Investments (Investimentos)

Valuation. General: Valuation of investments that are neither consolidated nor accounted for by the equity method depends on their classification as either temporary or permanent.

Temporary investments: Temporary investments are in either the current or long-term asset (ativo realizável a longo prazo) section of the balance sheet, depending on the intended holding period. These investments are carried at the lower of monetarily corrected cost or market value.

Permanent investments: Permanent investments are grouped in the permanent asset (ativo permanente) section of the balance sheet and are carried at the lower of monetarily corrected cost or market value. Classification as a permanent investment implies that management intends to hold the investments for an extended period of time. This valuation basis is also appropriate for investments in affiliates that do not meet the relevance test described in Section 4. Normally, cost is determined on an average basis. The lower of cost or market principle should be applied as follows:

□ A valuation reserve (provisão) is made only if the loss is deemed to be permanent.

□ The evaluation is made on an investment-by-investment basis.

□ Once an investment has been written down, the reduced amount becomes the new cost basis for future valuation tests. The write-down provision is not reversed.

Gains/Losses. Gains or losses on the sale of securities are recognized in results of operations for the period as nonoperating income or expense.

Disclosure. The following should be disclosed for investments:

□ Significant variations in market value after the balance sheet date.

☐ Basis of valuation (temporary or permanent) for each type of investment.
☐ Market value, if available.
☐ Components of the investment caption.
☐ Any restrictions on the sale of investments.
☐ Investments mortgaged, pledged or subject to liens.

Reference. Corporate Law 6,404, articles 179 and 183.

17. Accounts Receivable (Contas a Receber)

Accounting Treatment. Recognition: Revenues and the related receivables are recognized when title passes on goods sold or when services are performed, and reasonable assurance regarding measurement and collectibility of the consideration exists.
　　Discounts: Sales are recorded net of nonconditional discounts. Conditional discounts or optional discounts, such as early payment discounts, are classified as interest expense.
　　Allowances: **Accounts receivable** should be recorded at their **net realizable value**. No specific method is prescribed for calculating the allowance for bad debts. The method used should be based on an analysis of individual items in the account, if practical.

Factored Receivables. Where receivables are discounted with recourse, discounts are reflected as a reduction of accounts receivable. Other forms of factoring receivables are not common.

Disclosure. Accounts and notes receivable should be separately presented for trade accounts (contas a receber—clientes), related parties (partes relacionadas) and unusual items, if material. Trade accounts are generally further divided into local market and export receivables, if exports are material. Also, allowances and discounts are disclosed, generally in the notes. The valuation basis for accounts receivable is disclosed in the accounting policies note. Receivables pledged or subject to liens are disclosed.

Reference. Corporate Law 6,404, article 176, paragraph 5, and article 183.

18. Inventories and Work in Process (Estoques)

General Accounting Treatment. **Inventories** are carried at the lower of cost or market, generally determined on an item-by-item basis. Cost is the nominal local currency cost, without adjustment (except for public companies, as described in Section 7).
　　Market is defined in article 183 of Corporate Law 6,404 as follows:

☐ For raw materials (materias-primas) and supplies—**Replacement cost**.
☐ For work in process (produtos em processo) and finished goods (produtos acabados)—Net realizable value from sale in the normal course of business less applicable taxes and selling expenses and a normal profit margin. Costs of a general nature (general administrative and general marketing costs) that cannot be clearly attributed to specific inventory items or groups of items are not deducted in calculating net realizable value. Work in process in a very early stage can be broken down into its elements of raw material for comparison with replacement; otherwise estimated

costs to complete are added to costs incurred as of the balance sheet date to determine total cost for comparison with net realizable value.

FIFO, specific cost, **average cost** and **LIFO** are all acceptable cost flow assumptions. LIFO is not acceptable for local tax purposes and is therefore rarely used in practice. Because of inflation, the weighted-moving-average cost method is used by most companies.

The cost of manufactured inventories is determined using full **absorption costing** based on an entity's normal operating capacity.

Long-Term Contracts (Contratos de Longo Prazo). **Revenue** is generally recognized using the **percentage of completion method**. Costs incurred are accumulated in an inventory account not subject to adjustment. Unbilled receivables and advances are accounted for and presented separately on the balance sheet.

Disclosure. The inventory cost flow assumptions and valuation principles used are disclosed in the accounting policies note. The principal components of inventory, including any valuation reserves, are disclosed, generally in the notes. Inventories pledged or subject to liens are disclosed.

For long-term contracts, required disclosures include: the revenue recognition basis and methods used to estimate percentage completed, method and policy used to account for changes in estimates (including their effects) and contracts accounted for by the **completed contract method**. Any significant loss provisions, incentives or penalties recognized during the period and data regarding unrecorded events such as disputes, claims and contingencies are also disclosed. Suggested disclosures include a general description of all large contracts, specifying obligations, business risks, incentives, penalties, contract amendments and financing agreements, and comments regarding any significant contracts cancelled or reduced in scope. A general summary of backlog and of contracts in progress, together with projected completion dates, is also included.

Reference. Corporate Law 6,404, article 176, paragraph 5, and IBRACON Pronouncement, *Construction, Fabrication or Service Contracts.*

19. Current Liabilities (Passivo Circulante)

General Accounting Treatment. **Current liabilities** are amounts payable within one year from the date of the balance sheet or within the normal operating cycle, if longer than one year. Current liabilities are presented by main classes, for example, bank loans, including current portion of long-term debt; trade payables; accrued liabilities; wages and related fringe benefits; taxes other than income taxes; income taxes; dividends payable; advances from customers; and deferred revenue. Trade **accounts payable** include amounts owed to creditors for goods and services purchased on credit for which invoices have been received. Unbilled obligations are recorded as accrued liabilities (e.g., utility usage). Amounts received from customers or clients for goods or services to be provided should be recorded as advances and not as deferred revenue. Deferred revenue includes items such as rents received in advance and commissions; it may also include amounts received in advance on long-term contracts.

Creation of General and Specific Provisions.   Liabilities are recorded when incurred, known and measurable. Therefore, general provisions are not permitted. However, for specific industries (airlines, shipping, steel and sugar) or types of equipment, provisions for maintenance or overhaul are recorded between overhaul dates.

The main types of specific provisions are for income taxes, dividends, employee entitlements and future expenses such as warranties. For income taxes and dividends, the actual liability is usually determined at a later date by the taxation authorities or shareholders. Employee entitlements are estimates of current entitlements to future paid leave on the basis of past services. A proposed dividend is recorded on the year-end balance sheet following the requirements of Corporate Law (see Section 22). The proposed dividend must be approved by the shareholders before payment.

Disclosure.   The principal classifications of current liabilities are presented on the face of the balance sheet if amounts are material. Assets securing short-term obligations are disclosed in connection with those assets. Separate disclosure of short-term debt components is not required. Any amounts due in foreign currency are presented separately, if material.

Reference.   Corporate Law 6,404, articles 179, 180 and 184.

20. Long-Term Debt (Empréstimos e Financiamentos)

General Accounting Treatment.   The most common forms of long-term debt are debentures, mortgages and long-term loans from government agencies. Amounts are recorded at their face value.

Debt Restructuring and Debt Extinguishment.   There are no official Brazilian standards on debt restructuring and extinguishment. There is a lack of long-term credit markets in Brazil, and these situations are not normally encountered in practice.

Disclosure.   Disclosures for long-term debt include amounts outstanding, interest rates, short- and long-term portions and principal provisions of debt contracts, such as restrictive covenants and collateral or security. Amounts due in foreign currencies are disclosed separately.

Reference.   Corporate Law 6,404, article 176, paragraph 5.

21. Contingencies (Contingências)

Contingent Losses.   A loss contingency should be recorded when a loss is deemed probable and the amount of the loss can be estimated.

Contingent Gains.   A gain contingency is recorded when realized, that is, when the transaction creating the gain is settled.

Disclosure.   Losses: If a contingent loss is not accrued, its nature and an estimate of its financial statement effect are generally disclosed in a note unless the possibility of a loss is remote. If a reliable estimate of the financial statement effect cannot be made, this fact is disclosed. **Contingencies** that are accrued may warrant separate disclosure.

Gains: If there is a possibility of realization, the nature and estimated amount can be disclosed, provided that the disclosure would not result in erroneous inferences by readers of the financial statements.

Reference. IBRACON Pronouncement XXII and Corporate Law 6,404, article 176, paragraph 5.

22. Capital and Reserves (Patrimônio Líquido)

General. Corporate Law divides shareholders' equity as follows:

☐ Capital (Capital social)—Amounts either received from shareholders or generated by the company and formally incorporated into the capital (capitalized).

☐ Capital reserves (Reservas de capital)—Amounts received that did not flow through income as revenues.

☐ Appraisal reserves (Reservas de reavaliacão)—Amounts relating to the appraisal write-up of assets (see Section 3).

☐ Profit reserves (Reservas de lucros)—Profits retained for specifically defined objectives.

☐ Retained earnings (Lucros ou prejuízos acumulados)—Profits retained for which objective(s) are yet to be defined.

Share Capital. **Share capital** includes both ordinary and preferred shares, which may be issued with or without **par value**. The excess of the issue price over par value is accounted for in a capital reserve. Shares without par value, when issued, may be divided between share capital and a capital reserve. Corporate Law limits the issuance of non-voting preferred shares to two-thirds of total capital. Shares are not required to be paid in full on issue but must be paid if the balance is called by the directors. Shares subscribed but not yet paid (capital subscrito) are shown on the face of the balance sheet as shares to be paid, which is a reduction of capital. An entity's bylaws may or may not establish limits for the number of authorized capital shares. Corporate Law permits both repayment and retirement of shares as well as capital reductions; specific procedures must be followed and public companies are subject to certain restrictions. **Treasury shares** are accounted for at cost as a reduction of share capital.

As explained in Section 3, shareholders' equity accounts are adjusted for the effects of inflation. The adjustment of the share capital account is accounted for in the capital reserve from monetary correction of capital account (correcão monetária do capital realizado). Corporate Law restricts increases in the share capital account to resolutions approved by the shareholders and requires, in general, that this reserve be capitalized as part of share capital when the shareholders approve the financial statements for the year.

Reserves. The following is a summary of the principal types of reserves:

☐ Capital reserves—Created when shares are issued and also result from the monetary correction of capital until such time as the adjustment is capitalized. In general, capital reserves, except for the monetary correction of capital reserve, can be used only to offset accumulated losses that exceed retained earnings and profit reserves (appropriated retained earnings); repay, retire or purchase shares; increase share capital; and pay dividends to preferred shareholders when stipulated by the issue and specified in the bylaws.

□ Appraisal reserves (see Section 3).

□ Legal reserve—Five percent of net income for the year must be allocated to this reserve prior to any other usage until the reserve equals 20 percent of the adjusted amount of share capital, or until the legal reserve plus reserves specified in article 192, paragraph 1, of Corporate Law exceed 30 percent of share capital as adjusted. This reserve can be used only to offset accumulated losses or to increase share capital.

□ Statutory reserves—Profit appropriation reserve required by the bylaws of the company.

□ Contingency reserve—Reserve approved by the shareholders; not normally encountered in practice.

□ Profit retention reserve—A reserve approved by the shareholders to support future capital investment. Public companies must disclose in the notes justification for retention of profits, even if left in retained earnings. This reserve may include principal components of the company's capital budget for a period of up to five years.

□ Unrealized profit reserve—An optional appropriation of retained earnings, it limits dividends when such payments would jeopardize the stability of the company. If this risk does not exist, the reserve should not be created. Corporate Law requires the payment of minimum dividends (see below). A calculation of the reserve must be included in the notes for public companies and is recommended for nonpublic companies.

Total reserves, excluding the contingency and unrealized profit reserves, may not exceed share capital. The excess must be capitalized or distributed as a dividend, as approved by the shareholders.

Reference.   Corporate Law 6,404, articles 182 and 193–197.

Dividends.   Dividends are payable from current period net income, retained earnings and profit reserves. Preferred dividends can be paid with capital reserves resulting from the issue of shares.

A minimum dividend must be distributed. Most public company bylaws specify the minimum dividend required by law—25 percent of net income as adjusted for contingency reserves, legal reserves and unrealized profit reserve. The law allows a waiver in certain instances, which are infrequent. Nonpublic companies may distribute less than the minimum or no dividend, if no shareholder at the annual meeting objects.

For public companies, the CVM has formally recommended payment of dividends adjusted for the effects of inflation from the balance sheet date to the payment date, which can be up to six months after year-end.

Corporate Law requires allocation of all profits (net income) generated during the period to the specific reserves described above. Statutory reserves and profit retention reserves cannot be created to an extent that would result in payment of less than the obligatory minimum dividend.

There are also foreign exchange rules applicable to foreign shareholders in Brazilian companies. Such rules are not contained in Corporate Law, but are exchange restrictions imposed by another federal law.

Reference.   Corporate Law 6,404, articles 192, 198 and 201.

Disclosure.   The following should be disclosed for capital and reserves:

- [ ] Treasury shares held.
- [ ] Adjustments to beginning retained earnings.
- [ ] Authorized capital, if applicable.
- [ ] Share capital—Number, type and classes of shares authorized, issued and outstanding as well as any shares not yet paid.
- [ ] Dividend per share and basis for its determination.
- [ ] Options to purchase outstanding shares of the company approved and exercised during the period.
- [ ] Appraisal and appraisal reserve.
- [ ] Reserve details—Nature and explanation of reserves (e.g., contingency and statutory reserves).
- [ ] Unrealized profit reserve—Detailed calculation.
- [ ] Profit retention reserve—Detailed justification.

Options, rights, warrants and similar items are not encountered in the Brazilian capital markets.

Reference.   Corporate Law 6,404, articles 176 and 186, and CVM Instruction Nos. 10, 39 and 59.

ACCOUNTING PRINCIPLES FOR SPECIFIC ITEMS— INCOME STATEMENT

23. Revenue Recognition

General Principles.   Revenue is recognized when goods are sold or services performed and reasonable assurance regarding measurement and collectibility of the consideration exists. Revenue from a sales transaction is recognized when the seller has transferred to the buyer the significant risks and rewards of ownership of the goods sold. In deciding whether the significant risks and rewards have been transferred, consideration should be given to whether any significant acts of performance remain to be completed and whether the seller retains continuing involvement in, or effective control of, the goods transferred.

Revenue from service transactions is usually recognized when the service is performed.

Long-Term Contracts.   Revenue is recognized using the percentage of completion method, unless estimates of progress toward completion, revenue and costs are not reasonably determinable. In that event, the completed contract method is used.

Rights of Return.   There are no codified rules in Brazil; practice is similar to that in the United States. If customers have the right to return purchases for a refund or replacement, the transaction should not be included in revenue unless the potential cost of the right of return can be estimated reliably and accrued.

Product Financing.   Although Brazilian standards do not specifically address this topic, accounting for the transaction should be based on its substance and not its form. Practice normally parallels that in the United States, where **product financing arrangements** are accounted for as borrowings, not as sales.

Disclosure.   Gross revenues from the sale of goods and services, less nonconditional discounts and sales taxes, and net sales after the reductions are disclosed.

Long-term contract disclosure requirements are included in Section 18.

Reference.   Corporate Law 6,404, article 187.

24.   Government Grants and Assistance

Accounting Treatment.   Government assistance to private-sector companies is primarily through a reduction or exemption of income tax for companies operating in specific areas. The tax normally due is computed and reflected as period expense. The amount of the incentive is recorded as a reclassification from retained earnings to a capital reserve. Restrictions on the use of this reserve exist and are similar to those on capital reserves, described in Section 22.

Disclosure.   Disclosure requirements are the same as for capital reserves (see Section 22).

25.   Research and Development

Accounting Treatment.   If material, expenses for new products are deferred and amortized over the period of expected future benefit. Expenditures necessary to maintain the market position of existing products are expensed as incurred.

Disclosure.   The nature and amounts deferred and amortization period and method should be disclosed.

Reference.   IBRACON Pronouncement VIII, *Deferred Assets*.

26.   Capitalized Interest Costs

General.   It is not appropriate to capitalize interest under Brazilian GAAP unless the company is in a preoperating stage or has a significant expansion in a preoperating stage. In these circumstances, special rules apply.

27.   Imputed Interest

General.   For the basic financial statements, interest is imputed only in accounting for capital leases.

For the constant currency financial statements described in Section 7, interest may be imputed to discount noninterest-bearing monetary items to their present value.

Disclosure.   Disclosure is covered by the note on capital lease obligations or in the required disclosures for the supplemental constant currency statements.

28.   Extraordinary or Unusual Items

General.   Extraordinary items (itens extraordinários) are items that are both unusual and infrequent, when considered in relation to the entity's operating environment. They are unrelated to typical activities and would not be expected to recur in the foreseeable future.

Unusual items are material items that are either unusual or infrequent.

Disclosure.   Extraordinary items, net of applicable income tax, are shown separately in the income statement (or in the notes in certain cases) and are not included in operating results. The notes include a description of the nature of the extraordinary item. Unusual items are separately disclosed, but are not shown net of tax. Unusual items are identified as operating or nonoperating depending on their characteristics.

Reference.   IBRACON Pronouncement XIV, *Income and Expense—Results*, paragraphs 58–60.

29.   Income Taxes

The provision for income tax is based on accounting income for the period. The deferred tax provision is the difference between the total tax provision and the amount of taxes currently payable. Deferred tax balances are adjusted for subsequent changes in tax rates in accordance with the liability method.

Losses cannot be carried back under existing tax legislation. The future tax benefit of accounting loss carryforwards, to the extent that such amounts exceed existing net deferred tax credits at the balance sheet date, is almost always recognized at the time it is realized. Only in rare circumstances is it recognized in the period in which the loss is generated.

Disclosure.   The following disclosures are required for income taxes:

☐   Tax loss carryforwards (and their expiration dates) are disclosed in the notes.
☐   When losses reduce current period tax expense, the amount of the reduction is disclosed in the notes.
☐   Deferred tax assets and liabilities are presented separately on the balance sheet.

Reference.   IBRACON Pronouncement XX, *Deferred Taxes*.

30.   Postretirement Benefits

General.   No formal pronouncements exist on accounting for pension plans and for other postretirement benefits to employees.

Accounting Treatment. For defined benefit pension plans, the actuarially determined contribution required to fund the plan is considered a reasonable basis for recording periodic pension expense. Costs of other postretirement benefits, which normally are minimal, are recorded on the cash basis.

Pension Fund Surpluses. Under existing legislation, once a payment is made by the company, no refunds are possible.

Disclosure. The notes should contain the following information:

- ☐ Description of the existing plan.
- ☐ Actuarial method used to determine the periodic pension expense and contribution to the plan.
- ☐ Annual benefit expense.
- ☐ Defined obligation recorded on the balance sheet.
- ☐ Potential obligations, recorded or not recorded, with appropriate explanations.

Reference. CVM Orientation Opinion 18.

31. Discontinued Operations

Accounting Treatment. There is no prescribed accounting method for discontinued operations. The following description is based on the basic accounting concepts described in Section 3 and on preferred practice.

Reorganization and business closure costs are recognized when there is a firm commitment to reorganize or discontinue operations. All costs relating to a particular reorganization or closure should, as far as possible, be recognized at the same time. Thus it is usual to include such items as redundancy payments, write-downs of assets to net realizable values and the costs of settling claims from customers or suppliers. Uncertainties could arise, however, in the treatment of revenue and of expenses incurred from the date the reorganization is recognized to the final completion date. It is generally appropriate to include short-term costs related to the completion of work on hand or incurred to obtain the best realization of assets. General overhead expenses that are likely to continue after the reorganization or closure has been completed should not be included.

Disclosure. Material reorganization costs should be disclosed separately on the face of the income statement or in the notes, together with an explanation of their treatment. Such costs could qualify for treatment as an extraordinary item.

32. Earnings per Share

Definition. Earnings per share is defined as net income divided by the total outstanding shares of all classes.

Method of Calculation. Earnings per share is calculated based on the weighted average number of shares outstanding during the period by class, if differences exist between classes.

Disclosure.   Earnings per share must be disclosed. Earnings per share is generally presented on the face of the income statement unless the determination is complex, that is, there are various classes of stock outstanding. Normally, the accounting policies note should contain the method used to calculate earnings per share.

Reference.   Corporate Law 6,404, article 187.

Appendix
DO BRAZILIAN STANDARDS OR PREVALENT PRACTICE SUBSTANTIALLY COMPLY WITH INTERNATIONAL ACCOUNTING STANDARDS?

Section	Topic	Substantially complies with IAS?	Comments
3.	Basic accounting concepts and conventions	Yes	
	Contents of financial statements	Yes	
4.	Business combinations*	Yes	Except that consolidated financial statements are required to be prepared only by public companies, more than 30 percent of whose net worth is represented by investments in subsidiaries
5.	Joint ventures	Yes	
6.	Foreign currency translation*	No	
8.	Accounting changes*	Yes	
9.	Prior period adjustments*	Yes	
10.	Post balance sheet events	Yes	
11.	Related party transactions	Yes	
12.	Segmental information	No	
13.	Property, plant and equipment*	Yes	
15.	Leases	No	
16.	Investments	Yes	
17.	Accounts receivable	Yes	
18.	Inventories and work in progress*	No	The cost of inventories is not adjusted for the effect of hyperinflation
19.	Current liabilities	Yes	
20.	Long-term debt	Yes	
21.	Contingencies	Yes	
22.	Capital and reserves	Yes	
23.	Revenue recognition*	Yes	
24.	Government grants and assistance	No	
25.	Research and development*	Yes	

Appendix (*Continued*)

Section	Topic	Substantially complies with IAS?	Comments
26.	Capitalization of interest costs*	Yes	
28.	Extraordinary or unusual items*	Yes	
29.	Income tax**	Yes	
30.	Postretirement benefits*	Yes	

*These topics are subject to change as a result of the IASC Improvements Project—see the appendix to the International Accounting Standards chapter.

**The IAS on accounting for taxes on income is currently being revised, and an exposure draft has been issued.

Comparison in this table is made to International Accounting Standards in force at January 1, 1993. For further details, see the International Accounting Standards chapter.

CANADA

GENERAL NATIONAL INFORMATION

1. Source of Generally Accepted Accounting Principles

Generally Accepted Accounting Principles. **Generally accepted accounting principles** (GAAP) are derived from authoritative pronouncements, accounting literature and well-established practice, and are applicable to the majority of business entities in Canada.

Accounting Standards. **Accounting standards** in Canada are issued by the Canadian Institute of Chartered Accountants (CICA) and are codified as "Recommendations" in the CICA Handbook. All references to Canadian standards indicate the Handbook section. Where there is no accounting standard, general acceptability is based on less formal guidance issued by the CICA or on those principles and methods that have been established through practice as acceptable.

Financial statement presentation and disclosure, generally accepted accounting principles and their methods of application are similar in Canada and the United States; however, there remain some significant differences.

2. Audit and Public Company Requirements

Audits. Under the Canada Business Corporations Act (CBCA), shareholders of a corporation are required to appoint an auditor annually who is independent of the corporation and its affiliates. Generally, all public corporations and other corporations with consolidated gross revenues exceeding $10 million or consolidated assets exceeding $5 million are required to file audited comparative financial statements.

Corporations and securities laws do not establish minimum qualifications for auditors. Some provinces provide for licensing of auditors. Licenses are normally issued only to persons with specific professional qualifications and experience. All auditors, regardless of their qualifications, are required to follow generally accepted auditing standards as promulgated by the CICA.

Public Companies. The CBCA requires companies under federal jurisdiction to prepare annual financial statements in compliance with recommendations in the CICA Handbook. These financial statements are required to be distributed to all shareholders at least 21 days before the annual meeting. Most provincial companies and securities legislation requires similar compliance.

Corporations that seek to issue securities to the public must meet the applicable securities legislation requirements. The relevant securities and corporations acts and regulations are determined on the basis of the incorporating jurisdiction of the offeror and the jurisdiction(s) in which the offer is to be made. A prospectus offering is the predominant method of issuing securities to the public in Canada.

GENERAL ACCOUNTING

3. Financial Statements

Basic Accounting Concepts. Except in unusual circumstances, financial statements are prepared using the **historical cost** basis of measurement. Items recognized in financial statements are accounted for in accordance with the **accrual basis** of accounting using accounting policies applicable to a **going concern**.

Transactions and events should be accounted for and presented in a manner that conveys their substance rather than their legal or other form. The determination of the substance of a transaction or event is a matter of professional judgment in the circumstances.

Comparability in the financial statements of an entity is enhanced when the same **accounting policies** are used consistently from period to period. When a change in accounting policy is deemed to be appropriate (see Section 8), disclosure of the effects of the change may be necessary to maintain comparability.

Contents of Financial Statements. Financial statements normally include a balance sheet, income statement, statement of retained earnings and statement of changes in financial position (or cash flow statement). Notes to financial statements and supporting schedules to which the financial statements are cross-referenced are considered an integral part of the statements. Financial statements are considered to be the **consolidated financial statements** of the parent and its **subsidiaries**. Financial statements of the **parent company** only are rarely issued for **public companies**.

Format of Financial Statements. Financial statements should be prepared in such form and use such terminology and classification as makes them readily understandable. They should normally be prepared on a comparative basis, showing amounts for the corresponding prior period.

In the balance sheet, assets and liabilities are segregated between current and noncurrent, except where such a classification is not helpful (e.g., financial institutions and companies in the development stage). Short-term items expected to be refinanced are classified as long-term only if contractual arrangements for the refinancing have been made. Obligations that are callable but not expected to be called within one year are sometimes classified as long-term, if there is evidence that the creditor does not intend to call for repayment within one year.

The statement of changes in financial position (or cash flow statement) is usually prepared using the **indirect method** of reporting cash flows, although the **direct method** is also permitted. Cash flows are reported by operating, investing and financing activities. Dividends may be reported as operating or financing activities or as a distinct category.

Disclosure of Accounting Policies. An entity should identify and describe the accounting policies that are significant to its operations. As a minimum, disclosure should include areas where judgment has been exercised (i.e., where there is a choice between acceptable alternatives) and the use of accounting principles and methods that are peculiar to the industry in which the entity operates.

In unusual circumstances, a literal application of an authoritative pronouncement might render the financial statements misleading, in which case it is necessary to depart from the usual treatment. The practice followed and the reason for the departure should be disclosed in a note.

When a financial statement item is reclassified, it is common practice to include a note explaining that certain items in the prior year statements have been restated to conform to the current year's presentation.

Reference. CICA Handbook S.1000, 1500, 1505 and 1540.

4. Business Combinations

Principles of Consolidation. All subsidiaries, defined as controlled enterprises, should be consolidated. Consolidation should cease when control is lost. Any continuing investment in a former subsidiary should be accounted for in accordance with its nature.

Control. Control of an enterprise is indicated by the continuing ability to determine its strategic operating, investing and financing policies without the cooperation of others.

Ownership of shares conferring a right to elect a majority of the board of directors usually gives control; however, there may be instances where other arrangements provide control without ownership of majority voting power. Conversely, control may sometimes not be considered to exist despite majority voting power; for example, where there are severe statutory restrictions on activities or where the investment was acquired with an intent to dispose of it in the foreseeable future.

Accounting for Business Combinations. **Business combinations** include transactions in which one company obtains control of another company or of a group of assets that constitutes a business entity. Business combinations do not include transactions between companies under common control, such as between two subsidiaries of the same parent. Business combinations should normally be accounted for by the **purchase method**. In those rare circumstances where an acquirer cannot be identified, the **pooling of interests method** is used.

Purchase method: There are specific recommendations for allocating the cost of the purchase to the assets and liabilities acquired. The cost of the acquiring company's interest in identifiable assets and liabilities should be based on their fair values to the purchaser at the date of acquisition. The fair values attributed to most acquired assets and liabilities are often their carrying values on the acquired company's books. Intangible and other assets such as land and buildings, natural resources and nonmarketable securities may be attributed a fair value equal to their estimated or appraised value. The excess of the cost of the purchase over the acquiring company's interest in identifiable net assets should be recorded as an asset, **goodwill**, in the balance sheet. **Negative goodwill** is not recognized. If assigned values exceed the cost of the net assets acquired, the excess is eliminated by reducing amounts assigned to identifiable nonmonetary assets.

Pooling of interests method: If the pooling of interests method is used, the combined company includes the assets and liabilities in its balance sheet at the values recorded by the combining companies prior to the combination. Income for the period in which the combination occurs is reflected on a combined basis, as the parties are considered to have always been combined.

Goodwill.   Goodwill arising from business acquisitions, as described above, is reflected separately on the balance sheet as an **intangible asset** and should be amortized to income by the straight-line method over its estimated life, not to exceed 40 years. Any impairment in value that is other than temporary, results in the unamortized portion of goodwill being written down by a charge against income.

Equity Accounting.   The equity method of accounting should be used for investments in an enterprise if the investor has the ability to exercise ''significant influence'' over the strategic operating, investing and financing policies of the investee. Indications of significant influence include representation on the board of directors, participation in the policy-making processes, material intercompany transactions and the interchange of company personnel and technical information. Significant influence is usually presumed to exist when the investor holds 20 percent or more of the investee's voting shares.

Minority Interests.   The interests of minority shareholders in the assets and liabilities of consolidated subsidiaries should be reflected in terms of carrying values in the accounting records of the subsidiaries. **Minority interests** should be shown separately from shareholders' equity.

Disclosure.   If an investee in which a majority voting interest is not held is consolidated, or an investee in which a majority voting interest is held is not consolidated, the reasons should be disclosed.

For each business combination the accounting method used, the net assets brought into the combination and the consideration given should be disclosed. Combined information may be presented for a number of small combinations.

Purchase method: Information should include the name and description of the business acquired, the date of acquisition and the period for which results of operations of the acquired business are included in the consolidated income statement and, where shares are acquired, the percentage held and the amount of consideration given by way of **common shares**, **preferred shares**, debt, cash or other consideration and any contingent consideration.

Pooling of interests method: The information disclosed should include the name and description of each of the companies involved; the percentage of each company's voting shares exchanged to effect the combination; the effective date; net assets brought into the combination by each of the combining companies; a description and the fair value of each type of consideration received by the shareholders of each of the combining companies; and a description, nature and fair value of the combined companies' voting shares held by each company.

Equity accounting: Investments in companies accounted for by the **equity method** should be disclosed separately as a class. Total income calculated by the equity method should also be disclosed separately.

If the operations of a company accounted for by the equity method are an important factor in evaluating the operations of the investor, disclosure of summarized information about the assets and liabilities and results of operations of the investee is desirable.

Reference. CICA Handbook, S.1580, 1590, 1600 and 3050.

5. Joint Ventures

Accounting for Investments in Joint Ventures. Canadian accounting recommendations do not address the different forms of **joint venture** detailed in IAS 31, *Financial Reporting of Interests in Joint Ventures*; they do acknowledge that joint ventures may be incorporated or unincorporated.

Jointly Controlled Operations. The accounting treatment in IAS 31 would be appropriate in Canada.

Jointly Controlled Assets. The accounting treatment in IAS 31 would be appropriate in Canada.

Jointly Controlled Entities. **Joint control** renders consolidation accounting inappropriate, even though a venturer may hold a majority investment in the undertaking.

The usual method of accounting for joint ventures is the equity method since it recognizes income when earned, matches costs with revenues and gives appropriate treatment to transactions with the joint venture. However, where a substantial part of their operations is through joint ventures, venturers have the option of accounting for their investment in joint ventures by the **proportionate consolidation method**. In rare cases when the benefits of an investment in a joint venture are unlikely to accrue to the venturer, the cost method of accounting should be used.

Transactions Between Venturers and the Joint Venture. In general, the contribution of assets to a joint venture in exchange for an interest in the venture does not give rise to a gain or loss on disposal in the contributor's financial statements. Gains resulting from other transactions between the venturer and the joint venture should be recognized only to the extent of the interests of nonrelated venturers. However, losses should be recognized in their entirety.

Disclosure. Equity accounting: Where a significant portion of the venturer's activities is carried on through joint ventures, a summary of the venturer's share of the assets and liabilities, revenues and expenditures of the venture(s) should be presented. The information may be on a combined basis for all ventures.

Proportionate consolidation accounting: Similar to equity accounting, except that if substantially all of the venturer's activities are carried out through joint ventures, a statement to this effect is sufficient disclosure.

In addition, where the venturer is liable for any contingent liability or commitment with respect to the joint venture, this should be disclosed.

The Canadian requirements are consistent with IAS 31, except that the equity method of accounting for an investment in a jointly controlled entity is an **allowed alternative** to IAS 31's **benchmark treatment** of proportionate consolidation. Canadian recommendations for the treatment of transactions between the venturers and the joint venture, and for the recognition of **contingencies** and commitments of and related to the joint venture, are similar to those in IAS 31 except that normally a venturer may not recognize a gain on assets contributed to a venture in exchange for an interest therein.

Accounting by Joint Ventures. Generally accepted accounting principles apply to all assets and liabilities and operations of joint ventures. However, there is little guidance in Canada on accounting by joint ventures for assets contributed by the venturers. At present, there are three permitted alternatives:

☐ Fair value.
☐ The carrying value of the assets in the contributor's financial statements.
☐ The carrying value of the contributor's net investment in the joint venture.

Disclosure. The basis of valuation of the assets contributed should be disclosed.

Reference. CICA Handbook S. 3055, as interpreted.

6. Foreign Currency Translation

Bases of Translation. General: A distinction is made between translating **foreign currency** denominated **transactions** and balances of domestic operations and translating financial statements of foreign operations.

Domestic operations: The **temporal method** should be applied to foreign currency denominated transactions and balances—that is, **monetary items** (both hedged and un-hedged) and items carried at market values should be translated at current rates, and transactions and other balances at historical rates. Most exchange gains and losses are included in income immediately; however, exchange gains and losses arising from long-term monetary items with fixed or ascertainable lives should be deferred and amortized over the remaining life of the item.

Foreign operations: Foreign operations are classified as integrated or self-sustaining. Financial statements of **integrated foreign operations** should be translated using the temporal method. Financial statements of **self-sustaining foreign operations** should be translated using the **current rate method**, and exchange gains and losses should be accumulated separately, within shareholders' equity, in a translation adjustment account.

Hedges. Many entities seek to reduce or eliminate the risk of loss on exchange inherent in foreign transactions or operations by hedging. For a foreign exchange contract, asset, liability or future revenue stream to be recognized as a **hedge**, there must be reasonable assurance of its effectiveness as a hedge. If the hedge itself is a monetary item, when it is translated at the current rate any gain or loss will automatically offset the gain or loss on the transaction or balance hedged. If the hedge is a nonmonetary item, there will be no current exchange gain or loss on the nonmonetary item and any gain or loss arising from the translation of the hedged monetary item should be deferred until the settlement date. If the hedge is a foreign currency forward contract, any gain or loss is accrued to offset the gain or loss on the hedged item.

Disclosure. Any significant elements that give rise to changes in the translation ad-justment account in shareholders' equity should be disclosed. The amount of exchange gain or loss included in income does not have to be disclosed. The method of **amortization** of any deferred exchange gains and losses should be disclosed.

Reference. CICA Handbook S.1650.

7. Changing Prices/Inflation Accounting
No supplementary information is required to be disclosed.

8. Accounting Changes

Accounting Treatment. Changes in accounting policies are distinguished from changes in accounting estimates.

Accounting policies: Accounting policy changes should be made retroactively and comparative figures restated to give effect to the new policy, unless the necessary information is not determinable. A new accounting policy need not be preferable to the policy it replaces, so long as it is an acceptable alternative under GAAP. Changes arising from changes in accounting standards usually may be applied prospectively.

Accounting estimates: A change in an estimate arises from new information or developments. The effect of a change in an accounting estimate should be accounted for in the period in which the change occurs and applicable future periods.

Disclosure. A description of each change in accounting policy and its effect on the current period's financial statements should be disclosed.

Reference. CICA Handbook S.1506.

9. Prior Period Adjustments

Definition of Adjusting Items. Prior period financial statements are adjusted to correct for known errors. Prior years' earnings are also restated for gains or losses that clearly relate to the income of those periods, for example, the subsequent realization of a previously unrecorded contingent loss. To qualify for treatment as a **prior period adjustment** an item must be:

☐ Specifically identified with and directly related to the business activities of particular prior periods.

☐ Not attributable to economic events occurring subsequent to the date of the financial statements for such prior periods.

☐ Dependent primarily on decisions or determinations by persons other than management or owners.

☐ Not capable of being reasonably estimated prior to such decisions or determinations.

Accounting Treatment. Prior period adjustments should be excluded from the determination of net income for the current period, and the income statement of the prior periods to which the adjustments relate should be restated. The opening balances of retained earnings in subsequent periods, including the current period, are adjusted accordingly.

When income figures of the preceding period have been restated, the basic earnings per share of the preceding period should be based on the restated amounts.

Disclosure.   The nature of the adjustment and the effect of making the adjustment to the financial statements should be disclosed. Disclosure of the related per share amounts is not required.

Reference.   CICA Handbook S.3600.

10.   Post Balance Sheet Events

Definition.   Two different types of post balance sheet events are identified in Canadian accounting standards:

- [ ] Those that provide further evidence of conditions that existed at the financial statement date.
- [ ] Those that are indicative of conditions that arose subsequent to the financial statement date.

Accounting Treatment.   Conditions existing at the financial statement date: The financial statements should be adjusted for events occurring between the financial statement date and the date of their completion that provide additional information relating to conditions existing at the financial statement date.

Conditions arising after the financial statement date: Some events occurring after the financial statement date, but not relating to conditions existing at that date, may have a significant effect on the assets and liabilities or future operations of an entity in a subsequent period. The current period financial statements should not be adjusted for these items, which should, however, be disclosed.

Disclosure.   No disclosure is required for events relating to conditions existing at the financial statement date, since the financial statements are adjusted for these items. If material, events indicative of conditions arising after the financial statement date should be disclosed in a note, which should indicate the nature of the event and, when practicable, the estimated financial effect.

Reference.   CICA Handbook S.3820.

11.   Related Party Transactions

Definition.   Parties are considered related if one has the ability to exercise significant influence over the operating and financial decisions of the other or if the parties are subject to common significant influence by another party.

Accounting Treatment.   Canadian standards do not address measurement and accounting treatment pertaining to related party transactions. However, disclosure of the nature and extent of related party transactions is required to assist the user of financial statements in understanding the impact of such transactions.

Disclosure.   The following information should be disclosed:

☐   A description of the nature and extent of transactions.
☐   A description of the relationship.
☐   Amounts due to or from related parties.
☐   The terms of settlement, if not otherwise apparent.

No charge transactions between related parties should be disclosed. Management compensation arrangements and transactions eliminated on consolidation or in applying the equity method of accounting need not be disclosed.

When ongoing operations depend on a significant volume of business with another party (e.g., a major customer, supplier or lender), the economic dependence on that party should be disclosed and explained.

Reference.   CICA Handbook S.3840.

12.   Segmental Information

General.   In Canada, public companies (and all life insurance companies) should disclose segmental information. Reportable industry segments should cover a major portion (usually defined as at least 75 percent) of total operations, although judgment may be exercised in deciding what constitutes a segment. When substantially all (more than 90 percent) of operations are in one industry, that industry segment should be identified as dominant.

Disclosure.   The following information is to be disclosed for each reportable segment:

☐   Sales to outside customers.
☐   Intersegment sales or transfers.
☐   Operating profit or loss.
☐   Depreciation and amortization expense.
☐   Total carrying amount of identifiable assets.
☐   Capital expenditures for the period.

Reporting is also required by geographical segment, where significant (10 percent or more of total assets or total revenue).

Reference.   CICA Handbook S.1700.

ACCOUNTING PRINCIPLES FOR SPECIFIC ITEMS— BALANCE SHEET

13.   Property, Plant and Equipment

General.   Accounting standards address **capital assets**, which comprise property, plant and equipment as well as intangible properties. Capital assets are defined as identifiable assets that:

□ Are held for use in the production or supply of goods and services, for rental to others, for administrative purposes or for the development, construction, maintenance or repair of other capital assets.

□ Have been acquired, constructed or developed with the intention of being used on a continuing basis.

□ Are not intended for sale in the ordinary course of business.

Classification of Capital and Revenue Expenditure. Expenditures for capital assets that increase physical output or service capacity, decrease associated operating costs, extend useful life or improve the quality of output are capitalized as part of the cost of the related assets. Expenditures to maintain normal operating efficiency are expensed as incurred.

Basis of Valuation. Capital assets are normally accounted for on the basis of the purchase price and other acquisition costs, such as option costs, brokers' commissions and installation costs. Provisions are required for the impairment of capital assets when their net carrying amount exceeds the net recoverable amount. Write-downs should not be reversed if the net recoverable amount subsequently increases. Gains and losses arising on the disposal of capital assets are included in income. Capital assets may be recorded at appraised values only when the entire balance sheet is revalued as part of a financial reorganization.

Amortization. Amortization may be termed **depreciation** or depletion. Various amortization methods are found in practice (e.g., **straight-line**, **unit-of-production**, **declining balance**). Any method, consistently applied, that results in a rational and systematic allocation appropriate to the nature of the asset is acceptable. The overriding rule is that the total amount of amortization that should be charged to income is the greater of:

□ Cost less salvage value, over the life of the asset; or

□ Cost less residual value, over the useful life of the asset.

When the useful life of a capital asset, other than land, is expected to exceed 40 years but cannot be estimated and clearly demonstrated, the amortization period should be limited to 40 years. If an appraisal has been recorded in the past, subsequent charges for amortization should be based on the new values.

Disclosure. For each major category of capital assets, cost, accumulated amortization (including the amount of any write-down) and the amortization method used (including the depreciation period or rate) should be disclosed. The net carrying amount of a capital asset under construction, development or removal from service that is not being amortized should be disclosed. The income statement should disclose the amount of amortization and write-downs for the current period.

If any capital assets are carried at appraised values, the basis of the valuation, the date of the appraisal and the basis of any transfer of appraisal increases to **retained earnings** should be disclosed.

Where the entity has comprehensively revalued its assets and liabilities as a result of a financial reorganization, certain disclosures are required in the period in which the reorganization is effected and for three years thereafter.

Reference. CICA Handbook S.1625 and 3060.

14. Intangible Assets

The general principles covering intangible assets that fall within the definition of capital assets are set out in Section 13. Accounting principles relating to goodwill arising from business acquisitions and research and development expenditures are set forth in Sections 4 and 25, respectively.

15. Leases

Classification. Leases that transfer substantially all the benefits and risks of ownership to the lessee are accounted for as capital (**finance**) **leases**. Leases and contingent rental payments that are not capital leases should be accounted for as **operating leases**. Guidance, rather than rules, assists in the appropriate classification of leases as either capital or operating, as follows:

☐ If a lease results in ownership being transferred to the lessee by the end of the lease term, or if the lease provides for a bargain purchase option; or

☐ If the term of the lease is equal to 75 percent or more of the economic life of the leased property; or

☐ If the present value of the lease payments equals 90 percent or more of the fair market value of the leased property,

it is normally considered that the risks and benefits have been transferred and that the lease should be classified as a capital lease.

Accounting Treatment. Capital leases: Capital leases should be capitalized and accounted for as an asset and a matching obligation by the lessee, and as a sale or direct financing transaction by the lessor. The income tax effects of the transactions, including investment tax credits, may be considered by the lessor in accounting for direct financing leases. Initial direct costs in a direct financing lease should be expensed as incurred, and a portion of the unearned income equal to the initial direct costs should be recognized in income in the same period.

Operating leases: The rental payments are expensed by the lessee and recorded as revenue by the lessor in the periods to which they relate.

Leveraged Leases. There are no special rules for **leveraged leases**, largely because until recently tax laws did not make leveraged leases attractive. The lessor records the investment in the lease net of nonrecourse debt. The U.S. approach of netting the investment in financial leases and the related debt for financial statement presentation purposes is acceptable in Canada.

Disclosure. The lessee is required to disclose the future minimum lease payments, in the aggregate and for each of the next five years, under operating and capital leases. Assets leased under capital leases should be disclosed separately.

The lessor is required to disclose the cost of property held for leasing purposes and the related accumulated depreciation.

Reference. CICA Handbook S.3065.

16. Investments

Valuation. General: Valuation of investments that are neither consolidated nor accounted for by the equity method depends on their classification as short term (current) or long term (noncurrent).

Current investments: Investments held for the short term are usually carried at the lower of cost and market value. The lower of cost and market test may be applied to marketable investments individually or in the aggregate. Canadian practice is mixed with respect to reversals of write-downs when market value recovers. When short-term investments include securities of affiliated companies, these should be set out separately.

Noncurrent investments: Investments held for the long term should be carried at cost, and the quoted market value of marketable securities should be disclosed. They should be written down to recognize any declines in value that are other than temporary; write-downs may not be reversed if there is a subsequent increase in value.

Treatment of Valuation Reserves. Generally, reserves are not set up for declines in the valuation of investments.

Gains/Losses. The calculation of the gain or loss on the sale of part of a holding of securities should be based on the average carrying value.

Disclosure. The basis of valuation for long-term and short-term investments should be disclosed. Any securities issued by the parent and owned by subsidiaries excluded from consolidation should be disclosed in the parent company's financial statements.

Reference. CICA Handbook S.3010 and 3050.

17. Accounts Receivable

Accounting Treatment. Recognition: **Revenues**, and hence the related receivables, are recognized when performance is complete and reasonable assurance exists regarding measurement and collectibility of the consideration.

Discounts: Trade discounts are normally recorded as a reduction in sales revenues, and cash discounts either as a reduction in sales revenues or as an expense when taken by the customer.

Allowances: An adequate allowance should be established for doubtful accounts, although there is no requirement to make reference to or disclose the amount of the allowance. No specific basis is prescribed for calculating the allowance for doubtful accounts. Specific identification is the preferred basis, but when it is impracticable, other methods may be used.

Sale of Receivables. **Factoring** of receivables is not common in Canada.

A transfer of receivables can be recorded as a sale rather than as a financing transaction if the significant risks and rewards of ownership of the receivables have been transferred and reasonable assurance exists regarding the measurement of the consideration exchanged. If the purchaser is provided with recourse for bad debts incurred, such recourse must be reasonable in relation to the losses expected to be incurred and normally may not exceed 10 percent of the proceeds. If all these conditions are not met, the transaction would be in substance a borrowing and the proceeds should be recorded as a liability.

Disclosure.   Accounts and notes **receivable** should be segregated between trade accounts, amounts receivable from related parties and other unusual types of receivables.

Reference.   CICA Handbook S.3020.

18.   Inventories and Work in Progress

General Accounting Treatment.   **Inventories** are carried at the lower of cost and market. Commonly used methods of determining cost include **FIFO**, specific cost and **average cost**. **Standard cost** is acceptable only if it approximates one of these methods. **LIFO** is not prevalent since it is not acceptable for tax purposes. Direct costing is acceptable but is not common practice.

Market is determined by any method appropriate in the circumstances (e.g., **replacement cost, net realizable value** or net realizable value less a normal profit margin).

For work in progress and finished goods, costs should include the cost of materials, the cost of direct labor and an appropriate share of overhead expense chargeable to production. Abnormal costs, such as rehandling of goods and idle facilities, are usually excluded. Similarly, a portion of fixed overhead should be excluded if including it would distort the net income for the period because of a fluctuating volume of production.

Long-Term Contracts.   There are no specific standards in Canada on accounting for long-term contracts. Revenue recognition for long-term contracts is covered in Section 23. The excess of the amount of work in progress on long-term contracts over the related aggregate progress billings is disclosed as an asset on the balance sheet. Work in progress includes all costs that can be reasonably allocated to the contract plus an allowance for profit.

Disclosure.   It is common practice to disclose the amounts of raw materials, supplies, work in process and finished goods. In addition, the basis of valuing inventories should be disclosed.

Reference.   CICA Handbook S.3030.

19.   Current Liabilities

General Accounting Treatment.   As a balance sheet classification, **current liabilities** include amounts payable within one year from the date of the balance sheet or within the normal operating cycle, if longer than one year. Current liabilities should be segregated between main classes; for example, bank loans, **accounts payable** and accrued liabilities, loans payable, taxes payable, dividends payable, deferred revenues and current payments on long-term debt.

Accounts payable include amounts owed to creditors for goods and services that have been received.

Most expenses are recorded during an accounting period at the time they are incurred. Expenses incurred but not recorded because payment is not yet due, such as unpaid salaries and wages, are recorded as accrued liabilities.

Amounts received or due from customers or clients with respect to goods to be delivered or services to be performed should be recorded as deferred revenue.

Creation of General and Specific Provisions. It is not acceptable to create general provisions for future losses. Specific provision should be made for liabilities that are known but whose amount must be estimated, such as warranties and employee benefits.

Disclosure. Commitments to make expenditures that are abnormal in relation to the entity's financial position or usual business operations (e.g., commitments for substantial capital asset expenditures) and commitments that will govern the level of a certain type of expenditure for a considerable period into the future should be disclosed.

Any secured liabilities should be presented separately and the fact that they are secured should be indicated.

Reference. CICA Handbook S.1510 and 3280.

20. Long-Term Debt

General Accounting Treatment. Long-term debt includes bonds, debentures and similar securities. A premium or discount on long-term debt is shown as a deferred credit or a deferred charge, which is amortized over the term of the debt.

Debt Restructuring. There are no official Canadian standards addressing the question of accounting for troubled debt restructuring; practice normally parallels that of the United States. A troubled debt restructuring occurs when a creditor grants a concession because of the debtor's financial difficulties. The aggregate net gain or loss experienced by the debtor is included in net income. If the creditor is also a significant shareholder of the debtor, it may be appropriate to record the gain as a capital transaction. Where the debt restructuring takes place as part of a financial reorganization, any adjustments are recorded as **share capital** or **contributed surplus**, as appropriate.

Debt Extinguishment. There are no official Canadian standards addressing the question of accounting for debt extinguishment; practice normally parallels that of the United States. A gain or loss arises on early extinguishment of a debt when the reacquisition price and the net carrying amount of the debt extinguished before maturity are different. The gain or loss is included in income as a separate item when the debt is extinguished. The portion of the gain or loss that clearly relates to the change in the value of a share conversion privilege attached to convertible debt may be accounted for as a capital transaction.

The normal criteria apply to classifying such gains or losses as extraordinary (see Section 28).

In-substance **defeasance** refers to a situation where the debtor retains its primary obligation to repay the debt but is considered to have extinguished the debt if risk-free monetary assets are placed in an irrevocable trust solely for satisfying the debt and the possibility of the debtor having to make further payments is remote. Risk-free monetary assets are taken to mean cash or securities that are guaranteed, usually by the federal government, and irrevocable to mean that the debtor has no future rights to the trust assets. In order to meet the criteria, the timing and amount of payments must be reasonably determinable in advance; for example, floating-rate debt cannot be extinguished through in-substance defeasance because future debt service requirements may vary.

The accounting for in-substance defeasance is the same as for extinguishment of debt.

Disclosure. There are no specific disclosure requirements concerning debt extinguishment and debt restructuring. The nature and extent of disclosures for such transactions are guided by the general disclosure requirements in Canada—if the information is significant to understanding the financial position of the enterprise, details should be disclosed.

Reference. CICA Handbook S.1625 and 3210.

21. Contingencies

General. The accounting treatment and disclosure requirements for **contingencies** depend on the likelihood of occurrence or nonoccurrence of the future events that will determine the contingency.

Contingent Losses. If it is likely that a contingency existing at the financial statement date will result in a loss whose amount can be estimated, the loss must be accrued.

If there is a reasonable possibility that a loss may be incurred, but either the amount cannot be estimated or the exposure exceeds the amount already accrued, the existence of the contingent loss at the financial statement date should be disclosed but not accrued. Disclosure is also required if the likelihood of the occurrence cannot be determined.

Contingent Gains. Contingent gains should not be accrued in the financial statements, but if their realization is likely, they should be disclosed.

Disclosure. Disclosure of a contingent gain or loss should include a description of the contingency, an estimate of the amount or a statement that an estimate cannot be made, and whether any resulting settlement will be accounted for as a prior period adjustment or as a charge or credit to income of the period in which the settlement occurs. In practice, companies disclosing contingencies rarely indicate the accounting treatment that will be applied to any settlement expected in the future.

Reference. CICA Handbook S.3290.

22. Capital and Reserves

General. Shareholders' equity is generally divided between share capital and items of **surplus**. For items of surplus, distinction is made between those derived from earnings and those derived from contributions, usually classified as retained earnings and contributed surplus, respectively.

In Canadian terminology, the word ''reserve'' is substantially limited to discretionary reserves created by an appropriation of retained earnings. Reserves cannot be created, increased or decreased by charges or credits to income. There are no requirements to maintain reserves for specific purposes.

Unrealized foreign exchange gains and losses arising from the translation of the financial statements of self-sustaining foreign operations should be included as separate components of shareholders' equity (see Section 6).

Share Capital. Businesses incorporated under the CBCA must issue shares without nominal or **par value**. They must be in registered form (i.e., not in bearer form).

A company's share capital may consist of different classes of shares, each of which is characterized by its voting, dividend and capital repayment rights. For accounting purposes, **common shares** are those that represent the residual equity in the earnings of a company. All other types of capital shares are senior shares, including **preferred shares** that participate with common shares but whose participation rights are restricted.

If a company redeems or acquires its own shares and the cost is different from their stated or assigned values, the difference should be excluded from the determination of net income. A company's own shares that it has acquired should be carried at cost and shown as a deduction from shareholders' equity until cancelled or resold.

When a company cancels or redeems its own shares, the cost must be allocated among the components of shareholders' equity. If the cost of such shares is equal to or greater than their stated value, an amount equal to the stated value should be allocated to reduce share capital, any excess to reduce contributed surplus to the extent that it arises from transactions in the same class of shares, and any remaining excess to reduce retained earnings. If the cost is below the stated value, an amount equal to the stated value should be allocated to share capital.

Other Reserves.   Contributed surplus: Contributed surplus includes capital donations from shareholders and other sources, as well as items such as premiums on shares issued, gain on forfeited shares and proceeds arising from donated shares.

Retained earnings: Retained earnings is the accumulated balance of income less losses from operations, after taking into account dividends, refundable taxes and other amounts that may be charged or credited to it.

Distribution Restrictions.   Under the CBCA, a corporation cannot pay a dividend if the corporation would be unable to pay its liabilities as they become due or if the realizable value of the corporation's assets would thereby be less than its liabilities and stated capital combined.

Disclosure.   Details of authorized and issued share capital and of transactions during the period should be disclosed. Any commitments to issue or resell previously acquired shares and any conversion rights or share option privileges should be disclosed. If the distribution of retained earnings is restricted, the details should be disclosed.

Where the share capital and reserves of an entity have been restated as a result of a comprehensive revaluation of an entity's assets and liabilities in a financial reorganization, this should be disclosed in the period that the reorganization is effected and for three years thereafter.

Reference.   Handbook S.1625, 3240, 3250 and 3260.

ACCOUNTING PRINCIPLES FOR SPECIFIC ITEMS— INCOME STATEMENT

23. Revenue Recognition

General Principles.   Revenue is recognized when performance is complete and reasonable assurance exists regarding measurement and collectibility of the consideration. Revenue from sales of goods is recognized when the seller transfers to the buyer the significant risks and rewards of ownership of the goods. Whether any significant acts of performance remain to be completed and whether the seller retains any continuing involvement in, or effective control of, the goods transferred are factors in determining whether significant risks and rewards have been transferred.

Revenue from service transactions is usually recognized as the service is performed, using either the percentage of completion or the completed contract method.

Long-Term Contracts. Revenue from long-term contracts is usually recognized as the contract activity is performed, using either the percentage of completion or the completed contract method. Normally, the percentage of completion method is used when contract performance consists of more than one act, and revenue is recognized in proportion to each act performed. The completed contract method is appropriate only if performance consists of a single act or if the extent of progress toward completion cannot reasonably be estimated.

Instalment Sales. The instalment basis is an acceptable alternative when there is uncertainty as to the amount of consideration to be realized. Profit is recognized as sales proceeds are collected in the proportion that the proceeds bear to the total sales price.

Rights of Return. Where customers have the right to return their purchases for a refund or replacement, whether under the terms of the sales contract or as a matter of the entity's practice, prudence dictates that such sales not be included in revenue unless the potential cost of honoring the right of return privilege can be estimated reliably and accrued. There are no codified rules in Canada, and conditions similar to those in the United States would apply.

When a right of return exists, revenue can be recognized at the time of sale if:

☐ The price is substantially fixed or determinable.

☐ Any obligation to pay the purchase price is unconditional.

☐ The purchaser has economic substance apart from that provided by the vendor. (This condition relates primarily to buyers that exist on paper and its purpose is to prevent enterprises from recognizing sales on transactions with parties that the vendors have established primarily for the purpose of recognizing such sales.)

☐ The vendor has no significant obligations for future performance to directly bring about the product's resale.

☐ The amounts of future returns are accrued.

Transactions for which revenue is postponed should be recognized as sales when the right of return has expired.

Product Financing. Although Canadian standards do not specifically address this topic, the accounting for a product financing transaction should be based on its substance and not its form, and practice normally parallels that in the United States, where **product financing arrangements** are accounted for as borrowings and not as sales. Commitments to purchase products acquired on the entity's behalf are recorded as inventory and the purchase price as debt. The portion of the repurchase cost allocable to financing and carrying charges is accounted for in accordance with the vendor-repurchaser's normal policy of accounting for financing and carrying costs.

Disclosure. The amount of revenue recognized during the period should be disclosed in the income statement.

Reference. CICA Handbook S.3400.

24. Government Grants and Assistance

Accounting Treatment. Government assistance includes forgivable loans as well as grants. Government assistance for current expenses or revenues should be included in income. Government assistance related to expenses of future periods should be deferred and included in income as related expenses are incurred. Assistance related to **capital expenditures** should either be deducted from the cost of the related asset, with depreciation calculated on the net amount, or deferred and amortized to income on the same basis as the related asset.

Disclosure. The following disclosure of government assistance should be made:

☐ Amount of assistance received and receivable in the current period.
☐ Amount credited to income, deferred credit or capital assets in the current period.
☐ Terms and conditions applicable to the assistance.
☐ Amount of any contingent liability for repayment.

With respect to assistance received in prior periods for which a contingent liability for repayment exists, the amount of the contingent liability and the relevant terms and conditions should be disclosed.

Reference. CICA Handbook S.3800.

25. Research and Development

Definitions. Research is planned investigation undertaken with the hope of gaining new scientific or technical knowledge and understanding. It may or may not be directed toward a specific practical aim or application. Development is the translation of research findings into a plan or design for new or substantially improved materials, devices, products or services prior to the start of commercial production.

Accounting Treatment. In general, research costs should be expensed as incurred. Development costs must be deferred and amortized when all the criteria set out below are satisfied:

☐ The product or process is clearly defined and the costs attributed to it can be identified.
☐ The technical feasibility of the product or process has been established.
☐ Management has the intention to produce and market or use the product or process.
☐ The future market is clearly defined or the product's usefulness to the entity has been established depending on whether the product or process is to be sold or used internally.
☐ Adequate resources are available to complete the project.

Amortization of development costs commences with commercial production or use. The amortization period is determined by reference to the benefits expected to arise from the sale or use of the product or process and takes into account such uncertainties as technological change and competition.

The unamortized portion of deferred development costs should be reviewed at the end of each period to determine whether deferral is still appropriate. If doubt exists, the unamortized balance should be written off to income for the period. If deferral continues to be appropriate, the amount of the unamortized balance of development costs for each project should be analyzed in relation to its recovery from expected future revenues less related costs. Any excess unamortized costs should be written off.

Disclosure. The financial statements should disclose the amounts of:

☐ Unamortized deferred development costs.
☐ Development costs deferred during the period.
☐ Research and development costs charged to expense for the period.
☐ Amortization of deferred development costs charged to expense for the period.

Reference. CICA Handbook S.3450.

26. Capitalized Interest Costs

Accounting Treatment. There is no authoritative accounting guidance in Canada on the subject of capitalization of interest and practice varies. It is acceptable to capitalize interest as part of the cost of constructing assets during the construction period. In the case of inventory, interest capitalization is usually restricted to industries such as land development and heavy construction. Once a policy has been adopted, it should be followed consistently.

Disclosure. The amount of interest capitalized in the period should be disclosed.

Reference. CICA Handbook S.3850.

27. Imputed Interest

General. The recognition of **imputed interest** on transactions that are not in the normal course of business is for the most part optional, except in those rare circumstances when failure to discount would result in unfair presentation. There are three areas in which interest is currently imputed in practice: business combinations, capital leases and long-term debt.

Accounting Treatment. If the effective date of an acquisition predates the payment date, interest is imputed for this period at an appropriate rate to discount the purchase price and reduce the cost of the purchase and the net income of the acquirer from the effective date of acquisition.

In accounting for a capital lease, the discount rate used by the lessee in determining the present value of minimum lease payments is the lower of the lessee's rate of incremental borrowing and the interest rate implicit in the lease. In accounting for a sales-type or financing lease, calculations are discounted using an implicit rate of interest.

If the coupon rate on long-term debt differs from the effective interest rate (which is the interest rate implicit in the transaction), the amount recorded is the consideration transferred and not the face value of the debt instrument. This results in a discount or premium, which is amortized.

Disclosure.   Disclosure of the accounting policies is required if the transactions are material.

28.   Extraordinary or Unusual Items

Extraordinary Items.   Recent changes in accounting standards place greater restrictions on the criteria an item must meet to be classified as extraordinary. To be classified as extraordinary, an item should meet all of the following criteria:

- □   Not be expected to occur frequently over several years.
- □   Not be typical of the normal business activities of the entity.
- □   Not depend primarily on decisions or determinations by management or owners.

Unusual or Abnormal Items.   Canadian accounting standards prohibit items that do not have all the characteristics of an extraordinary item from being presented net of income tax. The use of the term ''unusual items'' is no longer allowed in the income statement. In addition, earnings per share information should not be presented for such items or for earnings before such items.

Disclosure.   Each extraordinary item and the amount of any applicable income taxes should be described and shown separately. Similar items may be combined. The income statement should distinguish between income before extraordinary items, extraordinary items net of applicable income taxes (the amount of which should be disclosed) and net income for the period.

Reference.   CICA Handbook S.3480.

29.   Income Taxes

The existing standards require the use of the **deferral method** of income tax allocation. The provision for income taxes is calculated on the basis of the accounting income for the period. The difference between the current tax provision and taxes currently payable is shown as deferred tax on the balance sheet. It is computed at current tax rates without subsequent adjustment of the accumulated tax allocation debit or credit balance for changes in tax rates.

The future tax benefit of tax losses carried forward can be recognized, ordinarily as a separate asset, if there is virtual certainty that it will be realized.

If a loss for tax purposes is carried back to recover taxes of a previous period, the recovery should be recorded in the period in which the loss occurs.

Disclosure.   Disclosure of the reasons for significant variations in the customary rela-tionships between income tax expense and pretax accounting income is required for public companies and other companies that file their annual financial statements with a securities commission.

30. Postretirement Benefits

Pensions

General. The accounting treatment for pensions depends on whether they relate to **defined benefit** or **defined contribution pension plans**. The objective in accounting for pension costs is distinctly different from the objective of funding a pension plan. The objective of accounting for pension costs is to provide a proper allocation of the cost of the plan to the years in which the related employee services are rendered. The objective of funding a pension plan is to provide cash or other consideration, discharge pension obligations and provide for pension security. Accordingly, the amount contributed to a pension fund in a period is not necessarily the appropriate amount to be recognized as pension expense of the period.

Defined Benefit Pension Plans. For defined benefit plans, the cost of pension benefits recorded in the period should be determined using the accrued benefit method, including salary projections prorated on service.

Past service costs, gains and losses on changes in actuarial assumptions and experience gains and losses should be deferred and amortized over an appropriate period, usually the expected average remaining service life of the employee group. Gains or losses on settlement or curtailment should be recognized immediately.

Differences between pension expense (income) and funding payments for the period should be shown as a pension accrual or deferred charge in the balance sheet.

Defined Contribution Pension Plans. The cost of pension benefits for current services is the employer's required contribution for the period.

Past service costs should be deferred and amortized over the expected average remaining service life of the employee group.

Pension Fund Surpluses. In Canada, there are legal questions regarding an employer's entitlement to pension surpluses, and some jurisdictions have placed a moratorium on withdrawal of surpluses. Pension surplus may be recognized provided that there is a reasonable expectation that the employer will obtain a benefit from it by either withdrawing funds or reducing future contributions. The amount recognized should be limited to the expected future benefit.

Disclosure. Defined benefit pension plans: Disclosure of the actuarial present value of accrued pension benefits and the value of pension fund assets is required.

Defined contribution pension plans: The present value of required future contributions for past service should be disclosed.

Postretirement Benefits Other Than Pensions. There is little guidance in Canada on accounting by employers for postretirement benefits other than pensions. Where such benefits are sufficiently significant as to affect the fair presentation of the financial statements, disclosure should be made of the method used. At present there are three permitted alternatives:

□ Current accrual method whereby a current service cost is actuarially determined and accrued in the accounts;

□ "Pay as you go" method under which costs are recognized as incurred by retirees and paid by the employer; and

□ A method under which an estimated liability for benefits to be provided is accrued at the time an employee retires.

Disclosure. The following should be disclosed:

□ A general description of the postretirement benefits other than pensions provided by the employer; and

□ A description of the accounting policy adopted for these benefits.

Reference. CICA Handbook S.3460, as interpreted.

31. Discontinued Operations

The results of discontinued operations of a business segment should be reported separately from continuing operations. "Business segment" means a component whose activities represent a separate line of business or class of customer. It need not be a separate entity, provided that its assets, results of operations and activities can be separately identified.

The results of discontinued operations would include and separately disclose, net of income taxes, the results of operations prior to the date of disposal (or formal plan of disposal) and the subsequent net gain or loss from discontinued operations. The amount would not be classified as an extraordinary item in the income statement.

The calculation of the net gain or loss from discontinued operations includes both the actual or estimated gain or loss on disposal and the actual or estimated results of operations between the date management commits itself to a formal plan of disposal and the disposal date. Costs and expenses that are a direct result of the decision to dispose of the segment are included in the calculation.

Disclosure. The following additional disclosures are required:

□ Identity and nature of discontinued segment.
□ Disposal date.
□ Manner of disposal.
□ Description and carrying value of any remaining assets and liabilities.
□ Revenue applicable to the discontinued operations.
□ Income or loss from the discontinued segment and any proceeds from disposal.

Reference. CICA Handbook S.3475.

32. Earnings per Share

Definition. Earnings per share represents the portion of the income for a period attributable to a share of issued capital of an enterprise.

Methods of Calculation. Earnings per share (EPS) information is generally calculated on two bases. The first calculation is based principally on the weighted average number of common shares actually issued and outstanding and is known as basic earnings per share. The second calculation takes into account any material reduction in earnings per common share that could arise if the various stock options, warrants, conversion privileges attaching to debt or other classes of shares or other similar rights were exercised. This is referred to as fully diluted EPS. Where debt or senior securities are converted into common shares during the period, a third set of calculations (adjusted basic EPS) is required as if the conversion had occurred at the beginning of the period.

Earnings figures used in the calculations should be the reported amounts adjusted for specific items relevant to basic, adjusted basic and fully diluted EPS calculations.

Disclosure. Basic EPS figures for the current and preceding years should be disclosed either on the face of the income statement or in a note by any enterprise with more than a few shareholders. Adjusted basic EPS, if materially different from basic EPS, should be disclosed in a note, cross-referenced to the income statement. Fully diluted EPS for the current year should be shown in a note, cross-referenced to the income statement. It is not necessary to disclose adjusted or fully diluted EPS for the preceding years.

Reference. CICA Handbook S.3500.

Appendix
DO CANADIAN STANDARDS OR PREVALENT PRACTICE SUBSTANTIALLY COMPLY WITH INTERNATIONAL ACCOUNTING STANDARDS?

Section	Topic	Substantially complies with IAS?	Comments
3.	Basic accounting concepts and conventions	Yes	
	Contents of financial statements	Yes	
4.	Business combinations*	Yes	
5.	Joint ventures	Yes	
6.	Foreign currency translation*	Yes	
8.	Accounting changes*	Yes	
9.	Prior period adjustments*	Yes	
10.	Post balance sheet events	Yes	
11.	Related party transactions	Yes	
12.	Segmental information	Yes	
13.	Property, plant and equipment*	Yes	
15.	Leases	Yes	
16.	Investments	Yes	
17.	Accounts receivable	Yes	
18.	Inventories and work in progress*	Yes	
19.	Current liabilities	Yes	
20.	Long-term debt	Yes	
21.	Contingencies	Yes	
22.	Capital and reserves	Yes	
23.	Revenue recognition*	Yes	
24.	Government grants and assistance	Yes	
25.	Research and development*	Yes	
26.	Capitalization of interest costs*	Yes	
28.	Extraordinary or unusual items*	Yes	

Appendix (*Continued*)

Section	Topic	Substantially complies with IAS?	Comments
29.	Income tax**	Yes	
30.	Postretirement benefits*	Yes	

*These topics are subject to change as a result of the IASC Improvements Project—see the appendix to the International Accounting Standards chapter.

**The IAS on accounting for taxes on income is currently being revised, and an exposure draft has been issued.

Comparison in this table is made to International Accounting Standards in force at January 1, 1993. For further details, see the International Accounting Standards chapter.

CHANNEL ISLANDS

GENERAL NATIONAL INFORMATION

1. Source of Generally Accepted Accounting Principles

Generally Accepted Accounting Principles. **Generally accepted accounting principles** in the Channel Islands are derived from the following sources:

- [ ] The Companies (Jersey) Law 1991 (Jersey Company Law).
- [ ] The Companies (Guernsey) Laws 1908 to 1990 (Guernsey Company Law).
- [ ] The Companies (Alderney) Laws 1894 to 1962 (Alderney Company Law).
- [ ] Statement of Channel Islands Accounting Practice 1988.
- [ ] United Kingdom GAAP.

The Jersey, Guernsey and Alderney Company Laws provide limited guidance with regard to information to be disclosed in financial statements to be presented to shareholders. The Jersey and Guernsey Societies of Chartered and Certified Accountants produced a joint statement in 1988, which provided that:

- [ ] Financial statements of Channel Island incorporated companies should normally be prepared in compliance with Statements of Standard Accounting Practice issued by the accountancy bodies in the United Kingdom (SSAPs).
- [ ] Financial statements of companies incorporated in jurisdictions other than the Channel Islands should be prepared in compliance with either the SSAPs, International Accounting Standards or **accounting standards** of other jurisdictions, as appropriate, and the accounting standards followed should be disclosed.

The Jersey Company Law permits the competent authority in Jersey to introduce subordinate legislation from time to time specifying the form and content of financial statements.

2. Audit and Public Company Requirements

Audits. Companies may be established under Jersey, Guernsey or Alderney Company Law. The Guernsey and Alderney Company Laws require each company's auditors to report to the shareholders on the accounts presented to them at the general meeting. Jersey Company Law requires such reporting for **public companies** only, although all companies must present accounts to a general meeting. For public companies, this must take place within seven months of the financial year end; other companies have up to ten months.

Public Companies.   No distinction is made under existing Guernsey or Alderney Company Law between public and private companies. Jersey Company Law, however, defines a public company as one that has more than 30 members (shareholders) or states that it is public.

All companies are required to file an annual return with the competent authorities in each island. This return details registered shareholders (who may be nominees) and in Guernsey also lists the names of directors. In Jersey, only public companies must list the names of directors.

There is no requirement in the Channel Islands for a company to file accounts with its annual return, except in Jersey Company Law, which requires public companies to file accounts with the registrar within seven months. Companies engaged in banking, insurance and collective investment schemes are regulated under other laws and are required to file accounts with the competent authorities.

GENERAL ACCOUNTING

3. Financial Statements

Basic Accounting Concepts.   As indicated above, basic **accounting concepts** are derived from those in the United Kingdom and include:

- [ ] The **prudence concept**.
- [ ] The **going concern concept**.
- [ ] The **accruals basis**.
- [ ] The consistency concept.

Financial statements are normally prepared on the **historical cost basis**. However, under the UK's "alternative accounting rules," the revaluation of certain assets is permitted.

Contents and Format of Financial Statements.   The content of financial statements is not defined in existing Jersey, Guernsey or Alderney Company Law. As noted above, the accounting profession has sought to define the basis on which financial statements should be prepared and has set minimum disclosure requirements, which are based on International Accounting Standard 5. The Statement of Channel Islands Accounting Practice requires the disclosure of **accounting policies**. Also as noted above, Jersey Company Law permits the form and content of financial statements to be defined.

4. Business Combinations

Principles of Consolidation.   The company laws are silent on the principles of consolidation; however, adoption of UK GAAP would require the **parent** undertaking of a group to prepare consolidated accounts that include all **subsidiary** undertakings, including unincorporated entities such as partnerships as well as limited companies. Control rather than legal ownership determines whether an undertaking is a subsidiary (see below).

Accounting for Business Combinations. A **business combination** arises where one undertaking buys shares in another undertaking, which becomes a subsidiary. There are two accounting methods that can be applied to business combinations in the Channel Islands. **Acquisition accounting** applies in the majority of situations. **Merger accounting**, which is equivalent to pooling, can be used, provided that certain conditions in SSAP 23 are complied with.

Acquisition Accounting. In acquisition accounting, the fair value of the consideration given in the acquisition is offset against the fair value of the net assets of the undertaking acquired. The difference represents **goodwill** or **negative goodwill**. All identifiable assets, including intangibles, of the undertaking acquired are valued.

Merger Accounting. Where merger accounting is used, the book values of assets and liabilities of the merged undertaking and of the group are consolidated without fair value adjustment. In addition, the profit and loss account for the entire period of the merged undertaking is included in the consolidated profit and loss account. Current and prior year amounts for both the profit and loss account and the balance sheet are shown as if the entities had always been combined.

Control. Control is indicated in a number of ways, as follows:

□ The parent holds a majority of the voting rights in an undertaking.

□ The parent is a member of the undertaking and has the right to appoint or remove a majority of the undertaking's board of directors.

□ The parent has the right to exercise dominant influence over the undertaking via provisions included in its memorandum or articles of association (the company's written rule book).

□ The parent has the right to exercise dominant influence over an undertaking via a control contract.

□ The parent is a member of the undertaking and controls, via an agreement with other shareholders, the majority of the voting rights in the undertaking.

□ The parent has a participating interest (over 20 percent) in the undertaking and actually exercises dominant influence over it.

□ The parent has a participating interest in the undertaking and both the parent and the undertaking are managed on a unified basis.

Goodwill. The treatment of purchased goodwill arising on consolidation is governed by SSAP 22, which, while giving options, indicates a preference for the immediate write-off of consolidation goodwill to reserves. Normally, this write-off is made directly to the profit and loss account reserve or the merger reserve, although some companies may create a negative reserve by writing off goodwill to a reserve that starts with a zero balance. Companies may also apply to the court to write goodwill off against their **share**

premium account. SSAP 22 also allows companies to amortize goodwill over a period not to exceed the goodwill's useful life. In practice, most companies write goodwill off immediately to reserves; however, some amortize goodwill over periods of up to 40 years. Where goodwill is written off to reserves on acquisition and the entity acquired is subsequently sold, the profit or loss on sale has to be calculated in accordance with UITF Abstract 3 to include the goodwill previously taken to reserves (thereby reducing the profit or increasing the loss on sale). Negative goodwill arising on consolidation is added to reserves.

Equity Accounting. If an investor has a participating interest in another undertaking and exercises significant influence over the undertaking's operating and financial policies, that undertaking should be treated as an **associated undertaking**. An investor that holds 20 percent or more of the voting rights in another undertaking is presumed to exercise significant influence unless there is evidence to the contrary. A number of factors may indicate significant influence in practice, such as board representation. All associated undertakings are normally accounted for by the **equity method**.

Minority Interests. **Minority interests** in the consolidated balance sheet show the amount of capital and reserves attributable to shares in subsidiaries included in the consolidation that are held by or on behalf of persons other than the parent and its subsidiaries. Similarly, minority interests in the consolidated profit and loss account include the amount of any profit or loss on ordinary activities attributable to shares in subsidiaries included in the consolidation that are held by or on behalf of persons other than the parent and its subsidiaries.

Disclosure. General: The names of the undertakings acquired or merged have to be disclosed, along with the accounting method used. In addition, the number and class of shares issued have to be disclosed, with details of any other consideration exchanged. For both acquisition and merger accounting, the fair value of the total consideration given has to be disclosed.

Acquisition accounting: Financial statements have to disclose the nature and amount of significant accounting adjustments necessary to achieve consistency of accounting policies. Details must be provided regarding the profit and loss accounts of the undertaking or group acquired from the beginning of the financial year to the date of acquisition and for its previous financial year. Sufficient information has to be disclosed about the acquired companies' results to enable users of financial statements to assess the acquisition's effect on the consolidated results.

For each material acquisition, a table must be given showing the book values of assets and liabilities acquired and their fair values at the date of acquisition. The table should present fair value adjustments, provisions for future trading losses foreseen at the time of purchase and other provisions needed to bring accounting policies into alignment. Adjustments made in future years to provisions created upon acquisition have to be divided between amounts used and amounts released, unused or applied for another purpose. In addition, adjustments may be made to the fair values provisionally used at the date of acquisition, during a period after the acquisition known as a "hindsight period," but these have to be explained.

The cumulative amount of goodwill written off in the current year and earlier years, net of any amounts attributable to subsidiaries sold, has to be disclosed.

Merger accounting: The nature and amount of any significant accounting adjustments have to be disclosed. The profit and loss account of the acquired undertaking from the beginning of the financial year to the date of the merger has to be shown, with that of the previous year. In addition, profit before extraordinary items both before and after the effective date of the merger is shown separately for the group, excluding the undertaking acquired, and for the undertaking acquired. Extraordinary items are presented both before and after the merger, indicating the party to which each item relates.

Reference.   UK GAAP.

5.   Joint Ventures

Accounting for Investments in Joint Ventures.   Channel Island accounting requirements do not address the different forms of **joint venture** detailed in International Accounting Standard (IAS) 31, *Financial Reporting of Interests in Joint Ventures*. Joint ventures may either be incorporated or unincorporated.

Jointly Controlled Entities.   If there is **joint control** of a venture, then consolidation accounting is inappropriate. However, if one party has more than a 50 percent share in the risks and rewards of the venture, then consolidation is required.

The usual method of accounting for joint ventures is the equity method since it recognizes income when earned, matches costs with revenues and gives appropriate treatment to transactions with the joint venture. Where a joint venture is incorporated, no alternative accounting treatment is allowed. However, where the joint venture is unincorporated, the investing company may choose between the equity accounting method and the **proportional consolidation method**. In joint ventures where the investment is below 20 percent and the investing company does not have significant influence over the joint venture, the investment should be recorded at cost or at its current cost (i.e., market value or share of net assets).

Jointly Controlled Operations.   The accounting treatment in IAS 31 would be appropriate in the Channel Islands.

Jointly Controlled Assets.   The accounting treatment in IAS 31 would be appropriate in the Channel Islands.

Transactions Between Venturers and the Joint Venture.   In general, the contribution of assets to a joint venture in exchange for an interest in the joint venture does not give rise to a gain or loss on disposal in the contributor's financial statements. Gains resulting from other transactions between the venturer and the joint venture should be recognized only to the extent of the interests of nonrelated venturers. However, losses should be recognized in their entirety.

Disclosure.   Equity accounting: Where the results or assets and liabilities of a joint venture or a group of ventures are so material in the context of the investing group, additional disclosure should be made of their turnover, depreciation, profit or loss before tax, profits or losses attributable to the investing group, tangible and intangible assets and liabilities.

Proportionate consolidation accounting: No specific additional disclosures are required, although similar disclosures to those required where a company is consolidated in full would generally be given.

In addition, where the venturer is liable for any contingent liability or commitment with respect to the joint venture, this should be disclosed.

Channel Island requirements are consistent with IAS 31, except that the equity method of accounting for an investment in a jointly controlled entity is the required treatment for joint venture companies. The **benchmark treatment** of proportionate consolidation is allowed only for unincorporated joint ventures. Channel Island requirements for the treatment of transactions between the venturers and the joint venture, and for the recognition of contingencies and commitments of and related to the joint venture, are similar to those in IAS 31 except that a venturer may not recognize a gain on assets contributed to a venture in exchange for an interest therein.

Accounting by Joint Ventures.   Generally accepted accounting principles apply to assets and liabilities and operations of incorporated joint ventures. Generally, such principles would also apply to unincorporated joint ventures, particularly where auditors report on their accounts in true and fair terms. There is no specific guidance in the Channel Islands on accounting by joint ventures for assets contributed to them by the venturers. Such transfers would generally be made at fair value, but carrying value of the assets in the contributor's financial statements in certain situations might alternatively be used.

Reference.   UK GAAP.

6. Foreign Currency Translation

Domestic Operations.   Revenue or costs arising from a transaction denominated in a foreign currency should be translated into the local currency at the exchange rate in effect on the date of the transaction. If a transaction is settled by a contracted rate, that rate should be used. No subsequent translation should normally be made once nonmonetary assets have been translated and recorded. At the balance sheet date, monetary assets and liabilities denominated in foreign currencies should be translated using the exchange rate on that date (the closing rate) or, where appropriate, the exchange rates contracted under the terms of the relevant transaction. All exchange gains and losses arising from these transactions should be taken to the profit and loss account.

Foreign Operations.   For consolidation purposes the accounts of a foreign enterprise should normally be translated using the **closing rate**/net investment **method**. Under this method, the profit and loss account would be translated at the closing rate or at an average rate for the period. The balance sheet of the foreign enterprise would be translated using the closing rate. The difference between the opening net investment in a foreign enterprise translated at the closing rate of the previous year and the closing rate of the current year should be reflected in the statement of total recognized gains and losses in accordance with FRS 3. Previously, such differences would have been taken directly to reserves. In certain circumstances, such as where a branch operates as an extension of the company and the branch's cash flows have a direct impact on those of the company, the **temporal method** of translation should be used.

Hedges. If an individual company has monetary assets denominated in a foreign currency that are matched with forward contracts, the exchange rates specified in those contracts should be used. If a company or group uses foreign currency borrowing to finance or provide a **hedge** against its foreign equity investments and certain conditions are complied with, the net exchange difference arising on translating the foreign currency borrowing and the investments may be offset as a reserve movement.

Disclosure. The accounting policies should disclose the methods used to translate the financial statements of foreign enterprises and the treatment of exchange differences. Where the offset procedure is used (as outlined above), the amount offset in reserves has to be disclosed together with the net amount charged or credited to the profit and loss account. All companies have to disclose the net movement on reserves arising from exchange differences.

Reference. UK GAAP.

7. Changing Prices/Inflation Accounting

General. There is no requirement in the Channel Islands to make any adjustments for inflation or changes in prices.

Methods of Calculating and Reporting the Effects of Inflation. The UK Accounting Standards Committee (ASC) handbook outlines two methods of calculating and reporting the effects of inflation. The ASC recommends that companies use current cost asset valuation together with either the operating or financial capital maintenance concepts. The other method the handbook details is the current purchasing power method of accounting for inflation.

Disclosure. Where current cost information is presented, it is normally as supplementary information to the company's or group's main financial statements.

Reference. UK GAAP.

8. Accounting Changes

Accounting Treatment. It is a fundamental accounting concept that accounting treatment be consistent within a period and from one period to the next. Consequently, a change in accounting policy can be justified only on the grounds that the new policy is preferable. If there has been a change in accounting policy, FRS 3 (previously SSAP 6) requires the amounts for the current and the corresponding periods to be restated on the basis of the new policy; that is, that the change be accounted for as a prior year adjustment (see Section 9).

Estimating future events requires the exercise of judgment. Since a change in estimate arises from new information, FRS 3 (previously SSAP 6) requires changes in estimates to be accounted for in the year that the change is made.

Disclosure. Changes in accounting policy should be disclosed in accordance with the disclosure for prior period adjustments (see Section 9).

Changes in accounting methods used (for example, changing from the **straight-line** depreciation method to the **sum-of-the-years'-digits method**), if material, may be disclosed as exceptional items (see Section 28).

Reference. UK GAAP.

9. Prior Period Adjustments

Definition of Adjusting Items. As mentioned above, a **prior period adjustment** must be made where there is a change in accounting policy. In addition, fundamental financial statement errors found at a later date should be accounted for as prior period adjustments. A fundamental error is one of such significance that it would destroy the true and fair view, and therefore the validity, of the company's financial statements.

Accounting Treatment. For both changes in accounting policy and correction of fundamental errors, the prior period profit and loss account and balance sheet have to be adjusted. The reserves note should present the reserves as previously reported, the prior year adjustment and the restated reserves. Under FRS 3, this restatement is reflected in the statement of total recognized gains and losses.

Earnings per Share. The earnings per share of the prior period would be restated for the adjustments.

Disclosure. Changes in accounting policies and fundamental errors should be fully explained in the notes. Furthermore, the effect of the prior year adjustment on the results of the preceding year should be disclosed where feasible.

Reference. UK GAAP.

10. Post Balance Sheet Events

Definition. SSAP 17 defines post balance sheet events as both favorable and unfavorable events that occur between the balance sheet date and the date on which the financial statements are approved by the board of directors. Post balance sheet events are split into two types, adjusting events and nonadjusting events.

Accounting Treatment. A post balance sheet adjusting event provides additional evidence of conditions existing at the balance sheet date and should be recorded in the current year financial statements. A nonadjusting event concerns conditions that did not exist at the balance sheet date. Such events are not reflected in the current year financial statements.

Disclosure. A post balance sheet nonadjusting event should be disclosed if it is so material that it would affect the ability of users of financial statements to reach a proper understanding of the company's financial position. The notes to the financial statements should disclose the nature of the event and give an estimate of the financial effect or state that it is not practicable to make an estimate.

Reference. UK GAAP.

11. Related Party Transactions

There is no general requirement for disclosing transactions with related parties.

The ASC issued ED 46, *Disclosure of Related Party Transactions*, in July 1989, which contains proposals for disclosure of abnormal transactions (i.e., transactions outside the ordinary course of business) with related parties and disclosure of the existence and nature of controlling related party relationships. These cover, in particular, transactions with directors and disclosures relating to substantial shareholders, group companies and related companies.

Reference. UK GAAP.

12. Segmental Information

SSAP 25 and the International Stock Exchange's Continuing Obligations (the **Yellow Book**) for UK listed companies both include requirements for segmental reporting. To determine the segments (classes of business or geographical segments), the directors must consider how the company's activities are organized. This involves analyzing the type of business, the geographical areas of production and geographical markets.

Disclosure. The Yellow Book requires a geographical analysis of **turnover** and contributions made by operations conducted outside the UK to trading (or operating) results. SSAP 25 requires public companies and large private companies to present the following additional disclosures:

- ☐ A definition of each reported business and geographical segment.
- ☐ **Turnover** by business and geographical segment on the origin basis (i.e., country of production) and destination basis (i.e., country of sale).
- ☐ Results by business and geographical segment before tax, minority interests and extraordinary items, and before or after accounting for interest, depending on the importance of interest to the segment.
- ☐ Intersegment turnover by geographical and business segment.
- ☐ Net assets by geographical and business segment.
- ☐ Segment information relating to associated entities.

If presenting the above information would seriously prejudice the interests of the company, it need not be disclosed, but the omission has to be disclosed.

Reference. UK GAAP.

ACCOUNTING PRINCIPLES FOR SPECIFIC ITEMS— BALANCE SHEET

13. Property, Plant and Equipment

Classification of Capital and Revenue Expenditure. Expenditures that give rise to **capital assets** are classified as **fixed assets**. Pretrading expenditures, expenses and commission relating to an issue of shares or debentures, and costs of research cannot be capitalized and are treated as expenses as incurred.

Basis of Valuation. Fixed assets are recorded at their purchase price or production cost, which includes any consideration given by the company to obtain them. Fixed assets other than goodwill can be revalued at current cost; any resulting surplus must be credited to a revaluation reserve. When assets are revalued, surpluses and deficits on individual assets have to be determined and accounted for separately. Under the provisions of FRS 3, revaluation surpluses and deficits are reflected in the statement of total recognized gains and losses in the year that the asset is revalued. Such gains and losses generally will then be taken to the revaluation reserve. When a revalued asset is sold, the profit on sale is computed by reference to the carrying value of the asset. Any revaluation gains or deficits that are realized on the sale are transferred to a realized reserve, but are not recorded through the profit and loss account (which was previously possible under SSAP 6) or the statement of total recognized gains and losses.

Investment Properties. Investment properties are interests in land or buildings with respect to which construction work and development have been completed and that are held for their investment potential, any rental income being negotiated at arm's length.

Investment properties should be carried on the balance sheet at open market value and not depreciated, with valuation adjustments accounted for on the same basis as those arising on the revaluation of fixed assets.

Depreciation. A fixed asset with a limited useful life has to be reduced by provisions for **depreciation** calculated to write off the asset systematically over its useful life. The depreciation base to be written off is the asset's purchase price, production cost or revalued amount less any residual value at the end of its useful life. Acceptable depreciation methods include the straight-line method, sum-of-the-years'-digits method, **annuity method** and methods based on the number of units produced. The useful life of an asset is defined in SSAP 12 as the period over which the present owner will derive economic benefit from the asset.

In order for the financial statements to give a true and fair view, depreciation should not be provided on investment properties, except for properties held under lease when the unexpired lease period is less than 20 years.

Disclosure. The following have to be disclosed for each major class of depreciable asset:

☐ The depreciation methods used.
☐ The useful lives or depreciation rates used.
☐ Total depreciation expense for the period.
☐ The gross amount of depreciable assets and the related accumulated depreciation at the balance sheet date.

Where there has been a change in depreciation method used, the effect, if material, and the reason for the change should be disclosed. If an asset has been revalued, the reason and the effect, based on both the revalued amount and the historical cost of the asset, must also be disclosed.

Reference. UK GAAP.

14. Intangible Assets

Accounting Treatment. **Intangible assets** such as patents, licenses, trademarks, brands, titles and other rights and assets may be capitalized if they are acquired for valuable consideration or are created by the company. However, a 1990 ASC proposal (ED 52) would restrict considerably the carrying of certain intangible assets. SSAP 22 requires that on the acquisition of a company, intangible assets should be separately identified from purchased goodwill. At the time of this writing, the ASB is further considering the ASC's proposal and is expected to issue a discussion paper on the subject.

Development costs may be capitalized, provided that specific conditions are met. Research costs must be expensed as incurred. The conditions for treatment of research and development costs are outlined in Section 25.

Purchased goodwill may also be capitalized and treated as other intangible assets.

Valuation. All intangible assets other than goodwill may be revalued. Any surplus or deficit arising on revaluation must be taken to the revaluation reserve.

Amortization. All intangible assets, including goodwill, should be amortized over their estimated useful lives. The **amortization** rules for intangible assets are the same as for tangible fixed assets, discussed above. There is no maximum amortization period.

Disclosure. The disclosure requirements for intangible assets are comparable to those for tangible assets, mentioned above.

Reference. UK GAAP.

15. Leases

Classification. Leases are classified as either **finance** or **operating leases**. SSAP 21 defines a finance lease as a lease that transfers substantially all the risks and rewards of ownership of the asset to the lessee. Such transfer of risks and rewards is presumed to occur if, at the beginning of the lease term, the present value of the minimum lease payments equals 90 percent or more of the fair value of the leased asset. An operating lease is defined as a lease other than a finance lease.

Accounting Treatment. Lessees: Lessees are required to capitalize finance leases and show lease obligations as a liability. For operating leases, lessees treat lease payments as a charge to revenue.

Lessors: Lessors treat finance leases as receivables (**debtors**) in their balance sheet. Operating lease assets are treated as fixed assets, and lease income is credited to the profit and loss account.

Disclosure. Lessees: The gross amount of assets held under finance leases, together with related accumulated depreciation, should be disclosed for each class of asset. Obligations owed under finance leases should be disclosed separately from other liabilities, either on the face of the balance sheet or in a note. Lease obligations are classified as amounts payable in the next year, amounts payable in the next two to five years and aggregate amounts payable thereafter. The aggregate finance charges for the period also have to be shown. Commitments that exist at the balance sheet date should be disclosed.

For operating leases, rent expense has to be disclosed. In addition, the lessee has to disclose the annual payments due on leases that expire during the next year, in the next two to five years and thereafter.

Lessors: The net investment in finance leases at the balance sheet date has to be disclosed. The gross amount of assets held for use in operating leases and the related accumulated depreciation have to be disclosed. The aggregate rent income received during the period for finance and operating leases and the costs of assets acquired for purposes of contracting out through finance leases also have to be shown.

Reference.   UK GAAP.

16.   Investments

Valuation Principles.   There is no accounting standard in the Channel Islands on investments, although there is a proposal by the ASC (ED 55), which may affect the future treatment of gains and losses on disposal.

Current asset investments: Current asset investments are normally stated at the lower of cost or market value, and marking to market is often used by financial institutions.

Fixed asset (noncurrent) investments: Fixed asset investments are normally stated at cost.

Gains/Losses.   Under FRS 3, surpluses and deficits on revaluation are reflected in the statement of total recognized gains and losses before adjusting the revaluation reserve. Gains or losses on sales of investments are computed based on the carrying value, and no adjustment is allowed in the profit and loss account for any element of the revaluation reserve that becomes realized. Such realized amounts are transferred to a realized reserve as a reserve movement. If such gains and losses are material, they should be shown as exceptional items before arriving at profit on ordinary activities before tax (see Section 28). For investments not acquired with the intention of resale, such as investments in subsidiaries, gains or losses arising on disposal may be taken to a capital reserve.

Disclosure.   Investments are normally classified as listed and unlisted; the market value of each category is shown. For investments exceeding 20 percent, required disclosures include the aggregate amount of capital and reserves of the investee and the profit or loss disclosed by the investee's financial statements. As explained earlier, undertakings of which over 20 percent is held may also be treated as either associated undertakings or subsidiaries, in which case additional disclosure is required and the accounting treatment will differ.

Reference.   UK GAAP.

17.   Accounts Receivable

Accounting Treatment.   Recognition: The recognition of revenues, and hence the related receivables, is described in Section 23.

Discounts: Receivables are normally recorded net of trade and quantity discounts. Cash discounts are recognized at time of payment.

Allowances: Adequate provision must be made for bad and doubtful accounts, but there are no formal methods for calculating such provisions.

Disclosure. An analysis of debtors should be disclosed, either in the balance sheet or the notes, under the following headings: trade debtors; amounts owed by group companies; amounts owed by undertakings in which the company has a participating interest; other debtors; prepayments and accrued income. In addition, debtors should be split between those receivable within one year of the balance sheet date and those receivable after one year. Where debtors receivable after one year are material, they should be disclosed separately on the face of the balance sheet in accordance with UITF Abstract 4.

Reference. UK GAAP.

18. Inventories and Work in Progress

General Accounting Treatment. SSAP 9 requires **stocks** to be carried at the lower of cost or **net realizable value**. Cost is defined as an expenditure that has been incurred in the normal course of business in bringing the product or service to its present location and condition. This includes costs of purchase and costs of conversion, which encompass direct expenditures, production overhead and a proportion of other overhead. Items of stock that are indistinguishable from one another may be valued using methods such as **FIFO**, **average cost** or any similar method. **LIFO** is not acceptable in the Channel Islands for tax purposes and is not commonly used. Net realizable value is the estimated selling price less all further costs of completion and all costs to be incurred in marketing, selling and distributing.

Long-Term Contracts. Long-term contracts should be assessed on a contract-by-contract basis and reflected in the profit and loss account by recording turnover and related costs as the contract activity progresses (i.e., the **percentage of completion method**). Turnover may include attributable profit to the extent that the outcome of the contract can be assessed with reasonable certainty. Long-term contract work in progress is reduced by the costs included in the profit and loss account, which are matched with turnover for the period.

Disclosure. The accounting policies applied have to be disclosed. Stocks are usually classified in the notes as raw materials and consumables, work in progress, finished goods and goods for resale, and payments on account.

The amount by which turnover on long-term contracts exceeds payments on account is classified as amounts recoverable on contracts and separately disclosed within debtors. If payments on account exceed turnover, the balance should be offset against long-term work in progress, and any excess classified as payments on account and separately disclosed within **creditors**. The note on long-term contracts should disclose separately both the net cost less foreseeable losses and the applicable payments on account.

Reference. UK GAAP.

19. Current Liabilities

General Accounting Treatment.   Creditors due within one year are usually separately disclosed for the following categories: debenture loans; bank loans and overdrafts; payments received on account; trade creditors; bills of exchange payable; amounts owed to group companies; amounts owed to companies in which the company has a participating interest; other creditors, including tax and social security; accruals and deferred income.

Creation of General and Specific Provisions.   There is often confusion about whether items should be accounted for as creditors and accruals or as provisions (which are disclosed separately). Provisions for liabilities or charges include reasonable amounts to provide for liabilities or losses that are either likely to be incurred, or certain to be incurred but uncertain as to amount or date, whereas creditors normally represent amounts actually owed to third parties. For some provisions, for example, bad debt provisions, it is correct to net the provision against the related assets.

Disclosure.   The aggregate amount of creditors is usually split between amounts payable in more than five years and amounts payable in instalments, any of which fall due after the end of the five-year period. The terms of payment or repayment and the applicable interest rate are given in general terms.

If the company has secured creditors, that is, liabilities that are secured by particular assets of the company, details of the security given and the total amount of secured creditors are usually disclosed.

Reference.   UK GAAP.

20. Long-Term Debt

General Accounting Treatment.   Creditors due after one year are usually disclosed separately from creditors due within one year. Furthermore, long-term creditors are disclosed under the same headings as for current liabilities, detailed above.

Disclosure.   The disclosure requirements for long-term debt are the same as those discussed above for current liabilities. Further proposals concerning additional disclosures for short- and long-term debt are included in Financial Reporting Exposure Draft (FRED) 3, *Accounting for Capital Instruments*.

Reference.   UK GAAP.

21. Contingencies

Contingent Losses.   A material contingent loss should be accrued if it is probable that a future event will confirm a loss that can be estimated with reasonable accuracy at the date on which the financial statements are approved. If a contingent loss is not accrued, it should be disclosed, unless the possibility of loss is remote.

Contingent Gains.   Contingent gains should not be accrued, and should be disclosed only if it is probable that a gain will be realized.

Disclosure. For each contingent loss or contingent gain that is disclosed, the required disclosures are: the nature of the contingency; the uncertainties that are expected to affect the ultimate outcome; and a prudent estimate of the financial effect, showing separately the amounts that have been accrued, or a statement that it is not feasible to make such an estimate.

Reference. UK GAAP.

22. Capital and Reserves

General. Shareholders' equity is divided between **share capital** and reserves. Reserves are usually classified as either capital reserves or revenue reserves.

Share Capital. Jersey, Guernsey and Alderney Company Laws require companies to include in their memorandum and articles of association the amount of their authorized share capital and its division into a number of shares of a fixed amount (**par value**). The authorized share capital sets the maximum limit on the shares that can be issued to shareholders.

Shares need not be issued at par, but any excess of the share issue price over par value must be credited to a share premium account. In Jersey, shares may not be issued at a discount. Redeemable **preference shares** may be issued, and the share premium account may be utilized to:

□ Pay up unissued shares as fully paid bonus shares.
□ Provide the premium payable on redemption of redeemable preference shares.

In Jersey, it may also be utilized to:

□ Write off preliminary expenses.
□ Write off commissions, discounts and expenses paid on share issues.

After shares have been issued, a company may not reduce its share capital except with the permission of the court.

Share capital may be divided into different classes, each characterized by its voting, dividend and capital repayment rights.

Other Reserves. Capital and revenue reserves are generally distributable.

Disclosure. Generally accepted practice dictates that companies disclose their authorized and issued share capital, detailing the number, class and par value of shares in existence. Details of any options, warrants or other rights with similar features would also generally be disclosed.

The origin of reserves and their availability for distribution should be disclosed, as appropriate.

FRED 3 proposes that shareholders' funds be split between those applicable to equity shareholders and those applicable to nonequity shareholders.

Reference. Jersey, Guernsey and Alderney Company Laws.

ACCOUNTING PRINCIPLES FOR SPECIFIC ITEMS— INCOME STATEMENT

23. Revenue Recognition

General Principles.   Although there is no accounting standard on the recognition of **revenue** earned from operations, there is now a draft Statement of Principles entitled *The Recognition of Items in Financial Statements*. The draft statement would allow revenue recognition where a change in assets is not offset by an equal change in liabilities and consequently a gain or loss results (unless the change relates to a transaction with owners, in which case a contribution from owners or distribution to owners would be recognized). The draft statement would require that gains and losses be recognized either in the profit and loss account or, under FRS 3, in the statement of total recognized gains and losses.

The only direct references in accounting standards to revenue recognition are contained in the definition of prudence in SSAP 2 and in the principles for recognition of revenue from long-term contracts (discussed below). In accordance with SSAP 2, revenue and profit should not be anticipated but should be recognized only when realized in the form of cash or other assets whose ultimate cash realization can be assessed with reasonable certainty. The concept of prudence is further embodied in the Act, which requires that only profits realized at the balance sheet date be included in the profit and loss account.

As there is no specific standard dealing with revenue recognition, the provisions outlined in the draft Statement of Principles can be regarded as best practice. Under the draft statement, gains should be recognized in the profit and loss account only when, in addition to the general recognition criteria being met, the following conditions are satisfied:

☐   The gain has been earned—that is, there is no material transaction, contract or other event that must occur before the change in the entity's assets or liabilities inherent in the gain will have occurred.

☐   The gain has been realized—that is, one of the following conditions has been met:
—A transaction whose value is measurable with sufficient reliability has occurred. In addition, for a transaction involving an exchange, the assets or liabilities exchanged must be dissimilar or monetary.
—The gain results from a change in an asset or liability of a type not held for continuing use in the business, and the resultant asset or liability is readily convertible to known amounts of cash or cash equivalents.
—The gain results from a liability expiring, being canceled or otherwise ceasing to exist.

In practice, the principles described below are normally followed in determining when to recognize revenue.

Revenue from a transaction involving the sale of goods is usually recognized when the seller has transferred to the buyer the significant risks and rewards of ownership of the goods. In most situations, the substance of the transaction rather than its legal form will determine the time of sale. If, however, goods are sold subject to conditions (e.g., consignment sales, cash on delivery), revenue is not recognized until the conditions have been complied with.

Revenue from the rendering of services is usually recognized as the services are performed. If the service is performed as a single act, revenue is recognized when the service is completed. If the service is provided over a period of time, revenue is recognized in a manner appropriate to the stage of completion of the service, provided that the outcome can be assessed with reasonable certainty.

Long-Term Contracts. The principles for the recognition of revenue on long-term contracts are contained in SSAP 9. In a long-term contract, the time taken to substantially complete the contract is such that the contract activity falls into different accounting periods. A contract accounted for as long term will usually extend beyond one year. However, a duration exceeding one year is not an essential feature of a long-term contract. Some contracts with a duration shorter than one year should be accounted for as long-term contracts (provided that the policy is applied consistently within the reporting entity and from year to year), if they are sufficiently material that not to record turnover and attributable profit would lead to a distortion such that the financial statements would not give a true and fair view.

Where the business has long-term contracts and the outcome can be assessed with reasonable certainty before their conclusion, profit would be recognized on the percentage of completion method as the contract activity progresses. If the outcome cannot be assessed with reasonable certainty, no profit would be reflected in the profit and loss account from those contracts; profit would be recognized when the contract is completed. If there will be a loss on a contract as a whole, the entire loss should be recorded as soon as it is foreseen, in accordance with the prudence concept. Initially, the foreseeable loss is deducted from work in progress, thus reducing it to net realizable value. Any loss in excess of the work in progress should be classified as an accrued liability or a provision for liabilities and charges, depending on the circumstances.

Instalment Sales. On **instalment sales**, revenue is normally recognized at the date of sale. If, however, collection is not reasonably assured, revenue is recognized as cash instalments are received.

Rights of Return. When goods are sold giving the buyer the right to return them for a refund or replacement, revenue may be recognized at the point of sale, provided that adequate provision is made for future returns. Even where goods are sold subject to a reservation of title clause, which enables the seller to have a lien on them until the purchaser has paid for them, revenue recognition is not deferred. If, however, the clause is likely to be acted upon, it is appropriate to create a provision for the doubtful debt.

Product Financing. Product financing occurs when goods are sold with a commitment to repurchase them at a later date. In a sale of goods with a commitment to repurchase, the original owner may retain the principal benefits and risks of ownership, if the repurchase price is predetermined and covers the cost, including interest, incurred by the other party in purchasing and holding the goods. In such a situation, the transaction should be accounted for as a financing rather than a sales transaction, leaving the asset and a corresponding liability on the balance sheet of the original owner.

Disclosure. A company should disclose in its profit and loss account, under the heading turnover, the amount it derives from providing goods and services from ordinary activities. The accounting policy for turnover should also be disclosed in the notes. The method of ascertaining turnover and attributable profit in relation to long-term contracts should also be stated.

Reference: UK GAAP.

24.   Government Grants and Assistance

Accounting Treatment.   SSAP 4 sets out the accounting treatment to be followed for government grants, which should be recognized when the expenditure that they are intended to contribute to is recognized.

SSAP 4 stipulates that government grants relating to fixed assets should be credited to revenue over the asset's expected useful life. This can be achieved in one of two ways:

☐   The grant may be deducted from the purchase price or production cost of the asset, thereby reducing depreciation expense.

☐   The grant may be treated as a deferred credit, of which a portion is credited to revenue annually.

Disclosure.   The following information must be disclosed in the financial statements:

☐   The accounting policy adopted for government grants.

☐   The effects of government grants on the results for the period and/or the financial position of the enterprise.

☐   Where the results of operations are materially affected by the receipt of government assistance other than grants, the effects of that assistance and its nature, to the extent that such effects can be measured.

Potential liabilities to repay grants in specified circumstances should, if necessary, be disclosed in accordance with SSAP 18, *Accounting for Contingencies*.

Reference.   UK GAAP.

25.   Research and Development

Definitions.   Research and development expenditures fall into one or more of the following broad categories:

☐   Pure or basic research—Experimental or theoretical work undertaken primarily to acquire new scientific or technical knowledge rather than directed toward any specific practical aim or application.

☐   Applied research—Original or critical investigation undertaken to gain new scientific or technical knowledge and directed toward a specific practical aim or objective.

☐   Development—Use of scientific or technical knowledge in order to produce new or substantially improved materials, devices, products or services; to install new processes or systems prior to the commencement of commercial production or commercial applications; or to improve substantially those already produced or installed.

Accounting Treatment. Research expenditures are expensed as incurred. SSAP 13 sets forth the following conditions that must be satisfied to capitalize development expenditures:

☐ There is a clearly defined project.

☐ The related expenditure is separately identifiable.

☐ The outcome of the project has been assessed with reasonable certainty as to both its technical feasibility and its ultimate commercial viability, considered in the light of factors such as likely market conditions (including competing products), public opinion and consumer and environmental legislation.

☐ The aggregate of the deferred development costs, any further development costs and related production, selling and administration costs is reasonably expected to be exceeded by related future sales or other revenues.

☐ Adequate resources exist, or are reasonably expected to be available, to enable the project to be completed and to provide any additional working capital needed as a result of the project.

Provided that these conditions are satisfied, a company can capitalize development expenditure, but only until commercial production begins. SSAP 13 requires a company to amortize the capitalized expenditure from the time commercial production of the product or service begins, which is when the company manufactures the product with a view to selling it commercially. Amortization of development expenditure must be allocated to each accounting period on a systematic basis over the production life of the product.

At the end of each accounting period, a company should review capitalized development expenditure. If the circumstances that justified the original deferral of an expenditure no longer apply or are considered doubtful, the company should write off the expenditure immediately to the extent it is considered irrecoverable.

Disclosure. The following disclosures should be made in the notes:

☐ The accounting policy adopted for research and development expenditure.

☐ The total amount of research and development expenditure charged to the profit and loss account in the period, both current year expenditure and amortization of deferred expenditure.

☐ Movements on deferred development expenditure and the amounts at the beginning and end of the period.

☐ The period over which capitalized development costs are being amortized, together with the reasons for capitalizing them.

Reference. UK GAAP.

26. Capitalized Interest Costs

Accounting Treatment. There is no accounting standard in the Channel Islands that deals with capitalization of interest. Interest on any capital borrowed to finance the production of an asset may be included in the production cost of the asset.

Disclosure.   The amount of capitalized interest included in production cost is usually stated in the notes.

Reference.   UK GAAP.

27.   Imputed Interest

General.   **Imputed interest** is not used widely in the preparation of financial statements in the Channel Islands. However, the principles of discounting account balances and transactions to their present value are recognized in some accounting standards, for example, SSAP 21 (Leasing) and SSAP 24 (Pension Costs).

Accounting Treatment.   Although there is no authoritative guidance on the use of discounting in financial statements in the Channel Islands, Technical Release (TR) 773 highlights instances where discounting may be required to enable financial statements to give a true and fair view. TR 773 identifies the following as the two main potential applications of discounting in financial reporting:

☐   Allocation of cash flows as revenues or expenses over accounting periods in a manner consistent with the time value of money.

☐   Valuation where no ready external market exists and no cash equivalent is available.

Disclosure.   TR 773 encourages disclosure in the financial statements of the accounting policy adopted where discounting has been used, in particular, the significant assumptions made regarding choice of interest rate and timing of cash flows.

Reference.   UK GAAP.

28.   Extraordinary or Unusual Items

Extraordinary Items.   The definition of extraordinary items has changed with the introduction of FRS 3 to relate to material items possessing a high degree of abnormality that arise from events or transactions that fall outside the ordinary activities of the reporting entity, and that are not expected to recur. Under FRS 3, extraordinary items will be extremely rare, and the ASB has stated that in view of the extreme rarity of such items it cannot provide any examples. Consequently, it is unlikely that extraordinary items will arise in the future.

Exceptional Items.   Exceptional items are defined in FRS 3 as material items that derive from events or transactions that fall within the ordinary activities of the company and that individually or, if of a similar type, in the aggregate need to be disclosed by virtue of their size or incidence if the financial statements are to give a true and fair view. The definition in FRS 3 encompasses those items that were disclosed as extraordinary under SSAP 6.

Disclosure.   Generally, exceptional items are recognized in the profit and loss account in arriving at profit or loss from ordinary activities. They should be attributed to continuing or discontinued operations, as appropriate. However, there are three exceptions to the general rule, which require separate disclosure after operating profit or loss, but before interest, under either continuing or discontinued operations, as follows:

☐ Profits or losses on the sale or termination of an operation.
☐ Costs of a fundamental reorganization or restructuring having a material effect on the nature and focus of the reporting entity's operations.
☐ Profits or losses on the disposal of fixed assets.

Reference. UK GAAP.

29. Income Taxes

Accounting Treatment. In the Channel Islands, companies that are resident for tax purposes pay income tax on the accounting income of the year adjusted for certain items, whether distributed or undistributed. In accordance with SSAP 15 (Deferred Taxation), companies are also required to account for deferred taxes. Deferred taxes should be computed under the **liability method**, which requires that tax deferred or accelerated because of timing differences be accounted for, but only to the extent that it is probable that a tax liability or asset will materialize (i.e., on a partial provision basis).

Deferred tax debit balances, including those arising from losses, should not be carried forward as assets, except to the extent that they are expected to be recoverable without replacement by equivalent debit balances. Recovery may be affected by, among other things, the period of time losses are available to be carried forward for tax purposes. Deferred tax assets arising from losses should be recognized only when recovery is assured beyond reasonable doubt.

Disclosure. The notes to the profit and loss account usually disclose the following:

☐ The amount of the income tax, specifying the charge on the income of the year.
☐ The amount of deferred tax relating to ordinary activities. (Similar disclosure is required for deferred tax relating to extraordinary items, which should be shown as part of the tax on extraordinary items.)
☐ The amount of any potential deferred tax that has not been provided for the period, divided into major components.
☐ Adjustments to deferred tax from changes in tax rates and tax allowances, which should normally be disclosed as part of the tax charge for the period.
☐ Under FRS 3, the tax on the three specific exceptional items set out in Section 28.

30. Postretirement Benefits

Accounting Treatment. SSAP 24 deals with both the measurement of pension costs and the disclosure of pension information in company financial statements. The accounting objective of SSAP 24 is that the expected cost of providing pensions should be recognized on a systematic and rational basis over the period during which an employer benefits from employees' services. Most pension plans (called schemes) in the Channel Islands are funded and are either **defined contribution** or **defined benefit schemes**.

Defined Benefit Pension Plans.   In a defined benefit scheme, rules determine the benefits to be paid, regardless of the contributions paid with respect to each employee. Employers' obligations are not capable of being defined in an absolute sense; instead, actuarial expertise is required to determine an appropriate level of contributions to fund the obligations. Consequently, the accounting objective is met by providing for periodic pension costs that are a substantially level percentage of the current and expected future pensionable earnings in the light of current actuarial assumptions.

Variations from regular costs because of experience, changes in actuarial methods or assumptions, or retroactive changes in benefits or membership should normally be spread forward over the expected remaining service lives of current employees. SSAP 24 does not suggest a period but states that it should be determined by the actuary.

Defined Contribution Pension Plans.   In a defined contribution scheme, the future benefits payable to employees are determined by the accumulated value of contributions paid in to the scheme. The employer's obligations are, therefore, normally discharged by an agreed level of contributions. Consequently, the company meets the accounting objective by charging against profits the amount of contributions payable to the scheme in the accounting period.

Pension Fund Surpluses.   Treatment of pension scheme surpluses is governed by the scheme's trust deed. It may be reflected in the form of either contribution holidays, a period of reduced contributions or cash refunds to employers.

Postretirement Benefits.   The UITF issued a statement in December 1992 that requires companies to account for postretirement benefits in a similar way to that prescribed for defined benefit pension plans in SSAP 24. Transitional provisions do not bring in the full requirement until December 1994 year ends. However, until that time, the potential liability has to be noted in the financial statements, where it is possible to determine the amounts involved.

Disclosure.   Defined contribution schemes must disclose: the nature of the scheme (i.e., defined contribution); the accounting policy; the pension cost charge for the period; and any outstanding or prepaid contribution at the balance sheet date.

In addition to the above disclosures, defined benefit schemes must disclose a significant amount of actuarial information, including:

□   The actuarial method used and the main actuarial assumptions.
□   The market value of the scheme assets at the date of their valuation or review.
□   The level of funding expressed as a percentage and comments on any material surplus or deficit.

In addition, details of the expected effects on future costs of any material changes in the group's and/or company's pension arrangements, together with any commitment to make additional payments over a limited number of years, should be disclosed.

Reference.   UK GAAP.

31. Discontinued Operations

The accounting treatment of terminated activities of business segments is dealt with in FRS 3 (see Section 28). The provisions of FRS 3 apply to accounting periods ending on or after June 22, 1993, and earlier adoption is encouraged (prior to the adoption of FRS 3, the provisions of SSAP 6 still apply).

Under FRS 3, discontinued operations are defined as operations of the reporting entity that are sold or terminated and that satisfy all of the following conditions:

☐ The sale or termination is completed either in the period covered by the financial statements, or before the earlier of three months after the commencement of the subsequent period and the date on which the financial statements are approved.

☐ If a termination, the former activities have ceased permanently.

☐ The sale or termination has a material effect on the nature and focus of the reporting entity's operations and represents a material reduction in its operating facilities resulting either from its withdrawal from a particular market (class of business or geographical) or from a material reduction in turnover in the reporting entity's continuing markets.

☐ The assets, liabilities, results of operations and activities are clearly distinguishable, physically, operationally and for financial reporting purposes.

If a decision has been made to sell or terminate an operation, any consequential provision should reflect the extent to which obligations have been incurred that are not expected to be covered by the future profits of the operation or the disposal of assets. The reporting entity should be demonstrably committed to the sale or termination and this should be evidenced by either a binding sale agreement or a detailed plan for termination. Only, however, if the operation qualifies as a discontinued operation (that is, satisfies the conditions above) would such amounts be shown under that category in the profit and loss account. If it does not satisfy those conditions, it must be shown as part of continuing operations. Where material, *discontinuing* (as opposed to discontinued) operations should be shown as a component of continuing operations.

Disclosure. Under FRS 3, if the operation qualifies as discontinued, any write-down of assets and any provisions should appear under discontinued operations in the profit and loss account. Otherwise, such amounts should appear under continuing operations in the profit and loss account. Where in the subsequent period an operation qualifies as discontinued under FRS 3, and provisions have previously been established under continuing operations, the provisions should be used to offset the results of the discontinued operation.

Reference. UK GAAP.

32. Earnings per Share

General. SSAP 3 requires **listed companies** and companies traded on the UK Unlisted Securities Market to show earnings per share (EPS) on the face of the profit and loss account.

Definition.   Under FRS 3, the definition of EPS in SSAP 3 has changed to include extraordinary items in the definition of earnings. Now EPS is defined as the amount of consolidated profit of the period, after tax and after deducting extraordinary items (in the unlikely event that there are any under FRS 3), minority interests and preference dividends, attributable to each equity share. FRS 3 allows alternative bases for calculating EPS as long as they are not given more prominence than the EPS required by SSAP 3.

Method of Calculation.   EPS is generally calculated on two bases. The first calculation uses the weighted-average share capital eligible for dividends in the period and is known as the basic earnings per share. The second calculation takes into account that companies often have equity shares in issue that are not eligible for a dividend but will be in the future. There may also be a future reduction in earnings if conversion rights attaching to debentures, loan stock, preference shares, or options or warrants to subscribe for equity shares are exercised. Where these situations exist, SSAP 3 requires that fully diluted earnings per share should also be calculated and disclosed on the face of the profit and loss account.

Disclosure.   EPS should be shown on the face of the profit and loss account both for the current period and for the corresponding previous period. The basis of calculating EPS should be disclosed either in the profit and loss account or in a note. In particular, the amount of earnings and the number of equity shares used in the calculation should be shown.

In addition to the basic EPS, the fully diluted EPS should be shown on the face of the profit and loss account. The basis of calculating the fully diluted EPS must be disclosed. The fully diluted EPS for the corresponding previous period should not be shown unless the assumptions on which it is based still apply. The fully diluted EPS need not be given if either it deviates from basic EPS by less than 5 percent or basic EPS is negative. Basic and fully diluted EPS, if both are disclosed, should be equally prominent.

Where under FRS 3 an alternative EPS figure is disclosed, the financial statements should reconcile the alternative figure to the EPS figure required by SSAP 3 on the face of the profit and loss account.

Reference.   UK GAAP.

Appendix
DO THE CHANNEL ISLAND STANDARDS OR PREVALENT PRACTICE SUBSTANTIALLY COMPLY WITH INTERNATIONAL ACCOUNTING STANDARDS?

Section	Topic	Substantially complies with IAS?	Comments
3.	Basic accounting concepts and conventions	Yes	
	Contents of financial statements	Yes	Except that cash flow statements are required only for large companies
4.	Business combinations*	Yes	
5.	Joint ventures	Yes	
6.	Foreign currency translation*	Yes	
8.	Accounting changes*	Yes	
9.	Prior period adjustments*	Yes	
10.	Post balance sheet events	Yes	
11.	Related party transactions	No	Those parties deemed to be related are fewer than under IAS 24
12.	Segmental information	Yes	
13.	Property, plant and equipment*	Yes	
15.	Leases	Yes	
16.	Investments	Yes	
17.	Accounts receivable	Ycs	
18.	Inventories and work in progress*	Yes	
19.	Current liabilities	Yes	
20.	Long-term debt	Yes	
21.	Contingencies	Yes	
22.	Capital and reserves	Yes	
23.	Revenue recognition*	Yes	
24.	Government grants and assistance	Yes	
25.	Research and development*	Yes	
26.	Capitalization of interest costs*	Yes	Capitalization is optional

Appendix (*Continued*)

Section	Topic	Substantially complies with IAS?	Comments
28.	Extraordinary or unusual items*	Yes	
29.	Income tax**	Yes	
30.	Postretirement benefits*	Yes	

*These topics are subject to change as a result of the IASC Improvements Project—see the appendix to the International Accounting Standards chapter.

**The IAS on accounting for taxes on income is currently being revised, and an exposure draft has been issued.

Comparison in this table is made to International Accounting Standards in force at January 1, 1993. For further details, see the International Accounting Standards chapter.

CHINA

GENERAL NATIONAL INFORMATION

1. Source of Generally Accepted Accounting Principles

In the People's Republic of China (PRC), different accounting regulations have been promulgated by the Ministry of Finance (MOF) applicable to different types of companies such as state enterprises, collective enterprises, joint stock limited companies, foreign investment companies and enterprises located in Shenzhen Special Economic Zone of PRC and engaged in specialized industries such as banking, agriculture, securities and manufacturing. This chapter describes **generally accepted accounting principles** applicable to Foreign Investment Enterprises (FIEs). The FIEs consist of Sino–Foreign Equity Joint Ventures (EJVs); Sino–Foreign Cooperative Joint Ventures (CJVs) and Wholly Foreign Owned Enterprises (WFOEs).

The PRC Accounting Systems and Practices for the FIEs (the Practices) promulgated by the MOF became effective on July 1, 1992. The Practices were issued together with the Rules of Administration of Financial Affairs for the FIEs (the Rules). The Practices set out the **accounting methods** and bases and, to a certain extent, the underlying **accounting principles** and **accounting policies**. The Rules set out the administration of the financial and accounting matters.

2. Audit of FIEs and Relevant Laws and Regulations

The FIEs are required to be audited annually by registered Chinese Certified Public Accountants according to the relevant laws and regulations. The auditors express an audit opinion on the truth and fairness of the financial statements in accordance with the Practices and the relevant laws and regulations.

The relevant laws and regulations for FIEs, in addition to the accounting regulations, are as follows:

☐ The PRC Sino–Foreign Equity Joint Venture Law (EJV Law), which was promulgated by the National People Congress (NPC) and became effective on July 8, 1979.

☐ Implementing Regulations of the EJV Law, which was promulgated by the State Council (SC) and became effective on September 20, 1983.

☐ The PRC Sino–Foreign Cooperative Joint Venture Law (CJV Law), which was promulgated by the NPC and became effective on April 13, 1988.

□ The PRC Wholly Foreign Owned Enterprises Law (WFOE Law), which was promulgated by the NPC and became effective on April 12, 1986.

□ Implementing Rules of the WFOE Law, which were promulgated by the SC and became effective on December 12, 1990.

□ The PRC Income Tax Law for FIEs and Foreign Enterprises (FIEs Income Tax Law), which was promulgated by the NPC and became effective on July 1, 1991.

□ Implementing Regulations of the FIEs Income Tax Law, which were promulgated by the SC and became effective on July 1, 1991.

GENERAL ACCOUNTING

3. Financial Statements

Basic Accounting Concepts. Financial statements are prepared primarily on the **historical cost basis**. In normal circumstances, the balances as at the balance sheet date are required to be stated at cost. The general accounting principles recognized by the Practices are: **going concern**, **accrual**, **matching**, consistency and, to a limited extent, **substance over form** and **prudence**. The accounting year should follow the calendar year.

Financial Statements. The Classification of Accounts and Accounting Statements for the PRC Industrial FIEs (the Financial Reportings) set out the chart of accounts and account codes; the explanatory notes for individual accounts; and the forms, format, layout, contents and frequency of reporting for financial statements. The format of financial statements and reporting requirements are determined by the MOF; prior approval from the finance authorities is required for departures from the rules and regulations.

Financial statements comprising a balance sheet and a profit and loss account are required monthly, quarterly and annually. A statement of changes in financial position and schedules supporting the balance sheet and the profit and loss account are required annually (with two exceptions, which are required quarterly).

Comparative figures for the previous period/year are required to be shown in the balance sheet and profit and loss account.

There is no requirement to either attach a directors' statement to the financial statements or disclose the accounting policies adopted in preparing the financial statements.

4. Business Combinations

Principles of Consolidation. If a FIE invests in another company and the investment exceeds 50 percent of the capital of the investee company, the FIE should consolidate the financial statements of the investee company into its financial statements.

FIEs need not consolidate an investee company's financial statements if the nature of operations is considered so different from that of the FIE and nonconsolidation has been approved by the responsible finance bureau or the relevant supervisory authorities under the State Council. When nonconsolidation is followed, the FIE may consider whether **equity accounting** should be adopted (see below).

In any event, the financial statements of the investee company must be submitted to the relevant authorities together with the financial statements of the investing company.

Reference.   Article 75 of the Practices.

Goodwill.   The Practices do not address the accounting treatment for goodwill arising on consolidation.

Equity Accounting.   If the investment in the investee company exceeds 25 percent of its capital, and the investing company can exercise significant influence over the operation and management of the investee company, equity accounting may be adopted. In practice, the cost method is generally used.

Reference.   Article 27 of the Practices.

Minority Interests.   There are no specific requirements for treatment of **minority interests**.

Disclosure.   There are no specific disclosure requirements.

Where equity accounting is used, there is no requirement to disclose which investments are accounted for using such method, or, if the results of operations of an investee company are material in evaluating the operations of the investor, the total income included and the assets and liabilities.

5. Joint Ventures

The common practice is to account for investments in **joint ventures** using the cost method. There are no specific provisions governing accounting for interests in joint ventures.

6. Foreign Currency Translation

Foreign Currency Denominated Transactions.   **Foreign currency** denominated **transactions** should be translated into the reporting currency using either the official exchange rate (average of the official buy and sell rates) at the date of the transaction or the official exchange rate on the first day of the month in which the transaction occurred.

Reference.   Article 61 of the Practices.

At month-end, foreign currency denominated balances (excluding those that are separately accounted for using the swap rate, described below) should be revalued at the month-end official exchange rate. Exchange differences arising from the revaluation should be included in the current month profit and loss account.

Net exchange losses arising during the preoperating period should be separately accounted for and amortized over five years on a straight-line basis from the commencement of production. The unamortized balance should be classified as other assets.

The Practices suggest the following three accounting treatments for net preoperating exchange gains:

□   Amortizing the net exchange gain over five years on a straight-line basis from the commencement of production;

□   Setting off the operating losses incurred after the commencement of production and operation; or

□ On liquidation of the company, including net exchange gains as a liquidation income item.

Net exchange gains arising during the preoperating period should be included in other liabilities.

Exchange gains or losses directly related to the acquisition or construction of fixed assets should be included as part of the purchase or construction cost of the fixed assets.

Reference. Articles 62 and 39 of the Practices.

FIEs can buy and sell foreign currencies/Renminbi (RMB, the national currency) at the swap rate through the swap centers. The swap rate, representing the market rate determined by demand and supply forces, is higher than the official rate. Transactions involving buying and selling foreign currencies in swap centers should be recorded at the swap rate. Any exchange gain or loss from selling foreign currency at the swap centers should be included in the profit and loss account of the period.

Foreign currency purchased through the swap centers should be recorded at the swap rate. When the foreign currency is utilized, it should be accounted for at the book carrying swap rate. The book swap rate can be determined using first in, first out or weighted-average methods.

Reference. Article 64 of the Practices.

Foreign Entities. If FIEs whose reporting currency is the RMB have overseas subsidiaries (including those in Hong Kong and Macau) whose financial statements are reported in foreign currency, the financial statements of the subsidiaries should be translated into RMB before consolidation.

Balance sheet items should be translated at the year-end official exchange rate. Balances originally stated in RMB should be stated at the original RMB amount. If the capital of an investee company is registered in RMB, the amount should be stated at the amount of RMB at the time the investment was made or the RMB equivalent amount of the foreign currency invested. If the capital is registered in foreign currency, it should be translated at the year-end official rate.

The profit and loss items of foreign subsidiaries should be translated using the weighted average exchange rate for the year.

The differences arising from translating the balance sheet and profit and loss account items at different rates would be treated as a foreign currency translation difference and should be separately disclosed as a reserve movement in the financial statements.

Reference. Articles 73 and 74 of the Practices.

Hedges. Forward contracts in foreign currencies, although available through foreign bank branches or designated Chinese organizations, are not common in the PRC. The Practices do not specify the accounting treatment for or disclosure of these forward contracts.

FIEs can, through the swap centers, buy foreign currencies and foreign exchange quotas (see below). To a certain extent, these can be utilized for the purpose of hedging to reduce the risk of currency fluctuation. The Practices require specific methods of translation for transactions made at the swap centers, as described above under foreign currency denominated transactions.

Foreign exchange quotas are rights that allow the holder to exchange RMB for foreign currency at the official rate. There is a market price for the quotas, which represents the difference between the market rate and official rate. Foreign exchange quotas purchased should be separately shown as **current assets** and should be recorded at their actual cost.

If the reporting currency is RMB, the foreign currency purchased using foreign exchange quotas should be recorded according to the book carrying cost of the foreign exchange quota plus the amount of RMB paid for the exchange of the foreign currency.

If the reporting currency is the foreign currency, the foreign currency purchased should be recorded at the actual amount of foreign currency received. If the foreign currency purchased is different from the reporting foreign currency, then the foreign currency amount received should be translated into the reporting foreign currency using the official exchange rate either at the date of receipt or on the first day of the month.

The difference between the proceeds received from the selling of the foreign exchange quota and the book cost should be accounted for as foreign exchange gain or loss.

The foreign exchange quota obtained as partial settlement of sales proceeds should be recorded separately in a memorandum register and disclosed in a note to the balance sheet. The income received from selling the quota through a swap center should be treated as foreign exchange gain for the period.

Disclosure. The net exchange differences included in general and administrative expenses should be disclosed in the profit and loss account.

The foreign exchange quota available as at the financial statement date should be disclosed in a note to the balance sheet.

The foreign currency capital amounts contributed by investors should be disclosed in the balance sheet under paid-in capital. The export sales in foreign currencies, together with the equivalent amount in reporting currency; and the domestic sales in foreign currencies, together with the equivalent amount in the reporting currency, and those domestic sales in foreign exchange certificates should be disclosed in a note to the profit and loss account.

There is no requirement to disclose foreign currency translation policies, the significant factors that give rise to changes in the capital translation difference included in the equity reserve or the amortization method for deferred exchange gains and losses.

Reference. Financial Reportings.

7. Changing Prices/Inflation Accounting

This is not covered by the Practices, and no supplementary information is required to be disclosed.

8. Accounting Changes

Accounting Treatment. The Practices do not cover accounting changes, and there is no distinction between changes in accounting policies and changes in accounting estimates.

Disclosure. There is no requirement for disclosing changes in any accounting policies or the related effect on the financial statements of the current period.

9. Prior Period Adjustments

Accounting Treatment. There are three accounting treatments for prior period adjustments:

- ☐ Adjustments required by the auditor that affect the profit for a prior period are made against the balance brought forward in the undistributed profits account.
- ☐ Adjustments required by tax authorities should be recorded in the undistributed profits account. Moreover, taxes payable and the undistributed profits account should also be adjusted accordingly.
- ☐ Subject to the approval of the tax authorities, adjustments related to prior years may be accounted for in the current year profit through nonoperating income or nonoperating expenses.

Disclosure. The adjustments should be reflected in the statement of profit appropriation and statement of nonoperating income and expenses.

The nature of the adjustment, the effect of making the adjustment to the financial statements and the related per share amount are not required to be disclosed.

Reference. Article 58 of the Practices, Financial Reportings.

10. Post Balance Sheet Events

Accounting Treatment. There is no specific discussion in the Practices on post balance sheet events. Adjusting events that provide further evidence of conditions that existed at the financial statement date but that are related to prior periods can either be adjusted in the current period through nonoperating income and expenses or be adjusted through the undistributed profits account (see Section 9).

Disclosure. There is no requirement to disclose post balance sheet events.

11. Related Party Transactions

Definition. Related party transactions are not defined in the Practices.

Accounting Treatment. Amounts due to and from **subsidiary** companies should be accounted for in the intercompany account, which should be eliminated upon consolidation.

Funds given to a subsidiary that is not a tax-independent-assessing entity should be accounted for in the funds to branches account. The subsidiary should, in its accounting records, account for the funds received in the funds from head office account.

Disclosure. There is no requirement to disclose in the financial statements the nature and extent of related party transactions, the relationship between the related parties, the amounts due to or from related parties, the terms of settlement and no-charge transactions between related parties. Even though the ongoing operations of the FIEs depend on a significant volume of business with another related party (e.g., a major supplier, customer or lender), the economic dependence on that party need not be disclosed.

Reference. Financial Reportings.

12. Segmental Information

General. Segmental reporting is not covered in the Practices.

Disclosure. No segmental information disclosure is required.

ACCOUNTING PRINCIPLES FOR SPECIFIC ITEMS— BALANCE SHEET

13. Property, Plant and Equipment

Classification of Capital and Revenue Expenditure. Expenditures are classified as capital when they benefit the company for more than one year. Expenditures that benefit the company only for the current year are classified as revenue expenditures.

Fixed assets include buildings, structures, plant and machinery, transportation vehicles, other equipment, utensils and tools related to production whose useful life is more than one year. Equipment that is not related to production but whose individual unit cost is over RMB 2000 and useful life is more than two years is also regarded as fixed assets.

Reference. Articles 10 and 16 of the Rules.

Basis of Valuation. Fixed assets should be stated in the balance sheet at historical cost. Cost of fixed assets contributed by investors should be based on the joint venture contract and the inspection list. Cost also includes transportation, loading and unloading expenses, insurance, tax and custom duties that are borne by the company.

The cost of fixed assets purchased by the company should include the purchase price plus the cost of transportation, loading and unloading expenses, insurance, custom duties and tax, and the cost of installation.

Fixed assets manufactured and constructed by the company are stated at the expenditure incurred during manufacture and construction.

The cost of donated fixed assets preferably should be determined based on the invoice price. If the invoice is not available, the company may record the asset by referring to either the domestic or international market price of the same type of asset. If the donated fixed asset is used, accumulated depreciation should be taken into consideration. The related costs of transportation, loading and unloading expenses, insurance, custom duties and tax should also be included.

In the case of expansion, replacement, renovation or reform of the technology, the original value of the fixed assets should be increased based on the actual expenditure incurred.

Reference. Article 30 of the Practices.

Depreciation. Generally, straight-line **depreciation** should be adopted. If the **straight-line method** is not appropriate, the production or service output method is also acceptable.

Depreciation charges should be computed based on the original cost of the fixed asset and the depreciation rate for the particular category of fixed assets. Specific depreciation rates for particular fixed assets can also be adopted. An estimated scrap value of not less than 10 percent of the original cost of the fixed assets should be provided for before calculating the depreciation charge.

The depreciation periods of various fixed asset categories are set out below:

☐ Buildings and structures: not less than 20 years.

☐ Trains, vessels, plant and machinery, and other production equipment: not less than ten years.

☐ Electronic equipment, transportation vehicles other than trains and vessels, and other production and operation related appliances, tools and furniture: not less than five years.

Acceptable accelerated depreciation methods are the **sum-of-years'-digits method** and the **double declining balance method**.

Depreciation should be computed on a monthly basis beginning the month following that in which the asset is placed in service. Depreciation is discontinued the month following that in which it is taken out of service.

If the value of a fixed asset has increased due to augmentation, replacement, renovation or technical reform, the depreciation charge is computed according to the adjusted value, the estimated scrap value, the depreciation already charged and the remaining useful life.

For fixed assets used during the preoperating period but not directly related to construction, the related depreciation charges should be included as preoperating expenses.

Except for buildings or structures, depreciation charges should cease if the assets have been idle for a long time. There is no requirement to write down idle or surplus fixed assets to their recoverable amount.

Reference.   Articles 19 and 31 of the Practices.

Fixed Asset Gains and Losses.   Gain or loss on disposal of fixed assets should be recorded in nonoperating income or nonoperating expenses, respectively.

Reference.   Article 32 of the Practices.

Construction in Progress.   Construction in progress includes construction engineering work and installation performed during the course of construction and completed construction work not handed over to the company.

For larger-scale construction projects lasting more than one year, construction in progress can be accounted for on an individual project basis.

A net loss attributable to damages and write-offs of construction in progress can be included in the cost of the ongoing construction work. The net loss is computed after taking into account the scrap value of the materials disposed of and any compensation received from an insurance company or other party.

If the damages and write-offs are due to extraordinary circumstances, the net loss should be included in preoperating expenses or nonoperating expenses, depending on whether the company is at the preoperating or production stage.

Before the commencement of production, expenses incurred for the trial operation can be included in construction in progress. Income from sale of the finished goods produced during the trial operation, net of relevant costs, can be applied to offset the cost of construction in progress.

If the total cost of construction cannot be ascertained at the commencement of production, the company should estimate the cost and transfer it to fixed assets and compute depreciation charges accordingly. Adjustments can be made when cost is known.

Reference.   Articles 23, 30, 33, 34 and 35 of the Practices.

Disclosure.   The total cost, accumulated depreciation and net book value of fixed assets and the value of construction in progress should be separately disclosed in the balance sheet.

Fixed assets depreciation, surplus or deficit of fixed assets count, gains or losses of fixed assets disposal, proceeds from disposal of fixed assets, capital contributions to other ventures in the form of fixed assets and additions to fixed assets should be disclosed in the statement of changes in financial position.

In the statement of fixed assets and accumulated depreciation, the opening and closing costs, opening and closing accumulated depreciation, depreciation rates and current period depreciation charges are disclosed for each major category of fixed assets. Also, the breakdown of additions due to acquisitions, completion of construction, capital contributions by shareholders in the form of fixed assets, fixed assets count surpluses and donated fixed assets received; and the breakdown of reductions due to disposals, scrapping, fixed assets count deficits, extraordinary losses, capital contributions to other ventures in the form of fixed assets and donated capital are to be disclosed.

The movement of construction in progress during the period, the status and breakdown by major projects of construction in progress are disclosed in the statement of construction in progress.

14. Intangible Assets

Intangible assets include industrial property rights, proprietary technology, site use rights, franchises and copyrights. Preoperating expenses, foreign exchange loss incurred during the preoperating period, deferred investment loss, deferred expenditure and **goodwill** that require periodic amortization are also regarded as intangible assets.

Preoperating expenses include registration expenses, salaries and wages, traveling and transportation expenses, staff training expenses, board of directors expenses and other expenses not included in the acquisition and construction cost of fixed assets or intangible assets.

Accounting Treatment.   Foreign exchange loss incurred during the preoperating period should be treated as other assets and separately disclosed in the balance sheet.

Deferred investment loss is the difference between the appraised value of assets invested and their book carrying value.

Other deferred expenditure should be recorded based on the expenditures incurred.

Goodwill may arise from the contribution of capital to FIEs or from the purchase of assets from third parties. It should be stated at cost.

Reference.   Article 38 of the Practices.

Valuation.   Intangible assets contributed by the investor are recorded at the agreed value between the investor and the company or the amount set out in the application document for incorporation of the company. The value should also include incidental expenses borne by the company.

The value of purchased intangible assets should be the amounts actually paid.

The value of intangible assets developed by the company should be the actual expenditure incurred in the course of the development.

For donated intangible assets such as industrial property rights, proprietary technology, site use rights, franchises and copyrights, the value should be the estimated market price of similar assets.

The valuation of intangible assets should be supported by relevant documentation, such as a copy of the certificate of ownership and the bases and standards of the valuation. Valued proprietary technology, franchises and goodwill should be appraised and their valuation affirmed by an organization with the authority to attest or by a Chinese registered certified public accountant.

Reference.   Article 36 of the Practices and article 22 of the Rules.

Amortization.   From the date the company starts to benefit from the intangible assets, the intangible assets should be amortized on straight-line basis, over the period specified in any contract or agreement. In the absence of a contract or agreement, **amortization** should be over the period during which the company may benefit from the intangible assets, subject to a minimum of ten years.

Preoperating expenses and foreign exchange loss incurred during the preoperating period should be amortized on a straight-line basis over a period of not less than five years from the date of commencement of operations.

Deferred investment loss should be amortized in accordance with the investment period or a period of not less than ten years on straight-line basis.

Deferred expenditure should be amortized on a straight-line basis over the estimated period that the company benefits from the expenditure, but not less than ten years.

The land grant fees paid by a company engaging in the development of large tracts of land should be amortized on a straight-line basis over the term for which the leasehold is granted. If the company requires a shorter amortization period because its term of operation is shorter than the term of the grant, this must be approved by the finance authorities in charge.

Goodwill should be amortized using the straight-line method over the period specified in the contract. If there is no contract term governing the period, it should be amortized over the estimated period of benefit, or if that period cannot be estimated, over ten years. Amortization expense should be charged to general and administration expenses—amortization of intangible assets.

Reference.   Articles 37, 39 of the Practices and article 23 of the Rules.

Disclosure.   Land use rights, industrial property rights and proprietary technology and other intangible assets should be separately disclosed under intangible assets. Preoperating expenses, foreign exchange loss incurred during the preoperating period, deferred investment loss and deferred expenditure that require periodic amortization should be separately disclosed under other assets.

15. Leases

Classification. There is no classification or definition in the Practices regarding **finance** or capital **leases** and **operating leases**.

Accounting Treatment. The cost of finance leased fixed assets in the lessee's accounting records is the contract price plus the cost of transportation, loading and unloading expenses, insurance, tax and custom duties. If the contract price includes interest expenses and handling charges, they should be excluded unless the contract price is not significant and the lease period involved is short.

Depreciation charges should be computed for fixed assets that are acquired under finance leases and fixed assets that have been leased out under operating leases.

Also, accumulated depreciation for fixed assets acquired under finance leases should be separately accounted for.

The Practices do not deal with the treatment of operating leases or the accounting for leases by lessors.

Disclosure. The amount of leased fixed assets should be disclosed as a note to the balance sheet.

Reference. Article 30 of the Practices.

16. Investments

Marketable securities represent short-term investments in shares and bonds to be disposed of for cash within one year.

Long-term investments include direct investments in other entities in the form of cash, tangible and intangible assets and shares and bonds to be held for over one year.

Valuation. Marketable securities should be accounted for at their purchase price plus related transaction expenses such as brokerage commissions.

Investments in other entities should be valued based on the actual amount paid or the prices of the tangible and intangible assets in accordance with the relevant investment contract and agreement.

The value of share investments can be determined either by actual payment or by the revaluation of the tangible and intangible assets invested plus any relevant expenses.

If the actual payment includes dividends declared or interest receivable, such dividends or interest should be excluded from the investment cost and be treated as temporary payment in other receivables.

For bonds purchased at a premium or discount, the difference between the actual payment and the **par value** of the bond should be periodically amortized until the maturity date. Also, the interest income and the book carrying cost of the long-term investment should be adjusted accordingly. The company can use the straight-line amortization method or effective interest rate amortization method.

The difference between the value of tangible and intangible assets invested and the book carrying value of the investment should be treated as deferred investment gain or loss and amortized evenly over the investment period and recorded in nonoperating income or nonoperating expenses, respectively.

The funds that a company allocates to a branch that keeps independent accounts but does not pay taxes independently should be valued according to the book carrying value of the cash, tangible assets and intangible assets actually allocated. These allocations should be included under long-term investment in the balance sheet.

Reference.   Articles 26 and 28 of the Practices.

Treatment of Valuation Reserves.   There is no requirement to set up reserves for the permanent diminution in value of investments. It is also not required to compare the cost and market value of short-term marketable securities.

Recognition of Gains or Losses on Investments Held and Disposed of.   Dividends and interest income from marketable securities should be accounted for as nonoperating income. The disposal gain or loss on securities or the difference between the actual amount received and the book carrying cost plus the recorded dividends and interest receivable upon maturity of the securities should be treated as investment gain or loss and be accounted for as nonoperating income or expenditure.

Where equity accounting is used for long-term investments, the corresponding changes in the book carrying cost of the long-term investments due to changes in equity of the investee company should be treated as nonoperating expenses or nonoperating income.

Reference.   Article 27 of the Practices.

Disclosure.   Marketable securities to be held for less than one year should be separately disclosed under current assets.

Long-term investments should be separately disclosed.

The net unamortized balance of the deferred investment gain or loss should be disclosed under other assets or other liabilities.

17. Accounts Receivable

Notes receivable, **accounts receivable**, short-term advances and other receivables should be separately accounted for.

Reference.   Articles 19 and 22 of the Practices.

Accounting Treatment.   The company can provide for bad and doubtful debts based on the year-end balances of accounts receivable, notes receivable or the outstanding advances as at year-end. However, the provision cannot exceed 3 percent of the receivable balances.

If the bad and doubtful debt provision computed for the current year is more than the book balance already provided, an additional provision can be recorded. Similarly, if the provision required is less than the book balance, the provision can be adjusted accordingly.

Bad debt expense should be included in general and administrative expenses. The amount of bad debt expenses incurred should be set off against the bad debt provision. If the company collects a debt previously written off to bad debt expenses, current period general and administrative expenses may be reduced accordingly.

Bad debt expenses incurred should be reported to the local tax authorities for examination and confirmation.

The finance authorities will approve bad debts arising from the following circumstances:

☐ The debtor enters bankruptcy and the amount due is not collectible even after the court's judgment of liquidation.

☐ The debtor dies and the debtor's estate is insufficient to repay the debt in full.

☐ The debtor has failed to repay the debt for more than two years and the debt is still not collectible.

Reference. Article 22 of the Practices and article 30 of the Rules.

Factored Receivables. Factoring of receivables is not common in the PRC and it is not covered in the Practices.

Disclosure. Provision for bad and doubtful debts should be separately disclosed in the balance sheet as a deduction from accounts receivable.

Discounted notes receivable of the company should be disclosed in a note to the balance sheet.

Reference. Article 22 of the Practices.

18. Inventories and Work in Progress

General Accounting Treatment. **Inventories** should be accounted for based on cost, including the purchase price, freight charges, loading and unloading charges, insurance, reasonable wastage during the course of transportation, relevant taxes payable and other expenses incurred before the inventories are placed at the warehouse. Merchandise purchased by commercial and service enterprises is stated at the purchase price plus relevant taxes payable.

Self-manufactured, self-produced and self-extracted inventories are stated at the total expenditure incurred during the course of manufacturing, production or extraction.

Inventories produced by subcontractors are stated at the sum of the cost of raw materials or semi-finished goods consumed, together with the cost of processing, freight, loading and unloading expenses, insurance and taxes payable.

Donated inventories should be valued according to the amount specified in the invoice plus the freight, insurance and taxes borne by the company. In the absence of an invoice, the company can value them based on the market price of similar inventories.

Companies should adopt the perpetual inventory system. Merchandise, raw materials, semi-finished goods and finished goods requisitioned or issued should be accounted for based on actual cost, using any of the following methods:

☐ **First in, first out**.
☐ **Weighted average**.
☐ Moving weighted average.
☐ **Last in, first out**.
☐ Batch actual.

If standard costing is adopted, an appropriate portion of the costing variance should be allocated periodically to the cost of the related issues or requisitions. Companies adopting standard costing for inventories should account for the differences between **standard cost** and actual cost.

Issue of low-value consumable and recurring-use packing materials should be accounted for using the method of one-time write-off or periodic amortization. Any significant issue of low-value consumable items during the initial period of commencement of production can be treated as other assets.

Inventory counts should be carried out periodically, at least once a year. Discrepancies between the physical count and the book balance should be investigated. Accounting adjustments are normally made at year-end. Gain on stocktaking should be recorded based on original cost.

As at year-end, the company can provide for obsolete, old, substandard or excessive merchandise, finished goods, and semi-finished goods if their book carrying costs are higher than their **net realizable value** after the approval of the financial authorities or the relevant department under the State Council. The loss can be charged to cost of sales, whereas the provision should be separately accounted for.

When the company sells inventories that have already been written down to their net realizable value, the provision should be offset against the cost of sales.

Net realizable value should be determined based on the estimated realizable income minus the necessary cost of additional work and repair.

Reference.   Articles 23, 24, 25 and 49 of the Practices.

Long-Term Contracts/Work in Progress.   Operating income from long-term contracts may be recognized according to the stage of completion.

Disclosure.   The inventory provision should be disclosed as a deduction from inventories. In the notes to the balance sheet, the company should disclose the amount of materials subcontracted for further processing; merchandise held for consignment sales; and materials and supplies held on behalf of third parties.

In the statement of inventories, details of inventories, including the current period balance, prior year comparative figure and the budget for each category of inventories, should be disclosed. The various categories are materials in warehouses (including raw materials, packaging materials and low-value consumables); materials in transit; materials subcontracted for further processing; work in process; semi-finished goods; finished goods and despatched merchandise on the **instalment sales** basis.

The company should also disclose in the notes to the statement of inventories, the average inventory balances, the inventories turnover statistics, the inventories written down, the inventories not written down but whose net realizable value is lower than cost, inventories pending disposal, inventory shortage and damaged, the actual cost, the net realizable value and the probable loss of these problem inventories.

19. Current Liabilities

Liabilities that are payable within one year from the balance sheet date are classified as **current liabilities** and include short-term borrowings, **accounts payable**, receipts in advance or deposits received, and accrued expenses.

General Accounting Treatment. Short-term borrowings, receipts in advance, deposits received and accrued expenses should be accounted for separately. Payables should be classified according to the categories of notes payable, accounts payable, wages payable, taxes payable, dividends payable and other payables.

Staff bonus and welfare fund should be treated as current liabilities.

Reference. Article 40 of the Practices.

Creation of General and Specific Provisions/Reserves. It is not acceptable to create general provisions for future losses except for the bad debt provision, mentioned earlier. Specific provisions such as for inventories are allowed for liabilities that are known but the amounts need to be estimated. General and specific reserves are covered in Section 22.

Disclosure. Short-term borrowings, notes payable, accounts payable, wages payable, taxes payable, dividends payable, receipts in advance, other payables, accrued expenses and the staff welfare and bonus fund are separately disclosed under current liabilities. There is no requirement to disclose significant commitments to make certain expenditures or any liabilities that are secured.

20. Long-Term Debt

General Accounting Treatment. Long-term liabilities include long-term borrowings, bonds issued and payables for leased assets.

Bonds issued should be recorded according to the face value of the bonds. The difference between the actual amount received and the face value of the bond should be separately accounted for as bond discount or bond premium.

If the amount received includes interest payable, it should be treated as a temporary receipt and be included in other payables.

Bond premium or discount should be amortized against interest expense using the straight-line method or effective interest rate method.

If the issue is through a financial institution, the handling charges paid should be accounted for as finance charges.

Reference. Articles 41, 42, 43 and 44 of the Practices.

Treatment of Debt Restructuring. The Practices do not cover the treatment of debt restructuring.

Treatment of Debt Extinguishment. The Practices do not cover the treatment of debt extinguishment.

Disclosure. Long-term borrowings, bonds issued, payables for leased fixed assets and bond premium and discount should be separately disclosed under long-term liabilities.

The preoperating period exchange gain and deferred investment income should be separately disclosed under other liabilities.

The portion of long-term liabilities payable within one year from the balance sheet date should be disclosed under current liabilities.

There is no specific disclosure requirement regarding debt restructuring and debt extinguishment.

21. Contingencies

General.   The Practices do not cover the accounting treatment and disclosure requirements for contingencies.

Contingent losses and gains usually are not accounted for or disclosed.

22. Capital and Reserves

Definition.   The equity interest of investors of FIEs includes paid-in capital, undistributed profits, reserves appropriated from post-tax profit (namely, the general reserve fund and the enterprise expansion reserve fund) and the capital reserves (namely, capital premium, capital translation difference and donated capital).

Paid-in capital represents the amount contributed by investors in accordance with any contract, agreement or the application to set up the FIEs.

Donated capital represents additional capital, unrelated to the registered capital, contributed to the FIEs in the form of cash or tangible assets.

Capital translation difference represents the difference between the asset accounts and the paid-in capital account arising from different exchange rates adopted for translation.

Capital premium represents the excess amount paid by investors over the amount of registered capital.

Reference.   Articles 45, 46 and 49 of the Practices.

Treatment of Share Capital.   The cash investment should be accounted for based on the actual amount received.

Investment contributions in the form of tangible assets should be accounted for based on the amounts shown in the contract, agreement or the application to set up the FIEs and the inspection list.

Investment contributions in the form of intangible assets should be accounted for based on the amount shown in the contract, agreement or the application to set up the FIEs.

If the paid-in capital recorded is different from the capital verification report issued by the Chinese registered public accountants as required by the relevant law, the difference should be adjusted in the accounts.

If the investment contributed is in foreign currency, it should be translated into the reporting currency. The relevant assets should be translated as described in Section 6. The paid-in capital should be translated based on the official State Administration of Foreign Exchange Control rate stated in the contract. If a rate is not stipulated in the contract, the translation should be based on the official rate on the date the amount is received.

If the capital contribution is received in instalments, and is in foreign currency, subsequent capital instalments received should be translated into the reporting currency based on the official exchange rate adopted for the translation of the first instalment.

If the value of assets contributed differs from the paid-in capital due to different exchange rates, the differences should be treated as a capital reserve.

Donated capital in the form of cash should be recorded based on the donated amount. If the donated capital is in the form of a tangible asset, it should be recorded based on the invoice attached or the domestic or international market price if there is no invoice.

If the donated capital is a used fixed asset, it should be recorded based on original cost less estimated depreciation.

Reference.   Articles 46, 47, 48 and 49 of the Practices.

Treatment of Other Reserves.   FIEs are required to make appropriations from post-tax profit to the general reserve fund, the staff bonus and welfare reserve fund and the enterprise expansion reserve fund. WFOEs are not required to create an enterprise expansion reserve fund.

Reference.   Article 57 of the Practices.

Restrictions on Dividends and Other Distributions.   The general reserve can be used for the setting off of losses incurred and the increase of capital. The enterprise expansion reserve fund can be used to increase the capital. The staff bonus and welfare reserve fund can be used for nonrecurring bonuses to staff or collective staff welfare such as the acquisition of staff quarters and other facilities. Such assets are not regarded as assets of the FIEs.

The profit after income tax and appropriation to general reserve fund, staff bonus and welfare reserve fund and enterprise expansion reserve fund is distributable to the investors.

Reference.   Article 57 of the Practices.

Disclosure.   The FIEs should disclose, under investor equity, the total original amount of investment, the paid-in capital in RMB and the original foreign currency amount (in the case of joint ventures, it should be split into the Chinese interest and the foreign interest), the investment returned, the capital reserve, the general reserve, the enterprise expansion reserve fund, the profit capitalized on return of investment, the current year profit and the undistributed profits.

The increase in capital and capital reserve should be reflected in the statement of changes in financial position.

Return of investment for a CJV should be disclosed as a deduction from paid-in capital.

ACCOUNTING PRINCIPLES FOR SPECIFIC ITEMS— INCOME STATEMENT

23.   Revenue Recognition

General Principles.   Generally, **revenues** are recognized at the time when the products or merchandise has been despatched; construction works have been handed over to the company; services or labor services have been provided; sales proceeds have been received; or the right to claim the sales proceeds has been obtained.

The right to claim the sales proceeds is obtained when:

☐ In the case of requesting a bank to collect the money, the necessary bank collection procedures have been completed.

☐ For consignment sales, the FIEs receive from the consignee the list of goods sold.

Reference. Article 54 of the Practices.

Long-Term Contracts. Revenue is recognized according to the progress of the construction work or the extent of actual work completed (**percentage of completion method**).

Reference. Article 54 of the Practices.

Instalment Sales. Revenue can be recognized according to the payment schedule stated in the contract.

Reference. Article 54 of the Practices.

Right of Return. Contracts with right of return are not common in China. In general, sales returns, whether related to the prior year or current year, should be offset against the sales income of the current period.

Product Financing. Product financing is not covered in the Practices.

Disclosure. The amount of revenue recognized during the period should be disclosed in the profit and loss account. The amount of export sales and sales discounts and allowances should also be disclosed. The sales analysis by major products should be included in the statement of production cost, sales and cost of sales for major products.

24. Government Grants and Assistance

Accounting Treatment. The Practices do not cover government grants and assistance. Although they may be treated as donated capital in substance, it is not clear in the Practices whether they should be amortized or how.

Disclosure. No disclosure of government grants and assistance information is required.

25. Research and Development

Definitions. Research and development are not defined in the Practices.

Accounting Treatment. There is no guidance in the Practices on the accounting treatment for research and development cost. However, the Practices do allow industrial FIEs to separately account for the external sales and cost of trial products produced during the course of research and development. If these products cannot be sold externally, the cost can be included in general and administrative expenses after deducting the scrap value; or it can be deferred and charged to cost of production after the commencement of production.

Disclosure. Research and development expenses should be separately disclosed under general and administrative expenses.

Reference. Articles 51 and 52 of the Practices.

26. Capitalized Interest Costs

Accounting Treatment. Interest expenses directly related to the acquisition and construction of a fixed asset should be capitalized. Other interest expenses incurred during the preoperating period should be charged to preoperating expenses. Interest expenses incurred after the commencement of operations should be charged to operating expenses for the current period.

Reference. Article 44 of the Practices.

Disclosure. The amount of interest capitalized during the period is not required to be disclosed.

27. Imputed Interest (Discounting)
Imputed interest is not common in the PRC and is not covered in the Practices.

28. Extraordinary or Unusual Items
Extraordinary items are not defined in the Practices.

Unusual/Abnormal/Exceptional Items. Income and expenses arising from extraordinary activities are classified as nonoperating income and nonoperating expenses. Non operating income includes investment income, gain on revaluation of investments, surplus of fixed assets count, gain on fixed asset disposal, penalty income and prior year income. Nonoperating expenses include investment loss, loss on revaluation of investments, shortage of fixed assets count, loss on disposal of fixed assets, penalty, donation, extraordinary loss and prior year loss.

Reference. Article 55 of the Practices.

Accounting Treatment. The above items should be separately accounted for under nonoperating income and nonoperating expenses.

Disclosure. Nonoperating income and nonoperating expenses should be separately disclosed in the profit and loss account. Also, the breakdown of nonoperating income and expenses by categories should be set out in the statement of nonoperating income and expenses.

29. Income Taxes

Accounting Treatment. The current year income tax payable computed based on current year profit and current year applicable tax rate should be charged to undistributed profits. Deferred income tax is not covered in the Practices.

Treatment of Tax Losses.   Tax losses can be carried forward for a maximum of five years.

Reference.   Article 11 of the FIEs Income Tax Law.

Disclosure.   Income tax provided should be separately disclosed in the statement of profit appropriation.

30.   Postretirement Benefits

Pensions.   Generally, FIEs in the PRC do not have pension plans. Companies are required to pay the retirement insurance premium to the designated insurance company for their Chinese personnel in accordance with the relevant national and local labor management regulations. Retirement insurance includes pension, medical and funeral expenses and pension benefits for the family of a disabled or deceased employee.

Accounting Treatment.   The cost of retirement insurance is accounted for in general and administrative expenses.

Rules.   Retirement insurance is governed by the national and local labor management regulations. In general, a specific percentage of the total wages of currently employed Chinese personnel is required to be paid as the retirement insurance premium. Appropriate adjustments to the insurance premium may be made if necessary, subject to the insurance company obtaining approval from the local authorities.

The retirement insurance fund is a separate fund with independent accounting; enterprises are prohibited from diverting the fund for other purposes.

Disclosure.   There is no requirement to disclose retirement insurance and other pension information.

Reference.   Provisions of the Ministry of Labour and Personnel of the PRC on the Autonomous Right of FIEs in the Hiring of Personnel and on Salaries and Wages, Insurance and Welfare Expenses; and respective local/municipal regulations on labor and personnel administration for Sino–Foreign EJVs.

Other Postretirement Benefits.   Other postretirement benefits are not provided in the PRC.

31.   Discontinued Operations
The Practices do not cover the accounting and disclosure requirements for discontinuance of part of a company's operations.

32.   Earnings per Share
This topic is not covered in the Practices.

Appendix
DO CHINESE STANDARDS OR PREVALENT PRACTICE SUBSTANTIALLY COMPLY WITH INTERNATIONAL ACCOUNTING STANDARDS?

Section	Topic	Substantially complies with IAS?	Comments
3.	Basic accounting concepts and conventions	Yes	Except prudence is not well recognized
	Contents of financial statements	No	There is no requirement to disclose accounting policies
4.	Business combinations*	Yes	
5.	Joint ventures	No	
6.	Foreign currency translation*	No	
8.	Accounting changes*	No	
9.	Prior period adjustments*	No	
10.	Post balance sheet events	No	
11.	Related party transactions	No	
12.	Segmental information	No	
13.	Property, plant and equipment*	Yes	
15.	Leases	No	
16.	Investments	Yes	
17.	Accounts receivable	Yes	Except for some restrictions, no doubtful debt provisions
18.	Inventories and work in progress*	Yes	Except for some restrictions on inventory provisions
19.	Current liabilities	Yes	
20.	Long-term debt	Yes	
21.	Contingencies	No	
22.	Capital and reserves	Yes	
23.	Revenue recognition*	Yes	
24.	Government grants and assistance	No	
25.	Research and development*	No	
26.	Capitalization of interest costs*	Yes	

Appendix (*Continued*)

Section	Topic	Substantially complies with IAS?	Comments
28.	Extraordinary or unusual items*	No	
29.	Income tax**	No	
30.	Postretirement benefits*	NCE	

*These topics are subject to change as a result of the IASC Improvements Project—see the appendix to the International Accounting Standards chapter.

**The IAS on accounting for taxes on income is currently being revised, and an exposure draft has been issued.

NCE—Not commonly encountered in the People's Republic of China.

Comparison in this table is made to International Accounting Standards in force at January 1, 1993. For further details, see the International Accounting Standards chapter.

CYPRUS

GENERAL NATIONAL INFORMATION

1. Source of Generally Accepted Accounting Principles

Generally Accepted Accounting Principles and Practices. **Generally accepted accounting principles** and practices are derived from the following sources:

☐ Companies Law Chapter 113 (the Companies Law). The Companies Law is virtually a replica of the United Kingdom 1948 Companies Act and provides that financial statements must consist of a directors' report, an auditors' report, a profit and loss account and a balance sheet. The Companies Law further provides that the financial statements presented to the shareholders must give a true and fair view. The details to be disclosed in the profit and loss account and the balance sheet (or the notes to the financial statements) are prescribed by the Companies Law. If a company has **subsidiaries**, group financial statements need to be prepared; normally these take the form of **consolidated financial statements**. Disclosure requirements for consolidated financial statements are also prescribed by the Companies Law.

☐ International Accounting Standards (IASs) issued by the International Accounting Standards Committee (IASC) are used where the Companies Law does not provide detailed guidance. IASs do not have the force of law, but it is generally accepted that they need to be followed if the financial statements are to show a true and fair view as required by the Companies Law. United Kingdom SSAPs are also used as a guide where there is no corresponding IAS. The Institute of Certified Public Accountants of Cyprus (ICPAC), whose members are also members of recognized United Kingdom accounting bodies, has adopted the IASs, and all its members are obligated to follow them.

2. Audit and Public Company Requirements

Audits. Every limited company is obligated to appoint auditors to hold office from one annual general meeting to the end of the next annual general meeting. No resolution is needed for reappointment. Auditors are required to report whether in their opinion:

☐ The balance sheet and the profit and loss account of the company and the consolidated financial statements, if prepared, have been properly prepared in accordance with the Companies Law.

□ A true and fair view is given by the financial statements of the state of the company's affairs at the end of the **financial year**, and of the company's profit or loss for the year.

□ If consolidated financial statements are presented, a true and fair view is given of the state of affairs and the profit or loss of the company and its subsidiaries.

□ The company has kept proper books and records, and the financial statements are in agreement therewith.

In addition, auditors have a statutory duty to include certain information in their report if the information is not otherwise disclosed in the financial statements. This includes information related to **directors' emoluments** (salaries and other benefits), pensions and compensation for loss of office (including noncash compensation).

Auditors are also required to report significant departures from the IASs, except when they concur with a departure.

Other duties and obligations of auditors are contained in International Standards on Auditing. These standards, issued by the International Auditing Practices Committee of the International Federation of Accountants, prescribe the basic principles and practices that members of the ICPAC are expected to follow when conducting an audit.

Public Companies.   Under the Companies Law, a company is a **public company** if it is not a private company. A private company is one that limits the right to transfer its shares, limits the number of its members to 50 and prohibits any invitation to the public to subscribe for its shares. Many private companies (which constitute the majority of companies in Cyprus) are exempt private companies. To qualify as an exempt private company, an entity must not have corporate shareholders (unless they are exempt themselves), corporate directors or nominee shareholders. Private exempt companies enjoy certain privileges, mainly that the auditor of the company need not qualify as an auditor under the Companies Law.

The directors of all companies, with the exception of exempt private companies, are required by law to file financial statements, including directors' and auditors' reports, each year with the Registrar of Companies. These reports are available for public inspection.

GENERAL ACCOUNTING

3. Financial Statements

Basic Accounting Concepts.   Financial statements are normally prepared on the **historical cost basis**. However, the Companies Law allows alternative accounting rules, which permit the revaluation of certain assets. Thus, companies base their financial statements on either the pure historical cost convention or the historical cost convention modified for the revaluation of certain assets. In practice, the majority of companies issue historical cost financial statements, with certain fixed assets revalued.

The assumptions underlying financial statements are the **going concern concept**, the consistency concept, the **prudence concept**, the **accruals concept** and the concept of separate determination of individual assets and liabilities.

It is a fundamental requirement that financial statements give a true and fair view. In certain circumstances, it is necessary to depart from the provisions of the Companies Law in order to give a true and fair view. Where this is necessary, the details of the departure, the reasons for it and its effect should be given in the notes to the financial statements.

Contents of Financial Statements.   Financial statements generally include a directors' report (a narrative supplement to the financial statements), a profit and loss account, a balance sheet, a statement of source and application of funds (although not required by the Companies Law), a statement of accounting policies and notes that are referenced to those financial statements.

There is no statutory requirement for the preparation or disclosure of a cash flow statement. However, the requirements of the recently issued IAS 7 (revised), *Cash Flow Statements*, will have to be complied with when the revised standard becomes effective (for periods beginning on or after January 1, 1994).

In the case of a group, the financial statements also include a consolidated balance sheet and a consolidated profit and loss account. In certain circumstances, the profit and loss account of the **parent company** need not form part of the consolidated financial statements.

Format of Financial Statements.   The Companies Law does not prescribe a format for either the profit and loss account or the balance sheet. Schedule Eight of the Companies Law, however, gives details of the items to be disclosed in the financial statements.

Disclosure of Accounting Policies. Both the Companies Law and IAS 1 require the company's **accounting policies** to be disclosed. Changes in accounting policies that have a material effect on the financial statements are also disclosed, together with the reason for and effect of the change.

4. Business Combinations

Principles of Consolidation.   The Companies Law requires the parent company of a group to prepare consolidated financial statements that include all subsidiary undertakings, including unincorporated entities such as partnerships, as well as limited companies.

Control rather than legal ownership determines whether a company is a subsidiary (see below). Consolidated financial statements are not required if in the opinion of the directors:

☐   Their preparation is impracticable or would be of no real value to the **members** of the company.
☐   The result would be misleading or harmful to the business of the company.
☐   The business of the holding company and that of the subsidiary are very dissimilar.

Accounting for Business Combinations.   A **business combination** arises where one company obtains an interest in another company, which becomes a subsidiary. The **purchase method** is used in the majority of cases. The **pooling of interests method** is used in rare circumstances in which neither party can be identified as the acquirer.

Control. As provided by the Companies Law, a company is a subsidiary of another where:

□ The parent holds the majority of the voting rights in a company.

□ The parent is a member of the company and has the right to appoint or remove the majority of the company's board of directors.

Goodwill. The treatment of purchased **goodwill** arising on consolidation is governed by IAS 22, which allows several options to be followed. Purchased goodwill can either be recognized as an asset in the consolidated financial statements or be immediately adjusted to shareholders' interests. One option given by IAS 22 has allowed entities to recognize goodwill as an asset and write it off over a number of years.

Equity Accounting. If an investor has a participating interest in another company and exercises significant influence over the company's operating and financial policies, that company should be treated as an **associated company**. An investor that holds at least 20 percent, directly or indirectly, of the voting rights in another company is presumed to exercise significant influence unless there is evidence to the contrary. A number of factors may indicate significant influence in practice, such as board representation. IAS 28 allows the use of the cost method instead of the **equity method** where the associate operates under severe long-term restrictions that significantly impair its ability to transfer funds to the investor. Investments in associates are also accounted for using the cost method when the investment is acquired and held exclusively with a view to its disposal in the near future.

Minority Interests. There are prescribed lines in the balance sheet and profit and loss account for **minority interests**. Minority interests in the consolidated balance sheet show the amount of capital and reserves attributable to interests in subsidiaries included in the consolidation that are held by or on behalf of persons other than the parent and its subsidiaries. Similarly, minority interests in the consolidated profit and loss account include the amount of any profit or loss on ordinary activities attributable to interests in subsidiaries included in the consolidation that are held by or on behalf of persons other than the parent and its subsidiaries.

Disclosure. Consolidation: The accounting method used and date of the combination should be disclosed. For the purchase method, the proportion of voting shares acquired, the purchase cost, details of the purchase consideration and the treatment of goodwill (if any) should be disclosed. For the pooling of interests method, details of the shares issued, assets and liabilities contributed and results of the enterprises before the combination should be disclosed. On an ongoing basis, detailed disclosure is required of the composition of the group.

Equity accounting: A description of significant associated companies and the proportion of ownership and voting power held should be given. Investments accounted for under the equity method should be shown as long-term assets in the consolidated balance sheet and the investor's share of results shown as a separate item in the consolidated profit and loss account.

5. Joint Ventures

Accounting for Investments in Joint Ventures.   In the absence of specific legislation on the subject, the accounting treatment of investments in **joint ventures** is governed by IAS 31.

Jointly Controlled Entities.   IAS 31 recommends the use of the **proportionate consolidation method**, rather than the equity method, as it better reflects the substance and economic reality of a venturer's interest in a jointly controlled entity. Nevertheless, IAS 31 does permit the use of the equity method as an **allowed alternative treatment**. The equity method reflects the position that it is inappropriate to combine controlled items with jointly controlled items. It also reflects the view that venturers have significant influence, rather than **joint control**, in a jointly controlled entity.

The use of either method is inappropriate when the interest in a jointly controlled entity is held exclusively with a view to its disposal in the near future or when the jointly controlled entity operates under severe long-term restrictions that significantly impair its ability to transfer funds to the venturer. Such interests are accounted for as investments in accordance with IAS 25.

Jointly Controlled Operations.   The venturer should recognize the assets under its control, the liabilities and expenses incurred and its share of the income it earns from the sale of goods or services by the joint venture.

Jointly Controlled Assets.   The venturer should recognize the following:

- ☐   Its share of the jointly controlled assets.
- ☐   Any liabilities it has incurred.
- ☐   Its share of any liabilities incurred jointly with other venturers.
- ☐   Its share of the income and expenses of the joint venture.
- ☐   Any expenses it has incurred with respect to its interest in the joint venture.

Transactions Between Venturers and the Joint Venture.   Generally, when a venturer contributes assets to a joint venture, it should recognize only the portion of any gains attributable to the interests of the other venturers. Any losses, however, should be recognized in full.

Disclosure.   A venturer should disclose any interests in significant joint ventures and the proportion of ownership interest held in jointly controlled entities. A venturer that reports its interests in jointly controlled entities using the line-by-line reporting format for proportionate consolidation or the equity method should disclose the aggregate amounts of current assets, long-term assets, current liabilities, long-term liabilities, income and expenses related to its interests in joint ventures.

In accordance with IAS 5 and IAS 10, the venturer should disclose any commitments or contingencies, except where the probability of loss is remote, with respect to its interests in joint ventures.

Accounting by Joint Ventures. There are no specific local requirements, and generally accepted accounting principles apply to the assets, liabilities and operations of joint ventures.

6. Foreign Currency Translation

Domestic Operations. Revenue or costs arising from a transaction denominated in a foreign currency should be translated into the local currency at the exchange rate in effect on the date of the transaction. If a transaction is settled by a contracted rate, that rate should be used. At the balance sheet date, monetary assets and liabilities denominated in foreign currencies should be translated using the exchange rate on that date (the closing rate) or, where appropriate, the exchange rates contracted under the terms of the relevant transactions. All exchange gains and losses arising from these transactions should be recorded in the profit and loss account.

Foreign Operations. For consolidation purposes the financial statements of a foreign enterprise should normally be translated using the closing rate/net investment method. Under this method, the profit and loss account is translated at the closing rate or at an average rate for the period, and the balance sheet of the foreign enterprise is translated using the closing rate. The difference between the opening net investment in a foreign enterprise translated at the closing rate of the previous year and the closing rate of the current year should be adjusted directly to reserves. In certain circumstances, such as where a branch operates as an extension of the company and the branch's cash flows have a direct impact on those of the company, the **temporal method** of translation should be used.

Hedges. When the reporting currency amount required to settle a foreign currency transaction is established by a forward exchange contract, the difference between the spot rate at inception and the forward rate is amortized over the life of the contract. If foreign currency loans and transactions are treated as a **hedge** against a net investment in a foreign entity, the related exchange differences should be included in shareholders' equity to the extent that they are covered by exchange differences arising on translation of the net investment.

Disclosure. The accounting policies should disclose the translation method used and the net exchange differences taken to income and shareholders' equity. It is also necessary to disclose whether the closing or average rate was used for translating the profit and loss account of foreign entities. Any deferred exchange differences should also be disclosed.

7. Changing Prices/Inflation Accounting

General. There is no requirement in Cyprus to make any adjustments for inflation or changes in prices. Current cost financial statements are very rarely prepared in Cyprus. This is because the economy has historically experienced very low levels of inflation.

8. Accounting Changes

Accounting Treatment. It is a fundamental **accounting concept** that accounting treatment be consistent within a period and from one period to the next. Consequently, a change in accounting policy can be justified only on the grounds that the new policy is preferable. If there has been a change in accounting policy, IAS 8 requires the amounts for the current and corresponding prior periods to be restated on the basis of the new policy; that is, that the change be accounted for as a prior year adjustment.

Estimating the financial impact of future events requires the exercise of judgment. Since a change in estimate arises from new information, IAS 8 requires changes in estimates to be accounted for in the year that the estimate is changed.

Disclosure. Changes in accounting policy should be disclosed in a manner similar to prior period adjustments.

Changes in **accounting methods** used (for example, changing from the straight-line depreciation method to the sum-of-the-years'-digits method), if material, may be disclosed as exceptional items.

9. Prior Period Adjustments

Definition of Adjusting Items. As mentioned above, a **prior period adjustment** must be made where there is a change in accounting policy. In addition, fundamental financial statement errors found at a later date should be accounted for as prior period adjustments. A fundamental error is one of such significance that it would destroy the true and fair view, and therefore the validity, of the company's financial statements.

Accounting Treatment. For both changes in accounting policy and corrections of fundamental errors, the prior period profit and loss account and balance sheet are normally adjusted. The reserves note should present the reserves as previously reported, the prior year adjustment and the restated reserves. Alternatively, as allowed by IAS 8, the adjustment can be separately disclosed in the current income statement as part of net income.

Disclosure. Changes in accounting policies and fundamental errors should be fully explained in the notes. Furthermore, the effect of the prior year adjustment on the results of the preceding year should be disclosed where feasible.

10. Post Balance Sheet Events

Definition. IAS 10 defines post balance sheet events as both favorable and unfavorable events that occur between the balance sheet date and the date on which the financial statements are authorized for issue. Post balance sheet events are split into two types, adjusting events and nonadjusting events.

Accounting Treatment. A post balance sheet adjusting event provides additional evidence of conditions existing at the balance sheet date and should be recorded in the current year financial statements. A nonadjusting event concerns conditions that did not exist at the balance sheet date and, accordingly, are not reflected in the current year financial statements.

Disclosure. A post balance sheet nonadjusting event should be disclosed if it is so material that it would affect the ability of users of financial statements to reach a proper understanding of the company's financial position. The notes to the financial statements should disclose the nature of the event and give an estimate of the financial effect or state that it is not practicable to make an estimate.

11. Related Party Transactions

Definition.   Parties are considered related if one party has the ability to control or exercise significant influence over the other's financial and operating decisions.

Accounting Treatment.   Transactions between related parties are accounted for on the basis of prices used by the two parties. There is no requirement to remeasure to an arm's-length basis.

Disclosure.   The identity of related parties should be disclosed even if there have been no transactions between them. If there have been related party transactions, it is necessary to disclose the type of transaction and sufficient additional information to allow a user of the financial statements to understand the effect of the transaction.

12. Segmental Information

IAS 14, which deals with financial reporting by segment, does not have much applicability in Cyprus. This is because even public companies are relatively small, and diversified activities tend to be limited.

ACCOUNTING PRINCIPLES FOR SPECIFIC ITEMS— BALANCE SHEET

13. Property, Plant and Equipment

Classification of Capital and Revenue Expenditure.   Expenditures that give rise to capital assets are classified as **fixed assets**. Pretrading expenditures, expenses and commissions relating to an issue of shares or debentures, and costs of research cannot be capitalized and are treated as expenses when incurred.

Basis of Valuation.   Fixed assets are recorded at their purchase price or production cost, which includes any consideration given by the company to obtain them. Fixed assets other than goodwill can be revalued to current cost, with any resulting surplus credited to a revaluation reserve. When assets are revalued, surpluses and deficits are determined for individual assets and accounted for separately. A deficit on the revaluation of an asset should be deducted from the revaluation reserve to the extent that there is a previous surplus that relates to that asset; any excess should be charged to the profit and loss account. Gains or losses on the sale of an asset are computed using its carrying value. However, if a revaluation has taken place previously, any remaining revaluation reserve surplus for that asset may be included as part of the profit from the sale of the asset.

Depreciation.   Fixed assets with limited useful lives are depreciated systematically over those useful lives. The **depreciation** base to be written off is an asset's purchase price, or production cost or revalued amount, less any residual value at the end of its useful life. Acceptable depreciation methods include the **straight-line method, sum-of-the-years'-digits method, annuity method** and methods based on the number of units produced. The useful life of an asset is defined in IAS 4 as the period over which the present owner will derive economic benefit from the asset.

Disclosure. The following has to be disclosed for each major class of depreciable asset:

- [ ] The depreciation method used.
- [ ] The useful lives or depreciation rates used.
- [ ] Total depreciation expense for the period.
- [ ] The gross amount of depreciable assets and the related accumulated depreciation at the balance sheet date.

Where there has been a change in depreciation method used, the effect, if material, and the reason for the change should be disclosed. If an asset has been revalued, the reason and the effect, based on both the revalued amount and the historical cost of the asset, must also be disclosed.

14. Intangible Assets

Accounting Treatment. **Intangible assets** such as patents, licenses, trademarks and other rights and assets may be capitalized if they are acquired for valuable consideration or are created by the company.

Purchased goodwill may also be capitalized and treated as other intangible assets. Capitalizing internally generated goodwill is not an accepted practice in Cyprus.

Valuation. All intangible assets other than goodwill may be revalued. Any surplus or deficit arising on revaluation must be adjusted to the revaluation reserve.

Amortization. All intangible assets, including goodwill, should be amortized over their estimated useful lives. The **amortization** rules for intangible assets are the same as for tangible fixed assets, discussed above. There is no maximum amortization period.

Disclosure. The disclosure requirements for intangible assets are comparable to those for tangible assets, mentioned above.

15. Leases

Classification. Leases are classified as either **finance** or **operating leases**. IAS 17 defines a finance lease as a lease that transfers substantially all the risks and rewards of ownership of the asset to the lessee. An operating lease is defined as a lease other than a finance lease.

Accounting Treatment. Lessees: Lessees are required to capitalize finance leases and show lease obligations as a liability. For operating leases, lessees treat lease payments as charges to income on a systematic basis.

Lessors: Lessors treat finance leases as receivables (**debtors**) in their balance sheet. Operating lease assets are treated as fixed assets, and lease income is credited to the profit and loss account.

Leveraged Leases. Such transactions are not common in Cyprus, and there is no specified accounting treatment.

Disclosure. Lessees: The gross amount of assets held under finance leases, together with related accumulated depreciation, should be disclosed for each class of asset. Obligations owed under finance leases should be disclosed separately from other liabilities, either on the face of the balance sheet or in a note. Lease obligations are classified as amounts payable in the next year and aggregate amounts payable thereafter. The aggregate finance charges for the period also have to be shown. Commitments that exist at the balance sheet date should be disclosed.

For operating leases, rent expense has to be disclosed.

Lessors: The net investment in finance leases at the balance sheet date has to be disclosed. The gross amount of assets held for use in operating leases and the related accumulated depreciation have to be disclosed. The aggregate rental income received during the period for finance and operating leases and the costs of assets acquired for purposes of contracting out through finance leases also have to be shown.

16. Investments

Valuation Principles. Current asset investments: **Current asset** investments are stated at market value or at the lower of cost and market value. When the latter is used, the carrying amount may be determined on an aggregate **portfolio basis**, in total or by category of investment, or on an individual investment basis.

Long-term investments: Long-term investments should be stated in the balance sheet at cost or revalued amounts or, for marketable securities, the lower of cost and market determined on a portfolio basis.

Treatment of Valuation Reserves. Surpluses arising on revaluation of investments should be credited to a revaluation reserve. Deficits may be charged to a revaluation reserve only to the extent of any surplus from a previous revaluation of the same asset. Any excess must be charged to the profit and loss account.

Gains/Losses. When investments are sold, the profit or loss on sale is normally computed using the carrying value of the investment; however, the revaluation surplus may be included in the profit or loss. If such profits and losses are material, they should be shown as exceptional items before arriving at profit on ordinary activities before taxes. For investments not acquired with the intention of resale, such as investments in subsidiaries, profits or losses arising on disposal may in certain circumstances be treated as extraordinary items.

Disclosure. The basis used to value long-term and current investments should be disclosed, as well as the treatment of gains and losses. In addition, there should be detailed disclosure of investments, including amounts included in income, market values of marketable investments, dates, frequency and basis of revaluations and changes in the revaluation reserve.

17. Accounts Receivable

Accounting Treatment. Recognition: The recognition of revenues, and hence the related receivables, is described in Section 23.

Discounts: Receivables are normally recorded net of trade and quantity discounts. Cash discounts are recognized at time of payment.

Allowances: Adequate provision must be made for bad and doubtful accounts, but there are no formal methods for calculating such provisions.

Factored Receivables.   This practice is rare in Cyprus, and no specified accounting treatment exists.

Disclosure.   An analysis of debtors has to be disclosed, either in the balance sheet or in the notes, under the following headings: trade debtors, amounts owed by group companies, amounts owed by undertakings in which the company has a participating interest, other debtors, prepayments and accrued income.

18.   Inventories and Work in Progress

General Accounting Treatment.   IAS 2 provides several methods for valuing stocks. Most companies, however, use **FIFO** or **average cost** for valuing stocks. Whichever method is used it is essential that stocks be stated in the financial statements at the lower of cost or **net realizable value. LIFO, base stock** and **latest purchase price** are not acceptable methods of valuing inventories. Costs include all expenses incurred in the normal course of business and any expenses incurred in the process of bringing the goods to their present location and condition.

Long-Term Contracts.   Long-term contracts should be assessed on a contract-by-contract basis and reflected in the profit and loss account by recording **turnover** and related costs as the contract activity progresses. Turnover may include attributable profit to the extent that the outcome of the contract can be assessed with reasonable certainty. Long-term contract work in progress is reduced by the costs included in the profit and loss account, which are matched with turnover for the period.

Disclosure.   The accounting policies applied have to be disclosed. It is usual practice for stocks to be classified in the notes as raw materials and consumables, work in progress, finished goods and goods for resale, and payments on account.

The amount by which turnover on long-term contracts exceeds payments on account is classified as amounts recoverable on contracts and separately disclosed within debtors. If payments on account exceed turnover, the balance should be offset against long-term work in progress, and any excess classified as payments on account and separately disclosed within **creditors**. The note on long-term contracts should disclose separately both the net cost less foreseeable losses and the applicable payments on account.

19.   Current Liabilities

General Accounting Treatment.   The following categories of creditors are separately disclosed: debenture loans; bank loans and overdrafts; payments received on account; trade creditors; bills of exchange payable; amounts owed to group companies; amounts owed to companies in which the company has a participating interest; other creditors, including tax; accruals; and deferred income.

Creation of General and Specific Provisions.   The creation of hidden reserves or excessive provisions is not permitted. Specific provisions for identified liabilities or **contingencies** should be made.

Disclosure. The terms of payment or repayment and the applicable interest rate have to be given in general terms. If the company has liabilities secured by particular assets, details of the security given and the total amount of secured creditors must be disclosed.

20. Long-Term Debt

General Accounting Treatment. Long-term debt is external financing due more than one year from the balance sheet date. Long-term debt includes bonds, debentures and term loans.

Debt Restructuring. There is no specified treatment for debt restructuring.

Debt Extinguishment. There is no specified treatment for debt extinguishment.

Disclosure. The disclosure requirements for long-term debt are the same as those for current liabilities.

21. Contingencies

Contingent Losses. A material contingent loss should be accrued if it is probable that a future event will confirm a loss that can be estimated with reasonable accuracy at the date on which the financial statements are approved. If a contingent loss is not accrued, it should be disclosed, unless the possibility of loss is remote.

Contingent Gains. Contingent gains should not be accrued and should be disclosed only if it is probable that a gain will be realized.

Disclosure. For each contingent loss or contingent gain that is disclosed, the required disclosures are: the nature of the contingency; the uncertainties that are expected to affect the ultimate outcome; and a prudent estimate of the financial effect, showing separately the amounts that have been accrued, or a statement that it is not feasible to make such an estimate.

22. Capital and Reserves

Share Capital. Called-up share capital has to be disclosed in the balance sheet and is the aggregate amount of the calls made on the company's shares, whether or not those calls have been paid. Called-up share capital not paid is shown as a debtor.

If share capital is issued at a premium, the premium is credited to a **share premium** account. The share premium account can be used only to issue fully paid bonus shares (i.e., stock splits), write off preliminary expenses of the company, write off expenses relating to the issue of shares or debentures, write off commissions paid or discounts allowed on any issue of shares or debentures and provide for the premiums payable on redemption of debentures.

Other Reserves. Only realized profits are credited to the profit and loss account. Unrealized profits are normally reflected in the revaluation reserve that is used to record surpluses from the revaluation of assets. Reserves are classified as either revaluation reserve, capital redemption reserve, profit and loss account reserve and other reserves.

Restrictions on Dividends and Other Distributions. Distributions can be paid only out of accumulated realized reserves after taking account of realized losses.

Disclosures. Share capital: The total issued capital, the amount of paid-up **share capital** and the authorized share capital have to be disclosed in a note. If any capital is redeemable, the dates and the terms of redemption and the amount of premium payable on redemption have to be given. If there are any rights attaching to shares, the number, description and amount of the shares must be disclosed, together with the period over which the rights can be exercised and the price to be paid for the shares allotted.

Reserves: The notes must disclose the aggregate amount of each reserve at the beginning and end of the year, any amounts transferred to or from reserves and the source and application of amounts transferred.

ACCOUNTING PRINCIPLES FOR SPECIFIC ITEMS—
INCOME STATEMENT

23. Revenue Recognition

General Principles. IAS 18 sets out the rules to be followed for recognizing **revenue** in the profit and loss account. Revenues are not to be recognized unless realized. IAS 18 clearly states the conditions that have to be satisfied for revenues to be considered realized. The following principles are normally followed in determining when to recognize revenue.

Revenue from a transaction involving the sale of goods is usually recognized when the seller has transferred to the buyer the significant risks and rewards of ownership of the goods. In most situations, the substance of the transaction rather than its legal form will determine the time of sale. If, however, goods are sold subject to conditions (e.g., consignment sales), revenue is not recognized until the conditions have been complied with.

Revenue from the rendering of services is usually recognized as the services are performed. If the service is performed as a single act, revenue is recognized when the service is completed. If the service is provided over a period of time, revenue is recognized in a manner appropriate to the stage of completion of the service, provided that the outcome can be assessed with reasonable certainty.

Long-Term Contracts. With the exception of construction contracts (see Section 18), there is no requirement for any special treatment, and long-term contracts are accounted for under the general provisions explained above.

Instalment Sales. Revenue is normally recognized at the date of sale. If, however, collection is not reasonably assured, revenue is recognized as cash instalments are received.

Rights of Return. When goods are sold giving the buyer the right to return them for a refund or replacement, revenue may be recognized at the point of sale, provided that adequate provision is made for future returns. Even where goods are sold subject to a reservation of title clause, which enables the seller to have a lien on them until the purchaser has paid for them, revenue recognition is not deferred. If, however, the clause is likely to be acted upon, it is appropriate to create a provision for the doubtful debt.

Product Financing.   These arrangements, which are rare in Cyprus, are accounted for as borrowings.

Disclosure.   In addition to the requirements for disclosure of accounting policies, the financial statements should provide information on the circumstances in which revenue recognition has been postponed pending the resolution of significant uncertainties. Sales or other operating revenue is normally disclosed separately in the profit and loss account.

24.   Government Grants and Assistance

Accounting Treatment.   IAS 20 sets out the accounting treatment to be followed for government grants. These should be recognized when the expenditure they are intended to contribute to is recognized.

IAS 20 stipulates that government grants relating to fixed assets should be credited to revenue over the asset's expected useful life. This can be achieved in one of two ways:

☐   The grant may be deducted from the purchase price or production cost of the asset, thereby reducing depreciation expense.

☐   The grant may be treated as a deferred credit, of which a portion is credited to revenue annually.

Disclosure.   The following information must be disclosed in the financial statements:

☐   The accounting policy adopted for government grants.

☐   The nature and extent of government grants recognized in the financial statements and an indication of other forms of government assistance from which the enterprise has directly benefited.

☐   Unfulfilled conditions and other contingencies attaching to government assistance that has been recognized.

25.   Research and Development

Definitions.   Research and development expenditures fall into one or both of the following broad categories:

☐   Research is original and planned investigation undertaken with the hope of gaining new scientific or technical knowledge and understanding.

☐   Development is the translation of research findings or other knowledge into a plan or design for the production of new or substantially improved materials, devices, products, processes, systems or services prior to commencement of commercial production.

Accounting Treatment.   The provisions of IAS 9 are followed. That standard allows for development costs to be capitalized provided the following criteria are met:

☐ The product or process is clearly defined and the cost attributable to it can be separately identified.

☐ The technical feasibility of the production process can be demonstrated.

☐ Management of the enterprise has indicated its intention to produce and market or use the product or process.

☐ There is a clear indication of a future market for the product or process or, if it is to be used internally rather than sold, its usefulness to the enterprise can be demonstrated.

☐ Adequate resources exist or are reasonably expected to be available to complete the project and market the product or process.

Provided that these conditions are satisfied, a company can capitalize development expenditure, but only until commercial production begins. IAS 9 requires a company to amortize the capitalized expenditure from the time commercial production of the product or service begins, which is when the company manufactures the product with a view to selling it commercially. Amortization of development expenditure must be allocated to each accounting period on a systematic basis over the production life of the product. At the end of each accounting period, a company should review capitalized development expenditure. If the circumstances that justified the original deferral of an expenditure no longer apply or are considered doubtful, the company should write off the expenditure immediately to the extent it is considered irrecoverable.

Disclosure.   The following disclosures should be made in the notes:

☐ The accounting policy adopted for research and development expenditure.

☐ The total research and development costs, including amortization of deferred development costs, charged as expense.

☐ The movement in and the balance of unamortized deferred development costs.

☐ The basis proposed or adopted for the amortization of development costs.

26. Capitalized Interest Costs

Accounting Treatment.   Borrowing costs may be capitalized as part of the cost of an asset by applying a capitalization rate to costs of acquisition, construction or production of assets that require a substantial amount of time to be made ready for use. Not capitalizing interest costs is also permitted. In either case, the policy followed should be applied consistently. The capitalization rate is determined by the ratio of borrowing costs to outstanding borrowings. When a new borrowing is associated with a specific asset, the capitalization rate may be determined on the basis of the actual borrowing cost incurred. Capitalization of borrowing costs ceases when the asset is ready for its intended use.

Disclosure.   The amount of borrowing costs capitalized in the period should be disclosed.

27. Imputed Interest

General.   Imputed interest is not used in the preparation of accounts in Cyprus except in relation to finance leases (see Section 15).

28. Extraordinary or Unusual Items

Unusual Items. Unusual items are defined in IAS 8 as items that derive from events or transactions that are distinct from the ordinary activities of the enterprise and therefore are not expected to recur frequently or regularly.

Disclosure. Unusual items are included in net income, and their nature and amount are disclosed separately in the notes to the financial statements.

29. Income Taxes

Accounting Treatment. In Cyprus, companies pay corporation tax on the accounting income of the year adjusted for certain items, whether distributed or undistributed. Corporation tax is payable on the basis of three provisional instalments and one self-assessment. If a company makes a distribution to shareholders, the company withholds income tax from the payment equal to 30 percent of the gross dividend. This tax is payable within a month of being withheld. An individual shareholder receiving a dividend is taxed on the amount of income equivalent to the gross dividend and is subsequently credited with the corresponding withholding tax.

In accordance with IAS 12, companies are also required to account for deferred taxes. Deferred taxes should be computed under either the **liability** or the **deferral method**. The **tax allocation** method used should normally apply to all timing differences. However, the tax expense for the period may exclude the tax effects of certain timing differences when there is reasonable evidence that these timing differences will not reverse for a considerable period and there is no indication that they are likely to reverse after this period.

Deferred tax assets should not be carried forward unless there is a reasonable expectation of realization.

Disclosure. The notes to the profit and loss account must disclose the following:

☐ The tax expense related to income from the ordinary activities of the enterprise.

☐ The tax expense relating to unusual items, to prior period items and to changes in accounting policy.

☐ The tax effects, if any, related to assets that have been revalued to amounts in excess of historical cost or previous revaluation.

30. Postretirement Benefits

Accounting Treatment. In Cyprus, the only common form of postretirement benefits are provident funds, which are **defined contribution plans** as defined by IAS 19.

Provident Funds. The amount to be paid as retirement benefits is determined by contributions to the fund together with investment earnings thereon. The level of contributions of both employees and employers is determined by the funds memorandum and is usually a percentage of the employee's salary. At retirement, employees receive a lump sum payment determined in the manner described above.

Disclosure. Sufficient disclosure is required to provide an understanding of the significance of pension costs to an enterprise.

31. Discontinued Operations

General. There is no prescribed treatment for discontinued operations.

Disclosure. Sufficient disclosure is necessary to make the financial statements clear and understandable.

32. Earnings per Share

There is no legal or other requirement in Cyprus to disclose any information, either for public or private companies, relating to earnings per share.

Appendix
DO CYPRIOT STANDARDS OR PREVALENT PRACTICE SUBSTANTIALLY COMPLY WITH INTERNATIONAL ACCOUNTING STANDARDS?

Section	Topic	Substantially complies with IAS?	Comments
3.	Basic accounting concepts and conventions	Yes	
	Contents of financial statements	Yes	
4.	Business combinations*	Yes	
5.	Joint ventures	Yes	
6.	Foreign currency translation*	Yes	
8.	Accounting changes*	Yes	
9.	Prior period adjustments*	Yes	
10.	Post balance sheet events	Yes	
11.	Related party transactions	Yes	
12.	Segmental information	Yes	
13.	Property, plant and equipment*	Yes	
15.	Leases	Yes	
16.	Investments	Yes	
17.	Accounts receivable	Yes	
18.	Inventories and work in progress*	Yes	
19.	Current liabilities	Yes	
20.	Long-term debt	Yes	
21.	Contingencies	Yes	
22.	Capital and reserves	Yes	
23.	Revenue recognition*	Yes	
24.	Government grants and assistance	Yes	
25.	Research and development*	Yes	
26.	Capitalization of interest costs*	Yes	
28.	Extraordinary or unusual items*	Yes	

Appendix (*Continued*)

Section	Topic	Substantially complies with IAS?	Comments
29.	Income tax**	Yes	
30.	Postretirement benefits*	Yes	

*These topics are subject to change as a result of the IASC Improvements Project—see the appendix to the International Accounting Standards chapter.

**The IAS on accounting for taxes on income is currently being revised, and an exposure draft has been issued.

Comparison in this table is made to International Accounting Standards in force at January 1, 1993. For further details, see the International Accounting Standards chapter.

DENMARK

GENERAL NATIONAL INFORMATION

1. Source of Accounting Standards

Generally Accepted Accounting Principles. **Generally accepted accounting principles** are derived from the following sources:

☐ European Community (EC) legislation in the form of Accounting Directives. This legislation contains certain rules for the carrying values of assets and liabilities and sets out various disclosure requirements for corporate entities.

☐ Accounts Presentation Act. This act sets forth accounting and disclosure requirements for private entities. Similar acts apply to specific industry sectors such as banking and insurance. The Accounts Presentation Act incorporates the EC Accounting Directives into national law.

☐ Danish Accounting Guidelines (DAGs). These are issued by the Institute of State Authorized Public Accountants (ISAPA) in Denmark, and compliance with them by directors and auditors who are members of this professional body is recommended. Currently, DAGs apply to private- and public-sector reporting entities, as relevant. Furthermore, companies quoted on the Copenhagen Stock Exchange must state in the financial statements that they comply with DAGs.

☐ International Accounting Standards (IASs). Issued by the International Accounting Standards Committee, each standard is translated, provided with a foreword and issued by the Institute of State Authorized Public Accountants in Denmark. The foreword explains deviations, if any, from current generally accepted Danish accounting practice and provides recommendations for compliance.

☐ Undocumented principles or national practices that are commonly accepted.

2. Audit and Public Company Requirements

Audits. The Companies Act requires that all companies be audited by state authorized or registered company auditors. The size of company that registered company auditors can audit is limited to companies that do not exceed two of the following three size criteria:

Total assets	DKK 50 million
Turnover	DKK 100 million
Average number of employees	250

State authorized and registered company auditors must be members of one of the two professional accounting bodies in Denmark and must fulfill the training requirements of these bodies. Those requirements include appropriate studies of accounting and company law, and at least three years of practical experience (including specific experience in auditing). State authorized public accountants must also have a master's degree in accounting and economics. Neither state authorized or registered company auditors can be officers of a company, or partners, employers or employees of an officer of the company, that they audit. They also cannot be indebted to the company.

The auditors are appointed by the shareholders at the annual general meeting and hold office until the next annual general meeting. They may be re-elected indefinitely.

The State Authorized Public Accountants Act and Accounts Presentation Act set out the duties and responsibilities of auditors, which relate principally to reporting to the shareholders on the truth and fairness of the accounts and on the company's compliance with applicable requirements. These obligations are amplified by the ISAPA, which issues Auditing Guidelines (AGs).

Compliance with the requirements of the professional guidelines is recommended for members of the professional bodies. In instances of disciplinary actions, noncompliance with professional guidelines will generally result in a State Authorized Public Accountants Act decision against the auditor.

Reference. Accounts Presentation Act (Arsregnskabsloven), chapter 8a; Companies Act (Aktieselskabsloven), sections 4, 5, 21, 26, 51, 84, 90, 103, 111, 130 and 131; and Professional Auditing Guidelines issued by the ISAPA.

Public Companies. **Public companies** wishing to trade their shares in Denmark must apply for listing with the Copenhagen Stock Exchange, which imposes certain reporting requirements and ethical rules for companies wishing to be listed. These requirements are in addition to the normal statutory requirements. The exchange has the authority to enforce compliance with its rules by delisting companies that do not meet its requirements.

The principal requirements for obtaining a listing on the Main Board of the Exchange (Bors I) are:

☐ A minimum number of shareholders (at least 500 of which must be the general public).

☐ Paid-up capital (including share premium) of at least DKK 15 million.

☐ The issuance of a prospectus, including annual accounts and other financial information.

☐ An expected initial trading value of the proposed issue of DKK 8.5 million.

Furthermore, the Stock Exchange Act established rules restricting the misuse of information (insider trading). These are also covered by the Stock Exchange Ethical Rules.

The reporting requirements include the production of half-yearly and annual financial information in Danish. The annual information includes the company's financial statements as prepared under the Accounts Presentation Act. Any information that can influence the share price must be communicated to the Stock Exchange without delay.

Listed public **companies** must file their financial statements with the stock exchange annually, at the latest eight days before the annual general meeting, and must provide unaudited details of their results every six months, within four months of the close of each half-yearly period. If the results in the annual financial statements deviate significantly from the expectations indicated in the half-yearly financial information, an explanation must be given.

Annual accounts, including **consolidated accounts** (four years comparable financial information and a statement of changes in financial position, usually derived from the annual accounts) must be approved at a directors' meeting, signed by the directors, have an audit report attached and be presented to and adopted at the company's annual general meeting within six months of year-end. They must then be filed with the Registrar of Companies and become available to the public. Listed public companies are required to be audited by two separate auditors, who must be state authorized public accountants. If a **subsidiary** of a public company is not audited by the **parent company** auditor or by a recognized international accounting firm, this fact must be clearly stated in the directors' report. Changes in **accounting policies** and other disclosures must be clearly stated and the effects quantified. Compliance with DAGs is compulsory.

Reference. Copenhagen Stock Exchange Act; Copenhagen Stock Exchange—Registration of Companies on the Copenhagen Stock Exchange; Stock Exchange Ethical Rules; and Obligations to publish information for issuers of shares on the Copenhagen Stock Exchange.

GENERAL ACCOUNTING

3. Financial Statement Concepts and Presentation (Regnskabets Koncepter og Indhold)

Basic Accounting Concepts. The basic concepts underlying the selection of accounting policies and the preparation and presentation of financial information in Denmark are contained in the Accounts Presentation Act. Guidance is also given in Danish Accounting Guidelines nos. 1 and 2. Financial statements must present a true and fair view and must comply with the basic **accounting concepts** of **going concern**, consistency and **accrual**. Furthermore, the considerations of **prudence**, **materiality** and **substance over form** must be applied in the selection of appropriate accounting policies and related presentations.

Contents of Financial Statements. Companies are required under the Accounts Presentation Act to present to the shareholders at the annual general meeting a profit and loss account, balance sheet and directors' report. The latter should include a short description of the activities of the company, including research and development activities and management's expectations as to the future; significant changes since year-end; and management's suggestion regarding the distribution of the profits for the year, including dividends where relevant.

The profit and loss account and balance sheet, together with any necessary supporting notes, must be prepared so as to give a true and fair view of the company's profit and loss and financial condition and must be signed by the board and management, and be accompanied by an auditors' report commenting on the truth and fairness of the information and indicating that the accounts are in accordance with the law. If the company is a parent company, additional information must also be presented for the group in the form of consolidated accounts. It is recommended that larger companies prepare a statement of changes in financial position, although this is mandatory only for public companies.

Format of Financial Statements.   The profit and loss account and balance sheet should, unless exceptional circumstances prevail, be prepared in accordance with approved **accounting standards** and the requirements of the Accounts Presentation Act. These rules prescribe a variety of information that must be disclosed and, in particular, require a fixed format for the profit and loss account and balance sheet. Departures from this format are permitted only if it can be demonstrated that adopting the fixed format would impair the true and fair view given by the accounts; supporting reasons must be given by the directors. Prior year comparative figures must be presented. The balance sheet should show intangible, tangible and financial fixed assets separately, as well as current assets. Debt is divided into long- and short-term debt. Provisions should be separately disclosed. The profit and loss account should separately disclose significant items of income and expense. Where necessary or required by law or generally accepted accounting practices, notes should be provided to explain individual profit and loss account and balance sheet items.

Disclosure of Accounting Policies.   All material accounting policies that have been adopted in the preparation of the accounts must be disclosed. However, the going concern and accrual bases need be mentioned only if they are not used and the effect is material. The summary of accounting policies is usually located as a separate section before the profit and loss account and balance sheet or in the initial section of the notes. Changes in the format of the accounts or in accounting policies must be presented in such a way that the consistency of presentation and disclosure is not adversely affected. Such changes must be adequately explained and their effects quantified in the summary of accounting policies.

Reference.   Accounts Presentation Act, chapter 1; Accounting Guideline nos. 1, 2 and 3; and Enactment No. 533—Preparation of Annual Financial Statements and Consolidated Financial Statements.

4.   Business Combinations (Virksomheds Sammenslutninger [Koncerner])

Principles of Consolidation.   The accounts of a group of companies (a parent company with one or more subsidiaries) usually consist of consolidated accounts prepared in the same format as the parent company accounts. If a company is not included in the consolidated accounts, the reason must be given in the notes and the extent to which the **group accounts** are significantly affected by transactions and balances between the excluded company and the rest of the group must be specified.

Control.   A subsidiary is defined by the Companies Act as a company in which the investor, who must in every case be a shareholder:

□ Holds more than 50 percent of the voting rights in the form of issued ordinary share capital;

□ Can control more than 50 percent of the votes at an annual general meeting; or

□ Exercises control through, for example, the board of directors or by agreement with other shareholders.

Companies listed on the Copenhagen Stock Exchange are required to submit consolidated accounts, if relevant.

Accounting for Business Combinations. The **purchase method** is normally used to account for **business combinations**, although the **pooling of interests method** is not specifically disallowed. The cost of acquisition, from the acquiring company's viewpoint, is determined by reference to the fair value of shares or assets given up.

Goodwill. A distinction is drawn between internally generated and purchased **goodwill**. Internally generated goodwill is not recognized in the accounts. Purchased goodwill can arise through the acquisition of a business entity or part thereof, the assets therein or some or all of the shares in another entity. It is measured as the excess of the fair value of the purchase consideration over the fair value of the identifiable net assets acquired.
Purchased goodwill should be:

□ Allocated on the basis of the fair values of the underlying assets acquired; then

□ Fully written off against reserves at the time of acquisition; or

□ Recognized as an intangible fixed asset in the financial statements at acquisition and amortized by systematic charges to income over the period during which benefits are expected to arise, which as a general rule should not exceed five years. (The reason for any extension of amortization period beyond five years must be explained in the notes.)

To the extent that the excess of the purchase consideration over the fair value of the net assets acquired does not represent goodwill (i.e., future benefits), it should be written off to the profit and loss account immediately.

Equity Accounting (Indre Vaerdi). Investments in **associated companies** are accounted for under the **equity method** in the consolidated accounts. The equity method may also be used to account for investments in subsidiaries in the accounts of the parent. Although there is no legislation to this effect, it is assumed that the equity method may also be used to account for investments in associated companies in the accounts of the parent.

An associated company is defined as an investee over which the investor has significant influence. Significant influence essentially involves the ability to affect a company's financial and operating policy decisions (including dividend policy), but not to control those policies. Representation on the board of directors is indicative of such participation, but is neither conclusive evidence of it nor the only method by which the investor may be capable of influencing policy decisions. If an investor holds 20 percent or more of the voting power, this is deemed to lead, in the absence of evidence to the contrary, to a presumption of significant influence.

Equity financial information is included in the balance sheet and profit and loss account of the investor. Increases in the value of investments accounted for on the equity basis must be allocated to a nondistributable equity reserve, which is reduced when the carrying value of the investments is reduced and when dividends are received. The notes must disclose the name and location of subsidiary and associated companies as well as the percentage of equity held.

Minority Interests (Minoritets Interesser). The minority share of operating profit and extraordinary items is shown as a separate line item deducted on the face of the consolidated profit and loss account in arriving at operating profit attributable to members of the parent company. This amount, as well as the minority share of share capital, retained earnings and reserves, is disclosed as a single line item in the shareholders' equity section of the consolidated balance sheet or between debt and shareholders' equity.

Disclosure. Consolidation: Detailed disclosures are required in the group accounts relating to subsidiaries, including acquisitions and disposals, percentage of equity held and, in exceptional cases where subsidiaries are not consolidated, the results and shareholders' equity as well as intercompany balances. The accounting policy adopted for goodwill and details of **amortization** are required to be disclosed.

If the parent company is in turn the subsidiary of another company that is incorporated within the EC and that also prepares consolidated accounts in accordance with the Seventh Directive, a "subgroup consolidation" need not be prepared by the Danish parent. The Danish company can submit its own accounts, accompanied by the consolidated accounts of its ultimate parent, to the Registrar of Companies. A note explaining the application of this exemption must appear in the financial statements of the Danish parent company.

Reference. Accounts Presentation Act, section 1 and chapter 8; Enactment No. 533— Preparation of Annual Financial Statements and Consolidated Financial Statements.

5. Joint Ventures

Accounting for Investments in Joint Ventures. Danish accounting recommendations do not address the different forms of joint venture detailed in International Accounting Standard (IAS) 31, *Financial Reporting of Interests in Joint Ventures*. Joint ventures may be incorporated or unincorporated in Denmark.

Jointly Controlled Entities. The usual method of accounting for joint ventures is the **proportionate consolidation method**. In rare cases when the benefits of the investment in the joint venture are unlikely to accrue to the venturer, the cost method of accounting should be used. The use of the equity method in accounting for jointly controlled entities is also an allowable method where the investment complies with the criteria for an associated company (see Section 4). The accounting treatment in IAS 31 for jointly controlled operations and jointly controlled assets would be appropriate in Denmark.

Transactions Between Venturers and the Joint Venture. In general, the contribution of assets to a joint venture in exchange for an interest in the joint venture does not give rise to a gain or loss on disposal in the contributor's financial statements. Gains resulting from other transactions between the venturer and the joint venture should be recognized only to the extent of the interests of nonrelated venturers. However, losses should be recognized in their entirety.

Disclosure. Disclosure requirements are the same as for full consolidation of subsidiaries or, in certain instances, associated companies.

In addition, where the venturer is liable for any contingent liability or commitment with respect to the joint venture, this should be disclosed.

Danish requirements are consistent with IAS 31. The equity method of accounting for an investment in a jointly controlled entity is an **allowed alternative** to IAS 31's **benchmark treatment** of proportionate consolidation. Danish recommendations for the treatment of transactions between the venturers and the joint venture, and for the recognition of **contingencies** and commitments of and related to the joint venture, are similar to those in IAS 31.

Accounting by Joint Ventures. Generally accepted accounting principles apply to all assets and liabilities and operations of joint ventures. However there is little guidance on accounting by joint ventures for assets contributed by the venturers. At present there are three permitted alternatives:

□ Fair value.

□ The carrying value of the assets in the contributor's financial statements.

□ The carrying value of the contributor's net investment in the joint venture.

Reference. Accounts Presentation Act, section 60.

6. Foreign Currency Translation (Omregning af Fremmed Valuta)

General. There are no pronouncements on accounting for foreign currency translation. Generally accepted accounting principles are based on perceived good accounting practice and international practice. The ISAPA has issued an Accounting Guideline Exposure Draft (49) on this subject. It is expected to be ratified before the end of 1993.

Foreign Currency Denominated Transactions. Each asset, liability, revenue or expense arising from entering into a **foreign currency transaction** should initially be measured and recorded in the domestic currency using the exchange rate in effect at the date of the transaction. Foreign currency **monetary items** outstanding at the balance sheet date should be translated at the rate applicable at that date (year-end rate). Exchange differences should be accounted for in the profit and loss account in the period in which the exchange rates change. In instances where foreign currency transactions have been covered by a forward currency contract, the covered transactions are translated at the rate applicable to the currency covered.

Foreign noncurrent loans generally are converted at exchange rates at the balance sheet date. Any valuation gains on foreign exchange can be recognized in profit and allocated to a foreign currency equalization reserve account. In some cases such unrealized gains are credited directly to the reserve account.

Foreign Operations. The balance sheet of a foreign operation is generally translated using the **current rate method**. Any exchange difference can be taken directly to a foreign currency translation reserve or adjusted against reserves in the consolidated accounts. The profit and loss account should be translated using the exchange rates on the dates of the individual transactions.

Foreign operations that are deemed to be **integrated foreign operations** should be translated using the historical rate for nonmonetary items.

Average or standard exchange rates may be used, provided that the effect of their application is not material and their use is disclosed in the notes.

The same principles of translation apply to foreign operations treated as associated companies.

In instances where the foreign operation trades in a country with high inflation, the financial statements should be adjusted for inflation before conversion to Danish krone.

Hedges (Termins Kontrakter). A transaction should be classified as a **hedge** of a specific foreign currency exposure only as long as it is expected to continue to be effective as a hedge. Exchange differences on transactions undertaken to hedge foreign currency exposure should, except as noted below, be recorded in the profit and loss account in the period in which the exchange rates change. Any losses or gains arising at the time of entering into hedge transactions should, if material, be accounted for separately from the exchange differences on the hedge transactions and be recorded in the profit and loss account over the lives of the hedge transactions.

For transactions intended to hedge the purchase or sale of goods or services, exchange differences (to the extent that they occur up to the date of purchase or sale) and losses or gains arising at the time of entering into the transactions can be deferred and included in the measurement of the purchase or sale.

Disclosure. The accounts and group accounts should disclose details of the treatment and amount of exchange differences, changes in the foreign currency translation reserve and foreign currency exposure at the balance sheet date. Where various categories of exchange differences are subject to different accounting treatments, the effects should be disclosed separately.

Reference. Accounts Presentation Act, sections 42 and 46; ISAPA Exposure Draft 49, *Accounting Treatment of Foreign Currency Translation.*

7. Changing Prices/Inflation Accounting (Inflations Regnskaber)

There are no standards or other provisions covering accounting for changing prices or inflation accounting in Denmark.

8. Accounting Changes (Aendringer i Regnskabs Principper)

Accounting Policies. Accounting policies are the specific accounting principles, bases or methods applied in preparing and presenting financial statements. These should be followed consistently from year to year.

Changes in accounting policies should be accounted for prospectively, except when a company changes an accounting policy to comply with a statutory requirement or with an accounting guideline that specifically requires an accounting entry to give retroactive effect to the changed method of accounting. The resulting gain or loss should be adjusted directly against retained profits or accumulated losses as at the beginning of the period in which the change is made. Comparative figures must also be restated, where relevant and possible.

Disclosure.   Adequate disclosure of a change in accounting policy should be made in the financial statements, including the nature of the change, reason and financial effect, if material or expected to become material.

Reference.   Accounting Guideline no. 3 and Accounts Presentation Act, sections 4, 7, 26, 26a and 42.

9.   Prior Period Adjustments (Reguleringer Vedrorende Tidligere Perioder)

Retrospective adjustments to prior period reported figures are not permitted, other than those arising in the circumstances described in Section 8 and those arising from reclassifications necessary to ensure consistency of presentation in the financial statements.

Accounting Treatment.   Adjustments applicable to prior years should be charged or credited to operating profit for the current period and, if material, separately disclosed in the notes or the profit and loss account, depending on the circumstances.

Disclosure.   If material, the notes should describe the adjustment and any effect it may have on future results.

Reference.   Accounting Guideline no. 3 and Accounts Presentation Act, sections 4, 7 and 24.

10.   Post Balance Sheet Events (Begivenheder Efter Balance Datoen)

Accounting Treatment.   Financial statements should be prepared on the basis of conditions existing at the balance sheet date. When an event occurs after the balance sheet date that relates to a condition that existed at that date, the financial effect of the event should be reflected in the financial statements.

Post balance sheet events that do not relate to conditions existing at the balance sheet date should not be recognized in the financial statements. However, such events must be disclosed in the directors' report, if material.

Disclosure.   Disclosure of material adjusting events is required in the directors' report. Disclosure for a nonadjusting event must include a description and an indication, where possible, of its financial effect, and a statement that the event occurred after the balance sheet date and that its financial effect has not been recognized in the financial statements. In addition, the directors' report must include details of any matters that have arisen since the end of the financial year that have affected or may significantly affect the company's and the group's operations, results and financial condition in any ensuing financial year.

Reference.   Accounts Presentation Act, section 56; and Accounting Guideline no. 4.

11. Related Party Transactions (Transaktioner Mellem Afhaengige Parter)

Definition. The term *related party* includes any company that at any time during the **financial period** had control or significant influence over another company, or was subject to such control or significant influence, either directly or through a controlled company. It also includes directors, spouses of directors, relatives of directors and companies under the control or significant influence of directors, spouses of directors or their relatives.

Accounting Treatment. Although there is no specific pronouncement on related party transactions, such transactions are usually accounted for in accordance with normal **accounting principles** and practices.

Disclosure. There is a general requirement in the Accounts Presentation Act that related party transactions should be disclosed.
Specific disclosure requirements include the following:

□ Details of guarantees and other sureties given on behalf of subsidiaries and other companies within a group.

□ Receivables and payables to and from group companies (must be disclosed in the balance sheet).

□ The names and addresses of shareholders who own more than 10 percent of the nominal share capital or control 10 percent or more of the votes, if the amount exceeds DKK 100,000.

□ Details of illegal related party transactions, such as guarantees on behalf of or loans to directors and shareholders, including the amounts involved and the conditions under which they were given.

Reference. Accounts Presentation Act, sections 46 and 46a; and Companies Act, sections 28a, 115 and 115a.

12. Segmental Information (Segmentopdelte Oplysninger)

General. All companies whose **turnover** and net asset value exceed prescribed minimum values should disclose segmental turnover by activity or industry and by geographical market. Only material segments are required to be disclosed in the financial statements. In certain instances this information can be omitted if disclosure could cause serious harm to the company. Similar rules apply to consolidated financial statements.

Reference. Accounts Presentation Act, section 49.

ACCOUNTING PRINCIPLES FOR SPECIFIC ITEMS— BALANCE SHEET

13. Property, Plant and Equipment (Materielle Anlaegs Aktiver)

Classification of Capital and Revenue Expenditure. An expenditure is classified as a **capital expenditure** when it gives rise to an asset held with a view either to disposal or to generate funds over the long term. All other expenditures are expensed as incurred.

Basis of Valuation.   While tangible **fixed assets** are generally required to be carried at depreciated **historical cost**, revaluations are permitted. If a company chooses to revalue its fixed assets upward, the entire class of assets must be revalued on a consistent basis to an amount that is not in excess of the recoverable amount. (For this purpose, recoverable amount means the amount expected to be recovered from the total cash inflows less relevant cash outflows from its continued use or through its sale.) Any accumulated **depreciation** relating to that class at the date of revaluation must be credited to the asset account and the net amount revalued. Depreciation should then be provided on the basis of the revalued amount. A downward valuation is permitted only if the carrying amount is greater than the recoverable amount; the asset should be revalued to its recoverable amount.

Revaluation surpluses must be transferred to the asset revaluation reserve (see Section 22) and may not be distributed as dividends until the revalued asset is disposed of.

Both purchased and self-constructed assets are permitted to be capitalized at a cost that fairly reflects the expenditure necessarily incurred to bring the assets to their present location and a condition ready for use. Thus interest and overhead on self-constructed assets may be capitalized, provided it can be demonstrated clearly that these are costs of making the asset ready for use.

If property, plant and equipment are disposed of, the proceeds should be compared with their net book value (based on depreciated original cost or revalued amount), and the resulting gain or loss (unless it qualifies as an extraordinary item) should be reflected in operating profit before income tax and disclosed separately, if material.

Depreciation.   The method of depreciation selected should be appropriate to the type of asset and best reflect the using up of the asset's service potential. The two most common methods are the **straight-line method** and the reducing (**declining**) **balance method**. Depreciation rates and the underlying assessment of useful life should be reviewed annually. Tax depreciation methods are not allowed for accounting purposes.

Disclosure.   The accounting policies adopted in relation to valuation and depreciation of fixed assets must be disclosed. In addition, details of cost, depreciation and valuations of each class of property, plant and equipment must be shown separately in the notes.

The latest public assessment of land and buildings must be disclosed in the notes.

Reference.   Accounts Presentation Act, sections 16, 17, 27–30, 42 and 47.

14.   Intangible Assets (Immaterielle Aktiver)

General.   Purchased goodwill and research and development costs are covered separately in Sections 4 and 25, respectively.

Accounting Treatment.   **Intangible assets** may be capitalized only if they have been acquired for cash consideration. The most common forms of intangible assets recognized in the balance sheet, apart from purchased goodwill and research and development costs, are technology-based (patents, trademarks, licenses), brand names and distribution rights.

Valuation.   Although intangible assets are valued essentially the same way as other noncurrent assets, they may not be revalued. Intangible assets are accounted for at their purchase price or production cost. They are carried forward on the balance sheet as long as they provide a measurable future economic benefit controlled by the entity.

Amortization. All intangible assets are assumed to have a finite useful life. Thus, it is usual practice to amortize intangible assets over their estimated useful life to the net amount expected to be recovered on disposal, if any.

Disclosure. Intangible assets are separately disclosed on the face of the balance sheet; the amounts of patents, trademarks and licenses included are shown separately. The total amount of amortization charged and the relevant accounting policies adopted are disclosed.

Reference. Accounts Presentation Act, sections 16, 17, 27–30, 36 and 42.

15. Leases (Leasede Aktiver)

Classification and Accounting Treatment. As a general rule, accounting practice does not differentiate between **finance** and **operating leases**, although it is becoming more usual for companies to classify and account for leases in accordance with international practice. In general, leases are treated as operating leases; the lessee charges lease payments to the profit and loss account in the periods in which they are incurred, and the lessor capitalizes leased assets and recognizes rental income when earned. Where finance leases are capitalized, companies generally apply International Accounting Standard 17, *Accounting for Leases.*

Disclosure. Lessees must disclose rental expense and lease commitments. If material, accounting policies should also be disclosed.

Lessors must disclose the value of assets held for lease and any related depreciation. The basis of valuation and depreciation should be disclosed in the same way as for other fixed assets.

Reference. Accounts Presentation Act, section 46; and IAS 17.

16. Investments (Kapitalandele og Vaerdipapirer)

Valuation. General: The valuation of investments depends on their classification as current (i.e., those representing a temporary investment of surplus funds) or noncurrent (i.e., those held for the medium or long term).

Current investments: Current investments should be stated at the lower of cost or **net realizable value**. Net realizable value is normally market value net of transaction costs. The comparison should be made on an individual investment basis and a provision made for each investment whose net realizable value is below cost. The resulting write-down should be recognized in operating profit and separately disclosed as an abnormal item, if material. Revaluations of current investments to reflect increases in market value above cost are permitted only for investments quoted on a recognized stock exchange. Any revaluations as a result of such write-ups must be allocated to a revaluation reserve and may not be distributed as dividends until the investment is disposed of.

Noncurrent investments: Noncurrent investments should be stated at cost adjusted as necessary for any provision for permanent diminution in value. Any write-down of noncurrent investments arising from a line-by-line assessment of the investment's recoverable amount should be recognized in the profit and loss account except when it reverses a previous revaluation increment that was credited to an asset revaluation reserve.

In these circumstances, the write-down should be charged to the reserve. Write-downs are normally charged to operating profit and separately disclosed as abnormal items, if material. Noncurrent investments may be revalued to reflect permanent increases in market value above cost on an individual basis. Revaluation increments must be credited directly to an asset revaluation reserve and may not be taken to income until the specific investment is disposed of.

Reversal of write-downs: If an investment has been written down in prior years either to reflect a permanent diminution in value for a noncurrent investment or to net realizable value for a current investment, the investment should be restored, either in whole or in part, to its original cost or to a revalued amount if the reasons for making the write-down have ceased to apply.

Capital gains tax: If there has been a decision to sell a revalued asset, the impact of capital gains tax should to be taken into account, preferably by revaluing the asset net of capital gains tax. If an asset has been revalued and it is likely that its primary benefit to the entity will be through a sale, the potential capital gains tax liability should be disclosed in a note.

Treatment of Valuation Reserves.   Reserves arising from the revaluation of investments are treated as revenue reserves (see Section 22).

Gains/Losses.   When investments are sold, the profit or loss to be recognized is measured as the difference between the net proceeds received for the investment and its carrying amount at the time of the sale. This gain or loss should generally be included in operating profit and disclosed as an abnormal item, if material. In calculating the profit or loss on disposal of part of a holding, the **average cost** method is used. Any amounts in the revaluation reserve relating to investments disposed of may be transferred to the profit and loss account.

Disclosure.   Detailed disclosure is required of each different type of investment held, including cost, valuations and amounts written off and accounting policies adopted. Further disclosure is required for quoted investments and capital gains tax effects on valuations.

Material gains and losses arising from the sale of noncurrent investments are required to be disclosed, together with the amounts charged to the profit and loss account arising from the depreciation, amortization or diminution in value of investments.

Reference.   Accounts Presentation Act, sections 17, 27, 29, 30, 31 and 42.

17. Accounts Receivable (Debitorer og Tilgodehavender)

Accounting Treatment.   Recognition: The recognition of **revenues**, and hence the related receivables, is described in Section 23.

Discounts: Sales and **debtors** are normally recorded net of trade and quantity discounts. Since the recognition of cash discounts occurs at the time of payment, it is not usually necessary to take account of potential cash discounts in determining the value to be attributed to a trade **account receivable**.

Allowances: There are two methods of computing a provision for doubtful accounts: specific assessment or by reference to a formula based on previous experience. If a formula is used, its continuing appropriateness should be kept under review.

Factored Receivables. Accounts receivable that have been factored to a finance company for cash consideration should be excluded from the balance sheet. Discounts given to the finance company should normally be accounted for in the same way as cash discounts. If the factor has recourse to the vendor for bad debts, disclosure of the contingent liability and provision for probable losses should be made. There may be cases where the continuing risk to the vendor is so great or so uncertain, that the transaction with the finance company may need to be accounted for as a loan rather than as a **factoring** of debt.

Disclosure. Receivables are segregated into various classes, such as trade debtors, bills receivable, prepayments, deposits and other debtors. Disclosure is required of current and noncurrent receivables (i.e., those amounts due within one year and after one year) for each class. Trading balances with related companies are disclosed separately as intercompany trade debtors.

Separate disclosure is also required showing the amounts charged to the profit and loss statement and provided in the balance sheet for bad and doubtful accounts, and the amount of any unearned revenue.

Reference. Accounts Presentation Act, sections 19, 33 and 42; and Enactment No. 533—Preparation of Annual Financial Statements and Consolidated Financial Statements.

18. Inventories and Work in Progress (Varelager og Igangvaerende Arbejder)

General Accounting Treatment. **Inventories** are generally valued at the lower of cost or net realizable value. (In determining the carrying amount of inventories, each item should be dealt with separately or, where this is impracticable, similar items should be dealt with as a group.) However, the Accounts Presentation Act allows for upward revaluations of inventory to its repurchase value. This provision is not widely used; if used, it should be disclosed in the notes.

The overriding consideration in choosing the bases for valuing inventories is that the basis chosen in a particular business should give a true and fair view of the position and results of the business, and be applied consistently from year to year. The basis for determining cost should also fairly reflect the expenditure actually incurred in bringing the inventory to its present location and condition.

In determining cost, the following methods are considered appropriate:

☐ **Specific identification**.
☐ Average cost.
☐ **FIFO**.
☐ **Standard cost**.

LIFO is not recommended in the Accounting Guideline. Replacement cost is not acceptable in historical cost accounting unless it approximates net realizable value (when it is lower than cost). However, the Accounts Presentation Act allows for valuing inventories at replacement cost, as noted above.

Direct labor and material costs usually form the basis of valuation for manufactured inventories. It is recommended that indirect production costs be allocated, using **absorption costing** techniques (based on an entity's normal operating capacity). Standard costing is acceptable, provided that the standards are realistically attainable, reviewed regularly and revised as necessary in the light of current conditions.

Net realizable value is the estimated proceeds of sale less all further costs to completion and marketing, selling and distribution costs. Costs of a general nature—for example, general administrative and general marketing costs—that cannot be clearly attributed to specific items or groups of items of inventory are normally not deducted in arriving at net realizable value.

Long-Term Contracts. The gross amount of construction work in progress and, as a deduction therefrom, the related aggregate progress billings should be disclosed. The gross amount of construction work in progress includes all costs that can reasonably be allocated to the contract plus any profits recorded in accordance with the **percentage of completion method**, less any foreseeable losses. Further guidance on recognizing revenue for long-term construction contracts is contained in Section 23. If a contract is expected to result in an overall loss, the expected loss should be determined as accurately as possible and provided for in full in the income statement.

In certain cases where the risks are deemed to be large or recording procedures are inadequate, construction work in progress is accounted for at cost and profits are not recorded until the project is completed (i.e., **completed contract method**).

Disclosure. Inventories: All significant accounting policies relating to inventories should be disclosed. More specifically, the general bases and methods adopted in inventory valuation, including methods of assigning costs, should be disclosed. The notes should disclose inventories in the following classifications:

☐ Raw materials and supplies.
☐ Work in progress.
☐ Finished goods.

No guidance is given on the criteria for inclusion in each classification; this is a matter of judgment in the particular circumstances of each business. Separate disclosure is required of any inventory valued other than at cost.

Construction work in progress: In addition to the requirement to disclose separately gross construction work in progress and the progress billings set out above, the aggregate of cash received and receivable as progress billings (including retention allowances) and advances on account of construction work in progress should be disclosed.

Reference. Accounts Presentation Act, sections 19, 31–34, 38 and 48; and Accounting Guideline nos. 6 and 8.

19. Current Liabilities (Kortfristet Gaeld)

General Accounting Treatment. A **current liability** is defined as a liability that, in the ordinary course of business, will be settled within the next 12 months. Liabilities are generally assumed to be legal obligations, but may arise from ethical or commercial considerations as well. Commitments such as purchase orders do not qualify as liabilities until the service to which they relate has been performed, and contingencies are accounted for as liabilities only when they become probable.

The most common forms of current liabilities are trade and other **creditors**, bank overdrafts, bills of exchange and promissory notes, the current portions of bank loans and debentures, and any unearned income.

Trade creditors include amounts payable to suppliers for goods and services and are measured at the face value of the money, goods or services that are to be applied in payment. The liability is recognized when the service is performed, regardless of whether an invoice has been received.

Bank overdrafts and other monetary liabilities are also measured at their face value and usually include accrued interest.

Where items such as promissory notes are issued at a discount, the face value remains on the balance sheet and the discount is treated as an offset and amortized over the life of the debt.

Income received in advance (deferred income), such as subscriptions, is recognized as revenue when earned; until that time it is deferred as a liability.

Disclosure. The Accounts Presentation Act requires that current liabilities be disclosed on the face of the balance sheet. Each material component should be listed separately. Trading balances with related companies are usually disclosed separately as intercompany trade creditors.

If any liabilities are secured by way of a registered or unregistered charge over assets, details of the amount and nature of the security must also be disclosed.

Creation of General and Specific Provisions. The term *provision* is used in Denmark to describe liabilities whose measurement involves a degree of subjective judgment, therefore making the values ascribed to them less precise.

General provisions are not permitted. To satisfy the definition of a liability, provisions must relate to a specific existing obligation. Similarly, provisions for future expenses or losses are not permitted unless the circumstances giving rise to the expense have occurred.

The main types of provisions are for deferred income tax, pensions and other employee benefits and those relating to known future expenses such as warranties.

Provisions for such items as reorganization costs are permitted only after a definite decision has been made to reorganize; provisions for future expenses relating to warranties and guarantees are recognized at the point of sale of the item under warranty.

Disclosure. Disclosure of each specific provision must be made separately in the balance sheet and explained in the notes, if the amounts are material.

Reference. Accounts Presentation Act, sections 19, 20, 42 and 46.

20. Long-Term Debt (Langfristet Gaeld)

General Accounting Treatment. The most common forms of long-term debt in Denmark are subordinated loan capital, debentures, convertible notes, foreign loans, mortgages and long-term bank loans. The general accounting treatment applied to these items is basically the same as for current liabilities, that is, they are included in the balance sheet at their face value as long as they continue to represent a present obligation of the entity. Interest is accrued and provided for up to the balance sheet date.

Debt Restructuring. There are no pronouncements dealing with accounting for the restructuring of debt other than conversion to equity. In practice, any gains or losses on restructuring would normally be recognized in the profit and loss account at the time of the restructuring.

Debt Extinguishment. A debt is accounted for as having been extinguished only if it has been:

☐ Settled by repayment, replacement with another liability or provision of assets.
☐ Subject to a legal **defeasance**.
☐ Converted to equity.

A legal defeasance occurs where the creditor formally acknowledges the release of the debtor from the primary obligation.

Debt may be converted to equity at par or at a lower value that states the resulting equity at its true nominal value.

Disclosure. General: Long-term debt is classified under appropriate headings on the face of the balance sheet. The notes must specify what portion of long-term debt is due after five years. If any long-term debt is secured, disclosure of the nature, terms and amount of the collateral is also required. The short-term portion of long-term debt must be classified separately under current liabilities.

Convertible notes are treated as liabilities. The notes to the financial statements must disclose the debt outstanding, the conversion rate and the dates when conversion can take place. Subordinated loan capital is treated as long-term debt and may not be classified as part of equity, although it is sometimes shown as a separate classification immediately after equity. The conditions under which subordinated loan capital is provided should be stated in the notes.

Debt extinguishment: The reasons for the conversion, as well as the reasons and dates of the incurrence of the debt to be converted, must be explained by the directors. The auditors must report on how the conversion is reflected in the books of the company and in its balance sheet.

Reference. Accounts Presentation Act, sections 19, 45 and 46; and Companies Act, section 33a.

21. Contingencies (Eventual Poster)

Contingent Losses. Material contingent losses should be accrued if at the balance sheet date it is probable that a loss will arise as a result of a past transaction or event and that loss can be reliably estimated at that time.

Contingent Gains. Contingent gains are recorded only if they result from the application of normal asset recognition and liability reduction criteria. Thus, contingent gains are not accrued in the accounts unless their realization is virtually certain.

Disclosure. If a material contingent loss has not been accrued, the details should be disclosed in the notes unless the possibility of loss is remote. Separate disclosure must be made of the total security given for subsidiary and other group undertakings. Certain contingencies must be disclosed by law, including guarantees, discounted bills of exchange and pension commitments.

Unrecorded contingent gains are disclosed in the notes if they are material and disclosure is considered necessary to ensure the presentation of a true and fair view. The notes must clearly disclose the nature of the contingency to ensure that a misleading impression is not given as to the likelihood that the amounts will be received.

Reference. Accounts Presentation Act, sections 46 and 46a; and Accounting Guideline no. 4.

22. Capital and Reserves (Selskabskapital og Reserver)

Shareholders' equity is generally divided between **share capital** (amounts contributed by shareholders) and reserves.

Share Capital. The Companies Act requires that a company include in its articles the amount of its share capital and the division of this into a number of shares of a fixed amount (**par value**). There is no distinction between authorized and issued share capital as all share capital must be issued.

Shares need not be issued at par, but any excess of the share issue price over its par value must be credited to a **share premium** reserve. The issue of shares at a discount from par is not permitted. Shares are not required to be paid for in full on issue, but the balance must be called by the directors within one year of issuance and must be paid or the shares forfeited. After issue, a company may not reduce its share capital except under special conditions, for example, the offset of accumulated losses against share capital. Legislation to permit companies to buy back their own shares provides for the right to hold up to 10 percent of a company's own shares. However, the shares must be stated at zero value, or an equivalent reserve must be set up against the value of the shares acquired.

A company's share capital may be divided into different classes, each characterized by its voting, dividend and capital repayment rights. The main classes of shares are usually 'A' and 'B' shares. The exact rights of each type are included in the company's articles. All shares have voting rights; it is, however, possible to differentiate the votes up to a ratio of 10:1 for the different classes of shares. **Preference shares** are usually described as such in the financial statements.

Other Reserves. The share premium reserve can be utilized only in certain circumstances and is generally distributable to shareholders on liquidation of the company. Revenue reserves, subject to any special limitations contained in the company's memorandum and articles, can be utilized in any manner the directors choose, with the exception of the asset and equity revaluation reserves, whose utilization is restricted by the Accounts Presentation Act.

The share premium reserve is required to be created when the issue price of shares exceeds their par value; the difference is credited to this reserve. The reserve can be used to issue bonus shares (shares issued from reserves in lieu of dividends) or write off company formation expenses or accumulated losses, provided that all distributable reserves have been utilized first.

The main types of revenue reserves are:

☐ Asset revaluation—This reserve arises as a result of the revaluation of noncurrent assets and can be dissolved only if specific assets subject to revaluation have been disposed of. The reserve can be transferred to share capital.

☐ Equity revaluation—This reserve results from the revaluation of subsidiary and associated companies carried in the books on an equity accounting basis. The reserve is dissolved only through the issuance of dividends, disposal of an associated company or reduction of equity value.

☐ Foreign currency translation—This reserve arises as a result of translating the financial statements of an overseas subsidiary.

☐ Foreign currency equalization—This reserve arises from translating noncurrent foreign currency account balances at year-end rates, resulting in unrealized gains.

The latter two types of revenue reserves are not required by law, but are often seen in Danish financial statements; there are no statutory rules governing the treatment of these reserves.

Dividends. Dividends are declared once a year on the recommendation of the directors and must be approved at the annual general meeting. Interim dividends are not allowed by law. Usually dividends declared are shown in the balance sheet as part of current debt.

Disclosure. Share capital: Companies must disclose details of any shares issued, including both number and class of shares, and the purpose of any issue during the year. If options have been granted requiring the issue of shares at a later date, relevant details must be disclosed, as must the terms and conditions of any preference shares, for example, dividend rate, date and conditions of redemption.

Earnings: The proposed distribution of annual earnings must be specified either in connection with the profit and loss account or in the directors' report.

Reserves: Companies must disclose the name and amount of each reserve and details of any transfers between or to and from those reserves.

Reference. Accounts Presentation Act, sections 30, 34, 39, 40, 44 and 54; and Companies Act, sections 40, 44a, 47, 110 and 111.

ACCOUNTING PRINCIPLES FOR SPECIFIC ITEMS— INCOME STATEMENT

23. Revenue Recognition (Indtaegts Kriteriet)

General Principles. The following broad principles are appropriate in determining when to recognize revenue.

Revenue from a transaction involving the sale of goods is usually recognized at the point when the seller has transferred to the buyer the significant risks and rewards of ownership of the asset sold. This requires an analysis of the substance of the transaction. In most cases, transfer of the legal title either results in or coincides with the passing of possession (e.g., most retail sales) or transfer of the risks and rewards of ownership to the buyer (e.g., the dispatch of goods without condition), and therefore revenue is usually recognized at this point. However, the seller may retain significant risks of ownership (e.g., liability for unsatisfactory performance in excess of the normal warranty), and revenue should not be recognized until those risks have been reduced or eliminated.

Revenue from service transactions is usually recognized as the service is performed.

Revenue should be recognized only when no significant uncertainty as to its collectibility or measurement exists (i.e., there is a reasonable expectation, at the time of sale or provision of the service, of ultimate realization). If uncertainty arises subsequent to the time of sale or the rendering of the service, recording a separate doubtful accounts provision is the appropriate treatment, rather than adjusting the original revenue recorded.

Long-Term Contracts.   Generally accepted accounting practice in Denmark calls for use of the percentage of completion method in recognizing revenue from long-term construction contracts when the outcome of a contract can be reliably estimated. This requires that reliable estimates of revenue, costs to date, stage of completion and costs to complete can be made. Where these conditions cannot be met, profit must not be recognized until such time as they can. This may mean that, in certain circumstances, no profit is recognized until the contract is completed.

If it is expected that there will be a loss on a contract as a whole, a provision should be made for the entire amount of the loss as soon as it is identified. This has the effect of reducing the cost attributable to the work done to date to its net realizable value. Where unprofitable contracts are of such magnitude that they can be expected to absorb a considerable part of the company's capacity for a substantial period, indirect costs (e.g., general administrative and selling costs) to be incurred during the period to completion of those contracts must also be included in the calculation of the provision for losses.

Instalment Sales.   The general principles of revenue recognition apply to **instalment sales**. Thus, if the significant risks and benefits of ownership pass to the buyer at the inception of the transaction, the fact that the purchase price is to be received in instalments will not prevent the seller from recognizing the transaction in full at that time and creating a receivable for the deferred payment. The only impact delayed payment would have in this instance is in relation to the interest component of the instalment sale, which should be reflected by the use of discounted cash flows in measuring revenue.

Rights of Return.   The fact that a buyer can return goods is not usually an ownership risk of significant magnitude to prevent a seller from recognizing a sale at the time possession initially passes to the buyer. In this instance the more appropriate accounting treatment would be to record a provision for returns (e.g., a provision for warranty) if this risk was considered to be material. However, if the right of return constituted a significant ownership risk, revenue recognition would be deferred until the risk was eliminated or sufficiently reduced.

Product Financing.   The broad general principles relating to the transfer of risks and benefits of ownership apply in determining the appropriate accounting treatment for **product financing arrangements**. If the nature of the agreements is such that substantially all the risks and benefits of ownership do not pass to the buyer, recognition of revenue would not be appropriate and the transaction should be treated as a financing transaction.

Disclosure. Companies are required to disclose total operating revenue, which must be segmented by activity and geographical market. Sales revenue includes revenue from the sale of goods or provision of services and usually represents revenue derived from the company's main trading activities. Other revenue includes the gross proceeds from any secondary activities, such as interest and rental income, and dividend income from investments. The segmented disclosure may be omitted if this information can cause significant damage to the company. A note to that effect should be included in the financial statements.

Small and medium-sized companies, as defined in the provisions of the Accounts Presentation Act, can elect not to disclose turnover for competitive reasons. This provision can be applied only when two of the following three conditions apply: The company's net assets do not exceed DKK 50 million, the turnover does not exceed DKK 100 million and the average number of employees does not exceed 250.

The basis used to recognize profit on construction contracts should be disclosed in the notes.

Reference. Accounts Presentation Act, sections 22, 25, 48 and 49; and Accounting Guideline nos. 1 and 6.

24. Government Grants and Assistance (Offentlige Tilskud og Assistance)

Accounting Treatment. There are no pronouncements dealing with accounting for government grants and assistance. Accordingly, practice is influenced by International Accounting Standard 20, *Accounting for Government Grants and Disclosure of Government Assistance*. As a general rule, however, government grants are not used to reduce the values of assets purchased, but may be recorded as income either immediately or on a deferral basis as related expenses are incurred.

Disclosure. The accounting policy adopted in relation to government grants and assistance should be disclosed where these are material.

Reference. IAS 20.

25. Research and Development (Forsknings- og Udviklingsomkostninger)

Definition. Research and development expenditure is not defined in the provisions of the Accounts Presentation Act. However, the Accounting Guideline defines such expenditure as costs incurred for the purpose of acquiring new knowledge, developing a new product or bringing about a significant improvement in an existing product.

Accounting Treatment. The most common treatment is to expense research and development costs as incurred. Although the Accounts Presentation Act permits deferral, the Accounting Guideline suggests that development costs should be capitalized only where there is a clear connection between the development costs and expected future earnings of the individual projects.

If capitalized, development costs must be amortized over a maximum of five years or in such a manner as to match the costs with related benefits, commencing with commercial production. Further, deferred development costs should be reviewed at each balance sheet date and, if the capitalized expenditure exceeds the recoverable amount, the excess should be written off immediately. Development expenditures that have been written off should not be reinstated, even if the uncertainties that led to their being written off no longer apply. Research costs should not be capitalized in any circumstances.

Grants received from government and other organizations for research and development should be treated in the same manner as the expenditure to which they are related. That is, if the related expenditure is deferred, the grant should be deducted from the carrying amount of the asset; if the related expenditure is expensed, the grant should also be taken to income.

Disclosure. The directors' report should disclose details of research and development costs expensed. Where relevant, the notes should disclose the amounts of development costs (for the period and cumulative) deferred and amortized, and the basis of amortization. The accounting treatment used should be explained.

Reference. Accounting Guideline no. 7 and Accounts Presentation Act, section 19.

26. Capitalized Interest Costs (Kapitaliserede Rente Omkostninger)

Accounting Treatment. There is no specific prescribed accounting guideline dealing with capitalization of interest. Interest is sometimes capitalized as part of the cost of an asset constructed for continuing use in the entity, if the interest is incurred in bringing the asset to the condition and location of its intended use.

Disclosure. Disclosure is required in the notes of the amount of interest capitalized by class of assets and, where interest capitalized is material, the accounting policy adopted.

Reference. Accounts Presentation Act, section 27; and IAS 23.

27. Imputed Interest (Beregnet Rente)

General. The use of **imputed interest** is not generally accepted in Denmark.

28. Extraordinary or Unusual Items (Ekstraordinaere og Udsaedvanlige Poster)

Extraordinary Items. Extraordinary items are defined as items of revenue and expense that are attributable to events or transactions outside the ordinary operations of the reporting entity and not of a recurring nature. They do not include items that, though exceptional on grounds of size and incidence (and which therefore require separate disclosure), derive from the ordinary activities of the business (i.e., abnormal items). They also do not include prior year items merely because they relate to a prior year.

Disclosure. Extraordinary items should be disclosed separately on the face of the profit and loss account, showing the total extraordinary items and related tax. Separate disclosure of details of each individual material component of extraordinary items is required in the notes and in the directors' report, if material.

Reference. Accounting Guideline no. 5 and Accounts Presentation Act, section 24.

29. Income Taxes (Indkomst Skatter)

Accounting Treatment. Although it is acceptable to account for deferred income tax under the **deferred** (historical) **method**, the **liability method** is normally used. Under the liability method, the tax effects of timing differences are regarded as liabilities for taxes payable in the future or as assets representing "prepaid" taxes. These liabilities or assets are subject to future adjustment if tax rates change or new taxes are imposed.

Deferred income tax may be computed on a comprehensive or partial basis. The partial basis recognizes only those timing differences that are expected to reverse in the foreseeable future.

The profit and loss statement should show the amount of income tax expense properly attributable to the transactions included in that statement. The income tax expense should be calculated on the pretax accounting profit adjusted for any permanent differences.

Where possible, future income tax benefits attributable to a tax loss may be offset against the deferred income tax provision to the extent that the provision relates to timing differences that will reverse in the period during which the tax loss benefit is available. Otherwise, a future income tax benefit may be carried forward as an asset only if the benefit can be regarded as being assured beyond any reasonable doubt. This would normally be the case only where a company is part of a group taxation arrangement where the income tax benefit can be utilized by the group and the benefit allocated to the company.

Disclosure. Details of income taxes charged to the profit and loss account, deferred income tax liability/future income tax benefit, income tax payable and the extent and treatment of tax losses should be disclosed. Income taxes relating to extraordinary items should be disclosed separately. The accounting policy for determining deferred taxes should be disclosed. Where deferred taxes are provided for on a partial basis, the notes should disclose the full deferred tax liability. Similarly, where tax is calculated using the deferred method, the deferred tax liability calculated according to the liability method should be disclosed in the notes. Any calculated future capital gains liabilities on disposal should also be disclosed in the notes.

Reference. Accounts Presentation Act, section 50.

30. Postretirement Benefits (Pensions Ydelser)

Accounting Treatment. There are no pronouncements on accounting for pensions or other postretirement benefits. However, actuarially determined contributions required to fund a pension plan are assumed to be a reasonable basis for recording the periodic expense. A liability would usually be recognized if the contributions were not made. Most plans in the private sector are fully insured.

Pension Fund Surpluses. Pension fund surpluses can arise only in relation to **defined benefit plans** and occur when the plan assets are in excess of the projected amount of defined benefits required to be paid.

The rules for the treatment of surpluses are determined by the fund's own trust deed. However, pension fund surpluses generally cannot be distributed to contributors until the pension fund is liquidated. The usual way in which overfunded situations are controlled is by the actuaries recommending that the sponsoring company decrease or cease to make contributions until the surplus is eroded.

Disclosure.   No particular disclosure requirements are stipulated other than those stated for contingent liabilities in general.

All companies are required to disclose pension contributions made to plans in connection with the retirement of directors and management.

Reference.   Accounts Presentation Act, section 46.

31.   Discontinued Operations (Standsning af Drift)

Accounting Treatment.   There is no prescribed accounting method for discontinued operations in Denmark, although there are detailed rules governing the liquidation and winding up of a company's activities. Consequently, the following comments are based on preferred practice for accounting for related costs arising from the discontinuation or reorganization of a business segment.

Reorganization and business closure costs are recognized when there is a firm commitment to reorganize or discontinue operations. All costs relating to a particular reorganization or closure should, as far as possible, be recognized at the same time. Thus it is usual to include, in the aggregate reorganization costs, such items as employee termination payments, write-downs of current assets, adjustments to fixed asset values and the costs of settling claims from customers or suppliers. Uncertainties may arise, however, in the treatment of revenue, expenses or operating losses incurred from the date the reorganization is recognized to the completion date. It is appropriate to include in reorganization costs short-term costs that are related to the completion of work in process or that are incurred to obtain the best realization of assets. General overhead expenses that are likely to continue after the reorganization or closure has been completed should not be included.

Disclosure.   Material reorganization costs should be classified as extraordinary items and explained separately in the notes. It is normally desirable for the accounting policies to explain the treatment of reorganization costs.

Reference.   Accounts Presentation Act, sections 26 and 46; and Accounting Guideline no. 2.

32.   Earnings per Share

General.   There is no pronouncement dealing with the computation and disclosure of earnings per share. Where this information is disclosed, however, it is usually calculated on the basis of ordinary income after tax and issued share capital in multiples of 100.

Appendix
DO DANISH STANDARDS OR PREVALENT PRACTICE SUBSTANTIALLY COMPLY WITH INTERNATIONAL ACCOUNTING STANDARDS?

Section	Topic	Substantially complies with IAS?	Comments
3.	Basic accounting concepts and conventions	Yes	
	Contents of financial statements	Yes	Except that a statement of changes in financial position is required only for publicly traded companies
4.	Business combinations*	Yes	
5.	Joint ventures	Yes	
6.	Foreign currency translation*	Yes	Except that unrealized gains on long-term loans may be taken directly to reserves
8.	Accounting changes*	Yes	
9.	Prior period adjustments*	Yes	
10.	Post balance sheet events	Yes	
11.	Related party transactions	No	
12.	Segmental information	No	
13.	Property, plant and equipment*	Yes	
15.	Leases	No	
16.	Investments	Yes	
17.	Accounts receivable	Yes	
18.	Inventories and work in progress*	Yes	
19.	Current liabilities	Yes	
20.	Long-term debt	Yes	
21.	Contingencies	Yes	
22.	Capital and reserves	Yes	
23.	Revenue recognition*	Yes	
24.	Government grants and assistance	Yes	
25.	Research and development*	Yes	
26.	Capitalization of interest costs*	Yes	

Appendix (*Continued*)

Section	Topic	Substantially complies with IAS?	Comments
28.	Extraordinary or unusual items*	Yes	
29.	Income tax**	Yes	
30.	Postretirement benefits*	No	

*These topics are subject to change as a result of the IASC Improvements Project—see the appendix to the International Accounting Standards chapter.

**The IAS on accounting for taxes on income is currently being revised, and an exposure draft has been issued.

Comparison in this table is made to International Accounting Standards in force at January 1, 1993. For further details, see the International Accounting Standards chapter.

FINLAND

GENERAL NATIONAL INFORMATION

1. Source of Generally Accepted Accounting Principles

Historically, Finnish tax legislation has had a significant influence on the preparation of financial statements. This influence has been most noticeable in the creation of special reserves (untaxed reserves) and depreciation deductions on fixed asset expenditures, which are driven by tax considerations and which must be reflected in the financial statements to be allowed in computing taxable income.

While most large and most listed Finnish companies have tended to separate tax appropriations in the income statement and in the balance sheet in order to avoid distorting accounting income and asset values, there was no legal requirement to do so, and other Finnish companies have, in practice, not made such a separation.

Historic reporting practices are changing significantly as entities reporting under **generally accepted accounting principles** in Finland adopt, beginning in 1993, new financial reporting legislation in the amended Companies Act and the amended Accounting Act. This amended legislation substantially reflects the content of the European Community's (EC) Fourth and Seventh Directives on company and group financial statements and also takes account of International Accounting Standards. The amended legislation requires, for the first time, that financial statements show a true and fair view. Among other matters, the legislation will require all reporting entities to clearly separate tax appropriations within the financial statements. At the same time, reform of the Finnish taxation system for companies is continuing. This is removing or reducing the availability of many of these tax appropriations.

Most large and **listed companies** with calendar year ends will be preparing financial statements under the new requirements for the year ended December 31, 1993. However, under transitional arrangements, the latest date for preparing financial statements under the new legislation is July 1, 1994. Further, certain specific provisions of the new legislation have later implementation dates, as noted in the relevant sections of this chapter.

In view of the significant changes taking place, and the fact that for the first 18 months there will in effect be parallel reporting requirements, this text, while based on the ''new'' accounting regime, also describes the ''old'' regime.

Generally accepted accounting principles (good accounting practice) in Finland are derived from the following sources:

□ The Accounting Act (Kirjanpitolaki 1973/655, KPL) and Accounting Ordinance (Kirjanpitoasetus 1992/1575), which establish general **accounting principles** for private-sector entities.

□ The Companies Act (Osakeyhtiölaki 1978/734, OYL). Chapter 11 of this legislation establishes accounting principles and information reporting requirements for limited liability companies, regardless of size or ownership, complementary to those included in the Accounting Act. Like the Accounting Act, Chapter 11 of the Companies Act has also been amended effective beginning January 1, 1993.

□ Recommendations issued by the Finnish Association of Authorized Public Accountants (KHT-yhdistyksen hyvää tilintarkastustapaa ja hyvää kirjanpitotapaa kartoittavat suositukset). These recommendations establish good accounting practice (generally accepted accounting principles).

□ General directions and statements (conventions) issued by the Finnish Accounting Board (Kirjanpitolautakunta, KILA). The KILA is a government body (under the Ministry of Trade and Industry, KTM) that develops generally accepted accounting principles. It prepares and issues general directions and statements on accounting matters and the preparation of financial statements.

□ Recommendation for Information Included in the Financial Statements of a Listed Company and Rules of the Helsinki Stock Exchange (both parts of Rules and Regulations of the Helsinki Stock Exchange) issued by the Helsinki Stock Exchange Cooperative (Helsingin Arvopaperipörssi Osuuskunta, pörssi). The Finnish Association of Authorized Public Accountants has recommended that other companies also comply with the recommendations of the Stock Exchange to the extent that they are applicable.

□ The Banking Supervision Office, which provides directions on the financial statements of banks.

□ The Insurance Department of the Ministry of Social Affairs and Health, which provides directions on the financial statements of insurance companies.

2. Audit and Public Company Requirements

Audits. The auditing profession in Finland is regulated by the Central Chamber of Commerce. A qualified accountant is a public accountant authorized by the Central Chamber of Commerce (KHT) or an approved accountant authorized by the Local Chamber of Commerce (HTM). The Ministry of Trade and Industry has overall public responsibility for the auditing profession.

An authorized public accountant must have a university degree in accounting and business administration, involving accountancy, company and taxation law. To become licensed, an authorized public accountant must also have passed the required examinations and have obtained at least five years of practical experience, mainly with an authorized firm or authorized accountant. An authorized approved accountant must meet corresponding requirements, except that a lower standard of higher education is acceptable.

The following audit requirements relate to limited liability companies as defined in the Companies Act.

All limited liability companies must be audited and must appoint one (or more) auditors, as provided by the articles of association. An auditor is elected at the general meeting. The auditor must be independent of the company.

At least one of the auditors must be a Finnish citizen living in Finland or an audit firm authorized by the Central or Local Chamber of Commerce. The auditor must have the requisite knowledge and experience of accounting and economics, considering the nature and scope of the company's operations. An audit firm authorized by the Central or Local Chamber of Commerce may be appointed auditor. In the case of a group, at least one of the **parent company's** auditors should, if possible, be appointed auditor of a subsidiary.

Where the restricted equity of a company exceeds 2 million Finnish Markka (FIM), at least one of the auditors appointed by the general meeting has to be an authorized public accountant or an authorized approved accountant.

At least one of the auditors appointed by the general meeting must be an authorized public accountant if:

☐   The company's shares are listed on the Helsinki Stock Exchange, or

☐   The company has, during the two preceding **financial periods**, had more than 500 employees, on average.

The auditors must examine, to the extent required by generally accepted auditing standards, the annual report, the accounts and the administration of the company. The primary purpose of the examination of the administration of the company is to determine whether there has been any act or omission that could give rise to a liability for damages on the part of a member of the board of directors or the managing director, or if a member of the board or the managing director has in any way acted in a manner in conflict with the Companies Act or the articles of association. The auditors' examination also covers management's controls over the business, including establishing whether there exists a reliable system of internal control. If the company is a parent company, the auditors examine the consolidated accounts and also the relationships between the group companies.

The auditors must submit an audit report to the general meeting, containing statements:

☐   That the audit has been carried out as required by generally accepted auditing standards.

☐   On whether the annual report has been prepared in accordance with the prevailing legislation.

☐   On the adoption of the income statement and balance sheet.

☐   On the proposal included in the directors' report as to the disposition of the company's profit or loss.

☐   On whether the members of the board and the managing director should be discharged from their liabilities for the financial period.

The basic obligations set out in the Companies Act are amplified by the Association of Authorized Public Accountants, which issues recommendations on generally accepted auditing standards (good auditing practice). These recommendations aim at providing authoritative guidance on the auditing procedures to be followed by members of the Association.

Public Companies.   Requirements for registration and listing: The board of directors of the Helsinki Stock Exchange decides, on the application of a Finnish or foreign limited liability company, whether to admit the company's shares for listing. Shares may be admitted to listing on the following conditions:

- ☐ The fully paid **share capital** amounts to at least FIM 10 million and shareholders' equity to at least FIM 20 million.
- ☐ A sufficient proportion of the share capital, generally not less than 10 percent, will be publicly traded on the Stock Exchange.
- ☐ The company is profitable and financially sound, has the ability to pay dividends and has competent management.
- ☐ The company has prepared audited financial statements for at least three accounting periods prior to its application for listing. However, subject to certain conditions, the Stock Exchange will consider applications where there are audited financial statements for only one accounting period of at least 12 months duration.
- ☐ The shares are freely transferable.
- ☐ Each type of share to be listed has at least 1000 shareholders. However, classes of shares with fewer than 500 shareholders may be admitted to listing, if the distribution of shareholdings is likely to ensure an adequate market in the shares.
- ☐ The voting rights of one shareholder do not exceed 80 percent of the total voting rights.

In connection with its application for listing, the company submits to the Stock Exchange a prospectus or a corresponding listing memorandum pursuant to the guidelines of the Securities Market Act and the Banking Supervision Office.

Bonds, debentures or other promissory notes intended for public subscription may be admitted to listing on the following conditions:

- ☐ The minimum amount of the loan is FIM 20 million or the equivalent in foreign currency.
- ☐ The bonds are freely transferable.

An applicant must sign a listing agreement with the Stock Exchange and must undertake to adhere to its rules and regulations. Prior to submitting its application for listing, a company must pay a registration fee, which is not refundable. When the securities have been admitted to listing, the supervisory board of the Stock Exchange may decide to require payment of an annual fee. A listed company must also be a member of the Helsinki Stock Exchange Cooperative.

Requirements to prepare financial statements: Rules of the Helsinki Stock Exchange impose particular publicity requirements on listed companies. There are further rules covering the information to be published in the financial statements of listed companies.

Where a listed company is the parent company of a group, the Stock Exchange's financial reporting requirements extend principally to the **consolidated financial statements**.

The financial statements of a listed company, according to the rules, must include the following in addition to the information prescribed in the Companies Act and the Accounting Act:

☐ An explanation of the **accounting policies** adopted in the financial statements and the consolidated financial statements, covering at least the definition of inventory costs, the useful lives of tangible and intangible fixed assets, pension expenses and the treatment of foreign exchange rate movements.

☐ Information on the results for the financial period before changes in untaxed reserves and direct taxes.

☐ Disclosure of the exceptional factors affecting the composition of the results and their treatment in the financial statements.

☐ Information on significant investments and the volume of orders.

☐ The future prospects of the company.

☐ Disclosure of any share issues during the financial period.

☐ A description of the ownership and distribution of the company's shares.

☐ Disclosure of any warrants and convertible bonds and their possible future effect on the company's share capital.

☐ The number of shares issued with a dividend entitlement.

☐ Information on the trend of share prices adjusted for share issues and share splits.

☐ Information on the results and dividends per share for the last five financial periods adjusted for share issues and share splits.

The annual report must also provide information on the ten largest shareholders by number of shares or voting rights and on each shareholder holding 5 percent or more of the company's shares or voting rights.

The annual report must also provide information on the proportion (if in excess of 5 percent) of the company's share capital or voting rights held by another listed company or an over the counter company.

Company announcements: A listed company must publish, without undue delay, all significant decisions or circumstances concerning the company's (or the group's) activities that may have a significant impact on the share price. The announcement must be sufficient to assess the likely impact of such decision or circumstances on the company's financial position or future activities. Where information already in the public domain has changed, the company must announce details of such change immediately.

A listed company must prepare either one interim report on its operations during the first six months of the financial period or at least two interim reports for periods of the same length, so that each report covers the operations of the financial period to date.

Reference. Rules of the Helsinki Stock Exchange.

GENERAL ACCOUNTING

3. Financial Statements

Basic Accounting Concepts. The Accounting Act requires that companies observe good accounting practice. The amendments to the Accounting Act include the obligation that the annual report (financial statements) present a true and fair view of the company's results and financial position. The main components of good accounting practice are the basic assumptions that the subject is an economic entity, the **going concern concept** and the **historical cost concept**; the central accounting principles of **realization, accrual accounting** and the **matching concept**; and the supplementary accounting principles of **prudence**, consistency, **materiality**, objectivity and **substance over form**.

Within the framework of the accounting legislation, there is scope for the application of different accounting policies. In order to maintain comparability, it is important to follow the chosen accounting policies consistently. If special circumstances arise requiring a change in accounting policy, the change and its effect on the results for the accounting period must be explained in the financial statements.

In Finland, tax legislation has a significant impact on the preparation of financial statements. For example, certain expenses and reserves must be included in the financial statements in order to be deductible in computing taxable income. The amendments to the Accounting Act did not change this linkage.

Contents of Financial Statements.   Limited liability companies are required under the Companies Act to issue an annual report containing an income statement, balance sheet and directors' report. Notes to the financial statements are considered an integral part of the statements. If the entity is a parent company, the annual report contains a consolidated income statement and balance sheet in addition to those of the parent company.

A statement of changes in financial position (or cash flow statement) must be attached to the directors' report of large companies (and groups) and is recommended for smaller companies. A company is considered large if its restricted equity capital exceeds FIM 2 million, if its shares are listed on the Stock Exchange, or if during the two preceding financial periods it has had more than 500 employees, on average. The form and content of the statement are not specified by law, and an enterprise should determine the most appropriate method of presentation for its business. The Association of Authorized Public Accountants has, however, issued two alternative models for the statement.

Other private-sector entities are required under the Accounting Act to issue annual reports similar to those issued by limited liability companies.

According to the Companies Act, the directors' report should contain:

☐ Information on any circumstances that are not specifically required to be disclosed in the income statement or balance sheet but that are considered to be important in understanding the results and financial position of the company.

☐ Information on any events of significance to the company, even if they occurred after the end of the financial period.

☐ Where the company has obtained control of another company or received assets and liabilities of another company through a merger during the financial period, an explanation thereof.

☐ Information on the average number of employees during the financial period and the total salaries and fees for the board of directors, the supervisory board, and the managing director and other employees. Bonuses to the board of directors and the managing director must be separately stated.

Where the financial statements are for a group, the directors' report must contain the above information with respect to the group.

☐ The proposal by the board of directors for the disposition of the profit or loss of the company for the financial period.

☐ A statement of changes in financial position (applies to large companies).

☐ Effective January 1, 1993, an explanation of significant changes in the business during the past financial period and an indication of likely developments during the current financial period. An explanation of the extent of research and development activities must also be given.

Where consolidated financial statements are presented, the directors' report of the parent company should include an explanation of the consolidation principles applied and the amount that group companies, in accordance with their articles of association, transfer from nonrestricted to restricted shareholders' equity. In the directors' report of a **subsidiary**, the identity of the parent company must be given.

Format of Financial Statements.   The company's financial statements must follow the formats specified by the Accounting Act and Ordinance and the Companies Act.

The general income statement format splits income and expenditure into items resulting from:

☐ Ordinary operations (**turnover** and costs of items sold).

☐ Other business operations.

☐ Financial operations.

☐ Extraordinary events and year-end adjustments for tax purposes (changes in untaxed reserves).

Companies that include production overheads in the cost of inventories must prepare an income statement based on a functional classification of expenses. Other companies may prepare an income statement classifying expenses by type.

Assets and liabilities are segregated into current and noncurrent in the balance sheet. Financial statements have to show corresponding figures for the preceding period.

Disclosure of Accounting Policies.   Disclosure of accounting policies in general is not required where fundamental **accounting concepts** and accounting principles are followed in the financial statements. Disclosure is, however, required of certain accounting policies; the information is usually included in the notes to the financial statements or in the directors' report.

Rules of the Helsinki Stock Exchange include disclosure requirements, which, according to the recommendations of the Association of Authorized Public Accountants, should be followed also by other companies, to the extent applicable. The accounting policies for at least the following should be disclosed by all limited liability companies:

☐ The principles used to prepare the consolidated financial statements.

☐ Foreign currency items and the treatment of differences in foreign exchange rates.

☐ The valuation of **inventories** and **fixed assets**, including **depreciation**. Where there has been a material change in the valuation principles for inventories, or if the amount or basis of depreciation of fixed assets for the financial period deviates significantly from the previous period, an explanation of the change or deviation must be given.

□ Pension plans and pension expenses.

□ Lease costs and sale-and-leaseback transactions.

□ Research and development costs.

Reference. Accounting Act, Chapter 3; Companies Act, Chapter 11; Rules of the Helsinki Stock Exchange; Recommendation for Information Included in the Financial Statements of a Listed Company; Recommendations issued by the Finnish Association of Authorized Public Accountants.

4. Business Combinations

Principles of Consolidation. Before the amendments to the Accounting Act and Companies Act, only parents that were limited liability companies had to prepare consolidated financial statements. Beginning January 1, 1993, other business enterprises are also required to prepare consolidated financial statements.

A parent company need not present consolidated financial statements if it is at least 90 percent owned by another enterprise that has to present consolidated financial statements and the parent obtains the approval of the owners of the **minority interest**. However, where a 90 percent or more owned parent distributes dividends, the adequacy of the nonrestricted equity of the subgroup must be proved and accordingly consolidated or equivalent financial statements must be prepared. Some small groups, as specified in the Act, are also excluded from the obligation to prepare consolidated financial statements.

The parent company and subsidiaries must have the same accounting period. According to the amendments to the Act, the financial statements of the subsidiaries must be amended, if possible, so that they are in accordance with the amended Accounting Act. All listed companies included in the consolidation must use uniform accounting policies.

The financial statements of the parent company have to be presented along with the consolidated financial statements.

Methods of Accounting for Business Combinations. A corporate combination, whereby two existing operating companies come together so that one becomes the parent and the other the subsidiary, can be described either as a true purchase from the parent company's view, or as a merger of the economic interests of both companies (**pooling of interests**). The treatment in consolidation, and therefore the valuation principles to be applied to the subsidiary's assets, depend on the type of consolidation. Normally, the combination is a true purchase and should be accounted for in accordance with the **purchase method**. When the combination is achieved by the issue of shares by the parent company and also meets certain other requirements for a merger (e.g., if neither of the companies dominates in size; the shareholders in the former companies exert proportionate influence over the combined entity so that there is continuity of ownership; and there is continuity of the combined entity's activities), the pooling of interests method is applicable.

Control. A business enterprise that exercises control (parent company) over another business enterprise or comparable foreign enterprise (subsidiary), has to prepare and include in its consolidated financial statements, the financial statements of the controlled entity.

Control is presumed to exist where a company:

☐ Owns more than one half of the voting power.

☐ Has the power to appoint the majority of the members of the board of directors or equivalent governing body under the articles of association (or equivalent agreement), together with the voting power by ownership (or membership).

☐ Has the power over more than one half of the voting rights or power to appoint the majority of the board or equivalent body by virtue of an agreement with other investors.

Control is also presumed to exist when a company jointly with one or several subsidiaries exercises the powers described above.

Goodwill.   Under the purchase method, the difference between the purchase cost of an acquired entity's shares and the acquiring company's interest in the book value of the net assets (equity) of the subsidiary should be determined at the acquisition date. A positive difference is allocated to specific identifiable assets or is recorded separately as **goodwill** in the consolidated balance sheet.

If the goodwill can be allocated, it is recorded as part of the carrying value of the assets in question, normally tangible assets, and is accounted for accordingly.

If the goodwill cannot be allocated, it is recorded separately in the consolidated balance sheet and must be amortized on a systematic basis over its useful life not exceeding 20 years. If it is found at any time that goodwill arising on acquisition is not supported by future income, it should, to the extent necessary, be charged immediately to income.

Negative goodwill is presented separately between shareholders' equity and liabilities.

Equity Accounting.   If a group company, alone or jointly with other group companies, has a significant ownership interest (at least 20 percent of shareholders' equity) and significant influence (20–50 percent of the voting power) in another business enterprise (**associated company**), the annual accounts of this enterprise have to be accounted for in the consolidated financial statements using the **equity method**. Before the January 1, 1993 amendments to the Accounting Act, only listed companies had to account for associated companies when calculating earnings per share information.

An investor that has investments in associates but does not have subsidiaries does not have to issue consolidated financial statements. The participating interest is recorded as other shares or other long-term investments in the financial statements of the investor company.

Minority Interests.   According to the Accounting Act, minority interests must be presented as a separate item in the consolidated balance sheet, recorded at the minority's share of the postacquisition values of the net identifiable assets involved. According to general directions issued by the KILA, the minority's share of the results for the financial period must be presented as a separate item in the consolidated income statement. Minority interests are separated before the elimination of intragroup items. Calculation of the minority interest takes account of direct interest, indirect interest and brought forward minority balances.

Following the January 1, 1993 amendments to the Accounting Act, the minority interest in untaxed reserves should be taken into account when deferred tax is imputed on untaxed reserves.

Disclosure.   According to the amended Accounting Act, the following must be disclosed in the consolidated financial statements: the names of subsidiaries that have been or have not been consolidated and, where relevant, the reasons for not consolidating; if group companies do not have the same year-end dates, a statement that permission has been granted by the KILA; an explanation of the principles used in preparing the consolidated financial statements (consolidation principles); information on the associated companies included in the consolidation and the related consolidation principles; deferred tax liabilities relating to voluntary reserves (untaxed reserves); and a listing of companies in which a group company alone or jointly with other group companies has significant ownership interests, including the name, percentage interest, the most recent results and amount of its equity.

According to the amended Accounting Act, the parent financial statements of a group company must present the following: financial income received from and expenses paid to other group companies; the totals of shares, participations and loans receivable included under long-term investments, related to both group companies and associated companies; receivables from, and liabilities to, group companies and associated companies; a listing of group companies and associated companies in which it has ownership interests, including the name, percentage interest and the most recent results, and also the equity of associates in which it has significant ownership interests (at least 20 percent of equity).

Reference.   Accounting Act, Chapter 3; General Directions for the Preparation of the Consolidated Financial Statements issued by the KILA.

5. Joint Ventures

In Finland, there is no prescribed **accounting standard** on accounting for interests in, or the consolidation of, joint ventures. Joint ventures are not covered by the amendments to the Accounting Act and Companies Act.

6. Foreign Currency Translation

Foreign Currency Denominated Transactions.   All **foreign currency transactions** are recorded on an accrual basis at the rates on the dates on which they occurred. The use of standard or average rates is, however, permitted, if it approximates the actual rate. The exchange differences between the amount originally recorded and the settlement amount are entered in the financial records according to their nature: Those connected with sales and purchases are recorded as adjustments to those items, and those connected with financial transactions are recorded as financing income and expenses.

According to the amended Accounting Act, all receivables and liabilities and other commitments in foreign currency are translated into local currency at the rate at the balance sheet date. If receivables or liabilities or other commitments are subject to a fixed rate of exchange by an agreement or otherwise, they may be translated at that rate.

The unrealized differences in exchange rates (transactions not settled at the balance sheet date) are generally recorded in the income statement according to the underlying transactions to which they relate, as described above. Also, differences in exchange rates that originate when translating long-term receivables or liabilities in the financial statements are usually included in the income statement. Unrealized exchange gains and losses on long-term monetary receivables and liabilities can, however, also be deferred as valuation items and recognized in income of future periods on a systematic basis over the remaining lives of the **monetary items** to which they relate. This treatment is, however, not recommended according to the explanatory memorandum issued by the government with the amendments to the Accounting Act. Before the legislative amendments, the KILA recommended that unrealized exchange losses be deferred, and unrealized exchange gains be deferred as valuation items.

Foreign Operations.   The Accounting Act and Companies Act do not specifically cover the translation of foreign subsidiaries' financial statements. The Finnish Association of Authorized Accountants recommends that international standards should be complied with as follows: For **independent foreign operations** (foreign entities), the **closing rate method** should be used, and the exchange difference resulting from translation should be taken to shareholders' equity. For **integrated foreign operations** (integral to the operations of the parent), the **monetary/nonmonetary method** should be used, and the exchange difference should be taken to income.

When translating income statement items, a weighted-average rate in effect during the period may be used.

Differences arising on the translation of the opening net investment in overseas subsidiaries are taken separately to the consolidated balance sheet either as a valuation item or as an exchange translation adjustment within the group's shareholders' equity.

Subsidiaries in countries with particularly high inflation rates give rise to special problems. Translating their financial statements using the current rate method usually results in an unrealistic picture of their financial position and results of operations. Accordingly, it is recommended that the monetary/nonmonetary method be used even for independent subsidiaries in such countries.

Hedges.   When a forward exchange contract is entered into to establish the amounts of the reporting currency required or available at the settlement day of **foreign currency transactions**, the difference between the forward rate and the spot rate at the inception of the contract should be recognized in income over the life of the contract. For short-term transactions, the forward rates specified in the related foreign exchange contracts should be used as the basis for measuring and reporting the transactions.

If foreign currency loans and other foreign currency transactions are designated as, and provide, an effective **hedge** against a net investment in a foreign entity, exchange differences arising on the loans or transactions should be taken to shareholders' equity (or to valuation items) to the extent that they are covered by exchange differences arising on the net investment.

Disclosure.   The basis of the rate of exchange used in the translation of receivables and liabilities and other commitments denominated in foreign currencies must be disclosed if the Bank of Finland rates on the balance sheet date (closing date) have not been used.

Exchange rate differences recorded as valuation items in the balance sheet, specifying the additions and deductions during the financial period, must be disclosed.

If exchange differences relating to long-term monetary items have been deferred, the nature and amount and the intended method of income recognition must be disclosed.

The methods used in translating the financial statements of foreign entities must be explained, if the accounting practice is not uniform.

Reference.   Accounting Act, Chapter 3; Statement on the Treatment of the Differences in Exchange Rates issued by the KILA; Recommendation on the Translation of Foreign

Currency Denominated Items issued by the Finnish Association of Authorized Accountants; Recommendation for Information Included in the Financial Statements of a Listed Company issued by the Helsinki Stock Exchange.

7. Changing Prices/Inflation Accounting

General. There is no prescribed accounting standard on accounting for changing prices. In the financial statements of a listed company, it is recommended that the effects of inflation, if they are significant, on the results for the accounting period, as well as the basis used in their evaluation, be disclosed.

Reference. Recommendation for Information Included in the Financial Statements of a Listed Company issued by the Helsinki Stock Exchange.

8. Changes in Accounting Policy

Accounting Treatment. There is no accounting standard on accounting for changes in accounting policy. The effects of changes in accounting policy are normally included in the income statement according to their nature. In exceptional cases, the effect of a change in accounting principle may be recorded as a reserve or valuation item and as extraordinary income or expenses.

Disclosure. The Accounting Act and Companies Act require disclosure of changes in the bases on which assets and liabilities are carried in the balance sheet if the changes are significant or have materially affected results for the period.

Reference. Companies Act, Chapter 11; Accounting Act.

9. Prior Period Adjustments

There is no accounting standard on accounting for prior period adjustments. Material prior period adjustments should be recorded as other income or expenses from business operations or as extraordinary income or expenses in the income statement for the current period rather than as adjustments of opening **retained earnings** in the financial statements for the current period.

In order to facilitate comparison between periods, amendments to comparative information with respect to prior periods should be made. Supplementary information may also be presented on a pro forma basis to show what the effect on income in prior periods would have been if the items had been reported in the period to which they relate.

Disclosure. The amount and nature of material prior period items should be disclosed.

10. Post Balance Sheet Events

The Companies Act requires that the directors' report include information on any events of significance to the company, even if they occurred after the end of the financial period, and an indication of developments in business activities after the balance sheet date.

Reference. Companies Act, Chapter 11.

11. Related Party Transactions

Definition. Parties are considered to be related if one party has the ability to control the other party or exercise significant influence over the other party in making financial and operating decisions. A related party transaction involves the transfer of resources or obligations between related parties, regardless of whether a price is charged.

Accounting Treatment. Accounting standards do not specifically address the measurement and accounting treatment of related party transactions. Nevertheless, the general principle is that related party transactions should be accounted for in accordance with normal principles and practices.

Disclosure. According to the Companies Act, the directors' report must include the total salaries and fees for the board of directors, the supervisory board and the managing director. Bonuses payable to the board of directors and the managing director must be separately stated.

According to the amended Companies Act, the notes to the financial statements must include future or agreed pension commitments for the members of the supervisory board and board of directors and the managing director and the subtotal of the loans granted to them and significant information about the terms and repayment of the loans.

The annual report of a listed company must include the total holdings of the company's shares and of the convertible instruments and bonds with equity warrants issued by the company to the members (including the deputy members) of the supervisory board, the company's board of directors, the managing director and deputy managing director, and their total voting rights obtainable through conversion or exercise of warrants.

Reference. Companies Act, Chapters 11 and 12; Accounting Act, Chapter 3; Rules and Regulations of the Helsinki Stock Exchange.

12. Segmental Information

According to the amended Accounting Act, turnover must be disclosed by segment in the notes. (There is no requirement to disclose profit or assets by segment.) Where there are foreign activities, turnover must also be disclosed by geographical market area, if the activities differ significantly from each other (unless this information is apparent from the information disclosed in the consolidated financial statements).

Reference. Accounting Act, Chapter 3; Recommendation for Information Included in the Financial Statements of a Listed Company issued by the Helsinki Stock Exchange.

ACCOUNTING PRINCIPLES FOR SPECIFIC ITEMS— BALANCE SHEET

13. Property, Plant and Equipment

Classification of Capital and Revenue Expenditure. Subsequent expenditure that substantially increases the future benefits from an existing asset beyond its previously assessed standard of performance should be capitalized as part of the cost of the asset.

Expenditure to maintain the normal operating standard (repairs) should be expensed as incurred. It is also, however, possible to capitalize significant repairs.

Basis of Valuation.   According to a general principle, the acquisition cost of an asset includes the variable cost of its purchase or construction plus other costs, as long as they can be justified by the nature of activities or other special reasons.

According to the amended Accounting Act, if fixed costs of purchase or construction represent a material part of the acquisition cost, these can be included in the carrying value, provided it is justifiable with respect to the nature of the business. Significant interest expenses that are attributable to an exceptionally large construction project incurred up to the completion of construction may also be capitalized (see Section 26).

If there is a permanent diminution in the value of an individual asset (such as a building) or a group of assets collectively (such as machinery and equipment), the net carrying amount should be reduced to the recoverable amount and the difference charged to income.

If the estimated lasting recoverable amount of land or water areas, buildings or other similar assets is materially higher than their cost, a revaluation up to the amount of the difference between the estimated recoverable amount and the net carrying value can be made. The estimated costs of disposal should be taken into consideration in the calculation. A revaluation is not possible, if the recoverable amount is not in excess of the original acquisition cost. An increase in net carrying amount arising on revaluation is credited directly to shareholders' equity under the heading revaluation fund (surplus) and is not available for distribution. No depreciation can be charged on the revalued portion of the carrying value.

A revaluation of machinery and equipment is not possible.

Gains or losses arising from the disposal of land and water areas, buildings and structures are recognized in the income statement according to their nature (usually as income or expenses from other business operations or as extraordinary items).

Depreciation.   Under the amended Accounting Act, the acquisition cost of tangible assets is depreciated over their estimated useful life. This is known as "depreciation according to plan" or "plan depreciation," which means that the depreciable amount must be allocated to each accounting period over the useful life on a systematic basis. When calculating plan depreciation, the **straight-line method** is usually applied. The selected policy, which includes the depreciation method and estimated useful life, should be changed only in exceptional circumstances.

Since 1986, it has been permissible to include in the financial statements depreciation according to plan, and in fact good accounting practice has recommended this approach. However, prior to the amended Accounting Act, it was also possible to allocate depreciation to each accounting period in variable amounts unrelated to the economic life or usage of the asset. Such allocations depended on the profitability of the enterprise and taxation considerations. Under the amended Accounting Act, enterprises must use plan depreciation for financial periods ending December 31, 1995 or earlier.

Despite this change in the accounting regime, depreciation claimed for tax purposes must still be recorded in the financial statements. This means that the financial statements include two depreciation entries—one for plan depreciation and a second representing depreciation claimed for tax purposes (fiscal depreciation), which may be higher or lower than plan depreciation.

For tax purposes, property, plant and equipment are generally depreciated using the **declining balance method**. Constructions such as bridges, railways, dams and docks are depreciated using the straight-line method over their estimated useful lives, the maximum period being 40 years. The cost of land may never be depreciated for tax purposes. The maximum fiscal rates of depreciation are defined in the Act on the Taxation of Income from Economic Activity, and they vary depending on the nature of the item. However, rates of depreciation are generally higher than rates for plan depreciation.

The difference between plan depreciation and fiscal depreciation for the period must be presented in the income statement before appropriations to or from untaxed reserves, and the accumulated differences must be included in liabilities in the balance sheet under untaxed reserves. According to the amended Accounting Act, the net carrying values for each category of fixed asset must be stated after deducting accumulated depreciation according to plan.

Disclosure. The net carrying values of tangible assets must be classified in the balance sheet as follows: land and water areas, buildings and structures, machinery and equipment, other tangible assets, prepayments and contracts in progress.

The financial statements must disclose information on how the tangible assets have been valued and depreciated (method, useful life and depreciation for tax purposes).

Under the amended Accounting Act, the notes to the financial statements must include for each category of tangible asset accumulated depreciation differences and changes in the gross acquisition costs, specifying gross acquisition cost at the beginning of the period, additions and disposals during the period and accumulated plan depreciation at the end of the period.

The taxation value of real property must also be disclosed according to balance sheet categories.

Reference. Accounting Act, Chapter 3; Accounting Ordinance; Act on the Taxation of Income from Economic Activity, Part III/Chapter 3 and Part IV.

14. Intangible Assets

Accounting Treatment and Valuation. Under a general principle, the acquisition cost of **intangible assets** includes the variable cost of their purchase (or development) and may also include other costs, which may be capitalized depending on the nature of activities or other special reasons.

Amortization. According to the Accounting Act, intangible assets must be amortized over their estimated useful lives according to plan. The straight-line method is used. According to the amended Companies Act, goodwill has to be amortized over five years or over a longer period, but not exceeding 20 years. The acquisition cost of patents, trademarks, other intangible assets and goodwill may, for tax purposes, be written down, using the straight-line method, over the estimated useful lives of the assets but not exceeding ten years.

Disclosure. The net carrying values of intangible assets must be classified in the balance sheet as follows: establishment and organization expenditure, research and development expenditure, intangible rights, goodwill, other long-term expenditure and prepayments.

Under the amended Accounting Act, the notes to the financial statements must include changes in the gross acquisition costs, specifying gross acquisition cost at the beginning of the period, additions and disposals during the period and accumulated depreciation at the end of the period.

Reference.   Accounting Act, Chapter 3; Accounting Ordinance; Companies Act, Chapter 11; Act on the Taxation of Income from Economic Activity, Part III/Chapter 3 and Part IV.

15. Leases

General.   Under Finnish accounting practice, no distinction is made between **finance** and **operating leases**, and all leases are accounted for as operating leases.

Assets held for leasing are recorded as property, plant and equipment in the balance sheet of the lessor. Rental income and expenses are recognized over the lease term on a systematic basis. The depreciation of leased assets is on a basis consistent with the lessor's normal depreciation policy for similar assets.

The accounting practice for leases is based on prudence and reflects the legal ownership of the assets.

The accounting treatment of a sale and leaseback transaction does not depend on the type of lease involved. Any profit or loss is recognized immediately at the time of a sale and leaseback transaction, regardless of the type of lease involved.

Disclosure.   According to Rules and Regulations of the Stock Exchange, if a listed company has significant future lease payment commitments, they must be disclosed as part of future liabilities (obligations) in the notes to the financial statements. Lease payments due in the next accounting period must be shown separately from the aggregate of future payments due.

In a sale and leaseback transaction, if the seller-lessee continues to bear a material economic risk connected to the ownership of the asset sold and leased back, this liability must be explained in the notes to the financial statements.

Although the above disclosure requirements apply only to listed companies, their adoption by other companies is recommended.

16. Investments

Valuation Principles.   In principle, current investments and noncurrent investments are valued and treated in the same way. Investments should be carried at the lower of cost or estimated recoverable amount. Investments in securities must be valued individually and not on a **portfolio basis**. A write-down should be recorded as an operating expense or a financial expense or, in particular circumstances, as an extraordinary item.

According to the Accounting Act, if at the balance sheet date the estimated lasting recoverable amount (**net realizable value**) of a security is materially higher than its acquisition cost, a revaluation up to the amount of the difference between the estimated recoverable amount and the net carrying value can be made. The estimated costs of disposal should be taken into consideration in the calculation. Reversals of previous write-downs are permitted. A revaluation is not possible if the recoverable amount is not in excess of the original acquisition cost.

Treatment of Revaluation Reserves. An increase in the net carrying amount arising on revaluation is credited directly to shareholders' equity under the heading of revaluation fund and is not available for distribution. The revaluation fund can be used only for the purposes described in Section 22.

Gains/Losses. When investments are sold, the profit or loss on sale is normally calculated using the carrying value of the investment; the revaluation surplus may not be included in the profit or loss. On sale of part of a holding of securities, the measurement of gain or loss should be based on the average carrying value. The gain or loss should be recorded as an operating item or a financial item or, in particular circumstances, as an extraordinary item.

Disclosure. In the amended balance sheet format, long-term investments are presented under noncurrent assets and short-term investments under **current assets**. Long-term investments are classified in the balance sheet as follows: shares and participations, loan receivables and other long-term investments.

The basis for valuation, revaluations and write-downs as well as the treatment of gains and losses should be explained in the notes.

According to the Companies Act, the taxation values of securities must be disclosed in the notes, specified according to balance sheet item.

Under the amended Accounting Act, a material difference between the carrying value and market value of shares and participations held as short-term investments must be disclosed in the notes to the financial statements.

Also under the amended Accounting Act, a group company has to separately disclose the amounts of shares, participations and loan receivables held as long-term investments relating to group companies and to associated companies.

Reference. Amendments to the Accounting Act, Chapter 3; and Accounting Ordinance.

17. Accounts Receivable

Accounting Treatment. Recognition: The recognition of revenues, and hence the related receivables, is described in Section 23.

Discounts: Revenues and the related receivables are normally recorded net of trade discounts. Where there are cash discounts, these are normally recognized on settlement.

Allowances: Under the amended Accounting Act, probable bad debts must be recorded in the income statement as adjustments to sales and in the balance sheet as deductions from receivables (or presented as an obligatory provision).

According to amendments to fiscal law, beginning January 1, 1993, probable bad debts (specific bad debt provisions) from trade receivables and only confirmed bad debts from other receivables are deductible for tax purposes.

Factored Receivables. Receivables that have been factored should not be included in the balance sheet. Where the factor has recourse to the vendor for doubtful accounts, disclosure of the contingent liability should be made if a provision for probable losses has not been recorded.

Disclosure. In the amended balance sheet format, receivables are classified as follows: trade receivables, loan receivables (current part), accrued receivables and other receivables.

Reference. Accounting Act, Chapter 3; Accounting Ordinance; Companies Act, Chapter 11.

18. Inventories and Work in Progress

General Accounting Treatment. Inventories are stated at the lower of historical cost or net realizable value. According to the Accounting Act, if the estimated **replacement cost** or realizable value at the balance sheet date is less than acquisition cost, inventories must be written down.

The general method of determining acquisition cost is **FIFO**, which is also the fiscal requirement, but the weighted-**average cost** method is also allowed and often used.

The general principle is that acquisition cost includes variable costs of purchase and manufacture.

According to the amended Accounting Act, if fixed production costs are material in relation to acquisition cost, these can also be included in acquisition cost. This means that production overheads that relate to bringing inventories to their present location and condition can also be included in inventory cost. The allocation of fixed production overheads is based on the normal level of production.

Long-Term Contracts/Work in Progress. Generally the **completed contract method** is used. However, under the amended Accounting Act, the **percentage of completion method** is also allowed for long-term contracts, where the profitability of each separate contract can be reliably estimated.

The preparatory work (documented in a written report) on which the amendments to the Accounting Act were based provided the following guidance on where the use of the percentage of completion method would be appropriate:

- [ ] Total contract revenues to be received can be reliably estimated.
- [ ] Both the costs to complete the contract and the stage of contract performance completed at the balance sheet date can be reliably estimated.
- [ ] The costs attributable to the contract can be reliably identified.
- [ ] The contract will affect at least two accounting periods and can therefore be considered long term.
- [ ] The contract is significant in scope.
- [ ] Prudence is observed in estimating costs.
- [ ] If the result for the contract as a whole, based on estimates, is negative, the entire loss has to be charged immediately to income.

Disclosure. The notes to the financial statements must describe the valuation principles used if they differ from the general principles. According to the Accounting Act, inventories must be classified appropriately in the balance sheet.

If production overheads are included in the cost of inventories, the company must categorize expenses by function in its income statement.

The notes should show the effect on results of using the percentage of completion method, and the criteria used when applying this method for long-term contracts.

Reference. Accounting Act, Chapter 3, Act on the Taxation of Income from Economic Activity, Part III/Chapter 2 and Part IV.

19. Current Liabilities

General Accounting Treatment. Items are included in **current liabilities** if they are payable at the demand of the creditor or are expected to be discharged within one year.

Current liabilities cannot be offset by current assets.

Creation of Specific and General Provisions. General provisions are not allowed, as provisions must relate to specific existing obligations. However, under the Accounting Act, certain reserves are allowed to be created in the financial statements—investment, operational, inventory and similar reserves. These reserves are not in the nature of accounting provisions, but generally represent appropriations of profits that would otherwise be taxable and are based on particular fiscal regulations. In order for these reserves to be allowable for tax purposes, they must be recorded in the financial statements. According to the amended Accounting Act, these untaxed reserves are classified as voluntary reserves.

After the reforms of business income tax effective beginning January 1, 1993, these reserves will mostly be abolished for tax purposes. In the amended balance sheet format, these untaxed reserves are shown as voluntary reserves. However, to the extent that untaxed reserves are required as accounting provisions, they should be shown separately in the balance sheet as obligatory provisions and not as voluntary reserves. Movements in voluntary reserves are presented in the income statement as appropriations to or from voluntary reserves.

The creation of specific provisions for future expenses and losses are described in Section 21.

Disclosure. In the amended balance sheet format, current liabilities are classified as follows: loans from financial institutions, loans from pension institutions, advances received, trade payables, accrued liabilities and other short-term loans.

Reference. Accounting Act, Chapter 3; Accounting Ordinance; Companies Act, Chapter 11; Act on the Taxation of Income from Economic Activity.

20. Long-Term Debt

The general accounting treatment applied to these items is basically the same as for current liabilities.

Contingent financial liabilities, such as pledges, mortgages and guarantees, are identified and disclosed in the notes to the financial statements. Contingencies are recognized as liabilities only when a loss becomes probable (see Section 21).

Disclosure. In the amended balance sheet format, long-term liabilities are classified as follows: debentures (bonds), convertible loans (bonds), loans from financial institutions, loans from pension institutions and other long-term liabilities.

According to the Accounting Act, group companies must disclose liabilities to other group companies and associated companies, according to balance sheet classification.

Pledges, mortgages for long-term loans, guarantees, loans and guarantees, and other commitments given must be disclosed in the notes to the financial statements. Where the company has convertible loans or bonds with equity warrants, both the date and terms of the conversion or the subscription must be disclosed for the outstanding amount of each loan.

Reference. Accounting Act, Chapter 3; Accounting Ordinance; Companies Act, Chapter 11.

21. Contingencies

General Accounting Treatment. The accounting treatment of a contingent loss is determined by the expected outcome of the **contingency**. If it is probable that a contingency will result in a loss, then it is prudent to accrue the loss in the financial statements. Contingent gains are not accrued.

Contingent Losses. According to the amended Accounting Act, future costs are charged to income, if it is probable that the associated income will not be realized. Probable future losses are also charged to income.

Future costs and losses that have not been realized by the balance sheet date have to be charged to income, if:

☐ It is probable that they will be realized on the basis of a commitment or decision.

☐ The amounts at which they are included can be estimated with reasonable accuracy (based on information available at the date on which the financial statements are authorized for issue).

According to the amended Accounting Act, such contingent losses are included in the balance sheet as a separate item, obligatory provisions, under reserves. The movements in such provisions are charged to expenses in the income statement according to their nature.

Contingent Gains. Contingent gains cannot be accrued in the financial statements. The existence and nature of contingent gains can be included in the directors' report, if they are significant and it is probable that the gain will be realized by the enterprise.

Disclosure. Contingent losses (obligatory provisions) have to be specified, where necessary, in the notes, if they have a significant effect on the results for the period.

Reference. Amendments to the Accounting Act, Chapter 3 (new section 16a).

22. Capital and Reserves

General. Under the Companies Act, shareholders' equity must be divided between restricted and nonrestricted equity. This distinction is made in order to clearly define those funds that are distributable to shareholders. Restricted equity consists of **share**

capital, reserve fund and revaluation fund. Other reserves are included in nonrestricted equity. The profit or loss for the period and retained earnings or losses from previous years are presented separately as additions to or deductions from distributable equity.

Share Capital.   Where the company has different classes of shares, the share capital has to be divided so that the amount of each class is disclosed. Where a company holds its own shares, the number of shares and their nominal value must be disclosed.

Restricted Reserves.   Two kinds of restricted reserves may appear in the balance sheet of a limited liability company.

Reserve fund: The following allocations should be made to the reserve fund:

☐   Any amount received in excess of nominal value on an issue of shares or on the conversion of convertible loans.

☐   Any amount paid by a subscriber whose shares have been declared forfeited.

☐   Any amount received in respect of bonus shares where the person entitled to the shares has not taken possession of them and they have been sold on the person's account.

☐   Any amount specifically allocated by the articles of association.

☐   Any amount specifically approved to be transferred from nonrestricted equity to the reserve fund at the general meeting of shareholders.

☐   A reduction in the share capital (optional).

Any reduction in the reserve fund requires approval at a general meeting of shareholders and may be made only for the following purposes:

☐   To cover losses that cannot be covered by nonrestricted equity.

☐   To increase share capital through a bonus issue or (in large companies) for a transfer to share capital to restore the value of new shares to their nominal value where a new issue has been made at a discount.

☐   For any other purpose if a court of law gives approval to the reduction.

Revaluation fund: This reserve results from the revaluation of land and water areas, buildings, securities and other similar items.

It may be used only for:

☐   Issuing bonus shares.

☐   A transfer to share capital to restore the value of new shares to their nominal value where a new issue has been made at a discount.

☐   Covering write-downs of assets that have previously been revalued.

Distribution Restrictions.   A distribution of a company's assets to shareholders may be made only in accordance with the regulations of the Companies Act on the payment of dividends, payments in connection with a reduction of the share capital or the reserve fund, and payments on the winding up of the company. As dividends are the most common form of distribution, only they are considered here.

The payment of dividends may not exceed the amount disclosed as distributable in the balance sheet approved by the board of directors. For a parent company, dividends may not exceed the amount of distributable equity shown in the consolidated balance sheet. The distributable amount includes the profit for the period, retained earnings from previous years and other nonrestricted reserves less (1) reported losses and (2) the amount that the articles of association require to be transferred to the reserve fund or that is otherwise to be left undistributed.

Dividends may not be distributed to the extent that it would be contrary to good business practice. The company's or the consolidated group's needs, cash needs or financial position in other respects should be considered. The distribution of dividends is approved at the general meeting of shareholders. The general meeting may not approve a dividend that is higher than the dividend proposed or approved by the board of directors.

If the total amount of a reduction in the share capital is used for the purposes of a transfer to the reserve fund or immediate coverage of losses for which the distributable equity is not sufficient, notice of the reduction must be registered. During a period of three years after the registration of such reduction, dividends may be declared only with the court's permission, unless in the meantime the share capital has been increased by at least an amount corresponding to the amount of the registered reduction.

Disclosure.   All changes in the components of capital and reserves since the previous balance sheet date have to be disclosed. Where shares have been issued but have not been registered or paid up, such amount has to be disclosed as a separate item.

Reference.   Companies Act, Chapters 11, 12, 6; Accounting Ordinance.

ACCOUNTING PRINCIPLES FOR SPECIFIC ITEMS— INCOME STATEMENT

23. Revenue Recognition

General Principles.   There is no specific revenue recognition accounting standard in Finland. The general principles for revenue recognition are the realization concept (and the accrual accounting concept) and the completed contract method. The percentage of completion method is also allowed in appropriate circumstances (see Section 18).

In a transaction involving the sale of goods or the rendering of services, the following conditions are, in principle, required to be fulfilled in determining whether **revenue** may be recognized:

☐   The seller of the goods or services has transferred to the buyer the significant risks and rewards of ownership.

☐   No significant uncertainty exists regarding: the acceptance of delivery of the goods or the rendering of the service; the associated costs incurred or to be incurred in producing or purchasing the goods or in rendering the service; the extent to which goods may be returned.

Interest is recognized on a time proportion basis (daily basis) taking account of the principal outstanding and the rate applicable; dividends from investments are recognized when the payment has actually been received (not when the right to receive payment is established); royalties are recognized on an accruals basis in accordance with the terms of the relevant agreement.

Where the sale is subject to installation and inspection, revenue should not be recognized until installation and inspection are completed and the customer accepts the delivery.

Long-Term Projects/Contracts. Revenue recognition on long-term projects and contracts is covered in Section 18.

Instalment Sales. The general principles of revenue recognition apply to **instalment sales**. Thus, if the significant risks and rewards of ownership are transferred to the buyer at inception of the transaction, the fact that the purchase price is to be received in instalments will not prevent the seller from recognizing the whole sales price at the date of sale (and creating a receivable for the deferred payment). The interest element should be recognized as revenue proportionately to the unpaid balance due to the seller. If collection is not reasonably assured, revenue should be recognized as cash instalments are received.

Rights of Return. Recognition of revenue will depend on the substance of the agreement. The fact that a buyer can return goods is usually not an ownership risk of significant magnitude to prevent a seller from recognizing a sale at the time possession initially is transferred to the buyer. However, if the right of return constitutes a significant ownership risk, revenue recognition should be deferred until the risk is eliminated or sufficiently reduced. General provisions for future returns (losses) are not allowed, if they are not probable and cannot be estimated with reasonable accuracy.

Product Financing. The general principles relating to the transfer of risks and rewards of ownership apply in determining the appropriate accounting treatment for **product financing arrangements**. Most of these agreements are in substance financing arrangements, and recognition of revenue would not be appropriate. Usually, the transaction should be treated as a financing transaction.

Disclosure. Under the amended Accounting Act, only net sales are required to be disclosed.

Reference. Accounting Act, Chapters 2, 3; Accounting Ordinance.

24. Government Grants and Assistance

Accounting Treatment. Government grants should be recognized in the income statement over the periods necessary to match them with the related costs that they are intended to compensate, on a systematic basis (income approach).

Grants related to income: Grants related to income are deducted in reporting the related expense; alternatively, they are presented in the income statement under "other income from business operations."

A government grant that becomes receivable as compensation for expenses or losses already incurred or for the purpose of giving immediate financial support to the enterprise, with no further related costs, should be recognized in the income statement of the period in which it becomes receivable, as an unusual item under "other income from business operations."

Grants related to assets: Government grants related to assets, including nonmonetary grants at fair value, should be presented in the balance sheet by deducting the grant in arriving at the carrying amount of the asset. A government grant that becomes repayable should be recorded by increasing the carrying amount.

Grants related to nondepreciable assets may require the fulfillment of certain obligations and should be amortized over the periods that bear the cost of meeting the obligations.

Disclosure. The nature and extent of significant grants related to income that are not disclosed in the income statement as a separate item and significant grants related to assets must be disclosed in the notes.

Reference. A statement (no. 563/1982) issued by the KILA.

25. Research and Development

Definitions. Research is original and planned investigation undertaken with the prospect of gaining new scientific or technical knowledge and understanding. Development is the translation of research findings or other knowledge into a plan or design for the production of new or substantially improved materials, devices, products, processes, systems or services prior to the commencement of commercial production or use.

Accounting Treatment. The allocation of costs of research and development activities to different accounting periods is determined by the relationship between the costs and the economic benefits that are expected to be derived from these activities. When, as a result of undertaking these activities, it is probable that the related costs will give rise to future economic benefits and the costs can be measured reliably, they qualify for recognition as an asset. The economic benefits include revenue from the sale of the product or process and cost savings resulting from the use of the product or process by the enterprise.

The research and development costs of a project recognized as an asset should be limited to the amount that, taken together with further research and development costs, related production costs, and selling and administration costs directly incurred in marketing the product, is probable of being recovered from future revenues. To the extent that research and development costs are not recognized as an asset, they must be recognized as an expense of the period in which they are incurred.

According to the Companies Act, expenditures arising from technical assistance, research and development activities, experimental operation, market research and other similar activities, if they have been capitalized, have to be amortized over a period of not more than five years, unless special reasons justify a longer period. According to a general principle in the Accounting Act, if other long-term expenditure (which would include research and development expenditure) has been capitalized, such amounts must be amortized over their economic lives.

Disclosure. According to the amended Accounting Act, the net carrying value of capitalized research and development expenditure is presented in the balance sheet as a separate item under intangible assets. Research and development expenses, including amortization, are included in the income statement under "other expenses from business operations." The notes must disclose changes in gross acquisition costs, specifying costs at the beginning of the period, additions and disposals during the period and accumulated amortization at the end of the period.

Reference. Accounting Act, Chapter 3; Companies Act, Chapter 11; Accounting Ordinance.

26. Capitalized Interest Costs

Accounting Treatment. According to a general principle in the Accounting Act, costs other than the acquisition costs of tangible assets may be capitalized, depending on the nature of activities or other special reasons.

According to a statement issued by the KILA, this general principle can be applied to interest costs attributable to construction projects that are incurred throughout the period of construction. In practice, this means that significant interest expenses that are attributable to an exceptionally large construction project for a tangible asset and that are incurred up to the completion of construction may be capitalized.

For taxation purposes, however, only interest related to the financing of the construction of a new power generation plant, mine or other industrial plant may be capitalized and amortized over a period of ten years or less.

Interest related to inventories may not be capitalized.

Disclosure. Valuation items and the additions and disposals to them during the period must be specified.

Reference. Accounting Act, Chapter 3; Act on the Taxation on Income from Economic Activity, Part III/Chapter 1; a statement (no. 563/1982) issued by the KILA.

27. Imputed Interest

There is no specific prescribed standard or recommendation dealing with **imputed interest**, and it is not recognized in practice.

28. Extraordinary or Unusual Items

Definition. Under the amended Accounting Act and Ordinance, "extraordinary income and expenses" is a new line item in the income statement. Entities should be very restrictive when classifying transactions as extraordinary items. The following three criteria have been put forward, all of which have to be met for an item to qualify as extraordinary:

☐ The event or transaction giving rise to the item has no evident relation to the ordinary operations of the business.

☐ The event or transaction is not expected to occur frequently or regularly.

☐ The item is material.

Disclosure. Extraordinary income and expense items are disclosed separately in the income statement. An explanation of the nature and amount of each extraordinary item is required in the notes. In the old format income statement, extraordinary items were included under the heading "other income and expenses" after "operating profit."

Reference. Amendments to the Accounting Ordinance; preparatory work on the amendments to the Accounting Act and Ordinance.

29. Income Taxes

Accounting Treatment. There is no specific accounting standard for income taxes. Deferred tax accounting is not recognized in the financial statements of a separate taxable legal entity. However, deferred tax accounting may be applied in consolidated financial statements, as explained below. The provision for income tax is calculated on the basis of the accounting income for the period and is presented as an accrued liability or an accrued asset in the balance sheet. Tax expense is presented as a separate item in the income statement before net results for the period.

According to the amended Accounting Act, in the consolidated financial statements, untaxed reserves may be deferred tax effected. Thus, untaxed reserves in the balance sheet may be divided between shareholders' equity and deferred tax liability, and changes in untaxed reserves for the financial period may be divided between results for the period and deferred tax charge or credit. This treatment is possible only in consolidated financial statements because a group is not a taxable entity; in entity financial statements, untaxed reserves must continue to be recorded. The KILA is expected to issue guidance on whether the **liability method** or the **deferral method** should be used for deferred tax accounting.

Treatment of Tax Losses. Losses may be carried forward and offset against future profits for ten subsequent years.

Reference. Accounting Ordinance.

30. Postretirement Benefits

Pensions. An employer's cost of postretirement benefits to employees results from receiving services from the employees who are entitled to receive such benefits.

Plans providing statutory pension benefits are usually arranged through insurance companies, and employers must pay statutory insurance premiums to the insurers. Pension liabilities are based on the level of pension benefits and actuarial assumptions established by the government and determined by comprehensive independent actuarial calculations performed on an annual basis. Postretirement benefits provided through insurance companies are fully funded, and the costs of providing such benefits are accrued in the financial statements as the premium contributions are paid.

However, plans to provide statutory postretirement benefits may be arranged and administrated through company-owned pension foundations or by the company itself. Contributions to company-owned foundations are reflected as a charge against income; however, the company can select the amount to be contributed and, as a result, liabilities for postretirement benefits may not be adequately funded. The only minimum requirement is that contributions should be sufficient to cover benefit payments to retired participants. Prior to the recent amendments to the Accounting Act, unfunded liabilities with respect to pension foundation administered plans or liabilities where the company itself assumed responsibility required only disclosure in the notes to the financial statements; no provision was required in the financial statements.

In the case of listed companies administering their retirement plans themselves or through company-owned pension foundations, unfunded liabilities for statutory (or other legally binding) pension commitments are required to be provided as a separate item within long-term liabilities. However, a counter item is allowed to be included as an asset under "valuation items." Listed companies may also account for voluntary additional pensions in this way and, if this is not done, the reasons for a different accounting treatment must be explained in the financial statements.

As explained below, as a result of the amended Accounting Act, all companies will be required to reflect fully the costs of providing postretirement benefits in their financial statements. The transitional period for companies to meet this new requirement extends until 2000.

Disclosure. The financial statements must include an explanation of the arrangements for providing employee postretirement plans. According to the amended Accounting Act, the costs of postretirement commitments and liabilities must be charged against income and provided in the balance sheet as an obligatory provision, by the latest in the financial statements for the period ending December 31, 2000.

Reference. Amendments to the Accounting Act, Chapter 3; Rules and Regulations of the Helsinki Stock Exchange; preparatory work on the amendments to the Accounting Act.

31. Discontinued Operations

Accounting Treatment. There is no prescribed accounting standard for discontinued operations. In practice, some entities prefer that gains or losses from disposals or discontinued operations of a significant business segment should be presented as an extraordinary item, while others prefer that discontinued operations be accounted for as part of business operations. The effect of normal changes and adjustments to a product line should be included in "other income from business operations."

Disclosure. An explanation of the nature and amount of discontinued operations is required in the notes.

Reference. Preparatory work on the amendments to the Accounting Act and Ordinance.

32. Earnings per Share

The Companies Act does not require companies to disclose earnings per share. However, according to rules of the Stock Exchange, listed companies must disclose various per share data for the previous five accounting periods. Earnings per share must be based on the information in the financial statements, or the consolidated financial statements in the case of a group. Earnings must be calculated as results before extraordinary items, plus or minus minority interest in profit or loss for the period, plus or minus share of results of associated companies, minus direct taxes.

The number of shares is the average adjusted number of shares in issue during the accounting period.

Disclosure.   Earnings per share during the last five years must be disclosed in the notes to the financial statements of listed companies. Also, the basis of calculating per share data must be described.

Reference.   Recommendations for Information Included in the Financial Statements of a Listed Company issued by the Helsinki Stock Exchange.

Appendix
DO FINNISH STANDARDS OR PREVALENT PRACTICE SUBSTANTIALLY COMPLY WITH INTERNATIONAL ACCOUNTING STANDARDS?

Section	Topic	Substantially complies with IAS?	Comments
3.	Basic accounting concepts and conventions	Yes	
	Contents of financial statements	Yes	Except that a statement of changes in financial position is required only for large companies and a statement of accounting policies is not generally required
4.	Business combinations*	Yes	
5.	Joint ventures	NS	
6.	Foreign currency translation*	Yes	
8.	Accounting changes*	Yes	
9.	Prior period adjustments*	Yes	
10.	Post balance sheet events	Yes	
11.	Related party transactions	No	Disclosures are limited to certain transactions and balances with directors and group companies
12.	Segmental information	No	
13.	Property, plant and equipment*	No	Additional depreciation is permitted to be charged
15.	Leases	No	
16.	Investments	Yes	
17.	Accounts receivable	Yes	
18.	Inventories and work in progress*	Yes	
19.	Current liabilities	Yes	
20.	Long-term debt	Yes	
21.	Contingencies	Yes	
22.	Capital and reserves	Yes	
23.	Revenue recognition*	Yes	
24.	Government grants and assistance	Yes	

Appendix (*Continued*)

Section	Topic	Substantially complies with IAS?	Comments
25.	Research and development*	Yes	
26.	Capitalization of interest costs*	Yes	
28.	Extraordinary or unusual items*	Yes	
29.	Income tax**	Yes	
30.	Postretirement benefits*	No	

*These topics are subject to change as a result of the IASC Improvements Project—see the appendix to the International Accounting Standards chapter.

**The IAS on accounting for taxes on income is currently being revised, and an exposure draft has been issued.

NS—No treatment specified.

Comparison in this table is made to International Accounting Standards in force at January 1, 1993. For further details, see the International Accounting Standards chapter.

FRANCE

GENERAL NATIONAL INFORMATION

1. Source of Generally Accepted Accounting Principles

French **accounting principles** are set out in national legislation and various regulatory texts, which are clarified and supplemented by authoritative pronouncements.

Generally Accepted Accounting Principles. **Generally accepted accounting principles** are derived from the following sources:

☐ Business Code (Code de Commerce). Accounting principles applicable to business entities are set out in Articles 8 to 17 of the Business Code. The text of these Articles is derived from the Law of April 30, 1983 and Articles 1 to 27 of the Decree dated November 29, 1983.

☐ General Accounting Plan (Plan Comptable Général). The General Accounting Plan consists of a detailed chart of accounts that must be used by all manufacturing and commercial entities, together with definitions and principles. The current General Accounting Plan, based on the Fourth European Community (EC) Directive (78/660/EC), was introduced in 1982 by Government Order dated April 27, 1982 and was modified in December 1986.

☐ Pronouncements and recommendations issued by the National Accounting Board (Conseil National de la Comptabilité), a consultative body attached to the ministry responsible for the economy.

Generally accepted consolidation principles are set out in the Law of July 24, 1966 (Articles L 357-1 to L 357-10) and the Decree of March 23, 1967 (Articles D 248 to D 248-13). The consolidation principles are based on the Seventh EC Directive (83/349/EC).

In most respects, the accounting principles applicable to the statutory financial statements of individual companies also apply to **consolidated financial statements** of groups. However, in specific instances, groups are either required or permitted to apply valuation methods that are not acceptable for statutory reporting purposes. These consolidation adjustments are designed to enable French groups to present consolidated financial statements that are in accordance with international accounting standards, while individual statutory accounts are still driven, to a greater or lesser degree, by tax considerations.

The differences between statutory and group valuation methods are outlined in the relevant sections of this chapter.

Accounting Standards.

☐ The Institute of Public Accountants and Authorized Accountants (Ordre des Experts Comptables et des Comptables Agréés) issues recommendations designed to assist members in the application of accounting legislation and regulations.

☐ The Stock Exchange Commission (Commission des Opérations de Bourse) participates in the development of accounting doctrine by publishing recommendations and opinions primarily designed to encourage **public companies** and their auditors to adopt good accounting and auditing practices. The Stock Exchange Commission also issues position papers that are published in its monthly bulletin and annual report.

2. Audit and Public Company Requirements

Audits.   According to the Companies Act of July 24, 1966 (the Act), all joint-stock corporations (sociétés anonymes—Article L 218) and all limited partnerships with share capital (sociétés en commandite par actions—Article L 254) are required to appoint independent auditors who are responsible for ensuring that the annual financial statements have been properly prepared and comply with the "true and fair view" principle. The same applies to closely held corporations (sociétés à responsabilité limitée—Articles L 64 and D 43) and to ordinary limited partnerships and general partnerships (sociétés en commandite simple and sociétés en nom collectif—Article L 17-1) that meet any two of the following three criteria at year-end:

☐ Total assets in excess of French francs (FRF) 10 million.
☐ Total sales in excess of FRF 20 million.
☐ Average number of employees in excess of 50.

Corporations required to publish consolidated financial statements (Article L 223, subparagraph 3) must appoint two independent auditors. This requirement applies to public companies and other corporations that meet any two of the following criteria:

☐ Total group assets in excess of FRF 100 million.
☐ Total group sales in excess of FRF 200 million.
☐ Average number of group employees in excess of 500.

Subgroups that are controlled by another corporation and are included in that corporation's consolidated accounts are exempt from the requirement to publish consolidated accounts (Article L 352-2), provided that the controlling group's consolidated accounts are prepared in accordance with the Seventh EC Directive, audited, published and made available to subgroup shareholders in French (Article D 248-13). Moreover, if the controlling group is from outside the European Community, the parent company of the French subgroup must supplement this information with certain disclosures concerning its own subconsolidation.

Only those persons or firms registered on a list kept by the Appeal Court in their district may be appointed as auditors (Article L 219). To be registered, they must have certain professional qualifications. French legislation includes strict conflict of interests rules designed to ensure that auditors are truly independent.

The auditors are appointed by the shareholders (Article L 223, subparagraph 1) for an initial term of six years. There is no limit on the number of times their appointment may be renewed. Statutory auditors may not be removed from office during the six-year term, except as a result of a court ruling in the case of serious professional misconduct or disqualification.

The Institute of Statutory Auditors (Compagnie Nationale des Commissaires aux Comptes) publishes professional standards that must be adhered to by all members, together with guidelines for auditors' use. These standards reflect the profession's opinion as to what constitutes "due diligence"; the standards are equivalent, in all material respects, to the International Standards on Auditing published by the International Federation of Accountants (IFAC).

Public Companies.   Public companies are defined as follows (Article L 72):

☐   Companies whose stock is traded on a recognized stock exchange or unlisted securities market.

☐   Companies that have offered to sell securities to the public (defined as representing at least 300 people).

Prospectuses issued by public companies in connection with public placings or public offers to acquire shares (takeover bids) must be submitted to the Stock Exchange Commission for prior approval. Listing requirements vary according to the market (official market for larger companies and "second marché" for medium-sized companies). As a general rule, audited consolidated financial statements covering the most recent two-year period are required to be presented in French (translation to be verified by a French auditor). If the listing occurs more than nine months after the last audited balance sheet, audited consolidated interim financial statements must be presented for the most recent half-year. Public companies are also required to file copies of published financial information with the Commission.

The financial reporting requirements for public companies are more comprehensive than for unlisted corporations. These requirements, which vary depending on whether the company's stock is quoted on a recognized or an unlisted securities market, include the publication of annual, semiannual and quarterly financial information.

Reference.   Companies Act of July 24, 1966.

GENERAL ACCOUNTING

3. Financial Statements

Basic Accounting Concepts.   The basic concepts underlying the selection of accounting policies and the preparation and presentation of financial information are derived from the Business Code and the General Accounting Plan. The basic concepts include:

☐ The **going concern concept** (Business Code, Article 14).

☐ The **accrual concept** (Business Code and the Act).

☐ The **historical cost** convention (Business Code, Article 12).

☐ The principle of **prudence** (Business Code, Article 14).

☐ The principle of consistency in accounting methods from period to period (Business Code, Article 11).

Assets and liabilities may not be offset in the balance sheet, and income and expenses may not be offset in the income statement (Business Code, Article 13).

The General Accounting Plan also stipulates that the opening balance sheet must agree with the closing balance sheet at the end of the previous **fiscal period**.

Two basic principles recognized by the International Accounting Standards Committee (IASC) are not explicitly included in French accounting law:

☐ Principle of **substance over form**: Certain transactions, such as leases, are accounted for in France in a manner that conveys their legal form, rather than their substance.

☐ Principle of **materiality** (relative importance): This principle is not explicitly mentioned in French accounting law; however, the Business Code (Article D 24) includes the concept of relative importance with regard to the contents of the notes to financial statements.

Contents of Financial Statements. The financial statements include the balance sheet, the income statement and the notes (known as the ''Annexe''), which form an integral part of the financial statements (Business Code, Article 8, subparagraph 3 for statutory financial statements; Article L 375-5, subparagraph 1 for consolidated financial statements). The financial statements, which are presented to shareholders at the annual general meeting, must be prepared in compliance with accounting regulations and give a true and fair view of the net assets, financial position and operating results of the business (Business Code, Article 9). Accounting regulations specify the information to be included in the notes, which varies depending on the size of the business.

The balance sheet and income statement should include comparative figures for the prior year (Business Code, Article 10).

A statement of changes in financial position is not compulsory.

The full set of **parent company** financial statements must be separately published even when the presentation of consolidated financial statements is required (see Section 2). The parent company financial statements are generally included in the same document as the consolidated statements (annual report), although the use of a separate document is also allowed.

Format of Financial Statements. All companies are required to present their balance sheet and income statement according to a standard format, which may be simplified for smaller businesses. French accounting regulations also specify the method of calculating each balance sheet and income and expense item, based on the accounts contained in the General Accounting Plan.

Assets and liabilities are not segregated between current and noncurrent, but this classification is required in the notes. Balance sheet items are classified on the basis of their purpose or origin (Business Code, Article D 10).

The income statement is presented by type of income and expense. However, as a departure from this rule, the consolidated income statement can be presented by function, provided that certain minimum requirements concerning content are adhered to.

There is no regulatory format for the statement of changes in financial position, which remains optional although its presentation is encouraged by the Stock Exchange Commission. Professional institutes (Institute of Public Accountants—Recommendation no. 1-22) now recommend presentation of a cash flow statement in the international format. Both the **direct** and the **indirect methods** of preparation are allowed, but, in practice, the indirect method is most commonly used.

Disclosure of Accounting Policies. The financial statements should include a description of the main accounting policies. Detailed information should be given if a choice has been made between acceptable alternatives, if the accounting policy adopted represents an exception to or a departure from the usual treatment or if the application of a generally accepted accounting principle would not give a "true and fair view." Differences in presentation or valuation methods from the previous year should also be explained.

Reference. Business Code and Companies Act of July 24, 1966.

4. Business Combinations (Regroupements d'Entreprises)

Principles of Consolidation. In general, all **subsidiaries** should be consolidated. However, there are three exceptions to this principle:

- □ Subsidiaries engaged in a business that is so dissimilar to that of the parent company, that their consolidation would result in a misleading presentation of the group's accounts, are accounted for by the **equity method**.
- □ If control by the parent company is seriously and permanently impaired, the cost method is used.
- □ Subsidiaries only temporarily controlled by the parent, subsidiaries not significant in relation to the group as a whole and subsidiaries whose financial statements are not produced in time for inclusion in the consolidated accounts are accounted for by the cost method.

Companies jointly controlled by a limited number of shareholders are consolidated by the proportional method, that is, on the basis of the consolidating entity's percentage share of assets, liabilities, income and expenses (see Section 5).

Accounting for Business Combinations. Only the **purchase method** is allowed. **Goodwill** (Ecart de première consolidation), representing the difference between the purchase price of the investment and the acquiring company's interest in the underlying net assets at the date of acquisition, is allocated as far as possible among identifiable assets and liabilities. The unallocated balance is recorded on a separate line of the balance sheet as goodwill or **negative goodwill**. In practice, goodwill is allocated primarily among noncurrent assets, including intangibles, and long-term debt. In no circumstances should the adjustments exceed the goodwill to be allocated.

Control.   Control is indicated by:

☐   Ownership of a majority of the voting rights.

☐   The designation of a majority of the members of the board of directors (conseil d'administration) in two consecutive years. (The investor is presumed to designate a majority of the members of the board if the investor holds more than 40 percent of the voting rights and no other shareholder owns an equivalent or greater percentage.)

☐   Being in a position to dominate decision making by virtue of a contract or clauses in the investee's articles of incorporation.

Goodwill (Ecart d'Acquisition).   Goodwill (and negative goodwill) is generally amortized over a period reflecting the assumptions and objectives prevailing at the time of the acquisition. If the original assumptions prove to be incorrect and the objectives for the acquired business are not met, resulting in a permanent, significant impairment in value, the amortization period must be shortened accordingly. French law does not specify a maximum amortization period.

Equity Accounting (Mise en Équivalence).   Companies over which the consolidating entity exercises significant influence are accounted for by the equity method. Significant influence over the management and financial policies of the investee is usually presumed to exist when the investor holds 20 percent or more of the voting shares.

Minority Interests (Intérêts Minoritaires).   **Minority interests** are shown separately in the consolidated balance sheet and income statement to clearly identify the net assets and net income (or loss) attributable to the parent company. However, if a subsidiary has negative shareholders' equity, the interest of minority shareholders is shown as attributable to the parent company.

When a subsidiary is consolidated for the first time, minority interests in the subsidiary's shareholders' equity should be determined on the basis of the fair values resulting from the allocation of goodwill among identifiable assets and liabilities.

Disclosure.   The notes should contain all significant information required to enable the reader to understand and form an opinion on the consolidated financial statements, including details of the companies consolidated, the consolidation principles and methods applied, the content of and changes in certain balance sheet and income statement items, an analysis of consolidated sales by industry segment and geographical area and information on companies accounted for by the equity method (summarized financial statements).

The notes should also include information on the amounts paid by consolidated companies to members of the board of directors of the parent company and commitments given by consolidated companies on behalf of board members.

A statement of changes in financial position and a statement of changes in shareholders' equity are recommended but not compulsory.

Reference.   Law of July 24, 1966 (Articles L 357-1 to L 357-10) and Decree of February 17, 1986 (Articles 248-12-11 and 248-12-12).

5. Joint Ventures

Accounting for Investments in Joint Ventures. French legislation acknowledges that **joint ventures** may be incorporated (enterprises sous contrôle conjoint) or unincorporated (sociétés en participation).

Jointly Controlled Entities. Companies jointly controlled by a limited number of shareholders are accounted for by the **proportional consolidation** method. **Joint control** is dependent not on an equal split of voting rights among venturers, but rather on the existence of a contractual agreement providing that decisions in all areas essential to the accomplishment of the goals of the joint venture require consent of all the venturers.

Jointly Controlled Operations (Individual Accounts of Venturers). Jointly controlled operations are conducted under a specific structure (société en participation) without legal existence. The venturers in charge of negotiating transactions with third parties are required to record such transactions as if they were achieved solely in their name. The net result of the joint venture is then allocated to the other venturers by use of specific accounts provided by the General Accounting Plan (quote part de résultats sur opérations faites en commun).

Jointly Controlled Assets (Individual Accounts of Venturers). When venturers contribute assets to a joint venture without legal existence (société en participation), they retain official ownership of those assets, which they must carry on their balance sheet at full historical cost. Conversely, assets that are undividedly owned by the venturers (for instance, assets purchased or created by the joint venture) are capitalized by each venturer according to its percentage in the joint venture.

Transactions Between Venturers and the Joint Venture. The contribution of assets to a joint venture in exchange for an interest in the joint venture does not give rise to a gain or loss on disposal in the contributor's financial statements. Gains resulting from other transactions between the venturer and the joint venture should be recognized only to the extent of the interests of nonrelated venturers. However, losses should be recognized in their entirety.

Accounting by Joint Ventures. Generally accepted accounting principles apply to incorporated joint ventures. Accounts of unincorporated joint ventures (sociétés en participation) exist only for use of the venturers and for tax purposes.

Disclosure. Jointly controlled entities included in consolidated accounts of the venturer must be identified, together with the method of consolidation used (normally proportional consolidation method) and the percentage interest owned.

Venturers in unincorporated joint ventures need only mention commitments with respect to the other venturers.

Reference. Law of July 24, 1966 (Articles L 357-1 and L 357-3); General Accounting Plan (par. 241.b and page II, 133 and 134); National Accounting Board (Recommendation no. 13).

6. Foreign Currency Translation (Conversion Monétaire)

Foreign Currency Denominated Transactions. **Foreign currency** denominated **transactions** are translated at the transaction date exchange rate, and foreign currency **monetary items** outstanding at the balance sheet date are revalued at the balance sheet date spot rate.

In the statutory financial statements, unrealized losses are generally charged against income; unrealized gains are not recorded. If a loan is taken out in a foreign currency to finance the acquisition of property, plant and equipment or an equity investment, any unrealized loss can be written off over the life of the loan. Unrealized gains may be netted against unrealized losses on foreign currency transactions in comparable currencies with comparable due dates.

In consolidated financial statements, companies may choose to include unrealized gains in income immediately, together with unrealized losses.

Foreign Operations. If a foreign operation is **self-sustaining**, its assets and liabilities are translated at the year-end exchange rate, and income and expense items are translated at either the year-end rate or the average rate for the year, whichever is more appropriate. The resulting translation differences are recorded as a separate component of shareholders' equity.

If a foreign operation is **integrated** with the reporting company, the monetary items in its balance sheet are translated at the year-end exchange rate and nonmonetary items are translated at the historical rate. Income and expense items are translated at the average exchange rate for the year. The resulting translation differences are recorded directly in income.

Hedges. A transaction is classified as a **hedge** of a foreign currency exposure only if there is a firm, clearly identified commitment and the transaction effectively eliminates any exchange risk. The hedged debt or receivable is translated at the forward exchange rate, and the difference between this rate and the historical rate is recorded directly in income.

Disclosure. The notes should include the following information on open hedging positions at year-end: type of transaction hedged (asset, liability, off balance sheet item), type of market on which the position has been taken (organized market, over-the-counter market) and impact on income of positions taken during the year (Stock Exchange Commission recommendation issued in October 1988, primarily applicable to public companies). Details concerning the method used to translate the financial statements of foreign subsidiaries should also be given in the notes to the consolidated financial statements.

Reference. Law of July 24, 1966 (Article L 357-8) and General Accounting Plan.

7. Changing Prices/Inflation Accounting (Variations de Prix/Inflation)

General. There is no obligation to account for changing prices in the statutory financial statements, nor are there any disclosure requirements. In the consolidated financial statements, assets and liabilities may be restated on a current cost basis, in which case the resulting difference is shown as a separate component of shareholders' equity; however, this method is rarely used by French corporations. In addition, as an exception to the normal treatment, depreciable property, plant and equipment and inventories may be restated at replacement cost in the consolidated financial statements.

Reference. Law of July 24, 1966 (Article L 357-8).

8. Accounting Changes (Changements de Principes Comptables)

Accounting Treatment. Accounting principles: The effect of a change on opening balances should be recorded in income for the year as an exceptional item (in accordance with the principle that the opening balance sheet must agree with the closing balance sheet at the end of the previous period). The only changes in accounting principles whose effects on opening balances can be shown as an adjustment to opening stockholders' equity (retroactive restatement) are those changes made compulsory by a change in the accounting regulations.

Accounting estimates: The effect of a change on opening balances should be recorded in income for the year.

In both cases, prior year figures should not be restated.

Disclosure. Changes in accounting principles should be described and explained in a note. The effect of the change on income should be shown as a nonrecurring (exceptional) item and explained in the notes, if necessary. The effect of changes in accounting estimates should be included in operating income.

Reference. Business Code (Article 11).

9. Prior Period Adjustments (Ajustements sur Exercices Antérieurs)

Definition of Adjusting Items. Adjusting items represent adjustments made to prior period financial statements to correct clerical errors, the use of inappropriate accounting principles or the incorrect application of accounting principles.

Accounting Treatment. The effect of the adjustment is included in nonrecurring income or expense for the current year.

Disclosure. Details of adjustments to correct significant prior period errors should be disclosed in a note.

Reference. Recommendation P.C.15 of the Institute of Public Accountants.

10. Post Balance Sheet Events (Evénements Postérieurs à la Clôture)

Definition. Post balance sheet events should be considered only if they indicate the existence of a risk or a loss. In addition, a distinction must be made between:

- ☐ Events relating to conditions that existed at the balance sheet date; and
- ☐ Events that are not directly connected with conditions existing at the balance sheet date.

Accounting Treatment. For conditions existing at the balance sheet date, the financial statements must be adjusted if the amount of the risk or loss can be reasonably estimated.

For conditions arising after the balance sheet date, the financial statements should not be adjusted.

Disclosure. For conditions existing at the balance sheet date, if the financial statements have not been adjusted, a note should indicate the type of event and the reason a reasonable estimate of the risk or the amount of the loss cannot be made; if the financial statements have been adjusted, disclosure is not compulsory, but material adjustments are normally described in a note.

Conditions arising after the balance sheet date that are likely to affect the company's ability to continue to operate as a going concern must be disclosed in a note; otherwise, disclosure is recommended but not compulsory.

Reference. Business Code (Article 14); General Accounting Plan; and Recommendation P.C.12 of the Institute of Public Accountants.

11. Related Party Transactions (Opérations Entre Parties Liées)

Definition. The Business Code and the Fourth and Seventh EC Directives define related parties as:

□ The dominant entity (parent company);
□ Dependent entities—that is, entities controlled, either directly or indirectly, by the parent company; or
□ **Associated companies**, over which the parent company exercises significant influence, either directly or indirectly.

For directors and board members, the following specific disclosures are required:

□ Total remuneration.
□ Loans and credit commitments.

Accounting Treatment. French accounting law does not include any provisions concerning the accounting treatment of related party transactions. However, following France's adoption of the Seventh EC Directive (consolidated financial statements), it is recommended that balances deriving from transactions with related parties be shown on a separate line of the balance sheet.

Disclosure. Where material, the following information should be disclosed:

□ Proportion of investments, debts, receivables, interest income and expense concerning related parties.
□ Amount of financial commitments given to or received from related parties.

Reference. Business Code (Article D 24) and General Accounting Plan.

12. Segmental Information (Informations Sectorielles)

French companies are required to disclose net sales by industry and geographical segment. If a company does not wish to disclose certain segmental information on the grounds that it would be damaging to its business interests, the relevant note should stipulate that the information given is incomplete. In addition, public companies must publish quarterly consolidated sales by industry segment.

French accounting law does not define industry or geographical segments. Corporations should, therefore, use judgment in deciding the basis to be used in presenting the information. However, the General Accounting Plan stipulates that the disclosure is necessary only if the company operates in several very dissimilar industries or markets. A segment may be considered to be sufficiently material to require disclosure if it represents more than 10 percent of sales, operating income or total assets.

Reference. Business Code (Article D 24); General Accounting Plan; and Decree of March 23, 1967 (Article D 297).

ACCOUNTING PRINCIPLES FOR SPECIFIC ITEMS— BALANCE SHEET

13. Property, Plant and Equipment (Immobilisations Corporelles)

Classification of Capital and Revenue Expenditure. An expenditure is classified as a **capital expenditure** when it gives rise to an asset. Expenditures related to existing assets are treated as follows:

☐ An expenditure to maintain assets in normal working condition until the end of their useful life is treated as an expense as incurred.

☐ An expenditure that significantly increases the value of an asset or extends an asset's useful life is capitalized.

Basis of Valuation. In general, fixed assets are stated at historical cost, as follows:

☐ Assets acquired for valuable consideration are stated at cost, including incidental purchasing costs.

☐ Self-constructed assets are stated at production cost, which includes capitalized interest, where applicable.

☐ Assets acquired at no cost to the company are stated at fair value at date of acquisition.

In 1945, 1959 and 1976 French corporations were permitted to perform a legal revaluation of assets, and the accounts of some companies may still include items carried at revalued amounts. Discretionary ("free") revaluations have been permitted since January 1, 1984, but only if all classes of property, plant and equipment and investments are revalued. The gain derived from the revaluation may not be credited to income but must be recorded as a separate component of shareholders' equity ("free revaluation reserve"). The reserve may be incorporated into capital stock but may not be written back to income at any time in the future. The reserve adjustment is subject to corporate income tax in the year in which the revaluation is performed. Upon sale of the revalued assets, a transfer to distributable reserves would be made.

At the time of disposal of an asset, the difference between the disposal proceeds and the net book value (i.e., historical or revalued cost, less accumulated depreciation) represents the gain or loss on disposal. The transaction is accounted for in nonrecurring income and expense from capital transactions, as follows:

☐ Net book value of the asset is a nonrecurring expense.

☐ Proceeds from sale are nonrecurring income.

Depreciation (Amortissements). Two methods of calculating **depreciation** are used:

☐ Book depreciation, which reflects the irreversible decline in value of an asset due to wear and tear, technological advances and so on. In practice, book depreciation consists of writing down the value of an asset over its estimated useful life, until the asset is entirely depreciated or reduced to its residual value, depending on the asset, according to a predetermined depreciation schedule. Accumulated depreciation is shown in the balance sheet as a reduction of the carrying value of the asset, and the depreciation charge (dotation aux amortissements) for the year is included in the income statement. The asset's estimated useful life is determined by management, based on past experience and industry practice. No specific depreciation method is recommended or prohibited but, in practice, the most common methods are **straight-line** (linéaire) and reducing (**declining**) **balance** (dégressif).

☐ Excess fiscal depreciation (amortissements dérogatoires), under which depreciation is charged solely to reduce the corporation's tax liability. Accumulated fiscal depreciation is included in shareholders' equity under the heading untaxed provisions (provisions réglementées), and the related charge for the year is classified as a nonrecurring expense in the income statement.

Temporary impairments in the carrying value of a fixed asset may be recognized through a provision for depreciation, which is deducted from the asset value. Reversals are written back to income.

Disclosure. Where material, the following information should be disclosed in the notes:

☐ Valuation methods applied, particularly those used to calculate depreciation.

☐ The effect of any fixed asset revaluation on the financial statements.

☐ An analysis of **fixed assets**, showing acquisitions and disposals for the year, and transfers between fixed asset categories.

☐ An analysis of accumulated depreciation and current year depreciation expense.

☐ Any capitalized interest included in the production cost of a self-constructed asset.

Reference. Business Code (Articles 12, D 7, D 8 and D 12) and General Accounting Plan.

14. Intangible Assets (Immobilisations Incorporelles)

Accounting Treatment. In general, the following are recorded as **intangible assets**:

☐ Start-up costs (i.e., incorporation expense and share capital issuance costs) that are essential to the existence, business or development of the entity but not attributable to the production of specific goods or services.

☐ Internal and external research and development expenditures, which may be capitalized in certain cases (see Section 25).

☐ Licenses, patents, trademarks, manufacturing processes and similar items, consisting of costs incurred to obtain the benefit represented by the legal protection granted to the inventor, author or holder of the right to exploit a patent, license and so on.

☐ Leasehold rights (droit au bail), which are amounts paid or due to a previous tenant as consideration for the transfer of a lease under a private agreement or the terms of legislation governing business property.

☐ Internally generated goodwill (fonds de commerce), representing the intangible components of a business (e.g., clientele) that are not valued and accounted for separately in the balance sheet but that contribute to maintaining or developing the company's business (purchased goodwill is accounted for separately).

☐ Purchased and internally developed software (logiciels) for internal use.

Valuation. Intangible assets are generally valued in accordance with the same principles as property, plant and equipment, that is, acquisition cost or production cost in the case of software and research and development expenditures. However, intangible assets may not be revalued, although internally generated goodwill could have been created under the 1976 legal revaluation.

Amortization. In principle, intangible assets are amortized if they have a finite useful life or are legally protected for a specified period. Intangibles that are deemed to have an infinite useful life, such as trademarks and internally generated goodwill, are not required to be amortized but any impairment in value should be recorded.

Disclosure. The following information must be disclosed:

☐ Valuation methods used.
☐ Changes in gross values, accumulated **amortization** and current year amortization expense.

Reference. Business Code (Article D 19) and General Accounting Plan.

15. Leases (Contrats de Location)

Classification. Leases are classified differently in the statutory financial statements and the consolidated financial statements.

☐ In the statutory financial statements, all leases are treated as **operating leases**.
☐ In the consolidated financial statements, **finance leases** may be capitalized. French law does not define finance leases, but they are generally understood to represent leases under which ownership is transferred at the end of the lease term, leases containing a bargain purchase option, leases whose term is equivalent to the useful life of the leased property or leases for which the present value of the minimum lease payments is equal to the fair value of the leased property at inception of the lease.

Accounting Treatment. Operating leases: The lease payments are expensed by the lessee and credited to income by the lessor in the period to which they relate.

Finance leases: The lessee records an asset and a debt, and the lease payments are allocated between interest expense and a reduction of debt. The lessor records a receivable, and the lease payments are allocated between interest income and a reduction of the receivable.

Leveraged Leases. **Leveraged leases** do not exist in France.

Disclosure. Statutory financial statements: The following information must be disclosed in a note:

☐ Value of the leased property at inception of the lease.

☐ Lease payments for the current and prior years.

☐ Depreciation expense for the current and prior years, as if the property had been acquired.

☐ Future minimum lease payments by due date and residual value at the end of the lease term, if applicable.

Consolidated financial statements: The following information must be disclosed:

☐ Capitalized values, by category.

☐ Depreciation method used.

☐ Amount of debt carried in the balance sheet, separated into current, due beyond one year and within five years, and due beyond five years.

Reference. Law of July 24, 1966 (Articles L 357-7 and L 357-8) and General Accounting Plan.

16. Investments (Placements)

Valuation. Investments, depending on their nature, are classified as current or noncurrent. Current investments (marketable securities) are investments that management intends to dispose of within a short time.

Current investments: Current investments are stated at the lower of cost or probable transaction value. This latter notion is defined for quoted investments as the investment's average market value for the final month of the accounting period; for unquoted investments, it is determined judgmentally. Provisions for declines in value are determined on an individual line-by-line basis. However, there are two situations where investments may be valued on an aggregate **(portfolio) basis**:

☐ If the investments are quoted and constitute a highly liquid portfolio.

☐ If market values have fallen abnormally and this decline appears to be temporary.

Noncurrent investments (Immobilisations financieres): Noncurrent investments are stated at the lower of cost or their useful value to the investor. This latter value is determined judgmentally. Investments are valued on an individual line-by-line basis and may not be valued on a portfolio basis.

Treatment of Valuation Reserves. As explained above, a decline in the value of noncurrent investments is provided for, but unrealized gains are not recognized. Investments cannot be revalued upward.

However, there is one exception to this principle; it concerns investments in companies under the control of a parent company that prepares consolidated financial statements (Articles L 340-4 and D 245). These investments can be valued in the parent company's individual financial statements on the basis of the parent's share in the underlying net assets (equity method); the difference arising from an upward adjustment of the share in net assets is not credited to income (and therefore not tax-effected) but is recorded as a separate component of shareholders' equity. However, if the parent company's share in net assets is adjusted downward, the difference is first applied to any reserve relating to a previous upward adjustment of the same investment and then charged against income. Companies that elect to use this method must apply it to all investments in companies over which they exercise control.

Gains/Losses. Gains or losses from the disposal of current investments are presented in the financial income/expense section of the income statement (résultat financier). For noncurrent investment disposals, the cost of the investment is shown as a nonrecurring expense and the proceeds from the sale as nonrecurring income. Prior investment value adjustments on investments sold are not taken into account in determining gains and losses on the sale; the reversal is shown as nonrecurring income (for noncurrent investments) or financial income (for current investments).

Disclosure. Disclosure requirements include a description of accounting policies, details of changes in noncurrent investments during the year and, for each shareholding in excess of 10 percent, details of the percentage interest held and the equity and latest results and financial position of the investee.

Reference. Business Code (Articles D 7, D 8 and D 15) and General Accounting Plan.

17. Accounts Receivable (Créances)

Accounting Treatment. Recognition of revenue, and hence the related receivable, is described in Section 23.

Discounts: Receivables are normally recorded net of trade discounts. Cash discounts are normally recorded at the time of payment.

Provision for doubtful accounts: No specific method is stipulated in determining a provision for doubtful accounts. General provisions are rare, and specific provisions tend to be calculated only in extreme cases. The reason for this lack of a consistent, general practice is the historical link in France between accounting treatment and treatment for tax purposes, which tended to permit a deduction only in cases of pending or proven receivership/liquidation. The position is evolving.

Factored receivables: Under French law, **factoring** is an arrangement that leads to a real transfer of the risk of nonpayment to the factor. Consequently, the trade receivables transferred are immediately removed from the accounts, and the related expenses and financing commission deducted by the factor are simultaneously charged against profit.

Disclosure. Receivables are classified in the notes as short term (receivable within one year) or long term. If there are discounted bills, the total value of such bills should be shown in the note on commitments.

Reference. General Accounting Plan.

18. Inventories and Work in Progress (Stocks et en-Cours)

General Accounting Treatment. **Inventories** are carried at the lower of cost or either realizable value or replacement cost. This comparison should be made on an item-by-item basis. Only two methods of determining cost are permitted for statutory financial statements: weighted average and **FIFO**. For consolidated financial statements the **LIFO method** can be used. If inventories are manufactured, costs are determined using **absorption costing**. If the actual activity for the period is less than normal, costs are imputed as if production were at normal operating levels; the excess overhead is expensed.

Long-Term Contracts. Revenue recognition for long-term contracts is covered in Section 23. Progress billings are not deducted from work in progress in the balance sheet. Losses expected at contract completion should be provided for when they become probable.

Disclosure. The basis of valuation and methods used to determine write-downs below cost are disclosed in the notes. Inventories are shown by category in the balance sheet; no further disclosure is required.

Reference. Business Code (Articles 7 and 8); General Accounting Plan; and Decree of March 23, 1967 (Article D 248-8).

19. Current Liabilities (Dettes à Court Terme)

General Accounting Treatment. **Current liabilities** are not shown separately in the balance sheet. However, in the notes, debts are disclosed separately by maturity under the headings current, due beyond one year and within five years, and due beyond five years.

In the statutory balance sheet, liabilities are separated into the following classes, which may be combined in the consolidated balance sheet:

- □ Customer advances.
- □ **Accounts payable**—trade (dettes fournisseurs et comptes rattachés), including accruals for goods received but not yet invoiced and net of accruals for credit notes and discounts (representing debts arising in the normal course of business).
- □ Accrued taxes, social security taxes and personnel costs.
- □ Other debts.
- □ Deferred income (produits constatés d'avance).

Creation of General and Specific Provisions. The creation of general provisions is not normally permitted in France. Known potential liabilities and charges that can be reasonably estimated are provided for on the balance sheet under provisions for **contingencies** (see Section 21). Known accrued charges about which there exists a degree of uncertainty concerning the due date or the exact amount are included in the balance sheet items listed above at the company's best estimate.

Disclosure.   In addition to debts by maturity date, information on accrued charges included in the different classes of liabilities and debts represented by trade notes should be presented in the notes.

Reference.   Business Code (Article D 23) and General Accounting Plan.

20.   Long-Term Debt (Dettes à Long Terme)

General Accounting Treatment.   As mentioned above, debts are not separated in the balance sheet between long and short term, but total current items and total noncurrent items are shown below the balance sheet total and a more detailed analysis is given in the notes. Similarly, bank overdrafts and short-term borrowings (concours bancaires courants) are included in bank borrowings (emprunts et dettes auprès des établissements de crédit) in the balance sheet, but the total is also indicated under the balance sheet total.

Debts are shown in the balance sheet by type (although certain items may be combined in the consolidated balance sheet), as follows:

☐   Convertible bonds (emprunts obligataires convertibles).
☐   Other bonds (autres emprunts obligataires).
☐   Bank borrowings.
☐   Other debts.

Accrued interest at period-end is included under the above headings.

Loans are always carried in the balance sheet at their outstanding principal amount. Bond redemption premiums (primes de remboursement des obligations) are included in assets and amortized pro rata to accrued interest or by the straight-line method over the life of the loan.

Debt Restructuring.   In France, there are no specific accounting principles related to debt restructuring. Normal practice consists of recording the resulting gains or losses in income at the time of the restructuring.

Debt Extinguishment.   For accounting purposes, a debt is considered extinguished when it has been repaid in full or has been subject to an in-substance **defeasance**.

An in-substance defeasance, which is a new concept in France inspired by US practice, must meet the following conditions to be recorded:

☐   The transfer of the debt to the trustee must be irrevocable.
☐   The securities transferred must be used solely to service the debt, they must be denominated in the same currency as the debt and the due dates for principal and interest payments must match those of the debt.

Under French accounting practice, commissions paid in connection with an in-substance defeasance and the difference between the value of the securities and the amount of the debt on the defeasance date are included in nonrecurring items.

Disclosure.   The notes should include a detailed breakdown of convertible bonds, indicating the number of bonds outstanding, the nominal amount and the rights attached to the bonds. Details of in-substance defeasances must be disclosed in a note in the year in which they occur; the outstanding balance must be disclosed annually until the debt has been repaid.

Reference.   Business Code (Article D 24); General Accounting Plan; and In-substance defeasances: Pronouncement No. 76 issued by the National Accounting Board.

21.   Contingencies (Eventualités)

Contingent Losses.   Contingent losses are provided for in the following instances:

- [ ]   The specific exposure or loss is clearly identifiable.
- [ ]   The probability of the exposure or loss occurring results from events in progress at year-end or known by management at the time of the year-end closing.

If the loss or exposure is not certain, general provisions for contingencies or provisions based on past experience may be set up.

Contingent Gains.   Contingent gains are not recognized in the financial statements.

Disclosure.   The existence of contingencies that have not been provided for must be disclosed in a note, indicating why no provision has been set up. Where possible, an estimate of the amount involved should be given or an explanation of why no estimate can be made.

Reference.   Business Code (Article 14) and General Accounting Plan.

22.   Capital and Reserves (Capitaux Propres)

General.   Shareholders' equity is generally divided between **share capital**, premiums, revaluation reserves and other reserves.

Share Capital (Capital Social).   The share capital (number of shares and **par value**) must be indicated in the company's articles of incorporation. At least one-quarter of the par value of the shares must be paid up for the shares to be considered subscribed. The share capital included in equity always corresponds to the subscribed capital; any uncalled (i.e., unpaid) fraction is shown on the asset side of the balance sheet.

A company's share capital may consist of different classes of shares, each class characterized by different voting and dividend rights.

A company may acquire its own shares to cancel them or to stabilize the price quoted on the stock market or for allocation to employees, for example, under stock option plans.

Premiums (Primes). Premiums represent the difference between the par value of shares and the price at which they are issued. The issue price must be at least equal to the par value. When a company acquires its own shares to cancel them, the difference between the price paid and the par value of the shares is charged to premiums.

The proceeds derived from the issue of unattached warrants (bons autonomes de souscription) are also included in premiums. However, if the warrants are attached to bonds, the proceeds are included in debt.

Revaluation Reserves.   (See Sections 13 and 16.)

Other Reserves.   Other reserves include:

☐ The legal reserve (Réserve légale)—Each year, 5 percent of net income must be appropriated to the legal reserve until the reserve equals 10 percent of share capital.

☐ Untaxed reserves (Réserves réglementées)—Untaxed reserves include primarily income taxed at a reduced rate; if the reserves are distributed, additional tax becomes payable.

☐ Other reserves—Appropriations to other reserves are decided by the shareholders.

☐ Special translation reserve (Ecarts de conversion) in the consolidated balance sheet— The special translation reserve, which is created only on consolidation, includes differences arising on translation of the financial statements of consolidated foreign subsidiaries (see Section 6).

Although they are not included in reserves, investment subsidies (subventions d'investissement) (see Section 24) and untaxed provisions (excess fiscal depreciation [see Section 13] and special provisions for tax purposes) are nevertheless included in shareholders' equity in the statutory financial statements. In the consolidated financial statements, these items are restated. This restatement involves reclassifying the investment subsidies and any deferred taxes connected with untaxed provisions as liabilities.

Other Equity.   Permanent capital raised on the money markets and repayable at the discretion of the company is classified as near equity (autres fonds propres). Near equity is shown on a separate line on the liability side of the balance sheet, between debt and shareholders' equity, if the company does not intend to effect repayment in the foreseeable future. However, in the consolidated balance sheet near equity may be included in shareholders' equity if no interest is payable because the issuer does not report adequate income.

Distribution Restrictions.   If start-up costs or research and development expenditures have been capitalized (see Section 25), and other reserves represent less than the unamortized value of these expenses, no dividend may be paid. In addition, the legal reserve may not be distributed in any circumstances.

Disclosure.   The breakdown of share capital by class of shares at the beginning and end of the period must be disclosed in a note. Changes in revaluation reserves should also be presented. If any stock options, warrants or equivalent securities are outstanding, the following information must be given:

□ Details of the issue—Amount, number, price and exercise period.

□ Number of securities outstanding and number of shares issued during the year.

Reference. Business Code (Article D 13); General Accounting Plan; and Pronouncement No. 75 issued by the National Accounting Board.

ACCOUNTING PRINCIPLES FOR SPECIFIC ITEMS— INCOME STATEMENT

23. Revenue Recognition (Constatation des Produits)

General Principles. Revenue is recognized when services have been provided or goods have been delivered.

The notion of delivery is generally considered to be the relinquishing of the item sold to the protection and possession of the purchaser. At this point, title to the goods normally transfers to the purchaser, and the vendor recognizes the sale as complete.

Long-Term Contracts (Contrats de Longue Durée). Revenue may be recognized by either the **completed contract method** (méthode de l'achèvement) or the **percentage of completion method** (méthode du pourcentage d'avancement), which is recommended by the Institute of Public Accountants (Avis P.C. 25). For the percentage of completion method to be acceptable, a number of conditions must be fulfilled:

□ The accounting system must be capable of determining the exact status of work in progress.

□ The purchaser must agree as to the work carried out.

□ Reliable forecast figures concerning the contract must exist.

□ It must be possible to calculate the overall profit with some degree of certainty.

Instalment Sales (Ventes à Tempérament). **Instalment sales** are generally recognized as outright sales when the goods are delivered to the purchaser.

Rights of Return. Recognition of revenue from sales where the right of return exists depends largely on the nature of the transaction or industry practice. If the likelihood of return is considered minimal, there would be no reason not to recognize the sale on delivery of the goods. However, it may be considered advisable to set up a provision for returns if prior experience shows that some goods are likely to be returned.

Sales with reservation of title (Ventes avec clause de réserve de propriété), that is, where the seller retains title to the goods, should be recognized based on commercial substance over legal form. Revenue should be recognized when the goods are delivered, with appropriate disclosure.

Product Financing. **Product financing arrangements**, which are agreements to sell a product and to buy it back at a later date, are not specifically dealt with in French standards. However, in this case legal form would take precedence over substance, and the transaction would be treated as a sale and not as a financing transaction.

Disclosure.   Revenue recognition methods for long-term contracts must be disclosed in the notes.

Reference.   General Accounting Plan and Institute of Public Accountants Recommendation P.C. 11 and Avis P.C. 25.

24. Government Grants and Assistance (Subventions et Aides Publiques)

Accounting Treatment.   Government grants and assistance are classified into two categories; the accounting treatment is different for each.

Operating subsidies (Subventions d'exploitation), which are grants to promote the creation of new employment and to promote research, are included in operating revenues when received; however, recognition may be deferred if the funds are used to finance capitalized research expenditures (see Section 25).

Investment subsidies (Subventions d'investissement), which are used to finance part of the cost of additions to fixed assets, may be either included in nonrecurring income when received or recorded as a separate component of shareholders' equity in the statutory accounts or as a noncurrent liability in the consolidated accounts (see Section 22) and written back to income to match the depreciation charged on the corresponding fixed assets.

Disclosure.   The method used to account for grants and assistance must be disclosed in the notes.

Reference.   General Accounting Plan.

25. Research and Development (Frais de Recherche et Développement)

Definition.   Research and development expenditures are defined as expenditures for work carried out by a company on its own behalf in the areas of basic and applied research and experimental development. This definition excludes expenses incorporated in the production cost of products ordered by third parties, which are normally expensed or included in work in progress.

Accounting Treatment.   Research and development expenditures are normally expensed as incurred. However, research and development expenditures may be capitalized as intangible assets if the following conditions are fulfilled:

☐   The project is clearly defined and the costs attributed to it can be identified.
☐   The technical or commercial feasibility of the product or process has been established.

Capitalized research and development expenditures must normally be amortized over a maximum of five years. There are no clearly established rules concerning the starting date for amortization; consequently, amortization may be charged either from the date on which the expenditure is capitalized or from the date on which the product or process is first marketed or used.

If the project subsequently proves to be unsuccessful, the unamortized capitalized costs are written off immediately as a nonrecurring expense. Once written off, expenditures should not be reinstated, even if the situation reverses.

Disclosure. The following information should be disclosed, if material:

☐ Components of capitalized research and development expenditures.

☐ Any departures from the rules providing for amortization over a maximum of five years.

☐ Valuation methods used to determine capitalized expenditures.

☐ Amortization method.

Reference. Institute of Public Accountants Information Note No. 3 and General Accounting Plan.

26. Capitalized Interest Costs (Incorporation de Charges Financières à des Eléments d'Actif)

Accounting Treatment. Inventory: If the production cycle exceeds 12 months (this specific condition does not apply to consolidated financial statements), the interest cost on funds borrowed to finance production may be included in the value of inventory. In practice, this principle applies only to a very limited number of industry segments (such as construction).

Property, plant and equipment: Interest costs incurred during the construction period of self-constructed assets and assets manufactured by subcontractors may be capitalized. However, the capitalized interest cost may not exceed the total interest expense incurred by the company during the period.

Disclosure. The amount of any interest capitalized, by class of asset, is required to be disclosed.

Reference. Business Code (Article D 7-2) and Institute of Public Accountants Recommendation P.C. 19.

27. Imputed Interest (Actualisation de Dettes ou Créances)

General. Interest is discounted only on loans and receivables granted at exceptionally favorable terms, including:

☐ Sales made with exceptional deferred payment terms.

☐ Long-term loans at exceptionally low interest rates.

Accounting Treatment. At present, there is a significant difference of opinion in France concerning the accounting treatment of **imputed interest**.

☐ The National Accounting Board believes that these loans and receivables should be stated at their nominal value, without discounting.

☐ The Institute of Public Accountants and the Stock Exchange Commission believe that they should be stated at fair value; that is, that they should be discounted so they produce a constant periodic rate of return approximating the market rate.

☐ The Institute of Statutory Auditors believes that these loans should be stated at their "useful" value and therefore can be written down.

In practice, companies may choose any one of these methods, although any discount provision would be disallowed for tax purposes.

Disclosure. If the amounts involved are material, the method used and its impact on the financial statements must be disclosed in a note.

28. Extraordinary or Unusual Items (Eléments Exceptionnels ou Inhabituels)

Definitions. Under French accounting standards, all events that do not relate to the day-to-day operation of the business are classified as exceptional or nonrecurring (résultat exceptionnel). This definition is very broad and includes both nonrecurring items and extraordinary or unusual items outside the ordinary operations of the reporting entity. In particular, nonrecurring income and expense includes:

☐ All forms of penalties paid or received.
☐ Gains and losses on disposals of fixed assets.
☐ Subsidies granted.

Accounting Treatment. Whatever the amount involved, nonrecurring items are reported in the nonrecurring income and expense section of the income statement. No distinction is made in the income statement between tax on nonrecurring items and tax on continuing operations.

Disclosure. The amount of any income taxes related to nonrecurring items must be disclosed in the notes.

Reference. Business Code (Article D 14).

29. Income Taxes (Impôts sur les Bénéfices)

Accounting Treatment. Income taxes are treated differently in the statutory financial statements and the consolidated financial statements.

Statutory financial statements: Despite the February 1987 recommendation by the Institute of Public Accountants that deferred taxes be accounted for, present French accounting principles require only current taxes (i.e., the amount currently payable) to be recorded.

In particular, the only tax losses that may give rise to the recognition of a deferred tax asset are those effectively eligible for carryback under French tax rules. In such cases, current tax profit is accounted for in the year in which the loss is incurred.

Consolidated financial statements: Deferred taxes are recorded in the consolidated financial statements. Companies may choose between the **deferral method** (méthode du report fixe) and the **liability method** (méthode du report variable) and between partial and full recognition of timing differences; the Institute of Public Accountants recommends the use of the liability method and full recognition of all timing differences.

The future tax benefits attributable to tax loss carryforwards may be recognized if it is probable that they will be realized. Reasonable probability is deemed to exist if:

- ☐ The losses can be offset against deferred tax liabilities.
- ☐ The losses correspond to an exceptional, nonrecurring loss.
- ☐ There is a strong probability that the company will earn profits in the future.

Disclosure. Statutory financial statements: The tax effect of timing differences should be disclosed.

Consolidated financial statements: The method used should be disclosed in a note.

Reference. Decree of March 23, 1967 (Articles D 248-11 and D 248-7).

30. Postretirement Benefits (Prestations de Retraite)

General. Two types of pension plans exist in France.

Defined contribution plans: These plans, which are always externally funded, may be compulsory (government-sponsored plans) or voluntary (initiated by the employer).

Defined benefit plans: These plans, which may be funded internally or externally, provide for the payment of either a life annuity or a lump sum upon retirement.

Other types of postretirement benefits generally do not exist. In specific instances where they exist, they should be accounted for in the same way as pensions.

Accounting Treatment. Defined contribution plans: These plans are funded by contributions made by both employees and employers based on current salaries. Employers' contributions are expensed when paid. Substantially all pension costs incurred by French companies are for defined contribution plans that are government sponsored.

Defined benefit plans: In the absence of specific rules, common practice is to distinguish between liabilities relating to retired employees, which are provided for, and commitments for employees who have not yet reached retirement age, which may or may not be provided for, at the discretion of the company. Provisions for pensions are calculated based on actuarial assumptions. The most common method used to provide for commitments for employees who have not yet reached retirement age is the accrued benefit method, prorated based on years of service.

The effect of changes in actuarial assumptions and the adoption of new plans on past service costs can be deferred and amortized over the expected average remaining service life of the employee group concerned.

Pension Fund Surpluses. As very few commitments under defined benefit plans are funded in France, no pronouncements have been issued on this topic.

Disclosure. Companies are required to disclose details of defined benefit pension plans and the accounting principles adopted for each such plan. The amount of any unfunded commitments must also be disclosed. The calculation method used for funded and unfunded commitments must be described, and directors' pension commitments must be disclosed separately.

Reference.   Business Code (Article 9); General Accounting Plan; Recommendation P.C. 16 of the Institute of Public Accountants; and Institute of Statutory Auditors Bulletin No. 62.

31.   Discontinued Operations (Arrêts d'Activité)

Accounting Treatment.   There is no prescribed accounting method for discontinued operations in France. However, in practice the total net cost resulting from a business closure or the reorganization of a business segment is normally recognized when the decision to discontinue operations is made. The net cost includes probable losses on the sale or scrapping of fixed assets (net of related gains), operating expenses up to the date of closure or reorganization and the cost of any planned layoffs.

Disclosure.   The net costs relating to discontinued operations are reported as nonrecurring expense. If material, the discontinued operations may be described in a note.

32.   Earnings per Share (Résultats par Action)

General.   There is no formal accounting standard prescribing the disclosure of earnings per share in the financial statements. However, this information must be given in the schedule included in the report of the board of directors summarizing the company's business results for the past five years. Earnings per share are generally computed by dividing net income by the number of shares outstanding.

If a company has issued warrants, diluted earnings per share must be disclosed in a note. There is no prescribed method for calculating diluted earnings per share. At present, earnings per share information is not disclosed by all French corporations.

Reference.   Warrants: National Accounting Board Pronouncement No. 75.

Appendix
DO FRENCH STANDARDS OR PREVALENT PRACTICE SUBSTANTIALLY COMPLY WITH INTERNATIONAL ACCOUNTING STANDARDS?

Section	Topic	Substantially complies with IAS?	Comments
3.	Basic accounting concepts and conventions	Yes	Except that accounting for a transaction follows its legal form in France rather than its substance
	Contents of financial statements	No	No cash flow statement or statement of changes in financial position is required
4.	Business combinations*	Yes	
5.	Joint ventures	Yes	
6.	Foreign currency translation*	Yes	Except that unrealized gains are generally deferred
8.	Accounting changes*	Yes	
9.	Prior period adjustments*	Yes	
10.	Post balance sheet events	Yes	Except that nonadjusting events are required to be disclosed only if they are likely to affect the going concern assumption
11.	Related party transactions	No	
12.	Segmental information	No	
13.	Property, plant and equipment*	Yes	Except that accelerated depreciation is permitted in the statutory financial statements
15.	Leases	No	Capitalization of finance leases occurs only in consolidated financial statements and remains optional
16.	Investments	Yes	
17.	Accounts receivable	Yes	
18.	Inventories and work in progress*	Yes	
19.	Current liabilities	Yes	

Appendix (*Continued*)

Section	Topic	Substantially complies with IAS?	Comments
20.	Long-term debt	Yes	
21.	Contingencies	Yes	
22.	Capital and reserves	Yes	
23.	Revenue recognition*	Yes	
24.	Government grants and assistance	Yes	
25.	Research and development*	Yes	
26.	Capitalization of interest costs*	Yes	
28.	Extraordinary or unusual items*	No	
29.	Income tax**	Yes	Except that tax effect accounting is required only in consolidated financial statements
30.	Postretirement benefits*	No	

*These topics are subject to change as a result of the IASC Improvements Project—see the appendix to the International Accounting Standards chapter.

**The IAS on accounting for taxes on income is currently being revised, and an exposure draft has been issued.

Comparison in this table is made to International Accounting Standards in force at January 1, 1993. For further details, see the International Accounting Standards chapter.

GERMANY

GENERAL NATIONAL INFORMATION

1. Source of Generally Accepted Accounting Principles (Quellen der Rechnungslegungsgrundsätze)

Generally Accepted Accounting Principles and Accounting Standards.   Both German **accounting principles** and **standards** are derived predominantly from the German Commercial Code, generally observed accounting practices that have developed in the form of uncodified standard practices and through tax court rulings, pronouncements of the German Institute of Certified Public Accountants (Institut der Wirtschaftsprüfer) and the German Stock Corporation Law and Limited Liability Companies Law as they pertain to companies with these legal structures.

2. Audit and Public Company Requirements (Prüfungs- und Publizitätspflichten)

Audits.   All medium-sized and large stock corporations and limited liability companies are required to have their annual financial statements audited. A company is classified as medium-sized or large if it meets two of the following three criteria for two successive years:

	Total assets in millions DM	Sales in millions DM	Number of employees
Medium-sized	3.9–15.5	8.0–32.0	51–250
Large	>15.5	>32.0	>250

Some partnerships and sole proprietorships, because of their size, are regulated by the Law on Disclosure Requirements for Large Enterprises and thus also require annual audits.

Shareholders of medium-sized and large enterprises are required to appoint independent auditors annually, who are then commissioned by management. Any German certified public accountant (Wirtschaftsprüfer) or association of certified public accountants in the form of a limited liability company or stock corporation is eligible for such appointment. Certified public accountants are required to be members of the German professional association.

The German Commercial Code requires independent auditors to report whether the financial statements comply with legal regulations, have been prepared in conformity with required accounting principles and give a true and fair view of the net worth, financial position and results of the enterprise. Within this legal framework, the German Institute of Certified Public Accountants is the auditing and reporting standard-setting body; it issues opinions and guidelines.

Public Companies. A German stock corporation wishing to have its shares traded on a German stock exchange requires the assistance of a credit institution that is represented on the exchange; the company must submit a listing application and a comprehensive listing prospectus to the exchange's admission panel. The stock exchanges do not impose significant continuing reporting requirements; rather, the reporting and publishing requirements for all **public companies**, listed and unlisted, are established in the German Commercial Code.

Publication and filing requirements vary according to the enterprise's size. Large companies must publish their financial statements, management report and appropriation of results in the German Federal Gazette and must file this material with the local Commercial Register within nine months after their fiscal year-end; medium-sized companies must file this material with the local Commercial Register within nine months, and notice of their compliance must be published in the Federal Gazette.

A German business entity's fiscal year cannot exceed 12 months.

GENERAL ACCOUNTING (ALLGEMEINES ZUR RECHNUNGSLEGUNG)

3. Financial Statements (Jahresabschluss)

Basic Accounting Concepts. Annual financial statements must be prepared using the **historical cost basis** of measurement and must strictly adhere to the **going concern** and **accrual concepts**. The **prudence concept** also has to be observed. It requires the recognition of all anticipated risks and losses arising up to the date of the balance sheet and becoming known up to the time of preparation of the financial statements, but prohibits recognition of any unrealized profits. The principle of individual valuation requires that an item-by-item approach be applied in any measuring process; offsetting assets against liabilities and income against expenses is not allowed.

Contents of Financial Statements. Financial statements of all companies include a balance sheet, income statement and notes, which are an integral part of the financial statements. A statement of retained earnings and a statement of cash flows or changes in financial position are not required. The Commercial Code requires that financial statements be prepared in a clear, understandable and complete manner; that both the balance sheet and income statement be presented for the current and preceding years; and that the beginning balance sheet agree with the closing balance sheet of the preceding year.

The notes to the financial statements must provide adequate explanations of the balance sheet and income statement and all additional details necessary for the financial statements to give a true and fair view of the net worth, financial position and results of the reporting entity. All companies are required by the Commercial Code to disclose certain information in the notes; medium-sized and large companies are required to make additional disclosures, and small companies may omit some disclosures.

The Commercial Code requires large and medium-sized stock corporations and limited liability companies to prepare an annual management report along with their financial statements. The management report must give a true and fair view of the company's economic progress and position and must also cover significant events that occurred subsequent to the balance sheet date and expected developments within the company and its markets. The management report is referred to in the independent auditors' report and must be submitted to shareholders. Large and medium-sized companies must publish the management report in the German Federal Gazette and/or file it with the local Commercial Register.

Format of Financial Statements. The format of German annual financial statements is prescribed by the Commercial Code, which reflects the provisions of the European Community (EC) Fourth Directive. While only one standard format is available for the balance sheet, the Code permits a choice between an operations-oriented format (disclosing cost of sales and gross profit) and a more general revenues-, costs- and expenses-oriented format for the income statement. There are four balance sheet captions that have not been incorporated into the standard balance sheet format but could gain significance in certain circumstances: unpaid contributions to subscribed capital, expenses incurred to start up or expand the business, deferred income tax assets, and deficit not covered by equity capital. In addition, a fifth balance sheet caption, special (liability) items, including an equity portion, while not included in the prescribed format, could gain significance in certain circumstances.

Disclosure of Accounting Policies. Among other prescribed disclosures, notes to financial statements must refer to the accounting policies and valuation methods used and provide justification for and quantification of any inconsistencies with the preceding year.

Reference. Commercial Code para. 284 et seq.

4. Business Combinations (Unternehmensverbindungen)

Principles of Consolidation. The Commercial Code requires in general that all domestic and foreign **subsidiaries** (i.e., companies over which the investor directly or indirectly exercises control) must be consolidated. In the **consolidated financial statements**, the net worth, financial position and results of the consolidated enterprises must be shown as if all enterprises formed a single business entity. The assets and liabilities of the enterprises included must be valued uniformly within the framework of methods available to the **parent company**. Deviations from the valuation methods applied in the parent's financial statements must be indicated and justified in the notes.

A parent company is exempted from preparing consolidated financial statements if total group assets or sales or the total number of employees does not meet certain size tests at the end of two successive years.

The Commercial Code also exempts parent companies from preparing consolidated financial statements if they are, in turn, subsidiaries of a parent company that is resident in a member state of the European Community and that prepares consolidated financial statements in accordance with the relevant provisions of the EC Directives, and provided that minority shareholders of the parent do not oppose the exemption.

A subsidiary may be excluded from consolidation if:

□ It is not significant in relation to the group's net worth, financial position and results;

□ Exercise of the parent company's rights in relation to the subsidiary's assets or management is seriously impaired;

□ The information required for consolidation purposes cannot be obtained without unreasonable expense or delay; or

□ The investment is held solely for the purpose of resale.

A subsidiary must be excluded from consolidation if its activities are so divergent from those of the other group enterprises that its inclusion would be detrimental to a true and fair presentation of the group's net worth, financial position and results.

Methods of Accounting for Business Combinations. Both the **purchase method** and the **pooling of interests method** are permitted. However, the pooling of interests method may be used only if at least 90 percent of the nominal value of the acquired shares was exchanged for shares in a group company and any cash consideration paid did not exceed 10 percent of the nominal value of the shares issued in the acquisition.

Control. Control is usually indicated if one of the following conditions is satisfied:

□ Ownership of the majority of voting rights.

□ Capacity of a shareholder to dominate the composition of the investee's management or supervisory board.

□ Capacity to exercise a dominating influence based on a contract of domination concluded with the investee company or based on its bylaws.

Goodwill. The difference between the fair value of the identifiable net assets acquired in a business combination and the fair value of the consideration given is recorded as **goodwill**. It may be capitalized as an intangible fixed asset and amortized either over four years or systematically over the years that the company is likely to benefit from it. (For income tax purposes, however, the amortization period is fixed at 15 years.) Alternatively, goodwill may be charged to reserves on the face of the consolidated balance sheet.

Negative goodwill is shown on the consolidated balance sheet as "difference arising on capital consolidation" and may be included in future income only if certain conditions are met.

Equity Accounting. If a company that is included in the consolidated financial statements of a group holds a participation in another (unconsolidated) enterprise for the purpose of establishing a long-term business connection with that enterprise, and if significant influence can be exercised over the business and financial policies of that enterprise, the investment is accounted for by the **equity method**. The existence of such significant influence is assumed if the investor holds at least 20 percent of the voting rights in the investee.

Minority Interests. The Commercial Code requires that **minority interests** in the equity of consolidated subsidiaries be separately disclosed in the equity section of the consolidated balance sheet and that the profit or loss attributable to such minority interests be shown separately in the consolidated income statement.

Disclosure. The Commercial Code prescribes the following minimum disclosures to be made in the notes to the consolidated financial statements:

- ☐ The accounting and valuation methods applied, inconsistencies, their justification and a quantification of their effects on the net worth, financial position and results of the group.
- ☐ The basis for translation of foreign currency financial statements.
- ☐ The name and legal seat of, and the size of the investment in, subsidiary companies included in the consolidation and companies accounted for by the equity method.
- ☐ Reasons for excluding from consolidation or equity accounting companies that would normally have been required to be included.

The consolidated financial statements must be supplemented by a group management report, which, among other disclosures, is required to give a true and fair view of the group's economic progress and position and also cover significant post balance sheet events and expected developments within the group and its markets. The group management report must be referred to in the independent auditors' report on the consolidated financial statements.

Reference. Commercial Code para. 313 et seq.

5. Joint Ventures

German accounting legislation and literature provide no precise definition of **joint ventures** (Gemeinschaftsunternehmen). As a result, it is not unusual for this term to be applied to a variety of situations. For purposes of this book, joint ventures are business undertakings that are jointly controlled by two or more enterprises, regardless of whether the joint ventures are incorporated and regardless of their purpose or intended duration.

Accounting by Joint Venture Entities. If joint ventures are organized as partnerships or corporations, their accounting is governed by the general accounting provisions of the German Commercial Code. Other joint ventures are subject only to bookkeeping rules for tax purposes. Normally, however, it is in the venturers' best interests to ensure that joint ventures observe general commercial rules.

Accounting for Joint Ventures in the Venturers' Single-Entity Financial Statements. Venturers would normally classify an investment as a "participating interest" on their balance sheet and carry it at cost; if the investment has declined in value it may be written down to current value, and must be written down if the decline is considered permanent. Accounting for an investment in joint ventures on the equity basis in single-entity financial statements is not permitted. Venturers organized as corporations and owning an interest of not less than 20 percent must disclose in the notes to their financial statements the name and domicile of joint ventures and the size of their interest. In the unusual event where the interest exceeds 50 percent, disclosure must also be made of the joint venture's net worth and its most recent annual profit or loss.

Accounting for Joint Ventures in the Venturers' Consolidated Financial Statements. The most common method of accounting for investments in joint ventures is the equity method (see Section 4). However, in this isolated case the Commercial Code also permits

proportionate consolidation (Quotenkonsolidierung). If a co-venturer belongs to the same group of companies, but has been excluded from consolidation as may be permitted or even required by the provisions of the Commercial Code in certain circumstances (Section 4), the interests of all group companies must be added together and, if the aggregate exceeds 50 percent, full consolidation in lieu of equity accounting or proportionate consolidation is mandatory.

Transactions Between Venturers and the Joint Venture.   Accounting for such transactions depends on whether the transaction is related to the venturer's position as such or is based on a separate contractual relationship. Transactions relating to the venturer's capacity as an investor in the joint venture are accounted for as investment costs. Accounting for other transactions is governed by general arm's-length principles. **Accounts receivable** and **payable** arising from such a contract must be disclosed in the venturer's balance sheet separately from the carrying value of the investment.

Reference.   Commercial Code para. 310.

6.   Foreign Currency Translation (Fremdwährungsumrechnung)

General.   A distinction is made between reporting **foreign currency** denominated **transactions** and balances of domestic operations and translating financial statements of foreign operations.

Foreign Currency Transactions.   While foreign currency receivables and payables are initially recorded using the exchange rate prevailing at the transaction date, the translation at year-end is governed by the prudence concept. Accordingly, receivables should generally be reported at the lower, and payables at the higher, of the historical or the year-end exchange rate.

Translation of Foreign Financial Statements.   No specific requirements exist in German law or accounting principles as to which method must be used. However, strict consistency in the translation method and adequate disclosure in the notes are required. Any gain or loss resulting from the translation of foreign currency denominated financial statements may be recognized in the income statement or recorded in the equity section of the balance sheet, as long as the treatment is consistent from year to year.

Hedges.   German law has not established specific rules on accounting for futures contracts. **Generally accepted accounting principles** require in most cases that futures contracts be valued at the balance sheet date. Unrealized losses must be recognized, but unrealized gains may not be recognized.

   If an enterprise has hedged against a specific foreign currency receivable and the exchange rate at the balance sheet date indicates that the receivable, if unhedged, would have to be reduced, it is permissible to offset an unrealized gain from the hedging transaction against the unrealized loss inherent in the receivable. This is one of the rare exceptions to the rule that gains should not be offset against losses.

Disclosure.   The treatment of exchange and translation differences is disclosed in the notes, but amounts are normally not shown separately in the financial statements.

Reference.   Commercial Code paras. 284 and 313.

7.   Changing Prices/Inflation Accounting (Inflationsbereinigung)

With the relatively low inflation rates in Germany since the introduction of the Deutsche Mark in 1948, there has been no need for development of any accounting or reporting standards or rules addressing this subject. The basic rule that the historical cost of assets is the valuation ceiling prevents asset revaluations.

8.   Accounting Changes (Änderungen in den Bilanzierungs- und Bewertungsmethoden)

General.   A distinction is made between changes in the exercise of options granted by the Commercial Code (e.g., the inclusion on the balance sheet of expenses incurred to start up or expand an enterprise's business) and changes in the application of general measurement and valuation principles.

With respect to changes in the exercise of options granted by the Commercial Code, the consistency principle does not apply.

With respect to changes in the application of general measurement and valuation principles, the consistency principle may be departed from only in justifiable, exceptional circumstances. An exception to this rule is made for the use of valuation methods that are triggered solely by income tax savings considerations but that, to be effective for such purposes, also have to be applied for financial reporting purposes.

Disclosure.   Inconsistencies in the exercise of options granted by the Commercial Code must be disclosed in the notes. Changes in the application of general measurement and valuation principles must be justified in the notes, and their effect on net worth, financial position and results must be disclosed. The extent to which results for the year were influenced by valuation measures adopted solely for income tax savings reasons must also be disclosed in the notes.

Reference.   Commercial Code paras. 284 and 313.

9.   Prior Period Adjustments (Berichtigung vorhergehender Jahresabschlüsse)

Retrospective adjustments to prior period reported figures, other than those arising from reclassifications of items necessary to ensure consistency of presentation with current figures, are not permitted. Errors discovered subsequent to the submission of the audit report are corrected in the following year.

If the financial statements or management report is changed after the audit report has been submitted, the auditor would have to re-examine the related documents and report on the results.

Reference.   Commercial Code para. 316.

10.   Post Balance Sheet Events (Vorgänge von besonderer Bedeutung nach dem Schluss des Geschäftsjahrs)

Definition.   Accounting practice differentiates between post balance sheet events that provide further evidence of conditions that existed at the balance sheet date and those that are indicative of conditions that arose subsequent to that date.

Accounting Treatment. Events providing further evidence of conditions that existed at the balance sheet date that become known prior to the preparation of the financial statements are adjusted for in the financial statements. They then need no further disclosure.

Disclosure. The Commercial Code requires that significant post balance sheet events that are indicative of conditions that arose subsequent to the balance sheet date be disclosed in the management report.

Reference. Commercial Code paras. 289 and 315.

11. Related Party Transactions (Geschäftsbeziehungen mit verbundenen Unternehmen)

Definition. The Commercial Code defines related parties as affiliated enterprises, which, in turn, are defined as enterprises that are, or would be in the absence of specific exemptions, included in consolidated financial statements.

Accounting Treatment. Related party transactions are usually accounted for in accordance with normal accounting principles and practices. In most cases, income tax considerations will be a prime inducement to adhere strictly to the arm's-length concept.

Disclosure. The standard formats for the balance sheet and income statement provide for separate disclosure of investments (both current and long term) with related parties, as well as separate disclosure of certain income and expenses (notably interest) pertaining to related parties.

Reference. Commercial Code paras. 266 and 275.

12. Segmental Information (Angaben nach Tätigkeits- und geographischen Bereichen)

General. The Commercial Code requires disclosure in the notes of sales by type of activity as well as by geographically defined markets, to the extent that these activities and markets differ significantly from one other. No further details are required.

Reference. Commercial Code paras. 285 and 314.

ACCOUNTING PRINCIPLES FOR SPECIFIC ITEMS— BALANCE SHEET (RECHNUNGSLEGUNGSGRUNDSÄTZE—BILANZ)

13. Property, Plant and Equipment (Sachanlagen)

Classification of Capital and Revenue Expenditure. An expenditure is considered to be of a capital nature when an asset is created that is held by an enterprise for permanent use. An expenditure that does not give rise to such an asset, or does not represent a betterment to or replacement of a fixed asset already in existence, is charged to current income. **Fixed assets** costing DM 800 or less may also be charged to current income.

Basis of Valuation. Fixed assets are carried at cost of acquisition or construction, net of accumulated systematic **depreciation**. Carrying fixed assets at appraised values is not permitted.

Depreciation. The following depreciation methods are acceptable in Germany: **straight-line, declining balance, sum-of-the-years'-digits, unit of production** and hours of use. Sinking fund depreciation or any other method that initially results in a lower annual depreciation expense than the amount determined by the straight-line method, as well as the composite life and group basis methods of depreciation, are generally considered inappropriate.

Disclosure. The Commercial Code requires that fixed assets, whether tangible, intangible or financial, be presented, either on the face of the balance sheet or in a note, in a "grid" setting forth the following information for each line item:

- [ ] Historical cost brought forward at the beginning of the year and additions (at cost) and disposals (at cost) during the year.
- [ ] Transfers between line items.
- [ ] Current year depreciation.
- [ ] Accumulated depreciation at year-end.
- [ ] Net book values at the preceding and current year-end.

Reference. Commercial Code para. 268.

14. Intangible Assets (Immaterielle Vermögensgegenstände)

Accounting Treatment and Valuation. **Intangible** fixed **assets** such as franchises, patents, licenses and similar rights must be capitalized at cost if they have been acquired for consideration. Capitalization of goodwill is optional. Capitalization of self-generated intangibles not acquired for consideration is not permitted by the Commercial Code.

Amortization. The Commercial Code requires **amortization** of capitalized intangible fixed assets over their estimated useful lives. If goodwill has been capitalized, it is amortized over four years or systematically over the years that the company is likely to benefit from it. For income tax purposes, the amortization period is fixed at 15 years, starting with the year of initial capitalization.

Disclosure. The same disclosure is required as for tangible fixed assets (see Section 13).

Reference. Commercial Code paras. 248, 253 and 255.

15. Leases (Leasingverhältnisse)

Classification. Leases that transfer substantially all the risks and benefits usually associated with ownership without transferring the legal ownership as well are considered **finance leases**. In contrast, an **operating lease** is one in which the lessor effectively retains all the risks and benefits of ownership. Leases that are, in effect, **instalment sales** are always considered finance leases.

Accounting Treatment.   Finance leases: In most cases the accounting treatment of a finance lease follows its treatment for income tax reporting purposes. Accordingly, the accounting treatment depends on complex tax rules. Whether the leased asset is to be capitalized by the lessor or the lessee depends on a wide range of circumstances. These include criteria such as whether there is full pay-out to the lessor during the noncancellable period, whether the noncancellable lease period covers at least 40 percent but not more than 90 percent of the leased asset's normal useful life and whether the lease agreement includes a purchase or lease renewal option at the end of the noncancellable period; if it does, the accounting depends on the terms of the option. Capitalization by lessor or lessee is further dependent on the nature of the leased asset; that is, whether it is land, a building or a movable fixed asset. Each lease has to be dealt with on an individual basis.

Operating leases: For operating leases, the rental payments are expensed by the lessee and recorded as income by the lessor in the periods to which they relate.

Leveraged Leases.   **Leveraged leasing** is relatively uncommon in Germany; the accounting treatment would be substantially the same as for finance leases.

Disclosure.   Lease commitments that do not appear on the balance sheet but are significant to the entity's financial position are required by the Commercial Code to be disclosed in the notes.

Reference.   Commercial Code paras. 285 and 314.

16.   Investments (Beteiligungen)

Valuation.   General: Valuation of investments depends on their classification as current (securities) or long term (financial assets).

Current investments: Current investments, that is, those that are not intended as permanent investments of capital and are marketable, are carried at the lower of acquisition cost or market. A lower value may be used as of the balance sheet date if this would avoid a valuation change in the near future as a result of value fluctuations, or if the company can thereby avail itself of a lower valuation permitted for income tax purposes. Write-downs to such lower values must be reversed when the reasons for them no longer exist, unless tax regulations permit the written down values to be retained.

Long-term investments: The Commercial Code requires long-term investments to be carried at cost; equity accounting is not used in single-entity financial statements. If an investment that has been carried at cost has declined in value, it may be written down to current value; it must be written down to current value if the decline is considered permanent. The lower valuation may not be retained if the reasons for the diminution in value have ceased to exist, unless tax regulations permit this.

Gains/Losses.   When investments are disposed of, the profit or loss to be recognized is measured, on an individual basis, as the difference between the proceeds received and the book value at the time of disposal. The gain or loss is included in results of ordinary activities.

Disclosure.   Disclosure of changes in long-term investments during the year is required, as described in Section 13.

Reference.   Commercial Code paras. 253 and 271.

17.   Accounts Receivable (Forderungen)

Accounting Treatment.   Recognition: The recognition of revenues, and hence the related receivables, is described in Section 23.

Receivables due after (generally) one year that are noninterest bearing or bear interest at a rate lower than the prevailing commercial rate should be written down to their present value.

Discounts: Receivables are recorded at the invoiced amounts; cash discounts are recorded at the time they are taken by customers.

Allowances: Uncollectible amounts must be written off. To provide against collection risks, a flat rate provision is generally established for general credit risks and, together with any allowances for specifically known risks, is deducted directly from the receivables.

Factored Receivables.   Where accounts receivable have been factored, the trade receivables are replaced by a receivable against the factor. If the factor has recourse for uncollectible amounts, disclosure of the contingent liability and provision for probable losses must be made.

Disclosure.   The balance sheet format prescribed by the Commercial Code shows receivables subdivided into trade accounts, receivables from affiliated companies and other receivables (shown as part of other assets); amounts with a remaining term of more than one year must be identified.

Trade notes receivable are included with trade receivables.

Reference.   Commercial Code paras. 255, 266 and 268.

18.   Inventories and Work in Progress (Vorräte einschliesslich unfertige Erzeugnisse und Leistungen)

General Accounting Treatment.   The Commercial Code requires **inventories** to be carried at the lower of cost or market, market generally being represented by **replacement cost** if the valuation is governed by the procurement market (raw materials, maintenance materials, supplies) or **net realizable value** (sales values reduced by costs of completion, disposal and, at the option of the company, profit) if the valuation is governed by the sales market (work in process, finished goods). If the replacement cost of work in process or finished goods is lower than the net realizable value, replacement cost may be used for valuation purposes. Goods purchased for resale are carried at the lower of cost, replacement cost or net realizable value.

Inventory costs consist of purchase or manufacturing cost. Purchase cost is calculated net of discounts and allowances. Manufacturing cost includes the cost of direct material and labor and any specific production costs such as special molds and tools and manufacturing license expenses; it may, and generally does, include manufacturing and material overheads. Certain general administrative expenses may also be included, but not selling expenses.

Inventory cost is generally determined by **specific identification**. If this is not possible or feasible, the moving-average method is generally used. **FIFO** and **LIFO** methods are also permitted. The use of **standard costs** is allowed, but the actual purchase or manfacturing cost must be used if it is lower.

Long-Term Contracts.   The **completed contract method** is used in almost all cases in Germany (see Section 23). Work in process is valued accordingly.

Disclosure.   The Commercial Code requires inventories to be shown subdivided into raw materials and supplies, work in process, finished goods and goods purchased for resale, and advance payments made on inventory purchases.

The methods used in valuing inventories must be disclosed in the notes.

Costs accumulated under long-term construction-type contracts may be included on the balance sheet in work in process. It is generally preferable, however, to show them as a separate item (e.g., uncompleted orders). As an exception to the general rule prohibiting the offsetting of assets and liabilities, it is permissible to deduct customers' advance payments from work in process, provided that they can be matched with related work in process.

Reference: Commercial Code paras. 253, 255, 266 and 284.

19.   Current Liabilities (Kurzfristige Verbindlichkeiten)

General Accounting Treatment.   There is no authoritative definition of **current liabilities**. The Commercial Code subdivides them into accruals (with separate captions for pensions, taxes and other accrued liabilities) and accounts payable (with separate captions for debenture loans, amounts owed to credit institutions, trade payables, notes payable, amounts owed to affiliates and other payables). If any category of accounts payable includes amounts with a remaining term of more than one year, these amounts must be disclosed in total. Further, disclosure is required in the notes of the total amount of liabilities with a remaining term of more than five years.

A careful distinction is made in Germany between accruals and accounts payable. If there is no uncertainty as to the existence and amount of an obligation, the item must be included in accounts payable; if there is any uncertainty about either existence or amount, the item must be included in other accruals. If only the due date of an obligation is uncertain, it is presented as a payable.

While the concept of matching expenditures with related income is fundamental in Germany, the concept of prudence has priority. Accordingly, accruals must be set up for uncertain liabilities, impending losses from uncompleted business transactions, repairs and maintenance expenses to be incurred in the first three months of the following year and warranties performed without legal obligation. Uncertain liabilities are estimated liabilities for which it is either known or probable that an asset has been impaired or a liability incurred as of the balance sheet date.

Accruals: Accrued taxes include accruals for all types of estimated current and deferred taxes. When tax assessment notices are received, the related amounts are adjusted and reclassified to accounts payable.

Accounts payable: Trade payables include amounts owed to suppliers of goods and services and are recorded on receipt of the goods and services or the invoice, whichever occurs earlier. Amounts owed to affiliates include all types of liabilities, irrespective of reason or origin. Other payables include such items as accrued payroll, payroll withholdings, assessed taxes, sales agents' commissions and credit balances in trade accounts receivable.

Deferred income: Income received in advance, such as prepaid rental or interest income, is recognized as income when earned. It is deferred as a liability until that time. The Commercial Code specifies that deferred income be shown separately on the balance sheet.

Disclosure.   The Commercial Code requires that the total amount of secured liabilities be disclosed in the notes, stating the type and form of security.

Reference.   Commercial Code paras. 253, 266 and 285.

20.   Long-Term Debt (Langfristige Verbindlichkeiten)

General Accounting Treatment.   The most common forms of long-term debt in Germany are debenture loans and long-term bank loans. The general accounting treatment of these items is basically the same as for current liabilities, that is, they are included on the balance sheet at their face value as long as they continue to represent a present obligation of the entity.

Debt Restructuring.   There are no standards or rules addressing accounting for debt or **troubled debt restructurings**.

Debt Extinguishment.   There are no specific standards or rules on the subject of debt extinguishment.

Disclosure.   The Commercial Code requires the disclosure of security for long-term debt (see Section 19). Since troubled debt restructurings and early debt extinguishments are very rare in Germany, there are no disclosure rules for these items.

Reference.   Commercial Code paras. 253 and 285.

21.   Contingencies (Haftungsverhältnisse)

Contingent Losses.   The accounting treatment (accrual or disclosure only) is governed by the concept of prudence (see Section 19). Accordingly, all contingent losses that are likely to occur must be accrued on an estimated basis.

Contingent Gains.   Contingent gains are normally not recorded or disclosed.

Disclosure.   A contingent liability that has not been accrued must be disclosed on the face of the balance sheet or in the notes. The Commercial Code requires that the disclosure differentiate between contingent liabilities relating to:

- ☐   The issuance and transfer of notes receivable.
- ☐   Guarantees.
- ☐   Warranties.
- ☐   Security granted for third party liabilities.

Disclosure is required regardless of the existence of any contingent assets of equal value available to offset a contingent liability.

Reference. Commercial Code para. 251.

22. Capital and Reserves (Kapital und Rücklagen)

General. Shareholders' equity is divided between **share capital** and reserves. Reserves are classified as either capital or revenue reserves.

Share Capital. Authorized and issued capital is recorded at its aggregate nominal amount as subscribed capital. If there are separate classes of shares (e.g., ordinary and **preferred shares**), each class must be presented separately. If shares with multiple voting rights exist, details must be disclosed on the balance sheet.

Capital Reserves. Capital reserves include:

- □ Amounts received for the issue of shares (and warrants) in excess of their nominal value.
- □ Amounts paid for conversion rights or options, in excess of the stated value of debentures.
- □ Additional amounts paid in by shareholders in consideration of preferences awarded by the company.
- □ Any other additional payments made by shareholders in respect of subscribed capital.

Revenue Reserves. The Commercial Code differentiates between:

- □ Legal reserve.
- □ Reserve for treasury stock.
- □ Reserves prescribed by the company's articles.
- □ Other revenue reserves.

Legal reserve: The requirement to set up a legal reserve pertains only to public stock corporations (Aktiengesellschaft) and is prescribed by the German Stock Corporation Law. Five percent of each year's profit must be allocated to this reserve until, together with certain components of the capital reserves, it is equal to 10 percent of the **par value** of the share capital or such larger amount as the corporation's articles may prescribe.

Reserve for treasury stock: The Commercial Code requires that any holding of **treasury stock** or investment in shares of a controlling company must be offset by a reserve in a corresponding amount.

Reserves prescribed by the company's articles: These reserves comprise appropriations of earnings as prescribed by a company's articles; they may, but need not, be earmarked for certain purposes.

Distribution Restrictions. If a company elects to capitalize expenses incurred to start up or expand the business or elects to capitalize a deferred tax asset, profits may be distributed only if, after such distribution, the freely available revenue reserves plus retained profits less any accumulated losses brought forward are at least equal to the capitalized amounts.

Disclosure. According to the provisions of the Commercial Code, all activities during the year in the capital and reserve accounts must be disclosed in the balance sheet or notes. Public stock corporations must also disclose in the notes all acquisitions and disposals of treasury stock during the year, including the prices and the application of the proceeds, and details of convertible loans and similar securities and the rights represented by them.

Reference. Commercial Code para. 272 and Stock Corporation Law para. 150 et seq.

ACCOUNTING PRINCIPLES FOR SPECIFIC ITEMS— INCOME STATEMENT (RECHNUNGSLEGUNGSGRUNDSÄTZE— GEWINN- UND VERLUSTRECHNUNG)

23. Revenue Recognition (Die Vereinnahmung von Erträgen)

General Principles. The only published rule or standard on revenue recognition is the general provision of the Commercial Code that sales **revenues** as shown on the income statement are to comprise revenues from the sale and rental or leasing of products and goods and from the performance of services that are typical of the ordinary sales and service activities of an entity, net of sales reductions and **value added tax**. Revenue recognition is governed by the prudence concept, which prohibits the recognition of unrealized profits but requires the recognition of all anticipated risks and losses.

Long-Term Contracts. The completed contract method is used in almost all cases and recognizing any profit prior to contract completion is rare.

Instalment Sales. The fact that a purchase price is to be received in instalments does not prevent the seller from recognizing the transaction in full at the time of sale. If the related receivable is noninterest or low-interest bearing, it would be appropriate to record the receivable at a reduced amount (i.e., less **imputed interest**).

Rights of Return. There are no codified rules on this topic in Germany. If the terms of a sales contract give the customer a right to return the purchase for a refund, generally accepted accounting practice prohibits the recognition of profit and requires all estimated expenses associated with the return to be accrued.

Product Financing. **Product financing arrangements**, whereby an entity sells and simultaneously either agrees to repurchase the same or a substantially identical product or guarantees the resale price to third parties, are rare in Germany. Accordingly, there are no codified rules on this subject; the accounting treatment for such a transaction would be governed by the prudence concept.

Disclosure. There are no particular disclosure requirements with respect to revenue recognition.

Reference. Commercial Code para. 277.

24. Government Grants and Assistance (Zulagen und Zuschüsse der öffentlichen Hand)

Accounting Treatment. There is no codified accounting standard covering government grants and assistance. In practice, the accounting treatment of grants related to **capital expenditures** is different from that of assistance toward current expenses.

Grants Related to Capital Expenditures. If these grants are subject to income tax, they are usually netted against the acquisition or manufacturing cost of the related fixed asset. If they are income tax free, they are usually included directly in income.

Assistance Toward Current Expenses. These grants are included in income in the period in which the corresponding expense is recorded; accordingly, government assistance related to expenses of future periods is deferred until the corresponding expense is incurred.

Disclosure. Grants related to capital expenditures and included directly in income are shown with other operating income. Assistance toward current expenses is also included in other operating income; it is not acceptable to net the income against any corresponding expenses.

The policy adopted for government grants and assistance must be disclosed in the notes.

25. Research and Development (Forschungs- und Entwicklungskosten)

General. Research and development expenses are normally not capitalizable.

Disclosure. While there is no requirement to disclose the annual amount of research and development expenses, medium-sized and large companies are required to include in their annual management report and, where applicable, group management report, a general discussion of their research and development activities.

26. Capitalized Interest Costs (Zinsen für Fremdkapital)

Accounting Treatment. The Commercial Code specifies that interest on loan capital is not part of manufacturing cost, unless there is a close and identifiable relationship between the loan capital and an asset whose manufacture extends over a long period of time. If these criteria are met, companies may, but need not, capitalize interest cost.

Disclosure. If any interest costs have been included in manufacturing cost accumulated on long-term construction-type contracts or self-manufactured fixed assets, the Commercial Code requires disclosure thereof in the notes.

Reference. Commercial Code paras. 255 and 284.

27. Imputed Interest (Ab- und Aufzinsungen)

General. Imputation of interest in Germany occurs for the most part only in connection with receivables due after one year that are noninterest bearing or bear interest at a rate lower than the prevailing commercial rate (Section 17); or in discounting long-term liabilities to present value, for instance, pension accruals, or in connection with certain categories of securities (e.g., zero bonds).

Accounting Treatment. The book value of the receivable or liability is adjusted to reflect its present value as at the balance sheet date.

Disclosure. No specific disclosures are required.

28. Extraordinary or Unusual Items (Ausserordentliche und ungewöhnliche Posten)

Extraordinary or Unusual Items. Extraordinary income and expense are defined in the Commercial Code as items that arise outside the ordinary activities of an entity.

Items that are unusual on account of size or incidence but arise within the ordinary activities of the enterprise are not subject to any specific disclosure requirements. However, it is conceivable that lack of any related disclosure could significantly detract from the true and fair view that the financial statements are to provide and that, therefore, disclosure in the management report would be required.

Disclosure. The Commercial Code requires that the nature and amounts of extraordinary items be disclosed in the notes.

Reference. Commercial Code paras. 277, 289 and 315.

29. Income Taxes (Steuern vom Einkommen und Ertrag)

There are many areas in the German income tax regulations where an accounting method chosen for income tax purposes is required to be used for financial reporting purposes as well. Accordingly, there are relatively few differences in Germany between taxable income for financial reporting purposes and for tax reporting purposes.

The Commercial Code requires a net deferred tax liability to be recorded using the **liability method** when taxable income under tax regulations is lower than pretax accounting income. The recording of a deferred tax asset is optional, but if it is done, profits may be distributed only if, after such distribution, the freely available revenue reserves plus retained profits less any accumulated losses brought forward are at least equal to the recorded tax asset.

If eliminations made in the consolidation process have an effect on income, a deferred tax asset or liability must be recorded.

If a loss for tax purposes is carried back to recover taxes of the previous period, the recovery is recorded in the period in which the loss occurs.

Disclosure. Income taxes and other taxes must be shown separately on the income statement; however, current and deferred income taxes need not be separately shown. There is no allocation of related income taxes to extraordinary items. Income tax deferrals resulting from the consolidation process must be disclosed separately on the consolidated balance sheet or in the notes.

Reference.   Commercial Code paras. 274 and 306.

30.   Postretirement Benefits (Altersversorgung)

General.   It is widespread practice in Germany to accrue future pension obligations; funding of pension obligations is the exception rather than the rule. The pension accruals must cover all pension benefits granted to individuals after December 31, 1986. Benefits granted on or before that date (and subsequent changes to such benefits) are often, but need not be, covered by an accrual.

Accounting Treatment.   If actuarial calculations are based, as they usually are, on German tax regulations, they measure individually for each pension plan participant the total benefit obligation as the present value of the future benefits, net of the present value of assumed future premiums that would be payable if a life insurance policy had been purchased. In lieu of taking personnel fluctuations into account, the entry age into the pension plan is assumed to be 30 years for all participants.

The difference in the sum of these calculations for all plan participants between the current year and the preceding year constitutes one part of the pension expense (or income) for the year. The other part consists of the actual benefit payments during the current year.

Tax regulations permit consideration of the following actuarial factors only: the assumed mortality ages of employees, the risk of disability and an assumed interest factor (discount rate) of 6 percent (5% for companies in Berlin) used to compute the present value. Companies may use different discount rates for financial statement purposes. The fact that employees will receive salary increases throughout their employment, which will result in higher pension payments being ultimately paid than those based on their current salary level, is not permitted to be considered as an actuarial factor. Nor is it normal to include employee turnover as an actuarial factor, unless turnover is particularly high. Salary increases and turnover are normally considered only when they occur.

Until December 31, 1986 a company could choose either to charge all past and prior service costs to expense immediately or to spread them over three years when adopting a new or amending an existing pension plan. While this alternative is not available for new pension rights granted after December 31, 1986, it is still permissible to spread over three years increases in pension benefits granted up to that date.

Under the actuarial method used in Germany, actuarial gains and losses are recognized currently as adjustments of pension expense rather than spread over a number of years.

Postretirement benefits other than pension payments are rather uncommon in Germany; accordingly, no accounting standards have been developed in this respect.

Disclosure.   Disclosure is required in the notes of the methods and the interest rate used in the calculation of the year-end pension accrual. If, in comparison with the value of the total future pension obligation, the accrual is deficient, the amount of the deficiency must be disclosed. If benefits granted on or before December 31, 1986 have not been accrued, the related aggregate amount must be disclosed in the notes.

Reference: Commercial Code para. 253.

31. Discontinued Operations (Aufgegebene Geschäftstätigkeiten)

There is no prescribed accounting method for discontinued operations in Germany. Accordingly, there is no requirement to report the results of discontinued operations separately from those of an entity's ordinary activities.

32. Earnings per Share (Gewinn je Aktie)

It is neither a requirement nor usual practice in Germany to calculate or disclose earnings per share information.

Appendix
DO GERMAN STANDARDS OR PREVALENT PRACTICE SUBSTANTIALLY COMPLY WITH INTERNATIONAL ACCOUNTING STANDARDS?

Section	Topic	Substantially complies with IAS?	Comments
3.	Basic accounting concepts and conventions	Yes	Except that in certain circumstances, a transaction is accounted for in accordance with its legal form rather than its economic substance
	Contents of financial statements	No	No cash flow statement or statement of changes in financial position is required
4.	Business combinations*	Yes	
5.	Joint ventures	Yes	
6.	Foreign currency translation*	No	
8.	Accounting changes*	Yes	
9.	Prior period adjustments*	No	
10.	Post balance sheet events	Yes	
11.	Related party transactions	No	
12.	Segmental information	No	
13.	Property, plant and equipment*	Yes	German standards do not permit property, plant and equipment to be carried at valuation
15.	Leases	No	
16.	Investments	Yes	
17.	Accounts receivable	Yes	
18.	Inventories and work in progress*	Yes	
19.	Current liabilities	Yes	
20.	Long-term debt	Yes	
21.	Contingencies	Yes	Except that there is no requirement to disclose the existence of contingent gains
22.	Capital and reserves	Yes	
23.	Revenue recognition*	Yes	

Appendix (*Continued*)

Section	Topic	Substantially complies with IAS?	Comments
24.	Government grants and assistance	Yes	
25.	Research and development*	Yes	
26.	Capitalization of interest costs*	Yes	
28.	Extraordinary or unusual items*	Yes	
29.	Income tax**	Yes	
30.	Postretirement benefits*	Yes	

*These topics are subject to change as a result of the IASC Improvements Project—see the appendix to the International Accounting Standards chapter.

**The IAS on accounting for taxes on income is currently being revised, and an exposure draft has been issued.

Comparison in this table is made to International Accounting Standards in force at January 1, 1993. For further details, see the International Accounting Standards chapter.

HONG KONG

GENERAL NATIONAL INFORMATION

1. Source of Generally Accepted Accounting Principles

Generally Accepted Accounting Principles. **Generally accepted accounting principles** in Hong Kong are derived from the following sources:

☐ Statements of Standard Accounting Practice (SSAPs) and Accounting Guidelines issued by the Hong Kong Society of Accountants (HKSA).

☐ Companies Ordinance—This is the principal ordinance governing the operations of companies incorporated in Hong Kong and those incorporated elsewhere but trading in Hong Kong as a branch. The ordinance contains rules on the maintenance of books and records, and the preparation of and disclosures required in financial statements.

☐ The Stock Exchange of Hong Kong Limited (SEHK)—The rules and regulations of the SEHK relate to accounting and reporting requirements for companies whose securities are listed on the Exchange.

Accounting Standards. **Accounting standards** in Hong Kong are issued by the HKSA, the professional accounting body in Hong Kong responsible for setting accounting standards. They are codified as SSAPs in the HKSA members' handbook. The HKSA was established in 1973 under the Professional Accountants Ordinance.

The HKSA is a member of the International Federation of Accountants and the International Accounting Standards Committee. Although compliance with statements issued by these two bodies is not mandatory for HKSA members, the Society nevertheless supports their objectives.

2. Audit and Public Company Requirements

Audit Requirements. The Companies Ordinance stipulates that every company incorporated in Hong Kong must appoint an independent auditor to report on the financial statements presented to its members at its annual general meeting. The auditor must be a member of the HKSA and hold a valid practicing certificate issued by the Society.

The auditor has a responsibility to report whether the financial statements prepared by the directors have been properly prepared in accordance with the requirements of the

Companies Ordinance and whether they show a true and fair view. The auditor has a professional responsibility to carry out his or her examination in accordance with auditing standards issued by the HKSA. The auditor must also report instances where the financial statements do not comply in any material respect with the SSAPs issued by the HKSA, except where, in the opinion of the auditor, such noncompliance is justified and disclosure is made of the departure in the notes to the financial statements.

Reference. Professional Accountants Ordinance—Section 29; Companies Ordinance—Section 140; and HKSA Statement No. 3.0.

Public Companies. The Companies Ordinance does not define a "**public company**" but instead defines a "private company." A private company is one that by its articles:

- ☐ Restricts the right to transfer its shares.
- ☐ Limits the number of its shareholders to 50.
- ☐ Prohibits any invitation to the public to subscribe for any shares or debentures of the company.

If a company ceases to be a private company, it is required to deliver to the Registrar of Companies for registration a prospectus containing the required information set out in the Second Schedule of the Companies Ordinance.

Nonprivate companies that want to have their securities listed on the SEHK must meet applicable securities legislation and SEHK requirements. These include the need to:

- ☐ Prepare annual financial statements in compliance with the disclosure requirements of the Companies Ordinance, together with additional detailed disclosures relating to properties and segmental information.
- ☐ Distribute financial statements to all shareholders at least 21 days before the annual general meeting.
- ☐ Prepare and publish in the local newspapers interim and final results.

Qualifications for listing on the SEHK include:

- ☐ Both the company and its business must be suitable for listing.
- ☐ Companies applying for listing must normally have a three-year trading record, although a shorter period may be accepted in certain circumstances.
- ☐ Minimum aggregate market value of a new listing applicant is HK$50 million, with at least HK$25 million in the hands of the public.
- ☐ Minimum expected initial market capitalization for each class of security is HK$30 million.
- ☐ At least 25 percent of any issue must be in the hands of the public at all times. This may be reduced to 10 percent in the case of very large companies with expected initial market capitalization of over HK$4,000 million.

Reference. Companies Ordinance—Sections 29 and 30, and SEHK Listing Rules—Chapter 8.

GENERAL ACCOUNTING

3. Financial Statements

Basic Accounting Concepts. Financial statements of companies incorporated in Hong Kong are prepared primarily under the **historical cost** convention and follow four fundamental accounting concepts, namely, **going concern**, **accruals**, consistency and **prudence**. The historical cost convention may be modified to state noncurrent assets at directors' or professional valuation.

Reference. HKSA Statement No. 2.101 (SSAP 1).

Contents of Financial Statements. The financial statements presented to shareholders at a company's annual general meeting normally include a balance sheet, a profit and loss account and a cash flow statement, together with accompanying notes. If the company is a **holding company** with **subsidiaries**, it is also normally required to present **group financial statements**, which are usually in the form of **consolidated financial statements**.

The financial statements are required to be accompanied by a directors' report and the report of the auditors.

A cash flow statement is required as part of all financial statements intended to give a true and fair view except for the following:

☐ Wholly owned subsidiaries where:
    (i) the holding company publishes consolidated financial statements that include the subsidiaries.
    (ii) a consolidated cash flow statement is presented for the group.
    (iii) the consolidated cash flow statement gives sufficient information to enable a user of the financial statements to derive the totals for the group required to be shown under each of the standard headings set out in SSAP 15.

☐ Banking, insurance and shipping companies that take advantage of the disclosure exemptions in Part III of the Tenth Schedule of the Companies Ordinance.

☐ Charities and nonprofit entities whose financial statements are prepared on a cash basis.

☐ Unlisted small entities with turnover less than HK$20 million per annum (with exceptions for companies in regulated industries).

A format for the cash flow statement is specified, and the statement is required to list the inflows and outflows of cash and cash equivalents for the period, grouped under the following "standard" headings:

☐ Operating activities.
☐ Returns on investments and servicing of finance.
☐ Taxation.
☐ Investing activities.
☐ Financing.

Cash flows from operating activities may be reported on a gross basis (the so-called "**direct method**") or a net basis (the so-called "**indirect method**"). The direct method is encouraged, but whichever method is used a reconciliation between operating profit reported in the profit and loss account and the net cash flow from operating activities should be given in a note to the cash flow statement.

Format of Financial Statements.   The financial statements should be prepared in accordance with the SSAPs and the requirements of the Tenth Schedule of the Companies Ordinance. Although there is no prescribed format for presenting the financial statements, these rules detail the minimum disclosures. Fixed assets, current assets and those that are neither fixed nor current are required to be disclosed separately. Similarly, liabilities are normally classified as current or noncurrent. The financial statements should be prepared on a comparative basis with amounts shown for the corresponding previous period. For companies listed on the SEHK, a five-year summary of the results and of the assets and liabilities of the group is also required.

Disclosure of Accounting Policies.   The principal **accounting policies** followed for items that are judged material in determining the profit or loss, and the company's financial position and changes therein, should be disclosed. Normally the disclosure of principal accounting policies is given as the first note to the financial statements.

Where accounting policies adopted are inconsistent with those recommended by the SSAPs, the departures and the reasons for them are required to be disclosed in the notes. If the auditor does not concur with the departures, he or she is obligated to state this in the audit report.

Reference.   Companies Ordinance—Sections 122 to 126, 161 and 161B, and Tenth Schedule; HKSA Statement Nos. 2.101 (SSAP 1) and 2.115 (SSAP 15); and SEHK Listing Rules—Appendix 7.

4.   Business Combinations

Principles of Consolidation.   Under the Companies Ordinance, holding companies are required to prepare group accounts, except where:

□   The holding company itself, at the end of the fiscal year, is a wholly owned subsidiary of another corporation (whether incorporated in Hong Kong or elsewhere); or

□   In the opinion of the directors, group accounts:
   (i)   are impracticable to prepare;
   (ii) would be of no real value to the members because of the insignificant amounts involved;
   (iii) would be disproportionately costly or time-consuming to prepare;
   (iv) would be misleading;
   (v)   would be harmful to the company or any of its subsidiaries; or
   (vi) are undesirable because the business of the holding company and subsidiary are so different that they cannot be treated as a single undertaking.

The Financial Secretary's approval is required for omission of group accounts for the reasons stated in (v) and (vi) above.

The group accounts usually take the form of consolidated financial statements that present the information contained in the separate financial statements of the holding company and its subsidiaries as if they were a single entity. Consolidated financial statements are the best means of achieving the objective of group accounts, which is to give a true and fair view of the profit or loss and the financial position of the group.

SSAP 7 requires that where group accounts are prepared in a form other than consolidated financial statements, the onus is on the directors to justify and state in the accounts the reasons for the conclusion that the resulting group accounts give a fairer view of the financial position of the group as a whole.

SSAP 7 also requires that a subsidiary be excluded from consolidation if:

☐ Its activities are so dissimilar to those of other companies in the group that consolidated financial statements would be misleading and that information for the holding company's shareholders and other users of the statements would be better provided by presenting separate financial statements for such subsidiary; or

☐ The holding company lacks effective control; that is, although it owns, directly or through other subsidiaries, more than half the equity share capital of the subsidiary, either:
— it does not own share capital carrying more than half the votes; or
— contractual or other restrictions are imposed on its ability to appoint the majority of the board of directors; or

☐ The subsidiary operates under severe restrictions, which significantly impair control by the holding company over the subsidiary's assets and operations for the foreseeable future; or

☐ Control is intended to be temporary.

Under the Companies Ordinance, a company is deemed to be a "subsidiary" of another company if:

(a) that other company:
(i) controls the composition of the board of directors of the first-mentioned company; or
(ii) controls more than half of the voting power of the first-mentioned company; or
(iii) holds more than half of the issued share capital of the first-mentioned company (excluding any part of it that carries no right to participate beyond a specified amount in a distribution of either profits or capital); or

(b) the first-mentioned company is a subsidiary of any company that is that other company's subsidiary.

The rules of the SEHK do not separately require group accounts, but refer to the accounts prepared pursuant to the Companies Ordinance.

Accounting for Business Combinations. **Business combinations** should normally be accounted for by the **purchase method**. Use of the **pooling of interests method** is rare. All intragroup balances and transactions and unrealized intragroup profits are eliminated.

Control. Control is usually indicated by ownership of over 50 percent of the voting shares carrying the right to elect a majority of the members of the board of directors.

H-6 □ HONG KONG

Reference. HKSA Statement No. 2.107 (SSAP 7).

Goodwill. There is no prescribed accounting standard on **goodwill**, but the HKSA has issued a nonmandatory accounting guideline setting out recommended practice, which is detailed below.

A distinction is made between purchased goodwill and internally generated goodwill. Internally generated goodwill should not be recorded.

Purchased goodwill results from the purchase of a business accounted for as an acquisition. Positive goodwill arising on an acquisition may be eliminated either immediately, directly against reserves or by amortization through the profit and loss account on a systematic basis over its estimated useful life. Under the amortization method, if there is a permanent diminution in value of goodwill, the unamortized balance should be written down immediately through the profit and loss account to its estimated recoverable amount. **Negative goodwill** should be credited directly to reserves.

The useful life of purchased goodwill is the best estimate of the life of such goodwill at the date of purchase.

Reference. HKSA Statement No. 2.204.

Equity Accounting. **Associated companies** should be accounted for under the **equity method** in the investing group's consolidated financial statements. An associated company is defined by SSAP 10 as a company that is not a subsidiary of the investing group or company and in which:

☐ The investing group's or company's interest is effectively that of a partner in an undertaking and the investing group or company is in a position to exercise significant influence over the company in which the investment is made; or

☐ The investing group's or company's interest is long term and substantial, and, with regard to the disposition of the other shareholdings, the investing group or company is in a position to exercise significant influence over the company in which the investment is made.

Significant influence over a company essentially involves participation in its financial and operating policy decisions (including dividend policy) but not necessarily control of those policies. Representation on the board of directors is indicative of such participation, but does not necessarily give conclusive evidence of it, nor is it the only method by which the investing company may participate in policy decisions.

Unless it can clearly be demonstrated otherwise, if the investing group or company holds 20 percent or more of the equity voting rights of a company, the investing group or company is presumed to have the ability to exercise significant influence over the company.

Where different companies in a group hold shares in a company, for the purposes of establishing whether or not significant influence is presumed to exist, the investment should be considered as the aggregate of the holdings of the investing company and of those of its subsidiaries but not its associated companies.

If a subsidiary is excluded from consolidation on the grounds of lack of effective control (see "Principles of Consolidation," above), SSAP 7 recommends that it be accounted for in the consolidated financial statements using the equity method. If a subsidiary is excluded from consolidation because it operates under severe restrictions that significantly impair control by the holding company over the subsidiary's assets and operations in the foreseeable future, the investment should be stated at the amount at which it would have been carried under the equity method at the date the restrictions became effective.

Minority Interests. **Minority interests'** share of operating profit and extraordinary items is shown as a separate line on the profit and loss account before arriving at operating profit attributable to **members** of the holding company. The minorities' share of share capital, retained earnings and reserves is disclosed as a separate single line in the liabilities section of the balance sheet.

Disclosure. Detailed disclosures are required in the group accounts, including:

☐ Accounting policy used in preparing the group accounts.

☐ Share of profits less losses in subsidiaries.

☐ Amount attributable to minority interests.

☐ Names and places of incorporation of subsidiaries and the nature of their principal activities.

☐ Percentage shareholdings in subsidiaries.

☐ Details of acquisitions and disposals of subsidiaries.

☐ Amounts due to and from subsidiaries.

☐ Details of subsidiaries excluded from the group accounts, including reason for exclusion.

☐ Details of restrictions on the holding company to distribute retained profits of the group.

Where equity accounting is adopted, the following information is required:

☐ Share of profits less losses in associated companies.

☐ The investing group's share of the net assets other than goodwill of associated companies, where possible after attributing fair values to the net assets at the time of acquisition of the interest in the associated companies.

☐ The investing group's share of any goodwill in the associated companies' own financial statements.

☐ The premium (or discount) paid on the acquisition of the interests in the associated companies to the extent that it has not already been written off or amortized (this and the previous item may be shown as one aggregate amount).

☐ Where the interest in associated companies is material to the investing group's financial statements, extracts from the financial statements of the associated companies.

Reference. Companies Ordinance—Sections 124 to 129 and Tenth Schedule and HKSA Statement Nos. 2.107 and 2.110 (SSAPs 7 and 10).

5. Joint Ventures

Accounting for Investments in Joint Ventures.   There are no specific rules on accounting for **joint ventures**, and reference is normally made to guidance provided in International Accounting Standard 31, *Financial Reporting of Interests in Joint Ventures.*

Accounting by Joint Ventures.   There is no prescribed standard for accounting by a joint venture for assets contributed by the venturers.

Reference.   International Accounting Standard 31.

6. Foreign Currency Translation

Bases of Translation.   Any currency may be used as the reporting currency. A distinction is made between translating **foreign currency** denominated **transactions** and balances of the domestic operations of an individual company, and translating financial statements of foreign operations for consolidation purposes.

Individual company: For an individual company, the **temporal method** should be used. The resulting exchange differences are included in operating results.

Consolidated financial statements: When preparing group accounts for an investing company and its foreign enterprises, the **closing rate** (net investment) **method** of translating the financial statements should normally be used. Exchange differences will arise if the closing rate differs from that used at the previous balance sheet date; these differences should be recorded as a change in the foreign currency translation reserve (see Section 22).

The profit and loss account of a foreign enterprise accounted for under the closing rate method is translated either at the closing rate or at the average rate for the period. If the average rate is used, the difference between the profit and loss account translated at the average rate and that translated at the closing rate should be recorded as a change in the foreign currency translation reserve.

If the trade of the foreign enterprise is more dependent on the economic circumstances of the investing company's reporting currency than on its own reporting currency, the temporal method should be used.

Hedges.   If a company has used foreign currency borrowings or forward contracts to finance, or provide a **hedge** against, its foreign currency assets, the following accounting applies, subject to the conditions set out below. The foreign currency assets are denominated in the appropriate foreign currencies and the carrying amounts translated at the end of each period at closing rates for inclusion in the company's financial statements. Any resulting exchange differences are recorded in reserves; the exchange gains or losses arising on the borrowings or the forward contracts are offset against those exchange differences. The conditions are as follows:

□   In any period, exchange gains or losses arising on the borrowings or the forward contracts should be offset only to the extent of exchange differences arising on the foreign currency assets.

□   The foreign currency borrowings or the forward contracts are designated and effective as a hedge against the foreign currency assets.

If a forward contract is used as a hedge of a foreign currency asset, the discount or premium on the contract should be either amortized in the profit and loss account over the period of the contract or recorded in reserves with the gain or loss.

Disclosure. The method used in the translation of the financial statements of foreign enterprises and the treatment of exchange differences should be disclosed in the financial statements.

The following information should also be disclosed in the financial statements of all companies other than licensed banking, insurance and shipping companies that take advantage of the disclosure exemptions permitted under Part III of the Tenth Schedule to the Companies Ordinance:

- The net amount of exchange gains and losses on foreign currency borrowings less deposits, identifying separately:
  —the amount offset directly against reserves with respect to hedges;
  —the net amount recorded in the profit and loss account.
- The net amount of exchange gains or losses on forward contracts, together with any associated discount or premium on these contracts, offset directly against reserves with respect to hedges.
- The net change in reserves arising from exchange differences.

Reference.   HKSA Statement No. 2.111 (SSAP 11).

7. Changing Prices/Inflation Accounting

There is no prescribed accounting standard relating to inflation accounting. Companies in Hong Kong have elected not to adopt International Accounting Standard 15, *Information Reflecting the Effects of Changing Prices*.

8. Accounting Changes

Accounting Treatment.   Changes in accounting policies are distinguished from changes in accounting estimates, which arise from new information or developments.

Change in accounting policy: In the case of a change in accounting policy, such as the issue of a statement that creates a new accounting basis or expresses a preference for a basis not presently used by the company, the cumulative adjustments applicable to prior years have no bearing on the results of the current year and, accordingly, should not be included in arriving at the profit for the current year. They should be accounted for by restating prior years' figures and adjusting the opening balance of retained profits brought forward.

Although a change from one accounting method to another would normally represent a change in accounting policy and would require a **prior year adjustment**, an exception to this rule is available in the case of **depreciation**. Where there is a change from one method of depreciation to another (e.g., from the reducing (**declining**) **balance method** to the **straight-line method**), the net book value of the asset should be written down to its residual value over the remaining useful life on the new basis, commencing with the period in which the change is made.

Change in accounting estimate: The effect of a change in estimate should be accounted for in the period the change occurs and applicable future periods. For example, if the estimate of the useful life of an asset is revised, the depreciation rate should be adjusted so as to allocate the depreciable amount of the asset less accumulated depreciation at the date of the change, over the remaining revised useful life of the asset.

Disclosure. The effect of a change in accounting policy should be disclosed where practicable by showing separately the amount involved in the restatement of the previous year's retained profit brought forward. Where material, the effect of a change in accounting estimate during the current period should be disclosed in the financial statements as an exceptional/abnormal item.

Reference. HKSA Statement Nos. 2.101, 2.102 and 2.106 (SSAPs 1, 2 and 6).

9. Prior Period Adjustments

Definition. Prior year adjustments are limited to the following items, if material:

☐ Corrections of errors in financial statements of prior periods.
☐ Changes in accounting policies.

Accounting Treatment. Prior year adjustments should be accounted for by restating prior year figures, with the result that the opening balance of retained profits brought forward is adjusted.

Disclosure. A statement of retained profits/reserves showing any prior year adjustments should immediately follow the profit and loss account for the year.

Reference. HKSA Statement No. 2.102 (SSAP 2).

10. Post Balance Sheet Events

Definition. There are two different types of post balance sheet events:

☐ Those that provide further evidence of conditions that existed at the balance sheet date.
☐ Those that are an indication of conditions that arose subsequent to the balance sheet date.

Accounting Treatment. The accounting treatment depends on the category that the event falls into.

If the event falls into the first category, it represents an adjusting event and the financial statements should be adjusted. An example of such an event would include the renegotiation of amounts due by debtors.

If the event falls into the second category, it should be treated as a nonadjusting event and should not be reflected in the financial statements. An exception to this rule occurs where the application of the going concern concept to the whole or a material part of the company is no longer appropriate. For example, a fire or flood occurring after the balance sheet date would normally be a nonadjusting event. However, if the extent of the damage is such that the company is no longer a going concern, the financial statements would be adjusted.

Disclosure. Normally, no specific disclosure is required for adjusting events. However, a material post balance sheet event should be disclosed if:

☐ It is a nonadjusting event of such **materiality** that its nondisclosure would affect the ability of the user of financial statements to reach a proper understanding of the financial position; or

☐ It is the reversal or maturity after year-end of a transaction entered into before year-end, the substance of which was primarily to alter the appearance of the company's balance sheet (i.e., window dressing).

Disclosures should include:

☐ The nature of the event.

☐ An estimate of the financial effect, or a statement that it is not practicable to make such an estimate.

Reference. HKSA Statement No. 2.109 (SSAP 9).

11. Related Party Transactions

General. In 1985, the HKSA issued a discussion paper on related party transactions. However, a definitive statement has yet to be issued and, accordingly, in practice only minimum information on related party transactions is disclosed.

Accounting Treatment. Related party transactions should be accounted for in accordance with normal accounting principles and practices.

Disclosure. The minimum requirements for the disclosure of specified related party information under the Companies Ordinance and under SSAP 7, "Group Accounts," include the disclosure of:

☐ **Directors' emoluments** and loans to officers.

☐ Details of intragroup indebtedness and amounts due to and from other subsidiaries.

☐ Details of subsidiaries and significant investments.

Reference. HKSA Discussion Paper November 22, 1985, "Related Party Transactions—Audit Implications"; Companies Ordinance—Sections 128, 129, 161 and 161B and Tenth Schedule; and HKSA Statement No. 2.107 (SSAP 7).

12. Segmental Information

General. The need to include disclosures of segmental information is restricted to companies listed on the SEHK. The Listing Rules of the SEHK require the disclosure by **listed companies** of certain segmental information in the annual report presented to members at the annual general meeting.

Disclosure. Segmental information is normally disclosed in the directors' report (in contrast to the financial statements) and includes:

□　For each principal activity of the company and its subsidiaries, the **turnover** and contribution to operating results attributable to it.

□　A geographical analysis of consolidated turnover and contribution to operating results of trading operations carried on by the company and its subsidiaries outside Hong Kong, unless such operations comprise less than 10 percent of the turnover and 10 percent of the operating results of the company and its subsidiaries.

Reference.　SEHK—Listing Rules, Appendix 7 and HKSA Statement No. 2.206.

ACCOUNTING PRINCIPLES FOR SPECIFIC ITEMS— BALANCE SHEET

13. Property, Plant and Equipment

Classification of Capital and Revenue Expenditure.　Expenditures are classified as capital when they give rise to an asset that will produce economic benefits in future periods.

Basis of Valuation.　Depreciable assets: Depreciable assets are stated at cost or valuation, after charging depreciation. Land and buildings should be accounted for separately; if the relative costs are not known, they should be estimated based on a professional valuation. Where depreciable assets are stated at valuation, any revaluation surplus should be credited directly to an asset revaluation reserve.

If depreciable assets are disposed of for an amount different from their net book value, the surplus or deficiency should be reflected in current operating results. Any remaining revaluation surplus relating to assets disposed of should be transferred from the asset revaluation reserve to distributable reserves through the profit and loss account or to another general distributable or nondistributable reserve.

Investment properties: Investment properties should be stated at their open market value at the balance sheet date. Changes in the value of investment properties should be treated as changes in the investment property revaluation reserve. If the total of this reserve is insufficient to cover a deficit on a **portfolio basis**, the excess should be charged to the profit and loss account.

Unlisted companies with investment properties whose carrying value is less than HK$50 million or 15 percent of total group assets may state investment properties at their net book value.

Expenditures that do not give rise to such assets are treated as expenses (revenue expenditure) and are charged directly to the profit and loss account.

Definitions.　Property, plant and equipment may be classified into two major categories:

□　Depreciable assets.
□　Investment properties.

Depreciable assets are defined as assets that:

□　Are expected to be used during more than one accounting period.

□ Have a limited useful life.

□ Are held by a company for use in the production or supply of goods and services, for rental to others or for administrative purposes.

An investment property is an interest in land and buildings on which construction work has been completed and that is held for its investment potential, with any rental income negotiated at arm's length. A property or part of a property owned and occupied by a company for its own use, or leased to and occupied by a group company, is not an investment property.

Depreciation. Depreciable assets: The depreciable amount should be allocated to the profit and loss account on a systematic basis over the useful life of the asset. Depreciable amount is defined as historical cost or other amount substituted for historical cost, less the estimated residual value. Useful life is the period over which a depreciable asset is expected to be used; it should be estimated after considering the expected physical wear and tear, obsolescence and any limits on the use of the asset.

If a depreciable asset is revalued, the provision for depreciation should be based on the revalued amount and the current estimate of its remaining useful life.

The method of depreciation selected should be appropriate to the type of asset and the utilization of the asset's service potential, and should be applied consistently from period to period. The two most common methods are the straight-line method and the reducing balance method. If there is a change in method, the net book value of the asset should be written down to the residual value over the remaining useful life on the new basis, commencing with the period in which the change is made.

Depreciation rates and the underlying assessment of useful life should be reviewed annually.

Land and buildings that are depreciable assets are subject to special treatment. Land in Hong Kong is mostly leasehold land; there is little freehold land. Where land is held and the relevant lease has an unexpired term of not less than 50 years (including the renewal period to the year 2047) at the balance sheet date, it is permissible not to amortize the depreciable amount of the land even though it is of a depreciable nature. Land held on leases with unexpired lease terms of less than 50 years should be amortized over the remaining period of the lease. Buildings are normally depreciated using the straight-line method over a maximum of 50 years.

Investment properties: Investment properties should not be depreciated unless the unexpired term of the lease is 20 years or less.

Disclosure. Depreciable assets: The following should be disclosed for each major class of depreciable asset:

□ The basis of arriving at the amounts at which the depreciable assets are stated in the financial statements.

□ The depreciation methods used.

□ The useful lives or the depreciation rates used.

□ Total depreciation charged in the accounting period.

□ The gross amount of depreciable assets and the related accumulated depreciation, distinguishing between assets included in the financial statements at cost and those included at valuation.

If the company's depreciable assets include land and buildings, the following information should be disclosed:

☐ The amount at which land and buildings are carried in the balance sheet.
☐ The location of the property, whether in Hong Kong or overseas, and whether the land is freehold.
☐ The balances of any revaluation reserve, together with details of changes during the accounting period.
☐ Any deficit on revaluation charged to the profit and loss account during the period.

The following should also be disclosed, if material:

☐ The reason for and effect of any change in depreciation method.
☐ The effect of any change in the estimated useful life of an asset.
☐ The effect of any revaluation of depreciable assets during the period.
☐ The surplus or deficiency on disposal of any depreciable assets.

If depreciable assets are revalued during the period or at the balance sheet date, the names of the persons making the valuation, or details of their qualifications, should be disclosed, together with the basis of valuation used. If a person making a valuation is an employee or officer of the company or group, this fact should be disclosed.

Investment properties: The following information should be disclosed:

☐ The carrying value of the investment properties.
☐ The balance of the investment property revaluation reserve, together with details of changes during the period.
☐ Any deficit on revaluation charged to the profit and loss account during the period.
☐ The surplus or deficiency on disposal of any investment properties.
☐ The names of the persons making the valuation, or details of their qualifications, together with the basis of valuation used. If a person making a valuation is an employee or officer of the company or group, this fact should be disclosed.

Reference.   HKSA Statement Nos. 2.106 and 2.113 (SSAPs 6 and 13).

14.   Intangible Assets

Accounting Treatment.   There is currently no accounting standard dealing with accounting for **intangible assets**. However, the HKSA has issued a nonmandatory accounting guideline on goodwill, and the principles included therein normally would be applicable to other intangibles. In addition, the HKSA has issued a nonmandatory accounting guideline on accounting for textile quota entitlements.

The most common forms of intangibles recognized in the balance sheet are technology based (patents, trademarks, licenses), media based (newspapers, magazine mastheads, TV programs, film rights and radio licenses), purchased permanent textile quota entitlements and distribution rights.

In determining whether it is appropriate to identify and capitalize an intangible asset, the following questions would normally be considered:

□ Does the intangible convey a right capable of enforcement?

□ Is it capable of producing revenue in its own right?

□ Is it capable of being sold separately without disposing of the business as a whole?

Valuation. Accounting principles applied to valuing intangibles are essentially the same as those applied to other noncurrent assets. The cost of the intangible is its purchase price or its production cost plus an appropriate portion of production overhead. The intangible may be carried forward in the balance sheet at this cost if it will provide measurable future economic benefits to the company. As in the case of noncurrent assets, intangibles may be revalued and stated at directors' valuation.

Amortization. If an intangible has a finite useful life, or it can be demonstrated that the recoverable amount is declining, the intangible may either be written off directly against reserves or amortized over its estimated useful life through the profit and loss account. It is not common practice for intangibles to be permanently retained in the balance sheet.

Disclosure. The accounting policy followed with respect to intangibles should be explained in the notes to the financial statements. Intangible assets should be separately disclosed. The amounts written off or amortized should be shown, and any changes in reserves from write-offs should be separately identified.

Reference. HKSA Statement Nos. 2.204 and 2.207.

15. Leases

Classification. Leases can be classified into **finance leases** or **operating leases**. A finance lease is one whereby the lessor transfers substantially all the risks and rewards incident to ownership to the lessee. An operating lease is a lease other than a finance lease.

The characteristics of a finance lease are as follows:

□ Ownership will be transferred by the end of the lease term.

□ The lease contains a bargain purchase option.

□ The lease term is for a major part of the asset's useful life.

□ At the inception of the lease the present value of minimum lease payments is at least 90 percent of the asset's fair value.

Accounting Treatment. Finance leases: Lessee: A finance lease should be recorded in the balance sheet of a lessee as an asset and as an obligation to pay future rentals. At the inception of the lease, the asset and liability should be equal to the present value of the minimum lease payments, calculated by discounting them at the interest rate implicit in the lease. In most cases, the fair value of the asset will closely approximate the present value of the minimum lease payments.

Rentals payable should be apportioned between the finance charge and a reduction of the outstanding obligation for future amounts payable. The total finance charge under a finance lease should be allocated to accounting periods during the lease term so as to produce a constant periodic rate of charge on the remaining balance of the obligation for each period, or a reasonable approximation thereof.

The asset under a finance lease should be depreciated over the shorter of the lease term or its useful life. However, in the case of a hire purchase contract, which has the characteristics of a finance lease, the asset should be depreciated over its useful life.

Lessor: The amount due from the lessee under a finance lease should be recorded in the balance sheet of a lessor as a receivable at the amount of the net investment in the lease after making provision for bad and doubtful rentals receivable. The total gross earnings under a finance lease should be allocated to accounting periods to give a constant periodic rate of return on the lessor's net cash investment.

Operating leases: Lessee: The rental under an operating lease should be charged on a straight-line basis over the lease term, even if payments are not made on such a basis, unless another systematic and rational basis is more appropriate.

Lessor: The asset relating to an operating lease should be recorded by the lessor as a fixed asset and depreciated over its useful life. Rental income from an operating lease should be recognized on a straight-line basis over the lease period.

Leveraged Leases.   Accounting standards do not specifically address **leveraged leases**. The lessor records the investment in a finance lease net of nonrecourse debt. The US approach of netting the investment in the finance lease and the related debt is acceptable in Hong Kong.

Disclosure.   The accounting policy adopted for leases should be disclosed. Where material, lessees should disclose detailed information with respect to finance leases, including amounts capitalized, **amortization**, finance charges and lease commitments. For operating leases, lessees should disclose rental expense and lease commitments.

Lessors are required to disclose the net investment in finance leases and hire purchase contracts; gross amounts of assets held for use in operating leases and related accumulated depreciation charges; the aggregate rentals receivable in relation to finance leases and operating leases; and the cost of assets acquired for the purpose of leasing under finance leases.

Reference.   HKSA Statement No. 2.114 (SSAP 14) and Companies Ordinance—Tenth Schedule.

16. Investments

Valuation.   The valuation of investments depends on their classification as noncurrent (i.e., held for the medium or long term) or current (i.e., temporary investments of surplus cash, normally held for less than 12 months).

Current investments: Current investments are stated at the lower of cost and **net realizable value**, either on a portfolio basis or an individual basis. The write-down to net realizable value should be recognized in operating profit and separately disclosed as an exceptional item, if material.

Noncurrent investments: Noncurrent investments are normally stated at cost; however, revaluation to market is permitted. Provision should be made in the event of a permanent diminution in value. The write-down of a noncurrent investment to its recoverable amount should be charged to the profit and loss account, except when it reverses a previous revaluation increment that was credited directly to an asset revaluation reserve. In this circumstance, the write-down should be charged to the revaluation reserve.

Accounting and disclosure requirements for investment properties are set out in Section 13.

Treatment of Revaluation Reserves. Reserves arising from the revaluation of non-current investments are included as part of shareholders' equity in the balance sheet. They are frequently used in stock dividends (bonus share issues).

Gains/Losses. When investments are sold, the profit or loss to be recognized is normally measured as the difference between the net proceeds received for the investment and its carrying amount at the time of sale. If such profits and losses are material, they should be included in operating profit and disclosed as an exceptional item. For investments not acquired with the intention of resale, such as investments in subsidiaries, profits or losses arising on disposal should in certain circumstances be treated as extraordinary items (see Section 28). In calculating the profit or loss on disposal of part of a holding, "**average cost**" is used.

Disclosure. The following should be disclosed:

☐ The policies adopted for accounting for investments.

☐ The amounts included in investment income, distinguishing between income from listed and unlisted investments, and rental income from land and buildings, where this is significant.

☐ The market value of marketable investments if they are not carried at market value.

☐ Significant restrictions on the realizability of investments or the remittance of income and proceeds of disposal.

☐ For listed companies, details such as address, usage and valuation of properties.

Reference. HKSA Statement Nos. 2.102, 2.103 and 2.113 (SSAPs 2, 3 and 13); International Accounting Standard 25; and Companies Ordinance—Tenth Schedule.

17. Accounts Receivable

Accounting Treatment. Recognition: The recognition of revenues, and hence the related receivables, is described in Section 23.

Discounts: Receivables are normally recorded net of trade and quantity discounts. Cash discounts are recognized at time of payment.

Allowances: Adequate provision must be made for bad and doubtful accounts, but there are no formal methods for calculating such provisions.

Factored Receivables. **Factoring** of receivables is not common in Hong Kong. Where **accounts receivable** have been factored or sold to a finance company for a cash consideration, the relevant debts, which then become due to the finance company, should be excluded from the balance sheet. Discounts given to the finance company should be accounted for in the same way as cash discounts. If the factor has recourse to the vendor for bad debts, disclosure of the contingent liability and provision for probable losses should be made.

Disclosure. Receivables are included in **current assets** to the extent that they are expected to be realized within one year. They are normally analyzed by major classes such as trade accounts receivable, bills receivable, deposits, prepayments and other accounts. Receivables due from subsidiaries, associates and fellow subsidiaries are separately disclosed. Amounts due after one year are classified as noncurrent assets.

Reference. HKSA Statement No. 2.101 (SSAP 1) and Companies Ordinance—Tenth Schedule.

18. Inventories and Work in Progress

General Accounting Treatment. **Inventories** should be valued at the lower of cost and net realizable value. In determining the carrying amount of inventories, generally each item should be dealt with separately; where this is impracticable, similar items may be dealt with as a group.

The overriding consideration in choosing a basis for cost is that the basis should be a fair reflection of the expenditure actually incurred in bringing the inventory to its present location and condition.

Commonly used methods of determining cost include specific cost, **FIFO** and average cost. **Standard costing** is acceptable if it approximates one of those methods. **LIFO, latest purchase price** and **base stock** are not normally used.

Cost includes cost of purchase and cost of conversion. Cost of purchase comprises purchase price, including import duties, inward transport and handling costs, and any other directly attributable costs, less trade discounts, rebates and subsidies. Cost of conversion includes costs specifically attributable to units of production (i.e., direct labor and expenses and subcontracted work), production overhead (i.e., overhead incurred with respect to materials, labor and services for production based on normal operating capacity) and any other overhead that can be attributed to the product.

Long-Term Contracts. A long-term contract is a contract entered into for the design, manufacture or construction of a single substantial asset or the provision of a service (or of a combination of assets or services that together constitute a single project) where the activity to substantially complete the contract falls into different accounting periods. A contract that is required to be accounted for as long term will usually extend for a period exceeding one year. However, a duration exceeding one year is not an essential feature of a long-term contract. Some contracts with a duration shorter than one year should be accounted for as long-term contracts if not recording their attributable profit would distort the period's results to such an extent that the financial statements would not give a true and fair view. The policy relating to accounting for long-term contracts must be applied consistently within the reporting entity and from year to year.

Long-term contract work in progress is stated in the financial statements at cost plus attributable profit, less any foreseeable losses and progress payments received and receivable. If, however, anticipated losses on individual contracts exceed the cost incurred to date less progress payments received and receivable, such excesses should be shown separately as provisions.

"Attributable profit" is the part of the total profit estimated to arise over the duration of the contract (after allowing for likely increases in costs not recoverable under the terms of the contract) that fairly reflects the profit attributable to the work performed at the balance sheet date. There can be no attributable profit until the outcome of the contract can be assessed with reasonable certainty.

"Foreseeable losses" are losses estimated to arise over the duration of the contract (after allowing for estimated remedial and maintenance costs, and increases in costs not recoverable under the terms of the contract).

Disclosure. The accounting policies used in calculating cost, net realizable value, attributable profit and foreseeable losses should be stated.

Inventory and work in progress should be subclassified in a manner appropriate to the business and so as to indicate the amounts held in each of the main categories.

In relation to long-term contracts, there should be stated:

☐ The amount of work in progress at cost plus attributable profit, less foreseeable losses.

☐ Cash received and receivable as progress payments on contracts in progress.

Reference. HKSA Statement No. 2.103 (SSAP 3).

19. Current Liabilities

General Accounting Treatment. In Hong Kong there is no prescribed accounting standard relating to accounting for **accounts payable**, accrued liabilities and deferred income. Nevertheless, balance sheets normally separately identify **current liabilities**, which include amounts payable within one year from the date of the balance sheet. Current liabilities are normally classified as bank overdrafts, accounts payable, bills payable, accrued liabilities, loans payable, taxes payable, dividends payable and deferred revenue and long-term debt due within one year of the balance sheet date.

Accounts payable and bills payable include amounts owed to creditors for goods and services bought on credit and for which invoices or bills have been received.

Most expenses are recorded at the time they are incurred. Expenses that have been incurred but not recorded because payment is not due, such as unpaid salaries, wages, electricity, telephone and other charges, are recorded as accrued liabilities.

Amounts received in advance of delivery of goods or performance of services are recorded as unearned or deferred revenue.

Creation of General and Specific Provisions. There is no requirement to create specific provisions for future expenses. Provisions are made at the discretion of management under the concept of prudence.

Provision is made for all known liabilities (expenses and losses). The amounts provided are the best estimates of the expense and loss, given the information available.

Amounts provided in excess of amounts required to write off assets (i.e., excess depreciation to replace assets) are regarded as reserves and are required to be separately identified.

Disclosure. The Companies Ordinance requires the following to be disclosed separately in the balance sheet:

☐ Bank loans and overdrafts.

☐ Amounts due to subsidiary companies, including loans.

☐ Amounts due to group companies, distinguishing between debentures and other indebtedness.

☐ The amount recommended for distribution as dividends.

☐ Taxes:
   —basis for providing Hong Kong profits tax;

—liability for profits tax on current period profits, shown either as a current liability or as a separate item, but not grouped with deferred taxes.

☐ Provisions classified under suitable headings.

☐ Changes in provisions.

☐ Reserves, representing amounts provided in excess of what, in the opinion of the directors, is reasonably necessary for the purpose.

☐ The fact that a liability is secured, if applicable.

Reference. Companies Ordinance—Tenth Schedule and HKSA Statement No. 2.101 (SSAP 1).

20. Long-Term Debt

General Accounting Treatment. The most common forms of long-term debt are debentures, mortgages and other long-term bank loans. The general accounting treatment for these items is basically the same as for current liabilities, that is, they are included in the balance sheet at face value as long as they continue to represent an obligation of the company.

There are no prescribed accounting standards or accounting guidelines with respect to debt restructuring and debt extinguishment. Guidance is normally sought from generally accepted accounting practices in other countries.

Disclosure. The Companies Ordinance requires the following to be disclosed:

☐ The aggregate amount of loans, bank loans and overdrafts, indicating the details of terms on which they are repayable and rates of interest.

☐ Dates and terms of redemption or conversion of debentures and other long-term indebtedness.

☐ Details of redeemed debentures that may be reissued.

☐ Accrued interest on mortgage debentures and secured loans, shown gross and added to debentures if interest is secured; included with current liabilities if not.

☐ Number, description and amount of debentures of the company held beneficially by its subsidiary companies.

☐ Nominal amount and book value of debentures of the company held by a nominee or trustee.

Reference. Companies Ordinance—Tenth Schedule.

21. Contingencies

General. The accounting treatment and disclosure of **contingencies** depend on the likelihood of occurrence of future events that will determine the contingency.

Contingent Losses. Material contingent losses should be accrued in financial statements where it is probable that a future event will confirm a loss that can be estimated with reasonable accuracy at the date on which the financial statements are approved by the board of directors.

If a material contingent loss has not been accrued, it should be disclosed in the notes to the financial statements, unless the possibility of loss is remote.

Contingent Gains. Contingent gains should not be accrued in the financial statements. A material contingent gain should be disclosed in the financial statements only if it is probable that it will be realized.

Disclosure. For each contingency required to be disclosed, the following information should be stated in a note to the financial statements:

☐ The nature of the contingency.

☐ The uncertainties expected to affect the ultimate outcome.

☐ A prudent estimate of the financial effect, made at the date on which the financial statements are approved by the board of directors, or a statement that it is not practicable to make such an estimate.

Reference. HKSA Statement No. 2.108 (SSAP 8).

22. Capital and Reserves

General. Shareholders' equity is generally divided between **share capital** (amounts contributed by shareholders) and reserves.

Share Capital. The Companies Ordinance requires that a company include in its memorandum and articles the amount of its share capital (authorized capital), divided into a number of shares of a fixed amount (**par value**). The number of shares that can be issued is limited by the authorized capital.

Shares need not be issued at par, but any excess of the issue price over par value must be credited to a **share premium** reserve (described below).

A company's share capital may be divided into different classes, each characterized by its voting, dividend and capital repayment rights. The main classes of shares are usually ordinary and **preference shares**. The exact rights of each type are included in the company's memorandum and articles. The Companies Ordinance provides that certain conditions must be met before preference shares are issued or shares are issued at a discount.

After issue, a company may not reduce its share capital except with the special permission of the court. After satisfying certain conditions, companies are permitted to buy back their own shares.

Reserves. All reserves are normally grouped together. However, it is possible to categorize them into nondistributable and other reserves. Nondistributable reserves include those that are required to be established under the Companies Ordinance, have legislative restrictions on their use or have been designated by management as not available for distribution.

The two main types of nondistributable reserves are:

☐ Share premium reserve—This reserve is created from the excess of the issue price of shares over their par value. The Companies Ordinance restricts its use to issuing stock dividends, writing off company formation expenses or providing for the premium payable on redemption of preference shares.

□ Capital redemption reserve—This reserve is required where a company issues redeemable shares that it intends to redeem other than by a new share issue.

These two reserves may be utilized only in certain circumstances and are generally distributable to shareholders only on liquidation.

The four main types of other reserves are:

□ Asset revaluation reserve—This reserve arises as a result of the revaluation of non-current assets.

□ Foreign currency translation reserve—This reserve arises as a result of translating the financial statements of overseas subsidiaries into the reporting currency of the holding company in the consolidated financial statements.

□ General reserve—This reserve represents an appropriation of profits from retained profits made at the discretion of the directors.

□ Retained profits—This represents the balance of profits earned that have not been transferred to other reserves or appropriated as dividends.

Restrictions on Dividends and Other Distributions.   Under the Companies Ordinance, companies are restricted from making distributions except out of profits available for the purpose of the distribution. The term "distribution" has been widely defined and includes distributions by cash and otherwise, with only a few exceptions. In effect, profits available for distribution are limited to a company's accumulated realized profits less its accumulated realized losses. Companies are required to make good retained losses brought forward before a distribution can be made.

Disclosure.   The following disclosures are required:

□ Summary of authorized and issued share capital.

□ Options on unissued shares—Number, description and amount of shares affected, option price and the period for which exercisable.

□ Amount of share capital on which interest has been paid out of capital during the fiscal year and the rate of interest, unless disclosed in the profit and loss account.

□ Number, description and amount of shares of the company held beneficially by its subsidiary companies.

□ Redeemable preference shares, showing:
 —amount and earliest and latest dates of redemption;
 —whether redemption is mandatory or at the company's option;
 —the premium, if any, payable on redemption.

□ Arrears of fixed cumulative dividends, showing:
 —amount for each class of shares;
 —the period for which in arrears.

□ Amount of the share premium reserve.

□ Where material, the source or application of any increase or decrease in the share premium reserve compared with the end of the immediately preceding fiscal year.

☐ Capital redemption reserve fund, if shares were redeemed other than from the proceeds of a new issue.

☐ Changes in reserves.

Reference. Companies Ordinance—Sections 47A–63, and Tenth Schedule.

ACCOUNTING PRINCIPLES FOR SPECIFIC ITEMS— INCOME STATEMENT

23. Revenue Recognition

General Principles. There is no specific accounting standard on the recognition of **revenue**, and reference is normally made to guidance provided in International Accounting Standard 18, *Revenue Recognition.*

Revenue from a transaction involving the sale of goods is usually recognized when the seller has transferred the significant risks and rewards of ownership to the buyer. In most cases, transfer of legal title either results in or coincides with the passing of possession (e.g., most retail sales) or the transfer of the risks and rewards of ownership (e.g., the dispatch of goods without condition) to the buyer, and therefore revenue would usually be recognized at this point.

Revenue from service transactions is usually recognized over the period in which the services are performed.

Revenue should be recognized only when no significant uncertainty as to its collectibility or measurement exists. If uncertainty arises subsequent to the time of sale or the rendering of services, a separate provision for doubtful accounts should be made, rather than adjusting the original revenue recorded.

If goods for resale or services performed are exchanged for nonmonetary assets, the fair value of the assets or services exchanged is normally used to determine the amount of revenue.

Long-Term Contracts. The percentage of completion method should be used in recognizing revenue from long-term construction contracts when the outcome of the contract can be reliably estimated. This requires reliable estimates of revenue, costs to date, state of completion and costs to complete. If these estimates cannot be made, no profit is recognized until the contract is complete. If, however, it is expected that there will be a loss on a contract, a provision should be made for the total amount of the loss as soon as it is identified. This has the effect of reducing the cost attributable to the work done to date to its net realizable value.

If unprofitable contracts are of such magnitude that they can be expected to absorb a considerable part of the company's capacity for a substantial period, indirect costs (e.g., general, administrative and selling costs) to be incurred during the period to the completion of those contracts should also be included in the provision for losses.

Instalment Sales. If the significant risks and benefits of ownership pass to the buyer at the inception of the transaction, the fact that the purchase price is to be received in instalments should not prevent the seller from recognizing the sale in full at that time and creating a receivable for the deferred payments. Profit is recognized as sale proceeds are collected in the proportion that the proceeds bear to the total sales price.

Rights of Return.   If a significant and predictable amount of goods is expected to be returned, it may be sufficient to make a provision therefor. If a significant but unpredictable amount of goods is expected to be returned, the criteria for recognition of revenue may not have been fully met and, accordingly, revenue recognition is postponed.

Product Financing.   The general principles relating to the transfer of risks and benefits of ownership apply in determining the appropriate accounting treatment for **product financing agreements**.

Disclosure.   Companies are required to disclose the components and total amount of turnover. For details of disclosures for long-term contracts, see Section 18.

Reference.   Companies Ordinance—Tenth Schedule and International Accounting Standard 18.

24.   Government Grants and Assistance

Accounting Treatment.   The government provides minimal direct assistance to industry, and there is no accounting standard dealing with accounting for government grants and assistance. If government assistance is given, reference is normally made to guidance provided in International Accounting Standard 20, *Accounting for Government Grants and Disclosure of Government Assistance*.

Disclosure.   The financial statements should disclose the accounting policy adopted for government grants and the amounts involved.

Reference.   International Accounting Standard 20.

25.   Research and Development

Accounting Treatment.   There is no accounting standard on accounting for research and development, and reference is normally made to guidance provided in International Accounting Standard 9, *Accounting for Research and Development Activities*.

Disclosure.   The accounting policy adopted for research and development costs should be disclosed. Total research and development cost, including amortization charged to the profit and loss account, and the changes in and balance of unamortized development costs should be disclosed.

Reference.   International Accounting Standard 9.

26.   Capitalized Interest Costs

Accounting Treatment.   There is no SSAP dealing with the capitalization of interest. However, the HKSA has issued a nonmandatory accounting guideline on capitalization of borrowing costs. The guideline recommends that, where borrowing costs are significant to a company, they should be capitalized as part of the cost of an asset that requires a substantial period of time to get it ready for use or sale by applying a capitalization rate to expenditures on the acquisition, construction or production of the asset. Borrowing costs, however, should not be capitalized for inventories that are routinely manufactured or otherwise produced in large quantities on a regular basis.

Disclosure. For an accounting period in which borrowing costs are capitalized, the total amount of borrowing costs incurred during the period and the amount capitalized should be disclosed.

Reference. HKSA Statement No. 2.205.

27. Imputed Interest

There is no accounting standard dealing with **imputed interest**, which is normally recognized only in accounting for finance lease transactions (see Section 15).

28. Extraordinary or Unusual Items

Extraordinary Items. Extraordinary items derive from events or transactions outside the ordinary activities of the business and are both material and expected not to recur frequently or regularly.

Exceptional Items. Exceptional items derive from events or transactions within the ordinary activities of the business and are both material and exceptional in terms of size and incidence.

Disclosure. Extraordinary items (less taxes attributable thereto) should be disclosed separately on the face of the profit and loss account. Separate disclosure of details of individual material extraordinary items is required in the notes.

Exceptional items should be included in profit for the year before taxes and extraordinary items, and their nature and size disclosed. The disclosure is normally made in the notes.

Reference. HKSA Statement No. 2.102 (SSAP 2).

29. Income Taxes

Accounting Treatment. Deferred tax should be computed under the **liability method**. Tax deferred or accelerated by the effect of timing differences should be accounted for to the extent that a liability or an asset is probable. The assessment of whether a deferred tax liability or asset will or will not arise should be based on reasonable assumptions that take into account all relevant information available up to the date on which the financial statements are approved by the board of directors and also on management's intentions.

Treatment of Tax Losses. Tax losses may not be carried back to recover taxes of previous periods, but may be carried forward indefinitely. Net deferred tax asset balances should not be recognized and carried forward, except to the extent that there is reasonable certainty as to their recoverability without replacement by equivalent asset balances.

Disclosure. Deferred tax relating to ordinary activities and extraordinary items should be shown separately. Adjustments to deferred tax arising from changes in tax rates and tax allowances should be disclosed separately as part of the tax charge for the period. However, the effect of a change in basis of taxation or government fiscal policy should be treated as an extraordinary item, if material.

The deferred tax balance and the amount of unprovided tax, classified by major components, should be disclosed in the financial statements.

Reference. HKSA Statement No. 2.112 (SSAP 12).

30. Postretirement Benefits

There is no accounting standard dealing with postretirement benefits, and reference is normally made to International Accounting Standard 19, *Accounting for Retirement Benefits in the Financial Statements of Employers*.

Reference. International Accounting Standard 19.

31. Discontinued Operations

Accounting Treatment. There is no prescribed accounting standard for discontinued operations.

Disclosure. The gain or loss on disposal of fixed assets should be disclosed, if material. If such disposals arise because of the discontinuance of a significant part of the business, they should be treated as extraordinary items.

Reference. HKSA Statement Nos. 2.102 and 2.106 (SSAPs 2 and 6); HKSA Technical Bulletin No. 6—October 1, 1985; and Companies Ordinance—Section 155A and Tenth Schedule.

32. Earnings per Share

Companies whose equity securities are listed on the SEHK are required to provide information relating to earnings per share.

Definition and Method of Calculation. SSAP 5 defines earnings per share as:

> ... the profit or loss in dollars and cents attributable to each equity share, based on the consolidated profit or loss of the period after tax and after deducting minority interests and preference dividends, but before taking into account extraordinary items, divided by the number of equity shares in issue and ranking for dividend in respect of the period.

Disclosure. Earnings per share should be disclosed on the face of the profit and loss account for both the current period and the corresponding prior period. The basis of calculation and the amount of earnings and number of equity shares used in the calculation should be shown.

In addition to the basic earnings per share, fully diluted earnings per share should be given, if the dilution is material. Dilution of earnings arises where a company has, at the balance sheet date, contracted to issue further shares after the end of the period, or where it has already issued shares on which dividends will be declared subsequently.

Reference. HKSA Statement No. 2.105 (SSAP 5) and Companies Ordinance—Tenth Schedule, Part III.

Appendix
DO HONG KONG STANDARDS OR PREVALENT PRACTICE SUBSTANTIALLY COMPLY WITH INTERNATIONAL ACCOUNTING STANDARDS?

Section	Topic	Substantially complies with IAS?	Comments
3.	Basic accounting concepts and conventions	Yes	
	Contents of financial statements	Yes	Except that a statement of cash flows is not required for certain small companies
4.	Business combinations*	Yes	
5.	Joint ventures	Yes	
6.	Foreign currency translation*	Yes	
8.	Accounting changes*	Yes	
9.	Prior period adjustments*	Yes	
10.	Post balance sheet events	Yes	
11.	Related party transactions	No	
12.	Segmental information	No	Segment reporting requirements extend only to listed companies and the required disclosures are more limited than IAS 14
13.	Property, plant and equipment*	Yes	
15.	Leases	Yes	
16.	Investments	Yes	
17.	Accounts receivable	Yes	
18.	Inventories and work in progress*	Yes	
19.	Current liabilities	Yes	
20.	Long-term debt	Yes	
21.	Contingencies	Yes	
22.	Capital and reserves	Yes	
23.	Revenue recognition*	Yes	
24.	Government grants and assistance	Yes	

Appendix (*Continued*)

Section	Topic	Substantially complies with IAS?	Comments
25.	Research and development*	Yes	
26.	Capitalization of interest costs*	Yes	
28.	Extraordinary or unusual items*	Yes	
29.	Income tax**	Yes	
30.	Postretirement benefits*	Yes	

*These topics are subject to change as a result of the IASC Improvements Project—see the appendix to the International Accounting Standards chapter.

**The IAS on accounting for taxes on income is currently being revised, and an exposure draft has been issued.

Comparison in this table is made to International Accounting Standards in force at January 1, 1993. For further details, see the International Accounting Standards chapter.

INDIA

GENERAL NATIONAL INFORMATION

1. Source of Generally Accepted Accounting Principles

Generally Accepted Accounting Principles.   **Generally accepted accounting principles (GAAP)** are derived from the following sources:

☐   The Companies Act 1956 (the Act), Schedule VI of which prescribes the form and content of the balance sheet, profit and loss statement and other information that must be disclosed by all companies except insurance, banking, electricity and other companies governed by acts that specify the form of their balance sheet. The Act also includes a number of general **accounting principles**. At the time of this writing, the Act is in the process of being revised.

☐   Accounting Standards (AS), issued by the Institute of Chartered Accountants of India (ICAI) (see below).

☐   Statements and Guidance Notes on Accounting Matters issued by the ICAI. Statements on Accounting Matters are issued with a view to securing compliance by members on matters that in the opinion of ICAI are critical to the proper discharge of their functions. Guidance Notes, on the other hand, are recommendations. They are designed primarily to provide guidance to members on matters that may arise in the course of their professional work and on which they may desire assistance in resolving complex issues.

The Accounting Standards Board of ICAI formulates **accounting standards**, taking into consideration applicable laws, customs, usage and business environment. Members of ICAI, industry, banks, the Company Law Board, the Central Board of Direct Taxes and the Comptroller and Auditor General of India are represented on the Accounting Standards Board. The council of ICAI has issued 12 standards, of which seven are now mandatory. Accounting standards are recommendatory in nature in their initial years and become mandatory on specified dates. In situations in which certain matters are covered by both a statement and an accounting standard, the statement prevails until the relevant accounting standard becomes mandatory. Once an accounting standard becomes mandatory, the related statement or relevant part thereof is automatically withdrawn. No legal support has yet been given to accounting standards issued by ICAI. On matters on which no standards or statements have been issued by ICAI, members have the option of consulting the International Accounting Standards (IASs).

In exceptional circumstances, where an accounting standard is not in agreement with the provisions of a statute, the provisions of law will prevail.

2. Audit and Public Company Requirements

Audits.   Every company at each annual general meeting is required to appoint an auditor to hold office from the conclusion of that meeting until the conclusion of the next annual general meeting. Where at an annual general meeting no auditor is appointed, the Central Government may appoint an auditor. The first auditor of a company is appointed by the board of directors within one month of the date of registration of the company; such auditor holds office until the conclusion of the first annual general meeting. If the board fails to exercise this power, the company may appoint the first auditor at a general meeting. The board may fill any casual vacancy in the office of auditor. However, any casual vacancy caused by the resignation of an auditor can be filled only by the shareholders at a general meeting. An auditor can be removed before the expiration of the term only by the shareholders at a general meeting, after obtaining approval of the government. However, government approval is not necessary for removal of the first auditor appointed by the board.

Only a chartered accountant or a firm of chartered accountants within the meaning of the Chartered Accountants Act 1949 can be appointed auditors of a company, including an Indian branch of a foreign company.

Statutory auditors are required to report whether:

☐   The accounts give the information required by the Act in the manner specified.

☐   The accounts give a true and fair view of the state of the company's affairs as at the end of the financial year and of the profit or loss for its financial year.

☐   They have obtained all the information and explanations that to the best of their knowledge and belief were necessary for the purposes of their audit.

☐   In their opinion proper books of account as required by law have been kept by the company, based on their examination of those books, and proper returns adequate for the purpose of their audit were received from branches not visited by them.

☐   Reports on the accounts of branch offices audited by other auditors have been forwarded to them, and how they dealt with those reports in preparing their report.

☐   The company's balance sheet and profit and loss statement reported on are in agreement with the books of account and returns.

The auditors' report also includes a statement on matters referred to in the Manufacturing and Other Companies (Auditor's Report) Order, 1988. The Order contains 27 questions on which the auditors have to comment, if applicable. The questions cover a wide range of matters, including maintenance of records; verification and valuation of assets; transactions and balances with certain related parties; internal control procedures on purchases and sales; compliance with rules in regard to deposits from the public; regularity of depositing provident funds and employee state insurance dues; and undisputed unpaid tax liabilities.

Where the answer to any of the matters on which the auditors are required to report is unfavorable or qualified, the auditors should state the reasons for such answer. Where the auditors are unable to express any opinion in answer to a particular question, their report should indicate such fact, together with the reasons therefor.

In conducting their audits, members of the ICAI are required to examine whether mandatory accounting standards and statements are complied with in the presentation of the financial statements. In the event of any deviation, adequate disclosure should be made in the audit report. Members should also ensure that they follow statements relating to auditing matters issued by ICAI. If for any reason they have not been able to perform the audit in accordance with such statements, their report should draw attention to the material departures therefrom. Members should ordinarily follow recommendations in Guidance Notes relating to auditing matters issued by ICAI, except where they are satisfied that it is not necessary to do so in the circumstances. Similarly, members should consider whether the recommendations given in recommendatory accounting standards or guidance notes relating to accounting matters have been followed. If they have not been, members should consider whether disclosure in the report is necessary.

Under the Act, the Central Government can prescribe the maintenance of cost records for a class of companies engaged in production, processing, manufacturing or mining activities and can direct that the cost accounts be audited. A statutory auditor may not be appointed as a cost auditor.

Companies whose **turnover** exceeds certain prescribed limits must file a tax audit report along with their tax return. The tax auditor must be a chartered accountant.

Public Companies. Companies can be listed on any of the recognized stock exchanges in India. Shares or debentures can be traded on the stock exchange after permission has been obtained from the stock exchange. All **listed companies** have to publish half-yearly results and file them with the stock exchanges on which their shares are quoted. All issues of shares and debentures have to be made in accordance with the guidelines issued by the Securities and Exchange Board of India.

At every annual general meeting of a company, the board of directors should present a balance sheet as at the end of the **financial period** and a profit and loss account for that period, which, except with special permission from the Registrar of Companies, may not exceed 15 months. The financial statements have to be placed before the general meeting within six months of the close of the financial period or within such extended period as the Registrar may allow. In the case of **holding companies**, certain documents (refer to Section 3) relating to **subsidiaries** are to be attached to the financial statements. A copy of the complete financial statements should be sent to every member of the company not less than 21 days before the date of the meeting. For listed companies, it is sufficient for a statement containing prescribed information, including the financial statements in abridged form, to be sent to every member, provided that copies of the documents mentioned above are available for inspection at the company's registered office during office hours for a period of 21 days before the meeting.

GENERAL ACCOUNTING

3. Financial Statements

Basic Accounting Concepts. Financial statements are normally prepared on the **historical cost** basis. Companies may base their financial statements on either the pure historical cost convention or the historical cost convention modified for the revaluation of **fixed assets**. **Current assets** are normally stated at the lower of historical cost or **net realizable value**. Certain fundamental accounting assumptions underlie the preparation and presentation of financial statements, as follows:

□ **Going concern**.
□ Consistency.
□ **Accrual concept**.

Contents of Financial Statements. Financial statements normally include a directors' report containing information required by the Act, a balance sheet and a profit and loss statement. Notes to financial statements, including a statement of accounting policies and supporting schedules to which the financial statements are cross-referenced, are considered an integral part of the statements. Comparative figures for the previous period are required to be shown. Cash flow statements are not required. AS-3, *Changes in Financial Position* (not mandatory), recommends that a statement of changes in financial position for the period be published along with the annual accounts. However, in practice this is not normally followed.

In addition, the following documents relating to each subsidiary are required to be attached to the balance sheet of a holding company:

□ Balance sheet.
□ Profit and loss statement.
□ Report of board of directors.
□ Auditors' report.
□ Statement of the holding company's interest, specifying the extent of interest and the net aggregate amount of subsidiaries' profits less losses as concerns the holding company, showing separately amounts included and not included in the holding company's financial statements.
□ Where the financial year of a subsidiary does not coincide with that of the holding company, information regarding changes in interests in the subsidiary during the intervening period and material changes in such period of the subsidiary's fixed assets, investments and moneys lent or borrowed for purposes other than meeting current liabilities.

Format of Financial Statements. Financial statements should be prepared in either vertical or horizontal form. The formats for the balance sheet and the disclosure requirements for the profit and loss statement are prescribed in the Act. There are strict rules governing the formats and when they can be amended. Certain required detailed information can be shown in the notes to the financial statements.

Disclosure of Accounting Policies. All significant **accounting policies** adopted in the preparation and presentation of financial statements should be disclosed in one place as part of the financial statements. When a fundamental accounting assumption is not followed, the fact should be disclosed.

Generally, accounting policies cover the basis of accounting; methods of depreciation, depletion or amortization; translation of foreign currency items; valuation of inventories; fixed assets, including goodwill; recognition of profit on long-term contracts, and so on.

Prudence, **substance over form**, and **materiality** are the major considerations governing the selection and application of accounting policies.

Reference. AS-1, Sections 211, 212, 217, and Schedule VI of the Act.

4. Business Combinations

Principles of Consolidation. In India there is no requirement to consolidate the financial statements of subsidiaries with those of the **parent company**. Subsidiaries are accounted for as investments by the parent company.

Accounting for Amalgamations. On an application made to it, a court can sanction a scheme for the amalgamation of two or more companies. The Act also gives authority to the Central Government to order the amalgamation of two or more companies into a single company.

In certain amalgamations there is a genuine pooling not merely of the assets and liabilities of the two companies, but also of the shareholders' interests and the businesses of the companies. Such amalgamations are in the nature of mergers.

Accounting for amalgamations in the nature of mergers: Subject to the identity of the reserves being preserved, the aggregate of the consideration and reserves is deducted from the book value of the net assets of the transferor company. If the result is positive, the amount is reflected in a capital reserve. If it is negative, it is recorded as **goodwill**.

Certain reserves may have been created by the transferor company pursuant to the requirements of the Income Tax Act or other statute (e.g., investment allowance reserve under the Income Tax Act). These statutes may require that these reserves be preserved for a specified period.

Where a company acquires the net assets, but not the shares, of another company, this is an amalgamation in the nature of a purchase.

Accounting for amalgamations in the nature of purchases: Only those reserves whose identity is required by statute to be preserved are so preserved. The aggregate of the consideration and the amount of reserves to be preserved is deducted from the book value of the assets acquired. If the result is positive, the amount is recorded as capital reserve; if negative, it is recorded as goodwill.

Goodwill. Goodwill arising from a **business combination** may be adjusted against any available capital reserve. As a matter of financial prudence, goodwill is frequently written off over a period of years. However, there is no prevalent practice and many companies do not write off goodwill.

Equity Accounting. There is no requirement for equity accounting.

Disclosure. Acquisitions of shares are accounted for as investments, with details of the number of shares, corresponding values and name of the investee company disclosed in the financial statements. If an investee company becomes a subsidiary, that fact should be disclosed in the schedule of investments.

In the case of amalgamations, goodwill should be disclosed under fixed assets. The terms of the amalgamation are disclosed in a note to the financial statements.

Reference. Guidance Note on Accounting Treatment of Reserves in Amalgamation; Section 394 and Schedule VI of the Act.

5. Joint Ventures

Accounting for Investments in Joint Ventures. ICAI has not issued any pronouncements addressing the different forms of **joint ventures** detailed in IAS 31.

Jointly Controlled Entities. Investments in jointly controlled entities should normally be classified as long-term investments and carried in the balance sheet at their original cost. However, the carrying amount should be reduced to recognize a decline that is other than temporary. All disclosure rules applicable to investments are also applicable to jointly controlled entities.

A jointly controlled entity operates in the same way as any other commercial enterprise and may have a basis of accounting distinct from that of the venturers.

Jointly Controlled Assets. When an enterprise owns fixed assets jointly with others (other than as a partner in a firm), the extent of ownership and the proportion of the original cost, accumulated depreciation and written down value generally are included separately in the enterprise's balance sheet. Alternatively, the pro rata cost of jointly owned assets is grouped together with fully owned assets, and details of the jointly owned assets are recorded separately.

Jointly Controlled Operations. There is no guidance by ICAI on accounting for jointly controlled operations. The accounting treatment in IAS 31 appears to be appropriate.

6. Foreign Currency Translation

General. AS-11, *Accounting for the Effects of Changes in Foreign Exchange Rates*, is being revised and ICAI has published a draft of the standard. The following paragraphs outline the accounting treatment in the draft.

Domestic Operations. A transaction in foreign currency should be translated into the local currency at the exchange rate prevailing at the date of the transaction (spot rate) or at an average rate (for example, an average rate for all transactions during a week or month). The same rate should be used to report a group of interrelated transactions.

At each balance sheet date, foreign currency **monetary items** should be reported using the **closing rate** except where a lower rate is appropriate due to lack of reasonable certainty as to ultimate collection or use. Nonmonetary items carried at historical cost are reported using the exchange rate on the date of the transaction except that any fluctuation in the value of a liability incurred for the purchase of a fixed asset is added to, or deducted from, the cost of the asset. Where the cost of a depreciable asset has been adjusted, **depreciation** on the revised depreciable amount should be provided prospectively over the residual value of the asset.

Exchange differences arising on **foreign currency transactions** should be recognized as income or expenses in the period in which they arise, except as stated above for fixed assets. If an enterprise enters into a forward exchange contract or any other financial instrument that is in substance a forward exchange contract to establish the amount of the reporting currency required or available at the settlement date, the difference between the forward rate and the exchange rate at the inception of the contract should be recognized as interest income or expense over the life of the contract, except where the contract relates to a fixed asset. Any profit or loss arising on cancellation of a forward exchange contract should be recognized as income or expense for the period, except with respect to fixed assets, in which case the profit or loss should be adjusted in the cost of the asset.

Foreign Operations.   Because **consolidated financial statements** are not required in India, foreign currency translation arises only with respect to the financial statements for foreign branches.

Revenue items, except for opening and closing **inventories** and depreciation, generally should be translated at an average rate; in appropriate circumstances (e.g., when income and expenses are not earned or incurred evenly during the accounting period or when there are exceptionally wide fluctuations in exchange rates during the period), the weighted-average rate may be applied. Opening and closing inventories should be translated at the rates prevalent at the beginning and end, respectively, of the accounting period. Depreciation should be translated at the rates used for translation of the related assets. Monetary items should be translated using the closing rate, except where a lower rate is appropriate due to lack of reasonable certainty as to ultimate realization or use. Nonmonetary items other than inventories should be translated using the exchange rate at the date of the transaction, except with respect to fixed assets, in which case the increase or reduction in liability on account of fluctuation in exchange rates is adjusted in the historical cost of the asset. The net exchange difference resulting from the translation of items in the financial statements should be recognized as income or expense for the period, except to the extent adjusted in the carrying value of fixed assets.

Disclosure.   The following should be disclosed:

☐   The amount of exchange differences included in net profit or loss for the period.
☐   The amount of exchange difference adjusted in the carrying amount of fixed assets.
☐   The amount of exchange difference relating to forward exchange contracts not included in profit or loss for the period.
☐   The enterprise's foreign currency risk management policy.

Reference.   AS-11 (not mandatory).

7. Changing Prices/Inflation Accounting

There is no requirement in India to make any adjustment for inflation or changes in prices. However, the ICAI recommends that while the primary financial statements should continue to be prepared and presented on the historical cost basis, supplementary information reflecting the impact of changes in prices may also be provided on a voluntary basis, particularly by large enterprises. Current cost accounting has been recommended as the most appropriate method in the context of the economic environment in India.

Reference.   Guidance Note on Accounting for Changing Prices.

8. Accounting Changes

Accounting Treatment.   A fundamental accounting assumption is that accounting treatment be consistent within a period and from one period to the next. A change in accounting policy should be made only in exceptional circumstances, that is, if the adoption of a different accounting policy is required by statute or for compliance with an accounting standard or if the change is considered to result in a more appropriate preparation or presentation of the financial statements.

Accounting Estimates.   The preparation of financial statements involves making estimates based on the circumstances existing at the time the statements are prepared. It may be necessary to revise the estimate in a subsequent period if there is a change in the circumstances on which the estimate was based. Changes in estimates are neither prior period items nor extraordinary items. Revision of an item that was treated as extraordinary is itself treated as extraordinary.

Disclosure.   Any change in accounting policy that has a material effect is disclosed. The impact of and the adjustment resulting from such changes, if material, on the current period's financial statements should also be disclosed. If the impact of a change on the financial statements is not ascertainable, that fact should be disclosed. If a change in accounting policy has no material effect on the financial statements for the current period but is reasonably expected to have a material effect in later periods, the fact of such change should be appropriately disclosed in the period in which the change is adopted.

A change in accounting estimate that has a material impact in the current period should be disclosed and quantified. A change in accounting estimate that is reasonably expected to have a material effect in later periods should also be disclosed.

Reference.   AS-5.

9. Prior Period Adjustments

Definition.   Prior period items are material charges or credits that arise in the current period as a result of errors or omissions in the preparation of financial statements in one or more prior periods. The charge or credit arising on the outcome of a **contingency**, which at the time of occurrence could not be estimated accurately, does not constitute the correction of an error, but a change in estimate.

Accounting Treatment.   Prior period items are included in the profit and loss statement for the current period.

Disclosure.   Separate disclosure of all prior period items is made, wherever applicable.

Reference.   AS-5.

10. Post Balance Sheet Events

Definition.   Post balance sheet events are significant events, both favorable and unfavorable, that occur between the balance sheet date and the date the financial statements are approved by the board of directors or other comparable authority. Two types of post balance sheet events are identified:

□   Those that provide further evidence of conditions that existed as at the balance sheet date.

☐ Those that are indicative of conditions that arose subsequent to the balance sheet date.

Accounting Treatment. Adjustments to assets and liabilities are required for significant events occurring after the balance sheet date that provide additional information materially affecting the determination of amounts relating to conditions existing at the balance sheet date. For example, an adjustment may be made for a loss on a trade account receivable that is confirmed by the insolvency of a customer occurring after the balance sheet date.

Adjustments to assets and liabilities are not appropriate for events occurring after the balance sheet date that do not relate to conditions existing at the balance sheet date.

Disclosure. Events indicative of conditions that arose subsequent to the balance sheet date are disclosed. The disclosure should cover the nature of the event and an estimate of its financial effects or a statement that such an estimate cannot be made. Disclosure is generally made of events in subsequent periods that represent unusual changes affecting the going concern assumption of the enterprise at the balance sheet date.

Reference. AS-4.

11. Related Party Transactions

Related parties are not defined in the Act. However, the Act requires certain transactions with certain parties to be disclosed. Such parties include:

☐ A director or relative, a firm in which such director or relative is a partner, any other partner in such a firm or a private company of which the director is a member or director.

☐ A manager, defined as an individual who subject to the superintendence, control and direction of the board of directors, manages all, or substantially all, of the affairs of a company.

☐ Companies under the same management.

☐ A holding company and an ultimate holding company.

Accounting Treatment. There is no prescribed accounting treatment pertaining to transactions with related parties.

Disclosure. The main disclosures required are:

☐ Transactions and balances with directors, managers and other parties connected with them, including loans and other balances due to or from the company, guarantees, fees, remuneration and commissions.

☐ Debts and loans and advances due from companies under the same management, with the names of the companies and, in the case of loans and advances, the maximum amount due at any time during the year, and investments in companies under the same management.

☐ Advances and loans to and from subsidiaries and investments in subsidiaries.

☐ Advances and loans to firms in which the company or a subsidiary is a partner.

☐ The number of shares held in subsidiaries by the holding company and the ultimate holding company and its subsidiaries.

Reference. Sections 2, 295, 370, and Schedule VI of the Act.

12. Segmental Information

There is no requirement for reporting financial information by major industry and geographical segments. However, the following details are required to be reported by product:

- ☐ Installed capacity.
- ☐ Licensed capacity.
- ☐ Production.
- ☐ Purchases of finished goods.
- ☐ Sales.
- ☐ Opening and closing finished goods inventories.
- ☐ Consumption of raw materials.

Reference. Schedule VI of the Act.

ACCOUNTING PRINCIPLES FOR SPECIFIC ITEMS— BALANCE SHEET

13. Property, Plant and Equipment

Classification of Capital and Revenue Expenditure. Fixed assets are assets held with the intention of being used for producing or providing goods or services and not for sale in the normal course of business. Subsequent expenditures related to a fixed asset are added to its book value only if they increase the future benefits from the existing asset beyond its previously assessed value.

Basis of Valuation. Fixed assets are generally carried at historical cost or at valuation. The cost of a fixed asset should comprise its purchase price and any attributable cost of bringing the asset to its working condition for its intended use. Financing costs relating to deferred credits or to borrowed funds attributable to construction or acquisition of fixed assets for the period up to completion of construction or acquisition should also be included in the value of the asset to which they relate. Expenditures incurred on start-up and commissioning of the asset, including test runs and experimental production, are usually capitalized as an indirect element of construction cost. Foreign exchange differences relating to amounts incurred for the acquisition of fixed assets are adjusted in the carrying amount of the fixed assets. Material items retired from active use and held for disposal are stated at the lower of their net book value or net realizable value and shown separately in the financial statements.

A commonly accepted and preferred method of revaluation is by appraisal, normally undertaken by competent valuers. Other methods sometimes used are indexation and reference to current prices; the results are cross-checked periodically by appraisal. When assets are revalued, the entire class of assets should be revalued or the selection should be made on a systematic basis, which should be disclosed. The revaluation of a class of assets should not result in net book value of that class being greater than the recoverable amount of assets of that class. An increase in net book value arising on revaluation of fixed assets is directly reflected in owners' equity in a revaluation reserve account except that to the extent such increase is related to and not greater than a decrease arising on devaluation previously charged to the profit and loss statement, it may be credited to the profit and loss statement. A decrease in net book value arising on revaluation is charged directly to the profit and loss statement except that to the extent such a decrease is related to an increase previously recorded in the revaluation reserve and not subsequently reversed or utilized, it may be charged directly to that account.

Gains or losses on sale of assets are normally recognized in the profit and loss statement. Any balance in the revaluation reserve relating to an asset sold is adjusted against the sales proceeds.

Depreciation. Fixed assets with limited useful lives are depreciated systematically over those useful lives. Land normally is not depreciated. The Act specifies the rates of depreciation for each category of assets using both the **straight-line method** and **diminishing balance method**, on single shift, double shift and triple shift working bases. For certain highly depreciable assets, 100 percent depreciation is prescribed. These rates are minimum rates and therefore a company is not permitted to charge depreciation at lower rates. However, on the basis of a *bona fide* technical evaluation, higher rates of depreciation are justified. Where assets have been revalued, depreciation on differential increases in value arising from revaluation can be recouped from the revaluation reserve.

Disclosure. The following information should be disclosed in the financial statements:

☐ The accounting policies adopted in relation to valuation and method of depreciation.

☐ Gross book and net book value at the beginning and end of the accounting period, showing additions and acquisitions, disposals and other movements, depreciation for the period and the related accumulated depreciation, and for each class of fixed assets distinguishing as far as possible between land, buildings, leaseholds, railway sidings, plant and machinery, furniture and fittings, development of property, livestock and vehicles.

☐ Expenditures incurred on fixed assets in the course of construction or acquisition.

☐ Depreciation rates or useful lives of the assets, if they are different from the principal rates specified in the statute governing the enterprise.

☐ For assets that have been revalued, the revalued amount substituted for historical cost. The date of revaluation, the method adopted to compute the revalued amount, the nature of indices used and whether an external valuer was involved should be disclosed in a note in the year of revaluation. The balance sheets for the first five years subsequent to the revaluation should also show the amount of increase or decrease. In addition, the amount of depreciation recouped from the revaluation reserve should be shown separately in the profit and loss statement, normally as a deduction from gross depreciation.

☐ The amount of exchange loss or gain included in the carrying amount of fixed assets.

Reference. AS-10 and 11; Circular from Department of Company Affairs dated March 7, 1989; Schedule VI of the Act.

14. Intangible Assets

Accounting Treatment.   **Intangible assets** such as patents and other rights and assets are capitalized only when some consideration in money has been paid for them or when they have been created by the company. Goodwill is recorded only when some consideration has been paid for it. Amounts paid for technical know-how, layout and design of buildings or designs of machinery are capitalized as part of the related asset.

Valuation.   Writing off patents (especially when they are developed in the company) in the profit and loss statement in the year incurred is a common practice. If they are capitalized, care is taken to revise the amount written off each year as the circumstances regarding the expected useful life of patents change.

Amortization.   As a matter of financial prudence, goodwill should be amortized over a period. However, many enterprises do not write off goodwill and retain it as an asset. Patents and other intangible assets are amortized over their legal term of validity or over their useful life, whichever is shorter.

Disclosure.   The accounting policy in relation to valuation and **amortization** should be disclosed. Goodwill and patents, trademarks and designs should be separately disclosed in the balance sheet.

Reference.   AS-10; Statement of Auditing Practices; Schedule VI of the Act.

15. Leases

General.   ICAI has not issued any accounting standard on accounting for leases. A Guidance Note was issued by ICAI in 1988 on the subject but has been kept in abeyance on the basis of a court order. In the introduction to the Guidance Note, ICAI stated that an accounting standard would be issued and that the guidance was being issued as an interim measure. Companies are not precluded from accounting for lease transactions in accordance with IAS 17.

However, in practice most companies in India do not distinguish between **finance** and **operating leases**. Lessees recognize lease rentals in the profit and loss statement. Lessors capitalize the assets on lease and charge depreciation thereon. Lease income is accounted for according to the terms of the agreement.

16. Investments
An accounting standard on Accounting for Investments is under formulation by ICAI.

Valuation.   Investments are ordinarily valued at cost, including transfer fees, stamp duty and similar fees, on an individual basis. When there is a permanent decline in the value of long-term investments, they are written down to realizable value. Premises acquired through purchase of shares in cooperative societies are treated as fixed assets and are subject to depreciation. For investment companies, investments meant for trading are shown under current assets and valued at the lower of cost and realizable value on the balance sheet date.

Recognition of Gains or Losses.   When investments are sold, the profit or loss on sale is computed using the carrying value of the investments.

Disclosure.   Investments should be disclosed showing the basis of valuation and the nature of the investments. The following distinctions are made:

☐   Government or trust securities.
☐   Shares, debentures or bonds, showing separately shares fully paid up and partly paid up and also distinguishing the different classes of shares (and showing similar details for investments in subsidiary companies).
☐   Immovable properties.
☐   Capital of partnership firms.

The aggregate amount of the company's quoted investments and unquoted investments and also the market value of quoted investments should be disclosed.

A statement of investments should be attached to the financial statements, distinguishing between trade investments (investments by a company in the shares or debentures of another company other than a subsidiary, for the purpose of promoting trade or business of the first company) and other investments, showing the nature and extent of each investment. For investments made in capital of partnership firms, the names of the firms (with the names of all their partners, total capital and the shares of each partner) should be given. Any uncalled liability on partly paid shares should be disclosed in a note to the financial statements.

Reference.   Statement of Auditing Practices; Schedule VI of the Act.

17.   Accounts Receivable

Accounting Treatment.   Recognition of revenue and hence the related receivables are dealt with in Section 23.

Discounts.   Receivables are normally recorded net of trade discounts and volume rebates. Cash discounts are normally treated as an expense when taken by the customer.

Provision for Doubtful Debts.   An adequate provision should be made for bad and doubtful accounts. No specific basis is prescribed for calculating the provision for doubtful debts.

Factored Receivables.   **Factoring** of receivables is not common in India. If trade **accounts receivable** have been factored for cash consideration, the relevant receivables should be excluded from the balance sheet. Discounts given should normally be expensed. If receivables have been sold with recourse, disclosure of the contingency and provision for losses should be made in the financial statements.

Disclosure.   **Debtors** should be segregated as follows:

☐   Debts considered good and in respect of which the company is fully secured.

□ Debts considered good for which the company holds no security other than the debtor's personal security.

□ Debts considered doubtful or bad.

These are further classified under:

□ Debts outstanding for a period exceeding six months.

□ Other debts.

All doubtful debts should be provided for and such provisions should be disclosed. All such doubtful debts and the related provision continue to be shown in the balance sheet until they are written off as bad debts.

With respect to bills accepted by customers and discounted with the company's bankers, if the practice is to credit customers' accounts, the related contingent liability is disclosed.

If in the opinion of the board of directors, the realizable value of debtors is not at least equal to the amount at which they are stated, that should be stated.

Reference.   AS-9; Schedule VI of the Act.

18.   Inventories and Work in Progress

Inventories are normally stated at the lower of historical cost or net realizable value. Consumable stores and maintenance supplies are normally stated at cost but in appropriate circumstances may be stated lower than cost.

Historical cost includes cost of purchase, cost of conversion and other costs incurred in the normal course of business in bringing the inventories to their present location and condition. The cost of conversion includes direct labor, direct expenses and production overheads but excludes expenses that relate to general administration, finance, research and development, and selling and distribution. The cost of inventories is normally determined using **FIFO, average cost** or **LIFO** formulas. However, the **specific identification method** may be used for inventories of items that are not ordinarily interchangeable or for goods manufactured and earmarked for a specific purpose. Adjusted selling price (**retail method**) may be used in retail businesses or in businesses where the inventory comprises items the individual cost of which is not readily ascertainable. The **standard cost** method may be used if the results approximate consistently the results that would be obtained under FIFO, average cost and LIFO formulas. The **base stock** method is used in exceptional circumstances. A fundamental aspect of valuation is consistency.

Long-Term Contracts.   The cost of long-term contracts should comprise costs that relate directly to a specific contract and those that are attributable to contract activities in general and can be allocated to specific contracts. Revenue recognition for long-term contracts is covered in Section 23.

Disclosure.   The accounting policy adopted for valuation of inventories, including the cost formulas used, should be disclosed. A change in the accounting policy, and its effects, if material, should also be disclosed. Inventories in the balance sheet are classified under stores and spare parts, loose tools, stock in trade (raw materials separately, wherever practicable) and work in progress. Detailed quantity and value information for finished goods is required to be disclosed in the profit and loss statement. Progress payments received and advances and retention on account of contracts included in construction work in progress and the amount receivable with respect to income accrued under cost plus contracts not included in construction work in progress are disclosed.

If in the opinion of the board of directors, the realizable value of inventories is not at least equal to the amount at which they are stated, that fact should be stated.

Reference.   AS-2 (not mandatory) and 7; Schedule VI of the Act.

19.   Current Liabilities

Current liabilities are distinguished from other balance sheet items. The following categories are presented and disclosed separately: acceptances (bills of exchange payable), sundry **creditors**, amounts due to subsidiaries, advance payments, unclaimed dividends, other liabilities (if any) and interest accrued but not due on loans.

Sundry creditors normally include all liabilities arising from the trading activities of the company.

Provisions.   Liabilities whose existence is certain, but whose value is estimated, are regarded as provisions, which are disclosed separately. They may include estimated liabilities for product warranties, service contracts and guarantees, taxes on income and gratuities. Provisions relating to assets, for example, bad debt provisions may be netted against the related assets. General or specific provisions or reserves may be created for contingencies but the movement in the provision should be separately disclosed in the profit and loss statement.

Disclosure.   In addition to the disclosure requirements referred above, provisions should be separately disclosed in the balance sheet as provisions for taxation, proposed dividends, contingencies, provident fund scheme, insurance, pension and similar staff benefit schemes, and other.

Reference.   Statement of Auditing Practices; Opinion by Expert Advisory Committee of ICAI; Schedule VI of the Act.

20.   Long-Term Debt

Long-term debt includes loans from banks and financial institutions, bonds, debentures and similar securities. Under the guidelines for the protection of interests of debenture-holders, before debenture redemption commences, the company should create a debenture redemption reserve (DRR) equivalent to 50 percent of the amount of debentures issued. The DRR may be used for redemption purposes only after 40 percent of the debenture liability has been redeemed by the company. The premium payable on the redemption of debentures or bonds can be either charged to the profit and loss statement over the term of such debentures or bonds or charged to the **share premium** account.

Disclosure.   Long-term debt is normally included in the balance sheet under secured loans or unsecured loans. Secured loans have to be disclosed separately as debentures, loans and advances from banks, loans and advances from subsidiaries and other loans and advances. Unsecured loans have to be separately disclosed as fixed deposits, loans and advances from subsidiaries, short-term loans and other loans and advances from banks and from others. The short-term portion (due within one year of the balance sheet date) of loans and advances from banks and from others is disclosed separately. Loans from directors and similar parties should be disclosed separately (see Section 11). Terms of redemption or conversion of debentures are to be stated together with the earliest date of redemption or conversion. Details of security against debt should be disclosed. Loans guaranteed by third parties in whose favor the assets of the company are mortgaged should be classified as secured only to the extent of the market value of the security.

Reference. Section 78 and Schedule VI of the Act; Guidelines for the Protection of Interest of Debenture-holders.

21. Contingencies

Contingent Losses. A material contingent loss may be accrued if it is probable at the balance sheet date that a future event will confirm a loss as at that date and a reasonable estimate of the loss can be made. The existence of a contingent loss should be disclosed in the financial statements if either of the above two conditions is not met, unless the possibility of loss is remote.

Contingent Gains. Contingent gains should not be accrued in the financial statements. The existence and nature of contingent gains are normally disclosed in the report of the board of directors if it is reasonably certain that the gains will be realized by the enterprise. However, it is important to avoid giving misleading implications as to the likelihood of realization.

Disclosure. Provisions for contingencies are disclosed separately in the profit and loss statement. For unprovided contingencies the required disclosures are: the nature of the contingency, the uncertainties that may affect the future outcome, an estimate of the financial effect or a statement that such an estimate cannot be made.

Reference. AS-4; Schedule VI of the Act.

22. Capital and Reserves

General. Shareholders' funds comprise **share capital** and reserves. Share capital refers to the aggregate amount of money paid or credited as paid on the shares of a corporate enterprise. A company's share capital may consist of equity shares and **preference shares**. Preference shares give the holder of the shares preferential rights with respect to dividends and repayment of capital. They may also have full or partial participating rights in surplus profit or surplus capital.

Reserves represent the portion of earnings, receipts or other surplus of an enterprise appropriated by the management for a general or specific purpose other than a provision for depreciation or diminution in the value of assets or for a known liability. Reserves are primarily of two types: capital reserves and revenue reserves. A capital reserve represents a reserve of a corporate enterprise that is not available for distribution as dividends. Revenue reserves are normally derived from earnings and available for distribution and are usually called free reserves.

Share Capital. The paid-up share capital is the aggregate amount of calls made on the company's shares reduced by calls in arrears. If shares are issued at a premium, the premium is credited to the share premium account. The share premium account can be used only to issue fully paid bonus shares, write off preliminary expenses, write off expense relating to the issue of shares or debentures, write off commission paid or discounts allowed on any issue of shares or debentures and provide for the premium payable on redemption of any redeemable preference shares or debentures. All preference shares are redeemable within ten years out of the profits of the company available for dividends or the proceeds of a new issue of shares made mainly for the purpose of redemption. Where such shares are redeemed otherwise than out of the proceeds of a new issue, a sum equal to the nominal amount of the shares redeemed should be transferred to a capital redemption reserve account, which can be utilized to issue fully paid bonus shares.

Reserves. Reserves and surplus are classified as capital reserve, capital redemption reserve, share premium account, sinking funds, other reserves and surplus (i.e., balance in profit and loss account after providing for proposed allocations). Surplus from the revaluation of assets is credited to a revaluation reserve and is shown under capital reserve. Reserves created by appropriation of profit for availing of benefits under the Income Tax Act are normally shown under other reserves and are reversed on the expiration of the benefit period under the tax law.

Distribution Restrictions. Dividends can be paid for any financial year only out of the profits of that year or any previous financial year, after providing for depreciation prescribed under the Act, including arrears, if any. However, dividends can be paid without providing for such depreciation, with permission from the Central Government. Before a dividend exceeding 10 percent is declared, a percentage of the profit for that year as prescribed in the Companies (Transfer of Profits to Reserves) Rules, 1975 is transferred to reserves. The percentages prescribed do not exceed 10 percent of the profits, and a voluntary transfer of a higher percentage is allowed subject to certain conditions given in the rules. In the event of inadequacy or absence of profit in any year, dividends can be paid out of accumulated profits earned in previous years and transferred to reserves, subject to certain conditions contained in the Companies (Declaration of Dividend out of Reserves) Rules, 1975.

Disclosure. Share capital: Share capital is disclosed, distinguishing between the various classes of shares and stating the total number of shares and the nominal value of each share. Any unpaid calls are shown as a deduction from called-up capital to arrive at paid-up capital. Calls unpaid by directors and others are disclosed. Details of shares allotted pursuant to a contract without payment in cash and shares allotted by way of fully paid-up bonus shares (specifying the source from which issued, e.g., capitalization of profits, reserves or share premium account) are disclosed. Terms of redemption or conversion of any redeemable share capital together with the earliest date of redemption or conversion and details of any options on unissued share capital are disclosed. For subsidiary companies, the number of shares held by the holding company as well as by the ultimate holding company and its subsidiaries should be separately stated.

Reserves and surplus: All reserves are disclosed separately, showing the aggregate amount of each reserve at the beginning and end of the year and giving the movements and showing the sources of such movements.

Reference. Guidance Note on Terms Used in Financial Statements, Sections 78, 80A, 205 and Schedule VI of the Act; Companies (Transfer of Profits to Reserves) Rules, 1975; Companies (Declaration of Dividend out of Reserves) Rules, 1975.

ACCOUNTING PRINCIPLES FOR SPECIFIC ITEMS— INCOME STATEMENT

23. Revenue Recognition

General Accounting Principles. As a general principle, revenue is recognized when performance is complete and reasonable assurance exists regarding measurement and collectibility of the consideration. Where revenue is not measurable or where it is unreasonable to expect ultimate collection, recognition is postponed.

Revenue from sale of goods is recognized when the seller has transferred the goods to the buyer for a price or all significant risks and rewards of ownership have been transferred to the buyer and the seller retains no effective control of the goods transferred and no significant uncertainty exists regarding the amount of consideration.

Revenue from service transactions is usually recognized when the service is performed, using either the **percentage of completion method** or the **completed contract method**. Performance is regarded as achieved when no significant uncertainty exists regarding the amount of consideration that will be derived from rendering the service.

Revenue in the form of interest, royalties and dividends is recognized when no uncertainty as to measurement or collectibility exists, using following bases:

- ☐ Interest: on a time proportion basis taking into account the amount outstanding and the rate applicable.
- ☐ Royalties: on an accrual basis in accordance with the terms of the agreement.
- ☐ Dividends: when the owner's right to receive payment is established.

Long-Term Contracts. Revenue from long-term contracts is usually recognized using either the percentage of completion or the completed contract method. When an entity uses a particular method of accounting for a contract, the same method is adopted for all other contracts meeting similar criteria.

The percentage of completion method is used if the outcome of the contract can be reliably estimated. When recognizing profit under the percentage of completion method, an appropriate allowance for future unforeseeable factors is made on either a specific or a percentage basis. For fixed price contracts profit is not recognized until the work has progressed to a reasonable extent. If there is a foreseeable loss on an entire contract, it should be provided for in the financial statements as it is foreseen irrespective of the amount of work done and the method of accounting followed.

Instalment Sales. On **instalment sales**, revenue is normally recognized on the date of sale.

Rights of Return. When goods are sold giving the buyer the right of return, recognition of revenue will depend on the substance of the agreement. For retail sales offering a guarantee, it is appropriate to recognize the sales but to make a suitable provision for returns based on previous experience. For consignment sales, revenue is not recognized until the goods are sold to a third party.

Product Financing. In cases where the seller concurrently agrees to repurchase the same goods at a later date, the transaction in substance is a financing agreement. The resulting cash inflow is not recognized as revenue.

Disclosure. The Act requires the following disclosures:

☐ The turnover, that is, the aggregate amount of sales effected by the company, giving sales for each class of goods whose value accounts for 10 percent of the total value and indicating quantities for each class.

☐ Gross income from services rendered.

☐ Income from investments, distinguishing between trade investments and other investments.

☐ Dividends from subsidiary companies.

☐ Interest income, specifying its nature.

☐ Profit on investments.

☐ Any exceptional or nonrecurring income, if material.

☐ Miscellaneous income.

The accounting policy for turnover and other income is disclosed. Where revenue recognition has been postponed pending resolution of significant uncertainties, the circumstances should be disclosed. The method of accounting for long-term contracts is disclosed. If a contractor changes from the percentage of completion method to the completed contract method for contracts in progress at the beginning of the year, it may not be possible to quantify the effect of the change. In such cases, disclosure should be made of the amount of attributable profits reported in prior years with respect to contracts in progress at the beginning of the accounting period.

Reference. AS-7 and 9; Schedule VI of the Act.

24. Government Grants and Assistance

Accounting Treatment. Government grants are not recognized until there is reasonable assurance that the enterprise will comply with the conditions attached to them and that the grants will be received. Normally, grants related to specific assets are shown as a deduction from the gross values of the assets. Alternatively, grants related to depreciable fixed assets may be treated as deferred income and recognized in the profit and loss statement over the useful life of the asset (e.g., in the same proportion as depreciation on related assets). Grants related to nondepreciable assets are recorded in capital reserves under this method. If a grant related to a nondepreciable asset requires fulfillment of certain obligations, the grant is reflected in income over the same period as the costs of meeting the obligation, and deferred income is separately disclosed. Grants related to revenue are recognized over the periods necessary to match them with the related costs. These grants are either shown separately under other income or deducted in reporting the related expenditures. Grants in the nature of promoters' contributions are recorded in capital reserves and treated as part of shareholders' funds. Grants in the form of monetary assets given at a concessionary rate are accounted for on the basis of their acquisition cost. If the asset is given free of charge, it is recorded at a nominal value. Government grants that become refundable are accounted for as extraordinary items. Grants in the nature of promoters' contributions that become refundable are charged to capital reserves.

Disclosure.   The accounting policy adopted for government grants and the nature and extent of government grants recognized in the financial statements, including grants of nonmonetary assets given at a concessionary rate or free of charge, are disclosed.

Reference.   AS-12 (not mandatory).

25.   Research and Development

Definition.   Research is original and planned investigation undertaken with the hope of gaining new scientific or technical knowledge and understanding. Development is the translation of research findings into a plan or design for the production of new or substantially improved materials, devices, products, processes, systems or services prior to the commencement of commercial production.

Accounting Treatment.   Research and development costs are charged as an expense of the period in which they are incurred except where such costs are permitted to be deferred. The following criteria should be met for research and development costs to be deferred to future periods:

- The product or process is clearly defined and the costs attributable to it can be separately identified.
- The technical feasibility of the product or process has been demonstrated.
- The management of the enterprise has indicated its intention to produce and market or use the product or process.
- There is a reasonable indication that current and future research and development costs to be incurred on the project, together with expected production, selling and administration costs, are likely to be more than covered by related future revenues or benefits.
- Adequate resources exist, or are reasonably expected to be available, to complete the project and market the product or process.

Where research and development costs are deferred, they are allocated on a systematic basis to future accounting periods by reference either to the sale or use of the product or process or to the time period over which the product or process is expected to be sold or used. At the end of each accounting period, the enterprise should review the deferred research and development costs of a project. If the criteria that justified the original deferral of the costs no longer apply, the unamortized balance is charged as an expense immediately. If the criteria continue to be met but the amount of unamortized balance exceeds the related expected future revenues or benefits, the excess is charged as an expense immediately.

If a policy of deferring research and development costs is adopted, it should be applied to all projects that meet the criteria.

Disclosure. The following should be disclosed:

☐ The accounting policy adopted for research and development expenditure should be disclosed.

☐ The total research and development cost, including the amortized portion of deferred cost, charged as expense should be disclosed in the profit and loss statement.

☐ The deferred portion of research and development expenditure should be separately disclosed in the balance sheet.

Reference. AS-8.

26. Capitalized Interest Costs

Accounting Treatment. Interest payable during the period of construction or installation of fixed assets is capitalized. This applies to actual interest charges or commitment fees but not to any notional or **imputed interest** charges that are not actually incurred. Interest actually paid on share capital during the period of construction in circumstances envisioned under section 208 of the Act may also be capitalized as part of the construction cost or as part of the cost of the relevant plant and equipment. However, interest payable on fixed assets purchased on a deferred payment basis or on moneys borrowed for acquisition of assets is not capitalized after such assets are put to use.

Disclosure. Although there is no statutory requirement, it is a practice in some companies to disclose the gross interest and show the capitalized interest as a deduction therefrom to arrive at the net charge in the profit and loss statement.

Reference. Guidance Note on Treatment of Interest on Deferred Payments; Guidance Note on Treatment of Expenditure during Construction Period; Section 208 of the Act.

27. Imputed Interest
Imputed interest is not used in the preparation of financial statements in India.

28. Extraordinary or Unusual Items

Definition. Extraordinary items are defined as ''gains or losses which arise from events or transactions that are distinct from the ordinary activity of the business and which are both material and expected not to recur frequently or regularly.'' They also include material adjustments necessitated by circumstances that, although related to a previous period, are determined in the current period.

Extraordinary items are sometimes termed unusual items. Examples are the sale of a significant part of the business, liabilities arising on account of legislative changes or judicial pronouncement and so forth. Income or expenses arising from the ordinary activities of the enterprise, although abnormal in amount and infrequent in occurrence, do not qualify as extraordinary. An example would be the write-off of a very large receivable from a regular trade customer.

Disclosure. Extraordinary items should be disclosed in the profit and loss statement as part of net income. The nature and amount of such items should be separately disclosed in a manner that indicates their relative significance and effect on the current operating results of the period.

Reference. AS-5.

29. Income Taxes

Accounting Treatment. There are two methods prescribed for accounting for tax liabilities: the tax payable method and **liability method**. Although ICAI encourages use of the liability method, the tax payable method is more commonly followed primarily because its application is relatively easier.

Where the liability method is used, it should be applied to all timing differences except where there is reasonable evidence that differences will not reverse for a considerable period (at least 5 years). A deferred tax debit balance should not be carried forward unless there is a reasonable expectation of realization. An adjustment for unabsorbed depreciation and carryforward tax losses should be made only to the extent that there is absolute certainty that future taxable profit will arise.

Under tax laws, losses are allowed to be carried forward for set-off against future profits for eight years, and unabsorbed depreciation is allowed to be carried forward indefinitely.

Disclosure. The amount of income tax and other taxation on profit should be disclosed in the profit and loss statement, distinguishing between them, where practicable.

The accounting policy regarding treatment of tax on income should be disclosed. Where the liability method is used, the tax effect of timing differences, both current and cumulative, not recognized should be disclosed. Deferred tax balances should be disclosed separately in the balance sheet.

Reference. Guidance Note on Accounting for Taxes on Income; Schedule VI of the Act; Income Tax Act (Sections 32 and 72).

30. Postretirement Benefits

General. It is a statutory requirement for both employers and employees to contribute to provident funds administered by a duly constituted and approved independent trust or government. Payment of retirement gratuity is also a statutory requirement. However, the statutory requirements are limited to employees whose salary is less than amounts specified by the rules. It is not necessary for employers to provide for pension payments. Nevertheless, it is common for companies to set up pension funds on the basis of contractual agreement with employees. In order to obtain tax benefits, funding is necessary for gratuity, pension and superannuation plans.

Pensions. When pensions are payable on the basis of contractual agreement, such liabilities are normally provided for in the accounts on the basis of an actuarial valuation and are funded.

Other Postretirement Benefits.   Contributions to a provident fund by employers are in an amount equal to the amount deducted from the wages of employees (which is normally 10 percent of basic wages); such contributions are charged in the profit and loss statement.

Gratuity to employees on their retirement is normally actuarially ascertained and the accruing liability for each year is charged in the accounts. It is normal practice to have a gratuity fund created even for employees who are not covered by the Payment of Gratuity Act.

Disclosure.   The accounting policy for retirement benefits should be stated. The profit and loss statement should show the contribution to provident and other funds. If the company does not provide for gratuity, statutory or contractual, that fact and the amount of the gratuity liability should be disclosed.

Reference.   Schedule VI of the Act; Payment of Gratuity Act 1972; Employees' Provident Funds and Miscellaneous Provisions Act, 1952.

31. Discontinued Operations

Neither the Act nor ICAI specifies any treatment for discontinued operations.

32. Earnings per Share

There is no requirement in India to present earnings per share data, and it is not a common disclosure.

Appendix
DO INDIAN STANDARDS OR PREVALENT PRACTICE SUBSTANTIALLY COMPLY WITH INTERNATIONAL ACCOUNTING STANDARDS?

Section	Topic	Substantially complies with IAS?	Comments
3.	Basic accounting concepts and conventions	Yes	
	Contents of financial statements	No	Normally, a statement of changes in financial position is not presented
4.	Business combinations*	No	
5.	Joint ventures	No	
6.	Foreign currency translation*	No	
8.	Accounting changes*	Yes	
9.	Prior period adjustments*	Yes	Retroactive restatement is not permitted
10.	Post balance sheet events	Yes	
11.	Related party transactions	No	
12.	Segmental information	No	
13.	Property, plant and equipment*	Yes	
15.	Leases	No	
16.	Investments	Yes	
17.	Accounts receivable	Yes	
18.	Inventories and work in progress*	Yes	
19.	Current liabilities	Yes	
20.	Long-term debt	Yes	
21.	Contingencies	Yes	
22.	Capital and reserves	Yes	
23.	Revenue recognition*	Yes	
24.	Government grants and assistance	Yes	
25.	Research and development*	Yes	
26.	Capitalization of interest costs*	Yes	

Appendix (*Continued*)

Section	Topic	Substantially complies with IAS?	Comments
28.	Extraordinary or unusual items*	Yes	
29.	Income tax**	No	
30.	Postretirement benefits*	Yes	

*These topics are subject to change as a result of the IASC Improvements Project—see the appendix to the International Accounting Standards chapter.

**The IAS on accounting for taxes on income is currently being revised, and an exposure draft has been issued.

Comparison in this table is made to International Accounting Standards in force at January 1, 1993. For further details, see the International Accounting Standards chapter.

INDONESIA

GENERAL NATIONAL INFORMATION

1. Source of Generally Accepted Accounting Principles

Generally Accepted Accounting Principles.   The general objectives and concepts of accounting are derived from Indonesian Accounting Principles (PAI) (Prinsip Akuntansi Indonesia), last codified in 1984.

It should be stressed that, even where topics are addressed by Indonesian **accounting principles**, it is not uncommon for the preferred accounting treatment as set down in this chapter to be recommended rather than prescribed. In such circumstances it is possible that alternative accounting treatments may be acceptable if they comply with general principles and common practice.

Accounting Standards.   **Accounting standards** in Indonesia are issued by the Steering Committee of the Indonesian Accountants Association (IAI) (Ikatan Akuntan Indonesia). The main set of principles, PAI, is supplemented by periodic accounting statements and interpretations covering specific issues. References in this chapter are as follows:

- [ ] PAI—Refers to 1984 Indonesian Accounting Principles.
- [ ] PAI Statement—Refers to Statements on Accounting Standards issued by IAI since 1984 (Nos. 1–7).
- [ ] IPAI—Refers to Interpretations of Indonesian Accounting Principles issued by IAI since 1984 (Nos. 1–9).
- [ ] BAPEPAM SE-24—Applies to **public companies** only and establishes Guidelines on the Format and Contents of a Financial Report [issued as Attachment V to circular of the Chairman of the Capital Market Executive Board (BAPEPAM) No. SE-24/PM/1987, dated December 24, 1987].

For topics not addressed in the PAI or subsequent statements, the previous Generally Accepted Accounting Principles of Indonesia (1973) are still considered to be authoritative. If neither apply, then recourse should be had to common practice. International Accounting Standards may be referred to, as the IAI is a member of the International Accounting Standards Committee.

2. Audit and Public Company Requirements

Audits.   There is no general annual audit or reporting requirement, although it is implicit in the Commercial Code of Indonesia that financial statements should be prepared annually for presentation to the annual general meeting.

Audits are required for companies listed on a stock exchange, banks, insurance companies, leasing companies, stockbrokers and underwriters. Foreign investment companies established under the authorization of the Capital Investment Coordinating Board (BKPM) are required to submit audited financial statements prepared in accordance with Indonesian accounting principles to BKPM and Bank Indonesia (the central bank) annually. **Parent company** accounts are not required to be filed with local Indonesian accounts. Audit opinions may be issued only by Indonesian registered public accountants.

Public Companies.   The Jakarta and Surabaya stock exchanges are regulated by the Capital Market Executive Board, as are companies operating therein, such as securities companies and brokers. BAPEPAM's function and powers were codified in Presidential Decree No. 53 of 1990. Audit and reporting regulations for public companies are still being developed, although Guidelines on the Format and Contents of a Financial Report were issued as an attachment to a circular of the Chairman of BAPEPAM (No. SE-24/PM/1987). These are consistent with Indonesian Accounting Principles, and in some areas they provide fuller definitions and expanded reporting requirements.

Where topics are not specifically addressed by Indonesian accounting principles, the general principles have been supplemented by pronouncements affecting public companies only, where these offer clearer definitions of terms or accounting practice. This summary does not, however, attempt to provide comprehensive guidance on detailed reporting requirements for public companies.

GENERAL ACCOUNTING

3. Financial Statements (Laporan Keuangan)

Basic Accounting Concepts.   Financial statements are prepared on the **historical cost basis**. They are also prepared on the basis of continuity (**going concern**), so that it is assumed that the economic entity will continue its activities. This assumption underlies the presentation of assets at acquisition cost rather than cash value or realizable value in a liquidation.

Income and expenses are determined by applying the **accrual** method, so that the measurement of assets and liabilities is related to the time of occurrence of transactions rather than to the date of payment of funds. Income and related costs are matched wherever possible, although it is recognized that some costs are not directly linked to income generation and should be reported in the period in which they are incurred.

Financial statements are conservative in the face of uncertain circumstances. Greater emphasis should be given to the economic substance of an event or transaction than to its legal form.

The principle of consistency is included within the seven qualities of financial information identified as necessary for that information to be useful. The seven qualities are relevance, comprehensibility, verifiability, neutrality, timeliness, comparability and completeness.

Contents of Financial Statements. Financial statements comprise a balance sheet (Neraca), profit and loss statement (Perhitungan Rugi/Laba), statement of changes in financial position (Perhitungan Perubahan Posisi Keuangan) and notes to the financial statements (Catatan atas Laporan Keuangan). No statement of cash flows is required.

Public companies are required to give additional information in the notes to the financial statements for any asset, liability or capital line item whose value exceeds 5 percent of total assets, liabilities or capital, respectively, and for any income or expense item exceeding 10 percent of the pretax profit. Further, any special item relevant to the nature of the industry should be disclosed, regardless of its value.

Format of Financial Statements. Assets on the balance sheet are classified by their liquidity ranking (current assets, investments, fixed assets, intangible assets, other assets), while liabilities are classified according to the date they fall due (current liabilities, long-term liabilities, other liabilities). The statement of changes in financial position should show the movement of the company's funds in the period, in terms of either cash or net working capital.

More detailed formats are provided in BAPEPAM regulations for public companies.

Disclosure of Accounting Policies. A summary of significant **accounting policies** adopted in the preparation of the financial statements should be disclosed. This should specify those accounting policies that affect the company's reported financial position and results.

Reference. PAI Sections I and II; BAPEPAM SE-24, Chapter III.1.

4. Business Combinations

Principles of Consolidation. Control of a **subsidiary** is an "indication" of the requirement to prepare consolidated statements, unless control is temporary or the subsidiary operates in a different field of activity from that of the **holding company**.

In practice, the interpretation of IAI members has been that consolidation is not mandatory, so many subsidiaries are accounted for using the **equity method** or even on the cost basis.

Accounting for Business Combinations. **Business combinations** may be categorized as either **purchases** or **poolings of interests**. The method of accounting should reflect the economic substance of the transaction and not merely its legal form.

Purchase method: This is viewed as the acquisition of a company, similar to the purchase of a group of assets. The assets and liabilities acquired should be recorded at their fundamentally real (fair) values. The difference between these values and the amount paid is recorded as **goodwill**.

Pooling of interests method: This is viewed as a combination of business entities in which the ownership of the companies is united, giving rise to no change in the basis of accounting. The balance sheets of the merged companies are combined by simple addition of assets, liabilities and retained earnings, with no goodwill arising.

Apart from these general principles, PAI does not lay down detailed guidelines for accounting for business combinations, except to state that adjustments should be made so as to ensure that the **consolidated financial statements** exclude intercompany account balances, intercompany transactions and any profits or losses arising thereon that are not realized outside the group.

Control.   Control is indicated by ownership of over 50 percent of the voting shares in an entity. For public companies, BAPEPAM specifies that ownership may be direct or indirect.

Goodwill.   Goodwill is included in intangible assets and is described as possibly having an unlimited useful life. There is no detailed guidance on how goodwill is calculated.

Equity Accounting.   The equity method of accounting is considered preferable to reflect the economic relationship between investor and investee companies where the investor holds shares with voting rights in the investee company in order to have significant influence over that company.

Under the equity method, an investment is recorded at acquisition cost, adjusted for the proportional share of the investee company's results. Dividends received from the investee company reduce the value of the investment account.

Minority Interests.   As consolidated financial statements are rarely prepared, Indonesian accounting principles do not specifically address disclosure of **minority interests**.

Disclosure.   The basis of consolidation must be disclosed in the financial statements or the notes thereto. It may be appropriate to prepare a special report as a supplement to the consolidated report to show the position of the parent company.

Reference.   PAI Section II, Articles 9 and 10; Section IV, Articles 3 and 5; BAPEPAM SE-24, Chapter I.11.

5. Joint Ventures

Accounting for Investments in Joint Ventures.   Indonesian accounting principles do not address the different forms of **joint venture** detailed in International Accounting Standard (IAS) 31, *Financial Reporting of Interests in Joint Ventures.*

Jointly Controlled Entities.   **Joint control** usually renders consolidation accounting inappropriate, even though a venturer may hold a majority investment in the undertaking. However, some exceptions exist.

The usual method of accounting for joint ventures is the equity method since it recognizes income when earned, matches costs with revenues and gives appropriate treatment to transactions with the joint venture. In rare cases, the cost method or **proportionate consolidation method** is used.

Indonesian requirements are consistent with IAS 31, except that the equity method of accounting for an investment in a jointly controlled entity is an **allowed alternative** (and the method commonly used in practice) to IAS 31's **benchmark treatment** of proportionate consolidation.

Jointly Controlled Operations.   The accounting treatment in IAS 31 would be appropriate in Indonesia.

Jointly Controlled Assets. The accounting treatment in IAS 31 would be appropriate in Indonesia.

Transactions Between Venturers and the Joint Venture. In general, the contribution of assets to a joint venture in exchange for an interest in the joint venture gives rise to a gain or loss on disposal in the contributor's financial statements. In accounting for other transactions between the venturer and the joint venture, if a gain or loss has resulted, it is recognized in its entirety.

Indonesian recommendations for the treatment of transactions between venturers and the joint venture, and for the recognition of contingencies and commitments of and related to the joint venture, are similar to those in IAS 31 except that normally a venturer may recognize a gain or loss on assets contributed to a venture in exchange for an interest therein.

Disclosure. Under equity accounting, if a significant portion of the venturer's activities is carried on through joint ventures, a summary of the venturer's share of the revenues and expenditures of the venture(s) is presented. Information about the venturer's share of the assets and liabilities is not disclosed.

In addition, where the venturer is liable for any contingent liability or commitment with respect to the joint venture, this should be disclosed.

Accounting by Joint Ventures. **Generally accepted accounting principles** apply to all assets and liabilities and operations of joint ventures. There is no guidance in Indonesia on accounting by the joint venture for assets contributed to the joint venture by the venturers. At present there are several alternatives:

☐ Fair value of the asset contributed.
☐ The value of the interest/benefit received in the venture (e.g., par value of stock received in new venture).
☐ The book value of the assets in the contributor's financial statements.

6. Foreign Currency Translation

Bases of Translation. The following general principles are laid down:

☐ Transactions in foreign currencies should be translated using the rate in effect at the date of the transaction.
☐ Monetary assets and liabilities denominated in foreign currencies should be translated to Indonesian rupiah using the closing rate.
☐ Exchange gains and losses arising from **foreign currency** denominated **transactions** and from year-end translations of monetary assets and liabilities in foreign currencies should be recognized in current income of the period.

Specific regulations apply in the case of a devaluation or revaluation arising directly from a government decision, as follows:

☐ Exchange gains or losses in respect of cash balances should be recognized in current income of the period.

□   Exchange gains or losses in respect of other monetary assets or liabilities may be recognized in current income of the period or deferred. If they are deferred (usually in the case of losses on long-term loans), they should be systematically amortized against the realization of the related liability.

If a forward contract is used as a **hedge** of a foreign currency asset or liability, the discount or premium on the contract should be amortized over the period of the forward contract.

A gain or loss on forward transactions arising from a devaluation should be treated consistently with the treatment of the balance that was hedged by the forward transaction.

Disclosure.   The accounting policy for foreign exchange should be disclosed in the notes to the financial statements. If exchange losses related to a devaluation are deferred, the related amortization policy should also be disclosed.

Reference.   PAI Section II, Article 7; PAI Statement No. 1.

7. Changing Prices/Inflation Accounting

General.   There is no requirement for inflation accounting, although PAI does indicate that where there is a significant fluctuation in monetary values, attention should be drawn to the fact that accounting information that does not reflect changes in the value of monetary units is less relevant for decision-making purposes.

Reference.   PAI Section I, Article 2.4.

8. Accounting Changes

Accounting Treatment.   When a company adopts a change in accounting principle, the cumulative effect of the change should be calculated and reported as a separate item in the profit and loss statement.

Where the method of inventory valuation is changed, it is recognized that it will usually be difficult to identify the cumulative effect of the change in accounting principle. The effects of such changes are therefore not usually disclosed in the financial statements.

Accounting estimates may change because of the occurrence of a new event, additional experience or new information received. Such changes in accounting estimates are of two types: those that require adjustment in the current period only and those that affect both the current and future periods.

Where there is a change in the structure of the reporting entity, as, for instance, in the event of a business combination accounted for as a pooling of interests, the prior financial statements should be retroactively restated.

Disclosure.   For changes in accounting principle, the financial statements should show the cumulative effect in the current year. The nature of and reasons for the change in accounting principle should also be disclosed.

Reference.   PAI Section II, Article 6.

9. Prior Period Adjustments

Definition and Accounting Treatment. There is no explicit provision for financial statements to be amended once issued. As noted above, the cumulative effect of changes in accounting principles should normally be reflected in the current period profit and loss statement rather than by restatement of prior period results.

Public companies are required to disclose, in a statement of retained earnings, details of errors or changes in accounting estimates in prior period financial reports. The notes should contain an explanation of the effects of the correction on reported profits and earnings per share.

Reference. PAI Section II, Article 6; BAPEPAM SE-24, Chapter III.E.

10. Post Balance Sheet Events

Accounting Treatment. This subject is not specifically addressed by published accounting principles in Indonesia. If the event is one providing more information about items existing at the balance sheet date, it would usually be reflected in the financial statements. This might happen, for instance, where a post balance sheet event made the occurrence of a contingent liability reasonably certain (see Section 21) or where it provided more information leading to the correction of an accounting estimate (see Section 8).

For public companies, if subsequent events provide more information about conditions existing at the balance sheet date, then the financial report should be adjusted. Subsequent events that do not reflect conditions existing at year-end require disclosure; examples are acquisitions of other companies, share issues and settlement of claims.

Reference. BAPEPAM SE-24, Chapter III.G.

11. Related Party Transactions

Definition. There is no formal definition of related parties, although their importance is implicit in certain areas of Indonesian Accounting Principles. For example, investments in subsidiaries and affiliates are required to be disclosed separately (see Section 16), although these terms are not defined.

For public companies, affiliated companies have been defined by BAPEPAM as those with direct or indirect ownership interests of 20 percent or more, while a special relationship is defined as any relationship that directly or indirectly influences the management of the company. Balances with such entities should be separately disclosed.

Accounting Treatment. There is no special accounting treatment for the recording of related party transactions.

Disclosure. As noted above, investments should be classified separately between investments in subsidiaries and investments in affiliates. Amounts due to directors or to affiliated companies are required to be disclosed separately as part of other liabilities (not current liabilities), while receivables from shareholders are classified as other assets.

Reference.   PAI Section IV, Article 6; Section V, Article 4; BAPEPAM SE-24, Chapter I.11.

12.   Segmental Information

This subject is not covered by published accounting principles in Indonesia. As a result, such information is not usually disclosed.

ACCOUNTING PRINCIPLES FOR SPECIFIC ITEMS— BALANCE SHEET

13.   Property, Plant and Equipment (Aktiva Tetap Berwujud)

Classification of Capital and Revenue Expenditure.   **Fixed assets** are tangible assets providing a benefit to the company for a period of more than one year. Expenditures that prolong the useful life of assets should be capitalized.

Basis of Valuation.   Tangible fixed assets are recorded at their acquisition cost. Assets that the company constructs for its own use are recorded as the total of all related costs incurred up to the point the asset is ready for use. Assets that are exchanged or donated may be recorded at an estimated price or their fair market value.

Revaluation of fixed assets is permitted only where allowed by government regulation. Such regulations have previously been issued only following devaluations of the Indonesian rupiah.

Depreciation (Penyusutan).   **Depreciation** of fixed assets should be based on an appropriate estimate of their useful lives and can be calculated using either the **straight-line** or **declining balance method**.

Gains/Losses (Rugi/Laba).   Gains or losses on disposal of fixed assets are recognized as other income or expense.

Disclosure.   Each fixed asset category should be stated separately in the financial statements or notes thereto. Accumulated depreciation on fixed assets may be shown by category or in total. The basis of valuation and method of depreciation should be disclosed in the notes, together with details of any fixed assets pledged as security.

Reference.   PAI Section IV, Article 4.

14.   Intangible Assets (Harta Tak Berwujud)

Definition and Accounting Treatment.   **Intangible assets** reflect a right, privilege or other favorable condition enjoyed by a company. Intangible assets may have a limited or an unlimited useful life. Intangible assets may be obtained through purchase or be developed by the company itself. Intangible assets may include all costs incurred prior to commercial operation/production; these costs are recognized as deferred preoperating costs.

Valuation.   Intangible assets are initially recorded at acquisition cost, which includes all costs incurred in relation to the acquisition of the asset.

Amortization (Amortisasi).   **Amortization** should be applied systematically over the asset's useful life, usually on a straight-line basis. If that life is unlimited, the amortization charge should be based on reasonable judgment. If the useful life is reassessed, the rate of amortization should be revised accordingly.

Disclosure.   Intangible assets should be presented in the balance sheet by type. The basis of valuation, amortization policy and related amounts should be disclosed in the notes.

Reference.   PAI Section IV, Article 5.

15.   Leases (Sewa)

Classification.   Companies are required to treat leases as **finance** (capital) **leases** if the lease contract meets all three of the following conditions:

☐   There is an option for the company to purchase the assets at the end of the lease period at a predetermined price.

☐   The regular lease payments, together with the final residual value settlement, are sufficient to repay the cost of the asset plus the interest on funds provided by the leasing company.

☐   The lease period is a minimum of two years.

All other leases are treated as **operating leases**.

Accounting Treatment.   Finance leases: The asset should be recorded at cost in the lessee's balance sheet and amortized over its useful life.

The related liability is calculated as the future lease instalments plus the residual payment. The company may choose the method of allocating interest, although the straight-line or reducing (declining) balance methods are suggested by PAI Statement No. 6.

Lessors should account for their investment in finance leases as a receivable, less deductions for unearned income. Income should be recognized on a consistent basis, using an appropriate rate of return. No guidance is given on the method to be used.

Operating leases: Lease costs should be treated as rentals on a straight-line basis by the lessee (even if the agreement provides for a different basis).

Operating lease income should be treated as rentals, with the assets shown as fixed assets of the lessor and depreciated over their useful lives.

Sale and leaseback agreements are treated following similar principles. The profit or loss arising can be amortized over the same period as the corresponding asset's lease.

Disclosure.   The accounting policy for leases should be disclosed in the notes to the financial statements.

Leased assets under finance leases should be disclosed separately from owned fixed assets, including disclosure of the related accumulated depreciation.

The depreciation charge for the year on leased assets should be disclosed.

Annual rentals for the next two years under operating leases should be disclosed.

For all leases, details of guarantees and major conditions of agreements should be disclosed, together with total lease instalments due within the next two years.

The profit or loss recognized on sale and leaseback transactions, and related amortization, should be disclosed.

Leasing companies should disclose the total lease receivables due within two years, the nature of security deposits held, any receivables pledged to third parties and any syndicated or **leveraged lease** transactions.

Reference.   PAI Statement No. 6.

16.   Investments (Investasi)

Valuation Principles.   Marketable investments should be recorded at the lower of acquisition cost, which is the total of the purchase price and any transaction costs such as commissions, and market price. Any payment for accrued interest included in a bond price should be accounted for separately from acquisition cost.

Long-term investments, defined as long-term holdings or holdings giving significant influence over another company, are generally stated at purchase price plus any transaction costs. Dividends are recorded as other income, except where they are made from pre-acquisition earnings, in which case they are recorded as a reduction of the investment account. Where a holding gives significant influence over another company, the equity method of accounting is considered preferable.

Treatment of Valuation Reserves.   For marketable securities, a reserve may be created if market price is below acquisition cost. If the market price subsequently rises, this will be reflected by a reduction in the reserve against investments.

For long-term investments recorded at cost, a reserve should be provided against the cost of the investment if the investee company suffers significant losses in asset value.

Gains/Losses.   In respect of marketable securities, the cost of securities sold should be determined on either the **FIFO** or **average cost** basis.

Profits or losses on disposals of any asset should normally be recognized on the transaction date.

Disclosure.   The accounting policy for investments should be disclosed in the notes to the financial statements. Whatever valuation policy is adopted, the financial statements should disclose both cost and market value information. Investments in subsidiaries or affiliates should be disclosed separately.

Reference.   PAI Section IV, Articles 2.2 and 3; IPAI 8.

17.   Accounts Receivable (Piutang Dagang)

Accounting Treatment.   **Debtors** are classified as either trade debtors or other debtors. Trade debtors arise from normal business trading activities. Notes receivable are receivables supported by a document containing a formal promise to pay.

Receivables are presented at gross value net of an estimate of uncollectible amounts.

Factored Receivables. These are not covered specifically by Indonesian Accounting Principles. Contingent liabilities for the sale of receivables with an agreement for repurchase should be disclosed.

Disclosure. Trade debtors, notes receivable and other debtors should be disclosed separately. Receivables should be disclosed gross, together with the amount of any provision for bad debts. The provision may be offset against the asset account, rather than recorded in liabilities. Credit balances, if material, should be classified as liabilities in the balance sheet.

The total amount of pledged receivables should be disclosed in the notes to the financial statements.

Reference. PAI Section IV, Article 2.3.

18. Inventories and Work in Progress (Persediaan dan Barang Dalam Process)

General Accounting Treatment. **Inventories** are defined as tangible goods that are available for sale, are in the process of production or are available to be used in production, whether such goods are on hand, on consignment or in transit.

Inventories are generally stated at their acquisition cost, inclusive of all direct and indirect costs incurred in getting them to their present state and location.

Cost should be based on either the **LIFO**, **FIFO** or **average cost** method. The method of valuation should be applied on a consistent basis.

Inventories should be valued at the lower of cost and market price, which is defined as **replacement value** that is not higher than **net realizable value** (selling price less selling expenses) and not lower than realizable value after deduction of an estimated normal profit. The comparison of cost and market price can be made for each item, by category of inventory or on total inventory. Unfavorable price variances arising from the comparison should be charged against current period income.

Inventory may be valued at net realizable value when the selling price can be determined with certainty, the selling expense is insignificant and the products are interchangeable, or cost is difficult to determine.

Long-Term Contracts. Long-term contracts should be stated at cost adjusted for the estimated profit to be recognized based on the **percentage of completion method**. Revenue on contracts may be recognized proportionately based on the stage of completion, calculated either on percentage of costs to date over estimated total costs or on the basis of physical completion.

Disclosure. The accounting policy for inventory valuation, including the valuation of long-term contracts, should be disclosed in the notes to the financial statements.

If inventories are pledged as collateral, this fact should be disclosed in the notes to the financial statements.

When material, the charge against profit arising from a write-down to market price should be disclosed separately in the notes to the financial statements and also be shown as a separate item in cost of sales in the profit and loss statement.

19. Current Liabilities (Hutang Jangka Pendek)

General Accounting Treatment.   **Current liabilities** are those obligations that are expected to be paid in full within one year. If the company's operating cycle is more than one year, the normal operating cycle may be used for determining which items are current. General principles for liabilities apply, namely, the liability should be recorded at the monetary value assigned to the economic sacrifice that will be incurred upon settlement of the obligation at the future due date.

Creation of General and Specific Provisions.   There are no specific rules for provisions beyond the general principles governing recognition of liabilities, outlined above.

Disclosure.   Current liabilities should be classified by when they fall due.

Reference.   PAI Section V, Articles 1 and 2.

20. Long-Term Debt (Hutang Jangka Panjang)

General Accounting Treatment.   Long-term debt is defined as debt that is not due within one year. General principles for liabilities apply, as noted above.

   If any bond premium or discount is created on the issue of debt, it should be amortized over the life of the bond.

Debt Restructuring/Extinguishing.   These are not covered by Indonesian Accounting Principles. As financial instruments become more sophisticated, reference is generally made to applicable International Accounting Standards or US GAAP.

Disclosure.   Disclosure should be made of each type and amount of debt and the principal components of the loan agreement, such as security or guarantees and terms, including interest rate. The amount due within one year should be shown separately in current liabilities, unless the repayment will not utilize **current assets** or will create another long-term loan.

Reference.   PAI Section V, Articles 1 and 3.

21. Contingencies (Kewajiban Bersyarat)

General.   A provision for contingent losses should be recognized in the financial statements only if there is a strong indication that the value of an asset has declined or that a liability has arisen at the balance sheet date and the total losses incurred can be reasonably estimated.

   There is no consideration of any recognition of contingent gains.

Disclosure.   Details of the circumstances giving rise to the **contingency** and the estimate of its amount should be disclosed in the notes to the financial statements.

Reference.   PAI Section III, Article 12; Section V, Article 6.

22. Capital and Reserves (Modal Sendiri)

General. **Share capital** includes **preference shares**, ordinary shares and **additional paid-in capital**. The latter includes any excess of share proceeds over their **par value**, or any other difference arising between the par value of the shares issued and the benefit to the company, such as exchange differences or returned shares. Share issue costs are not required to be written off against this premium, but may be carried forward in other assets and amortized systematically.

The only reserves that are defined by Indonesian Accounting Principles are **retained earnings**, which are the accumulation of periodic results after distributions.

Share Capital. Issued capital is recorded at par value, with any surplus recorded as additional paid-in capital. Shares may be issued in exchange for noncash assets or for the rendering of services, with the value being determined as the more readily identifiable value of either the related assets/services or the shares themselves.

Returned shares can be accounted for by a deduction from capital either at cost (the original issue value of the shares) or at par. If the company pays in excess of the original issue value, the excess cost should be debited to retained earnings.

Donated shares, which are shares returned by shareholders for no consideration, are normally accounted for as a deduction from capital at their original share issue cost. If donated shares are subsequently sold, the proceeds would be credited to the donated shares account; this is very rare in practice.

Other Reserves. Additional paid-in capital, as already described, is a **share premium** account, and, like the revaluation reserve, is regarded as permanent capital of the company. There is no provision for excess depreciation arising as a result of a revaluation to be offset against the revaluation reserve.

Under Article 47 of the Indonesian Commercial Code, if a PT (limited liability) company has accumulated losses in excess of 75 percent of its capital, it may apply to have its limited liability status withdrawn. If it continues to trade, it effectively loses its limited liability status and the directors become jointly and severally liable for its acts. The practical implications of Article 47 remain untested.

Restrictions on Distributions. The balance of retained earnings is considered to be available for distribution, unless it has been specifically allocated to a reserve account to meet the company's commitments. Distributions are recognized at the time they are declared, and it is at this point that dividends are appropriated from retained earnings.

If a company declares a stock dividend, retained earnings should be reduced by the fair value of the shares, as determined by the related shareholders' meeting.

Disclosure. Authorized, issued and paid-up capital should be disclosed, together with the par value and number of shares outstanding for each class of stock. Preferential rights regarding distributions, or in the event of a liquidation, should be disclosed. Any unpaid dividends on cumulative preference shares should be disclosed, including the total dividends relating to prior periods. Any change in the company's capital during the year should be disclosed. A company's Articles of Association may include additional disclosure requirements.

Any balance of retained earnings restricted as to distributions should be disclosed, with the reason for the restriction. Any dividend that represents a repayment of capital to the shareholders must be disclosed in the notes to the financial statements. A dividend that takes the form of a distribution of noncash assets requires disclosure as to the basis of valuation.

Loss of limited liability arising from breach of Article 47 of the Commercial Code should be disclosed.

Reference. PAI Section VI; IPAI 9.

ACCOUNTING PRINCIPLES FOR SPECIFIC ITEMS— INCOME STATEMENT

23. Revenue Recognition (Pengakuan Penjualan)

General Principles. Sales and profits should not be anticipated and income should be recognized at the time of realization. For product sales this is the date of sale, which is usually the date of delivery, while for services it is when the service is performed. Compensation for use of assets, such as rentals, interest or royalties, is recognized as the asset is used.

Exceptions may be allowed for specific products with a fixed sales price and secure market, such as precious metals or agricultural products, where revenue could be recognized upon completion of production, especially if production cost is difficult to determine. Where recoverability is very uncertain, by contrast, it may be appropriate to recognize revenue only at the date of payment.

Revenue on contracts may be recognized proportionately on the stage of production, based on either percentage of cost or physical completion.

Disclosure. There are no specific disclosure requirements, although relevant accounting policies should be disclosed in the notes to the financial statements.

Reference. PAI Section III, Article 1.

24. Government Grants and Assistance (Bantuan Pemerintah)

Accounting Treatment. This topic is not specifically addressed by Indonesian Accounting Principles. Disclosure would be usual, especially since activities funded by government grants frequently attract tax concessions.

25. Research and Development (Penelitian dan Pengembangan)

Accounting Treatment. This topic is not specifically addressed by Indonesian Accounting Principles. Similar principles would be applied to those set out for intangible assets (see Section 14).

Development costs should be expensed except when related to specifically identifiable assets of continuing benefit to the company.

26. Capitalized Interest Costs (Kapitalisasi Biaya Bunga)

Accounting Treatment. Interest may be capitalized if the following conditions are met:

- ☐ The construction cost of the asset can be separately identified.
- ☐ Construction of the asset requires a sufficiently long time period (the necessary period, however, is not specified).
- ☐ The cost of construction results in an increased interest cost to the company.
- ☐ Assets must be qualifying assets, defined as excluding inventories, assets already in use or ready for use and assets not used to earn profit. Qualifying assets may be constructed by the business itself or by contractors.

The interest capitalized is that part of interest expense that could be avoided if the asset were not constructed. This is calculated either based on the actual interest charged on a specific loan to finance construction or by applying the weighted-average interest rate to the accumulated average expenditure on construction.

Interest capitalization begins when preparation for construction begins and should end when the asset is substantially completed and ready for use.

Disclosure. Disclosure should be made of the accounting policy adopted, the total interest accruing in the period, the total interest paid in the period and the total interest capitalized.

Reference. PAI Statement No. 2.

27. Imputed Interest and Discounting

Accounting Treatment. This topic is not specifically addressed by Indonesian Accounting Principles. An **imputed interest** rate may, however, be applied in calculations for finance leases, but this is not a requirement (see Section 15).

28. Extraordinary or Unusual Items (Transaksi Luar Biasa)

Extraordinary Items. Extraordinary items are defined as those that are abnormal in nature, are not related to the business' daily activities and occur rarely.

Extraordinary items as defined above should be distinguished from the ordinary operating results in the profit and loss statement. The related tax effects are generally also shown separately from ordinary operating results.

Disclosure. The nature and amount of an extraordinary item should be disclosed in a note to the financial statements.

Reference. PAI Section III, Article 7.

29. Income Taxes (Pajak Penghasilan)

Accounting Treatment. Normally only current taxes are recorded in the financial statements as there is no requirement to provide for deferred taxation. It is permissible, however, for companies to provide deferred taxation arising on timing differences between accounting and taxable income. Deferred tax is usually calculated using the **liability method**. Deferred tax benefits should be created only if recovery of the asset is reasonably certain. Tax losses, for instance, may be carried forward only up to five years. Deferred tax benefits should be shown among other assets in the balance sheet; a deferred tax provision should be disclosed among other liabilities.

Under Indonesian tax law, losses can be offset against taxable profits in the succeeding five years. The resulting deferred tax benefit is usually not recognized as an asset in the balance sheet.

Disclosure. The policy adopted for accounting for income tax should be disclosed in the notes to the financial statements.

Reference. PAI Section III, Article 9; Section IV, Article 6; Section V, Article 4.

30. Postretirement Benefits (Tunjangan Pension)

Accounting Treatment. Pension accounting has not been specifically addressed by Indonesian Accounting Principles. Accordingly, costs are usually recognized on a cash basis. However, as a result of the new pension law enacted in 1992 by the government, it is expected that a pronouncement from the steering committee of the Indonesian Accountants Association will be forthcoming.

Public companies are required to disclose accounting treatment and funding policy and the effect of any changes in accounting, changes in actuarial assumptions or changes in the pension plan.

Reference. BAPEPAM SE-24, Chapter III.32.

31. Discontinued Operations

Accounting Treatment and Disclosure. There is no specific statement in respect to discontinued operations. General principles of conservatism would govern the recognition of foreseeable losses in the financial statements. Contingent losses should be recognized when there is a strong indication that a liability exists and a reasonable basis for determining its value (see Section 21).

Public companies are required to record all costs and income related to the discontinuance of a business segment separately in the profit and loss statement, and any assets relating to the segment separately in other assets. A further explanation of the calculation of profits and losses should be recorded in the notes.

Reference. BAPEPAM SE-24, Chapter II.3.D.5.

32. Earnings per Share (Laba per Saham)

Definition and Accounting Treatment.   There is no general requirement for earnings per share to be calculated and disclosed in financial statements in Indonesia, although such disclosure may be made.

Public companies are required to disclose earnings per share, based on operating profits per share, profits before extraordinary items per share and net profit after taxation per share. If more than one class of shares exists, the calculation should be adjusted to reflect their respective rights. The basis of calculation should be disclosed.

Reference.   BAPEPAM SE-24, Chapter II.3.D.9.

Appendix
DO INDONESIAN STANDARDS OR PREVALENT PRACTICE SUBSTANTIALLY COMPLY WITH INTERNATIONAL ACCOUNTING STANDARDS?

Section	Topic	Substantially complies with IAS?	Comments
3.	Basic accounting concepts and conventions	Yes	
	Contents of financial statements	Yes	
4.	Business combinations*	No	
5.	Joint ventures	No	
6.	Foreign currency translation*	No	
8.	Accounting changes*	Yes	
9.	Prior period adjustments*	Yes	
10.	Post balance sheet events	Yes	
11.	Related party transactions	No	
12.	Segmental information	No	
13.	Property, plant and equipment*	Yes	
15.	Leases	Yes	
16.	Investments	Yes	
17.	Accounts receivable	Yes	
18.	Inventories and work in progress*	Yes	Except that inventory may be stated at net realizable value
19.	Current liabilities	Yes	
20.	Long-term debt	Yes	
21.	Contingencies	Yes	Except that there is no requirement to disclose contingent gains
22.	Capital and reserves	Yes	
23.	Revenue recognition*	Yes	
24.	Government grants and assistance	No	
25.	Research and development*	No	
26.	Capitalization of interest costs*	Yes	

Appendix (*Continued*)

Section	Topic	Substantially complies with IAS?	Comments
28.	Extraordinary or unusual items*	Yes	
29.	Income tax**	Yes	
30.	Postretirement benefits*	No	

*These topics are subject to change as a result of the IASC Improvements Project—see the appendix to the International Accounting Standards chapter.

**The IAS on accounting for taxes on income is currently being revised, and an exposure draft has been issued.

Comparison in this table is made to International Accounting Standards in force at January 1, 1993. For further details, see the International Accounting Standards chapter.

REPUBLIC OF IRELAND

GENERAL NATIONAL INFORMATION

1. Source of Generally Accepted Accounting Principles

Generally Accepted Accounting Principles and Practices.   Generally accepted accounting principles and practices are derived from the following sources:

☐ The Companies Act 1963 (as amended by the Companies [Amendment] Act 1986 [the Act], the Companies Act 1990 [1990 Act] and the EC [Group Accounts] Regulations 1992 [the 1992 Regulations]) defines formats for profit and loss accounts and balance sheets. It also includes valuation rules for historical cost accounts and separate valuation rules that apply specifically to assets included in the accounts at a value other than historical cost. Furthermore, the Act includes a number of general accounting rules and detailed disclosure requirements. The 1992 Regulations implement the Seventh EC Directive on company (group) accounts. The 1990 Act defines connected and related parties, among other things.

☐ Statements of Standard Accounting Practice (SSAPs) issued by the Accounting Standards Committee (ASC) (see below).

☐ Financial Reporting Standards (FRSs) issued by the Accounting Standards Board (ASB).

☐ Statements of Recommended Practice (SORPs) issued by the ASC. These statements are developed when there is a need for guidance on a specific topic, but not a SSAP. Adherence to these statements is not mandatory, but they are an indication of best accounting practice and companies are encouraged to comply with them.

☐ Approved ("franked") SORPs are issued by certain specialized industries and indicate recommended accounting practice on specific topics. Adherence to franked SORPs is not mandatory, although companies in those industries generally comply with their requirements.

☐ The United Kingdom's International Stock Exchange's Continuing Obligations (the **Yellow Book**), with a special supplement for companies registered in Ireland, includes accounting disclosure requirements for companies listed on the Stock Exchange; its General Undertaking includes similar requirements for companies traded on a second-tier market known as the Unlisted Securities Market (USM).

□ Technical Releases issued by professional accounting bodies (see below) indicate best accounting practice and often precede an exposure draft of an accounting standard.

Accounting Standards. Previously, **accounting standards** in the Republic of Ireland, known as SSAPs, were developed by the ASC, a committee of the Consultative Committee of Accounting Bodies Limited (CCAB). They were then issued by the governing councils of the Institute of Chartered Accountants in England and Wales (ICAEW), the Institute of Chartered Accountants of Scotland (ICAS), the Institute of Chartered Accountants in Ireland (ICAI), the Chartered Association of Certified Accountants (CACA), the Chartered Institute of Public Finance and Accountancy (CIPFA) and the Chartered Institute of Management Accountants (CIMA). Currently, accounting standards are developed and issued by an independent Accounting Standards Board (ASB). While the FRSs issued by the ASB do not have the force of law in Ireland (as they do in the UK), the obligation to prepare financial statements that give a true and fair view means that a company should follow applicable accounting standards unless there are good reasons not to do so.

2. Audit and Public Company Requirements

Audits. Every limited company is obligated to appoint auditors at each general meeting at which the company's financial statements are presented. Where auditors are appointed, they are required to report that they have obtained all the information and explanations they considered necessary, and whether in their opinion:

□ The balance sheet and the profit and loss account of the company and the **consolidated financial statements**, if prepared, have been properly prepared in accordance with the Act.

□ A true and fair view is given by the financial statements of the state of the company's affairs at the end of the financial year, and of the company's profit or loss for that year.

□ If consolidated financial statements are presented, a true and fair view is given of the state of affairs and the profit or loss of the company and its **subsidiaries**.

□ The company has kept proper books and records and whether the financial statements are in agreement therewith.

□ A financial situation exists in the company whereby the net assets have fallen to less than half the called-up share capital.

□ The financial information provided in the directors' report is consistent with the financial statements.

In addition, auditors have a statutory duty to include certain information in their report if the information is not disclosed in the financial statements. This includes information related to:

□ The **directors' emoluments** (salaries and other benefits), pensions and compensation for loss of office (including noncash assets).

□ Loans and other transactions benefiting directors.

Auditors are also required to report significant departures from the SSAPs or FRSs, except where they concur with any such departures.

Other duties and obligations of auditors are contained in Auditing Standards and Guidelines. These standards and guidelines are developed by the Auditing Practices Committee (APC), a committee of the CCAB, and are issued by five professional bodies (the CCAB bodies outlined above, excluding CIMA). Auditing standards prescribe the basic principles and practices that members of the issuing organizations are expected to follow when conducting an audit. The Auditing Practices Committee has been replaced by the Auditing Practices Board; however, the procedures remain the same.

Public Companies. In order for a company to be a **public company** under the Act, it must maintain a minimum allotted **share capital** of £30,000, of which one-quarter must be paid up.

A public limited company may become a listed public company if any part of its shares or debt securities have been admitted to the Official List of the International Stock Exchange. Alternatively, it may become a quoted public company if any of its shares are quoted on the USM. The regulatory requirements for registration and listing as a public company are set out in the Act and the Yellow Book.

The Yellow Book states that the market value of securities must be at least £700,000 in the case of shares and £200,000 in the case of debt. This provides a guideline for the marketability of the company. In addition, the Yellow Book stipulates that 25 percent of any class of shares must be in the hands of the public for a public company to be listed.

The reporting requirements for a public company do not differ significantly from those for a private limited company, apart from the requirement for certain additional financial statement disclosures imposed by the International Stock Exchange's Continuing Obligations or, for USM companies, its General Undertaking.

A company is required by the Act to deliver accounts to the Registrar of Companies within 11 months after the end of the relevant accounting period.

GENERAL ACCOUNTING

3. Financial Statements

Basic Accounting Concepts. Financial statements are normally prepared on the **historical cost basis**. However, the Act allows alternative accounting rules. These rules allow the revaluation of certain assets, as follows:

☐ **Intangible** fixed **assets** may be stated at their **current cost**, determined in accordance with the ASC handbook entitled *Accounting for the Effects of Changing Prices*.

☐ Tangible **fixed assets** may be stated either at their market value on the date when they were last valued or at their current cost.

☐ Fixed asset investments may be shown either at their market value on the date at which they were last valued or at a value determined on a basis the directors consider appropriate if market values are not available.

☐ **Current asset** investments may be stated at their current cost (as defined below).

☐ Stocks may be stated at their current cost.

Current cost is defined as the lower of an asset's net current **replacement cost** or its recoverable amount. Recoverable amount is the higher of the asset's **net realizable value** or the amount recoverable from its future use.

Thus, companies may base their financial statements on either the pure historical cost convention, the historical cost convention modified for the revaluation of certain assets, or current cost. Several companies issue modified historical cost financial statements, with certain fixed assets revalued.

Where there is a material difference between the profit recognized in financial statements based on modified historical costs and the profit that would arise on an historical cost basis, FRS 3 requires a statement of profit or loss based on historical cost to follow the profit and loss account. A note to the financial statements should include a reconciliation showing the items giving rise to the difference.

The assumptions underlying financial statements are governed by the Act, which identifies the **going concern concept**, the consistency concept, the **prudence concept**, the **accruals concept** and the concept of separate determination of individual assets and liabilities. The latter concept requires that each asset and each liability be separately determined and valued. SSAP 2 also prescribes these concepts, except for the separate determination concept.

In addition, as mentioned in Section 2, it is a fundamental requirement that financial statements give a true and fair view. In certain circumstances, it is necessary to depart from the provisions of the Act in order to give a true and fair view. Where this is necessary, the particulars of the departure, the reasons for it and its effect should be given in the notes to the financial statements.

When a company uses a method such as FIFO and the resulting valuation differs materially from the "relevant alternative amount" of the items, the difference should be disclosed in a note to the financial statements.

The "relevant alternative amount" is the amount of the assets determined according to their replacement cost as at the balance sheet date. The replacement cost will normally be the current cost, but it may instead be the most recent actual purchase price or production cost.

Contents of Financial Statements. Financial statements generally include a directors' report (a narrative supplement to the financial statements), a profit and loss account, a balance sheet, a statement of cash flows, a statement of accounting policies and notes that are referenced to those financial statements.

In the case of a group, the financial statements also include a consolidated balance sheet, a consolidated profit and loss account and a consolidated statement of cash flows. The profit and loss account of the **parent company** need not be reproduced in the consolidated financial statements if the omission is noted in the financial statements.

Format of Financial Statements. The Fourth EC Directive, enacted in the Republic of Ireland by the Companies (Amendment) Act 1986, details two balance sheet formats and four profit and loss account formats, which are standard throughout the EC. The company's directors may choose the particular formats to follow. There are strict rules governing the use of the formats and when they can be amended. Certain required detailed information can be relegated to the notes to the financial statements. There is no set format for the statement of cash flows, although specific headings are defined in FRS 1.

FRS 3 requires the inclusion of two additional statements for financial statements prepared for accounting periods ending on or after June 22, 1993. These statements are:

☐ Statement of total recognized gains and losses. This statement shows, in one place, all gains and losses recognized during the year, whether they are recorded in the profit and loss account or through reserves. Its purpose is to show the total performance of the company for the year.

☐ Reconciliation of movements in shareholders' funds. This statement may be included as a note to the financial statements or as a primary statement and shows items not included in the statement of total recognized gains and losses, such as an issue of shares or write-off of goodwill directly to reserves.

Disclosure of Accounting Policies. Both the Act and SSAP 2 require the company's **accounting policies** to be disclosed. Accounting policies would include the basis of accounting; the treatment of **associated companies**; research and development; intangible assets; goodwill; fixed asset valuations; investment properties; leased assets and obligations; the treatment of government grants; valuation of fixed asset investments; valuation of stocks and long-term contracts; the treatment of deferred tax; pension costs; foreign currency translation; and the basis on which **turnover** is stated.

Ryan Commission Proposals. A commission established by the Institute of Chartered Accountants in Ireland under the Chairmanship of Dr. Loudan Ryan has made a series of proposals for improving the quality of public reporting. Among the proposals are the inclusion of a directors' responsibility statement in the annual report, together with greater disclosures of fees earned by the directors and the auditors.

Reference. Companies (Amendment) Act 1986.

4. Business Combinations

Principles of Consolidation. Consolidated financial statements are the normal way in which **group accounts** are presented. Consolidated financial statements include the accounts of the parent company and its subsidiaries, which are entities in which the parent controls, either directly or indirectly, 50 percent or more of the voting rights, has a right to appoint or remove directors having a majority of the voting rights at meetings of the board or has a right to exercise dominant influence over the subsidiary. Subsidiaries should be excluded from consolidation if they meet any of the following criteria:

☐ Severe long-term restrictions substantially hinder the parent's exercise of its rights over the assets or management of the subsidiary.

☐ The interest of the parent is held exclusively with a view to subsequent resale and the subsidiary has not previously been included in the consolidated financial statements.

☐ The activities of one or more subsidiaries are so different from those of the other subsidiaries that their inclusion would be incompatible with the obligation to give a true and fair view. (This exemption does not, in itself, exclude banking and insurance subsidiaries.)

While FRS 2 requires exclusion of subsidiaries that meet any of the above criteria, it permits the exclusion of nonmaterial subsidiaries. However, two or more subsidiaries may be excluded only if, taken together, they are not **material**. The 1992 Regulations permit exclusion of a subsidiary if the relevant information cannot be obtained without incurring disproportionate expense or undue delay. FRS 2 does not permit an exclusion on this ground.

Exemption from Preparing Consolidated Financial Statements. FRS 2 and the 1992 Regulations permit parent companies to opt not to prepare consolidated financial statements in the following circumstances:

□   The group is a small or medium-sized group, as defined by the Act.
□   They are intermediate parent companies.
□   All of the subsidiaries are permitted or required to be excluded from consolidation.

Accounting for Business Combinations. A **business combination** arises where one undertaking buys shares in another undertaking, which becomes a subsidiary. There are two accounting methods that can be applied to business combinations in the Republic of Ireland. **Acquisition accounting** applies in the majority of situations. **Merger accounting**, which is equivalent to pooling, can be used, provided that certain conditions in the Act and in SSAP 23 are complied with. Due to the absence of merger relief (see United Kingdom chapter, Section 4) in Irish legislation, the use of merger accounting is rare in Ireland.

Acquisition Accounting. In acquisition accounting, the fair value of the consideration given in the acquisition is offset against the fair value of the net assets of the undertaking acquired. The difference represents **goodwill** or **negative goodwill**. All identifiable assets, including intangibles, of the undertaking acquired are valued. Fair value adjustments can be made either on consolidation or in the books of the acquired company. This applies with the exception of the valuation of stocks and long-term contracts, which have to be adjusted on consolidation.

Merger Accounting. Where merger accounting is used, the book values of assets and liabilities of the merged undertaking and of the group are consolidated without restatement to fair value. In addition, the profit and loss account for the entire period of the merged undertaking is included in the consolidated profit and loss account. Current and prior year amounts for both the profit and loss account and the balance sheet are shown as if the entities had always been combined. Shares issued above par will, however, generate a **share premium** and, consequently, goodwill due to the absence of merger relief.

Goodwill. The treatment of purchased goodwill arising on consolidation is governed by SSAP 22, which, while giving options, indicates a preference for the immediate write-off of consolidation goodwill to reserves. Normally, this write-off is made to the profit and loss account reserve or the merger reserve, although some companies may create a negative reserve by writing off goodwill to a reserve that starts with a zero balance. Companies may also apply to the High Court to form general reserves from their share premium account against which goodwill can be written off. SSAP 22 also allows companies to amortize goodwill over a period not to exceed the goodwill's useful life. In practice, most companies write goodwill off immediately to reserves; however, some amortize goodwill over periods of up to 40 years. This question is now under review by the ASB. Negative goodwill arising on consolidation is added to consolidated reserves.

Equity Accounting. If an investor has a participating interest (of less than 50 percent) in another undertaking and exercises significant influence over the undertaking's operating and financial policies, that undertaking should be treated as an associated undertaking unless it satisfies one of the tests for a subsidiary undertaking. An investor that holds 20 percent or more of the voting rights in another undertaking is presumed to exercise significant influence unless there is evidence to the contrary. A number of factors may indicate significant influence in practice, such as board representation. All associated undertakings are required by the Act to be accounted for by the **equity method**.

Minority Interests. There are prescribed lines in the balance sheet and profit and loss account formats for **minority interests**. Minority interests in the consolidated balance sheet show the amount of capital and reserves attributable to shares in subsidiaries included in the consolidation that are held by or on behalf of persons other than the parent and its subsidiaries. Similarly, minority interests in the consolidated profit and loss account include the amount of any profit or loss on ordinary activities attributable to shares in subsidiaries included in the consolidation that are held by or on behalf of persons other than the parent and its subsidiaries.

Date of Changes in Group Membership. The date for accounting for an undertaking becoming a subsidiary is the date on which control passes to the parent. This may be earlier than the date upon which consideration passes or the offer becomes unconditional. An undertaking ceases to be a subsidiary from the date upon which control is relinquished. Control is defined as the ability of an undertaking to direct the financial and operating policies of the subsidiary with a view to gaining economic benefits from its activities.

Disclosure. General: The names of the undertakings acquired or merged have to be disclosed, along with the accounting method used. In addition, the number and class of shares issued have to be disclosed, with details of any other consideration exchanged. For both acquisition and merger accounting, the fair value of the total consideration given has to be disclosed.

Acquisition accounting: Financial statements have to disclose the nature and amount of significant accounting adjustments necessary to achieve consistency of accounting policies. Sufficient information has to be disclosed about the acquired companies' results to enable users of financial statements to assess the acquisition's effect on the consolidated results.

For each material acquisition, a table must be given showing the book values of assets and liabilities acquired and their fair values at the date of acquisition. The table should present fair value adjustments, provisions for future trading losses foreseen at the time of purchase and other provisions needed to bring accounting policies into alignment. Adjustments made in future years to provisions created upon acquisition have to be divided between amounts used and amounts released, unused or applied for another purpose. In addition, adjustments may be made to the fair values provisionally used at the date of acquisition, during a period after the acquisition known as a "hindsight period," but these have to be explained.

The cumulative amount of goodwill written off in the current year and earlier years, net of any amounts attributable to subsidiaries sold, has to be disclosed. Goodwill written off to reserves with respect to subsidiaries subsequently disposed of must be taken into account in calculating the profit or loss on disposal.

Merger accounting: The nature and amount of any significant accounting adjustments have to be disclosed. The profit and loss account of the acquired undertaking from the beginning of the financial year to the date of the merger has to be shown, with that of the previous year. In addition, profit before extraordinary items both before and after the effective date of the merger is shown separately for the group, excluding the undertaking acquired, and for the undertaking acquired. Extraordinary items are presented both before and after the merger, indicating the party to which each item relates.

Reference.   FRS 2; SSAPs 22 and 23; Companies Act 1963; Companies (Amendment) Act 1986; and 1992 Regulations.

5. Joint Ventures

In Ireland, there is limited coverage of accounting for **joint ventures** in the accounting recommendations. SSAP 1 states that where the interest of an investing group or company is effectively that of a partner in a joint venture and the investor is in a position to exercise significant influence over the company in which the investment is made, the interest should be treated as an associated company and accounted for on an equity basis. SSAP 1 acknowledges that this treatment need not be applied to noncorporate joint ventures that have features that justify accounting for a proportionate share of individual assets and liabilities as well as profits and losses.

ED 50 repeated the guidance set out above; however, it proposed that where the substance of an unincorporated joint venture is that of an associated company, it should be accounted for on the equity basis of accounting. Where the substance of a corporate joint venture would make **proportionate consolidation** a more appropriate accounting approach, ED 50 recognized that such an approach is not in accordance with the Act. The changes made in the 1992 Regulations would facilitate proportionate consolidation in certain circumstances.

The parts of ED 50 relating to joint ventures and partnerships have not yet been issued as an FRS and remain nonmandatory guidance.

Reference.   SSAP 1, ED 50 and 1992 Regulations.

6. Foreign Currency Translation

Domestic Operations.   Revenue or costs arising from a transaction denominated in a foreign currency should be translated into the local currency at the exchange rate in effect on the date of the transaction. If a transaction is settled by a contracted rate, that rate should be used. No subsequent translation should normally be made once monetary assets have been translated and recorded. At the balance sheet date, monetary assets and liabilities denominated in foreign currencies should be translated using the exchange rate on that date (the closing rate) or, where appropriate, the exchange rates contracted under the terms of the relevant transaction. All exchange gains and losses arising from these transactions should be recorded in the profit and loss account.

Foreign Operations.   For consolidation purposes the accounts of a foreign enterprise should normally be translated using the closing rate/net investment method. Under this method, the profit and loss account would be translated at the closing rate or at an average rate for the period. The balance sheet of the foreign enterprise would be translated using the closing rate. Exchange differences arising from the retranslation of the opening net investment of a foreign enterprise at the closing rate should be recorded directly in reserves. In certain circumstances, such as where a branch operates as an extension of the company and the branch's cash flows have a direct impact on those of the company, the **temporal method** of translation should be used. The mechanics of this method are identical to those used in preparing the financial statements of an individual company.

Hedges. If an individual company has monetary assets denominated in a foreign currency that are matched with forward contracts, the exchange rates specified in those contracts should be used. If a company or group uses foreign currency borrowing to finance or provide a **hedge** against its foreign equity investments and certain conditions are complied with, the net exchange difference arising on translating the foreign currency borrowing and the investments may be offset as a reserve movement.

Disclosure. The accounting policies should disclose the methods used to translate the financial statements of foreign enterprises and the treatment of exchange differences. Where the offset procedure is used (as outlined above), the amount offset in reserves has to be disclosed together with the net amount recorded in the profit and loss account. All companies have to disclose the net movement on reserves arising from exchange differences.

Reference. SSAP 20.

7. Changing Prices/Inflation Accounting

General. There is no requirement in the Republic of Ireland to make any adjustments for inflation or changes in prices. However, as mentioned in Section 3, companies may revalue their assets using the alternative accounting rules.

Current cost financial statements based on the methods outlined in the ASC handbook entitled *Accounting for the Effects of Changing Prices* are rarely prepared, except in some nationalized industries.

Methods of Calculating and Reporting the Effects of Inflation. The ASC handbook outlines two methods of calculating and reporting the effects of inflation. The ASC recommends that companies use current cost asset valuation based on either the operating or financial capital maintenance concept. The other method the handbook details is the current purchasing power method of accounting for inflation.

Disclosure. Where current cost information is presented, it is normally as supplementary information to the company's or group's main financial statements.

Reference. SSAP 16 (withdrawn) and ASC handbook.

8. Accounting Changes

Accounting Treatment. It is a fundamental **accounting concept** that accounting treatment be consistent within a period and from one period to the next. Consequently, a change in accounting policy can be justified only on the grounds that the new policy is preferable. If there has been a change in accounting policy, SSAP 6 requires the amounts for the current and the corresponding periods to be restated on the basis of the new policy; that is, that the change be accounted for as a prior year adjustment (see Section 9).

Estimating future events requires the exercise of judgment. Since a change in estimate arises from new information, SSAP 6 requires changes in estimates to be accounted for in the year that the change is made, without retrospective effect.

Disclosure.   Changes in accounting policy should be disclosed in accordance with the disclosure for prior period adjustments (see Section 9).

Changes in **accounting methods** used (for example, changing from the straight-line depreciation method to the sum-of-the-years'-digits method), if material, may be disclosed as exceptional items (see Section 28).

Reference.   SSAP 6; Companies Act 1963; and Companies (Amendment) Act 1986.

9.   Prior Period Adjustments

Definition of Adjusting Items.   As mentioned above, a **prior period adjustment** must be made where there is a change in accounting policy. In addition, fundamental financial statement errors found at a later date should be accounted for as prior period adjustments. A fundamental error is one of such significance that it would destroy the true and fair view, and therefore the validity, of the company's financial statements.

Accounting Treatment.   For both changes in accounting policy and correction of fundamental errors, the prior period profit and loss account and balance sheet have to be adjusted. The reserves note should present the reserves as previously reported, the prior year adjustment and the restated reserves.

Earnings per Share.   The earnings per share of the prior period would be restated for the adjustments.

Disclosure.   Changes in accounting policies and fundamental errors should be fully explained in the notes. Furthermore, the effect of the prior year adjustment on the results of the preceding year should be disclosed where feasible.

Reference.   SSAP 6.

10.   Post Balance Sheet Events

Definition.   SSAP 17 defines post balance sheet events as both favorable and unfavorable events that occur between the balance sheet date and the date on which the financial statements are approved by the board of directors. Post balance sheet events are split into two types, adjusting events and nonadjusting events.

Accounting Treatment.   A post balance sheet adjusting event provides additional evidence of conditions existing at the balance sheet date and should be recorded in the current year financial statements. A nonadjusting event concerns conditions that did not exist at the balance sheet date. Such events are not reflected in the current year financial statements.

Disclosure. A post balance sheet nonadjusting event should be disclosed if it is so material that it would affect the ability of users of financial statements to reach a proper understanding of the company's financial position. The notes to the financial statements should disclose the nature of the event and give an estimate of the financial effect or state that it is not practicable to make an estimate.

Reference. SSAP 17.

11. Related Party Transactions

There is no general requirement for disclosing transactions with related parties, although there are specific requirements in the International Stock Exchange Yellow Book that capture the majority of related party transactions that would be reported in other countries. These requirements, which apply to listed companies, relate specifically to transactions with directors and persons connected with directors, such as:

☐ Transactions in which a director has a material interest have to be disclosed.

☐ Loans and credit transactions with directors and persons connected with them, whether legal or not, have to be disclosed and the directors concerned identified.

☐ Transactions in which a director sells assets to or buys assets from the company have to be disclosed to the Stock Exchange as well as in the directors' report or notes to the financial statements.

In addition, disclosures of transactions with and interests in affiliated companies are as described in Section 4.

The ASC issued ED 46, *Disclosure of Related Party Transactions*, in July 1989, which contains proposals for disclosure of abnormal transactions (i.e., transactions outside the ordinary course of business) with related parties and disclosure of the existence and nature of controlling related party relationships. These cover, in particular, transactions with directors and disclosures relating to substantial shareholders, group companies and related companies.

The Companies Act 1963 requires certain disclosures relating to emoluments and loans to directors. The Companies Act 1990 also contains significant provisions with respect to transactions involving directors.

Reference. Companies Act 1963; Companies Act 1990; and International Stock Exchange Yellow Book.

12. Segmental Information

The Act, SSAP 25 and the International Stock Exchange Yellow Book for listed companies all include requirements for segmental reporting. To determine the segments (classes of business or geographical segments), the directors must consider how the company's activities are organized. This involves analyzing the type of business, the geographical areas of production and geographical markets.

Disclosure. The Act requires that, if the company has conducted business in two or more segments during the year, a description of each segment, its turnover and its profit or loss before tax be disclosed in the notes. Furthermore, if a company has supplied goods and services within two or more markets during the year, the turnover must also be disaggregated between the markets. The Yellow Book requires a geographical analysis of turnover and contributions made by operations conducted outside the Republic of Ireland to trading (or operating) results. SSAP 25 requires public companies and large private companies to present the following additional disclosures:

☐ A definition of each reported business and geographical segment.

☐ Turnover by business and geographical segment on the origin basis (i.e., country of production) and destination basis (i.e., country of sale).

☐ Results by business and geographical segment before tax, minority interests and extraordinary items, and before or after accounting for interest, depending on the importance of interest to the segment.

☐ Intersegment turnover by geographical and business segment.

☐ Net assets by geographical and business segment.

☐ Segment information relating to associated entities.

Both the Act and SSAP 25 provide an exception from these disclosures: If presenting the above information would seriously prejudice the interests of the company, it need not be disclosed, but the omission and the reason for it have to be disclosed.

Reference. Companies (Amendment) Act 1986 and SSAP 25.

ACCOUNTING PRINCIPLES FOR SPECIFIC ITEMS— BALANCE SHEET

13. Property, Plant and Equipment

Classification of Capital and Revenue Expenditure. Expenditures that give rise to **capital assets** are classified as fixed assets. Pre-trading expenditures, expenses and commission relating to an issue of shares or debentures, and costs of research cannot be capitalized and are treated as expenses as incurred.

Basis of Valuation. Fixed assets are recorded at their purchase price or production cost, which includes any consideration given by the company to obtain them. Transfers of assets from current to fixed assets should be made at the lower of cost or net realizable value (UITF 5). Fixed assets other than goodwill can be revalued at current cost; any resulting surplus must be credited to a revaluation reserve. Because of the valuation rules explained in Section 3, when assets are revalued, surpluses and deficits on individual assets have to be determined and accounted for separately. A deficit on the revaluation of an asset should be deducted from the revaluation reserve to the extent that there is a previous surplus that relates to that asset; any excess should be charged to the profit and loss account. Gains or losses on sale are computed using the carrying value of the asset. However, if a revaluation has taken place previously, any remaining revaluation reserve surplus for that asset may be included as part of the profit from the sale of the asset.

Investment Properties. Investment properties are interests in land or buildings with respect to which construction work and development have been completed and that are held for their investment potential, any rental income being negotiated at arm's length.

Investment properties should be carried on the balance sheet at open market value and valuation adjustments accounted for on the same basis as those arising on the revaluation of fixed assets.

Depreciation. Fixed assets with limited useful lives are depreciated systematically over those useful lives. The **depreciation** base to be written off is an asset's purchase price, production cost or revalued amount, less any residual value at the end of its useful life. Acceptable depreciation methods include the **straight-line method, sum-of-the-years'-digits method, annuity method** and methods based on the number of units produced. The useful life of an asset is defined in SSAP 12 as the period over which the present owner will derive economic benefit from the asset.

In order for the financial statements to give a true and fair view, depreciation should not be provided on investment properties, except for properties held on lease when the unexpired lease period is less than 20 years.

Disclosure. The following has to be disclosed for each major class of depreciable asset:

☐ The depreciation method used.
☐ The useful lives or depreciation rates used.
☐ Total depreciation expense for the period.
☐ The gross amount of depreciable assets and the related accumulated depreciation at the balance sheet date.

Where there has been a change in depreciation method used, the effect, if material, and the reason for the change should be disclosed. If an asset has been revalued, the reason and the effect, based on both the revalued amount and the historical cost of the asset, must also be disclosed.

Reference. SSAPs 12 and 19; UITF 5, Companies Act 1963; and Companies (Amendment) Act 1986.

14. Intangible Assets

Accounting Treatment. Intangible assets such as patents, licenses, trademarks and other rights and assets may be capitalized if they are acquired for valuable consideration or are created by the company. However, a 1990 ASB proposal (ED 52) would considerably restrict the capitalization of certain intangible assets. SSAP 22 requires that on the acquisition of a company, intangible assets should be separately identified from purchased goodwill.

Development costs may be capitalized, provided that specific conditions are met. Research costs must be expensed as incurred. The conditions for treatment of research and development costs are outlined in Section 25.

Purchased goodwill may also be capitalized and treated as other intangible assets.

Valuation. All intangible assets other than goodwill may be revalued. Any surplus or deficit arising on revaluation must be recorded in the revaluation reserve.

Amortization. All intangible assets, including goodwill, should be amortized over their estimated useful lives. The **amortization** rules for intangible assets are the same as for tangible fixed assets, discussed above. There is no maximum amortization period.

Disclosure. The disclosure requirements for intangible assets are comparable to those for tangible assets, mentioned above.

Reference. SSAPs 12 and 13 and Companies (Amendment) Act 1986.

15. Leases

Classification. Leases are classified as either **finance** or **operating leases**. SSAP 21 defines a finance lease as a lease that transfers substantially all the risks and rewards of ownership of the asset to the lessee. Such transfer of risks and rewards is presumed to occur if, at the beginning of the lease term, the present value of the minimum lease payments equals 90 percent or more of the fair value of the leased asset. An operating lease is defined as a lease other than a finance lease.

Accounting Treatment. Lessees: Lessees are required to capitalize finance leases and show lease obligations as a liability. For operating leases, lessees treat lease payments as charges to revenue.

Lessors: Lessors treat finance leases as receivables (**debtors**) in their balance sheet. Operating lease assets are treated as fixed assets, and lease income is credited to the profit and loss account. The fixed assets are depreciated in accordance with their useful life.

Leveraged Leases. Current Irish GAAP do not provide a specific method of dealing with **leveraged leases**, as these transactions are not common in the Republic of Ireland. At present, the asset and liability relating to leveraged lease arrangements should be shown in full on the balance sheet; no right of offset exists between the two components.

Disclosure. Lessees: The gross amount of assets held under finance leases, together with related accumulated depreciation, should be disclosed for each class of asset. Obligations owed under finance leases should be disclosed separately from other liabilities, either on the face of the balance sheet or in a note. Lease obligations are classified as amounts payable in the next year, amounts payable in the next two to five years and aggregate amounts payable thereafter. The aggregate finance charges for the period also have to be shown. Commitments that exist at the balance sheet date should be disclosed.

For operating leases, rent expense has to be disclosed. In addition, the lessee has to disclose the annual payments due on leases that expire during the next year, in the next two to five years and thereafter.

Lessors: The net investment in finance leases at the balance sheet date has to be disclosed. The gross amount of assets held for use in operating leases and the related accumulated depreciation have to be disclosed. The aggregate rental income received during the period for finance and operating leases and the costs of assets acquired for purposes of contracting out through finance leases also have to be shown.

Reference. SSAP 21 and Companies Act 1963 (Sixth Schedule).

16. Investments

Valuation Principles.   There is no accounting standard in the Republic of Ireland on investments, although there is a proposal (ED 55). Under the "separate valuation" concept in the Act, investments should be valued individually rather than on a **portfolio basis**.

Current asset investments: Current asset investments are normally stated at the lower of cost or market value; the alternative accounting rules (see Section 3) permit revaluation at current cost.

Fixed asset (noncurrent) investments: Fixed asset investments are normally stated at cost; however, the alternative accounting rules (see Section 3) permit revaluation either at their market value on the date at which they were last valued, or at a value determined on a basis the directors consider appropriate.

Treatment of Valuation Reserves.   Surpluses arising on revaluation of investments under the alternative accounting rules should be credited to a revaluation reserve. Deficits may be charged to a revaluation reserve only to the extent of any surplus from a previous revaluation of the same asset. Any excess must be charged to the profit and loss account.

Gains/Losses.   When investments are sold, the profit or loss on sale is normally computed using the carrying value of the investment; however, the revaluation surplus may be included in the profit or loss. If such profits and losses are material, they should be shown as exceptional items before arriving at profit on ordinary activities before tax (see Section 28). For investments not acquired with the intention of resale, such as investments in subsidiaries, profits or losses arising on disposal may in certain circumstances be treated as extraordinary items.

Disclosure.   Investments of less than 20 percent of the equity of a company are carried in the balance sheet at the lower of cost or market value, with no separate disclosure of the details of individual investments. The total value of investments listed on a recognized stock exchange (and their market value, where different) should be included in a note. As explained earlier, undertakings of which over 20 percent is held may also be treated as either associated undertakings or subsidiaries, in which case additional disclosure is required and the accounting treatment will be on the basis of equity accounting or full consolidation.

Reference.   Companies (Amendment) Act 1986.

17. Accounts Receivable

Accounting Treatment.   Recognition: The recognition of **revenues**, and hence the related receivables, is described in Section 23.

Discounts: Receivables are normally recorded net of trade and quantity discounts. Cash discounts are recognized at time of payment.

Allowances: Adequate provision must be made for bad and doubtful accounts, but there are no formal methods for calculating such provisions.

Factored Receivables.   There is no accounting standard that relates to factored receivables, but proposals are being developed. Where the seller of the debt is in substance a borrower, the debtor should normally be recorded on the balance sheet and a loan recorded for amounts advanced by the factor. The interest element of the factor's charges should be accrued and recorded as interest expense. The notes to the accounts should explain the arrangements and, in particular, the amounts of receivables that have been sold.

Disclosure. An analysis of debtors has to be disclosed, either in the balance sheet or the notes, under the following headings: trade debtors; amounts owed by group companies; amounts owed by undertakings in which the company has a participating interest; other debtors; prepayments; and accrued income. In addition, debtors must be split between those receivable within one year of the balance sheet date and those receivable after one year. This analysis can be given in the notes, except where the element of receivables due after one year is so substantial to the receivables figure as to distort the view given by the balance sheet (UITF 6).

Reference. UITF 6 and Companies (Amendment) Act 1986.

18. Inventories and Work in Progress

General Accounting Treatment. The Act and SSAP 9 require **stocks** to be carried at the lower of cost or net realizable value. SSAP 9 defines cost as an expenditure that has been incurred in the normal course of business in bringing the product or service to its present location and condition. This includes costs of purchase and costs of conversion, which encompass direct expenditures, production overhead and a proportion of other overhead. Items of stock that are indistinguishable from one another may be valued using methods such as **FIFO**, **average cost** or any similar method. **LIFO** is not acceptable in the Republic of Ireland for tax purposes and is not commonly used. Net realizable value is the estimated selling price less all further costs of completion and all costs to be incurred in marketing, selling and distributing. Stocks are shown at a valuation using the alternative accounting rules when the financial statements are prepared on a current cost basis.

Long-Term Contracts. Long-term contracts should be assessed on a contract-by-contract basis and reflected in the profit and loss account by recording turnover and related costs as the contract activity progresses. Turnover may include attributable profit to the extent that the outcome of the contract can be assessed with reasonable certainty. Long-term contract work in progress is reduced by the costs included in the profit and loss account, which are matched with turnover for the period.

Disclosure. The accounting policies applied have to be disclosed. The Act requires stocks to be classified in the notes as raw materials and consumables, work in progress, finished goods and goods for resale, and payments on account.

The amount by which turnover on long-term contracts exceeds payments on account is classified as amounts recoverable on contracts and separately disclosed within debtors. If payments on account exceed turnover, the balance should be offset against long-term work in progress, and any excess classified as payments on account and separately disclosed within creditors. The note on long-term contracts should disclose separately both the net cost less foreseeable losses and the applicable payments on account.

Reference. SSAP 9 and Companies (Amendment) Act 1986.

19. Current Liabilities

General Accounting Treatment. The Act requires **creditors** due within one year to be separately disclosed for the following categories: debenture loans; bank loans and overdrafts; payments received on account; trade creditors; bills of exchange payable; amounts owed to group companies; amounts owed to companies in which the company has a participating interest; other creditors, including tax and social security; accruals; and deferred income.

Creation of General and Specific Provisions. There is often confusion about whether items should be accounted for as creditors and accruals or as provisions (which are disclosed separately). Provisions for liabilities or charges include reasonable amounts to provide for liabilities or losses that are either likely to be incurred, or certain to be incurred but uncertain as to amount or date, whereas creditors normally represent amounts actually owed to third parties. For some provisions, for example, bad debt provisions, it is correct to net the provision against the related assets.

Disclosure. The aggregate amount of creditors has to be split between amounts payable in more than five years and amounts payable in instalments, any of which fall due after the end of the five-year period. The terms of payment or repayment and the applicable interest rate have to be given in general terms. The Stock Exchange Yellow Book also requires bank loans and other borrowings to be separately disclosed for amounts repayable within one year or on demand; between one year and two years; between two years and five years; and after five years.

If the company has secured creditors, that is, liabilities that are secured by particular assets of the company, details of the security given and the total amount of secured creditors must be disclosed.

Reference. Companies (Amendment) Act 1986 and Companies Act 1963 (Sixth Schedule).

20. Long-Term Debt

General Accounting Treatment. Creditors due after one year are disclosed separately from creditors due within one year. Furthermore, long-term creditors have to be disclosed under the same headings as for **current liabilities**, detailed in Section 19.

Debt Restructuring. There are no accounting standards dealing with debt restructuring in the Republic of Ireland, but the Act contains a number of rules that relate to the procedures to be followed when arrangements of this nature are made. Normally, such debt restructuring arrangements would involve the debt holders taking shares in the company and possibly cancelling part of their debt.

Disclosure. The disclosure requirements for long-term debt are the same as those discussed for current liabilities in Section 19.

Reference. Companies Act 1963.

21.   Contingencies

Contingent Losses.   A material contingent loss should be accrued if it is probable that a future event will confirm a loss that can be estimated with reasonable accuracy at the date on which the financial statements are approved. If a contingent loss is not accrued, it should be disclosed, unless the possibility of loss is remote.

Contingent Gains.   Contingent gains should not be accrued, and should be disclosed only if it is probable that a gain will be realized.

Disclosure.   For each contingent loss or contingent gain that is disclosed, the required disclosures are: the nature of the **contingency**; the uncertainties that are expected to affect the ultimate outcome; and a prudent estimate of the financial effect, showing separately the amounts that have been accrued or a statement that it is not feasible to make such an estimate.

Reference.   SSAP 18 and Companies Act 1963 (Sixth Schedule).

22.   Capital and Reserves

Share Capital.   Called-up share capital is the amount of capital that has to be disclosed in the balance sheet. Called-up share capital is the aggregate amount of the calls made on the company's shares, whether or not those calls have been paid. Called-up share capital not paid is shown as a debtor.

If share capital is issued at a premium, the premium is credited to a share premium account. The share premium account can be used only to issue fully paid bonus shares (i.e., stock splits), write off preliminary expenses and write off expenses relating to the issue of shares.

Other Reserves.   Only realized profits are credited to the profit and loss account. Unrealized profits are normally reflected in the revaluation reserve that is used to record surpluses from the revaluation of assets under the alternative accounting rules (explained in Section 3). The Act does not require reserves to be disclosed as either realized or unrealized. Reserves are classified as revaluation reserve; capital redemption reserve; reserve for own shares; reserves provided for by the articles of association; other reserves; and the profit and loss account reserve.

Restrictions on Dividends and Other Distributions.   Distributions can be paid only out of accumulated realized reserves after taking account of realized and unrealized losses. In addition, public companies can make a distribution only if it does not reduce net assets below the aggregate of called-up share capital plus undistributable reserves.

Disclosure.   Share capital: The total allotted (i.e., issued) capital, the amount of paid-up share capital and the authorized share capital have to be disclosed in a note. If shares have been allotted, the notes must show the number and aggregate value of those shares. If any capital is redeemable, the dates and terms of redemption and the amount of premium payable on redemption have to be given. If there are any rights attaching to shares, the number, description and amount of the shares must be disclosed, together with the period over which the rights can be exercised and the price to be paid for the shares allotted.

Reserves: The notes must disclose the aggregate amount of each reserve at the beginning and end of the year, any amounts transferred to or from reserves and the source and application of amounts transferred.

Reference. Companies Act 1963; Companies (Amendment) Act 1983; Companies (Amendment) Act 1986; and Companies (Amendment) Act 1990.

ACCOUNTING PRINCIPLES FOR SPECIFIC ITEMS— INCOME STATEMENT

23. Revenue Recognition

General Principles. At present, there is no accounting standard on the recognition of revenue earned from operations. The only direct reference to revenue recognition is contained in the definition of prudence in SSAP 2. In accordance with SSAP 2, revenue and profit should not be anticipated but should be recognized only when realized in the form of cash or other assets whose ultimate cash realization can be assessed with reasonable certainty. The concept of prudence is further embodied in the Act, which requires that only profits realized at the balance sheet date be included in the profit and loss account. Other than those two references and principles for recognition of revenue from long-term contracts (discussed below), there is no specific guidance in the Republic of Ireland on recognition criteria. However, the following principles are normally followed in determining when to recognize revenue.

Revenue from a transaction involving the sale of goods is usually recognized when the seller has transferred to the buyer the significant risks and rewards of ownership of the goods. In most situations, the substance of the transaction rather than its legal form will determine the time of sale. If, however, goods are sold subject to conditions (e.g., consignment sales, cash on delivery), revenue is not recognized until the conditions have been complied with.

Revenue from the rendering of services is usually recognized as the services are performed. If the service is performed as a single act, revenue is recognized when the service is completed. If the service is provided over a period of time, revenue is recognized in a manner appropriate to the stage of completion of the service, provided that the outcome can be assessed with reasonable certainty.

The ASB is developing accounting guidance for revenue recognition.

Long-Term Contracts. The principles for the recognition of revenue on long-term contracts are contained in SSAP 9. In a long-term contract, the time taken to substantially complete the contract is such that the contract activity falls into different accounting periods. A contract accounted for as long term will usually extend beyond one year. However, a duration exceeding one year is not an essential feature of a long-term contract. Some contracts with a duration shorter than one year should be accounted for as long-term contracts (provided that the policy is applied consistently within the reporting entity and from year to year), if they are sufficiently material that not to record turnover and attributable profit would lead to a distortion such that the financial statements would not give a true and fair view.

Where the business has long-term contracts and the outcome can be assessed with reasonable certainty before their conclusion, profit is recognized on the **percentage of completion method** as the contract activity progresses. If the outcome cannot be assessed with reasonable certainty, no profit is reflected in the profit and loss account from those contracts; profit is recognized when the contract is completed. If there will be a loss on a contract as a whole, the entire loss should be recorded as soon as it is foreseen, in accordance with the prudence concept. Initially, the foreseeable loss is deducted from work in progress, thus reducing it to net realizable value. Any loss in excess of the work in progress should be classified as an accrued liability or a provision for liabilities and charges, depending on the circumstances.

Instalment Sales.   On **instalment sales**, revenue is normally recognized at the date of sale. If, however, collection is not reasonably assured, revenue is recognized as cash instalments are received.

Rights of Return.   When goods are sold giving the buyer the right to return them for a refund or replacement, revenue may be recognized at the point of sale, provided that adequate provision is made for future returns. Even where goods are sold subject to a reservation of title clause, which enables the seller to have a lien on them until the purchaser has paid for them, revenue recognition is not deferred. If, however, the clause is likely to be acted upon, it is appropriate to create a provision for the doubtful debt.

Product Financing.   **Product financing** occurs when goods are sold with a commitment to repurchase them at a later date. In a sale of goods with a commitment to repurchase, the original owner may retain the principal benefits and risks of ownership, if the repurchase price is predetermined and covers the cost, including interest, incurred by the other party in purchasing and holding the goods. In such a situation, the transaction should be accounted for as a financing rather than a sales transaction, leaving the asset and a corresponding liability on the balance sheet of the original owner.

Disclosure.   A company must disclose in its profit and loss account, under the heading turnover, the amount it derives from providing goods and services from ordinary activities, after deducting the **value added tax** and other taxes. The accounting policy for turnover should also be disclosed in the notes. The method of ascertaining turnover and attributable profit in relation to long-term contracts must also be stated.

Reference.   SSAP 9 and Companies (Amendment) Act 1986.

24. Government Grants and Assistance

Accounting Treatment.   SSAP 4 sets out the accounting treatment to be followed for government grants, which should be recognized when the expenditure that they are intended to contribute to is recognized.

SSAP 4 stipulates that government grants relating to fixed assets should be credited to revenue over the asset's expected useful life. This can be achieved in one of two ways:

□ The grant may be deducted from the purchase price or production cost of the asset, thereby reducing depreciation expense.

□ The grant may be treated as a deferred credit, of which a portion is credited to revenue annually.

The ASC has received legal opinion, however, that the option to deduct government grants from the purchase price or production cost of fixed assets is not available to companies governed by the accounting and reporting requirements of the Act (i.e., the majority of companies that prepare accounts).

Disclosure. The following information must be disclosed in the financial statements:

□ The accounting policy adopted for government grants.

□ The effects of government grants on the results for the period and/or the financial position of the enterprise.

□ Where the results of operations are materially affected by the receipt of government assistance other than grants, the effects of that assistance and its nature, to the extent that such effects can be measured.

Potential liabilities to repay grants in specified circumstances should, if necessary, be disclosed in accordance with paragraph 16 of SSAP 18, *Accounting for Contingencies*.

Reference. SSAP 4 and Companies (Amendment) Act 1986.

25. Research and Development

Definitions. Research and development expenditures fall into one or more of the following broad categories (except to the extent that expenditures relate to locating or exploiting oil, gas or mineral deposits or are reimbursable by third parties either directly or under the terms of a firm contract to develop and manufacture at an agreed price calculated to reimburse both elements of the expenditure):

□ Pure or basic research—Experimental or theoretical work undertaken primarily to acquire new scientific or technical knowledge rather than directed toward any specific practical aim or application.

□ Applied research—Original or critical investigation undertaken to gain new scientific or technical knowledge and directed toward a specific practical aim or objective.

□ Development—Use of scientific or technical knowledge in order to produce new or substantially improved materials, devices, products or services; to install new processes or systems prior to the commencement of commercial production or commercial applications; or to improve substantially those already produced or installed.

Accounting Treatment. The Act permits only development costs to be capitalized, and only in special circumstances. All research costs must be expensed as incurred. The Act does not define the special circumstances in which development costs may be capitalized, but SSAP 13 sets forth the following conditions that must be satisfied to capitalize development expenditures:

☐ There is a clearly defined project.

☐ The related expenditure is separately identifiable.

☐ The outcome of the project has been assessed with reasonable certainty as to both its technical feasibility and its ultimate commercial viability, considered in the light of factors such as likely market conditions (including competing products), public opinion and consumer and environmental legislation.

☐ The aggregate of the deferred development costs, any further development costs and related production, selling and administration costs is reasonably expected to be exceeded by related future sales or other revenues.

☐ Adequate resources exist, or are reasonably expected to be available, to enable the project to be completed and to provide any additional working capital needed as a result of the project.

Provided that these conditions are satisfied, a company can capitalize development expenditure, but only until commercial production begins. SSAP 13 requires a company to amortize the capitalized expenditure from the time commercial production of the product or service begins, which is when the company manufactures the product with a view to selling it commercially. Amortization of development expenditure must be allocated to each accounting period on a systematic basis over the production life of the product.

At the end of each accounting period, a company should review capitalized development expenditure. If the circumstances that justified the original deferral of an expenditure no longer apply or are considered doubtful, the company should write off the expenditure immediately to the extent it is considered irrecoverable.

Disclosure. The following disclosures should be made in the notes:

☐ The accounting policy adopted for research and development expenditure.

☐ The total amount of research and development expenditure charged to the profit and loss account in the period, both current year expenditure and amortization of deferred expenditure.

☐ Movements on deferred development expenditure fixed asset balances and the amounts at the beginning and end of the period.

☐ The period over which capitalized development costs are being amortized, together with the reasons for capitalizing them.

Reference. SSAP 13 and Companies (Amendment) Act 1986.

26. Capitalized Interest Costs

Accounting Treatment. There is no accounting standard in the Republic of Ireland that deals with capitalization of interest. However, the Act allows interest on any capital borrowed to finance the production of an asset to be included in the production cost of the asset. Views differ as to whether the amount to be capitalized should be shown gross or net of taxes. The ASB is currently reviewing this issue.

Disclosure. The amount of capitalized interest included in production cost must be stated in the notes.

Reference. Companies (Amendment) Act 1986.

27. Imputed Interest

General. Imputed interest is not used widely in the preparation of financial statements in the Republic of Ireland. However, the principles of discounting account balances and transactions to their present value are recognized in some accounting standards, for example, accounting for lease transactions (SSAP 21) and accounting for pension liabilities (SSAP 24).

Accounting Treatment. Although there is no authoritative guidance on the use of discounting in financial statements in the Republic of Ireland, Technical Release (TR) 773 highlights instances where discounting may be required to enable financial statements to give a true and fair view. TR 773 identifies the following as the two main potential applications of discounting in financial reporting:

☐ Allocation of cash flows as revenues or expenses over accounting periods in a manner consistent with the time value of money.

☐ Valuation where no ready external market exists and no cash equivalent is available.

Disclosure. TR 773 encourages disclosure in the financial statements of the accounting policy adopted where discounting has been used, in particular, the significant assumptions made regarding choice of interest rate and timing of cash flows.

Reference. TR 773.

28. Extraordinary or Unusual Items

Extraordinary Items. Extraordinary items are defined in FRS 3 as items that derive from events or transactions that fall outside the ordinary activities of the company and that are therefore expected not to recur frequently or regularly. Extraordinary items do not include exceptional items, nor do they include prior year items merely because they relate to a prior year. Under the definition in FRS 3, extraordinary items are very rare.

Exceptional Items. Exceptional items are defined in FRS 3 as material items that derive from events or transactions that fall within the ordinary activities of the company, but need to be disclosed separately because of their size or incidence in order for the financial statements to give a true and fair view.

The following exceptional items are required to be disclosed separately on the face of the profit and loss account after operating profit and before interest:

☐ Profit or losses on the sale or termination of a business.

☐ Costs of a fundamental reorganization or restructuring.

☐ Profits or losses on a disposal of a fixed asset.

Disclosure. Exceptional items should generally be disclosed in a note, except as described above. An adequate description has to be given of each exceptional item.

Extraordinary items are disclosed in the profit and loss account under the four headings of: extraordinary income; extraordinary charges; extraordinary profit or loss; and tax on extraordinary profit or loss. This breakdown may be given in a note, rather than on the face of the profit and loss account, and in practice many companies adopt this form of disclosure.

Reference. FRS 3; Companies Act 1963; and Companies (Amendment) Act 1986.

29. Income Taxes

Accounting Treatment. In the Republic of Ireland, companies pay corporation tax on the accounting income of the year adjusted for certain items, whether distributed or undistributed. In the absence of a dividend, corporation tax is payable seven months after the end of the accounting period. If a company makes a distribution to shareholders, the company does not withhold any income tax from the payment, but is required to make an advance payment of corporation tax (ACT). This ACT is normally offset against the company's total liability for corporation tax on its income, but not on its chargeable (taxable) gains on the sale of capital items, in the period. The resulting net liability is known as the mainstream liability. An individual shareholder receiving a dividend is taxed on the amount of income equivalent to the dividend plus the imputed tax credit. This is known as the imputation system of corporation tax and is covered in SSAP 8.

In accordance with SSAP 15, companies are also required to account for deferred taxes. Deferred taxes should be computed under the **liability method**, which requires that tax deferred or accelerated because of timing differences be accounted for, but only to the extent that it is probable that a tax liability or asset will materialize (i.e., on a partial provision basis). The provision for deferred tax liabilities should be reduced by any deferred tax debit balances arising from separate categories of timing differences and any ACT that is available to offset those liabilities.

Deferred tax debit balances, including those arising from losses, should not be carried forward as assets, except to the extent that they are expected to be recoverable without replacement by equivalent debit balances. Recovery may be affected by, among other things, the period of time losses are available to be carried forward for tax purposes. Deferred tax assets arising from losses should be recognized only when recovery is assured beyond a reasonable doubt.

Disclosure. The notes to the profit and loss account must disclose the following:

☐   The amount of corporation tax, specifying:
  — The charge for corporation tax on the income of the year. (If the corporation tax includes material transfers between the deferred tax account and the profit and loss account, these also should be separately disclosed.)
  — Tax attributable to **franked investment income**.
  — Irrecoverable ACT.
  — Relief for overseas taxation.
☐   The total overseas tax, relieved or unrelieved, specifying the portion of the unrelieved overseas tax arising from the payment or proposed payment of dividends.

☐ The amount of deferred tax relating to ordinary activities. (Similar disclosure is required for deferred tax relating to extraordinary items, which should be shown as part of the tax on extraordinary items.)

☐ The amount of any potential deferred tax that has not been provided for the period, divided into major components.

☐ Adjustments to deferred tax from changes in tax rates and tax allowances, which should normally be disclosed as part of the tax charge for the period. However, the effect of a change in the basis of taxation or a significant change in government fiscal policy should be treated as an extraordinary item, if material.

Reference. SSAPs 8 and 15; Companies Act 1963 (Sixth Schedule); and Companies (Amendment) Act 1986.

30. Postretirement Benefits

Accounting Treatment. SSAP 24 deals with both the measurement of pension costs and the disclosure of pension information in company financial statements. The accounting objective of SSAP 24 is that the expected cost of providing pensions should be recognized on a systematic and rational basis over the period during which an employer benefits from employees' services. Most pension plans (called schemes) in the Republic of Ireland are funded and are either **defined contribution** or **defined benefit schemes**.

Defined Benefit Pension Plans. In a defined benefit scheme, rules determine the benefits to be paid, regardless of the contributions paid with respect to each employee. The employer's obligations are not capable of being defined in an absolute sense; instead, actuarial expertise is required to determine an appropriate level of contributions to fund the obligations. Consequently, the accounting objective is met by providing for periodic pension costs that are a substantially level percentage of the current and expected future pensionable earnings in the light of current actuarial assumptions.

Variations from regular costs because of experience, changes in actuarial methods or assumptions, or retroactive changes in benefits or membership should normally be spread forward over the expected remaining service lives of current employees. SSAP 24 does not suggest a period, but states that it should be determined by the actuary.

Defined Contribution Pension Plans. In a defined contribution scheme, the future benefits payable to employees are determined by the accumulated value of contributions paid in to the scheme. The employer's obligations are, therefore, normally discharged by an agreed level of contributions. Consequently, the company meets the accounting objective by charging against profits the amount of contributions payable to the scheme in the accounting period.

Pension Fund Surpluses. Treatment of pension scheme surpluses is governed by the scheme's trust deed. It may be reflected in the form of either contribution holidays, a period of reduced contributions or cash refunds to employers.

UITF 6 deals with accounting for postretirement benefits other than pensions. It requires that obligations with respect to such benefits be recognized in the financial statements and that the principles of SSAP 24 be applied to the accounting for such benefits. This requirement applies to financial statements for periods ending on or after December

23, 1994. Until that date, disclosure of the benefits is required. It would be rare for an Irish company to have such obligations.

Disclosure.   Defined contribution schemes must disclose: the nature of the scheme (i.e., defined contribution); the accounting policy; the pension cost charge for the period; and any outstanding or prepaid contribution at the balance sheet date.

In addition to the above disclosures, defined benefit schemes must disclose a significant amount of actuarial information, including:

☐   Whether the scheme is funded or unfunded.

☐   Whether the pension cost and provision (or asset) are assessed in accordance with the advice of a professionally qualified actuary and, if so, the date of the most recent formal actuarial valuation or later formal review used for this purpose.

☐   Explanation of significant changes in the pension cost charge compared with the previous period.

☐   The amount of any deficiency on a current funding basis, indicating the action, if any, to be taken (applicable beginning in January 1993 to companies unquoted on the Stock Exchange).

☐   Outline of results of the most recent formal actuarial valuation or later formal review, including:
   — The actuarial method used and the main actuarial assumptions.
   — The market value of the scheme assets at the date of their valuation or review.
   — The level of funding expressed as a percentage and comments on any material surplus or deficit.

In addition, details of the expected effects on future costs of any material changes in the group's and/or company's pension arrangements, together with any commitment to make additional payments over a limited number of years, should be disclosed.

Reference.   SSAP 24; UITF 6; and Companies (Amendment) Act 1986.

31.   Discontinued Operations

FRS 3 requires that an analysis be provided on the face of the profit and loss account of, at a minimum, turnover and operating profit between amounts attributable to:

☐   Continuing operations.
☐   Acquisition as a component of continuing operations.
☐   Discontinued operations.

The notes to the profit and loss account should include an analysis of the other statutory profit and loss account headings under the same categories. Alternatively, this information can be given on the face of the profit and loss account.

In the year in which the decision to discontinue or sell a segment of the business is made, the profit and loss account should contain details of provisions made in relation to the disposal or sale. The provisions should reflect the extent to which obligations have been incurred that are not expected to be covered by the future profits of the operation or the disposal of its assets. The decision as to when the provisions should be booked should be based on the time at which the company becomes demonstrably committed to the disposal or sale.

Reference. FRS 3 (for accounting periods ending on or after June 22, 1993) and Companies Act 1986.

32. Earnings per Share

General. The Act does not require earnings per share (EPS) information to be given. However, SSAP 3 requires listed companies and companies traded on the USM to show EPS on the face of the profit and loss account.

Definition. EPS is defined in FRS 3 as the amount of consolidated profit of the period, after tax and after deducting minority interests and preference dividends, attributable to each equity share.

Method of Calculation. EPS is generally calculated on two bases. The first calculation uses the weighted-average share capital eligible for dividends in the period and is known as the basic earnings per share. The second calculation takes into account that companies often have equity shares in issue that are not eligible for a dividend but will be in the future. There may also be a future reduction in earnings if conversion rights attaching to debentures, loan stock, **preference shares**, or options or warrants to subscribe for equity shares are exercised. Where these situations exist, SSAP 3 requires that fully diluted earnings per share should also be calculated and disclosed on the face of the profit and loss account.

Under the imputation system of corporation tax, the tax charge used in determining EPS should include any irrecoverable ACT and any unrelieved overseas tax from payment or proposed payment of dividends. This is known as the net basis as opposed to the nil basis, which excludes irrecoverable ACT and unrelieved overseas tax (except insofar as they relate to preference dividends).

Disclosure. EPS should be shown on the face of the profit and loss account on the net basis both for the current period and for the corresponding previous period. If the calculation of EPS on the nil basis is materially different from the net basis, the nil basis figure should also be disclosed. The basis of calculating EPS should be disclosed either in the profit and loss account or in a note. In particular, the amount of earnings and the number of equity shares used in the calculation should be shown.

In addition to the basic EPS, the fully diluted EPS should be shown on the face of the profit and loss account. The basis of calculating the fully diluted EPS must be disclosed. The fully diluted EPS for the corresponding previous period should not be shown unless the assumptions on which it is based still apply. The fully diluted EPS need not be given if either the dilution is less than 5 percent of basic EPS or basic EPS is negative. Basic and fully diluted EPS, if both are disclosed, should be equally prominent.

FRS 3 allows EPS to be calculated on alternative bases, provided the disclosure is not given more prominence than that based on the above definitions.

Reference. SSAP 3 and FRS 3.

Appendix
DO IRISH STANDARDS OR PREVALENT PRACTICE SUBSTANTIALLY COMPLY WITH INTERNATIONAL ACCOUNTING STANDARDS?

Section	Topic	Substantially complies with IAS?	Comments
3.	Basic accounting concepts and conventions	Yes	
	Contents of financial statements	Yes	
4.	Business combinations*	Yes	
5.	Joint ventures	No	Normally equity accounting is used to account for all types of joint ventures
6.	Foreign currency translation*	Yes	
8.	Accounting changes*	Yes	
9.	Prior period adjustments*	Yes	
10.	Post balance sheet events	Yes	
11.	Related party transactions	No	Both the definition of related party and the transactions that need to be disclosed are more restricted than in IAS 24
12.	Segmental information	Yes	
13.	Property, plant and equipment*	Yes	
15.	Leases	Yes	
16.	Investments	Yes	
17.	Accounts receivable	Yes	
18.	Inventories and work in progress*	Yes	
19.	Current liabilities	Yes	
20.	Long-term debt	Yes	
21.	Contingencies	Yes	
22.	Capital and reserves	Yes	
23.	Revenue recognition*	Yes	
24.	Government grants and assistance	Yes	
25.	Research and development*	Yes	

Appendix (*Continued*)

Section	Topic	Substantially complies with IAS?	Comments
26.	Capitalization of interest costs*	Yes	
28.	Extraordinary or unusual items*	Yes	
29.	Income tax**	Yes	
30.	Postretirement benefits*	Yes	

*These topics are subject to change as a result of the IASC Improvements Project—see the appendix to the International Accounting Standards chapter.

**The IAS on accounting for taxes on income is currently being revised, and an exposure draft has been issued.

Comparison in this table is made to International Accounting Standards in force at January 1, 1993. For further details, see the International Accounting Standards chapter.

ISRAEL

GENERAL NATIONAL INFORMATION

1. Source of Generally Accepted Accounting Principles

Generally accepted accounting principles (GAAP) and auditing standards in Israel are derived from the following sources:

☐ The Israeli Securities Law, 1968, and the Securities (Preparation of Annual Financial Statements) Regulations, 1992 (Securities Regulations), under that Law. These set out reporting requirements for companies whose securities are traded on the Israeli Stock Exchange. These reporting requirements serve also as guidelines for the preparation of financial statements by private companies.

☐ Israeli Accounting Standards. Professional principles, procedures and guidelines (Opinions) are issued by the Institute of Certified Public Accountants in Israel (the Israeli Institute or the Institute) and are binding on all certified public accountants.

☐ The Auditors (Mode of Performance) Regulations, 1973, published under the Auditors' Law, 1955. These provide that the audit, by a certified public accountant, be made in accordance with generally accepted auditing standards and procedures and prescribe the manner of the expression of the auditor's opinion on the financial statements, including qualifications and disclaimer of opinion.

☐ The International Accounting Standards (IASs) published by the International Accounting Standards Committee (IASC). These standards apply in cases where there are no specific pronouncements or generally accepted accounting principles in Israel. Most of the new Opinions issued by the Israeli Institute take into account the provisions of existing IASs; the Institute also endeavors to ensure that the principles incorporated in such Opinions are not contrary to US GAAP.

☐ Israeli Companies Legislation (known as the Companies Ordinance [New Version], 1983). Under this legislation, companies in Israel are required to prepare financial statements (balance sheet and income statement) and provide certain financial statement disclosures.

☐ Undocumented principles or practices that are commonly accepted. It should be noted that a great emphasis is placed on principles and practices that are accepted by the profession in the United States (including SEC rules).

2. Audit and Public Companies

Audit.   The Companies Ordinance requires that the annual financial statements of all companies (whether private or public) be audited by independent public accountants.

Under the Auditors' Law, 1955, which regulates the CPA profession in Israel, the grant of a license to practice is conditional upon the candidate being at least 23 years of age, having passed the qualifying examinations and having two years approved work experience either in Israel or abroad. A candidate need not be the holder of an academic degree. In practice, however, almost all candidates in recent years have academic training. Independent public accountants cannot be directors or officers of the audited company, nor can they be partners of an officer of the company or employees of the company (except in the case of a private company).

The Institute and the Securities Authority (which was established under the Israeli Securities Law) have published guidelines regarding independence. The guidelines published by the Securities Authority apply to auditors of companies whose securities are traded and are substantially similar to those applicable in the United States.

The auditors are appointed by the company at a general meeting of the shareholders and remain in service until the next annual general meeting. Removal of an auditor is likewise made at a general meeting.

The Companies Ordinance sets out the basic duties and responsibilities of auditors, which relate principally to examining the financial statements (consisting of a balance sheet and a statement of income) of the company and to reporting to the shareholders on the fairness of the those statements and on the company's compliance with the requirements of the Companies Ordinance.

Auditing standards and procedures are prescribed by the Israeli Institute and incorporated in the Auditors (Mode of Performance) Regulations, 1973. The basic format of the auditors' report is also prescribed by the Israeli Institute. The above auditing standards and procedures are included in the Members' Guide published by the Israeli Institute.

While membership in the Israeli Institute is voluntary, most accountants in Israel are members.

Reference.   Companies Ordinance, s. 211, 215–216, 129; Auditors' Law, s. 4.

Public Companies.   **Public companies** seeking to register their securities in Israel must apply for listing on the Tel-Aviv Stock Exchange, which is the only stock exchange in Israel. The Securities Authority plays a dominant role in the process of approving prospectuses of such companies. Companies whose securities are quoted on the stock exchange have to comply with the reporting requirements prescribed by the Securities Law, 1968 and the Securities Regulations thereunder. These requirements are in addition to the normal statutory reporting requirements.

The requirements for obtaining a listing on the Stock Exchange vary depending on the type of listing (main list or parallel list). The principal requirements for listing a company under the main list (according to three possibilities) are:

Paid-up capital—in millions	A	B	C
	US dollars		
Prior to listing	12	6	2
Subsequent to listing	12	8	4

	A	B	C
		US dollars	
Net income—in thousands			
For latest year	800	600	400
Another year in the 4 years prior to listing		600	400
Revenues—in the year preceding the listing and another year in the 4 years prior to listing—in millions			7.5
Annual added value—in the year preceding the listing—in millions			2.5

Under the parallel list, the minimum equity is $2 million; also, companies are required to be in operation for at least one year. There are no requirements concerning net income or revenues.

Once admitted, a company is required to submit immediate reports on certain events as prescribed by regulations, and periodic reports, accompanied by audited annual financial statements, as well as quarterly financial statements (reviewed by the auditor). The above statements and reports are to be submitted to the Securities Authority, the Stock Exchange and the Registrar of Companies. As a condition for listing securities, the Stock Exchange requires companies to circulate their annual financial statements, as well as the above quarterly financial statements, accompanied by the directors' report, to all registered shareholders. Such statements must also be available for perusal at offices of members of the Stock Exchange. The filing of the above periodic and immediate reports is under the supervision of the Securities Authority.

Listed public **companies** must submit their annual financial statements within four months of the end of their financial year, and their quarterly statements within two months of the period end.

Reference. Stock Exchange Rules and Guidelines—Chapter 10, and Securities Law—Chapter 6.

GENERAL ACCOUNTING

3. Financial Statements

Basic Accounting Concepts. Inflation accounting has been adopted as a basic **accounting concept**, as explained in Section 7. The following accounting concepts, which stem from common practice, underlie financial statements:

☐ Financial statements are prepared on the assumption that the entity is a **going concern**; different bases of measurement may be appropriate when the entity is not expected to continue in operation for the foreseeable future (considered to be one year from the balance sheet date).

☐ **Revenues** and profits are recognized only when realized or when they can be assessed with reasonable certainty. Provision is made for all known liabilities if it is probable that future events will confirm that a liability has been incurred at the balance sheet date, and a reasonable estimate of the resulting loss can be made (if the chances for incurrence of a liability are remote, the existence of such a loss should only be disclosed).

□ Revenues and costs are accounted for on the **accrual basis**, except where collection is not assured, in which case revenues are recognized only upon actual receipt.

□ Accounting for similar items within an accounting period and from one period to the next should be consistent. Consistency is a major factor in creating comparability.

□ Transactions and other events should be accounted for and presented in accordance with their substance and not merely their legal form.

□ Financial statements should disclose all items that are **material** enough to affect users' evaluations or decisions.

Contents of Financial Statements. In accordance with the Securities Regulations, companies whose securities are traded on the Stock Exchange are required to prepare and publish full financial statements, which include a balance sheet and statements of income, changes in shareholders' equity and cash flows. **Consolidated financial statements** as well as separate statements of the **parent company** are required.

In practice, financial statements prepared by nonpublic companies differ from those of public companies mainly with respect to the extent of disclosure given in certain areas (e.g., related parties, composition of certain balance sheet and income statement items).

Format of Financial Statements. In 1965, the Israeli Institute published accounting and reporting rules relating in general to industrial enterprises incorporated as limited companies. These rules specify the format of the financial statements and classification of items included therein, as well as the additional information to be included in those statements. Also, the Israeli Institute has published Sample Financial Statements for entities in various fields of operations (industrial, commercial, building construction, banks, insurance). Comparative figures are required for the previous year; companies whose securities are quoted on the Stock Exchange are required to present comparative figures for the two previous years in the income statement and the statements of changes in shareholders' equity and cash flows. The Securities Regulations include specific provisions regarding the format of the statements and classification and presentation of the financial statement items according to a specified order (unless the activities of the entity require different classification and presentation).

Disclosure of Accounting Policies. The financial statements include a note (usually the first note) describing all material **accounting policies** that have been adopted in their preparation, including changes in the application of accounting policies in the reporting period in comparison with prior periods.

Reference. Securities Regulations, 1 and 8, Member's Guide published by the Israeli Institute, parts B and C.

4. Business Combinations

Principles of Consolidation. The Israeli Institute requires preparation of consolidated financial statements. Consolidation is also required under the Securities Regulations.

Accounting for Business Combinations.   **Business combinations** are generally treated as **purchases**. The **pooling of interests** concept is rarely used.

In Israel, transactions involving the transfer of net assets or exchange of shares between companies under common control are accounted for in accordance with US rules (APB Opinion No. 16), that is, the assets and liabilities so transferred are accounted for at **historical cost** in a manner similar to pooling of interests accounting.

Control.   The condition for consolidation of a **subsidiary** is that the parent company has direct or indirect control. Such control exists when the parent holds more than 50 percent of the subsidiary's shares conferring voting rights, or when the parent is entitled to nominate the majority of the directors.

Consolidation is not permitted when:

- ☐   Control is temporary.
- ☐   The subsidiary operates abroad under economic and monetary restrictions that significantly limit its ability to transfer funds to the parent company.
- ☐   The parent company does not actually have formal control because the subsidiary is insolvent and has been abandoned or transferred to a liquidator or receiver.
- ☐   Minority shareholders hold a substantial part (75 percent or more) of the subsidiary's shares conferring a right for receipt of profits.

Goodwill.   **Goodwill** represents the difference between the cost of investment in investees and the fair value of their identified assets net of liabilities at the date of acquisition.

Where the fair value of identified net assets at the date of acquisition exceeds the cost of investment, such excess is first deducted from intangible assets of the investee, and the balance is deducted from nonmonetary depreciable assets in proportion to the fair value of these assets. Any remaining excess represents **negative goodwill.**

Goodwill should be amortized over a period of five years (in rare cases, which should be explained, 20 years). In practice, goodwill is amortized over a longer period, up to 40 years.

Equity Accounting.   The **equity method** of accounting is used for investments in investee companies if the investor has the ability to influence the operating and financial policies of those companies (significant influence). Significant influence is presumed to exist when shares conferring more than 25 percent of the voting rights or the right to nominate directors in the investee are held. The equity basis may also be used if significant influence is clearly demonstrated, even if the voting rights in the investee are 25 percent or less.

Minority Interests.   The interests of minority shareholders in shareholders' equity of consolidated subsidiaries are to be presented as a separate item before the shareholders' equity section in the balance sheet. The interests of minority shareholders in profits of those subsidiaries are to be presented as a separate item in the income statement, while their interests in extraordinary items are to be deducted from such items.

The minority shareholders are not charged with their share of the excess of accumulated deficit over share capital and surplus of the subsidiary, as it is not legally possible to force the minority shareholders to bear their share in such deficit.

Reference. Opinion 15, s. 2, 3, 7–10, 18; Opinion 22, s. 2.1 and 2.3.

Disclosure. Consolidation: The following disclosures are required in the consolidated financial statements: principles of consolidation; the basis of inclusion of investments in unconsolidated subsidiaries and of determining their operating results; the accounting treatment of "excess cost" relating to consolidated and unconsolidated subsidiaries; information regarding balance sheet dates of subsidiaries that are different from that of the group; description of translation method of foreign currency financial statements of subsidiaries; information regarding unconsolidated subsidiaries, such as percentage of shareholding and reasons for nonconsolidation; data (assets, liabilities and revenues) relating to subsidiaries consolidated for the first time and to companies excluded from consolidation in the reported year.

Equity accounting: Companies whose securities are quoted on the stock exchange are required to provide the following data relating to unconsolidated subsidiaries and **associated companies**: details of investments and long-term loans and other indebtedness, classified by currency of repayment, linkage terms and interest rates; investments in marketable securities, which are to be presented separately, stating their quoted value; details of total "excess cost" not attributed to specific items, the original amount of goodwill and the balance, after amortization, at the balance sheet date.

Also, the above companies are required to submit, upon filing their financial statements, audited financial statements of significant unconsolidated subsidiaries.

Reference. Opinion 15, s. 24; Securities Regulations, 22.

5. Joint Ventures

Accounting for Investments in Joint Ventures. There are no rules in Israel for accounting for investments in **joint ventures**. Accordingly, the provisions of IAS 31, *Financial Reporting of Interests in Joint Ventures*, apply in Israel.

Jointly Controlled Entities. The most common arrangement in Israel whereby two or more parties undertake an economic activity that is subject to **joint control** relates to joint building ventures, which are not established as incorporated joint entities.

Investments in joint building ventures are accounted for by the **proportionate consolidation method** in the consolidated financial statements of a venturer. Under this method, the venturer reports its share in the assets, liabilities, income and expenses of the joint venture according to the venturer's proportionate interests (using the line-by-line reporting format or the separate line items format). Investments in joint ventures that are established as a corporation are usually accounted for by the equity method.

Transactions Between Venturers and the Joint Venture. When assets are contributed to a joint venture in exchange for an interest in the joint venture, a gain should be recognized in the venturer's statements to the extent of the interests of nonrelated venturers. However, losses should be recognized in their entirety.

Disclosure. A venturer should disclose a listing and description of interests in significant joint ventures and the proportion of ownership interest held in jointly controlled entities. A venturer that reports its interest in jointly controlled entities by the line-by-line reporting format should disclose the aggregate amounts of current assets, noncurrent assets, current liabilities, long-term liabilities, income and expenses.

In addition, where the venturer is liable for any contingent liability or commitment with respect to the joint venture, this should be disclosed.

Accounting by Joint Ventures.   Generally accepted accounting principles apply to all assets and liabilities and to operations of joint ventures. Accounting by the joint venture for assets contributed by the venturers is rare in Israel; if assets were so contributed, they would be accounted for by the joint venture at fair value.

Reference.   IAS 31.

6.   Foreign Currency Translation

Foreign Currency Denominated Transactions.   Transactions in **foreign currency** are measured and recorded at the domestic exchange rate in effect on the transaction date. Monetary (as distinct from nonmonetary) foreign currency balances outstanding at the balance sheet date are stated at the prevailing domestic exchange rate as of the balance sheet date. Resulting exchange differences are recognized in the income statement in the period in which the exchange rate changes.

Foreign Operations.   Foreign operations are classified as **self-sustaining** (i.e., operating independently) or **integrated** (with those of the parent company). For the purpose of consolidation or inclusion on the equity basis, the amounts (in foreign currency terms) included in the statements of investee companies are treated as follows:

□   If the investee is self-sustaining, its balance sheet items at the end of the year and its results of operations for the year are translated at the exchange rate of the relevant foreign currency at the end of the year; balance sheet items at the beginning of the year and changes in shareholders' equity items during the year should be reflected in the parent company's (and consolidated) financial statements on a "restate and then translate" basis. In practice, where the results are not significantly different, these items are translated at the relevant exchange rate at the beginning of the year or at the date of each change and then adjusted on basis of the changes in the Israeli consumer price index through the end of the year (see also Section 7).

   Differences resulting from the above treatment are carried as a separate item under shareholders' equity (differences on translation of financial statements of investee companies in foreign currency).

□   If the investee is integrated (i.e., its activities are an integral part of the activities of the investor), its financial statements are translated into Israeli currency using the **temporal method**; that is, **monetary items** and items carried at market value should be translated at current rates, and transactions and other balances, at historical rates. Resulting exchange differences are recognized in the income statement in the period in which the exchange rates change.

Hedges.   Certain entities hedge against possible consequences of foreign currency risks. Financial instruments should be accounted for based on whether they are speculative or designated, and effective, as a **hedge**. A speculative instrument is required to be marked to market, with unrealized gains or losses recognized currently. Unrealized gains or losses on financial instruments that hedge a currency exposure are deferred and follow the recognition of the item being hedged.

Disclosure. Disclosure is made in the financial statements of the exchange rate as of the balance sheet date of the Israeli currency relative to the applicable foreign currency (usually, the US dollar); the accounting treatment relating to foreign operations and movements in the "differences on translation of financial statements of investee companies in foreign currency" account; the accounting treatment of hedge transactions and details of commitments with respect to forward foreign currency exchange contracts.

Reference. Interpretation no. 8 to Opinion 36; IAS 21, s. 10; Statement 52 of the FASB.

7. Changing Prices/Inflation Accounting

General. As a result of the high rates of inflation that Israel experienced through 1985, financial statements in nominal Israeli currency (historical cost) were difficult to comprehend or analyze, particularly with regard to the carrying value of nonmonetary assets and the year to year comparison of operating results. Accordingly, since 1985, financial statements have been adjusted to reflect changes in the general purchasing power of the Israeli currency (new Israeli shekel—NIS). The adjustment is calculated on the basis of the Israeli consumer price index (CPI) and results in financial statements presented in a constant general purchasing power unit of measure, the "adjusted NIS" (referred to as adjusted statements).

Smaller nonpublic companies may provide, in lieu of full adjusted statements, information on the effect of inflation as additional information in notes to their financial statements.

However, certain companies are entitled to base their adjusted statements on the changes in the rate of exchange of foreign currency (usually the US dollar), provided one of the following conditions is met:

☐ The revenues (or the main part thereof) are receivable in foreign currency and the **fixed assets** (or the main part thereof) were purchased in foreign currency.

☐ The reporting company's securities are traded on the stock exchange of a foreign country.

Accounting Treatment. The balance sheet items are classified into monetary and nonmonetary items.

Monetary items—which represent items that reflect updated values or realizable values at the balance sheet date—are not adjusted (presented at an amount equal to their nominal value at the balance sheet date); however, comparative figures are adjusted to reflect the changes in the CPI during the year. Nonmonetary items—items that reflect historical values at date of acquisition or origination (mainly, property, plant and equipment, inventories and shareholders' equity items derived from cash flow from shareholders)—are adjusted on the basis of the CPI or the foreign currency exchange rate, as the case may be, at the time the related transactions took place; the income statement components relating to these items (mainly depreciation and changes in inventories) are adjusted on the same basis as that applied for adjusting the related balance sheet items. The components of the statement of income (except financing) relating to transactions carried out during the year—sales, purchases, labor costs, etc.—are adjusted on the basis of the CPI (or the exchange rate) for the month in which the transaction occurred.

So that the financial statements are presented on a uniform basis (i.e., in Israeli currency reflecting the changes in the purchasing power of that currency), comparative figures (including those relating to monetary items) included in the financial statements should be adjusted to the changes in the CPI (or the foreign currency exchange rate) during the year.

The erosion of net monetary items is included in net income (among financial expenses or income, except in certain cases, such as where it is feasible to accurately allocate it to the related transactions). The financing item in the income statement consists of two components: financial expenses and income in real terms, and the erosion of monetary balances during the year. Since it is difficult to analyze these components, the gain or loss on net monetary items is not separately disclosed, except for the expense, in real terms, relating to long-term liabilities.

The accounting treatment for adjusted statements, as described above, is consistent in all respects with the provisions of IAS 29, *Financial Reporting in Hyperinflationary Economies* (except for the requirement under IAS 29 to disclose separately the gain or loss on net monetary items, as noted in the preceding paragraph).

The term "cost" referred to in the following sections signifies cost in adjusted Israeli currency.

Reference.   Opinions 23, 34, 36, 37 and 50.

8. Accounting Changes

Accounting Treatment.   Changes in accounting policy resulting from a new pronouncement of the Israeli Institute are accounted for in accordance with specific instructions included in the new pronouncement. Accounting changes made for other reasons are usually treated in accordance with US rules (APB Opinion No. 20).

Accounting policy changes are usually treated as a catch-up adjustment to the current year's income for the cumulative effect of the change on prior periods.

A change in an accounting estimate is accounted for in the period in which the change occurs and applicable future periods.

A company may restate its financial statements prior to an initial public offering. The Israeli Securities Authority will usually ask the registrant to disclose the effect of such restatement. A reference to the restatement will also be made in the auditors' report.

Disclosure.   A description of the accounting change, the justification for the change and its effect on pretax income, on net income and on per share earnings are to be provided if the effect is material.

Reference.   IAS 8, s. 22–23; Securities Regulations, 6.

9. Prior Period Adjustments

Accounting Treatment.   Adjustments applicable to prior years are treated as part of net income for the current year and, if the amount is material, should be disclosed as a separate item in the income statement or as part of other income (expenses).

Reference. IAS 8, s. 19.

10. Post Balance Sheet Events

Definition. Two different types of post balance sheet events are identified in Israeli accounting rules.

☐ Those that relate to conditions that existed at the balance sheet date and provide additional evidence regarding the financial position of the company at that date and the operating results for the period then ended.

☐ Those that are indicative of conditions that arose subsequent to the balance sheet date and that might have a significant influence on the financial position and operating results subsequent to the balance sheet date.

Accounting Treatment. Recognition should be given in the current period financial statements to events relating to conditions existing at the balance sheet date.

The current year financial statements should not be adjusted for events that are indicative of conditions that arose subsequent to the balance sheet date.

Disclosure. If material, events that are indicative of conditions arising after the balance sheet date should be disclosed in a note to the financial statements, which should indicate the nature of the event and, if practical, the estimated financial effect.

Reference. Opinion 11, s. 5–7.

11. Related Party Disclosures

Definition. Parties are considered related if one has the ability to control or to exercise significant influence over the operating or financial decisions of the other, or if the parties are subject to control or significant influence of a third party.

Related parties under Opinion 29 of the Israeli Institute include:

☐ Parties one of which (directly or indirectly):
  —Holds 10 percent or more of the issued **share capital** of the other, or the voting rights therein, or has the right to appoint directors in that party, or
  —Has the right to appoint the general manager, or
  —Serves as a director or general manager.
☐ Any corporation in which a party as described above holds 25 percent or more of the issued share capital or of the voting rights or the right to appoint directors.
☐ Spouses and offspring who are minors.

Under the Securities Regulations, related parties are referred to as "interested parties." The definition according to those regulations is similar to that in Opinion 29, except that the percentage of issued share capital is 5 percent or more, and investee companies (e.g., subsidiaries and associated companies) are not considered to be related parties.

Accounting Treatment. The relevant Israeli Opinion and Securities Regulations relate only to disclosure of the nature and extent of related party transactions, and not to the accounting treatment thereof.

Disclosure.   The following information should be disclosed:

☐   A description of the nature and extent (**turnover** and results) of transactions that are not conducted in the ordinary course of business.

☐   The extent of transactions in the ordinary course of business if in the aggregate it exceeds 10 percent of turnover.

☐   Transactions without any consideration.

☐   Balances outstanding during the period (including those settled before the balance sheet date) of loans and guarantees to related parties.

☐   Directors' fees (including related expenses), except for amounts payable for services connected with filling a position with the company.

☐   Other items (such as management fees, participation in expenses and interest) payable to, or receivable from, related parties.

When the operations conducted by the reporting party depend on a significant volume of business with another party (e.g., a major customer, supplier, etc.), the economic dependence on that party should be disclosed and explained.

The disclosure requirements for companies whose securities are quoted on the stock exchange include details relating to short- and long-term liabilities to related parties, investments in such parties (including details of long-term loans granted, other receivables and guarantees given in their favor), benefits to those parties—whether employed by the reporting entity or not so employed (including the number of persons to whom such benefits relate), and a description of the nature and extent of transactions (including amounts, pricing methods, credit and other terms), whether or not they are conducted in the ordinary course of business.

Reference.   Opinion 29, s. 3–4, 8, 10; Securities Regulations, 1, 62–64.

12. Segmental Information

General.   Enterprises whose securities are publicly traded and other economically significant entities (including subsidiaries) should disclose segmental information; other economically significant entities represent entities whose levels of revenues, profits, assets or employment are significant in the countries in which their major operations are conducted. When both parent company and consolidated financial statements are presented, the above information need be presented only in the consolidated financial statements.

The bases for presenting information on operations by segment are industry segments and geographical segments. An enterprise would present information on both bases if both are applicable to its operations, provided such segments are considered to be significant to the enterprise.

Industry segment information is usually presented on the basis of general groupings of related products and services, or by types of customer. Geographical segment information is presented on the basis of the location of operations of the enterprise, on the basis of markets or on both bases (an enterprise's domestic operations are generally considered to be a separate geographical segment).

A rate of 10 percent of consolidated revenue, or operating profit or total assets, may serve as a guideline on how material a segment should be before it is reported separately.

Disclosure. For each reported segment, the following information is generally provided:

☐ A description of the activities of the segment and an indication of the composition of each reported geographical area.

☐ Sales or other operating revenues, distinguishing between revenue derived from customers outside the enterprise and revenue derived from other segments.

☐ Segment results.

☐ Segment assets employed.

☐ The basis of intersegment pricing.

Reconciliations should be provided of the sum of the information on individual segments and the aggregate information in the financial statements.

Reference. IAS 14.

ACCOUNTING PRINCIPLES FOR SPECIFIC ITEMS— BALANCE SHEET

13. Property, Plant and Equipment

Classification of Capital and Revenue Expenditure. An expenditure is classified as a capital expenditure when it gives rise to an asset. All other expenditures are charged to income as incurred.

Basis of Valuation. Property, plant and equipment are recorded at cost (in adjusted Israeli currency—see Section 7), net of related government investment grants (see also Section 24).

In previous years, due to inflation, some companies (mainly those first going public) adopted the practice of revaluing fixed assets in their nominal Israeli currency statements; depreciation was accordingly computed on the basis of the revaluation. In the adjusted financial statements, no recognition is given to revaluation of assets.

Depreciation. **Depreciation** is generally computed by the **straight-line method**. The residual value of scrap is not accounted for, except by shipping companies.

Disclosure. The accounting policies adopted in relation to valuation and depreciation of fixed assets are to be disclosed (including the depreciation period or rate). In addition, details are provided for cost and accumulated depreciation of each class of fixed assets, for expenses capitalized in cost of fixed assets (including the amounts deducted from the relevant expenses included in the income statement) and for rights in immovable property (ownership or lease rights and whether registered in Land Registry).

Companies whose securities are quoted on the stock exchange are also required to disclose, for each class of depreciable assets, movements during the period in cost and accumulated depreciation, and any provision made during the period for decline in value of each fixed asset item.

Reference. IAS 4, 16 and 23; Securities Regulations, 18–20.

14. Intangible Assets

Accounting Treatment. There are currently no accounting rules in Israel dealing with accounting for **intangible assets** (other than goodwill arising from business acquisitions and research and development expenses—see Sections 4 and 25, respectively).

In practice, other intangibles are treated as follows:

☐ Patents and know-how are amortized over a period not exceeding their legal period or useful life.

☐ Debenture issue costs are amortized over the period of the debentures, in proportion to the balance of debentures outstanding.

☐ Company organization expenses are generally charged against income as incurred; in some cases, they are deferred and amortized over a period of three–five years.

Disclosure. The financial statements should disclose the accounting policies regarding the recording of intangible assets and **amortization** method adopted, the original amounts and the unamortized balances as of the balance sheet date.

Reference. Securities Regulations, 21.

15. Leases

Classification. The classification of leases is based on the extent to which risks and rewards incidental to ownership of a leased asset lie with the lessor or the lessee. A lease is classified as a **finance** (or capital) **lease** if it transfers substantially all the risks and rewards of ownership; if all the risks and rewards are not transferred, the lease is classified as an **operating lease**.

The following guidelines are used in Israel for classification of a lease as a finance lease:

☐ The lease term is 75 percent or more of the economic life of the leased property, or

☐ The present value of the lease payments equals 90 percent or more of the fair value of the leased property.

Accounting Treatment. Finance leases (lessee): A finance lease should be capitalized and accounted for as an asset and obligation at amounts equal, at the inception of the lease, to the fair value of the leased property (net of grants and tax credits receivable by the lessor) or, if lower, at the present value of the minimum lease payments. A finance lease gives rise to a depreciation charge for the asset (consistent with depreciation for owned assets) as well as a finance charge for each accounting period.

Finance leases (lessor): In the financial statements of the lessor, finance income is allocated over the lease term on a systematic and rational basis; a finance lease of an asset by a manufacturer or dealer gives rise to two types of income: profit or loss from sale and finance income over the lease term.

Operating leases: Rental payments are expensed by the lessee and recorded as revenue by the lessor in the period to which they relate.

Rights to land owned by the Israeli Lands Authority and leased for a long period (between 25 and 999 years) in consideration of rental are treated as operating leases.

Sale-leaseback transactions: Gains on sale of assets that are leased back under operating leases for a limited period are recognized in the year of sale.

Disclosure. Lessees disclose accounting policies for finance leases, as well as balances of cost and accumulated depreciation at the balance sheet date for assets leased under those leases, and the balance of the related obligations.

Commitments for minimum lease payments under finance leases and under noncancellable operating leases with a term of more than one year should be disclosed in summary form giving the amounts and periods in which the payments will become due. Lessors should disclose, at each balance sheet date, the gross investment in leases reported as finance leases and the related unearned finance income. The basis used for allocating income should also be disclosed.

Reference. IAS 17.

16. Investments

Valuation. For investments that are neither consolidated nor accounted for by the equity method, a distinction is made between investments designated for realization in the short term, which constitute a part of liquid resources (current investments), and investments that are intended to be held for longer periods (permanent investments). Investments designated as current investments should be presented among **current assets**, while those designated as permanent investments should be presented as noncurrent items. Current investments are carried at market value; permanent investments are carried at cost (in adjusted Israeli currency), plus accrued interest for debentures, unless a decrease in their value that is not temporary has occurred, in which case the investments are written down. Decreases in value are considered separately for each security. Where a permanent investment was written down and subsequent circumstances indicate that there has been a rise in its value, the rise is carried back to the income statement to the extent of the previous charge.

The entire change in value of marketable investments for the year is carried to income.

Gains/Losses. Gains or losses on realization of current investments form part of the adjustment of those investments to market value at the end of the year; such adjustment is presented in the income statement among financial income or expenses.

Disclosure. Investments are classified according to main categories: debentures, shares, participation certificates in mutual funds, and so forth. Disclosure is required of the accounting policies regarding valuation and treatment of changes in market value, income (if material) from investments included in the income statement and any restrictions on the negotiability of securities or on receipt of income therefrom.

Reference. Opinion 44.

17. Accounts Receivable

Accounting Treatment. Recognition: Revenues, and hence the related receivables, are recognized when performance is complete and reasonable assurance exists regarding measurement and collectibility of the consideration.

Discounts: Sales and **accounts receivable** are normally recorded net of trade and quantity discounts. Since the recognition of cash discounts occurs at the time of payment, it is usually not necessary to consider potential cash discounts in determining the amount of a trade receivable.

Allowances: The allowance for doubtful accounts is generally determined on basis of assessment of specific doubtful debts or, in some cases, as a fixed percentage of outstanding trade and other receivables.

Factored Receivables. **Factoring** of receivables is not common in Israel.

Disclosure. Receivables are segregated into various classes, such as trade receivables, employees and employee institutions, "interested parties" (see Section 11), subsidiary and associated companies, prepayments and other receivables. The accounting policy regarding the allowance for doubtful accounts should be disclosed.

Companies whose securities are quoted on the stock exchange are required to disclose the balances of allowances for doubtful accounts (amounts deducted from trade receivables are to be separately stated) and the amounts of doubtful and bad debts charged in the income statement. Also, such companies are required to state separately any receivable that exceeds 5 percent of total current assets.

Reference. Securities Regulations, 13 and 52.

18. Inventories and Work in Progress

General Accounting Treatment. **Inventories** are valued at the lower of cost (in adjusted Israeli currency) or market. Cost is generally determined on the basis of **FIFO** or **average cost**. Items such as tools and implements, spare parts and the like are generally valued on the **base stock** method. The **LIFO** method of inventory is not applied, as it is not acceptable for tax purposes.

"Market" means **net realizable value**. Comparison between cost and market is made by item or group of like items.

For work in process and finished goods, costs include the cost of materials and direct labor and an appropriate share of overhead expense chargeable to production.

Long-Term Contracts. The net amount of contracting work in progress in excess of related customer advances is presented in the balance sheet among assets, while the net amount of customer advances in excess of the related contracting work in progress is presented among liabilities. The gross amount of contracting work in progress includes all costs that can reasonably be allocated to the contract plus any profits recorded in accordance with the **percentage of completion method,** less any anticipated losses. For revenue recognition for long-term contracts, see Section 23.

Disclosure. The basis of valuation of inventories and contracting work in progress (including the method of determining cost of inventories) should be disclosed. Details are to be provided regarding inventory components (including raw materials and supplies, work in process and finished products).

Reference. IAS 2; Securities Regulations, 14 and 30.

19. Current Liabilities

General Accounting Treatment.   **Current liabilities** include:

☐   Liabilities that are payable within one year from the balance sheet date or within the normal operating cycle if longer than one year (in such case, the operating cycle should be stated).

☐   Customer advances, income received in advance and unrealized profits that are likely to be recorded as income in the income statement within the above-stated period.

Current liabilities should be presented and classified according to the following categories: bank credit, classified according to interest rates and linkage basis; current maturities of long-term liabilities; amounts payable to suppliers of goods and services; income received in advance, customer advances and unrealized profits; employee liabilities and other liabilities in respect of wages and salaries; institutions; "interested parties" (see Section 11); subsidiary and associated companies; dividends declared or proposed; and other current liabilities.

The current portion of a long-term liability may be excluded from current liabilities if the reporting entity intends to refinance the obligation on a long-term basis and there is reasonable assurance that the entity will be able to do so.

Creation of General and Specific Provisions.   It is not acceptable to create general provisions for future losses. Specific provision should be made for liabilities that are known and whose amount can be estimated, such as warranties and employee benefits.

Disclosure.   When a reporting entity excludes a liability from the current classification as stated above, the amount of the liability and the terms of the refinancing should be disclosed.

If liabilities are secured by pledges on assets or are subject to restrictions, the amounts of such liabilities, as well as details regarding the assets pledged and nature of the security, should be disclosed.

Companies whose securities are quoted on the stock exchange are required to state separately any liability that exceeds 5 percent of total current liabilities.

Reference.   IAS 13, s. 22–24; Securities Regulations, 26–27, 38.

20. Long-Term Debt

General Accounting Treatment.   Long-term debt includes debentures and similar securities (including those convertible into shares), loans from banks and other financial institutions, liabilities to "interested parties" and to subsidiary and associated companies, obligations under finance leases, deferred income and unrealized profits and other liabilities.

Debentures are presented at the amount of the liability at the balance sheet date, with the addition of the premium or net of the discount not yet amortized at the balance sheet date, in accordance with the issue terms. The premium or discount is amortized either over the period of the debentures (in proportion to the balance of debentures outstanding) or by the "interest" method.

Debentures convertible into shares are presented among long-term debt if they are not expected to be converted; if conversion is expected, the debentures are presented as a separate balance sheet item between shareholders' equity and long-term debt.

Debt Restructuring.   There are no official Israeli rules addressing the issue of accounting for troubled debt restructuring; in some cases US rules are adopted.

Debt Extinguishment.   There are no official Israeli rules addressing the issue of accounting for debt extinguishment; in some cases US rules are adopted.

Disclosure.   Details are provided for long-term debt balances (before deduction of current maturities) by currency of repayment, linkage terms and interest rates and by maturity in the five years after the balance sheet date and thereafter.

If liabilities are secured by pledges on assets or are subject to restrictions, the amounts of such liabilities, as well as details regarding the assets pledged and nature of security, should be disclosed.

Companies whose securities are quoted on the stock exchange are required:

- ☐   To state separately any liability that exceeds 5 percent of total long-term debt.
- ☐   If during the period there are circumstances that may accelerate the repayment date of a liability, but such acceleration has not yet taken place, to disclose those circumstances and the amount of such liability.
- ☐   If during the period the repayment date of a liability was accelerated, to disclose the amount of such liability and details regarding the repayment date and the main terms relating thereto.
- ☐   If there is a condition with respect to a liability that restricts the entity's use of its assets, the grant of a credit or other operations, to disclose such condition.

Reference.   Securities Regulations, 34–35, 38.

21.   Contingencies

Contingent Losses.   The amount of a contingent loss should be accrued if it is probable that future events will confirm that an asset had been impaired or a liability incurred at the balance sheet date, and a reasonable estimate of the amount of the resulting loss can be made.

The existence of a contingent loss should be disclosed in the financial statements if the above conditions are not met, unless the possibility of loss is remote.

Contingent Gains.   Contingent gains should not be accrued in the financial statements. The existence of contingent gains should be disclosed if it is probable that a gain will be realized.

Disclosure.   Disclosure of a contingent loss or gain should include a description of the nature of the **contingency**, the uncertain factors that may affect the future outcome and an estimate of the financial effect or a statement that such an estimate cannot be made (in such a case, reference is usually made to a legal opinion).

Companies whose securities are quoted on the stock exchange are also required to provide details regarding contingencies whose prospects of realization are remote, but where the liability or possible loss may raise doubts as to the entity's continued operations.

Reference. IAS 10, s. 27–28, 33; Securities Regulations, 36.

22. Capital and Reserves

General. Shareholders' equity is generally divided between share capital (including receipts on account thereof) and items of **surplus**. Items of surplus are classified as either capital surplus or **retained earnings** (including reserves created by an appropriation of retained earnings, provided that such creation is stipulated in the company's articles of association).

Differences arising from translation of financial statements of self-sustaining foreign operations are included as a separate component of shareholders' equity (see Section 6).

Share Capital. The Companies Ordinance requires that a company specify in its memorandum and articles the amount of its share capital (authorized capital), i.e., the total **par value** of share capital that it is authorized to issue and the division of the share capital into a number of shares of a fixed amount (par value).

Shares are not required to be paid for in full on issue. The unpaid capital represents share capital called up by the directors but not yet paid; the company is entitled to enforce the payment thereof or forfeit the unpaid shares. A company may reduce its share capital, in accordance with a special resolution of the shareholders, subject to the approval of the court.

A company's share capital may be divided into different classes, characterized by voting rights, rights to dividends and to repayment of capital, or participation in surplus assets upon liquidation. The main classes of shares are ordinary and **preference shares** (redeemable preference shares may be redeemed only out of earnings available for distribution of dividends or out of proceeds from a new share issue). The exact rights of each type are included in the company's memorandum and articles.

Except in the case of redemption by a company of redeemable preference shares (see ''Other Reserves'' below), a company is prohibited from acquiring, directly or indirectly, its own shares; also, a company may not provide, directly or indirectly, financial assistance to acquire its shares.

When a subsidiary purchases shares of its parent company (using the subsidiary's own resources), the cost of such shares will be presented as a deduction from the equity section. Gains and losses, net of related tax, on sale of these shares are also recognized in the equity section.

Other Reserves. Capital surplus represents capital donated by shareholders and from other sources that is not available for distribution in cash. The other sources are mainly:

☐ Premium on shares representing the excess of proceeds from a share issue over par value of the shares issued.

☐ Capital redemption reserve—Upon redemption of redeemable preference shares out of earnings available for distribution, a company must transfer from its retained earnings to the capital redemption reserve an amount equal to the par value of the shares redeemed.

Retained earnings (including reserves that are not part of capital surplus) consist of the accumulated balance of income, less losses from operations, after taking into account dividends and other amounts that may be recorded in retained earnings.

Disclosure. Share capital: Companies must disclose details at the balance sheet date of their authorized, issued and paid capital—the nominal amount and the number of shares, divided into the relevant classes. Companies whose securities are quoted on the stock exchange are required to disclose the main rights applicable to each class (including the redemption terms relating to redeemable preference shares). The amount of dividends in arrears (not declared) on cumulative preference shares should be stated.

If option notes have been granted conferring on the holder the right to acquire shares to be allotted by the company, relevant details must be disclosed, as must the conditions of any commitment to issue shares.

Reserves: If the distribution of retained earnings is restricted, the restriction and the related amounts should be disclosed.

Reference. Companies Ordinance, s. 5, 139, 141–143; Securities Regulations, 39–42, 44–45.

ACCOUNTING PRINCIPLES FOR SPECIFIC ITEMS— INCOME STATEMENT

23. Revenue Recognition

General Principles. Revenue is recognized when performance is complete and reasonable assurance exists regarding measurement and ultimate collection of the consideration. Revenue from a transaction involving the sale of goods is usually recognized when the seller of goods has transferred to the buyer the significant risks and rewards of ownership. The main considerations in deciding whether significant risks and rewards have been so transferred are whether any significant acts remain to be completed; and whether the seller retains continuing managerial involvement in, or effective control of, the goods transferred to a degree usually associated with ownership.

Revenue from service transactions is usually recognized as the service is performed.

Long-Term Contracts. For the purpose of timing the recording of income, a distinction is drawn between income from construction of buildings for sale and income from contracting work.

Income from construction of buildings for sale is recognized when construction of the building unit has been completed or substantially completed and at least 75 percent of the apartments in the building unit have been sold.

Income from contracting work is accounted for by either the percentage of completion method or the **completed contract method**. The percentage of completion method should be used in recognizing income from contracting work when a material portion of the work has been performed and there is sufficient and reliable data about the work remaining until completion (stage of completion, cost and consideration for the total work).

Adequate provision is to be made for any anticipated losses.

Administrative, general and financial expenses are period costs. Where the completed contract method is applied, such expenses may be capitalized only in those cases where noncapitalization would cause improper **matching** between costs and revenues.

Instalment Sales.   There are no specific guidelines in Israel on this matter.

Rights of Return.   There are no rules in Israel on this subject.

In certain cases, where a company grants its customers a certain period to evaluate the product, prior to purchase, the practice is usually not to recognize sales revenue until such products are actually purchased.

Product Financing.   Product financing is not common in Israel.

Disclosure.   The accounting policies regarding revenue recognition should be disclosed, as well as the circumstances in which revenue recognition has been postponed pending the resolution of significant uncertainties.

Where administrative, general and financial expenses have been capitalized, the amount so capitalized should be presented as a deduction from the relevant expense items in the income statement, and the reasons for capitalization should be explained.

Companies whose securities are quoted on the stock exchange are required to provide details on revenues, costs, provisions for losses and profit for the reported period in respect of long-term contracting works.

Reference.   IAS 18; Opinion 6; Securities Regulations, 50.

24.   Government Grants and Assistance

Accounting Treatment.   Government grants should not be recognized until there is reasonable assurance that the company will comply with the conditions attaching to them and the grants will be received.

Government grants related to fixed assets are to be included in the financial statements for the year in which the related investments were executed. The grants are to be presented as a deduction from the cost of fixed assets; depreciation is to be computed on basis of the net amount.

Government assistance for research and development programs is deducted from the related research and development expense.

Other grants related to income (as discussed in IAS 20, *Accounting for Government Grants and Disclosure of Government Assistance*) are not common in Israel.

Disclosure.   The following disclosure of government assistance should be made:

- □   The accounting policy adopted and the nature and extent of government grants recognized in the financial statements.
- □   Terms and conditions applicable to the assistance, including charges registered as security for compliance with the terms attaching to the grants.
- □   Unfulfilled conditions and other contingencies attaching to government assistance that has been recognized.

Reference.   Opinion 35; IAS 20; Securities Regulations, 18(d).

25. Research and Development

Definitions. Research is original and planned investigation undertaken with the hope of gaining new scientific or technical knowledge and understanding. It may or may not be directed toward a specific practical aim or application. Development is the translation of research findings or other knowledge into a plan or design for the production of new or substantially improved materials, devices, products, processes, systems or services prior to the start of commercial production.

Accounting Treatment. Research costs should be charged as an expense of the period in which they are incurred; development costs of a project may be deferred to future periods if all of the following criteria are satisfied:

- ☐ The product or process is clearly defined and the costs attributable to it can be separately identified.
- ☐ The technical feasibility of the product or process has been demonstrated.
- ☐ Management has indicated its intention to produce and market, or use, the product or process.
- ☐ There is a clear indication of a future market for the product or process or, if it is to be used internally, its usefulness to the entity can be demonstrated.
- ☐ Adequate resources exist, or are reasonably expected to be available, to complete the project and market the product or process.

Amortization of development costs is to be made on a systematic basis by reference either to the sale or use of the product or process or to the period over which the product or process is expected to be sold or used.

The deferred development costs should be reviewed at the end of each accounting period to determine whether deferral is still appropriate. When the criteria that previously justified the deferral of the costs no longer apply, the unamortized balance should be charged as an expense immediately. When the criteria for deferral continue to be met but the unamortized balance of such costs exceeds the amount of deferred development costs that can reasonably be expected to be recovered from related future revenues, the excess should be charged as an expense immediately.

Disclosure. The financial statements should disclose:

- ☐ The accounting policy regarding research and development costs and the amortization method relating to deferred development costs.
- ☐ The total research and development costs (including amortization of deferred development costs), net of grants and participations, charged to expense for the period.
- ☐ The movement in, and the balance of, unamortized deferred development costs.

Companies whose securities are quoted on the stock exchange are also required to disclose the circumstances that made it necessary to defer expenses during the period and the method of computing the deferral.

Reference. IAS 9, s. 3, 16–17, 20–21, 23–24; Securities Regulations, 54.

26. Capitalized Interest Costs

Accounting Treatment. There are no specific accounting rules dealing with capitalization of interest. It is, however, accepted practice to capitalize financial expenses in cost of fixed assets only during the construction period of the assets (prior to the operation thereof); the amount capitalized generally relates to loans and credit for financing purchase or construction of the assets (specific financing).

Disclosure. The financial statements should disclose the cumulative amount of financial expenses capitalized, including the amount capitalized in the current period, and, where financial expenses capitalized are material, the accounting policy adopted.

Companies whose securities are quoted on the stock exchange should also disclose the circumstances that made it necessary to capitalize and the method of computation.

Reference. Securities Regulations, 54.

27. Imputed Interest

General. **Imputed interest** is used in Israel in considering the probability of exercise and conversion of convertible securities (warrants and liabilities convertible into shares).

The present value of warrants and convertible liabilities (which are composed, from an economic standpoint, of a regular liability and an option to purchase shares) is computed:

- ☐ In determining the probability of conversion, which is based on the share price ratio (the share price at any given date divided by the present value of the exercise increment as of that date).
- ☐ In determining the exercise increment of warrants and the conversion price of convertible liabilities, if they are in Israeli currency that is not linked; the computation takes into account the remaining period through exercise of the warrants or through redemption of the convertible liabilities.

Disclosure. Disclosure of the accounting policies used is required where transactions are material.

Reference. Opinions 48 and 53.

28. Extraordinary or Unusual Items

General. No guidance on the matter has been published in Israel.

Extraordinary Items. In practice, it is generally customary in Israel to follow the US definition of extraordinary items, i.e., to regard as extraordinary items events and transactions that are distinguished by their unusual nature and the infrequency of their occurrence.

Unusual Items. Under the Securities Regulations, profits or losses arising from events or transactions that are unusual or infrequent should be presented as other income and expenses.

Disclosure. Each extraordinary item and the applicable income taxes should be disclosed separately in the income statement (and the corresponding per share amounts). Separate disclosure of the details of each extraordinary or unusual item is required in the notes.

Reference. IAS 8; Securities Regulations, 46–47.

29. Income Taxes

General. In Israel, tax losses may usually be carried forward indefinitely. However, no carryback of losses is permitted.

Accounting Treatment. No comprehensive guidance on this matter has been published in Israel. In practice, deferred income tax is accounted for by the **liability method** and provided for differences between the book basis (in adjusted financial statements—see Section 7) and the tax basis (which is also measured in real terms) of assets and liabilities. The effects of such differences are regarded as future tax liabilities or as assets representing "prepaid" taxes. These liabilities or assets are subject to adjustments if tax rates change or new tax legislation is enacted.

Deferred tax balances are computed at the tax rate expected to be in effect at the time of release to income from the deferred tax accounts. The amount of deferred taxes presented in the income statement represents changes in the balances during the period.

The setting up of a deferred tax asset is supportable where there is a reasonable prospect that the company will, in future years, realize chargeable income that will permit utilization of the related amounts. On the other hand, no recognition as an asset is given to the future tax saving resulting from availability of carryforward losses for tax purposes. Nevertheless, carryforward tax losses are taken into account in determining the balance of deferred taxes carried as a liability.

Disclosure. The accounting policy adopted regarding **tax allocation** should be disclosed, as well as the policy for taxes that may be payable upon realization of investments in subsidiaries and associated companies or in the event of intercompany dividends distributed by those companies. Details should also be provided about deferred tax balances in the balance sheet, distinguishing between current portion (either as a current asset or a current liability) and noncurrent portion; composition of income taxes included in the income statement (including the tax rates applied in computing such taxes); tax exemptions or reliefs to which the company is entitled (including the terms with which the company is required to comply); differences relating to assets (such as goodwill, passenger cars and certain depreciable fixed assets), the depreciation or amortization of which is not deductible for tax purposes; the balance of carryforward tax losses and the balance of losses for which deferred taxes were not provided; and final tax assessments received and tax assessments in dispute.

Companies whose securities are quoted on the stock exchange are also required to prepare a theoretical tax computation that accounts for variations between the theoretical tax (assuming income is taxed at the statutory tax rate) and income tax expense as reflected in the income statement for the period, and to provide details regarding the movement during the period in deferred tax accounts according to material types of differences that resulted in the recording of deferred taxes.

Reference.   Opinion 40, Clarifications of Accounting Treatment—no. 2 and 3; Securities Regulations, 32, 57.

30. Postretirement Benefits

General.   Under Israeli law and labor agreements, companies are required to make severance and pension payments to dismissed employees and to employees terminating employment in certain other circumstances. The liability for severance pay and pensions is, in most cases, also funded.

There are no pronouncements in Israel on accounting for **defined benefit** and **defined contribution pension plans**. Pension plans are relatively rare in Israel (companies are usually relieved of their pension liability through deposits with pension funds), and where applicable these matters are dealt with in accordance with IAS 19.

Accounting Treatment.   Except where, under the terms of labor agreements, funding of the related amounts relieves the employer of any further liability, the treatment of severance pay and pensions is as follows:

☐   The amounts provided are adjusted yearly on the basis of employees' most recent salaries.

☐   The provision for pensions is for the full amount of pension liability, including for past service; the amount provided is generally determined based on an actuarial computation.

Pension Fund Surpluses.   There are no published rules in Israel regarding accounting for a pension fund surplus.

Disclosure.   Disclosure of the existing arrangements for covering severance pay and pension liabilities and for covering the unfunded balance, if any, by the balance sheet accrual is required. Where the accrued liability for pensions to employees who have already retired is based on an actuarial computation, the discount rate used in the computation and the latest date of computation should be disclosed. The amounts of the balance sheet accrual for severance pay and pension liabilities and the portion funded should be stated.

Reference.   Opinion 20.

31. Discontinued Operations

Accounting Treatment.   Rules have not been published in Israel for accounting for discontinued operations.

Companies whose securities are quoted on the stock exchange are required to present as a separate item in the income statement, following income after income taxes, profits or losses from discontinued operations, net of related income taxes.

Certain companies in Israel apply the relevant US reporting rules (APB Opinion No. 30), whereby the results of continuing operations should be reported separately from discontinued operations, and any gain or loss from disposal of a segment of a business should be reported in conjunction with the related results of discontinued operations and not as an extraordinary item. Amounts of income taxes applicable to the results of discontinued operations and the gain or loss from disposal of the segment should be disclosed in the income statement or in related notes.

Reference. Securities Regulations, 46(a).

32. Earnings per Share

General. Companies whose securities are quoted on the stock exchange and other companies that publish per share data are required to compute earnings per share (EPS) in accordance with rules published by the Israeli Institute.

Definition. EPS represents the portion of net income or loss for a period attributable to a share of issued capital. The per share data is expressed as a monetary amount per one NIS of par value of share capital, based on the par value of shares outstanding.

Methods of Calculation. EPS is determined on basis of the weighted-average par value of share capital outstanding during the year, after giving retroactive effect to distributions of bonus shares (stock dividends). The per share data includes both primary (basic) and fully diluted earnings per share. For the primary EPS computation, account is also taken of shares issuable upon exercise or conversion of convertible securities (warrants, convertible debentures), if the exercise or conversion is expected at each balance sheet date (even if the effect is antidilutive); for the fully diluted EPS computation, account is also taken of convertible securities not expected to be exercised or converted if the effect is dilutive.

Earnings figures used in the calculations should be the amounts reported in the income statement adjusted for specific items relevant to the primary and fully diluted EPS calculations.

Distinction is made between EPS before extraordinary items and EPS relating to such items.

Disclosure. Companies are required to disclose the methods of computation of primary and fully diluted EPS and the data relating to net income or loss and to the par value of shares used in the computation of EPS; such data is disclosed either in the income statement or in a note. The difference between primary and fully diluted EPS should be explained (provided such difference is material).

Companies whose securities are quoted on the stock exchange are required to state the effect on EPS of changes in accounting principles and accounting estimates and of changes resulting from restatement of prior years' financial statements.

Reference. Opinion 55; Securities Regulations, 6(c)–(e).

Appendix
DO ISRAELI STANDARDS OR PREVALENT PRACTICE SUBSTANTIALLY COMPLY WITH INTERNATIONAL ACCOUNTING STANDARDS?

Section	Topic	Substantially complies with IAS?	Comments
3.	Basic accounting concepts and conventions	Yes	Inflation accounting is a basic concept in the preparation of Israeli financial statements
	Contents of financial statements	Yes	
4.	Business combinations*	Yes	
5.	Joint ventures	Yes	
6.	Foreign currency translation*	Yes	
8.	Accounting changes*	Yes	
9.	Prior period adjustments*	Yes	
10.	Post balance sheet events	Yes	
11.	Related party transactions	Yes	Except that the definition of related party is somewhat different from that in IAS 24
12.	Segmental information	Yes	
13.	Property, plant and equipment*	Yes	
15.	Leases	Yes	
16.	Investments	Yes	
17.	Accounts receivable	Yes	
18.	Inventories and work in progress*	Yes	
19.	Current liabilities	Yes	
20.	Long-term debt	Yes	
21.	Contingencies	Yes	
22.	Capital and reserves	Yes	
23.	Revenue recognition*	Yes	
24.	Government grants and assistance	Yes	
25.	Research and development*	Yes	

Appendix (*Continued*)

Section	Topic	Substantially complies with IAS?	Comments
26.	Capitalization of interest costs*	Yes	
28.	Extraordinary or unusual items*	Yes	
29.	Income tax**	Yes	
30.	Postretirement benefits*	Yes	

*These topics are subject to change as a result of the IASC Improvements Project—see the appendix to the International Accounting Standards chapter.

**The IAS on accounting for taxes on income is currently being revised, and an exposure draft has been issued.

Comparison in this table is made to International Accounting Standards in force at January 1, 1993. For further details, see the International Accounting Standards chapter.

ITALY

GENERAL NATIONAL INFORMATION

1. Source of Generally Accepted Accounting Principles

Generally Accepted Accounting Principles.   **Generally accepted accounting principles** are derived from the civil code, fiscal law and the **accounting standards** issued by the representative body of the accounting profession (Consiglio Nazionale dei Dottori Commercialisti e dei Ragionieri [CNDCR]). Italian tax law requires that for an expense to be deductible it must be recorded in the statutory financial statements; many accounting treatments are influenced by this rule.

Accounting Standards.   The accounting standards issued by the CNDCR supplement the civil code rules, which are very broad and generic. They have been recognized by the stock exchange commission (Commissione Nazionale per le Societa e la Borsa [CONSOB]) and are generally applied to financial statements of companies subject to regulation by CONSOB.

A law published on April 17, 1991 enacted the Fourth and Seventh European Community Directives, substantially changing the civil code. The new rules will come into effect for financial statements for years ending between April 17, 1993 and April 16, 1994 (in the majority of cases, December 31, 1993) relating to the application of the Fourth Directive and one year later for the Seventh Directive.

2. Audit and Public Company Requirements

Audits.   The law requires that all companies quoted on the stock exchange, publishing companies, insurance companies, state-controlled companies, many financial companies and certain other companies be audited by registered auditing firms.

Registered auditing firms are those registered with CONSOB. Among the requirements for registration is that the majority of partners must be members of the Italian accounting profession or equivalent foreign bodies. The firm must be established as a partnership with unlimited liability of the partners, and partners and employees must be independent.

The auditing firm is appointed at the shareholders' meeting for three years; the appointment can be renewed for two additional three-year periods. Subsequently, the firm cannot be reappointed until five years have elapsed.

The law sets out the basic duties and responsibilities of the auditing firm, which relate principally to reporting to the shareholders on the truth and fairness of the accounts and their compliance with the civil code regulations.

Auditing standards are established and issued by CNDCR, which provides authoritative guidance on the auditing procedures to be followed. Auditing procedures are not compulsory. The audit report format included in these standards is not accepted by CONSOB, which requires a different format.

Public Companies. **Public companies** wishing to offer their shares to the public in Italy must apply for listing with the stock exchange via CONSOB. CONSOB enforces certain reporting requirements and regulates the trading of shares of **listed companies**. These requirements supplement normal company law and statutory requirements. CONSOB has the power to enforce compliance with the rules by delisting companies that do not meet its requirements. In general the main requirements for listing on the stock exchange are:

- □ A net book value of at least Lira 10 billion.
- □ At least 25 percent of the capital distributed to the public.
- □ At least 500 shareholders.
- □ Profits in the last three years (before extraordinary items).
- □ Audited financial statements.

CONSOB, however, may authorize exceptions to the above requirements.

Reference. Decree of the President of the Republic (DPR) 31.3.75 No. 136 and Principi di revisione issued by CNDCR.

GENERAL ACCOUNTING

3. Financial Statements

Basic Accounting Concepts. Financial statements are normally prepared in accordance with the **historical cost** basis of measurement. Financial statements are prepared on the assumption that the entity is a **going concern**.

Items recognized in financial statements are accounted for in compliance with the **accrual basis** of accounting.

Transactions and events are normally accounted for and presented in a manner consistent with their legal form. In particular instances (e.g., leases), the substance may be different.

Contents of Financial Statements. The civil code requires companies to present to their shareholders a balance sheet, a profit and loss statement, a directors' report, a schedule of investments in controlled and **associated companies** (associated companies are those in which the investor owns more than 10 percent of the share capital if not quoted and more than 5 percent if quoted on the stock exchange), the latest approved financial statements of controlled companies and certain significant balance sheet data relating to associated companies.

In many instances, although it is not compulsory, a balance sheet and an income statement, reclassified in accordance with the principles established by CNDCR (which correspond to US practice), and a cash flow statement and statement of changes in shareholders' equity are also presented. The cash flow statement, when presented, is prepared using the **indirect method**.

In addition, if investments in **subsidiaries** are significant, **consolidated financial statements** with explanatory notes may also be presented as additional disclosure to the statutory financial statements.

Format of Financial Statements.   The format of the statutory balance sheet and profit and loss statement is prescribed by the civil code, which indicates the assets, liabilities and shareholders' equity accounts to be disclosed as a minimum in the balance sheet, and the revenues and costs to be disclosed as a minimum in the profit and loss statement.

No classification between current and noncurrent assets is required, and all reserves and provisions are classified as liabilities. The profit and loss statement follows a conventional format, with costs on one side and revenues on the other. Costs and revenues are classified by their nature.

Disclosure of Accounting Policies.   Companies are required to disclose in the directors' report the **accounting policies** used in the valuation of assets and in depreciation, amortization and accruals; changes in accounting policies must also be disclosed in the directors' report.

Reference.   Civil code articles 2359, 2424, 2425bis and 2429bis; and CNDCR No. 2.

4. Business Combinations

Principles of Consolidation.   Although consolidation is not required by law, companies quoted on the stock exchange are required to present consolidated financial statements, and other companies may also do so.

In those instances all controlled companies, that is, companies that are controlled by virtue of the number of shares owned or by contractual agreements or other arrangements, are consolidated, unless the business of a controlled company is substantially different from that of the rest of the group. This may be the case for banks or insurance companies in a group of industrial companies, or vice versa. In these cases the investment in the company excluded from consolidation is accounted for by the **equity method**.

Accounting for Business Combinations.   Accounting for **business combinations** depends on whether the transaction is a merger or an acquisition. In a merger the companies merge into a single legal entity, whereas in an acquisition the companies retain their separate legal identities.

When a company merges with a controlled company, the excess of the value of the investment in the controlled company over its net book value is allocated on the basis of the fair values of assets and to **goodwill**. If the value of the investment is less than the net book value of the subsidiary, the difference is allocated to **retained earnings** (no **negative goodwill** or liabilities are recognized). If a merger takes place between two companies neither of which controls the other, the values recorded in the balance sheet of the new company are normally the book values of the merged companies before the combination. Acquisitions are accounted for in the books of the acquiring company on the same basis as other investments (see Section 16) and, where required, are consolidated using the **purchase method**.

Control.   Control is defined by article 2359 of the civil code, which states that a company is controlled if:

☐   The **holding company** has a number of shares sufficient to control the majority of votes at the shareholders' meeting (normally 50 percent plus one share); or

☐   The controlled company is dominated directly or indirectly because of the number of shares owned by the holding company or because of a contractual agreement.

Goodwill (Avviamento).   Goodwill is recorded in the statutory financial statements of a company in Italy when an amount has been paid for it in an acquisition and the price is clearly indicated in the purchase contract. In addition, as mentioned above, goodwill may be recorded if there is a merger of two companies. Such goodwill is amortized on the basis of its utility as estimated by the directors and the statutory auditors. Goodwill is normally amortized over a five- to ten-year period.

Goodwill recorded in consolidated financial statements is the difference between the value of the consideration paid in the acquisition of a subsidiary and the fair value of the identifiable assets acquired. Goodwill may be recorded as a long-term asset and amortized over a period that is normally no longer than 10 years or may be written off directly against retained earnings. A negative difference may arise if the cost of an acquisition is less than the aggregate net fair value of identifiable assets and liabilities acquired. In this case, in accordance with International Accounting Standards, the difference may be treated as deferred income and recognized as income systematically over a period of time; alternatively, it may be allocated to individual depreciable nonmonetary assets acquired. If the principles issued by CNDCR are followed, a negative difference reduces fixed assets acquired; any remaining difference is either recorded in retained earnings or deferred and recognized as income over a period not greater than five years.

Equity Accounting.   The equity method of accounting should be used in consolidated financial statements prepared in accordance with the principles issued by CNDCR when the investor has significant influence over the investee, as may be indicated by representation on the board of directors and/or participation in the policy-making process.

The equity method of accounting may also be used to value investments included in unconsolidated financial statements prepared in conformity with the civil code requirements. However, because application of the equity method would result in taxation of equity income recorded, it is normally not used in statutory financial statements.

Minority Interests (Interessenze Minoritarie).   The interests of minority shareholders in a consolidated subsidiary's net assets are disclosed as a line item, sometimes separately from both liabilities and shareholders' equity and sometimes included within liabilities. **Minority interests** in operating results are included as a separate item in the profit and loss statement before net profit.

Disclosure.   Detailed disclosures are made in the consolidated financial statements, including a reconciliation of net equity and net income shown in the financial statements of the holding company prepared in accordance with the civil code and those reflected in the consolidated statements. Additional disclosures include the method of consolidation, any changes in the companies consolidated and the reasons for excluding any controlled subsidiaries from the consolidation. The accounting policy adopted for goodwill and its amortization is also disclosed.

For companies included under the equity method, details are normally given of the companies and their transactions with fully consolidated companies.

Reference. Civil code articles 2359, 2427 and 2501; CNDCR No. 8; and Law No. 216/74.

5. Joint Ventures

Accounting for Investments in Joint Ventures. The civil code and CNDCR principles do not address accounting for investments in **joint ventures**; therefore, all methods of accounting, provided they are reasonable, are acceptable for joint ventures.

Jointly Controlled Entities. Jointly controlled entities may be accounted for by either the **proportionate consolidation** or the equity method.

Intercompany profits are eliminated according to the normal rules. Where proportionate consolidation is used, gains generally are recognized to the extent of the interest of nonrelated venturers. Losses are recognized in their entirety.

Jointly Controlled Operations. The accounting treatment in International Accounting Standard (IAS) 31 would be appropriate in Italy.

Jointly Controlled Assets. The accounting treatment in IAS 31 would be appropriate in Italy.

Disclosure. If a venturer's interest in a joint venture is equivalent to that of an interest in an associated company (see Section 4), certain balance sheet data must be included in the holding company's directors' report. Contingent liabilities and commitments with respect to the joint venture are also required to be disclosed in the directors' report.

Accounting by Joint Ventures. The same accounting principles applicable to all companies, as dictated by the civil code and supplemented by CNDCR principles, are applicable to joint ventures.

Reference. Civil code article 2424.

6. Foreign Currency Translation

Foreign Currency Denominated Transactions. Each asset, liability, revenue or expense arising from **foreign currency transactions** is measured in the domestic currency using the exchange rate in effect at the date of the transaction. Foreign currency **monetary items** outstanding at the balance sheet date are normally translated at the average exchange rate during the last month of the financial year.

Foreign Operations. Foreign operations may relate to a branch, a subsidiary or a joint venture. Financial statements of a branch are translated at the current rate, and differences resulting from translation are recorded in the income statement.

Financial statements of a foreign company or joint venture are translated only for the purpose of preparing consolidated financial statements. There are no specific rules in Italy and those of IAS 21 are applied.

Hedges.   Many entities seek to reduce or eliminate the risk of loss on exchange inherent in foreign transactions or operations by hedging. Profit or loss from hedging transactions is normally recognized when the transaction is closed.

Disclosure.   No specific disclosures are required by law; however, many companies disclose the accounting policies used for foreign currency conversion and translations in the directors' report.

Reference.   DPR 22.12.86 No. 917 article 72.

7.   Changing Prices/Inflation Accounting

Supplementary information on changing prices is not required to be disclosed, and it is not common practice to disclose such information.

8.   Accounting Changes

The civil code does not distinguish between changes in accounting policies and changes in accounting methods. When a change in accounting policy or method is made, its effect is included in current year income, since no retroactive adjustment is permitted.

Disclosure.   The civil code requires that changes in accounting policies and methods be indicated in the directors' report. This is often interpreted as also requiring disclosure of the effect of the change.

Reference.   Civil code article 2429bis.

9.   Prior Period Adjustments

Prior period adjustments are not made in financial statements for any reason.

10.   Post Balance Sheet Events

The civil code requires only that material post balance sheet events be described in the directors' report. The principles issued by CNDCR identify different types of post balance sheet events, as follows:

- ☐   Those that provide further evidence of conditions that existed at the financial statement date.
- ☐   Those that relate to conditions that arose after the date of the financial statements.

Accounting Treatment.   The financial statements are normally adjusted for events relating to both conditions that existed at the financial statement date and conditions that arose between the financial statement date and the date of their completion by the board of directors.

Disclosure.   Disclosure should be made in a note in the directors' report for all material events that occurred after the financial statement date.

Reference. Civil code article 2429bis and CNDCR No. 2.

11. Related Party Transactions

Definition. The civil code indicates that related parties are companies that control one another. The principles issued by CNDCR further define related parties as companies that are under common control.

Accounting Treatment. The civil code and CNDCR principles do not require any particular accounting treatment pertaining to related party transactions, and they are usually treated in accordance with normal **accounting principles** and practices.

Disclosure. The civil code requires that balances with controlled and associated companies be specifically indicated in the balance sheet. The directors' report must also include a description of transactions with controlling, controlled and associated companies, as well as any changes in investments and **accounts receivable** and **payable** involving those companies.

Reference. Civil code articles 2424 and 2429bis.

12. Segmental Information
Segmental information is not required by the civil code and normally is not presented.

ACCOUNTING PRINCIPLES FOR SPECIFIC ITEMS— BALANCE SHEET

13. Property, Plant and Equipment (Cespiti/Immobilizzazioni Techniche)

Classification of Capital and Revenue Expenditure. An expenditure is considered a capital item if it relates to a tangible asset used to produce further revenues or if it increases the useful life, productivity or security of an existing asset. Expenditures to maintain normal operating efficiency are expensed as incurred.

Basis of Valuation. Property, plant and equipment are normally carried at cost increased by the revaluations (monetary revaluations) permitted or required by special laws (the last of which occurred in 1991). In companies originated by a spin-off (scorporo), which occurs when a company transfers certain of its assets and liabilities to another company incorporated for this purpose, **fixed assets** are normally valued at appraised values; the spin-off reserve is subject to taxation. The monetary revaluation reserve is included in shareholders' equity and, if distributed, is subject to income taxes.

Depreciation (Ammortamento). **Depreciation** is normally computed using the **straight-line method** at the rates permitted by tax law, which are considered adequate to write off the assets over their useful lives.

In addition to normal depreciation, additional depreciation ("anticipated depreciation") is frequently provided as permitted by tax law. The maximum amount of anticipated depreciation has varied over time. Anticipated depreciation can be recorded only during the first three years of fixed asset service lives. Normally, anticipated depreciation is not shown separately in the depreciation reserve.

Disclosure. The method and rates used for depreciation, as well as any revaluation of fixed assets, should be outlined in the directors' report.

Reference. Civil code articles 2425 and 2429bis; CNDCR No. 4; DPR 12.22.86 No. 917 article 67; and Ministerial Decree (D.M.) 31.12.88.

14. Intangible Assets (Oneri Pluriennali)

Accounting Treatment. **Intangible assets** arise from **capitalized expenditures** that are considered to provide future benefits. Examples include patents, trademarks, licenses, research and development and goodwill. In rare instances advertising expenses are capitalized.

Valuation. The civil code requires that patents, trademarks and licenses be valued at cost. Normally, all other intangible assets are also valued at cost.

Amortization (Ammortamento). Intangible assets are amortized over varying periods depending on their nature. **Amortization** periods are normally within the limits specified by tax law.

Disclosure. The directors' report should describe the nature and amount of intangible assets capitalized and the method of amortization.

Reference. Civil code articles 2425 and 2429bis, and DPR 12.22.86 No. 917 articles 68 and 74.

15. Leases

Classification and Accounting Treatment. There are no standards or civil code requirements relating to leases. All leases are recorded as **operating leases**. Material commitments are recorded in memorandum accounts.

Disclosure. There are no specific disclosure requirements relating to leases. However, disclosures are sometimes made in accordance with IAS provisions.

16. Investments (Partecipazioni)

Valuation. In accordance with the civil code, investments in shares and fixed income securities may be recorded at directors' valuation, after applying prudent judgment and taking into consideration the trend of market quotations for listed securities. However, investments are generally valued on an individual investment basis, as follows:

☐ Investments in corporate entities are valued at the lower of cost or market value.
☐ Investments in other securities are valued at cost unless there is a permanent diminution in value, in which case a reserve is set up in the balance sheet for the shortfall in value.

☐ Nonstock participations (i.e., investments represented by quotas recorded in the shareholders' book and not by share certificates) are valued at cost unless the investor's share of net book value in the investee's latest balance sheet is lower, in which case a reserve is set up in the balance sheet or the value is reduced.

When an investment in a single type of share or security has been accumulated through several purchases, the **LIFO** method of valuation is normally used.

Gains/Losses.   When investments are sold, the profit or loss to be recognized is measured as the difference between the net proceeds received and the carrying amount.

Disclosure.   The directors' report discloses the method of valuation and any changes since the preceding year. A schedule of investments in controlled and associated companies (see Section 3) and copies of the latest financial statements of controlled companies and significant balance sheet data relating to associated companies are annexed to the financial statements.

Reference.   Civil code articles 2424, 2425 and 2429bis.

17.   Accounts Receivable (Crediti/Clienti)

Accounting Treatment.   **Revenues**, and hence the related receivables, are recognized when title to goods sold has been transferred or services have been performed.

Discounts.   Sales are recorded gross of any discounts other than those reflected in invoices. Cash discounts are usually recorded at the time of payment and are reported separately in the income statement.

Allowances.   Allowances for bad or doubtful debts are recorded as a liability in the balance sheet. The reserve may be computed by any practical method, provided that the reserve is adequate.

Factored Receivables.   In accordance with CNDCR principles, a transfer of receivables can be recorded as a sale rather than as financing when the transferor has transferred the significant risks associated with the receivables. However, since the CNDCR principles are not binding, practice varies and receivables factored with full recourse are sometimes treated as sales.

Disclosure.   When receivables are factored with recourse, the amount at risk is recorded in memorandum accounts and disclosed in the directors' report.

Reference.   CNDCR No. 6.

18.   Inventories and Work in Progress (Inventario/Magazzino e Lavori in Corso/ Semilavorati)

General Accounting Treatment.   **Inventories** are carried at the lower of cost or market value. In determining the carrying amount of inventories, each item should be considered individually. Commonly used methods of determining cost are LIFO, **FIFO**, specific cost and **average cost**. **Standard cost** is acceptable only if it approximates one of these methods. Market value is determined by replacement cost or **net realizable value**, depending on the circumstances. General marketing expenses, advertising expenses and other selling expenses not directly attributable to the product are not considered. For work in progress and finished goods, cost includes the cost of materials plus the cost of direct labor and an appropriate share of production overhead expenses.

Long-Term Contracts. The only Italian standard on long-term contracts is that included in the tax law; it permits both the **completed contract method** and the **percentage of completion method**. In practice, the latter is more commonly used. If a loss is foreseen on a contract, the entire loss is normally provided for in the financial statements of the year in which it is foreseen. The loss is not deductible for tax purposes until it is realized. Long-term contracts that are valued using the percentage of completion method are frequently subject to a provision of 2 percent (for contracts in Italy) or 4 percent (for contracts abroad) for contractual risks, as permitted by tax law.

Disclosure. It is common practice to disclose amounts of raw materials, supplies, work in progress and finished goods. In addition, the basis of valuing inventories and any changes thereto should be disclosed in the directors' report.

Reference. Civil code 2425; CNDCR No. 3; and DPR 12.22.86 No. 917 articles 59 and 60.

19. Current Liabilities (Passivita' Correnti)

General Accounting Treatment. The civil code does not require classification of liabilities between current and noncurrent. Accordingly, in the statutory balance sheet such distinction is normally not made. When reclassified financial statements are presented, a distinction is made between **current** and noncurrent **liabilities**. Current liabilities are generally segregated into main classes, for example, bank overdrafts, accounts payable (trade **creditors**), accrued liabilities, taxes payable, current portion of long-term debt, advances from customers and payables to related companies.

Trade creditors include amounts payable to suppliers for goods and services received and normally also include invoices to be received. Trade creditors are measured at the face value of the invoices or of the purchase orders (if the invoice has not yet been received). Interest payable on bank overdrafts may be included in bank overdrafts or in accrued liabilities.

Creation of General and Specific Provisions. General provisions are not permitted. A provision must relate to a specific existing obligation or to a probable contingent liability.

The main types of provisions relate to income taxes, bonus discounts to customers and warranties.

Disclosure. Amounts owed to controlled or associated companies are indicated separately; the directors' report should describe and comment on changes during the year.

Reference. Civil code articles 2424 and 2429bis.

20. Long-Term Debt

General Accounting Treatment. Long-term debt (generally represented by mortgage loans, debentures and other long-term bank loans) is normally recorded at face value. A premium or discount on long-term debt is shown as a deferred credit or charge and is amortized over the term of the debt. The current portion of long-term debt is normally not separately disclosed in the statutory financial statements. Interest accrued on long-term debt is recorded separately.

Debt Restructuring. Debt restructuring is not addressed by the civil code or by CNDCR principles, and is rare in practice.

Debt Extinguishment. There are no requirements in the civil code or in the CNDCR principles regarding extinguishment of debt. A gain or loss arises on early extinguishment of a debt when the negotiated price and the net carrying amount of the debt extinguished before maturity are different. The gain or loss is included in income as part of other income or other deductions when the debt is extinguished.

Disclosure. The change in the amount of debt during the year is described in the directors' report.

Reference. Civil code article 2229bis and CNDCR No. 7.

21. Contingencies

General. **Contingencies** are not addressed by the civil code, but are addressed by the CNDCR principles. The accounting treatment of contingencies depends on their probability and determinability.

Contingent Losses. Contingent losses are normally accrued in the accounts if, at the date the financial statements are completed by the board of directors, it is probable that a loss will arise as a result of a past transaction or event and the loss can be reasonably estimated.

Contingent Gains. Contingent gains are normally not recorded prior to realization.

Disclosure. Disclosure must be made in the balance sheet under the caption "Memorandum accounts" of guarantees given or received, bills discounted with recourse and obligations undertaken.

Reference. CNDCR No. 2 and civil code article 2423.

22. Capital and Reserves (Capitale e Riserve)

General. Shareholders' equity is frequently not clearly indicated in the balance sheet prepared in accordance with the civil code. Accumulated losses and a current year loss are reflected as assets on the debit side of the balance sheet. If reclassified financial statements are prepared, shareholders' equity is separately shown, divided into reserves and retained earnings.

Share Capital.   The civil code requires that the articles of association indicate the amount of **share capital**, the number of shares and their nominal **(par) value**. Increases or decreases in share capital must be approved at a shareholders' meeting. The subscription price of shares may exceed par value. Any excess of the share price over par value is credited to a specific **share premium** reserve. Issuance of shares at a discount from par is not permitted. A company may buy its own shares according to certain rules in the civil code. **Treasury shares** are recorded as assets and are accounted for in accordance with rules applicable to investments. A company's share capital may be divided into different classes of shares, each characterized by its rights. The main classes of shares are **common shares**, **preference shares** and "savings" shares, which have no voting rights whatsoever.

Other Reserves.   Legal reserve (Riserva legale): This reserve is created by accumulating each year 5 percent of profit until the reserve reaches 20 percent of the share capital. The legal reserve is not distributable and can be utilized only to cover losses after all other available reserves have been used.

Revaluation reserves: These reserves are created following revaluation of assets permitted or required by special laws, the latest of which relates to 1991. The reserves are distributable, in which case they are subject to income taxes unless taxes had to be paid at the time of revaluation.

Share premium reserve (Riserva sovrapprezzo azioni): This reserve is created when the issue price of shares exceeds their par value. The reserve is distributable when the legal reserve is equal to 20 percent of share capital.

Other: Other reserves created through the accumulation of profits are distributable. However, those created before December 1, 1983 are subject to an equalization tax of 15 percent of the amount distributed, and those created with income exempt from tax are subject to an equalization tax of 56.25 percent of the amount distributed.

Disclosure.   The directors' report should indicate changes in the amount of reserves and also the amounts of reserves that, in the event of distribution, are subject to income tax or equalization tax.

Reference.   Civil code articles 2328, 2357, 2428 and 2430; and Law No. 649/83.

ACCOUNTING PRINCIPLES FOR SPECIFIC ITEMS— INCOME STATEMENT

23. Revenue Recognition

General Principles.   Revenue is recognized when services have been performed or an exchange of goods has taken place. Revenue from a transaction involving the sale of goods is recognized when the seller has transferred title to the goods to the buyer. Because uncertainties often arise in determining the transfer of ownership, normally sales are recognized at the time of delivery or shipment of the goods. Revenue from service transactions is usually recognized when the service has been performed.

Instalment Sales. Instalment sales are treated in accordance with general principles. Thus, if the goods have been delivered and substantially all the significant risks and benefits of ownership have been transferred to the buyer, the fact that the purchase price is to be received on an instalment basis does not prevent the seller from recognizing the transaction in full at the time of delivery. Often **instalment sales** include a clause under which legal title to goods is not transferred until full payment has been made. However, as required by tax law, the sale is fully recognized at the time of delivery.

Rights of Return. When the buyer has the right to return goods for a refund or replacement, whether under the terms of the sale contract or as a commercial practice, the seller recognizes the sale at the time the goods are delivered. If the amount of returns is likely to be material, however, a provision is made to eliminate gross profit on sales of goods expected to be returned.

Product Financing. **Product financing arrangements** are extremely rare in Italy and are not specifically addressed by the civil code, tax law or CNDCR principles. The general principles relating to the transfer of ownership apply in determining the appropriate accounting principles, and therefore product financing arrangements are normally recorded as sales. However, because of the agreement to repurchase the goods, any profit on the sale is not recognized.

Disclosure. There are no specific requirements of the civil code in this area. The amount of revenue recognized from transactions arising from product financing agreements during the period would normally be separately indicated in the income statement.

Reference. CNDCR No. 6 and DPR 12.22.86 No. 917 articles 60 and 75.

24. Government Grants and Assistance

Accounting Treatment. Government grants and assistance include loans at special interest rates, contributions to capital expenditures and contributions to current expenses. The accounting treatment of grants is normally dictated by the laws that establish the grants and indicate how they should be accounted for to avoid being subject to taxation. When the law does not specify an accounting treatment, in the absence of any accounting standard in the civil code and in the CNDCR principles, IAS 20, *Accounting for Government Grants and Disclosure of Government Assistance*, is normally followed.

Disclosure. Grants received during the year and their accounting treatment should be disclosed in the directors' report.

25. Research and Development (Ricerca e Sviluppo)

Definition. Research and development expenditures are not defined by the civil code or the CNDCR principles. Research and development is normally understood to be studies and experimentation carried on for the purpose of acquiring new knowledge, developing a new product or bringing about a significant improvement in an existing product.

Accounting Treatment. In accordance with tax law, research and development costs may be expensed in the year in which they were incurred or capitalized and amortized over a five-year period. If research and development expenses have been capitalized and at any year-end are judged to be irrecoverable, the unamortized balance is expensed. Research and development grants received from the state or public entities are recorded as liabilities, as permitted by tax law in order to be exempt from taxes.

Disclosure. The amount of research and development charged as an expense and the accounting policies followed in its valuation and amortization should be disclosed in the directors' report.

Reference. DPR 12.22.86 article 74.

26. Capitalized Interest Costs

Accounting Treatment. In accordance with the CNDCR principles, it is acceptable to capitalize interest incurred during the construction period as a component of the cost of fixed assets. Capitalization of interest relating to inventory is not permitted except for products that require several years of warehousing before sale, such as brandy.

Tax law requires that interest on loans obtained specifically for the acquisition or construction of a fixed asset be capitalized as a component of the fixed asset cost.

Disclosure. The accounting policy adopted is normally disclosed in the directors' report.

Reference. CNDCR Nos. 3 and 4 and DPR 12.22.86 No. 917 article 76.

27. Imputed Interest

General. **Imputed interest** is dealt with in the CNDCR principles in relation to:

☐ Receivables that have abnormal collection terms and bear no interest or interest at a rate significantly below the market rate.

☐ Payables with the above characteristics, provided that they originate from a transaction relevant to the purchase of goods and services.

Imputed interest is not addressed by the civil code or by tax law.

Accounting Treatment. Since imputed interest is not addressed by tax regulations, general tax rules apply. Imputed interest on payables is not recorded, whereas imputed interest on receivables is recorded in many cases, although there is no prevailing practice.

Disclosure. If imputed interest is computed, disclosure is normally made in the directors' report.

28. Extraordinary or Unusual Items

Extraordinary items are not addressed by the CNDCR principles or by the civil code, and such items are not normally separately classified in the financial statements. No distinctions are made between extraordinary items and unusual or exceptional items in the financial statements. In practice, extraordinary and exceptional items are normally disclosed in the directors' report. In reclassified and consolidated financial statements, extraordinary and exceptional items often are separately classified in the income statement.

29. Income Taxes (Imposte)

General. Tax law normally subjects any profit recorded in the financial statements to taxation, even if that profit is not required to be recorded by tax regulations (e.g., equity income from investments). Costs or losses that are not recognized as deductible by tax law may be recorded in the financial statements but cannot be deducted in the tax return.

Accounting Treatment. Normally, only current taxes are recorded in the financial statements. However, in the case of profit on sales of fixed assets or investments, the tax law permits the profit to be recorded in one year and taxed in subsequent years; the relevant deferred tax liability is often accrued. The future tax benefits of tax loss carryforwards are not recognized.

IAS 12, *Accounting for Taxes on Income*, is often applied in consolidated financial statements. In such cases deferred taxation is accounted for using the **liability method**.

Disclosure. No special disclosure is required by the civil code.

30. Postretirement Benefits (Truttamento di Fine Rapporto)

Private pension plans are rare in Italy, and there are no particular rules for accounting for such plans. Normally, costs are charged to expense as incurred. Pensions are paid by the state, which receives contributions from companies based on their payroll; these contributions are expensed as incurred.

All employees are entitled to receive deferred compensation on terminating their employment. The entitlement is approximately one month's pay for each year worked, adjusted for inflation. All amounts matured for service rendered during the year are expensed. The liability at each year-end is the amount that would have been payable if all employees had left the company at that date.

Other postretirement benefits are very rare and are not dealt with by the civil code or the CNDCR principles.

31. Discontinued Operations

General. There is no prescribed accounting method for discontinued operations in the civil code or in the CNDCR principles; as a consequence, practice varies. In most cases, reorganization and business closure costs are recognized when there is a firm commitment to discontinue operations; sometimes such costs are recognized when incurred.

Disclosure. Reorganization or business closure costs should be described in the directors' report.

32. Earnings per Share

General.   There is no requirement in the civil code or in the CNDCR principles to compute and disclose earnings per share. Consequently, earnings per share normally is not disclosed. In some instances, earnings per share is computed and disclosed in the directors' report. Earnings per share may be computed simply on the basis of the average number of common shares issued and outstanding or by taking into account the various stock options, warranties and conversion privileges attaching to debt.

Disclosure.   No disclosure is required of earnings per share.

Appendix
DO ITALIAN STANDARDS OR PREVALENT PRACTICE SUBSTANTIALLY COMPLY WITH INTERNATIONAL ACCOUNTING STANDARDS?

Section	Topic	Substantially complies with IAS?	Comments
3.	Basic accounting concepts and conventions	Yes	Except that transactions are usually accounted for based on their legal form rather than their substance
	Contents of financial statements	No	No cash flow statement or statement of changes in financial position is required
4.	Business combinations*	Yes	Except that consolidated financial statements are required only for publicly traded companies
5.	Joint ventures	Yes	
6.	Foreign currency translation*	No	
8.	Accounting changes*	Yes	
9.	Prior period adjustments*	Yes	
10.	Post balance sheet events	Yes	
11.	Related party transactions	No	
12.	Segmental information	No	
13.	Property, plant and equipment*	Yes	Except accelerated depreciation is permitted
15.	Leases	No	
16.	Investments	Yes	
17.	Accounts receivable	Yes	
18.	Inventories and work in progress*	Yes	
19.	Current liabilities	Yes	
20.	Long-term debt	Yes	
21.	Contingencies	Yes	Except that there is no requirement to disclose contingent gains
22.	Capital and reserves	Yes	
23.	Revenue recognition*	Yes	
24.	Government grants and assistance	Yes	

Appendix (*Continued*)

Section	Topic	Substantially complies with IAS?	Comments
25.	Research and development*	Yes	
26.	Capitalization of interest costs*	Yes	
28.	Extraordinary or unusual items*	No	
29.	Income tax**	No	
30.	Postretirement benefits*	No	

*These topics are subject to change as a result of the IASC Improvements Project—see the appendix to the International Accounting Standards chapter.

**The IAS on accounting for taxes on income is currently being revised, and an exposure draft has been issued.

Comparison in this table is made to International Accounting Standards in force at January 1, 1993. For further details, see the International Accounting Standards chapter.

JAPAN

GENERAL NATIONAL INFORMATION

1. Source of Generally Accepted Accounting Principles

Generally Accepted Accounting Principles. Generally accepted accounting principles in Japan are derived from legal provisions, authoritative pronouncements, accounting literature and well-established practice.

Accounting Standards. Accounting standards promulgated by law and stipulated by authoritative organizations are as follows:

☐ Commercial Code (Shoho)—The Commercial Code provides general rules of valuation of assets and liabilities, recording of deferred assets, provision of reserves, accounting for legal and capital reserves, and other fundamental matters.

☐ Income Tax Law (Zeiho)—Income Tax Law provides general and specific provisions for determination of taxable income. All expenses and write-downs of assets for tax purposes must be recorded for accounting purposes.

☐ Financial Accounting Standards for Business Enterprises promulgated by the Business Accounting Deliberation Council (BADC)—The BADC, an advisory body to the Ministry of Finance, has issued a concise, comprehensive set of standards that cover general standards, income statement standards and balance sheet standards. The BADC has also issued standards relating to consolidated financial statements, interim financial statements, cost accounting and translation of foreign currency transactions.

☐ Pronouncements by the Audit Committee of the Japanese Institute of Certified Public Accountants (JICPA)—The Audit Committee of the JICPA has issued a number of papers relating to preferable accounting practices, specific auditing procedures and requirements for qualified or adverse opinions if such practices are not followed.

2. Audit and Public Company Requirements

Audits Under the Commercial Code. The Commercial Code requires every joint-stock corporation (Kabushiki Kaisha) to elect one or more statutory auditors (Kansayaku) at a general shareholders' meeting. No professional qualifications have been established for statutory auditors, who can be re-elected for two-year terms.

The financial statements and supporting schedules of a large corporation, defined as a corporation with capital stock of Y500 million or more or total liabilities of Y20 billion or more, are subject to audit not only by statutory auditors but also by independent auditors (Kaikeikansanin), who are either independent CPAs or audit corporations (Kansahojin). The statutory auditors examine principally the managerial actions of the directors; the independent auditors examine the accounting records and financial statements.

The directors of a corporation must submit the financial statements to the statutory and independent auditors at least eight weeks before the designated date of the annual shareholders' meeting, and supporting schedules within three weeks after submitting the financial statements.

Under the Commercial Code, an annual shareholders' meeting must be held within three months after the fiscal year-end. The independent auditors are required to submit the audit report to the statutory auditors and the directors within four weeks after receiving the financial statements. The statutory auditors' report must be submitted to the directors and the independent auditors within one week after receiving the independent auditors' report.

In principle, the balance sheet, income statement and proposal for appropriation of retained earnings require the approval of the shareholders at the annual general meeting. However, if the independent auditors submit an unqualified audit report, the shareholders' approval for the balance sheet and income statement is not required.

Audits Under the Securities and Exchange Law.   Under the Securities and Exchange Law (Shokentorihikiho), corporations that offer securities to the public or whose outstanding securities are traded publicly must file financial statements (Zaimushohyo) as part of a registration statement, securities report or interim securities report with the Securities Bureau of the Ministry of Finance (MOF). Those financial statements must be audited by independent auditors. The auditors' independence and reporting requirements are set out by the "Ordinance Concerning Audit Certification of Financial Statements," MOF Ordinance No. 12 of 1957, as amended.

Except where the total amount involved is less than Y500 million or there are fewer than 50 subscribers, corporations that offer their shares or bonds to the public are required to file a registration statement (Yukashoken Todokeidesho) with the Securities Bureau of the MOF. The registration statement includes individual financial statements of the **parent company** for the two most recent fiscal years, **consolidated financial statements** (Renketsu Zaimushohyo) for the same period and semiannual financial statements (Chukan Zaimushohyo) for the current year, if applicable. Those financial statements must be audited by independent auditors.

Corporations that have offered securities and have filed a registration statement in the past or whose securities are listed on stock exchanges or traded in the over-the-counter market are required to file a securities report annually and an interim securities report every six months with the MOF. The annual securities report includes individual financial statements of the parent company and consolidated financial statements that have been audited by independent auditors.

When a joint-stock corporation goes public, it must submit a securities report for listing application to the Stock Exchange or the Securities Dealers Association of Japan (SDAJ) containing the following audited financial statements: (a) individual financial statements of the parent company for the three most recent fiscal years, (b) individual interim financial statements of the parent company for the two most recent fiscal years, (c) consolidated financial statements for the two most recent fiscal years and (d) individual financial statements of major affiliated corporations for the most recent fiscal year.

The form and content of the registration statement, annual securities report and semiannual securities report are prescribed by the Ordinance Concerning Corporate Disclosure, MOF Ordinance No. 5 of 1973, as amended.

Reference. Commercial Code; Law for Special Exceptions to the Commercial Code Concerning Audit, etc., of Joint Stock Corporations; Securities and Exchange Law; Ordinance Concerning Audit Certification of Financial Statements; and Ordinance Concerning Corporate Disclosure.

GENERAL ACCOUNTING

3. Financial Statements

Financial Statements Under the Commercial Code. Under the Commercial Code, a joint-stock corporation is required to prepare the following financial statements and data as of each fiscal year-end: balance sheet (Taishaku Taishohyo), income statement (Soneki Keisansho), business report (Eigyo Hokokusho), proposal for appropriation of retained earnings (Riekikin Shobunan) and supporting schedules (Fuzoku Meisaisho). The business report contains an outline of the business, operations and financial position and operating results.

The form and content of financial statements required under the Commercial Code are dictated by the Regulations Concerning the Balance Sheet, Income Statement, Business Report and Supporting Schedules of Joint Stock Corporations, Ministry of Justice Ordinance No. 31 of 1963, as amended.

The underlying objective of financial statements prepared in accordance with the Commercial Code is to protect creditors and current investors. Accordingly, disclosures on the availability of earnings for dividend distributions, credit worthiness and earning power are of primary importance. The emphasis is on proper presentation of the company's financial position and results of operations in accordance with the law and the company's articles of incorporation. The statements and supporting schedules are prepared for a single year and for the parent company only. A statement of changes in financial position or of cash flows is not required.

Financial statements are prepared primarily using the **historical cost** basis and the **going concern concept**. Income and expenses are recognized when realized or incurred following the **accrual concept**. Disclosure of significant **accounting policies** and other matters is required in the notes to the financial statements.

Financial Statements Under the Securities and Exchange Law. In addition to the financial statements required under the Commercial Code, corporations whose shares are listed on the stock exchanges or traded in the over-the-counter market are required by the Securities and Exchange Law (SEL) to prepare financial statements to be included in two periodic securities reports: the Annual Securities Reports (Yukashoken Hokokusho) filed with the MOF within three months after the fiscal year-end and the Semiannual Securities Report (Hanki Hokokusho) filed within three months after the semiannual period-end. The annual securities report must include consolidated financial statements. Copies of these securities reports are also submitted to the Stock Exchange or the Securities Dealers Association for public inspection.

The form and content of the financial statements required under the SEL are prescribed by the Regulations Concerning Financial Statements and Related Matters, MOF Ordinance No. 59 of 1963, as amended; the Regulations Concerning Consolidated Financial Statements, MOF Ordinance No. 28 of 1976, as amended; and the Regulations Concerning Interim Financial Statements, MOF Ordinance No. 38 of 1977, as amended.

Although the basic financial statements required under the SEL are the same as those required under the Commercial Code, the terminology, form and content of the financial statements and supporting schedules are more precisely defined in the SEL financial regulations. These regulations require, in most instances, additional detail and reclassification of certain items from the Commercial Code financial statements. However, net income and shareholders' equity do not change as a result of the reclassification.

The balance sheet is divided into assets, liabilities and shareholders' equity sections. Assets are classified as **current assets**, noncurrent assets and deferred charges, with noncurrent assets further divided into tangible **fixed assets, intangible** fixed **assets** and investments. Liabilities are classified as current and noncurrent. Shareholders' equity is divided into **capital stock**, capital surplus, legal reserves and **retained earnings**.

The income statement is divided into ordinary income (or loss) and extraordinary gain (or loss). Ordinary income is subdivided into operating income and nonoperating income. Extraordinary gain (or loss) includes **prior period adjustments**, gain (or loss) on sale of fixed assets and other items. Income taxes are deducted from income (or loss) before income taxes to arrive at net income (or loss).

A cash flow statement, including a cash flow forecast, is included as supplemental information in annual and semiannual securities reports; however, it is not considered a basic financial statement and thus is not subject to audit. The form and content of the statement of "cash flow conditions" is prescribed by regulations and rulings. The statement reconciles the net change in cash and cash equivalents to cash flows, segregated between operating and financing activities. This statement includes actual cash flow information for two comparative periods and a cash flow forecast for the next six-month period. The actual cash flow information may be determined by either the **direct method** or the **indirect method**.

The SEL financial statements present two-year comparative data and include details of major accounting policies and other appropriate footnote disclosures.

Reference. Regulations Concerning the Balance Sheet, Income Statement, Business Report and Supporting Schedule of Joint Stock Corporations; Regulations Concerning Financial Statements and Related Matters; Regulations Concerning Consolidated Financial Statements; and Regulations Concerning Interim Financial Statements.

4. Business Combinations

Principles of Consolidation. The parent company's ownership interest in **subsidiaries** and affiliated companies determines whether they are consolidated or accounted for using the **equity method**. Generally, management control is not a basis for those determinations.

Subsidiaries are generally consolidated. A subsidiary is a company of which more than half of the voting power is owned directly or indirectly by a parent company.

A subsidiary is excluded from consolidation if:

- [ ] It is no longer effectively under the parent's control (e.g., loss of effective control because of a reorganization);
- [ ] It is not considered to be a going concern because of bankruptcy or liquidation;
- [ ] The voting power in the subsidiary is owned on a temporary basis; or
- [ ] There are adequate reasons why including the subsidiary in the consolidation would be misleading to interested parties.

In addition, if a subsidiary comprises less than 10 percent of total group assets or sales, it may be excluded from consolidation on the basis of **materiality**.

The Securities and Exchange Law requires listed companies to issue consolidated financial statements as supplementary information to the financial statements of the parent company. ''Financial Accounting Standards on Consolidated Financial Statements,'' published by the BADC, describes the standards to be used to prepare the consolidated financial statements. The form and content of consolidated financial statements are prescribed by the MOF Ordinance, Regulations Concerning Consolidated Financial Statements.

Accounting for Business Combinations. Mergers are usually effected by an exchange of shares between an acquired company and an acquiring company (money may also be exchanged). Mergers are generally accounted for by the **pooling of interests method**. The excess of transferred assets and liabilities over increased capital as a result of a merger is recorded as capital surplus.

An acquisition is regarded as an investment in the acquired company. The shares acquired are recorded at their cost to the acquiring company.

Goodwill. The difference between the cost of an investment in a subsidiary and the parent's share of the subsidiary's equity is allocated principally to accounts such as tangible fixed assets and **goodwill**. The goodwill is amortized using the **straight-line method** over a reasonable period (normally five years), or charged to income at acquisition if it is not significant. **Negative goodwill** may also be recognized.

Equity Accounting. Investments in **associated companies** and unconsolidated subsidiaries generally are accounted for in the consolidated financial statements using the equity method. An associated company is a company in which between 20 and 50 percent of the voting power is directly or indirectly owned by the parent company.

Minority Interests. The **minority interest** is the part of a subsidiary's equity that is attributable to shares held by entities other than the parent company. Losses applicable to minority interests in excess of shareholders' equity of the subsidiary are charged against the parent's interest in the equity of the subsidiary.

Disclosure. There are no specific disclosures required for business combinations. Disclosure requirements in the notes to consolidated financial statements are as follows:

- [ ] Consolidation policy—policies adopted with respect to inclusion of subsidiaries in consolidation, application of the equity method for unconsolidated subsidiaries and associated companies, other significant matters and a description of and reasons for any significant changes.

□ Difference in fiscal year-end—if the fiscal year-end of a subsidiary is different from the date of the consolidation, the subsidiary's fiscal year-end and an outline of any special adjustments made for consolidation purposes.

□ **Accounting principles** and practices—valuation basis and depreciation or amortization method for significant assets, method used to eliminate unrealized intercompany profits, and significant differences in the accounting principles and practices adopted by a subsidiary.

□ Appropriated retained earnings—treatment of appropriated retained earnings in consolidation.

□ Items translated in the financial statements of foreign subsidiaries—translation method adopted for foreign subsidiaries and associated companies included in consolidated financial statements.

□ Other material matters—any other significant matters necessary for adequate interpretation of the financial position and results of operations of the consolidated entity.

Reference. Financial Accounting Standards on Consolidated Financial Statements (BADC) and Regulations Concerning Consolidated Financial Statements.

5. Joint Ventures

General. In Japan, there are both jointly controlled operations and jointly controlled entities as defined by International Accounting Standard 31.

Accounting for Jointly Controlled Operations. The most common examples of jointly controlled operations in Japan are related to large construction projects. Such operations involve the use of the assets and other resources of the individual venturers; that is, each venturer uses its own property, plant and equipment and carries its own inventories. The **joint venture** agreement usually provides a means by which revenue from contracts and any costs and expenses incurred in common are shared among the venturers.

With respect to its interests in jointly controlled operations, each venturer records in its accounting records:

□ The assets that it controls and the liabilities that it incurs.

□ The costs and expenses that it incurs directly and its share of revenue earned from contracts.

Accounting for Jointly Controlled Entities. Jointly controlled entities in Japan are normally established in corporate form, and each venturer owns shares of stock representing its interest in the joint venture entity. The jointly controlled entity owns the assets of the joint venture, incurs liabilities and expenses and earns income. Each venturer is entitled to a share of the results of the jointly controlled entity, which is distributed in the form of dividends.

Venturers record investments in the joint venture entity at acquisition cost, the same as any investment in the equity shares of a company.

Investments in jointly controlled entities are generally accounted for in a venturer's consolidated financial statements using the equity method. Application of the **proportionate consolidation** method is not allowed in Japan.

Disclosures. There are no particular disclosure requirements for joint ventures.

Reference. Financial Accounting Standards for Business Enterprises (BADC); Financial Accounting Standards on Consolidated Financial Statements (BADC); and Regulations Concerning Consolidated Financial Statements.

6. Foreign Currency Translation

General. The prescribed accounting method for foreign currency translation is the "modified **temporal method**."

Foreign Currency Transactions. **Foreign currency transactions** are translated at the rate in effect when the transaction occurred. However, foreign currency transactions with a fixed yen value—for example, a forward exchange contract—are recorded using the fixed yen amount. Differences arising from the settlement of foreign currency monetary rights or obligations are accounted for as exchange gains or losses in the period of settlement.

Short-term monetary rights or obligations are translated at the rate of exchange in effect at the balance sheet date. However, convertible debentures for which the conversion period has not yet expired are translated using the exchange rate in effect when they were issued.

Long-term foreign currency monetary rights or obligations are translated at the rate of exchange in effect when the rights were acquired or obligations incurred. However, application of this basic principle may be modified to allow the use of year-end exchange rates where there is a significant change in exchange rates.

Differences arising from translation at the balance sheet date are recorded in income as exchange gains or losses.

Foreign Currency Financial Statements. Short-term monetary rights or obligations are translated at the rate in effect at the balance sheet date. Long-term monetary rights or obligations are translated at the rate in effect when the rights were acquired or obligations incurred. Securities, inventories and tangible fixed assets are translated at the rate in effect when they were acquired. If these assets were not recorded at acquisition cost, the asset values are translated into yen at the rate in effect at the time their value was determined. In applying the lower of cost or market method for securities and inventories, market value is the foreign currency market value multiplied by the rate in effect at the balance sheet date.

Revenue and expenses are translated at the rate effective when they are recognized or an average rate for the period, except that amounts charged to income from asset accounts, such as inventories and tangible fixed assets, are translated at the rate in effect when the assets were acquired.

Net income and retained earnings are translated at the rate in effect at the balance sheet date, with the resulting differences reflected in translation adjustment accounts on the income statement and statement of retained earnings.

Differences arising from translating foreign currency balance sheet accounts are recorded in a translation adjustment account, which is shown as a net asset or liability on the balance sheet.

Hedges.   The establishment of accounting standards for futures and option transactions for stocks, bonds, interest and foreign currencies, including the accounting treatment of related **hedges**, is an important current issue in Japan.

The BADC issued an interim accounting standard on May 29, 1990, but concluded that further study would be required to establish concrete standards.

However, proper disclosure in relation to futures and option transactions, including carrying value, contract amount, market value and unrealized profit or loss, is required. Also see disclosure requirements discussed in Section 16.

Disclosure.   The bases used to translate foreign currency assets and liabilities into yen and to translate financial statements of foreign consolidated subsidiaries are disclosed in the accounting policy note. Assets and liabilities denominated in foreign currencies are disclosed in the notes. Long-term monetary rights or obligations translated into yen at the rate in effect at the end of the period are required to be disclosed.

Reference.   Accounting Standards for Foreign Currency Transactions, etc. (BADC).

7.   Changing Prices/Inflation Accounting

There is no accounting standard or disclosure requirements for changing prices in Japan.

8.   Accounting Changes

Accounting Treatment for Changes in Accounting Principles.   The effect of changes in accounting principles is the difference between:

- □   The amount of the current year's income or expense based on the newly adopted accounting principle, without considering the retroactive effect of the change on the opening balances of related balance sheet items; and
- □   The amount of the current year's income or expense based on the previous accounting policy.

The cumulative effect at the time of the change in accounting principle is not required to be retroactively accounted for; accordingly, prior years' financial statements are not restated for a newly adopted accounting principle.

A change in accounting estimate is distinguished from a change in accounting principle. If the effect of a change in accounting estimate on prior period amounts is material, the amount is shown as an extraordinary gain or loss (described as a prior period adjustment) in the year of recognition.

Disclosure.   Any material change in accounting principles, the reason for the change and its effect on the financial statements must be disclosed in the notes. Similar disclosure is required for changes in accounting estimates.

Reference.   Financial Accounting Standards for Business Enterprises (BADC); Regulations Concerning the Balance Sheet, Income Statement, Business Report and Supporting

Schedule of Joint Stock Corporations; and Regulations Concerning Financial Statements and Related Matters.

9. Prior Period Adjustments

Accounting Treatment. Retroactive adjustments of prior period reported amounts are not permitted. Adjustments for known errors attributable to prior periods are recorded in current income.

Disclosure. Prior period adjustments are presented as extraordinary gains or losses in the income statement. Explanation of the nature of the adjustment is required in the notes.

Reference. Financial Accounting Standards for Business Enterprises (BADC) and Regulations Concerning Financial Statements and Related Matters.

10. Post Balance Sheet Events

Definition. Post balance sheet events are events that occur between the balance sheet date and the date the financial statements are authorized. There are two types of post balance sheet events: (a) those relating to conditions that existed at the balance sheet date and (b) those relating to conditions that did not exist at the balance sheet date.

Accounting Treatment. The financial statements are adjusted to reflect the effects of material post balance sheet events of the type described in (a) above.

Disclosure. Where material, disclosure of post balance sheet events of the type described in (b) above is required in the notes.

Reference. Financial Accounting Standards for Business Enterprises (BADC) and Regulations Concerning Financial Statements and Related Matters.

11. Related Party Transactions

Definition and Accounting Treatment. Related parties include the parent company, subsidiaries, affiliated companies, shareholders, directors and statutory auditors. Transactions between the reporting company and related parties are accounted for in accordance with normal accounting principles and practices.

Disclosure. Related party account balances must be presented separately in the balance sheet or disclosed in the notes, if material. Sales, purchases and other related party transactions must be presented separately in the income statement or disclosed in the notes.

Disclosure of related party transactions is required in the annual securities report to appropriately describe transactions among business entities within the same financial group. The definition of related parties is similar to that in US Statement of Financial Accounting Standards No. 57. Transactions during the period and account balances at year-end are presented in tabular form under the caption ''Condition of Business Group.''

Reference. Regulations Concerning the Balance Sheet, Income Statement, Business Report and Supporting Schedule of Joint Stock Corporations; and Regulations Concerning Financial Statements and Related Matters.

12. Segmental Information

General. Companies that file consolidated information with their annual securities report must provide segmental information.

The following segmental information is disclosed:

(a) Segment by industry—Sales and operating profit (or loss) by segment, determined as follows: If a segment's sales exceed 10 percent of total sales or its operating profit exceeds 10 percent of total operating profit, the segment is presented separately.

(b) Segment by domestic and overseas location—Sales and operating profit (or loss) by location (domestic or overseas) of parent and subsidiaries.

(c) Overseas sales—Sales if overseas sales exceed 10 percent of consolidated sales.

Disclosure. For (a) and (b) above, external sales, intrasegment sales, allocated cost and expenses, unallocated expenses and operating profit (or loss) are presented in table form for each segment. The major product names for each industrial segment must be disclosed.

Reference. Ordinance Concerning Corporate Disclosure and Disclosure of Segment Information under the Securities and Exchange Law (MOF Ruling).

ACCOUNTING PRINCIPLES FOR SPECIFIC ITEMS— BALANCE SHEET

13. Property, Plant and Equipment (Yukei Kotei Shisan)

Classification of Capital and Revenue Expenditure. A **capital expenditure** increases the useful life and capacity of the related assets and is recorded as part of the cost of the assets. Tangible fixed assets include buildings, structures, machinery, ships, vehicles, tools, furniture and fixtures, land and construction in progress.

Repair and maintenance expenses are charged to income as incurred. Renewals and improvements are capitalized; however, minor items are expensed, as allowed by tax law.

Basis of Valuation. Fixed assets are generally carried at acquisition cost, which is determined as follows:

☐ Purchase—invoice price plus incidental expenses.
☐ Self-construction—cost computed on a cost accounting basis.
☐ Exchange—fair value of assets given in exchange.

Interest on funds used during construction cannot be capitalized. Upward revaluation is not accepted, but downward revaluation is permitted in certain circumstances.

Depreciation. The following **depreciation** methods are used:

- [ ] Straight-line method.
- [ ] **Declining balance method.**
- [ ] **Sum-of-the-years'-digits method.**
- [ ] **Unit-of-production method.**

Useful lives of tangible fixed assets are estimated by considering various economic factors such as technological changes. However, in practice, many companies adopt useful lives specified by the income tax law. The declining balance method is the most common method used because it results in higher depreciation charges in the early years of an asset's life.

Gains or losses on sales or disposals of assets are generally recorded as extraordinary items in the income statement.

Disclosure. Accumulated depreciation is presented in the balance sheet or in the notes. The depreciation method adopted is disclosed in the accounting policy note.

Reference. Financial Accounting Standards for Business Enterprises (BADC); Commercial Code; Regulations Concerning the Balance Sheet, Income Statement, Business Report and Supporting Schedule of Joint Stock Corporations; Regulations Concerning Financial Statements and Related Matters; and Income Tax Law.

14. Intangible Assets (Mukei Kotei Shisan)

Accounting Treatment. Intangible assets are classified as legal rights and goodwill, according to their identifiable characteristics. Intangible assets are recorded at cost. The cost of patents, utility model rights and design rights includes registration and license tax, patent attorney fees and expenses paid for research. Purchased goodwill is recorded in the accounts as an intangible asset, but internally developed goodwill is not recognized as an asset.

Amortization. The cost of intangibles, except for property rights, which are not amortized, is normally amortized on a straight-line basis over their useful life or over the number of years prescribed by the income tax law. Purchased goodwill is amortized within five years using the straight-line method, in accordance with the Commercial Code.

Disclosure. Intangible assets, net of **amortization**, are presented in the balance sheet. The amortization method adopted is disclosed in the accounting policy note.

Reference. See Section 13.

15. Leases

Classification and Accounting Treatment. No standard or regulation has been issued on accounting for **financing leases**. All lease transactions are accounted for by both lessees and lessors as **operating leases**. Lessees expense lease or rental payments in the period to which they relate. The lessor credits income as it is earned.

There are special tax rulings relating to sale and leaseback transactions and **leveraged leases**. According to the definition given by the tax ruling, a sale and leaseback transaction is treated as a financing lease for tax purposes. A leveraged lease, according to the definition given by the tax ruling, is treated as a financing lease or sale and purchase transaction, depending on the substance of the transaction. These tax rules, which apply to both the lessor and the lessee, do not necessarily have to be followed for financial reporting purposes.

Disclosure.   Lessees disclose major tangible fixed assets held under a lease contract in the notes. Lessees also disclose details of leased assets in a supporting schedule, in accordance with the Commercial Code.

Reference.   Regulations Concerning the Balance Sheet, Income Statement, Business Report and Supporting Schedule of Joint Stock Corporations; and Income Tax Rulings, 1978 and 1988.

16. Investments (Toshi)

Classification.   Securities are generally classified as specified by the Securities and Exchange Law. Examples are:

- [ ] Government bonds.
- [ ] Local government bonds.
- [ ] Corporate bonds.
- [ ] Equity stock.

Bonds include convertible bonds and bonds carrying a warrant for stock.

Marketable securities and/or investments held for short-term investment purposes are classified as current assets. Securities held for long-term investment purposes are classified as investment securities. Investment securities include securities issued by affiliated companies.

Valuation.   Securities acquired are recorded at cost, which includes the consideration given and related incidental costs such as commissions. Equity (i.e., **common**) **stocks** acquired through conversion of securities already held are valued at the same cost as the securities converted.

Marketable securities are carried at either cost or the lower of cost or market. In applying the lower of cost or market method, market value means repurchase price, that is, the quoted price plus purchase commission. The cost of each security is determined using the moving-**average cost** or other acceptable methods. If the market price of securities carried at cost is less than 50 percent of that cost, the carrying value must be reduced to the market price unless recovery of the original carrying value is expected.

Investment securities are stated at acquisition cost, determined using the moving-average cost or other acceptable methods. The moving-average method is most common. Other methods, such as **FIFO**, weighted-average and **specific identification**, are acceptable. The lower of cost or market method may be adopted for quoted investment securities, except for investments in subsidiaries. If the market value or equity value is substantially lower than cost, the investment must be written down to the market or equity value. Equity value as shown in the investee company financial statements is used if there is no readily available market value.

Bonds are carried at their purchase price, which may include a premium or discount. The premium or discount is amortized over the remaining life of the bonds.

Gains/Losses.   Gains or losses on the sale of marketable securities are generally recorded as nonoperating income or expenses. Gains or losses on the sale of investment securities are recorded as extraordinary gains or losses.

Disclosure.   Disclosure of the basis used for the valuation of marketable securities and investment securities is required in the accounting policy note. Disclosure of the market value of marketable securities at the balance sheet date is required.

The notes must include a table that shows the balance sheet value and unrealized profit or loss by classification of current assets (stocks, bonds and others) and noncurrent assets (stocks, bonds and others).

The contract amount, market value and unrealized profit or loss relating to future transactions for stocks, bonds and interest are required to be disclosed in the notes. Also, the market value and unrealized profit or loss relating to option transactions for stocks, bonds and interest are required to be disclosed in the notes.

Reference.   See Section 13.

17. Accounts Receivable (Eigyo Saiken)

Accounting Treatment.   Recognition: Revenue recognition is described in Section 23.

Classification: Trade receivables owed by customers for goods and services sold or provided as part of the normal operation of the business are presented as current assets in the balance sheet. Trade receivables are classified as **accounts receivable** or notes receivable.

Promissory notes receivable are often used in Japanese business to settle accounts receivable. Notes receivable normally have terms of 60 to 180 days; they are discounted at a bank and disclosed as contingent liabilities. The difference between the face value of notes and the discounted proceeds is recorded as a discount charge on the income statement.

Discounts: Accounts receivable are recorded net of trade discounts. Cash discounts for early payment are recognized when payment is received and are recorded as sales discounts in the income statement.

Factored Receivables.   **Factoring** of receivables is not common in Japan.

Allowance for Doubtful Accounts.   At the balance sheet date, an allowance for uncollectible accounts is provided based on past experience and is recorded as a reduction of receivables. The amount provided depends on the particular business circumstances of each company. However, it is common for the allowance for doubtful accounts to equal the limit prescribed by the income tax laws and regulations.

Disclosure.   Disclosure of the basis of the allowance for doubtful accounts is required in the accounting policy note. Any loss **contingencies** that exist on receivables and receivables assigned or pledged as collateral are disclosed in the notes.

Reference. See Section 13.

18. Inventories and Work in Progress (Tanaoroshi Shisan)

Classification of Inventories. The term **inventory** includes items that are (a) held for sale in the normal course of business, (b) in production, (c) shortly to be consumed in the production of goods or services for sale and (d) shortly to be consumed in the process of sale or general administrative activities.

Inventories are normally classified as follows:

- □ Merchandise.
- □ Finished goods.
- □ Semi-finished goods.
- □ Raw materials.
- □ Work in progress.
- □ Office and manufacturing supplies.

General Accounting Treatment. The cost of purchased inventory is the invoice price, net of quantity discount, plus incidental costs such as transportation, import duty, handling and insurance.

The cost of manufactured inventory is the actual manufacturing cost computed in accordance with Cost Accounting Standards issued by BADC. All direct and overhead costs are included in determining manufacturing cost. Direct cost accounting is not acceptable. A **standard cost** basis may be acceptable if the standard cost is reasonably determined. There is an income tax regulation specifying that if standard cost variances do not exceed 5 percent of total production cost for the period, the variances can be included in the cost of sales and need not be added to or deducted from product cost at the prescribed standard cost.

Inventories are valued at either cost or lower of cost or market. Under the lower of cost or market method, market value is usually the repurchase price. In accordance with the Commercial Code, if inventory is stated at cost and the market price is significantly less than cost, inventory must be valued at market unless recovery of the shortfall is reasonably assured.

The following inventory costing methods are commonly used:

- □ Individual cost.
- □ First-in, first-out (FIFO).
- □ **Last-in, first-out (LIFO)**.
- □ Weighted-average.
- □ Moving-average.
- □ **Latest purchase price**.

Damaged or obsolete inventories are normally valued at **net realizable value**. The write-down is either directly deducted from the inventory value or an allowance is credited.

Long-Term Contracts. Accumulated costs incurred on a long-term contract are essentially no different from other inventory costs. Costs not clearly related, either directly or indirectly, to a long-term contract should be excluded from inventory and treated as period costs. Refer to Section 23 for a discussion of revenue recognition for long-term contracts.

Disclosure.   The basis of valuing inventories is disclosed in the accounting policy note.

Reference.   Financial Accounting Standards for Business Enterprises (BADC); Cost Accounting Standards (BADC); Commercial Code; Regulations Concerning the Balance Sheet, Income Statement, Business Report and Supporting Schedule of Joint Stock Corporations; Regulations Concerning Financial Statements and Related Matters; and Income Tax Law.

19.   Current Liabilities (Ryudo Fusai)

General Accounting Treatment.   **Current liabilities** are normally classified on the balance sheet as follows:

☐   Notes payable.
☐   Trade **accounts payable**.
☐   Short-term loans, current portion of long-term debt.
☐   Other accounts payable.
☐   Accrued expenses.
☐   Advances received, deposits received, deferred income.
☐   Reserves.

Trade accounts payable include amounts owed to suppliers of goods and services in the normal operation of the business. Promissory notes are often issued for settlement of accounts payable.

Most expenses are recorded when incurred. Expenses incurred but not recorded because payment is not yet due, such as unpaid salaries and wages, are recorded as accrued expenses.

Amounts received from or due to customers for goods to be delivered or services to be performed are recorded as advances received, deposits received or deferred income, depending on the nature of the liability.

Creation of General and Specific Provisions.   Certain expenses or losses that will be incurred in future periods should be charged to current income as expenses or losses by providing a reserve in the liabilities section of the balance sheet. Such reserves should be provided when expenses or losses are attributable to the current or prior periods, if it is probable that they will occur and if their amount can be reasonably estimated. Examples of such expenses and losses are sales rebates, sales returns, employee bonuses and repairs. Certain reserves are required to comply with specialized industry laws, such as public utility regulations.

Disclosure.   Disclosure of the basis of recording reserves is required in the accounting policy note.

Reference.   See Section 13.

20. Long-Term Debt (Choki Fusai)

General Accounting Treatment. Long-term debt is normally classified on the balance sheet as follows:

□ Bonds, convertible bonds.
□ Long-term loans.

Long-term debt includes liabilities that mature after one year. The current portion of long-term debt is classified as a current liability.

Bonds, whether or not convertible or interest bearing, are recorded at face value. Bonds with detachable warrants are also recorded at face value. Bond discounts are recorded as deferred charges in the balance sheet and amortized over the redemption period. Bond issue costs are normally recorded as deferred assets and amortized within three years or the redemption period, whichever is shorter.

Loans payable are recorded at face value or contractual settlement value. Interest payable is generally recorded as an accrued expense. Debt restructuring and debt extinguishment are rare; there are no official standards on accounting for these transactions in Japan.

Disclosure. Long-term debt is disclosed by account classification in a schedule to the balance sheet. The information disclosed includes maturity date, interest rate and collateral.

Reference. See Section 13.

21. Contingencies (Guhatsu Saimu)

General. The term contingency designates a possible liability that arises from a past condition, circumstance or action. Examples are notes discounted or endorsed, guarantees on loans, product warranties, future sales and purchases.

Accounting Treatment. Contingent losses must be either accrued and reported in the financial statements or disclosed in the notes, depending on their nature. Contingent gains are not accrued in the financial statements.

An estimated loss must be accrued if both of the following conditions are met: (1) information available prior to the issuance of the financial statements indicates it is probable that an asset had been impaired or a liability had been incurred at the date of the balance sheet and (2) the amount of loss can be reasonably estimated.

If no accrual is made because one or both of the above conditions are not met, the contingency must be disclosed when there is at least a reasonable possibility that an unrecorded loss may have been incurred.

Disclosure. Footnote disclosure should include details of the contingency.

Reference. Regulations Concerning Financial Statements and Related Matters.

22. Capital and Reserves (Shihon/Joyokin)

Classification.   Shareholders' equity is classified on the balance sheet as follows:

☐   Capital stock.
☐   Capital reserve.
☐   Legal reserve.
☐   Retained earnings.

Capital Stock.   Capital stock includes common and **preferred shares** with or without **par value**. When a company issues shares with par value for cash, all or part of the proceeds are recorded as capital stock. The amount recorded as capital stock should not be less than half of the proceeds or more than the par value of the shares. The remainder is recorded in the paid in **surplus** account included in the capital reserve component of shareholders' equity. The issue of shares at a price less than par value is prohibited under the Commercial Code. When shares without par value are issued, more than half of the proceeds should be recorded as capital stock.

When bonds are converted to common shares, more than half of the prescribed conversion price is recorded as capital stock; the remainder is accounted for as paid in surplus.

Distributions of shares without consideration normally are accounted for by transferring an amount equivalent to the par value of the shares from paid in surplus to capital stock. The amount appropriated for stock dividends is transferred from retained earnings to capital stock. Stock splits do not affect the capital stock account.

The acquisition of **treasury stock** is prohibited except for certain situations stipulated by the Commercial Code, such as a purchase for cancellation of stock and a merger or business acquisition. A decrease in capital stock exceeding the redeemed amount is credited to capital reserve as a gain on reduction in capital stock.

Capital Reserve.   The capital reserve includes paid in surplus, gain on reduction in capital stock and gain arising from mergers.

Legal Reserve.   The legal reserve consists of retained earnings set aside under the Commercial Code, which requires that an amount equal to at least 10 percent of the sum of cash dividends and officers' bonuses paid be set aside until the reserve is equal to 25 percent of the capital stock account. The legal reserve cannot be transferred to capital stock or offset against accumulated deficit.

Retained Earnings.   In Japan it is common to appropriate a certain amount of retained earnings for special purposes.

Dividends and Distribution Restrictions.   Under the Commercial Code, retained earnings available for dividends is limited to total shareholders' equity less capital stock, capital reserve, legal reserve, legal reserve to be set up in the current year, and deferred preoperating and research and development costs.

Disclosure.   Details of authorized and issued shares should be disclosed in the notes. Details of dividend restrictions, if any, must also be disclosed.

Reference.   Financial Accounting Standards for Business Enterprises (BADC); Commercial Code; Regulations Concerning the Balance Sheet, Income Statement, Business Report and Supporting Schedule of Joint Stock Corporations; and Regulations Concerning Financial Statements and Related Matters.

ACCOUNTING PRINCIPLES FOR SPECIFIC ITEMS— INCOME STATEMENT

23. Revenue Recognition

General Principles.   **Revenue** is generally defined as the gross increase in assets or gross decrease in liabilities during the period from delivering or producing goods, rendering services or other earning activities of an enterprise. Revenue for the period is generally recognized when the earning process is complete or virtually complete and an exchange transaction has taken place. Revenue from selling products is recognized at the date of the sale, usually interpreted as the date of delivery to customers. Revenue from services rendered is recognized when services have been performed and are billable.

Long-Term Contracts.   Long-term contract revenue is accounted for by either the **percentage of completion method** or the **completed contract method**.

Instalment Sales.   Revenue from **instalment sales** is principally recognized at the time the goods are delivered. However, if future collection of instalment sales is uncertain, sales profit may be based on the instalment sales method. Under this method, current profit is recognized for that portion of the profit calculated to be collectible during the current period divided by the total receivables on instalment sales.

Consignment Sales and Other Types of Sales.   Under consignment sales agreements, the consignor recognizes a sale when the consignee sells the consigned goods. Accordingly, consignment sales revenue for the period includes all sales revenue supported by sales advices from consignees.

Sales on approval are recorded when a purchase notification is received or at the notification due date. Subscription sales revenue is recognized as goods are delivered or services rendered.

Rights of Return and Product Financing.   Sales transactions with the right of return and **product financing arrangements** are rare in Japan.

Disclosure.   Sales of goods and of services are presented separately in the income statement. Details of cost of sales are also presented. Selling, general and administrative expenses are deducted from gross profit to arrive at operating income.

The use of the percentage of completion method to record long-term contracts or the instalment sales method for recognizing instalment sales profit should be disclosed in the accounting policy note.

Reference.   Financial Accounting Standards for Business Enterprises (BADC); Regulations Concerning the Balance Sheet, Income Statement, Business Report and Supporting

Schedule of Joint Stock Corporations; and Regulations Concerning Financial Statements and Related Matters.

24. Government Grants and Assistance

Accounting Treatment. Government grants and assistance for capital expenditures are principally deducted from the cost of the related fixed assets. Depreciation is then calculated on the net cost. Government assistance for current expenses is recorded as current income.

Disclosure. Government grants and assistance received and deducted from the cost of fixed assets are disclosed in the notes.

Reference. Financial Accounting Standards for Business Enterprises (BADC).

25. Research and Development

Accounting Treatment. The Commercial Code provides that certain research and development costs may be recorded as deferred charges. The costs must be amortized within five years, at least one-fifth in each period.
  Research and development costs for the following purposes may be capitalized:

- [ ] Research on new goods or new techniques.
- [ ] Adoption of new techniques or new managing systems.
- [ ] Exploitation of resources.
- [ ] Development of markets.

Research and development costs paid in the ordinary course of business must be expensed as incurred.

Disclosure. The unamortized balance of deferred research and development costs is separately shown on the balance sheet. If research and development costs are recorded as deferred assets, the amortization method used must be disclosed in the accounting policy note.

Reference. See Section 13.

26. Capitalized Interest Costs
Capitalization of interest cost is not general practice in Japan, except for real estate development companies.

27. Imputed Interest
The recognition of **imputed interest** is not general practice in Japan.

28. Extraordinary or Unusual Items

Extraordinary Items. Extraordinary items consist of prior period adjustments, gains or losses on sale of fixed assets and other gains or losses.

Other extraordinary gains or losses include gains or losses from the disposal of securities or other assets not originally acquired for resale, write-off of deferred charges with no expected future benefit and other losses resulting from events or transactions that are not normal. Extraordinary items are not restricted to events and transactions distinguished by their unusual nature and infrequency.

Disclosure.   Extraordinary gains and losses are presented after ordinary income (or loss) to arrive at the amount of income before income taxes in the income statement. The nature of extraordinary gains and losses is disclosed.

Reference.   See Section 23.

29.   Income Taxes

Accounting Treatment.   Income taxes shown in the income statement are the taxes levied on taxable income for the period by the national and local governments. A business tax based on income is also levied on most industries, but is recorded as selling, general and administrative expenses.

Income taxes shown on the balance sheet are amounts currently payable, net of the tax effect of a loss brought forward. The potential tax effect of a loss carryforward is not recognized.

Interperiod income tax allocation is not acceptable for preparing individual or consolidated financial statements. However, recognition of the tax effects of eliminating intercompany unrealized profits on consolidation is considered meaningful in certain cases. Accordingly, income **tax allocation** is permitted in consolidated financial statements in these circumstances.

Disclosure.   Income taxes paid or payable resulting from an examination by the tax authority are presented separately from current income taxes.

Reference.   See Section 23.

30.   Postretirement Benefits

General.   Historically, Japanese companies have adopted employee retirement and severance benefit plans under which the employees are entitled to lump-sum payments generally based on rate of pay and length of service at their termination. Because of the existence of government-sponsored programs, other forms of postretirement benefits are generally not provided by Japanese companies.

In the past, employee retirement and severance plans were generally not funded, but there is now a tendency to partially fund such plans. Most large companies have adopted pension plans that are funded through a financial institution. There are several annuity type pensions for different employer sizes, pension participants or methods of future pension payments. Contributions to a pension fund are deductible for tax purposes for those plans meeting the requirements of the tax regulations.

Accounting Treatment.   According to Opinion 2 of the BADC, "Establishment of Liability for Retirement Allowance," there are three methods of computing the amount of the company's liability for lump-sum benefits.

(1) Estimated future payment method—Liability is accrued based on the estimated lump-sum future payments.

(2) Year-end necessary payment method—Liability is accrued as if all employees were to leave at the end of the period.

(3) Present value method—The present value of the liability computed based on either method (1) or (2) above is accrued.

Tax regulations limit the deductibility of employee retirement and severance benefit liabilities to a maximum of 40 percent of the voluntary severance liability computed as of the balance sheet date. Therefore, most companies that have adopted lump-sum payment plans provide a reserve for retirement on a tax basis; the increase in reserve and amount paid to retired employees are charged to income.

Because contributions to pension plans are tax-deductible expenses, most companies record pension expense equal to the contribution paid during the period. The contributions normally include past service costs, which are computed by actuaries based on the company's funding policy.

Disclosure. The basis of providing the reserve for retirement must be disclosed in the accounting policy note. An outline of the plan and either total funded assets or present value of past service cost must be disclosed. The amortization period of past service cost should also be disclosed.

Reference. Financial Accounting Standards for Business Enterprises (BADC); Establishment of Liability for Retirement Allowance (BADC); Regulations Concerning the Balance Sheet, Income Statement, Business Report and Supporting Schedule of Joint Stock Corporations; and Regulations Concerning Financial Statements and Related Matters.

31. Discontinued Operations

There is no accounting standard or disclosure requirement for discontinued operations in Japan.

32. Earnings per Share

Method of Calculation. Earnings per share (EPS) information is calculated as net income for the year divided by the weighted-average number of common shares issued and outstanding during the year. No diluted EPS information is required in Japan.

For financial statements prepared under the Securities and Exchange Law, net assets per share information is also required to be disclosed. Net assets per share is calculated using net assets as of the balance sheet date divided by the number of common shares issued and outstanding as of that date.

Disclosure. Both earnings per share and net assets per share are disclosed in the notes. The number of authorized shares and issued shares are also disclosed in the notes.

Reference. Regulations Concerning the Balance Sheet, Income Statement, Business Report and Supporting Schedule of Joint Stock Corporations; and Regulations Concerning Financial Statements and Related Matters.

Appendix
DO JAPANESE STANDARDS OR PREVALENT PRACTICE SUBSTANTIALLY COMPLY WITH INTERNATIONAL ACCOUNTING STANDARDS?

Section	Topic	Substantially complies with IAS?	Comments
3.	Basic accounting concepts and conventions	Yes	
	Contents of financial statements	Yes	Except that comparative figures for the previous period and a cash flow statement are required only for publicly traded companies
4.	Business combinations*	Yes	Except that consolidated financial statements are required only for publicly traded companies
5.	Joint ventures	Yes	
6.	Foreign currency translation*	No	
8.	Accounting changes*	Yes	
9.	Prior period adjustments*	No	Adjustments are disclosed as extraordinary items in Japan
10.	Post balance sheet events	Yes	
11.	Related party transactions	Yes	
12.	Segmental information	Yes	Except that segment assets and the basis of intersegment pricing are not required to be disclosed
13.	Property, plant and equipment*	Yes	
15.	Leases	No	
16.	Investments	Yes	
17.	Accounts receivable	Yes	Except that it is common for the provision for doubtful debts to be determined as the maximum allowed for tax purposes
18.	Inventories and work in progress*	Yes	

Appendix (*Continued*)

Section	Topic	Substantially complies with IAS?	Comments
19.	Current liabilities	Yes	
20.	Long-term debt	Yes	
21.	Contingencies	Yes	
22.	Capital and reserves	Yes	
23.	Revenue recognition*	Yes	
24.	Government grants and assistance	Yes	
25.	Research and development*	No	The range of costs that may be deferred in Japan is in excess of that allowed under IAS 9
26.	Capitalization of interest costs*	Yes	
28.	Extraordinary or unusual items*	No	
29.	Income tax**	No	
30.	Postretirement benefits*	Yes	

*These topics are subject to change as a result of the IASC Improvements Project—see the appendix to the International Accounting Standards chapter.

**The IAS on accounting for taxes on income is currently being revised, and an exposure draft has been issued.

Comparison in this table is made to International Accounting Standards in force at January 1, 1993. For further details, see the International Accounting Standards chapter.

REPUBLIC OF KOREA

GENERAL NATIONAL INFORMATION

1. Source of Generally Accepted Accounting Principles

Generally Accepted Accounting Principles. **Generally accepted accounting principles (GAAP)** in Korea have been developed in the form of decrees and regulations by the Ministry of Finance (MOF: JAE-MOO BU) and the Securities and Exchange Commission (SEC: JEUNG-KWON KAM-DOK-WON). In January 1982, the SEC issued a regulation, with approval of the MOF, describing the Financial Accounting Standards (FAS: KI-UP HOE-KYE KI-JOON) to be followed by all business enterprises. This regulation, as amended several times, most recently in March 1990, encompasses all prior accounting rules and regulations. Where there is no applicable regulation in FAS, special rules incorporated in other laws and regulations and **accounting principles** and methods established through general practice are followed. In addition, Korean GAAP contain many provisions derived from taxation principles.

2. Audit and Public Company Requirements

Audits (Oe-Bu Kam-Sa). Under the External Audit of Joint-Stock Companies Act, representatives of a corporation are required annually to appoint an external auditor, who is independent of the corporation and all of its affiliates, through a proposal by the internal auditor, resolution of the board of directors and approval at the general shareholders' meeting. Generally, all corporations with total assets exceeding W4,000 million are required to file audited comparative financial statements. External auditors must be members of the Korean Institute of Certified Public Accountants (KICPA). There are restrictions relating to the size of client to which auditors may be appointed. Such restrictions depend on the size of the accounting firm or number of associates. Audits are conducted in accordance with generally accepted auditing standards, as established by the SEC.

The Korean Commercial Code requires companies under its jurisdiction to prepare annual financial statements in compliance with FAS. These financial statements are distributed to all shareholders at least one week prior to the annual meeting. Most provincial companies legislation and securities legislation have similar requirements.

Public Companies (Sang-Jang Hoe-Sa). Corporations that want to issue securities to the public must meet the requirements of and obtain approval from the Securities and

Exchange Commission. The Securities Exchange Act (Jeung-Kwon Keo-Rae-Beop) and relevant regulations cover the public offering procedures, conditions and institutions through which a public offering is made.

The requirements for a company to make a public offering of its equity securities include the following:

- ☐ Incorporated at least five years.
- ☐ **Capital stock** must be more than W3000 million.
- ☐ Greater than 300,000 issued and outstanding shares.
- ☐ Greater than 30 percent of outstanding shares offered to the public.
- ☐ Liability ratio less than 1.5 times the industry average.
- ☐ Operating income, ordinary income and net income to capital stock ratios more than 1.5 times commercial banks' interest rate for time deposits with a maturity of one year.
- ☐ Independent auditors' reports on the financial statements for the previous three years that do not contain an adverse opinion or a disclaimer.

Public companies are required to file audited financial statements with the SEC at least one week before the annual shareholders' meeting, which should be held within three months after the financial year-end. The operating report, which includes the auditors' report and explanation of the company's operating results, must also be presented.

GENERAL ACCOUNTING

3. Financial Statements (Jae-Mu Jei-Pyo)

Basic Accounting Concepts. Accounting information should be prepared and fairly reported on the basis of objective data and evidence. Use of the **historical cost** basis of measurement (modified for revaluation of **fixed assets** in terms of the Asset Revaluation Law [see Section 13]) is required, and transactions and events are recognized in the financial statements at the amounts paid or received or at the fair value ascribed to the transactions when they occurred. The assumption that the entity is a **going concern** is an important concept for comparability of the financial statements and the historical cost basis of measurement. When the entity is not expected to continue in operation for the foreseeable future, a liquidation value basis of measurement should be used.

All revenues and expenses should be reported in the period during which the related transactions occurred (**accrual basis**). However, revenue should be recognized only at the time it is earned (realized); unearned revenue should be excluded from income.

The accounting policies and practices of business enterprises should provide the users of financial statements with an adequate basis for making judgments about the substance of the business operations. However, when reasonable support exists for alternative accounting principles or methods of application, the option that most conservatively presents the financial position should be chosen.

Accounting policies and **procedures** should be applied in a manner consistent with that of the preceding period to provide for comparability between periods, and they should not be changed without appropriate justification.

Contents of Financial Statements. Basic financial statements consist of a balance sheet, statement of income, statement of changes in financial position and statement of (proposed) appropriation of retained earnings or disposition of deficit. A statement of retained earnings, statement of cost of goods manufactured and other schedules should be attached to the financial statements as supplementary schedules if applicable. Significant accounting policies and relevant accounting information should be described in annotations shown in brackets on the face of the financial statements and in notes to the financial statements.

Format of Financial Statements. The format, description of account titles and notes to the financial statements should be clear and concise. Accounts and amounts disclosed in the financial statements should be determined based on **materiality**.

Financial statements should be prepared in a comparative format with those of the preceding year.

Disclosure of Accounting Policies. Significant accounting policies and relevant financial information should be fully disclosed in the notes to the financial statements.

Reference. FAS Articles 2, 3, 4, 5, 65 and 118.

4. Business Combinations (Yeon-Kyeol, Hap-Byeong)

Principles of Consolidation. In principle, a controlling company should prepare **consolidated financial statements**, including the accounts of **subsidiary** or controlled companies, as supplementary financial information. In practice, however, to date companies generally have not prepared consolidated financial statements, and have recorded investments in subsidiary companies on a cost basis. Consolidated financial statements have not been required as the company's primary financial statements. Similarly the **equity method** of accounting has not been required in the primary financial statements, and investments have been carried at cost. The requirement for consolidated financial statements is being enforced by the SEC beginning in 1993.

Accounting for Business Combinations. Accounting for **business combinations** is based on the **purchase method**, unless any relevant regulation requires application of the **pooling of interests method**. Whichever method is used, deferred charges and deferred credits should be treated as zero. However, the value of deferred credits actually payable (e.g., long-term unearned income) should be recorded based on their book value. In addition, **treasury stock** should be recorded at the acquired company's book value.

Control. A controlled company is a company (referred to as "B" corporation or "C" corporation in this paragraph) that has one of the following relationships with another corporation (referred to as "A" corporation in this paragraph):

☐ "A" corporation owns more than half of the total issued and outstanding voting shares of "B" corporation.
☐ "A" corporation owns more than half of the total issued and outstanding voting shares of "B" corporation, and "B" corporation owns more than half of the total issued and outstanding voting shares of "C" corporation.

- □ "A" corporation controls "B" corporation and the aggregate shareholdings of "A" and "B" corporations are more than half of the total issued and outstanding voting shares of "C" corporation.

- □ A corporation should be considered a controlled company if each of the controlling companies and other controlled companies under the two items immediately above owns more than half of the total issued and outstanding voting shares of that corporation or exercises substantial control over that corporation.

- □ A company falling into one of the following categories should be regarded as a controlling company on the basis that it exercises substantial control over the other company, unless other factors, such as stock distribution status, clearly evidence that the company does not exercise substantial control:

   — A company that owns more shares than any other shareholder and owns more than 30 percent of the total outstanding voting capital stock of the controlled company.

   — A company that is not only the largest shareholder of the other company, but the total amount of loans, collateral and payment guarantees made for the other company is more than 30 percent of the controlling company's capital stock.

Goodwill (Young-Up-Kwon). When the acquisition cost is greater than the fair value of the acquired net assets, the difference is identified as **goodwill**. In the contrary case, the excess net asset value over acquisition cost is **negative goodwill** or gain on business combination.

Only purchased goodwill should be recorded in the financial statements. Purchased goodwill can arise through mergers, acquisitions, the purchase of partial business operations or the purchase of leasehold rights. If the excess of acquisition cost over the fair value of the acquired net assets is due to an accumulated deficit in the acquired company, it should not be recorded as goodwill, but as a combination deficit, which is recorded as an adjustment to capital.

Negative goodwill is treated as a gain on business combination in the year of combination; it includes the excess of the value of the assets acquired over the value of the liabilities assumed plus the cash or capital stock (at par value) given in connection with the acquisition. A gain on business combination should be recorded as capital **surplus** in the balance sheet.

Goodwill is reported in the balance sheet as an intangible asset and should be amortized using the straight-line method over no more than five years.

Equity Accounting (Ji-Boon-Beop). An investment in a controlled company that is excluded from consolidation, or in a company of which between 20 and 50 percent of the issued and outstanding shares is owned by the controlling company, should be accounted for in accordance with the equity method in the consolidated financial statements. However, except for the purpose of preparing consolidated financial statements, valuation of the investment account should be based on the historical cost principle.

Minority Interests (So-Soo Ju-Ju Ji-Boon). The portion of a subsidiary's capital that is not attributable to the controlling company should be presented as a **minority interest** in the consolidated balance sheet.

When a net loss attributable to a minority interest exceeds the minority interest, the excess should be charged to the equity of the controlling company. If the subsidiary subsequently earns income, that income should be added to the equity of the controlling company until the earlier net loss has been recovered.

Net income or loss attributable to minority interests should be deducted from or added to net income or loss in the consolidated statement of income.

Disclosure. The following disclosures should be made for consolidations and business combinations.

Consolidations:

☐ Consolidation policies—The names of controlled companies included in and excluded from consolidation; and a description of the business of companies newly consolidated and a description of and reasons for changes, if any, in the consolidation policies.

☐ Accounting policies—The method of offsetting the investment account of the controlling company with the capital account of the controlled company.

☐ The method used to value the investment account.

Business combinations:

☐ Summary of the business combination—The name, representatives and summary of operations of the acquired company; total number of securities issued at combination; stock exchange ratio and any additional cash payment.

☐ Combination policy.

☐ Combination accounting treatment.

Reference. FAS Articles 36 and 94; Consolidated Financial Statements Standard Articles 2, 3, 4, 5, 13, 14, 15, 20 and 21; and Combination Accounting Standard Articles 5, 6, 8 and 13.

5. Joint Ventures (Hab-Jak Hoe-Sa)

There are no specific prescribed accounting standards for **joint ventures**.

Generally, joint ventures prepare their financial statements in accordance with Korean generally accepted accounting principles.

Joint venture financial statements intended for foreign investors may be converted into generally accepted accounting principles of the foreign investors.

6. Foreign Currency Translation (Oe-Hwa Pyeong-Ka, Hwan-San)

Basis of Translation. Domestic operations: Monetary assets and liabilities denominated in a foreign currency should be valued in Korean Won at the exchange rate in effect at the balance sheet date. Foreign exchange gains or losses should be treated as current revenue or expense.

Monetary assets and liabilities generally comprise assets and liabilities that are contractually fixed in specific currency units and do not fluctuate with currency value changes, such as cash on hand, bank deposits, **accounts receivable**, **accounts payable** and loans. However, certain assets and liabilities of both a monetary and nonmonetary nature, such as marketable securities, may be classified and valued as **monetary items** based on the nature and purpose of their ownership.

Foreign subsidiaries: Assets and liabilities of foreign subsidiaries should be translated at the exchange rate as of the balance sheet date, and income and expense should be translated at the average exchange rate during the reporting period.

Foreign operations (foreign branches or offices): The **monetary/nonmonetary method** should be used for translating foreign currency assets and liabilities into Korean Won. However, when translating foreign currency assets and liabilities into Korean Won for the purpose of combining financial statements of foreign operations with those of controlling domestic operations, assets and liabilities of foreign operations may be translated at the exchange rate as of the balance sheet date, and income and expense may be translated at the average exchange rate during the reporting period. Gains or losses from translation of assets and liabilities of foreign operations should be offset against each other, and the difference should be recorded as an overseas business translation debit or credit, which is reported in the equity section of the balance sheet.

The overseas business translation debit or credit should not be amortized, but should be offset against similar debits or credits in following reporting periods. When the foreign operation is closed, the net debit or credit is recognized as an extraordinary gain or loss in that period.

Hedges. When forward exchange contracts, swaps, futures contracts, options and similar contracts are entered into for the purpose of decreasing the risk from future changes in exchange rates or interest rates, the asset or liability arising from the **hedged** transaction should be recorded on the basis of the exchange rate or interest rate fixed in the contracts.

Disclosure. Changes in the overseas business translation debit or credit should be disclosed in the notes to the financial statements. The details of foreign currency assets and liabilities, translation method and translation gains or losses should also be disclosed in the notes.

Reference. FAS Articles 103, 103-2, 103-3 and 118.

7. Changing Prices/Inflation Accounting (Mool-Ka Byeon-Dong Hoe-Kye)

There are no accounting standards specifically covering changing prices or inflation. The historical cost principle is the fundamental **accounting concept** followed in practice.

8. Accounting Changes (Hoe-Kye Byeon-Kyeong)

Accounting Treatment. Changes in accounting principles and accounting estimates are allowed only when the changes result in more objectively reliable financial statements or when the changes are required by new accounting principles. Changes in accounting principles and accounting estimates are applied only prospectively.

Disclosure. The description of the change, reason for the change and effect on the financial statements should be disclosed in the notes.

Reference. FAS Article 111.

9. Prior Period Adjustments (Jeon-Ki Son-Ik Soo-Jeong)

Definition of Adjusting Items. Accounting errors treated as **prior period adjustments** include errors in the application of accounting principles, errors in developing accounting estimates, errors in classification, computational errors, omission of facts and misuse of facts. Any changes in accounting policies or adjustments due to changes in accounting estimates that are based on new events and additional information or experience and are not corrections of accounting errors should not be recorded as prior period adjustments.

Accounting Treatment. Prior period adjustments should include any gains or losses arising from the correction of errors attributable to prior years' financial statements. Gains and losses should be classified separately and recorded as an adjustment of unappropriated retained earnings at the end of the prior year.

Disclosure. The cause and description of the prior period adjustment and the adjusted net income of each adjusted preceding period should be disclosed in the notes.

Reference. FAS Article 110.

10. Post Balance Sheet Events (Dae-Cha-Dae-Jo-Pyo I-Hu Sa-Keon)

Definition. Post balance sheet events can be classified as those that provide further evidence of conditions existing at the balance sheet date and those that are indicative of conditions that arose subsequent to the balance sheet date.

Accounting Treatment. Post balance sheet events providing further evidence of conditions that existed at the balance sheet date should be reflected in those financial statements. Significant post balance sheet events indicative of conditions that arose subsequent to the balance sheet date should be disclosed in the notes.

Disclosure. The nature of material post balance sheet events affecting the financial statements should be disclosed in the notes.

Reference. FAS Article 118-3.

11. Related Party Transactions (Teuk-Su Kwan-Kye-Ja-Wa-Eui Keo-Rae)

Definition. Related parties include the following:

☐ Affiliated companies—Companies that have one of the following relationships:
  — One company owns 20 percent or more of the total issued and outstanding shares of the other company or has an investment of 20 percent or more of its total shareholders' equity.
  — Companies in which the same person owns 50 percent or more of the issued and outstanding shares, or has an investment in both companies equal to 50 percent or more of the respective companies' total shareholders' equity.
  — One company has the ability to control the management of the other.
☐ Related companies—Companies (other than affiliated companies) that have a significant interest, either direct or indirect, in one another. For example, companies that have relationships with each other through the supply of raw materials, lending or borrowing, and affiliation between owners of one company and those of another company.

□ Shareholders, directors and employees—A shareholder who owns shares equal to or greater than 1 percent of the total issued and outstanding shares is considered to be a related party.

Accounting Treatment. Korean standards do not address measurement and accounting treatment of related party transactions. However, certain disclosures are required to assist the user of the financial statements in understanding the impact of such transactions.

Disclosure. Transactions with related parties should be recorded and reported separately. Examples include the following:

□ Investment in equity and debt securities of affiliated companies.
□ Investments in unincorporated affiliates.
□ Short-term and long-term loans to affiliated companies, shareholders, directors and employees.
□ Short-term and long-term loans from affiliated companies, shareholders, directors and employees.
□ Sales to affiliated companies.
□ Purchases from affiliated companies.

The following should be disclosed in the notes to the financial statements:

□ The names of affiliated companies and amounts of related assets and liabilities.
□ Significant transactions with affiliated companies.
□ The names of related companies.
□ Significant transactions with related companies.

The following schedules should be prepared as supplements to the financial statements:

□ Schedule of assets and liabilities of affiliated companies.
□ Schedule of receivables from and payables to shareholders, directors and employees.

Reference. FAS Articles 6, 9, 22, 25, 44, 45, 94 and 118.

12. Segmental Information (Boo-Moon-Byeol Jeong-Bo)

General. There are no prescribed accounting standards for segmental information. However, there are certain disclosure requirements.

Disclosure. Sales and cost of sales may be presented separately for each operating segment. Sales of semifinished goods, by-products and scrap; sales of services; sales to related companies; export sales; and long-term instalment sales that are significant in nature or amount should be presented separately in the income statement, unless supplementary schedules of sales and cost of sales including that information are provided.

Reference. FAS Articles 6-2, 68 and 70.

ACCOUNTING PRINCIPLES FOR SPECIFIC ITEMS—BALANCE SHEET

13. Property, Plant and Equipment (You-Hyeong Ko-Jeong Ja-San)

Classification of Capital and Revenue Expenditure. Expenditures that prolong the useful lives of fixed assets or increase the value of fixed assets should be capitalized and added to the cost of the related fixed assets. Expenditures for restoring fixed assets to their original condition or for maintaining their efficiency should be expensed as incurred.

Basis of Valuation. Fixed assets should be stated at acquisition cost, except for assets appraised in accordance with the Asset Revaluation Law, which should be stated at their appraisal value. When there is a significant difference between the face value and present value of debt related to the acquisition of fixed assets, the assets should be restated at present value.

If a company revalues fixed assets in accordance with the Asset Revaluation Law, they should be recorded at the revalued amount and the asset revaluation surplus should be recorded as a separate component of shareholders' equity.

Cost of property, plant and equipment includes all direct costs of self-constructed assets and purchase costs. Assets acquired in exchange for shares should be valued at the value of the shares issued. Assets acquired in exchange for other assets should be valued at the fair market value of the assets received.

Interest costs, finance charges and similar costs on debt directly related to the manufacture, purchase or construction of property, plant and equipment should be capitalized as part of the cost of the related assets. Interest income from the temporary deposit of funds related to the debt should be offset against the interest costs to be capitalized.

Depreciation (Kam-Ka Sang-Kak). **Depreciation** of property, plant and equipment should be based on the **straight-line**, **declining balance** or **unit-of-production method**.

Additional depreciation is allowed for machinery and equipment that is highly utilized for production during the year or is placed in operation to meet requirements relating to energy saving, new technology implementation, antipollution and similar purposes. A company that elects to record such additional depreciation for qualifying machinery and equipment should record and report it in a special depreciation account. Special depreciation is classified as an extraordinary loss, except for special depreciation based on usage in excess of ordinary working hours, which is classified as manufacturing cost.

Assets that have been fully depreciated should be recorded at salvage value or nominal value. Accumulated depreciation on property, plant and equipment is presented as a deduction from the corresponding fixed asset account, or, if more appropriate, the total accumulated depreciation may be presented in the aggregate as a deduction from total property, plant and equipment.

Disclosure. Interest costs, finance charges and similar costs on debt directly related to the manufacture, purchase or construction of property, plant and equipment should be disclosed in the notes to the financial statements. The nature, basis and amount of special depreciation should also be disclosed. A schedule of property, plant and equipment and a schedule of depreciation should be prepared as supplementary information to the financial statements.

The date of revaluation, net book value by asset category before revaluation, revaluation amount and accounting treatment for revaluation increments should be disclosed in the notes. In years subsequent to the year of revaluation, only the date of revaluation and revaluation increment need be disclosed.

Reference. FAS Articles 30, 76, 87, 87-2, 91, 91-2, 96 and 120; and Asset Revaluation Law.

14. Intangible Assets (Moo-Hyeong Ja-San)

General. **Intangible assets** consist of intangible fixed assets (Mu-Hyeong Ko-Jeong Ja-San) and deferred charges (I-Yeon Ja-San). Intangible fixed assets include goodwill, patents, utility model rights, design rights, trademarks, mining rights, fishing rights and land use rights. Deferred charges include organization costs, preoperating costs, stock issue costs, bond issue costs and research and development costs.

There is no prescribed basis of valuation for intangible assets. They should be valued using the same historical cost accounting principles as used for purchased tangible assets.

Amortization. **Amortization** of intangible assets should be based on the straight-line method or unit-of-production method.

Goodwill and other intangible fixed assets should be amortized using the straight-line method over no more than five years.

Organization costs should be amortized over no more than five years using the straight-line method, starting in the year of incorporation or the year after the final preoperating dividend is paid. Preoperating and stock issue costs should be amortized over no more than three years using the straight-line method, starting in the year operations commence. Bond issue costs should be amortized over no more than three fiscal years using the straight-line method, starting in the year the bonds are issued. If the repayment period of the bonds is less than three years, amortization should be over that period. Research and development costs should be amortized over no more than five years using the straight-line method, starting in the year incurred.

Disclosure. Intangible fixed assets and deferred charges are presented as separate line items in the balance sheet, net of related amortization. A schedule of intangible fixed assets should be presented as supplementary information to the financial statements.

A schedule of deferred charges may be prepared as supplementary information to the financial statements.

Reference. FAS Articles 36, 37, 38, 39, 97, 98 and 120.

15. Leases

Classification. A lease that has noncancellable terms and meets one or more of the following three criteria should be classified as a **financing lease**. Otherwise, it should be classified as an **operating lease**.

- [ ] The lessor transfers ownership of the leased property to the lessee at the end of the lease term.
- [ ] The lease contains a bargain purchase option.
- [ ] The lease term approximates the estimated useful life of the leased property.

Accounting Treatment. A financing lease is accounted for as an instalment purchase by the lessee and as a lending activity by the lessor. Under an operating lease, the leased property is recorded as an asset by the lessor and the lease payments are accounted for as rental income and expense by the lessor and lessee, respectively.

Leveraged Leases. **Leveraged leasing** is rare in Korea.

Disclosure. The lessee is required to disclose future lease payments to be made under both operating leases and financing leases, and the gross amount of assets in use under financing leases. A general description of the lessee's leasing arrangements should be presented for both operating and financing leases. The lessor is required to disclose the acquisition cost of leased property, future lease rentals receivable and the description and amount of assets under operating and financing leases.

Reference. FAS Article 131 and Financial Accounting Standards for Leasing Transactions.

16. Investments (You-Ka Jeung-Kwon & Tu-Ja Ja-San)

Valuation. General: Investments are carried in the financial statements at acquisition cost computed using either the weighted-average or moving-average method. Valuation of investments depends on their classification as current or noncurrent.

Current investments: Current investments are usually carried at the lower of aggregate cost or market value.

Noncurrent investments: If the value of equity securities has declined below their book value, they should be written down to market value (marketable securities) or net asset value (nonmarketable securities). However, investments in affiliated companies, where the investing company exercises significant influence over the investee, may, at the election of the company, be stated at acquisition cost, even if market or net asset value has declined below book value.

Gains/Losses: The calculation of the gain or loss arising from sale of securities should be based on the moving-average or the weighted-average method.

Disclosure. The method of valuation for current and noncurrent investments should be disclosed. For investments in securities, including those of affiliated companies, where the investing company exercises significant influence over the investee, the difference between book value and market value (or net asset value) should be disclosed when those investments have fallen below book value but the company has elected not to devalue the investments to market value or net asset value.

Reference. FAS Articles 12, 13, 22, 24, 92, 94, 118-3 and 120.

17. Accounts Receivable (Mae-Chool Chae-Kwon)

Accounting Treatment. Recognition: The recognition of **revenue** and the related receivables is covered in Section 23.

Discounts (Mae-Chool E-Noo-Ri & Mae-Chool Hal-In): Sales of merchandise or finished goods should be presented net of sales allowances and returns. Trade discounts such as sales price reductions granted to customers based on quantities or amounts transacted during a certain period are recorded as sales allowances when offered. Cash discounts are recorded when early payments are received and are classified as nonoperating expenses.

Allowances for doubtful accounts (Dae-Son Choong-Dang-Keum): There are two methods of computing a provision for doubtful accounts: analysis of individual accounts or prior years' experience.

Once a method is selected, consistency of application should be maintained until use of the method is no longer appropriate.

Factored Receivables.   Accounts receivable that have been factored should be excluded from accounts receivable.

Disclosure.   Receivables are classified as accounts receivable (trade), notes receivable (trade), accounts receivable (other), accrued receivables and other accounts. The description and amounts of notes receivable discounted or endorsed should be disclosed in the financial statements.

Reference.   FAS Articles 13, 14, 15, 68, 75, 81 and 120.

18.   Inventories (Jae-Ko Ja-San) and Work in Progress (Jae-Kong-Poom)

General Accounting Treatment.   **Inventories** such as merchandise, finished goods, semifinished goods, work in process, raw materials and supplies should be stated in the balance sheet at production cost computed using any of the following methods: **specific identification, first-in first-out, last-in first-out**, weighted-average or **retail pricing**.

If the market value of any inventory item has declined below cost, the inventory should be valued at market. Inventory should be written down for quality deterioration, obsolescence and spoilage.

Market value is based on a price survey index published by a reputable price survey institute and represents the average wholesale price for one month preceding the balance sheet date. If a relevant market price is not included in the price survey index, the inventory should be valued at **net realizable value**, which is defined as the estimated proceeds of sale of the inventory less estimated costs of sale.

Long-Term Contracts (Jang-Ki Keon-Seol Kong-Sa Kye-Yak).   Revenue recognition for long-term contracts is covered in Section 23. Construction costs incurred during the year on contracts in progress at the financial year-end are recorded as work in progress in the balance sheet, less any amounts charged to the income statement under the **percentage of completion method** of accounting for long-term contracts, if applicable.

Disclosure.   Required footnote disclosures for inventory include the following:

☐   Accounting policies relating to inventory.
☐   The basis of valuing inventory.
☐   The amounts of significant losses arising from revaluation of inventory.

Reference.   FAS Articles 16, 67, 81, 93, 118-3 and 120.

19. Current Liabilities (You-Dong Bu-Chae)

General Accounting Treatment.   **Current liabilities** should include amounts payable within one year from the date of the balance sheet. Current liabilities should be classified as follows: trade accounts payable, trade notes payable, bank overdrafts, short-term borrowings, other accounts payable, advance receipts, withholdings, accrued expenses, accrued income taxes, short-term loans, current portion of long-term debt, unearned income and allowances to be written off within one year (which should be presented in accounts descriptive of their purposes). Contra accounts and other memorandum accounts should not be presented in the balance sheet as liabilities.

Creation of General and Specific Provisions (Bu-Chae-Seong Choong-Dang-Keum). Provisions for future expenses (i.e., expenses not related to current revenues) are not permitted. However, expenses related to current revenues that are certain of being paid after the balance sheet date and may reasonably be estimated should be accrued as allowances of a liability nature. Such allowances include provisions for severance pay, repairs and maintenance, product warranties and guarantees and similar items. Allowances that are to be written off proportionately over several years, or for which it is difficult to reasonably estimate the period of write-off, may be classified as long-term liabilities.

Disclosure.   Short-term borrowings and other accounts payable represented by promissory notes should be disclosed in the financial statements.

Reference.   FAS Articles 44, 47, 47-2, 53, 99, 118-3 and 120.

20. Long-Term Debt (Ko-Jeong Bu-Chae)

General Accounting Treatment.   Long-term debt includes bonds, convertible bonds, other long-term borrowings and provisions for severance pay. The general accounting treatment applied to these items is basically the same as for current liabilities.

In situations where the difference between the face value and present value of debt arising from transactions on a long-term deferred payment basis or similar transactions is significant, the debt should be valued at present value. A premium or discount on bonds issued, if any, should be presented as a deduction from the recorded bond amount.

A premium or discount on bonds should be amortized using the effective interest method over the period the bond is expected to be outstanding. Amortization of premium or discount should be added to or subtracted from interest on bonds. Treasury bonds acquired with the intention of resale, such as those acquired for the temporary use of idle cash, should be presented as a separate component of other current assets. However, if treasury bonds were acquired in order to extinguish debt, they should be deducted from the related bond account.

Debt Restructuring.   There are no official accounting standards for **troubled debt restructurings**. The aggregate net gain or loss from debt restructuring is generally included in net income. Where the creditor is also a significant shareholder of the debtor, it may be appropriate to record the gain as a capital transaction.

Debt Extinguishment.   There are no official accounting standards for early debt extinguishment; however, Korean practice normally parallels that in the United States. A gain or loss arises on early extinguishment of a debt when the reacquisition price and the net carrying amount of the debt extinguished before maturity are different. The gain or loss should be included in income as an extraordinary item when the debt is extinguished.

Disclosure.   Convertible bonds should be presented separately; their terms should be disclosed in the notes to the financial statements. The purpose for acquisition of treasury bonds and other pertinent data should be disclosed in a note. There are no specific disclosure requirements concerning debt restructuring and early debt extinguishment. There should be footnote disclosure of the amount of the estimated severance benefits payable to officers and employees as of the balance sheet date, the amount recorded, amounts paid during the year and the accounting treatment for severance pay.

Reference.   FAS Articles 45, 47, 47-2, 48, 102-2, 118-3 and 120.

21.   Contingencies (U-Bal Sa-Hang)

General.   **Contingencies** are not accrued in the financial statements.

Contingent Losses (U-Bal Son-Sil).   If the occurrence of a loss becomes probable and the amount of the loss is estimable, the amount and nature of the contingent liability should be disclosed in the notes. A description of assets pledged as collateral for either the company or others should also be disclosed in the notes.

Contingent Gains (U-Bal I-Ik).   If the occurrence of a contingent gain is likely, its existence should be disclosed in the notes. For example, the nature and prospect of pending litigation should be disclosed.

Disclosure.   Disclosure of a contingent gain or loss should include sufficient details to provide a general understanding of the contingency.

Reference.   FAS Article 118-3.

22.   Capital (Ja-Bon) and Reserves (Ing-Yeo-Keum)

General.   Shareholders' equity is generally classified into **share capital**, capital surplus, **retained earnings** and capital adjustments.

Share Capital (Ja-Bon-Keum).   Share capital consists of different classes of capital stock, each class characterized by its voting, dividend and capital repayment rights. **Common shares** are those that represent the residual equity in the earnings of a company. Senior shares are all other types of capital stock, including **preferred shares** that participate with common shares but whose participation rights are effectively restricted.
   A company's own shares acquired should be carried at cost and shown as a deduction from shareholders' equity until they are cancelled or resold.

Other Reserves. Capital surplus (Ja-Bon Ing-Yeo-Keum): Capital surplus includes capital reserves and asset revaluation surplus. Capital reserves are further classified as:

- ☐ Paid-in capital in excess of **par value**.
- ☐ Gain on retirement of capital stock.
- ☐ Gain on business combinations.
- ☐ Other capital surplus.

Other capital surplus includes government subsidies, contributions for capital construction, gains from insurance settlements on fixed assets, capital contributions and liabilities forgiven for recovery of capital deficiencies, gain on sale of **treasury stock** and other similar items.

Retained earnings (I-Ik Ing-Yeo-Keum): Retained earnings include legal reserves, other statutory reserves, discretionary reserves and unappropriated retained earnings or undisposed deficit. Unappropriated retained earnings or undisposed deficit should present separately the adjusted prior year's unappropriated retained earnings or undisposed deficit and the current year's net income or loss.

Capital adjustments (Ja-Bon Jo-Jeong Kye-Jeong): Capital adjustments include discounts on stock issued, treasury stock, prepaid dividends during preoperating periods, stock rights, convertible rights and overseas business translation debit or credit.

Dividends (Bae-Dang Keum): Dividends can be declared only from unappropriated retained earnings, except for dividends paid by the issue of shares, which can be declared from either restricted reserves (capital surplus, legal reserves or other statutory reserves) or unappropriated retained earnings.

Disclosure. Each legal class of share capital should be presented separately, along with disclosure of the par value and number of shares authorized, issued and outstanding. Subscriptions received for issuance of new share capital should be presented in a separate account in the shareholders' equity section of the balance sheet. The number of the new shares to be issued, due date for payment of subscriptions and amount, if any, to be retained as additional capital should be disclosed in the notes. There should also be footnote disclosure of the amount of asset revaluation surplus and related details established pursuant to the Asset Revaluation Law. In addition, the following items should be disclosed in the notes:

- ☐ Surplus, if any, restricted from cash dividends in accordance with the provisions of laws or other regulations, other than capital reserves, asset revaluation surplus and legal reserves.
- ☐ The account names and amounts of additional capital or retained earnings applied to dispose of a deficit, within two years prior to the beginning of the current fiscal year, and the date of the general shareholders' meeting approving such disposition.
- ☐ The details of shares mutually owned among affiliated companies and other types of shares that are restricted as to voting rights in accordance with the provisions of other laws or regulations.

Reference. FAS Articles 54, 55, 56, 57, 57-2, 60, 61, 62, 62-2, 95, 104, 105, 106 and 118-3.

ACCOUNTING PRINCIPLES FOR SPECIFIC ITEMS—
INCOME STATEMENT

23. Revenue Recognition (Su-Ik In-Sik)

General Principles. Revenue is recognized when performance has occurred and reasonable assurance exists regarding measurement and collectibility of the consideration to be received. Revenue from a transaction involving the sale of goods would be recognized when the seller has transferred to the buyer the significant risks and rewards of ownership of the goods.

Under Korean GAAP, sales revenue should be recognized at the time of selling goods or rendering services, except for consignment sales, **instalment sales**, conditional sales, subscription sales and construction contracts.

Sales of merchandise or finished goods should be presented net of sales allowances and returns. Discounts granted to customers based on quantities or amounts transacted during a certain period should be included in sales allowances.

Long-Term Contracts (Jang-Ki Keon-Seol Kong-Sa Kye-Yak). Contract sales should be recognized when merchandise is physically delivered or service is rendered. However, for long-term contract sales, revenue may be realized based on the percentage of completion method. Revenue from construction contracts should be realized based on either the percentage of completion method or the **completed contract method**. The percentage of completion method is applied when revenues, costs and percentage of completion relating to construction work in progress can be reasonably estimated.

Instalment Sales (Hal-Boo Mae-Chool). Instalment sales should be recognized when the merchandise is physically delivered. However, long-term instalment sales may be recognized when each instalment becomes due.

Rights of Return. In Korea, a buyer's right to return goods is not usually an ownership risk of significant magnitude to prevent a seller from recognizing a sale at the time possession initially passes to the buyer. The more appropriate accounting treatment would be to record a provision—for example, a provision for warranty—when this risk is considered to be significant.

Product Financing. A **product financing arrangement** occurs when an entity sells and simultaneously either agrees to repurchase the same or substantially identical products or guarantees the resale price to third parties. It also includes situations where an intermediary purchases items on the entity's behalf and the entity simultaneously purchases them from the intermediary. In Korea, product financing is rare.

Disclosure. The amount of revenue recognized during the period should be disclosed in the income statement.

Reference. FAS Articles 67 and 68.

24. Government Grants and Assistance (Jeong-Bu Bo-Jo-Keum)

Accounting Treatment. In Korea, there are no accounting standards specifically dealing with accounting for government grants and assistance. Government assistance related to **capital expenditures** is generally included in capital reserves.

Disclosure. Under Korean GAAP, assets of other parties (including the government) provided as collateral on behalf of a company or guarantees extended by other parties on behalf of a company should be disclosed in the notes.

Reference. FAS Articles 57 and 118-3.

25. Research and Development (Yeon-Ku Kae-Bal-Bi)

Definitions. Research is a planned and creative searching activity designed to discover new scientific knowledge or to develop new applications for existing scientific knowledge for a certain practical purpose. Development is a planned and systematic activity designed to devise, manufacture and test a new or significantly improved product or process using the research findings or other knowledge. New product or new technology means product or technology newly introduced by a company, including services, raw materials, processes, equipment, and so on. Costs related to research and development are the total costs incurred, directly or indirectly, for research and development activities.

Accounting Treatment. Research and development costs should be deferred and amortized over future years if they meet the following criteria: (a) they are incurred in relation to a particular product or technology; (b) each element of the costs is identifiable; and (c) future benefits sufficient in amount to recover the related costs are reasonably expected. Other research and development costs should be expensed in the year they are incurred.

Expenses incurred in connection with the development of new markets or adoption of new management systems should be recorded as expenses in the year when they are incurred. When an agreement related to new products or new technology satisfies the following conditions, related expenses, depending on their nature, may be recorded as intangible assets: (a) the legal or economic right to manufacture the related product or use the related technology is secured by the agreement; and (b) future benefits to recover the related expenses are secured by the agreement.

Intangible assets recorded pursuant to the above provision should be amortized by the straight-line method from the year when production of the related product or use of the related technology begins through the year in which the agreement expires.

Disclosure. Fixed assets used for research and development activities should be disclosed separately.

Reference. FAS Article 38 and Financial Accounting Standards for Research and Development Costs.

26. Capitalized Interest Costs (Keon-Seol Ja-Keum I-Ja)

Accounting Treatment. Interest expense and other financing charges for debt directly related to the manufacture, purchase or construction of fixed assets and incurred prior to completion of the assets should be capitalized as part of their cost. However, capitalized interest expense should be reduced by the interest income earned on temporary investment of the proceeds of the debt.

Disclosure. The amount and nature of any interest capitalized should be disclosed in the notes.

Reference. FAS Article 96.

27. Imputed Interest (You-Hyo I-Ja)

General. **Imputed interest** on the use of equity funds is not a general accounting practice in Korea.

Accounting Treatment. When the difference between the face value and present value of debt or assets arising from transactions on a long-term deferred payment basis or similar transactions is significant, the debt or the asset should be recorded at present value. Present value should represent the fair value or discounted value of future cash flows.

Disclosure. The interest rate applied in discounting future cash flows and the accounting method used should be disclosed in the notes.

Reference. FAS Article 102-2.

28. Extraordinary or Unusual Items (Teuk-Byeol Son-Ik)

Extraordinary Items. Korean GAAP specify certain transactions that must be recorded as extraordinary gains or losses, including:

- □ Gain or loss on disposition of investments.
- □ Gain or loss on disposition of fixed assets.
- □ Gain from collection of receivables previously written off.
- □ Casualty losses.
- □ Special depreciation.

Disclosure. Extraordinary or unusual items are presented separately, on a pretax basis, in the income statement after ordinary income or loss. As noted above, Korean GAAP specify items that must be classified separately as extraordinary items in the income statement.

Reference. FAS Articles 86, 87 and 87-2.

29. Income Taxes (Beop-In-Sei Deung)

Accounting Treatment. The provision for income taxes is based on the corporation tax and resident tax surcharges currently payable. No deferred income taxes are provided for **temporary differences** between accounting income and taxable income. The additional payment or refund of taxes related to a prior year is recorded as a prior period adjustment. Operating loss carryforwards or carrybacks are not required to be disclosed under Korean GAAP.

Disclosure. A supplementary schedule of income taxes should be prepared.

Reference. FAS Articles 89 and 120.

30. Postretirement Benefits (Yeon-Keum Hoe-Kye)

General. There are no formal accounting practices for pensions in Korea, nor have any pronouncements been issued on this topic. At present, a severance benefit plan exists under the Korean Labor Standards Law, which entitles employees with more than one year of service to receive a lump-sum payment upon termination of employment. The amount of benefit is based on the length of service and rate of pay (i.e., it is a **defined benefit plan**). A National Pension Scheme came into effect in 1988, which is a **defined contribution plan**.

To date, Korean companies have not established supplemental retirement benefit plans for their employees. Korean GAAP require that companies set up a severance accrual at the balance sheet date assuming all employees terminated their employment as of that date. The full amount of the current year's increase in the severance obligation should be recorded. Prior years' underaccrued liabilities should be fully accrued within ten years.

31. Discontinued Operations (Joong-Dan Young-Eop Jeong-Bo)

An accounting standard for discontinued operations has not been developed in Korea, and thus no additional disclosure is required unless the discontinued operations are significant.

32. Earnings per Share (Ju-Dang I-Ik)

Definition. Earnings per share represent the portion of income for a period attributable to a share of issued capital stock.

Methods of Calculation. Earnings per share (EPS) information is required to be calculated on the basis of the weighted-average number of common shares issued and outstanding. Adjusted or diluted EPS is not required to be disclosed; however, in the case of a complex capital structure, the footnotes should disclose that EPS could be lower due to the exercise or conversion of dilutive securities.

Disclosure. Earnings per share should be disclosed in the income statement. The method of calculating EPS should be disclosed in the notes. It is not necessary to disclose adjusted or fully diluted EPS.

Reference. FAS Article 90-2.

Appendix

DO KOREAN STANDARDS OR PREVALENT PRACTICE SUBSTANTIALLY COMPLY WITH INTERNATIONAL ACCOUNTING STANDARDS?

Section	Topic	Substantially complies with IAS?	Comments
3.	Basic accounting concepts and conventions	Yes	
	Contents of financial statements	Yes	
4.	Business combinations*	Yes	The requirement to prepare consolidated financial statements began to be enforced in 1993
5.	Joint ventures	No	
6.	Foreign currency translation*	Yes	
8.	Accounting changes*	Yes	
9.	Prior period adjustments*	Yes	
10.	Post balance sheet events	Yes	
11.	Related party transactions	Yes	
12.	Segmental information	No	
13.	Property, plant and equipment*	Yes	Except accelerated depreciation is permitted
15.	Leases	Yes	
16.	Investments	Yes	
17.	Accounts receivable	Yes	
18.	Inventories and work in progress*	Yes	
19.	Current liabilities	Yes	
20.	Long-term debt	Yes	
21.	Contingencies	Yes	
22.	Capital and reserves	Yes	
23.	Revenue recognition*	Yes	
24.	Government grants and assistance	No	
25.	Research and development*	Yes	
26.	Capitalization of interest costs*	Yes	

Appendix (*Continued*)

Section	Topic	Substantially complies with IAS?	Comments
28.	Extraordinary or unusual items*	No	
29.	Income tax**	No	
30.	Postretirement benefits*	No	

*These topics are subject to change as a result of the IASC Improvements Project—see the appendix to the International Accounting Standards chapter.

**The IAS on accounting for taxes on income is currently being revised, and an exposure draft has been issued.

Comparison in this table is made to International Accounting Standards in force at January 1, 1993. For further details, see the International Accounting Standards chapter.

LUXEMBOURG

GENERAL NATIONAL INFORMATION

1. Source of Generally Accepted Accounting Principles

Generally accepted accounting principles are essentially established by law. The basic accounting law of May 4, 1984 was introduced to accommodate the provisions of the Fourth Directive of the European Community (EC). The law of July 11, 1988 sets out generally accepted consolidation principles and is based on the Seventh EC Directive.

In the absence of any Luxembourg **accounting standards** or **principles** on a specific subject, companies generally refer to International Accounting Standards (IASs) or, if applicable and not in contradiction with general Luxembourg accounting standards or principles, to the accounting standards of the **parent company**.

The Luxembourg Companies Law (loi fondamentale concernant les sociétés commerciales) contains provisions regarding profit appropriation, preparation and publication of financial statements and the appointment of auditors.

2. Audit and Public Company Requirements

Audits. The Companies Law requires that substantially all companies be audited by a statutory auditor (commissaire) or by an independent auditor (réviseur d'entreprises). The size of companies that a statutory auditor can audit is limited to companies that do not exceed two of the following three criteria:

Total assets	LUF 77 million
Turnover	LUF 160 million
Average number of employees	50

An independent auditor must be a member of the Luxembourg Auditors Institute (Institut des Réviseurs d'Entreprises—IRE) and must fulfill its training and examination requirements. Those requirements include an appropriate university degree or its equivalent in economic and financial studies, and a three-year training period with an independent auditor and a passing grade on the Institute's examinations.

Independent auditors are generally elected either by the annual general meeting of shareholders or by the board of directors. The auditors should be independent, competent and individuals of professional integrity. The responsibilities of independent auditors are to give an opinion on the financial statements presented by the company, including whether the financial statements present a true and fair view of the financial position and results of operations and whether the directors' report is in accordance with the financial statements.

Compliance with the requirements of the professional guidelines issued by the Luxembourg Auditors Institute is compulsory for its members acting in the capacity of independent auditors.

Exact filing requirements vary with the size of the company. Furthermore, exemptions are granted for:

□ The financial statements of Luxembourg **subsidiaries** if the parent company, which has to be located in the EC, has assumed responsibility for the liabilities of the subsidiary.

□ The **consolidated financial statements** of Luxembourg intermediate holdings and subholdings.

In both cases, the consolidated financial statements of the parent company must be filed and must include the financial statements of the subsidiary or the consolidated financial statements of the intermediate holding or subholding company.

Public Companies. The Commissariat aux Bourses (Exchange Supervisory Commission), which acts as the national supervisory authority (under the jurisdiction of the Finance Minister), is mainly responsible for the regulation and control of all organized markets. The Société de la Bourse de Luxembourg (the Luxembourg Stock Exchange), established in 1927, is responsible for day-to-day management of the exchange, under the supervision of the Commissariat.

The issue and listing of securities are governed by applicable legal and regulatory provisions, which require an issuer to publish a prospectus containing the terms and conditions of the issue, and giving information on the issuer's financial status, activities, management and future prospects. Ensuring compliance with these and other provisions is the responsibility of the Commissariat and the Bourse. All applications must be made through an approved member of the Bourse and require approval by the Commissariat.

The public offering prospectus and the listing particulars are required to contain the information that, according to the nature of the issuer and of the securities concerned, is necessary to enable investors and their investment advisors to make an informed assessment of the assets and liabilities, financial position, profits and losses, prospects and status of the issuer and of the rights and obligations attaching to the securities. Financial information for at least the past two years is generally required. Any additional information deemed useful or necessary to provide full and fair disclosure to the public may also be requested. The Commissariat may recognize, under certain conditions, the public offering prospectus approved by a competent authority of another EC Member State as listing particulars for admission to listing on the Luxembourg Bourse.

Regular financial information, including audited annual financial statements, must be presented as required by the law. Additional information may be requested by the authorities where considered necessary to provide a full understanding of the company's financial status and activities. The law specifies the format and minimum necessary disclosures for such financial information.

Reference. Company Law—Section XIII—Law of May 4, 1984; RGD (Grand-Ducal Decree) of December 28, 1990 (Admission to Stock Exchange).

GENERAL ACCOUNTING

3. Financial Statements (Comptes Annuels)

Basic Accounting Concepts. The fundamental **accounting concepts** for the preparation of financial statements are:

- ☐ **going concern**
- ☐ **prudence**
- ☐ consistency
- ☐ **matching**
- ☐ **accruals**

No offset between assets and liabilities, and income and expenses is allowed.

Financial statements are prepared using the **historical cost** basis. Revaluation of fixed assets or financial assets is currently not allowed although subsidiaries and participating interests (greater than 20 percent owned) can be accounted for on the equity basis. Noncompliance with the basic accounting concepts is allowed only in exceptional circumstances and if it can be justified. The justification and the impact of the noncompliance on the net equity and on the results have to be disclosed in the notes to the accounts.

Contents of Financial Statements. The annual financial statements include a balance sheet, income statement and notes thereto. A statement of changes in financial position or of cash flows is not required. The auditors' report must be included in the published financial statements. A directors' report, commenting on important developments during the year and other specified matters, must either be published with the financial statements or be available on request at the company's registered office. The financial statements must be prepared so as to give a true and fair view of the company's financial position at the end of the period and of its results for the period. Certain specific information not directly related to the balance sheet or the income statement must also be disclosed in the notes (e.g., contingent liabilities, average number of employees, remuneration of, loans to and guarantees given for present or former supervisory and management board members).

Format of Financial Statements. The financial statements must be prepared in accordance with one of the formats prescribed by law. Departures from these formats are permitted only if it can be demonstrated that adopting the fixed formats would impair the true and fair view given by the accounts; supporting reasons must be disclosed in the notes. Prior year comparative figures must be presented.

Disclosure of Accounting Policies. The principles underlying the valuation of assets and the determination of operating results must be disclosed for each item. The principles used in translating foreign currency and the treatment of exchange differences must also be disclosed. In exceptional cases, where application of accounting policies set out in the law would result in the financial statements not giving a true and fair view, these policies may be departed from. The details and justification of any such departure must be explained in the notes, and the differences resulting from the departure must be indicated.

Reference. Company Law—Section XIII—Law of May 4, 1984; RGD of June 29, 1984 (Holdings).

4. Business Combinations

Principles of Consolidation. All parent companies must prepare, in addition to their own financial statements, consolidated financial statements consisting of a balance sheet, income statement and notes. A consolidated directors' report should also be prepared.

A parent company is exempt from preparing consolidated financial statements if:

☐ It is a subsidiary of a company that prepares and publishes audited consolidated financial statements; or

☐ On a consolidated basis, it does not exceed two of the following three limits:

Total assets	LUF 775 million
Turnover	LUF 1600 million
Average number of employees	500

This exemption does not apply if any of the companies of the group is listed on a stock exchange in the EC.

A financial holding company is exempt from preparing consolidated financial statements if:

☐ During the year, it has not intervened directly or indirectly in the management of its subsidiaries.

☐ During the current and the five previous years, it has not used its voting rights with respect to the nomination of a member of the supervisory or management board, or when its voting rights had to be exercised, no majority shareholder or partner of the **holding company** nor any of its supervisory or management board members was a member of the supervisory or management board of the subsidiary and the so-appointed members exercise their duties without interference of the holding company or of one of its subsidiaries.

☐ It has granted loans only to companies in which it holds a participating interest. If loans were granted to other beneficiaries, these loans had to have been reimbursed at the previous year-end.

☐ The exemption has been approved by the appropriate regulatory body after verification of compliance with the previous three requirements.

In general, all subsidiaries should be consolidated. However, in certain circumstances, as set out below, a subsidiary can be accounted for using the **equity method**.

A subsidiary need not be included in the consolidated financial statements if:

☐ It is not **material** to the consolidated position (two or more subsidiaries satisfying this requirement are considered in the aggregate); or

☐ Serious long-term restrictions substantially hinder the effective control over the subsidiary or the use of its assets; or

☐ The information necessary for inclusion of the subsidiary in the consolidated financial statements cannot be obtained without disproportionate expense or undue delays; or

☐ The shares are held exclusively with a view to their subsequent sale.

Accounting for Business Combinations. The **purchase method** is normally used to account for **business combinations**. The **pooling of interests method** can be used if specific requirements are met.

Proportional consolidation of an entity is permitted when one or more group companies are entitled to jointly exercise rights of authority.

Control. A subsidiary is defined as a company in which the investor:

☐ Holds more than 50 percent of the voting rights of the shareholders or partners; or

☐ Is authorized to appoint or discharge more than half of the members of the management or supervisory board and is at the same time a shareholder or partner of that company; or

☐ Is a shareholder or partner and exercises (as a consequence of an agreement with others entitled to vote) more than half of the voting rights of the shareholders or partners.

A participating interest (**associated company**) is a legal entity to which the investing company has provided capital for the purposes of furthering its own business activities by establishing a long-term relationship, regardless of the percentage of ownership. If an interest of at least 20 percent of the issued capital of an entity is held, it will automatically be presumed to be a participating interest of the investing company.

Goodwill. **Goodwill**, positive or negative, is based on the difference between the value of consideration given and the book value of the net assets acquired at the acquisition date. Goodwill should be allocated, as far as possible, to assets and liabilities with market values above or below their carrying values. Any remaining difference is included in the consolidated balance sheet under an appropriate heading as an asset if positive or as a liability if negative.

A positive consolidation difference must be written off in the consolidated income statement over a maximum of five years. However, goodwill can be amortized over a longer period, provided it does not exceed the estimated useful life of the goodwill, but this must be justified in the notes.

A positive consolidation difference can also be charged directly to shareholders' equity.

A negative consolidation difference can be included in the consolidated income statement only if:

☐ It arises from the expectation of unfavorable future results of the subsidiary or from charges that the subsidiary may incur in the future; or

☐ It represents a realized capital gain.

Equity Accounting. Participating interests (associated companies) must be accounted for using the equity method if the investor exercises significant influence over the commercial and financial policies. Significant influence is presumed to exist if 20 percent or more of the total voting rights is owned.

Subsidiaries are accounted for by the equity method if their activities are so different that consolidation would impair the true and fair view of the group's financial statements. This has to be duly explained in the notes. Moreover, if the financial statements of the subsidiaries are not published in Luxembourg, copies must be attached to the consolidated financial statements or made available to the public at the registered office of the parent company.

When the equity method is used, an undistributable reserve must be set up for the investor's share of income reported by participating interests, less dividends received or whose payment can be claimed from them.

Minority Interests.   **Minority interests** in fully consolidated companies are disclosed separately in the balance sheet immediately after shareholders' equity, and in the income statement as a deduction from the total net group income.

Disclosure.   The consolidation policy, including the criteria on which it is based, must be disclosed. The parent company must disclose the names, registered offices and level of participation in the issued share capital of all subsidiaries and other group companies. For nonconsolidated interests, net equity and results also have to be disclosed.

The information stated above need not be included in the notes if:

- ☐ It has been filed with the Office of the Clerk of the District Court (Greffe du Tribunal d'Arrondissement) and that fact has been stated in the notes; or
- ☐ This disclosure would harm severely one of the companies and that fact has been stated in the notes.

If subsidiaries are not consolidated, the reasons for their exclusion must be given.

Movements in consolidation differences and in differences arising from the application of the equity method must be disclosed in the notes.

Reference.   Company Law—Section XVI—Law of July 11, 1988.

5. Joint Ventures

Accounting for Investments in Joint Ventures.   Luxembourg regulations do not specifically address accounting for **joint ventures**. Joint ventures may be incorporated or unincorporated. Generally, companies follow International Accounting Standards.

Jointly Controlled Entities.   The usual methods of accounting for joint ventures are either the equity method or proportionate consolidation.

Jointly Controlled Operations.   The accounting treatment in IAS 31 would be appropriate in Luxembourg.

Jointly Controlled Assets.   The accounting treatment in IAS 31 would be appropriate in Luxembourg.

Transactions Between Venturers and the Joint Venture. In general, the contribution of assets to a joint venture in exchange for an interest in the venture does not give rise to a gain or loss on disposal in the contributor's financial statements. Gains resulting from other transactions between the venturer and the joint venture should be recognized only to the extent of the interests of nonrelated venturers until the assets are sold to third parties. However, losses should be recognized in their entirety.

When a venturer purchases assets from a joint venture, the venturer does not recognize its share of the related profits of the joint venture until it resells the assets to an independent party. A venturer recognizes its share of losses resulting from these transactions in the same way as profits except that losses are recognized immediately when they represent a reduction in the **net realizable value** of **current assets** or a decline, other than temporary, in the carrying amount of long-term assets.

Disclosure. Generally, a venture would disclose a listing and description of interests in significant joint ventures and the proportion of ownership interest held in jointly controlled entities.

Where the venturer is liable for any contingent liability or commitment with respect to the joint venture, this should be disclosed.

Accounting by Joint Ventures. Generally accepted accounting principles apply to all assets and liabilities and operations of joint ventures. However, there is little guidance in Luxembourg on accounting by joint ventures for assets contributed by the venturers. At present there are two permitted alternatives:

☐ Fair value.
☐ The carrying value of the assets in the contributor's financial statements.

6. Foreign Currency Translation

General. There are no pronouncements on accounting for foreign currency translation. Generally accepted accounting principles are based on tax laws, perceived good accounting practice and international practice.

Foreign Currency Denominated Transactions. Transactions in foreign currencies should be recorded at the exchange rate prevailing at the transaction date. Foreign currency **monetary items** outstanding at the balance sheet date should be translated at exchange rates prevailing at the balance sheet date. Unrealized exchange losses should be expensed. Unrealized exchange gains can be deferred or taken to income.

Foreign Operations. The financial statements of foreign subsidiaries included in consolidated financial statements must be translated into the reporting currency using either the **monetary/nonmonetary method** (for operations in hyperinflationary environments) or the **closing rate method**. Under the monetary/nonmonetary method, nonmonetary assets are translated at the rate applicable when these amounts were recorded as assets. Monetary assets and liabilities, monetary rights and commitments are translated at the closing (balance sheet date) rate. Under the closing rate method, all monetary and nonmonetary assets, liabilities, rights and commitments are translated at the closing rate.

Income and expenses are translated at the rates applicable when they were recorded or at an average rate for the **financial period**.

If the monetary/nonmonetary method is used, translation differences must be recorded in the income statement. Unrealized exchange differences may, however, be treated using the methods applied by the consolidating company.

If the closing rate method is applied, exchange differences must be recorded in the liabilities section of the balance sheet under an appropriate heading.

Hedges. Monetary assets or liabilities denominated in foreign currencies and **hedged** through a foreign currency forward contract are generally translated into the reporting currency at the hedging rate.

Disclosure. The methods used to translate foreign currency items and financial statements of foreign subsidiaries and associated enterprises into the reporting currency must be disclosed. The treatment of differences arising on translation should also be disclosed.

Reference. Company Law—Section XIII—Law of May 4, 1984.

7. Changing Prices/Inflation Accounting

There is no legal requirement and it is not standard practice to provide for the effect of inflation in financial statements.

8. Accounting Changes

Accounting Treatment. Changes in accounting principles may be made only for well-founded reasons. The effect of changes in valuation rules is generally accounted for prospectively.

Disclosure. Any changes in the valuation rules must be disclosed and justified in the notes. An evaluation of the effect on the financial position and results must also be given in the period in which the change occurs.

9. Prior Period Adjustments

All items that relate to prior periods are generally included in the income statement of the current year. However, the notes should disclose if income or expenses of the current year are significantly affected by those relating to a previous period.

Reference. Company Law—Section XIII—Law of May 4, 1984.

10. Post Balance Sheet Events

Definition. A distinction is made in information that becomes known after the balance sheet date between that which:

(a) provides further details on the financial position at that date.

(b) gives no further data on the situation at the balance sheet date.

Accounting Treatment. Information of type (a) should be accounted for in the financial statements. Information of type (b) should not be accounted for in the financial statements unless it casts doubt on the assumption of the entity's ability to continue as a going concern.

Disclosure. Information of type (b) that becomes known after the balance sheet date and that has important financial consequences (either favorable or unfavorable) should be disclosed in the additional information. This disclosure should include the nature of the event(s) and an estimate of the financial statement effects. If an estimate is not considered possible, this should be indicated. Information must also be given in the directors' report.

Reference. IRE recommendation No. 13.

11. Related Party Transactions

Definition. Parties are considered to be related if one party has the ability to control the other party or exercise significant influence over the other party in making financial and operating decisions. A related party transaction is a transfer of resources or obligations between related parties, regardless of whether a price is charged.

Accounting Treatment. No specific rules govern the accounting treatment of related party transactions, and normal accounting principles and practices are followed. In most cases, income tax considerations are a prime inducement to adhere strictly to the arm's-length basis.

Disclosure. The standard formats for the financial statements provide for separate disclosure of investments (both current and long term) with related parties, as well as separate disclosure of certain income and expenses (notably interest) pertaining to related parties.

Reference. Company Law—Section XIII—Law of May 4, 1984.

12. Segmental Information

Disclosure. An analysis of **turnover** by activity and geographical markets must be disclosed, where significant.

Reference. Company Law—Section XIII—Law of May 4, 1984.

ACCOUNTING PRINCIPLES FOR SPECIFIC ITEMS— BALANCE SHEET (BILAN)

13. Property, Plant and Equipment

Classification of Capital and Revenue Expenditure. Physical items that have a useful life of more than one year and are not regarded as inventories are considered tangible **fixed assets**. For reasons of efficiency, tangible assets of low value are usually expensed in the period of acquisition.

Expenditures to maintain operations should be expensed when incurred.

Basis of Valuation. Property, plant and equipment are stated at acquisition cost less **depreciation**. Revaluations are currently not permitted.

Both purchased and self-constructed assets are permitted to be capitalized at a cost that fairly reflects the expenditure necessarily incurred to bring the assets to a location and condition ready for use. Thus interest and overhead on self-constructed assets may be capitalized, provided it can be demonstrated that these are costs of making the assets ready for use.

Depreciation. The method of depreciation selected should be appropriate to the type of asset and best reflect the use of the asset's service potential. The two most common methods are the **straight-line method** and the **diminishing balance method**.

Fixed assets with limited or unlimited useful lives are subject to supplementary or exceptional depreciation when their book values exceed their value to the company and if this reduction in value is of a durable nature.

Disclosure. The valuation and depreciation accounting policies adopted must be disclosed in the notes. Details of the depreciation methods and the rates of depreciation must also be disclosed. Capitalization of interest must be disclosed.

A summary by main category of tangible fixed assets (land and buildings, plant and machinery, other fixtures and fittings, tools and equipment, payments on account and tangible assets under construction) is required, showing additions, disposals and transfers during the year, accumulated depreciation and correction of previous depreciation.

Reference. Company Law—Section XIII—Law of May 4, 1984.

14. Intangible Assets

Accounting Treatment. The following **intangible** fixed **assets** are shown separately:

□ Research and development costs.
□ Concessions, patents, licenses, trademarks and similar rights and assets, if they were:
  —Acquired for valuable consideration;
  —Created by the company itself.
□ Goodwill, to the extent that it was acquired for valuable consideration.
□ Payments on account.

Formation expenses, which include costs relating to capital increases, are disclosed under a separate heading.

Valuation. Intangible fixed assets are recorded at cost, provided that cost does not exceed the value of their estimated usefulness or future contribution to the company.

Amortization. Formation expenses are amortized over no more than five years. Insofar as formation expenses have not been completely amortized, no distribution of profits is permitted unless the amount of reserves available for distribution and profits brought forward is at least equal to the unamortized formation expenses.

Intangible assets are amortized over their useful lives. The rules that apply to the depreciation of tangible fixed assets (see Section 13) also apply to the **amortization** of intangible fixed assets, except that research and development costs and goodwill should normally be amortized over a period of five years. In exceptional circumstances, amortization of these assets is spread over a longer period; the reasons for the use of an extended amortization period should be given in the notes.

Disclosure. The amounts of formation expenses must be explained in the notes. The valuation rules must indicate the basis of valuation and the amortization policies.

A summary by main category of intangible fixed assets is required, showing additions, disposals and transfers during the year, accumulated depreciation and corrections of previous depreciation.

Reference. Company Law—Section XIII—Law of May 4, 1984.

15. Leases

General. There are no pronouncements on accounting for leases. The most common practice follows fiscal rules.

Classification. Leases that transfer substantially all the risks and benefits usually associated with ownership without transferring legal ownership as well are considered **finance leases**. In contrast, an **operating lease** is one in which the lessor effectively retains all the risks and benefits of ownership. Leases that are, in effect, **instalment sales** are always considered finance leases.

Accounting Treatment. Finance leases: In most cases the accounting treatment of a finance lease follows its treatment for income tax reporting purposes. Accordingly, the accounting treatment depends on complex tax rules. Whether the leased asset is capitalized by the lessor or the lessee depends on a wide range of circumstances. These include criteria such as whether there is full payout to the lessor during the noncancellable period, whether the noncancellable lease period covers at least 40 percent but no more than 90 percent of the leased asset's normal useful life and whether the lease agreement includes a purchase or lease renewal option at the end of the noncancellable period; if it does include such an option, the accounting depends on the terms of the option. Capitalization by lessor or lessee is further dependent on the nature of the leased asset; that is, whether it is land, a building or a movable fixed asset. Each lease is dealt with on an individual basis.

Operating leases: Rental payments are recorded as expenses by the lessee and as income by the lessor in the periods to which they relate.

Leveraged Leases. **Leveraged leasing** is relatively uncommon in Luxembourg; the accounting treatment would be substantially the same as for finance leases.

Disclosure. Lease commitments that do not appear on the balance sheet but are significant to the entity's financial position are required to be disclosed in the notes.

16. Investments

General. Investments are classified as fixed (noncurrent) or current assets.

Valuation.   Noncurrent investments: Financial fixed assets can be valued by one of the following three methods:

☐   Acquisition cost less value adjustment for any reduction in value (even temporary).
☐   Acquisition cost less value adjustment for any reduction in value considered to be of a durable nature.
☐   Net equity (if the investment is a subsidiary or an associated company over which the investor exercises significant influence).

Previously recorded value adjustment is reversed when the underlying reasons for the value adjustment have ceased to apply.

Financial fixed assets may not be revalued to reflect permanent increases in market value above cost, except when these assets are valued at net equity.

Current investments: Current investments should be stated at the lower of cost or net realizable value. The comparison should be made on an individual investment basis and a provision made for each investment whose net realizable value is below cost. Revaluation of current investments to reflect increases in market value above cost is not permitted. If an investment has been written down in prior years, it is generally restored, either in whole or in part, to its original cost if the reasons for the write-down have ceased to apply.

Gains/Losses.   Gains or losses on the sale of part of an investment are usually calculated on the basis of weighted-average prices.

Disclosure.   Disclosure requirements include a description of accounting policies, details of changes in noncurrent investments during the year and, for each shareholding in excess of 20 percent, the name and registered office, the percentage interest held and the equity and latest results of the investor.

The disclosure requirements can be limited to a description of the accounting policies and the details of changes in noncurrent investments during the year on a global basis if:

☐   The investor is a holding company; or
☐   The other information has been filed separately and that fact has been stated in the notes; or
☐   This disclosure would harm severely one of the companies and that fact has been stated in the notes.

Reference.   Company Law—Section XIII—Law of May 4, 1984.

17. Accounts Receivable

Accounting Treatment.   Recognition: The recognition of **revenues**, and hence the related receivables, is described in Section 23.

Discounts: Trade receivables are recorded net of trade discounts. Cash discounts are recorded as financial charges when payment is received within the stipulated period.

Allowances: Receivables should be valued at their nominal value, after deduction of any provisions for bad debts and discounts allowed. Both **specific identification** and general formula-based provisions are permitted.

Factored Receivables. When trade receivables are factored, they are excluded from the balance sheet. If the factor has recourse to the vendor for bad debts, disclosure of the contingent liabilities and a provision for probable losses should be made.

Disclosure. Separate disclosure is required of amounts receivable from trade debtors, affiliated companies, associated companies and other debtors. The different categories of receivables are separated into amounts receivable within and after one year.

Reference. Company Law—Section XIII—Law of May 4, 1984.

18. Inventories and Work in Progress

General Accounting Treatment. **Inventories** are stated at the lower of historical cost (purchase price or production cost) or market value.

Accepted methods for the valuation of inventories are specific cost, weighted average, **FIFO** and **LIFO**.

The difference between the valuation by one of these methods and the **replacement value** must be disclosed in the notes, if substantial.

When valuing inventories, it is not permissible to make allowance for costs that are not incurred until sale and delivery. Production cost comprises the purchase price of raw materials and consumables used and other expenses directly attributable to the production of the asset. Production cost may also include a reasonable proportion of indirect costs and interest on capital borrowed over the period attributable to the production of the asset; in that case, the notes must state that such interest has been included.

Long-Term Contracts. No differentiation is made between short-term and long-term contracts in Luxembourg accounting law. Although valued at production cost, contracts in progress may include a portion of the profit to be earned on the contract, based on the state of completion, provided that the profit is reasonably assured. Alternatively, a company may record contracts in progress or specific types of such contracts at production cost until completion and sale.

Work in progress and contracts in progress should be written down when production cost, increased by the estimated expenses still to be incurred, exceeds either the expected net selling price at the balance sheet date or the contract price.

Disclosure. The following categories of inventories must be shown separately: raw materials and consumables, work in progress, finished goods and goods for sale, and payments on account.

The notes should disclose the basis on which inventories are valued.

Reference. Company Law—Section XIII—Law of May 4, 1984.

19. Current Liabilities

General Accounting Treatment. **Current liabilities** do not need to be shown separately in the balance sheet. However, if they are not, the maturity of the debts should be disclosed in the notes under the headings current, due beyond one year and within five years, and due beyond five years.

Liabilities are classified into the following categories:

- □ Debenture loans, showing convertible loans separately.
- □ Amounts owed to credit institutions.
- □ Payments received on account of orders insofar as they are not shown separately as a deduction from inventories.
- □ Trade creditors.
- □ Bills of exchange payable.
- □ Amounts owed to affiliated companies.
- □ Amounts owed to group companies.
- □ Other creditors, including tax and social security.

Where the amount repayable on account of any debt is greater than the amount received, the difference may be shown as an asset. It must be shown separately in the balance sheet or in the notes. This difference should be written off by a reasonable amount each year and completely written off no later than the time of repayment of the debt.

Deferred income is shown separately in the balance sheet under an appropriate heading.

Creation of General and Specific Provisions.   Provisions for liabilities and charges are recorded for charges that have their origin in the current or previous financial year and for specific expenses or losses whose nature is clearly defined and that at the date of the balance sheet are either likely to be incurred, or certain to be incurred but uncertain as to amount or as to the date on which they will arise.

Provisions relating to a specific asset should be deducted from that asset.

Disclosure.   If current liabilities are not shown separately on the balance sheet, they need to be disclosed in the notes.

For each item mentioned, the amount and nature of any collateral must be disclosed.

If the company has accepted liability for the debts of others, obligations arising from these commitments should be disclosed in accordance with the terms of the commitments. Commitments relating to pensions or entered into for the benefit of group companies must be disclosed separately.

Provisions for risks and charges have to be separately presented for pensions and similar obligations, tax claims and other liabilities.

Reference.   Company Law—Section XIII—Law of May 4, 1984.

20.   Long-Term Debt

General Accounting Treatment.   Generally, long-term debt is accounted for in the same manner as current liabilities, that is, debts are included in the balance sheet at their face value as long as they continue to represent a present obligation of the company.

Disclosure.   The various categories of debts and disclosure requirements are detailed in Section 19.

Reference.   Company Law—Section XIII—Law of May 4, 1984.

21. Contingencies

Contingent Gains.   Luxembourg accounting regulations do not specifically address contingent gains. Such gains would not be accrued but, if significant, could be mentioned in the notes.

Contingent Losses.   Contingent losses should be provided for in the financial statements if the amount can be estimated. Otherwise, the loss should be disclosed in a note.

Disclosure.   Disclosure is required of all significant rights and commitments not reflected in the balance sheet, such as guarantees given, assets pledged, significant commitments and **contingencies**, litigation and pension commitments.

Where no provision can be shown in the balance sheet for a contingent loss because it is not possible to make a reasonable estimate of the amount of the obligation, disclosure should be made in the notes of the nature of the contingent liability, the uncertain factors affecting future outcome and the fact that a reasonable estimate is not possible.

Reference.   Company Law—Section XIII—Law of May 4, 1984.

22. Capital and Reserves

General.   Shareholders' equity includes issued **share capital**, **share premium**, revaluation reserves, reserves and profits or losses brought forward.

Share Capital.   The authorized capital has to be detailed in the articles of the company and does not have to be completely issued. For a **public company**, at least 25 percent of the issued capital must be paid up. When the contributions are in kind, the total contribution must be made within five years.

The total issued capital subscribed to by the shareholders, whether called or uncalled, has to be disclosed. The unpaid subscribed capital is shown on the asset side of the balance sheet. The called but not yet paid portion must appear separately on the asset side.

Shares can be either bearer or nominal shares. Shares may be issued without a **par value** and can be subdivided into different classes with different dividend rights and voting rights.

Capital may be paid in cash or in kind. Contributions in kind must be capable of being economically appraised. An independent auditor must report on contributions in kind, expressing an opinion as to whether the fair value of contributions in kind is at least equal to the value of the shares received.

Shares may be issued at a premium.

Reductions of share capital are not uncommon in Luxembourg. There are, however, legal requirements protecting the creditors and third party rights.

Share capital is not reduced by shares owned by the company itself or by its subsidiaries. Moreover, there are some restrictions concerning these holdings.

Reserves.   The following reserves have to be separately disclosed:

□   Share premium.

☐ Revaluation surplus (see also Sections 13 and 16).

☐ Legal reserve. At least 5 percent of the profit available for appropriation has to be transferred to the legal reserve until the reserve equals 10 percent of the subscribed capital.

☐ Reserve for own shares. When acquiring its own shares, the company must transfer from **retained earnings** an amount equal to the nominal or par value of the shares bought (for redeemable shares) or cost (for other shares). This reserve can be used for a capital increase by incorporation of reserve.

☐ Reserves provided for by the articles of association.

☐ Other reserves, including the equity reserve (see Section 16).

☐ Profits or losses brought forward.

The profit or loss for the year is presented separately on the asset side (loss) or liability side (profit) of the balance sheet.

Distribution Restrictions. The distribution of the legal reserve is restricted. The reserve for own shares becomes distributable after reduction of the subscribed capital. No dividend distribution is permitted if it would result in the net assets of the company being reduced below the amount of the share capital increased by the undistributable reserves.

Insofar as formation expenses, research and development costs and goodwill have not been completely written off, no dividend distribution is permitted unless the amount of the reserves available for distribution and profits brought forward is at least equal to that of the expenses not written off.

Interim dividends are allowed under specific conditions.

Disclosure. The notes to the financial statements must disclose:

☐ The number and the nominal value or, in the absence of a nominal value, the accounting par value of the shares subscribed during the financial year within the limits of the authorized capital.

☐ Where there is more than one class of shares, the number and the nominal value or, in the absence of a nominal value, the accounting par value for each class.

☐ Commitments to issue shares, indicating the amount of outstanding convertible loans, the number of outstanding subscription rights, the maximum number of shares to be issued and the corresponding amount of capital to be subscribed.

☐ The amount of authorized capital not issued.

Reference. Company Law—Section XIII—Law of May 4, 1984.

ACCOUNTING PRINCIPLES FOR SPECIFIC ITEMS— INCOME STATEMENT (COMPTE DE PROFITS ET PERTES)

23. Revenue Recognition

General Principles. There is no accounting pronouncement specifically addressing revenue recognition in Luxembourg. The accounting law indicates that income must be accounted for irrespective of the date received, unless collection is uncertain.

In general, revenue from the sale of goods is recognized when the risks and rewards of ownership are transferred. Revenue from services is recognized when the services are performed. Invoicing generally occurs during the same period.

Long-Term Contracts. Long-term contract revenue may be recognized using both the **percentage of completion method** and the **completed contract method**. Contract profit must be reasonably assured if the percentage of completion method is used. If the contract is expected to result in a loss, a provision should be recorded immediately.

Instalment Sales. Sales revenue is generally recognized when ownership has passed to the buyer. Interest on instalment sales is included in income over the period of the sales contract.

Rights of Return. There are no specific rules in Luxembourg on sales transactions where the right of return exists. Revenue is generally recognized upon delivery to the customer even though performance warranties may exist.

Product Financing. **Product financing** is not common in Luxembourg, and hence there are no specific accounting rules in this area. Such arrangements would normally be treated as financing transactions if the risks and benefits of ownership have not passed to the buyer.

Disclosure. Total operating revenue is disclosed, together with the details of turnover. Other operating revenue includes operating income that does not result from the sale of goods or services in the normal course of business and that does not have the characteristics of financial or extraordinary income.

24. Government Grants and Assistance

Accounting Treatment. There is no accounting pronouncement specifically addressing this topic in Luxembourg.

Investment grants for the acquisition of tangible fixed assets are generally deducted from the investment itself.

Interest subsidies are generally recorded on receipt as financial income.

Disclosure. The notes should state the nature and extent of subsidies and how they have been accounted for.

25. Research and Development

Definitions. Research and development costs are not defined in the accounting law but they are generally understood to include the cost of developing prototypes and research and experimentation that will benefit the company through new knowledge, developing new products and improving the production process.

Accounting Treatment. Research and development costs may be capitalized as intangible fixed assets only to the extent that they do not exceed a prudent estimate of their useful value or their future profit contribution to the enterprise.

Capitalized research and development costs must normally be depreciated over five years.

If research and development costs are subsidized by government authorities, the subsidy is generally deducted from the capitalized costs.

Disclosure. The valuation rules adopted to capitalize research and development costs have to be disclosed. Depreciation spread over more than five years must be justified.

Reference. Company Law—Section XIII—Law of May 4, 1984.

26. Capitalized Interest Costs

Accounting Treatment. The acquisition cost of tangible and intangible fixed assets may include interest, for the period preceding their being ready for their intended use, on capital borrowed to finance the acquisition. The cost of inventory and contracts in progress may also include interest, if the normal production or construction period exceeds one year. Interest expense in the income statement is shown net of capitalized interest.

Disclosure. Interest included in the cost of tangible or intangible fixed assets and in production costs of inventory or contracts in progress must be disclosed in the valuation rules. The amount of interest capitalized is generally disclosed separately in the notes.

Reference. Company Law—Section XIII—Law of May 4, 1984.

27. Imputed Interest

General. **Imputed interest** is not a common feature of accounting in Luxembourg.

Accounting Treatment. An exception is the provision for pensions, which are valued at their discounted present value.

Disclosure. Imputed interest charges on provisions for pensions are generally classified as pension costs in the profit and loss account and are not accounted for as interest charges.

28. Extraordinary or Unusual Items (Résultats Exceptionnels)

General. Extraordinary income and expenses arise other than in the ordinary course of an entity's business. This may include income and charges arising from acts and events of a nonrecurring nature. An explanation of the nature and extent of material extraordinary income and expenses must be given in the notes.

Disclosure. The amounts of extraordinary items should be shown before tax, according to their nature. The tax on extraordinary results has to be disclosed separately.

Reference. Company Law—Section XIII—Law of May 4, 1984.

29. Income Taxes

Accounting Treatment. Income tax expense is based on taxable net income. There is presently no requirement to account for deferred taxes in statutory financial statements. However, it is mandatory for consolidated accounts. Companies may choose between the **deferred method** and the **liability method**. Deferred taxes may either be recorded together with current taxes or be disclosed in the balance sheet as a separate item with an appropriate heading. If the company does not account for deferred taxes in its statutory financial statements, adequate disclosure of the deferred tax amounts should be given in the notes.

Tax Losses. Luxembourg tax legislation authorizes the carryforward of losses for deduction from future taxable profits. Carryforward can be made without time limit for accounting years ended from 1991 onwards. For years prior to 1991, carryforward was limited to five years. Carryback of losses to previous years is prohibited.

Disclosure. The income statement should show separately the tax attributable to ordinary activities, the tax related to extraordinary items and other taxes. The notes must disclose an explanation of the way in which tax effects arising from differences between the valuation for tax purposes and the accounting valuation have been accounted for.

The amount of deferred taxes should be disclosed, if not presented in the balance sheet as a separate item.

Reference. Company Law—Section XIII—Law of May 4, 1984.

30. Postretirement Benefits

Accounting Treatment. Company Law does not specify any accounting treatment for pensions or other postretirement benefits. The practice is based on the fiscal regulations.

Typically, book reserves are used to finance pension benefits. Allocation to a book reserve in the employer's balance sheet must be calculated in accordance with generally recognized actuarial valuation methods using an interest rate of 5 percent a year and a standard mortality table. Pensions must be financed over the period from when the commitment is made until the employee's retirement. There is no past service liability to be met on an employee's entry to the plan. Salary may be anticipated if there is a defined scale of increases. Otherwise, increases in pensions resulting from salary increases must be spread over the employee's future career.

Book reserves are often partly or wholly reinsured by the employer. If the retirement benefits are reinsured, the surrender value of the insurance contracts, calculated on an interest rate of 3.5 percent a year, must be shown as an asset in the balance sheet.

A pension fund is effectively a private insurance company and is subject to the same requirements as insured plans.

Disclosure. Financial commitments concerning pensions that are not shown in the balance sheet should be disclosed separately for personnel and for current or former board members. Pension costs are presented separately under personnel costs in the income statement.

Reference. LIR 24 (fiscal regulations) and Company Law, Section XIII—Law of May 4, 1984.

31. Discontinued Operations

Luxembourg accounting legislation does not specifically address discontinued operations. Generally, if part of a company's operations are discontinued, the relevant costs are recognized when the decision to discontinue is made. These costs may be capitalized when they are clearly defined and relate to a substantial change in the structure or organization of the enterprise, provided that the change is intended to have a lasting and favorable effect on the profitability of the enterprise. A statement of compliance with these conditions must be given in the notes. These capitalized costs generally include termination, write-downs of current assets, extraordinary depreciation of fixed assets, provision for liabilities and charges resulting from claims.

Capitalized amounts must be included with formation expenses and should be depreciated following the valuation rules of the enterprise.

Disclosure. Formation expenses should be disclosed in the notes, including changes in cost, depreciation and net book value. Details on the amount of reorganization costs recorded should also be disclosed.

32. Earnings per Share

There is no requirement to disclose earnings per share in Luxembourg, and such disclosure is uncommon.

Appendix
DO LUXEMBOURG STANDARDS OR PREVALENT PRACTICE SUBSTANTIALLY COMPLY WITH INTERNATIONAL ACCOUNTING STANDARDS?

Section	Topic	Substantially complies with IAS?	Comments
3.	Basic accounting concepts and conventions	Yes	
	Contents of financial statements	No	No cash flow statement or statement of changes in financial position is required
4.	Business combinations*	Yes	
5.	Joint ventures	Yes	
6.	Foreign currency translation*	No	Gains on translation of monetary assets or liabilities may be deferred and the financial statements of self-sustaining subsidiaries may be translated using the monetary/nonmonetary method
8.	Accounting changes*	Yes	
9.	Prior period adjustments*	Yes	
10.	Post balance sheet events	Yes	
11.	Related party transactions	No	
12.	Segmental information	No	
13.	Property, plant and equipment*	Yes	
15.	Leases	No	The criteria for capitalization of finance leases are based largely on income tax regulations
16.	Investments	Yes	
17.	Accounts receivable	Yes	
18.	Inventories and work in progress*	Yes	
19.	Current liabilities	Yes	
20.	Long-term debt	Yes	
21.	Contingencies	Yes	

Appendix (*Continued*)

Section	Topic	Substantially complies with IAS?	Comments
22.	Capital and reserves	Yes	
23.	Revenue recognition*	Yes	
24.	Government grants and assistance	Yes	
25.	Research and development*	Yes	
26.	Capitalization of interest costs*	Yes	
28.	Extraordinary or unusual items*	Yes	
29.	Income tax**	No	Tax effect accounting is not mandatory
30.	Postretirement benefits*	No	

*These topics are subject to change as a result of the IASC Improvements Project—see the appendix to the International Accounting Standards chapter.

**The IAS on accounting for taxes on income is currently being revised, and an exposure draft has been issued.

Comparison in this table is made to International Accounting Standards in force at January 1, 1993. For further details, see the International Accounting Standards chapter.

MEXICO

GENERAL NATIONAL INFORMATION

1. Source of Generally Accepted Accounting Principles

Accounting standards in Mexico are issued by the Mexican Institute of Public Accountants (Instituto Mexicano de Contadores Públicos), after review and comment by its members. The study, preparation and presentation of **accounting principles** are carried out through the Institute's Accounting Principles Commission (Comisión de Principios de Contabilidad), which consists of independent public accountants, business executives and representatives of several financial institutions.

The accounting standards approved by the Accounting Principles Commission are classified in the following statements:

- [ ] Series A—Basic accounting principles
- [ ] Series B—Principles related to financial statements
- [ ] Series C—Rules applicable to specific items or captions
- [ ] Series D—Special issues on determining income

The International Accounting Standards issued by the International Accounting Standards Committee or the Statements of Financial Accounting Standards (SFASs) issued by the US Financial Accounting Standards Board are generally followed in situations where no published Mexican accounting standards exist for a particular topic.

2. Audit and Public Company Requirements

Audits (Auditorías). Under specific legal and tax provisions, companies (empresas) that meet any of the following criteria are required to have their financial statements audited for tax purposes:

- [ ] Cumulative income above New MP 5,850,000 (approximately US $1,828,125) in one year.
- [ ] Assets, determined under the terms of the Tax on Assets Law, above New MP 11,700,000 (approximately US $3,656,250).
- [ ] More than 300 employees in each month of the year.

The above obligation also applies to companies integrated as economic groups—holding companies and affiliates—when the aggregate operations meet any of the afore-mentioned criteria.

Companies not meeting any of the above criteria are not required to have audited financial statements for tax purposes.

Audits should be performed by an independent public accountant (contador público) appointed by the stockholders (accionistas). The Code of Professional Ethics of the Mexican Institute of Public Accountants requires independent auditors who sign audit reports to be certified public accountants.

Audits should be performed in accordance with the auditing standards issued by the Auditing Standards and Procedures Commission of the Mexican Institute of Public Accountants.

Public Companies (Compañías Públicas). The main requirements for **public companies** relate to the delivery of annual (audited) and quarterly (unaudited) financial information to the Mexican Stock Exchange. Annual reports should be sent to the Exchange within four months of the balance sheet date.

GENERAL ACCOUNTING

3. Financial Statements (Estados Financieros)

Basic Accounting Concepts. Inflation accounting has been adopted as a basic accounting concept, as explained in Section 7. Other basic concepts underlying the presentation of financial statements include **going concern**, **realization**, **matching**, consistency and **materiality**. In addition, financial statements are required to present fairly the financial position of the enterprise.

Contents of Financial Statements. Financial statements include a balance sheet (balance general), income statement (estado de resultados), statement of changes in stockholders' equity (estado de variaciones en el capital contable), statement of changes in financial position (estado de cambios en la situación financiera) and explanatory notes, which are referenced to, and are an integral part of, the financial statements.

Format of Financial Statements. Financial statements should be prepared using readily understandable terminology and classification. They should normally be prepared on a comparative basis, showing amounts for the corresponding prior period, and should clearly distinguish between short-term and long-term items.

The typical income statement shows net sales and expenses categorized by type of expenditure. Separate disclosure is made of the "Integral cost of financing" (Costo integral de financiamiento), which consists of financial expense (gastos financieros), exchange loss/gain (pérdida/utilidad en cambios) and gain/loss from monetary position (utilidad/pérdida por posición monetaria) (see Section 7).

The balance sheet should separately identify assets (activo), liabilities (pasivo) and stockholders' equity (capital contable).

Disclosure of Accounting Policies. Companies should disclose **accounting policies** that are significant to the preparation of their financial statements. This information is usually included in the first note to the financial statements. As a minimum, all **accounting** principles and **methods** used that are peculiar to the industry in which the entity operates should be disclosed.

Reference.   Statements A-11 and B-1.

4. Business Combinations

Principles of Consolidation.   Normally, **subsidiaries** must be consolidated. Companies in which the **parent** has a direct or an indirect interest of more than 50 percent of participating stock are considered subsidiaries, unless control is not exercised. Also, a company can be considered a subsidiary if the parent has 50 percent or less of participating stock but exercises control.

The following subsidiaries may be excluded from consolidation:

(a)   Foreign subsidiaries where there is exchange control limitation on the payment of dividends or monetary instability.

(b)   Subsidiaries in a suspension-of-payments (bankruptcy) situation.

If subsidiaries in the above cases are excluded from consolidation, the investments must be valued at the lower of equity value or **net realizable value**.

Accounting for Business Combinations.   **Business combinations** are accounted for under the **purchase method**.

For the preparation of **consolidated financial statements**, both when the **equity method** (see below) is applied and when the financial statements are combined, the following rules should be followed:

☐   Individual financial statements must be prepared as of the same date as, or with a difference not exceeding three months from the date of, the consolidated financial statements.

☐   The results of subsidiaries acquired or sold during the period must be included in the income statement during the time they belong to the group.

☐   Accounting principles used by the companies included must be uniform in similar circumstances.

☐   Intercompany transactions must be eliminated, including unrealized profits included in assets.

☐   Intercompany balances, as well as the investments in **capital stock** within the group, must be eliminated.

Control.   Control is indicated by the ability to govern a company's operating and financing policies, as a means to benefit from its activities.

Goodwill (Crédito Mercantil).   When the acquisition cost is higher than the stockholders' equity of the subsidiary, the excess, after attribution of fair values to the net identifiable assets acquired, may be considered an **intangible asset**, subject to **amortization** over a reasonable period not exceeding 20 years. To the extent that the excess of the acquisition cost over the fair values of the acquired net assets does not represent

goodwill, such excess should be written off directly through the income statement. If the company's share in the net assets acquired is higher than the acquisition cost, the excess is considered **negative goodwill**, subject to amortization over a period not exceeding five years.

Equity Accounting.   The equity method must be used when the investor has the ability to influence the decisions of the company without exercising control. This is normally taken to be when stock participation is over 10 percent. The equity method should also be used when stock participation is 10 percent or less, but influence is exercised.

Minority Interests (Intereses Minoritarios).   Under accounting principles, **minority interests** should be included as part of stockholders' equity.

Disclosure.   Consolidation: The basis of consolidation, details of any capitalized earnings in subsidiaries and the method and period of amortization of any recorded goodwill should be disclosed. Where subsidiaries are excluded from consolidation, the reasons for nonconsolidation should be given, together with a summary of assets, liabilities and income of the subsidiaries.

Equity accounting: The method used to account for investments and the amount of **retained earnings**, operating results and dividends received from companies accounted for under the equity method should be disclosed.

Reference.   Statement B-8.

5.   Joint Ventures

There are no prescribed standards in Mexico regarding accounting for and reporting of **joint ventures** (asociaciones en participación). Joint ventures in Mexico take the form of legal private agreements and are not considered legal entities; however, they are treated in practice as economic entities for both accounting and auditing purposes. Since joint ventures are agreements, the parties share the results of the business on an agreed-upon basis.

6.   Foreign Currency Translation

There are no published accounting principles or regulations in Mexico governing the translation of financial statements into a foreign currency or for the translation of foreign currency financial statements into Mexican currency.

However, the treatment of certain foreign currency denominated balances, such as investments and accounts receivable, is addressed by specific accounting statements. These require that those balances be valued at the exchange rate in effect at the date of the financial statements.

In the absence of any Mexican accounting principles, SFAS No. 52 is normally used, although it is not mandatory. Where SFAS No. 52 is not used, practice varies.

7.   Inflation Accounting

General.   All companies are required to adjust their financial statements, including those for prior years, for the effects of inflation so as to report in the current value of Mexican pesos at the closing date of the period being reported on.

Accounting Treatment. Two different bases may be used for calculating the adjusted figures:

- ☐ Changes in general price levels, based on the indices of the National Consumer Price Index; or
- ☐ Replacement cost, which may be used only to restate inventories and fixed assets.

The replacement cost method is compulsory, for the applicable balances, for public companies. Other companies may use either method, but the two should not be applied to the same item.

The main items subject to restatement are:

- ☐ Inventories and cost of sales.
- ☐ Fixed assets, accumulated depreciation and depreciation for the period.
- ☐ Stockholders' equity.
- ☐ The determination of the gain or loss from monetary position and the gain or loss from holding nonmonetary assets (the latter may be determined only when the replacement cost method is applied).

The gain or loss from monetary position for the year is included in the income statement under the caption "Integral cost of financing."

Disclosure. Disclosure should be made of the method used (indices or replacement cost) to restate inventories, net fixed assets and stockholders' equity. It should also be disclosed that the currency value in which figures are stated shows the purchasing power effective at the date of the financial statements.

Reference. Statement B-10.

8. Accounting Changes

Accounting Treatment. Changes in accounting policies and estimates are not applied retroactively; the full effect is taken in the current year's income. There is no restatement of comparative financial statements. This treatment has been adopted mainly for legal reasons.

Disclosure. Changes in accounting principles, together with their financial effect, are disclosed in the notes; they are also mentioned in the auditor's report.

Reference. Statement A-7.

9. Prior Period Adjustments (Ajustes de Años Anteriores)

Definition. **Prior period adjustments** include specifically identified items that:

- ☐ Were not correctly reflected in the prior period financial statements.

□ Are not attributable to economic events occurring subsequent to the date of such prior period financial statements.

□ Are derived from third-party decisions.

Accounting Treatment. Prior period items must be included in the financial statements as an adjustment to opening retained earnings, net of the related income tax effect.

Disclosure. Comparative financial statements must be adjusted, and disclosure of the adjustment made.

Reference. Statement A-7.

10. Post Balance Sheet Events (Eventos Subsecuentes)

Accounting Treatment. This subject is not covered by published accounting principles in Mexico. In practice, however, the following criteria are used:

□ For an event occurring between the date of the financial statements and the date on which they are issued, the financial statements are adjusted if the event relates to conditions existing at the financial statement date.

□ If a material or unusual event occurs after the financial statement date, but is not related to conditions existing at that date, the event must be disclosed in the financial statements so as to provide the reader with adequate financial information.

□ If an event has not occurred before the financial statements are issued but relates to a condition existing at the balance sheet date, the accounting principles applicable to **contingencies** (see Section 21) are followed.

11. Related Party Transactions (Transacciones con Partes Relacionadas)

Definition. Parties are considered related if one party, either an individual or a corporation, has the ability to exercise significant influence over the operation or decisions of the other. This includes both directors and affiliated companies.

Accounting Treatment. Transactions with related parties require no special accounting treatment; they are recorded as usual. However, additional disclosures, as shown below, are necessary.

Disclosure. The following should be disclosed with respect to related party transactions:

□ The nature of the relationship.
□ A description of the transactions, even if they are at no cost or charge.
□ Amount of such transactions.
□ Effect of changes in recurring transactions.
□ Balances with related parties, indicating whether they are assets or liabilities.
□ Any other information that could be helpful to a better understanding of the transaction.

Reference. Statement C-13.

12. Segmental Information

This subject is not governed by published accounting principles in Mexico. Consequently, it is not common for Mexican companies to disclose such information.

ACCOUNTING PRINCIPLES FOR SPECIFIC ITEMS— BALANCE SHEET

13. Property, Plant and Equipment (Inmuebles, Maquinaria y Equipo)

Classification of Capital and Revenue Expenditure. Classification of **capital** and **revenue expenditure** depends on the materiality of the expenditure. Those improvements that extend the expected useful life of assets should be capitalized.

Basis of Valuation. All **fixed assets** (activo fijo) are initially accounted for at their acquisition cost and then restated to current values at the balance sheet date, using indices or **replacement value**, as described in Section 7.

Interest, foreign exchange variations and the monetary gains arising from the financing of fixed asset acquisitions are capitalized until such fixed assets become productive.

Depreciation (Depreciación): **Depreciation** for the period is determined based on fixed asset restated values and on their estimated useful lives. The most common form of depreciation is the **straight-line method**. Depreciation should be allocated to cost of sales or administrative expense, depending on the type of asset.

Gains/Losses. Gains or losses arising from the disposal of fixed assets are normally included in other income.

Disclosure. Disclosure should be made of the following:

☐ The method used to restate fixed assets and accumulated depreciation.
☐ Depreciation charged for the year.
☐ The types of fixed assets.
☐ If applicable, any changes in their estimated useful lives.

Reference. Statements B-10 and C-6.

14. Intangible Assets (Activos Intangibles)

Accounting Treatment. Intangible assets must be capitalized when they have been purchased, internally developed or otherwise acquired; however, items whose amounts cannot be objectively determined should not be capitalized.

Valuation. Intangible assets are initially accounted for at their acquisition cost, together with any additional expenditures entailed in their acquisition. They are then restated at the balance sheet date based on the consumer price index.

Amortization (Amortización). Intangible assets must be amortized, based on their restated value and taking into account their useful lives (which may not exceed 20 years) and the future periods that will benefit from those assets.

Disclosure. Intangible assets should be shown in the balance sheet as the last group of assets (other assets). The amortization method and period should be disclosed.

Reference. Statement C-8.

15. Leases (Arrendamientos)

Accounting Treatment. Leases are classified as capital (**finance**) **leases** or **operating leases**, based on whether they transfer substantially all the benefits and risks of ownership. Principal and financing interest associated with capital leases are accounted for by lessees as fixed assets and prepayments, respectively.

Operating leases are expensed by lessees in the income statement.

For *operating* leases, lessors record the leased property in the balance sheet, and record depreciation in accordance with their normal depreciation policy. Lessors also report rent, generally on a straight-line basis over the lease term.

For *capital* leases, lessors record as gross investment in the lease, the minimum lease payments plus the unguaranteed residual value accruing to the benefit of the lessor. The difference between the gross investment and the sum of the present value of the two components of gross investment is recorded as unearned income.

Disclosure. A general description of leasing arrangements is required for both lessees and lessors.

Required disclosures for lessees include the following:

☐ Capital leases—Assets recorded by major classes; future minimum lease payments in the aggregate and for each of the succeeding five years, with deductions from the total to arrive at present value.

☐ Operating leases—Future minimum rental payments required in the aggregate and in each of the five succeeding years, and total rental expense included in each income statement presented.

Required disclosures for lessors include:

☐ Capital leases—Components of the net investment and future minimum lease payments to be received.

☐ Operating leases—Cost of property held for lease by major class, total accumulated depreciation and minimum future rentals in the aggregate and for each of the five succeeding years.

Reference. Statement D-5.

16. Investments (Inversiones)

Accounting Treatment. Only the treatment of temporary investments is covered by published accounting principles. Temporary investments are those that are purchased with an intent to resell and are classified as either marketable securities (valores nego-ciables) (securities listed on the stock exchanges or managed by the financial system) or other investment securities (instrumentos de inversión). Both are initially recorded at acquisition cost and, depending on their availability or purpose, are included in either **current** or noncurrent **assets**.

Investments in affiliated companies are treated as business combinations (see Section 4).

Valuation.   Investments in marketable securities are carried in the financial statements at net realizable value, and those in other securities at the lower of cost or net estimated realizable value. If the investment is denominated in foreign currency, it should be translated at the rate of exchange in effect at the balance sheet date.

Gains/Losses.   The difference between cost and net realizable value is taken directly to income as part of the integral cost of financing. Therefore, gains arising from adjust-ments to net realizable value are distributable to shareholders.

Disclosure.   Disclosure should be made of the types of investment, the rates of exchange used for their translation (if applicable) and the effect of any decrease in net realizable value of marketable securities between the financial statement date and the date on which the financial statements are issued.

Reference.   Statement C-1.

17.   Accounts Receivable (Cuentas por Cobrar)

Accounting Treatment.   **Accounts receivable** represent demandable rights arising from sales, services rendered, loans or any other similar items. They are accounted for at their originally agreed to value and are recognized under the **accrual** basis.

Valuation.   The originally agreed to value must be modified to reflect what is expected to be received in cash, kind, credit or services; this is accomplished by recording re-ceivables net of trade and other discounts and by establishing an allowance for doubtful accounts. Accounts receivable denominated in foreign currency are valued at the rate of exchange in effect at the balance sheet date.

Factored Receivables (Cuentas por Cobrar Descontadas).   The treatment of factored receivables is not covered by published accounting principles in Mexico. However, they are generally accounted for as a contingent liability, with disclosure of the factored amount.

Disclosure.   Short-term and long-term accounts receivable should be disclosed sepa-rately, as should those related to customers (trade) and those receivable from other debtors. In addition, the following should be identified:

☐   Accounts receivable from **holding** or affiliated **companies**.
☐   Material accounts receivable from an individual or company.
☐   The amount of the allowance for doubtful accounts.

☐ Where applicable, any lien, contingency or restriction to which accounts receivable are subject.

☐ The amount of foreign currency accounts receivable.

Reference. Statement C-3.

18. Inventories (Inventarios) and Work in Progress (Producción en Proceso)

General Accounting Treatment. **Inventories** and work in progress are initially recorded at their acquisition or production cost and then restated at the balance sheet date based either on changes in the general price (index) level or on replacement costs, as described in Section 7. When indices are used for restating, the same valuation method (see below) that was used for the initial cost must continue to be used.

Inventories and work in progress are valued at the lower of restated or realizable value; if applicable, an allowance for obsolescence is created. Acceptable valuation methods are **LIFO**, **FIFO**, **average cost**, specific cost and **last purchase price**. **Absorption** or direct **costing** may also be used, based on historical or **standard costs**. Where standard costs are used, they should approximate historical costs before the restatement for inflation accounting is made.

Long-Term Contracts. The treatment of long-term contracts is not covered by published accounting principles in Mexico. In practice, the **percentage of completion method** is generally used.

Disclosure. Inventories are included in current assets, with disclosure of:

☐ The various inventory components (e.g., raw materials [materias primas], work in progress [producción en proceso] and finished goods [productos terminados]).

☐ The restatement method used—replacement costs or indices.

☐ Where required, the amount of the adjustment to market valuation or provision for obsolescence.

☐ If direct costing is used, the amount of fixed production costs absorbed in the period.

☐ Any liens to which inventories may be subject.

☐ If applicable, any change in the method used to restate inventories, indicating the effect on income for the period.

Reference. Statement C-4.

19. Current Liabilities (Pasivo a Corto Plazo)

General Accounting Treatment. **Current liabilities** include obligations that are due to mature within one year or the normal operating cycle of the business. They may include obligations to suppliers, advance payments from customers, tax obligations and financing in the form of loans or advances from credit institutions, affiliates, stockholders and so forth. Current liabilities are accounted for based on the amount originally agreed to, plus accrued interest, when applicable.

Current liabilities must be recognized when incurred and/or demandable. When it is not possible to accurately determine the amount, they must be reasonably estimated. Foreign currency liabilities are valued at the rate of exchange in effect at the balance sheet date.

Creation of General or Specific Provisions.   Consistent with the accrual concept, provisions should be created on a reasonable basis for the financial effect of transactions or events that occurred in the past. Specific provisions required by Mexican published accounting principles include:

☐ Indemnities and seniority premiums payable to employees in case of dismissal or any other circumstances stated by the Federal Labor Law.

☐ Pension plans and retirement payments.

Disclosure.   Disclosure should be made of the following:

☐ Separate identification of liabilities to each of the following: suppliers, affiliated companies, income tax (net of corresponding advance payments), employees' profit sharing and bank loans.

☐ Any restrictions or obligations on the company arising from the contracts it has entered into.

☐ The amount of liabilities denominated in foreign currencies.

Reference.   Statement C-9.

20.   Long-Term Debt (Deuda a Largo Plazo)

Accounting Treatment.   Long-term debt includes obligations that are due to mature after one year or the normal operating cycle of the business. As for current liabilities, they may include obligations to suppliers, advance payments from customers, tax obligations and financing in the form of loans or advances from credit institutions, affiliates, stockholders and so forth. Long-term liabilities are accounted for based on the amount originally agreed to, plus accrued interest, when applicable.

Long-term debt must be recognized when incurred and/or demandable. When it is not possible to accurately determine the amount, it should be reasonably estimated. Foreign currency liabilities are valued at the rate of exchange in effect at the balance sheet date.

Debt Restructuring.   Debt restructuring is not covered by Mexican published accounting principles.

Debt Extinguishment.   Debt extinguishment is not covered by Mexican published accounting principles.

Disclosure.   Disclosure should be made of the following:

☐ Separate identification of long-term liabilities to each of the following: suppliers, affiliates, income tax (net of corresponding advance payments), employees' profit sharing and bank loans.

☐ Any restrictions or obligations on the company arising from the contracts it has entered into.

☐ The amount of long-term debt denominated in foreign currencies.

Reference. Statement C-9.

21. Contingencies (Contingencias)

General Accounting Treatment. The accounting treatment and disclosure requirements for contingencies depend on the likelihood of their occurrence. They are classified as either recurring and measurable based on past experience (e.g., warranty claims) or nonrecurring but capable of being fairly measured based on judgment. Both types of contingent losses should be provided for in the financial statements using fair estimates. Contingent gains should not be recorded until they are realized. If a contingency cannot be fairly estimated based on objective criteria, it should not be provided for in the accounts, but disclosure should be made.

Disclosure. Disclosure of both recorded and unrecorded contingencies must be sufficient to enable readers to understand the nature of the contingencies.

Reference. Statement C-12.

22. Capital and Reserves (Capital Contable)

General. Stockholders' equity is divided into two different categories: capital contributions from stockholders and earned capital. The amounts included in the financial statements for both categories should include recognition of the effects of inflation.

To classify stockholders' advance payments as stockholders' equity, a resolution must be passed at the stockholders' or partners' meeting; otherwise, advance payments are considered a liability of the entity. Changes in contributed or earned capital, and the amount of dividends per share and the form of payment, must be reported.

Contributed capital (Capital contribuído): Contributed capital is represented by capital stock (capital social), contributions for future capital increases, premium on sale of stock and capital gifts to the company. (Nonmonetary capital gifts are initially recorded at their market value.)

Earned capital (Capital ganado): This is represented by retained earnings, including amounts applied to capital reserves, accumulated losses and the excess (shortfall) in the restatement of stockholders' equity for the effects of inflation.

In addition to the above, Mexican Corporate Law requires that 5 percent of net income be appropriated to a legal reserve, until the reserve is equal to 20 percent of capital stock.

Accounting Treatment. All stockholders' equity items should be stated in units of purchasing power as at the balance sheet date. Each specific item is therefore stated at its original value plus restatement amount.

Dividends (Dividendos) declared are considered liabilities in the financial statements.

Distributions made are considered as dividends as long as they do not exceed retained earnings, including its restatement. With the exception of maintaining the minimum capital stock authorized under Mexican Corporate Law, there are no restrictions on distributions, including those of capital stock.

Capital stock may be reduced by the redemption of shares. However, if the redemption amount exceeds the **par value** of the stock, earned capital should be reduced for the excess. Alternatively, if provided for in the corporation charter and intended to reduce the number of shares only, shares may be redeemed through a reduction of retained earnings (with the amount of capital stock remaining the same).

Disclosure.   Disclosure should be made of:

☐ Contributed capital and earned capital.

☐ The amount of capital not fully paid for, which reduces the value of subscribed capital in stockholders' equity, even though the related account receivable is represented by credit instruments (notes receivable).

☐ The characteristics of the stock—**common** or **preferred**—or partners' interests.

☐ The classes and series of stock.

☐ The minimum and maximum capital stock, including its restatement.

☐ The number of shares issued and subscribed, indicating their par value or the absence of it.

☐ Stockholders' equity restrictions due to legal or contractual provisions or to a resolution passed by the stockholders.

☐ Types of taxes to which reimbursements or distributions are subject.

Reference.   Statement C-11.

ACCOUNTING PRINCIPLES FOR SPECIFIC ITEMS— INCOME STATEMENT

23. Revenue (Ingresos) Recognition

This subject is not covered by published accounting principles in Mexico. However, under the accrual basis of accounting, **revenue** should be reflected in the period in which it is considered to have been earned.

Instalment Sales, Rights of Return and Product Financing.   There are no generally accepted accounting treatments for the recognition of revenue or profit on any of these arrangements in Mexico and practice varies.

24. Government Grants and Assistance (Donativos y Asistencia del Gobierno)

Accounting Treatment.   Government grants are not common in Mexico and their treatment is not covered by published accounting principles. However, where a subsidy from the government exists, disclosure should be made in a note, revealing the nature, amount and term, together with any impact on the results of operations.

25. Research and Development (Investigación y Desarrollo)

Accounting Treatment.   All research and development costs are expensed as incurred.

Disclosure.   Where material, the amount and characteristics of research and development expenses incurred during the period should be disclosed.

Reference.   Statement C-8.

26.   Capitalized Interest Costs (Intereses Capitalizados)

Accounting Treatment.   Interest accrued during the period of construction and installation of fixed assets may be capitalized, in conjunction with any exchange differences and monetary gain arising from the liability that financed the acquisition of the asset, by charging all of these items (''integral cost of financing'' under inflation accounting) to the cost of the asset until the asset is available for operations. The main objective is to maintain a fair relationship between cost and revenues.

Disclosure.   The amount of interest or integral cost of financing capitalized, as well as how and over what period it is being applied to income, must be disclosed.

Reference.   Statements B-10 and C-6.

27.   Imputed Interest (Interés Asociado)
The use of **imputed interest** is rare in Mexico and is not covered by published accounting principles.

28.   Extraordinary or Unusual Items (Partidas Extraordinarias o Inusuales)
There are no specific definitions of extraordinary or unusual items in Mexican accounting principles. However, the benefit from utilization of tax loss carryforwards must be disclosed as an extraordinary item (meaning that it must be separate from any other captions in the income statement). Also, in practice, operations different from the normal activity of the enterprise are considered extraordinary items.

Any income or expense, such as the gain or loss on the sale of fixed assets, arising from transactions that are not part of the entity's operating or financing activities are included in other income.

29.   Income Taxes (Impuestos Sobre la Renta)

Accounting Treatment.   Income taxes (including employees' profit sharing) are determined using the partial **liability method**. Under this method, deferred taxes (impuestos diferidos) should be provided, using estimates of tax rates applicable to the time of reversal, for all material timing differences that are considered likely to materialize (reverse) in a reasonable period and that have been fully identified. Nonreversible or permanent differences are not subject to deferred tax. Deferred taxes must be reviewed each year for compliance with the above principles. Deferred tax assets may be maintained only when it is certain that the differences will materialize.

Tax Losses (Pérdidas Fiscales).   The benefit from utilization of tax loss carryforwards may be recognized only in the year in which they are offset; it must be disclosed and treated as an extraordinary item.

Disclosure.   The following disclosure is required:

☐   The income tax liability, net of any advance payments made.

☐   Separate presentation of deferred and current taxes in the income statement and balance sheet.

☐   Classification of the deferred tax as current or noncurrent, depending on the reversal period of timing items.

☐   Tax loss carryforwards and their tax effect.

☐   Timing differences for which no deferred tax was determined.

Profit Sharing.   According to the Mexican Labor Law, an employee profit sharing should be determined by each company equal to 10 percent of taxable income for a year computed in accordance with the Mexican Income Tax Law. The recognition of this item in the income statement is following income before taxes.

Reference.   Statement D-4.

30.   Postretirement Benefits (Remuneraciones al Retiro)

Accounting Treatment: Pension plans in Mexico are generally **defined benefit plans**. The accounting treatment set out below does not therefore deal with **defined contribution pension plans**.

The cost and liability related to pensions must be recorded during the time eligible services are rendered. The determination of the obligation must be based on a logical, systematic and consistent actuarial valuation (valuación actuarial), which must be performed at least every three years. The pension liability must be sufficient to meet payments to employees who are eligible for benefits.

When a pension plan (plan de pensiones) is established, the cost of past services must be reasonably applied to future years.

The refund of pension plan surplus to the company is not permitted.

A new basis for accounting for pensions was promulgated in the third quarter of 1992, effective for periods beginning on January 1, 1993. Under this basis, accounting for pensions in Mexico is similar to that under US SFAS No. 87.

Disclosure.   The following disclosure is required:

☐   A description of the characteristics of the plan.

☐   Whether the plan is funded or not.

☐   If applicable, the deferred charge corresponding to past services and the amortization period thereof.

☐   Any changes in the plan, in the determination of the actuarial computation or in circumstances affecting the plan or the actuarial computations.

☐   If the plan has established a fund, the pension liability net of such fund, shown separately from short-term liabilities.

Reference.   Statement D-3.

31. Discontinued Operations (Operaciones Descontinuadas)

Accounting Treatment.   Published accounting principles in Mexico provide no specific guidance for the treatment of discontinued operations. However, under the criteria for recognition of losses, a provision should be set up for losses to be incurred when a decision is made to close a part of the business.

32. Earnings per Share (Utilidad por Acción)

There are no requirements to disclose earnings per share figures in Mexico.

Appendix
DO MEXICAN STANDARDS OR PREVALENT PRACTICE SUBSTANTIALLY COMPLY WITH INTERNATIONAL ACCOUNTING STANDARDS?

Section	Topic	Substantially complies with IAS?	Comments
3.	Basic accounting concepts and conventions	Yes	
	Contents of financial statements	Yes	
4.	Business combinations*	Yes	
5.	Joint ventures	NS	
6.	Foreign currency translation*	NS	
8.	Accounting changes*	Yes	
9.	Prior period adjustments*	Yes	
10.	Post balance sheet events	Yes	
11.	Related party transactions	Yes	
12.	Segmental information	NS	
13.	Property, plant and equipment*	Yes	
15.	Leases	Yes	
16.	Investments	Yes	
17.	Accounts receivable	Yes	
18.	Inventories and work in progress*	Yes	
19.	Current liabilities	Yes	
20.	Long-term debt	Yes	
21.	Contingencies	Yes	
22.	Capital and reserves	Yes	
23.	Revenue recognition*	Yes	
24.	Government grants and assistance	NCE	
25.	Research and development*	Yes	
26.	Capitalization of interest costs*	Yes	
28.	Extraordinary or unusual items*	Yes	

Appendix (*Continued*)

Section	Topic	Substantially complies with IAS?	Comments
29.	Income tax**	Yes	
30.	Postretirement benefits*	Yes	

*These topics are subject to change as a result of the IASC Improvements Project—see the appendix to the International Accounting Standards chapter.

**The IAS on accounting for taxes on income is currently being revised, and an exposure draft has been issued.

NCE—Not commonly encountered in Mexico.

NS—No treatment specified.

Comparison in this table is made to International Accounting Standards in force at January 1, 1993. For further details, see the International Accounting Standards chapter.

NETHERLANDS

GENERAL NATIONAL INFORMATION

1. Source of Generally Accepted Accounting Principles

Generally Accepted Accounting Principles. The requirements for annual reports of companies have been established by an Act of Parliament and are included in Title 9 of Book 2 of the Civil Code. This Title has been introduced to accommodate the provisions of the Fourth Directive of the European Community (EC). In addition, the Title provides a framework for the objectives and contents of annual financial statements. Alternatively, if justified by its international connections, a company may prepare its financial statements according to the standards accepted in one of the other EC member states. If this is done, it must be disclosed.

A committee consisting of representatives of the accounting profession (users, preparers and auditors of financial statements) is working on a draft of **accounting principles** acceptable in the Netherlands. This committee, the Council for Annual Reporting (Raad voor de Jaarverslaggeving, CAR), has issued Accounting and Reporting Guidelines (Richtlijnen voor de Jaarverslaggeving) on a number of subjects, consisting of what the Council considers **generally acceptable accounting principles** in the Netherlands, taking into account International Accounting Standards (IASs).

The Minister of Justice may assign or, where necessary, issue regulations for financial statements, provided that they are equivalent to the regulations of the EC's Seventh Directive.

Enforcement of accounting requirements is vested in the Enterprise Chamber (Ondernemingskamer, OK) of the Amsterdam Court of Appeal. On request, the OK issues court orders to be followed by the management board of a company in preparing its annual report. Judgments of the OK can be appealed to the Supreme Court.

2. Audit and Public Company Requirements

Audits. A statutory audit may be carried out by either a member of the Netherlands Institute of Registered Accountants or a foreign auditor who has been authorized by the Minister of Economic Affairs.

The requirements described in this chapter apply to the following legal entities (hereafter called companies):

□ Public limited liability companies (Naamloze Vennootschappen, NV).

□ Private limited liability companies (Besloten Vennootschappen, BV).

□ Cooperatives (Coöperaties), the participants in which are referred to as "members."

□ Mutual guarantee companies (Onderlinge Waarborgmaatschappijen, OWM).

All companies have to be audited except for:

□ Small companies (as defined below).

□ Companies whose financial data has been included in the **consolidated financial statements** of another company (exemption is subject to certain conditions).

Companies are divided into the following categories:

□ Small companies, which satisfy at least two of the following requirements:
— The value of the assets according to the balance sheet and the notes thereto does not exceed 5 million guilders (NLG);
— The net **turnover** for the financial year does not exceed 10 million NLG; or
— The average number of employees during the financial year is less than 50.

□ Medium-sized companies, which satisfy at least two of the following requirements:
— The value of the assets according to the balance sheet and the notes thereto does not exceed 20 million NLG;
— The net turnover for the financial year does not exceed 40 million NLG; or
— The average number of employees during the financial year is less than 250.

□ Large companies, that is, all other companies.

For a group of companies, the above requirements are applied to the group as a whole. To determine the category a company falls into, the value of its assets must be calculated on the basis of purchase price or production cost.

A Dutch annual report is composed of the financial statements (jaarrekening), a directors' report (jaarverslag) and additional information (overige gegevens). The additional information includes the auditors' report, the provisions in the corporation's articles of association concerning the appropriation of annual earnings and a statement of post balance sheet events and the extent of their consequences.

In addition to expressing an opinion on the financial statements, the independent auditors are also required to ascertain whether the directors' report has, insofar as they can judge, been drawn up in accordance with Title 9 and is consistent with the financial statements. Furthermore, the auditors have to establish whether the required additional information has been included. The auditors' report should be attached to the financial statements unless the additional information discloses a legal basis for not including it.

Apart from the auditors' report to the shareholders and the public, auditors report separately on their examination to the company's supervisory board (a board of supervisory directors or nonexecutive directors), if applicable. The financial statements may not be finalized or approved if the auditors' report is not made available to the supervisory board.

In general, companies have to prepare their financial statements within five months of the end of the financial year (six months for a cooperative) and have to file their financial statements at the Trade Register within eight days of their adoption by the supervisory board and approval by the shareholders at a general meeting. In specific cases, some extension of these terms is possible.

In principle, the information to be filed has to be in the Dutch language, although English, French or German is also acceptable. The financial statements presented to the Workers Council (a board consisting of employees) must always be in Dutch.

Exact filing requirements vary with the size of the company. Furthermore, exemptions are granted for:

- [ ] The financial statements of **subsidiaries** if the **parent company** has assumed responsibility for the liabilities of the subsidiary.
- [ ] The consolidated financial statements of intermediate holdings and subholdings.

In both cases, the consolidated financial statements of the parent company must be filed and must include the financial statements of the subsidiary or the consolidated financial statements of the intermediate holding or subholding company.

Public Companies.   In addition to normal reporting requirements, the Regulations for Quoted Securities stipulate that **public companies** must publish quantitative information, including notes with respect to their activities and operating results for the first six months of the financial year. This half-yearly report, which has to be published within four months after the end of the reporting period, is required to:

- [ ] Provide all relevant information to investors in order to enable them to form a judgment about the company's activities and operating results.
- [ ] Disclose all special factors that affected those activities and operating results.
- [ ] Enable a comparison to be made with the corresponding period of the previous year.

Insofar as possible, the developments expected for the full year should be described in the notes.

GENERAL ACCOUNTING

3. Financial Statements (Jaarrekening)

Basic Accounting Concepts.   The general requirements included in Title 9 indicate the **accounting concepts** and principles to be used in the preparation of financial statements. The most important requirement is to furnish the "insight" required to enable a sound judgment to be formed regarding the entity's:

- [ ] Financial position and results.
- [ ] Solvency and liquidity (to the extent that the nature of the financial statements permits).

In addition, Title 9 requires application of the **matching, realization, going concern, accruals** and **prudence concepts**.

Title 9 allows purchase price or production cost to be used for valuation purposes. For tangible and financial fixed assets and inventories, current value is also permitted. Current value accounting is further described in Section 7.

Contents of Financial Statements. Financial statements include a balance sheet, income statement and notes thereto. Presentation of the financial statements of the parent company (statutory financial statements) along with the consolidated financial statements is required by law.

Cash flow statements are not required by Dutch law, but are normally also included in the financial statements, as recommended by CAR Guidelines. Normally the **indirect method** is used, but some companies apply the **direct method**. In the latter instance, CAR Guidelines recommend that a reconciliation of the cash flow statement to the balance sheet and income statement be presented. Various formats are used for cash flow statements. The formats prescribed in IAS 7 (revised) would be appropriate in the Netherlands.

Title 9 contains requirements (varying with size of company) for the contents of the balance sheet, the income statement and notes thereto. Certain specific information not directly related to the balance sheet or the income statement must also be disclosed in the notes (e.g., contingent liabilities; average number of employees of the company and its subsidiaries; and remuneration of, loans to and guarantees given for present and former supervisory and management board members). The income statement of the parent company may be abbreviated if consolidated financial statements are presented.

Format of Financial Statements. Various formats are prescribed for the balance sheet and the income statement, according to the size of the company. Most major companies, however, use a two-sided balance sheet and a vertical income statement.

Disclosure of Accounting Policies. The principles underlying the valuation of assets and the determination of operating results must be disclosed for each item. The principles used in translating foreign currency and the treatment of exchange differences must also be disclosed.

Reference. Articles 361, 362, 402 and 405 of Title 9; and Guidelines 1.02, 1.03, 1.05, 1.06, 1.08 and 4.20 (draft) of CAR.

4. Business Combinations (Groepsverhoudingen)

Principles of Consolidation. There are three categories of group relationships: subsidiaries, participating interests and group companies. (These categories are defined later in this section, under "Control.")

The financial data of all group companies, as well as of the parent company, must be included in the consolidated financial statements of the group, which must comply with all the requirements of Title 9.

If, because of a difference in activities, consolidation would conflict with the requirement of providing appropriate insight, the (individual or subgroup) financial statements of subsidiaries and other group companies should be included separately. In addition, consolidation is not required of group companies:

□ Whose total significance is negligible;

☐ Whose financial data can be obtained or estimated only at disproportionate costs or great delay; or

☐ That are to be disposed of.

Consolidation is also not required if the limits applicable to small companies would not be exceeded if consolidation took place.

Consolidation of a subgroup may be omitted (with disclosure in the notes) if all of the following conditions are fulfilled:

☐ No written notices of objection have been lodged with the legal entity within six months of the beginning of the financial year by at least 10 percent of the members (for a cooperative) or by the holders of at least 10 percent of the issued **share capital**.

☐ The financial data required to be consolidated by the legal entity is included in the consolidated financial statements of a larger group.

☐ The consolidated financial statements and report of the management board have been prepared in accordance with the regulations of the EC's Seventh Directive or, if these regulations need not be observed, in an equivalent way.

☐ The consolidated financial statements, together with the auditors' report, have been prepared in or translated into Dutch, French, German or English.

☐ Within six months after the balance sheet date or within one month after an authorized later publishing date, the documents or translations referred to above have been filed with the office of the Trade Register in the place where the legal entity has its statutory seat, or reference has been made to the office of the Trade Register where they have been filed.

Proportional consolidation of an entity is permitted when one or more group companies are entitled to jointly exercise rights of authority, pursuant to an agreement of cooperation with the other investors, in that joint venture, and the legal requirement of insight is met (see Section 5).

Accounting for Business Combinations. **Business combinations** should normally be accounted for by the **purchase method**. In the rare circumstance where an acquirer cannot be identified, the **pooling of interests method** is used.

The initial book value of the investment is determined on the basis of the net asset value (the intrinsic value of the participating interest) based on the accounting principles used by the acquiring company or, if this net asset value cannot be determined because of a lack of information, the net asset value according to the participating interest's own balance sheet or the cost of the shares acquired.

Control. The concept of control can be derived from the following definitions of subsidiary company, participating interest and group company.

A subsidiary is one of the following:

☐ A legal entity in which the investing company (alone or together with one or more group companies) is authorized to exercise (including as a consequence of an agreement with others entitled to vote) more than half of the voting rights at a general meeting of shareholders.

□ A legal entity in which the investing company is authorized to appoint or discharge more than half of the members of the management or supervisory board under the same conditions as described above.

□ A partnership of which the investing company is a fully liable partner.

A participating interest is one of the following:

□ A legal entity to which the investing company (or one or more of its subsidiaries) has provided capital for the purpose of furthering its own business activities by establishing a long-term relationship.

□ An interest in a partnership for whose liabilities the investing company, or one of its subsidiaries, accepts full responsibility as a partner.

□ An interest in a partnership in which the investing company, or one of its subsidiaries, is a partner for the purpose of furthering its own business activities by establishing a long-term relationship.

When an interest has the characteristics described above, the legal entity or partnership is considered to be a participating interest, regardless of the percentage of ownership. If an interest of at least 20 percent of the issued share capital of an entity is held, it will automatically be presumed to be a participating interest of the investing company.

A group company is defined as a legal entity or partnership that is associated in a group with one or more other legal entities. The law defines a group as an organizational and economic unity of legal entities and companies.

Goodwill. **Goodwill** may be charged directly to the income statement, charged directly to shareholders' equity or capitalized as an **intangible** fixed **asset**. In all cases, the amount of goodwill should be disclosed separately.

Capitalized goodwill must be amortized over its expected economic life. **Amortization** is charged to the income statement. If it is possible to allocate goodwill to a period longer than five years, it may be amortized over that longer period, although the reasons for this extension and the amortization period must be disclosed in the notes. A revaluation reserve should be set up for the amount of any **negative goodwill**.

Equity Accounting. Equity accounting in the Netherlands usually is applied by increasing or decreasing the net asset value of the participating interest at acquisition date by the pro rata share of the postacquisition earnings or losses. Participating interests must be accounted for using the **equity method** if the investor's influence over the commercial and financial policies of these interests is deemed to be considerable. Considerable influence is presumed to exist legally if the investor company, together with its subsidiaries, exercises at least 20 percent of the votes at the shareholders' meeting. Valuation at cost or, less likely, at current value is mandatory if the influence is not considerable.

When the equity method is used, a legal reserve must be set up for the investor's share of income reported by participating interests, less dividends received from them. However, if dividends can be distributed to the parent company in the Netherlands without any prohibition and their declaration depends solely on the parent company's decision, this legal reserve does not have to be formed or maintained. The treatment of taxation on future dividends must be set out in the notes.

Minority Interests.   **Minority interests** in fully consolidated companies are disclosed separately in the balance sheet immediately after shareholders' equity, and in the income statement as a deduction from the total net group income.

Disclosure.   The parent company must disclose the names, statutory domiciles and participation in the issued share capital of all subsidiaries and other group companies. For nonconsolidated interests, net equity and results also have to be disclosed if these interests are valued at cost or at current value. This information is not required if the equity method is used.

The information stated above need not be included in the notes if it has been filed with the Trade Register and that fact has been stated in the notes, as well as in the list filed with the Trade Register.

Information on changes in the value of participating interests must be disclosed in the statutory accounts of the parent company.

There are no specific disclosure requirements for goodwill, except those relating to amortization, as described in Section 14.

Reference.   Sections 11, 12 and 13 of Title 9; and Guideline 2.03 (draft) of CAR.

5.   Joint Ventures

Accounting for Investments in Joint Ventures.   Dutch accounting principles do not address the different forms of **joint venture** detailed in International Accounting Standard (IAS) 31, *Financial Reporting of Interests in Joint Ventures*; they do acknowledge that joint ventures may be incorporated or unincorporated.

Jointly Controlled Operations.   The accounting treatment in IAS 31 would be appropriate in the Netherlands.

Jointly Controlled Assets.   The accounting treatment in IAS 31 would be appropriate in the Netherlands.

Jointly Controlled Entities.   Venturers have the option of accounting for investments in joint ventures by the proportionate consolidation method, provided it furnishes the required insight (see Section 3). If not, joint ventures should be accounted for by the equity method. These requirements are consistent with IAS 31.

Transactions Between Venturers and the Joint Venture.   There are no specific rules for accounting for transactions between venturers and the joint venture.

Disclosure

□   Equity accounting: Disclosure requirements for joint ventures are the same as for participating interests (see Section 4).

□   Proportionate consolidation accounting: The venturer must disclose the names and statutory domiciles of the joint ventures included in the consolidated financial statements and the reasons for such inclusion.

In addition, if the venturer is liable for any contingent liability or commitment with respect to the joint venture, this should be disclosed.

There are no specific Dutch requirements or recommendations for the treatment of transactions between venturers and the joint venture or for the recognition of **contingencies** and commitments of and related to the joint venture. In general, the requirements of IAS 31 would be appropriate in the Netherlands.

Accounting by Joint Ventures.   Generally accepted accounting principles apply to all assets and liabilities and operations of joint ventures.

Reference.   Articles 409 and 414 of Title 9 and Guideline 2.03 (draft) of CAR.

6.   Foreign Currency Translation (Verwerking van Vreemde Valuta)

Bases of Translation: In accounting for exchange differences, a distinction is made between transactions in foreign currencies and foreign-based operations.

Transactions in foreign currencies: Transactions in foreign currencies settled during the accounting period should be reported in the financial statements at the settlement rate. Receivables or payables arising from transactions not settled by the balance sheet date should be carried in the balance sheet at the rate of exchange prevailing at the balance sheet date, except where forward transactions have been concluded as a **hedge** against the difference on exchange. In general, exchange losses on short-term and long-term transactions should be recognized in income in the period in which they arise. While it is preferable to record exchange gains on long-term transactions in income in the period in which they arise, it is also acceptable as an alternative to allocate gains on long-term transactions systematically over the remaining period until maturity, showing the unallocated portion in the balance sheet as a deferred gain.

Foreign-based operations: There are two types of foreign-based operations: activities of foreign entities (**self-sustaining**) and direct (**integrated**) **foreign operations**.

The parent company is assumed to have an exchange risk with respect to its net investment in activities of foreign entities, irrespective of the assets into which that net investment has been converted. Assets and liabilities are translated at the rate of exchange prevailing at the balance sheet date, and exchange differences are transferred directly to net equity (reserves). Income statement items are translated either at the rate of exchange prevailing at the balance sheet date or at an average exchange rate for the period; exchange differences are either taken to income or transferred directly to reserves.

The parent company considers direct operations primarily from the standpoint of its own currency, because it regards foreign subsidiaries' assets and liabilities as its own. Assets and liabilities are translated at the rate of exchange prevailing at the balance sheet date, except for fixed assets and inventories valued at historical cost, which are translated at the exchange rate in effect at the date of acquisition of the assets. Income statement items are translated at exchange rates in effect at the date of settlement of the transactions or at an average exchange rate for the accounting period. All exchange differences are taken to income.

Hedges.   If forward transactions have been concluded as a hedge against the exchange risk inherent in long-term **foreign currency transactions**, valuation at the forward rate may lead to a difference between the discounted (present) rate at the time the forward transaction is concluded and the forward rate at which the transaction will be settled.

This difference is mainly a result of differences in interest rates. Consequently, if an exchange difference is involved, it should be allocated over the duration of the forward transaction. If loans or forward transactions have been concluded to cover future cash flows in foreign currencies, and if and to the extent that it may reasonably be assumed that the exchange risks to which the principal of such loans is exposed will be covered by those future cash flows, it is permissible for any related exchange losses at the balance sheet date to be recognized only when the loans have been repaid or the forward trans-actions settled.

Disclosure.   The accounting policies used for the translation of foreign currencies and the treatment of exchange differences should be disclosed.

Reference.   Guideline 1.03.9 of CAR and Article 384 paragraph 5 of Title 9.

7. Changing Prices/Inflation Accounting (Prijswijzigingen/Actuele Waarde)

General.   There is no legal requirement and it is not standard practice to provide for the effects of inflation in financial statements. However, information based on current value is generally necessary to enable a sound judgment to be formed about the company's financial position and operating results. At present, generally accepted accounting standards allow information to be furnished on the following bases:

- ☐ The balance sheet and income statement at current value.
- ☐ The balance sheet and income statement at **historical cost**, with supplementary current value information in the notes.
- ☐ If supplementary current value information cannot be determined with sufficient accuracy or certainty, an indication of the effect of the current values will suffice.

If the balance sheet and income statement prepared on the historical cost basis do not differ substantially from those calculated on a current value basis, or if no indication of current value can be given, it is recommended that this be disclosed in the notes.

The current value to be used for tangible assets and inventories in specific situations is set out in the Ministerial Decree on Current Value, although the main text of the Decree gives no specific indication as to how these values should be determined. **Replacement, going concern** and realizable **values** are therefore used, depending on their appropriateness for the particular asset in providing the degree of insight required. Where the going concern value is used, the explanatory notes to the Decree prescribe the use of discounted (present) values.

Where assets are valued at current value, a nondistributable revaluation reserve must be set up.

Supplementary Information Disclosed.   If the balance sheet and income statement have been prepared on the basis of historical cost, consideration should be given to presenting in the notes to the balance sheet and the income statement, information by item (or for each heading) on the basis of current value.

Disclosure.   The notes must disclose the way in which current values of assets have been determined.

Reference. Price convention, Guideline 1.03 of CAR.

8. Accounting Changes (Stelselwijzigingen)

Accounting Treatment. Changes in **accounting policies** may be made only for well-founded reasons. When a change is made, insight must be given into the effect of the change on the financial position and results by presenting adjusted figures for the financial year or the preceding financial year. The net effect of the change is deducted from or added to net equity.

Disclosure. The reason for the change and the financial effect must be set out in the notes.

Reference. Guideline 1.06 of CAR and Articles 363 and 384 of Title 9.

9. Prior Period Adjustments (Resultaten Voorgaande Jaren)

Accounting Treatment. The nature and amount of income and expenses that relate to prior financial years should be disclosed (unless minor).

This does not apply to adjustments arising from further assessments or adjustments made on the basis of information not available when the previous financial statements were prepared. (Adjustments relating to changes in accounting policies are covered in Section 8.)

Reference. Guideline 2.71.2 (210) of CAR.

10. Post Balance Sheet Events (Gebeurtenissen na Balansdatum)

Definition. A distinction is made between information that becomes known after the balance sheet date that:

(a) Provides further details of the financial position at that date.
(b) Gives no further data on the situation at the balance sheet date.

Accounting Treatment. Information of type (a) should be accounted for in the financial statements. Information of type (b) should not be accounted for in the financial statements unless it casts doubt on the assumption of the entity's ability to continue as a going concern.

If, subsequent to their issue, it is found that the financial statements are seriously deficient in furnishing the insight required, management must inform the **members** or shareholders without delay and must file notice at the office of the Trade Register; this notice must be accompanied by an auditors' certificate if the financial statements have been examined.

Disclosure. Information of type (b) above that becomes known after the balance sheet date and that has important financial consequences (either favorable or unfavorable) should be disclosed in the additional information (see Section 2). This disclosure should include the nature of the events and an estimate of their financial statement effects. If an estimate is not considered possible, this should be indicated. Information must also be given in the directors' report.

Reference. Guideline 4.03 (draft) of CAR and Articles 362 paragraph 6 and 392 of Title 9.

11. Related Party Transactions (Transacties Tussen Verbonden Partijen)

Definition. Parties are considered to be related if one party has the ability to control the other party or exercise significant influence over the other party in making financial and operating decisions. A related party transaction is a transfer of resources or obligations between related parties, regardless of whether a price is charged.

Accounting Treatment. Measurement of related party transactions is not specifically addressed in Title 9. Therefore, they are treated in accordance with normal accounting principles and practices.

Disclosure. There is no specific requirement in Title 9 to disclose related party transactions. The article regarding the required insight is decisive for this matter. In addition, CAR states that names of related parties should be disclosed, together with the nature and extent of transactions, pricing policy and other conditions.

Reference. Guideline 1.19.3 (draft) of CAR.

12. Segmental Information (Informatie per Onderdeel)

General. If the legal entity's business is divided into various industry sectors, insight must be provided, in quantitative terms, concerning the extent to which each type of activity has contributed toward net turnover. Net turnover must similarly be broken down by the various geographical areas in which the legal entity supplies goods and services. This requirement applies to large companies (see Section 2).

The Minister of Economic Affairs may, on request, grant exemption from this obligation, if there are grounds for believing that disclosure might be seriously prejudicial. Such exemption may be given for successive periods up to a maximum of five years. The notes must state that exemption has been granted or requested.

Disclosure. If the net turnover in a sector of business or certain geographical area exceeds 10 percent of the total net turnover, separate disclosure should be made. The required information about the composition of net turnover should be given in amounts of money or ratios in relation to the group total.

Reference. Article 380 of Title 9 and Guideline 2.71.6 (draft) of CAR.

ACCOUNTING PRINCIPLES FOR SPECIFIC ITEMS— BALANCE SHEET

13. Property, Plant and Equipment (Onroerend Goed, Machines en Inventaris)

Classification of Capital and Revenue Expenditure. Physical items that have a useful life of more than one year and are not regarded as inventories are considered tangible **fixed assets**. They include land and buildings and nonoperating tangible fixed assets that are held as long-term investments. For reasons of efficiency, tangible fixed assets of low value are usually accounted for as expenses in the period of acquisition. Economic ownership, not legal ownership, is the decisive factor in determining whether an item is considered a tangible fixed asset.

Basis of Valuation.   Tangible fixed assets may be valued at historical cost (purchase price or production cost) or at current value.

Current value may be determined as replacement value, going concern value (the value of the net turnover attributable to the asset that may be generated by continued operation of the business) or realizable value, depending on the circumstances. If it may reasonably be assumed that goods forming part of tangible assets will be replaced by goods of equal economic significance for the purpose of business activities, they are valued at replacement value. If it may reasonably be assumed that goods forming part of tangible assets will not be replaced, they are valued at their going concern value if they are still employed in, or intended for, business activities. In the remaining cases, they are valued at their realizable value. In choosing a valuation policy, the company should be guided by the rules of required insight.

In the valuation of fixed assets, allowance must be made for any reduction in their value that is expected to be permanent. Consistency requires that, once a pricing convention has been adopted, it should, insofar as possible, be maintained in subsequent periods. This also applies to the method of calculating current value or historical cost.

Depreciation.   **Depreciation** must be applied irrespective of the results for the financial year. Fixed assets with limited useful economic lives must be written down annually in accordance with a system that takes account of their expected useful future lives. The requirement of consistency implies that the depreciation method chosen should fulfill the general requirements of insight. The most customary method of depreciation is **straight-line** depreciation, although the sinking fund method, the **declining balance method** and the **unit-of-production method** are also used. If tangible fixed assets have undergone a permanent reduction in value, additional depreciation must be provided.

As the expectations regarding the total useful life of an asset change, it is necessary to determine new depreciation amounts on the basis of the new expectations. This is done by spreading the total amount to be written off over the reassessed total useful life. A change in depreciation method is regarded as a change in accounting estimate.

Disclosure.   Tangible fixed assets should be separately disclosed as land and buildings, plant and machinery, other operating fixed assets (such as technical and office equipment), fixed assets under construction and payments on account, and tangible fixed assets not used in the production process.

If the company has only a limited right to the permanent use of tangible fixed assets, this must be stated. Movements in each category of fixed asset during the financial year must be recorded in a reconciling statement showing the related amounts of depreciation, downward valuations and unrealized revaluations.

The methods of calculating depreciation must be stated in the notes. The amount of depreciation on tangible fixed assets and any revaluations and reversals have to be disclosed separately in the income statement.

Reference.   Articles 364 paragraph 2, 366, 368 paragraphs 1 and 2, 377 paragraphs 1 to 4, 386, 387 paragraphs 4 and 5, and 388 paragraph 2 of Title 9; and Guideline 2.02 of CAR.

14. Intangible Assets (Immateriële Vaste Activa)

Accounting Treatment.   The following intangible fixed assets are shown separately:

(a) Incorporation and share issue expenses.

(b) Research and development costs (see Section 25).

(c) Expenses relating to concessions, licenses and intellectual property rights.

(d) Cost of goodwill acquired from third parties for valuable consideration (see Section 4).

(e) Advance payments from third parties on intangible fixed assets.

(f) Other intangible fixed assets, such as preparatory and startup costs, rights to trade names and membership rights.

Explanatory notes must be furnished for costs referred to in categories (a) and (b) above. In addition, a legal reserve must be included in the balance sheet equal to the amount of intangible assets capitalized in these categories.

Valuation.   Intangible fixed assets may be capitalized only if there is a well-founded expectation that they will have future benefits. They should be capitalized up to the amount of their related expenditure costs or purchase price, less an allowance for amortization.

Amortization.   Intangible fixed assets should be amortized consistently. (Amortization in proportion to the sale or the use of the product or process meets this requirement.) At the end of each accounting period, a review of the remaining unamortized amount should be made to determine whether it is still supported by the estimated useful lives of the assets or whether it should be written off more quickly (by charging additional amortization).

Incorporation and share issue expenses should be amortized over no more than five years. Amortization applied to intangible assets in the past should not be reversed, unless it relates to a reversal of additional amortization.

Disclosure.   Intangible fixed assets should be shown separately in the balance sheet. Movements in each intangible fixed asset should be recorded in a reconciling statement. The cumulative amortization, including any additional amortization, should be stated for each intangible fixed asset.

The costs of amortizing intangible fixed assets should be included in the income statement. Additional amortization and reversals thereof should be shown separately in the income statement or the notes.

The principles of valuation for each of the items shown under intangible fixed assets should be indicated, including the methods of amortization. If goodwill is amortized over more than five years, this should be disclosed, together with the reasons. If the costs of intangible fixed assets are charged to expense in the year of their origin, those costs may not be classified as amortization expense.

Reference.   Articles 364 paragraph 2, 365, 368 paragraphs 1 and 2, 377 paragraphs 3 and 4, 387 paragraphs 4 and 5, 386, and 391 of Title 9; and Guideline 2.01 (draft) of CAR.

15. Leases (Leasing)

Classification. A distinction is made between **finance leases** and **operating leases**. Finance leasing is in essence a form of financing in which the legal ownership of the assets generally remains with the lender but the economic risks are borne entirely or almost entirely by the borrower. An operating lease is similar to a "huurovereenkomst" in Dutch law, that is, the lessee has the benefit and use of the asset, and the economic risks remain (almost) entirely with the lessor. Between these two forms there are a number of intermediate forms. The nature of any specific arrangement will have to be deduced from the terms of the contract as a whole.

Accounting Treatment. If it is evident from the terms of the contract that a finance lease is involved, the leased assets should be capitalized by the lessee. In principle, these assets and the related liabilities are shown in the balance sheet at their cash price. If this price is not known, the discounted value is calculated. In many types of finance leasing, a finance company is involved. The finance company should show the outstanding rentals in its balance sheet under **accounts receivable** and not under fixed assets. Where the lessor's legal ownership of the asset serves as security for the receivable, the asset should be included in the lessor's balance sheet if it is certain or likely that the lessee cannot or will not meet the obligation.

Under an operating lease, the lessee treats rental payments as an expense, while the lessor carries the leased items in its balance sheet as tangible fixed assets and treats rental income as **revenue**.

Leveraged Leases. There are no special rules for **leveraged leases** in the Netherlands.

Disclosure. Lessee: If the company has entered into operating lease commitments for substantial sums of money for rather long periods, this should be disclosed in the notes. In the case of finance leases, the lessee includes the leased assets in the tangible fixed assets section of the balance sheet and the future obligations under liabilities. It should be disclosed in the balance sheet or the notes that the company is the economic but not the legal owner.

Lessor: A note to the lessor's balance sheet should disclose the extent to which the legal ownership of assets serves as security for the receivables.

Reference. Guideline 1.05, paragraphs 121 to 127, of CAR.

16. Investments (Beleggingen)

General. Investments are classified as financial fixed assets, if the intention is to keep them for a long time, and as **current assets** if they are not expected to be kept for more than a year. This section does not cover investments in participating interests, group companies and subsidiaries, which are discussed in Section 4.

Valuation. Financial fixed assets: Financial fixed assets may be valued at their purchase price or current value. If securities carried at purchase price have undergone a permanent reduction in value, they must be revalued at their **net realizable value**; no downward revaluation is necessary if the reduction in value is considered temporary. The most common valuation policy is the lower of purchase price or net realizable value (or market value). Current value is determined as net realizable value. If net realizable value has been estimated, the method of estimation must be explained in the notes. When current value is used, all reductions in value must be accounted for.

Current assets: Current assets must be valued at market value if it is lower than the purchase price at the balance sheet date. Where an exceptional reduction in the value of current assets in the near future is foreseeable, this may be taken into account in their valuation. Value adjustments and any reversals thereof must be disclosed separately in the income statement or the notes. Valuation at current value is not allowed.

Treatment of Revaluation Reserve. If an asset is revalued upward, the amount of the revaluation should be added to a revaluation reserve; it may be either gross or net of taxes, depending on whether and in what way allowance has been made for deferred taxes (see Section 29). The reserve is shown separately under shareholders' equity. Reductions in the value of assets, other than periodic depreciation, may be deducted from the revaluation reserve. If the revaluation reserve is insufficient, the reduction is charged to income. The revaluation reserve may be reduced to the extent that amounts included in it relating to assets that are still held by the company at the balance sheet date are no longer necessary.

Gains/Losses. Gains or losses on the sale of part of an investment should be calculated on the basis of weighted-average prices, the FIFO method, the LIFO method or a similar method.

Disclosure. Reductions in the revaluation reserve that are recognized in the income statement must be shown separately or disclosed in the notes. The notes must disclose whether and in what way allowance has been made for the tax effect of the revaluation. If the market value of investments classified as current assets is higher than the carrying value, the market value should be disclosed in the notes.

Disclosure must be made of the aggregate value of other securities included as current assets and listed on a Dutch or foreign stock exchange. The extent to which securities are not at the company's free disposal must be stated. Changes in financial fixed assets must be presented in a reconciling statement.

Reference. Guidelines 2.03 (draft), 2.13 and 2.41 of CAR; and Articles 367, 368, 371, 373 paragraph 1, 385 paragraph 2, 387, and 390 of Title 9.

17. Accounts Receivable (Vorderingen)

Accounting Treatment. Recognition: The recognition of revenues, and hence the related receivables, is described in Section 23.

Discounts: Discounts and credit restriction surcharges should be deducted or added in accordance with the method of determining net sales. Discounts allowed to customers may be deducted from turnover or treated as interest charges.

Allowances: Receivables should be valued at their nominal value, after deduction of any provisions for bad debts and discounts allowed. Both **specific identification** and general formula based provisions are permitted.

Factored Receivables. If accounts receivable have been factored to a finance company for cash consideration, the relevant debts should be excluded from the balance sheet. If the factor has recourse to the vendor for bad debts, disclosure of the contingent liability and a provision for probable losses should be made.

Disclosure. Separate disclosure is required of amounts receivable from trade **debtors**, group companies and other debtors. Separate identification is also necessary for unpaid called-up share capital and amounts receivable from shareholders and amounts receivable (such as loans, advances and guarantees) from directors and members of the supervisory board.

For each category of receivables, any amount due after more than one year must be indicated.

Reference. Guideline 2.12 of CAR and Articles 370 and 383 paragraph 2 of Title 9.

18. Inventories and Work in Progress (Voorraden en Onderhanden Werk)

General Accounting Treatment. **Inventories** are valued at either the lower of historical cost (purchase price or production cost) or market value, or at current value.

Historical cost may be determined using the **LIFO**, **FIFO** or **base stock** method. Where the LIFO and base stock methods are used, the current value of the inventories should also be disclosed.

Current value is determined by replacement value, if it is assumed that inventories will be replaced and the net realizable value is not lower than the replacement value.

It is customary to capitalize physical inventories instead of economic inventories, such as forward purchase contracts. In certain circumstances, information is required concerning economic inventories, either by capitalizing them or giving details in the notes.

When valuing inventories, it is not permissible to make allowance for costs that are not incurred until sale and delivery. Production cost comprises the purchase price of raw materials and consumables used and other expenses directly attributable to the production of the asset. Production cost may also include a reasonable proportion of indirect costs and interest on capital borrowed over the period attributable to the production of the asset; in that case, the notes must state that such interest has been included and must disclose in general terms the indirect costs included.

Long-Term Contracts. The **percentage of completion method** is formally in contravention of the law. However, if a separate identifiable part of work in progress has been finished and sold and the revenue has been received, the percentage of completion method can be considered acceptable because the realization principle has been met. Alternatively, the **completed contract method** may be used. The policy applied must be indicated clearly.

All foreseeable and quantifiable losses on work in progress should be recognized in accordance with the prudence concept.

Disclosure. The following must be shown separately under the current asset heading "Inventories": raw materials and consumables; work in progress; finished goods and goods for sale; and payments on account of inventories.

Prepayments received after the year-end relating to work in progress are often deducted from the value of the work in progress at the balance sheet date, although the amounts received post year-end must be disclosed separately.

Reference. Guideline 2.11 of CAR and Articles 369, 375 paragraph 1c, 385 paragraphs 1 to 3, 388 and 410 paragraph 2 of Title 9.

19. Current Liabilities (Schulden op Korte Termijn)

General Accounting Treatment. Liabilities are generally included in the balance sheet at their face value.

Accruals and deferred income should include amounts received in advance for income to be recognized in subsequent periods and amounts to be paid after the balance sheet date relating to expenses incurred in a prior period.

Creation of General and Specific Provisions. Provisions may be created only when the following conditions are satisfied:

☐ There are concrete, specific risks attached to particular business activities, and those risks go beyond the general risk usually inherent in entrepreneurial activity.

☐ The risks must exist on the balance sheet date, and must arise from events that took place, acts performed or commitments entered into before that date.

☐ The extent of the provision, if uncertain, can reasonably be estimated.

A consistent policy should be established for creating provisions. Provisions relating to a specific asset should be deducted from that asset. Other provisions should be shown separately in the balance sheet as liabilities. A provision or part of a provision expected to be settled within one year should be regarded as short term.

Provisions may be calculated on either a specific identification or general formula basis.

Disclosure. Separate disclosure is required for different groups of liabilities, such as amounts owed to trade **creditors**, group companies, tax authorities, pension schemes, credit institutions and other creditors. Separate disclosure should also be made of debentures, mortgages, payments on account and bills of exchange. Amounts due after one year should be indicated separately for each category, as should amounts due after five years (see Section 20). For each item mentioned, the amount and nature of any collateral must be indicated.

For convertible loans, the terms of conversion must be stated. If the company has accepted liability for the debts of others, obligations arising from these commitments should be disclosed in accordance with the terms of the commitments. Commitments entered into for the benefit of group companies must be disclosed separately.

Reference. Guidelines 2.51, 2.53, 2.55 and 2.62 of CAR; and Articles 364 paragraph 4, 370, 374, 375 and 376 of Title 9.

20. Long-Term Debt (Schulden op Lange Termijn)

General Accounting Treatment. Generally, long-term debt is accounted for in the same manner as **current liabilities**, that is, debts are included in the balance sheet at their face value as long as they continue to represent a present obligation of the company.

Disclosure. The various categories of debts and disclosure requirements are detailed in Section 19.

For loans due after one year from the balance sheet date, the rate of interest and amount of instalments due within one year from the balance sheet date must be disclosed.

Reference. Guidelines 2.51, 2.53, 2.54 and 2.62 of CAR; and Articles 374 and 375 of Title 9.

21. Contingencies (Voorwaardelijke Baten en Lasten)

General. Contingent income should not be recorded unless it is almost certain that it will be received.

Contingent losses, however, should be provided for in the financial statements to cover the risk of the liability becoming unconditional.

Disclosure. If it is probable that a contingent gain will be realized, the existence of the contingent gain should be disclosed in the notes, together with information about its nature and the uncertain factors that may affect the future outcome.

Where no provision can be shown in the balance sheet for a contingent loss because it is not possible to make a reasonable estimate of the amount of the obligation, disclosure should be made in the notes of the nature of the contingent liability, the uncertain factors affecting future outcome and the fact that a reasonable estimate is not possible.

Reference. Guidelines 1.05, 2.02, 2.14 and 2.65 of CAR; and Article 376 of Title 9.

22. Capital and Reserves (Aandelenkapitaal en Reserves)

General. Shareholders' equity includes issued share capital, **share premium**, revaluation reserves, statutory reserves, other legally required reserves, other reserves and retained profits, all of which should be disclosed separately in the statutory financial statements.

Treatment of Share Capital. If the issued share capital has not been fully paid up, the amount actually paid must be disclosed. The issued share capital is also stated. Share capital is not reduced by shares owned by the company itself or by its subsidiaries.

If financial statements are prepared in a foreign currency, the issued share capital is recorded in this currency at the rate prevailing at the balance sheet date. The rate and the amount in Dutch guilders should also be shown.

Treatment of Other Reserves. The Civil Code requires a number of legal reserves to be established. These reserves are intended to protect the company's equity and, by doing so, third parties' interests.

Legally required reserves must be created for:

□ Capitalized share issue expenses and research and development costs.
□ Share of income, less dividends, of equity accounted participating interests where distribution restrictions exist. (This reserve may be converted into share capital and is further explained in Section 4 under "Equity Accounting.")
□ Negative goodwill. (This reserve may be converted into share capital.)
□ Upward revaluations. (This reserve may be converted into share capital.)

□ Shortage in the legally required minimum equity of a BV. (The aggregate of share capital, legal and statutory reserves must be at least 40,000 NLG.)

□ Loans granted by a BV for the purpose of acquisition of its share capital.

Distribution Restrictions. None of the legal reserves, as shown above, may be distributed. Redemption of share capital is restricted to a certain percentage of share capital (BV, 50%; NV, 90%). Share premium may be distributed with the approval of the shareholders.

Disclosure. All categories of capital and reserves should be disclosed separately in the statutory financial statements. The consolidated financial statements need not make this disclosure, although any differences between shareholders' equity on the statutory and consolidated balance sheets must be explained and minority interests in consolidated equity disclosed.

A schedule should be prepared showing the movements throughout the year of each type of shareholders' equity and, in the case of share capital, subdivided into the classes of paid-up or called-up shares.

Separate disclosure must be made of all shares and trust certificates reacquired by the company itself or by a subsidiary. An NV must disclose every acquisition and disposal for its own account of its own shares and trust certificates, stating the reasons, the number, **par value** and agreed price of the shares and trust certificates involved in each transaction, and the proportion of the capital they represent.

Stock options (including conversion rights) granted to shareholders, employees or others should be disclosed in the notes. If cumulative **preference shares** have been issued, it should be indicated in the notes whether, and if so to what extent, dividends are in arrears. Where a payment to the shareholders charged to the share premium account might give rise to tax being payable by the recipient, it should be detailed in the notes which part of the premium is included in a tax claim and which part is not. Corresponding details should be given about the part of the paid-up and called-up capital that is not recognized as fully paid up for tax purposes. In addition, a statement of the number of profit-sharing certificates and similar instruments should be included, with an indication of the rights they confer, and a list of persons to whom a special right to control the company is granted by the articles of incorporation and a description of the nature of that right. If the right is embodied in shares, the number of shares held by each person should also be stated. Where such a right vests in a company, partnership, cooperative association, mutual guarantee company or foundation, the names of the latter's board members must also be disclosed.

Reference. Guideline 2.41 of CAR and Articles 364 paragraph 4, 373, 378 and 411 of Title 9.

ACCOUNTING PRINCIPLES FOR SPECIFIC ITEMS— INCOME STATEMENT

23. Revenue Recognition (Resultaatbepaling)

General Principles. Income is allocated to the period in which sales transactions occur, usually in the form of supplying goods or services or transferring ownership. Invoicing generally occurs during the same period.

Long-Term Contracts. Revenue from long-term contracts is recognized using either the percentage of completion method or the completed contract method. The percentage of completion method may be used only when the different stages of performance of the long-term contract can be distinguished (see Section 18).

Instalment Sales. For transactions based on hire purchase, finance leasing or credit sales, a distinction may be made between profit from transactions and remuneration for deferred payment. Profit from transactions should be recorded at the time of the sale, and remuneration for providing credit should be allocated to the instalments.

Product Financing. In a sale and leaseback transaction, economic ownership generally remains with the seller, so the transaction is, in substance, a financing arrangement. The selling price received should be treated as a loan, secured by the related asset and repayable in lease instalments.

Disclosure. In the income statement, income from ordinary activities and extraordinary income must be shown separately. Separate disclosure must be made of net turnover, other operating income, income from participating interests, income from other financial assets, other interest and similar income.

Reference. Guideline 2.71 of CAR and Article 377 of Title 9.

24. Government Grants and Assistance (Overheidssubsidies)

Accounting Treatment. Government grants and assistance may be in the form of operating and investment subsidies, finance facilities or development credits.

Operating subsidies are subsidies for current expenses, certain lost revenues or general operating deficits. The amount of the subsidy should be recorded in income in the year in which either the subsidized expenditures are charged, the revenues were lost or the operating deficit occurred.

Investment subsidies are subsidies for expenditures that are allocated over the number of years in which they are considered to be of benefit. The subsidy should either be included separately as a provision under liabilities, or be deducted from the investment itself or from the tax charge.

Finance facilities are linked to a type of credit—for instance, subordination, remission subject to certain conditions or interest rates lower than market value.

Development credits are obtained to finance development costs. Repayment is generally conditional on the financial results of the project. In the event of failure, the debt is cancelled after a number of years. If the project is successful, the entrepreneur must repay the principal plus interest. Repayment is generally linked to the turnover resulting from the development activities. Amounts received on development credits are offset against development costs incurred. Repayments of development credits are reflected as cost of sales.

It is not permissible to record a subsidy directly in shareholders' equity.

Disclosure. The notes should state the nature and extent of subsidies, how they have been accounted for, the basis of allocation to subsequent financial years and the conditions on which any development credits have been obtained.

Reference. Guideline 3.01 of CAR.

25. Research and Development (Onderzoek en Ontwikkeling)

Definition. Research and development generally refers to the systematic activity of obtaining new scientific knowledge and insight (research), and of translating the results of the research or other knowledge into a plan or design for new or essentially improved products or processes before commercial production is started (development). Research and development costs include personnel costs, cost of materials consumed, depreciation of durable capital goods, patent and license costs, other direct costs and an appropriate allocation of indirect costs.

Accounting Treatment. Research and development costs are capitalized in the balance sheet only if there is a well-founded expectation that they will have future benefits. Research and development costs meet this requirement only if:

☐ The product or process is accurately defined and the specific costs to be allocated can be determined.

☐ The technical feasibility of the product or process has been proved.

☐ Management has decided to introduce the new product or process and begin marketing it or to start using it.

☐ There is a clear indication of a future market for the product or process or, if it is to be used internally, its usefulness to the company can be proved.

☐ Sufficient funds are available or can reasonably be expected to become available for completion of the process and for the marketing (or the internal use) of the product or process.

Costs of basic research often do not qualify for capitalization, since there is normally no potential for commercial operation at the research stage.

Other research and development costs are intangible fixed assets, which should be amortized consistently. Amortization in proportion to sale or use of the product or process meets this requirement. At the end of each accounting period, the remaining unamortized amount should be reviewed to determine whether additional amortization should be charged.

Disclosure. The total amount of research and development costs expensed in the financial year should be disclosed.

Reference. Guideline 2.01 of CAR and Article 365 of Title 9.

26. Capitalized Interest Costs (Geactiveerde Rente)

Accounting Treatment. Production cost of an asset may include interest on capital borrowed over the period attributable to the production of the asset. A consistent policy should be followed for the costs attributable to an asset and for the capitalization of interest.

Disclosure. The notes must state that capitalized interest has been included in the cost of assets and the amount capitalized in the current year.

Reference. Article 388 paragraph 2 of Title 9.

27. Imputed Interest (Gecalculeerde Rente)

General. **Imputed interest** is not a common feature of accounting in the Netherlands.

Accounting Treatment. An exception to this is provisions for pensions, which are valued at their discounted (present) value. The discounted value may also be used, in addition to the face value, for provisions for deferred taxes and provisions for early retirement plans.

Disclosure. Imputed interest charges on provisions for pensions are classified as pension costs in the income statement and are not accounted for as interest charges.

Reference. Guideline 1.03 of CAR.

28. Extraordinary or Unusual Items (Buitengewone Resultaten)

General. Extraordinary income and expense arise other than in the ordinary course of an entity's business. This may include income and charges arising from acts and events of a nonrecurring nature. An explanation of the nature and extent of material extraordinary income and expenses must be given in the notes.

Disclosure. Extraordinary income and extraordinary expenses should be distinguished according to their nature. The amount should be shown before and after tax.

Reference. Guideline 2.71.2 of CAR and Article 377 of Title 9.

29. Income Taxes (Belastingen)

Accounting Treatment. The tax on income recognized in the income statement for a year is the amount arising from the application of the effective rate or rates to the profit before tax, after allowing for the effect of tax-exempt income, nondeductible expenses, certain tax reliefs and other differences. If the proportion of the amount of tax on income compared with income before taxation differs substantially from the statutory tax rate, an indication of the reasons for this difference is recommended.

Deferred taxes are generally accounted for on a full allocation basis using the **liability method**. They may be valued in the balance sheet at either their nominal or present value. Deferred tax assets should be included only to the extent that there is reasonable assurance of recovery and to the extent that there are also deferred tax liabilities of the same duration and of at least the same amount. Specific circumstances are outlined in paragraph 512 of Guideline 2.53.5 (draft) of CAR. Where deferred tax assets and liabilities are of the same duration, the net figure should be shown in the balance sheet. An insight into the composition of deferred taxes should be given by grouping deferred taxes as far as possible according to their duration.

Tax Losses. Netherlands tax legislation permits offsetting losses arising in any year against the profits of a limited number of preceding years (tax loss carrybacks) and against profits of a limited number of subsequent years (tax loss carryforwards); startup losses may be offset against the profits of subsequent years for an unlimited number of years.

Disclosure. The income statement should show separately the tax attributable to ordinary activities, the tax related to extraordinary items and other taxes. There must be separate disclosure of provisions for tax liabilities that may arise after the current year but are chargeable to that year or to a preceding year, including provision for taxes that may arise from a valuation above purchase price or production cost. The notes must disclose whether and in what way allowance has been made for the tax effect of the revaluation, and an explanation of the way in which tax effects arising from differences between the valuation for tax purposes and the accounting valuation have been accounted for. The amount of loss qualifying as a tax loss carryforward, but not included in the provision for deferred taxes, should be stated in the notes.

Reference. Guideline 2.53.5 paragraph 512 (draft) of CAR and Articles 374 paragraph 4, 377 paragraph 1, and 390 paragraph 5 of Title 9.

30. Postretirement Benefits

Dutch pension plans are regulated in the Act on Pension- and Savingfunds. The basic principle of this act is that vested pension rights of employees must be reinsured with a life insurance company that is independent from the employer, or placed in a pension fund (legally, a foundation) that must also be independent from the employer.

Most Dutch pension plans are **defined benefit plans** usually on a final pay basis, although other benefit plans are also possible.

In principle, pension liabilities are calculated by the static method or by the dynamic method. Under both methods valuation should be at discounted (present) value.

Under the static method, the liabilities associated with accrued pension entitlements should, whatever the method of financing, be imputed to the years in which related employee services were performed. This may not parallel the payment of lump-sum premiums or periodic contributions under the financing plan.

Under the dynamic method, the intention is for the liabilities of the pension scheme for a body of employees to show an even trend over the years, for instance, in relation to annual wages. Therefore, there may be a timing difference between actual payments of contributions and contributions expensed to the income statement.

If pension rights have not already been financed, unconditional entitlements should be shown in the balance sheet, valued using actuarial principles. If a legal entity, at its own expense, awards former employees pensions or pension supplements that are deemed irrevocable, these should be treated as unconditional entitlements. Entitlements to be granted on the basis of a legal entity's intention to make legally enforceable pension arrangements should be disclosed in the financial statements. Provision for possible deficits in pension funds that can legally be claimed from the company should be made in the company's balance sheet.

Charges arising from pension entitlements are part of operating results, except for prior service charges arising from new plans or changes in the way pension entitlements are regulated. Prior service charges are either considered extraordinary charges or charged directly to net equity.

Disclosure. Pension expenses and provisions for pension liabilities must be stated separately. The notes must distinguish between:

☐ Prior service obligations of reinsured pensions.
☐ Pension obligations not reinsured.
☐ Unreinsured obligations of pension allowances for retired employees.

Separate disclosure must be made in the income statement or notes thereto of social security costs, distinguishing between those relating to pensions and others.

Reference. Guideline 2.53.3 of CAR and Articles 374 paragraph 4, 375 paragraph 1, 377, 382, 383 paragraph 1 and 410 of Title 9.

31. Discontinued Operations (Discontinuiteit)

Accounting Treatment. If it may reasonably be assumed that the operation for which assets are used (or intended) will be discontinued in the near future, they are valued at net realizable value.

Disclosure. Where, due to the expected discontinuance of operations, assets and liabilities are stated in the accounts at their net realizable value, this fact must be disclosed in the notes.

Reference. Guideline 1.03.6 of CAR and Article 384 paragraph 3 of Title 9.

32. Earnings per Share (Winst per Aandeel)

General. Although there is no formal disclosure rule regarding earnings per share, it is not uncommon for this information to be disclosed.

Definition. Earnings per share is the profit accruing, whether by distribution or retention, to the holders of ordinary shares, divided by the number of shares entitled to that profit. Profit means the net profit on the income statement, less any amounts not accruing to the holders of ordinary shares (e.g., payments to the holders of preference shares).

Disclosure. Disclosure of earnings per share is recommended.

Reference. Guideline 4.24 of CAR.

Appendix
DO DUTCH STANDARDS OR PREVALENT PRACTICE SUBSTANTIALLY COMPLY WITH INTERNATIONAL ACCOUNTING STANDARDS?

Section	Topic	Substantially complies with IAS?	Comments
3.	Basic accounting concepts and conventions	Yes	
	Contents of financial statements	Yes	A cash flow statement is not a legal requirement, but normally is presented
4.	Business combinations*	Yes	Except that a subsidiary may be excluded from consolidation for the reason that its business activities are dissimilar
5.	Joint ventures	Yes	
6.	Foreign currency translation*	Yes	
8.	Accounting changes*	Yes	
9.	Prior period adjustments*	Yes	
10.	Post balance sheet events	Yes	
11.	Related party transactions	Yes	
12.	Segmental information	No	
13.	Property, plant and equipment*	Yes	
15.	Leases	Yes	
16.	Investments	Yes	
17.	Accounts receivable	Yes	
18.	Inventories and work in progress*	Yes	
19.	Current liabilities	Yes	
20.	Long-term debt	Yes	
21.	Contingencies	Yes	
22.	Capital and reserves	Yes	
23.	Revenue recognition*	Yes	
24.	Government grants and assistance	Yes	Except that government subsidies may be shown as a deduction from the tax charge
25.	Research and development*	Yes	

Appendix (*Continued*)

Section	Topic	Substantially complies with IAS?	Comments
26.	Capitalization of interest costs*	Yes	
28.	Extraordinary or unusual items*	Yes	
29.	Income tax**	Yes	Except that the rules for the recognition of deferred tax assets are less strict
30.	Postretirement benefits*	Yes	

*These topics are subject to change as a result of the IASC Improvements Project—see the appendix to the International Accounting Standards chapter.

**The IAS on accounting for taxes on income is currently being revised, and an exposure draft has been issued.

Comparison in this table is made to International Accounting Standards in force at January 1, 1993. For further details, see the International Accounting Standards chapter.

NEW ZEALAND

GENERAL NATIONAL INFORMATION

1. Source of Generally Accepted Accounting Principles

Generally Accepted Accounting Principles and Accounting Standards. Generally accepted accounting principles are derived primarily from the following sources as well as from well-established commercial practice:

☐ The Companies Act 1955. This act sets out in the Eighth Schedule certain disclosure requirements for corporate entities. At the time of this writing, company legislation is the subject of a wide-ranging review, and two bills, the Companies Bill 1990 and the Financial Reporting Bill 1991, are before parliament. It is anticipated that these will become law by the end of 1993.

Significant proposals in the Companies Bill include:

—A solvency test to determine whether a company may make a distribution.

—Abolition of the concept of par and nominal values of shares and provision for a company to purchase its own shares.

—Repeal of the Eighth Schedule. However, financial statements will still be required to show a "true and fair view."

Under the proposals contained in the Financial Reporting Bill, all "issuers" (issuers of securities to which the Securities Act 1978 applies) will be required to comply with approved **accounting standards**.

☐ Financial Reporting Standards (FRSs). These standards are approved and issued by the Council of the New Zealand Society of Accountants (NZSA) and apply (unless specifically restricted) to all financial statements intended to give a true and fair view of an entity's financial position and its profit or loss for the period. Prior to 1992, accounting standards were called Statements of Standard Accounting Practice (SSAPs). These standards will continue to be referred to as SSAPs until they are revised.

At present, there is no legislation requiring the application of FRSs or SSAPs; however, as explained above, the Financial Reporting Bill proposes that issuers will have to comply with accounting standards approved by a new body to be formed (the Accounting Standards Review Board [ASRB]).

☐ Technical Practice Aids (TPAs). These are issued by the Accounting Research and Standards Board of the NZSA for general information and guidance. The Council of the NZSA does not approve them.

☐ Research Bulletins. These are published under the authority of the Accounting Research and Standards Board for the purpose of promoting wider discussion, but do not purport to represent official NZSA recommendations.

At the time of this writing, the NZSA has issued a series of exposure drafts, collectively entitled "A Proposed Framework for Financial Reporting in New Zealand" (ED 59 to 65). These exposure drafts encompass broad principles and concepts for general purpose financial reporting for both the private and public sectors and a differential reporting framework.

2. Audit and Public Company Requirements

Audit. The Companies Act requires that every company appoint auditors at each annual general shareholders' meeting. There is an exception for certain private companies, which may, by a unanimous shareholder resolution, vote at the annual general meeting not to appoint auditors for the following year. Private companies may not have more than 25 shareholders. The exception does not apply to a private company that is a subsidiary of a company that is not a private company or to a nonexempt private company, which is a private company 25 percent or more of whose voting rights are controlled by persons or companies not ordinarily resident or incorporated in New Zealand or a private company that is indebted to any person for any deposit or loan to which the Securities Act 1978 applies. In addition, New Zealand branches of overseas companies are required to file audited financial statements in New Zealand.

Auditors must be members of either the NZSA or an association of accountants constituted within the Commonwealth that is approved by the Minister of Justice. An auditor may not be an officer or employee of the company, a partner or an employee of an officer or employee of the company (**public companies** only) or a corporate entity.

A company's initial auditors may be appointed by the directors before the first annual general meeting. Thereafter the shareholders appoint the auditors at the annual general meetings, although the directors may fill a vacancy.

Auditing Standards (ASs) are issued by the NZSA. These standards define the fundamental principles of auditing and are supplemented by Auditing Guidelines (AGs), which deal with auditing techniques and procedures.

Reference. Companies Act 1955, Sections 163, 165 and 354, Schedule 8; Auditing Standards, AS 1 to 10; and Auditing Guidelines, AG 1 to 23.

Public Companies. All companies are required to present financial statements for shareholder approval at the annual general meeting, at least once in every calendar year and not more than 15 months after the previous annual general meeting. There is one exception to this requirement, which applies in a company's first reporting period, when the first annual general meeting must be held within 18 months of incorporation.

Most companies are required to file their financial statements with the Registrar of Companies within 30 days of their approval at the annual general meeting. Private companies, except nonexempt private companies (see above), need not file financial statements.

There is only one stock exchange in New Zealand, although there are a number of branches, principally in Auckland and Wellington.

For a new listing to be considered, the total paid up value of the securities to be quoted must be at least NZ $10,000,000. A class of equity securities normally will not be considered for quotation unless at least 200 members of the public hold a minimum of 25 percent of the class or 500 members of the public hold a minimum of 15 percent. If these criteria are not met, a company may be granted a "Non-Standard" listing.

Listed companies are required to make preliminary announcements of their results of operations, financial position and cash flows within three months of the end of their fiscal year and fiscal half-year. Preliminary announcements need not be audited. A printed and audited annual report is required to be issued to securityholders within four months of the end of the fiscal year. Unaudited half-year reports must be issued within three months of the end of the fiscal half-year.

Reference. Companies Act 1955, Sections 133, 152, 354 and 402; and New Zealand Stock Exchange Listing Requirements, July 1989.

GENERAL ACCOUNTING

3. Financial Statements

Basic Accounting Concepts. Financial statements are prepared primarily using the **historical cost** convention, whereby transactions and events are recognized at the amount of cash or cash equivalent consideration paid or received, or the fair value ascribed when the transactions took place. However, revaluation of assets is permitted, following what is frequently referred to as the modified historical cost convention.

Financial statements are prepared on the assumptions that the entity is a **going concern** and that **accrual** accounting has been used. Where the going concern assumption is invalid and an alternative basis of accounting is used, this should be explained in the notes to the financial statements.

Contents of Financial Statements. Financial statements normally include a balance sheet, income statement and cash flow statement. Notes to the financial statements are an integral part of the statements.

The financial statements are required by the Companies Act to give a true and fair view of the state of affairs of the company as of its fiscal year-end and of its profit or loss for the year then ended. A **holding company** must also prepare **group accounts** that show a true and fair view. The holding company's separate balance sheet must also be presented, but a separate income statement is not required. In addition, a directors' report must be attached to every balance sheet presented to a general meeting.

Format of Financial Statements. There is no prescribed format for financial statements, except for the cash flow statement. However, there are a number of specific requirements in the Eighth Schedule of the Companies Act, supplemented by the requirements of various accounting standards, in particular SSAP 9, *Information to Be Disclosed in Company Balance Sheets and Profit or Loss Accounts.* Assets and liabilities are classified as current or noncurrent; reserves, as capital or revenue reserves. Comparative figures for the previous period are required to be shown.

Cash flow statements should reconcile cash at the beginning and end of the period and should show major sources and uses of cash relating to operating activities, investing activities and financing activities.

Cash flows from operating activities should be presented using the **direct method**, showing gross cash flows from customers and to suppliers. In addition, a reconciliation of the reported operating surplus with the cash generated from operating activities is required. Interest paid is shown separately as part of cash flows from operating activities.

Disclosure of Accounting Policies.   An entity is required to disclose all significant **accounting policies**. The disclosure statement, which may be either a separate statement or a note to the financial statements, should include:

- ☐   General accounting policies with respect to measurement base and **matching** of expenses and revenues.
- ☐   Specific accounting policies used.
- ☐   Changes in accounting policies or a statement that there have been no changes.

Reference.   Companies Act 1955, Sections 152 to 161, Schedule 8; and SSAPs 1 and 9; and FRS 10.

4. Business Combinations

Principles of Consolidation.   The financial statements of groups of companies (holding company with one or more **subsidiaries** or in-substance subsidiaries) usually are consolidated, although directors may produce the same or equivalent information in another form if they consider it preferable. An alternative form showing separate consolidations of nonfinance and finance subsidiaries is sometimes used by conglomerate groups. Group financial statements need not be prepared if, at the end of the year, a holding company is a wholly owned subsidiary of a company incorporated in New Zealand.

A company is a subsidiary of another company, as defined in the Companies Act, if:

- ☐   The **parent**
    — is a shareholder of the subsidiary and controls the composition of the subsidiary's board of directors; or
    — holds more than 50 percent of the subsidiary's voting share capital; or
- ☐   The subsidiary is a subsidiary of a company that is itself a subsidiary of the parent.

SSAP 8 extends this definition to cover in-substance subsidiaries, which are companies or other entities in which the investor has the risks and rewards associated with majority ownership, even if they do not meet the conditions above. Essentially the concept behind this definition is to include all entities controlled by the investor.

Subsidiaries may be excluded from group financial statements if including the subsidiaries would be:

- (a)   Impracticable or of no real value because amounts are immaterial; or
- (b)   Excessively expensive or would result in an excessive delay; or

(c)   Misleading or harmful; or

(d)   Unreasonable because the business of the investor and subsidiary are so different.

Approval of the Governor General in Council is required for (c) and (d) above.

Accounting for Business Combinations.   **Business combinations** are usually accounted for by the **purchase method**. The **pooling of interests method** is permitted in the rare circumstances in which neither party can be identified as the acquirer.

Control.   Control is defined as the power to govern, directly or indirectly, the financial and operating policies of the management of the investee so as to obtain the majority of the benefits from its activities. Usually ownership of more than 50 percent of the voting power of the investee is needed to achieve this.

Goodwill.   **Goodwill** arising on consolidation is separately disclosed and amortized over the period of expected benefits. The **amortization** period normally does not exceed 10 years and should never exceed 20 years. Unamortized goodwill should be reviewed regularly and written down for any permanent impairment.

Negative goodwill is eliminated by reducing proportionately the fair values of nonmonetary assets acquired. If negative goodwill remains after all nonmonetary assets have been written off, the remaining balance is classified as a gain in the income statement.

Equity Accounting.   Investments in **associated companies** are accounted for using the **equity method**.

Goodwill, or negative goodwill, is calculated on the acquisition of an associate by comparing the fair value of the net identifiable assets acquired with the cost of the investment to the group, in the same manner as for subsidiaries. The accounting treatment for this goodwill, or negative goodwill, is also the same as for subsidiaries. If it is not practical to determine fair values, book values may be used.

Minority Interests.   **Minority interests** are shown separately from shareholders' equity in the consolidated balance sheet. Minority interests in the profit or loss for the period are shown as a separate item in the consolidated income statement.

Disclosure.   The statement of accounting policies should include a description of the methods used to account for subsidiaries, in-substance subsidiaries and associates. If a merger was reflected in the financial statements by the pooling of interests method, this should be disclosed, together with the reasons for using the pooling method.

The financial statements for the period in which an investment was acquired should disclose the name and a brief description of the investee and the period for which the results of the investee are included in the consolidated income statement.

If a subsidiary or in-substance subsidiary was acquired or disposed of during the period, the financial statements should disclose:

☐   The increase or decrease in individual assets and liabilities of the group.

☐   The purchase price or proceeds of sale and how the sale was or will be settled.

This information may be shown in the aggregate where there is more than one acquisition or disposal, unless separate disclosure is required for presentation of a true and fair view. Gains or losses on disposals should be separately disclosed.

The following disclosures are also required:

□ A listing and description of all significant subsidiaries, in-substance subsidiaries and associates, including the ownership interest held and balance sheet date of each investee.

□ Why a subsidiary was not consolidated or why the equity method was not used to account for an associate.

□ Any statutory or contractual restrictions on the resources of the group.

□ Information needed to identify and evaluate exposure to exceptional risks of operating or borrowing in other countries.

For investments accounted for using the equity method, the following, by class of entity, should be disclosed:

□ Dividends received and receivable.

□ The investor's share of retained profits less losses of investees for the year (both before and after tax), which is disclosed after group operating profit after tax and after deducting minority interests.

□ The investor's share of postacquisition profits less losses carried forward by investees.

□ The investor's interest in postacquisition capital and revenue reserves, excluding retained earnings, of investees, which is disclosed separately as part of capital and reserves.

□ The investor's aggregate interest in investees.

□ Advances and other balances between the investor and investees.

Reference. Companies Act 1955, Sections 154 to 158; and SSAP 8.

5. Joint Ventures

Accounting for Investments in Joint Ventures. **Joint ventures** are a form of joint arrangement in which there is a contractual association, other than a partnership, between two or more parties to undertake a specific business project in which the venturers have several liability with respect to the costs and liabilities of the project and share any resulting output. There is no distinction in New Zealand accounting standards between the different types of joint venture arrangements addressed in International Accounting Standard 31, *Financial Reporting of Interests in Joint Ventures*.

Venturers account for joint ventures by the **proportionate consolidation method**.

Transactions Between Venturers and the Joint Venture. Where venturers contribute noncash resources in proportions different from their agreed share of the output, the assets should be recognized at their fair values, together with any associated goodwill or discount. In accounting for other transactions between the venturer and joint venture, where the substance of the transaction is that a gain has resulted, the gain should be recognized only to the extent of the interests of nonrelated venturers. Losses should be recognized in their entirety.

Disclosure. The following should be disclosed:

☐ A description, in the statement of accounting policies, of the method of accounting for joint ventures.

☐ A listing and description of significant joint ventures, including names, interests in the joint ventures and their principal activities.

☐ Amounts relating to any significant unadjusted transactions occurring between the balance sheet date of the venturer and the balance sheet date of the joint venture.

☐ The venturer's share of contingencies and capital commitments of the joint venture.

☐ The period for which the joint venture's results are included in the profit and loss account.

☐ A summary of assets, liabilities, revenues and expenses relating to joint ventures included in the financial statements, if they represent a material proportion of the venturer's assets, liabilities or income.

Accounting by Joint Ventures. Generally accepted accounting principles apply to all assets and liabilities and operations of joint ventures.

Reference. SSAP 25.

6. Foreign Currency Translation

Bases of Translation. Foreign currency denominated transactions: **Foreign currency transactions** are recorded using the rate of exchange at the transaction date. Foreign currency **monetary items** outstanding at the balance sheet date are translated at the rate in effect at the balance sheet date (closing rate); nonmonetary items are translated at historical rates. Exchange rate adjustments are recorded in the income statement.

Foreign operations: Foreign operations are classified as either integrated or independent. The financial statements of an **integrated foreign operation** are translated as though the underlying transactions had been entered into by the reporting entity. The financial statements of an independent (**self-sustaining**) **foreign operation** are translated at the closing rate. Exchange rate adjustments arising from translating the opening net investment at a different rate than previously used should be recorded in the foreign currency translation reserve account.

Hedges. A **hedge** is undertaken to fix the price of a purchase or sale transaction. The premium, discount or other costs associated with a hedge should be deferred and recorded as part of the purchase or sale transaction. If a foreign currency liability is a hedge of a nonmonetary asset, or vice versa, the asset should be translated at the closing rate and the exchange rate adjustment recorded in the foreign currency translation reserve account. The exchange rate adjustment on the liability should also be included in the foreign currency translation reserve account to the extent that it is offset by the exchange rate adjustment on the asset. If a foreign currency monetary liability is a hedge of a net investment in an independent foreign operation, any exchange rate adjustment on the liability should be recorded in the foreign currency translation reserve account to the extent that it is offset by the exchange rate adjustment on the net investment.

If a future income (expense) stream is a hedge of a foreign liability (asset), or vice versa, and the stream is expected to accumulate over the next 12 months to at least equal to the amount of the item being hedged, the liability (asset) should be translated at the closing rate and the exchange rate adjustment deferred and amortized. The amount amortized should equal the adjustment resulting from translating the hedged item at the weighted-mean rate for the current 12-month period and the previous period.

Disclosure.   The financial statements should disclose the translation methods used, the net exchange rate adjustments included in the income statement for the period, a reconciliation of the foreign currency translation reserve and the amount of any unamortized exchange rate adjustment resulting from hedging a foreign currency liability (asset).

Reference.   SSAP 21.

7. Changing Prices/Inflation Accounting

General.   There is no requirement to present information on the effects of changing prices.

8. Accounting Changes

Accounting Treatment.   Accounting policies: A change in accounting policy is permitted only if the new policy is preferable to the old because it will give a fairer presentation of the results of operations and financial position of the entity. All changes in accounting policy that affect the measurement of financial performance should be recognized in the statement of financial performance in the period in which the decisions to change the accounting policies are made and applied, except where an FRS or statutory requirement specifically requires the change in policy to be accounted for retrospectively. Where material, such adjustments should be disclosed separately.

Accounting estimates: A change in accounting estimate arises from new information or developments. Its effect is accounted for in the period of the change and applicable future periods.

Disclosure.   The nature of a change in accounting policy, the reason for the change and the monetary effect, if quantifiable, on the financial position and results of operations should be disclosed.

Reference.   SSAPs 1 and 7 (subject to ED 57A).

9. Prior Period Adjustments

Definition of Adjusting Items.   Prior period adjustments arise from the correction of fundamental errors or from changes in accounting policy that are required by an FRS or a statutory requirement to be accounted for retrospectively. Fundamental errors are errors that are currently identified in previously issued financial statements and are so significant that they destroy the fair presentation of the financial statements taken as a whole.

Accounting Treatment. Prior period adjustments are accounted for by restating prior period financial statements.

Effect on Previously Reported Earnings per Share. Earnings per share are recalculated using the restated earnings.

Disclosure. The adjustment and its effect should be separately disclosed.

Reference. SSAP 7 (subject to ED 57A).

10. Post Balance Sheet Events

Definition. Two types of post balance sheet events are identified:

☐ Adjustable events, which provide evidence or clarify conditions that existed at the balance sheet date.
☐ Nonadjustable events, which relate to conditions that arose subsequent to the balance sheet date.

Accounting Treatment. Adjustable events: Appropriate adjustments are made to the financial statements to recognize the financial effects of the events.

Nonadjustable events: Financial statements should not be adjusted to record the effects of nonadjustable post balance sheet events. However, events that may influence a reader's evaluation of the entity's future viability should be disclosed in a note.

Disclosure. No separate disclosure is required for adjustable events. The note disclosing a nonadjustable event should state that the event occurred subsequent to the balance sheet date and, where possible, should disclose its financial effects.

Reference. SSAP 5.

11. Related Party Transactions

Definition. Parties are considered to be related if one party has the ability, directly or indirectly, to control or exercise significant influence over the operating, investing and financing decisions of the other party. Parties are also considered related if they are subject to common outside control or significant influence. Other parties that may be regarded as related, depending on the substance of the relationship, include directors, key management personnel, major shareholders and close family relatives of or entities controlled by any of the above.

Accounting Treatment. Related party transactions are reported at the values at which the transactions were recorded. There is no requirement to remeasure to an arm's-length value.

Disclosure. If there were material related party transactions during the period, the following should be disclosed:

☐ The identity of each related party and the nature of the relationship.

☐   The types of transactions involved.

☐   The recorded value of the transactions either in monetary terms or as a percentage of the value of all transactions of each type for the period.

☐   The related party balances outstanding, together with repayment terms.

☐   The total debts with related parties written off during the period.

If related party transactions occurred at no apparent or nominal value, this should be disclosed, together with a general description of such transactions.

If an entity is controlled by another entity, the name of the controlling entity and, if applicable, the name of the entity ultimately controlling that party should be disclosed.

In addition, the aggregate of directors' fees paid during the period and balances due to and from directors at the balance sheet date must be disclosed.

Reference.   SSAPs 9 and 22, and Companies Act 1955, Section 197.

12. Segmental Information

General.   The financial statements of all entities, other than wholly owned subsidiaries of New Zealand companies, are required to disclose segmental information by both industry and geographical location. A reportable segment is generally defined as one whose revenue, results of operations or assets exceed 10 percent of the total revenue (including intersegmental revenue), total results of operations (segments that had a profit and those that had a loss are considered separately) or total assets for all segments. Reportable segments should cover a substantial proportion of total operations, generally at least 75 percent of the entity's external revenue. If an entity operates predominantly (greater than 90%) in one industry or geographical location, only that industry or geographical segment need be disclosed.

Disclosure.   For each industry and geographical segment, segment revenue (distinguishing between external and intersegmental revenue), segment results, carrying value of segment assets, the basis of intersegmental pricing and abnormal items should be disclosed. In addition, segment revenue, segment results of operations and segment assets should be aggregated and reconciled to the related information in the financial statements.

Reference.   SSAP 23.

ACCOUNTING PRINCIPLES FOR SPECIFIC ITEMS— BALANCE SHEET

13. Property, Plant and Equipment

Classification of Capital and Revenue Expenditure.   The initial amount capitalized for a **fixed asset** is the consideration given to acquire or create the asset and any directly attributable costs of preparing the asset for its intended use. Expenditures that are expected to increase the service potential of a fixed asset are also capitalized. Other expenditures, including repairs and maintenance, are expensed as incurred.

Basis of Valuation.   Fixed assets either are carried at depreciated historical cost or are revalued.

When the modified historical cost system of accounting is adopted, fixed assets should be revalued by class on a systematic basis, preferably annually, and at least every three years (the cyclical method).

A class of fixed assets consists of fixed assets that have a similar nature or function in the reporting entity. Assets are revalued normally to net current value, but the value should not exceed the recoverable amount. When a fixed asset is revalued, accumulated depreciation should first be deducted from the asset. The valuation adjustment should be made against an asset revaluation reserve account, unless a net deficit in the revaluation reserve of a class results, in which case the net deficit must be recognized immediately in the income statement. However, to the extent that a revaluation gain reverses a previous deficit for the same asset class, the gain may be credited to the income statement. Periodic **depreciation** is calculated on the revalued amount and is charged to the income statement.

When the asset is sold, the related revaluation reserve is transferred directly to **retained earnings**. The gain or loss is recognized in the income statement.

Depreciation.   The depreciable amount is allocated to the income statement on a systematic basis over the useful life of the asset. The most commonly used method of allocation is **straight-line**, but the reducing (**declining**) **balance method** is also sometimes used. Land is not depreciated.

Disclosure.   The depreciation methods and rates should be disclosed. In addition, for each asset class, cost or valuation (clearly distinguishing the two) and accumulated depreciation should be disclosed. The amount of depreciation expense in the income statement should also be disclosed. For each class of fixed asset, it should be disclosed whether the class has been revalued, intervals at which revaluations take place, dates and amounts of valuations, names and qualifications of the valuers, the basis of the valuations, and, where the cyclical method of valuation has been adopted, this should be disclosed and the method explained. The aggregate latest available valuation of land and buildings should also be disclosed.

Reference.   SSAPs 3, 9 and 28.

14.   Intangible Assets

Accounting Treatment.   There is currently no accounting pronouncement on **intangible assets** in New Zealand, although there is a pronouncement on the deferral of certain development costs (see Section 25).

Normally, identifiable intangible assets acquired from third parties, including purchased goodwill, are recorded at cost. Internally generated goodwill is not recognized in financial statements in New Zealand.

Valuation.   Revaluation of either externally purchased or internally developed intangible assets has not been a common accounting practice.

Where a revaluation is recorded, accounting rules similar to those for the revaluation of fixed assets apply.

Amortization.   Intangible assets are amortized to income on a systematic basis over their expected useful life.

Disclosure.   The accounting policy for intangible assets, the unamortized balances of intangible assets and the amount of purchased goodwill amortized in the period should be disclosed.

Reference.   SSAPs 3 and 11.

15.   Leases

Classification.   Leases are classified as either **finance** (capital) **leases** or **operating leases**. A lease is classified as a finance lease if substantially all the risks and rewards of ownership are transferred to the lessee. The following usually indicate that a lease is a finance lease:

☐   The lease may not be cancelled.
☐   Collection of the minimum lease payments is reasonably predictable.
☐   Unreimbursed costs yet to be incurred by the lessor are reasonably predictable.
☐   Ownership passes to the lessee at the end of the lease, the lessee has a bargain purchase option, the lease is for a major portion (normally at least 75%) of the asset's useful life or the present value, at the inception of the lease, of the minimum lease payments is not less than substantially all (normally at least 90%) of the asset's fair value.

All other leases are classified as operating leases.
Classification of leases is generally, but not necessarily, the same for the lessor and lessee.

Accounting Treatment.   Finance leases: A finance lease should be accounted for by the lessee as an asset and a liability calculated on the basis of the fair value of the asset or the present value of the minimum lease payments, whichever is lower. A finance lease is treated as a sale and receivable by the lessor.

Operating leases: For the lessee, the rental payments are expensed on a systematic basis corresponding to the time pattern of the lessee's benefit. For the lessor, the leased asset should be capitalized and the rental income recognized on a straight-line basis over the term of the lease, unless another systematic basis is more representative of the earnings process.

Leveraged leases: The lessor records the investment in the lease net of nonrecourse debt and of related finance costs to the third party lender. Finance income is recognized on the basis of the lessor's net investment.

Disclosure.   Lessees: The amount of assets subject to finance leases, by major asset class, together with the related accumulated depreciation should be disclosed. The aggregate current and long-term liabilities relating to finance leases should be separately disclosed. Interest charged during the period on finance leases, depreciation charged on leased assets and operating lease rental expense should also be disclosed. Lease commitments at the balance sheet date, classified as up to one year, one to two years, two to five years and over five years, should be disclosed separately for finance and operating leases.

Lessors: The gross investment in finance leases should be disclosed, together with related unearned finance income. The financial statements should also disclose the basis used to allocate income. Assets held for leasing under operating leases should be separately disclosed as part of fixed assets, together with any related accumulated depreciation.

Reference. SSAP 18.

16. Investments

Valuation. There are no specific pronouncements in New Zealand dealing with investments other than investment properties. The usual valuation for short-term investments is the lower of cost or market value. Long-term investments are usually stated at either market value or cost adjusted for any permanent impairment in value.

Investment properties, which are defined as property held primarily for capital growth or rental or similar income, should be revalued annually to their net current value. Increments or decrements in value are transferred to an investment property revaluation reserve either directly or indirectly through the income statement, at the choice of the reporting entity. In the latter instance, the increment or decrement is separately disclosed below ordinary operating income and extraordinary items. The method used should be applied consistently for all investment properties.

Treatment of Revaluation Reserves. Reserves for revaluation of investments are shown as part of shareholders' equity. Debit balances in these reserves are not permitted.

Gains/Losses. For investments other than property investments, profit or loss on disposal is most commonly calculated using the lower of historical cost or carrying value. Profit, including any revaluation reserve relating to the investment, or loss is reflected on the income statement. Where part of a holding of securities is sold, various methods of calculating cost, including FIFO and weighted average, are acceptable.

For investment properties, the treatment of the gain or loss on disposal depends on how previous revaluations were recorded. If the revaluation adjustments were recognized in the income statement, only the gain or loss measured against the carrying value of the property is shown on the income statement, as part of ordinary activities. Any balance relating to the property remaining in the revaluation reserve is transferred directly to retained earnings. If revaluation increments or decrements were recorded directly to a revaluation reserve, the entire gain, including any element remaining in the revaluation reserve relating to that property, may be shown on the income statement as part of ordinary activities.

Disclosure. The bases of accounting for all types of investments should be disclosed.

There should be separate disclosure of long-term investments in subsidiaries, associated companies, other companies, government or local authority stocks and other investments. In addition, the market value of quoted securities should be disclosed. Either market value or (for investments without a market value) value as estimated by the directors, or gross cost or valuation and the aggregate amounts written off since the date of acquisition or valuation should be disclosed for unquoted securities.

For short-term investments, quoted and unquoted securities are disclosed separately. Market value of quoted securities is shown.

For property investments, the revaluation reserve and changes during the period should be disclosed. The carrying value of investment properties should be separately disclosed in the balance sheet. The name of each appraiser employed, the total valuation and the dates of valuations are disclosed. Any changes in investment value included in the income statement should also be disclosed.

Reference. Companies Act 1955, Schedule 8, and SSAPs 9 and 17.

17. Accounts Receivable

Accounting Treatment. Recognition: **Revenues**, and hence receivables, are generally recognized when goods are delivered or services performed and there is reasonable assurance regarding measurement and collectibility of the consideration.

Discounts: Receivables are normally recorded net of trade discounts; prompt payment discounts are recorded when the receivables are settled. However, some entities also provide for anticipated prompt payment discounts on receivables and show the net receivable on the balance sheet.

Allowances and provisions: Provisions should be established for doubtful accounts. No particular method of calculating the provision is prescribed. Frequently specific identification and formula-based methods are used.

Factored Receivables. If **accounts receivable** have been factored to a finance company for cash consideration, the relevant receivables should be excluded from the balance sheet. Discounts given to finance companies should normally be accounted for in the same way as cash discounts. If the finance company has recourse to the entity for bad debts, disclosure of the contingent liability and provision for probable losses should be made. If the continuing risk to the entity is **material** or uncertain, the transaction with the finance company may need to be accounted for as a loan rather than as a **factoring** of receivables.

Disclosure. Accounts receivable should be classified as current or noncurrent. Trade receivables, receivables from directors, intercompany receivables, receivables from associated companies and other receivables are also separately disclosed. There is no requirement to show separately the amounts provided for doubtful accounts or the amounts written off during the period.

Reference. Companies Act 1955, Schedule 8; and SSAP 9.

18. Inventories and Work in Progress

General Accounting Treatment. **Inventories** are stated at the lower of cost or **net realizable value**.

Cost is determined using **FIFO**, weighted-**average cost**, **specific identification** or other similar methods. **LIFO** and **base stock** are not acceptable methods. Overhead that relates to bringing inventories to their present location and condition should be allocated to the cost of inventory systematically. General administration, finance, marketing and distribution expenditures are specifically excluded from inventory cost.

Net realizable value should be considered on an item-by-item basis or by groups of similar items.

Long-Term Contracts.   Profits on long-term contracts are recorded using the **percentage of completion method**. Profits may be recognized only if there is an unconditional sales contract and the final outcome of the contract can be reliably estimated. Potential losses must be provided for in full at the time they are first foreseen.

Disclosure.   Inventories should be disclosed in financial statements in classifications appropriate to the business. Typically raw materials, work in progress and finished goods are separately disclosed. The basis for valuing inventories should also be disclosed.

The amount of progress payments received and receivable should be disclosed separately as a deduction from the gross amount of contract work in progress.

Reference.   SSAPs 4, 9, 14 and 17.

19. Current Liabilities

General Accounting Treatment.   There are no specific pronouncements on **current liabilities** in New Zealand. Current liabilities generally include all obligations existing at the balance sheet date for which settlement is due within one year. Current liabilities should be classified under the appropriate headings, including bank loans and overdrafts, current portion of long-term debt, trade payables, intergroup balances, amounts due to associated companies, amounts due to directors and proposed dividends.

Creation of General and Specific Provisions.   If a decision such as one to reorganize the entity has been made, it is usual for a provision to be created to cover the estimated future costs to be incurred as a result of that decision.

For construction contracts, a provision is made for all future losses on a contract at the date the potential losses are first foreseen.

Disclosure.   Current liabilities must be classified separately under appropriate headings. Secured liabilities should be separately identified, and the notes should show the nature of the collateral given.

Companies are required to disclose the estimated amount of contracted future **capital expenditures**.

The Companies Act requires that provisions, other than for depreciation, renewals or diminution in value of assets, be appropriately classified and shown separately.

Reference.   Companies Act 1955, Schedule 8; and SSAP 9.

20. Long-Term Debt

General Accounting Treatment.   Bank loans, mortgages, debentures and convertible notes are the most common forms of long-term debt in New Zealand. The general accounting treatment applied to these items is basically the same as for current liabilities.

Debt Restructuring.   There is no pronouncement on debt restructuring in New Zealand. Practice normally follows US practice. Any gain resulting from debt restructuring would be shown on the income statement, possibly as an extraordinary item.

Debt Extinguishment.   A debt is accounted for as extinguished only if it has been:

☐   Settled through repayment or replacement by another liability;
☐   Subject to a legal **defeasance**; or
☐   Subject to an in-substance defeasance.

In a legal defeasance, the debtor is released from the primary obligation for the debt, and this is either formally acknowledged by the creditor or established by legal judgment.

An in-substance defeasance is a defeasance in which the debtor effectively achieves release from the primary obligation for a debt, either by placing irrevocably in a trust risk-free assets that are adequate to meet both the interest and principal service requirements of the debt, or by having a risk-free entity assume responsibility for the servicing requirements. For an in-substance defeasance to be effective, there must be virtual certainty that the debtor will not have to reassume the primary obligation. Risk-free assets are limited to securities of a risk-free entity denominated in the same currency as the debt. A risk-free entity is a credit worthy government or a body guaranteed under statute by a credit worthy government.

Partial defeasances of both principal and interest and instantaneous defeasances are permitted to be accounted for as defeasances, provided that they meet the above criteria.

Disclosure.   When a defeasance takes place, the financial statements should disclose the aggregate carrying amounts of assets given up and of debt extinguished by defeasance, and the net gain or loss recognized in the income statement. For all defeased debts, details of amounts defeased that are outstanding and any outstanding guarantees, indemnities or similar undertakings given by or on behalf of the debtor are disclosed.

Reference.   Companies Act 1955, Schedule 8; and SSAPs 9 and 26.

21. Contingencies

Contingent Losses.   Contingent losses should be accrued if future events are expected to confirm that either the value of an asset has been impaired or a liability has been incurred and a reasonable estimate can be made of the likely loss. If both of these conditions are not met, the contingent loss should be disclosed in the notes.

Contingent Gains.   Contingent gains should not be accrued, but their existence should be disclosed if it is probable that a gain will be realized.

Disclosure.   Where a **contingency** exists at the balance sheet date, a note should disclose the nature of the contingency, a description of the uncertain factors that may affect the future outcome, an estimate of the financial effect (net of taxation) or a statement that no estimate can be made, and the existence of any counterclaims that could reduce the effect of the exposure.

Reference.   Companies Act 1955, Schedule 8; and SSAP 15.

22.   Capital and Reserves

General.   Shareholders' equity is divided between **share capital** and reserves. Reserves are classified as revenue reserves or capital reserves.

Share Capital.   The amount of authorized share capital and its division into a number of shares of fixed amount (**par value**) are stated in the company's memorandum of association (constitution). The authorized capital may be increased at any time by an ordinary resolution of the shareholders. A company may issue shares only up to the number authorized; for a private company, all authorized share capital must be issued. A company is not permitted to repurchase its own shares. Shares may be issued at any value, although shares may be issued at a discount only in specified circumstances and with the sanction of the court. Calls on shares can be made progressively, and shares need not be paid for in full on issue.

A company may authorize and issue different classes of shares. Each class is characterized by its voting, dividend and capital repayment rights. The main classes of shares are ordinary shares and **preference shares**.

The concept of share capital will be subject to extensive change with the passing of the Companies Bill (see Section 1).

Reserves.   Share premium account: When a share is issued for more than its par value, the excess over par value is transferred to a reserve called the **share premium** account. The share premium account may be used only to pay for additional shares issued proportionally to existing shareholders for no consideration (bonus shares), pay for any unpaid or partly paid shares issued to shareholders, write off preliminary expenses incurred in the formation of the company or expenses, commissions or discounts on the issue of shares or debentures, or provide for the premium payable on redemption of redeemable preference shares or debentures of the company.

Capital redemption reserve fund: When preference shares are redeemed other than from the proceeds of a new issue of shares, the company must establish a capital redemption reserve in an amount equal to the par value of the shares redeemed. The capital redemption reserve is created by transfer of profits that would otherwise be available for distribution as dividends. The capital redemption reserve fund is subject to the same restrictions as share capital.

Asset revaluation reserve: This reserve arises from the revaluation of noncurrent assets.

Foreign currency translation reserve: This reserve arises from the translation of the financial statements of independent foreign subsidiaries.

Other reserves: Other reserves may be established by the directors for various reasons.

Retained earnings: Retained earnings is the balance of accumulated net profits that have not been distributed as dividends or appropriated for any purpose.

Distribution Restrictions.   The rules regarding distributions are not set out in the legislation but have evolved in case law. The overriding rules are that dividends may be paid only out of profits, and the company must remain in a position to be able to pay its liabilities as they fall due. "Profits" have been widely interpreted in the law. Prior period losses do not necessarily have to be made up before a distribution can be made out of current period profit.

Disclosure.   Share capital: The number, par value and amount of shares authorized, issued and paid should be disclosed, together with any changes during the period. All rights, preferences, restrictions and preferred dividends in arrears should be stated. For redeemable preference shares, the earliest redemption date should be disclosed, together with whether redemption is at the option of the company or the shareholder.

Options: For options on unissued shares, the number, description and amount of shares affected, the option price and period exercisable are disclosed.

Reserves: Reserves must be classified under their specified headings and changes in each reserve shown. Any restriction on distribution should be described.

Reference.   Companies Act 1955, Sections 60 to 94, Schedule 8; SSAPs 9, 17, 21 and 28.

ACCOUNTING PRINCIPLES FOR SPECIFIC ITEMS— INCOME STATEMENT

23. Revenue Recognition

General Principles.   There are no pronouncements in New Zealand on revenue recognition, except for long-term contracts and properties developed for resale. The substance of a transaction is therefore used to determine the point at which a sale takes place. This will usually be when substantially all the risks and rewards of ownership of an asset are transferred or the time at which service is performed.

Long-Term Contracts.   Profits from long-term contracts, or any contract that extends over more than one accounting period, are determined by the percentage of completion method. Profit may be recognized only when the outcome of the project can be reliably estimated. If a loss on a contract is foreseen, the full amount of the loss, both for the stage of completion reached and for future work, must be recognized immediately.

Instalment Sales.   To determine the appropriate accounting treatment for an **instalment sale**, the general principles stated above would be considered. If it is determined that the risks and rewards of ownership passed at the inception of the transaction, the full sale would be recognized and a deferred receivable recorded. If material, an interest element is usually imputed to the deferred settlement arrangements.

Rights of Return.   If purchasers have a right of refund or replacement for goods returned under a sales contract, the timing of recognition of revenue varies depending on the circumstances. If a company customarily trades in volume under such terms and the likely level of returns can be reasonably estimated, the revenue would normally be recorded at the date of the original sale and an appropriate provision established for expected returns. However, if a company makes only occasional sales on a right of return basis, recognition of the sale is normally deferred until it is determined that the right will not be exercised.

Product Financing. A **product financing arrangement** exists when an entity sells and simultaneously agrees to repurchase the same or substantially identical products, or guarantees the resale price to a third party. Such transactions are, in substance, financing transactions and are accounted for accordingly.

Disclosure. Sales or gross operating revenues for the period should be disclosed. Gross cash received should be shown in the cash flow statement.

Reference. SSAPs 9, 14 and 17; and FRS 10.

24. Government Grants and Assistance

Accounting Treatment. Government grants are recognized in the income statement on a systematic basis. They should not be recognized until the primary conditions attached to them have been complied with. If losses or increased costs are expected in connection with government grants, losses or costs should be recognized over the period in which they are expected to be incurred.

A grant forgiving a loan may be recognized in the income statement once the conditions for forgiveness have been met.

For a grant of nonmonetary assets, the fair value of the assets should be used to record the transaction.

Disclosure. The financial statements should disclose the accounting policies adopted, the nature and extent of government grants recorded in the period and the extent to which government grants for which all the conditions have not been fulfilled have been recognized in the financial statements, together with the amount of any relevant original liabilities.

25. Research and Development

Definitions. Research is original and planned investigation undertaken with the hope of gaining new scientific or technical knowledge and understanding.

Development is the translation of research findings or other knowledge into a plan or design for the production of new or substantially improved materials, devices, products, processes, systems or services prior to the commencement of commercial production.

Accounting Treatment. Research expenditures should be expensed as incurred. Development expenditures may be deferred and amortized in future periods if all of the following criteria are met:

☐ The product or process is clearly defined and costs attributable to it can be separately identified.

☐ Technical feasibility of the product or process has been demonstrated.

☐ The management of the entity has indicated its intention to produce and market or use the product or process.

☐ There is a clear indication that a future market exists for the product or, if it is to be used internally, its usefulness to the entity can be demonstrated.

☐ There are, or are expected to be, adequate resources to complete the project.

The amount of deferred expenditure may not exceed the amount that can reasonably be expected to be recovered from future revenues.

Deferred development costs should be amortized on a systematic basis either by reference to the sale or use of the product or process, or to the time period over which the process or product is expected to be sold or used.

Unamortized deferred expenditures should be reviewed at each balance sheet date to ensure that the criteria for deferral are still being met and that the balance does not exceed anticipated benefits. Any excess expenditure should be written off to the income statement. Once written off, deferred expenditures should not be reinstated even if uncertainties cease to exist.

Disclosure. The accounting policy adopted for research and development expenditures and, where expenditures are deferred, the basis of amortization should be disclosed. In addition, the balances of unamortized deferred expenditures and changes therein, and total research and development costs, including any amount amortized, should be disclosed.

Reference. SSAP 13.

26. Capitalized Interest Costs

Accounting Treatment. Practice regarding capitalization of interest varies. For fixed assets, finance costs directly attributable to purchase or construction may be capitalized. The period of capitalization begins when financing costs are incurred, expenditures for the asset are incurred and activities necessary to prepare the asset for its intended use are in progress. The period ends when the asset is complete and ready for its intended use.

Interest capitalization on inventory is not common, but is recorded for major projects, such as property development, where finance costs are directly attributable to a project.

Disclosure. When interest is capitalized in fixed assets, the accounting policy and the amount capitalized during the period are disclosed.

Reference. SSAP 28.

27. Imputed Interest

General. Interest imputation is specifically addressed in accounting standards in New Zealand for finance leases and the purchase or sale of a subsidiary or associated company.

Accounting Treatment. If the settlement date and date of acquisition or disposal do not coincide, the cost of the subsidiary or associated company or proceeds of disposal are adjusted for **imputed interest**. The rate used is the investor's average borrowing rate before tax.

For finance leases, a lessee should use the interest rate implicit in the lease or, if this is not practical to determine, the incremental borrowing rate. For the lessor, the interest rate implicit in the lease should be used, unless it is artificially low. In that event, a commercial rate should be used.

For other deferred purchase or sale agreements, usually the future cash flows are discounted at the interest rates implicit in the transactions, although no accounting pronouncement specifically requires this.

Disclosure.   For finance lease disclosures, see Section 15.

Reference.   SSAPs 8 and 18.

28.   Extraordinary or Unusual Items

Extraordinary Items.   Extraordinary items arise from events or transactions that are distinct from the ordinary activities of the entity, are not expected to recur frequently or regularly and are outside the control or influence of managers and owners. Items are not classified as extraordinary merely because of their size or because they relate to a prior year.

Abnormal Items.   Abnormal items arise from ordinary activities of the entity, but because of their size or incidence, require separate disclosure for the financial statements to provide a true and fair view.

Disclosure.   Extraordinary items: Extraordinary items should be separately disclosed on the face of the income statement following profit after tax from ordinary activities and minority interests. A description, pretax amount and applicable tax effect of each extraordinary item should be presented.
Abnormal items: Abnormal items should be included in profit from ordinary activities. The amount and a description of each abnormal item should be disclosed.

Reference.   SSAP 7 (subject to ED 57A).

29.   Income Taxes

Accounting Treatment.   Income tax expense is calculated using the **liability method**. Generally, deferred tax is recorded for all timing differences (comprehensive method). However, if it can be demonstrated with reasonable probability that the tax liability will not result for certain timing differences, they may be excluded (partial method). The conditions that demonstrate reasonable probability are:

☐   The entity is a going concern.
☐   There is reasonable evidence that the timing differences will not reverse for a considerable time (at least three years).
☐   There is no evidence that the situation is likely to change thereafter.

Whether the comprehensive or the partial method is used, it should be consistently applied to all timing differences from year to year.
Deferred tax debit balances, including debit balances arising from tax losses, should be recognized only when there is virtual certainty of recovery in future periods.
The conditions that establish virtual certainty for the recognition of deferred tax debits are:

☐ Future assessable income will be sufficient for the income tax liability arising from that income to absorb the debit balance in the deferred tax account; and

☐ The income tax liabilities arising will occur in such periods as will enable that ˍbsorption to take place.

The conditions that establish virtual certainty of recovery of deferred tax debits arising from tax losses are:

☐ The loss arose from an identifiable and nonrecurring item.

☐ A record of assessable income has been established over a long period, and occasional losses have been more than offset by assessable income in subsequent years (there is no provision for carrying back losses under tax legislation).

☐ There is assurance beyond a reasonable doubt that there will be sufficient assessable income to offset the loss in the carryforward period permitted by law.

Disclosure. The accounting policy adopted (i.e., the comprehensive or partial method) should be disclosed.

Companies should explain and reconcile, in a note, the difference between income tax expense in the income statement and the accounting profit multiplied by the current tax rate. A reconciliation between the opening and closing deferred tax balances should also be shown. Any unrecognized income tax losses available to offset taxes payable in future years should be disclosed. In addition, the full potential tax effect of unrecognized timing differences, including the tax effect of any fixed asset revaluations, should be shown (e.g., a tax liability that might arise if an asset was sold for its revalued amount).

The movements during the period in the imputation credit account and dividend withholding payments account of the parent company should be disclosed, along with the credits available to shareholders of the parent company at the balance sheet date:

☐ Through their shareholdings in the parent company; and

☐ Through their indirect interests in subsidiaries and in-substance subsidiaries.

Reference.   SSAP 12.

30.   Postretirement Benefits

Accounting Treatment.   There are no pronouncements on accounting for pensions or other postretirement benefits in New Zealand. Employer contributions are commonly expensed as incurred. If a **defined benefit** type **plan** has an unfunded liability, normally the increased employer contributions are also expensed. Usually, pension funds are formally valued by actuaries once every three years.

Pension Fund Surpluses.   The ultimate distribution of a pension fund surplus generally depends on the pension trust deed.

Disclosure.   There are no formal pension or other postretirement benefit disclosure requirements.

31. Discontinued Operations

Accounting Treatment.   Generally a provision is established at the balance sheet date to reflect the consequences of decisions made to discontinue or reorganize a business segment. The provision includes, for example, employee termination payments, estimated profit or loss from the disposal of assets, pension costs, operating results after implementation of the decision and any losses due to penalty clauses in contracts.

Disclosure.   There are no formal disclosure requirements.

32. Earnings per Share

General.   The only requirement for companies to publish earnings per share (EPS) information is contained in the Listing Requirements of the New Zealand Stock Exchange. Companies party to a listing agreement are required to publish annualized EPS, after tax and before extraordinary items. Recommendations for calculating EPS are contained in TPA 4, but practice varies.

Methods of Calculation.   TPA 4 recommends that both basic and diluted EPS be calculated.

Basic: Basic EPS is calculated by dividing consolidated profit after tax, minority interests and preference dividends for the period by the weighted-average number of shares issued. Any bonus shares (stock splits) issued during the period are deemed to have been issued on the first day of the accounting period, and comparative figures for prior years are adjusted to reflect the bonus issue.

Diluted: Diluted EPS takes account of the potential dilutive effect of all convertible securities and options. For options, imputed earnings, calculated by reference to the bank overdraft rate (reduced for income tax), are credited to profit before the calculation is made.

EPS calculated on profit after extraordinary items should also be calculated for both basic and diluted EPS, where the difference is material from EPS before extraordinary items.

Disclosure.   Basic and diluted EPS for both the current and prior years should be disclosed. If the figures are materially different, both EPS calculations should also be disclosed using profit after extraordinary items. The amounts of earnings and number of shares used in the calculations should be disclosed.

Reference.   New Zealand Stock Exchange Listing Requirements, July 1989; and TPA 4.

Appendix
DO NEW ZEALAND STANDARDS OR PREVALENT PRACTICE SUBSTANTIALLY COMPLY WITH INTERNATIONAL ACCOUNTING STANDARDS?

Section	Topic	Substantially complies with IAS?	Comments
3.	Basic accounting concepts and conventions	Yes	
	Contents of financial statements	Yes	
4.	Business combinations*	Yes	
5.	Joint ventures	Yes	
6.	Foreign currency translation*	Yes	
8.	Accounting changes*	Yes	
9.	Prior period adjustments*	Yes	
10.	Post balance sheet events	Yes	
11.	Related party transactions	Yes	
12.	Segmental information	Yes	
13.	Property, plant and equipment*	Yes	
15.	Leases	Yes	
16.	Investments	Yes	Except that increases resulting from the revaluation of investment properties may be taken to the income statement
17.	Accounts receivable	Yes	
18.	Inventories and work in progress*	Yes	
19.	Current liabilities	Yes	
20.	Long-term debt	Yes	
21.	Contingencies	Yes	
22.	Capital and reserves	Yes	
23.	Revenue recognition*	Yes	
24.	Government grants and assistance	Yes	
25.	Research and development*	Yes	
26.	Capitalization of interest costs*	Yes	

Appendix (*Continued*)

Section	Topic	Substantially complies with IAS?	Comments
28.	Extraordinary or unusual items*	Yes	
29.	Income tax**	Yes	
30.	Postretirement benefits*	No	

*These topics are subject to change as a result of the IASC Improvements Project—see the appendix to the International Accounting Standards chapter.

**The IAS on accounting for taxes on income is currently being revised, and an exposure draft has been issued.

Comparison in this table is made to International Accounting Standards in force at January 1, 1993. For further details, see the International Accounting Standards chapter.

NIGERIA

GENERAL NATIONAL INFORMATION

1. Source of Generally Accepted Accounting Principles

Generally Accepted Accounting Principles.   **Generally accepted accounting principles** are derived from authoritative pronouncements, accounting literature and well-established practice.

Accounting Standards.   **Accounting standards** in Nigeria are issued by the Nigerian Accounting Standards Board (NASB) as Statements of Accountancy Standards (SASs). Where there is no accounting standard, the provisions of relevant International Accounting Standards (IAS) are adopted; where the two are in conflict, the local standard takes precedence.

For historical reasons, financial statement presentation and disclosure, general **accounting principles** and methods of application are very similar in Nigeria and the United Kingdom. Despite the many similarities, however, there are some significant differences.

2. Audit and Public Company Requirements

Audits.   Under the Nigerian Companies and Allied Matters Act (the Act) of 1990, shareholders of a company are required to appoint auditors annually who are independent of the company and its affiliates. Generally, all companies are required to file audited comparative financial statements. Under the Act, only licensed members of the Institute of Chartered Accountants of Nigeria are qualified to be appointed as auditors of companies and are required to comply with auditing standards issued by the Institute.

Public Companies.   The Act requires all companies to prepare annual financial statements in compliance with provisions of the SASs. These financial statements should be distributed to all shareholders at least 21 days before the annual general meeting.

Companies that seek to issue securities to the public must meet the applicable requirements of the Securities and Exchange Decree of 1988 and the regulations of the Nigerian Stock Exchange, in addition to the provisions of the Act.

GENERAL ACCOUNTING

3. Financial Statements

Basic Accounting Concepts. Financial statements are prepared primarily using the **historical cost** basis of measurement, whereby transactions and events are recognized in financial statements at the amount of cash or cash equivalents paid or received or the fair value ascribed to them when they took place. Financial statements are prepared on the assumption that the entity is a **going concern**. Different measurement bases may be appropriate when the entity is not expected to continue to operate for the foreseeable future.

Items recognized in financial statements are accounted for on the **accrual basis**.

Transactions and events should be accounted for and presented in a manner that conveys their substance rather than their legal or other form. The determination of the substance of a transaction or event is a matter of professional judgment.

Comparability of financial statements is enhanced when the same **accounting policies** are used consistently from period to period. When a change in accounting policy is deemed appropriate (see Section 8), disclosure of the effects of the change may be necessary to maintain comparability.

Contents of Financial Statements. Financial statements normally include a balance sheet, income statement, statement of retained earnings and statement of changes in financial position. Notes to financial statements and supporting schedules to which the financial statements are cross-referenced are considered an integral part of the statements. **Public company** financial statements should also include a value added statement, a five-year financial summary and, in the case of a **holding company**, **group financial statements**. There is currently no requirement to prepare a cash flow statement as an integral part of the financial statements in accordance with the revised IAS 7.

Format of Financial Statements. Financial statements should be readily understandable. They should normally be prepared on a comparative basis, showing amounts for the corresponding prior period. Assets and liabilities are segregated between current and noncurrent in the balance sheet, except where such a classification is not helpful (e.g., financial institutions and companies in the development stage). Short-term items expected to be refinanced are classified as long-term if contractual arrangements for the refinancing have been made. Obligations that are callable but are not expected to be called within one year are sometimes classified as long-term if there is evidence that the creditor does not intend to call for repayment within one year.

Disclosure of Accounting Policies. An entity should identify and describe the accounting policies that are significant to its operations. As a minimum, disclosure should include areas where judgment has been exercised (i.e., where there is a choice between acceptable alternatives) and those accounting principles and methods that are peculiar to the industry in which the entity operates.

In unusual circumstances, literal application of an authoritative pronouncement might render the financial statements misleading, so that it is necessary to depart from the usual treatment. The practice followed and the reason for the departure should be disclosed in a note.

When a financial statement item is reclassified, commonly a note explains that certain items in the prior year financial statements have been restated to conform to the current year's presentation.

Reference. SAS 1.

4. Business Combinations

Principles of Consolidation. In general, all **subsidiaries** should be consolidated. Exceptions to this rule may be permitted or required when:

- [ ] Increases in equity are not likely to accrue to the **parent**—Use of the cost method is required.
- [ ] Control by the parent is temporary—The investment is accounted for at estimated **net realizable value** or its carrying value as determined by the **equity method**.
- [ ] Control by the parent is seriously impaired—Use of the cost method is required.
- [ ] Financial statement components of a subsidiary are so dissimilar to those of other companies in the consolidated group that inclusion in the **consolidated financial statements** would not provide the most informative presentation—Use of the equity method is required.

Accounting for Business Combinations. **Business combinations** should normally be accounted for by the **purchase method**. In those rare circumstances where an acquirer cannot be identified, the **pooling of interests method** is used.

Transactions between companies under common control, such as between two subsidiaries of the same parent, do not constitute business combinations.

Control. Control is usually indicated by ownership of over 50 percent of an entity's voting shares and the right to elect a majority of the members of the board of directors.

Goodwill. **Goodwill**, arising from business acquisitions, is reflected separately on the balance sheet as an intangible asset and should be amortized to income using the straight-line method over its estimated life. The unamortized portion of goodwill should be adjusted for any permanent impairment in value.

The fair values attributed to most acquired assets and liabilities would be the acquired company's book values. Intangible and other assets, including land, natural resources and nonmarketable securities, may be valued at an estimated or appraised value.

Equity Accounting. The equity method of accounting should be used for investments in common stock if the investor has the ability to significantly influence the decisions of the investee. Significant influence may be indicated by representation on the board of directors, participation in policy-making processes and common management. Significant influence is usually presumed to exist when the investor holds 20 percent or more of the voting shares.

Minority Interests. The interests of minority shareholders in consolidated subsidiaries' assets and liabilities should be shown separately from shareholders' equity.

Disclosure.   For each business combination, the accounting method used, the net assets brought into the combination and the consideration exchanged should be disclosed. Aggregated information may be presented for a number of small combinations.

When a subsidiary is excluded from consolidation, the reason for the exclusion should be disclosed.

Purchase method: Information should include the name and description of the business acquired; the date of acquisition and the period for which operating results of the acquired business are included in the combined income statement; and, where stock has been acquired, the percentage held and the ordinary shares, preferred shares, debt, cash or other consideration and any contingent consideration exchanged.

Pooling of interests method: The information disclosed should include the name and description of each of the companies involved; the percentage of each company's voting shares exchanged to effect the combination; the effective date of the combination; the assets brought into the combination by each of the combining companies; a description and the fair value of each type of consideration received by the shareholders of the combining companies; and a description of the nature and the fair value of the combined companies' voting shares held by each company.

Equity accounting: Investments in companies accounted for by the equity method should be disclosed separately as a class. Total income calculated by the equity method should also be disclosed separately.

If the operations of a company accounted for by the equity method are an important factor in evaluating the operations of the investor, disclosure of summarized information about the assets and liabilities and operating results of the investee is usually desirable.

Reference: SASs 1 and 2, and IAS 3, 22, 27 and 28.

5. Joint Ventures

There is currently no Nigerian standard on financial reporting of interests in **joint ventures**. The provisions of IAS 31, *Financial Reporting of Interests in Joint Ventures*, would be appropriate in Nigeria.

6. Foreign Currency Translation

Bases of Translation.   General: A distinction is made between translating **foreign currency denominated transactions** and balances of domestic operations and translating financial statements of foreign operations.

Domestic operations: The **temporal method** should be applied to foreign currency denominated transactions and balances—that is, **monetary items** (both hedged and unhedged) and items carried at market values should be translated at current rates, and transactions and other balances at historical rates. Most exchange gains and losses are included in income immediately; however, exchange gains and losses arising from long-term monetary items with fixed or ascertainable lives should be deferred and amortized over the remaining life of the related item.

Foreign operations: Foreign operations are classified as integrated or self-sustaining. Financial statements of **integrated foreign operations** should be translated using the temporal method. Financial statements of **self-sustaining foreign operations** should be translated using the **current rate method**, and exchange gains and losses should be accumulated separately in a translation adjustment account.

Hedges. Many entities seek to reduce or eliminate the risk of loss on exchange inherent in foreign transactions or operations by hedging. For a foreign exchange contract, asset, liability or future revenue stream to be recognized as a **hedge**, there must be reasonable assurance of its effectiveness as a hedge. If the hedge is a monetary item, when it is translated at the current rate any gain and loss will automatically offset the loss or gain on the transaction or balance hedged. If the hedge is a nonmonetary item, there will be no current exchange gain or loss, and any loss or gain arising from translation of the hedged item should be deferred until the settlement date. If the hedge is a foreign currency forward contract, any gain or loss is accrued to offset the loss or gain on the hedged item.

Disclosure. Any significant changes in the translation adjustment account should be disclosed. The amount of exchange gain or loss included in income does not have to be disclosed. The method used to amortize any deferred exchange gains and losses should be disclosed.

Reference. SAS 7.

7. Changing Prices/Inflation Accounting

General. There are no requirements to provide information on the effects of changes in the price level on financial statements in Nigeria. If companies revalue their fixed assets to reflect current values, the basis of valuation is disclosed.

8. Accounting Changes

Accounting Treatment. Changes in accounting policies are distinguished from changes in accounting estimates.

Accounting policies: Accounting policy changes may be made retroactively and comparative figures restated to give effect to the new policy, unless the necessary information is not determinable. Alternatively, accounting policy changes may be made without retroactive effect; in that event, the effect of the change on current income must be disclosed, if material. A change in accounting policy is recommended if the new policy will enhance the true and fair value of the financial statements. A new accounting policy need not be preferable to the policy it replaces, provided that it is an acceptable alternative under NASB. Changes arising from changes in accounting standards usually may be applied prospectively only.

Accounting estimates: A change in an estimate arises from new information or developments. The effect of a change in an accounting estimate should be accounted for in the period in which the change occurs and applicable future periods.

Disclosure. A description of a change in accounting policy and its effect on the current period's financial statements should be disclosed.

Reference. SAS 1.

9. Prior Period Adjustments

Definition of Adjusting Items. Prior period financial statements are adjusted to correct for known errors. Prior years' earnings are also restated for gains or losses that clearly relate to those periods, for example, subsequent realization of a previously unrecorded contingent loss. To qualify for treatment as a **prior period adjustment**, an item must meet the following specific criteria:

☐ It must be specifically identified with and directly related to the business activities of particular prior periods.

☐ It must not be attributable to economic events occurring subsequent to the date of the prior period financial statements.

☐ It must depend primarily on decisions by persons other than management or owners.

☐ It must not have been reasonably estimable prior to such decisions.

Accounting Treatment.   Prior period adjustments should be excluded from the determination of net income for the current period; the income statement of the affected prior period should be restated. The opening balances of **retained earnings** in subsequent periods, including the current period, are adjusted accordingly. When income figures of the preceding period are restated, the basic earnings per share of the preceding period should be based on the restated amounts.

Disclosure.   The nature of the adjustment and its effect on the financial statements should be disclosed. Disclosure of the related per share amounts is not required.

Reference.   SAS 6.

10.   Post Balance Sheet Events

Definition.   Two different types of post balance sheet events are identified in Nigerian accounting standards:

☐ Those that provide further evidence of conditions that existed at the financial statement date.

☐ Those that are indicative of conditions that arose subsequent to the financial statement date.

Accounting Treatment.   Conditions existing at the financial statement date: The financial statements should be adjusted for events occurring between the financial statement date and the date of their completion (i.e., the date they are signed by the directors) that provide additional information relating to conditions existing at the financial statement date.

Conditions arising after the financial statement date: Some events occurring after the financial statement date and relating to conditions not existing at that date (e.g., an uninsured loss from fire) may have a significant effect on the assets and liabilities or future operations of an entity in a subsequent period. Current period financial statements should not be adjusted for these items.

Disclosure.   If **material**, post balance sheet events that are indicative of conditions that arose subsequent to the financial statement date should be disclosed in a note. Both the nature of the event and, when practicable, its estimated financial statement effect should be indicated.

Reference. SAS 6.

11. Related Party Transactions

Definition. Parties are considered related if one has the ability to significantly influence the operating and financial decisions of the other or if the parties are subject to common significant influence by another party.

Accounting Treatment. Nigerian standards do not address measurement and accounting treatment pertaining to related party transactions. Such transactions are treated in accordance with the provisions of IAS 24 and normal accounting principles and practices.

Disclosure. The following information should be disclosed:

- [ ] A description of the nature and extent of transactions.
- [ ] A description of the relationship.
- [ ] Amounts due to or from related parties.
- [ ] The terms of settlement, if not otherwise apparent.

No charge transactions between related parties should be disclosed. Management compensation arrangements and transactions eliminated on consolidation or in applying the equity method of accounting need not be disclosed.

When ongoing operations depend on a significant volume of business with another party (e.g., a major customer, supplier or lender), that situation should be disclosed and explained.

Reference. IAS 24.

12. Segmental Information

General. There is currently no Nigerian standard on reporting by segments, and the provisions of IAS 14 are followed. The Act requires that if a company is engaged in more than one line of business, the **turnover** and profit of each line should be disclosed separately.

Disclosure. The following information is disclosed for each reportable segment:

- [ ] Sales to outside customers.
- [ ] Intersegment sales or transfers.
- [ ] Operating profit or loss.
- [ ] **Capital expenditures** for the period.

Reporting by geographical segment is also required, if material.

Reference. IAS 14 and the Act.

ACCOUNTING PRINCIPLES FOR SPECIFIC ITEMS— BALANCE SHEET

13. Property, Plant and Equipment

Classification of Capital and Revenue Expenditure. Expenditures for **capital assets** that significantly increase their useful life and capacity are capitalized as part of their cost. Expenditures to maintain normal operating efficiency are expensed as incurred.

Basis of Valuation. Property, plant and equipment are normally accounted for at their historical cost. Occasionally, such as in a significant restructuring of the business, **fixed assets** may be recorded at appraised values based on the current market value or on their value to the business.

Appraisal increases should be shown as a separate item in the shareholders' equity section of the balance sheet. An appraisal increase either remains indefinitely on the balance sheet or is transferred to retained earnings when amounts are realized through sale.

Provisions are occasionally made for possible impairment in the carrying value of fixed assets. These provisions are sometimes reversed if they are no longer considered necessary. Gains and losses arising on the disposal of property, plant and equipment are included in income for the period.

Depreciation. Various **depreciation** methods are used in practice (e.g., **straight-line**, **unit-of-production** and **declining balance**). Any consistently applied method that produces a reasonable and systematic allocation over the asset's useful life is acceptable. If an appraisal has been recorded, subsequent depreciation expense should be based on the new values.

Disclosure. The depreciation methods and rates and accumulated depreciation should be disclosed. The income statement should disclose depreciation expense for the year.

If any fixed assets are carried at appraised values, the date of the appraisal should be stated. The identity of the appraiser, the basis of valuation and the disposition of the appraisal adjustment, if not otherwise apparent, need to be disclosed.

Reference. SASs 3 and 9.

14. Intangible Assets

Accounting Treatment. **Intangible assets** acquired from a third party are recognized in the balance sheet. Other intangibles are recognized only to the extent of direct costs related to the use of an asset (e.g., patent registration costs can be recognized but not the costs related to development of the patented product).

Valuation. There is no prescribed basis of valuation for intangible assets. They are valued in the same manner as purchased tangible assets using historical cost accounting.

Amortization. There is no clearly defined requirement in Nigerian accounting literature to amortize intangible assets not having a fixed or determinable life, other than goodwill.

However, a majority of companies that record intangible assets amortize all or part of the assets over a number of years.

Disclosure. If intangibles are amortized, the basis of **amortization** and the expense for the current period should be disclosed. The major intangible assets should be shown separately (e.g., goodwill, franchises, patents) and the basis of valuation for each should be disclosed.

15. Leases

Classification. Two forms of leases are recognized: **finance leases** and **operating leases**. The main criterion for the classification of a lease as a finance lease is whether the risks and benefits associated with the lease have been substantially transferred to the lessee. A lease qualifies as a finance lease if it is noncancellable and its term covers substantially (80% or more) the useful life of the assets, or the net present value of the lease at its inception, using minimum lease payments and the implicit interest rate, is equal to or greater than the fair value of the leased assets, or the lease has a purchase option that is likely to be exercised. A lease that does not qualify as a finance lease is usually treated as an operating lease.

Accounting Treatment. Finance leases: Finance leases should be capitalized and accounted for as an asset and a matching obligation by the lessee, and as a sale or financing transaction by the lessor. Alternatively, the lessee may treat each finance lease payment as an expense of the period in which it is incurred. The income tax effects of the transactions, including investment tax credits, may be considered by the lessor in accounting for direct finance leases. Initial direct costs in a direct finance lease should be expensed as incurred, and a portion of the unearned income equal to the initial direct costs should be recognized in income in the same period.

Operating leases: The rental payments are expensed by the lessee and recorded as revenue by the lessor in the periods to which they relate. Leases of land and buildings are usually operating leases.

Leveraged Leases. There are no special rules for **leveraged leases** in Nigeria. The lessor records the investment in the lease net of nonrecourse debt. The US approach of netting the investment in finance leases and the related debt for financial statement presentation purposes is acceptable in Nigeria.

Disclosure. The following disclosures should be made by lessees:

☐ The amount and the major classes of assets under lease at the balance sheet date. Liabilities related to leased assets should be separately disclosed from other liabilities and should be separated into current and long-term liabilities.

☐ Commitments for minimum lease payments with a term in excess of one year, in summary, stating the aggregate amount and the payments due in each year.

☐ Any significant financing restrictions, renewal or purchase options, contingent rentals and other contingencies arising from leases.

Lessors should disclose the following:

□ The gross investment in leases classified as finance leases, the related deferred income and the unguaranteed residual values of the leased assets at the balance sheet date.

□ The net investment in leases, split between current and noncurrent portions.

□ The basis or bases used to allocate income.

□ For assets under operating leases, the amount of assets in each category and the accumulated depreciation at the balance sheet date.

Reference. SAS 11 and IAS 17.

16. Investments

Valuation. General: Valuation of investments that are neither consolidated nor accounted for by the equity method depends on their classification as current or noncurrent.

Current investments: Temporary (current) investments are usually recorded at the lower of cost or market value. The lower of cost or market test may be applied to marketable investments individually or in the aggregate.

Noncurrent (long-term) investments: Long-term investments should be recorded at cost, and quoted market value of marketable securities should be disclosed. Long-term investments should be written down to recognize any permanent decline in value; write-downs may not be reversed if there is a subsequent increase in value.

Gains/Losses. The calculation of a gain or loss on the sale of part of a holding of securities should be based on the weighted-average carrying value.

Disclosure. The basis used to value long-term and temporary investments should be disclosed. Any securities issued by the parent company and owned by subsidiaries excluded from consolidation should be disclosed in the parent company's financial statements.

Reference. IAS 25.

17. Accounts Receivable

Accounting Treatment. Recognition: **Revenues**, and hence the related receivables, are recognized when performance is complete and reasonable assurance exists regarding measurement and collectibility of the consideration.

Discounts: Sales revenues are normally recorded net of cash discounts.

Allowances: An adequate allowance should be recorded for doubtful accounts, although there is no requirement to make reference to or disclose the amount of the allowance. No specific basis is prescribed for calculating the allowance for doubtful accounts. **Specific identification** is the preferred method, but when it is impracticable, other methods may be used.

Factored Receivables. **Factoring of receivables** is not common in Nigeria.

A transfer of receivables can be recorded as a sale rather than as a financing transaction if the significant risks and rewards of ownership of the receivables have been transferred and reasonable assurance exists regarding the measurement of the consideration exchanged. If receivables are transferred with recourse, it must be reasonable in relation to the losses expected to be incurred and normally may not exceed 10 percent of the proceeds. If all of these conditions are not met, the transaction would be, in substance, a borrowing and the proceeds should be recorded as a liability.

Disclosure. Accounts and notes **receivable** should be segregated between trade accounts, amounts receivable from related parties and other types of receivables.

Reference. IAS 25.

18. Inventories and Work in Progress

General Accounting Treatment. **Inventories** are carried at the lower of cost or net realizable value. Commonly used methods of determining cost include **FIFO**, specific cost and **average cost**. **Standard cost** is acceptable only if it approximates one of these methods.

LIFO, **base stock** and **latest purchase price** are not acceptable methods of valuing inventory.

For work in progress and finished goods, inventory costs include materials, direct labor and an appropriate share of overhead expense chargeable to production. Abnormal costs, such as rehandling of goods and idle facilities, are usually excluded. Similarly, a portion of fixed overhead should be excluded if including it would distort net income for the period because of a fluctuating production volume.

Long-Term Contracts. The **completed contract** and **percentage of completion methods** are alternative methods used for recognizing long-term contract revenue. Under the completed contract method, profit on long-term contracts is recorded only when the contract is completed. Under the percentage of completion method, profit is recorded in proportion to work completed.

Disclosure. Inventories are disclosed by classification, for example, raw materials, supplies, work in process and finished goods. In addition, the basis of valuing different classes of inventories should be disclosed. Long-term contracts in progress and the methods used for recognizing revenue should also be disclosed.

Reference. SASs 4 and 5.

19. Current Liabilities

General Accounting Treatment. **Current liabilities** include amounts payable within one year from the date of the balance sheet or within the normal operating cycle, if longer than one year. Current liabilities should be segregated into main classes, for example, bank loans, **accounts payable** and accrued liabilities, loans payable, taxes payable, dividends payable, deferred revenues and current portion of long-term debt.

Accounts payable include amounts owed to creditors for goods and services for which invoices or bills have been received.

Most expenses are recorded when incurred. Expenses incurred but not recorded because payment is not yet due, such as for salaries and wages, are recorded as accrued liabilities. Amounts received from customers or clients for goods to be delivered or services to be performed should be recorded as deferred revenue.

Creation of General and Specific Provisions. There is no requirement to create specific provisions for future expenses. Reserves may be created at the discretion of management for such purposes as general contingencies or future plant expansion.

Disclosure. Any secured liabilities should be separately presented. Commitments for abnormal expenditures or unusual business operations (e.g., commitments for substantial fixed asset expenditures) and commitments establishing the level of a specific expenditure for a future period should be disclosed.

Reference. IAS 13.

20. Long-Term Debt

General Accounting Treatment. Long-term debt includes bonds, debentures and similar securities. A premium or discount on long-term debt is shown as a deferred credit or charge and should be amortized over the term of the debt.

Debt Restructuring. There are no published standards on debt restructuring in Nigeria.

Debt Extinguishment. There are no published Nigerian standards on accounting for debt extinguishment or waiver. A gain or loss arises on early extinguishment or waiver of debt when the reacquisition price and the net carrying amount of the debt are different. The gain or loss is included in income, as a separate item. It may be classified as an extraordinary item, if it meets the criteria for such treatment (see Section 28).

Accounting for in-substance **defeasances** is the same as for extinguishment of debt. An in-substance defeasance is a transaction in which the debtor remains obligated to repay debt, but the debt is considered to have been extinguished because risk-free monetary assets have been placed in an irrevocable trust solely to satisfy the debt repayment terms, and the possibility that the debtor will be required to make further payments is remote. Risk-free monetary assets are cash or securities that are guaranteed, usually by the federal government. Irrevocable means the debtor has no future rights to the trust assets. To meet the criteria for an in-substance defeasance, the timing and amount of payments must be reasonably determinable in advance; for example, floating-rate debt cannot be extinguished through in-substance defeasance because future debt service requirements may vary.

Disclosure. There are no specific disclosure requirements concerning debt restructuring or debt extinguishment. If information is significant to understanding the financial position of the enterprise, details should be disclosed.

21. Contingencies

General. The accounting treatment and disclosure requirements for **contingencies** depend on the likelihood of occurrence or nonoccurrence of the future events that will determine the contingency.

Contingent Losses. If it is likely that a contingency existing at the financial statement date will result in a loss whose amount can be estimated, the loss must be accrued. If there is a reasonable possibility that a loss may be incurred, but either the amount cannot be estimated or the exposure exceeds the amount already accrued, the existence of the contingent loss at the financial statement date should be disclosed but not accrued. Disclosure is also required if the likelihood of occurrence cannot be determined.

Contingent Gains. Contingent gains should not be accrued in the financial statements, but if their realization is likely, they should be disclosed.

Disclosure. Disclosure of a contingent gain or loss should include a description of the contingency, an estimate of the amount or a statement that an estimate cannot be made and whether any resulting settlement will be accounted for as a prior period adjustment or as a charge or credit to income when settlement occurs. In practice, companies disclosing contingencies rarely indicate the accounting treatment that will be applied to any settlement expected in the future.

22. Capital and Reserves

General. Shareholders' equity is generally divided into **share capital** and **surplus** items. For surplus items, distinction is made between those derived from earnings and those derived from capital contributions, usually classified as retained earnings and **contributed surplus**, respectively. In Nigeria, reserves are substantially limited to discretionary reserves created by an appropriation of retained earnings. There are no requirements to maintain reserves for specific purposes. Reserves cannot be created, increased or decreased by charges or credits to income. Unrealized increases in the value of fixed assets and foreign exchange gains and losses arising from the translation of the financial statements of foreign entities should be included as separate components of shareholders' equity (see Sections 13 and 6).

Share Capital. Businesses incorporated under the Act must issue shares with a nominal or **par value**.

A company's share capital may consist of different classes of shares, each of which is characterized by its voting, dividend and capital repayment rights. For accounting purposes, **common shares** are those that represent the residual equity in the earnings of a company. All other types of capital shares are senior shares, including **preferred shares** that participate with common shares but whose participation rights are restricted.

If a company redeems or acquires its own shares at a cost different from the par, stated or assigned value of the shares, the difference should be excluded from net income. A company's own shares that it has acquired should be carried at their original cost and shown as a deduction from shareholders' equity until they are cancelled or resold.

Other Reserves. Contributed surplus consists of capital donations from shareholders and other sources, including premiums on shares issued, gain on reissuance of forfeited shares and proceeds from donated shares.

Retained earnings is the accumulated balance of income less losses from operations, after dividends, refundable taxes and other amounts.

Distribution Restrictions.   Currently there are no legislative restrictions on dividends declared from retained earnings. Capital distributions are not permitted.

Disclosure.   Details of authorized and issued share capital and of transactions during the period should be disclosed. Any commitments to issue or resell previously acquired shares and any conversion rights or share option privileges should be presented. If the distribution of retained earnings is restricted, the details should be disclosed.

ACCOUNTING PRINCIPLES FOR SPECIFIC ITEMS— INCOME STATEMENT

23. Revenue Recognition

General Principles.   Revenue is recognized when performance is complete and reasonable assurance regarding measurement and collectibility of the consideration exists. Revenue from sales is recognized when the seller transfers to the buyer the significant risks and rewards of ownership of the goods. Whether any significant acts of performance remain to be completed and whether the seller retains any continuing involvement in, or effective control of, the goods transferred may determine whether significant risks and rewards have been transferred.

Revenue from service transactions is usually recognized as the service is performed, using either the percentage of completion or completed contract method.

Long-Term Contracts.   Revenue from long-term contracts is usually recognized as the contract activity is performed, using either the percentage of completion or completed contract method. Normally, the percentage of completion method is used when contract performance consists of more than one act, and revenue is recognized in proportion to each act performed. The completed contract method is appropriate only if performance consists of a single act or if the extent of progress toward completion cannot reasonably be estimated.

Instalment Sales.   The instalment basis is an acceptable alternative in circumstances where immediate recognition of the full profit may be inappropriate. Profit is recognized as sale proceeds are collected in the proportion that the proceeds bear to the total sales price.

Rights of Return.   When a right of return exists, revenue can be recognized at the time of sale if:

☐   The price is substantially fixed or determinable.
☐   Any obligation to pay the purchase price is unconditional.
☐   The vendor has no significant obligations for future performance to directly bring about the product's resale.
☐   The amounts of potential future returns are accrued.

Product Financing.   **Product financing** is not common in Nigeria.

Reference.   SAS 1.

24. Government Grants and Assistance

Accounting Treatment. Government assistance includes forgivable loans as well as grants. Government grants for current expenses should be included in income. Government grants related to future period expenses should be deferred and included in income as the related expenses are incurred. Assistance related to capital expenditures should be either deducted from the cost of the related fixed asset, with depreciation calculated on the net amount, or deferred and amortized to income on the same basis as the related asset. Government loans should be treated as either long-term or short-term loans, depending on the loan term. If a loan is forgiven, the amount should be included in income and disclosed, if material.

Disclosure. The following disclosure of government assistance should be made:

- ☐ Amount of grants received and receivable in the current period.
- ☐ Amount credited to income, deferred credits or fixed assets in the current period.
- ☐ Amount of any loan outstanding at the balance sheet date, separated into current and long-term portions.

Reference. IAS 20.

25. Research and Development

Definitions. Research is planned investigation undertaken with the hope of gaining new scientific or technical knowledge and understanding. It may or may not be directed toward a specific practical aim or application. Development is the translation of research findings into a plan or design for new or substantially improved materials, devices, products or services prior to the start of commercial production.

Accounting Treatment. In general, research costs should be expensed as incurred. Development costs may be deferred and amortized if all the criteria below are satisfied:

- ☐ The product or process is clearly defined and attributed costs can be identified.
- ☐ The technical feasibility of the product or process has been established.
- ☐ Management intends to produce and market or use the product or process.
- ☐ The future market is clearly defined or the product's usefulness to the entity has been established.
- ☐ Adequate resources are available to complete the project.

Amortization of development costs commences with commercial production or use. The amortization period is based on the benefits expected to arise from the sale or use of the product or process, taking into account such uncertainties as technological change and competition.

The unamortized portion of deferred development costs should be reviewed at the end of each period to determine whether deferral is still appropriate. If doubt exists, the unamortized balance should be written off to income. If deferral continues to be appropriate, the unamortized balance of development costs for each project should be analyzed in relation to its recovery from expected future revenues less related costs. Any excess unamortized costs should be written off.

Disclosure. The financial statements should disclose the amounts of:

□ Unamortized deferred development costs.
□ Development costs deferred during the period.
□ Research and development costs charged to expense for the period.
□ Amortization of deferred development costs charged to expense for the period.

Reference. IAS 9.

26. Capitalized Interest Costs

Accounting Treatment. There is no Nigerian authoritative accounting guidance on interest capitalization and the IAS on this topic has been adopted. The Act allows the payment and capitalization of interest on contributions to share capital under certain specified conditions. Interest may be capitalized as part of the cost of constructing assets during the construction period. Inventory interest capitalization is usually restricted to industries such as land development and heavy construction. Once a policy has been adopted, it should be followed consistently.

Disclosure. The amount of interest capitalized during the period should be disclosed.

Reference. IAS 23.

27. Imputed Interest

General. **Imputed interest** is recognized only with respect to finance leases.

Accounting Treatment. The discount factor used in computing the present value of the minimum lease payments is the interest rate implicit in the lease or, if it is not practicable to determine this rate, the lessee's incremental borrowing rate.

Reference. IAS 17.

28. Extraordinary or Unusual Items

Extraordinary Items. Recent changes to accounting standards place greater restrictions on the criteria an item must meet to be classified as extraordinary. Those criteria are that an item:

□ Not be expected to occur frequently over several years.
□ Not be typical of the normal business activities of the entity.
□ Not depend primarily on decisions or determinations by management or owners.

Exceptional Items.   Exceptional items occur within the ordinary activities of an enterprise but are not expected to recur frequently—for example, a sale of property that results in a significant gain.

Unusual or Abnormal Items.   Nigerian accounting standards specifically prohibit items that do not have all the characteristics of an extraordinary item from being presented net of income tax. A separate unusual items classification is no longer allowed in the income statement. In addition, earnings per share information should not be presented for such items or for earnings before such items.

Disclosure.   Each extraordinary item and the amount of any applicable income taxes should be described and shown separately. Similar items may be combined. The income statement should distinguish between income before extraordinary items, extraordinary items net of applicable income taxes (the amount of which should be disclosed) and net income for the period. Exceptional items, before consideration of any associated taxes, should be disclosed in the profit and loss account.

Reference.   SAS 6.

29.   Income Taxes

Accounting Treatment.   The tax expense for the period should be determined using tax-effect accounting, under either the **deferral method** or the **liability method**. All timing differences should normally be taken into account. However, if there is reasonable evidence that timing differences will not reverse for at least three years and no indication that they will subsequently reverse, they may be excluded. Timing differences that result in a debit to the deferred tax balance should not be carried forward as an asset unless there is a reasonable expectation of realization.

If a tax loss is carried back to recover taxes of a previous period, the recovery should be recorded in the period in which the loss occurs.

Disclosure.   The following disclosures are required:

☐   The amount of the income tax provision on profit on a segment basis.
☐   The amount of deferred taxes recorded or not recorded.
☐   The method of calculating tax liabilities, that is, the deferral or liability method.
☐   The contingent tax liability arising from fixed asset revaluation.
☐   Unused losses and capital allowances carried forward.

30.   Postretirement Benefits

General.   Nigerian accounting standards cover employee retirement schemes or provident pension plans in which there are formal or implied contracts between employers and employees specifying benefits or specific amounts due to employees upon the attainment of a retirement age or due to disability, early leaving or death. These include unfunded plans, insured and uninsured plans, trust fund plans, **defined contribution plans** and **defined benefit plans**.

Defined Benefit Plans.   For defined benefit plans, the cost of pension benefits recorded in the period should be determined using the accrued benefit method, including salary projections prorated on services.

Past service costs, gains and losses on changes in actuarial assumptions and experience gains and losses should be deferred and amortized over an appropriate period, usually the expected average remaining service life of the employee group. Gains or losses on settlement or curtailment should be recognized immediately.

Differences between pension expense (income) and funding payments for the period should be recorded as accrued pension costs or deferred charges.

Defined Contribution Plans.   The cost of pension benefits for current services is the employer's required contribution for the period.

Past service costs should be deferred and amortized over the expected average remaining service life of the employee group.

Pension Fund Surpluses.   In Nigeria, there are legal questions regarding employer entitlement to pension surpluses, and some jurisdictions have placed restrictions on withdrawing surpluses. Pension surplus may be recognized provided that there is a reasonable expectation that the employer will obtain a benefit from it, by either withdrawing funds or reducing future contributions. The amount recognized should be limited to the expected future benefit.

Disclosure.   The following information should be disclosed in the notes to the financial statements:

☐ The existence of a retirement, provident or pension plan and the categories of employees covered.
☐ The accounting, actuarial and funding methods used, and changes thereto, for a defined contribution or benefit plan.
☐ The provisions made for retirement, provident or pension costs for the year.

Reference.   SAS 8, IAS 19 and 26.

31. Discontinued Operations

There is no requirement in Nigeria to disclose the results of discontinued operations of a business segment separately from continuing operations.

32. Earnings per Share

Earnings per share represents the portion of income for a period attributable to one common share of issued capital of an enterprise.

Methods of Calculation.   Earnings per share (EPS) information is generally calculated on two bases. The first calculation is based principally on the weighted-average number of common shares actually issued and outstanding and is known as basic earnings per share. The second calculation takes into account any material reduction in earnings per common share that could arise if the various stock options, warrants, conversion privileges attaching to debt or other classes of shares or other similar rights were exercised.

This is referred to as fully diluted EPS. Where debt or senior securities are converted into common shares during the period, a third set of calculations (adjusted basic EPS) is required as if the conversion had occurred at the beginning of the period.

Earnings figures used in the calculations should be the reported amounts adjusted for specific items relevant to basic, adjusted basic and fully diluted EPS calculations.

Disclosure. Basic EPS figures for the current and preceding years should be disclosed either on the face of the income statement or in a note. Adjusted basic EPS, if materially different from the basic EPS, should be disclosed in a note, cross-referenced to the income statement. Fully diluted EPS for the current year should be shown in a note, cross-referenced to the income statement. It is not necessary to disclose adjusted or fully diluted EPS for the preceding year.

Reference. SAS 2.

Appendix
DO NIGERIAN STANDARDS OR PREVALENT PRACTICE SUBSTANTIALLY COMPLY WITH INTERNATIONAL ACCOUNTING STANDARDS?

Section	Topic	Substantially complies with IAS?	Comments
3.	Basic accounting concepts and conventions	Yes	
	Contents of financial statements	Yes	
4.	Business combinations*	Yes	
5.	Joint ventures	Yes	
6.	Foreign currency translation*	Yes	
8.	Accounting changes*	Yes	
9.	Prior period adjustments*	Yes	
10.	Post balance sheet events	Yes	
11.	Related party transactions	Yes	
12.	Segmental information	Yes	
13.	Property, plant and equipment*	Yes	
15.	Leases	Yes	Except there is an option not to capitalize finance leases
16.	Investments	Yes	
17.	Accounts receivable	Yes	
18.	Inventories and work in progress*	Yes	
19.	Current liabilities	Yes	
20.	Long-term debt	Yes	
21.	Contingencies	Yes	
22.	Capital and reserves	Yes	
23.	Revenue recognition*	Yes	
24.	Government grants and assistance	Yes	
25.	Research and development*	Yes	
26.	Capitalization of interest costs*	Yes	
28.	Extraordinary or unusual items*	Yes	

Appendix (*Continued*)

Section	Topic	Substantially complies with IAS?	Comments
29.	Income tax**	Yes	
30.	Postretirement benefits*	Yes	

*These topics are subject to change as a result of the IASC Improvements Project—see the appendix to the International Accounting Standards chapter.

**The IAS on accounting for taxes on income is currently being revised, and an exposure draft has been issued.

Comparison in this table is made to International Accounting Standards in force at January 1, 1993. For further details, see the International Accounting Standards chapter.

NORWAY

GENERAL NATIONAL INFORMATION

1. Source of Generally Accepted Accounting Principles

Generally Accepted Accounting Principles. **Generally accepted accounting principles** in Norway are derived from the following sources:

- The Norwegian Accounting Act (Regnskapsloven, 1977), which establishes general accounting principles for most private-sector entities, except limited companies.
- The Norwegian Joint Stock Companies Act (Lov om aksjeselskaper 1976), which establishes general accounting principles for limited companies.
- **Accounting standards** issued by the Norwegian Accounting Standards Board (NRS, Norsk RegnskapsStiftelse), with the participation of major organizations interested in the development of accounting standards in Norway.
- Recommendations issued by the Norwegian Institute of State Authorized Accountants (NSRF, Norges Statsautoriserte Revisorers Forening), which are still valid in areas where the NRS has not yet issued standards.
- Accounting Bulletins issued by the Oslo Stock Exchange for **listed companies**.
- Recommendations issued by the Accountancy Advisory Group (Regnskapsrådet).

Norway is in the process of a major international harmonization effort, under which Norwegian legislation is being revised to conform with the European Community directives. Other major changes will also be included in the revised legislation, and will affect accounting standards. In addition, as noted in Section 29, beginning in 1992, companies are required to account for deferred taxes. The revision process will take place mainly in the period from 1992 to 1995 and will be led by a governmental committee (Regnskapslovutvalget) and a new standard-setting body, authorized in the Accounting Act. An exposure draft has been issued proposing that the accounting rules (the Norwegian Accounting Act and the Norwegian Joint Stock Companies Act) be categorized into three groups, one for larger and **public companies**, one for medium-sized companies and one for smaller companies. This is not expected to be approved before 1994. Accounting standards published by the NRS now distinguish the requirements for larger and public companies, and medium-sized companies. This chapter deals with these two groups, but not smaller companies.

2. Audit and Public Company Requirements

Audits.   According to the Joint Stock Companies Act all limited companies must be audited by a qualified accountant. Large companies (those with more than 200 employees) and/or listed companies must be audited by a State Authorized Public Accountant (Statsautorisert revisor). Other companies, except enterprises with an annual turnover of less than NOK 2 million, may be audited by either a Registered Public Accountant (Registrert revisor) or a State Authorized Public Accountant. The NOK 2 million limit is expected to be raised to NOK 5 million in 1994.

The auditing profession in Norway is regulated by the Norwegian Audit Act (Revisorloven, 1964) and the Joint Stock Companies Act. Auditing standards are issued by the NSRF. The NSRF has also issued Rules of Professional Ethics for the profession.

The Ministry of Finance (Finansdepartementet) has overall public responsibility for the auditing profession. On behalf of the Ministry, The Banking, Insurance and Securities Commission (Kredittilsynet) carries out the day-to-day supervision of the profession.

State Authorized Public Accountants must have a special university qualification (Høyere revisoreksamen) as well as at least two years of practice experience.

Registered Public Accountants must have a commercial college-level qualification and two years practice experience.

The auditor must be independent of the company. A person cannot be elected as auditor if he or she is:

□   An owner or a participant in the enterprise.

□   A lender to the company, unless the amount does not exceed the fees for the two preceding years.

□   A member of the company's board.

□   Employed by the company, or in other ways dependent on the company.

□   Married or closely related to a person holding one of the above-mentioned positions.

The auditor is appointed by the general meeting of the shareholders and remains in office until the general meeting appoints another auditor.

The auditor shall, to the extent required by generally accepted auditing standards, examine the company's annual report, the accounts and the administration of the company. In particular, the auditor shall verify that the accounts are in accordance with laws and regulations, and that the annual report is complete and meets the informational needs of shareholders, lenders, management and employees, as well as the public.

The auditor shall submit an audit report to the general meeting, stating:

□   That the audit has been carried out as required by generally accepted auditing standards.

□   Whether the annual report meets the requirements stated by the law and generally accepted accounting principles.

□   Whether the proposed appropriation of the year's profit or loss is in accordance with the law.

Public Companies.   There is no distinction between public and private companies in Norway.

Companies wanting to go public and to trade their shares must apply for listing on the Oslo Stock Exchange (Oslo Børs).

Listing requirements are partly governed by law. Minimum requirements for listing shares are normally as follows:

☐ The corporation must have existed for at least one year.
☐ The share capital must be at least NOK 10 million.
☐ The number of shares issued must be at least 200,000 and there must be at least 500 shareholders.

Less stringent requirements apply for smaller companies included on a special list (SMB-Listen).

In addition, shares in nonresident corporations cannot be listed without the approval of the Ministry of Finance.

The procedure for listing consists of filing an application with the stock exchange's board. An application for listing shares must contain:

☐ The share capital.
☐ Par value of the shares.
☐ The number of shareholders.
☐ Dividend distributions for the past two years.
☐ Five copies of the corporation's bylaws.
☐ Five copies of the financial statements for the past two years.

The board of the stock exchange may require information in addition to that mentioned above.

Companies (or other entities having issued bonds) are obligated to furnish the stock exchange with five copies of each year's financial statements. Any information that may have an impact on the securities' market value, including specifically decisions on dividend distributions, the issuance of shares or bonds and capitalization of reserves, must be furnished.

An exposure draft of new regulations for listed companies was issued by the Oslo Stock Exchange in 1991.

Reference. Audit Act, Chapters I and II; Joint Stock Companies Act, Chapter 10; NSRF, Recommendations on generally accepted auditing standards; Regulations for Public Listing on the Stock Exchange; Oslo Stock Exchange, Accounting Recommendations for Listed Companies.

GENERAL ACCOUNTING

3. Financial Statements

Basic Accounting Concepts. Norwegian **accounting principles** are based on the principles of **historical cost accounting, going concern concept**, lower of cost and market valuation and congruity. **Current assets** are stated at the lower of cost and market value. **Fixed assets** are valued on the basis of historical cost, but if a permanently lower value has been identified, the asset should be written down to that value. Revaluation of fixed assets is allowed, with certain restrictions. The principle of congruity means that all movements in equity capital, except those deriving from new share capital or the payment of dividends to shareholders, should be reported in the income statement; for example, a correction of an error in a prior period is included in the current year's income as an extraordinary item.

Contents of Financial Statements. Limited companies are required under the Joint Stock Companies Act to issue an annual report containing an income statement, a balance sheet and notes. A written statement from the board (board's report) is an obligatory part of the annual report.

For large companies (companies with assets totaling more than NOK 10 million, with more than 200 employees or whose shares are listed) the annual report includes a statement of changes in financial position or cash flows.

Where the entity is a **parent company**, the annual report also contains a consolidated income statement, balance sheet, statement of changes in financial position for the group and notes.

Other private enterprises are required under the Accounting Act to issue similar annual reports.

The board's report includes relevant additional information about the company's financial position and operations, including information on matters occurring after the year-end date, if material. The report also includes information about the number of employees and about compensation paid to members of the board and the managing director. The report gives information about the auditor's fee, split between audit and consulting. The report also contains information about the number of shareholders and shareholders owning more than 20 percent of the share capital, as well as the number of shares owned by members of the board, the managing director, the auditor (auditors are not permitted to own shares, but the fact that they own none must be reported) and close relatives. The report contains the board's proposal for appropriating the profit or loss of the company. Information about external pollution and waste resulting from the company's operations and what is done to eliminate such pollution, and, if the company has more than 10 employees, information about the company's internal working conditions is required.

Large companies are required to issue at least a half-year report (and listed companies, quarterly or four-monthly reports), containing a summary income statement and summary of changes in liquidity and financial position.

The general meeting is required to approve the annual report within six months of the year-end date. For 1992, the opening balance, restated to reflect the new deferred tax accounting standard (see Section 29), is also required to be approved by the general meeting. Within one month after the general meeting's approval the full annual report, including the auditor's report, is submitted to a public accounts register (Regnskapsregisteret) where it is publicly available.

Format of Financial Statements. The company's annual report should follow the format specified by the Accounting Act and the Joint Stock Companies Act. Exceptions called for by the nature and extent of the business are permitted, but are normally not used.

Income and costs are segregated into those resulting from ordinary operations, those resulting from financial operations, those resulting from extraordinary events and taxes.

Assets and liabilities are segregated into current and noncurrent in the balance sheet. A noncurrent asset is defined as an asset intended for continuous use or possession by the entity. All other assets are current assets. The one-year rule is the criterion for classifying receivables as current or noncurrent.

Large companies are required to issue a statement of changes in financial position or a cash flow statement.

Disclosure of Accounting Policies. Disclosure of **accounting policies** in general is not required. Disclosure is, however, required of valuation principles used in connection with current assets, as well as changes in these principles. Information about participation in other enterprises (other than limited companies) should include the name of the enterprise, the share owned by the company and the method used for including it in the accounts. Principles used in connection with the preparation of **consolidated financial statements** should be disclosed.

Reference. Accounting Act, Chapter 3; Joint Stock Companies Act, Chapter 11.

4. Business Combinations

Principles of Consolidation. Under the Joint Stock Companies Act, parent companies that are limited companies must present consolidated accounts. Other private enterprises are also required, under the Accounting Act, to present consolidated accounts.

The consolidated accounts cover the same period as those of the parent and comprise an income statement, a balance sheet and a statement of changes in financial position or cash flows, based on the accounting principles used by the parent company. The board's report of the parent company presents additional information on the economic situation and market trends for the group as well as for the parent company.

The Banking, Insurance and Securities Commission normally grants exemption from the requirement to present subconsolidated accounts if the parent company is itself a **subsidiary**.

Accounting for Business Combinations. Until 1988 there were no accounting standards relating to **business combinations** in Norway. That year a committee issued a recommendation on **accounting methods** for business combinations. This recommendation covers both the consolidation of a parent company and its subsidiaries, as well as company mergers.

The basic principle of this recommendation is that the accounting method shall reflect the economic substance. Thus, if from the acquirer's point of view, the combination is a purchase, the **purchase method** should be used. If the combination is a merger of the economic interests of both companies, the **pooling of interests method** should be used.

The formal merger of two companies is regulated by the Joint Stock Companies Act, Chapter 14. There is a general understanding that this law requires the pooling of interests method to be used in the case of a formal merger.

Control. A parent–subsidiary relationship is defined by the Joint Stock Companies Act as follows:

☐ Where a company is holder of such a number of shares of another company, or such a fraction of another private enterprise, that it represents the majority of the votes at the general meeting, the former company is a parent company and the latter is a subsidiary. If a parent company and a subsidiary together hold such a number of shares or fraction of another company, then the latter also is a subsidiary.

□ Where a company has, by virtue of its holding of shares or participation or by virtue of agreement, a decisive influence over another company or private entity, and a considerable share in its results, the company is a parent company and the other is a subsidiary.

The Joint Stock Companies Act will be revised during the 1990s. The definitions of parent company and subsidiary will be changed to conform to the European Community directives.

Goodwill.   Under the purchase method, an analysis of the fair values of assets and liabilities should be made at the time of purchase. The differences between the purchase value and the book value should be allocated to the identified assets and liabilities in the consolidated balance sheet.

Where the difference has been identified as **goodwill**, the value should be recorded as such in the consolidated balance sheet. According to the Joint Stock Companies Act and Accounting Act, goodwill is subject to annual **amortization** of 20 percent on the **straight-line** basis. Amortization can be based on a longer period, limited to a maximum of 20 years (5 percent).

Equity Accounting.   An entity is normally defined as being associated with another company if the latter holds shares in the entity to the extent that it controls 20 percent or more of the voting power but less than 50 percent. However, the level of ownership is not the sole criterion for defining a company as being associated with another. A company may not be considered associated even though it holds more than 20 percent of the voting power, if:

□ There is doubt about whether the ownership is in compliance with the company's articles of association.

□ The investor is denied board representation in the company.

□ There is another dominating owner or group of owners, preventing the investor's influence.

□ Other restrictions prevent the exercise of the investor's influence.

The Joint Stock Companies Act allows the use of the **equity method** in consolidated accounts but not in the accounts of individual entities. Investments in entities other than limited companies are accounted for by one of three methods:

□ **Proportional consolidation** (bruttometoden).

□ Equity accounting.

□ **Historical cost**.

However, a draft recommendation from the NRS recommends the use of equity accounting and will probably lead to more uniform practice.

Minority Interests.   At the time of purchase the **minority interest** is the minority's share of the subsidiary's equity capital and differences identified through the analysis of fair values, except goodwill.

The minority's share of the consolidated income is its part of the subsidiary's results after dividends, adjusted for internal gains and losses and the allocation of fair value differences to the group's profit and loss account.

The minority interest is disclosed between long-term liabilities and shareholders' equity in the balance sheet.

Disclosure. Consolidation: The Joint Stock Companies Act and Accounting Act require the annual report to disclose the names of subsidiaries, as well as the share capital owned. The method used for consolidation should also be disclosed. This information is normally given in the notes to the consolidated accounts.

Equity accounting: Information about participation in other enterprises should include the name of the enterprise, the share owned by the company and the method used for including it in the accounts.

Reference. Joint Stock Companies Act, Chapter 11; Recommended accounting methods for business combinations; NRS, Draft Recommendation on Accounting Methods for Associated Enterprises.

5. Joint Ventures

The accounting regulation and treatment comply with IAS 31, except that proportionate consolidation is the only allowed accounting treatment. Jointly controlled operations in which the venturers have contractually agreed to share control over an economic activity should follow the draft standard for jointly controlled operations.

Contractual arrangements normally cover:

☐ The activity and duration of the **joint venture**.

☐ Capital contribution by the venturers.

☐ Appointment of the board of directors or equivalent governing body and the voting rights of the venturers.

☐ The sharing by the venturers of the output, income, expenses or results of the joint venture.

A joint venture can be carried out through jointly controlled operations (which also includes jointly controlled assets) or jointly controlled entities. The definitions comply with IAS 31.

In a joint venture, the proportionate consolidation method is required to be used in the venturers' accounts and/or the consolidated accounts. The proportionate method cannot be used for interests in limited joint stock companies; the cost method has to be used. For such companies, disclosure of the effect of using proportionate consolidation should be made in the notes to the financial statements.

Two reporting formats are used: either the line-by-line basis or combining the share of each of the assets, liabilities, income and expenses in the joint venture with the similar items in the venturer's financial statements. When reporting an interest in a joint venture, it is essential that a venturer reflect the substance and economic reality of the arrangement.

Transactions Between a Venturer and a Joint Venture. As long as the assets are retained by the joint venture, and provided the venturer has transferred the significant risks and rewards of ownership, the venturer recognizes only that portion of a gain attributable to the interests of the other venturers. The venturer recognizes the full amount of any loss when the contribution or sale provides evidence of a reduction in the **net realizable value** of current assets or a decline (other than temporary) in the carrying amount of long-term assets.

When a venturer purchases assets from a joint venture, the venturer does not recognize its share of the profits of the joint venture from the transaction until it resells the assets to an independent party. A venturer recognizes its share of losses resulting from these transactions in the same way as profits, except that losses are recognized immediately when they represent a reduction in the net realizable value of current assets or a decline (other than temporary) in the carrying amount of long-term assets. Other transactions between a venturer and a joint venture should also be eliminated (the venturer's portion).

Disclosure. Disclosure requirements are similar to those for equity accounting (see Section 4).

Accounting by Joint Ventures. The joint venture recognizes all assets, both acquired and contributed by venturers, at the purchase price to the joint venture.

Reference. NRS, Draft Accounting Standard for Financial Reporting of Jointly Controlled Operations.

6. Foreign Currency Translation

Foreign Currency Denominated Transactions. The treatment of **foreign currency denominated transactions** is based on the general valuation rules in the Joint Stock Companies Act and Accounting Act and on a recommendation (NSRF No. 11) on the valuation of receivables and payables denominated in foreign currency. Receivables denominated in foreign currency should be translated at the lower of the transaction date rate or the closing rate. Payables should be translated at the higher of the transaction date rate or the closing rate. Receivables and payables can be translated at the closing rate if the unrealized income thus reported is set off against an unrealized loss on other items denominated in the same currency. Cash and bank deposits may be translated at the closing rate.

All differences resulting from translation of foreign currency denominated transactions should be reported in the income statement.

Foreign Operations. The Joint Stock Companies Act does not specify any method for translating foreign subsidiaries' financial statements for consolidation purposes. However, according to prevalent practice, the income statement should be translated at the average rate for the year, and the balance sheet at the closing rate. Translation differences are normally taken directly to the group's equity.

Hedges. If a receivable or payable denominated in foreign currency is effectively hedged, the item should be translated at the exchange rate of the hedging contract.

Disclosure. The company should disclose the principles used for foreign currency translation. In addition, there should be disclosure of the company's currency exposure and the steps taken to reduce it.

Reference. Joint Stock Companies Act, Chapter 11; NSRF, Recommendation on Accounting Principles for Foreign Currency Items (No. 11).

7. Changing Prices/Inflation Accounting

General. In Norway there is no standard or recommendation on accounting practice for changing prices. Current value accounting is normally not used in company annual reports.

8. Accounting Changes

Accounting Treatment. The effects of accounting changes are normally included in the income statement and accounted for as extraordinary items. In the case of a fundamental change in accounting principles, however, the effect may be charged directly to shareholders' equity.

Disclosure. The Joint Stock Companies Act and Accounting Act require disclosure of changes in the bases on which assets and liabilities are carried in the balance sheet if the changes are significant or have materially affected income for the year.

It is further required that a change in the grouping or classification of the items in the financial statements or any other change that will affect comparability between years be disclosed.

Reference. Joint Stock Companies Act, paragraph 11; Accounting Act, Section 19; NRS, Draft Accounting Standard for Extraordinary Items.

9. Prior Period Adjustments
Prior period adjustments should, according to the congruity principle, be disclosed in the income statement. Material prior period adjustments are classified as extraordinary items.

Reference. NRS, Draft Accounting Standard for Extraordinary Items.

10. Post Balance Sheet Events
The Joint Stock Companies Act requires that the board's report include additional information about events material to the company, and not included in the income statement or the balance sheet, even if they occurred after the end of the accounting period.

Reference. Joint Stock Companies Act, Chapter 11, Section 12; NRS, Accounting Standard 3, Contingencies.

11. Related Party Transactions

Definition. Norwegian Accounting Laws do not include a clear definition of related parties or related party transactions. According to the Joint Stock Companies Act, transactions between the company and certain related parties such as group companies, shareholders, the managing director and members of the board should be disclosed.

General.   A company may not grant loans to a shareholder, member of the board or the managing director if the company does not have nonrestricted shareholders' funds at least equaling such loans. Adequate security must also be provided for the loans. Guarantees are treated in the same way. The same rule applies to persons who are married or closely related to a shareholder, member of the board or the managing director.

Accounting Treatment.   Generally, related party transactions should be accounted for in accordance with normal accounting principles. Shares in subsidiaries should be disclosed in the balance sheet. The same applies to receivables from and loans to another company or companies in a group. Interest paid to or received from group companies should also be disclosed. Salary paid to the managing director and the members of the board must be disclosed in the board's report.

Listed companies must, according to accounting recommendations issued by the Oslo Stock Exchange, disclose fuller information on related party transactions, including:

☐   The nature of related party interests.

☐   A description of the transactions involved and their effect on the accounts.

☐   Receivables and payables between the company and related parties on the closing date.

Listed companies should disclose the existence of related party interests even if transactions have not occurred during the accounting period.

Reference.   Joint Stock Companies Act, Chapter 11; Oslo Stock Exchange, Accounting Recommendations for Listed Companies.

12. Segmental Information

General.   Segmental information is not required according to Norwegian Accounting Regulations.

Accounting Treatment.   The Oslo Stock Exchange and the Norwegian Society of Financial Analysts recommend that listed companies include such information in their annual reports.

Reference.   Oslo Stock Exchange, Accounting Recommendations for Listed Companies.

ACCOUNTING PRINCIPLES FOR SPECIFIC ITEMS— BALANCE SHEET

13. Property, Plant and Equipment

Classification of Capital and Revenue Expenditure.   Expenditures for **capital assets** that result in a lasting improvement of the asset and thereby increase its value should be capitalized as part of the cost of the asset. Expenditures to maintain normal operating efficiency are expensed as incurred.

Basis of Valuation. Generally, fixed assets are carried at depreciated historical cost. However, a fixed asset that has a lasting value substantially in excess of the amount at which it was carried in the preceding balance sheet may be written up to the amount of its value. The amount written up is treated as a revaluation reserve that may be used only for a necessary write-down of the value of fixed assets, covering of loss on disposal of other fixed assets or a bonus share issue.

If the value of a fixed asset in the balance sheet substantially exceeds the lasting value, the fixed asset should be written down.

Depreciation. The Accounting Act requires fixed assets to be depreciated according to "an appropriate **depreciation** plan." Such a plan should, according to the NSRF's recommendations on accounting for tangible assets, be based on the historical cost concept, the estimated useful life of the asset and an appropriate allocation method. The most commonly used method is the straight-line method. However, any method consistently applied that produces a reasonable and systematic allocation of depreciation over the asset's useful life is acceptable. If sufficient depreciation has already been recorded, a change in the depreciation plan would be preferable to omitting depreciation. If an entity revalues its fixed assets upward, the revalued amount should then be depreciated.

Disclosure. The accounting policies adopted regarding the valuation and depreciation of fixed assets must be disclosed. Accumulated additional depreciation allowed for tax purposes should be disclosed as untaxed reserves in the balance sheet. The income statement should disclose the amount of depreciation charged for the accounting period. Details of cost, accumulated depreciation, remainder of earlier years' write-up and net book value of each class of assets must be disclosed in the notes.

Reference. Accounting Act, Chapter 3; Joint Stock Companies Act, Chapter 11; NSRF, Recommendation on Accounting for Depreciation of Tangible Fixed Assets.

14. Intangible Assets

Expenditures for technical assistance, research and development, trial runs, market research and similar activities may be recognized as **intangible assets**, provided that the expenditures will benefit the entity during future years. Such assets should be amortized by an appropriate amount, generally at least 20 percent annually, unless it is clear that the value of the intangible assets will last for a longer period.

Trademarks are amortized over their economic life.

Reference. Accounting Act, Chapter 3; Joint Stock Companies Act, Chapter 11; NSRF, Recommendation on Accounting for Research and Development and Recommendation on Accounting for Goodwill.

15. Leases

Classification. Leases that transfer substantially all the benefits and risks of ownership to the lessee should be accounted for as capital (**finance**) **leases**. Leases and contingent rental payments that are not capital leases should be accounted for as **operating leases**. Guidance, rather than rules, exists for the appropriate classification of leases as either capital or operating. In the following circumstances, it is normally considered that the risks and benefits have been transferred and that the lease should be classified as a capital lease:

☐ The lease results in ownership being transferred to the lessee by the end of the lease term, or the lease provides for a bargain purchase option; or

☐ The term of the lease is equal to 75 percent or more of the economic life of the leased property; or

☐ The present value of the lease payments equals 90 percent or more of the fair market value of the leased property.

Accounting Treatment. Capital leases: Capital leases should be capitalized and accounted for as an asset and a matching obligation by the lessee, and as a sale or a direct financing transaction by the lessor. The leased asset should be depreciated by the lessee in the same manner as other fixed assets.

Operating leases: The rental payments are expensed by the lessee and recorded as revenue by the lessor in the periods to which they relate.

In practice, many lease contracts are disclosed as operating leases even though by their nature they are capital leases.

Disclosure. If a significant portion of the company's fixed assets are held under leases, the leasing terms should be disclosed in a note to the balance sheet.

Reference. Accounting Act, Section 3; Joint Stock Companies Act, Chapter 11; NSRF, Recommendation on Accounting for Leasing Agreements (No. 17).

16. Investments

General. This section deals with investments held by companies, other than investments in subsidiaries, **associated companies** or interests in partnerships, which are discussed in Section 4. The valuation of investments depends on their classification as current or noncurrent.

Valuation. Current investments: Current investments should be carried at the lower of cost and market value. The lower of cost and market test may be applied to marketable investments individually or on a **portfolio basis**. Reversals of previous write-downs are permitted.

Noncurrent investments: Noncurrent investments should be carried at cost adjusted for any permanent diminution in value. Reversals of write-downs of noncurrent investments to reflect increases in market value are not permitted, except in those instances where the requirements of Chapter 3 of the Accounting Act and Chapter 11 of the Joint Stock Companies Act for revaluation of fixed assets are met.

Gains/Losses. The calculation of the gain or loss on the sale of part of a holding of securities should be based on the average carrying value.

Disclosure. Information on investments in other companies should be disclosed in the notes as required by paragraph 19 of the Accounting Act and paragraph 11-8 of the Joint Stock Companies Act.

Reference. Accounting Act, Chapter 3; Joint Stock Companies Act, Chapter 11.

17. Accounts Receivable

Accounting Treatment.   Recognition: The recognition of **revenues**, and hence the related receivables, is described in Section 23.

Discounts: Revenues and the related receivables are normally recorded net of trade discounts. Since the recognition of cash discounts occurs at the time of payment, it is not usual to take account of potential cash discounts in determining the value to be attributed to a trade **account receivable**.

Allowances: There are two methods of computing a provision for doubtful accounts: specific assessment and by a general assessment of exposure based on previous experience.

Factored Receivables.   Receivables that have been factored should not be included in the balance sheet. However, if the factor has recourse to the vendor for doubtful accounts, the transaction should be considered a loan.

Disclosure.   Accounts and notes receivable should be segregated between trade accounts, prepaid expenses, accrued income and other receivables. The total provision for doubtful accounts and recorded losses, divided into realized losses and change in provision, should be disclosed in the notes.

Trading balances with group companies are disclosed separately as intercompany trade **debtors**.

Reference.   Accounting Act, Chapter 3; Joint Stock Companies Act, Chapter 11; NSRF, Recommendation on Accounting for Valuation and Disclosure of Current Receivables (No. 16).

18. Inventories and Work in Progress

General Accounting Treatment.   **Inventories** should be carried at the lower of cost and market; **FIFO** and **average cost** are acceptable methods of determining cost. Market is determined by expected net market value at the time of sale, which, if material, is discounted to present value.

For work in progress and finished goods, cost should include the cost of materials, the cost of direct labor and an appropriate share of overhead expense chargeable to production. Interest should be excluded. Similarly, fixed overhead should be excluded to the extent that including it would distort the net income for the period because of a fluctuating volume of production. Medium-sized companies have the option of using direct cost for work in progress.

Long-Term Contracts.   The **benchmark treatment** for long-term contracts by larger and public companies is the **percentage of completion method**. Profit should not be included where the final outcome of the contract is uncertain. Expected losses should be provided for in full in the income statement. The **completed contract method** is also an allowed method.

Disclosure.   Inventories should be divided into raw materials and supplies, work in progress and finished goods, and long-term contracts. In addition, the basis of valuing inventories should be disclosed.

Reference.   Accounting Act, Chapter 3; Joint Stock Companies Act, Chapter 11; NRS, Accounting Standard 1, Inventories, and Accounting Standard 2, Long-Term Contracts.

19. Current Liabilities

General Accounting Treatment.   **Accounts payable** and liabilities due within the operating cycle are classified as **current liabilities**. As a balance sheet classification, other current liabilities include amounts payable within one year from the date of the balance sheet.

Creation of General and Specific Provisions.   General provisions are not permitted, as provisions must relate to a specific existing obligation. Provisions for future expenses or losses are not permitted unless the circumstances giving rise to them have occurred.

Provisions for future expenses relating to warranties should be recognized at the time of sale of the item under warranty.

Disclosure.   Current liabilities should be segregated between main classes; for example, bills of exchange payable, bank overdrafts, accounts payable, taxes payable, dividends payable and other current liabilities.

Payables to subsidiary and parent entities should be disclosed as a separate line item in the balance sheet.

Reference.   Accounting Act, Chapter 3; Joint Stock Companies Act, Chapter 11; NSRF, Recommendation on the Segregation Between Current and Noncurrent Assets, and Between Current and Long-Term Debt.

20. Long-Term Debt

General Accounting Treatment.   The most common forms of long-term debt in Norway are mortgages, bonds, debentures and other forms of long-term bank credit.

The general accounting treatment applied to these items is basically the same as for current liabilities, i.e., they are carried in the balance sheet at cost.

Disclosure.   Long-term debt should be segregated in the balance sheet between mortgages and other long-term loans. Long-term payables to subsidiary and parent entities should also be disclosed in the balance sheet.

Subordinated loans should be disclosed in the balance sheet under long-term debt, and details of the agreement should be disclosed in the notes, including any rights of conversion to equity capital.

Reference.   Accounting Act, Chapter 3; Joint Stock Companies Act, Chapter 11; NSRF, Recommendation on Disclosure of Subordinated Loans.

21. Contingencies

Contingent Losses.   The accounting treatment of contingent liabilities depends on the probability of occurrence of the future events that will determine the **contingency**. If the probability is high, the contingencies should be included among liabilities.

Contingent Gains. Contingent gains should not be accrued in the financial statements, but if their realization is likely, they should be disclosed in the notes.

Disclosure. The Accounting Act requires contingent liabilities to be disclosed under the headings discounted bills, guarantees and other contingent liabilities, and pension obligations that are not reported as a liability or covered by assets of a pension fund.

Contingencies are disclosed as memorandum items below the balance sheet or in the notes.

Reference. Accounting Act, Chapter 3; Joint Stock Companies Act, Chapter 11; NRS, Accounting Standard 3, Contingencies.

22. Capital and Reserves

General. Equity is accounted for in somewhat different ways by private firms, partnerships and limited companies. This chapter concentrates on limited companies. Equity is generally divided between restricted equity and nonrestricted equity or accumulated deficit. Restricted equity is divided among **share capital**, legal reserve, revaluation reserve and temporary restricted reserve.

Share Capital. Where the company's share capital is divided into several classes, the amount of each class should be disclosed. If there are differences between shares' voting rights, those rights should be disclosed.

Holdings of a company's own shares should be disclosed on a separate line as a deduction from the company's equity.

Restricted Reserves. Two kinds of restricted reserves may appear in a limited company's balance sheet.

Legal reserve: The following allocations should be made to the legal reserve:

☐ At least 10 percent of the net income for the year after deduction of any deficit brought forward. Such allocation must continue until the reserve equals 20 percent of the share capital, and restricted reserves and share capital must at least cover the company's total liabilities at the end of the fiscal year.

☐ At least as much as the amount paid in dividends that exceed 10 percent of restricted reserves and share capital at the beginning of the fiscal year.

☐ Any amount received in excess of the nominal value of issued shares.

A reduction in legal reserve may be made only for the following purposes:

☐ To cover losses that cannot be covered by nonrestricted equity.

☐ To increase share capital through a bonus share issue.

Revaluation reserve: This reserve results from the revaluation of fixed assets. It may be used only for a necessary write-down of the value of noncurrent assets, covering of loss on other fixed assets or bonus share issue.

Temporary Restricted Reserve.   As an effect of the tax reform in 1991/92, a part of the retained profit from previous years is allocated to a special capital surplus, temporary restricted reserve. Annually 20 percent is transferred to earned surplus/**retained earnings**.

Dividends.   Dividends to shareholders may not exceed the amount distributable according to the balance sheet approved by the board. The distributable amount includes net income for the year and retained earnings less reported losses and the amount allocated to legal reserve.

Dividends may not be distributed to an extent that would be contrary to good business practice, and losses that have occurred or may occur after the balance sheet date should be considered.

The general meeting of the shareholders may not declare a dividend that is higher than the dividend proposed or approved by the board of directors.

Reference.   Accounting Act; Joint Stock Companies Act.

ACCOUNTING PRINCIPLES FOR SPECIFIC ITEMS— INCOME STATEMENT

23. Revenue Recognition

General Principles.   There is no specific revenue recognition accounting standard in Norway, but the NRS has an ongoing project on this topic. Revenue is recognized when it is earned and its realization is reasonably assured. Revenue is generally recognized when the seller has transferred significant risks and rewards of the assets sold. These conditions are usually met by the time products or merchandise are delivered or services are rendered to customers.

Long-Term Projects/Contracts.   The benchmark treatment (for larger and public companies) is to recognize revenue as work progresses (the percentage of completion method) if the outcome of the contract can be reasonably determined. If the outcome of the contract is uncertain, recognition of revenue should not include profit. If a loss on the contract as a whole is expected, a provision should be made for the entire amount of the loss as soon as it is identified. The interest element should be recognized separately as interest income or expense.

Long-term projects where no sales contract exists at the time of commencement should be treated as production for inventory.

The completed contract method may also be used (allowed treatment).

Instalment Sales.   Revenue is normally recognized in full at the date of sale. However, if **instalment sales** are substantial, the implicit interest component should be recorded using discounted cash flow techniques.

Rights of Return.   If the right of return constitutes a significant ownership risk, either revenue recognition is deferred or revenue is recognized immediately and the risk reflected by a provision for returns until the risk is eliminated or sufficiently reduced.

Product Financing. A **product financing arrangement** is a transaction in which the price at the time of purchase is the same as at the time of sale, except for financing or other similar costs. Because the substantial risks and benefits of ownership do not pass to the buyer, such arrangements must be reflected as financing transactions rather than as sales.

Disclosure. Companies must disclose total operating revenue in the income statement. Disclosure of accounting policies for long-term projects/contracts is also required.

Reference. Accounting Act, Chapters 2 and 3; Joint Stock Companies Act, Chapter 11; Assumptions and Background for NSRF Recommendations on Good Accounting Practice (No. 0); Regnskapsrådet, Recommendation U1/91; NRS, Accounting Standard 2, Long-Term Contracts.

24. Government Grants and Assistance

Accounting Treatment. Revenue grants: Government assistance should be reported in the income statement under the same heading as the related expense, in a consistent manner from period to period. Compensation for reduced income should be reported as income.

Grants for fixed assets: The cost of the fixed assets should be reduced by the amount of the grant, or should be taken to income as an offsetting element against depreciation expense. Special investment grants to certain specific areas in Norway (from Distriktenes Utbyggingsfond) are reported as income.

Disclosure. Grants or assistance of substantial size must be disclosed either in the income statement or in the notes. Grants that are not fully disclosed in the income statement or grants that are difficult to quantify must be disclosed in the notes.

Reference. NSRF, Recommendation on Public Subsidies and Charges (No. 4); Oslo Stock Exchange, Accounting Recommendations 1990.

25. Research and Development

Definitions. Research is fundamental, planned research to acquire new technological or scientific innovation with a possible economic potential. Development is the translation of research findings or other knowledge into a plan or design for new or improved products or processes intended for sale or use.

Also included in the definition of research and development (R&D) is technical assistance, experimental operation and market research.

Accounting Treatment. Costs connected to R&D can be capitalized only to the extent that they relate to a profitable new activity or a more profitable existing activity. The company must intend to and be able to complete the investments, or there must be the possibility of selling the results. The use of the R&D-related work must add substantial and permanent value to the business.

Capitalization is limited to the lower of initial cost and actual value. If capitalized, R&D costs must be amortized over a period of five years, unless it is evident that the costs will represent a commercial value for a longer period. Deferred R&D costs should be reviewed at each balance sheet date, and if the capitalized amount exceeds the recoverable amount, the excess should be written off immediately. Research and development expenditures that have been expensed as incurred or written off can be revalued in certain restricted circumstances.

Disclosure. Amortization must be disclosed in the income statement and specified in the notes. Additional information concerning principles for estimating capitalized costs and amortization must be given.

If substantial R&D costs of permanent value to the business are expensed as incurred, they should be disclosed in the income statement or in the notes.

Reference. Accounting Act, paragraph 21; Joint Stock Companies Act, paragraph 11-11; NSRF, Recommendation on Accounting Treatment of Research and Development Costs (No. 14).

26. Capitalized Interest Costs

Accounting Treatment. There are no guidelines dealing with capitalization of interest.

Interest paid as part of the cost of an asset for continuing use by the entity may be capitalized. According to the accounting standard for long-term contracts/projects, interest costs related to long-term contracts/projects may be capitalized if the entity is involved in only a few substantial projects. **Imputed interest** on the entity's equity may not be capitalized.

Disclosure. Although there is no specific requirement for disclosure, the policy adopted for capitalization of interest is generally disclosed in the notes to the financial statements.

Reference. NRS, Accounting Standard 2, Long-Term Contracts.

27. Imputed Interest

General. Imputed interest is not widely used in the preparation of financial statements in Norway. However, the principles of discounting account balances and transactions to their present value are recognized in the accounting standard dealing with business combinations and in a recommendation of the Accountancy Advisory Group (Regnskapsrådet) dealing with sales and revenues.

Accounting Treatment

☐ Business combinations. If there is a difference between the time of purchase of a company and payment, the payment must be discounted and the interest component reported as a financing charge. This principle also extends to deferred settlement agreements for the sale of a company.

☐ Sales and revenues. If no interest or interest lower than the going rate is charged, the interest component should be reflected in income and determined by the use of discounted cash flow techniques in measuring revenue. This will apply only if the element interest is substantial to the business.

Disclosure. The accounting policy concerning business combinations should specifically disclose how imputed interest has been accounted for, if applicable. The same applies to credit sales if sales have been discounted.

Reference. Recommended accounting methods for business combinations; Regnskapsrådet, Recommendation U1/91.

28. Extraordinary or Unusual Items

Definition. Extraordinary items are events or transactions that are distinguished by their unusual nature, the infrequency of their occurrence and their **materiality**. They are unrelated to the typical activities of the entity and would not be expected to occur often or regularly. An extraordinary item may derive from an ordinary activity of the entity if it is the result of an abnormal exposure.

Corrections of material errors or omissions from previous years must be corrected in the income statement as extraordinary items.

Changes in accounting principles must also be classified as extraordinary items in the income statement.

Disclosure. Extraordinary revenues and expenses should be disclosed separately in the income statement. Separate disclosure of each extraordinary item is required in the notes. If an extraordinary item is a result of changes in accounting principles or disposals or discontinued operations of a significant business segment, it should be described as such. If there is a fundamental change in accounting policy, the extraordinary item may be adjusted against opening equity.

Reference. NRS, Draft Accounting Standard for Extraordinary Items.

29. Income Taxes

Accounting Treatment. In accordance with NRS Draft Accounting Standard for Taxes (1992), companies are required to account for deferred taxes. Accounting for deferred taxes covers limited companies and other operating businesses that are subject to income tax.

Deferred tax assets, including those arising from losses, should not be carried forward as assets, except to the extent that they are expected to be recoverable. Such balances should in most cases be deducted from deferred tax liabilities. A company or group cannot report deferred tax assets in an amount higher than the deferred tax liabilities reported.

Disclosure. The notes must disclose the following:

☐ Difference between profit before taxes and tax basis. Permanent and **temporary differences** should be specified.

☐ Specification of the relationship between the deferred tax basis and the tax rate.

☐ Specification of tax expense, including refund to active owners of the company's taxes paid by them.

☐ The total Norwegian and overseas tax.

□ The amount of deferred tax relating to ordinary activities and the amount relating to extraordinary items.

□ Adjustments to deferred tax from changes in tax rates and tax allowances.

□ The tax effect of items charged directly against equity.

□ Deferred tax on consolidated profit or profit-sharing according to the equity method.

□ The basis for tax assets in the balance sheet.

□ The effect of tax assets on the pension liability.

Listed companies and larger companies should additionally disclose:

□ The effect of tax on permanent and temporary differences during the year.

□ Losses to be brought forward and the year they will expire.

□ The share of losses to be brought forward, less reversed portion, and how much is shown in the balance sheet as a deferred tax asset.

For consolidated accounts, the disclosure requirements are not so comprehensive.

Companies other than limited companies should disclose the following, even though they do not account for deferred tax:

□ Difference between profit before tax and income according to the Companies Tax Act.

□ Permanent and temporary differences during the year.

□ Difference between accounting and tax values.

□ Deferred tax on revaluation.

Transitional Rules.   All temporary differences in the restated balance at January 1, 1992 should be identified. Untaxed reserves in the balance sheet from 1991 should be divided between deferred tax and distributable funds, or temporary restricted reserve. Other positive or negative temporary differences should be disclosed as deferred tax assets or liabilities.

If deferred tax has previously been reduced in the revaluation account, the fixed asset should be restated gross of tax. Companies that previously did not use the gross method for deferred taxes should change to the purchase method beginning in 1992.

Reference.   Accounting Act, Chapter 3, Joint Stock Companies Act, Chapter 11; NRS, Draft Accounting Standard for Taxes.

30. Postretirement Benefits

General.   Two systems of accounting for pensions are normally used in Norway: (1) actuarially computed premiums paid to an independent insurance company or (2) provision for the actual pension liability, computed by an external actuary or the company itself. If alternative (2) is used, a salary progression rate should be determined and the pension liability must be discounted according to actuarial principles. Future tax reductions may be deferred only if the company will be able to deduct pension costs in the future. Both systems are normally in substance "**defined benefit**" **plans**.

Accounting Treatment. Pensions of type (1) are treated as an operating expense with no further specification or information. Actuarially determined contributions required to fund a pension plan are assumed to be a reasonable basis for recording the periodic expense. Pensions of type (2) can be either presented as a long-term liability or disclosed as an off-balance sheet item. If presented as a long-term liability, changes in the liability from year to year will be deducted as operating expenses in the statement of income. Other postretirement benefits are rare in Norway.

The existing accounting standard will be replaced by a new standard. A proposed accounting standard was published as an exposure draft in 1991 and represents a fundamental change in accounting principles.

The new accounting principles will be in line with International Accounting Standards and US GAAP. The implementation timetable has not yet been determined.

Pension Fund Surpluses. Pension fund surpluses can be utilized only to cover expenses related to pensions, such as premiums or improved pension coverage.

Disclosure. For pensions of type (2), the following must be disclosed in the notes:

- [ ] Number of employees covered.
- [ ] Method of capitalization.
- [ ] Discount rate.
- [ ] Details of how taxation has influenced the estimate.

Pension fund surpluses may be reported as untaxed reserves, and yearly changes as year-end adjustments.

Reference. NSRF, Recommendation on Pension Liabilities (No. 13); NRS, Exposure draft on pension costs.

31. Discontinued Operations

Accounting Treatment. There is no prescribed accounting standard for discontinued operations. The Draft Accounting Standard for Extraordinary Items prescribes the accounting method for discontinued operations or sales of a significant business segment, but not the business as a whole. Gains or losses relating to such operations should be reported as an extraordinary item. All costs connected with the discontinued operations should be included.

Disclosure. Details of extraordinary items should be disclosed in the notes.

Reference. NRS, Draft Accounting Standard for Extraordinary Items.

32. Earnings per Share

Definition. Earnings per share are defined as ordinary income after tax payable, divided by shares issued.

Disclosure. Companies are not required to disclose earnings per share, but it is expected that stock exchange requirements will soon be introduced. There are requirements regarding disclosure of the number of shares and their nominal value, which makes it possible for analysts to make their own computations.

Reference. NFF, Recommendation on Key Figures and Segment Reporting from the Financial Analysts Organization.

Appendix
DO NORWEGIAN STANDARDS OR PREVALENT PRACTICE SUBSTANTIALLY COMPLY WITH INTERNATIONAL ACCOUNTING STANDARDS?

Section	Topic	Substantially complies with IAS?	Comments
3.	Basic accounting concepts and conventions	Yes	
	Contents of financial statements	Yes	Except that a statement of changes in financial position or statement of cash flows is required only for large companies
4.	Business combinations*	Yes	Except that the pooling of interests method may be used for legal mergers
5.	Joint ventures	Yes	
6.	Foreign currency translation*	No	
8.	Accounting changes*	Yes	Except that the effect of an accounting change is normally recorded as an extraordinary item
9.	Prior period adjustments*	Yes	Except that the effect of a prior period adjustment is normally recorded as an extraordinary item
10.	Post balance sheet events	Yes	
11.	Related party transactions	No	
12.	Segmental information	No	
13.	Property, plant and equipment*	Yes	Except that the rules for revaluation are different
15.	Leases	Yes	Except, in practice, many finance leases are accounted for as operating leases
16.	Investments	Yes	
17.	Accounts receivable	Yes	
18.	Inventories and work in progress*	Yes	
19.	Current liabilities	Yes	
20.	Long-term debt	Yes	

Appendix (*Continued*)

Section	Topic	Substantially complies with IAS?	Comments
21.	Contingencies	Yes	
22.	Capital and reserves	Yes	
23.	Revenue recognition*	Yes	
24.	Government grants and assistance	No	
25.	Research and development*	Yes	Research costs may be capitalized
26.	Capitalization of interest costs*	Yes	
28.	Extraordinary or unusual items*	No	The range of items that may be classed as extraordinary is wider than is permitted by IAS 8
29.	Income tax**	Yes	
30.	Postretirement benefits*	No	

*These topics are subject to change as a result of the IASC Improvements Project—see the appendix to the International Accounting Standards chapter.

**The IAS on accounting for taxes on income is currently being revised, and an exposure draft has been issued.

Comparison in this table is made to International Accounting Standards in force at January 1, 1993. For further details, see the International Accounting Standards chapter.

SINGAPORE

GENERAL NATIONAL INFORMATION

1. Source of Generally Accepted Accounting Principles

Generally Accepted Accounting Principles.   **Generally accepted accounting principles** are derived from authoritative pronouncements, accounting literature and well-established practice.

Accounting Standards.   In Singapore, generally accepted **accounting** and reporting **standards** are set out in Statements of Accounting Standard (SASs) issued by the Institute of Certified Public Accountants of Singapore (ICPAS). In addition, ICPAS issues statements of Recommended Accounting Practice (RAPs). Members of ICPAS who assume responsibility for financial statements of any commercial, industrial or business enterprise are obligated to observe the SASs. The SASs and RAPs are set out in the ICPAS Members' Handbook. While compliance with generally accepted accounting principles is expected, the SASs are not intended to be a comprehensive code of rigid rules, and professional judgment should be exercised in their application.

SASs are generally identical to International Accounting Standards published by the International Accounting Standards Committee. Most SASs have an introductory section that provides guidance as to the interpretation of the terms used in the standard as well as examples of their application.

2. Audit and Public Company Requirements

Audits.   Under the Singapore Companies Act, Chapter 50, all registered companies, except for exempt private companies (those owned by not more than 20 persons and with no corporate shareholders), are required to file audited financial statements with the Registrar of Companies. The first auditors of a company should be appointed by the directors within three months of incorporation. Thereafter, the appointment or reappointment is by shareholders' resolution passed at the annual general meeting.

No person can be appointed as auditor unless the Minister of Finance is satisfied that the applicant is of good character and competent to perform the duties of an auditor. The Minister has delegated the power to make this determination to the ICPAS. However, persons who are indebted to the company or its related corporations for an amount exceeding S$2,500 or who are related to the corporation or any of its affiliates, either directly or indirectly, cannot be appointed as auditors of the company.

Exempt private companies are required to have their financial statements audited; however, for the purpose of filing with the Registrar of Companies, instead of the audited financial statements, they are required to submit a certificate signed by a director, the company secretary and the auditors, confirming the solvency of the company.

All auditors are expected to adhere to the Statements of Auditing Guideline (SAGs) and Practice (SAPs) issued by the ICPAS, which set out generally accepted auditing practices and the form and content of audit reports. These statements are based on International Standards on Auditing published by the International Auditing Practices Committee of the International Federation of Accountants, amended where appropriate to reflect local circumstances.

Reference. Singapore Companies Act, and Statements of Auditing Guideline and Practice.

Public Companies. Companies seeking a listing on the Stock Exchange of Singapore (main board) or the Stock Exchange of Singapore Dealing & Automated Quotation Market (SESDAQ) (secondary board) must meet the requirements set out by the Stock Exchange. Approval of the listing application is at the sole discretion of the Exchange. A prospectus offering is the method usually employed to issue securities to the public.

All publicly **listed companies** are required to file semiannual financial statements with the Stock Exchange. The operating results for the fiscal year must be announced publicly before the financial statements are published and distributed. Audited financial statements must be distributed to shareholders at least 14 days before the annual general meeting. Annual financial statements and semiannual reports must be submitted to the Stock Exchange within three months of the end of the **fiscal period**.

Reference. Stock Exchange of Singapore Listing Manual, and Corporate Disclosure Policy.

GENERAL ACCOUNTING

3. Financial Statements

Basic Accounting Concepts. Financial statements are prepared in accordance with the **historical cost** convention, modified to allow certain assets—for example, property, plant and equipment—to be revalued. Fundamental accounting assumptions are that an enterprise will continue in operation for the foreseeable future, that the **accounting policies** are consistent from one period to another and that revenues and costs are recognized as they are earned or incurred and are recorded in the financial statements of the periods to which they relate. When a fundamental accounting assumption is not adhered to, the departure should be disclosed, together with the reasons. **Prudence, substance over form**, and **materiality** should govern the selection and application of accounting policies in the preparation of financial statements.

Contents of Financial Statements. Financial statements usually include a balance sheet, income statement, statement of changes in financial position and accompanying notes, which are identified as being part of the financial statements. The statement of changes in financial position is required only if **turnover** is equal to or more than S$1 million or where accounts are required to be published in a government periodical ("gazetted"). The **direct method** of reporting cash flows is not used. For a group of companies the **consolidated financial statements** would generally comprise both consolidated and **parent company** balance sheets and income statements, and only a consolidated statement of changes in financial position. In certain circumstances, a parent company may attach, rather than consolidate, the financial statements of a **subsidiary** or subsidiaries.

The financial statements must be accompanied by a directors' report, which contains specified information, including an overview of the company's performance, as well as by a statement by the directors that is signed by two directors on behalf of all the directors. The statement is a declaration that, in the opinion of the directors, the accounts are true and fair and that the company will be able to pay its debts when they fall due.

Format of Financial Statements.   Generally, all material information necessary to make the financial statements clear and understandable should be disclosed. Corresponding figures for the preceding period should also be presented. When a reclassification of a financial statement item occurs, a note is commonly included explaining that certain comparative figures have been reclassified to conform with the current year's presentation. The name of the enterprise, country of incorporation, balance sheet date and period covered by the financial statements should be given. A brief description of the nature of the activities of the enterprise, its legal form and the currency in which the financial statements are expressed should be given, if not otherwise apparent. The amounts and classification of items should be supplemented, if necessary for the sake of clarity, by additional information. Significant items should not be included with, or offset against, other items in the financial statements unless there is a legal right of offset. Assets and liabilities should generally be classified into current and noncurrent and, within each classification, specific items of information should be separately disclosed. Certain specific information is required to be disclosed in financial statements by the Companies Act (Ninth Schedule) and SAS 5.

Disclosure of Accounting Policies.   All significant accounting policies adopted in the preparation of financial statements should be disclosed as an integral part of the financial statements. Normally, this information is presented in one place in the statements. Accounting policies should be consistently applied from year to year. Any accounting policy change that has a material effect in either the current or subsequent years should be disclosed, together with the reason for the change. The effect of the change should, if material, be disclosed and quantified.

In unusual circumstances, a literal application of an authoritative pronouncement might render the financial statements misleading, and it is necessary to depart from the usual treatment. In such circumstances, the practice followed and the reason for the departure should be disclosed in a note.

Reference.   SAS 1—Disclosure of Accounting Policies; SAS 5—Information to Be Disclosed in Financial Statements; and Companies Act (Ninth Schedule).

4. Business Combinations

Principles of Consolidation.   SAS 26 deals with the preparation and presentation of consolidated financial statements for a group of enterprises under the control of a parent.

A parent that is a wholly owned, or virtually wholly owned, subsidiary need not present consolidated financial statements provided, in the case of one that is virtually wholly owned, approval of the minority shareholder(s) is obtained. "Virtually wholly owned" is taken to mean that the parent is itself owned by an entity that controls 90 percent or more of the voting power. The Companies Act, however, requires that **group financial statements** be prepared unless the parent is a wholly owned subsidiary of another corporation incorporated in Singapore. Group financial statements can, for this purpose, comprise either consolidated financial statements or the financial statements of the parent with those of the subsidiaries attached, provided that the extent of intercompany balances and transactions is indicated.

Consolidated financial statements should include all subsidiaries, unless:

☐ The parent's control is intended to be temporary; or

☐ The subsidiary operates under conditions in which severe long-term restrictions on the transfer of funds impair the parent's control over the subsidiary's assets and operations.

Exclusion of a subsidiary from consolidation on the grounds of dissimilar business activities is not acceptable.

Enterprises may be consolidated, although they are not subsidiaries, if the parent has the ability to control, by statute or agreement, the financial and operating policies of the investee, with or without more than half of the equity interest. Such control is usually attained when there is control of the board of directors.

Accounting for Business Combinations.   **Business combinations** are the result of an enterprise acquiring control of one or more other enterprises or the uniting of interests of two or more enterprises. Business combinations should be accounted for under the **purchase method**, except in the rare circumstance when a combination is deemed to be a uniting of interests, in which event the **pooling of interests method** may be used.

Control.   Control is the power to govern the financial and operating policies of an enterprise so as to obtain benefits from its activities. Control is presumed to exist when the parent owns, directly or indirectly through subsidiaries, more than half of the voting power of an enterprise.

Goodwill.   If not adjusted immediately against shareholders' equity, **goodwill** arising on acquisition should be recognized as an intangible asset in the consolidated balance sheet. It should be amortized to income on a systematic basis over its useful life. In the event that the value of goodwill is not supported by the potential for future income, it should be written off immediately.

Equity Accounting.   Under SAS 27, an **associate** is an enterprise in which the investor has significant influence but that is neither a subsidiary nor a **joint venture** of the investor. Significant influence is normally deemed to exist when an investor holds, directly or indirectly through subsidiaries, 20 percent or more of the voting power of the investee.

The existence of significant influence by an investor is also evidenced in one or more of the following ways:

□ Representation on the board of directors or equivalent governing body of the investee;

□ Participation in policy-making processes;

□ Material transactions between the investor and the investee;

□ Interchange of managerial personnel; or

□ Provision of essential technical information.

Investments in associates should be included in the consolidated financial statements under the **equity method** of accounting. However, a wholly owned subsidiary that is exempt from issuing consolidated financial statements is also exempt from applying the equity method to account for investments in associates.

On acquisition of an associate, any difference (whether positive or negative) between the cost of acquisition and the investor's share of the fair values of the net identifiable assets of the associate is accounted for in accordance with SAS 22. Appropriate adjustments to the investor's share of the profits and losses after acquisition are made to account for:

□ **Depreciation** of depreciable assets, based on their fair values.

□ Where applicable, **amortization** of the difference between the cost of the investment and the investor's share of the fair value of the net identifiable assets (i.e., goodwill on acquisition).

If an associate uses accounting policies other than those adopted by the investor for transactions and events in similar circumstances, appropriate adjustments are made to the associate's financial statements when they are used by the investor in applying the equity method.

Under the following conditions, the cost method is adopted:

□ Severe long-term restrictions significantly impair the associate's ability to transfer funds to the investor.

□ The investment is acquired and held exclusively with a view to its disposal in the near future.

Minority Interests. **Minority interests** are that portion of the net operating results or net assets of a subsidiary attributable to shares owned other than by the parent company or another subsidiary. Minority interests should be classified in the consolidated balance sheet as a separate item and should not be shown as part of shareholders' equity. Minority interests in current year profits or losses should be shown separately in the consolidated income statement.

Disclosure. For all business combinations, the following disclosures should be made in the financial statements immediately following the combination:

□ Names and descriptions of the combining enterprises.

□ Effective date of the combination for accounting purposes.

□ The method of accounting used to reflect the combination.

For business combinations accounted for under the purchase method, the following additional disclosures in the first financial statements following the combination are required:

- ☐ The percentage of voting shares acquired.
- ☐ The cost of acquisition and a description of the purchase consideration paid or contingently payable.
- ☐ The amount of any difference between the cost of acquisition and the aggregate fair value of net identifiable assets acquired, and the treatment thereof, including the period of amortization of any goodwill arising on acquisition.

For business combinations accounted for under the pooling of interests method, additional disclosures in the first financial statements following the combination are as follows:

- ☐ Description and number of shares issued, together with the percentage of each enterprise's voting shares exchanged to effect the combination.
- ☐ Amounts of assets and liabilities contributed by each enterprise.
- ☐ Details of the results of operations of the enterprises prior to the date of the combination that are included in the net income shown by the combined financial statements.

Consolidated financial statements must disclose the following:

- ☐ A listing of significant subsidiaries, including the name, country of incorporation and proportion of ownership interest and, if different, proportion of voting power held.
- ☐ A description of the method used to account for subsidiaries.
- ☐ The reasons for not consolidating a subsidiary.
- ☐ The nature of the relationship between the parent and a subsidiary of which the parent does not own, directly or indirectly through subsidiaries, more than half of the voting power.
- ☐ The name of any enterprise in which more than half of the voting power is owned, directly or indirectly through subsidiaries, but that, because of the absence of control, is not a subsidiary.
- ☐ The effect of the acquisition and disposal of subsidiaries on the financial position at the reporting date, on the results for the reporting period and on the corresponding amounts for the preceding period.

Where equity accounting is adopted, the following disclosures are required:

- ☐ A listing and description of significant associates, including the proportion of ownership interest and, if different, the proportion of voting power held.
- ☐ The investor's share of profits or losses, including unusual or prior period items, of associates.

Reference. SAS 22—Accounting for Business Combinations; SAS 26—Consolidated Financial Statements and Accounting for Investments in Subsidiaries; and SAS 27—Accounting for Investments in Associates.

5. Joint Ventures

There are no published standards on accounting for joint ventures in Singapore. In the absence of an SAS, reference would normally be made to IAS 31, *Financial Reporting of Interests in Joint Ventures*. Alternatively, the equity method would be used to account for an interest in a **jointly controlled** entity.

6. Foreign Currency Translation

Bases of Translation. General: A distinction is made between (1) accounting for **foreign currency transactions** in the financial statements of domestic operations and (2) translating the financial statements of foreign operations into a single reporting currency for inclusion in the financial statements of the reporting enterprise.

Domestic operations: A transaction in a foreign currency should be recorded in the currency of the reporting entity by applying the exchange rate, or an approximation of it, at the time of the transaction. At each balance sheet date, foreign currency **monetary items** should be reported at the exchange rate at that date (the closing rate).

Foreign operations: The method of translating the financial statements of foreign operations is determined by the operating and financial characteristics of those operations. Foreign operations fall into one of two categories:

☐ **Self-sustaining foreign operations** that accumulate cash and other monetary items, incur expenses and costs, realize revenues and arrange borrowings, all substantially in the local currency.

☐ **Integrated foreign operations**.

In translating the financial statements of a self-sustaining foreign operation, the assets and liabilities, both monetary and nonmonetary, are translated at the closing rate. Income statement items are translated either at the closing rate or at a rate that approximates it (e.g., average monthly or annual rates). Any differences arising from translating the net assets at the acquisition date at current rates as opposed to their historical rate are taken to shareholders' equity.

For integrated foreign operations, all monetary assets and liabilities are translated at the closing rate, and nonmonetary items are translated at the exchange rates in effect when the relevant transactions occurred. Income statement items are translated at exchange rates at the date of the underlying transactions or the average rates during the period.

Hedges. To record a transaction as a **hedge**, there must be reasonable assurance of its effectiveness as a hedge. If the hedge itself is a monetary item, any gain or loss on its translation will automatically offset the loss or gain on the transaction or balance hedged. If the hedge is a nonmonetary item, there will be no current exchange gain or loss and any gain or loss arising from the translation of the hedged monetary item should be deferred until the settlement date. If the hedge is a foreign currency forward contract, any gain or loss is accrued to offset the loss or gain on the hedged item.

Disclosure. The method used to translate amounts in foreign currencies to the currency in which the financial statements are expressed should be disclosed. Exchange differences for the period recorded in shareholders' equity or income should also be disclosed.

Reference. SAS 20—Accounting for the Effects of Changes in Foreign Exchange Rates.

7. Changing Prices/Inflation Accounting

The ICPAS has not adopted or issued any accounting standard on inflation accounting, and there is no statutory requirement to report the effects of inflation in published financial statements. Accordingly, inflation adjusted financial statement information is not prepared in Singapore.

8. Accounting Changes

Accounting Treatment. Changes in accounting policies should be made only if the adoption of a different accounting policy is required by statute or by an accounting standard-setting body, or if the change results in a more appropriate presentation of the financial statements. Prior period items and the amount of the adjustments, if any, resulting from changes in accounting policies should be either:

□ Reported by adjusting opening retained earnings in the current period financial statements and amending prior year financial statements included for comparative purposes; or

□ Separately disclosed in the current income statement as part of net income.

A change in accounting estimate should be distinguished from a change in accounting policy. Changes in accounting estimates arise from new information or developments and should be accounted for in the income statement in the period of the change.

Disclosure. When there is a change in an accounting policy, the effect of the change should be disclosed and quantified, together with the reasons for the change.

If a change in accounting estimate has a material effect on the current or subsequent periods, the effect should be disclosed and quantified.

Reference. SAS 8—Unusual and Prior Period Items and Changes in Accounting Policies.

9. Prior Period Adjustments

Definition of Adjusting Items. Prior period items are charges or credits that arise in the current period as a result of errors or omissions in the preparation of prior period financial statements.

Prior period adjustments resulting from changes in accounting policies are covered in Section 8.

Accounting Treatment. Prior period adjustments are made either by adjusting the opening retained earnings for the current period and amending the comparative financial statements, or by including them as a separate item of net income in the current income statement.

Disclosure. The nature and effect of prior period adjustments should be disclosed in the financial statements.

Reference. SAS 8—Unusual and Prior Period Items and Changes in Accounting Policies.

10. Post Balance Sheet Events

Definition. Post balance sheet events are events that occur between the balance sheet date and the date of issuance of the financial statements. Two types of events can be identified:

- ☐ Those that provide further evidence of conditions existing at the balance sheet date.
- ☐ Those that indicate conditions that arose after the balance sheet date.

Accounting Treatment. Adjustments should be recorded for conditions that existed at the balance sheet date. No adjustments should be recorded for conditions arising after the balance sheet date.

Disclosure. For material conditions arising after the balance sheet date, the nature of the event and an estimate of its financial effect, or a statement that such an estimate cannot be made, should be presented. No disclosure is required for events indicating conditions that existed at the balance sheet date.

Reference. SAS 10—Contingencies and Events Occurring After the Balance Sheet Date.

11. Related Party Transactions

Definition. Parties are related if one party has the ability to control the other party or exercise significant influence over the other party's financial and operating decisions.

Accounting Treatment. Related party transactions are recorded in accordance with normal accounting principles and practices. No special treatment is required, except for disclosure of the nature and extent of these transactions.

Disclosure. Related party relationships should be disclosed irrespective of whether there were transactions between the parties. For transactions between related parties, the reporting enterprise should disclose the types of transactions (including no charge transactions) and the elements of the transactions necessary for an understanding of the financial statements. Similar items may be disclosed in the aggregate except when separate disclosure is necessary for an understanding of their financial statement effects.

Disclosure of transactions between members of a group is unnecessary in consolidated financial statements because consolidated financial statements present the parent and subsidiaries as a single reporting enterprise. Transactions with associated enterprises accounted for under the equity method are not eliminated and therefore require separate disclosure.

Reference. SAS 21—Related Party Disclosures.

12. Segmental Information

General. Publicly listed companies and other economically significant entities (i.e., those meeting certain criteria for revenues, profits, assets and employment), including subsidiaries, should report financial information by major industry and geographical segments. Industry segments are the distinguishable components of an enterprise in terms of products or services provided. Geographical segments are the distinguishable components of an enterprise engaged in operations in particular geographical areas. When both parent company and consolidated financial statements are presented, segment information needs to be presented only for the consolidated financial statements.

Disclosure. The following information relating to segments should be disclosed in the notes:

- [ ] Description of the activities of each reported industry segment and delineation of each reported geographical area.
- [ ] Segment sales or other operating revenues separated into revenue derived from customers outside the enterprise and revenue derived from other segments.
- [ ] Segment profits or losses.
- [ ] Segment assets employed.
- [ ] Basis of intersegment pricing.
- [ ] A reconciliation between the total of individual segment information and the aggregate in the financial statements.
- [ ] Changes in segment grouping and in accounting practices used to report segment information, including the reasons for the change and its effect on the financial statements.

Reference. SAS 23—Reporting Financial Information by Segment.

ACCOUNTING PRINCIPLES FOR SPECIFIC ITEMS— BALANCE SHEET

13. Property, Plant and Equipment

Classification of Capital and Revenue Expenditure. A **revenue expenditure** benefits the company for one accounting period and is charged against revenue earned in that period. If the expenditure benefits the company for two or more periods, it is a **capital expenditure**. Purchases of property, plant and equipment are considered capital expenditures.

Basis of Valuation. Property, plant and equipment should be carried either at historical cost or at an amount established by a revaluation. If property, plant and equipment are revalued in financial statements, the revaluation should be for an entire class of assets and the selection of assets for revaluation should be made on a systematic basis.

A revaluation adjustment increasing the asset value should be credited directly to a capital reserve entitled revaluation surplus. Accumulated depreciation at the date of revaluation should not be credited to income. A revaluation to decrease the asset value should be charged to income unless there is a balance in the capital reserve from a previous upward revaluation of the same asset or class of assets.

Property, plant and equipment should be eliminated from the financial statements on disposal or when no further benefit is expected from their use. Gains or losses from the retirement or disposal of assets should be recognized in the income statement. On disposal of a previously revalued item of property, plant and equipment, the difference between the net proceeds and the net carrying amount is normally charged or credited to income. The related balance in the revaluation surplus account following the retirement or disposal of an asset may be transferred to **retained earnings**.

Depreciation.   The depreciable amount of an asset should be amortized on a systematic basis over its useful life. Various methods are used in practice, the most common of which is the **straight-line method**. The method used should be consistently applied over the asset's useful life.

Disclosure.   Fixed assets and accumulated depreciation by major category should be disclosed. The basis of valuation and depreciation policy should be indicated in all cases. Furthermore, cost or, where assets have been revalued, valuation amounts for each category of fixed assets should be shown separately. In the case of a revaluation, the method adopted, policy with regard to frequency of revaluation, year of an appraisal and whether an independent external appraiser was involved should also be disclosed.

Reference.   SAS 14—Accounting for Property, Plant and Equipment; and SAS 4—Depreciation Accounting.

14. Intangible Assets

Accounting Treatment.   There is no accounting standard in Singapore on **intangible assets**, although the standard on accounting for business combinations deals with goodwill, and RAP 1 recommends that material intangible assets be shown separately.

Valuation.   Generally, intangible assets are stated at cost less amortization. If an intangible asset is acquired other than through payment of cash or its equivalent, recommended practice is to fully disclose the basis of valuation.

Amortization.   Intangible assets with a limited useful life should be amortized over that life.

Disclosure.   Intangible assets should be disclosed separately. The basis of valuation and period and method of amortization should also be presented.

Reference.   RAP 1—Standards of Disclosure in Financial Statements.

15. Leases

Classification.   The substance rather than the form of a lease agreement determines the classification of the lease. Leases that transfer substantially all the benefits and risks of ownership to the lessee are accounted for as **finance leases**. Leases are classified as **operating leases** if substantially all the risks and rewards of ownership are not transferred.

Accounting Treatment: Lessees.   Finance leases: A lessee reflects a finance lease in the balance sheet by recording an asset and a corresponding liability at the beginning of the lease. Rental payments are apportioned between the finance charge and reduction of the outstanding liability, using a finance charge that reflects a constant periodic rate of interest on the outstanding liability. A finance lease gives rise to a depreciation charge for the asset as well as a finance charge for each accounting period. The depreciation policy for leased assets should be consistent with that for similar depreciable assets that are owned.

Operating leases: For operating leases, the charge to income each year is the rental expense for that year. This is recognized on a systematic basis corresponding to the time pattern of the user's benefit. There is no recognition of an asset or a related liability.

Disclosure: The assets subject to finance leases at each balance sheet date should be disclosed. Related liabilities should be shown separately from other liabilities, differentiating between the current and long-term portions. Commitments for minimum lease payments under finance leases and under noncancellable operating leases with a term of more than one year should be summarized. The amounts and periods in which payments will be due, significant restrictions, renewal or purchase options, contingent rentals and other **contingencies** arising from leases should be disclosed.

Accounting Treatment: Lessors.   Finance leases: A lessor records an asset under a finance lease in the balance sheet as a receivable equal to the net investment in the lease. Subject to the consideration of prudence, finance income should be recognized based on a pattern reflecting a constant periodic rate of return on either the lessor's net investment or the net cash investment in the finance lease. Manufacturer or dealer lessors should include selling profit or loss in income in accordance with the policy normally followed for outright sales.

Operating leases: Under an operating lease, the asset continues to be recorded as a depreciable asset by the lessor. Rental income is included as income on a straight-line basis over the lease term, and the related costs incurred are charged accordingly. Depreciation is provided on the leased asset consistent with the lessor's normal depreciation policy for similar assets. Initial direct costs incurred may be either deferred and allocated to income over the lease period in proportion to the recognition of the rental income or written off when incurred.

Disclosure: The gross investment in finance leases and related unearned finance income and unguaranteed residual values of leased assets should be disclosed at each balance sheet date. The bases used to allocate income to produce a constant periodic rate of return should also be disclosed. When a significant part of the lessor's business comprises operating leases, the amount of assets leased by major class, together with the related accumulated depreciation at each balance sheet date, should be disclosed.

Leveraged Leases.   **Leveraged leases** are not common in Singapore and their accounting treatment is not covered in published pronouncements.

Reference. SAS 15—Accounting for Leases.

16. Investments

Valuation. The basis of valuation of investments depends on their classification as current or long term. Current investments are readily realizable and intended to be held for not more than one year. All other investments are long term.

Current investments: Investments classified as **current assets** should be carried in the balance sheet at either market value or the lower of cost or market value. If current investments are carried at the lower of cost or market value, the carrying amount may be determined on either an aggregate **portfolio basis** or an individual investment basis.

Long-term investments: Investments classified as long-term assets should be carried in the balance sheet at either cost or revalued amounts or, for marketable equity securities, the lower of cost or market value determined on a portfolio basis. If revalued amounts are used, a policy for the frequency of revaluations should be adopted and an entire category of long-term investments should be revalued at the same time. The carrying amount of long-term investments should be reduced to recognize a decline in value that is other than temporary; that determination should be made for each investment individually.

Long-term investments may include investment properties, which, alternatively, may be accounted for as fixed assets and depreciated (see Section 13).

Treatment of Valuation Reserves. For long-term investments, an increase in carrying amount arising from revaluation should be credited to shareholders' equity as a revaluation surplus. To the extent that a decrease in carrying amount offsets a previous increase for the same investment, the decrease should be charged to the revaluation surplus. An increase in carrying amount that is directly related to a previous decrease for the same investment that was charged to income should be credited to income to the extent that it offsets the previously recorded decrease. If current investments are carried at market value, increases or decreases in carrying amount should be either included in income or accounted for in the same manner as long-term investments.

Gains/Losses. Gains or losses on disposal of investments should be credited or charged to income. If the investment was a current asset carried on a portfolio basis at the lower of cost or market value, the profit or loss on sale should be based on cost. If the investment was previously revalued, or was carried at market value and an increase in carrying amount was transferred to revaluation surplus, the enterprise should credit any remaining related revaluation surplus to either income or retained earnings. This policy should be applied consistently.

Disclosure. The following should be disclosed:

☐ The accounting policies adopted to determine the carrying amount of investments, the treatment of changes in market value of current investments carried at market value and the treatment of revaluation surplus on the sale of a revalued investment.

☐ Significant amounts included in income, including interest income, royalties, dividends and rentals on long-term and current investments, and profits and losses on disposal of current investments and changes in value of investments.

☐ The market value of marketable investments not carried at market.

□ The fair value of investment properties accounted for as long-term investments and not carried at fair value.

□ Significant restrictions on the realizability of investments or the remittance of income and proceeds of disposal.

□ For long-term investments stated at revalued amounts, the policy for the frequency of revaluations, the date of the latest revaluation and the basis of revaluation and whether an external appraiser was involved.

□ The movements for the period in revaluation surplus and the nature of such movements.

□ For enterprises whose main business is the holding of investments, an analysis of the investment portfolio.

Reference. SAS 25—Accounting for Investments.

17. Accounts Receivable

Accounting Treatment. Recognition: **Revenue** and the corresponding receivable usually are recognized when products or services are provided to the customer and reasonable assurance exists regarding measurement and collectibility of the consideration exchanged.

Discounts: Sales and **accounts receivable** are normally recorded net of discounts offered.

Allowances: The allowance for doubtful accounts can be computed by specific assessment of each account or by reference to a formula based on previous experience. If a formula is used, its continuing appropriateness should be reviewed.

Factored Receivables. If trade accounts receivable have been factored to a finance company for cash consideration, the relevant receivables should be excluded from the balance sheet. Discounts given to the finance company should normally be expensed against current income. If the receivables have been sold with recourse, disclosure of the loss contingency and provision for possible losses should be made in the entity's financial statements.

Disclosure. Trade accounts and notes receivable should be segregated from other receivables. If material, accounts receivable should be subdivided into trade accounts receivable, bills receivable and hire-purchase (i.e., finance lease) receivables. Loans and advances to directors should be separately disclosed. Trade accounts receivable normally include all receivables arising from sales or revenue-earning activities. The allowance for doubtful accounts should be separately disclosed and deducted from the total balance to which it applies.

Reference. RAP 1—Standards of Disclosure in Financial Statements; and SAS 16—Revenue Recognition.

18. Inventories and Work in Progress

General Accounting Treatment. **Inventories** should be valued at the lower of historical cost or **net realizable value**. Historical cost includes a systematic allocation of production overhead cost, based on the capacity of the facilities, relating to producing and delivering the inventories to their present condition and location. Overhead other than production overhead should be included in inventory cost only to the extent that it meets that objective. Exceptional spoilage and idle capacity should not be included in inventory cost.

Cost should be determined using the **FIFO** or weighted-**average cost** method. Where appropriate, the **specific identification method** may be used. The **LIFO** or **base stock** method may be used, provided that there is disclosure of the difference between the resulting amount of the inventories and the amount based on the lower of FIFO or weighted-average cost, or net realizable value. Inventories should be written down to net realizable value item by item or by groups of similar items. The above applies to manufacturing and trading inventories but not to inventories under long-term contracts.

Long-Term Contracts.   Long-term contracts should be stated at cost net of provision for foreseeable losses. Cost comprises those costs that relate directly to a specific contract and those that are attributable to contract activity in general and can be allocated to a specific contract. A provision for foreseeable loss on a contract should be based on the cost to complete the contract.

Disclosure.   General: In the balance sheet or notes, inventories should be classified in a manner appropriate to the business (e.g., materials, work in progress, finished goods, merchandise, production supplies). Accounting policies adopted, the cost formula used to value the inventory and provision for inventory write-down should also be disclosed.

Long-term contracts: There should be disclosure in the financial statements of:

☐   The amount of work in progress.
☐   Cash received and receivable as progress payments, advances and retentions on account of contracts included in construction work in progress.
☐   The amount receivable under cost-plus contracts not included in construction work in progress.

Reference.   SAS 2—Valuation and Presentation of Inventories in the Context of the Historical Cost System.

19. Current Liabilities

General Accounting Treatment.   **Current liabilities** should include all liabilities payable within one year from the date of the balance sheet or within the normal operating cycle, if longer than one year. Current liabilities should be segregated into main classes, including trade **accounts payable**, other payables, short-term loans, bank loans and overdrafts, income tax payable, provision for specific revenue commitments and contingencies, proposed dividends and current portions of long-term liabilities.

Accounts payable include amounts owed to creditors at the balance sheet date for goods and services received.

Accrued liabilities relate to amounts owed to creditors for goods and services for which invoices have not been received.

Deferred income represents amounts received or receivable from customers or clients with respect to goods to be delivered or services to be performed.

Creation of General and Specific Provisions.   Provisions are amounts set aside to meet specific expenses or losses or to cover expected losses that cannot be specifically identified and for the diminution in values of assets existing at the balance sheet date.

Provisions for diminution in values of assets should be shown in the balance sheet as deductions from the assets to which they relate.

Disclosure.   Bank loans and overdrafts, current portions of long-term liabilities and payables such as accounts and notes payable, payables to directors, and intercompany and associated company payables should be disclosed separately. Significant items included in other liabilities, provisions and accruals such as deferred taxes, deferred income and provisions for pensions should be separately disclosed.

Reference.   SAS 13—Presentation of Current Assets and Current Liabilities.

20. Long-Term Debt

General Accounting Treatment.   Long-term debt is external financing due more than one year from the balance sheet date. Long-term debt includes bonds, debentures, floating rate notes, loan stocks and term loans. A premium or discount on long-term debt is shown as a deferred credit or charge and should be amortized over the term of the debt.

Debt Restructuring.   There is no published standard on accounting for **troubled debt restructuring** in Singapore. In practice, the debtor's aggregate net gain or loss is included in the income statement. If the creditor is also a significant shareholder of the debtor, the gain on debt forgiven is commonly recorded as an extraordinary item.

Debt Extinguishment.   There is no published standard on accounting for debt extinguishment in Singapore. The accounting treatment of a gain or loss on debt extinguishment is similar to that for debt restructuring. The gain or loss is included in income as a separate item, and the normal criteria apply as to classifying the gain or loss as an extraordinary item.

Disclosure.   Secured and unsecured loans and intercompany and associated loans should be disclosed separately, excluding the portion repayable within one year. A summary of debt interest rates, repayment terms, covenants, subordinations, conversion features and amounts of unamortized premium or discount should be shown.

Reference.   SAS 5—Information to Be Disclosed in Financial Statements.

21. Contingencies

Contingent Losses.   The amount of a contingent loss should be accrued by a charge in the income statement if it is probable that the loss will be incurred and a reasonable estimate of the amount of loss can be made.

Contingent Gains.   Contingent gains should not be accrued in financial statements. The existence of contingent gains should be disclosed if it is probable that a gain will be realized.

Disclosure.   If a contingent loss is not accrued in the accounts, the existence of the contingency should be disclosed in the notes unless the possibility of loss is remote. The nature of the contingency, the factors affecting the future outcome and an estimate of the financial effect or a statement that such an estimate cannot be made should be provided in the financial statements.

Reference. SAS 10—Contingencies and Events Occurring After the Balance Sheet Date.

22. Capital and Reserves

General. Shareholders' equity is generally divided into **share capital** and reserves.

Share Capital. A company's share capital may be divided into different classes, each characterized by its dividend policy, voting rights and capital rights, including priority for repayment in the event of liquidation. The amounts of each class authorized for issue, together with the precise rights of each class, are set out in the company's articles of association. The most common classes of share capital are ordinary shares and **preference shares**.

Reserves. Capital reserves: Capital reserves are reserves that, for statutory reasons or because of provisions in a company's articles or for other legal reasons, are not free for distribution through the profit and loss account.

    Share premium reserves: If a company issues shares for which a premium is received, the premium should be separately shown in the balance sheet. The basis of calculating the premium should also be disclosed. The use of the share premium account is restricted by the Companies Act, Chapter 50.

    Revaluation surplus reserves: Revaluation adjustments relating to property, plant and equipment and to long-term investments are credited to revaluation surplus accounts. See Sections 13 and 16 for further details.

    Revenue reserves (including retained earnings): Revenue reserves arise from the retention of distributable profits for general use in the business and are not created in accordance with statutory requirements or in pursuance of any obligation or policy. Any restriction on distribution or use of this reserve should be disclosed and quantified, if material.

Disclosure. For each class of share capital, the number or amount of shares authorized, issued and outstanding, together with the **par value** of each share; changes in the share capital account during the year; rights; preferences; and restrictions on distribution should be disclosed. For reserves, changes during the period and any restrictions on distribution should be disclosed.

Reference. RAP 1—Standards of Disclosure in Financial Statements.

ACCOUNTING PRINCIPLES FOR SPECIFIC ITEMS— INCOME STATEMENT

23. Revenue Recognition

General Principles. Sales revenue should be recognized when the seller has transferred the significant risks and rewards of ownership to the buyer and there is no significant uncertainty regarding the consideration to be derived, the cost incurred or the extent to which goods may be returned. Revenue from service transactions is usually recognized as the service is performed, using either the **completed contract** or **percentage of completion method**.

Long-Term Contracts. Revenue from long-term contracts is recognized using either the percentage of completion or completed contract method. The accounting method used depends on the uncertainty of estimating contract costs and revenues. The percentage of completion method should be used only when the outcome of the contract can be reliably estimated. If the level of uncertainty is significant in relation to the revenue and costs incurred, use of the completed contract method would be appropriate.

Instalment Sales. When consideration is receivable in instalments, revenue attributable to the sales price, excluding interest, should be recognized on the date of sale. The interest element should be recognized as revenue in proportion to the unpaid balance. If collection is not reasonably assured, revenue should be recognized as cash instalments are received.

Rights of Return. Recognition of revenue on sales that give the buyer a right of return depends on the substance of the agreement. For normal retail sales, it may be appropriate to recognize the sale but to make a suitable provision for returns based on past experience. In other cases, the substance of the agreement may amount to a sale on consignment. In such circumstances, revenue would be recognized only when the goods are sold to a third party.

Product Financing. A **product financing arrangement** is a repurchase agreement in which the seller concurrently agrees to repurchase the goods at a later date. These arrangements are accounted for as borrowings rather than as sales; disclosure is made of the product collateralized.

Disclosure. In addition to disclosing the method of revenue recognition, as required under SAS 1, an enterprise should also disclose the circumstances in which revenue recognition has been postponed pending the resolution of significant uncertainties.

Reference. SAS 16—Revenue Recognition; and SAS 11—Accounting for Construction Contracts.

24. Government Grants and Assistance

Accounting Treatment. Government grants should not be recognized in the income statement until there is reasonable assurance that the enterprise will comply with the conditions attaching to the grants and that the grants will be received. Crediting grants directly to shareholders' equity is not permitted. Grants should be recognized in the income statement on a systematic basis over the period in which related costs are recorded. Grants compensating losses or expenses already incurred, or giving immediate financial support to an enterprise, are recognized as income when they become receivable. A grant of or for the purchase of an asset may be set up as deferred income and amortized over the life of the asset, or deducted in arriving at the carrying amount of the asset.

Grants that become repayable constitute changes in accounting estimates. Repayments of grants related to income are first applied against any related deferred credit and are then charged to income. Repayments of grants related to assets increase the asset carrying amount or decrease the deferred income balance; the cumulative additional depreciation that would have been charged to date in the absence of the grant is charged to income.

Disclosure. The accounting policy adopted and the method of presenting government grants should be disclosed in the financial statements. The nature and extent of grants recognized, and an indication of other forms of government assistance from which the enterprise has directly benefited, should be disclosed. Disclosure should also be made of unfulfilled conditions and other contingencies attached to government grants that have been recognized.

Reference. SAS 18—Accounting for Government Grants and Disclosure of Government Assistance.

25. Research and Development

Definitions. Research is original and planned investigation undertaken with the hope of gaining new scientific or technical knowledge and understanding.

Development is the translation of research findings into a plan or design with the intention of producing new or substantially improved materials, devices or products prior to commencement of commercial production.

Accounting Treatment. Research costs should be expensed in the period incurred. Development costs may be deferred to future periods and amortized if all the following criteria are satisfied:

☐ The product or process is clearly defined and the costs attributable to it can be separately identified.

☐ The technical feasibility of the product or process has been demonstrated.

☐ Management of the enterprise has indicated its intention to produce and market, or use, the product or process.

☐ There is a clear indication that a future market for the product or process exists or, if it is to be used internally rather than sold, its usefulness to the enterprise can be demonstrated.

☐ Adequate resources exist, or are reasonably expected to be available, to complete and market the product or process.

Deferred development costs should be amortized over the period in which the product or process is expected to be sold or used. Deferred development costs should be reviewed at the end of each accounting period; if the criteria for deferral no longer apply, the unamortized balance should be expensed immediately. If the criteria for deferral continue to be met but the unamortized balance of deferred development and other relevant costs exceeds the amounts that can be expected to be recovered from related revenues, the excess should be expensed immediately. Development costs that have been written off cannot be reinstated.

Disclosure. The total research and development costs, including amortization of deferred development costs, charged to expense should be disclosed. Changes in and the balance of unamortized deferred development costs should be disclosed. The basis, proposed or adopted, of amortization should also be disclosed.

Reference. SAS 9—Accounting for Research and Development Activities.

26. Capitalized Interest Costs

Accounting Treatment. An enterprise that has incurred interest costs on the construction of assets that require a substantial period of time to be completed should adopt and consistently apply a policy of either capitalizing or not capitalizing interest costs.

The capitalization rate is determined either by relating the total interest costs incurred during the period to the borrowings outstanding during that period, to arrive at an average rate for the period, or by using the rate associated with new borrowing specifically relating to the acquisition of the asset.

Capitalization of interest costs should begin when expenditures for the asset are being incurred, borrowings are outstanding and activities necessary to prepare the asset for its use or sale are in progress. In all cases, capitalization should be suspended when active development ceases. Capitalization should end when the asset is ready for its intended use or sale or, for investment assets (e.g., properties developed for rental to third parties), when the investee begins its planned principal operations.

If capitalization of interest costs results in a total capitalized asset cost that exceeds the recoverable amount or net realizable value, an adjustment is made to reduce the carrying amount to the recoverable amount or net realizable value.

Disclosure. Enterprises adopting a policy of capitalizing interest costs must disclose the amount of interest costs that have been capitalized during the period.

Reference. SAS 19—Capitalization of Borrowing Costs.

27. Imputed Interest

General. Interest is commonly imputed in Singapore only in accounting for finance leases.

Accounting Treatment. The discount factor used to compute the present value of the minimum lease payments is the interest rate implicit in the lease or, if this is not practicable to determine, the lessee's incremental borrowing rate.

Disclosure. Disclosure for accounting for leases is covered in Section 15.

Reference. SAS 15—Accounting for Leases.

28. Extraordinary or Unusual Items

Extraordinary Items. Extraordinary items are gains or losses that derive from events or transactions that are distinct from the ordinary activities of the enterprise and, therefore, are not expected to recur frequently or regularly.

Disclosure. Extraordinary items are disclosed separately, with an explanation of their nature.

Reference. SAS 8—Unusual and Prior Period Items and Changes in Accounting Policies.

29. Income Taxes

The tax expense for a financial period should be determined on the basis of **tax-effect accounting,** using either the **deferral** or the **liability method.** The method used should be disclosed and applied to all timing differences. However, tax expense for the period may exclude the tax effects of certain timing differences if there is reasonable evidence that the timing differences will not reverse within three years and there is no indication that they are likely to reverse subsequently. The amount of current and cumulative timing differences not recorded should be disclosed. The tax effect of timing differences resulting in a deferred tax asset should not be recorded unless there is a reasonable expectation of realization. Deferred tax balances should be presented in the balance sheet separate from shareholders' equity. A potential tax saving relating to a loss carryforward may be included in the determination of net income for the period of a loss if there is assurance beyond a reasonable doubt that future taxable income will be sufficient to allow the benefit to be realized.

Disclosure. Disclosure of the following is required:

- ☐ The tax on income from ordinary activities.
- ☐ The tax on unusual items, prior period adjustments and changes in accounting policy.
- ☐ The tax effects relating to asset revaluations.
- ☐ An explanation of the relationship between tax expense and accounting income, if not explained by the current corporate tax rate.
- ☐ The amount of tax saving included in the period of a loss.
- ☐ The amount of tax saving included in net income for the current period as a result of the realization of a tax loss carryforward that had not been accounted for in the year of the loss.
- ☐ The amount and future availability of tax losses for which the related tax effects have not been included in the net income of any period.

Reference. SAS 12—Accounting for Taxes on Income.

30. Postretirement Benefits

General. It is a statutory requirement for both employers and employees to contribute to the Central Provident Fund, which is a reserve to meet the financial needs of people of retirement age. As a result, it is rare for companies to have a separate retirement benefit plan. However, when there is a separate retirement benefit plan, the objective is to ensure that the cost of benefits is allocated to accounting periods on a systematic basis related to the employees' services, as set forth below.

Defined Benefit Pension Plans. For **defined benefit plans,** either an accrued benefit valuation method or a projected benefit valuation method should be used consistently to determine the cost of retirement benefits. Current service costs should be charged to income systematically over the expected remaining years of service of employees covered by the plan. Past service costs, experience adjustments and the effects of changes in actuarial assumptions should be charged or credited to income as they arise, or allocated systematically over a period not exceeding the expected remaining years of service of employees. The employer's costs must be estimated, since many factors influence the ultimate benefits and their costs.

Defined Contribution Pension Plans. In a **defined contribution plan** the employer's cost is determined by a formula stated in the plan, and it can normally be calculated with certainty.

Pension Fund Surpluses. Accounting for a pension fund surplus is not covered by a published pronouncement.

Disclosure. The accounting policies adopted for retirement benefit plan costs, matters affecting comparability with prior periods and differences between amounts funded and those charged to income should be disclosed in the financial statements. In addition, for defined benefit plans, any shortfall of fund assets from the actuarially determined value of vested benefits, the funding approach adopted and the date of the latest actuarial valuation should be disclosed.

Reference. SAS 17—Accounting for Retirement Benefits in the Financial Statements of Employers.

31. Discontinued Operations

There are no published standards in Singapore on accounting for discontinued operations.

Disclosure. In practice, the effect of discontinued operations, if material, is disclosed in the notes.

32. Earnings per Share

Definition. Earnings per share is defined as the profit in cents attributable to each ordinary share.

Methods of Calculation. Earnings per share is calculated by dividing net profit after tax, minority interests and preference share dividends but before extraordinary items, by the number of ordinary shares issued and eligible to receive dividends. This is known as basic earnings per share. Fully diluted earnings per share should also be disclosed if a company issues options, warrants, debentures or convertible loan stocks that may result in the issue of ordinary shares in the future, or a separate class of ordinary shares that are not eligible to receive dividends currently but may be in the future. However, fully diluted earnings per share need not be disclosed unless dilution is 5 percent or more of the basic earnings per share.

Disclosure.   Earnings per share should be disclosed in the income statement, for both the current period and the corresponding previous period. The basis of calculating earnings per share should be disclosed in the income statement or in a note.

For fully diluted earnings per share, the basis of computation should be disclosed. The disclosure of basic and fully diluted earnings per share must be equally prominent.

Reference.   SAS 6—Earnings per Share.

Appendix
DO SINGAPOREAN STANDARDS OR PREVALENT PRACTICE SUBSTANTIALLY COMPLY WITH INTERNATIONAL ACCOUNTING STANDARDS?

Section	Topic	Substantially complies with IAS?	Comments
3.	Basic accounting concepts and conventions	Yes	
	Contents of financial statements	Yes	Except that a statement of changes in financial position is required only by large companies
4.	Business combinations*	Yes	
5.	Joint ventures	Yes	Not yet adopted, but in practice the IAS on joint ventures is followed
6.	Foreign currency translation*	Yes	
8.	Accounting changes*	Yes	
9.	Prior period adjustments*	Yes	
10.	Post balance sheet events	Yes	
11.	Related party transactions	Yes	
12.	Segmental information	Yes	
13.	Property, plant and equipment*	Yes	
15.	Leases	Yes	
16.	Investments	Yes	
17.	Accounts receivable	Yes	
18.	Inventories and work in progress*	Yes	
19.	Current liabilities	Yes	
20.	Long-term debt	Yes	
21.	Contingencies	Yes	
22.	Capital and reserves	Yes	
23.	Revenue recognition*	Yes	
24.	Government grants and assistance	Yes	
25.	Research and development*	Yes	
26.	Capitalization of interest costs*	Yes	

Appendix (*Continued*)

Section	Topic	Substantially complies with IAS?	Comments
28.	Extraordinary or unusual items*	Yes	
29.	Income tax**	Yes	
30.	Postretirement benefits*	Yes	

*These topics are subject to change as a result of the IASC Improvements Project—see the appendix to the International Accounting Standards chapter.

**The IAS on accounting for taxes on income is currently being revised, and an exposure draft has been issued.

Comparison in this table is made to International Accounting Standards in force at January 1, 1993. For further details, see the International Accounting Standards chapter.

REPUBLIC OF SOUTH AFRICA

GENERAL NATIONAL INFORMATION

1. Source of Generally Accepted Accounting Principles

Generally Accepted Accounting Principles. **Generally accepted accounting principles (GAAP)** are derived from accounting statements, accounting guidelines, accounting literature and well-established practice. Accounting statements in South Africa are known as AC100 series, and accounting guidelines as AC200 series. AC300 opinions are issued on the appropriate accounting treatment for particular issues that are or could be subject to divergent or unacceptable treatment in practice.

The Companies Act 1973 (the Act) requires that annual financial statements fairly present, in conformity with generally accepted accounting practice, the state of affairs of the company and its business at the end of its financial year and its profit or loss for the year. The overriding requirement is that of fair presentation.

The Act also deals with the requirement for **group** annual **financial statements** and establishes, in Schedule 4, minimum financial statement disclosures. Companies may apply for exemption from, or the Minister of Finance, Trade and Industry may prohibit any company from, disclosing any particular information or fact concerning their affairs or business that is otherwise required to be disclosed, if nondisclosure is in the national or public interest or in the company's own interest.

Accounting Standards. **Accounting standards** in South Africa are approved by the Accounting Practices Board (APB), following a process of drafting and exposure by the South African Institute of Chartered Accountants (SAICA). On matters not covered by local standards, guidance is usually obtained from standards issued by the International Accounting Standards Committee (IASC). The SAICA is a member of the IASC and is obligated to use its best endeavors to ensure compliance with International Accounting Standards (IAS) or to obtain disclosure of the extent of noncompliance. US and UK GAAP are also sources of reference in South Africa.

In August 1990, the APB adopted the IASC's *Framework for the Preparation and Presentation of Financial Statements*, which sets out the objectives and concepts underlying the preparation of future accounting statements. Adoption of the Framework could affect the revision of existing South African GAAP, some elements of which are inconsistent with the Framework. As with IAS, South African accounting statements prescribe the principles applicable to the recognition and measurement of the items dealt with in the standards, as well as the related financial statement disclosure requirements.

A proposal for a new standard-setting process, based on the United Kingdom's, has been approved in principle. The APB will become the Accounting Standards Council, which will be given authority under the Act to set and monitor compliance with accounting standards.

2. Audit and Public Company Requirements

Audits.   The Act requires companies, both private and public, to appoint auditors who are independent of the company and any of its subsidiaries. All companies are required to issue to their shareholders copies of their audited annual financial statements and, if relevant, group annual financial statements.

The Public Accountants' and Auditors' Act (PAA Act) governs the practice of public accounting and auditing in South Africa. Under its terms, following qualification and obtaining membership in the SAICA, accountants entering public practice in South Africa must register with the Public Accountants' and Auditors' Board (PAAB). The PAA Act prohibits persons not registered with the PAAB from holding themselves out as public accountants and auditors. However, anyone may provide accounting and tax services.

Public Companies.   Any seven or more persons may form a **public company** by registering its memorandum and articles of association in compliance with the Act. A copy of the annual financial statements of public companies must be filed with the Registrar of Companies. A public company may be listed only if it complies with the listing requirements of The Johannesburg Stock Exchange (the JSE), the sole stock exchange in South Africa.

The following are the current criteria for a listing on the main board of the JSE:

☐   Subscribed capital of at least R2 million divided into at least 1 million issued shares.

☐   Satisfactory profit history for the preceding three years, with a current audited profit level of at least R1 million, before tax (other than mining).

☐   Thirty percent of the first million shares and an agreed percentage of the balance held by the public.

☐   At least 300 shareholders.

☐   Minimum initial issue price of not less than 100 cents per share.

The criteria for a listing on the Development Capital Market (DCM) of the JSE are less stringent and require only, for example, an acceptable trading record for two years, with a current audited profit level of R500,000, before tax (other than mining). The DCM is intended as a fund-raising vehicle for smaller companies that do not qualify for the main board.

Certain disclosure requirements are imposed by the JSE.

Reference.   Companies Act, PAA Act and listing requirements of the JSE.

GENERAL ACCOUNTING

3. Financial Statements

Basic Accounting Concepts. Financial statements are prepared primarily using the **historical cost** basis of **accounting**. Revaluation of noncurrent assets is acceptable in South Africa. The following four fundamental **accounting concepts** underlie the financial statements:

□ The **going concern concept**.
□ The **prudence concept**.
□ The **matching concept**.
□ The consistency concept. Accounting for similar items within an accounting period and from one period to the next should be consistent.

The following two considerations affect the application of accounting statements in particular circumstances:

□ **Substance over form**.
□ **Materiality**.

Contents of Financial Statements. The annual financial statements required by the Act consist of a balance sheet, an income statement, a cash flow statement, a directors' report (except where the company is a wholly owned subsidiary of a company incorporated in South Africa) and an auditors' report. Information may be included in notes that form an integral part of the financial statements. The directors' report presents certain specified information, including a review of the company's business and operations.

Format of Financial Statements. The balance sheet of the company should, in conformity with GAAP, fairly present the state of affairs of the company and its business as at the end of its financial year. For this purpose, reserves, provisions, liabilities and assets are to be classified under headings and subheadings appropriate to the business. **Fixed assets, current assets** and assets that are neither fixed nor current are separately identified, and liabilities are summarized and described as necessary to disclose their general nature.

The income statement should, in conformity with GAAP, fairly present the profit or loss of the company for the financial year.

The **direct method** (i.e., gross cash flows from receipts and payments) of reporting cash flow information is not used. The cash flow statement commences with net operating income adjusted for noncash items and is in a format that separately identifies:

□ Cash generated by operating activities.
□ Cash effects of finance costs and taxation.
□ Cash effects of distributions to owners.
□ Cash effects of investing activities.
□ Cash effects of financing activities.

Comparative figures for the preceding **financial period** (regrouped if necessary) are shown for all items in the balance sheet, income statement, cash flow statement and directors' report.

Disclosure of Accounting Policies.   The **accounting policies** followed for items that are judged material or critical in determining profit or loss for the period and in stating the company's financial position should be disclosed in a note. The explanations should be clear, fair and as concise as possible.

The accounting policies note should be prefaced by a paragraph indicating:

☐   Whether the policies are consistent with those of the previous period and, if not, how they have changed.

☐   Whether the historical cost basis has been used and, if not, which noncurrent asset categories have been revalued.

Reference.   AC100, AC101, AC118 and Companies Act.

4.   Business Combinations

Principles of Consolidation.   Under the Act, unless they are wholly owned **subsidiaries** of other companies incorporated in South Africa, **parent companies** have to publish group annual financial statements, along with their own financial statements. Although **consolidated financial statements** are presumed, "group annual financial statements" is a comprehensive term covering the information shown in the annual financial statements of the parent and its subsidiaries, in whichever form the directors decide to use. If consolidated financial statements for the whole group are not presented, either of the following forms, or a combination thereof, may be appropriate:

☐   Group annual financial statements consisting of the financial statements of one or more subsidiaries and the financial statements of the parent company.

☐   Group annual financial statements consisting of:
—Consolidated financial statements covering the parent and certain subsidiaries.
—One or more sets of consolidated financial statements covering the other subsidiaries.

Group annual financial statements need not include a subsidiary if control is temporary, or if the directors of the parent believe that including the subsidiary in the group's statements:

☐   Is impracticable;
☐   Would be of no real value to shareholders of the parent, in view of the insignificant amounts involved; or
☐   Would entail undue expense or delay.

In each of these cases, the auditors of the parent company should report on such decisions of the directors in the audit report.

In addition, subject to the approval of the Registrar of Companies, group annual financial statements need not include a subsidiary if the directors of the parent believe that:

☐ Including the subsidiary in the group financial statements would be misleading or harmful to the business of the parent or any of its subsidiaries; or
☐ The business of the parent and that of the subsidiary are so different that they cannot reasonably be treated as a single undertaking.

The parent company's auditors are not required to report on such decisions of the directors.

Accounting for Business Combinations. **Business combinations** are accounted for under the **purchase method**. Under the Act, the **pooling of interests method** is not permitted. The difference between the purchase price and the fair value of the acquired company's net identifiable assets is charged or credited to **goodwill** arising on consolidation or to a nondistributable reserve account.

Control. A company is a subsidiary of another company (the parent) if:

☐ The parent is a shareholder and either:
　　—holds the majority of the voting rights in the company; or
　　—has the right to appoint or remove directors holding a majority of the voting rights at board meetings; or
　　—has the sole control of a majority of the voting rights in the company, whether in accordance with an agreement with the other shareholders or otherwise.
☐ The company is a subsidiary of a subsidiary of the parent.
☐ Subsidiaries of the parent, or the parent and its subsidiaries, together hold the majority of the voting rights in the company.

Goodwill. Purchased goodwill arising from business acquisitions is recognized, but it is not generally accepted to recognize inherent or internally generated goodwill. However, there is no established method of accounting for goodwill and practice varies. The alternative accounting treatments used for purchased goodwill are as follows:

☐ Carried unamortized in the balance sheet.
☐ Carried in the balance sheet and amortized over its estimated useful life.
☐ Written down periodically to reflect economic worth.
☐ Shown as a deduction from shareholders' equity in the balance sheet.
☐ Written off against reserves on acquisition.
☐ Offset against the share premium account (in the case of an exchange of shares).

If goodwill is written off to reflect a permanent decline in value, the write-off is included in the income statement, normally as an extraordinary item.

Equity Accounting. Investments in **associates** and nonconsolidated subsidiaries are accounted for using the **equity method**. An associate is an incorporated or unincorporated enterprise in which an investor has long-term interests and over which it has the ability to exercise significant influence and that is neither a subsidiary nor a **joint venture** of the investor. An investor holding directly or indirectly 20 percent or more of the voting power of the investee is presumed to be able to exercise significant influence, unless the contrary can be demonstrated. Significant influence may also be indicated by representation on the board of directors, participation in policy making, material intercompany transactions, management interchange or provision of essential technical information.

Minority Interests. **Minority interests** in consolidated subsidiaries are shown separately from shareholders' equity in the consolidated balance sheet.

The minority share of subsidiaries' income is shown separately in the income statement in arriving at consolidated net income.

Disclosure. Consolidation: The basis of consolidation is disclosed. If a subsidiary is not included in the consolidated annual financial statements, the reason should be given, along with additional financial information about the subsidiary, as prescribed by the Act.

The parent company is required to disclose separately, normally in the directors' report, its interest in the aggregate profits and losses, after tax, of its subsidiaries.

The parent company is also required to disclose the following for each subsidiary:

☐ Its name and, if foreign, country of incorporation.

☐ Issued share capital, class, percentage held directly by the parent company or through a nominee or subsidiary and any changes during the period.

☐ The parent's interest in the subsidiary, distinguishing between shares and indebtedness, and any changes in such interest during the period.

Equity accounting: In addition to the equity accounting information in the balance sheet and income statement, the principal investees, including names and nature of business together with percentage and number of shares of each class held by the investor, should be disclosed.

Reference. AC110 and Companies Act.

5. Joint Ventures

Accounting for Joint Ventures. Joint ventures take many different forms, but there are three broad types: jointly controlled operations, jointly controlled assets and jointly controlled entities. The following characteristics are common to all joint ventures:

☐ Two or more venturers are bound by a contractual arrangement.

☐ The contractual arrangement effectively establishes **joint control**.

With respect to its interests in jointly controlled operations or jointly controlled assets, a venturer recognizes in its own financial statements:

☐ The assets it controls or its share of the jointly controlled assets, classified according to the nature of the assets.

☐ The liabilities it incurs or its share of liabilities incurred jointly with the other venturers.

Jointly Controlled Entities. A venturer usually reports its interest in a jointly controlled entity using the **proportionate consolidation method** of accounting. However, there may be exceptional circumstances (for example, when a voting pool agreement used to bind the interests of investors having significant influence creates joint control, but there is no intention by investors of acting as joint venturers) in which it would be more appropriate to use the equity method.

If the accounting policies of the jointly controlled entity and those of the venturer are different, appropriate adjustments should be made to align the policies of the jointly controlled entity to those of the venturer. If it is not practicable, that fact should be disclosed together with an estimate of the effect or significance thereof.

Transactions Between Venturers and the Joint Venture. In general, gains on contributions or sales of assets to a jointly controlled entity are recognized by a venturer only to the extent attributable to the interests of the other venturers who are not related parties. However, losses are recognized in their entirety.

Disclosure. South African disclosure requirements are consistent with IAS 31, *Financial Reporting of Interests in Joint Ventures*. The following must be disclosed: **contingencies** and commitments, a listing and description of significant joint ventures, the proportion of ownership interest held in jointly controlled entities and aggregate amounts of current assets, long-term assets, **current liabilities**, long-term liabilities, income and expenses of such entities that have been proportionately consolidated and are significant to the results of operations and/or the financial position and cash flows of the venturer.

In addition, disclosure is made of any other significant information relating to joint ventures, for example, post balance sheet events, retirement benefit information and uncovered foreign currency exchange exposure.

Accounting by Jointly Controlled Entities. Generally accepted accounting principles apply to all assets, liabilities and operations of jointly controlled entities. There is no special rule that requires the entity to adopt the same accounting policies as the venturers.

Reference. AC119.

6. Foreign Currency Translation

Bases of Translation. Two types of procedures are addressed separately: translating transactions in foreign currencies and translating foreign operations.

Transactions in foreign currencies: **Foreign currency denominated transactions** are translated at the actual or spot rates existing at the transaction dates. Where a foreign currency denominated transaction is covered by a forward exchange contract entered into prior to, at or immediately after the transaction date, the spot rate specified in the forward exchange contract should be used to record the transaction. The premium or discount should be amortized over the term of the contract.

At each balance sheet date, **monetary items** denominated in a foreign currency are translated at the rate in effect at the balance sheet date (closing rate). If there is a forward exchange contract covering a monetary item, the forward rate is used. Exchange differences arising on the settlement of monetary items or on the translation of unsettled monetary items denominated in a foreign currency at rates different from those at which they were previously translated are recognized in income for the period.

Foreign operations: Foreign operations may be classified either as **integrated foreign operations** of the reporting entity or as foreign entities.

The financial statements of an integrated foreign operation are translated using the **temporal method**. Exchange differences are included in income.

The financial statements of foreign entities (**self-sustaining foreign operations**) are normally translated using the closing rate for all items. Income statement items are translated at the exchange rates at the dates of the transactions or at an appropriately weighted-average rate. The closing rate may also be used if it is more appropriate for fair presentation. Exchange differences are recorded in a foreign currency translation reserve account, which is separately disclosed as part of nondistributable reserves.

Disclosure. The basis of foreign currency translation of financial statements of foreign operations and the net exchange difference for the period taken directly to foreign currency translation reserve are disclosed. Details of foreign currency exposure at the balance sheet date and any forward exchange contracts that do not relate to specific balance sheet items are also disclosed.

With regard to the income statement, foreign exchange gains and losses relating to foreign currency loans should be disclosed. Exchange differences included as financing costs should be separately identified.

Reference. AC112 and Companies Act.

7. Changing Prices/Inflation Accounting

General. In practice, the majority of South African companies do not disclose the effects of changing prices on financial statements. There is no requirement to produce this supplementary information and it does not form part of the statutory financial statements.

Supplementary Information. The guideline, "Disclosure of Effects of Changing Prices on Financial Results," issued by the SAICA, recommends disclosing in a supplementary **current cost** income statement, the major effects of price changes on operating results. The guideline recommends adjusting depreciation, cost of sales and financing provided by outside sources (financial gearing). The supplementary income statement measures current cost income as:

☐ Operating income, which is calculated in relation to the assets employed in the business and does not take into account the financial gearing adjustment.

☐ Owners' income, which adjusts operating income for the effects of financial gearing.

If consolidated financial statements are presented, the supplementary current cost income statement should be presented for consolidated financial results only. A current cost balance sheet is not dealt with in the guideline.

Reference. AC201.

8. Accounting Changes

Accounting Treatment. Change in accounting policy: A change in accounting policy should not be made unless it can be justified on the ground that the new policy is preferable to the one it replaces. Changes in accounting policies are accounted for by restating comparative amounts, including earnings per share, and the opening balance of retained income for the previous period.

Change in accounting estimate: A change in accounting estimate arises from new information or developments, and its effect is recorded prospectively in the period of change, without retroactive restatement.

Disclosure. A description of a change in accounting policy and its effect on the previous year's statements are disclosed, generally by restating comparative amounts. If it is not practical to restate comparative amounts, this is explained and the effect of applying the new policy in the current year is disclosed. The reason for the change is also disclosed in a note.

Reference. AC103.

9. Prior Period Adjustments

Definition. **Prior period adjustments** arise either from changes in accounting policies or from the correction of fundamental errors. Fundamental errors are those considered to be of such significance as to make the financial statements misleading and that would have led to their amendment had the errors been recognized in time. They do not include normal recurring corrections and adjustments of accounting estimates made in prior periods.

Accounting Treatment. Prior period adjustments are accounted for by restating the comparative amounts, including earnings per share, and the opening balance of retained income for the previous period.

Disclosure. The effect of the adjustment is disclosed, showing the amounts involved, either through restating of comparative prior amounts or in a note.

Reference. AC103.

10. Post Balance Sheet Events

Definition. Post balance sheet events are events that occur between the balance sheet date and the date on which the financial statements are authorized for issue. Two types of events are identified:

☐ Those that provide additional evidence of conditions that existed at the balance sheet date.

☐ Those that are indicative of conditions that arose subsequent to the balance sheet date.

Accounting Treatment. Conditions that existed at the balance sheet date: Financial statements are adjusted for events occurring after the balance sheet date that provide additional evidence of conditions existing at the balance sheet date or that indicate that the going concern assumption is no longer appropriate.

Conditions that arose subsequent to the balance sheet date: Financial statements are not adjusted for events occurring after the balance sheet date that do not affect the condition of assets and liabilities at that date.

In marginal cases, where it is difficult to decide whether an adjustment should be made for an event that occurred after the balance sheet date, the concept of prudence prevails.

Disclosure. Events occurring after the balance sheet date that do not affect the condition of the assets or liabilities at the balance sheet date, if material, are disclosed. The following information is provided for these subsequent events:

☐ The nature of the event.
☐ An estimate of the financial effect, both before and after tax, or, if an estimate cannot be made, a statement to that effect.

Reference. AC107.

11. Related Party Transactions

Definition. Parties are considered related if one party has the ability to control the other or to exercise significant influence over its financial and operating decisions.

Accounting Treatment. South African standards do not address measurement and accounting treatment pertaining to related party transactions. Such transactions are treated in accordance with the normal accounting principles and practices applied to other transactions.

Disclosure. The disclosure requirements relating to subsidiaries and associates, outlined in Section 4, meet most of the requirements of IAS 24. If minority interests are involved, additional disclosure is usually made for transactions not at arm's length.

In addition, the Act requires companies to disclose total directors' salaries and the details of loans to directors and managers.

12. Segmental Information

General. Listed companies and other economically significant entities whose financial statements are widely available must report financial information by segment, specifically by industries and geographical areas in which they operate.

Disclosure. Segmental information need not be disclosed if such disclosure would be seriously prejudicial to the interests of the enterprise. If such information has not been disclosed, that fact must be stated.

If segmental information is reported, the entity should describe the activities of each reported industry segment and indicate the composition of each reported geographical area.

For each industry and geographical segment, the following information, expressed either in monetary terms or as percentages of consolidated totals, is disclosed:

- [ ] Sales or other operating revenues.
- [ ] Segment operating results.
- [ ] Segment assets employed.

Intrasegment transactions and the basis of intrasegment pricing are also disclosed.

Where necessary, the entity should reconcile the sum of the information on individual segments to the aggregated information in the financial statements. Any change in the segments identified, the accounting practices used in reporting segment information or the accounting policies of segments should also be disclosed. Unless impracticable, comparative amounts should be restated.

Reference. AC115.

ACCOUNTING PRINCIPLES FOR SPECIFIC ITEMS— BALANCE SHEET

13. Property, Plant and Equipment

Classification of Capital and Revenue Expenditure. Expenditure on fixed assets that are held by an entity for use in the production or supply of goods and services, for rental or for administrative purposes is capitalized. Expenditure on improvements that extend an asset's useful life or increase its capacity or quality of output is also capitalized. Expenditures to maintain normal operating efficiency are expensed as incurred.

Basis of Valuation. Property, plant and equipment are generally carried at depreciated historical cost or valuation. The substitution of valuations for historical cost of fixed assets is permitted by the Act. Valuations may be determined using various criteria, such as current **replacement value** or market value. Valuations should not exceed the amount that can be expected to be recovered from the asset's continued use and, where relevant, its ultimate disposal.

Surpluses arising on revaluations are credited directly to a nondistributable reserve. Deficits are charged to income and disclosed as abnormal or extraordinary, depending on the circumstances.

If a valuation reverses a previous valuation, the accounting is the reverse of that employed previously. If a deficit exceeds the balance available in a nondistributable reserve arising from a previous valuation, the difference is charged to income.

If a deficit is determined to be temporary, it does not have to be charged to income. However, disclosure of the amount of the deficit and the circumstances should be disclosed.

Gains or losses on disposals, based on carrying amounts, are included in income as extraordinary or abnormal items, depending on the circumstances. Nondistributable reserve balances may be transferred to distributable reserve accounts to the extent that they relate to assets sold; such transfers should not be reflected in income for the period.

Investment Properties. Investment properties are properties that, based on intention and the particular circumstances, are classified as such by management. This definition provides management with wide latitude in deciding whether or not to depreciate buildings. However, it is unlikely that specialized property—that is, property that, due to the specialized nature of the buildings, their construction, arrangement, size, location or other features, is rarely, if ever, sold, except by way of a sale of the business in occupation—would be regarded as an investment property.

Two accounting treatments are permitted: The buildings on the property may be treated as depreciable assets and depreciated accordingly, or the whole property may be regarded as an investment, in which case it is carried in the balance sheet at open market value, which is determined at intervals of not more than five years.

Depreciation.   **Depreciation** is allocated on a systematic basis to each accounting period during the useful life of the asset. The depreciation method selected, which is normally the **straight-line** or **declining balance method**, should be applied consistently from period to period, unless altered circumstances justify a change. Investment properties need not be depreciated.

Disclosure.   The valuation bases used to determine the amounts at which depreciable assets are stated and the depreciation methods used are included in the accounting policies note. The following are also disclosed, for each major category of fixed assets:

□   Total depreciation charged in arriving at income for the period.
□   Total depreciation provided for the period.
□   Gross amount of depreciable assets and accumulated depreciation.

The objectives of revaluations and their intended frequency generally should be disclosed if the company has a policy of replacing historical cost with valuations. The date and basis of the latest valuation are disclosed. In the period that assets are revalued, the names and qualifications of the persons making the valuation and whether it was independent or internal should also be disclosed.

If investment properties, such as buildings, are not treated as depreciable assets, their carrying values and most recently established market values are disclosed, together with the effective date of valuation and whether the valuation was independent or internal.

Reference.   AC106, AC202 and Companies Act.

14.   Intangible Assets

Accounting Treatment.   No guideline or standard on **intangible assets** exists in South Africa and practice varies.

Disclosure.   Where applicable, the basis of **amortization** is disclosed. Intangible assets, if not written off, are shown as a single item in the balance sheet.

Reference.   Companies Act.

15.   Leases

Classification.   If substantially all the risks and rewards associated with ownership are transferred by the lessor to the lessee, the lease is considered to be a **finance lease**, whether or not title to the leased asset is transferred. **Operating leases** are leases other than finance leases. Any one of the following conditions may indicate that a lease transfers substantially all the risks and rewards of ownership:

□ The lease transfers ownership of the asset to the lessee at the end of the lease term;

□ The lease contains an option for the lessee to purchase the leased asset at a price that is sufficiently lower than its expected market value to make it reasonably certain that the option will be exercised;

□ The lease term is equal to or greater than 75 percent of the estimated economic life of the leased asset; or

□ The present value at the commencement of the lease is equal to or greater than substantially all (usually 90 percent or more) of the market value of the leased asset.

Accounting Treatment. Lessee: Assets held under finance leases are capitalized in the lessee's financial statements and a related liability is recorded. The amount capitalized is the market value of the asset, which is normally the cash price stated in the lease agreement. The difference between the total minimum lease payments and the capitalized value of the leased asset is the total finance charge, which is charged to income over the lease period. The capitalized value is depreciated over the leased asset's expected useful life or over the shorter of the lease term or the asset's useful life, if ownership at the end of the lease term is not reasonably certain.

Payments under operating leases are charged to income on a systematic basis related to the benefit derived from the leased asset.

Lessor: Under finance leases, profits on transfers of assets are recognized immediately, and the leases are recorded as receivables. The recognition of finance income reflects a constant periodic rate of return on the lessor's net cash investment. Receipts under operating leases are recognized as income on a systematic basis, and assets leased are recorded as fixed assets.

Sale and Leaseback Transactions. Where the sale and leaseback transaction gives rise to a finance lease, the carrying value of the asset does not change. The consideration received is recognized as a liability, and the finance charge is expensed over the lease term.

If the leaseback is an operating lease, a profit or loss is recognized immediately, except that future lease payments are adjusted for any difference between the sale price and the market value.

Leveraged Leases. **Leveraged leases** are not common in South Africa.

Disclosure. Lessee: The lessee should disclose the carrying amount of capitalized leased assets by major categories of fixed assets. The corresponding liabilities are disclosed, with details of interest rates and repayment dates. The current portions of lease liabilities are disclosed as current liabilities.

Operating lease payments charged to income are disclosed by major categories of assets. Sale and leaseback transactions that give rise to operating leases require the following additional disclosures:

□ Profit or loss arising from the sale after adjustment for any difference between the sale price and market value.

☐ Where the difference between the sale price and market value is recognized as a liability or prepayment, the amount settled or expensed for the period and the balance remaining.

☐ Details of any related repurchase commitments, contingencies or options.

Lessor: Lessors should disclose the gross investment in finance leases, the related unearned finance income and unguaranteed residual values of leased assets. The basis used for allocating income to produce a constant periodic rate of return is disclosed.

If a significant part of the lessor's business consists of operating leases, the lessor should disclose the amount of assets leased, by major class, together with the related accumulated depreciation.

When an enterprise is a participant in a leveraged lease, disclosure should be made of the effect of the participation and the manner in which it has been accounted for.

Reference. AC105 and AC113.

16. Investments

Valuation. There is no South African standard on accounting for investments. However, an exposure draft (ED) was issued by the SAICA in June 1992.

Definition. A trading investment, according to the ED, is an investment that:

☐ Is not intended to be held for use on a continuing basis in the activities of the enterprise.

☐ Is readily tradable and, therefore, has a fair value that can be calculated and readily established.

A nontrading investment is an investment other than a trading investment.

Trading investments held as current assets are generally accounted for at the lower of cost or **net realizable value**, which is normally market value or directors' valuation for unlisted securities. The ED requires these to be measured and reported at fair value.

Nontrading investments are usually carried at cost. The ED allows an option for these to be measured and reported at fair value. The **portfolio basis** of valuing nontrading investments is permissible.

Treatment of Valuation Reserves. If nontrading investments are revalued, a set policy for doing so should be established. Any revaluation above the carrying amount is credited to a revaluation reserve included in nondistributable reserves. Nontemporary reductions are charged to income unless they offset a previous revaluation surplus. If there is a rise in value, any previous reductions may be reversed.

Gains/Losses. On the sale of an investment, the difference between the carrying amount and sales proceeds, net of related expenses, is included in income.

If the investment sold had previously been revalued and the revaluation surplus credited to a revaluation reserve, the surplus may be transferred to a distributable reserve.

Disclosure. The aggregate fair values of nontrading investments, analyzed between listed and unlisted investments, need to be shown, if different from carrying values.

For nontrading investments stated at revalued amounts, the policy for frequency of revaluations, the date of the latest revaluation and the basis of revaluation are disclosed.

For each nontrading investment, the following is disclosed:

□ Name of company.
□ Number and class of shares held in a listed investment, or percentage ownership and voting power held, if different, in a listed or unlisted investment.

Gains and losses on investment transactions are disclosed. Income from investments, distinguishing between listed and unlisted investments, and among interest, dividends and other specified income, is also disclosed.

Reference. Companies Act and ED 86.

17. Accounts Receivable

Accounting Treatment. Recognition: The recognition of **revenues**, and hence the related receivables, is described in Section 23.

Discounts: Receivables are recorded net of trade and quantity discounts. Cash discounts are recognized at the time of payment.

Allowances: There is no required method used to calculate the allowance for doubtful accounts. Specific assessment of each account or a formula based on previous experience are commonly used methods.

Factored Receivables. If **accounts receivable** have been factored to a finance company for cash consideration, the relevant receivables are excluded from the balance sheet. Discounts given to the finance company are normally accounted for in the same way as cash discounts. If the receivables are sold with recourse, a provision for probable losses is recorded and the contingent liability is disclosed.

Disclosure. Accounts receivable are shown separately from other current assets. Noncurrent receivables are also shown separately. The allowance for doubtful accounts does not need to be disclosed or referred to.

Reference. Companies Act.

18. Inventories and Work in Progress

General Accounting Treatment. **Inventories** are valued at the lower of historical cost and net realizable value. Historical cost is the aggregate of cost of purchase, cost of conversion and other costs incurred in bringing inventories to their present location and condition.

Net realizable value is the estimated selling price in the ordinary course of business less costs of completion and selling costs. If inventories are written down to net realizable value, it should be done item by item or by groups of similar items. The method used should be consistently applied.

The historical cost of inventories is determined using the **first-in first-out (FIFO)** method or a weighted-average method, subject to the following exceptions:

□ Items of inventory not ordinarily interchangeable or goods manufactured and segregated for specific projects are accounted for by the specific identification method.

□ The **last-in first-out (LIFO)** method or **base stock** method may be used, provided
that there is disclosure of the difference between the carrying amount of inventories
and either:
—the lower of the FIFO/weighted-average value and net realizable value;
  or
—the lower of replacement cost at the balance sheet date and net realizable value.

□ Byproducts whose cost is not separable from that of main products may be valued
at net realizable value, provided that the cost of the main products is calculated
after deducting the value of byproducts.

Inventory costing techniques such as the **standard cost** method for valuing products
or the **retail method** for merchandise may be used for convenience if they consistently
approximate the results that would be obtained by using the lower of historical cost and
net realizable value.

Historical cost of manufactured inventory comprises the cost of materials, labor and
variable overheads. Cost also includes an allocation of fixed production overheads, based
on the capacity of the facilities, not on the actual level of output. If not directly related
to producing or delivering inventory to its present location or condition, fixed production
overheads may be excluded, provided that this exclusion is disclosed.

Long-Term Contracts. Revenue recognition for long-term contracts is covered in
Section 23.

Contract costs comprise costs that relate directly to specific contracts and those that
relate to contract activity in general and can be allocated to specific contracts.

Provision is made for losses relating to the stage of completion reached on the contract
and for foreseeable losses on the remainder of the contract.

Disclosure. Inventories and work in progress: Inventories and work in progress should
be shown separately and, if material to operating results or financial position, should be
classified under appropriate subheadings. Inventory subheadings include, where applicable:

□ Raw materials, including component parts.
□ Finished goods.
□ Merchandise, under subheadings if appropriate.
□ Consumables, including maintenance spares.
□ Work in progress.
□ Contracts in progress.

The accounting policies and costing methods adopted to value inventories and work in
progress are disclosed.

Long-term contracts: The following is disclosed for long-term contracts:

(a) The amount of contracts in progress (cost plus profit to date less any provision
for losses).

(b) Progress payments, advances or retentions received and receivable.

(c) Whether contract profits or losses have been recorded and, if so, to what extent.

(d) The method of calculating **turnover**.

If separate disclosure of the information in items (a) and (b) is considered misleading, the net amount only should be disclosed.

Reference. AC108, AC109 and Companies Act.

19. Current Liabilities

General Accounting Treatment. Current liabilities include amounts payable within 12 months from the financial year-end. Trade **accounts payable** are liabilities to suppliers for goods supplied or services rendered, irrespective of whether invoices or bills have been received. Provisions are amounts recorded for known liabilities, the amounts of which cannot be determined with substantial accuracy.

Current amounts owed to subsidiary or associated companies are normally classified as current liabilities. If part of a long-term loan is repayable within 12 months of the balance sheet date, it should be treated as a current liability. An exception may be made if the funds to finance the repayment will be provided from further long-term borrowings and thus the entity's liquidity will not be affected by the repayment.

Income received in advance, for example, payments from customers for goods and services not yet delivered, is treated as deferred income and is recognized as income when it is earned.

Creation of General and Specific Provisions. Most liabilities and accruals can be estimated with substantial accuracy and are classified as accounts payable. Circumstances arise, however, in which known liabilities cannot be closely estimated because some factors are uncertain. An example is a claim for breach of contract or faulty workmanship, in which the liability is acknowledged but the amount owed is in dispute.

Provisions recorded should be specific. If a provision is in excess of what, in the opinion of the directors, is reasonably necessary for its purpose, the excess is treated as an equity reserve. The auditors report if they disagree with the directors' determination in these matters.

Disclosure. Current liabilities are summarized as necessary to disclose their general nature and are classified under headings appropriate to the entity's business. The following items should be shown separately in the balance sheet:

☐ Bank overdrafts and short-term loans.

☐ Dividends declared or recommended, including dividends declared or recommended after the balance sheet date.

☐ Tax liability.

☐ Current portion of long-term liabilities, including liabilities relating to capitalized finance leases.

☐ Remaining liabilities of discontinued operations.

Generally, when a material provision is recorded in the financial statements, the amount of the provision is separately disclosed. If it is not subsequently used for the purpose intended, any material reversal or application of the excess is also disclosed in the financial statements.

Reference.   AC105, AC117 and Companies Act.

20.   Long-Term Debt

General Accounting Treatment.   Long-term debt is repayable either wholly or in part more than 12 months from the financial year-end. Secured long-term debt in South Africa is usually in the form of mortgages, debentures, suspensive sale (instalment sale in which ownership does not pass to the debtor until the last instalment has been paid) liabilities or bank loans. Loan **defeasance** transactions are not common in South Africa.

Debt Restructuring.   There is no South African standard on accounting for debt restructuring. Any gain or loss would normally be included in income at the time of the restructuring.

Debt Extinguishment.   There is no South African standard on accounting for debt extinguishment. Any gain or loss would be included in income when the debt is extinguished.

Disclosure.   The interest rate or basis of determining it, and repayment dates of long-term loans, including debentures, must be stated. If repayable in instalments, the amounts and due dates are stated.

Any liability secured by any asset of the company, other than by law (e.g., lien), should be disclosed.

For debentures, the following are also disclosed:

☐   The amounts and classes of debentures issued.

☐   For convertible debentures, the conditions and dates of conversion or, if the conditions are numerous, a note as to where the debentures may be inspected.

☐   The nominal amount of the company's own debentures held via a nominee or trustee and the amount at which they are recorded.

☐   Details of any redeemed debentures that the company has the authority to reissue.

☐   The number, description and amount of any debentures held by a subsidiary or nominee.

Reference.   Companies Act.

21.   Contingencies

Contingent Losses.   The amount of a contingent loss, after taking into account any related probable recovery, is provided for by a charge in the income statement if:

☐ It is probable that future events will confirm that the value of an asset has been impaired or a liability has been incurred at the balance sheet date.

☐ A reasonable estimate of the amount of the resulting loss can be made.

If a contingent loss is not recorded, its existence is disclosed, unless the possibility of a loss is remote and the disclosure would be misleading. While a contingent loss is not required by AC107 to be recorded or disclosed if it is regarded as remote, there is no exception for remoteness allowed by the Act. Accordingly, guarantees and bills discounted with recourse, for example, are disclosed by companies even though the likelihood of a loss being incurred is remote. If the possibility of loss is remote, reference may be made to the fact that no loss is expected, to avoid the possibility of giving a misleading impression.

Contingent Gains.   Contingent gains are not accrued in the financial statements. The existence of contingent gains is disclosed only if it is probable that they will be realized.

Disclosure.   The following information is presented for contingent losses that are disclosed:

☐ The nature of the contingency.

☐ The uncertain factors that may affect the future outcome.

☐ The estimated amount and the financial effect, if any, both before and after tax; if estimates cannot be made, a statement to that effect is made.

Reference.   AC107 and Companies Act.

22.   Capital and Reserves

General.   Shareholders' equity is generally divided into **share capital** and **share premium** (amounts contributed by shareholders) and reserves. Reserves are usually classified as either nondistributable or distributable.

Share Capital.   Share capital of a company may be divided into different classes, each characterized by dividend and voting rights and capital rights, including priority for repayment in the event of liquidation. The amount of each class authorized for issue and the precise rights of each class are set out in the company's memorandum and articles of association. The classes of share capital most commonly issued are **preference shares** and ordinary (equity) shares. Shares may not be allotted or issued unless consideration has been received in full (partly paid shares are prohibited).

Share capital, whether preference or ordinary, may consist of **par value** shares or no par value shares, provide that the entire class is the same. For no par value shares, all proceeds are included in the stated capital account, which may be used to write off:

☐ The preliminary (or formation) expenses of the company.

☐ The expenses of or commission paid on the creation or issue of any no par value shares.

If shares having no par value are issued for consideration other than cash, the value of the consideration as determined by the directors is transferred to the stated capital account.

If par value shares are converted to no par value shares, the par value of the shares and any existing share premium attributable to the shares should be transferred to the stated capital account.

If a company issues shares at a premium, the amount of the premium is transferred to the share premium account; the provisions of the Act relating to the reduction of the share capital apply, with certain exceptions, as if the share premium account were paid-up share capital. These exceptions allow the share premium account to be applied to:

☐ Issue fully paid capitalization (or bonus) shares.
☐ Write off:
—the preliminary expenses of the company;
—the expenses of or commission paid or discount allowed on any issue of shares of the company.
☐ Provide for the premium payable on redemption of any redeemable preference shares of the company, but only where such premium is payable in terms of both the issue of these shares and the articles. In the case of ordinary shares converted to redeemable preference shares, the premium payable on redemption is limited to the premium received on the issue of such ordinary shares.

If shares are issued to acquire a business or any other asset and the value of the consideration is not recorded in the purchase agreement, the assets acquired should be valued and the premium on the shares issued calculated by reference to such value.

Shares issued at a discount: A company may issue at a discount par value shares of a class already issued, if certain conditions of the Act have been complied with, primarily sanction by the Court. A special resolution is required to issue no par value shares at a discount, that is, at a price lower than the previous average issue price.

Redemption of redeemable preference shares: A company may issue redeemable preference shares, including shares having no par value. The shares may be redeemed at a fixed or determinable date or at the option of the company or the shareholders. They may be redeemed only from distributable profits of the company or the proceeds, including any premium, of shares issued specifically to provide funds for the redemption. If shares are redeemed at a premium, the premium should be provided from profits or a share premium account.

If the redemption is made from profits, the nominal value of the shares redeemed or, for no par value shares, an amount equal to their book value should be transferred to a capital redemption reserve fund. That fund may be used to pay up shares to be issued to **members** as fully paid-up capitalization shares.

Reserves. Distributable reserves may be credited to income and distributed through a dividend. However, Exchange Control Regulations currently restrict the free remittance of dividends to nonresident shareholders to noncapital income earned since January 1, 1984.

All other reserves are nondistributable reserves and may include the following:

☐ Reserves arising on consolidation.

☐ Unrealized surpluses on revaluation of noncurrent assets or on translation of the financial statements of foreign entities owned by the company.

☐ Amounts prohibited from being distributed by the articles of association.

☐ Reserves that the directors have set aside as not available for distribution, for example, amounts set aside for the increased cost of replacement of fixed assets.

☐ Capital redemption reserve fund.

Disclosure.   Separate disclosure of the authorized and issued share capital is required, together with any changes therein. Authorized and issued par value shares are recorded at their nominal value. For no par value shares, the stated capital account is shown separately. The share premium account is grouped with share capital and separately disclosed. Aggregate reserves are disclosed under separate headings, distinguishing between nondistributable and distributable reserves. Material changes in reserves are disclosed, including sources and applications. Options or preferential rights on unissued shares, including the number, description and amount of shares affected, are disclosed. The option price and period for which they are exercisable are also disclosed.

Normally, details of retained income not remittable to nonresident shareholders are disclosed.

Reference.   Companies Act and Exchange Control Regulations.

ACCOUNTING PRINCIPLES FOR SPECIFIC ITEMS— INCOME STATEMENT

23. Revenue Recognition

General Principles.   Revenue from sales or service transactions is recognized only after performance and measurement requirements have been satisfied and collectibility is reasonably assured, or uncollectible amounts can be reasonably estimated.

For revenue to be recognized from a transaction involving the sale of goods, the buyer must have assumed from the seller the significant risks and rewards of ownership. The following considerations are relevant to this determination:

☐ Whether any significant performance remains to be completed.

☐ Whether the seller retains any continuing managerial involvement in or effective control of the goods transferred to a degree usually associated with ownership.

☐ Whether the payment of the debt relating to the goods transferred depends on revenue earned by the buyer from the goods.

Revenue is recognized for services on the basis of performance. Performance may be evidenced through the execution of an act or through the passage of time. For example, long-term contract revenue may be recognized according to the **percentage of completion method** or the **completed contract method**.

Long-Term Contracts.   A contractor may use both the percentage of completion method and the completed contract method simultaneously for different contracts, but all contracts that meet similar criteria should be accounted for by the same method.

The percentage of completion method may be used for fixed price contracts, only if both of the following conditions are satisfied:

□ The stage of contract performance completed at the reporting date can be estimated with reasonable assurance.
□ Costs attributable to the contract can be clearly identified so that actual experience can be compared with prior estimates.

For cost plus contracts, the following conditions must be satisfied to use the percentage of completion method:

□ Costs attributable to the contract can be clearly identified.
□ Costs that will not be specifically reimbursable under the contract can be estimated with reasonable assurance.

Under the percentage of completion method, profit may be recognized only when the outcome of the contract can be estimated with reasonable assurance.

Instalment Sales. If consideration is receivable in instalments, revenue attributable to the sales price, exclusive of finance charges, is normally recognized at the date of sale. If collection is not reasonably assured, revenue is recognized only as cash instalments are received. The finance charge element is recognized as revenue proportionately to the unpaid balance.

Rights of Return. Recognition of revenue will depend on the substance of the agreement. For normal retail sales, it is appropriate to recognize the sale, but to record a provision for returns based on previous experience. If the substance of the agreement amounts to a sale on consignment, it should be treated as such.

Product Financing. **Product financing** occurs when a seller sells goods and concurrently agrees to repurchase the same goods at a later date. If such transactions are, in substance, financing arrangements, the sales proceeds are not recognized as revenue.

Disclosure. The aggregate amount of turnover for the period is disclosed, together with the basis on which turnover is determined.

Any circumstances in which revenue recognition has been postponed pending the resolution of significant uncertainties should be disclosed.

Reference. AC109, AC111 and Companies Act.

24. Government Grants and Assistance

Accounting Treatment. There is no South African standard on accounting for government grants and assistance. Government assistance for current expenditures is included in income, but is not offset against the relevant expenditure. There is no government assistance for **capital expenditures** in South Africa, other than tax incentives.

Disclosure. If material, the extent of government assistance is disclosed, together with the accounting policy adopted.

25. Research and Development

Definitions. Research is original and planned investigation undertaken with the hope of gaining new scientific or technical knowledge and understanding.

Development is the translation of research findings or other knowledge into a plan or design for the production of new or substantially improved materials, devices, products, processes, systems or services prior to the commencement of commercial production.

Accounting Treatment. In South Africa, research and development costs of a productive entity are normally expensed when incurred. This approach is compatible with IAS 9. If the criteria set out in IAS 9 are satisfied, it is acceptable to defer development costs (but not research costs), with appropriate disclosure.

Disclosure. The accounting policy for research and development costs and the expenditure charged to income should be disclosed. The amount of amortization of deferred expenditures also should be disclosed.

Reference. IAS 9.

26. Capitalized Interest Costs

Accounting Treatment. Interest costs may be capitalized only for assets that require a substantial period of time, usually longer than one year, to be prepared for sale or intended use. The policy followed with respect to capitalizing interest costs should be consistent.

The amount of interest cost capitalized is the amount of the interest costs incurred that would have been avoided if the expenditure had not been made.

The amount of interest costs capitalized during a period should not exceed the total amount of interest costs incurred. Interest capitalization should cease when the asset is ready for sale or intended use. Capitalization should also cease during extended periods in which active development is suspended.

Disclosure. The financial statements should disclose, where relevant:

☐ Whether interest costs are capitalized or not capitalized, and the major classification of assets to which the policy of capitalizing interest costs is applied.

☐ The amount of interest costs incurred during the period, identifying the portion, if any, capitalized during the period.

Reference. AC114 and Companies Act.

27. Imputed Interest

General. The recognition of **imputed interest** is not generally accepted in South Africa.

28. Extraordinary or Unusual Items

Extraordinary Items. Extraordinary items are material income and expense items resulting from transactions that are not typical of the ordinary trading or operating activities of the entity.

Unusual or Abnormal Items. Abnormal items are material income and expense items that are abnormal in amount and result from the ordinary trading or operating activities of the entity.

Abnormal items are included in the earnings per share calculation, but extraordinary items are not.

Disclosure. Extraordinary items, less related taxes and amounts attributable to minority interests, are aggregated and shown separately in the income statement after results from ordinary operations. Extraordinary items are explained in a note.

Abnormal items are also shown separately in the income statement or in a note.

Reference. AC103.

29. Income Taxes

Provisions are recorded for both current and deferred taxes. Deferred tax is computed using the **liability method** on either the comprehensive or the partial basis. The comprehensive basis recognizes the tax effects of all timing differences, whereas the partial basis recognizes only the tax effects of timing differences that will reverse in the foreseeable future without being replaced.

The partial basis may be used only if:

- ☐ The entity is a going concern.
- ☐ Management is able to reasonably estimate the tax that will become payable for at least three years as a result of applying the partial basis.
- ☐ Further tax liabilities are not likely to arise subsequently.

A tax loss is carried forward indefinitely and offset against future income until the loss has been recouped. A tax loss cannot be carried back in South Africa. The potential tax saving from a tax loss is recognized in the income statement only if there is assurance beyond a reasonable doubt that future taxable income will be sufficient for the tax benefit of the loss to be realized.

Disclosure. The accounting policy used to determine deferred taxes is disclosed together with details of current and deferred taxes attributable to income for the period, income taxes payable, deferred tax liability/asset shown by major category of timing difference and the existence and treatment of tax losses. If the effective tax rate is different from the standard rate, separate disclosure and quantification of significant reconciling items are required.

Where the partial basis is used, the effect on the amounts recorded for deferred taxes for the period had the comprehensive basis been used, should also be disclosed.

Reference. AC102 and Companies Act.

30. Postretirement Benefits

General. The Pension Funds Act governs most contractual retirement benefit plans in South Africa and sets down rules regarding the funding and the frequency and method of valuation of plans. Under this Act, a pension fund is a legal entity and has assets, rights, liabilities and obligations of its own.

Accounting Treatment. Although a South African standard exists for retirement benefit information, it does not establish standard practice for calculating the charge to income. The standard presents guidelines only on the disclosure of retirement benefit information and gives accounting alternatives for two types of pension plans. However, SAICA is addressing the matter and is likely to propose a new standard, based on IAS E47, for all postretirement benefits.

Unfunded obligations do not normally arise in **defined contribution plans**. Obligations to current and future pensioners under **defined benefit plans** are measured actuarially, but their value depends significantly on the basis of valuation and assumptions made. Accounting for the cost of benefit plans, therefore, depends on forecast estimates. New costs arising from experience adjustments are usually accounted for over future periods, perhaps the expected remaining working lives of the participating employees, or are charged immediately to income.

Postretirement benefits other than pensions, for example, health care benefits, are usually treated on a pay-as-you-go (cash) basis, but this is presently a controversial issue.

Pension Fund Surpluses. Pension fund surpluses arise only in relation to defined benefit plans and cannot be distributed to contributors until the pension fund is terminated or the pension fund rules permit such distribution. Employers usually can obtain the benefit of any surplus in the pension fund by decreasing or suspending contributions until the surplus is eliminated. This does not affect contributions by employees.

Disclosure. The financial statements should disclose sufficient information concerning pension plans to enable users of the financial statements to gain a broad understanding of the significance of retirement benefit costs in the accounting period and the actual and contingent liabilities and commitments at the balance sheet date. To meet the general objective of fair presentation, the financial statements should disclose at least the information required by the existing accounting standard. Reasonable summaries may be provided if there are a number of different pension plans. For group financial statements, the impact of the pension plans on minority interests is disclosed. Any further information that has a material impact on the entity's pension expense is also disclosed.

Reference. AC116.

31. Discontinued Operations

Discontinued operations are a significant identifiable part of an entity that has been committed by management to a formal plan of discontinuance, whether by sale or abandonment. The assets and operating results of the part of the entity should be clearly distinguished physically, operationally and for financial reporting purposes from the other assets and operations of the entity.

Accounting Treatment. If material, the results of discontinued operations prior to the discontinuance date are disclosed separately from the results of the other operations, but not as an extraordinary item. The discontinuance date is the date on which management has reasonable assurance as to the eventual execution of the plan of discontinuance.

The profit or loss on discontinuance, which is determined from the discontinuance date, is based on information available at the reporting date. The profit or loss on discontinuance should not include any amount recognized prior to the discontinuance, but should include estimated results to the expected disposal date, all costs directly associated with discontinuance and profits or losses on disposal of related assets and liabilities.

If a loss is expected from the discontinuance, provision is recorded for the full loss. An expected profit is recognized only when realized or when realization is reasonably certain.

Disclosure. If the results of discontinued operations prior to the discontinuance date are separately disclosed, the estimated attributable tax charge or savings and the effect on minority interests are similarly identified.

Any material profit or loss on discontinuance is disclosed as an extraordinary item. If a profit or loss on discontinuance is not known and cannot be estimated, this fact is disclosed. The following additional disclosure is required:

- ☐ Identity of the discontinued operation.
- ☐ Expected disposal date, if determinable.
- ☐ Remaining assets and liabilities of the discontinued operation.

Reference. AC117.

32. Earnings per Share

Definition. Earnings per share (EPS) for any class of equity shares is the earnings attributable to that class for the period, divided by the weighted average number of shares of that class. Earnings are the net income after deducting tax, outside shareholders' interest and preference dividends, but before taking into account extraordinary items and transfers to and from reserves; they include the retained equity income or deficit for the period that has been equity accounted.

Disclosure. Earnings or loss per share and dividends per share (in cents), together with comparative figures, are disclosed in the income statement of **listed companies**, companies the shares of which are publicly traded and other companies that choose to disclose EPS. Banks and insurance companies are not exempted from the disclosure requirements. The earnings and the weighted-average number of shares for each class of equity shares used in the calculation are also disclosed.

Future Dilution. A company may be committed to issue equity shares in the future as a result of having issued:

- ☐ Options to subscribe for equity shares or shares involving issues contingent on future events; or
- ☐ Debentures, loan stock, preference shares or other financial instruments convertible into equity shares; or
- ☐ Separate classes of equity shares that do not rank for dividends but will do so in the future.

In those circumstances, fully diluted EPS is disclosed to reflect the maximum potential dilution of current EPS as if the dilution had already taken place. Details relating to the rights attaching to the above and any other financial instruments that may result in a dilution of EPS are disclosed.

Where there has been a capitalization issue, a bonus issue as part of a rights issue, a share split, a share consolidation or a reduction affecting the number of shares issued, without a corresponding refund of capital, the corresponding EPS and dividends per share disclosed for all earlier periods should be proportionately adjusted.

Reference. AC104.

Appendix
DO SOUTH AFRICAN STANDARDS OR PREVALENT PRACTICE SUBSTANTIALLY COMPLY WITH INTERNATIONAL ACCOUNTING STANDARDS?

Section	Topic	Substantially complies with IAS?	Comments
3.	Basic accounting concepts and conventions	Yes	
	Contents of financial statements	Yes	
4.	Business combinations*	Yes	Except that other treatments for goodwill arising on consolidation are permitted in South Africa
5.	Joint ventures	Yes	
6.	Foreign currency translation*	Yes	
8.	Accounting changes*	Yes	
9.	Prior period adjustments*	Yes	
10.	Post balance sheet events	Yes	
11.	Related party transactions	No	
12.	Segmental information	Yes	Except that segmental information need not be disclosed where such disclosure would be seriously prejudicial to the enterprise
13.	Property, plant and equipment*	Yes	Except that a deficit arising on a valuation of an asset need not be charged to income if it is determined to be temporary, having regard to the life of the asset
15.	Leases	Yes	
16.	Investments	Yes	
17.	Accounts receivable	Yes	
18.	Inventories and work in progress*	Yes	
19.	Current liabilities	Yes	
20.	Long-term debt	Yes	

Appendix (*Continued*)

Section	Topic	Substantially complies with IAS?	Comments
21.	Contingencies	Yes	
22.	Capital and reserves	Yes	
23.	Revenue recognition*	Yes	
24.	Government grants and assistance	Yes	
25.	Research and development*	Yes	
26.	Capitalization of interest costs*	Yes	
28.	Extraordinary or unusual items*	Yes	
29.	Income tax**	Yes	
30.	Postretirement benefits*	Yes	

*These topics are subject to change as a result of the IASC Improvements Project—see the appendix to the International Accounting Standards chapter.

**The IAS on accounting for taxes on income is currently being revised, and an exposure draft has been issued.

Comparison in this table is made to International Accounting Standards in force at January 1, 1993. For further details, see the International Accounting Standards chapter.

SPAIN

GENERAL NATIONAL INFORMATION

1. Source of Generally Accepted Accounting Principles (Fuentes de Principios Contables)

Legislative Changes.   Spanish company law, financial reporting and auditing requirements have recently undergone major reform. On admission to full membership in the European Community (EC) on January 1, 1986, Spain accepted the obligation to adapt existing legislation to comply with the EC Directives on company law. The process began with the promulgation of both the Audit Law (Eighth Directive) and Company Law Reform Act (First, Second, Third, Fourth, Sixth and Seventh Directives), which both took effect in 1990. The process was completed with the issuance of a revised General Chart of Accounts (including details of **generally accepted accounting principles [GAAP]** and the form and content of accounts), in December 1990 and rules for the preparation of consolidated accounts in December 1991. This legislation represented a significant advance over the previous situation.

The pace of change has been rapid and a number of ambiguities in the legislation still require clarification. The regulatory body (ICAC; see below) is producing a series of pronouncements to narrow the scope for interpretation, as a result of which the contents of this chapter are subject to a higher-than-usual rate of obsolescence.

In Spain, the Fourth Directive is applicable to Sociedades Anónimas (SA; Limited Liability Corporations) and to Sociedades Limitadas (SL; Private Limited Liability Corporations). With regard to other types of companies, such as insurance or finance companies, separate rules derived from EC Directives are prepared and supervised by the appropriate regulatory body.

Spanish Terminology.   The Spanish translations used in this chapter are not necessarily those which have been in most common use, but they are the relevant account captions introduced by the new legislation. Further information on Spanish terminology is available from a Spanish-English, English-Spanish Dictionary of Financial Reporting, prepared by Coopers & Lybrand (Spain), specifically aimed at the translation of financial statements, for which purpose it is generally regarded as the standard work. The book is available from the publishers, Ediciones Deusto, Barraincúa 14, 48009 Bilbao, Spain, or through the Coopers & Lybrand Madrid office.

Generally Accepted Accounting Principles.   Historically, Spain has had no corpus of generally accepted accounting principles. Instead, there has been a rigid body of tax law that sought to override GAAP, leading to the belief that tax reporting and financial reporting were the same and that the financial position and results of operations determined in accordance with tax rules were the only appropriate ones for an entity to publish. This situation, for a long time, held Spanish financial reporting back. Tax law even went so far as to prescribe that any entity that published accounts differing from those prepared in accordance with tax legislation could be presumed to maintain two sets of books. Such presumption (i.e., of tax evasion) would have been difficult to avoid and would have entailed steep penalties.

Company law now requires that a company's accounts comply with the Plan General de Contabilidad (PGC; General Chart of Accounts) and reflect a true and fair view of its financial position and results.

Statutory requirements for financial statement presentation and disclosure, general **accounting principles** and their methods of application are now similar in Spain to those of other EC countries. The main sources of Spanish GAAP are as follows:

☐ Código de Comercio (CCom; Commercial Code or fundamental text of mercantile law). The relevant portions were radically amended as a part of the 1990 reform of company law.

☐ Texto Refundido de la Ley sobre el Régimen Jurídico de las Sociedades Anónimas (LSA; Company Law). The reformed LSA establishes certain accounting principles, the observance of which is obligatory for all companies.

☐ Plan General de Contabilidad. This is a statutory chart of accounts introduced in 1973 and revised and reissued in December 1990. The PGC is based on, and mirrors very closely, the French Plan Comptable Général. The sections relating to format and content of accounts and accounting principles (Criterios de Valoración) are obligatory for all SA companies. The PGC, or general chart of accounts, of 1973 was used as the basis for development of about a dozen specialized industry charts, setting out accounting principles and account formats that are mandatory for the industry in question. These charts are now in the process of revision to adapt them to the new requirements, but they remain in force to the extent they do not contradict the principles enunciated in the revised PGC.

☐ Normas para la Formulación de las Cuentas Consolidadas. These are the rules, issued in December 1991, governing the preparation of consolidated accounts. Prior to that time, presentation of consolidated accounts by groups of companies was not obligatory and was in fact uncommon.

☐ Instituto de Contabilidad y Auditoría de Cuentas (ICAC; Institute of Accounting and Auditing of Accounts—a government body under the Finance Ministry, created under the 1988 Audit Law). The Royal Decree introducing the PGC establishes that this body may adopt and issue accounting principles as and when it deems necessary, compliance with which will be obligatory. The ICAC may propose amendments to the PGC, which are subject to review by the Finance Ministry (Ministerio de Economía y Hacienda). The PGC empowers the ICAC to issue pronouncements that clarify or develop the PGC in the areas of accounting principles, rules for the preparation of annual accounts and the adaptation of those rules for specialized industries. The ICAC publishes a quarterly official bulletin (the

BOICAC) in which its pronouncements, resolutions, responses to queries and exposure drafts all appear.

☐   Asociación Española de Contabilidad y Administración (AECA). This is a private body incorporating a number of professional accountants and representatives from the business and academic worlds. Membership is voluntary and observance of its pronouncements is not obligatory. Nevertheless, until the reform of company law, it was effectively the only body promoting the development of advanced accounting principles in Spain. All 15 pronouncements previously issued by AECA have been revised to reflect the changes brought about by the process of reform and reissued. Generally, AECA requirements are not given in this chapter because they have no explicit legal recognition since official bodies in Spain do not follow the practice of giving recognition to private organizations.

2.   Audit and Public Company Requirements (Requerimientos en Cuanto a Auditoría y Empresas con Cotización Oficial)

Audits.   Under the LSA, companies are required to appoint state-recognized auditors, who must comply with strict criteria of independence vis à vis the client. This requirement took effect for financial years ending after June 30, 1990 and affects all corporations except those that satisfy at least two of the following conditions for two consecutive years.

Total assets less than pesetas (Ptas.) 230 million.
Turnover less than Ptas. 480 million.
Work force less than 50 employees.

Auditors are appointed by the company (i.e., the shareholders) in general meeting for a period of not less than three, nor more than nine, years. On termination of their period of office they may not be reappointed for a period of three years; however, it would appear that shorter contracts may be renewed up to a maximum of nine years. The auditors' fees, or the basis of their calculation, must be fixed for the entire period of the contract. Once appointed, auditors may not resign, or be removed without "just cause." What constitutes a "just cause" is not, however, defined.

Only persons whose names are inscribed in the Registro Oficial de Auditores de Cuentas (ROAC; Official Register of Auditors of Accounts), which is maintained by the ICAC, are eligible for appointment as statutory auditors. Inscription in the ROAC is open to all Spanish economics graduates who meet certain experience requirements, as well as to other similarly qualified EC nationals.

Auditing standards are established by the three professional bodies into which public accountants are grouped: the Instituto de Censores Jurados de Cuentas de Espana (ICJCE; Spanish Institute of Auditors), the Registro de Economistas Auditores (REA; Register of Economics-Graduate Auditors) and the Registro General de Auditores de Cuentas Titulares Mercantiles (REGA; Register of Commerce Graduate Auditors). However, under the Audit Law, their standards do not become effective until approved by the ICAC and published in its official bulletin. Although far less developed, the pronouncements of REA and ICJCE tend to adhere closely to International Standards on Auditing. The REA pronouncements, in particular, state that, in case of doubt, reference should be made to International Standards on Auditing or the standards of other leading national standard-setting bodies.

In addition to reporting on the accounts themselves, auditors are obligated to report on whether the Directors' Report (Informe de Gestion) is in agreement with the information contained in the accounts. The auditor is also required by law to make specific mention of post balance sheet events "which affect the operations of the business" and "any infractions of law or of the company's bylaws which come to light in the course of his or her work and which might affect the true and fair view the accounts must present."

Public Companies (Empresas con Cotización Oficial). There are no additional accounting rules or disclosure requirements for companies quoted on the Spanish Stock Exchange, though various rules regarding the filing of accounts apply. Audited annual accounts must be filed with the Comisión Nacional del Mercado de Valores (CNMV; the state body supervising the stock exchange) within two months of their approval by the shareholders, which, in turn, must be within six months of the year-end. Quarterly financial information must also be provided.

To issue shares to the public, a company is required to have a minimum of 100 shareholders and a minimum share capital of Ptas. 200 million. If any individual owns more than 25 percent of the capital, that capital is not taken into account in determining the minimum capital. The most recent annual accounts must have been audited, and profit sufficient to permit payment of a dividend of at least 6 percent of share capital must have been made in the last two years or in at least three of the last five years.

Admission to quotation requires the prior consent of the CNMV. To retain quotation, a minimum capital of Ptas. 25 million is required and, although there is no minimum number of shareholders, at least 20 percent of the shares must be traded on the market. The company must have a contract with a broker (sociedad de contrapartida) who undertakes to provide a market in the shares.

Reference. LSA Articles 203–207; RLA Articles 5 and 17–23; RB1 Article 32; SM1 RD 710/1986.

GENERAL ACCOUNTING (CONTABILIDAD EN GENERAL)

3. Financial Statements

Basic Accounting Concepts. Company law does not distinguish among fundamental or basic **accounting concepts**, underlying assumptions and accounting conventions. The PGC enunciates a series of fundamental accounting principles (principios contables) and establishes specific accounting principles (normas de valoración, or valuation rules) for each asset and liability. The principios contables are as follows:

☐ The **prudence, going concern, accrual, matching** and consistency principles.
☐ Recording—Transactions are recorded in the period in which the rights or obligations arise.
☐ **Historical cost**—All rights and assets are recorded at historical cost except where permitted otherwise by law (for an important exception, see Section 13). Liabilities are recorded at the amount at which they are to be settled.
☐ No offset—Items of income and expense may not be offset against one another, nor

may assets and liabilities. Each individual asset and liability must be valued separately.

☐ Conflict of principles—Where mandatory accounting principles conflict, priority is given to the principle that better produces the true and fair view.

☐ **Materiality**—Divergence from the above is acceptable where the effect is immaterial.

☐ Precedence—Without prejudice to the foregoing, the prudence principle always has precedence.

Format and Content of Financial Statements. Annual accounts comprise a balance sheet, a profit and loss account and the notes, or "memoria" (see below). They must be drawn up "with clarity" and must present a true and fair view ("faithful image") of the net worth, financial position and results of operations of the company.

In the absence of any specialized industry requirements, the formats of the balance sheet and the profit and loss account must conform to the formats established in the LSA and amplified in the PGC. The balance sheet and profit and loss account should be in the same format from one accounting period to the next, although, in exceptional cases, the format may be changed, but the fact must be indicated in the notes together with the reasons therefor. Captions in the standard form of accounts may be subdivided, or grouped and the analysis presented in the memoria, provided that the overall format is followed and the main headings are disclosed.

The standard form of accounts specified by the PGC is in itself a form of disclosure checklist. The assets side of the balance sheet contains some 72 captions, which must appear either on the face of the balance sheet or in the notes, if the related figure is material.

Recent legislation has created at least momentary confusion in nomenclature because of the use of the word *memoria* to denote "notes to the accounts." Previously, the word was used for "annual report." For clarity, memoria is generally translated as notes in this chapter.

The law treats **consolidated financial statements** as separate from the individual statements of the **parent company**, to be approved and filed separately. Some reporting entities are merging these to form a single set of financial statements, but it is too early to state which will be the prevailing format.

The statement of source and application of funds is described in the PGC as an obligatory element of the memoria. It is not clear why, under the legislation, this statement has not been given the status of a basic financial statement. The statement of source and application of funds has a tabular format, which does not use the **direct method** but rather adjusts net income for transactions of a noncash nature. The statement, which must show comparative figures for the prior year, lists in separate columns all sources and applications of funds, lists the net source/application and then separately discloses all individual changes in working capital. Prior year figures must be restated to conform with the current year presentation. (There is no requirement to present comparative figures in the memoria other than in the statement of source and application of funds.)

Small companies may present abridged accounts. The rules distinguish between presentation of an abridged balance sheet and memoria on the one hand and an abridged profit and loss account on the other. A statement of source and application of funds is not required in consolidated financial statements, nor in the statements of companies entitled to file an abridged balance sheet. To qualify as a small company, companies must meet at least two of the following three criteria in both of the preceding two years:

	Abridged balance sheet and memoria	Abridged profit and loss account
Total assets at year-end must not exceed	Ptas. 230 million	Ptas. 920 million
Turnover for the year must not exceed	Ptas. 480 million	Ptas. 1920 million
Average number of employees during the year must not exceed	50 persons	250 persons

Businesses incorporated other than as an SA and sole traders must, at a minimum, present abridged accounts.

Disclosure of Accounting Policies.   The PGC lists substantially all the account captions for which the **accounting policies** must be disclosed. In unusual circumstances, if a literal application of an authoritative pronouncement might render the financial statements misleading, it is necessary to depart from the usual treatment. The practice followed and the reason for and effect on income and financial position of the departure should be disclosed in a note.

Reference.   CCom Articles 34–38; PGC Parts 1.4 and 5; LSA Articles 173–201.

4.   Business Combinations (Fusiones y Adquisiciones)

Principles of Consolidation.   Under company law, the presentation of audited consolidated accounts became obligatory for financial years ended after December 31, 1990. The **purchase method** of consolidation is the usual method of accounting for **business combinations**, as "**poolings of interests**" are unusual in Spain. Whichever method of consolidation is used, the accounts of all group companies must be adjusted prior to consolidation to comply with the accounting principles followed by the parent.
The rules for preparation of consolidated accounts were published in December 1991.

Definition of Control.   Consolidated financial statements must be prepared when the company holds investments in other companies if:

☐   It owns the majority of the voting rights;
☐   It has the power to appoint or remove the majority of the members of the board of directors;
☐   It controls, by virtue of agreements with other shareholders, the majority of the voting rights; or
☐   It has appointed, by its sole vote, the majority of the members of the board of directors serving at the time the accounts are to be prepared and who have so served during the preceding two years.

The most significant exemption from the requirement to present consolidated accounts is when, at the end of the parent's financial year, the consolidated figures do not exceed the following limits:

	Until December 31, 1999	Beginning January 1, 2000
Total assets at year-end	Ptas. 2300 million	Ptas. 920 million
Turnover for the year	Ptas. 4800 million	Ptas. 1920 million
Average numbers of employees for the year	500 persons	250 persons

Alternatively, these limits are increased by 20 percent and applied to the total of the corresponding figures of the group companies. A further exemption arises when the reporting entity is at least 90 percent owned by an entity domiciled in Spain or elsewhere in the EC, and a majority of any minority shareholders agree to it. In such cases, the consolidated financial statements of the ultimate parent, translated into Spanish where appropriate, must be filed.

Similarly, a parent company may account on the equity basis for a **subsidiary** that it would otherwise be obligated to consolidate on the line-by-line basis if the subsidiary:

☐ Is immaterial;

☐ Is subject to judicial intervention or receivership, effectively prohibiting preparation of consolidated accounts by the parent or affecting the parent's rights over the equity or the management of the subsidiary;

☐ Cannot provide the information necessary for the preparation of consolidated accounts except at a disproportionate cost, or would delay the preparation of such accounts beyond the established time limits;

☐ Has been acquired solely with the objective of resale in the near future; or

☐ Has activities very different from those of the parent, as a result of which its inclusion would not facilitate an understanding of the group's financial position or results of operations. This exemption is, however, available only if the subsidiary is a bank or finance entity subject to specific regulation.

Goodwill (Fondo de Comercio).   Where the purchase price exceeds net book value of net assets acquired, such excess may be allocated to the various assets up to their fair market value. The remaining excess is shown in the balance sheet as **goodwill** and amortized over a period not exceeding five years or, in exceptional circumstances and where justified in the notes, not exceeding ten years.

Negative goodwill is classified as a separate balance sheet item, below **minority interests.** It may be released to income only (a) to offset losses foreseen at the time of acquisition or (b) to the extent the underlying capital gain has been realized.

Transitional arrangements for a group's first consolidated financial statements permitted negative consolidation differences to be reported as shareholders' funds.

No guidance is given as to the basis for attribution of fair value to acquired assets, nor is any obligation imposed to obtain an independent professional valuation. It remains to be seen, therefore, how it will be treated in practice.

Equity Method (Metodo de Puesta en Equivalencia).   **Associated companies** must be accounted for under the **equity method**. An associated company is defined as one in which the reporting entity holds shares, with which it enjoys a lasting relationship and to whose development it contributes. A company is presumed to be associated when the reporting entity holds at least 20 percent of the share capital (voting rights), or only 3 percent if the company is quoted.

Proportional Method (Metodo de Integración Proporcional). The proportional method of accounting is also available under Spanish law for **joint ventures** with other companies managed jointly by the venturers (see Section 5). Such entities are referred to as "multigroup" companies. Under this method, the financial statements of the multigroup company are first consolidated with those of any subsidiaries it may have, then adjusted for elimination of intercompany items and to bring them into line with the accounting principles of the parent. The resulting financial statements are then reduced, line by line, to reflect the reporting entity's proportional interest in the company and then added, line by line, to its statements.

Treatment of Minority Interests. In the consolidated balance sheet, that part of the net worth of subsidiaries attributable to outside shareholders must be shown separately (net of any unpaid calls on capital), immediately below shareholders' equity. The minority's share of income is shown in the profit and loss account as a deduction from after-tax income. If the subsidiary has a deficiency in assets, the entire deficiency must be ascribed to the parent company, unless the minority has agreed to make good its part.

Disclosure. The notes must contain for all subsidiary, associated and multigroup companies, whether consolidated or not, details of that company, the nature of ownership, "reserves" held, consolidation treatment, the net worth and net income of associated companies, and details of payables and receivables with unconsolidated group companies. A separate analysis should be given by company of movements in the carrying value of companies accounted for by the equity method. Disclosure should also be made of the accounting policy for amortization of goodwill, and a schedule of movements in goodwill (with an analysis by originating investment) should be shown.

In addition, the following should be separately disclosed: shares of any company in the group that are quoted; movements in minority interests (by company); and the company's investment in its own shares (either directly or through any consolidated subsidiary or nominees).

Where there have been significant changes during a year in the composition of the group, the necessary information must be included in the notes to the accounts to enable suitable comparisons of the balance sheet, the profit and loss account and the statement of source and application of funds to be made.

Reference. BOICAC Issue 2; CCom Articles 25–49.

5. Joint Ventures

Accounting for Investments in Joint Ventures. For **jointly controlled** entities, if the joint venture is incorporated, the venturers account for it in their individual annual accounts as an investment, at the lower of cost and market. In the consolidated accounts (if any) of the venturers, the venture would generally be consolidated using the proportional method (see Section 4) or, alternatively, the equity method. The case of unincorporated joint ventures is less clear but, to the extent that the venture has no corporate identity, the venturers may incorporate into their financial statements the appropriate percentages of the venture's assets, liabilities, income and expenses, as in the case of **proportionate consolidation**.

For jointly controlled operations and jointly controlled assets, the accounting treatment in IAS 31 would be appropriate in Spain.

Transactions Between Venturers and the Joint Venture. The contribution of assets to a joint venture does not give rise to a gain on disposal in the contributor's financial statements. A loss would be recognizable on contribution to an incorporated joint venture where the deed of constitution attributed a lower value to the asset than its carrying value in the books of the contributor. This would not necessarily be the case if the venture was unincorporated. In accounting for other transactions between the venturers and the joint venture, the treatment would differ in the individual and consolidated accounts of the venturer according to whether the venture was incorporated or unincorporated, with preference for deferral of recognition of profit and immediate recognition of any loss.

Disclosure. For incorporated joint ventures, the notes to the consolidated financial statements must include the following:

☐ Name and address of joint venture.
☐ Amount of investment and percentage interest held.
☐ Method of accounting used (if equity, a justification is required).
☐ Activities of the joint venture.
☐ Names of other venturers.

If any joint ventures are excluded from consolidation, all of the above information is also required, together with the reason and justification for exclusion, and capital, reserves and results of the last available year.

Accounting by Joint Ventures. Accounting by unincorporated joint ventures is an unregulated area. Generally, it may be assumed that such joint ventures between SA companies would apply the accounting principles in the PGC, although there may be justification for applying fair values to assets contributed. In June 1992, the ICAC designated a task force to work on an adaptation of the PGC to regulate accounting and reporting by joint ventures.

Incorporated joint ventures would follow the accounting principles in the PGC.

Reference. Consolidation Rules—Memoria 2.

6. Foreign Currency Translation (Conversión de Divisas)

Foreign Operations. The **current rate method** is used, except where the operations of the foreign subsidiary are such that they constitute "a mere extension of the activities of one of the group's Spanish companies," in which case the **temporal method** is prescribed. Under the current rate method, assets and liabilities are translated at the closing exchange rate; the profit and loss account is translated at the actual (or average) rate. The resulting difference in the balance sheet is taken to an "exchange difference" reserve (diferencias de conversión). Under the temporal method, nonmonetary balance sheet items are translated at the historical rate, whereas the remaining items are translated at the closing rate. Translation differences, both positive and negative, are recorded in income in a special caption; alternatively, they may be treated in the same way as the parent company accounts for normal exchange differences.

Accounts of associated companies reported under the equity method are translated under the current rate method. Accounts of subsidiaries in highly inflationary countries should be translated under the temporal method or adjusted first in the foreign currency for changes in purchasing power.

Domestic Operations.   The PGC stipulates the method of translation for all balance sheet items denominated in foreign currencies. Fixed assets, stock and variable return investments are translated at historical rates. All other balance sheet items are translated at the year-end rate. Transactions in foreign currencies are recorded in pesetas either at the rate prevailing at the time of the transaction or at an average rate for the period.

The rules are complex, but fundamentally the net unrealized exchange differences are, if positive, deferred and, if negative, charged to income. If, however, losses have been expensed in prior years, a gain may be recorded up to the amount of the previously reported loss. Deferred gains are taken to income when realized or used to offset subsequent losses.

Subject to certain conditions, exchange differences on loans financing assets under construction may be capitalized.

Transitional Arrangements for Foreign Exchange Differences.   As a transitional measure, the PGC permits exchange differences that arose prior to January 1, 1990 to be written off over a period not exceeding three years or the duration of the operation that gave rise to them, if less.

Hedging Transactions.   Company law is silent on accounting for **hedging** transactions. It can be assumed that the minority of companies actually engaging in such transactions would account for them broadly along US lines.

Disclosure.   The translation policy for foreign subsidiaries must be disclosed, together with the treatment of translation differences, which should be shown separately for each foreign entity.

The basis of translation of balances denominated in foreign currencies must be disclosed, together with the policy for treatment of exchange differences. If assets and liabilities were originally recorded in a foreign currency, the basis of translation must similarly be disclosed.

As the standard profit and loss account format contains the captions for exchange profits and losses, the amounts recorded in income for the year must be disclosed, unless immaterial. Further, foreign currency lendings and borrowings (by currency), with details of hedging arrangements, must be disclosed.

Reference.   PGC Part 4.

7. Changing Prices/Inflation Accounting (Contabilidad para la Inflación)

General.   Spain has no requirement to publish inflation-adjusted financial information, and the practice is generally unknown.

8. Accounting Changes (Cambios en Criterios de Valoración)

Accounting Treatment.   The treatment in financial statements of a change in accounting policy is not regulated in company law. However, a number of accounting rules emphasize the principle of consistency, indicating that where an accounting policy has been adopted, it must be followed consistently.

As a transitional measure for the first financial year beginning after December 31, 1990, companies were allowed to adapt to the new accounting rules by charging the cumulative effect of changes in accounting policies directly to reserves in certain circumstances (see "Finance Lease" in Section 15).

Regarding restatement of comparative figures for the preceding year, the legal texts are open to different interpretations stating that "where they are not comparable, the preceding year's figures will be adjusted for the purpose of their presentation in the current year." It is thought that this requirement affects only reclassification to conform with current year presentation and does not imply restatement of previously reported results.

The cumulative effect at the beginning of the year of changes in accounting policies and methods should, in the author's view, be accounted for as extraordinary items (see Section 28) in the year of change; changes in accounting estimates should be accounted for prospectively, except for the transitional measures mentioned earlier.

Disclosure.   The notes must disclose the reason for the change and its effect on the financial statements. The CCom also requires an explanation in the notes if financial statements are not comparable with those of preceding years.

Reference.   CCom Articles 35 and 44; PGC Part 4.

9. Prior Period Adjustments (Gastos e Ingresos de Otros Fjercicios)

Definition of Adjusting Items.   It would appear that in no case should previously reported results or reserves be adjusted, although reclassifications not affecting equity of a prior year's financial statements should be made to conform with the current year's presentation. The standard PGC profit and loss account format incorporates prior period items as an element of extraordinary items (see Section 28) entering into the determination of current year income.

Accounting Treatment.   The PGC includes captions under the general heading of extraordinary items (resultados extraordinarios) for reflecting income and expense of prior years. Only material items should be reported under this caption; minor items should be classified as ordinary expense for the year. Prior year reported **retained earnings** are not adjusted.

Disclosure.   Adequate explanation is to be given of prior year items, which are shown separately in the income statement.

Reference.   CCom Article 35; PGC Part 4.

10.   Post Balance Sheet Events (Acontecimientos Posteriores al Cierre)

Definition.   Company law provides no definition of post balance sheet events, but classifies them in two categories:

(a)   Events that do not affect the accounts, but knowledge of which is useful to the user.

(b)   Events that affect the applicability of the going concern basis.

Accounting Treatment.   Financial statements should be prepared based on conditions existing at the balance sheet date. Information regarding such conditions that comes to light during the preparation of the financial statements should be taken into account. Other material events should be disclosed.

Disclosure.   Separate disclosure is required of information relating to any post balance sheet events that fall into either category (a) or (b) above.

Reference.   PGC Part 4.

11.   Related Party Transactions (Transacciones con Partes Vinculadas)

Definition.   No definition of related parties is given in the law, although specific disclosure of certain types of transactions is required.

Accounting Treatment.   Transactions with related parties are accounted for using the same principles as for nonrelated party transactions. For purposes of tax assessment, the inspectorate may restate transactions with related parties on an arm's-length basis.

Disclosure.   The only related parties for which disclosure is required are subsidiary, associated and multigroup companies, and directors of all companies included in the reporting entity.

For directors, disclosure is required of the amount of salary, fees and any other form of remuneration from all consolidated companies, for whatever reason, classified by type of remuneration; insurance premiums paid or the amount of any pension obligations (for present or former members), classified by type; and loans and advances (made by either the parent company or any consolidated company) together with related interest and any guarantee issued in their favor.

For subsidiaries, disclosure should be made of total transactions, classified by type (i.e., sales, purchases and related year-end rebates, services received or given, interest received or charged, dividends or other profit distributions). For associated companies, disclosure is required of the amount of receivables/payables falling due in each of the following five years and the balance thereafter, appearing under each of the statutory balance sheet captions for receivables and payables.

Reference. PGC Part 4; CCom Article 48.

12. Segmental Information (Información por Categoria de Actividades)

General. All companies are required to report segmental information by activity and geographical area. The criteria for an activity or a geographical area are subjective, based on the reporting entity's operations.

Segmental information may be omitted if its publication could prejudice the entity or if the entity may publish an abbreviated profit and loss account.

Disclosure. The notes must present a breakdown of turnover by activity and geographical area.

Reference. PGC Part 4; LSA Article 200.

ACCOUNTING PRINCIPLES FOR SPECIFIC ITEMS— BALANCE SHEET

13. Property, Plant and Equipment (Inmovilizaciones Materiales)

Classification of Capital and Revenue Expenditure. No specific guidance is given for determining whether to capitalize or expense an expenditure, and in practice tax criteria have prevailed to date. The definition of assets to be recorded in specific PGC accounts gives some guidance, as does the section on accounting principles (normas de valoración). However, many grey areas remain.

Basis of Valuation. Company law explicitly states that the only basis for the carrying value of **fixed assets** is cost, with the single exception of legal "actualizations" (see below). However, in the past many businesses that have experienced continuing losses have revalued assets, crediting the surplus to the profit and loss account, rather than see the tax losses expire or become statute-barred. In recognition of the acquired rights of companies that had recorded such "voluntary revaluations" of assets prior to December 31, 1989, the amount recorded in the books at that date is regarded as "equivalent to cost." Accordingly, the carrying value of assets may be cost, "actualization" or revaluation, depending on the circumstances.

Write-downs of assets (other than normal **depreciation**) are unusual, although contemplated in the PGC. They must be reported separately in the profit and loss account and a provision set up until such time as the loss in value proves permanent, when they are written off against the asset.

On disposal of assets, the cost and accumulated depreciation accounts are adjusted and the profit or loss on sale is recorded in income as an extraordinary item (see Section 28).

Actualization (Actualización). Actualization, although now of decreasing significance, is a means of compensating businesses for the erosive effects of inflation. The government has, from time to time (most recently in 1979, 1981 and 1983), enacted legislation permitting optional revaluation of fixed assets by the application of specified coefficients based on the acquisition date of the assets and related annual depreciation. Revaluations were credited to an actualization (revaluation) reserve that was part of shareholders' equity.

Application of the coefficients was legally subject to the overriding condition that the resulting carrying value not exceed the "real" value of the asset. In practice, however, most businesses applied the full coefficient without regard to that criterion, in order to maximize the benefit of future tax-deductible depreciation expense. There was no requirement to maintain separate cost and "actualized" data, so that it would not be possible to reconstruct the historical cost and cost-based depreciation from accounting records. In addition, since most small and medium-sized Spanish businesses did not maintain fixed asset registers, the law permitted the coefficients to be applied to "homogeneous groups of assets."

The final use of the actualization reserve, after approval by the tax inspectorate or the lapse of a stated time, was specified in the legislation. Although capitalization was encouraged by exemption from related capital transfer tax, earlier actualization laws permitted the transfer of the actualization reserve to voluntary reserves and, hence, its distribution in the form of dividends.

Thus, although with the passing of time, growth, inflation and the depreciation or sale of revalued assets, actualization surpluses are of diminishing importance, there remain nondistributable reserves or parts of share capital that have their origin in a revaluation.

Meanwhile, the government of the Autonomous Basque Region passed a law in 1990, applicable only to companies in the Basque Region, permitting actualization. Although many companies availed themselves of this possibility, the constitutionality of this law is being challenged by the central government.

Depreciation.   Under the company law reform, companies are now required to allow for depreciation at rates calculated to write the cost of an asset down to its estimated **net realizable value** at the end of its economically useful life.

The depreciation method used is almost universally the **straight-line method** (subject to the variations explained below), although the reducing **(declining) balance method** is also acceptable.

As many medium-sized Spanish businesses lack detailed fixed asset registers, depreciation charges are often calculated on total acquisitions in each year.

Depreciation has traditionally been an area of conflict between tax law and the true and fair view concept. Many companies will probably continue to apply fiscal rates of depreciation that, while generally adequate, are by international standards low for such items as motor vehicles and EDP equipment.

Tax law contains tables of maximum depreciable lives and maximum depreciation rates for all types of industries and assets. Considerable latitude was allowed, provided that the expense in any one year did not exceed the maximum rate and that the asset was fully written off by the end of the maximum life. Any depreciation expense not meeting these criteria is not tax deductible, but provided the criteria are met, there is no obligation to apply the rate consistently. Consequently, in many companies, the charge for depreciation has in the past been a function of the "bottom line." Although this practice is tending to disappear, in those companies, the net book value of fixed assets will for some years vary, possibly materially, from amounts that would have arisen under more standard and consistent depreciation methods.

Disclosure.   A movements schedule must be presented for all tangible fixed asset accounts. Depreciation rates and, for each class of assets, details regarding assets acquired from group companies should be disclosed. A new disclosure, which may be difficult for many businesses to comply with, is the requirement to indicate the net unamortized portion of earlier revaluations or "actualizations" and the revaluation-related amortization charge for the year.

Other disclosure requirements include the cost and accumulated depreciation of assets located abroad; the amount of any interest expense or exchange differences capitalized during the year; cost and accumulated depreciation of assets not used in operations; nature and amount of assets fully amortized, technically obsolete or not in use; assets subject to any mortgage, lien or reversion; firm purchase (and sale) commitments for fixed assets and expected sources of financing; and any other relevant information (such as rental of premises, insurance, lawsuits and embargoes).

Reference.   PGC Part 5; LSA Article 195.

14.   Intangible Assets (Inmovilizaciones Inmateriales)

Accounting Treatment.   In general, **intangible assets** are recorded at cost, and, except where they conflict with specific rules, the same rules apply as for tangible fixed assets. Cost may include capitalization of internal costs, if applicable. Treatments of specific types of intangible assets are as follows:

☐   Patents and trademarks (Propiedad industrial)—This heading includes any amounts paid for the ownership or right to use patents or trademarks. It also includes any research and development expenses, together with any registration or similar costs. All of those costs are capitalized under this heading once the patent/trademark is registered. No **amortization** rules are mentioned in the PGC but, in practice, they will be the same as for research and development (see Section 25).

☐   Lease premiums (Derechos de traspaso)—Lease premiums are recorded at cost and written off over the period in which they contribute to the generation of income.

☐   Software—Software is recorded at cost and amortized as a research and development expense (see Section 25). Software maintenance may not be capitalized. The cost of producing software in house may be capitalized "only in cases where it is expected to be used over various years."

☐   Preliminary, formation and capital increase expenses (Gastos de establecimiento, de constitución y de ampliación de capital)—These are reported as startup expenses, a deferred expense, rather than as intangible fixed assets. Preliminary expenses are defined as the cost of initial technical and economic viability studies, launching publicity, initial recruitment and training of personnel. Formation expenses are defined as the legal and fiscal costs of incorporation; costs of printing share certificates, prospectuses and similar items; and related publicity expense. Similar types of cost arising from increases in share capital are also included in this heading. Such expenses must be amortized systematically over a period not exceeding five years. While unamortized expenses of this kind remain in the balance sheet, distribution of profits is restricted (see Section 22).

☐   Goodwill (Fondo de comercio)—Goodwill can be included as an asset only when it has been acquired for valuable consideration. It must be depreciated over its useful life, with a maximum of ten years. Where the period of depreciation exceeds five years, justification for the excess period must be included in the notes to the accounts.

□ Loan formalization expenses (Gastos de formalización de deudas)—Loan formalization expenses are reported as a deferred expense, rather than as intangible assets. Expensing in the year incurred is encouraged, but they may be amortized over the life of the loan.

The PGC also includes as intangible fixed assets leasing rights (see Section 15), research and development expenditures (see Section 25) and payments in advance on intangible assets.

Disclosure. A movements schedule is required for each category of intangible assets, and explanatory information must be given on material items.

Reference. PGC Parts 4 and 5; LSA Articles 194 and 195.

15. Leases (Arrendamiento Financiero)

Classification. The PGC is deliberately vague on the treatment of leased assets, indicating merely that "where it is evident from the economic terms of a leasing arrangement that it is an acquisition, it must be accounted for as such under intangible assets."

The ICAC has provided guidance on the subject, to the effect that an asset acquired under a lease may be considered a finance lease and capitalized provided:

□ The leasing contract includes an option to purchase.
□ There is "no reasonable doubt" that such an option will be exercised.

The following examples of "no reasonable doubt" are given:

□ When at the time of signing the contract, the option to purchase is less than the estimated value of the asset at the time of exercising the option.
□ When the option price at the time of signing the contract is insignificant with respect to the total lease contract amount.

Accounting Treatment in Financial Statements of Lessees. Finance lease: Total instalments due under a **finance lease** are credited to appropriate long- and short-term **creditors (accounts payable)**, the cash cost of the item is capitalized as an intangible asset in account 217, "rights over leased assets," and the balance is recorded as deferred interest. The asset cost is amortized normally, and the deferred interest is written off to expense as each instalment is paid on a financial basis (e.g., sum-of-the-digits).

Before the reform, lease payments were almost universally expensed as paid.

Transitional arrangements for finance leases in effect at the beginning of the first financial year commencing after December 31, 1990 provided that companies could, at their option, either capitalize finance lease assets retroactively, with an adjustment to reserves, or continue to expense the lease payments as incurred.

Operating lease: Rental payments for **operating leases** should be expensed as incurred.

Sale and leaseback operations: If in substance a sale and leaseback transaction is a financing operation, it must be reported as a loan. No further guidance is given in this area.

Disclosure.   The accounting policy used for assets acquired under finance leases must be disclosed. For all leases, disclosure must be made of the original cost, contract duration (including years expired), purchase option price and total leasing payments (shown separately for amounts paid in prior periods, paid during the year and outstanding).

Accounting Treatment in Financial Statements of Lessors.   Leased assets, whether subject to finance or operating leases, are separately identified in the balance sheet under the property, plant and equipment caption and depreciated on either the straight-line or financial basis (e.g., **sum-of-the-digits**).

The total future leasing payments are recorded immediately in the customer account, with a credit to a deferred interest account and the balance to the future leasing instalments account. As each payment is made, an appropriate portion of the deferred interest account is released to income. At the same time, an amount equivalent to the balance of the payment is released from the future leasing instalments account. When a financial method is used for depreciation of the asset, the monthly charge is equivalent to the amount released from the future leasing instalments account. As stated, however, the lessor has the alternative of recording depreciation on a straight-line basis, in which case losses would be reported in the earlier months of the contract.

Disclosure.   The accounting policy for assets sold under leasing arrangements must be disclosed. The assets subject to leasing are disclosed separately from operating assets and by appropriate category. Both the receivable and the future leasing instalments accounts must be analyzed by the year in which they fall due.

Leveraged Leases.   **Leveraged leases** are very uncommon in Spain and no specific pronouncement exists in this area.

Reference.   PGC Parts 4 and 5; AECA Documento 2.

16.   Investments (Inmovilizaciones e Inversiones Financieras)

Valuation.   Treatment of long- and short-term investments is similar. Both are reported at the lower of cost or market value. Cost includes costs of acquisition and purchase of subscription rights. Where subscription rights attaching to shares are sold, the cost of such rights reduces the carrying value of the shares. Market value is the lower of the year-end quotation or the average quotation for the last quarter. In determining the market value of unquoted investments, "reasonable" criteria should be used. In comparing cost with market value of fixed interest securities, accrued interest should be considered. Special accounting rules apply to **treasury stock** (own shares held), which are dealt with in Section 22.

Treatment of Valuation Reserve.   The amount of any necessary provisions to reduce the carrying value of investments to market value must be shown in the profit and loss account separately for long- and short-term investments. Any provision established in this connection may not be carried forward when the conditions dictating its creation cease to exist.

Gains/Losses.   The difference between the net book value and the selling price of an investment is recognized in income when the investment is sold. There is no rule for determining cost on a partial sale, but generally the practice would be to follow tax rules and use **average cost**. The profit or loss so determined is reported as an extraordinary item.

Disclosure.   A schedule showing the movements of investments, by account category, should be provided. In addition, the notes are required to present detailed disclosures related to investments, such as any associated pledges or commitments, the currencies of issue, hedging arrangements, maturity dates and yields.

Reference.   PGC Parts 4 and 5.

17.   Accounts Receivable (Deudores)

Accounting Treatment.   Receivables are recorded at their face value; any necessary provisions, such as for noncollection, are shown separately.

Recognition: The recognition of **revenue**, and hence the related receivable, is as described in Section 23.

Discounts and rebates: Cash discounts are relatively infrequent, but are accounted for when payment is made. Year-end rebates for achieving target levels of purchases are more frequent, and separate provision is made. Trade discounts are deducted on the face of the invoice and the sale recorded net.

Allowances: No specific method of calculating the provision for doubtful accounts is prescribed in the PGC.

Tax legislation is very specific in this area. Only the following are tax deductible:

□   Receivables from customers in receivership.

□   Receivables from slow-paying customers, either according to established parameters (25 percent of debts older than six months, 50 percent of debts older than one year and 100 percent of debts older than two years) or a general one-half percent provision.

Factored Receivables (Factoring).   **Factoring of receivables** is not common in Spain, but the discounting of receivables with banks is widespread. Most commercial transactions are for settlement in 90 days, and the most common means of settlement is by "letra," an unaccepted bill of exchange drawn by the supplier and generally negotiated with the bank for immediate use of the funds. At maturity it is processed through the clearing system and presented to the customer. If it is not honored, the bank has recourse to the supplier, whose account is debited. The PGC requires the recognition of the substance of the transaction; that is, the transaction should be accounted for as a bank loan secured against future cash flows, and **accounts receivable** should not be credited until the customer makes payment. In almost all cases, the up-front interest charge on discounting is not apportioned between accounting periods, although this treatment does not strictly conform with the matching principle.

Disclosure.   Standard captions in the PGC require separate disclosure of trade receivables (third parties); accounts receivable from group and associated companies; sundry **debtors**; employees; state entities; and advances received from customers.

Provisions for doubtful accounts and other allowances must be separately disclosed, as must the charge for the year, split between increases in the provision and write-offs.

Reference.   PGC Parts 3, 4 and 5.

18.   Inventories (Existencias)

General Accounting Treatment.   Under the PGC, **inventory** is categorized as follows:

- ☐   Goods purchased for resale without processing.
- ☐   Finished goods manufactured by the company and ready for sale.
- ☐   Work in progress, whatever its stage of manufacture, where destined for incorporation into finished products.
- ☐   Raw materials for incorporation into the production process.
- ☐   Other supplies, such as fuel, lubricants, packing materials and spares, that do not fall into any of the foregoing categories, plus salable scrap and byproducts.
- ☐   Provisions (such as for obsolescence).
- ☐   Advances to suppliers for purchase of inventory items.

Valuation.   Inventory is valued at the lower of cost or market value. The cost of purchased raw materials includes direct expenses incurred to the point at which the goods enter the warehouse (such as transportation, customs duties and insurance), but excludes interest, storage and other internal expenses. Cost of items manufactured by the company includes all direct costs plus certain production overheads.

The PGC implies that the preferred method of valuation is specific identification, but when this is impractical, weighted average should be used. In addition, **FIFO, LIFO** "or other analogous methods are acceptable if the reporting entity considers them more appropriate." Previously, LIFO had been unacceptable for financial reporting and remains so for tax purposes. Certain inventories, such as spares, may be carried at a fixed amount provided that they move quickly, the overall value and the composition do not fluctuate to any great extent and the amount is not material to the accounts. Where this approach is used, it must be explained and justified in the notes.

Market value of goods purchased from third parties is their replacement value or net realizable value, if less. Market value of manufactured items is their net realizable value. For work in progress, market value is defined as the net realizable value of the related finished product less costs to be incurred in its completion.

Long-Term Contracts.   The method of valuation of long-term contracts is not prescribed by legislation, although it is understood that the ICAC is developing a specialized industry Accounting Chart that will regulate this area. At present, the **percentage of completion method** is widely, though loosely, followed, while the **completed contract method** is also utilized because of the implicit deferral of tax outflows. The AECA stipulates the percentage of completion method. Balance sheet presentation of long-term contracts and associated accounts, such as advances, billings and accrued profit, is not regulated and there is no clear prevalent practice.

Disclosure.   The basis of valuation of inventory and the method of determining provisions for obsolescence should be disclosed. In the balance sheet, there should be separate presentation of the different types of inventory listed above, followed by any related provisions for obsolescence. The profit and loss account must also show separately the purchases made during the year, together with the changes in inventory and provisions for obsolescence. It should be noted that the PGC profit and loss account format does not disclose (or permit calculation of) a cost of goods sold figure. Other disclosures include details of significant purchase and sales agreements, and details (with values) of any charges or liens on inventory or goods on consignment.

There are no specific disclosure requirements for long-term contracts.

Reference.   PGC Parts 4 and 5.

19.   Current Liabilities (Pasivo Circulante)

Accounting Treatment.   **Current liabilities**, as defined by the PGC, include short-term loans and debts arising from the purchase of services or goods. The criterion for long-term/short-term distinction is now 12 months (under the old PGC, it was 18 months). The PGC provides specific captions for the presentation of liabilities whose maturity exceeds 12 months. Liabilities must be reflected at their face value. Accrued liabilities are reflected in a separate caption. Income received in advance (deferred income) is recognized as income when it accrues; until that time, it is shown as a long- or short-term liability.

Loans are shown at the amount drawn down; any undrawn balance is disclosed in a note.

Generally, proposed dividends are not provided for in the accounts, but there is an obligation to disclose them in the notes.

Creation of General and Specific Provisions.   Previously, a general provision "for risks and responsibilities," disclosed between shareholders' equity and long-term debt in the balance sheet, was largely unregulated and the risks it covered were rarely disclosed. Under the new PGC its use is restricted to specific, certain or probable risks; in addition to information on the risks covered, a movements schedule must be provided. General provisions are therefore no longer permitted.

Disclosure.   The format of the standard PGC balance sheet provides for separate disclosure, where material, of the short-term portion of debentures (split between convertible, nonconvertible, other debt and accrued interest), borrowings (loans and accrued interest), related party liabilities, commercial **creditors** (customer advances, trade creditors and debts represented by bills of exchange), nontrade creditors (state entities, debts represented by bills of exchange, accrued payroll, short-term deposits and others), provisions for guarantees and sales returns, accrued expenses and short-term deferred income. In addition, details of significant purchase commitments, circumstances that might give rise to lawsuits and details of guaranteed liabilities should be disclosed.

Reference. PGC Parts 4 and 5.

20. Long-Term Debt (Acreedores a Largo Plazo)

Accounting Treatment. Long-term debt is reported at the amount at which it is to be repaid, including premium, if any. The discount on issuance plus the repayment premium, if any, are reported as a deferred charge and are written off on a suitable basis.

Companies are encouraged to write off expenses of issuance in the year incurred, although "exceptionally" they may be written off over the life of the issue.

Any portion of loan principal repayable within 12 months of the balance sheet date is classified as a current liability. Under the 1973 PGC, the criterion was 18 months, and reclassification of the short-term portion to current liabilities was not permitted.

Debt Restructuring/Extinguishment (Restructuración y Amortización Anticipada de Deuda). Neither company law nor the AECA has dealt with this subject. Previously, the accounting treatment of such transactions would have been primarily dictated by tax considerations.

Disclosure. The standard balance sheet format requires separate disclosure of 14 different categories of debt, distinguishing among various types of debentures, loans, bills of exchange and other debt arrangements. The amount of principal repayable should be analyzed for each of the following five years and the total amount thereafter for each debt category; the total should be broken down by group, associated and other companies.

In addition, disclosure is required of the amount of unpaid accrued interest; details of mortgages securing debt; details of each issue of debentures or bonds (such as interest rate, repayment date, security given and conversion particulars); and details of unused lines of credit.

Reference. LSA Article 197; PGC Parts 4 and 5.

21. Contingent Liabilities (Pasivos Contingentes)

General Accounting Treatment. Accounting law gives little guidance on the treatment of loss **contingencies** and is silent on gain contingencies. Most quoted companies appear to have been broadly following US principles.

Disclosure. The amounts of any guarantees given with respect to third parties must be disclosed, analyzed by type of guarantee and broken down by group, associated and other companies. For each, the amount, if any, provided in the accounts must be disclosed.

Generally, for each contingency, there must be disclosure of its nature, the basis on which it is evaluated, factors on which it depends and its potential impact on net worth or an explanation of why it cannot be quantified, indicating maximum and minimum risks.

Reference. PGC Part 4.

22. Capital and Reserves (Fondos Propios)

General.   Capital and reserves constitute the shareholders' contribution to the financing of operations. In Spain, the minimum capital for an SA is Ptas. 10 million. The PGC contemplates shareholders' equity being divided into **share capital**, **share premium**, legal reserve, reserves for the purchase of its own (or parent company) shares, reserves from retained earnings, and profit or loss for the year less dividends paid on account during the year.

Share Capital (Capital Social).   Businesses incorporated under the LSA may issue shares in either registered or bearer form; shares issued in the latter form must be fully paid. Shares must have a **par value**, expressed in pesetas. A company's share capital may consist of different classes of shares, each with differing voting, dividend and capital repayment rights. Unpaid capital is shown as an asset, representing the company's rights against the shareholders. Uncalled amounts are shown above (i.e., as less liquid than) fixed assets, while called but unpaid amounts are shown as the first item in current assets.

No company may subscribe to its own shares or to those of its parent on issuance, but may acquire them on the market subsequently, provided that (a) they are fully paid; (b) the holding does not exceed 10 percent; and (c) the acquisition is authorized by the parent company in a general meeting.

Share Premium (Reserva de Prima de Emisión).   The share premium account is credited with the proceeds in excess of par value of new share issues. The law imposes no restriction on its use, merely indicating that it may be used to increase capital.

Legal Reserve (Reserva Legal).   Company law requires that 10 percent of the net profit in each year be appropriated to this reserve until such time as the balance equals 20 percent of the share capital. This reserve is not available for distribution (except to the extent that it exceeds 20 percent of share capital) but may be used to offset losses where no other reserves are available. It may also be used to increase capital, but only if, after the increase, the balance of the reserve is not less than 10 percent of the new capital.

Reserves (for Purchase of Own, or Related Company, Shares).   A company may not subscribe on issuance for either its own shares or shares issued by its parent company.

A company may, however, acquire its own shares or those of its parent company provided the following conditions are met:

☐ Acquisition is approved by a shareholders' meeting that sets the maximum and minimum price, maximum number of shares that can be acquired and the duration of the authority, which cannot exceed 18 months.

☐ The nominal value of the shares acquired, including those already held by the company and its subsidiaries, may not exceed 10 percent of share capital (5 percent if shares are quoted).

☐ The shares acquired have been fully paid up.

☐ A reserve must be created without reducing capital or undistributable reserves equal to the carrying value of the company's own shares or of the shares of the parent company. Such a reserve must be maintained until the shares are sold.

Crossholdings of shares also give rise to the obligation to set up a reserve. Thus, if a company (''A'') acquires, directly or indirectly, more than 10 percent of the shares in another (''B''), it must immediately notify that other company of the fact. Where crossholdings in excess of 10 percent arise involuntarily, the company that is first notified of the fact (say, B) must reduce its holding in the company issuing the notification (in this case A) below 10 percent. Until it has disposed of the excess, B must set up a ''reserve for crossholdings'' equal to the cost of that part of its holding in A that exceeds 10 percent. The reserve may be released when the excess is disposed of.

The transfers to and from the reserves listed above are recorded in one of the distributable reserves.

Dividends Paid on Account (Dividendo a Cuenta).   Dividends paid on account during the year are shown separately on the face of the balance sheet as a deduction under capital and reserves. (Proposed dividends are not recognized as a liability but disclosed by note.) Where a dividend has been paid on account, the notes must include an ''accounting forecast'' covering the 12 months from payment. The nature of this forecast is undefined.

Disclosure.   Details of authorized and issued share capital, including rights associated with founders' shares and convertible debentures, with a schedule of movements during the period should be provided. If capital is increased, details of the shares issued should be given. The amount of any authorized and unissued capital and restrictions on distribution of reserves should also be disclosed. The notes should disclose details of own shares held, directly or indirectly, indicating their ultimate use and amount of reserve. Holdings in excess of 10 percent of a reporting entity's capital should be disclosed.

Distribution Restrictions.   Companies may distribute shares out of the post-tax profits reflected in the official books of account unless:

☐   The distribution would reduce the remaining reserves to an amount less than the sum of the unamortized balance of preliminary and formation expenses plus research and development expenses (see Sections 14 and 25); or

☐   The actualization reserve (see Section 13) remains in the balance sheet, in which case dividends must not be distributed of such an amount as would reduce remaining reserves to an amount less than those exisiting at December 31, 1983.

Reference.   LSA Articles 49–54, 75–84, 157 and 214; BOICAC No. 2; and PGC Part 4.

ACCOUNTING PRINCIPLES FOR SPECIFIC ITEMS— INCOME STATEMENT

23.   Revenue Recognition (Reconocimiento de Ingresos)

General Principles.   Income is recorded when a service has been provided, the transfer of ownership in an asset has been effected or the right to the income arises. Normally, in the case of sale of goods, the time of recognition of income is on delivery of the goods. In the case of income from services, income is recognized when the services are completed. Income is recorded at its gross amount, and deductions for discounts or other rebates are shown separately. Interest income must be shown separately.

Long-Term Contracts. Revenue recognition for long-term contracts is described in Section 18.

Instalment Sales (Ventas a Plazo). Receivables on **instalment sales** are recorded at face value. If a credit sale extends over more than 12 months, the interest element is credited to a deferred income account and written back to income on a financial basis (e.g., sum-of-the-digits).

Rights of Return (Ventas con Derecho de Devolución). Sales where a right of return exists are generally recorded as firm sales, and appropriate provision is made for probable returns. No specific requirements exist, however, in this area.

Product Financing. **Product financing arrangements** are infrequent in Spain, and no accounting treatment is specified.

Disclosure. The principal income captions in the profit and loss account distinguish between income arising from the sale of goods or the provision of services, deductions for rebates and returns, investment income (various categories), profit on translation or conversion, extraordinary income, work on own assets and increases in inventory of finished and in-process stock.

The effect on income of any change in valuation criteria or method of presentation of income should also be shown.

Reference. AECA Documento 13; PGC Parts 4 and 5.

24. Government Grants and Assistance (Subvenciones Recibidas)

Accounting Treatment. Nonreimbursable capital grants (i.e., grants whose conditions have been fulfilled or where there is no reasonable doubt as to their being fulfilled) are generally deferred in a special balance sheet caption and written off to income at the same rate as the related assets. It is also theoretically possible to credit the entire grant against the cost of the related asset.

In addition to capital grants in cash, there are also operating grants, grants of land and total or partial relief from state or local taxes. All such grants are accounted for as a reduction of the related expense.

Disclosure. The amount, description and conditions attaching to subsidies and grants received, the unamortized balance, amount amortized during the period and accounting policy used must be disclosed. If the grant assists the purchase of property, plant and equipment, details of the grant must be provided under that caption.

Reference. PGC Part 4.

25. Research and Development (Investigación y Desarrollo)

Definitions of Research and Development Expenses. Research and development expenses are defined as expenses incurred for the purpose of improving technological and scientific know-how, perfection of new applications, improvement of the business or similar activity. As long as unamortized cost of this type remains in the balance sheet, distribution of profits is restricted as set out in Section 22.

Accounting Treatment. Research and development expenditures may be capitalized when:

☐ The projects are specifically identified and costs clearly defined so that they may be amortized.

☐ There is good reason to believe that the projects will be successful and the product profitable.

Amortization should be over as short a period as possible, with a maximum of five years from the end of the development project. If any doubt as to the commercial viability of the project arises, costs must be expensed immediately. When the process or product becomes protected by patent or otherwise, the related deferred costs should be transferred to the caption patents and trademarks (propiedad industrial); see Section 14.

Disclosure. A schedule of movements of the research and development account should be provided, and the criteria followed for the deferral and amortization disclosed.

Reference. PGC Parts 4 and 5.

26. Capitalized Interest Costs (Intereses Capitalizados)

Accounting Treatment. In the case of inventories, the general rule is that interest must not be capitalized. In the case of fixed assets, purchase cost may include interest accrued prior to the date of the asset becoming ready to be put into use. The amount of interest capitalized is restricted to interest charged by the supplier and interest and commissions on loans for financing the acquisition.

Disclosure. The interest capitalization policy and the amount capitalized during the year should be disclosed.

Reference. PGC Parts 4 and 5.

27. Imputed Interest (Intereses Imputados)

Accounting Treatment. Debt is stated at the amount at which it is to be repaid, and any excess over the actual proceeds of the loan is reported as deferred interest and written off to expense on a financial basis (e.g., sum-of-the-digits). While there is no specific requirement to write down loans or other long-term debt to net present value where agreements are entered into at lower-than-market rates of interest, this might be required on occasion in order to present a true and fair view.

Disclosure. The method of recognizing **imputed interest** must be disclosed. In addition, disclosure of the net amount outstanding and interest rate imputed would appear to be required under the caption "any other significant information."

Reference. PGC Parts 4 and 5.

28. Extraordinary or Unusual Items (Resultados Extraordinarios)

Definition. Terminology used for extraordinary items in Spain may be confusing, as two levels of extraordinary items are reported. Under the PGC, virtually all items of income and expense not relating to operating and financing activities are identified separately as extraordinary (resultados extraordinarios), on both the income and expense sides of the profit and loss account. "Resultados extraordinarios" include the following captions:

☐ Extraordinary results—positive:
  —Profit on sale of fixed assets.
  —Profit on dealings in own shares.
  —Grants transferred to income.
  —Extraordinary income.
  —Prior year items.
☐ Extraordinary results—negative:
  —Asset write-downs.
  —Loss on sale of fixed assets.
  —Loss on dealings in own shares.
  —Extraordinary expenses.
  —Prior year items.

As may be seen, within the above there are further specific captions for extraordinary income and expenses. These should record "those profits or losses of material amount which a user or reader of the financial statement would consider nonrecurring when estimating likely future results of operations." Generally, an income or expense is considered an extraordinary item if it originates from events or transactions that are outside the normal activities of the business and there is a reasonable expectation that they will not recur with frequency. The PGC gives various examples of transactions to be recorded as extraordinary items, such as losses arising from flood, fire or other accidents; costs of an unsuccessful takeover bid; fines; fiscal and legal penalties; and recovery of receivables previously considered irrecoverable. The list is not all-inclusive.

Disclosure. Apart from disclosure in specific captions of the income statement as described above, an explanation of the nature of any type of extraordinary income or expense should be given.

Reference. PGC Account Definitions of Part 4.

29. Income Taxes (Impuesto Sobre Sociedadas)

Accounting Treatment. Prior to the company law reform, income tax was treated for financial reporting purposes as a distribution of profit, and the amount, if disclosed, appeared only as part of the directors' proposal for distribution of profits. The new PGC, however, requires that income tax be accounted for as an expense and the liability disclosed on the balance sheet.

Deferred taxes are recognized under the **liability method**, and deferred tax assets are carried forward only to the extent that their recovery is reasonably assured. To date, deferred tax accounting has been practiced in Spain only by entities reporting to foreign parents or overseas stock exchanges; when appropriate, relevant overseas or international accounting principles have been applied. Therefore, the precise methods by which the liability method will be applied are unknown. There is, however, no explicit relief permitting the nonprovision for liabilities that are not expected to reverse in the foreseeable future. The full provision method, therefore, is likely to be used.

The recognition of deferred tax assets arising from loss carryforwards, tax credits and on-account payments is contemplated in the PGC, but they may be carried forward only if their recovery is "reasonably assured."

Tax losses may, subject to approval, be offset against profits for the succeeding five tax years. However, there is no provision in Spanish tax law for carryback (even on liquidation). Benefit for a tax loss is generally taken to the extent, and in the year, it is offset; the effect of the offset is disclosed in a note rather than as an extraordinary item.

Disclosure. Disclosure should include a reconciliation of the reported pretax income and taxable income, details of tax loss carryforwards and tax incentives/credits (including commitments therefor) and any other material information relating to the tax position (such as which years are open to inspection by the tax authorities—a major factor in assessing the financial position of a Spanish company). A schedule analyzing movement in the deferred tax provision should be shown.

Reference. PGC Parts 4 and 5.

30. Postretirement Benefits (Pensiones y Obligaciones Similares)

Accounting Treatment. The requirement for recognition in the financial statements of the future liability for retirement benefits is recent in Spain and, consequently, the accounting rules are relatively undeveloped. The PGC provides an account entitled "provision for pensions and other liabilities," under which should be reported sums set aside to cover legal or contractual pension obligations.

As a transitional arrangement, companies that at their year-end immediately preceding January 1, 1990 had incurred pension obligations are required to quantify the related actuarial liability at that date and to amortize it as follows:

□ Portion relating to active employees — over 15 years.
□ Portion relating to retired employees — over seven years.

In both cases, the method of amortization must be "systematic" (i.e., in most cases, straight line).

Some confusion in the area of accounting for the pension liability not provided for as of January 1, 1990 was introduced by an order of the ICAC of June 30, 1991, which, while specifically relating only to electrical utilities, set out in its preamble certain principles of generalized application. The prime objective of the order was to extend the above transitional periods to 20 and 10 years, respectively; however, it introduced the principle that the annual amortization should be charged to reserves to the extent possible and, only where those are insufficient, to profit for the year. The preamble to the order raised this to a principle to be applied in other business enterprises, but it is not known to what extent reporting entities outside the electrical sector will seek to apply it.

The requirement to account for postretirement benefits mentions only pensions. It may be assumed that other benefits should be similarly accounted for but, in the absence of explicit requirements, it is doubtful whether this is extensively followed in practice.

Pension Fund Surpluses.   In the past, pension costs were not accounted for under the accrual concept. The PGC states that any "excess provision" is to be credited to other operating income.

Disclosure.   In addition to the accounting policy, "a general description of the method of calculation" of the liability must be disclosed. A schedule of movements on the pension provision should also be given.

Reference.   PGC Part 5 and Transitional Provisions.

31.   Discontinued Operations (Actividades Abandonadas)

Accounting law does not specify any treatment for discontinued operations. Similarly, no pronouncement has been issued by the AECA.

32.   Earnings per Share (Beneficio por Acción)

There is no requirement in Spain to present earnings per share data and it is not a common disclosure.

Appendix
DO SPANISH STANDARDS OR PREVALENT PRACTICE SUBSTANTIALLY COMPLY WITH INTERNATIONAL ACCOUNTING STANDARDS?

Section	Topic	Substantially complies with IAS?	Comments
3.	Basic accounting concepts and conventions	Yes	
	Contents of financial statements	Yes	
4.	Business combinations*	Yes	
5.	Joint ventures	Yes	
6.	Foreign currency translation*	Yes	
8.	Accounting changes*	Yes	
9.	Prior period adjustments*	Yes	
10.	Post balance sheet events	Yes	
11.	Related party transactions	No	The definition of related party and the extent of disclosure are more limited than in IAS 24
12.	Segmental information	No	Industry and geographical analysis is required for sales only
13.	Property, plant and equipment*	Yes	
15.	Leases	Yes	
16.	Investments	Yes	
17.	Accounts receivable	Yes	
18.	Inventories and work in progress*	Yes	
19.	Current liabilities	Yes	
20.	Long-term debt	Yes	
21.	Contingencies	Yes	Except that there is no disclosure of contingent gains
22.	Capital and reserves	Yes	
23.	Revenue recognition*	Yes	
24.	Government grants and assistance	Yes	
25.	Research and development*	Yes	

Appendix (*Continued*)

Section	Topic	Substantially complies with IAS?	Comments
26.	Capitalization of interest costs*	Yes	
28.	Extraordinary or unusual items*	No	The range of items that may be classified as extraordinary is wider than is permitted by IAS 8
29.	Income tax**	Yes	Except that disclosure of the tax effect of unusual items, prior period items and changes in accounting policy is not required
30.	Postretirement benefits*	Yes	Except that transitional arrangements for unamortized past service costs at the time the standard came into force are different from IAS 19

*These topics are subject to change as a result of the IASC Improvements Project—see the appendix to the International Accounting Standards chapter.
**The IAS on accounting for taxes on income is currently being revised, and an exposure draft has been issued.

Comparison in this table is made to International Accounting Standards in force at January 1, 1993. For further details, see the International Accounting Standards chapter.

SWEDEN

GENERAL NATIONAL INFORMATION

1. Source of Generally Accepted Accounting Principles

Generally Accepted Accounting Principles. **Generally accepted accounting principles** in Sweden are derived from the following sources:

☐ The Swedish Accounting Act (Bokföringslagen 1974:125, BL), which establishes general accounting requirements for private-sector entities.

☐ The Swedish Companies Act (Aktiebolagslagen 1975:1385, AL), which sets forth accounting regulations for corporate annual reports, consolidated accounts, interim reports, appropriations and dividend distribution, and audit requirements.

☐ Accounting Standards prepared and adopted by the Swedish Financial Accounting Standards Board (Redovisningsrådet, RR). The main objective of the RR is to issue recommendations and to deal with accounting issues related to **public companies**.

☐ Recommendations on Accounting Matters issued by the Swedish Institute of Authorized Public Accountants (Föreningen Auktoriserade Revisorer, FAR), which describes generally accepted accounting principles and interprets certain regulations in the Swedish Companies Act and Swedish Accounting Act.

☐ Recommendations on accounting matters issued by the Swedish Accounting Standards Board (Bokföringsnämnden, BFN). The BFN is a government body that develops generally accepted accounting principles for use in corporate accounting and annual reports. The BFN also prepares and issues general advice on accounting matters and the preparation of financial statements.

☐ Recommendations issued by the Business Community's Stock Exchange Committee (Näringslivets Börskommitté, NBK) for Swedish quoted companies. The NBK was formed by the Stockholm Chamber of Commerce (Stockholms Handelskammare) and the Swedish Federation of Industries (Sveriges Industriförbund, SI) to issue recommendations concerning information provided to the stock exchange by quoted companies.

Swedish tax legislation has a significant impact on the preparation of single-entity financial statements; special deductions and allowances for tax purposes (tax appropriations) must be included in the income statement to be allowed in computing taxable income. To avoid distorting accounting income and asset values, tax appropriations are separately reported in the income statement and reflected as movements in untaxed reserves in the balance sheet. These untaxed reserves are considered a mixture of equity and deferred tax. They cannot be distributed as dividends, unless they are reversed to the income statement and thereby included in taxable income.

The practice described above will not be used in the future in consolidated accounts, as a result of the new Recommendation RR 01:91 on Consolidated Accounts (see Section 29).

2. Audit and Public Company Requirements

Audits.   All limited companies (aktiebolag, AB) must be audited by a qualified accountant, that is, an authorized public accountant or an approved accountant. Cooperatives, banks, insurance companies, branches of foreign corporations, public utilities, large private firms and partnerships are also required to be audited by a qualified accountant.

The auditing profession in Sweden is regulated by a government authority (Kommerskollegium), which acts as both a licensing and sanctioning body. There are no special professional examinations required, but all authorized public accountants must have a university degree in business administration involving three and a half years of study; accounting, company law and taxation are compulsory. To be licensed, an authorized accountant must also have five years of practical experience, mainly with an authorized firm or authorized accountant. An approved accountant must meet the same practical experience requirements, but is only required to study at university level for two years.

Qualified accountants are not allowed to carry out any activities incompatible with their professional duties as independent auditors. They must consistently observe the Rules of Professional Ethics in carrying out their professional duties. These rules closely correspond to those recommended by the International Federation of Accountants, of which the FAR is a member.

The auditor is appointed at a general meeting of shareholders and remains in office for the period prescribed in the articles of association (no maximum period is set by law and auditors may hold office indefinitely). The Swedish Companies Act sets out the basic duties and responsibilities of the auditor, which are as follows:

□   The auditor shall, to the extent required by generally accepted auditing standards, examine the annual report, the accounts and the administration of the company by the board of directors and the managing director. The primary purpose of the examination of the administration of the company is to determine whether there has been any act or omission that could give rise to a liability for damages on the part of a member of the board of directors or the managing director, or if a member of the board or the managing director has in any manner acted in conflict with the Companies Act or the company's statutes.[1] The examination also covers management's controls over operations, which include a satisfactory system of internal and budgetary control. If the company is a **parent company**, the auditor shall also examine the consolidated accounts and the relationships (transactions and agreements) between the **subsidiary** companies.

---

[1] This examination, together with the statement in the audit report regarding the board members' and the managing director's discharge from liability, has a very long tradition in Sweden as an integral part of the statutory audit.

□ The auditor shall submit an audit report to the general meeting, stating:
— That the audit has been carried out as required by generally accepted auditing standards.
— Whether the annual report has been prepared in accordance with the Swedish Companies Act.
— Whether the proposed appropriation of the year's profit or loss is in accordance with the law.
— Whether the auditor has found an act or an omission on the part of a member of the board or the managing director that may result in liabilities for damages, or whether a member of the board or the managing director has otherwise acted contrary to the Swedish Companies Act or the articles of association.
— Whether the members of the board and the managing director will be discharged from liability (based on the findings above).

The basic obligations set out in the Swedish Companies Act are amplified by the FAR, which issues Rules of Professional Ethics and Recommendations on Auditing Matters. The recommendations aim at providing authoritative guidance on the auditing procedures to be followed by members of the Institute.

Public Companies.   General: The Stockholm Stock Exchange (Stockholms Fondbörs AB) is at present the only authorized stock exchange for shares. Public companies must apply to the exchange if they wish to be listed there.

Registration requirements are stipulated by the Financial Supervisory Authority (Finansinspektionen) and state that at least 25 percent of the shares must be placed on the market and that the expected market value of the company must exceed 10 million SEK. Companies must agree to disclosure requirements and rules for tender offers and must maintain a share register on the Central Security Register System (Värdepapperscentralen, VPC). The Financial Supervisory Authority further regulates requirements regarding the contents and publishing of prospectuses for listing.

Reporting requirements: The Act governing stock exchanges requires **listed companies** to provide:

□ Published information on the company's activities to enable the public to assess the price of the company's shares.

□ Information that the stock exchange considers necessary to carry out its obligations under the Act or other ordinances. This information is provided to the stock exchange but is not made public.

According to the rules of the listing contract entered into by all companies listed on the Stockholm Stock Exchange, the company undertakes to publish and also to send to the Stockholm Stock Exchange promptly an approved year-end release setting out all significant facts to be contained in the annual accounts. This release includes:

□ The company's results from ordinary activities, or, for a parent company, the consolidated results.

□ Extraordinary revenues and expenses, where significant to the assessment of the company or the group.

☐ Earnings per share, including and excluding extraordinary items and adjusted to show the effect of the potential conversion of outstanding convertible bonds, if any.

☐ The proposed dividend.

☐ Any proposal for issue of stock or other securities.

☐ The location where the complete annual report will be available to the public.

The Act governing stock exchanges stipulates that a listed company must publish a half-yearly report. The requirements regarding the contents are determined by the Financial Supervisory Authority.

According to the rules of the listing contract, the contents of the half-yearly report must comply with the requirements in the Companies Act regarding interim reports. In addition, it is required to contain information regarding earnings per share, including and excluding extraordinary items and any adjustment to show the effect of the potential conversion of outstanding convertible bonds, if any.

The half-yearly report, other interim reports and forecasts relating to the company's results for the current fiscal year, as well as announcements about forthcoming annual accounts, should be made public and are also sent to the Stockholm Stock Exchange promptly after approval by the board of directors or the managing director.

Any disciplinary reminder sent by the auditors to the board of directors or the managing director of the company must be promptly reported by the company to the Stockholm Stock Exchange if the disciplinary reminder relates to circumstances that may be significant in valuing the company's shares.

Reference. The Act governing stock exchanges (Lag 1992:543 om börs- och clearingverksamhet); Listing contract approved by the Board of Directors of the Stockholm Stock Exchange; and the Financial Supervisory Authority's regulation on listing of financial instruments (Finansinspektionens föreskrifter om inregistrering av fondpapper m.m. FFFS 1992:24).

GENERAL ACCOUNTING

3. Financial Statements

Basic Accounting Concepts. Financial statements are prepared on the assumption that the entity is a **going concern** and items recognized in financial statements are accounted for in accordance with the **accrual** basis of accounting.

The **historical cost** basis is the primary measurement used when preparing financial statements. Revaluations of **fixed assets** are permitted provided that there is no effect on income or distributable earnings. The valuation of **current assets** at the lower of cost or market value forms part of this measurement basis.

Comparability in an entity's financial statements is improved when the same **accounting concepts** and **procedures** are used from period to period. Several requirements contained in the Companies Act and the Accounting Act support this concept.

Contents of Financial Statements. Limited companies are required under the Companies Act to provide shareholders with an annual report containing an administration report, balance sheet, income statement and statement of changes in financial position.

It is a common practice to present the statement of changes in financial position in terms of sources and applications of funds. Lately, however, there has been an increasing tendency to present cash flow statements using the **indirect method**. Notes to the financial statements are considered an integral part of the statements. Where the entity is a parent company, the annual report also contains a consolidated income statement, balance sheet and statement of changes in financial position for the group.

The administration report contains:

☐ Information on any circumstances that are not specifically required to be disclosed in the income statement or balance sheet but that are considered to be important in assessing the results and financial position of the company.

☐ Information on any significant events that occurred after the end of the financial year.

☐ Information with respect to the average number of employees.

☐ The total remuneration paid to the board of directors and the managing director and to other employees.

☐ A proposal for dealing with the profit or loss of the company.

Format of Financial Statements.   The income statement and balance sheet should follow the format specified in the Accounting Act, Sections 18 and 19, respectively. Departures called for by the nature and extent of the business are permitted. Assets and liabilities are segregated into current and noncurrent in the balance sheet. A noncurrent asset is defined as an asset intended for continuous use or possession by the entity. All other assets are current assets. The one-year rule is the criterion for classifying receivables and payables as current or noncurrent; receivables and payables that fall due within one year from the balance sheet date are classified as **current** assets or **liabilities**.

Disclosure of Accounting Policies.   Valuation principles used in connection with assets and liabilities should be disclosed as well as changes in valuation principles that have a material effect on income for the year. This information should be disclosed primarily for items such as inventories, receivables or payables denominated in foreign currencies; work in progress; and tangible and intangible fixed assets. The principles of revenue recognition in various industries such as consulting, construction and leasing should be disclosed.

Depreciation principles applying to various classifications of fixed assets should be disclosed, together with any material changes in these principles.

If a revaluation of fixed assets has taken place during the year, it should be disclosed, together with the revaluation amount and how it is recorded.

Any changes in the balance sheet or the income statement, regarding groupings of items or otherwise, that affect the comparability between years should be disclosed.

Reference.   Accounting Act—Sections 18, 19 and 20; Companies Act—Chapter 11; and Recommendation on the Annual Report of Limited Companies (FAR).

4. Business Combinations

General.   Consolidated accounts were first regulated in the Companies Act formally released in 1944. This regulation aimed to protect creditors of a parent company against a dividend distribution that was not supported by the economic situation of the group as a whole. There was no requirement to make the consolidated accounts public. However, they had to be presented to the auditor, who had to evaluate whether the dividend proposal was appropriate in view of the financial position of the group as a whole, using the consolidated accounts as the primary information tool. The auditor's opinion was then disclosed in the audit report.

Today, the **consolidated financial statements** are made public to enable shareholders, creditors, stock analysts and the general public to make their own assessment of the results and financial position of the group. However, the consolidated financial statements are still an instrument for evaluating the dividend proposal of the parent company.

Principles of Consolidation. Under the Companies Act, each parent company must present consolidated accounts comprising a consolidated income statement and balance sheet. The Act specifies the contents of the consolidated accounts, which in principle should be the same as the parent company's own financial statements.

Accounting Treatment of Business Combinations. A corporate combination, whereby two existing operating companies come together so that one becomes the parent and the other the subsidiary, can be described either as a true purchase from the parent company's view, or as a merger of the economic interests of both companies (pooling of interests). The treatment in consolidation and, therefore, the valuation principles to be applied to the subsidiary's assets depend on the type of combination. Normally, the combination is a true purchase and should be accounted for in accordance with the **purchase method**. When the combination is achieved by the issue of shares by one of the companies and also meets other requirements for a merger, the **pooling of interests method** is applicable. The criteria for merger accounting are: At least 90 percent of the outstanding shares of one company must be exchanged for shares of the other company; the combination must be effected in a single transaction or a series of transactions during a one-year period; the two companies must have been autonomous for at least two years prior to the combination; and shareholders must be neither deprived nor restricted in exercising voting rights in the resulting combined company for a certain period. Further, there are significant limitations on the cash consideration to be paid. Continuity of the combined companies' activities is also a requirement.

Control. A parent–subsidiary relation is defined by the Companies Act as follows:

□   Where a company is holder of such a number of shares or fractions of shares of a Swedish or foreign legal person that the holding represents more than half of the votes of the shares or the fractions of shares, the company is a parent company and the legal person a subsidiary. Where a subsidiary, a parent company jointly with one or several subsidiaries, or several subsidiaries jointly hold such a number of shares or fractions of shares of a legal person as mentioned above, that legal person is also a subsidiary of the parent company.

□   Where a company has otherwise, by virtue of its holdings of shares or parts or by virtue of agreement, a decisive influence over a legal person and a considerable share in its results, the company is a parent company and the legal person a subsidiary.

Goodwill.   At the acquisition date the difference between the purchase cost of an entity's shares and the fair values of the net identifiable assets acquired should be determined. A positive difference is recognized as **goodwill** arising on acquisition. Swedish accounting standards require goodwill to be recorded as an **intangible asset** in the consolidated balance sheet and to be amortized over its useful life, which should normally not exceed ten years. A maximum of 20 years is allowed. The reason for any extension of the amortization period beyond ten years must be disclosed in the notes. Adjustments against equity are not allowed.

If the difference is negative, it should be deducted from net assets acquired or classified as **negative goodwill**.

Equity Accounting.   An entity is defined as being associated with another company (the investor) if the investor holds shares in the entity to the extent that it controls 20 percent or more of the voting power but less than 50 percent.

Equity accounting in single-entity accounts does not comply with the Accounting Act. However, the FAR has issued an exposure draft recommending that equity accounting be applied in consolidated financial statements. An important requirement of the recommendation is that the equity accounted share of the **associated company's** undistributed earnings must be classified as nondistributable reserves in the consolidated financial statements.

The exposure draft on equity accounting represents a departure from the fundamental principle of applying the same approach in the preparation of consolidated accounts as in single-entity accounts.

Minority Interests.   **Minority interests** are separately identified and disclosed in the balance sheet, usually between long-term liabilities and the group's equity. The minority share of income after tax is deducted in determining consolidated net income and is shown as one of the last items in the income statement. Information about the minority share of income after financial income and expenses, extraordinary items and tax is disclosed in the notes to financial statements.

Disclosure.   Consolidation: The Companies Act requires the annual report to disclose the methods and valuation principles applied in preparing the consolidated financial statements. This information is most frequently included in the statement of **accounting policies**, which includes a more or less comprehensive description of the method of accounting for **business combinations** and the principles for translating the financial statements of foreign subsidiaries.

Equity accounting: As mentioned above, equity accounting is not permitted in the financial statements of a parent company or a single company. However, disclosure of the entity's share in the earnings of associated companies is recommended.

Reference.   Companies Act—Chapter 11; Accounting Act; Recommendation RR 01:91 on Consolidated Accounts; and Draft Recommendation on Equity Accounting (FAR).

5. Joint Ventures

Accounting for Investments in Joint Ventures.   Swedish accounting recommendations do not address the different forms of **joint ventures** detailed in IAS 31, *Financial Reporting of Interests in Joint Ventures*.

Jointly Controlled Entities. The usual method of accounting for joint ventures in the consolidated financial statements of a venturer has been the **equity method**. However, in the Draft Recommendation on Equity Accounting, FAR recommends the **proportionate consolidation** method of accounting for an investment in a **jointly controlled** entity as the **benchmark treatment**, with the equity method as an **allowed alternative**.

Jointly Controlled Operations and Jointly Controlled Assets. There are no recommendations in Sweden dealing with jointly controlled operations and jointly controlled assets.

Accounting by Joint Ventures. Generally accepted accounting principles apply to all assets and liabilities and operations of joint ventures. However, there is little guidance in Sweden on accounting by the joint venture for assets contributed to the joint venture by the venturers.

Disclosure. The methods applied in preparing the financial statements should be disclosed.

References. Draft Recommendation on Equity Accounting (FAR).

6. Foreign Currency Translation

Foreign Currency Denominated Transactions. There are no explicit rules in the Accounting Act for the valuation of receivables and payables denominated in foreign currencies. Consequently, the accounting treatment of **foreign currency denominated transactions** was not consistent prior to the BFN issuing Recommendation BFN R7 on Valuation of Receivables and Payables Denominated in Foreign Currency, which became effective in 1990. This requires that foreign currency monetary items be reported in the balance sheet at the closing rates. The exchange difference between the historical rates (or the closing rates at the previous balance sheet date) and the current closing rates should, with one minor exception, be reflected in net income in the period in which the exchange rates change. Unrealized exchange gains arising from long-term receivables and payables should be recorded in an untaxed currency reserve in the balance sheet. This reserve is not available for distribution as dividends.

Foreign Operations. The Companies Act does not specifically regulate translation of foreign subsidiaries' financial statements for consolidation purposes. However, a Proposed Recommendation on Translation of Foreign Subsidiaries' Financial Statements issued by the FAR in 1988 has standardized practice. This recommendation, which is still in draft form, differentiates between ''independent'' and ''**integrated**'' **foreign operations**.

''Independent subsidiary companies'' are subsidiaries whose income and expenses are received and paid principally in local currency and whose monetary assets and liabilities are expressed principally in that currency. Operations are substantially independent of the parent company, even if they are in the same business.

''Integrated subsidiary companies'' are subsidiaries whose operations are closely linked to the parent company, usually with a material portion of income and expenses relating to transactions with the parent company or other group companies. Integrated subsidiaries are usually dependent on the parent company for a major part of their financing (e.g., loans, equity or trade credit).

If a foreign subsidiary is *independent* (self-sustaining), its financial statements should be translated using the **current rate method**, and the translation difference, if any, should be taken directly to equity. The translation difference for the year should be separately disclosed in the note describing changes in consolidated equity. If a subsidiary has untaxed reserves, the translation differences on these reserves should be disclosed in a note.

If a foreign operation is *integrated* with the reporting company, its accounts should be translated using the **temporal method**, and resulting exchange differences arising from translation of **monetary items** should be included in consolidated income for the year.

Subsidiaries in countries with particularly high inflation rates give rise to special problems. Translating their financial statements using the current rate method usually results in an unrealistic picture of their financial position and results of operations. Accordingly, the temporal method should be used even for independent subsidiaries in such countries. Alternatively, inflation-adjusted financial statements may be translated using the current rate method.

The Companies Act requires the consolidated balance sheet to disclose the amount of unrestricted equity or the accumulated deficit of the group after deduction of unrealized intergroup profits. Therefore, it is necessary to determine how the accumulated translation differences should be divided between restricted and unrestricted equity or accumulated deficit.

Hedge Accounting. A transaction should be classified as a **hedge** only when it was entered into with that intention. If a receivable or payable denominated in foreign currency is effectively hedged, a change in the currency rate has no effect on the value of the item in the balance sheet. If the hedge is a foreign currency forward contract, the spot rate at the date of inception of the forward contract should be used for valuation of the underlying receivable or payable. The discount or premium on a forward contract should be recognized in income over the life of the contract. For contracts with a duration not exceeding three months, the forward rate may be used as an alternative for valuation of the underlying receivable or payable. Any other form of hedge that is effective as a forward contract should be treated in the same manner as a forward contract.

Disclosure. The effect of changes in exchange rates on trade receivables and payables should be disclosed in the income statement.

Changes in exchange rates that are **material** to the company's income and financial position should be disclosed in the administration report if the effect is not obvious from the income statement or a note.

The company should disclose the principles applied in valuing receivables and payables in a foreign currency. The disclosure should include the company's currency exposure and the steps taken to reduce it.

If there are changes in exchange rates after the end of the accounting year that are significant to the company's operations, the changes should be disclosed in the administration report.

A change in the method of translating the financial statements of foreign subsidiaries must be disclosed. If the effect of the change is significant, it is necessary to give effect to the change in the consolidated balance sheet for the preceding year and to present it with the balance sheet for the current year.

Reference. Companies Act—Chapter 11; Recommendation on Valuation of Receivables and Payables Denominated in Foreign Currency (BFN); and Proposed Recommendation on Translation of Foreign Subsidiaries' Financial Statements (FAR).

7. Changing Prices/Inflation Accounting

General. There is no prescribed standard on accounting for changing prices. In the late 1970s, a period of high inflation in Sweden, it was not unusual to find supplementary current value accounting information in the annual reports of listed companies. However, this practice has not been continued.

8. Accounting Changes

Accounting Treatment. Accounting changes are normally accounted for prospectively.

In exceptional cases, the effect of a major change in accounting principle may be charged against equity in the consolidated accounts.

Disclosure. The Accounting Act requires disclosure of changes in the bases on which assets and liabilities are carried in the balance sheet if the changes are significant or have materially affected income for the year.

The Companies Act further requires that a change in the grouping or classification of the items in the financial statements or any other change that will affect comparability between years be disclosed.

Neither the Accounting Act nor the Companies Act requires that the reason for the changes be disclosed, and this information is not always disclosed in practice.

Reference. Accounting Act; Companies Act—Chapter 11.

9. Prior Period Adjustments

Neither the Accounting Act nor the Companies Act contains any regulation regarding **prior period adjustments**.

However, the FAR Recommendation on Accounting for Extraordinary Items states that material prior period adjustments should be recorded as extraordinary items in the income statement for the current period rather than as adjustments of opening equity.

Reference. Recommendation on Accounting for Extraordinary Items (FAR).

10. Post Balance Sheet Events

The Companies Act requires that the administration report include information on events material to the company that occurred after the end of the accounting period—for example, major acquisitions or disposals—or events that significantly affect the company's dividend-paying capacity.

Reference. Companies Act—Chapter 11.

11. Related Party Transactions

Definition. Parties are considered related if one party has the ability to control the other party or to exercise significant influence over the other party in making financial and operating decisions. A related party transaction is one that transfers resources or obligations between related parties, regardless of whether a price is charged.

General. A company may not grant cash loans to a person who owns shares in the company or who is a member of the board or the managing director of the company or of another entity in the same group. The same rule applies to persons who are closely related to a shareholder, a member of the board or the managing director of the company.

Accounting Treatment. Swedish standards do not specifically address the measurement and accounting treatment of related party transactions. Nevertheless, the general principle is that related party transactions should be accounted for in accordance with normal accounting principles and practices.

Disclosure. The Companies Act requires the parent company and subsidiaries to disclose the proportion of purchases and sales that relate to other companies in the group. Payments made to directors in the form of salary and benefits must also be disclosed in the administration report.

Furthermore, listed companies should, in accordance with the registration contract, promptly make public and inform the Stock Exchange of decisions regarding transactions or other agreements with related parties if the transactions or agreements are significant to an assessment of the financial position and operating results of the company or to the company's relations with its shareholders.

Reference. Companies Act—Chapter 11; and contract of registration approved by the Board of Directors of the Stockholm Stock Exchange.

12. Segmental Information

The Companies Act requires companies engaged in different lines of business that are essentially independent of each other to report the operating income or loss of each line separately. This segmental information may be disclosed on the face of the income statement or in a note.

Reference. Companies Act—Chapter 11.

ACCOUNTING PRINCIPLES FOR SPECIFIC ITEMS— BALANCE SHEET

13. Property, Plant and Equipment

Classification of Capital and Revenue Expenditure. Expenditures for **capital assets** that result in a lasting improvement of the asset and, thereby, increase its value should be capitalized as part of the cost of the asset. Expenditures to maintain normal operating efficiency should be expensed.

Basis of Valuation. Generally, fixed assets may not be carried at a value higher than cost. However, a fixed asset that has a lasting value substantially in excess of the amount at which it was carried in the preceding balance sheet may be written up to an amount not in excess of its value. Under the regulations of the Accounting Act, this revaluation may be made only if the amount of the revaluation is required to offset a write-down of other fixed assets and there are special reasons for the offset. The Companies Act modifies these regulations to allow revaluations of fixed assets to be used for bonus share issues or for appropriations to a nondistributable revaluation reserve.

Fixed assets that continuously decline in value due to age, use or other comparable causes are subject to annual **depreciation** following an appropriate depreciation plan, unless it is obvious that sufficient depreciation has already been recorded.

If the value of a fixed asset has permanently declined, the asset should be written down.

Depreciation. The Accounting Act requires fixed assets to be depreciated according to "an appropriate depreciation plan." Such a plan should, according to the FAR's recommendations on accounting for tangible assets, be based on the historical cost concept, the estimated useful life of the asset and an appropriate allocation method. The most commonly used method is the **straight-line method**. However, any method consistently applied that produces a reasonable and systematic allocation over the asset's useful life is acceptable.

If an entity revalues its fixed assets upward, the depreciation should then be applied to the revalued amount.

Disclosure. The accounting policies adopted regarding the valuation and depreciation of fixed assets must be disclosed. If any fixed assets are carried at appraised values, this must also be disclosed. The income statement should disclose the amount of depreciation charged for the accounting period. Details of cost, accumulated depreciation and net book value of each class of assets must be disclosed in the notes.

Reference. Accounting Act—Section 15; Companies Act—Chapter 11; and Recommendation on Accounting for Tangible Assets (FAR).

14. Intangible Assets

If an entity has acquired a business for consideration that exceeds the value of the acquired assets, the difference may be recognized as an intangible asset to the extent that it represents goodwill. This asset should be amortized by an appropriate amount, at least 10 percent annually.

Expenditures for technical assistance, research and development, trial runs, market research and similar activities may be recognized as intangible assets, provided that the expenditures will benefit the entity during future years. Such assets should be amortized by an appropriate amount, generally at least 20 percent annually; in special circumstances, **amortization** at a lower rate may be considered to be in accordance with generally accepted accounting principles.

Reference. Accounting Act—Section 17; and BFN R1 on Accounting for Research and Development.

15. Leases

General. Neither the Accounting Act nor the Companies Act regulates accounting for leasing agreements. However, the FAR has issued a recommendation on this topic.

Accounting Treatment. When a lease contract includes an obligation to acquire ownership rights to the leased asset after a specific period and at terms agreed to in the lease contract, the leased asset should be recognized as a fixed asset in the lessee's balance sheet. The face value of payments due under the lease should be recognized as a liability, and the leased asset should be depreciated and included in pledged assets at net book value.

However, if the lease contract does not include an obligation but only a right to acquire the asset after a specified period, it is not necessary to recognize the leased asset in the lessee's balance sheet.

The lessor should separately report leased assets in the balance sheet if its leasing activities are significant in relation to total operations.

Disclosure. If a significant proportion of the company's fixed assets are held under leases, the leasing terms should be disclosed in the administration report or in a note to the balance sheet.

Reference. Recommendation on Accounting for Leasing Agreements (FAR).

16. Investments

General. This section deals with investments held by companies, other than investments in subsidiaries, associated companies or interests in partnerships, which are discussed in Section 4. The valuation of investments depends on their classification as current or noncurrent.

Valuation. Current investments: Current investments should be carried at the lower of cost or **net realizable value** (i.e., market value net of transaction costs). According to the FAR Recommendation on Accounting for Investments, the lower of cost or market concept may be applied on a total **portfolio basis** to marketable securities. The write-down, if any, should be reported as an operating expense or as a financial expense or, in particular circumstances, as an extraordinary item. Reversals of previous write-downs are permitted.

Noncurrent investments: Noncurrent investments should be carried at cost adjusted for any permanent diminution in value. Investments need not be assessed individually if they are considered as a portfolio. Any write-down should be reported as an operating expense or as a financial expense or, in particular circumstances, as an extraordinary item. Reversals of write-downs of noncurrent investments to reflect increases in market value are not permitted, except in those instances where the requirements of Section 15 of the Accounting Act for revaluation of fixed assets are met.

Gains/Losses. The measurement of the gain or loss on sale of part of a holding of securities should be based on average carrying value.

Disclosure. The market value of marketable securities should be disclosed in a note to the balance sheet.

When a noncurrent marketable security is carried at a value above market, the reason for this should be disclosed in a note to the balance sheet.

Reference. Accounting Act—Sections 14 and 15; Companies Act—Chapter 11; Recommendation No. 12 on Accounting for Investments (FAR); and Statement BFN U 88:5 on Disclosure of Securities (BFN).

17. Accounts Receivable

Accounting Treatment. Recognition: The recognition of **revenues**, and hence the related receivables, is described in Section 23.

Discounts: Revenues and the related receivables are normally recorded net of trade discounts. Cash discounts as an incentive to pay earlier or on time are not used frequently. In the mid-1970s businesses introduced interest on overdue receivables instead. When cash discounts are used, they are normally recognized when payment is received.

Allowances: Adequate allowances should be established for doubtful accounts, although there is no requirement to refer to or disclose the amount. No specific basis is required for calculating the allowance for doubtful accounts. **Specific identification** is the preferred basis, but when it is impracticable other methods may be used. Taxation authorities generally do not accept any basis other than specific identification.

Factored Receivables. Receivables that have been factored should not be included in the balance sheet. When the factor has recourse to the vendor for doubtful accounts, disclosure of the contingent liability should be made if provision for probable losses has not been recorded.

Disclosure. Receivables should be segregated in the balance sheet between bills receivable, **accounts receivable**, prepaid expenses and accrued income, amounts receivable from related parties and other receivables. Separate disclosure is required of current and noncurrent receivables as well as of receivables from subsidiary and parent entities.

The value of accounts receivable, trade or other, that are pledged should be separately reported as a line item in the balance sheet. The value of pledged receivables should also be disclosed at the bottom of the balance sheet.

Factoring arrangements should be disclosed in a note to the balance sheet or in the administration report.

Reference. Accounting Act—Section 19; Companies Act—Chapter 11; and Recommendation on Accounting for Factored Receivables (FAR).

18. Inventories and Work in Progress

General Accounting Treatment. **Inventories** should be carried at the lower of cost or real value. Real value is defined as net realizable value, but replacement cost, less allowance for obsolescence where appropriate, is permissible for raw materials and semi-finished products. Net realizable value is the estimated proceeds from the sale of the inventory, less all further costs necessary for marketing, selling and distribution to customers and an appropriate share of the entity's administration expenses.

FIFO is the most common method of determining cost and is recommended by the RR. It is also prescribed by the tax law.

To determine the carrying amount of inventory, each item should be analyzed separately; where this is impracticable, similar items may be dealt with in the aggregate.

When inventories are manufactured, cost should be determined using **absorption**

costing based on the entity's normal operating capacity. Cost relating to abnormal circumstances, such as idle facilities, should be excluded.

Long-Term Contracts.   Long-term construction and installation contracts are usually accounted for on the **completed contract** basis, but the **percentage of completion method** appears to be slowly gaining acceptance in practice. In the preparatory work (work documented in written reports supporting a bill to be tabled in parliament) of the Accounting Act, long-term contracts are used as an example of a situation where a departure from the lower of cost or market concept is permissible. However, this deviation should be limited to companies that carry out a few large projects that take a long time to complete. FAR Recommendation No. 2 on Inventories and Work in Progress permits the percentage of completion method, provided that the revenue and the costs to complete are determinable.

Reference.   Accounting Act—Section 14; Recommendation RR 02:92 on Accounting for Inventories; and Recommendation No. 2 on Inventories and Work in Progress (FAR).

19. Current Liabilities

General Accounting Treatment.   Current liabilities include amounts payable within one year from the date of the balance sheet.

Commitments such as purchase orders or other kinds of contractual obligations do not qualify as liabilities until the service has been performed. **Contingencies** are accounted for as liabilities only when they become probable.

Creation of General and Specific Provisions.   General provisions are not permitted, as provisions must relate to a specific existing obligation. Provisions for future expenses or losses are not permitted unless the circumstances giving rise to them have occurred.

Provisions for future expenses relating to warranties should be recognized at the time of sale of the item under warranty.

Disclosure.   Current liabilities should be segregated between bills payable; trade **creditors**; taxes payable, accrued liabilities and deferred revenues; advances from customers; and other current liabilities. Payables to subsidiary and parent entities should be disclosed as a separate line item in the balance sheet.

Reference.   Accounting Act—Section 19; and Companies Act—Chapter 11.

20. Long-Term Debt

General Accounting Treatment.   The most common forms of long-term debt in Sweden are debentures, bonds, mortgages and other forms of long-term bank credit. The general accounting treatment applied to these items is basically the same as for current liabilities, that is, they are carried in the balance sheet at face value. However, premium and discount on bonds and similar obligations should be reflected as an addition to or deduction from long-term debt. When convertible debt is issued, the portion of the proceeds allocated to the conversion option should be accounted for as restricted equity. The debt portion will be increased over the life of the liability using the interest method.

Disclosure. As with current liabilities, long-term debt must be segregated on the face of the balance sheet between debentures, bonds, bank overdrafts, construction credits, other long-term liabilities and pension provisions. Long-term payables to subsidiary and parent companies should also be disclosed in the balance sheet.

Where a company has issued convertible bonds or bonds containing an option to subscribe for new shares, the amount not yet converted and the time and conditions for conversion or subscription should be disclosed for each loan. The amount still outstanding on participating debentures and the interest provisions should be disclosed.

Reference. Accounting Act; Companies Act; Recommendation on Accounting for Loan Agreements (FAR); and RR 03:92 Accounting for Interest on Receivables and Payables.

21. Contingencies

Contingent Losses. The accounting treatment of contingent liabilities depends on the probability of occurrence of the future events that will determine the contingency. If the probability is high, the contingencies should be included among liabilities.

Contingent Gains. Contingent gains should not be accrued in the financial statements, but if occurrence is likely, their existence should be disclosed.

Disclosure. The Accounting Act requires contingent liabilities to be disclosed under the headings discounted bills, guaranties and other contingent liabilities and pension obligations that are not reported as a liability or covered by the assets of a pension fund. Contingencies are disclosed as memorandum items at the bottom of the balance sheet.

Reference. Accounting Act.

22. Capital and Reserves

General. Equity is accounted for in somewhat different ways by private firms, partnerships and limited companies. This chapter concentrates on limited companies. Shareholders' equity is generally divided between restricted equity and nonrestricted equity or accumulated deficit. Restricted equity includes **share capital**, legal reserve and revaluation reserve. Nonrestricted equity includes nonrestricted reserves, **retained earnings** forward and net income for the year, each of which is disclosed separately.

Share Capital. Where the company's share capital is divided into several classes, the amount of each class should be disclosed. The number of shares and the face value of each share should also be reported.

Holdings of the company's own shares should be recorded as an asset having no value; the aggregate face value of the holdings should be disclosed, preferably on the face of the balance sheet.

All changes in amounts under various equity headings since the preceding balance sheet date should be explained in a note to the balance sheet.

In accordance with the Companies Act, the disclosure requirements for a single entity's equity also apply to consolidated accounts, where appropriate.

Restricted Reserves. Two kinds of restricted reserves may appear in a limited company's balance sheet.

Statutory (legal) reserve: The following allocations should be made to the statutory reserve:

- [ ] At least 10 percent of the net income for the year after deduction of any deficit brought forward. Such allocation must continue until the reserve equals 20 percent of the share capital.
- [ ] Any amount received in excess of the nominal value of issued shares.
- [ ] Any amount paid by a person whose shares have been declared forfeited.
- [ ] Any amount specifically allocated by the articles of association or approved by the shareholders at a general meeting.

Any reduction in the statutory reserve requires a decision at a general meeting of the shareholders and may be made only for the following purposes:

- [ ] To cover losses that cannot be covered by nonrestricted equity.
- [ ] To increase share capital through a bonus share issue.
- [ ] For any other purpose, provided that the court gives consent.

Revaluation reserve: This reserve results from the revaluation of noncurrent assets. It may be used only for a necessary write-down of the value of noncurrent assets or for a bonus share issue or to cover a deficit in a balance sheet approved at a general meeting of shareholders, provided that the deficit cannot be covered by available unrestricted equity. Utilizing the revaluation reserve to cover a deficit requires consultation with the auditors. Unless the court has given consent, the company is prevented from declaring dividends for three years if the share capital is not increased by an amount at least equal to the deficit covered by the revaluation reserve.

Dividends. Dividends to shareholders may not exceed the amount distributable according to the balance sheet approved by the board. For a parent company, the consolidated balance sheet must also be considered in determining the distributable amount. The distributable amount includes net income for the year, retained earnings and nonrestricted reserves less (1) reported losses, (2) the amount allocated according to the Companies Act or articles of association to restricted equity and (3) the amount that, according to the articles of association, is to be used for other purposes.

Dividends may not be distributed to an extent that would be contrary to good business practice. The company's or the consolidated group's needs, cash needs or financial position in other respects should be considered.

The general meeting of the shareholders may not declare a dividend that is higher than the dividend proposed or approved by the board of directors unless provided for in the articles of association.

Reference. Accounting Act; Companies Act; and Recommendations on Accounting Matters (FAR).

ACCOUNTING PRINCIPLES FOR SPECIFIC ITEMS— INCOME STATEMENT

23. Revenue Recognition

General Principles. There is no specific revenue recognition accounting standard in Sweden. However, the **realization** principle requires that revenue be earned before it is recognized. Revenue is generally recognized when the earning process is complete and an exchange has taken place.

Long-Term Contracts. Revenue recognition for long-term contracts is covered in Section 18.

24. Government Grants and Assistance

Accounting Treatment. The BFN has issued a recommendation on accounting for government grants and assistance.

Revenue grants: Government assistance should be reported in the income statement under the same heading as the related expenses, in a consistent manner from period to period.

Grants for fixed assets: The cost of the fixed assets should be reduced by the amount of the government grant.

Disclosure. The accounting policy for government grants and assistance should be disclosed if the amounts are material. Benefits or commitments covering several periods should continue to be disclosed as long as they remain in effect.

Revenue grants: The effect on the company's operating results and financial position should be recognized in any summary of results covering a number of years.

Grants for fixed assets: The gross value of the assets and the amount of the grant should be disclosed in a note.

Reference. Recommendation BFN R5 on Accounting for Government Grants and Assistance (BFN).

25. Research and Development

Accounting Treatment. Under the Accounting Act, expenditures for technical assistance and for research and development (R&D) may be recognized as fixed assets if they will benefit the company in future years. The recorded asset should be amortized annually by an appropriate amount not less than 20 percent of its original value unless there are special circumstances in which amortization at a lower rate may be used in accordance with generally accepted accounting principles.

There is no uniformity in reporting practice in this area. The BFN recently issued a Recommendation on Accounting for Research and Development with the aim of conforming Swedish practice with international accounting practice (IAS 9). The general rule requires that research and development expenditures be expensed as incurred, unless the criteria set out below are satisfied:

□   The R&D project and the expenditures attributed to it are clearly defined.

□ The technical feasibility of the R&D project has been demonstrated.

□ The products or process resulting from the R&D project is intended for sale or internal use.

□ The expected revenue or cost savings resulting from the R&D project are known with reasonable probability.

□ There are adequate resources to complete the project.

If capitalized, research and development costs must be amortized annually according to the rules stated in the Accounting Act, that is, at least 20 percent annually.

Disclosure. The financial statements, on their face or in notes, should disclose:

□ The accounting policy for R&D.

□ The R&D expenditures expensed in the current year and the amortization of R&D expenditures capitalized in previous years.

□ The total R&D expenditures capitalized and the related accumulated amortization.

Reference. Accounting Act and Recommendation BFN R1 on Accounting for Research and Development (BFN).

26. Capitalized Interest Costs

Accounting Treatment. According to FAR Recommendation No. 3 on Accounting for Tangible Assets, it is acceptable to capitalize interest paid as part of the cost of construction of assets and machinery during the construction and installation period. **Imputed interest** on the entity's equity may not be capitalized.

On the contrary, interest costs incurred by the company in the processing or manufacture of inventory may not be capitalized except when the processing time is long.

Reference. Recommendation on Accounting for Tangible Assets (FAR) and Recommendation RR 02:92 on Accounting for Inventories.

27. Imputed Interest

General. Interest imputation is required in certain circumstances. As a general rule, when one party exchanges goods or services in return for a second party's obligation to pay cash in the future and the stated interest rate is not substantially equal to prevailing interest rates, the stated principal amount of the transaction should be adjusted so that it is substantially equal to the present value of all future payments discounted at the prevailing interest rate. The prevailing interest rate depends largely on the borrower's credit standing and the repayment terms, collateral and other pertinent factors.

This general rule has several exceptions, among them the one-year rule, which exempts receivables and payables arising in the normal course of business that are due within approximately one year. Certain other receivables and payables are also exempt, such as parent–subsidiary transactions.

Accounting Treatment. When imputed interest is required, the seller should record the sale and the purchaser the asset at the adjusted principal amount. Any resulting discount or premium is amortized as interest expense or income over the life of the note using the interest method.

Disclosure.   The face amount of the note and the effective interest rate are to be disclosed; the discount or premium is reported as a direct deduction from or addition to the face amount of the note.

Reference.   Recommendation RR 03:92 on Accounting for Interest on Receivables and Payables.

28. Extraordinary or Unusual Items

Extraordinary Items.   According to the preparatory work on the Accounting Act, entities should be very restrictive when classifying transactions as extraordinary items. In Recommendation No. 13 on Accounting for Extraordinary Items, the FAR has put forward the following three criteria, all of which have to be met for an item to qualify as extraordinary:

☐   The event or transaction originating the item has no evident relation to the ordinary operations of the entity.
☐   The event or transaction is not expected to occur frequently or regularly.
☐   The item is material in value.

Disclosure.   Extraordinary revenues and expenses should be disclosed separately on the face of the income statement. Netting revenues and expenses is not in accordance with generally accepted accounting principles. Separate disclosure of details of extraordinary items is required in the notes.

Reference.   Recommendation on Accounting for Extraordinary Items (FAR).

29. Income Taxes

General.   The Accounting Act and the Companies Act do not recognize deferred tax accounting. However, according to Recommendation RR 01:91 on Consolidated Accounts, deferred taxes should be recognized in the consolidated balance sheet. The method recommended is essentially the **liability method**. Increases (decreases) in the tax liability result in increases (decreases) in tax expense for the year. This also means that changes in the tax liability because of tax rate changes have an effect on tax expense in the period when the rate changes. If material, this tax component should be disclosed.

The treatment of income taxes in consolidated accounts is quite different from that in single-entity accounts, as described in Section 1.

Reference.   Recommendation RR 01:91 on Consolidated Accounts.

30. Postretirement Benefits

General.   Pension plans for white-collar employees are governed by nationwide union–employer organization agreements. Mainly, two systems are used: (1) actuarially computed premiums paid to an independent pension insurance company and (2) provision for the actual liability, which is computed by an independent organization. Under the latter system the liability is reported as a long-term liability.

Pension expenses for blue-collar employees are financed by direct charges and recorded as related salary costs under operating expenses.

Accounting standards for postretirement benefits other than pensions, such as continuing health care and other welfare benefits, have not been developed.

Accounting Treatment.   In general, the Accounting Act requires pension provisions to be separately disclosed on the face of the balance sheet as a long-term liability. However, it is acceptable to disclose the actuarially computed amount of such commitments as a contingent liability. This alternative treatment is used mainly for older commitments, often relating to former owners. The amounts involved are usually relatively insignificant from a balance sheet point of view.

The FAR Recommendation on Accounting for Pension Liabilities and Pension Expenses requires companies to charge actual pension expenses for the year to operating income. The recommendation also requires companies to calculate the interest cost on the benefit obligation. The interest cost is equal to the increase in the amount of the benefit obligation due to the passage of time. The interest cost component should be deducted from operating expenses and reported as financial expenses. The effect of any extraordinary circumstances on pension expenses should be reported as an extraordinary item.

Reference.   Accounting Act and Recommendation on Accounting for Pension Liabilities and Pension Expenses (FAR).

31. Discontinued Operations

Accounting Treatment.   There is no prescribed accounting standard for discontinued operations. However, the FAR Recommendation on Accounting for Extraordinary Items states that gains or losses from disposals or discontinued operations of a significant business segment should be reported as an extraordinary item. The effect of normal changes and adjustments of product line, market mix and so on should, however, be included in operating income.

Disclosure.   Details of extraordinary expenses from discontinued operations may be disclosed in a note. Disclosure of the details of write-downs of fixed assets is mandatory.

Reference.   Recommendation on Accounting for Extraordinary Items (FAR).

32. Earnings per Share

General.   The Companies Act does not require companies to disclose earnings per share (EPS). There are requirements regarding disclosure of the number of shares and their nominal value, which makes it possible for analysts to make their own computations. In 1983, the NBK issued a Recommendation on the Format of Income Statement and Financial Ratios containing a definition of EPS. The NBK recommended that EPS be disclosed, both including and excluding extraordinary items. If extraordinary items are insignificant, disclosing only EPS including extraordinary items is adequate. In addition, the income base used in the computation is calculated using a comprehensive tax expense for the year, that is, the current tax charge plus or minus changes in the imputed deferred tax.

Reference.   Recommendation on the Format of Income Statement and Financial Ratios (NBK).

Appendix
DO SWEDISH STANDARDS OR PREVALENT PRACTICE SUBSTANTIALLY COMPLY WITH INTERNATIONAL ACCOUNTING STANDARDS?

Section	Topic	Substantially complies with IAS?	Comments
3.	Basic accounting concepts and conventions	Yes	
	Contents of financial statements	Yes	
4.	Business combinations*	Yes	
5.	Joint ventures	No	There are no Swedish accounting standards addressing the treatment of jointly controlled assets or jointly controlled operations
6.	Foreign currency translation*	Yes	
8.	Accounting changes*	Yes	
9.	Prior period adjustments*	No	Adjustments are disclosed as extraordinary items in Sweden
10.	Post balance sheet events	Yes	
11.	Related party transactions	No	
12.	Segmental information	No	
13.	Property, plant and equipment*	Yes	
15.	Leases	No	
16.	Investments	Yes	
17.	Accounts receivable	Yes	
18.	Inventories and work in progress*	Yes	
19.	Current liabilities	Yes	
20.	Long-term debt	Yes	
21.	Contingencies	Yes	
22.	Capital and reserves	Yes	
23.	Revenue recognition*	Yes	For long-term contracts the percentage of completion method is permitted only to a limited extent

Appendix (*Continued*)

Section	Topic	Substantially complies with IAS?	Comments
24.	Government grants and assistance	Yes	
25.	Research and development*	Yes	
26.	Capitalization of interest costs*	Yes	
28.	Extraordinary or unusual items*	Yes	
29.	Income tax**	No	Tax effect accounting is required only in consolidated financial statements
30.	Postretirement benefits*	Yes	

*These topics are subject to change as a result of the IASC Improvements Project—see the appendix to the International Accounting Standards chapter.

**The IAS on accounting for taxes on income is currently being revised, and an exposure draft has been issued.

Comparison in this table is made to International Accounting Standards in force at January 1, 1993. For further details, see the International Accounting Standards chapter.

SWITZERLAND

GENERAL NATIONAL INFORMATION

1. Source of Generally Accepted Accounting Principles

Generally Accepted Accounting Principles. **Generally accepted accounting principles** in Switzerland are derived from Swiss Company Law, the Code of Obligations (Obligationenrecht [G], Code des Obligations [F][1]). This law has recently been amended substantially, with new requirements introduced for unconsolidated financial statements for financial periods commencing after July 1, 1992 and, for the first time, contains a requirement for companies exceeding a certain size to produce audited **consolidated financial statements** for financial periods commencing after July 1, 1993. This chapter describes the requirements of this new law.

Although not mandatory, the Accounting and Reporting Recommendations (ARR) (FER [G], RPC [F]) of the Foundation for Accounting and Reporting Recommendations, the independent Swiss standard-setting body, are gaining increasing recognition. These recommendations exceed the minimum required by the new law and in many instances approach the requirements of the International Accounting Standards (IAS) or European Community (EC) Directives. It is likely that these recommendations, which at present are being amended substantially, will form a minimum framework in the future for Swiss quoted companies.

The Swiss Institute of Accountants (Treuhand-Kammer [G], Chambre fiduciaire [F]) issues auditing and accounting recommendations in its Handbook (Revisionshandbuch der Schweiz [G], Manuel suisse de revision comptable [F]) and in technical circulars (Fachmitteilung [G], Communication professionnelle [F]). The Institute's recommendations serve to clarify legal requirements as well as to provide further guidance on areas not covered in the law. While they do not constitute binding rules, they are increasingly used as a reference by the accounting profession, as well as by the courts.

In addition, Swiss generally accepted accounting principles for unconsolidated financial statements are heavily influenced by federal and cantonal tax legislation, since those statements usually form the basis for a company's tax returns.

---

[1][G]—German term; [F]—French term.

2. Audit and Public Company Requirements

Audits.   The Code of Obligations requires that all companies (AG or Aktiengesellschaft [G], SA or société anonyme [F]) appoint statutory auditors (Revisionstelle [G], organe de révision [F]); the appointment must be recorded in the publicly accessible Commercial Register. The auditors of companies that meet minimum size conditions or that are required to produce consolidated financial statements or are publicly traded must fulfill special qualifications determined by the Swiss Federal Council. The auditors of banks and certain other financial institutions with banking characteristics also need to be approved by the Swiss Federal Banking Commission.

If a company appoints more than one auditor, at least one must be of Swiss domicile or have an office or branch office registered in Switzerland. Auditors must be independent of the board of directors and of shareholders holding the voting majority. In particular, they may neither be employed by the company to be examined nor perform work that is incompatible with the audit assignment. If requested by a shareholder or creditor, they must be independent of companies belonging to the same group. Auditors can be appointed for periods of a maximum of three years, with reelection possible.

The auditors are required by law to examine the books of account and the annual unconsolidated and, where required, consolidated financial statements and report whether these and the proposal for the appropriation of available retained earnings are in accordance with the law and the company's articles of incorporation.

The auditors of companies or groups that exceed certain minimum limits are required to produce a report addressed to the board of directors that provides details of the audit procedures performed on the unconsolidated or, where required, consolidated financial statements and the findings.

The auditors must report to the shareholders, recommending either the acceptance of the financial statements, with or without qualification, or their return to the board of directors for correction.

It is also the duty of auditors, when examining unconsolidated financial statements, to bring to the attention of the board of directors its obligations when accumulated losses exceed 50 percent of the company's share capital. This is discussed in more detail in Section 22.

The law does not prescribe the auditing procedures to be followed; however, the auditing standards issued by the Swiss Institute are used as a reference for good practice by the courts.

Public Companies.   **Public companies** must be audited by specially qualified auditors and, where applicable, produce audited consolidated financial statements. In addition to all the legal disclosure requirements for nonpublic companies, they must also disclose any shareholders who hold more than 5 percent of the voting rights or a lower limit if specified in the company's articles of incorporation. It is also highly likely that public companies will have to adopt the ARR requirements. In particular, this will result in a requirement for "fairly presented" consolidated financial statements, since the ARR introduce the major concepts found in the IASs or EC Directives; the ARR, however, do not mandate the choice of **accounting principle** options to be adopted or disclosures to be made.

Reference.   Code of Obligations, articles 663c, 727–729 and 731.

GENERAL ACCOUNTING

3. Financial Statements

Basic Accounting Concepts—General. Swiss annual financial statements, whether unconsolidated or consolidated, are to be produced according to Swiss "generally accepted commercial principles" so that the financial position and results of the company can be assessed as reliably as possible. They should be denominated in Swiss francs, and prior year information should be provided. If the shareholders agree, the statements do not necessarily have to be in the country's national languages of German, French or Italian.

Swiss generally accepted commercial principles imply that the following general concepts are applied in preparing annual financial statements:

- ☐ They are complete.
- ☐ The information is clearly presented and covers all **material** aspects.
- ☐ They have been prudently prepared.
- ☐ They assume the company is a **going concern**.
- ☐ They use consistent presentation and valuation principles.
- ☐ They do not offset assets with liabilities or income with expenses.

Deviations from the going concern and consistency assumptions and the lack of offsetting are permissible if justified; however, adequate disclosure must then be provided in the notes to the financial statements.

Reference. Code of Obligations, article 662a.

Basic Accounting Concepts—Consolidated Financial Statements. Swiss company law allows companies the option of not complying fully with best international practice as the notion that the financial statements should present the results and financial position "as reliably as possible" implies that a large measure of prudence can be utilized and, in general, a lower level of disclosure is required.

It is therefore permissible to create "hidden" reserves by valuing assets below their economic values, usually by using tax acceptable values (e.g., creating a provision allowed for taxation purposes on inventory of up to 33 percent), and to be excessively prudent in creating provisions. Nevertheless, there is a requirement that valuation principles be consistent from period to period, and the auditors must be informed of all changes in "hidden" reserves. It is necessary to disclose in the financial statements any net release that has a significant beneficial impact on the company's results. The law permits the undervaluation of assets and the overstatement of provisions "to the extent necessary to ensure the continued prosperity of the company and to distribute as equal a dividend as possible taking into account the interests of the shareholders." The overriding principle is that the balance sheet should be prudently prepared, providing for unrealized losses while deferring unrealized gains (the **"imparity" principle**).

Furthermore, the company's valuation principles apply to each item disclosed in the financial statements taken as a whole. At the detailed level within a balance sheet caption, variations in valuation principles or offsetting of gains and losses is acceptable as long as the valuation principles for the balance sheet caption as a whole are respected.

Basic Accounting Concepts—Unconsolidated Financial Statements.   Swiss unconsolidated accounts may be prepared using different accounting principles from those used in the consolidated financial statements. The accounting principles used for unconsolidated accounts are also used for tax filing purposes; in particular, any tax-deductible allowance must be reflected in order for it to be allowed for tax purposes (e.g., accelerated depreciation or general provisions to reduce the value of inventory or receivables). Provisions in excess of those allowed for tax purposes may also be included. The new law, however, requires disclosure in the notes, as for the consolidated financial statements, of the total net amount of released replacement and other "hidden" reserves insofar as they exceed the total amount of any such newly formed "hidden" reserves, if as a consequence of these releases the business results are significantly improved.

Reference.   Code of Obligations, article 663b-8.

Contents of Financial Statements.   The directors of a company are obligated to produce an annual report (Geschäftsbericht [G], Rapport annuel [F]), which consists of the business report (Jahresbericht [G], Rapport annuel de gestion [F]) and the financial statements (income statement, balance sheet and notes to the financial statements). The auditor's report is usually attached. Where applicable, companies exceeding a certain size need to produce, and have audited, consolidated financial statements.

Presentation of the income statement and balance sheet is based on the general format guidelines of the Fourth EC Directive. The income statement must show operating, nonoperating and exceptional income and expenses and, within these categories, some further minimal disclosures.

The balance sheet should be divided into **current** and long-term **assets**, third party liabilities and shareholders' equity. Again, some further disclosure within each caption is required.

Transactions with group companies and with major shareholders must be separately disclosed.

The notes to the financial statements also include a number of disclosures in the areas of guarantees, securities, commitments and contingencies, group and capital structure, revaluations and net decrease of "hidden reserves." When consolidated financial statements are prepared, the notes include the consolidation and valuation principles.

Reference.   Code of Obligations, article 663g.

4. Business Combinations

Large companies must publish consolidated financial statements. There is no generally accepted methodology for producing such statements, although the current trend is to adopt a methodology close to that set out in the IASs. The Foundation for Accounting and Reporting Recommendations has also issued recommendations for preparing consolidated statements, which broadly follow international methodology.

In its unconsolidated accounts, a company accounts for investments in **subsidiaries** at cost less any provisions necessary to reflect a permanent impairment of value. **Goodwill** forms part of the carrying value of the investment and is not identified separately. There is thus no requirement to write off goodwill, provided that it can be demonstrated that there is no permanent impairment of value.

5. Joint Ventures

Swiss company law requires that investments in a **joint venture** of between 20 and 50 percent of the voting capital would be considered as an **associated company**. The law does not cover in detail investments in unincorporated joint ventures. Accounting for joint venture investments in consolidated financial statements may be on the cost, **equity** or **proportionate consolidation** basis. In unconsolidated financial statements, joint ventures should be accounted for at cost, less any permanent diminution in value.

6. Foreign Currency Translation

There are no specific legal requirements regarding foreign currency translation. Many companies use the exchange rates published annually by the Swiss Federal Tax Administration as of January 1 (the average rates for December) and used for tax purposes, although companies may use different rates (e.g., year-end rates) and methodologies, provided they are prudent.

A technical circular of the Swiss Institute of Accountants proposes that any of four accepted translation methods can be used: current/noncurrent, **monetary/nonmonetary**, modified monetary, or **current rate**. In applying each of these methods it is necessary to ensure that, in general, the imparity principle (recognition of unrealized losses and deferral of unrealized gains) is respected and that assets are stated at the lower of cost or market value. The following additional guidelines of the Swiss Institute exist for individual balance sheet items:

☐ Cash and sight deposits and overdrafts—These may be translated at the year-end rate since the gains and losses can be considered realized.

☐ Other short-term assets and liabilities—Unrealized gains and losses can be offset to arrive at a net position which, if a gain, should be deferred.

☐ Marketable securities—Since such securities can be adjusted to year-end market price, the related exchange gain or loss should be recorded, even if it results in recording an unrealized gain.

☐ Long-term loans receivable and payable—Unrealized gains and losses can be offset provided that they are in the same currency and have the same maturity. A net gain would be deferred and a net loss recognized in accordance with the imparity principle.

☐ Long-term investments—Long-term investments should be translated at **historical cost**, although any unfavorable changes in exchange rates should be taken into account in assessing whether there has been any permanent impairment in value.

Hedges. There is no specific guidance on the treatment of **hedges**. However, normally an exchange gain or loss arising from a hedging operation is offset against the related gain or loss arising from the translation of the balance hedged.

Disclosure. There are no specific disclosure requirements.

Reference. Swiss Institute Handbook, section 2.2.

7. Changing Prices/Inflation Accounting
There are no requirements to provide information on the effects of changes in the price level on financial statements, and most companies do not provide this information.

8. Accounting Changes
Material changes in **accounting policies** must be mentioned in the notes and the effect quantified.

Reference. Code of Obligations, article 662a.

9. Prior Period Adjustments
In unconsolidated financial statements, all adjustments, whether or not they relate to the prior year, must be reflected in current net income, since reserves can be adjusted directly only for transactions of a capital nature that have been approved by the shareholders (e.g., dividends). There is a requirement for separate disclosure of material prior period items in current net income as exceptional items.

For consolidated financial statements, there is at present no specific guidance relating to accounting for **prior period adjustments**.

10. Post Balance Sheet Events
Current Swiss practice is to reflect in the financial statements any losses arising between the balance sheet date and the date the financial statements are prepared, to the extent that they originate from events prior to the balance sheet date. In accordance with the imparity principle, adjustments should be made only with respect to losses, not profits. The Swiss Institute also recommends that similar losses arising after the financial statements are prepared but prior to the shareholders' meeting also be brought to the attention of the shareholders. This is particularly important in cases where this could result in the company's net assets not covering share capital and legal reserves. In addition, disclosure should be made of any matters that have arisen since the balance sheet date that might affect the going concern assumption.

Reference. Swiss Institute Handbook, section 2.2; Swiss Institute Auditing Standard No. 8.

11. Related Party Transactions
Specific disclosure is required of year-end balances with group companies and major shareholders. Receivables from shareholders or related parties should be carefully assessed to ensure that they do not constitute a repayment of share capital in accordance with article 680 of the Code of Obligations.

Reference. Code of Obligations, article 663a.

12. Segmental Information
There are no specific accounting or disclosure requirements for segmental information.

ACCOUNTING PRINCIPLES FOR SPECIFIC ITEMS—
BALANCE SHEET

13. Property, Plant and Equipment

Classification of Capital and Revenue Expenditure. Expenditures that are expected to provide future economic benefits to the company are capitalized; expenditures to maintain normal operating efficiency are expensed as incurred. However, many companies tend to expense certain capital items, such as major renovations, in their unconsolidated financial statements in order to benefit from an immediate tax deduction. Such a policy is inherently prudent and, as such, is acceptable under Swiss accounting principles. These items may be capitalized in the consolidated financial statements.

Basis of Valuation. Company law requires that assets permanently used for the conduct of the business (such as land, buildings, power installations, machinery, transportation equipment, tools and movable property) be valued in the unconsolidated balance sheet at no higher than their purchase price or cost, less adequate **depreciation**.

For buildings, construction interest paid to third parties can be capitalized. Interest paid to shareholders can also be capitalized during the construction period until the company reaches full operating capacity.

Revaluation of **fixed assets** is allowed in unconsolidated financial statements only to cover the deficiency caused by the net assets of the company no longer covering half of its share capital and its legal reserves. In this situation, fixed assets can be revalued up to a maximum of their current value. Any revaluation has to be reviewed and approved by the auditors and the amount of the revaluation has to be allocated to a separate nondistributable revaluation reserve and mentioned in the notes.

In the consolidated financial statements, current or replacement costs may also be used to value property, plant and equipment.

Reference. Code of Obligations, article 670.

Depreciation. Depreciation should be recorded according to generally accepted commercial principles, which imply use of either the **straight-line** or reducing (**declining**) **balance** methods. Replacement reserves over and above these amounts may be created by the board of directors, as can additional undisclosed reserves. The auditors must be notified of the creation and release of replacement and undisclosed reserves, and the notes to the financial statements must mention any material net release of undisclosed reserves.

Reference. Code of Obligations, article 669.

Disclosure. Fixed assets may be shown net of separately disclosed accumulated depreciation, or accumulated depreciation may be shown separately on the liabilities side of the balance sheet. The latter treatment is increasingly less common.

Tangible fixed assets can be presented as one caption in the balance sheet. Further analysis is optional. The fire insurance value of fixed assets should be disclosed in a note.

Reference. Code of Obligations, article 663a.

14. Intangible Assets

Valuation. Company law distinguishes between *intangible fixed assets (Immaterielle Güter [G], immobilisations immatérielles [F])* and *organization costs (Organisations- kosten [G], frais d'organisation [F])*.

Examples of **intangible** fixed **assets** are rights, concessions, patents, special manu- facturing processes, licenses and trademarks. Purchased intangible fixed assets can be capitalized. Organization costs for incorporation of a company, an extension of the scope of the business or a reorganization of the business can be capitalized as long as a clause in the company's bylaws or a resolution of a shareholders' meeting provides for such treatment. The 3 percent stamp duty payable on issuing the company's share capital can be included in organization costs without any special provision or resolution.

Research and development costs are not capitalized unless they can be attributed to a specific product from which it is probable that a profit will result. Purchased goodwill can be capitalized, but self-created goodwill cannot be attributed a value in the balance sheet.

Amortization. Intangible fixed assets should be written off over their economic useful lives. Organization costs must be written off over no more than five years.

Disclosure. Intangible fixed assets and organization costs must be shown separately in the balance sheet.

Reference. Code of Obligations, article 664.

15. Leases

Accounting Treatment. Swiss practice does not make any distinction between **finance** and **operating leases**; all lease payments are treated as period operating expenses. The alternative approach for finance leases—that is, recognizing an asset and a matching liability—is permitted (and encouraged) by the Swiss Institute, but is not generally adopted.

The total amount of leasing obligations not included in the balance sheet must be shown in the notes.

Reference. Code of Obligations, article 663b; Swiss Institute Handbook, section 2.2.

16. Investments

Valuation. Company law requires that *quoted securities* may not be valued at a price higher than their average stock exchange price during the month prior to the date of the balance sheet. *Unquoted securities* may not be valued at higher than cost, and appropriate consideration should be given to whether their current return supports such cost, as well as to any possible decrease in value. The valuation policy may be applied on either an individual investment basis or a **portfolio basis**. Revaluation to current values in uncon- solidated financial statements is possible only if there is a capital deficiency (see Section 13).

Disclosure. Investments in the balance sheet should be split between short term and long term, based on the nature of the holding and management's intention.

Investments in subsidiaries are discussed in Section 4.

Reference. Code of Obligations, article 667.

17. Accounts Receivable

Accounting Treatment. Recognition: The recognition of **revenues**, and hence the related receivables, is outlined in Section 23.

Discounts: Sales and related receivables are normally recorded net of trade and quantity discounts. Cash discounts are usually recognized as an expense at the time of payment.

Allowances: Companies usually make specific provisions for doubtful accounts based on normal commercial criteria as to collection risk. In addition, general provisions are often made, usually up to the maximum allowed for tax purposes (normally 5 percent on domestic receivables and 10 percent on foreign receivables). Many companies do not formally write off a receivable, but fully provide for it, until its irrevocability has been conclusively demonstrated (e.g., receipt of loss certificate from the liquidator).

Factored Receivables. **Factoring of receivables** is not common in Switzerland. When receivables have been factored, they are normally excluded from the balance sheet. If a recourse provision exists, the Swiss Institute recommends that it be disclosed as a contingent liability on the balance sheet.

Disclosure. Receivables are segregated between trade accounts and prepayments/other receivables. Receivables from group companies must be shown separately.

18. Inventories and Work in Progress

General Accounting Treatment. **Inventories** are carried at the lower of cost or market. Commonly used methods of determining cost include **FIFO**, specific cost, **average cost** and **standard cost** (provided the latter gives a prudent valuation). Market is determined by any appropriate method (e.g., **replacement cost, net realizable value**).

For work in progress and finished goods, cost can include direct labor and overhead expenses, although these expenses may be excluded. The Swiss tax authorities permit a one-third general provision against inventory in addition to any specific provisions; many companies take the general provision and reflect it as a reduction of the balance sheet value of inventory in both the unconsolidated and consolidated financial statements, with no additional disclosure.

Long-Term Contracts. There are no specific accounting requirements, and both the **completed contract** and **percentage of completion methods** are acceptable.

Disclosure. There are no specific disclosure requirements.

Reference. Code of Obligations, article 666.

19. Current Liabilities

General Accounting Treatment. Companies must distinguish between **current liabilities** and long-term liabilities.

Trade **accounts payable** normally include amounts payable to suppliers for goods and services for which an invoice has been received. Where no invoice has been received at the time of closing the books, it is usual to include an estimate in accrued liabilities, although sometimes the amounts are classified as provisions. Balances with related companies or significant shareholders must be disclosed separately.

Creation of General and Specific Provisions. General provisions and value adjustments may be made that exceed generally accepted commercial principles. See Section 3 for the reporting and disclosure of these amounts.

20. Long-Term Debt

General Accounting Treatment. The most common forms of long-term debt are loans, bonds and mortgages. They are generally included in the balance sheet at their face value as long as they continue to represent a present obligation to the entity. In particular, company law addresses the treatment of bonds, which must be shown as a liability for the full amount repayable and indicated separately in the balance sheet, with interest rates and repayment dates included in the notes.

If bonds are repayable at a premium, the amount of the premium may be recorded as a liability and an asset, and the asset may be amortized by charges to income over the period to the maturity date. If the bonds are repayable in equal annual instalments, any premium can be expensed as the bonds are repaid.

Debt Extinguishment. Any gain or loss would be included in income when the debt is extinguished.

Disclosure. Where a loan (either long term or short term) is subordinated, that fact should be indicated and the amount shown separately in the notes.

Reference. Code of Obligations, article 663b.

21. Contingencies

General. **Contingencies** are accounted for in accordance with the imparity principle. This means that contingent losses that can be estimated at the balance sheet date and are likely to occur should be provided for. Company law specifically requires provisions to be made for any foreseeable losses in connection with suretyships, guarantees and other securities granted in favor of third parties, or with the performance of contracts for delivery or acceptance of goods or services and similar contracts not yet performed. Contingent gains, regardless of their probability, should be deferred.

Disclosure. If a provision has been made for a contingent loss, no further disclosure is normally made in the financial statements. Disclosure must be made of a loss contingency that cannot reasonably be quantified. The disclosure might be made in the auditors' report in a statement following the auditors' approval of the financial statements.

Company law requires disclosure of the following contingent liabilities in the notes: suretyships, guarantees and other securities granted in favor of third parties.

Reference. Code of Obligations, article 663b.

22. Capital and Reserves

General. Shareholders' equity must be divided into **share capital**, legal reserves and **retained earnings**.

Share Capital. Company law requires new companies to have a minimum share capital of SFr. 100,000, divided into shares of a minimum nominal value of SFr. 10. Shares can be either registered or bearer. Certain shares can also be accorded preferred rights (such as to dividends) or privileged voting rights based on equal voting rights for shares of differing nominal values. The company may also issue participation certificates, with or without **par value**, which are similar to nonvoting stock (Partizipationsscheine [G], bons de participation [F]).

Authorized and conditional share capital may be issued. In the case of authorized share capital, the board of directors is authorized to increase the capital up to the predetermined amount within two years. Conditional share capital can be utilized only for convertible bonds or option rights, or to create employee shares.

Shares may be issued in excess of nominal value; the premium, after deduction of expenses, is allocated to the general legal reserve. At least 20 percent of the share capital, or a minimum of SFr. 50,000, must be paid in. The unpaid share capital must be shown as an asset on the balance sheet. Contributions in kind, such as buildings and machinery, must be specifically itemized in the company's bylaws. A company and subsidiaries may own up to 10 percent of the company's own shares (**treasury stock**). A reduction of share capital requires a special report from specially qualified auditors, assuring that the claims of creditors are fully covered. The share capital cannot be reduced below SFr. 100,000.

Legal Reserves. General reserve: A first allocation of 5 percent of net profit must be made to the general reserve each year until this reserve reaches 20 percent of share capital. A second allocation is made of the following amounts:

☐ Any **share premium**, as mentioned above.

☐ The excess of the amount paid in on cancelled shares over a lower issue price of replacement shares.

☐ 10 percent of any dividend distribution in excess of a 5 percent annual dividend.

There is a ceiling of 50 percent of share capital, over which amount no further allocation to the general reserve need be made (the allocation should be made formally but it can subsequently be released). Below 50 percent, the legal reserve can be used only to cover losses, to support the company through periods of depressed business or to relieve unemployment or mitigate its consequences.

Holding companies are not required to make the second allocation with respect to dividend distributions.

Revaluation reserves: Where revaluations of fixed assets or investments have been made to make good capital deficiencies, the amount must be allocated to the legally prescribed revaluation reserve.

Reserve for own shares: Where a company has acquired its own shares, a legal reserve equal to the acquisition value of those shares must be established.

Other reserves: Other reserves may be established as required by the company's bylaws. Allocations and releases can be decided only by a shareholders' meeting.

Distribution Restrictions.   Dividends may be paid only from retained earnings or reserves specially created for this purpose. They require approval at a shareholders' meeting. Dividends from current earnings are not permitted.

Disclosure.   Companies must show the separate categories of share capital on the face of the balance sheet; any capital increases, purchase or sale of own shares, and authorized and conditional share capital must be disclosed in the notes. The proposal of the board of directors to the annual shareholders' meeting for the appropriation of retained earnings and other reserves is shown in a separate schedule, on which the auditors must confirm compliance with the law and the company's bylaws.

If half the share capital is no longer covered by assets, the board of directors must call a shareholders' meeting and make this known. If there are reasonable grounds for assuming insolvency, an interim balance sheet must be prepared based on realizable values. If the company's assets no longer cover its liabilities, the board must inform the relevant commercial court. The auditors must call attention to such a situation in their audit report in order to make readers aware of the situation and remind the board of its obligations.

Reference.   Code of Obligations, article 725.

ACCOUNTING PRINCIPLES FOR SPECIFIC ITEMS— INCOME STATEMENT

23. Revenue Recognition

General Principles.   There are no formal standards dealing with revenue recognition. In practice, revenue is recognized for the sale of goods when significant risks and rewards of ownership have been transferred; for service transactions, when the service is performed.

Long-Term Contracts.   Swiss companies may apply either the completed contract method or the percentage of completion method.

Instalment Sales.   The general principles enumerated above normally apply, although following the principle of prudence, companies often defer recognizing revenue until the due date of payment for the **instalment sale.**

Rights of Return.   Normally, a right of return provision is taken into account in assessing the need for warranty and other provisions, and influences the recognition of a sale only if it is usual for this option to be exercised to a significant extent.

Product Financing. Normally, an agreement to sell and repurchase at a later date means that the risks and benefits of ownership have not passed to the buyer; thus, revenue should not be recognized and the transaction should be treated as a financing transaction.

Disclosure. Total revenues must be disclosed in the income statement, separated into operating, nonoperating and exceptional revenues and between revenue from sales of goods or services, financial income and sales of fixed assets.

24. Government Grants and Assistance

Accounting Treatment. No specific accounting practice has developed in Switzerland since direct government grants and investment subsidies are rare.

25. Research and Development

Definition. No specific definition exists in Swiss accounting practice.

Accounting Treatment. Research and development costs should be expensed when incurred unless they can be attributed to a specific product from which it is probable that a profit will result. Normally, however, Swiss companies write off such costs as they arise.

Disclosure. There are no specific disclosure requirements.

Reference. Swiss Institute Handbook, section 2.2.

26. Capitalized Interest Costs

Accounting Treatment. This is discussed in Section 13. Normally, interest is capitalized only on construction projects, if at all.

Disclosure. There are no specific disclosure requirements.

27. Imputed Interest

General. Interest is normally imputed only with respect to a long-term loan receivable that either does not bear interest or where the interest rate is obviously too low. In this circumstance it is acceptable to discount the loan to its present value using an appropriate interest rate, in accordance with the imparity principle.

Reference. Swiss Institute Handbook, section 2.2.

28. Extraordinary or Unusual Items

Definition. No specific definition of extraordinary or unusual items exists in Switzerland, and it would be normal to refer to definitions in other sources of **accounting standards**.

Disclosure. Extraordinary or unusual items should be separately disclosed in the income statement.

Reference. Code of Obligations, article 663.

29. Income Taxes

Accounting Treatment. Deferred income tax in itself does not arise in Swiss unconsolidated accounts since there are usually no timing differences between these accounts and the tax accounts (tax-deductible provisions must be reflected in the unconsolidated accounts). Clearly, where provisions in the unconsolidated accounts exceed those in the tax accounts (or where the disallowance of a provision is probable), tax on the amount should be included in the current tax provision. A deferred tax asset would usually not be recorded in these circumstances.

For unconsolidated purposes, companies need provide only for taxes due for the current year assessment. Since until 1994 federal and certain cantonal income taxes are based on the results of periods prior to the current one, the tax provisions may not include an amount for taxes arising in the future on current income. There may therefore be an incomplete matching of pretax income and income tax expense. The preferred, and increasingly prevalent, practice is, however, to provide for future taxes on current earnings in the unconsolidated accounts.

Swiss tax legislation does not provide for loss carrybacks, except to the extent that one year's loss can offset the previous year's profit in tax jurisdictions where two-year assessment periods exist. It is not usual to give any accounting recognition to the future benefit of loss carryforwards.

There are no further accounting principles specified in this area for consolidated financial statements, although an increasing number of major Swiss companies follow IAS requirements.

Disclosure. Taxes do not have to be shown as a separate caption in either the income statement or the balance sheet.

30. Postretirement Benefits

Accounting Treatment. Companies normally treat as a period expense the actual amounts paid or due to the pension fund during the year. Provision is also normally made for any underfunding, as a matter of prudence. The concept of allocating payments in excess of an actuarially determined net periodic pension cost to a future period is unusual when preparing unconsolidated financial statements. This even extends to large single payments made to pension funds in excess of current requirements, which are usually made to enable the company to avail itself of a tax deduction. When preparing consolidated financial statements, however, many major Swiss companies are voluntarily using actuarially calculated amounts for the pension liability and pension expense, and it can be expected that the use of such methods will increase in the future.

Pension Fund Surpluses. Pension fund contributions are required to be paid into plans that are independent of the company. Surpluses cannot be repaid to the company. To the extent that such surpluses can be attributed to past employer contributions in excess of those required, they may in certain circumstances be used by the company to reduce or replace future contributions. However, accounting recognition should be limited to reducing or eliminating pension expense in a particular year. No deferred asset should be recorded.

Disclosure. Pension fund and similar liabilities need to be disclosed separately in the notes to the financial statements.

31. Discontinued Operations
There are no specific accounting or disclosure requirements for discontinued operations.

32. Earnings per Share
The definition and computation of earnings per share information are drawn from international practice. Such information is not required to be disclosed.

Appendix
DO SWISS STANDARDS OR PREVALENT PRACTICE SUBSTANTIALLY COMPLY WITH INTERNATIONAL ACCOUNTING STANDARDS?

Section	Topic	Substantially complies with IAS?	Comments
3.	Basic accounting concepts and conventions	Yes	Except that excessive prudence is permitted in creating provisions and, in certain circumstances, the legal form rather than its substance is followed
	Contents of financial statements	No	No cash flow statement or statement of changes in financial position is required
4.	Business combinations*	Yes	The current trend is to follow international methodology, although this is not universal
5.	Joint ventures	No	
6.	Foreign currency translation*	No	
8.	Accounting changes*	Yes	Required only after the introduction of the new law
9.	Prior period adjustments*	Yes	Required only after the introduction of the new law
10.	Post balance sheet events	Yes	
11.	Related party transactions	No	The new law requires disclosure of related party items in the balance sheet
12.	Segmental information	No	
13.	Property, plant and equipment*	Yes	Except accelerated depreciation is permitted
15.	Leases	No	
16.	Investments	Yes	
17.	Accounts receivable	Yes	
18.	Inventories and work in progress*	Yes	

Appendix (*Continued*)

Section	Topic	Substantially complies with IAS?	Comments
19.	Current liabilities	No	General provisions in excess of commercial requirements may be created
20.	Long-term debt	No	See current liabilities
21.	Contingencies	Yes	Except that there is no requirement to disclose contingent gains
22.	Capital and reserves	Yes	
23.	Revenue recognition*	Yes	
24.	Government grants and assistance	No	
25.	Research and development*	Yes	
26.	Capitalization of interest costs*	Yes	
28.	Extraordinary or unusual items*	Yes	The new law requires disclosure, but extraordinary items are not specifically defined
29.	Income tax**	No	
30.	Postretirement benefits*	No	

*These topics are subject to change as a result of the IASC Improvements Project—see the appendix to the International Accounting Standards chapter.

**The IAS on accounting for taxes on income is currently being revised, and an exposure draft has been issued.

Comparison in this table is made to International Accounting Standards in force at January 1, 1993. For further details, see the International Accounting Standards chapter.

UNITED KINGDOM

GENERAL NATIONAL INFORMATION

1. Source of Generally Accepted Accounting Principles

Generally Accepted Accounting Principles and Practices. **Generally accepted accounting principles** and practices are derived from the following sources:

☐ The Companies Act 1985 (as amended by the Companies Act 1989) (the Act) defines formats for profit and loss accounts and balance sheets. It also includes valuation rules for historical cost accounts and separate valuation rules that apply specifically to assets included in the accounts at a value other than historical cost. Furthermore, the Act includes a number of general accounting rules, detailed rules that apply to consolidations and detailed disclosure requirements. This legislation applies to Great Britain. Similar legislation for Northern Ireland is embodied in the Companies (Northern Ireland) Order 1986.

☐ Financial Reporting Standards (FRSs) issued by the Accounting Standards Board (ASB) and Statements of Standard Accounting Practice (SSAPs) issued by the ASB's predecessor body, the Accounting Standards Committee (ASC) and adopted by the ASB.

☐ Abstracts issued by the Urgent Issues Task Force (UITF). These abstracts deal with particular issues brought to the attention of the UITF. Although they do not have the statutory backing of **accounting standards,** they are considered to be part of UK GAAP, and the ASB considers compliance with them necessary to give a true and fair view.

☐ Statements of Recommended Practice (SORPs) issued by the ASC. These statements are developed when there is a need for guidance on a specific topic, but not an FRS. Adherence to these statements is not mandatory, but they are an indication of best accounting practice and companies are encouraged to comply with them. Some SORPs have been backed by legislation, and noncompliance has to be disclosed.

☐ Approved (''franked'') SORPs are issued by certain specialized industries and indicate recommended accounting practice on specific topics. Adherence to franked SORPs is not mandatory, although companies in those industries generally comply with their requirements.

□ The United Kingdom's International Stock Exchange's Continuing Obligations (the **Yellow Book**) includes accounting disclosure requirements for companies listed on the Stock Exchange; its General Undertaking includes similar requirements for companies traded on a second-tier market known as the Unlisted Securities Market (USM).

□ Technical Releases issued by professional accounting bodies (see below) indicate best accounting practice and often precede an exposure draft of an accounting standard.

Accounting Standards. Previously, accounting standards in the United Kingdom, known as SSAPs, were developed by the ASC, a committee of the Consultative Committee of Accounting Bodies Limited (CCAB). They were then issued by the governing councils of the Institute of Chartered Accountants in England and Wales (ICAEW), the Institute of Chartered Accountants of Scotland (ICAS), the Institute of Chartered Accountants in Ireland (ICAI), the Chartered Association of Certified Accountants (CACA), the Chartered Institute of Public Finance and Accountancy (CIPFA) and the Chartered Institute of Management Accountants (CIMA). Currently, accounting standards are developed and issued by an independent Accounting Standards Board. The obligation to prepare financial statements that give a true and fair view means that a company should follow applicable accounting standards unless there are good reasons not to do so.

2. Audit and Public Company Requirements

Audits. Every limited company, except a dormant company that has passed a resolution not to do so, is obligated to appoint auditors at each general meeting at which the company's financial statements are presented. In certain circumstances, a private company may elect, by resolution, not to reappoint its auditors annually. Where auditors are appointed, they are required to report whether in their opinion:

□ The balance sheet and the profit and loss account of the company and the **consolidated financial statements**, if prepared, have been properly prepared in accordance with the Act.

□ A true and fair view is given by the financial statements of the state of the company's affairs at the end of the financial year, and of the company's profit or loss for that year.

□ If consolidated financial statements are presented, a true and fair view is given of the state of affairs and the profit or loss of the company and its **subsidiaries**.

The auditors also assess whether the company has kept proper accounting records, whether they have received adequate audit evidence in the form of ''proper returns'' regarding those branches they did not visit and whether the financial statements agree with the accounting records. If any matters are not complied with, the noncompliance should be specifically reported in the auditors' report.

In addition, auditors have a statutory duty to include certain information in their report if the information is not disclosed in the financial statements. This includes information related to:

□ The **directors' emoluments** (salaries and other benefits), pensions and compensation for loss of office (including noncash assets).

□ Loans and other transactions benefiting directors.

Auditors are also required to report significant departures from FRSs and SSAPs, except where they concur with any departure from an FRS or a SSAP.

Other duties and obligations of auditors are contained in Auditing Standards and Guidelines. These standards and guidelines are developed and issued by the Auditing Practices Board (APB), previously known as the Auditing Practices Committee (APC), a committee of the CCAB. Auditing standards prescribe the basic principles and practices that members of the issuing organizations are expected to follow when conducting an audit.

The Companies Act 1989 implemented the European Community's (EC) Eighth Directive, which seeks to harmonize the qualifications of those entitled to carry out audits in the EC. The Act separates the authorization and supervision functions, undertaken by Recognized Supervisory Bodies (RSBs), from the examination and training functions, undertaken by Recognized Qualifying Bodies (RQBs). Any professional body may apply to become an RSB and/or an RQB. The ICAEW, ICAS, ICAI and CACA are all RSBs and RQBs. RPBs regulate the auditing profession, and RQBs oversee qualifications.

Public Companies. In order for a company to be a **public company** under the Act, it must maintain a minimum allotted share capital of £50,000, of which one-quarter must be paid up.

A public limited company may become a **listed** public **company** if any part of its shares or debt securities have been admitted to the Official List of the International Stock Exchange. Alternatively, it may become a quoted public company if any of its shares are quoted on the USM. The regulatory requirements for registration and listing as a public company are set out in the Act and the Yellow Book. The Yellow Book states that the market value of securities must be at least £700,000 in the case of shares and £200,000 in the case of debt. This provides a guideline for the marketability of the company. In addition, the Yellow Book stipulates that 25 percent of any class of shares must be in the hands of the public for a public company to be listed.

The reporting requirements for a public company do not differ significantly from those for a private limited company, except that for listed companies there are requirements for certain additional financial statement disclosures imposed by the International Stock Exchange's Continuing Obligations or, for USM companies, its General Undertaking.

A public company is required by the Act to deliver accounts to the Registrar of Companies within seven months after the end of the relevant accounting period. The equivalent period for private companies is 10 months. Fixed penalties apply for noncompliance with this requirement.

Small and Medium-Sized Companies. Small companies are defined as those companies that fall within two of the following three criteria:

□ **Turnover** less than £2.8m.
□ Balance sheet total less than £1.4m.
□ Employees fewer than 50.

There are various concessions in the Act, which exempt small companies from some of the detailed disclosures required in the balance sheet and profit and loss account and in the notes.

In addition, small and medium-sized companies may file abbreviated financial statements with the Registrar of Companies, although they are still required to issue full financial statements to their shareholders (subject to the concessions mentioned above for small companies).

Summary Financial Statements.　In certain circumstances, shareholders in listed companies may elect to receive summary financial statements instead of full financial statements. Whether a listed company's shareholders are sent full or summary financial statements, every listed company is required to file with the Registrar full financial statements.

GENERAL ACCOUNTING

3.　Financial Statements

Basic Accounting Concepts.　Financial statements are normally prepared on the **historical cost accounting** basis. However, the Companies Act 1985 allows alternative accounting rules. These rules allow the revaluation of certain assets, as follows:

- □　**Intangible** fixed **assets** may be stated at their current cost, determined in accordance with the ASC handbook entitled *Accounting for the Effects of Changing Prices*.
- □　Tangible **fixed assets** may be stated either at their market value on the date when they were last valued or at their current cost.
- □　Fixed asset investments may be shown either at their market value on the date at which they were last valued or at a value determined on a basis the directors consider appropriate if market values are not available.
- □　**Current asset** investments may be stated at their current cost (as defined below).
- □　**Stocks** may be stated at their current cost.

Current cost was defined by the ASC as the lower of an asset's net current replacement cost or its recoverable amount. Recoverable amount is the higher of the asset's **net realizable value** or the amount recoverable from its future use.

Thus, companies may base their financial statements on either the pure historical cost convention, the historical cost convention modified for the revaluation of certain assets, or current cost. The majority of companies issue modified historical cost financial statements, with certain fixed assets revalued.

The assumptions underlying financial statements are governed by the Act, which identifies the **going concern concept**, the consistency concept, the **prudence concept**, the **accruals concept** and the **individual evaluation concept** for assets and liabilities. SSAP 2 also prescribes these concepts, except for the individual evaluation concept. Furthermore, the concept of **substance over form** is now generally accepted, although not yet the subject of an accounting standard. An exposure draft on off balance sheet finance, Financial Reporting Exposure Draft No. 4 (FRED 4), which deals with the concept of substance over form, was published in February 1993.

In addition, as mentioned in Section 2, it is a fundamental requirement that financial statements give a true and fair view. In certain circumstances, it is necessary to depart from the provisions of the Act in order to give a true and fair view. Where this is necessary, the particulars of the departure, the reasons for it and its effect should be given in the notes to the financial statements. UITF Abstract 7 details how this disclosure should be made.

When a company uses a method such as FIFO and the resulting valuation differs materially from the "relevant alternative amount" of the items, the difference should be disclosed in a note to the financial statements.

The "relevant alternative amount" is the amount of the assets determined according to their replacement cost as at the balance sheet date. The replacement cost will normally be the current cost, but it may instead be the most recent actual purchase price or production cost.

Contents of Financial Statements. Financial statements generally include a directors' report (a narrative supplement to the financial statements), a profit and loss account, a balance sheet, a cash flow statement (required by FRS 1), a statement of total recognized gains and losses (required by FRS 3), a statement of accounting policies and notes that are referenced to those financial statements.

In the case of a group, the financial statements also include a consolidated balance sheet, a consolidated profit and loss account, a consolidated cash flow statement and a consolidated statement of total recognized gains and losses. In certain circumstances, the profit and loss account of the **parent company** need not be reproduced in the consolidated financial statements if the omission is explained in the notes, nor is there a requirement to include a cash flow statement or a statement of total recognized gains and losses for the parent. Therefore, generally the only statement of the parent company to appear in a set of consolidated financial statements is its own balance sheet in addition to the group's consolidated balance sheet.

Format of Financial Statements. The Fourth EC Directive, enacted in the UK by the Companies Act 1981, details two balance sheet formats and four profit and loss account formats, which are standard throughout the EC. The company's directors may choose the particular formats to follow. There are strict rules governing the use of the formats and when they can be amended. Certain required detailed information can be shown in the notes to the financial statements. As mentioned above, small companies may present amounts relating to certain specified items in the aggregate. Examples of the format of cash flow statements are given in the appendix to FRS 1, which requires cash flows to be shown under the following standard headings:

☐ Operating activities.
☐ Returns on investments and servicing finance.
☐ Taxation.
☐ Investing.
☐ Financing.
☐ Movement in cash and cash equivalents.

The cash inflow/outflow from operating activities can be shown as a single line item, or the detailed cash flows making up the figure (i.e., the **direct method**) may also be given, but this is not mandatory. A reconciliation also has to be given, in a note, between the operating profit and the cash inflow/outflow from operating activities. Totals must be given for each heading in the cash flow statement and for the net cash flow before financing. The analysis of the movement in cash and cash equivalents is given as a note.

Disclosure of Accounting Policies. Both the Act and SSAP 2 require the company's **accounting policies** to be disclosed. For example, accounting policies would include the basis of accounting; the treatment of **associated companies**; research and development; intangible assets; goodwill; fixed asset valuations; investment properties; leased assets and obligations; the treatment of government grants; valuation of fixed asset investments; valuation of stocks and long-term contracts; the treatment of deferred tax; pension costs; foreign currency translation; and the basis on which turnover is stated. The Act also requires companies to state in their financial statements whether they comply with "applicable accounting standards."

4. Business Combinations

Principles of Consolidation. The Companies Act 1989 and FRS 2 require the parent undertaking of a group to prepare consolidated accounts that include all subsidiary undertakings, including unincorporated entities such as partnerships as well as limited companies.

Control rather than legal ownership determines whether an undertaking is a subsidiary (see below). Under the Act subsidiaries *may* be excluded from consolidation for the following reasons:

□ The subsidiary is not **material**; however, two or more subsidiaries can be excluded only if they are not material taken together.

□ Severe long-term restrictions substantially hinder the parent's exercise of its rights over the assets or management of the subsidiary. FRS 2 *requires* exclusion where this restriction applies because control can no longer be exercised.

□ The interest of the parent is held exclusively with a view to subsequent resale and the subsidiary has not previously been included in the consolidated financial statements. FRS 2 has added that a purchaser must have been sought or must be being sought and the subsidiary must be reasonably expected to be disposed of within approximately one year of its date of acquisition.

□ The activities of one or more subsidiaries are so different from those of the other subsidiaries that their inclusion would be incompatible with the obligation to give a true and fair view. FRS 2 has restricted the use of this exemption as the ASB has been unable to identify any particular contrast of activities where the necessary incompatibility with the true and fair view generally occurs.

Accounting for Business Combinations. A **business combination** arises where one undertaking buys shares in another undertaking, which becomes a subsidiary. There are two accounting methods that can be applied to business combinations in the UK. **Acquisition accounting** applies in the majority of situations. **Merger accounting**, which is equivalent to pooling, can be used, provided that certain conditions in the Act and in SSAP 23 are complied with. Merger relief is an exemption, granted by statute, that eliminates the need for the acquiring company to account for the premium on the issue of shares given as consideration for the purchase of another company. Merger relief is available to the company regardless of whether acquisition accounting or merger accounting is used for the combination.

Acquisition Accounting. In acquisition accounting, the fair value of the consideration given in the acquisition is offset against the fair value of the net assets of the undertaking acquired. The difference represents goodwill or negative goodwill. All identifiable assets, including intangibles, of the undertaking acquired are valued. This practice has led recently to intangibles such as brand names being separately identified in consolidated financial statements. Fair value adjustments can be made either on consolidation or in the books of the acquired company. This applies with the exception of the valuation of stocks and long-term contracts, which have to be adjusted on consolidation.

Merger Accounting. Where merger accounting is used, the book values of assets and liabilities of the merged undertaking and of the group are consolidated without fair value adjustment. In addition, the profit and loss account for the entire period of the merged undertaking is included in the consolidated profit and loss account. Current and prior year amounts for both the profit and loss account and the balance sheet are shown as if the entities had always been combined.

Control. Control is indicated in a number of ways, as follows:

☐   The parent holds a majority of the voting rights in an undertaking.

☐   The parent is a **member** (shareholder) of the undertaking and has the right to appoint or remove a majority of the undertaking's board of directors.

☐   The parent has the right to exercise dominant influence over the undertaking via provisions included in its memorandum or articles of association (the company's written rule book).

☐   The parent has the right to exercise dominant influence over an undertaking via a control contract.

☐   The parent is a member of the undertaking and controls, via an agreement with other shareholders, the majority of the voting rights in the undertaking.

☐   The parent has a participating interest (over 20%) in the undertaking and actually exercises dominant influence over it.

☐   The parent has a participating interest in the undertaking and both the parent and the undertaking are managed on a unified basis.

Goodwill. The treatment of purchased **goodwill** arising on consolidation is governed by SSAP 22, which, while giving options, indicates a preference for the immediate write-off of consolidation goodwill to reserves. Normally, this write-off is made directly to the profit and loss account reserve or the merger reserve, although some companies may create a negative reserve by writing off goodwill to a reserve that starts with a zero balance. Companies may also apply to the court to form general reserves from their share premium account against which goodwill can be written off. SSAP 22 also allows companies to amortize goodwill over a period not to exceed the goodwill's useful life. In practice, most companies write goodwill off immediately to reserves; however, some amortize goodwill over periods of up to 40 years. Where goodwill is written off to reserves on acquisition and the entity acquired is subsequently sold, the profit or loss on sale has to be calculated in accordance with UITF Abstract 3 to include the goodwill previously taken to reserves (thereby reducing the profit or increasing the loss on sale). **Negative goodwill** arising on consolidation is added to reserves.

Equity Accounting.   If an investor has a participating interest in another undertaking and exercises significant influence over the undertaking's operating and financial policies, that undertaking should be treated as an associated undertaking. An investor that holds 20 percent or more of the voting rights in another undertaking is presumed to exercise significant influence unless there is evidence to the contrary. A number of factors may indicate significant influence in practice, such as board representation. All associated undertakings are required by the Act to be accounted for by the **equity method**.

Minority Interests.   There are prescribed lines in the balance sheet and profit and loss account for **minority interests**. Minority interests in the consolidated balance sheet show the amount of capital and reserves attributable to shares in subsidiaries included in the consolidation that are held by or on behalf of persons other than the parent and its subsidiaries. Similarly, minority interests in the consolidated profit and loss account include the amount of any profit or loss on ordinary activities attributable to shares in subsidiaries included in the consolidation that are held by or on behalf of persons other than the parent and its subsidiaries.

Disclosure.   General: The names of the undertakings acquired or merged have to be disclosed, along with the accounting method used. In addition, the number and class of shares issued have to be disclosed, with details of any other consideration exchanged. For both acquisition and merger accounting, the fair value of the total consideration given has to be disclosed.

Acquisition accounting: Financial statements have to disclose the nature and amount of significant accounting adjustments necessary to achieve consistency of accounting policies. Details must be provided regarding the profit and loss accounts of the undertaking or group acquired from the beginning of the financial year to the date of acquisition and for its previous financial year. Sufficient information has to be disclosed about the acquired companies' results to enable users of financial statements to assess the acquisition's effect on the consolidated results.

For each material acquisition, a table must be given showing the book values of assets and liabilities acquired and their fair values at the date of acquisition. The table should present fair value adjustments, provisions for future trading losses foreseen at the time of purchase and other provisions needed to bring accounting policies into alignment. Adjustments made in future years to provisions created upon acquisition have to be divided between amounts used and amounts released, unused or applied for another purpose. In addition, adjustments may be made to the fair values provisionally used at the date of acquisition, during a period after the acquisition known as a ''hindsight period,'' but these have to be explained.

The cumulative amount of goodwill written off in the current year and earlier years, net of any amounts attributable to subsidiaries sold, has to be disclosed.

Merger accounting: The nature and amount of any significant accounting adjustments have to be disclosed. The profit and loss account of the acquired undertaking from the beginning of the financial year to the date of the merger has to be shown, with that of the previous year. In addition, profit before extraordinary items both before and after the effective date of the merger is shown separately for the group, excluding the undertaking acquired, and for the undertaking acquired. Extraordinary items are presented both before and after the merger, indicating the party to which each item relates.

5. Joint Ventures

Accounting for Investments in Joint Ventures. UK accounting requirements do not address the different forms of **joint venture** detailed in International Accounting Standard (IAS) 31, *Financial Reporting of Interests in Joint Ventures*. Joint ventures may either be incorporated or unincorporated.

Jointly Controlled Entities. If there is **joint control** of a venture, then consolidation accounting is inappropriate. However, there must be a sharing of risks and rewards. If one party has more than a 50 percent share in the risks and rewards of the venture, then consolidation is required.

The usual method of accounting for joint ventures is the equity method since it recognizes income when earned, matches costs with revenues and gives appropriate treatment to transactions with the joint venture. Where a joint venture is incorporated, no alternative accounting treatment is allowed. However, where the joint venture is unincorporated the investing company may choose between the equity accounting method and the **proportional consolidation method**. In joint ventures where the investment is below 20 percent and the investing company does not have significant influence over the joint venture, the investment should be recorded at cost or at its current cost (i.e., market value or share of net assets).

Jointly Controlled Operations. The accounting treatment in IAS 31 would be appropriate in the UK.

Jointly Controlled Assets. The accounting treatment in IAS 31 would be appropriate in the UK.

Transactions Between Venturers and the Joint Venture. In general, the contribution of assets to a joint venture in exchange for an interest in the joint venture does not give rise to a gain or loss on disposal in the contributor's financial statements. Gains resulting from other transactions between the venturer and the joint venture should be recognized only to the extent of the interests of nonrelated venturers. However, losses should be recognized in their entirety.

Disclosure. Equity accounting: Where the results or assets and liabilities of a joint venture or a group of ventures are so material in the context of the investing group, additional disclosure should be made of their turnover, depreciation, profit or loss before tax, profits or losses attributable to the investing group, tangible and intangible assets and liabilities.

Proportional consolidation accounting: No specific additional disclosures are required, although similar disclosures to those required where a company is consolidated in full would generally be given.

In addition, where the venturer is liable for any contingent liability or commitment with respect to the joint venture, this should be disclosed.

UK requirements are consistent with IAS 31, except that the equity method of accounting for an investment in a jointly controlled entity is the required treatment for joint venture companies. The **benchmark treatment** of proportionate consolidation is allowed only for unincorporated joint ventures. UK requirements for the treatment of transactions between the venturers and the joint venture, and for the recognition of **contingencies** and commitments of and related to the joint venture, are similar to those in IAS 31 except that a venturer may not recognize a gain on assets contributed to a venture in exchange for an interest therein.

Accounting by Joint Ventures. Generally accepted accounting principles apply to assets and liabilities and operations of incorporated joint ventures. Generally, such principles would also apply to unincorporated joint ventures, particularly where auditors report on their accounts in true and fair terms. There is no specific guidance in the UK on accounting by joint ventures for assets contributed to them by the venturers. Such transfers would generally be made at fair value, but carrying value of the assets in the contributor's financial statements in certain situations might alternatively be used.

6. Foreign Currency Translation

Domestic Operations. Revenue or costs arising from a transaction denominated in a foreign currency should be translated into the local currency at the exchange rate in effect on the date of the transaction. If a transaction is settled by a contracted rate, that rate should be used. No subsequent translation should normally be made once nonmonetary assets have been translated and recorded. At the balance sheet date, monetary assets and liabilities denominated in foreign currencies should be translated using the exchange rate on that date (the closing rate) or, where appropriate, the exchange rates contracted under the terms of the relevant transaction. All exchange gains and losses arising from these transactions should be taken to the profit and loss account.

Foreign Operations. For consolidation purposes the accounts of a foreign enterprise should normally be translated using the **closing rate**/net investment **method**. Under this method, the profit and loss account would be translated at the closing rate or at an average rate for the period. The balance sheet of the foreign enterprise would be translated using the closing rate. The difference between the opening net investment in a foreign enterprise translated at the closing rate of the previous year and the closing rate of the current year should be adjusted to the statement of total recognized gains and losses in accordance with FRS 3. Previously, such differences would have been taken directly to reserves. In certain circumstances, such as where a branch operates as an extension of the company and the branch's cash flows have a direct impact on those of the company, the **temporal method** of translation should be used.

Hedges. If an individual company has monetary assets denominated in a foreign currency that are matched with forward contracts, the exchange rates specified in those contracts should be used. If a company or group uses foreign currency borrowing to finance or provide a **hedge** against its foreign equity investments and certain conditions are complied with, the net exchange difference arising on translating the foreign currency borrowing and the investments may be offset as a reserve movement.

Disclosure. The accounting policies should disclose the methods used to translate the financial statements of foreign enterprises and the treatment of exchange differences. Where the offset procedure is used (as outlined above), the amount offset in reserves has to be disclosed together with the net amount taken to the profit and loss account. All companies have to disclose the net movement on reserves arising from exchange differences.

7. Changing Prices/Inflation Accounting

General.   There is no requirement in the UK to make any adjustments for inflation or changes in prices. However, as mentioned in Section 3, companies may revalue their assets using the alternative accounting rules.

Current cost financial statements based on the methods outlined in the ASC handbook entitled *Accounting for the Effects of Changing Prices* are rarely prepared, except in some nationalized industries.

Methods of Calculating and Reporting the Effects of Inflation.   The ASC handbook outlines two methods of calculating and reporting the effects of inflation. The ASC recommends that companies use current cost asset valuation together with either the operating or financial capital maintenance concept. The other method the handbook details is the current purchasing power method of accounting for inflation.

Disclosure.   Where current cost information is presented, it is normally as supplementary information to the company's or group's main financial statements.

8. Accounting Changes

Accounting Treatment.   It is a fundamental **accounting concept** that accounting treatment be consistent within a period and from one period to the next. Consequently, a change in accounting policy can be justified only on the grounds that the new policy is preferable. If there has been a change in accounting policy, FRS 3 (previously SSAP 6) requires the amounts for the current and the corresponding periods to be restated on the basis of the new policy; that is, that the change be accounted for as a prior year adjustment (see Section 9).

Estimating future events requires the exercise of judgment. Since a change in estimate arises from new information, FRS 3 (previously SSAP 6) requires changes in estimates to be accounted for in the year that the change is made.

Disclosure.   Changes in accounting policy should be disclosed in accordance with the disclosure for prior period adjustments (see Section 9).

Changes in accounting methods used (for example, changing from the **straight-line** depreciation **method** to the **sum-of-the-years'-digits method**), if material, may be disclosed as exceptional items (see Section 28).

9. Prior Period Adjustments

Definition of Adjusting Items.   As mentioned above, a **prior period adjustment** must be made where there is a change in accounting policy. In addition, fundamental financial statement errors found at a later date should be accounted for as prior period adjustments. A fundamental error is one of such significance that it would destroy the true and fair view, and therefore the validity, of the company's financial statements.

Accounting Treatment. For both changes in accounting policy and correction of fundamental errors, the prior period profit and loss account and balance sheet have to be adjusted. The reserves note should present the reserves as previously reported, the prior year adjustment and the restated reserves. Under FRS 3, this restatement is recognized in the statement of total recognized gains and losses.

Earnings per Share. The earnings per share of the prior period would be restated for the adjustments.

Disclosure. Changes in accounting policies and fundamental errors should be fully explained in the notes. Furthermore, the effect of the prior year adjustment on the results of the preceding year should be disclosed where feasible.

10. Post Balance Sheet Events

Definition. SSAP 17 defines post balance sheet events as both favorable and unfavorable events that occur between the balance sheet date and the date on which the financial statements are approved by the board of directors. Post balance sheet events are split into two types, adjusting events and nonadjusting events.

Accounting Treatment. A post balance sheet adjusting event provides additional evidence of conditions existing at the balance sheet date and should be recorded in the current year financial statements. A nonadjusting event concerns conditions that did not exist at the balance sheet date. Such events are not reflected in the current year financial statements.

Disclosure. A post balance sheet nonadjusting event should be disclosed if it is so material that it would affect the ability of users of financial statements to reach a proper understanding of the company's financial position. The notes to the financial statements should disclose the nature of the event and give an estimate of the financial effect or state that it is not practicable to make an estimate.

11. Related Party Transactions

There is no general requirement for disclosing transactions with related parties, although there are specific requirements in the Act and the Yellow Book that capture the majority of related party transactions that would be reported in other countries. These requirements relate specifically to transactions with directors and persons connected with directors, such as:

- Transactions in which a director has a material interest have to be disclosed.
- Loans and credit transactions with directors and persons connected with them, whether legal or not, have to be disclosed and the directors concerned identified.
- Transactions in which a director sells assets to or buys assets from the company have to be disclosed to the Stock Exchange as well as in the accounts.

In addition, disclosures of transactions with and interests in affiliated companies are as described in Section 4.

The ASC issued ED 46, *Disclosure of Related Party Transactions*, in July 1989, which contains proposals for disclosure of abnormal transactions (i.e., transactions outside the ordinary course of business) with related parties and disclosure of the existence and nature of controlling related party relationships. These cover, in particular, transactions with directors and disclosures relating to substantial shareholders, group companies and related companies.

12. Segmental Information

The Act, SSAP 25 and the International Stock Exchange's Yellow Book for listed companies all include requirements for segmental reporting. To determine the segments (classes of business or geographical segments), the directors must consider how the company's activities are organized. This involves analyzing the type of business, the geographical areas of production and geographical markets.

Disclosure.   The Act requires that, if the company has conducted business in two or more segments during the year, a description of each segment, its turnover and its profit or loss before tax be disclosed in the notes. The Yellow Book requires a geographical analysis of turnover and contributions made by operations conducted outside the UK to trading (or operating) results. SSAP 25 requires public companies and large private companies to present the following additional disclosures:

☐   A definition of each reported business and geographical segment.

☐   Turnover by business and geographical segment on the origin basis (i.e., country of production) and destination basis (i.e., country of sale).

☐   Results by business and geographical segment before tax, minority interests and extraordinary items, and before or after accounting for interest, depending on the importance of interest to the segment.

☐   Intersegment turnover by geographical and business segment.

☐   Net assets by geographical and business segment.

☐   Segment information relating to associated entities.

If presenting the above information would seriously prejudice the interests of the company, it need not be disclosed, but the omission has to be disclosed.

ACCOUNTING PRINCIPLES FOR SPECIFIC ITEMS— BALANCE SHEET

13. Property, Plant and Equipment

Classification of Capital and Revenue Expenditure.   Expenditures that give rise to **capital assets** are classified as fixed assets. Pre-trading expenditures, expenses and commission relating to an issue of shares or debentures, and costs of research cannot be capitalized and are treated as expenses as incurred.

Basis of Valuation.   Fixed assets are recorded at their purchase price or production cost, which includes any consideration given by the company to obtain them. Fixed assets other than goodwill can be revalued at current cost; any resulting surplus must be credited to a revaluation reserve. Because of the valuation rules explained in Section 3, when assets are revalued, surpluses and deficits on individual assets have to be determined and accounted for separately. Under the provisions of FRS 3, revaluation surpluses and deficits are recognized in the statement of total recognized gains and losses in the year that the asset is revalued. Such gains and losses generally will then be taken to the revaluation reserve. When a revalued asset is sold, the profit on sale is computed by reference to the carrying value of the asset. Any revaluation gains or deficits that are realized on the sale are transferred to a realized reserve, but are not recorded through the profit and loss account (which was previously possible under SSAP 6) or the statement of total recognized gains and losses.

Investment Properties. Investment properties are interests in land or buildings with respect to which construction work and development have been completed and that are held for their investment potential, any rental income being negotiated at arm's length.

Investment properties should be carried on the balance sheet at open market value and not depreciated, with valuation adjustments accounted for on the same basis as those arising on the revaluation of fixed assets.

Depreciation. Fixed assets with limited useful lives are depreciated systematically over those useful lives. The **depreciation** base to be written off is an asset's purchase price, production cost or revalued amount less any residual value at the end of its useful life. Acceptable depreciation methods include the straight-line method, sum-of-the-years'-digits method, **annuity method** and methods based on the number of units produced. The useful life of an asset is defined in SSAP 12 as the period over which the present owner will derive economic benefit from the asset.

In order for the financial statements to give a true and fair view, depreciation should not be provided on investment properties, except for properties held on lease when the unexpired lease period is less than 20 years.

Disclosure. The following has to be disclosed for each major class of depreciable asset:

- □ The depreciation methods used.
- □ The useful lives or depreciation rates used.
- □ Total depreciation expense for the period.
- □ The gross amount of depreciable assets and the related accumulated depreciation at the balance sheet date.

Where there has been a change in depreciation method used, the effect, if material, and the reason for the change should be disclosed. If an asset has been revalued, the reason and the effect, based on both the revalued amount and the historical cost of the asset, must also be disclosed.

14. Intangible Assets

Accounting Treatment. Intangible assets such as patents, licenses, trademarks, brands, titles and other rights and assets may be capitalized if they are acquired for valuable consideration or are created by the company. However, a 1990 ASC proposal (ED 52) would considerably restrict the capitalization of certain intangible assets. SSAP 22 requires that on the acquisition of a company, intangible assets should be separately identified from purchased goodwill. At the time of this writing, the ASB is further considering the ASC's proposal and is expected to issue a discussion paper on the subject.

Development costs may be capitalized, provided that specific conditions are met. Research costs must be expensed as incurred. The conditions for treatment of research and development costs are outlined in Section 25.

Purchased goodwill may also be capitalized and treated as other intangible assets.

Valuation.   All intangible assets other than goodwill may be revalued. Any surplus or deficit arising on revaluation must be credited or charged to the revaluation reserve via the statement of total recognized gains and losses.

Amortization.   All intangible assets, including goodwill, should be amortized over their estimated useful lives. The **amortization** rules for intangible assets are the same as for tangible fixed assets, discussed above. There is no maximum amortization period.

Disclosure.   The disclosure requirements for intangible assets are comparable to those for tangible assets, mentioned above.

15.   Leases

Classification.   Leases are classified as either **finance** or **operating leases**. SSAP 21 defines a finance lease as a lease that transfers substantially all the risks and rewards of ownership of the asset to the lessee. Such transfer of risks and rewards is presumed to occur if, at the beginning of the lease term, the present value of the minimum lease payments equals 90 percent or more of the fair value of the leased asset. An operating lease is defined as a lease other than a finance lease.

Accounting Treatment.   Lessees: Lessees are required to capitalize finance leases and show lease obligations as a liability. For operating leases, lessees treat lease payments as charges to **revenue**.

Lessors: Lessors treat finance leases as receivables (**debtors**) in their balance sheet. Operating lease assets are treated as fixed assets, and lease income is credited to the profit and loss account.

Leveraged Leases.   Current UK GAAP do not provide a specific method of dealing with **leveraged leases**, as these transactions are not common in the UK. At present, the asset and liability relating to leveraged lease arrangements should be shown in full on the balance sheet; no right of offset exists between the two components.

Disclosure.   Lessees: The gross amount of assets held under finance leases, together with related accumulated depreciation, should be disclosed for each class of asset. Obligations owed under finance leases should be disclosed separately from other liabilities, either on the face of the balance sheet or in a note. Lease obligations are classified as amounts payable in the next year, amounts payable in the next two to five years and aggregate amounts payable thereafter. The aggregate finance charges for the period also have to be shown. Commitments that exist at the balance sheet date should be disclosed.

For operating leases, rent expense has to be disclosed. In addition, the lessee has to disclose the annual payments due on leases that expire during the next year, in the next two to five years and thereafter.

Lessors: The net investment in finance leases at the balance sheet date has to be disclosed. The gross amount of assets held for use in operating leases and the related accumulated depreciation have to be disclosed. The aggregate rental income received during the period for finance and operating leases and the costs of assets acquired for purposes of contracting out through finance leases also have to be shown.

16. Investments

Valuation Principles.   There is no accounting standard in the UK on investments, although there is a proposal (ED 55). Under the individual evaluation concept in the Act, investments should be valued individually rather than on a **portfolio basis**.

Current asset investments: Current asset investments are normally stated at the lower of cost or market value; the alternative accounting rules (see Section 3) permit revaluation at current cost, and marking to market is often used by financial institutions.

Fixed asset (noncurrent) investments: Fixed asset investments are normally stated at cost; however, the alternative accounting rules (see Section 3) permit revaluation either at their market value on the date at which they were last valued, or at a value determined on a basis the directors consider appropriate.

Treatment of Valuation Reserves.   Surpluses arising on revaluation of investments under the alternative accounting rules should be credited to a revaluation reserve. Deficits may be charged to a revaluation reserve only to the extent of any surplus from a previous revaluation of the same asset. Any excess must be charged to the profit and loss account. Under FRS 3, such surpluses and deficits on revaluation are recognized through the statement of total recognized gains and losses before adjusting the revaluation reserve.

Gains/Losses.   Under FRS 3, the gain or loss on sale of an investment is computed based on the carrying value, and no adjustment is allowed in the profit and loss account for any element of the revaluation reserve that becomes realized. Such realized amounts are transferred to a realized reserve as a reserve movement. If such gains and losses are material, they should be shown as exceptional items before arriving at profit on ordinary activities before tax (see Section 28).

Disclosure.   The Act requires a substantial amount of information to be disclosed concerning investments. Disclosure requirements increase with the percentage holding. For investments exceeding 10 percent, the following must be disclosed: the name of the investee; its country of incorporation; each class of shares the investor holds and the proportion of each class of shares held. For investments exceeding 20 percent, required disclosures include the aggregate amount of capital and reserves of the investee and the profit or loss disclosed by the investee's financial statements. As explained earlier, undertakings of which over 20 percent is held may also be treated as either associated undertakings or subsidiaries, in which case additional disclosure is required and the accounting treatment will differ.

17. Accounts Receivable

Accounting Treatment.   Recognition: The recognition of revenues, and hence the related receivables, is described in Section 23.

Discounts: Receivables are normally recorded net of trade and quantity discounts. Cash discounts are recognized at time of payment.

Allowances: Adequate provision must be made for bad and doubtful accounts, but there are no formal methods for calculating such provisions.

Factored Receivables. There is no accounting standard that relates to **factored receivables**, but proposals are being developed. Where the seller of the debt is in substance a borrower, the debtor should normally be recorded on the balance sheet and a loan recorded for amounts advanced by the factor. The interest element of the factor's charges should be accrued and recorded as interest expense. The notes should explain the arrangements and, in particular, the amounts of receivables that have been sold.

Disclosure. An analysis of debtors has to be disclosed, either in the balance sheet or the notes, under the following headings: trade debtors; amounts owed by group companies; amounts owed by undertakings in which the company has a participating interest; other debtors; prepayments; and accrued income. In addition, debtors must be split between those receivable within one year of the balance sheet date and those receivable after one year. Where debtors receivable after one year are material, they should be disclosed separately on the face of the balance sheet in accordance with UITF Abstract 4.

18. Inventories and Work in Progress

General Accounting Treatment. The Act and SSAP 9 require stocks to be carried at the lower of cost or net realizable value. SSAP 9 defines cost as an expenditure that has been incurred in the normal course of business in bringing the product or service to its present location and condition. This includes costs of purchase and costs of conversion, which encompass direct expenditures, production overhead and a proportion of other overhead. Items of stock that are indistinguishable from one another may be valued using methods such as **FIFO, average cost** or any similar method. **LIFO** is not acceptable in the UK for tax purposes and is not commonly used. Net realizable value is the estimated selling price less all further costs of completion and all costs to be incurred in marketing, selling and distributing. Stocks are shown at a valuation using the alternative accounting rules when the financial statements are prepared on a current cost basis.

Long-Term Contracts. Long-term contracts should be assessed on a contract-by-contract basis and reflected in the profit and loss account by recording turnover and related costs as the contract activity progresses (i.e., the **percentage of completion method**). Turnover may include attributable profit to the extent that the outcome of the contract can be assessed with reasonable certainty. Long-term contract work in progress is reduced by the costs included in the profit and loss account, which are matched with turnover for the period.

Disclosure. The accounting policies applied have to be disclosed. The Act requires stocks to be classified in the notes as raw materials and consumables, work in progress, finished goods and goods for resale and payments on account.

The amount by which turnover on long-term contracts exceeds payments on account is classified as amounts recoverable on contracts and separately disclosed within debtors.

If payments on account exceed turnover, the balance should be offset against long-term work in progress, and any excess classified as payments on account and separately disclosed within **creditors**. The note on long-term contracts should disclose separately both the net cost less foreseeable losses and the applicable payments on account.

19. Current Liabilities

General Accounting Treatment. The Act requires creditors due within one year to be separately disclosed for the following categories: debenture loans; bank loans and overdrafts; payments received on account; trade creditors; bills of exchange payable; amounts owed to group companies; amounts owed to companies in which the company has a participating interest; other creditors, including tax and social security; accruals; and deferred income.

Creation of General and Specific Provisions. There is often confusion about whether items should be accounted for as creditors and accruals or as provisions (which are disclosed separately). Provisions for liabilities or charges include reasonable amounts to provide for liabilities or losses that are either likely to be incurred, or certain to be incurred but uncertain as to amount or date, whereas creditors normally represent amounts actually owed to third parties. For some provisions, for example, bad debt provisions, it is correct to net the provision against the related assets.

Disclosure. The aggregate amount of creditors has to be split between amounts payable in more than five years and amounts payable in instalments, any of which fall due after the end of the five-year period. The terms of payment or repayment and the applicable interest rate have to be given in general terms. The Stock Exchange Yellow Book also requires bank loans and other borrowings to be separately disclosed for amounts repayable within one year or on demand; between one year and two years; between two years and five years; and after five years.

   If the company has secured creditors, that is, liabilities that are secured by particular assets of the company, details of the security given and the total amount of secured creditors must be disclosed.

20. Long-Term Debt

General Accounting Treatment. Creditors due after one year are disclosed separately from creditors due within one year. Furthermore, long-term creditors have to be disclosed under the same headings as for **current liabilities**, detailed in Section 19.

Debt Restructuring. There are no accounting standards dealing with debt restructuring in the UK, but the Act contains a number of rules that relate to the procedures to be followed when arrangements of this nature are made. Normally, such debt restructuring arrangements would involve the debt holders taking shares in the company and possibly cancelling part of their debt.

Disclosure. The disclosure requirements for long-term debt are the same as those discussed for current liabilities in Section 19. Further proposals concerning additional disclosures for short- and long-term debt are included in FRED 3, *Accounting for Capital Instruments*.

21. Contingencies

Contingent Losses. A material contingent loss should be accrued if it is probable that a future event will confirm a loss that can be estimated with reasonable accuracy at the date on which the financial statements are approved. If a contingent loss is not accrued, it should be disclosed, unless the possibility of loss is remote.

Contingent Gains. Contingent gains should not be accrued, and should be disclosed only if it is probable that a gain will be realized.

Disclosure. For each contingent loss or contingent gain that is disclosed, the required disclosures are: the nature of the contingency; the uncertainties that are expected to affect the ultimate outcome; and a prudent estimate of the financial effect, showing separately the amounts that have been accrued, or a statement that it is not feasible to make such an estimate.

22. Capital and Reserves

Share Capital. Called-up **share capital** is the amount of capital that has to be disclosed in the balance sheet. Called-up share capital is the aggregate amount of the calls made on the company's shares, whether or not those calls have been paid. Called-up share capital not paid is shown as a debtor.

   If share capital is issued at a premium, the premium is credited to a **share premium** account. The share premium account can be used only to issue fully paid bonus shares (i.e., stock split); write off preliminary expenses; write off expenses relating to the issue of shares or debentures; write off commissions paid or discounts allowed on any issue of shares or debentures; and provide for the premiums payable on redemption of debentures.

Other Reserves. Only realized profits are credited to the profit and loss account. Unrealized profits are normally reflected in the revaluation reserve that is used to record surpluses from the revaluation of assets under the alternative accounting rules (explained in Section 3). The Act does not require reserves to be disclosed as either realized or unrealized. Reserves are classified as revaluation reserve; capital redemption reserve; reserve for own shares; reserves provided for by the articles of association; other reserves; and the profit and loss account reserve.

Restrictions on Dividends and Other Distributions. Distributions can be paid only out of accumulated realized reserves after taking account of realized losses. In addition, public companies can make a distribution only if it does not reduce net assets below the aggregate of called-up share capital plus undistributable reserves.

Disclosure. Share capital: The total allotted (i.e., issued) capital, the amount of paid-up share capital and the authorized share capital have to be disclosed in a note. If shares have been allotted, the notes must show the number and aggregate value of those shares. If any capital is redeemable, the dates and terms of redemption and the amount of premium payable on redemption have to be given. If there are any rights attaching to shares, the number, description and amount of the shares must be disclosed, together with the period over which the rights can be exercised and the price to be paid for the shares allotted.

Reserves: The notes must disclose the aggregate amount of each reserve at the beginning and end of the year, any amounts transferred to or from reserves and the source and application of amounts transferred.

FRED 3 proposes that shareholders' funds be split between those applicable to equity shareholders and those applicable to nonequity shareholders.

ACCOUNTING PRINCIPLES FOR SPECIFIC ITEMS— INCOME STATEMENT

23. Revenue Recognition

General Principles.   Although there is no accounting standard on the recognition of revenue earned from operations, there is now a draft Statement of Principles entitled *The Recognition of Items in Financial Statements*. The draft statement would allow revenue recognition where a change in assets is not offset by an equal change in liabilities and consequently a gain or loss results (unless the change relates to a transaction with owners, in which case a contribution from owners or distribution to owners would be recognized). The draft statement would require that gains and losses be recognized either in the profit and loss account or, under FRS 3, in the statement of total recognized gains and losses.

The only direct references in accounting standards to revenue recognition are contained in the definition of prudence in SSAP 2 and in the principles for recognition of revenue from long-term contracts (discussed below). In accordance with SSAP 2, revenue and profit should not be anticipated but should be recognized only when realized in the form of cash or other assets whose ultimate cash realization can be assessed with reasonable certainty. The concept of prudence is further embodied in the Act, which requires that only profits realized at the balance sheet date be included in the profit and loss account.

As there is no specific standard dealing with revenue recognition, the provisions outlined in the draft Statement of Principles can be regarded as best practice. Under the draft statement, gains should be recognized in the profit and loss account only when, in addition to the general recognition criteria being met, the following conditions are satisfied:

☐   The gain has been earned—that is, there is no material transaction, contract or other event that must occur before the change in the entity's assets or liabilities inherent in the gain will have occurred.

☐   The gain has been realized—that is, one of the following conditions has been met:
—A transaction whose value is measurable with sufficient reliability has occurred. In addition, for a transaction involving an exchange, the assets or liabilities exchanged must be dissimilar or monetary.
—The gain results from a change in an asset or liability of a type not held for continuing use in the business, and the resultant asset or liability is readily convertible to known amounts of cash or cash equivalents.
—The gain results from a liability expiring, being cancelled or otherwise ceasing to exist.

In practice, the principles described below are normally followed in determining when to recognize revenue.

Revenue from a transaction involving the sale of goods is usually recognized when the seller has transferred to the buyer the significant risks and rewards of ownership of the goods. In most situations, the substance of the transaction rather than its legal form will determine the time of sale. If, however, goods are sold subject to conditions (e.g., consignment sales, cash on delivery), revenue is not recognized until the conditions have been complied with.

Revenue from the rendering of services is usually recognized as the services are performed. If the service is performed as a single act, revenue is recognized when the service is completed. If the service is provided over a period of time, revenue is recognized in a manner appropriate to the stage of completion of the service, provided that the outcome can be assessed with reasonable certainty.

Long-Term Contracts. The principles for the recognition of revenue on long-term contracts are contained in SSAP 9. In a long-term contract, the time taken to substantially complete the contract is such that the contract activity falls into different accounting periods. A contract accounted for as long term will usually extend beyond one year. However, a duration exceeding one year is not an essential feature of a long-term contract. Some contracts with a duration shorter than one year should be accounted for as long-term contracts (provided that the policy is applied consistently within the reporting entity and from year to year), if they are sufficiently material that not to record turnover and attributable profit would lead to a distortion such that the financial statements would not give a true and fair view.

Where the business has long-term contracts and the outcome can be assessed with reasonable certainty before their conclusion, profit is recognized on the percentage of completion method as the contract activity progresses. If the outcome cannot be assessed with reasonable certainty, no profit is reflected in the profit and loss account from those contracts; profit is recognized when the contract is completed. If there will be a loss on a contract as a whole, the entire loss should be recorded as soon as it is foreseen, in accordance with the prudence concept. Initially, the foreseeable loss is deducted from work in progress, thus reducing it to net realizable value. Any loss in excess of the work in progress should be classified as an accrued liability or a provision for liabilities and charges, depending on the circumstances.

Instalment Sales. On **instalment sales**, revenue is normally recognized at the date of sale. If, however, collection is not reasonably assured, revenue is recognized as cash instalments are received.

Rights of Return. When goods are sold giving the buyer the right to return them for a refund or replacement, revenue may be recognized at the point of sale, provided that adequate provision is made for future returns. Even where goods are sold subject to a reservation of title clause, which enables the seller to have a lien on them until the purchaser has paid for them, revenue recognition is not deferred. If, however, the clause is likely to be acted upon, it is appropriate to create a provision for the doubtful debt.

Product Financing. **Product financing** occurs when goods are sold with a commitment to repurchase them at a later date. In a sale of goods with a commitment to repurchase, the original owner may retain the principal benefits and risks of ownership, if the re-purchase price is predetermined and covers the cost, including interest, incurred by the other party in purchasing and holding the goods. In such a situation, the transaction should be accounted for as a financing rather than a sales transaction, leaving the asset and a corresponding liability on the balance sheet of the original owner.

Disclosure.   A company must disclose in its profit and loss account, under the heading turnover, the amount it derives from providing goods and services from ordinary activities, after deducting the **value added tax** and other taxes. The accounting policy for turnover should also be disclosed in the notes. The method of ascertaining turnover and attributable profit in relation to long-term contracts must also be stated.

24.   Government Grants and Assistance

Accounting Treatment.   SSAP 4 sets out the accounting treatment to be followed for government grants, which should be recognized when the expenditure that they are intended to contribute to is recognized.

SSAP 4 stipulates that government grants relating to fixed assets should be credited to revenue over the asset's expected useful life. This can be achieved in one of two ways:

☐   The grant may be deducted from the purchase price or production cost of the asset, thereby reducing depreciation expense.

☐   The grant may be treated as a deferred credit, of which a portion is credited to revenue annually.

The ASC received legal advice, however, that the option to deduct government grants from the purchase price or production cost of fixed assets is not available to companies governed by the accounting and reporting requirements of the Act.

Disclosure.   The following information must be disclosed in the financial statements:

☐   The accounting policy adopted for government grants.

☐   The effects of government grants on the results for the period and/or the financial position of the enterprise.

☐   Where the results of operations are materially affected by the receipt of government assistance other than grants, the effects of that assistance and its nature, to the extent that such effects can be measured.

Potential liabilities to repay grants in specified circumstances should, if necessary, be disclosed in accordance with SSAP 18, *Accounting for Contingencies*.

25.   Research and Development

Definitions.   Research and development expenditures fall into one or more of the following broad categories (except to the extent that expenditures relate to locating or exploiting oil, gas or mineral deposits or are reimbursable by third parties either directly or under the terms of a firm contract to develop and manufacture at an agreed price calculated to reimburse both elements of the expenditure):

□ Pure or basic research—Experimental or theoretical work undertaken primarily to acquire new scientific or technical knowledge rather than directed toward any specific practical aim or application.

□ Applied research—Original or critical investigation undertaken to gain new scientific or technical knowledge and directed toward a specific practical aim or objective.

□ Development—Use of scientific or technical knowledge in order to produce new or substantially improved materials, devices, products or services; to install new processes or systems prior to the commencement of commercial production or commercial applications; or to improve substantially those already produced or installed.

Accounting Treatment. The Act permits only development costs to be capitalized, and only in special circumstances. All research costs must be expensed as incurred. The Act does not define the special circumstances in which development costs may be capitalized, but SSAP 13 sets forth the following conditions that must be satisfied to capitalize development expenditures:

□ There is a clearly defined project.

□ The related expenditure is separately identifiable.

□ The outcome of the project has been assessed with reasonable certainty as to both its technical feasibility and its ultimate commercial viability, considered in the light of factors such as likely market conditions (including competing products), public opinion and consumer and environmental legislation.

□ The aggregate of the deferred development costs, any further development costs and related production, selling and administration costs is reasonably expected to be exceeded by related future sales or other revenues.

□ Adequate resources exist, or are reasonably expected to be available, to enable the project to be completed and to provide any additional working capital needed as a result of the project.

Provided that these conditions are satisfied, a company can capitalize development expenditure, but only until commercial production begins. SSAP 13 requires a company to amortize the capitalized expenditure from the time commercial production of the product or service begins, which is when the company manufactures the product with a view to selling it commercially. Amortization of development expenditure must be allocated to each accounting period on a systematic basis over the production life of the product.

At the end of each accounting period, a company should review capitalized development expenditure. If the circumstances that justified the original deferral of an expenditure no longer apply or are considered doubtful, the company should write off the expenditure immediately to the extent it is considered irrecoverable.

Disclosure. The following disclosures should be made in the notes:

□ The accounting policy adopted for research and development expenditure.

□ The total amount of research and development expenditure charged to the profit and loss account in the period, both current year expenditure and amortization of deferred expenditure.

□ Movements on deferred development expenditure and the amounts at the beginning and end of the period.

□   The period over which capitalized development costs are being amortized, together with the reasons for capitalizing them.

26.   Capitalized Interest Costs

Accounting Treatment.   There is no accounting standard in the UK that deals with capitalization of interest. However, the Act allows interest on any capital borrowed to finance the production of an asset to be included in the production cost of the asset. Views differ as to whether the amount to be capitalized should be shown gross or net of taxes.

Disclosure.   The amount of capitalized interest included in production cost must be stated in the notes.

27.   Imputed Interest

General.   **Imputed interest** is not used widely in the preparation of financial statements in the UK. However, the principles of discounting account balances and transactions to their present value are recognized in some accounting standards, for example, SSAP 21 (Leasing) and SSAP 24 (Pension Costs).

Accounting Treatment.   Although there is no authoritative guidance on the use of discounting in financial statements in the UK, Technical Release (TR) 773 highlights instances where discounting may be required to enable financial statements to give a true and fair view. TR 773 identifies the following as the two main potential applications of discounting in financial reporting:

□   Allocation of cash flows as revenues or expenses over accounting periods in a manner consistent with the time value of money.

□   Valuation where no ready external market exists and no cash equivalent is available.

Disclosure.   TR 773 encourages disclosure in the financial statements of the accounting policy adopted where discounting has been used, in particular, the significant assumptions made regarding choice of interest rate and timing of cash flows.

28.   Extraordinary or Unusual Items

Extraordinary Items.   The definition of extraordinary items has changed with the introduction of FRS 3 to relate to material items possessing a high degree of abnormality that arise from events or transactions that fall outside the ordinary activities of the reporting entity, and that are not expected to recur. Under FRS 3 extraordinary items will be extremely rare, and the ASB has stated that in view of the extreme rarity of such items it cannot provide any examples. Consequently, it is unlikely that UK companies will disclose any extraordinary items in the future.

Exceptional Items.   Exceptional items are defined in FRS 3 as material items that derive from events or transactions that fall within the ordinary activities of the company and that individually or, if of a similar type, in the aggregate need to be disclosed by virtue of their size or incidence if the financial statements are to give a true and fair view. The definition in FRS 3 encompasses those items that were disclosed as extraordinary under SSAP 6.

Disclosure. The disclosure of exceptional items under FRS 3 has changed from that under SSAP 6. Generally, exceptional items are charged or credited in the profit and loss account in arriving at profit or loss from ordinary activities. They should be attributed to continuing or discontinued operations, as appropriate. However, there are three exceptions to the general rule, which require separate disclosure after operating profit or loss, but before interest, under either continuing or discontinued operations, as follows:

☐ Profits or losses on the sale or termination of an operation.

☐ Costs of a fundamental reorganization or restructuring having a material effect on the nature and focus of the reporting entity's operations.

☐ Profits or losses on the disposal of fixed assets.

29. Income Taxes

Accounting Treatment. In the UK, companies pay corporation tax on the accounting income of the year adjusted for certain items, whether distributed or undistributed. In the absence of a dividend, corporation tax is payable nine months after the end of the accounting period. If a company makes a distribution to shareholders, the company does not withhold any income tax from the payment, but is required to make an advance payment of corporation tax (ACT). This ACT is normally offset against the company's total liability for corporation tax on its income, but not on its chargeable (taxable) gains on the sale of capital items, of the period. The resulting net liability is known as the mainstream liability. An individual shareholder receiving a dividend is taxed on the amount of income equivalent to the dividend plus the imputed tax credit. This is known as the imputation system of corporation tax and is covered in SSAP 8.

In accordance with SSAP 15 (Deferred Taxation), companies are also required to account for deferred taxes. Deferred taxes should be computed under the **liability method**, which requires that tax deferred or accelerated because of timing differences be accounted for, but only to the extent that it is probable that a tax liability or asset will materialize (i.e., on a partial provision basis). The provision for deferred tax liabilities should be reduced by any deferred tax debit balances arising from separate categories of timing differences and any ACT that is available to offset those liabilities.

Deferred tax debit balances, including those arising from losses, should not be carried forward as assets, except to the extent that they are expected to be recoverable without replacement by equivalent debit balances. Recovery may be affected by, among other things, the period of time losses are available to be carried forward for tax purposes. Deferred tax assets arising from losses should be recognized only when recovery is assured beyond reasonable doubt.

Disclosure. The notes to the profit and loss account must disclose the following:

☐ The amount of the UK corporation tax, specifying:
  — The charge for corporation tax on the income of the year. (If the corporation tax includes material transfers between the deferred tax account and the profit and loss account, these also should be separately disclosed.)
  — Tax attributable to **franked investment income**.

—Irrecoverable ACT.

—Relief for overseas taxation.

☐ The total overseas tax, relieved or unrelieved, specifying the portion of the unrelieved overseas tax arising from the payment or proposed payment of dividends.

☐ The amount of deferred tax relating to ordinary activities. (Similar disclosure is required for deferred tax relating to extraordinary items, which should be shown as part of the tax on extraordinary items.)

☐ The amount of any potential deferred tax that has not been provided for the period, divided into major components.

☐ Adjustments to deferred tax from changes in tax rates and tax allowances, which should normally be disclosed as part of the tax charge for the period.

☐ Under FRS 3, the tax on the three specific exceptional items set out in Section 28.

30. Postretirement Benefits

Accounting Treatment.   SSAP 24 deals with both the measurement of pension costs and the disclosure of pension information in company financial statements. The accounting objective of SSAP 24 is that the expected cost of providing pensions should be recognized on a systematic and rational basis over the period during which an employer benefits from employees' services. Most pension plans (called schemes) in the UK are funded and are either defined contribution or defined benefit schemes.

Defined Benefit Pension Plans.   In a **defined benefit scheme**, rules determine the benefits to be paid, regardless of the contributions paid with respect to each employee. The employer's obligations are not capable of being defined in an absolute sense; instead, actuarial expertise is required to determine an appropriate level of contributions to fund the obligations. Consequently, the accounting objective is met by providing for periodic pension costs that are a substantially level percentage of the current and expected future pensionable earnings in the light of current actuarial assumptions.

Variations from regular costs because of experience, changes in actuarial methods or assumptions, or retroactive changes in benefits or membership should normally be spread forward over the expected remaining service lives of current employees. SSAP 24 does not suggest a period, but states that it should be determined by the actuary.

Defined Contribution Pension Plans.   In a **defined contribution scheme**, the future benefits payable to employees are determined by the accumulated value of contributions paid in to the scheme. The employer's obligations are, therefore, normally discharged by an agreed level of contributions. Consequently, the company meets the accounting objective by charging against profits the amount of contributions payable to the scheme in the accounting period.

Pension Fund Surpluses.   Treatment of pension scheme surpluses is governed by the scheme's trust deed. It may be reflected in the form of either contribution holidays, a period of reduced contributions or cash refunds to employers.

Postretirement Benefits.   The UITF issued a statement in December 1992 that requires companies to account for postretirement benefits in a similar way to that prescribed for defined benefit pension plans in SSAP 24. Transitional provisions do not bring in the full requirement until December 1994 year-ends. However, until that time the potential liability has to be noted in the financial statements where it is possible to determine the amounts involved. In addition, compliance with the requirements of US SFAS No. 106 will fulfill the requirements of SSAP 24.

Disclosure. Defined contribution schemes must disclose: the nature of the scheme (i.e., defined contribution); the accounting policy; the pension cost charge for the period; and any outstanding or prepaid contribution at the balance sheet date.

In addition to the above disclosures, defined benefit schemes must disclose a significant amount of actuarial information, including:

☐ The actuarial method used and the main actuarial assumptions.

☐ The market value of the scheme assets at the date of their valuation or review.

☐ The level of funding expressed as a percentage and comments on any material surplus or deficit.

In addition, details of the expected effects on future costs of any material changes in the group's and/or company's pension arrangements, together with any commitment to make additional payments over a limited number of years, should be disclosed.

31. Discontinued Operations

The accounting treatment of terminated activities of business segments is dealt with in FRS 3 (see Section 28). The provisions of FRS 3 apply to accounting periods ending on or after June 22, 1993 and earlier adoption is encouraged. Because of the significant changes in these provisions, both the rules of FRS 3 and SSAP 6 relating to discontinued operations are given below.

Under FRS 3, discontinued operations are defined as operations of the reporting entity that are sold or terminated and that satisfy all of the following conditions:

☐ The sale or termination is completed either in the period covered by the financial statements, or before the earlier of three months after the commencement of the subsequent period and the date on which the financial statements are approved.

☐ If a termination, the former activities have ceased permanently.

☐ The sale or termination has a material effect on the nature and focus of the reporting entity's operations and represents a material reduction in its operating facilities resulting either from its withdrawal from a particular market (class of business or geographical) or from a material reduction in turnover in the reporting entity's continuing markets.

☐ The assets, liabilities, results of operations and activities are clearly distinguishable, physically, operationally and for financial reporting purposes.

If a decision has been made to sell or terminate an operation, any consequential provision should reflect the extent to which obligations have been incurred that are not expected to be covered by the future profits of the operation or the disposal of assets. The reporting entity should be demonstrably committed to the sale or termination and this should be evidenced by either a binding sale agreement or a detailed plan for termination. Only, however, if the operation qualifies as a discontinued operation (that is, satisfies the conditions above) would such amounts be shown under that category in the profit and loss account. If it does not satisfy those conditions, it must be shown as part of continuing operations. Where material, *discontinuing* (as opposed to discontinued) operations should be shown as a component of continuing operations.

In SSAP 6, a business segment is defined as a material and separately identifiable component of the business operations of a company or group whose activities, assets and results can be clearly distinguished from the remainder of activities. A business segment normally has separate product lines or markets.

If a decision has been made to discontinue a business segment or if a significant business segment has been terminated, SSAP 6 requires that a provision be made for the consequences of all decisions made up to the balance sheet date. Such a provision should be disclosed as an extraordinary item and usually includes some or all of the following costs:

☐ Redundancy costs, that is, costs of terminating employment (net of government contributions).

☐ Costs of retaining key personnel during the run down period.

☐ Profits or losses from the disposal of assets, including anticipated costs such as rent, rates (local property taxes) and security.

☐ Pension costs.

☐ Bad and doubtful debts arising from the decision to close.

☐ All debits and credits arising from business operations after implementation of the plan to discontinue.

☐ Any losses due to penalty clauses in contracts.

Such provisions are not precluded from being treated as extraordinary items merely because they occur and are recognized over a number of accounting periods, where this is either the ongoing result of a single decision or because of a number of separate decisions. Profits and losses from terminated activities occurring before implementation of the plan to discontinue are part of the operating results for the year and are therefore not extraordinary. However, because they derive from a business segment that has been discontinued, they may require separate disclosure to enable the results of continuing operations to be ascertained.

Reorganization programs that do not represent a discontinuance of a business segment are part of the normal business process, and their related costs should be included in the results of the company's ordinary activities.

Disclosure.   Under FRS 3, if the operation qualifies as discontinued, any write-down of assets and any provisions should appear under discontinued operations in the profit and loss account. Otherwise, such amounts should appear under continuing operations in the profit and loss account. Where in the subsequent period an operation qualifies as discontinued under FRS 3, and provisions have previously been established under continuing operations, the provisions should be used to offset the results of the discontinued operation. Previously under SSAP 6, all profits and losses resulting from discontinuing a business segment should be separately disclosed as extraordinary items. Material reorganization costs not related to the discontinuance of a business segment should be disclosed separately as exceptional items. The accounting policy for reorganization costs should be disclosed.

32. Earnings per Share

General. The Act does not require earnings per share (EPS) information to be given. However, SSAP 3 requires listed companies and companies traded on the USM to show EPS on the face of the profit and loss account.

Definition. Under FRS 3, the definition of EPS in SSAP 3 has changed to include extraordinary items in the definition of earnings. Now EPS is defined as the amount of consolidated profit of the period, after tax and after deducting extraordinary items (in the unlikely event that there are any under FRS 3), minority interests and preference dividends, attributable to each equity share. FRS 3 allows alternative bases for calculating EPS as long as they are not given more prominence than the EPS required by SSAP 3.

Method of Calculation. EPS is generally calculated on two bases. The first calculation uses the weighted-average share capital eligible for dividends in the period and is known as the basic earnings per share. The second calculation takes into account that companies often have equity shares in issue that are not eligible for a dividend but will be in the future. There may also be a future reduction in earnings if conversion rights attaching to debentures, loan stock, **preference shares**, or options or warrants to subscribe for equity shares are exercised. Where these situations exist, SSAP 3 requires that fully diluted earnings per share should also be calculated and disclosed on the face of the profit and loss account.

Under the imputation system of corporation tax, the tax charge used in determining EPS should include any irrecoverable ACT and any unrelieved overseas tax from payment or proposed payment of dividends. This is known as the net basis as opposed to the nil basis, which excludes irrecoverable ACT and unrelieved overseas tax (except insofar as they relate to preference dividends).

Disclosure. EPS should be shown on the face of the profit and loss account on the net basis both for the current period and for the corresponding previous period. If the calculation of EPS on the nil basis is materially different from the net basis, the nil basis figure should also be disclosed. The basis of calculating EPS should be disclosed either in the profit and loss account or in a note. In particular, the amount of earnings and the number of equity shares used in the calculation should be shown.

In addition to the basic EPS, the fully diluted EPS should be shown on the face of the profit and loss account. The basis of calculating the fully diluted EPS must be disclosed. The fully diluted EPS for the corresponding previous period should not be shown unless the assumptions on which it is based still apply. The fully diluted EPS need not be given if either it deviates from basic EPS by less than 5 percent or basic EPS is negative. Basic and fully diluted EPS, if both are disclosed, should be equally prominent.

Where under FRS 3 an alternative EPS figure is disclosed, the financial statements should reconcile the alternative figure to the EPS figure required by SSAP 3 on the face of the profit and loss account.

Appendix
DO UNITED KINGDOM STANDARDS OR PREVALENT PRACTICE SUBSTANTIALLY COMPLY WITH INTERNATIONAL ACCOUNTING STANDARDS?

Section	Topic	Substantially complies with IAS?	Comments
3.	Basic accounting concepts and conventions	Yes	
	Contents of financial statements	Yes	Except that cash flow statements are required only for large companies
4.	Business combinations*	Yes	
5.	Joint ventures	Yes	
6.	Foreign currency translation*	Yes	
8.	Accounting changes*	Yes	
9.	Prior period adjustments*	Yes	
10.	Post balance sheet events	Yes	
11.	Related party transactions	No	Those parties deemed to be related are fewer than under IAS 24
12.	Segmental information	Yes	
13.	Property, plant and equipment*	Yes	
15.	Leases	Yes	
16.	Investments	Yes	
17.	Accounts receivable	Yes	
18.	Inventories and work in progress*	Yes	
19.	Current liabilities	Yes	
20.	Long-term debt	Yes	
21.	Contingencies	Yes	
22.	Capital and reserves	Yes	
23.	Revenue recognition*	Yes	Not covered by UK accounting standards, but the principles are applied in a similar way
24.	Government grants and assistance	Yes	
25.	Research and development*	Yes	

Appendix (*Continued*)

Section	Topic	Substantially complies with IAS?	Comments
26.	Capitalization of interest costs*	Yes	Capitalization is optional
28.	Extraordinary or unusual items*	Yes	
29.	Income tax**	Yes	
30.	Postretirement benefits*	Yes	

*These topics are subject to change as a result of the IASC Improvements Project—see the appendix to the International Accounting Standards chapter.

**The IAS on accounting for taxes on income is currently being revised, and an exposure draft has been issued.

Comparison in this table is made to International Accounting Standards in force at January 1, 1993. For further details, see the International Accounting Standards chapter.

UNITED STATES

GENERAL NATIONAL INFORMATION

1. Source of Generally Accepted Accounting Principles

Generally Accepted Accounting Principles. **Generally accepted accounting principles (GAAP)** are derived from authoritative pronouncements, the pronouncements of bodies of expert accountants that follow a due process procedure, practices or pronouncements that represent prevalent practice in a particular industry or in specific circumstances, and other accounting literature.

Accounting Standards. **Accounting standards** in the United States come primarily from the following sources:

☐ Financial Accounting Standards Board (FASB). The FASB establishes standards of financial accounting and reporting that generally apply to all public and nonpublic enterprises except state and local governmental entities. Such pronouncements are primarily in the form of Statements of Financial Accounting Standards (SFAS).

☐ Governmental Accounting Standards Board (GASB). The GASB establishes financial accounting and reporting standards for activities and transactions of state and local governmental entities.

The American Institute of Certified Public Accountants (AICPA) has designated the FASB (and its predecessors, whose pronouncements it has endorsed) and GASB as authoritative standard-setting bodies under the AICPA's Code of Professional Conduct. AICPA members are prohibited from expressing an opinion or stating affirmatively that financial statements are presented in conformity with GAAP or stating that they are not aware of any material modifications that should be made to such statements in order for them to be in conformity with GAAP, if the statements contain any material departure from an accounting principle promulgated by the FASB or GASB.

Accounting standards are also issued by:

☐ The AICPA, which currently issues, principally through its Accounting Standards Executive Committee (AcSEC), Statements of Position (SOPs) on **accounting principles** in specific areas, usually after receiving concurrence from the FASB.

☐ The Securities and Exchange Commission (SEC), a federal agency, which has the statutory authority to establish the form and content of and requirements for financial statements of publicly held companies whose securities are registered with it. These are governed by SEC Regulation S-X. The SEC also has the authority to establish accounting standards, but generally has not exercised this authority. The SEC issues Financial Reporting Releases that are used to adopt, amend or interpret rules and regulations relating to accounting and auditing issues or financial statement disclosures. The staff of the SEC issues Staff Accounting Bulletins (SABs) to publicize the interpretations and practices it follows in administering the requirements of the federal securities laws.

□   Emerging Issues Task Force (EITF), a task force established by the FASB to provide timely guidance on implementation questions and emerging accounting issues.

The following summarizes the GAAP hierarchy in the United States:

GAAP Hierarchy Summary

	Nongovernmental Entities	State and Local Governments
Category (A)	FASB Statements and Interpretations, Accounting Principles Board (APB) Opinions and AICPA Accounting Research Bulletins (ARBs)	GASB Statements and Interpretations, as well as AICPA and FASB pronouncements specifically made applicable to state and local governmental entities by GASB Statements or Interpretations
Category (B)	FASB Technical Bulletins and, if cleared by the FASB, AICPA Industry Audit and Accounting Guides, and AICPA Statements of Position	GASB Technical Bulletins and, if specifically made applicable to state and local governmental entities by the AICPA and cleared by the GASB, AICPA Industry Audit and Accounting Guides, and AICPA Statements of Position
Category (C)	Consensus positions of the EITF and AICPA AcSEC Practice Bulletins that have been cleared by the FASB	AICPA AcSEC Practice Bulletins if specifically made applicable to state and local governmental entities and cleared by the GASB, as well as consensus positions of a group of accountants organized by the GASB that attempts to reach consensus positions on accounting issues applicable to state and local governmental entities
Category (D)	AICPA accounting interpretations and implementation guides (''Q's and A's'') published by the FASB staff, as well as practices that are widely recognized and prevalent either generally or in the industry	Implementation guides (''Q's and A's'') published by the GASB staff as well as practices that are widely recognized and prevalent in state and local government

In the absence of an accounting standard set forth in the above categories, other accounting literature may be considered, depending on its relevance in the circumstances.

Accounting standards set forth in Category (A) carry the greatest weight in determining the appropriate accounting treatment of a transaction or event. If accounting standards from one or more sources in Category (B), (C) or (D) conflict, the accounting treatment specified by the source in the higher category (e.g., Category (B) over Category (C)) should be followed.

2. Audit and Public Company Requirements

Audits. The AICPA has approved and adopted 10 broad standards collectively entitled "generally accepted auditing standards" (GAAS), which stipulate the personal qualities that an auditor should possess, how an audit should be conducted and the form and content of the auditor's report. The Auditing Standards Board (ASB) is the senior technical body of the AICPA responsible for promulgating auditing standards and procedures to be observed by AICPA members in accordance with the Institute's Code of Professional Conduct. The Auditing Standards Division (ASD), through the ASB, formally exposes proposed statements for comment and then issues Statements on Auditing Standards (SASs) and interpretations on the application of ASB pronouncements.

Several groups or organizations have the power to require audited financial statements. Lending institutions and other creditors may request audited financial statements in order to make financing decisions. The SEC and various stock exchanges require audited financial statements on behalf of investors. Independent auditors are generally appointed by directors of nonpublic companies and by stockholder approval for **public companies**.

In general, the SEC and state boards of accountancy require audits to be performed and reports to be signed by licensed independent certified public accountants (CPAs).

Membership in the AICPA is voluntary; by accepting membership, a CPA assumes obligations of self-discipline beyond the requirements of laws and regulations.

Public Companies. The SEC is the principal securities regulatory authority in the United States. A detailed registration statement must be filed with, and approved by, the SEC prior to the public offering of nonexempt securities. An initial registration statement generally requires audited financial statements for the preceding three years, and financial statements, which may be unaudited, as of a date within approximately 135 days of the registration filing. In addition, foreign company financial statements included in the registration must present a reconciliation to US GAAP.

Stock exchange listing requirements include an approved application by an exchange and the filing of a registration statement with the SEC. In addition, certain minimum requirements must be met for a company's publicly held stock value, tangible assets and pretax earnings, which differ among exchanges and for US and foreign companies.

The SEC requires registered companies to submit periodic reports to it and to shareholders. These include annual reports containing audited financial statements (two-year balance sheets, three-year statements of income, retained earnings and cash flows), which are due within 90 days after year-end, and a report containing less detailed, unaudited financial information, due within 45 days after the end of each of the first three fiscal quarters. In general, required quarterly data for foreign issuers consists of information made available in their own country. In addition, information must be filed with the SEC within 15 calendar days of the occurrence of certain significant events, which relate to bankruptcy or changes in control, assets, fiscal years or any other significant event that a prudent investor should know about. Changes in a company's auditor or directors must be filed within five business days.

Reference.   AICPA Statements on Auditing Standards, AICPA Code of Professional Conduct, State CPA Requirement Listings and Stock Exchange Listing Manuals.

GENERAL ACCOUNTING

3.   Financial Statements

Basic Accounting Concepts.   The basic concepts underlying the presentation of financial statements include:

☐   **Historical cost**.
☐   **Accrual** accounting.
☐   **Going concern**.
☐   Consistency and comparability—**Accounting policies** and **procedures** are to be consistently applied in order to enhance comparability between periods and with other entities.

Contents of Financial Statements.   Financial statements normally include a balance sheet, statement of income and retained earnings, statement of cash flows, and statement of changes in stockholders' equity. Footnotes are considered an integral part of the financial statements. The presentation of comparative financial statements for more than one period is generally preferable, and is required for publicly held companies registered with the SEC.

Format of Financial Statements.   The balance sheet consists of assets, liabilities, and equity. Assets and liabilities are usually further subdivided into current and long-term classifications.

   Some flexibility in the format of the income statement is allowed. However, specific rules govern the display of certain items such as extraordinary items and changes in accounting principles.

   The statement of cash flows provides information about the cash receipts and cash payments for the period, and is classified into operating, financing and investing activities. Companies are encouraged, but not required, to report major classes of cash flows from operating activities using the **direct method**. Companies that utilize the direct method are required to disclose, at a minimum, the following:

☐   Cash collected from customers.
☐   Interest and dividends received.
☐   Other operating cash receipts, if any.
☐   Cash paid to employees and other suppliers of goods or services.
☐   Interest paid.
☐   Income taxes paid.
☐   Other operating cash payments, if any.

Companies electing the **indirect method** for reporting operating cash receipts and payments determine and report the same amount for net cash flow from operating activities as under the direct method by adjusting net income for transactions of a noncash nature. In addition, if the indirect method is elected, amounts paid for interest and income taxes are required to be disclosed.

The statement of changes in stockholders' equity discloses changes in the components of stockholders' equity. Alternatively, this information may be disclosed in the footnotes.

When a company has subsidiaries, financial statements of the **parent company** alone are not deemed to be in conformity with GAAP and are not appropriate for issuance to shareholders as the financial statements of the primary reporting entity. Occasionally, the existence of preferred stockholders, loan or other agreements, or other special requirements will necessitate the preparation of financial statements for the parent company alone. In these cases, the parent company financial statements should be included in the same document as the **consolidated financial statements** (i.e., the primary financial statements) in order for the parent company statements to be in conformity with GAAP. The parent company statements may be side by side with the consolidated statements or in separate sections of the document and should indicate that they are those of the parent company only. In addition, the shareholders' equity reported in the parent company financial statements should be the same amount as reported in the consolidated financial statements. The parent company statements should indicate that the company publishes consolidated financial statements that are its primary financial statements and that the parent company statements are therefore not intended to be the primary financial statements.

Disclosure of Accounting Policies. Disclosure of significant accounting policies is required if alternative principles may be used, if the policy in use is peculiar to the industry in which the entity operates or if the policy or its application is unusual or innovative.

Reference. ARBs and APB Opinions and SFAS No. 95.

4. Business Combinations

Principles of Consolidation. Consolidated financial statements are considered more meaningful and are generally necessary for a fair presentation when one entity has a controlling financial interest in other entities of a group. Consolidation is required in substantially all cases in which a parent directly or indirectly owns the majority voting interest of a **subsidiary**, except when the control is temporary (as evidenced by an expressed intent to divest) or there is significant doubt concerning the parent's ability to control the subsidiary (such as bankruptcy or foreign exchange restrictions). The consolidation process includes the elimination of intercompany balances and profits.

Methods of Accounting for Business Combinations. Both the **pooling of interests method** and the **purchase method** are acceptable, although not as alternatives.

The pooling of interests method is acceptable when certain criteria are met: At least 90 percent of the outstanding voting common stock interest of one company must be exchanged for voting common stock of the other company; the combination must be effected in a single transaction; the two companies must have been autonomous for at least two years prior to the initiation of the plan of combination and stockholders must be neither deprived nor restricted in exercising voting rights in the resulting combined company for a certain period. Further, there are significant limitations on cash consideration to be paid.

All **business combinations** that do not meet the criteria for pooling of interests accounting are treated as acquisitions accounted for by the purchase method. Under the purchase method the acquiring company records the acquired assets less assumed liabilities at its purchase cost, with any difference between cost and fair value of net assets acquired recorded as **goodwill**. Under the purchase method the acquiring company includes in its income the acquired company's income only for the period subsequent to the acquisition date. Similarly, net assets acquired are combined as of the acquisition date.

Control.   In general, a controlling financial interest for consolidation purposes results from the ownership, directly or indirectly, of over 50 percent of the voting shares of another company. The SEC extends the definition of control to "the possession, direct or indirect, of the power to cause the direction of the management and policies of a person, whether through the ownership of voting shares, by control, or otherwise."

Goodwill.   In a business combination accounted for as a purchase, the difference between the purchase price and the fair value of net assets acquired must be amortized. The purchase price is allocated to identifiable individual assets and assumed liabilities based on fair values, with the unallocated amount attributed to goodwill. If the fair values of net assets are in excess of the purchase price, noncurrent assets, except for long-term investments in marketable securities, are reduced. If they are reduced to zero, the remainder of the purchase price is recorded as **negative goodwill**. Negative goodwill is generally displayed between liabilities and stockholders' equity. Goodwill and negative goodwill must be amortized to income over a reasonable period up to a maximum of 40 years, generally using the straight-line method. In practice, shorter amortization periods are frequently utilized.

Equity Accounting.   The **equity method** of accounting is followed for investments in joint ventures and 50 percent or less owned companies over whose operating and financial policies an investor has the ability to exercise significant influence. Although judgment is required to determine significant influence, an investment (direct or indirect) of 20 percent or more of the voting stock of a company creates a presumption of such influence.

A series of operating losses of an investee, as well as other factors that indicate a decrease in value that is other than temporary, may result in the reduction or elimination of the carrying amount of the investment. A difference between the carrying amount of an investment and the underlying equity in net assets of the investee is accounted for as if the investee were a consolidated subsidiary, resulting in amortization of goodwill or negative goodwill.

Minority Interests.   **Minority interests** arising in consolidation of subsidiaries not wholly owned should normally be shown immediately preceding stockholders' equity. Minority interests in the income of such subsidiaries are deducted in determining consolidated net income and are generally shown as one of the last items in the income statement. Dividends on preferred stock minority interests are similarly charged to the consolidated income statement.

Disclosure.　The consolidation policy, including the nature and description of business combinations, and the period of goodwill amortization must be disclosed.

For poolings of interests, required disclosures include: (a) the name and description of companies pooled during the latest period, the number of shares issued and the basis of presentation and restatements; (b) revenues, extraordinary items and net income of separate companies from the beginning of the period to the date of consummation; and (c) the nature of any adjustments to conform accounting practices.

Required disclosures for purchases include: (a) the name and a brief description of businesses purchased during the latest period, cost and, if applicable, number of shares issued or issuable and amount assigned thereto, and the period for which results of operations are included in the income statement; (b) contingent payments, options or commitments; (c) amortization period of any acquired goodwill or negative goodwill; and (d) supplemental pro forma information on results of operations for the current and immediately preceding period (if presented) as though the companies had combined at the beginning of the current period.

Summarized financial information (assets, liabilities and results of operations) is required to be presented for equity investees. For SEC purposes, separate financial statements of the investees are required to be presented in some instances.

Reference.　ARB No. 51; APB Opinion Nos. 16, 17 and 18; SFAS No. 94 and FASB Interpretation No. 35; and SEC Regulation S-X.

5.　Joint Ventures

Accounting for Investments in Joint Ventures.　US accounting literature contains little guidance related to investments in **joint ventures**. US GAAP acknowledge that joint ventures may be incorporated or unincorporated.

Jointly Controlled Operations.　US GAAP do not address any specific accounting.

Jointly Controlled Assets.　If an entity that otherwise meets the definition of a joint venture is not subject to **joint control**, by reason of each venturer owning an undivided interest in each asset and being proportionately liable for its share of each liability, investments in these arrangements are accounted for by the **proportionate consolidation method**. The proportionate consolidation method is also used in other limited circumstances, such as where it is the established industry practice (e.g., some oil and gas venture accounting).

Jointly Controlled Entities.　In those instances where joint control exists, investments in joint ventures are generally accounted for by the equity method. In certain limited circumstances the proportionate consolidation method (see jointly controlled assets above) is used. The equity method is used for both incorporated and unincorporated ventures that are subject to joint control. If a parent–subsidiary arrangement exists because of unilateral control, a venture should be consolidated.

Transactions Between Venturers and the Joint Venture.　Contributions of property, intangible assets and services to a joint venture by a venturer should generally be recognized in the venturer's investment account at the net book value of such assets unless there is an indicated impairment in value. However, there is diversity in practice in this area. In rare instances, a venturer can recognize a gain for appreciated assets contributed to a joint venture provided certain conditions exist, such as the receipt of cash in connection with the transfer. There are also limitations on the amount of any such gain. However, losses on transfers are fully recognized.

Disclosure. The following should be disclosed by a venturer:

- ☐ Accounting policies of the venturer with respect to its investment in the joint venture.
- ☐ Difference, if any, between the amount at which an investment is carried and the underlying equity in net assets, and the accounting treatment of the difference.
- ☐ If the investment is accounted for under the equity method and is material in the aggregate to the financial position or results of operations of the venturer, summarized information as to assets, liabilities and results of operations of the joint venture; this information is presented in the footnotes or in separate statements, either individually or in groups.
- ☐ Nature and amount of commitments and guarantees related to the joint venture.
- ☐ Basis of consolidation, if the proportionate consolidation method is used.
- ☐ Name of each joint venture and percentage ownership.

Accounting by Joint Ventures. Generally accepted accounting principles apply to the financial statements of joint ventures. However, there is limited authoritative literature on assets contributed to joint ventures. Generally, except in unusual circumstances, assets contributed are not revalued, and the predecessor basis of the contributing venturer is utilized.

Disclosure. There are no specific disclosure requirements for a joint venture, and customary generally accepted accounting principles apply.

Reference. APB Opinion 18, as interpreted; AICPA SOP 78-9; and SEC SABs 51 and 84.

6. Foreign Currency Translation

Bases of Translation. Currency exchange rate changes that affect cash flows are distinguished from those that do not. Those that do, require settlement in a currency other than the entity's "functional currency" (see below) and result in *transaction* adjustments. These are reported as transaction gains or losses during the period in which the transaction is settled or a change in the exchange rate takes place, and are included in net income. Those that do not are reported as *translation* adjustments and are excluded from net income. Translation adjustments are accumulated in a separate component of equity until the foreign investment is liquidated or is partly or fully sold by the parent. When this occurs, they are removed from equity and reported as part of the gain or loss on the liquidation or sale.

Implementation of this approach requires the determination of the functional currency of the foreign unit whose financial statements are to be translated. An entity's functional currency is the currency of the primary economic environment in which the entity operates. It can be the US dollar or a foreign currency, depending on the facts, and will normally be the currency of the economic environment in which cash is generated and expended by the entity.

If a company's functional currency is a foreign currency, the process of translating its financial statements into the reporting currency results in translation adjustments. All elements of financial statements are translated using a **current exchange rate**.

In highly inflationary economies in which the local currency has lost much of its value, use of the local currency as the functional currency may distort financial statements. In these cases, SFAS No. 52 requires the use of the reporting currency (normally the US dollar) as the functional currency. SFAS No. 52 defines a highly inflationary economy as one that has cumulative inflation of about 100 percent or more over a three-year period, but states that the trend of inflation might be as important as the absolute rate and that the definition of a highly inflationary economy should be applied with judgment.

If a company's records are not in its functional currency, the financial statements must be remeasured into that currency before they are translated into the reporting currency. In these circumstances, including where the reporting currency (usually the US dollar) is designated as the functional currency, the **monetary/nonmonetary** method will be used (with certain exceptions) to translate amounts. All translation and transaction adjustments are included in net income.

Exchange gains or losses on intercompany transactions are included in income unless they are of a long-term investment nature where settlement is not planned or anticipated in the foreseeable future. In that event, they are reflected as translation adjustments.

Hedge Transactions. **Foreign currency transactions** are treated as translation adjustments if they are designated as, and are "effective" as, economic **hedges** of a net investment in a foreign entity. An example would be a US parent company with a net investment in a subsidiary located in Switzerland whose functional currency is the Swiss franc. The US parent might also borrow Swiss francs and designate the loan as a hedge of the net investment in the Swiss subsidiary. The net effect of the translation adjustments related to the Swiss franc debt and the subsidiary's balance sheet would be included in the separate translation adjustment component of equity.

A gain or loss on a forward contract or other foreign currency transaction intended to hedge an identifiable foreign currency commitment is generally deferred and included in the measurement of the related foreign currency transaction.

Disclosure. Disclosure is required of:

☐ The aggregate transaction gain or loss included in determining net income for the period.

☐ An analysis of changes during the period in the cumulative translation adjustment component of equity.

☐ Rate changes that occur after the date of the financial statements and their effects on unsettled balances pertaining to foreign currency transactions, if significant.

Reference. SFAS No. 52.

7. Changing Prices/Inflation Accounting

General. Business enterprises are encouraged, but are not required, to disclose supplementary information on the effects of changing prices on selected income statement and balance sheet items. SFAS No. 89 provides measurement ("current cost/constant purchasing power'') and presentation guidance for companies that elect to disclose supplementary information on changing prices. However, companies need not follow that guidance, but may experiment with other forms of disclosure.

Due to lower inflation rates since the early 1980s, and a perceived limited use of this supplementary information by financial statement readers, most US companies do not disclose this information.

Reference.   SFAS No. 89.

8. Accounting Changes

Accounting Treatment.   Changes in accounting principles result from the adoption of a generally accepted accounting principle different from the one previously used for reporting purposes, although only when use of the new principle can be justified.

Changes in accounting principles can be mandatory, resulting from changes made to conform with new FASB or other pronouncements, or discretionary. Guidance for implementing mandatory accounting changes is provided in the relevant new pronouncement. Discretionary accounting changes are defined as changes in accounting principles, estimates or the reporting entity.

Except for certain discretionary changes, the cumulative effect (net of tax) of a change in accounting principle should be recorded in the year of change and shown in the income statement between extraordinary items and net income, without restating prior period statements. Changes that are not recognized as a cumulative effect adjustment are reflected retroactively and include a change from the LIFO method of accounting for inventory to another method, a change in the method of accounting for long-term construction-type contracts, and a change from or to the ''full cost'' method of accounting used in extractive industries.

Changes in accounting estimates occur as a result of new information or as additional experience is acquired. The effect of a change in accounting estimate (e.g., change in depreciable lives) is recorded prospectively in the period of change without retroactive restatement.

Changes in the reporting entity involve a difference in an entity's financial reporting since the prior period, such as a change in specific subsidiaries included in a consolidated group. Reporting entity changes are accounted for by restating all prior years presented to conform with the current entity structure.

Disclosure.   Disclosures required by new FASB or other pronouncements are specified in the pronouncement. Required disclosures of discretionary changes are specified by APB Opinion No. 20. They include, for changes requiring restatement, the nature of the change, justification for the change and effects on income before extraordinary items and on net income for all periods presented. Similar data is required for changes not requiring restatement, as well as the cumulative effect of the change (or the reason for omitting the cumulative effect) and pro forma effects of retroactive application on income before extraordinary items and net income. Other required disclosures depend on whether the accounting change is a change in accounting estimate or in the reporting entity.

Discretionary changes in accounting principles by public companies require an independent accountant's comment letter regarding preferability of the change to be filed with the SEC.

Reference.   APB Opinion No. 20 and SEC Regulation S-K.

9.   Prior Period Adjustments

Accounting Treatment.   **Prior period adjustments** are charged or credited to the opening balance of **retained earnings**, net of tax. Prior period financial statements presented are restated.

Effect of Prior Period Adjustments on Previously Reported Earnings per Share. The effect of the restatement on prior periods' earnings per share should be disclosed.

Disclosure.   The nature of an error in previously issued financial statements and the effect of its correction on income before extraordinary items, net income and the related per share amounts, both gross and net of applicable income tax, should be disclosed for all periods presented.

Reference.   APB Opinion Nos. 9 and 20, and SFAS No. 16.

10.   Post Balance Sheet Events

Definition.   Two types of events that occur after the date of the entity's financial statements but before the issuance of its financial statements (commonly referred to as "subsequent events") are distinguished.

- □   "Type 1" subsequent events—Events that provide additional evidence with respect to conditions that existed at the balance sheet date and affect the estimates inherent in the process of preparing financial statements. Examples would be credit losses resulting from a customer's deteriorating financial condition and settlement of a liability that previously had been estimated at a different amount.
- □   "Type 2" subsequent events—Events that provide evidence of conditions that did not exist at the balance sheet date but arose after that date. Examples would be sales of securities, business combinations and catastrophic losses.

Accounting Treatment.   Type 1 subsequent events should be considered, with other information that becomes available prior to the issuance of the financial statements, in management's evaluation of the conditions on which estimates were based. The financial statements should be adjusted for any changes in estimates resulting from the use of such evidence.

Type 2 subsequent events do not result in adjustment of the financial statements.

Disclosure.   For Type 2 subsequent events, footnote disclosure may be necessary to keep the financial statements from being misleading. Occasionally, disclosure may best be made by supplementing the historical financial statements with pro forma financial data (usually a balance sheet), giving effect to the event as if it had occurred at the date of the financial statements.

Reference.   SFAS No. 5 and AICPA Statement on Auditing Standards (SAS) No. 1, Section 560.

11. Related Party Transactions

Definition. A related party is defined as any party with which the reporting entity deals and one party controls or can significantly influence the management or operating policies of the other. Examples include affiliates of the reporting entity; principal owners, management and immediate family members of owners or management; entities in which investments are accounted for by the equity method by the entity; and pension trusts that are managed by the entity's management.

Accounting Treatment. Established accounting principles ordinarily do not require transactions with related parties to be accounted for differently from transactions with parties that are not related. However, the financial statements should recognize the substance of particular transactions rather than merely their legal form.

Disclosure. Disclosure of material related party transactions is required, including:

☐ The nature of the relationship(s).

☐ A description of the transactions(s), including transactions to which no amounts were ascribed, for each income statement presented.

☐ The dollar amount of transactions for each income statement presented.

☐ The effects of any change in the method of establishing terms from that used in the preceding period.

☐ Amounts due from or to related parties as of the date of each balance sheet presented and the terms and manner of settlement.

Reference. SFAS No. 57.

12. Segmental Information

General. Certain financial segment information regarding different industries and foreign operations and sales to major customers is required when a complete set of annual financial statements is presented.

Reportable industry segments are determined by identifying the individual products and services from which an enterprise derives its revenue, and grouping those products and services by industry lines into segments that are significant to the company as a whole.

In general, a reportable segment is defined as a segment that accounts for 10 percent or more of the combined segment revenue, operating profit or loss, or identifiable assets. The number of reportable segments should equal at least 75 percent of combined revenue from sales to unaffiliated customers of all industry segments, with all other segments, subject to certain limitations, combined under the caption "other."

Disclosure. For each reportable segment, information is presented relating to revenue, profitability, identifiable assets, depreciation and amortization, **capital expenditures**, equity in operations of certain investees and any changes in accounting principles.

Information relating to revenue, profitability and identifiable assets is also provided by geographic areas for operations located outside the home country. Export sales from the home country and major customer revenue should be disclosed, if significant.

The reporting of segmental information has been suspended for nonpublic companies.

Reference.   SFAS Nos. 14 and 21, and SEC Regulation S-K.

ACCOUNTING PRINCIPLES FOR SPECIFIC ITEMS— BALANCE SHEET

13.   Property, Plant and Equipment

Classification of Capital and Revenue Expenditure.   An expenditure is classified as a **fixed asset** when it gives rise to a **capital asset**, represents a significant improvement to an existing asset or significantly increases an asset's useful life. Expenditures for repairs or maintenance are treated as expenses as incurred.

Basis of Valuation.   Fixed assets are carried at cost and include expenditures incurred in preparing them for use. Gains or losses are generally reflected in income when assets are retired or disposed of. Write-up of asset costs to reflect appraisals or current value is not acceptable.

The accounting for long-term assets whose value is considered to be impaired is currently under consideration. However, to the extent that carrying values are not considered to be recoverable, an adjustment to reduce asset values should be made and charged against income.

Depreciation.   Fixed assets are depreciated based on an estimated useful life; generally, an anticipated salvage value is considered. **Depreciation** methods considered acceptable include **straight-line**, **declining balance**, **sum-of-the-years'-digits**, **unit of production** or hours of use. **Annuity method** depreciation is not considered acceptable.

Disclosure.   Balances of major classes of assets, and the corresponding accumulated depreciation either by asset class or in total, must be disclosed. Depreciation expense for each period presented, along with the method used in computing depreciation and the capitalization policy, should be disclosed. In addition, property pledged, mortgaged or subject to lien should be disclosed.

Reference.   ARB No. 43 and APB Opinion Nos. 6 and 12.

14.   Intangible Assets

Accounting Treatment.   **Intangible assets** acquired from others should be recorded on the balance sheet at cost. The costs to develop, maintain or restore intangible assets that are not specifically identifiable, have indeterminate lives or are inherent in a continuing business, such as goodwill, should be expensed. Aside from computer software, for which specific rules apply, the costs to develop specifically identifiable intangible assets may be recorded as assets if the periods of expected future benefit are reasonably determinable and recovery is reasonably assured.

Valuation.   Individual intangible assets should be recorded at cost at the date of acquisition. Cost is generally the amount of cash disbursed, the fair value of other assets distributed, the present value of amounts to be paid for liabilities incurred or the fair value of consideration received for stock issued. It is not acceptable to capitalize research and development expenditures as intangible assets (see Section 25).

Intangible assets acquired as part of a group of assets or as part of an acquired company should also be recorded at cost at the date of acquisition. The cost of identifiable intangible assets is a designated amount of the total cost of the group of assets or entity acquired, which is generally based on the fair values of individual assets. The cost of unidentifiable intangible assets (goodwill) is generally the difference between the cost of the group of assets acquired and the sum of the designated costs of individual tangible and identifiable intangible assets acquired less liabilities assumed.

Amortization.   Recorded costs of intangible assets should be amortized by systematic charges to income over the estimated life of each specific asset. The period of **amortization** should not exceed 40 years for goodwill; generally, much shorter periods are used for other intangible assets.

The straight-line method of amortization should be applied over estimated useful lives unless another systematic method can be demonstrated to be more appropriate. The period of amortization should be continually evaluated to determine whether later events or circumstances warrant revised estimates of useful lives.

Disclosure.   Major classes of intangible assets and the amount of accumulated amortization should be stated separately; the basis on which they are stated and amortized should be disclosed.

Reference.   APB Opinion No. 17 and SEC Regulation S-X.

15. Leases

Classification.   Classification of leases is based on whether a lease transfers substantially all of the benefits and risks of ownership.

In general, a *lessee* classifies a lease as a capital (**finance**) **lease** if any of the following criteria are met:

- □ The lease transfers ownership of the property to the lessee by the end of the lease term.
- □ The lease contains a bargain purchase option.
- □ The lease term is at least 75 percent of the property's economic life.
- □ The present value at the beginning of the lease term of the minimum lease payments (less executory costs) is at least 90 percent of the fair value of the leased property.

A *lessor* classifies a lease as a sales-type or direct financing lease, as appropriate, if it meets any of the four criteria above and if collectibility of minimum lease payments is reasonably predictable and no important uncertainties exist about unreimbursable costs yet to be incurred by the lessor under the lease.

A sales-type lease gives rise to a dealer's or manufacturer's profit (or loss). Normally, sales-type leases arise when dealers or manufacturers use leasing as a means of marketing their products. SFAS No. 66, *Accounting for Sales of Real Estate*, contains requirements for a sales-type lease involving real estate.

A direct financing lease is a lease other than a **leveraged lease** (see below) that does not give rise to a manufacturer's or dealer's profit (or loss) but otherwise meets the criteria for a sales-type lease. These normally occur when lessors are engaged primarily in financing operations, such as banks and insurance companies.

A leveraged lease is a direct financing lease in which (a) at least three parties—a lessee, a long-term creditor and a lessor—are involved, (b) the financing is nonrecourse as to the general credit of the lessor and is sufficient to provide the lessor with substantial leverage in the transaction and (c) the lessor's net investment declines during the early years and rises during the later years of the lease.

Leases that are not classified as capital, sales-type, direct financing or leveraged leases are **operating leases**.

Accounting Treatment. For operating leases, lessees normally charge rentals to expense when the rent becomes payable. Even if rental payments are not made on a straight-line basis, rental expense is generally recognized on a straight-line basis. Lessors record the leased property in the balance sheet. Lessors also record depreciation in accordance with their normal depreciation policy and report rent generally on a straight-line basis over the lease term. Lease incentives for a lessee to sign an operating lease must be recognized on a straight-line basis over the term of the lease.

A lessee records a capital lease as an asset and a liability at an amount equal to the present value at the beginning of the lease term of minimum lease payments during the lease term, exclusive of executory costs. The asset is amortized over either the life of the asset or the lease term, depending on the circumstances. Lessors' accounting is as follows:

☐ Sales-type leases—The minimum lease payments (net of executory costs) plus the unguaranteed residual value accruing to the benefit of the lessor are recorded as the gross investment in the lease. The difference between the gross investment and the sum of the present value of the two components of gross investment is recorded as unearned income. The net investment is the gross investment less unearned income. The present value of the minimum lease payments at the rate implied in the lease, net of executory costs, is recorded as the sale price. The cost or carrying amount, if different, of the leased property, plus any initial direct costs, less the present value of the unguaranteed residual value accruing to the benefit of the lessor, is charged against income in the same period. Unearned income is amortized to income over the lease term to produce a constant periodic rate of return on the net investment in the lease.

☐ Direct financing leases (other than leveraged leases)—The gross investment in the lease is recorded as in sales-type capital leases. The difference between the gross investment and the cost or carrying amount of the leased property is recorded as unearned income. The net investment is the gross investment less unearned income. Unearned income is amortized in the same manner as for a sales-type lease.

☐ Leveraged leases—The investment is recorded net of nonrecourse debt. The lessor's net investment in leveraged leases for purposes of computing periodic net income is the investment less applicable deferred taxes. Net income recognized is composed of three elements: pretax lease income, investment tax credit and the tax effect of pretax income recognized.

Accounting for a sale-leaseback transaction involving real estate generally depends on whether the seller-lessee has continuing involvement. If there is none, "sale-leaseback accounting" must be used; otherwise, the transaction is accounted for by the deposit method or as a financing, whichever is appropriate. If a sale-leaseback does not involve real estate and is a capital lease, the seller-lessee amortizes any profit or loss in proportion to the amortization of the leased asset. If it is an operating lease, the seller-lessor records amortization in proportion to the related gross rental charged to expense over the lease term.

Disclosure.   Required disclosures for lessees include the following:

- ☐   Capital leases—Assets recorded by major classes and future minimum lease payments in the aggregate, and for each of five succeeding years, with deductions from the total to arrive at present value.
- ☐   Operating leases—Future minimum rental payments required in the aggregate and each of five succeeding years and total rental expense for each income statement presented.
- ☐   A general description of leasing arrangements.

Required disclosures for lessors include the following:

- ☐   Sales-type and direct financing leases—The components of the net investment and future minimum lease payments to be received for each of the five succeeding years.
- ☐   Operating leases—Cost of property held for lease by major class with total accumulated depreciation and minimum future rentals in the aggregate and for each of five succeeding years.
- ☐   A general description of leasing arrangements.

Required disclosures for leveraged leases include the following:

- ☐   Pretax income from the leveraged lease, the tax effect of pretax income and the amount of investment tax credit recognized as income during the period.
- ☐   The components of the net investment balance, which consist of rentals receivable (net of principal and interest on the nonrecourse debt), estimated residual value of the leased asset, unearned and deferred income and deferred taxes arising from the leveraged lease.

Reference.   SFAS No. 13, as amended and interpreted, and SFAS Nos. 66 and 98.

16.   Investments

Valuation.   Investments that are inherently short term, readily marketable or represent part of a company's working capital may be classified as current assets. Investments made for purposes of control, affiliation or other long-term purpose, or that are not readily marketable, generally should not be considered current.

Marketable equity securities are grouped into separate portfolios according to current or noncurrent classifications for the purpose of comparing aggregate cost and market value, and to determine the resulting carrying amount. "Marketable" means the security has a publicly reported sales price. An "equity" security is an investment that represents ownership in a company (e.g., common stock) or the right to acquire such ownership at a fixed or determinable price (e.g., warrants and options). The carrying amount of a marketable equity securities portfolio should be the lower of its aggregate cost or market value, determined at the balance sheet date. An excess of aggregate cost over market value should be recorded as a valuation allowance. Generally, transfers between current and noncurrent portfolios are recorded at the lower of cost or market for the security.

Securities other than marketable equity securities are generally carried at cost. For those classified as current, a write-down to market value is required if a decline in value takes place, unless there is persuasive evidence of market recovery subsequent to year-end. For those classified as noncurrent, a write-down is required if evidence indicates cost will not be recovered.

Treatment of Valuation Allowances. Valuation allowances are deducted from the related balance sheet amounts. For current marketable equity securities, changes in the valuation allowance should be included in the determination of net income; for noncurrent marketable equity securities, in the equity section of the balance sheet.

For marketable equity securities included as noncurrent assets, a determination must be made as to whether a decline in market value below cost as of the balance sheet date is other than temporary. If it is considered to be other than temporary, the security should be reduced to a new cost basis. The amount of the adjustment should be accounted for as a realized loss by a charge to income; the new cost basis should not be changed for subsequent recoveries in market value.

Write-downs to market value for securities other than marketable equity securities are included in the determination of net income and establish a new cost basis for the securities.

Gains/Losses. Realized gains and losses represent the difference between net proceeds on sale and cost and are included in net income.

Disclosure. Required disclosures for all securities include their aggregate cost, market value and carrying amount, the valuation allowance deducted from the related investment portfolio and any hypothecation or other pledging. For marketable equity securities, gross unrealized gains and losses must also be disclosed.

For each income statement presented, net realized gains or losses included in the determination of net income, the basis on which cost was determined in computing realized gains or losses, the change in the valuation allowance included in net income (or equity section, as applicable) and significant net realized and unrealized gains and losses subsequent to the balance sheet date should also be disclosed.

Reference. APB Opinion No. 12, SFAS No. 12 and SEC Regulation S-X.

17. Accounts Receivable

Accounting Treatment. Recognition: **Accounts receivable** are recognized when the related **revenue** is recognized (see Section 23), generally based on the sale of assets or performance of services.

Discounts: Receivables and sales may be recorded at either the gross amount or net of trade or quantity discounts. Cash discounts are usually recorded when taken by the customer.

Allowances: The allowances for doubtful accounts should be deducted from the related receivables in the balance sheet, with appropriate disclosure. While there is no specific method for calculating the allowance, its adequacy should be reviewed periodically by evaluating the collectibility of the receivables.

Factored Receivables.   Receivables may be sold with or without recourse. When they are sold without recourse, the seller records the transaction as a sale of assets, and the difference between the receivable and the proceeds received is recorded as a gain or loss. When they are sold with recourse, they may be recognized as a sale if all the following conditions are met:

□   The transferor surrenders its control of the future economic benefits embodied in the receivables.

□   The transferor's obligation under the recourse provisions can be reasonably estimated.

□   The transferee cannot return the receivables to the transferor except pursuant to the recourse provisions.

If any of the above conditions is not met, the proceeds from the transfer of receivables should be reported as a liability.

Disclosure.   Disclosure requirements include:

□   Current and noncurrent receivables.
□   Allowance for doubtful accounts.
□   Related party amounts.
□   Receivables from trade customers and any other significant classes.
□   Receivables pledged as collateral for loans.
□   Proceeds from transfers of receivables with recourse, as well as information related to uncollected balances.

Reference.   ARB No. 43, Chapter 3A; APB Opinion No. 12; and SFAS Nos. 5, 57, 77 and 105.

18.   Inventories and Work in Progress

General Accounting Treatment.   **Inventories** should be stated at the lower of cost or market value. Methods of determining cost are usually either the **first-in first-out (FIFO)** method, **last-in first-out (LIFO)** method, **average-cost** method or **specific identification** method. Cost includes materials, labor and overhead, except for general corporate overhead, which should be expensed. Direct costing, or the exclusion of all elements of manufacturing overhead, is not considered to be in accordance with US GAAP.

The term "market" as used in "lower of cost or market" is defined as current replacement cost (by purchase or reproduction), provided that it is not (1) greater than **net realizable value** and (2) less than net realizable value reduced by an approximately normal profit margin.

Long-Term Contracts. Under the **percentage of completion method**, which is considered preferable in most circumstances, construction in process consists of costs incurred plus the estimated gross profit to date. Under the **completed contract method**, construction in process consists of costs incurred to date (see Section 23). For long-term contracts, the difference between construction in process and billings to date is reported in the balance sheet as an asset or a liability.

Disclosure. Major classes of inventories should be disclosed, as well as the basis for determining inventory amounts (e.g., lower of cost or market) and the method of determining cost (e.g., LIFO, FIFO, average cost). Disclosures should also include **hypothecation** or other pledging and, if LIFO is used, the excess of current or replacement cost over LIFO value and the income statement effect of a material LIFO inventory liquidation. The method of accounting for long-term contracts should be disclosed.

Reference. ARB No. 43, Chapters 3 and 4; ARB No. 45; and SEC Regulation S-X.

19. Current Liabilities

General Accounting Treatment. Liabilities payable within one year of the balance sheet date or whose liquidation is expected to require the use of **current assets**, are generally classified as **current liabilities**. The current liability classification should also include obligations that, by their terms, are due on demand or will be due on demand within one year of the balance sheet date, even though liquidation may not be expected within that period.

Accounts payable and significant accrued or other liabilities should be shown separately. Payments received in advance are recognized when earned, recorded as deferred revenue and presented in the balance sheet either as part of liabilities or between liabilities and equity.

Creation of General and Specific Provisions. General provisions or reserves for future losses are not permitted.

Specific provisions can be recorded for estimated liabilities and generally relate to such items as warranties, employee benefits, severance indemnities, environmental liabilities, and litigation, claims and assessments.

Disclosure. Generally, significant individual liabilities and accrued amounts are disclosed separately and include amounts payable for borrowings, trade payables, dividends, compensation arrangements, warranties and deferred taxes. Further, public companies are required to separately disclose all items that exceed 5 percent of total liabilities.

Reference. ARB No. 43, Chapter 3A; SFAS Nos. 5 and 109; and SEC Regulation S-X.

20. Long-Term Debt

General Accounting Treatment. Long-term debt is a liability due more than one year from the balance sheet date and is generally evidenced by notes, debentures, mortgages or similar obligations. Any premium or discount is reflected as an addition to or a deduction from the long-term debt.

Debt Restructuring. Certain transactions are considered **troubled debt restructurings** if a creditor, for reasons related to the debtor's financial difficulties, grants a concession to the debtor that it would not otherwise consider. That concession either stems from an agreement between the creditor and the debtor or is imposed by law or a court. A troubled debt restructuring may include asset transfers, the granting of equity interest or certain modifications of debt terms.

Accounting for a troubled debt restructuring is based on the type of the restructuring: (a) If it is a transfer of assets or granting of equity interest in full settlement of a debt and the value of the assets or equity interest is less than the carrying value of the debt, the difference generally is an extraordinary gain to the debtor and ordinary loss to the creditor. The debtor must also recognize a gain or loss for any difference between the carrying value of the assets transferred and their fair value. (b) If it is a modification of terms, it is accounted for prospectively from the time of the restructuring. No gain or loss is recorded at the time of the restructuring unless the carrying amount of the debt exceeds the total future cash payments (or receipts) specified by the new terms.

Debt Extinguishment. In certain circumstances debt is considered to be extinguished for financial reporting purposes; these circumstances are the repayment of the debt, a legal release from the primary obligation and the completion of an in-substance **defeasance**. In-substance defeasance accounting does not apply when the assets placed in trust were acquired at about the same time that the debt was incurred (instantaneous defeasance).

Any difference between the reacquisition price and net carrying amount of debt, however extinguished, should be recognized in the period of extinguishment and classified as an extraordinary item, net of the related income tax effect.

In certain circumstances, conversion privileges in a convertible debt instrument are changed or additional consideration is paid to debt holders for the purpose of inducing prompt conversion of the debt to equity securities (sometimes referred to as a convertible debt "sweetener"). The changed terms may involve reduction of the original conversion price, resulting in the issuance of additional shares of stock, issuance of warrants or other securities not provided for in the original conversion terms, or payment of cash or other consideration to debt holders who convert during a specified period. When convertible debt is converted to equity of the debtor pursuant to such an inducement offer, the debtor recognizes an expense equal to the fair value of all securities and other consideration transferred in the transaction in excess of the fair value of securities issuable pursuant to the original conversion terms. This expense is not reported as an extraordinary item.

Disclosure. The following disclosures are generally made for long-term debt: interest rate, due dates, call prices, combined aggregate amount of maturities for each of the next five years, whether any subordination exists, any conversion terms, any assets pledged as collateral, restrictive covenants and any contingencies regarding the payment of principal or interest.

For an extinguishment of debt, disclosures should include a description of the transaction, the income tax effect, the per share amount of the aggregate gain or loss and, in the case of an in-substance defeasance, the amount considered extinguished at the end of each period during which the debt is outstanding.

Reference. APB Opinion No. 26; SFAS Nos. 4, 15, 47, 76 and 84; SEC Regulation S-X; and FASB Technical Bulletin Nos. 80-1 and 84-4.

21. Contingencies

General. Whether a **contingency** results in a provision for loss or only disclosure is based on an assessment as to the probability of a measurable loss having occurred.

Contingent Losses. The accounting and reporting for loss contingencies is based on the likelihood that a future event will confirm the loss or impairment of an asset or the incurrence of a liability. The following are the ranges of likelihood and the criteria for classification:

- Probable—The future event is likely to occur.
- Reasonably possible—The chance of the future event occurring is more than remote but less than likely.
- Remote—The chance of the future event occurring is slight.

A liability for a loss contingency should be accrued when both of the following conditions are met:

- Information available prior to the issuance of financial statements indicates that it is probable that an asset had been impaired or a liability had been incurred at the date of the financial statements.
- The amount of loss can be reasonably estimated.

If the first condition is met and the estimate of loss is a range, the best estimate of the loss should be accrued. If no amount within the range is a better estimate than any other amount, the minimum amount in the range should be accrued.

Contingent Gains. Contingencies that might result in gains usually are not recorded, although adequate disclosure of such contingencies should be made. Misleading implications as to the likelihood of realization should be avoided.

Disclosure. Disclosure of the nature and, in some circumstances, the amount of accruals for estimated losses may be necessary. Also, disclosure of the nature of a contingency is required when there is at least a reasonable possibility that a loss or, in the case of a contingency that has been accrued, an additional loss may have been incurred at the date of the financial statements. An estimate of the possible loss or range of loss or a statement that an estimate cannot be made is also required.

Certain commitments, typically in the form of guarantees, should be disclosed even though the possibility of loss may be remote. Examples include the following:

- Guarantees of indebtedness of others.
- Unused letters of credit.
- Guarantees to repurchase receivables.
- Commitments for plant acquisition.
- Guarantees relating to the sale of a business or operating assets to a highly leveraged entity.

Disclosure of information about financial instruments with off-balance sheet risk of accounting loss is required. A financial instrument represents any contract that gives rise to both a (recognized or unrecognized) financial asset of one enterprise and a (recognized or unrecognized) financial liability or equity instrument of another enterprise. The required disclosures include the face, contract or notional principal amount; the nature and terms of the instruments and a discussion of their credit and market risk, cash requirements and related accounting policies; the accounting loss the entity would incur if any party to the financial instrument failed to perform according to the terms of the contract; the entity's policy for requiring collateral on financial instruments it accepts; and a description of collateral presently held. Disclosure is also required for significant concentration of credit risks from individual or groups of counterparties. In addition, all companies are required to disclose the fair value of financial instruments (both assets and liabilities recognized and not recognized in the balance sheet) for which it is practicable to estimate that value, and the methods and significant assumptions used to estimate the fair value.

Reference. SFAS Nos. 5, 105 and 107; SEC SAB No. 81; and SEC Regulation S-X.

22. Capital and Reserves

General. Ownership interest consists of capital contributed by shareholders and earnings that have been retained by the entity. These are usually included under the caption "stockholders' equity," although other descriptive titles may be used. Titles that are normally used for components of stockholders' equity are **capital stock**, **additional paid in capital** and retained earnings. These may be further divided, depending on the situation—for example, capital stock may be divided into **common stock** and **preferred stock**, and reduced by **stock** reacquired by the company (**treasury stock**).

Share Capital. State laws govern the incorporation of businesses and the issuance of stock. If a company has one class of stock, it is referred to as common stock. However, companies may issue other classes of stock having rights and privileges that differ from those attached to the common stock. These rights and privileges may vary but often pertain to shareholder voting, dividend preferences and capital repayment.

Generally, companies may issue stock at **par value** or without par value. Par value establishes the minimum amount a shareholder must pay for the shares to be fully paid, although companies may receive more than par value for the shares.

Other Reserves. Retained earnings may be restricted externally—for example, by loan covenants—or internally appropriated by management. The stockholders' equity section of the balance sheet may also include foreign currency translation adjustments (see Section 6).

Distribution Restrictions. In general, state laws prohibit distributions to shareholders unless the company's legal minimum capital remains intact. Dividends are usually paid from unrestricted retained earnings.

Disclosure. Companies must disclose in the balance sheet or footnotes, as appropriate, the par or stated value per share, the number of shares issued and outstanding, the number of shares authorized and convertibility features for each class of preferred and common stock. Companies should also disclose redemption data, dividend arrearages and the nature of preferences for each class of preferred stock. Descriptions of warrants, options or rights outstanding are required. Companies must also disclose the amount of retained earnings from which dividends may be paid and the reasons for any restriction on retained earnings.

Reference. ARB No. 43, Chapter 1A; APB Opinion Nos. 6, 10 and 15; SFAS No. 47; and SEC Regulation S-X.

ACCOUNTING PRINCIPLES FOR SPECIFIC ITEMS—INCOME STATEMENT

23. Revenue Recognition

General Principles. Revenues are generally not recognized until they are realized and earned. They are realized when products, goods or services, merchandise or other assets are exchanged for cash or claims to cash. They are earned when the entity has substantially accomplished what it must do to be entitled to payment. These conditions are usually met by the time products or merchandise is delivered or services are rendered to customers.

Long-Term Projects/Contracts. Long-term projects are generally for a specific customer pursuant to a contract. The existence of enforceable rights, such as the right to specific performance and progress payments, suggests a continuous sale occurs as the work progresses. GAAP generally call for the recognition of revenue as work progresses (the percentage of completion method) when estimates of progress toward completion, revenues and costs are reasonably dependable; the contract specifies the goods and services to be exchanged and the terms of settlement; and the buyer and contractor can be expected to perform under the contract. Otherwise revenue should be recognized when the contract is substantially completed (the completed contract method). Under either method, expected losses should be recognized as soon as they are known.

Instalment Sales. The instalment method of accounting, in which income is recognized pro rata as a long-term instalment receivable is collected, is not generally accepted except in certain circumstances outlined in SFAS No. 66, *Accounting for Sales of Real Estate*, and in other exceptional situations.

Rights of Return. When as a result of contractual arrangement or industry practice, the customer has the right to return items purchased, the transaction should not be recognized as a sale unless the following specified criteria have been met: sale price has been fixed, payment has been made in full or is not contingent on resale by the customer, customer's obligation is not affected by theft or damage to product, customer has economic substance, seller is not obligated to assist with resale of the product and future product returns can be reasonably predicted. Transactions for which revenue is postponed should be recognized as sales when the return privilege has expired.

Product Financing. A **product financing arrangement** is a transaction in which an enterprise sells and agrees to repurchase inventory, with the repurchase price equal to the original sale price plus carrying and financing costs, or other similar transactions. These arrangements are required to be accounted for as borrowings rather than as sales.

Disclosure.   Revenue from sales of products and services is generally separately disclosed in the income statement. Disclosure of accounting policies for long-term construction contracts is required. Significant transactions where the right of return exists must also be disclosed.

Reference.   ARB No. 45; APB Opinion No. 10; and SFAS Nos. 48, 49 and 66.

24.   Government Grants and Assistance

Accounting Treatment.   There is no authoritative standard dealing with government grants or assistance. The AICPA has, however, issued certain informal guidance with respect to grants. The basic issues in accounting for government grants are (1) whether the benefits should be credited to capital or income and (2) if to income, over what periods should they be recognized.

For business entities, the AICPA has recommended that grants be recognized in income, and that the period of recognition depends on the type of grant.

☐   Grants related to revenue, such as certain export subsidies and price control subsidies, should be recognized in the period of the related events.

☐   Grants to reimburse current expenditures, such as research and development costs, wages, training costs and transportation costs, should be treated as a reduction of current or future related expense, depending on when the related expense is recognized.

☐   Grants related to developing property, such as timberlands or mineral reserves, should be recognized over the useful lives of the assets.

If the benefits of the grant are received before the conditions of the grant are fulfilled, the enterprise should record the benefits as deferred revenue.

Disclosure.   The AICPA recommends that business enterprises consider the following disclosures:

☐   Grant amounts received during the period, recorded in income and deferred.
☐   Relevant terms of the grant.
☐   Contingencies related to the grant.

Reference.   AICPA Issues Paper, *Accounting for Grants Received from Governments*, October 16, 1979.

25.   Research and Development

Definitions.   Research is planned search or critical investigation aimed at discovery of new knowledge that will be useful in developing new products, services or processes or significantly improve existing products or processes. Development is the translation of research findings or other knowledge into a plan or design for new or improved products and processes intended for sale or use.

Accounting Treatment. Except for specialized rules relating to computer software, research and development costs, as defined, should be charged to expense when incurred. In certain circumstances in business combinations, purchased research and development is also charged to expense.

Disclosure. Research and development costs should be disclosed for each income statement presented.

Reference. SFAS Nos. 2 and 86 and FASB Interpretation No. 4.

26. Capitalized Interest Costs

Accounting Treatment. Interest costs are capitalizable, if material, for assets that require a period of time to be prepared for their intended use. Examples are assets an enterprise constructs for its own use (facilities) or intended for sale or lease that are constructed as discrete projects (real estate projects); however, interest cost is not capitalized for assets routinely manufactured or produced in large quantities on a repetitive basis. The amount capitalized is the interest incurred during the acquisition period that theoretically would have been avoided if the capital expenditures had not been made. The amount is determined by applying an interest rate, based on the rates on outstanding borrowings, to the average amount of accumulated expenditures for the asset during the period. Capitalization ceases when the asset is substantially complete and ready for use; the disposition of the capitalized interest cost is the same as for the other cost components.

Disclosure: Interest costs incurred and the amount capitalized are disclosed for all periods presented.

Reference. SFAS No. 34.

27. Imputed Interest

General. Interest imputation is required in certain circumstances. As a general rule, when one party exchanges goods or services in return for a second party's obligation to pay, in part or in full, cash (or other valuable consideration) in the future and the stated interest rate is not substantially equal to prevailing interest rates, the stated principal amount of the transaction should be adjusted so that it is substantially equal to the present value of all future payments discounted at the prevailing interest rate. The prevailing interest rate depends largely on the borrower's credit standing and the repayment terms, collateral and other pertinent factors.

This general rule has several exceptions, among them the "one-year rule," which exempts receivables and payables arising in the normal course of business that are due in not more than approximately one year. Certain other receivables and payables are also exempt, such as (1) advance payments for property, goods or services, (2) security deposits and retainages, (3) customary loans of financial institutions, (4) transactions in which interest rates are affected by tax attributes or legal restrictions prescribed by a government agency, and (5) parent–subsidiary transactions.

Accounting Treatment. When **imputed interest** is required, the seller should record the sale and the purchaser the asset (or expense) at the adjusted principal amount. Any resulting discount or premium is amortized as interest expense or income over the life of the note using the interest method, that is, so as to result in a constant rate of interest when applied to the amount outstanding at the beginning of any given period.

Disclosure. The face amount of the note and the effective interest rate are to be disclosed; the discount or premium is reported as a direct deduction from or addition to the face amount of the note.

Reference. APB Opinion No. 21.

28. Extraordinary or Unusual Items

Definition. Extraordinary items are events or transactions that are distinguished by both their unusual nature and the infrequency of their occurrence, when considered in relation to an entity's operating environment. They are unrelated to the typical activities of the entity and would not be expected to recur in the foreseeable future.

In addition, early extinguishment of debt gives rise to an extraordinary item.

Accounting Treatment. Extraordinary items are segregated from the results of continuing operations, as a separate line item, net of the applicable tax effects, on the face of the statement of income.

Disclosure. The nature, tax effect, effect on earnings per share and principal items entering into the determination of the gain or loss should be disclosed.

Significant events or transactions that are either unusual or infrequent but not both should be reflected separately as part of continuing operations or disclosed in the notes to the financial statements. Such items should not be reported net of income taxes, nor should the per share effects be disclosed.

Reference. APB Opinion Nos. 9 and 30.

29. Income Taxes

General. In February 1992, the FASB issued SFAS No. 109, *Accounting for Income Taxes.* SFAS No. 109 supersedes what were the two primary standards on accounting for income taxes, APB Opinion No. 11 and SFAS No. 96. SFAS No. 109 is effective for fiscal years beginning after December 15, 1992.

Accounting Treatment. Under SFAS No. 109, similar to SFAS No. 96, income taxes are accounted for under the **liability method**. Under the liability method, a current tax asset or liability is recognized for the estimated taxes refundable or payable on tax returns for the current year. A deferred tax asset or liability is determined for the estimated future tax effects attributable to **temporary differences** and carryforwards. The measurement of current and deferred tax assets or liabilities is based on regular tax rates and provisions of enacted tax laws expected to apply to taxable income in the periods in which the deferred tax asset or liability is expected to be realized or settled. The effects of anticipated changes in the tax laws or rates are not considered.

Under SFAS No. 109, unlike SFAS No. 96, expectations related to future taxable income are considered. A deferred tax asset is initially recognized for the estimated future tax effects of deductible temporary differences and for operating loss and other credit carryforwards. A deferred tax asset would be reduced by a valuation allowance if based on the weight of evidence, it is more likely than not that some or all of the potential deferred tax asset will not be realized. Under SFAS No. 109, tax-planning strategies are another source of taxable income that should be considered when determining the amount of a valuation allowance for deferred tax assets. Tax-planning strategies that are prudent and feasible are strategies that a company has the ability to implement and expects to implement, unless the need is eliminated in future years, to realize a future deductible amount such as an operating loss or tax credit carryforward. However, the tax benefit recognized as a result of a tax-planning strategy should be net of any significant expenses or losses that would be recognized if the strategy is implemented.

Forming a conclusion that a valuation allowance is not required is difficult when there is tangible, negative evidence such as cumulative losses in recent years. Other examples of tangible, negative evidence include (but are not limited to):

- ☐ A history of operating loss or tax credit carryforwards expiring unused.
- ☐ Losses expected in early future years (by a presently profitable entity).
- ☐ Unsettled circumstances that, if unfavorably resolved, would adversely affect future operations and profits.
- ☐ A carryback or carryforward period that is so brief that it would limit realization of tax benefits if a significant deductible temporary difference is expected to reverse in a single year or the company operates in a traditionally cyclical business.

Judgment must be used to determine whether negative evidence is outweighed by positive evidence. Examples of positive evidence that might support a conclusion that no valuation allowance is needed when there is negative evidence include (but are not limited to):

- ☐ Existing contracts or firm sales backlog that will produce more than enough taxable income to realize the deferred tax asset based on existing sales prices and cost structures.
- ☐ An excess of appreciated asset value over the tax basis of the company's net assets in an amount sufficient to realize the deferred tax asset.
- ☐ A strong earnings history, exclusive of the loss that created the future deductible amount, coupled with evidence indicating that the loss is an aberration rather than a continuing condition.

Deferred tax assets and liabilities are classified as current or noncurrent in a company's balance sheet based on the classification of the assets or liabilities related to the temporary differences. A deferred tax asset or liability that is not related to an asset or liability (e.g., a deferred tax asset related to a net operating loss carryforward) should be classified according to the expected reversal date of the temporary difference.

Disclosure. Under SFAS No. 109, the components of the net deferred tax asset or liability recognized in a company's balance sheet should be disclosed as follows:

☐ The total of all deferred tax assets.
☐ The total of all deferred tax liabilities.
☐ The total valuation allowance recognized for deferred tax assets.

In addition, any net change during the year in the total valuation allowance and the types of temporary differences, carryforwards or carrybacks that give rise to significant portions of deferred tax assets or liabilities should be disclosed. Public companies are required to disclose the approximate tax effect of each type of temporary difference and carryforward item.

In general, the significant components of income tax expense are disclosed, including the current and deferred portions, the benefits of operating loss carryforwards, adjustments of deferred tax assets or liabilities for enacted changes in tax laws or rates, and adjustments of the beginning-of-the-year balance of a valuation allowance because of a change in circumstances that causes a change in judgment about the realizability of the related deferred tax asset in future years.

Public companies are required to disclose a reconciliation (using percentages or dollar amounts) of the reported amount of income tax expense attributable to continuing operations for the year to the amount of income tax expense that would result from applying domestic federal **statutory tax rates** to pretax income from continuing operations. The statutory tax rates should be the regular tax rates if there are alternative tax systems. The estimated amount and the nature of each significant reconciling item should be disclosed. A nonpublic company should disclose the nature of significant reconciling items, but may omit a numerical reconciliation.

Companies are required to disclose the amounts and expiration dates of operating loss and tax credit carryforwards for tax purposes. In addition, the amount of the unrecognized deferred tax liability for any temporary differences related to investments in foreign subsidiaries and foreign corporate joint ventures is required to be disclosed.

Reference. SFAS No. 109.

30. Postretirement Benefits

General. Postretirement benefits are defined as all postretirement benefits offered to employees, including pension, health and other welfare benefits. The basic premise of accounting for postretirement benefits is that accrual accounting provides more relevant and useful information than does accounting based on cash funding decisions. Except for pension plan benefits, prior to 1993 US GAAP did not require the use of accrual accounting for postretirement benefits. The issuance of SFAS No. 106 mandates the use of accrual accounting for postretirement benefits other than pensions and is effective for fiscal years beginning after December 15, 1992 for all public companies and other employers who have US plans with more than 500 participants. All other employers, including those with plans outside the United States, must comply with the requirements of SFAS No. 106 no later than fiscal years beginning after December 15, 1994.

At the date of adoption of SFAS No. 106, an employer may elect to record the full amount of the transition obligation as an expense in the income statement as the effect of a change in accounting principle. However, as an alternative to immediate recognition of the transition obligation, an employer may recognize the obligation on a delayed basis. Under this approach, the transition obligation will generally be amortized on a straight-line basis over the greater of the average remaining service period of active plan participants or 20 years.

Pension Benefits:

Accounting Treatment.   Net pension expense for **defined benefit pension plans** includes the following components:

- ☐ Service cost calculated using a mandated actuarial cost method (either the unit credit method or the projected unit credit method).
- ☐ Interest cost—interest accrued on the beginning-of-the-year balance of the projected benefit obligation.
- ☐ Return on plan assets—a reduction in pension cost for the expected earnings on plan assets.
- ☐ Amortization of prior service cost using a method that results in a declining pattern of amortization, generally over the remaining service period of active plan participants.
- ☐ Amortization of gains and losses using any systematic and rational method, subject to certain limitations.
- ☐ Amortization of a transition asset or liability.

Existing standards contain specific guidance on selecting certain actuarial assumptions:

- ☐ Assumed interest (discount) rate used to measure the projected benefit obligation.
- ☐ Salary progression rate.
- ☐ Assumed rate of return on plan assets.

A pension liability (or asset) is recorded if the employer's cumulative contributions to the pension plan are different from the cumulative pension expense. An additional liability (generally along with a corresponding intangible asset) is recognized when unfunded accumulated benefits exceed the balance sheet liability for accrued pension costs.

Pension expense for **defined contribution pension plans** for a period is the contribution called for in that period.

Pension Fund Surpluses.   Surplus assets of a defined benefit pension plan may revert to the employer after all liabilities to participants and their beneficiaries have been satisfied. The US Internal Revenue Service, the Department of Labor and the Pension Benefit Guaranty Corporation have issued joint implementation guidelines for use in processing asset reversions.

Pension Settlements and Curtailments. Specific principles are followed for the measurement of immediate gains or losses arising from **pension plan settlements** or **curtailments** as discussed in SFAS No. 88.

Disclosure. For single-employer defined benefit plans, the following, among other matters, must be disclosed:

☐ A description of the plan, including employee groups covered, type of benefit formula, funding policy, types of assets held, significant nonbenefit liabilities (if any) and the nature and effect of significant matters affecting comparability of information for all periods presented.

☐ Net pension expense for the period, showing separately the service cost component, the interest cost component, the actual return on assets for the period and the net total of other components.

☐ A schedule reconciling the funded status of the plan with amounts reported in the employer's balance sheet, showing separately:
—The fair value of plan assets.
—The projected benefit obligation, identifying the accumulated benefit obligation and the vested benefit obligation.
—The amount of unrecognized prior service cost.
—The amount of unrecognized net gain or loss from changes in the amount of either the projected benefit obligation or plan assets resulting from experience different from that assumed and from changes in assumptions.
—The balance of the unrecognized transition asset or liability.
—The amount of any additional minimum liability required to be recognized if an unfunded accumulated benefit obligation exists.
—The amount of net pension asset or liability recognized in the employer's balance sheet (the net result of combining the preceding items).

☐ The weighted-average assumed settlement (discount) and earnings rates and the rate of compensation increase used.

For multiemployer plans, employers must disclose a description of the plan(s), including employee groups covered; the type of benefits provided (defined benefit or defined contribution); the nature and effect of significant matters affecting comparability of information; and the amount of cost recognized for the period. Required disclosures for defined contribution benefit plans also include the basis of determining contributions.

Companies that recognize a gain or loss on settlement of a pension obligation or curtailment of a plan must disclose the nature of the event and the amount of gain or loss recognized.

Postretirement Benefits Other Than Pensions:

Accounting Treatment. The accounting treatment and related disclosure for postretirement benefits other than pensions set forth in SFAS No. 106 are similar in many respects to the pension plan accounting and disclosure requirements set forth in SFAS Nos. 87 and 88. Net expense recognized can consist of a number of components such as service cost, interest cost, expected return on plan assets and amortization of the transition obligation or asset. The liability or asset to be recognized in the employer's balance sheet is the difference between the cumulative expense recognized and the actual amount of benefits paid or funded.

Key actuarial assumptions used to determine expense for postretirement benefits other than pensions and the related liability include the following:

☐ Assumed interest (discount) rate used to measure the expected postretirement benefit obligation.

☐ The salary progression rate for pay-related plans.

☐ Assumed health care cost trend rate.

Disclosure. Major disclosures required by SFAS No. 106 include:

☐ A description of the substantive plan that is the basis for the accounting, including the nature of the plan, any modifications of existing cost-sharing provisions, employee groups covered, types of benefits provided, funding policy and types of assets held, among others.

☐ Net expense for the period, showing separately the service cost component, interest cost component, actual return on plan assets for the period, amortization of the unrecognized transition obligation or asset and the net total of other components.

☐ A schedule reconciling the funded status of the plan with amounts reported in the employer's balance sheet, showing separately:
  —The fair value of plan assets.
  —The accumulated postretirement benefit obligation, identifying separately the portion attributable to retirees, other fully eligible plan participants and other active plan participants.
  —The amount of unrecognized prior service cost.
  —The amount of unrecognized net gain or loss.
  —The amount of any remaining unrecognized transition obligation or asset.
  —The amount of the net asset or liability recognized in the employer's balance sheet, which is the net result of combining the preceding items.

☐ The assumed health care cost trend rate used to measure the expected cost of benefits covered by the plan for the next year and a general description of the direction and pattern of change in the assumed trend rate thereafter, together with the ultimate trend rate and when that rate is expected to be achieved.

☐ The weighted average of the assumed discount rate and rate of compensation increase used to measure the accumulated postretirement benefit obligation, and the weighted average of the expected long-term rate of return on plan assets.

☐ The effect of a one-percentage-point increase in the assumed health care cost trend rates for each future year on the aggregate of the service and interest cost components, and the accumulated postretirement benefit obligation.

For multiemployer plans, employers must disclose a description of the plan, including the employee groups covered, the types of benefits provided, the nature and effect of significant matters affecting comparability of information for all periods presented and the amount of expense recognized during the period. For defined contribution plans, employers must disclose a description of the plan, including the employee groups covered, the basis for determining contributions, the nature and effect of significant matters affecting comparability of information for all periods presented and the amount of expense recognized during the period.

Employers that recognize a gain or loss on settlement of an obligation or curtailment of a plan must disclose the nature of the event and the amount of gain or loss recognized.

Postemployment Benefits:

In addition to postretirement benefits, many companies provide postemployment benefits to former or inactive employees after employment but before retirement. SFAS No. 112, which is effective for fiscal years beginning after December 15, 1993, establishes standards of financial accounting and reporting for the estimated costs of such benefits. Postemployment benefits are all types of benefits provided to former or inactive employees, their beneficiaries and covered dependents. Inactive employees are those who are not currently rendering service to the employer and who have not been terminated. They include those who have been laid off and those on disability leave, regardless of whether they are expected to return to active status. Postemployment benefits include, but are not limited to, salary continuation, supplemental unemployment benefits, severance benefits, disability-related benefits (including worker's compensation), job training and counseling, and continuation of benefits such as health care benefits and life insurance coverage.

A liability should be accrued for postemployment benefits if all of the following conditions are met:

□ The employer's obligation relating to employees' rights to receive compensation for future absences is attributable to employee services already rendered.

□ The obligation relates to rights that vest or accumulate.

□ Payment of the compensation is probable.

□ The amount of the obligation can be reasonably estimated.

Postemployment benefits that do not meet the above conditions and are not covered by other specific standards are accounted for in accordance with SFAS No. 5.

Disclosure. If an obligation for postemployment benefits is not accrued only because the amount cannot be reasonably estimated, this fact should be disclosed.

Reference. SFAS Nos. 87, 88, 106 and 112.

31. Discontinued Operations

Accounting Treatment. Discontinued operations of business segments are reported separately from continuing operations. A business segment refers to a component of an entity whose activities represent a separate major line of business or class of customer.

A formal plan to dispose of the segment is necessary to establish a measurement date. The formal plan should state the assets to be disposed of, the expected method and period to complete the disposal, the estimated results of operations to the disposal date and proceeds and salvage. An expected loss on disposal should be provided for at the measurement date; an expected gain should be recognized only when realized.

Costs and expenses directly associated with the decision to dispose, such as severance, relocation and future rentals, should be included in the determination of gain or loss on disposal. Operating income or loss of the segment from the measurement date to the disposal date should also be included in the determination of gain or loss on disposal. However, gain can be recognized only to the extent of losses recognized. Any excess gain is recognized when it is realized.

Disclosure.   The loss from operations and the expected loss on disposal should be disclosed separately, net of tax, in the statement of income before extraordinary items and the cumulative effect of accounting changes, but after income from continuing operations. All prior period financial statements presented should be reclassified to reflect this presentation for the discontinued segment.

The description of the business segment, the expected disposal date, manner of disposal, remaining assets and liabilities, any proceeds from disposition and the revenue applicable to the discontinued operations should be disclosed.

Reference.   APB Opinion No. 30.

32. Earnings per Share

Definition.   Earnings per share is defined as the amount of earnings attributable to each share of common stock.

Bases of Computation and Financial Statement Presentation.   Enterprises with simple capital structures (consisting of only common stock or including no potentially dilutive convertible securities, options, warrants or other rights that could in the aggregate dilute earnings per common share) present primary earnings per share data, based on the weighted-average common stock outstanding during the period and common stock equivalents that are not dilutive. Common stock equivalents are securities, such as stock options and warrants, that give their owners the right to acquire common stock. Their effect is not considered dilutive if their exercise or conversion would not have reduced primary earnings per share by at least 3 percent in the aggregate. Net income or loss adjusted for claims of senior securities, such as preferred stock dividends, is divided by the weighted-average number of shares outstanding.

Enterprises with complex capital structures generally present two types of earnings per share data: primary earnings per share and fully diluted earnings per share. Dual calculations are required if shares of common stock (a) were issued during the period upon conversions, exercise of options and so forth, or (b) were contingently issuable at the close of any period presented and if primary earnings per share for such period would have been affected (either dilutively or incrementally) had the shares been issued at the beginning of the period or would have been reduced had the contingent issuances taken place at the beginning of the period. The above contingencies may result from the existence of (a) senior stock or debt that is convertible into common shares but is not a common stock equivalent, (b) options or warrants, or (c) agreements for the issuance of common shares upon satisfaction of certain conditions. Anti-dilutive securities are excluded from the calculation if they result in an increase in the per share amount or a decrease in the loss per share amount.

Stock options and warrants and their equivalents enter earnings per share computations under the treasury stock method. Under that method, exercise of options or warrants is assumed at the beginning of the period (or time of issuance, if later) and proceeds from the exercise are assumed to be used to repurchase common stock for the treasury. Common stock outstanding is assumed to increase by the difference between the number of shares assumed to be issued and purchased.

Convertible securities are included in earnings per share computations under the if-converted method. Under that method, the security is assumed to have been converted into common stock at the beginning of the period (or at issuance, if later). Interest deductions, net of related income taxes, relating to convertible debt and dividends on convertible preferred stock are taken into consideration in determining income applicable to common stock.

Disclosure.   For primary and (when applicable) fully diluted calculations, disclosure is required of the basis of calculation and per share amounts of (a) income from continuing operations, (b) income before extraordinary items, (c) cumulative effect of a change in accounting principles and (d) net income. Other required disclosures include the pro forma effects of the retroactive application of a change in accounting principles on earnings per share and the per share effect of restatement of net income of a prior period. The presentation of earnings per share information is not required in the financial statements of nonpublic companies.

Reference.   APB Opinion No. 15, as amended and interpreted.

Appendix
DO UNITED STATES STANDARDS OR PREVALENT PRACTICE SUBSTANTIALLY COMPLY WITH INTERNATIONAL ACCOUNTING STANDARDS?

Section	Topic	Substantially complies with IAS?	Comments
3.	Basic accounting concepts and conventions	Yes	
	Contents of financial statements	Yes	
4.	Business combinations*	Yes	The US criteria for a pooling of interests are more detailed
5.	Joint ventures	Yes	
6.	Foreign currency translation*	Yes	Translation adjustments related to an operation whose functional currency is a foreign currency are recorded in equity
8.	Accounting changes*	Yes	
9.	Prior period adjustments*	Yes	
10.	Post balance sheet events	Yes	
11.	Related party transactions	Yes	
12.	Segmental information	Yes	
13.	Property, plant and equipment*	Yes	US standards do not permit property, plant and equipment to be carried at valuation
15.	Leases	Yes	
16.	Investments	Yes	All marketable securities are carried at the lower of cost or market on an aggregate portfolio basis. Other securities are generally carried at cost with adjustments for impairments
17.	Accounts receivable	Yes	
18.	Inventories and work in progress*	Yes	
19.	Current liabilities	Yes	
20.	Long-term debt	Yes	
21.	Contingencies	Yes	

Appendix (*Continued*)

Section	Topic	Substantially complies with IAS?	Comments
22.	Capital and reserves	Yes	Surplus revaluation accounts are not recorded
23.	Revenue recognition*	Yes	
24.	Government grants and assistance	Yes	No authoritative guidance has been provided in accounting standards, but predominant practice complies with IAS
25.	Research and development*	Yes	
26.	Capitalization of interest costs*	Yes	
28.	Extraordinary or unusual items*	Yes	In the US, extraordinary items are recognized as a separate component of net income, net of the applicable tax effects
29.	Income tax**	Yes	
30.	Postretirement benefits*	Yes	Specific guidance is provided in the US for postretirement and postemployment benefits

*These topics are subject to change as a result of the IASC Improvements Project—see the appendix to the International Accounting Standards chapter.

**The IAS on accounting for taxes on income is currently being revised, and an exposure draft has been issued.

Comparison in this table is made to International Accounting Standards in force at January 1, 1993. For further details, see the International Accounting Standards chapter.

MATRICES

This section of the publication summarizes accounting principles adopted by each country. The matrices are arranged by accounting topics, thus enabling comparison between the countries and with the requirements of International Accounting Standards or European Directives.

As a cautionary note, although they show a great deal of information, the matrices have necessarily been compiled at a high level and the accounting principles shown may not be applicable in all situations. Reference to the individual chapters is therefore advised when more detailed information is required. In addition, the matrices show accounting principles in effect on January 1, 1993. For countries such as Spain and Finland, where accounting principles are undergoing radical revision, care should be taken to avoid confusion with accounting principles in effect in previous years.

SECTION 2: AUDIT REQUIREMENTS

Country	Companies to be audited
International	Not applicable (national requirements are followed)
European Directives	Medium-sized and large companies
Argentina	All corporations (with minor exceptions)
Australia	All companies (with minor exceptions)
Belgium	Public companies, large limited liability companies and any company forming part of a group deemed to be large
Brazil	Public companies
Canada	Public and large private companies
Channel Islands	Guernsey and Alderney—all companies; Jersey—public companies
China, People's Republic of	All joint stock companies and foreign investment enterprises
Cyprus	All companies
Denmark	All companies
Finland	All limited liability companies (other companies with minor exceptions)
France	All companies except small partnerships and small closely held corporations
Germany	All medium-sized and large stock corporations and limited liability companies
Hong Kong	All companies
India	All companies
Indonesia	Public companies, banks, insurance companies, leasing companies, stockbrokers, underwriters and foreign investment companies
Ireland, Republic of	All companies
Israel	All companies
Italy	Listed, government owned and other companies as required by special laws
Japan	Joint-stock companies
Korea, Republic of	Joint-stock companies
Luxembourg	All companies
Mexico	All companies (with minor exceptions)
Netherlands	Medium-sized and large companies
New Zealand	All companies (with minor exceptions)
Nigeria	All companies
Norway	All companies (with minor exceptions)
Singapore	All companies
South Africa, Republic of	All companies
Spain	All medium-sized and large companies
Sweden	All limited liability companies
Switzerland	All companies
United Kingdom	All companies (with minor exceptions)
United States	Public and listed companies

SECTION 3: BASIC ACCOUNTING CONCEPTS/CONVENTIONS

Country	Cost convention	Accrual	Going concern	Substance over form
International	HR	R	R	S
European Directives	HR	R	R	LS
Argentina	CC	R	R	S
Australia	HR	R	R	S
Belgium	HR	R	R	S
Brazil	HP	R	R	S
Canada	HC	R	R	S
Channel Islands	HR	R	R	S
China, People's Republic of	HC	R	R	LS
Cyprus	HR	R	R	S
Denmark	HC	R	R	S
Finland	HR(1)	R	R	S
France	HR	R	R	L
Germany	HC	R	R	LS
Hong Kong	HR	R	R	S
India	HR	R	R	S
Indonesia	HR(1)	R	R	S
Ireland, Republic of	HR	R	R	S
Israel	HP	R	R	S
Italy	HR	R	R	L
Japan	HC	R	R	LS
Korea, Republic of	HR	R	R	S
Luxembourg	HC	R	R	S
Mexico	CC/HP	R	R	S
Netherlands	HR	R	R	S
New Zealand	HR	R	R	S
Nigeria	HR	R	R	S
Norway	HR	R	R	S
Singapore	HR	R	R	S
South Africa, Republic of	HR	R	R	S
Spain	HC	R	R	S
Sweden	HR	R	R	L
Switzerland	HR(1)	R	R	LS
United Kingdom	HR	R	R	S
United States	HC	R	R	S

CC   — Current cost
HC   — Historical cost
HP   — Historical cost with price level adjustments
HR   — Historical cost with optional revaluation
HR(1) — Historical cost with revaluation in restricted circumstances only

R   — Required

L   — Legal form generally followed
LS   — Mixture of legal form and substance
S   — Substance over form generally followed

SECTION 3: CONTENTS OF FINANCIAL STATEMENTS

Country	Balance sheet	Income statement	Statement of funds/ cash flows	Disclosure of accounting policies
International	R	R	R	R
European Directives	R	R	O	R
Argentina	R	R	RL, RP	R
Australia	R	R	R	R
Belgium	R	R	O	R
Brazil	R	R	R	R
Canada	R	R	R	R
Channel Islands	R	R	RL	R
China, People's Republic of	R	R	R	O
Cyprus	R	R	R	R
Denmark	R	R	RP	R
Finland	R	R	RL	R
France	R	R	O	R
Germany	R	R	O	R
Hong Kong	R	R	RL	R
India	R	R	O	R
Indonesia	R	R	R	R
Ireland, Republic of	R	R	RL	R
Israel	R	R	R	R
Italy	R	R	O	R
Japan	R	R	RP	R
Korea, Republic of	R	R	R	R
Luxembourg	R	R	O	R
Mexico	R	R	R	R
Netherlands	R	R	O	R
New Zealand	R	R	R	R
Nigeria	R	R	R	R
Norway	R	R	RL	O
Singapore	R	R	RL	R
South Africa, Republic of	R	R	R	R
Spain	R	R	R	R
Sweden	R	R	RL	R
Switzerland	R	R	O	R
United Kingdom	R	R	RL	R
United States	R	R	R	R

O —Optional

R —Required

RL— Required for large companies only

RP— Required for publicly traded companies only

SECTION 4: BUSINESS COMBINATIONS

Country	Con-solidated accounts	Con-solidation method for subsidiaries	Treatment of goodwill	Equity method for significant investments, based on significant influence
International	R	PM	B, W	R
European Directives	R	PM	B, W	R
Argentina	R	P	B	R
Australia	R	P	B(20)	R(D)
Belgium	R	P	B	R
Brazil	L	PM	B	R
Canada	R	PM	B(40)	R
Channel Islands	R	PM	B, W	R
China, People's Republic of	R	P	B	O
Cyprus	R	PM	B, W	R
Denmark	R	PM	B, W	R
Finland	R	PM	B(20)	R
France	R	P	B	R
Germany	R	PM	B, W	R
Hong Kong	R	PM	B, W	R
India	NR	NA	NA	NR
Indonesia	O	PM	B	O
Ireland, Republic of	R	PM	B, W	R
Israel	R	PM	B(40)	R
Italy	L	PM	B, W	R
Japan	L	PM	B(5)	R
Korea, Republic of	R	PM	B(5)	R
Luxembourg	R	PM	B, W	R
Mexico	R	P	B(20)	R
Netherlands	R	PM	B, W	R
New Zealand	R	PM	B(20)	R
Nigeria	R	PM	B	R
Norway	R	PM	B(20)	R
Singapore	R	PM	B, W	R
South Africa, Republic of	R	P	B, W, OT	R
Spain	R	P	B(10)	R
Sweden	R	PM	B(20)	O
Switzerland	R	PM	B, W	O

SECTION 4: *Continued*

Country	Con-solidated accounts	Con-solidation method for subsidiaries	Treatment of goodwill	Equity method for significant investments, based on significant influence
United Kingdom	R	PM	B, W	R
United States	R	PM	B(40)	R

L   —Listed parent companies only (exceptions may exist)

O   —Optional

R   —Required for all ultimate holding companies (exceptions may exist)

P   —Purchase (acquisition) method only permitted

PM —Usually purchase (acquisition) method, but merger accounting (pooling of interests method) also permitted

B(#)—Capitalized on balance sheet and amortized through profit and loss (maximum amortization period in parentheses)

OT —Other treatments available; refer to individual chapter

W   —Written off directly to reserves

R(D)—Disclosure of information is required in the accounts or consolidated accounts

NA —Not applicable

NR —Not required

SECTION 5: JOINT VENTURES

Country	Method of accounting for		
	Jointly controlled operations	Jointly controlled assets	Jointly controlled entities
International	A	S	E, P
European Directives	E, P	NS	E, P
Argentina	A	S	E, P
Australia	A	S	E
Belgium	A	NS	E, P
Brazil	A	S	E
Canada	A	S	E, P
Channel Islands	A	S	E, P
China, People's Republic of	I	NS	NS
Cyprus	A	S	E, P
Denmark	A	S	E, P
Finland	NS	NS	NS
France	A	S	P
Germany	A	S	E, P
Hong Kong	A	S	E, P
India	A	S	I
Indonesia	A	S	C, E, P
Ireland, Republic of	E	E	E
Israel	A	S	E, P
Italy	NS	NS	E, P
Japan	A	NS	E
Korea, Republic of	NS	NS	NS
Luxembourg	A	S	E, P
Mexico	NS	NS	NS
Netherlands	A	S	E, P
New Zealand	A	S	E
Nigeria	A	S	E, P
Norway	A	S	P
Singapore	A	S	E, P
South Africa, Republic of	A	S	P

SECTION 5: *Continued*

| | Method of accounting for | | |
Country	Jointly controlled operations	Jointly controlled assets	Jointly controlled entities
Spain	A	S	E, P
Sweden	NS	NS	E, P
Switzerland	NS	NS	C, E, P
United Kingdom	A	S	E, P
United States	NS	P	E

A — Venturer includes assets it controls, liabilities it incurs, expenses it incurs and its output or share of income earned

C — Cost

E — Equity accounting

I — Accounted for as an investment (see Section 16)

P — Proportionate consolidation

S — Venturer includes its share of jointly controlled assets, jointly incurred liabilities, income from shared output and expenses from shared expenses

NS — No treatment specified

SECTION 6: FOREIGN CURRENCY TRANSACTION AND TRANSLATION ADJUSTMENTS

Country	Treatment of exchange differences		Self-sustaining foreign operations*
	Foreign currency transactions*		
	Short-term monetary items	Long-term monetary items	
International	I	D	R
European Directives	NS	NS	NS
Argentina	I	I	I
Australia	I	I	R
Belgium	GD	GD	R
Brazil	I	I	I
Canada	I	D	R
Channel Islands	I	I	R
China, People's Republic of	I	I	R
Cyprus	I	I	R
Denmark	I	GD, I	R
Finland	I	D, I	R
France	GD, I	GD, I	R
Germany	GD, I	GD	NS
Hong Kong	I	I	R
India	I(F)	I(F)	NS
Indonesia	I	I	NS
Ireland, Republic of	I	I	R
Israel	I	I	R
Italy	I	I	NS
Japan	I	I	D
Korea, Republic of	I	I	R
Luxembourg	NS	NS	NS
Mexico	I	I	NS
Netherlands	I	I	R
New Zealand	I	I	R
Nigeria	I	D	R
Norway	I	I	R
Singapore	I	D, I	R

SECTION 6: *Continued*

Country	Treatment of exchange differences		
	Foreign currency transactions*		Self-sustaining foreign operations*
	Short-term monetary items	Long-term monetary items	
South Africa, Republic of	I	I	R
Spain	GD, I	GD	R
Sweden	I	GD	R
Switzerland	GD	GD	NS
United Kingdom	I	I	R
United States	I	I	R

*Some countries, such as the United States, refer to the "functional currency" of operations. For the purpose of this matrix, it has been assumed that for "Foreign currency transactions" the functional currency is the reporting currency, whereas for "Self-sustaining foreign operations" the functional currency is the local currency. Further reference should be made to relevant chapters. Similarly, reference should be made to individual chapters for the exchange rate methods permitted for foreign currency translation and for the accounting treatment of hedging transactions.

D —Deferral of exchange differences permitted or required

GD—Exchange gains deferred; losses recognized in income (except to the extent of previously deferred gains)

I —Exchange differences recognized in income

I(F)—Exchange differences recognized in income, except differences on liabilities incurred in the purchase of fixed assets are taken to the cost of the asset

R —Exchange differences taken to reserves

NS —No treatment specified

SECTION 7: CHANGING PRICES/INFLATION ACCOUNTING

Country	Inflation accounting requirements
International	Supplementary or primary current cost information (optional)
European Directives	Additional inflation accounting information is optional
Argentina	Inflation accounting is standard practice
Australia	Supplementary current cost information (optional)
Belgium	No requirements
Brazil	Constant currency financial statements required for all public companies
Canada	No requirements
Channel Islands	Supplementary current cost information (optional)
China, People's Republic of	No requirements
Cyprus	No requirements
Denmark	No requirements
Finland	No requirements
France	Supplementary current cost information (optional)
Germany	No requirements
Hong Kong	No requirements
India	Supplementary current cost information (optional)
Indonesia	No requirements
Ireland, Republic of	Supplementary current cost information (optional)
Israel	Inflation accounting is standard practice
Italy	No requirements
Japan	No requirements
Korea, Republic of	No requirements
Luxembourg	No requirements
Mexico	Inflation accounting is standard practice
Netherlands	Supplementary current cost information (optional)
New Zealand	No requirements
Nigeria	No requirements
Norway	No requirements
Singapore	No requirements
South Africa, Republic of	Supplementary current cost information (optional)
Spain	No requirements
Sweden	No requirements
Switzerland	No requirements
United Kingdom	Supplementary current cost information (optional)
United States	Supplementary current cost information (optional)

SECTIONS 8 AND 9: ACCOUNTING CHANGES AND PRIOR PERIOD ADJUSTMENTS

Country	Change in policy	Change in estimate	Prior period adjustments
International	CD, RA	CD	CD, RA
European Directives	NS	NS	NS
Argentina	RA(1)	CD	RA(1)
Australia	CD	CD	CD
Belgium	CD	CP	CD
Brazil	RA	CP	RA
Canada	RA	CP	RA
Channel Islands	RA	CP	RA
China, People's Republic of	NS	NS	U
Cyprus	RA	CD	RA
Denmark	CD(S)	CD	CD
Finland	CP	CP	CD
France	CD	CP	CD
Germany	CD	CD	CP
Hong Kong	RA	CD	RA
India	CD	CD	CD
Indonesia	CD	CP	CD
Ireland, Republic of	RA	CP	RA
Israel	CD, RA	CD	CP
Italy	CD	CD	CD
Japan	CD	CP	CD
Korea, Republic of	CP	CP	RA
Luxembourg	CD	CP	CD
Mexico	CP	CP	RA
Netherlands	RA	CD	CD
New Zealand	CD(S)	CP	RA
Nigeria	CD, RA	CP	RA
Norway	CD	CP	CD
Singapore	RA	CP	CD, RA

SECTIONS 8 AND 9: *Continued*

Country	Change in policy	Change in estimate	Prior period adjustments
South Africa, Republic of	RA	CD	RA
Spain	CD(T)	CP	CD
Sweden	CP	CP	CD
Switzerland	CD(T)	CP	CD(T)
United Kingdom	RA	CP	RA
United States	CD, RA	CP	RA

CD — Adjustments made to current period income and the effect of adjustments on current and/or prior period income disclosed

CD(S)— Adjustment made to current period income and the effect of adjustments on current and/or prior period income disclosed, except where required by law or an accounting standard to account for adjustments retrospectively

CD(T)— Adjustments made to current period income and the effect of adjustments on current and/or prior period income disclosed, although as a transitional measure certain changes necessitated by recent company law reform may be charged or credited to reserves

CP — Adjustments made to current period income

RA — Adjustments accounted for retroactively

RA(1) — Recognition of adjustments limited to disclosure if the prior year financial statements have already been approved at a shareholders' meeting

U — Adjustment made to undistributed profit account brought forward from the previous year

NS — No treatment specified

SECTION 10: POST BALANCE SHEET EVENTS

Country	Evidence of conditions existing at balance sheet date	Not evidence of conditions existing at balance sheet date
International	A	N
European Directives	NS	DR
Argentina	A	N
Australia	A	N
Belgium	A	DR, N
Brazil	A	N
Canada	A	N
Channel Islands	A	DR, N
China, People's Republic of	NS	NS
Cyprus	A	N
Denmark	A	DR
Finland	A	DR
France	A	GC
Germany	A	DR
Hong Kong	A	N
India	A	N
Indonesia	A	N
Ireland, Republic of	A	DR, N
Israel	A	N
Italy	A, DR	A, DR
Japan	A	N
Korea, Republic of	A	N
Luxembourg	A	DR, N
Mexico	A	N
Netherlands	A	DR, N
New Zealand	A	N
Nigeria	A	N
Norway	A	DR
Singapore	A	N
South Africa, Republic of	A	DR, N
Spain	A	N
Sweden	A	DR
Switzerland	A	DR, N
United Kingdom	A	DR, N
United States	A	N

A — Adjust financial statements

DR— Disclose in directors' or other managerial report (if material)

GC— Disclose in the notes to the financial statements only if the going concern assumption might be affected

N — Disclose in the notes to the financial statements (if material)

NS — No treatment specified

SECTION 11: RELATED PARTY TRANSACTIONS

Country	Related parties include directors?	Disclosure of related party transactions
International	Yes	A
European Directives	Yes	D, G
Argentina	No	G
Australia	Yes	D, M
Belgium	Yes	D, G
Brazil	Yes	A
Canada	Yes	A
Channel Islands	Yes	D
China, People's Republic of	NR	NR
Cyprus	Yes	A
Denmark	Yes	D, G, S
Finland	Yes	D, G
France	Yes	M
Germany	No	A
Hong Kong	Yes	D, G
India	Yes	D, G
Indonesia	Yes	D, G
Ireland, Republic of	Yes	D
Israel	Yes	M
Italy	No	A
Japan	Yes	M
Korea, Republic of	Yes	D, G, S
Luxembourg	Yes	D, G
Mexico	Yes	M
Netherlands	Yes	A
New Zealand	Yes	D, M
Nigeria	Yes	A
Norway	Yes	D, G
Singapore	Yes	M
South Africa, Republic of	Yes	D, G
Spain	Yes	D, G
Sweden	Yes	G, M
Switzerland	No	G, S
United Kingdom	Yes	D
United States	Yes	M

A —Certain details for all related party transactions (subject to certain exceptions)
D —Details of certain transactions with directors (and other specified personnel)
G —Certain information relating to affiliated/group companies
M —All material transactions with related parties
S —Details of certain transactions with shareholders

NR—No related party requirements

SECTION 12: SEGMENTAL INFORMATION

Country	Segments to be disclosed	Companies for which applicable
International	G, I	Listed or "economically significant"
European Directives	G, I	All
Argentina	I	Recommended for all
Australia	G, I	"Reporting entities"
Belgium	G, I	All
Brazil	N	—
Canada	G, I	Listed and life insurance
Channel Islands	G, I	Large
China, People's Republic of	N	—
Cyprus	G, I	Listed or "economically significant"
Denmark	G, I	Medium-sized and large
Finland	G, I	All
France	G, I	All
Germany	G, I	Medium-sized and large
Hong Kong	G, I	Listed
India	N	—
Indonesia	N	—
Ireland, Republic of	G, I	All
Israel	G, I	Publicly traded and "economically significant"
Italy	N	—
Japan	G, I	Listed
Korea, Republic of	N	—
Luxembourg	G, I	All
Mexico	N	—
Netherlands	G, I	Large
New Zealand	G, I	All
Nigeria	G, I	All
Norway	N	—
Singapore	G, I	Listed or "economically significant"
South Africa, Republic of	G, I	Listed or "economically significant"
Spain	G, I	Large
Sweden	I	All
Switzerland	N	—
United Kingdom	G, I	All
United States	G, I	Public and listed

G—Geographical location
I —Industry/business activity

N—No segmental information requirements

SECTION 13: PROPERTY, PLANT AND EQUIPMENT

Country	Revaluation permitted?	Depreciation method	Additional accelerated depreciation permitted?	Disclosure of current value of land and buildings
International	Yes	A	No	NR
European Directives	Yes	A	Yes	NR
Argentina	Yes	A	No	NR
Australia	Yes	A	No	RL
Belgium	Yes	A	Yes	NR
Brazil	Yes	A	No	NR
Canada	No	A	No	NR
Channel Islands	Yes	A	No	NR
China, People's Republic of	No	S, UP, SY, DDB	No	NR
Cyprus	Yes	DB, S, SY, UP	No	NR
Denmark	Yes	A	No	R
Finland	Limited	S, DB	Yes	NR
France	Limited	A	Yes	NR
Germany	No	DB, S, SY, UP	RD	NR
Hong Kong	Yes	A	No	NR
India	Yes	S, DB	No	NR
Indonesia	Limited	S, DB	No	NR
Ireland, Republic of	Yes	A	No	DR
Israel	Limited	S	No	NR
Italy	Limited	S	Yes	NR
Japan	No	DB, S, SY, UP	No	NR
Korea, Republic of	Yes	DB, S, UP	Yes	NR
Luxembourg	No	A	No	NR
Mexico	Yes	A	No	NR
Netherlands	Yes	A	No	R
New Zealand	Yes	A	No	R
Nigeria	Yes	A	No	NR
Norway	Yes	A	No	NR
Singapore	Yes	A	No	NR
South Africa, Republic of	Yes	A	No	NR
Spain	No	DB, S	No	NR
Sweden	Limited	A	No	NR

SECTION 13: *Continued*

Country	Revaluation permitted?	Depreciation method	Additional accelerated depreciation permitted?	Disclosure of current value of land and buildings
Switzerland	No	A	Yes	FI
United Kingdom	Yes	A	No	DR
United States	No	DB, S, SY, UP	No	NR

A   — Any appropriate systematic allocation over the assets' useful life
DB — Declining balance method
DDB— Double declining balance method
S   — Straight-line method
SY — Sum-of-the-years'-digits method
UP — Unit-of-production method

RD — Regional differences

DR — Current value disclosed in directors' report if significantly different from book value
FI   — Fire insurance value disclosed
NR — Not generally required
R   — Required
RL — Required for certain companies including listed and borrowing companies

SECTION 14: INTANGIBLE ASSETS
(EXCLUDING GOODWILL AND RESEARCH AND DEVELOPMENT COSTS)

Country	Intangibles capitalized		Amortization requirement	Revalu-ation
	Pur-chased	Internally developed		
International	NS	NS	U	NS
European Directives	P	P	U	P
Argentina	R	NP	U	P
Australia	R	P	U	P
Belgium	R	P	U	NP
Brazil	R	P	U	R
Canada	R	P	U	NP
Channel Islands	P	P	U	P
China, People's Republic of	P	P	UM	NP
Cyprus	P	P	U	P
Denmark	P	P	U	NP
Finland	P	P	U	NP
France	P	P	U	NP
Germany	R	NP	U	NP
Hong Kong	P	P	U	P
India	P	P	U	P
Indonesia	P	P	U	NP
Ireland, Republic of	P	P	U	P
Israel	R	P	U	NP
Italy	P	P	T, U	NP
Japan	R	NP	T, U	NP
Korea, Republic of	R	PD	U	NP
Luxembourg	P	P	U	NP
Mexico	R	P	U	P
Netherlands	P	P	U	NP
New Zealand	P	P	U	P
Nigeria	R	PD	U	NP
Norway	P	P	U	P
Singapore	P	PD	U	NP
South Africa, Republic of	P	P	U	P
Spain	P	P	U	NP

SECTION 14: *Continued*

Country	Intangibles capitalized		Amortization requirement	Revalu- ation
	Pur- chased	Internally developed		
Sweden	P	NP	U	NP
Switzerland	P	NP	U	NP
United Kingdom	P	P	U	P
United States	R	P	U	NP

NP — Not permitted
P   — Permitted
PD — Permitted to the extent of direct costs only
R   — Required

T   — Amortization period dependent on local tax laws
U   — Amortized over expected useful life (some countries give maximum period)
UM— Amortized over expected useful life, subject to minimum periods

NS — No treatment specified

SECTION 15: LEASES

Country	Do criteria exist for capitalization of finance leases?
International	Yes—C
European Directives	No treatment specified
Argentina	Yes—C
Australia	Yes—C
Belgium	Yes—C
Brazil	No—special rules apply for public companies and regulated financial institutions in the leasing business
Canada	Yes—C
Channel Islands	Yes—C
China, People's Republic of	No
Cyprus	Yes—C
Denmark	Yes—O
Finland	No
France	No, except in consolidated accounts, where it remains optional
Germany	Yes—depending on tax laws
Hong Kong	Yes—C
India	No
Indonesia	Yes—C
Ireland, Republic of	Yes—C
Israel	Yes—C
Italy	No
Japan	No
Korea, Republic of	Yes—C
Luxembourg	Yes—C (based largely on income tax regulations)
Mexico	Yes—C
Netherlands	Yes—C
New Zealand	Yes—C
Nigeria	Yes—C
Norway	Yes—C
Singapore	Yes—C
South Africa, Republic of	Yes—C
Spain	Yes—C (but in transition stage)
Sweden	Yes—O
Switzerland	Yes—O
United Kingdom	Yes—C
United States	Yes—C

C—Capitalization compulsory if criteria are met (the definition and criteria for capitalization of a finance lease vary from country to country—refer to individual chapters)

O—Capitalization optional

SECTION 16: INVESTMENTS

Country	Current investments	Noncurrent investments	Is portfolio basis of valuation permitted for current investments?
International	CM, M	CM, CP, M	Yes
European Directives	CM	CP, M	NS
Argentina	M	M, E, CPP	NA
Australia	CM, M	CP, M	No
Belgium	CM	CP	No
Brazil	CM	ACM	No
Canada	CM	CP	Yes
Channel Islands	CM, M	CP, M	No
China, People's Republic of	C	C	NA
Cyprus	CM, M	CM, CP, M	Yes
Denmark	CM	CP	No
Finland	CM	CP	No
France	CM	CI	Yes
Germany	CM	CP	No
Hong Kong	CM	CP, M	NS
India	CM	CP	NS
Indonesia	CM	CP	Yes
Ireland, Republic of	CM	CP, M	No
Israel	M	CP	NA
Italy	V	V	No
Japan	CM, CP	CP	No
Korea, Republic of	CM	CM	Yes
Luxembourg	CM	CM, CP	No
Mexico	CM, M	CM, M	NS
Netherlands	CM	CM, M	No
New Zealand	CM	CP, M	Yes
Nigeria	CM	CP	Yes
Norway	CM	CP	Yes
Singapore	CM, M	CP, M	Yes
South Africa, Republic of	CM, M	CP, M	Yes
Spain	CM	CM	No

SECTION 16: *Continued*

Country	Current investments	Noncurrent investments	Is portfolio basis of valuation permitted for current investments?
Sweden	CM	CP	Yes
Switzerland	CM, M	CP, M	Yes
United Kingdom	CM, M	CP, M	No
United States	CM	CM, CP	Yes

ACM—Lower of monetary adjusted cost or market value
C   —Cost
CI   —Lower of cost or useful value to investor
CM   —Lower of cost or market value
CP   —Cost adjusted for permanent diminutions in value
CPP —Cost adjusted for closing purchasing power
E   —Accounted for using the equity method
M   —Market value
V   —Varies according to type of investment

NA   —Not applicable
NS   —No treatment specified

SECTION 17: ACCOUNTS RECEIVABLE

Country	Treatment of trade discounts and rebates	Allowance for doubtful accounts	
		Method	Disclosure
International	NS	A	NS
European Directives	NS	NS	NS
Argentina	N	A	B, W
Australia	N	F, S	W
Belgium	N	A	W
Brazil	N	A	B
Canada	N	A	NS
Channel Islands	N	A	NS
China, People's Republic of	NS	AM	B
Cyprus	N	A	NS
Denmark	N	F, S	NS
Finland	G, N	S	NS
France	N	A	NS
Germany	G	F, S	NS
Hong Kong	N	A	NS
India	N	A	B, W
Indonesia	G, N	F, S	B
Ireland, Republic of	N	A	NS
Israel	N	F, S	B
Italy	G	A	NS
Japan	N	F, S	B
Korea, Republic of	N	F, S	B
Luxembourg	N	F, S	NS
Mexico	N	A	B
Netherlands	N	F, S	NS
New Zealand	N	A	NS
Nigeria	N	A	NS
Norway	N	F, S	NS
Singapore	N	F, S	B, W
South Africa, Republic of	N	A	NS

SECTION 17: *Continued*

Country	Treatment of trade discounts and rebates	Allowance for doubtful accounts	
		Method	Disclosure
Spain	N	A	B, W
Sweden	N	A	NS
Switzerland	G, N	F, S	NS
United Kingdom	N	A	NS
United States	G, N	A	B

G — Recorded at gross invoiced amounts
N — Balance shown net of discount/rebate/allowance on balance sheet

A — Any practical method
AM — Any practical method, but allowance cannot exceed a certain percentage of accounts receivable
F — General formula
S — Specific identification

B — Balance of allowances disclosed
W — Amount written off/written back in period disclosed

NS — No treatment specified

SECTION 18: INVENTORIES AND LONG-TERM CONTRACTS

Country	Inventories		Valuation method for long-term contracts
	Valuation method	LIFO costing permitted?	
International	CN	Yes	C, P
European Directives	CM	Yes	NS
Argentina	RN	Yes	C, P
Australia	CN	No	P
Belgium	CN	Yes	C, P
Brazil	CM	Yes	P
Canada	CM	Yes	C, P
Channel Islands	CN	No	P
China, People's Republic of	CNL	Yes	P
Cyprus	CN	No	P
Denmark	CN	Yes	C, P
Finland	CN	No	C, P
France	CN	CO	C, P
Germany	CM	Yes	C
Hong Kong	CN	No	P
India	CN	Yes	C, P
Indonesia	CM	Yes	C, P
Ireland, Republic of	CN	No	P
Israel	CM	No	C, P
Italy	CM	Yes	C, P
Japan	CM	Yes	C, P
Korea, Republic of	CM	Yes	C, P
Luxembourg	CM	Yes	C, P
Mexico	RR	Yes	P
Netherlands	CM, CV	Yes	C, P
New Zealand	CN	No	P
Nigeria	CN	No	C, P
Norway	CM	No	C, P
Singapore	CN	No	C, P
South Africa, Republic of	CN	Yes	C, P
Spain	CM	Yes	C, P
Sweden	CN	No	C, P

SECTION 18: *Continued*

| Country | Inventories | | Valuation method for long-term contracts |
	Valuation method	LIFO costing permitted?	
Switzerland	CM	No	C, P
United Kingdom	CN	No	P
United States	CM	Yes	C, P

CM —Lower of cost or market

CN —Lower of cost or net realizable value

CNL—Lower of cost or net realizable value (with some minor restrictions)

CV —Current value

RN —Lower of replacement cost or net realizable value (with some exceptions)

RR —Lower of restated or realizable value

CO —Consolidated accounts only

C —Completed contract method

P —Percentage of completion method

NS —No treatment specified

SECTIONS 19 AND 21: CURRENT LIABILITIES AND CONTINGENCIES

Country	Hidden/discretionary provisions permitted?	Treatment of contingencies	
		Losses	Gains
International	No	A	D
European Directives	NS	NS	NS
Argentina	No	A	AC
Australia	No	A	D
Belgium	No	A	D
Brazil	No	A	D
Canada	No	A	D
Channel Islands	No	A	D
China, People's Republic of	No	NS	NS
Cyprus	No	A	D
Denmark	No	A	D
Finland	No	A	D
France	No	A	D
Germany	No	A	ND
Hong Kong	No	A	D
India	No	A	D
Indonesia	No	A	ND
Ireland, Republic of	No	A	D
Israel	No	A	D
Italy	No	A	ND
Japan	No	A	D
Korea, Republic of	Yes	A	D
Luxembourg	No	A	ND
Mexico	No	A	D
Netherlands	No	A	D
New Zealand	No	A	D
Nigeria	No	A	D
Norway	No	A	D
Singapore	No	A	D
South Africa, Republic of	No	A	D
Spain	No	A	ND
Sweden	No	A	ND
Switzerland	Yes	A	ND
United Kingdom	No	A	D
United States	No	A	D

A — Accrued if likely/probable, otherwise disclosed in notes
AC — Accrued if highly probable, otherwise disclosed in notes
D — Disclosed if likely/probable, but not accrued prior to realization
ND — Not disclosed or accrued prior to realization

NS — No treatment specified

SECTIONS 24 AND 25: TREATMENT OF GOVERNMENT GRANTS AND RESEARCH AND DEVELOPMENT COSTS

Country	Government grants	Research and development
International	DI, N	D
European Directives	NS	RD
Argentina	NS	RD
Australia	CE, R	RD
Belgium	DI	RD
Brazil	CR	RD
Canada	DI, N	D
Channel Islands	DI, N	D
China, People's Republic of	NS	NS
Cyprus	DI, N	D
Denmark	DI	D
Finland	DI, N	RD
France	DI	RD
Germany	DI, N	E
Hong Kong	NS	D
India	DI, N	RD
Indonesia	NS	NS
Ireland, Republic of	DI	D
Israel	DI, N	D
Italy	L	RD
Japan	N	RD
Korea, Republic of	CR	RD
Luxembourg	DI, N	RD
Mexico	NS	E
Netherlands	DI, N, T	RD
New Zealand	DI	D
Nigeria	DI, N	D
Norway	DI, N	RD
Singapore	DI, N	D
South Africa, Republic of	NS	D
Spain	DI	RD

SECTIONS 24 AND 25: *Continued*

Country	Government grants	Research and development
Sweden	DI	RD
Switzerland	NS	RD
United Kingdom	DI	D
United States	DI	E

CE —Credited to equity if the grant is in the nature of a contribution by an owner

CR —Credited to a special reserve account that may or may not be released to revenue

DI —Deferred, if applicable to more than one period, and taken to income as related expenses are incurred

L —Legal requirements of grant followed

N —Netted against acquisition cost of related asset

R —Recognized immediately as revenues

T —Deducted from tax charge

D —Capitalization of development expenditure only is permitted or required (if specific criteria are met)

E —Expensed as incurred

RD—Capitalization of research and development expenditure is permitted or required (if specific criteria are met)

NS —No treatment specified

SECTIONS 26 AND 27: TREATMENT OF CAPITALIZED INTEREST COSTS AND IMPUTED INTEREST

Country	Capitalized interest costs	Imputed interest
International	CA	PR
European Directives	CA	NS
Argentina	CA	PR
Australia	CA	NG
Belgium	CA	PR
Brazil	NC	NG
Canada	CA	PR
Channel Islands	CA	NG
China, People's Republic of	CA	NG
Cyprus	CA	NP
Denmark	CA	NG
Finland	CA	NG
France	CA	PR
Germany	CA	PR
Hong Kong	CA	NG
India	CA	NP
Indonesia	CA	NG
Ireland, Republic of	CA	NG
Israel	CA	NG
Italy	CA	PR
Japan	NC	NG
Korea, Republic of	CA	NG
Luxembourg	CA	NG
Mexico	CA	NG
Netherlands	CA	NG
New Zealand	CA	NG
Nigeria	CA	NG
Norway	CA	NG
Singapore	CA	NG
South Africa, Republic of	CA	NG
Spain	CA	NG
Sweden	CA	PR
Switzerland	CA	NG
United Kingdom	CA	NP
United States	CA	PR

CA — Capitalization of interest as part of the cost of an asset permitted
NC — No capitalization of interest costs permitted

NG — Not generally used
NP — Not permitted
PR — Imputed interest used for payables and/or receivables granted under favorable conditions

NS — No treatment specified

SECTION 28: EXTRAORDINARY OR UNUSUAL ITEMS

Country	Are items that are not part of normal activities separately disclosed? If so, how are they described?
International	Yes—unusual
European Directives	Yes—extraordinary
Argentina	Yes—extraordinary
Australia	Yes—extraordinary
Belgium	Yes—exceptional
Brazil	Yes—extraordinary
Canada	Yes—extraordinary
Channel Islands	Yes—exceptional
China, People's Republic of	Yes—extraordinary (within nonoperating expenses)
Cyprus	Yes—unusual
Denmark	Yes—extraordinary
Finland	Yes—extraordinary
France	Yes—exceptional or nonrecurring
Germany	Yes—extraordinary
Hong Kong	Yes—extraordinary
India	Yes—extraordinary
Indonesia	Yes—extraordinary
Ireland, Republic of	Yes—extraordinary
Israel	Yes—extraordinary
Italy	No
Japan	Yes—extraordinary
Korea, Republic of	Yes—extraordinary
Luxembourg	Yes—exceptional
Mexico	Yes—extraordinary or nonrecurring
Netherlands	Yes—extraordinary
New Zealand	Yes—extraordinary
Nigeria	Yes—exceptional
Norway	Yes—extraordinary
Singapore	Yes—extraordinary
South Africa, Republic of	Yes—extraordinary
Spain	Yes—extraordinary
Sweden	Yes—extraordinary
Switzerland	Yes—exceptional
United Kingdom	Yes—exceptional
United States	Yes—extraordinary or nonrecurring

SECTION 29: INCOME TAXES

Country	Recognition of deferred taxes
International	Deferred or liability method
European Directives	No treatment specified
Argentina	Deferred or liability method (generally not recognized)
Australia	Liability method
Belgium	Liability method (consolidated accounts only, for the most part)
Brazil	Liability method
Canada	Deferred method
Channel Islands	Liability method
China, People's Republic of	No deferred tax
Cyprus	Deferred or liability method
Denmark	Deferred or liability method (must be disclosed in notes)
Finland	Liability method (consolidated accounts only)
France	Deferred or liability method (consolidated accounts only)
Germany	Liability method
Hong Kong	Liability method
India	Liability method (generally not recognized)
Indonesia	Liability method
Ireland, Republic of	Liability method
Israel	Liability method
Italy	Liability method (generally not recognized)
Japan	No deferred tax
Korea, Republic of	No deferred tax
Luxembourg	Deferred or liability method (consolidated accounts only)
Mexico	Liability method (generally not recognized)
Netherlands	Liability method
New Zealand	Liability method
Nigeria	Liability method
Norway	Liability method
Singapore	Deferred or liability method
South Africa, Republic of	Liability method
Spain	Liability method
Sweden	Liability method (consolidated accounts only)
Switzerland	No treatment specified
United Kingdom	Liability method
United States	Liability method

SECTION 30: POSTRETIREMENT BENEFITS

Country	Occurrence of external pension plans	Pension costs covered by accounting standards?	Refund of pension fund surplus permitted	Other postretirement benefits covered by accounting standards?
International	NA	Yes	NA	No
European Directives	NA	No	NA	No
Argentina	Rare	No	NS	No
Australia	Common	No	WU	No
Belgium	Common	No	SL	No
Brazil	Rare	No	NR	No
Canada	Common	Yes	SL	No
Channel Islands	Common	Yes	SL	No
China, People's Republic of	Rare	No	NA	No
Cyprus	Rare	Yes	NA	No
Denmark	Common	No	TD, WU	No
Finland	Common	No	NR	No
France	Rare	Yes	NS	No
Germany	Rare	Yes	BS	No
Hong Kong	Rare	No	NS	No
India	Common	No	NA	No
Indonesia	Rare	No	NS	No
Ireland, Republic of	Common	Yes	SL, TD	Yes
Israel	Rare	No	NS	No

Italy	Rare	No	NS	No
Japan	Common	Yes	NS	No
Korea, Republic of	Rare	No	BS	No
Luxembourg	Common	No	NS	No
Mexico	Common	Yes	BS	No
Netherlands	Common	Yes	NS	No
New Zealand	Common	No	TD	No
Nigeria	Common	Yes	SL	Yes
Norway	Common	Yes	SL	No
Singapore	Rare	Yes	NS	No
South Africa, Republic of	Common	Yes	TD, WU	No
Spain	Rare	Yes	OI	No
Sweden	Common	Yes	SL	No
Switzerland	Common	No	NR	No
United Kingdom	Common	Yes	SL	Yes
United States	Common	Yes	SL	Yes

Note: The treatment of pensions/retirement benefits is frequently complex, and the results of applying different treatments are often material. In particular, care is required when dealing with the standards now in effect in the United Kingdom or the United States.

BS — Generally not applicable as pension funding/commitments are included as part of the balance sheet
NR — No refund possible
OI — Surplus taken to other income
SL — Refund possible, subject to legal/revenue restrictions
TD — Refund dependent on trust deed
WU — Distributable only on winding up of the plan

NA — Not applicable
NS — No treatment specified

SECTION 31: DISCONTINUED OPERATIONS

Country	Accounting treatment	Costs separately disclosed (if material)?
International	NS	NS
European Directives	NS	NS
Argentina	IE	Yes
Australia	I, T	Yes
Belgium	T	Yes
Brazil	IE, T	Yes
Canada	I, T	Yes
Channel Islands	IE, T	Yes
China, People's Republic of	NS	NS
Cyprus	NS	NS
Denmark	IE, T	Yes
Finland	NS	Yes
France	IE, T	Yes
Germany	I	No
Hong Kong	IE	Yes
India	NS	NS
Indonesia	I	Yes
Ireland, Republic of	I, T	Yes
Israel	NS	NS
Italy	I	Yes (directors' report)
Japan	NS	No
Korea, Republic of	I	No
Luxembourg	I, T	Yes
Mexico	I	Yes
Netherlands	I	Yes
New Zealand	I, T	Yes
Nigeria	I	Yes
Norway	IE	Yes
Singapore	IE	Yes
South Africa, Republic of	IE, T	Yes
Spain	NS	NS
Sweden	IE, T	Yes
Switzerland	IE	Yes
United Kingdom	I, T	Yes
United States	I, T	Yes

I — Relevant amounts taken to income statement

IE — Relevant amounts taken to income statement and separately disclosed as an extraordinary item

T — Costs recognized at the time the decision is made

NS — No treatment specified

SECTION 32: EARNINGS PER SHARE

Country	Companies for which earnings per share should be disclosed
International	No requirement
European Directives	No requirement
Argentina	No requirement
Australia	Listed
Belgium	No requirement
Brazil	All corporations (SA)
Canada	All with more than a few shareholders
Channel Islands	Listed
China, People's Republic of	No requirement
Cyprus	No requirement
Denmark	Listed
Finland	Listed
France	All (disclosure in directors' report)
Germany	No requirement
Hong Kong	Listed
India	No requirement
Indonesia	Listed
Ireland, Republic of	Listed
Israel	Listed
Italy	No requirement
Japan	All
Korea, Republic of	All
Luxembourg	No requirement
Mexico	No requirement
Netherlands	No requirement
New Zealand	Listed
Nigeria	Listed
Norway	No requirement
Singapore	Listed
South Africa, Republic of	Listed and publicly traded
Spain	No requirement
Sweden	No requirement
Switzerland	No requirement
United Kingdom	Listed (also required for Unlisted Securities Market)
United States	Public

INTERNATIONAL ACCOUNTING STANDARDS COMPLIANCE CHECKLIST

Introduction

This checklist is directed at financial statements prepared in conformity with International Accounting Standards (IASs) issued by the International Accounting Standards Committee (IASC). It covers all IASs in effect at September 30, 1993, except IAS 26, *Accounting and Reporting by Retirement Benefit Plans*, and IAS 30, *Disclosure in the Financial Statements of Banks and Similar Financial Institutions*. The checklist does not cover exposure drafts issued by the IASC.

While every effort has been made to make the checklist accurate and comprehensive, it is necessarily general in nature and does not purport to be complete in all respects. This checklist is not a substitute for reading the original standards.

Each step in the checklist is cross-referenced to the appropriate paragraph in the applicable IAS. For example, 1-16 refers to IAS 1, paragraph 16, and Fr-7 refers to paragraph 7 of the Framework for the Preparation and Presentation of Financial Statements.

The checklist should be completed by answering each question "yes," "no" or "N/A" (not applicable), as appropriate. A "yes" answer indicates that an IAS requirement has been complied with, and a "no" answer indicates it has not.

IASC's Statement of Intent

The IASC has adopted a comprehensive Statement of Intent, "Comparability of Financial Statements," which will eliminate many of the choices of accounting treatments permitted under current IASs. An IASC project, the "Improvements Project," is underway to implement the Statement of Intent. In relation to the Improvements Project, exposure drafts of revised IASs have been issued on the following:

Research and Development Activities
Inventories
Capitalization of Borrowing Costs
Revenue Recognition
Construction Contracts

Property, Plant and Equipment
The Effects of Changes in Foreign Exchange Rates
Extraordinary Items, Fundamental Errors and Changes in Accounting Policies
Retirement Benefit Costs

The board of the IASC has considered the responses to many of these exposure drafts and, for certain of them, has agreed and announced changes that will be incorporated into the final standards.

A summary of the principal impacts of the Statement of Intent (as at the time of this writing) is included as an appendix to the chapter on International Accounting Standards. The Improvements Project is expected to be complete by the end of 1993.

This checklist does not incorporate the changes currently being proposed either by the Improvements Project, except insofar as revised standards have been issued by September 30, 1993, or in other areas, i.e., accounting for income taxes and financial instruments.

INDEX

Item	Description	IAS Ref.	Yes, no or N/A
GENERAL FUNDAMENTAL ASSUMPTIONS			
1	Have the following fundamental accounting assumptions been followed in the preparation of the financial statements: • Going concern? • Consistency? • Accrual?	1-16	
2	If a fundamental accounting assumption has not been followed, are that fact and the reasons disclosed?	1-16	
FINANCIAL STATEMENTS			
3	Do the financial statements contain: • A balance sheet? • An income statement? • A statement of changes in financial position or statement of cash flows? • Notes and other statements and explanatory material?	Fr-7	
4	Are comparative figures for the preceding period shown?	Fr-42, 1-21 and 5-9	
5	Are the following disclosed: • Name of the reporting entity? • Country of incorporation? • Balance sheet date? • Period covered by the financial statements? • Brief description of the nature of activities of the entity, its legal form and the currency in terms of which the financial statements are expressed, if not otherwise apparent?	5-7	
6	Is all material information that is necessary to make the financial statements clear and understandable disclosed?	5-6	
7	Are amounts and classifications supplemented where necessary by additional information to make their meanings clear?	5-8	
8	Are all significant items separately identified and not included with, or offset against, other items?	5-8	

Source: Taken from International Accounting Standards © 1993, International Accounting Standards Committee, 167 Fleet Street, London EC4A 2ES, England. Used with permission.

Item Description	IAS Ref.	Yes, no or N/A
ACCOUNTING POLICIES		
9 Have prudence, substance over form and materiality governed the selection and application of accounting policies?	1-17	
10 Are all significant accounting policies clearly and concisely disclosed (normally in one place) as an integral part of the financial statements?	1-18, 1-19 and 1-20	
Note: Wrong or inappropriate treatment of items in the balance sheet, income statement or other statements is not rectified either by disclosure of accounting policies used or by notes or explanatory material.		
Change in accounting policy		
11 Is a change in accounting policy made only where a different policy is required by statute or by an accounting standard-setting body or where it is considered that the change results in a more appropriate presentation of the financial statements?	8-20	
12 If there has been a change in accounting policy that has a material effect in the current period or may have a material effect in subsequent periods, are the following disclosed: • The change in accounting policy together with the reasons for the change? • The quantified effect, if material?	1-22 and 8-21	
BALANCE SHEET GENERAL **Restrictions on title**		
13 Are restrictions on the title to assets disclosed?	5-10	
Security for liabilities		
14 Is disclosure made of security given in respect of liabilities?	5-10	
Current/Noncurrent distinction		
Note: Each enterprise should determine whether or not to present current assets and current liabilities as separate classifications in its financial statements.	13-19	

Item	Description	IAS Ref.	Yes, no or N/A
15	If the current/noncurrent distinction is not made, are no subtotals of the amounts of assets and of liabilities given that would imply that such distinction is made?	13-20	

Set-off and netting

Item	Description	IAS Ref.	Yes, no or N/A
16	Are current assets and current liabilities reduced by other current liabilities or current assets only where a legal right of set-off exists and the off-setting represents the expectation as to the realization of the asset or settlement of the liability?	13-25	

Foreign currency translation

Item	Description	IAS Ref.	Yes, no or N/A
17	Except for transactions dealt with in 19 below, are foreign currency denominated transactions recorded in the reporting currency at the actual rate at the date of the transaction or a rate that approximates the actual rate?	21-24	
18	Except for transactions dealt with in 19 below, are foreign currency monetary items at the balance sheet date reported at the closing rate?	21-25	
19	When a forward exchange contract has been entered into to establish the amount of the reporting currency required or available at the settlement date, is the difference between the forward rate and the spot rate at the inception of the contract recognized in income over the life of the contract? *Note: For short-term transactions, the forward rates specified in the related foreign exchange contracts may be used as the basis for measuring and reporting the transaction.*	21-26	
20	Except as dealt with in 22 and 289 below, are exchange differences arising on settlement of monetary items or in reporting short-term foreign currency monetary items at different rates from those at which they were recorded during the period or presented in previous financial statements recognized in income for the period? *Note: An exchange difference that results from a severe devaluation or from depreciation of a*	21-27 21-31	

Item	Description	IAS Ref.	Yes, no or N/A
	currency against which there is no practical means of hedging and that affects liabilities arising directly on the recent acquisition of assets invoiced in the foreign currency may be included in the carrying amount of the related assets provided the carrying amount does not exceed the lower of replacement cost and the recoverable amount of the asset.		
21	Except as dealt with in the note to 20 above, are exchange differences arising on long-term foreign currency monetary items recognized in income?	21-28	
	Note: Exchange differences on long-term foreign currency monetary items may be deferred and recognized in income on a systematic basis over the remaining lives of the items to which they relate, except that exchange losses should not be deferred if it is reasonable to expect that recurring exchange losses will arise on those items in the future.		
22	Are exchange differences arising on loans and other foreign currency transactions designated and effective as a hedge against a net investment in a foreign entity taken to shareholders' interests to the extent that they are covered by exchange differences arising on the net investment?	21-30	

Disclosure

Item	Description	IAS Ref.	Yes, no or N/A
23	If exchange differences on long-term monetary items resulting from foreign currency transactions or from translating the financial statements of foreign operations that are integral to the operations of the parent are deferred, is the cumulative deferred amount still to be charged or credited to income disclosed?	21-35	
24	If exchange differences arising on liabilities associated with the acquisition of assets have been included in the carrying amount of the related assets (see the note to 20, above), is the amount that arose in the period disclosed?	21-36	

Item	Description	IAS Ref.	Yes, no or N/A
	LONG-TERM ASSETS **Property, plant and equipment**		
25	Does property, plant and equipment include tangible assets that: • Are held for use in the production or supply of goods and services, for rental to others, or for administrative purposes (may include items for the maintenance and repair of such assets)? • Have been acquired or constructed with the intention of being used on a continuing basis? • Are not intended for sale in the ordinary course of business?	16-35	
26	The gross carrying amount of a fixed asset should be either its historical cost or a revaluation. Are the valuation bases used for determining the amounts at which depreciable assets are stated disclosed in the accounting policies?	4-17 and 16-36	
27	Are the following items disclosed: • Land and buildings? • Plant and equipment? • Other categories of assets, suitably identified? • Accumulated depreciation? *Note: Separate disclosure should be made of leaseholds and of assets being acquired on instalment purchase plans.*	5-11	
28	Are the bases used for determining the gross carrying amounts of property, plant and equipment disclosed?	16-50	
29	If more than one basis for determining the gross carrying amount has been used, is the gross carrying amount for each category given?	16-50	
	Assets carried at historical cost		
30	Has the cost of a fixed asset been determined in accordance with the following rules?		
	For a purchased asset—Its purchase price and any attributable costs of bringing the asset to a working condition for its intended use.	16-37	
	For a self-constructed asset—The costs that relate directly to the specific asset and those that are	16-38	

Item	Description	IAS Ref.	Yes, no or N/A
	attributable to the construction activity in general and can be allocated to the specific asset. Cost inefficiencies should not be included as a part of such costs.		
	For an asset acquired in exchange or partial exchange for another asset—The fair value or net carrying value of the asset given up, adjusted for any balancing payment or receipt.	16-39	
31	Are gains or losses from the retirement or disposal of a fixed asset carried at historical cost recognized in the income statement?	16-43	

Assets carried at revalued amounts

Item	Description	IAS Ref.	Yes, no or N/A
32	If property, plant and equipment are stated at revalued amounts, are the following disclosed: • The method used to compute the amounts? • The policy in regard to the frequency of revaluations? • The nature of any indices used? • The year of any appraisal made? • Whether an external valuer was involved?	16-50	
33	Has an entire class of assets been revalued or, if not, has the selection of assets for revaluation been made on a systematic basis and has that basis been disclosed?	16-44	
34	When fixed assets are revalued upward, any accumulated depreciation should not be credited to income. Has this been complied with?	16-46	
35	Does the recoverable amount of a class of revalued assets exceed the net carrying amount of that class of assets?	16-45	
36	Has an increase in net carrying amount been credited directly to shareholders' interest under the heading revaluation surplus (except that, to the extent such an increase is related to and not greater than a decrease arising on a revaluation previously charged to income, it may be credited to income)?	16-47	
37	Has a decrease in net carrying amount been charged directly to income (except that, to the	16-47	

Item	Description	IAS Ref.	Yes, no or N/A
	extent such a decrease is the reversal of a previous increase that was credited to revaluation surplus and has not subsequently been reversed or utilized, it should be charged directly to that account)?		
38	On retirement or disposal of a previously revalued fixed asset, is the difference between the net disposal proceeds and the net carrying amount charged or credited to income?	16-49	

General provisions

Item	Description	IAS Ref.	Yes, no or N/A
39	Are subsequent expenditures relating to a fixed asset added to its carrying amount only if they increase the future benefits from the asset?	16-40	
40	Is the net carrying amount of a fixed asset reduced to its recoverable amount for any permanent impairment that caused the recoverable amount to fall below its net carrying amount, and has the difference been charged to income?	16-41	
41	Is the net carrying amount of a fixed asset retired from active use and held for disposal reduced to its recoverable amount where this is lower than its net carrying amount, and has the difference been charged to income?	16-41	
42	Are all fixed assets that have been disposed of or from which no future benefit is expected to be derived eliminated from the financial statements?	16-42	

Depreciation

Item	Description	IAS Ref.	Yes, no or N/A
43	Are the following disclosed for each major class of depreciable asset: • Depreciation methods used? • Useful lives or depreciation rates used? • Total depreciation allocated for the period? • Gross amount of depreciable assets and the related accumulated depreciation?	4-18	
44	Is the depreciable amount of all depreciable assets allocated on a systematic basis to each accounting period during the useful life of the assets?	4-13	

Item	Description	IAS Ref.	Yes, no or N/A
45	Has the depreciation method been applied consistently from period to period?	4-14	
46	If circumstances justify a change in depreciation method, has the effect of the change been quantified and disclosed and the reason stated?	4-14	
47	Are the useful lives of depreciable assets estimated after considering: • Expected physical wear and tear? • Obsolescence? • Legal or other limits on the use of the assets?	4-15	
48	Are the useful lives of major depreciable assets or classes of depreciable assets reviewed periodically?	4-16	
49	If the rates of depreciation required adjustment as a result of the review of useful lives, is the effect of the change disclosed?	4-16	

Leased assets

In the financial statements of lessees—Finance leases

Item	Description	IAS Ref.	Yes, no or N/A
50	Are finance leases reflected in the balance sheet by recording an asset and a liability at amounts equal at the inception of the lease to the fair value of the leased property net of grants and tax credits receivable by the lessor or, if lower, at the present value of the minimum lease payments? *Note: In calculating the minimum lease payments the discount factor is the interest rate implicit in the lease, if this is practicable to determine; if not, the lessee's incremental borrowing rate should be used.*	17-44	
51	Are rentals apportioned between the finance charge and the reduction of the outstanding liability? *Note: The finance charge should be allocated to periods during the lease term so as to present a constant periodic rate of interest on the remaining balance of the liabilities for each period.*	17-45	

Item	Description	IAS Ref.	Yes, no or N/A
52	Is depreciation charged on finance leases in a manner consistent with that for owned assets?	17-46	
	Note: If there is no certainty that the lessee will obtain ownership by the end of the lease term, the asset should be fully depreciated over the shorter of the lease term or the asset's useful life.		
53	Is the amount of assets subject to finance leases disclosed?	17-57	

In the financial statements of lessees—General

54	Are the following disclosed: • Significant financing restrictions? • Renewal or purchase options? • Contingent rentals or other contingencies arising from leases?	17-59	

In the financial statements of lessors—Finance leases

55	Are assets held under finance leases recorded as a receivable, at an amount equal to the net investment in the lease, and not as property, plant and equipment?	17-48	
56	Are the following disclosed: • The gross investment in leases reported as finance leases? • The related unearned finance income? • The related unguaranteed residual values of leased assets?	17-60	

In the financial statements of lessors—Operating leases

57	Are assets held for operating leases recorded as property, plant and equipment?	17-51	
58	Is depreciation calculated on a basis consistent with the normal depreciation policy for similar assets?	17-53	
59	If a significant part of the enterprise's business consists of operating leases, are the amounts of assets, by each major class, disclosed, together with the related accumulated depreciation?	17-62	

Item	Description	IAS Ref.	Yes, no or N/A
	Sale and leaseback transactions		
60	If the transaction resulted in a finance lease, any excess of sales proceeds over the carrying amount should not be recognized immediately in income. If such an excess is recognized, is it deferred and amortized over the lease term?	17-54	
61	If the transaction resulted in an operating lease and it is clear that the transaction was established at fair value, is any profit or loss recognized immediately?	17-55	
62	If the transaction resulted in an operating lease and the sale price was below fair value, is any profit or loss recognized immediately (except that, if the loss is compensated by future rentals below market price, it should be deferred and amortized in proportion to the rental payments over the period the asset is expected to be used)?	17-55	
63	If the transaction resulted in an operating lease and the sale price was above fair value, is any excess above fair value deferred and amortized in proportion to the rental payments over the period the asset is expected to be used?	17-55	
64	If the transaction resulted in an operating lease and the fair value at the time of the transaction was less than the carrying amount of the asset, is the difference between the carrying amount and the fair value recognized immediately?	17-56	
	OTHER LONG-TERM ASSETS		
65	Are the following disclosed separately, including, if applicable, the method and period of depreciation and any unusual write-offs during the period: • Long-term investments— Investments in subsidiaries? Investments in associated companies? Other investments? • Long-term receivables— Accounts and notes receivable—trade? Receivables from directors? Intercompany receivables?	5-12	

Item	Description	IAS Ref.	Yes, no or N/A
	Associated company receivables?		
	Other?		
	• Goodwill?		
	• Patents, trademarks and similar assets?		
	• Expenditures carried forward, e.g., preliminary expenses, reorganization expenses and deferred taxes?		
	Long-term investments		
	Note: An enterprise that does not distinguish between long-term and current assets in its balance sheet should nevertheless make a distinction between long-term and current investments for measurement purposes.	25-44	
66	Long-term investments should be carried in the balance sheet at:	25-47	
	• Cost, or		
	• Revalued amounts, or		
	• In the case of marketable securities, the lower of cost or market value determined on a portfolio basis.		
	Is the accounting policy used for determining the carrying amount disclosed?	25-55	
67	Is the carrying value of any long-term investment reduced to recognize a decline that is other than temporary in the value of the investment (each investment should be assessed individually)?	25-47	
68	If marketable securities or investments are not carried at market value, is market value disclosed?	5-12 and 25-55	
69	Are any significant restrictions on the realizability of investments or the remittance of income and proceeds of disposal disclosed?	25-55	
70	Are any investments reclassified from current to long-term transferred at the lower of cost or market value, or at market value if they were previously stated at that value?	25-52	
	Investments carried at revalued amounts		
71	Are the following disclosed:	25-55	
	• Policy for the frequency of revaluations?		

Item	Description	IAS Ref.	Yes, no or N/A
	• Date of the latest revaluation?		
	• Basis of revaluation and whether an external valuer was involved?		
	• Movements for the period in revaluation surplus and the nature of the movements?		
	• Policy for the treatment of a revaluation surplus on sale of a revalued investment?		
	• For enterprises whose main business is the holding of investments, an analysis of the portfolio of investments?		
	Note: The enterprise should adopt a policy for the frequency of revaluations; an entire category of long-term investments should be revalued at the same time.	25-47	
72	Has an increase in carrying amount been credited directly to shareholders' interests under the heading revaluation surplus (except that, to the extent such an increase is directly related to a previous decrease in carrying amount for the same investment that was previously charged to income, it should be credited to income)?	25-48	
73	Has a decrease in net carrying amount been charged directly to income (except that, to the extent such a decrease is the reversal of a previous increase, for the same investment, that was credited to revaluation surplus and has not subsequently been reversed or utilized, it should be charged directly to that account)?	25-48	

Investment properties

Item	Description	IAS Ref.	Yes, no or N/A
74	An enterprise holding investment properties should either treat them as property, plant and equipment and depreciate them, or account for them as long-term investments. Has the policy adopted been applied consistently?	25-45	
75	If investment properties are not carried at fair value, is the fair value disclosed?	25-55	

Specialized investment enterprises

Item	Description	IAS Ref.	Yes, no or N/A
76	Specialized investment enterprises that are prohibited from distributing profits on the disposal of	25-54	

Item	Description	IAS Ref.	Yes, no or N/A
	investments may exclude from income changes in value of investments, whether realized or not, provided they carry their investments at fair value. Where such an enterprise has so excluded from income changes in value, is a summary of all movements in value of investments for the period included in the financial statements?		

Disposal of long-term investments

Item	Description	IAS Ref.	Yes, no or N/A
77	Is the difference between net disposal proceeds and the carrying amount charged or credited to income?	25-50	
78	If the investment was previously revalued or carried at market value and the increase was transferred to a revaluation surplus, the enterprise should establish a policy either of crediting the remaining revaluation surplus to income or transferring it to retained earnings. Is the policy applied consistently?	25-50	

Subsidiaries

Item	Description	IAS Ref.	Yes, no or N/A
79	In a parent's separate financial statements, investments in subsidiaries should be: • For subsidiaries that are included in the consolidated financial statements, either: (i) accounted for using the equity method; or (ii) carried at cost or revalued amounts under the parent's accounting policy for long-term investments. • For subsidiaries that are excluded from consolidation, carried at cost or revalued amounts under the parent's accounting policy for long-term investments. Is the method used to account for subsidiaries disclosed?	27-35, 27-36 and 27-37	
80	Where a parent does not produce consolidated financial statements because it is a wholly owned, or virtually wholly owned, subsidiary, are the following disclosed: • The reasons consolidated financial statements have not been presented? • The bases on which subsidiaries are accounted for in the parent's separate financial statements?	27-27	

Item	Description	IAS Ref.	Yes, no or N/A
	• The name and registered office of its parent that publishes consolidated financial statements?		
	Associates		
81	An investment in an associate included in the separate financial statements of an investor that issues consolidated financial statements should be either: • Accounted for using the cost or equity method, whichever is used for the associate in the consolidated financial statements; or • Carried at cost or revalued amount under the accounting policy for long-term investments. Is this complied with?	28-26	
82	An investment in an associate included in the separate financial statements of an investor that does not issue consolidated financial statements should be either: • Accounted for using the cost or equity method, whichever would be appropriate for the associate if the investor issued consolidated financial statements; or • Carried at cost or revalued amount under the accounting policy for long-term investments. Is this complied with?	28-27	
83	Where the investor does not issue consolidated financial statements and does not use the equity method (although it would have been the appropriate accounting method for the associate if consolidated financial statements were issued), is the effect had the equity method been applied disclosed?	28-27	
84	Is the carrying value of an investment in an associate reduced to recognize a decline that is other than temporary (determined for each investment individually)?	28-28	
85	Are the following disclosed: • An appropriate listing of significant associates, including the proportion of ownership interest and, if different, proportion of voting power held? • The methods used to account for associates?	28-29	

Item	Description	IAS Ref.	Yes, no or N/A
86	Are investments in associates accounted for using the equity method classified as long-term assets and disclosed as a separate item in the balance sheet?	28-30	

Joint ventures

Jointly controlled operations

| 87 | Are the following recognized in the enterprise's separate financial statements (and consequently in the consolidated financial statements, if any):
• The assets that it controls and the liabilities that it incurs?
• The expenses that it incurs and its share of the income earned from the sale of goods or services by the joint venture? | 31-40 | |

Jointly controlled assets

| 88 | Are the following recognized in the enterprise's separate financial statements (and consequently in the consolidated financial statements, if any):
• Its share of the jointly controlled assets, classified according to the nature of the assets?
• Any liabilities that it has incurred?
• Its share of any liabilities incurred jointly with the other venturers in relation to the joint venture?
• Any income from the sale or use of its share of the output of the joint venture?
• Its share of any expenses incurred by the joint venture?
• Any expenses it has incurred in respect of its interest in the joint venture? | 31-41 | |

Jointly controlled entities

| | *Note: IAS 31 does not indicate a preference for any particular accounting treatment for reporting interests in jointly controlled entities in the separate financial statements of a venturer.*

The treatment in the consolidated financial statements is dealt with in 282–288 below. | 31-31 | |

Transactions between a venturer and a joint venture

| 89 | When the venturer contributes or sells assets to a joint venture, is the substance of the transaction | 31-46 | |

Item	Description	IAS Ref.	Yes, no or N/A
	used to reflect recognition of any portion of a gain or loss?		
	Note: While the asset is retained and provided the significant risks and rewards of ownership have been transferred, the venturer should recognize only that portion of the gain that is attributable to the interests of the other venturers.		
	The full amount of a loss should be recognized when there is evidence of a reduction in the net realizable value of a current asset or a decline that is other than temporary in the carrying amount of a long-term asset.		
90	When the venturer purchases assets from a joint venture, is recognition of the venturer's share of any profit of the joint venture deferred until the assets are resold to an independent third party?	31-47	
91	When the venturer purchases assets from a joint venture, is recognition of the venturer's share of any loss of the joint venture deferred until the assets are resold to an independent third party, except that the loss should be recognized immediately where it represents: • A reduction in the net realizable value of current assets; or • A decline that is other than temporary in the carrying amount of long-term assets?	31-47	
	Interests in joint ventures in which the venturer does not have joint control		
92	Is an interest in a joint venture in which the venturer does not have joint control accounted for: • As an investment; or • As an associate, where the venturer has significant influence in the joint venture?	31-48	
	Disclosure		
93	If consolidated financial statements are not issued because the enterprise does not have subsidiaries, is the information required in 180, 183 and 288 below disclosed in the separate financial statements?	31-53	

Item	Description	IAS Ref.	Yes, no or N/A
	Deferred development costs		
	Note: Research and development costs should include:	9-15	
	a) the salaries, wages and other related costs of personnel engaged in research and development activities;		
	b) the costs of materials and services consumed in research and development activities;		
	c) the depreciation of equipment and facilities to the extent that they are used on research and development activities;		
	d) overhead costs related to research and development activities; and		
	e) other costs related to research and development activities, such as the amortization of patents and licenses.		
94	Research and development costs should be charged as an expense as they are incurred, except that certain development costs may be deferred. Are development costs deferred only where the following criteria apply: • The product or process is clearly defined and the costs attributable to it can be separately identified? • The technical feasibility of the product or process has been demonstrated? • Management has indicated its intention to produce and market, or use, the product or process? • There is a clear indication of a future market for the product or process or, if it is to be used internally, its use to the enterprise can be demonstrated? • Adequate resources exist, or are reasonably expected to be available, to complete the project and market the product or process?	9-16 and 9-17	
95	Where an accounting policy of deferral of development costs is adopted, is it applied consistently to all development projects that meet the criteria for deferral?	9-19	
96	Are development costs deferred only to the extent that, taken together with further development and	9-18	

Item	Description	IAS Ref.	Yes, no or N/A
	other related costs, their recovery from related future revenues is reasonably assured?		
97	Are deferred development costs amortized on a systematic basis to future accounting periods by reference either to the sale or use of the product or process or to the time period in which the product or process is expected to be sold or used?	9-20	
98	Are deferred development costs of each project reviewed at the end of the accounting period, and where the criteria in 94 above no longer apply, is the unamortized balance charged as an expense immediately?	9-21	
	Note: Once written off, development costs should not be reinstated even where the uncertainties that led to their being written off no longer exist.	9-22	
99	When the criteria in 94 continue to be met but the amount of deferred development costs, together with further development and other related costs, exceeds the amount expected to be recovered from related future revenues, is the excess charged as an expense immediately?	9-21	
100	Are the following disclosed: • The movement in and the balance of unamortized deferred development costs? • The basis, proposed or adopted, for the amortization of the unamortized balance?	9-24	

Capitalized borrowing costs

Item	Description	IAS Ref.	Yes, no or N/A
101	If the enterprise incurs borrowing costs and incurs expenditures on assets that take a substantial period of time to get ready for their intended use, has a policy been established of either capitalizing borrowing costs or not capitalizing borrowing costs and is the policy applied consistently?	23-21	

When the policy is to capitalize borrowing costs

Item	Description	IAS Ref.	Yes, no or N/A
102	Are borrowing costs capitalized as part of the cost of an asset by applying a capitalization rate to expenditures on the acquisition, construction or production of assets that require a substantial period of time to get ready for their intended use or sale?	23-22	

Item	Description	IAS Ref.	Yes, no or N/A
103	Is the capitalization rate determined by relating the borrowing costs incurred during the period to the borrowings outstanding during the period? *Note: When a new borrowing is associated with the acquisition, construction or production of specific assets, the capitalization rate may be based on the actual borrowing costs.*	23-23	
104	For assets other than investments, does capitalization commence when: • Expenditures for the asset are being incurred; • Activities necessary to prepare the asset for its intended use or sale are in progress; and • Borrowing costs are being incurred?	23-24	
105	For investments, does capitalization commence when: • Expenditures for the investment are being incurred; • Activities necessary to commence the investment's principal operations are in progress; and • Borrowing costs are being incurred?	23-24	
106	Does capitalization cease when: • The asset is ready for its intended use or sale; or • For an investment, the principal operations are started?	23-25	
107	Is capitalization suspended during extended periods in which active development is interrupted?	23-25	
108	Where the construction of an asset is completed in parts that are capable of being used while construction continues on other parts, does capitalization cease on each part as it is completed?	23-26	
109	The amount of borrowing costs should not exceed the total borrowing costs incurred during the period. Is this requirement complied with? *Note: In consolidated financial statements the limitation applies to the consolidated amount of borrowing costs.*	23-27	

Item	Description	IAS Ref.	Yes, no or N/A
110	Is the amount of capitalized borrowing costs disclosed?	23-28	
	Government grants		
111	Are government grants, including nonmonetary grants at fair value, recognized only after there is reasonable assurance that: • The enterprise will comply with the conditions attaching to them; and • The grants will be received?	20-37	
112	Are government grants, including nonmonetary grants at fair value, presented in the balance sheet by either: • Setting the grant up as deferred income; or • Deducting the grant in arriving at the carrying amount of the asset?	20-39	
113	Are the following disclosed: • The accounting policy adopted for government grants, including the method of presentation adopted in the financial statements? • The nature and extent of government grants recognized in the financial statements and an indication of other forms of government assistance from which the enterprise has benefitted? • Unfulfilled conditions and other contingencies attaching to government assistance that has been recognized?	20-42	
	CURRENT ASSETS		
114	Are the following items included in current assets: • Cash and bank balances available for current operations? • Securities not intended to be retained and capable of being readily realized? • Trade and other receivables expected to be realized within one year of the balance sheet date? • Inventories? • Advance payments on the purchase of current assets? • Prepaid expense expected to be used up within one year of the balance sheet date?	13-21	
115	Is the total amount of current assets disclosed?	13-27	

Item	Description	IAS Ref.	Yes, no or N/A
	Inventories		
116	Is the total of inventories disclosed and subclassified in the balance sheet or in the notes to the financial statements in a manner that is appropriate to the business and that indicates the amounts held in each of the main categories?	2-33 and 5-13	
	Note: If items, other than tangible property held for sale in the ordinary course of business, in the process of production for such sale or to be consumed in the production of goods or services for sale, are shown under the caption "Inventories," their nature, amounts and basis of valuation should be disclosed.	2-35	
117	Is the accounting policy adopted for the purpose of valuation of inventories, including the cost formula used, disclosed?	2-34	
118	Are inventories stated at the lower of cost or net realizable value?	2-20	
	Cost of inventories		
119	Does the cost of manufactured inventories include a systematic allocation of those production overhead costs that relate to bringing the inventories to their present location and condition?	2-21	
120	Is the allocation of fixed production overhead to the costs of conversion based on the capacity of the facilities?	2-21	
121	If fixed production overhead is entirely or substantially excluded from the valuation of inventories on the grounds that it does not directly relate to bringing the inventories to their present location and condition, is this fact disclosed?	2-21	
122	Are overheads other than production overheads included as part of inventory cost only to the extent that they clearly relate to bringing the inventories to their present location and condition?	2-22	
123	Are exceptional amounts of wasted material, labor and other expenses excluded from inventory cost?	2-23	

Item	Description	IAS Ref.	Yes, no or N/A
124	Is the cost of inventory determined using: • FIFO, weighted average cost, LIFO or base stock formulae; or • Specific identification for items of inventory that are not ordinarily interchangeable or goods that are manufactured and segregated for specific projects?	2-24, 2-25 and 2-26	
	Note: Techniques such as the standard cost method of valuing products or the retail method of valuing merchandise may be used if the results approximate those that would be obtained using FIFO or weighted average cost formulae.	2-27	
125	Where LIFO or base stock formulae have been used, is disclosure made of the difference between the valuation used and either: • The valuation that would have been obtained using the lower of either FIFO or the weighted average cost method, and net realizable value; or • The lower of current cost at the balance sheet date and net realizable value?	2-26	
	Net realizable value of inventories		
126	Are estimates of net realizable value based on the most reliable evidence available at the time the estimates are made of what the inventories are expected to realize and not on temporary fluctuations of price or cost?	2-28	
127	Inventories should be written down to net realizable value item by item or by groups of similar items. Is the method used applied consistently?	2-29	
128	Is the net realizable value of a quantity of inventory held to satisfy firm sales contracts based on the contract price?	2-30	
	Note: Assessment of net realizable value of inventory quantities held in excess of sales contracts should be based on general market prices.		
129	Where a decline in the price of materials and other supplies held for incorporation in the production	2-31	

Item	Description	IAS Ref.	Yes, no or N/A

of finished goods indicates that the historical cost of finished products to be produced will exceed net realizable value, is the value of the materials written down (e.g., replacement cost may be the best measure of net realizable value)?

Note: If the finished goods are expected to realize more than historical cost, normal quantities of materials and other supplies should not be written down.

Construction contracts

130   Is either the completed contract method or the percentage of completion method used to account for construction contracts?   11-42

Note: The percentage of completion method may be used only if the outcome of the contract can be reliably estimated.   11-43

131   Do costs included in the amount at which construction contract work is stated comprise those costs directly related to a specific contract and those that are attributable to contract activity in general and can be allocated to specific contracts?   11-44

132   Is the same accounting method used for all contracts that meet similar criteria?   11-45

133   Is provision made for a foreseeable loss on a contract, both for the stage of completion reached and for future work on the contract?   11-46

134   Are the following disclosed: 11-47 and 13-26
- The amount of construction work in progress (analyzed to disclose separately the amounts attributable to contracts accounted for under the percentage of completion method and the completed contract method, where applicable)?
- Cash received and receivable as progress payments, advances and retentions on account of contracts included in contract work in progress (this amount may be deducted from the amount of related construction work in progress, provided the amount is disclosed)?

Item	Description	IAS Ref.	Yes, no or N/A
	• The amount receivable under cost plus contracts not included in construction work in progress?		
135	Where a change has been made from the percentage of completion method to the completed contract method for contracts in progress at the beginning of the year and it is not possible to quantify the effect of the change in accounting policy, is the amount of attributable profits reported in prior years in respect of contracts in progress at the beginning of the accounting period disclosed?	11-48	

Cash

Item	Description	IAS Ref.	Yes, no or N/A
136	Is the amount of cash and bank balances available for current operations, including cash on hand and current and other accounts with banks, disclosed? *Note: Cash or bank balances whose use for current operations is subject to restrictions should be included as a current asset only if the duration of the restrictions is limited to the term of an obligation that is classified as a current liability or if the restrictions lapse within one year.*	5-13 and 13-21	
137	Is the amount of cash not immediately available for use, e.g., balances frozen in foreign banks by exchange restrictions, disclosed?	5-13	

Current investments

Item	Description	IAS Ref.	Yes, no or N/A
	Note: An enterprise that does not distinguish between long-term and current assets in its balance sheet should nevertheless make a distinction between long-term and current investments for measurement purposes.	25-44	
138	Investments classified as current assets should be carried in the balance sheet at either: • Market value, or • The lower of cost and market value (determined either on an aggregate portfolio basis, in total or by category of investment, or on an individual investment basis).	25-46	
	Is the accounting policy used for the basis of determining the carrying amount disclosed?	25-55	

Item	Description	IAS Ref.	Yes, no or N/A
139	Is the amount of marketable securities, other than long-term investments, separately disclosed?	5-13	
140	If the carrying amount of marketable securities or investments, other than long-term investments, is different from the market value, is the market value disclosed?	5-13 and 25-55	
141	Are any significant restrictions on the realizability of investments or the remittance of income and proceeds of disposal disclosed?	25-55	
142	Are investments reclassified from long-term to current transferred at either: • The lower of cost or carrying amount, if current investments are carried at the lower of cost or market value (if the investment was previously revalued, any remaining related revaluation surplus should be reversed on the transfer); or • Carrying amount if current investments are carried at market value (if changes in market value of current investments are included in income, any remaining related revaluation surplus should be transferred to income)?	25-51	

Investments carried at market value

Item	Description	IAS Ref.	Yes, no or N/A
143	Increases or decreases in the carrying amount of investments should be either: • Included in income, or • Taken to reserves. Is the policy chosen applied consistently?	25-49	
144	Is the accounting policy for the treatment of changes in market value disclosed?	25-55	
145	Are the movements for the period in revaluation surplus and the nature of such movements disclosed?	25-55	
146	If increases or decreases are taken to reserves, has an increase in net carrying amount been credited directly to shareholders' interests under the heading revaluation surplus (except that, to the extent such an increase is directly related to a previous	25-48	

Item	Description	IAS Ref.	Yes, no or N/A
	decrease in carrying amount for the same investment that was previously charged to income, it should be credited to income)?		
147	If increases or decreases are taken to reserves, has a decrease in net carrying amount been charged directly to income (except that, to the extent such a decrease is the reversal of a previous increase, for the same investment, that was credited to revaluation surplus and has not subsequently been reversed or utilized, it should be charged directly to that account)?	25-48	
148	For an enterprise whose main business is the holding of investments, is an analysis of the portfolio of investments disclosed?	25-55	

Specialized investment enterprises

Item	Description	IAS Ref.	Yes, no or N/A
149	Specialized investment enterprises that are prohibited from distributing profits on the disposal of investments may exclude from income changes in value of investments, whether realized or not, provided they carry their investments at fair value. Where such an enterprise has so excluded from income changes in value, is a summary of all movements in value of investments for the period included in the financial statements?	25-54	

Disposal of current investments

Item	Description	IAS Ref.	Yes, no or N/A
150	Is the difference between net disposal proceeds and the carrying amount charged or credited to income?	25-50	
	Note: If the investment was carried at the lower of cost or market value on a portfolio basis, the profit or loss on sale should be based on cost.		
151	If the enterprise's policy is to carry investments at market value and to take increases or decreases in value to reserves, the enterprise should establish a policy of either crediting the remaining revaluation surplus to income or transferring it to retained earnings. Is the policy applied consistently?	25-50	

Item Description	IAS Ref.	Yes, no or N/A
Trade and other receivables		
152 Are the following disclosed: • Accounts and notes receivable—trade? • Receivables from directors? • Intercompany receivables? • Associated company receivables? • Other receivables and prepaid expenses?	5-13	
153 If trade receivables included in current assets include amounts falling due after one year, is that amount disclosed?	13-21	
LONG-TERM LIABILITIES		
154 Are the following, excluding the portion repayable within one year, separately disclosed: • Secured loans? • Unsecured loans? • Intercompany loans? • Loans from associated companies?	5-14	
155 Is a summary of interest rates, repayment terms, covenants, subordinations, conversion features and amounts of unamortized premium or discount shown?	5-14	
Leases		
In the financial statements of lessees		
156 Is the long-term portion of liabilities related to leased assets shown separately?	17-57	
Taxation		
157 Are deferred tax balances presented in the balance sheet separately from shareholders' interests?	12-45	
158 Are taxes on income relating to an item that is charged or credited to shareholders' interests accounted for in the same manner as the relevant item and is the amount disclosed?	12-41	
159 Are the tax effects, if any, related to assets that have been revalued to amounts in excess of historical cost or previous revaluation separately disclosed?	12-53	

Item	Description	IAS Ref.	Yes, no or N/A
	Retirement benefits		
160	Is the following information disclosed:	19-50 and 5-10	
	• The accounting policies adopted for retirement benefit plan costs, including a general description of the valuation method or methods used?		
	• Any other significant matters related to retirement benefits that affect comparability with the prior period?		
	• If the amounts funded since the inception of the plan are different from the amounts charged to income (or to retained earnings due to a change in accounting policy) over the same period, the amount of the resulting liability or deferred charge and the funding approach adopted (if there is no systematic policy of funding)? (Where there is more than one plan and this results in both a liability and a deferred charge, the liability and deferred charge should not be netted.)		
	• For a defined benefit plan—		
	(i) the amount of the shortfall (if any) of the net realizable value of the fund assets, together with the liability or deferred charge (if any) as described above, from the actuarially determined value of the vested benefits, and		
	(ii) a statement of the funding approach adopted? (When there is more than one plan, a shortfall of plan assets from the vested benefits of one plan should be disclosed without offsetting an excess of assets over vested benefit liabilities of another plan.)		
	• For a defined benefit plan, the date of the latest actuarial valuation?		
	Note: When there is more than one retirement benefit plan, this information may be reported in total for all plans, separately for each plan, or in such groupings as are considered to be the most useful.		
	Defined benefit plans		
161	Is an accrued benefit valuation method or a projected benefit valuation method used consistently,	19-45	

Item	Description	IAS Ref.	Yes, no or N/A
	together with appropriate and compatible assumptions, to determine the cost of retirement benefits?		
	Note: The pay-as-you-go and terminal funding methods should not be used in accounting for the cost of retirement benefits.		
162	Are current service costs charged to income systematically over the expected remaining working lives of employees covered by the plan?	19-45	
163	Are past service costs, experience adjustments and the effects of changes in actuarial assumptions on retirement benefit costs either charged or credited to income as they arise or allocated systematically over a period not exceeding the expected remaining lives of the participating employees?	19-45	
164	Is the effect of a change in actuarial method that effects the charge to income in the current period or may affect the charge in subsequent periods accounted for and disclosed in accordance with IAS 8, *Unusual Items and Prior Period Items and Changes in Accounting Policies*?	19-45	

Defined contribution plans

165	Is the employer's contribution for the period charged to income? (If the plan includes an element of past service costs, such element should be accounted for in accordance with 161–164 above.)	19-46	

General

166	If a retirement plan is amended so that additional benefits are provided for retired employees, is the cost accounted for in accordance with 163 above?	19-47	
167	If benefits supplemental to a plan that constitutes a continuing commitment have been promised to retired employees, is the present value of the cost of the supplemental benefits charged to income at the time the promise is made?	19-48	
168	If a plan has been terminated or if it is probable that a plan will be terminated, is the cost of any	19-49	

Item	Description	IAS Ref.	Yes, no or N/A
	unfulfilled obligation accrued and charged to income, unless the remaining obligation is transferred to another plan?		

CURRENT LIABILITIES

Item	Description	IAS Ref.	Yes, no or N/A
169	Do current liabilities include obligations payable at the demand of the creditor and those parts of the following obligations whose liquidation is expected within one year of the balance sheet date: • Bank and other loans? • The current portion of long-term loans? • Trade liabilities and accrued expenses? • Provision for taxes payable? • Dividends payable? • Deferred revenue and advances from customers? • Accruals for contingencies? *Note: For bank and other loans, if a loan is repayable in accordance with a schedule of repayment agreed with the creditor, the loan may be classified in accordance therewith, notwithstanding a right of the creditor to demand current payment.*	13-22	
170	Is the total amount of current liabilities disclosed?	13-27	
171	Are the following separately disclosed: • Bank loans and overdrafts? • Current portions of long-term liabilities? • Payables Accounts and notes payable—trade? Payables to directors? Intercompany payables? Associated company payables? Taxes on income? Dividends payable? Other payables and accrued expenses?	5-15	
172	Where an enterprise has excluded the current portion of a long-term liability from the current classification on the basis that it intends to refinance the obligation on a long-term basis and there is reasonable assurance that it will be able to do so, are the amount of the liability and the terms of the refinancing disclosed?	13-24	

Item Description	IAS Ref.	Yes, no or N/A
Leases		
In the financial statements of lessees		
173 Is the short-term portion of liabilities related to leased assets shown separately?	17-57	
OTHER LIABILITIES AND PROVISIONS		
174 Are significant items included in other liabilities and in provisions and accruals (e.g., deferred taxes, deferred income and provisions for pensions) separately disclosed?	5-16	
CONTINGENCIES		
175 Are all contingencies accrued by a charge to income where: • It is probable that future events will confirm that, after taking into account any related probable recovery, an asset has been impaired or a liability incurred at the balance sheet date; and • A reasonable estimate of the resulting loss can be made?	10-27	
176 Are all other contingent losses disclosed, except where the possibility of loss is remote?	10-28 and 5-10	
177 If it is probable that a contingent gain will be realized, is its existence disclosed?	10-29 and 5-10	
Note: Contingent gains should not be accrued in the financial statements.	10-29	
178 If disclosure of a contingency is required, are the following disclosed: • The nature of the contingency? • The uncertain factors that may affect its outcome? • An estimate of the financial effect or a statement that such an estimate cannot be made?	10-33	
179 Are taxes on income not related to ordinary activities, unusual items, prior period items, changes in accounting policy or revaluation of assets dealt with as contingencies?	12-54	
180 Unless the probability of loss is remote, are the following contingencies disclosed separately from other contingencies: • Contingencies that the venturer has incurred in relation to its interests in joint ventures and its	31-50	

Item	Description	IAS Ref.	Yes, no or N/A
	share of each contingency that has been incurred jointly with other venturers?		
	• The venturer's share of the contingencies of the joint ventures themselves for which it is contingently liable?		
	• Contingencies that arise because the venturer is contingently liable for the liabilities of the other venturers of a joint venture?		

COMMITMENTS

Item	Description	IAS Ref.	Yes, no or N/A
181	Are amounts committed for future capital expenditure disclosed?	5-10	
182	Are commitments for minimum lease payments under finance leases and noncancelable operating leases with a term of more than one year disclosed, giving in summary form the amounts and periods in which the payments will become due?	17-58	
183	Are the following aggregate amounts in respect of interests in joint ventures disclosed separately from other commitments:	31-51	
	• Any capital commitments of the venturer in relation to its interests in joint ventures and its share of capital commitments that have been incurred jointly with other venturers?		
	• The venturer's share of the capital commitments of the joint ventures themselves?		

SHAREHOLDERS' EQUITY
Share capital

Item	Description	IAS Ref.	Yes, no or N/A
184	For each class of capital, is the following disclosed:	5-17	
	• Number and amount of shares authorized, issued and outstanding?		
	• Capital not yet paid in?		
	• Par or legal value per share?		
	• Movement in share capital accounts during the period?		
	• Rights, preferences and restrictions with respect to the distribution of dividends and to the repayment of capital?		
	• Cumulative preference dividends in arrears?		
	• Reacquired shares?		
	• Shares reserved for future issuance under options and sales contracts, including the terms and amounts?		

Item	Description	IAS Ref.	Yes, no or N/A
	Other equity		
185	Are the movements for the period and any restrictions on distribution disclosed for: • Paid-in capital in excess of par value (share premium)? • Revaluation surplus? • Reserves? • Retained earnings?	5-17	
186	Government grants, including nonmonetary grants at fair value, should not be credited directly to shareholders' interests. Has this requirement been complied with?	20-37	
	POST BALANCE SHEET EVENTS		
187	Are the financial statements adjusted for events occurring after the balance sheet date that provide additional evidence to assist in estimating amounts relating to conditions existing at the balance sheet date or that indicate that the going concern assumption in relation to the whole or a part of the enterprise is not appropriate?	10-30	
188	Are dividends for the period covered by the financial statements and that are proposed or declared after the balance sheet date, but before approval of the financial statements, either adjusted for or disclosed?	10-31	
189	Are the following disclosed in relation to events that occurred after the balance sheet date that do not affect the condition of assets or liabilities at the balance sheet date, but are of such importance that nondisclosure would affect the ability of the users of the financial statements to make proper evaluations and decisions: • The nature of the event? • An estimate of the financial effect or a statement that such an estimate cannot be made?	10-32 and 10-34	
	INCOME STATEMENT		
190	Are the following disclosed: • Sales or other operating income? • Depreciation?	5-18, 9-23, 25-55 and 28-30	

Item	Description	IAS Ref.	Yes, no or N/A
	• Research and development costs, including amortization of deferred development costs, charged as expense? • Interest income? • Income from investments, including significant amounts included in income for: (i) Interest, royalties, dividends and rentals on long-term and current investments? (ii) Profits and losses on disposal of current investments, and changes in value of such investments? • Share of profits or losses of associates accounted for under the equity method? • Interest expense? • Taxes on income? • Unusual charges? • Unusual credits? • Significant intercompany transactions? • Net income?		

Revenue

Note: Revenue should be recognized only if, at the time of performance, it is not unreasonable to expect ultimate collection. Otherwise, revenue recognition should be deferred. — 18-22

Sale of goods

| 191 | Are sales of goods recorded only after:
• The significant risks and rewards of ownership have been transferred to the buyer; and
• No significant uncertainty exists regarding:
  (i) The consideration that will be derived from the sale;
  (ii) The associated costs incurred or to be incurred in producing or purchasing the goods; and
  (iii) The extent to which goods may be returned? | 18-23 | |

Rendering of services

| 192 | Is either the completed contract method or the percentage of completion method (whichever relates the revenue to the work accomplished) used to measure the performance of services? | 18-24 | |

Item	Description	IAS Ref.	Yes, no or N/A
193	Whichever method is used to recognize revenue, is performance regarded as being achieved when no significant uncertainty exists regarding: • The consideration that will be derived from rendering the service; and • The associated costs incurred or to be incurred in rendering the service?	18-24	

Interest, royalties, dividends and other investment income

Item	Description	IAS Ref.	Yes, no or N/A
194	Are the following included in income: • Investment income arising from: (i) Interest, royalties, dividends and rentals on long-term and current investments? (ii) Profits and losses on disposal of current investments? (iii) Unrealized gains and losses on current investments carried at market value? (iv) Reductions to market value and reversals of such reductions required to state current investments at the lower of cost or market value? • Reductions in the carrying amount for other than a temporary decline in value of long-term investments, and reversals of such reductions? • Profits and losses on long-term investments?	25-53	
195	Is revenue arising from use by others of the enterprise's resources yielding interest, royalties or dividends recognized on the following bases when no significant uncertainty exists as to measurement or collectibility: *Interest:* On a time proportion basis, taking into account the principal outstanding and the rate applicable? *Royalties:* On an accrual basis in accordance with the terms of the relevant agreement? *Dividends from investments not accounted for under the equity method of accounting:* When the right to receive the payment is established?	18-25	

Government grants

Item	Description	IAS Ref.	Yes, no or N/A
196	Are government grants, including nonmonetary grants at fair value, recognized only after there is reasonable assurance that:	20-37	

Item	Description	IAS Ref.	Yes, no or N/A
	• The enterprise will comply with the conditions attaching to them; and • The grants will be received?		
197	Are government grants recognized in the income statement on a systematic basis over the periods necessary to match them with the related costs that they are intended to compensate?	20-38	
198	Where a government grant becomes receivable as compensation for expenses or losses already incurred or for the purpose of giving immediate financial support to the enterprise with no further related costs, is the amount recognized in the income statement in the period it becomes receivable? *Note: If appropriate, the amount may need to be shown as an unusual item.*	20-40	

Operators of joint ventures

199	Are fees received by operators or managers of a joint venture accounted for as revenue?	31-49	

General

200	If revenue recognition has been postponed pending the resolution of significant uncertainties, are the circumstances disclosed?	18-26	

Cost of inventories

201	Are the amounts of inventories sold or used (unless allocated to other asset accounts) and of any writedown in the period to net realizable value charged to income for the period?	2-32	

Leases
In the financial statements of lessees—Operating leases

202	Is the rental expense for the period recognized on a systematic basis that is representative of the time pattern of the benefit from the lease?	17-47	

In the financial statements of lessors—Finance leases

203	Is the method used to recognize finance income based on a pattern reflecting a constant periodic rate of return on either the net investment out-	17-49	

Item	Description	IAS Ref.	Yes, no or N/A
	standing or the net cash investment outstanding in respect of the lease (applied consistently to leases of a similar financial nature)?		
204	Is the basis or bases used for allocating income disclosed?	17-61	
205	If the enterprise is a manufacturer or dealer, is the selling profit or loss included in income in accordance with the policy normally followed for outright sales?	17-50	
	Note: If artificially low rates of interest are quoted, selling profit should be restricted to that which would apply if a commercial rate of interest were charged.		

In the financial statements of lessors—Operating leases

Item	Description	IAS Ref.	Yes, no or N/A
206	Is rental income recognized on a straight-line basis over the lease term, unless a more systematic basis is more representative of the time pattern of the earnings process contained in the lease?	17-52	

Change in accounting estimates

Item	Description	IAS Ref.	Yes, no or N/A
207	If there is a change in an accounting estimate that has a material effect in the current period or may have a material effect in future periods, is the effect of the change disclosed and quantified?	8-23	
	Note: A change in an accounting estimate should be accounted for as part of income from ordinary activities, unless it relates to an item that was reported as unusual, in which case it should itself be reported as unusual.	8-22	
208	Is any government grant that became repayable accounted for as a revision to an accounting estimate?	20-41	

Associates

Item	Description	IAS Ref.	Yes, no or N/A
209	Is the investor's share of profits or losses from investments in associates accounted for using the equity method disclosed as a separate line item in the income statement?	28-30	

Item	Description	IAS Ref.	Yes, no or N/A
Taxation			
210	The tax expense for the period should be included in the determination of net income and determined on the basis of tax effect accounting, using either the deferral or the liability method. Is the method used disclosed?	12-40 and 12-42	
211	If the tax effect accounting method has not been applied to all timing differences, are the tax effects excluded only for timing differences that are not expected, based on reasonable evidence, to reverse for a considerable time period (at least 3 years) and for which there is no indication that they are likely to reverse after this period?	12-43	
212	Is the amount of timing differences, both current and cumulative, not accounted for disclosed?	12-43	
213	Is there a reasonable expectation that a debit balance, or a debit to the deferred tax balance carried forward, will be realized?	12-44	
214	Are taxes relating to a previous period that are recovered as a result of carrying back a tax loss included in net income in the period of the loss?	12-46	
215	Are potential tax savings relating to a loss carryforward included in the determination of net income for the period of the loss only: • Where there is assurance beyond a reasonable doubt that future taxable income will be sufficient to allow the benefit to be realized; or • To the extent of the net credits in the deferred tax balance that will reverse within the period during which the loss can be claimed as a tax benefit?	12-47, 12-48 and 12-49	
216	Are the following disclosed: • The amount of tax saving included in net income in the period of the loss, in accordance with the criteria set out in 215 above? • The amount of tax saving included in net income for the current period as a result of the realization of a tax loss carryforward that had not been accounted for in the year of loss?	12-50	

Item	Description	IAS Ref.	Yes, no or N/A
	• The amount and future availability of tax losses for which the related tax effects have not been included in the net income of any period?		
217	Are taxes payable by either the parent or subsidiaries on distribution to the parent company of the undistributed profits of subsidiaries accrued, unless it is reasonable to assume that those profits will not be distributed or that a distribution will not give rise to a tax liability?	12-51	
218	Are taxes that would be payable on distribution to the investor of its share of the undistributed profits of an associate accounted for under the equity method accrued when the profits are recognized by the investor, except when it is reasonable to assume that those profits will not be distributed or that a distribution will not give rise to a tax liability?	12-52	
219	Are the following disclosed separately: • The tax expense relating to ordinary activities? • The tax expense relating to unusual items? • The tax expense relating to prior period items? • The tax expense relating to changes in accounting policies? • The tax effects, if any, related to assets that have been revalued to amounts in excess of historical cost or previous revaluation? • An explanation of the relationship between the tax expense and accounting income, if not explained by the tax rates effective in the country of the reporting enterprise?	12-53	

Prior period items and changes in accounting policy

Item	Description	IAS Ref.	Yes, no or N/A
220	Are prior period items or the amount of adjustments resulting from changes in accounting policies either: • Reported by adjusting opening retained earnings in the financial statements for the current period and amending the comparative information; or • Separately disclosed in the income statement as a part of net income?	8-19	
221	Is the disclosure adequate to facilitate comparisons of the figures for the periods presented?	8-19	

Item	Description	IAS Ref.	Yes, no or N/A
222	Is the investor's share of any prior period items of associates accounted for under the equity method separately disclosed?	28-30	

Unusual items

223	Are unusual items included in net income and the nature and amount of each item separately disclosed?	8-18	
224	Is the investor's share of any unusual items of associates accounted for under the equity method separately disclosed?	28-30	

CASH FLOW STATEMENT

Note: Revised IAS 7, Cash Flow Statements, becomes effective for financial statements covering periods beginning on or after January 1, 1994 and will supersede IAS 7, Statement of Changes in Financial Position.

225	Is a cash flow statement presented as an integral part of the financial statements for each period for which financial statements are presented?	7-1 (revised)	
226	Does the cash flow statement report cash flows during the period classified by operating, investing and financing activities?	7-10 (revised)	

Operating activities

227	Are cash flows from operating activities reported using either: • The direct method; or • The indirect method?	7-18 (revised)	
	Note: Enterprises are encouraged to report cash flows from operating activities using the direct method.	7-19 (revised)	
228	Are cash flows arising from taxes on income separately disclosed and classified as cash flows from operating activities, unless they can be specifically identified with financing and investing activities?	7-35 (revised)	

Cash flows from investing and financing activities

229	Are the major classes of gross cash receipts and gross cash payments arising from investing and financing activities reported separately?	7-21 (revised)	

Item	Description	IAS Ref.	Yes, no or N/A
	Note: Cash flows arising from the following activities may be reported on a net basis: • *Cash receipts and payments on behalf of customers when the cash flows reflect the activities of customers;* • *Cash receipts and payments for items in which the turnover is quick, the amounts are large and the maturities are short.*	7-22 (revised)	
	And for a financial institution: • *Cash payments and receipts for the acceptance and repayment of deposits with a fixed maturity date;* • *The placement of deposits with and withdrawal of deposits from other financial institutions; and* • *Cash advances and loans made to customers and the repayment of those advances and loans.*	7-24 (revised)	
	Interest and dividends		
230	Are cash flows from interest and dividends received and paid disclosed separately?	7-31 (revised)	
	Note: Each should be classified in a consistent manner from period to period as either operating, investing or financing.		
	Foreign currency cash flows		
231	Are cash flows arising from transactions in foreign currency translated into the reporting currency at the rate of exchange at the date of the cash flow?	7-25 (revised)	
232	In the consolidated cash flow statement, are the cash flows of foreign subsidiaries translated at the rate of exchange at the date of the cash flow?	7-26 (revised)	
	Extraordinary items		
233	Are cash flows associated with extraordinary items classified appropriately as arising from operating, investing or financing activities and disclosed separately?	7-29 (revised)	
	Acquisition and disposal of subsidiaries and other business units		
234	Are the aggregate cash flows arising from acquisitions and disposals of subsidiaries presented separately and classified as investing activities?	7-39 (revised)	

Item	Description	IAS Ref.	Yes, no or N/A
235	Are each of the following disclosed, in the aggregate, in respect of both acquisitions and disposals of subsidiaries and other business units in the period: • The total purchase or disposal consideration? • The portion of the purchase or disposal consideration discharged by means of cash and cash equivalents? • The amount of cash and cash equivalents in the subsidiary or business unit acquired or disposed of? • The amount of assets and liabilities other than cash or cash equivalents in the subsidiary or business unit acquired or disposed of, summarized by major category?	7-40 (revised)	

Noncash transactions

236	Are investing and financing transactions that do not require the use of cash or cash equivalents excluded from the cash flow statement and disclosed elsewhere in the financial statements in a way that provides all the relevant information about the related activities?	7-43 (revised)	

Other disclosures

237	Are the components of cash and cash equivalents disclosed and presented as a reconciliation of the amounts in the cash flow statement to the equivalent items in the balance sheet?	7-45 (revised)	
	Note: Cash comprises cash on hand and short-term deposits. Cash equivalents are short-term, highly liquid investments that are convertible to known amounts of cash and which are subject to an insignificant risk of changes in value.	7-6 (revised)	
238	Is the amount of cash and cash equivalent balances held, but not available for use by the group, disclosed, together with a commentary by management?	7-48 (revised)	

STATEMENT OF CHANGES IN FINANCIAL POSITION

Note: Revised IAS 7, Cash Flow Statements, becomes effective for financial statements covering

Item	Description	IAS Ref.	Yes, no or N/A
	periods beginning on or after January 1, 1994 and will supersede IAS 7, Statement of Changes in Financial Position.		
239	Is a statement of changes in financial position presented as an integral part of the financial statements for each period for which financial statements are presented?	7-20 (old)	
240	Are funds provided from or used in the operations presented separately from other sources or uses of funds?	7-21 (old)	
241	Are unusual items that are not part of ordinary activities disclosed separately?	7-21 (old)	
242	Is the form of presentation for the statement of changes in financial position the most informative in the circumstances?	7-22 (old)	

OTHER MATTERS
SEGMENTAL REPORTING

Item	Description	IAS Ref.	Yes, no or N/A
	Note: Only enterprises whose securities are publicly quoted and other economically significant entities, including subsidiaries, are required to present segmental information.	14-20	
	When both parent entity and consolidated financial statements are presented, only segmental information based on consolidated information need be presented. In the first period in respect of which segmental information is presented, comparative information need not be presented if it is not readily available.	14-25	
243	Are the activities of each reported industry segment described and the composition of each reported geographical segment indicated?	14-21	
244	Is the following information reported for each industry and geographical segment: • Sales or other operating revenues, distinguishing between revenue derived from customers and revenue derived from other segments? • Segment results? • Segment assets employed, expressed either in	14-22	

Item	Description	IAS Ref.	Yes, no or N/A
	monetary amounts or as a percentage of the consolidated totals? • The basis of intersegment pricing?		
245	Are the totals of the information on individual segments reconciled to the information in the financial statements?	14-23	
246	Is the following disclosed for any changes in identification of segments or changes in accounting practices used in reporting segment information that have a material effect on the segment information: • Description of the nature of the change? • Explanation of the reasons for the change? • Where the information is reasonably determinable, the effect of the change?	14-24	

RELATED PARTY DISCLOSURES

Item	Description	IAS Ref.	Yes, no or N/A
247	Are related party relationships where control exists disclosed, irrespective of whether there have been transactions between the related parties?	24-25	
248	If there have been transactions between related parties, are the following disclosed: • The nature of the related party relationship? • The types of transactions? • The elements of the transactions necessary for an understanding of the financial statements? *Note: Items of similar nature may be aggregated except when separate disclosure is necessary for an understanding of the effects of related party transactions on the financial statements.*	24-26 and 24-27	

CONSOLIDATIONS AND BUSINESS COMBINATIONS
Consolidations and general

Item	Description	IAS Ref.	Yes, no or N/A
249	A parent should present consolidated financial statements unless it is a wholly owned subsidiary, or is virtually wholly owned and has obtained the approval of the minority interests. In this case the parent should disclose the reasons consolidated financial statements have not been presented, the bases on which subsidiaries are accounted for in	27-26 and 27-27	

Item	Description	IAS Ref.	Yes, no or N/A
	its separate financial statements, and the name and registered office of its parent that publishes consolidated financial statements. Have these requirements been complied with?		
250	Are all subsidiaries, foreign and domestic, included in the consolidation other than subsidiaries: • For which control is intended to be temporary because the subsidiary was acquired and is held exclusively with a view to disposal in the near future; or • That operate under severe long-term restrictions that significantly impair their ability to transfer funds to the parent?	27-28 and 27-29	
251	Are subsidiaries excluded from consolidation for the reasons set out in 250 above accounted for as investments?	27-29	
252	Are all intragroup balances and intragroup transactions and resulting unrealized profits or unrealized losses (except to the extent that cost cannot be recovered) eliminated in full?	27-30	
253	If financial statements used in the consolidation are prepared as of different reporting dates, are adjustments made for the effects of significant transactions or other events that occur between those dates and the date of the parent's financial statements? *Note: The difference in reporting dates should be no more than 3 months.*	27-31	
254	Are uniform accounting policies used for like transactions and other events in similar circumstances, or, if this is not practicable, is this fact disclosed, together with the proportions of the items in the consolidated financial statements to which different accounting policies have been applied?	27-32	
255	Are minority interests presented in the consolidated balance sheet separately from liabilities and the parent shareholders' equity?	27-33	

Item	Description	IAS Ref.	Yes, no or N/A
256	Are minority interests in the income of the group presented separately?	27-33	
257	In the consolidated financial statements, are the following disclosed: • A listing of significant subsidiaries, including the name, country of incorporation or residence, proportion of ownership interest and, if different, proportion of voting power held? • The reasons for not consolidating a subsidiary? • The nature of the relationship between the parent and a subsidiary of which the parent does not own, directly or indirectly, more than half of the voting power? • The name of an enterprise in which more than half of the voting power is owned, directly or indirectly, but that, because of the absence of control, is not a subsidiary? • The effect of the acquisition and disposal of subsidiaries on the financial position at the reporting date, the results for the reporting period and the corresponding amounts for the preceding period?	27-37	

Accounting method for business combinations

Item	Description	IAS Ref.	Yes, no or N/A
258	Is the business combination accounted for using: • The purchase method? • The pooling of interests method? (see note)	22-36	
	Note: The pooling of interests method may be used only in the rare circumstances when the business combination is deemed to be a uniting of interests. This is the case when the shareholders of the combining enterprises achieve a continuing mutual sharing in the risks and benefits attaching to the combined enterprise, and • *The basis of the transaction is principally an exchange of voting common shares of the enterprises involved; and* • *All, or effectively all, of the net assets and operations of the combining enterprises are commingled in one enterprise.*	22-37 and 22-38	
259	In the first financial statements following a combination, are the following disclosed:	22-50	

Item	Description	IAS Ref.	Yes, no or N/A
	• The names and descriptions of the combining enterprises?		
	• The effective date of the combination for accounting purposes?		
	• The method of accounting used to reflect the combination?		

Purchase method

Item	Description	IAS Ref.	Yes, no or N/A
260	Does the cost of acquisition include any noncash elements at fair value?	22-43	
261	Are the identifiable assets and liabilities of an acquired enterprise restated to their fair values at the date of acquisition?	22-39	
262	Is the difference (either positive or negative) between the cost of acquisitions and the fair values of the net identifiable assets acquired either: • Recognized in income (see 263 and 265 below); or • Immediately adjusted against shareholders' interests?	22-40	
263	If the policy is to recognize differences in income, is a positive difference recognized in the consolidated balance sheet as goodwill arising on acquisition and amortized to income on a systematic basis over its useful life?	22-41	
264	Is any goodwill arising on acquisition that is found not to be supported by future income charged immediately to income, to the extent necessary?	22-41	
265	If the policy is to recognize differences in income, is a negative difference either: • Treated as deferred income and recognized in income on a systematic basis? • Allocated to individual depreciable non-monetary assets acquired in proportion to their fair values?	22-42	
266	When the acquisition agreement provides for an adjustment to the purchase consideration contingent on one or more future events, is the amount: • Included in the cost of acquisition if payment	22-44	

Item	Description	IAS Ref.	Yes, no or N/A
	is probable and a reasonable estimate of the amount can be made? • Recognized, in all other cases, as soon as the amount is determinable, in accordance with the provisions of IAS 10, *Contingencies and Events Occurring After the Balance Sheet Date?*		
267	Is any minority interest that has arisen on a business combination stated at either: • The appropriate proportion of the postacquisition fair values of the net identifiable assets of the subsidiary; or • The appropriate proportion of the pre-acquisition carrying amounts of the net assets of the subsidiary?	22-45	
268	In the first financial statements following a combination, are the following disclosed: • The percentage of the voting shares acquired? • The cost of acquisition and a description of the purchase consideration paid or contingently payable? • The amount of any difference between cost of acquisition and the aggregate fair value of net identifiable assets acquired, and the treatment thereof, including the period of amortization of any goodwill arising on consolidation?	22-51	
269	Is a subsidiary that ceases to fall within the definition of a subsidiary and does not become an associate accounted for as an investment from that date?	27-34	

Pooling of interests method

Item	Description	IAS Ref.	Yes, no or N/A
270	Are the assets and liabilities and the revenues and expenses for the period in which the combination occurs and for any comparative periods included in the financial statements of the combined enterprises as if they had been combined from the start of those periods?	22-46	
271	Is the difference between the amount recorded as share capital issued (plus any additional consideration in the form of cash or other assets) and the amount recorded for the share capital acquired, adjusted against shareholders' interests?	22-47	

Item	Description	IAS Ref.	Yes, no or N/A
272	In the first financial statements following a combination accounted for under the pooling of interests method, are the following disclosed: • Description and number of shares issued, together with the percentage of each enterprise's voting shares exchanged to effect the combination? • The amounts of assets and liabilities contributed by each enterprise? • Details of the results of operations of the enterprises prior to the date of the combination that are included in net income in the combined financial statements (including details of sales, other operating revenues, unusual items and net income)?	22-52	

Treatment of taxes on income

Item	Description	IAS Ref.	Yes, no or N/A
273	Are permanent and timing differences between income and expenses recognized for financial reporting and for tax purposes dealt with on the basis of tax effect accounting in accordance with IAS 21, *Accounting for Taxes on Income.*	22-48	
274	When the benefits of any tax loss carryforwards that existed but were not recognized as an asset at the date of acquisition are received, is the carrying amount of goodwill arising on acquisition reassessed to identify any amount attributable to the benefits received?	22-49	
275	If part of the goodwill is found to be attributable to the tax benefits received as outlined in 274 above, is the amount: • Adjusted against shareholders' interests, where goodwill is immediately adjusted against reserves; or • Charged to income in all other cases?	22-49	

Business combinations after the balance sheet date

Item	Description	IAS Ref.	Yes, no or N/A
276	The financial statements should not incorporate a business combination the date of which is after the balance sheet date. Is this requirement complied with?	22-53	
277	If business combinations effected after the balance sheet date are of such importance that nondisclo-	22-54	

Item	Description	IAS Ref.	Yes, no or N/A
	sure would affect the ability of users of the financial statements to make proper evaluations and decisions, are the matters set out in 259, 268 and 272 above, as can be estimated, disclosed?		
	Note: If no estimate can be made, this fact should be disclosed.		
	Associates in consolidated financial statements		
278	Are associates, other than those acquired and held exclusively with a view to disposal in the near future, accounted for in the consolidated financial statements under the equity method?	28-24	
279	Are associates acquired and held exclusively with a view to disposal in the near future accounted for in the consolidated financial statements under the cost method?	28-24	
280	Is use of the equity method discontinued from the date that: • The investor ceases to have significant influence in an associate (but still retains all or part of its investment)? • Use of the equity method becomes inappropriate because the associate is operating under severe long-term restrictions that significantly impair its ability to transfer funds to the investor?	28-25	
281	Where the equity method has been discontinued, is the carrying amount of the investment at the date of discontinuance regarded as cost thereafter?	28-25	
	Joint ventures in consolidated financial statements ***Jointly controlled entities*** *Benchmark treatment*		
282	Is an interest in a jointly controlled entity reported in the consolidated financial statements using one of the two reporting formats for proportionate consolidation?	31-42	
	Note: The two reporting formats are: *(i) The venturer combines its share of each of the assets, liabilities, income and expenses of the jointly controlled entity with similar assets in*		

Item	Description	IAS Ref.	Yes, no or N/A
	the consolidated financial statements on a line-by-line basis. *(ii) The venturer shows as separate line items its share of the assets, liabilities, income and expenses of the jointly controlled entity in the consolidated financial statements.*		
283	Is proportionate consolidation discontinued from the date that the venturer ceases to have joint control over a jointly controlled entity?	31-44	
	Allowed alternative treatment		
284	Is an interest in a jointly controlled entity reported in the consolidated financial statements using the equity method?	31-42	
285	Is the use of the equity method discontinued from the date that the venturer ceases to have joint control over, or significant influence in, a jointly controlled entity?	31-44	
	Other requirements		
286	Is an interest in a jointly controlled entity accounted for as an investment (under IAS 25) where: • It is acquired and held exclusively with a view to its subsequent disposal in the near future? • It operates under severe long-term restrictions that significantly impair its ability to transfer funds to the venturer?	31-43	
287	If an interest in a jointly controlled entity became that of a subsidiary, is it accounted for as a subsidiary from the date it became one?	31-45	
	Disclosure		
288	Are the following disclosed: • A listing and description of interests in significant joint ventures? • The proportion of ownership interest held in jointly controlled entities? • For jointly controlled entities reported using the line-by-line format for proportionate consolidation or the equity method, the aggregate amounts of current assets, long-term assets, current liabilities, long-term liabilities, income	31-52	

Item	Description	IAS Ref.	Yes, no or N/A
	and expenses related to interests in joint ventures?		

Translation of the financial statements of foreign operations

Item	Description	IAS Ref.	Yes, no or N/A
289	Are exchange differences arising on an intercompany monetary item that is in effect an extension to or deduction from a parent's net investment in a foreign entity taken to shareholders' interests in the consolidated financial statements?	21-29	

Foreign entity (Independent operations)

Item	Description	IAS Ref.	Yes, no or N/A
290	Are the following procedures applied in translating the financial statements of a foreign entity: • Assets and liabilities, both monetary and non-monetary, are translated at the closing rate? • The exchange difference resulting from translating the opening net investment at an exchange rate different from that at which it was previously reported is taken to shareholders' interests? • The income statement is translated at the closing rate, the exchange rates at the dates of the transactions or a rate that approximates the actual rates? • The differences resulting from translating the income statement at a rate other than the closing rate are taken either to shareholders' interests or to income? • Exchange differences arising on other changes to shareholders' interests are recognized in shareholders' interests?	21-32	
	Note: The financial statements of a foreign entity that is affected by high rates of inflation should be adjusted for the effects of changing prices before the translation process is undertaken. Alternatively, the procedures in 291 below may be applied.	21-33	

Integrated operations

Item	Description	IAS Ref.	Yes, no or N/A
291	Are the following procedures applied in translating the financial statements of a foreign operation integral to the operations of the parent: • Monetary items are translated at the closing rate, except that those covered by forward ex-	21-34	

Item	Description	IAS Ref.	Yes, no or N/A
	change contracts in the parent's currency are translated at: (i) the closing rate (if gains and losses on forward contracts are separately measured); (ii) the spot rate existing at the inception of the forward contract (adjusted by any amortized discount or premium on the contract); or (iii) for short-term transactions, the forward contract rate? • Nonmonetary items that are recorded in terms of past events, e.g., historical cost, are translated at the exchange rates at the date the transactions occurred? • Nonmonetary items that are revalued in the foreign financial statements are translated at the exchange rates at the date of the revaluation? • Income statement items are translated at exchange rates at the dates of the underlying transactions (an average rate may be used if it approximates actual rates)?		
292	Exchange differences on long-term foreign currency monetary items may be deferred and recognized in income on a systematic basis over the remaining lives of the items to which they relate, except that exchange losses should not be deferred if it is reasonable to expect that recurring exchange losses will arise on those items in the future. Except when they are so deferred, are exchange differences arising on the translation of the financial statements of integrated foreign operations recognized in income for the period?	21-34	
	Note: An exchange difference that results from a severe devaluation or from depreciation of a currency against which there is no practical means of hedging and that affects liabilities arising directly on the recent acquisition of assets invoiced in the foreign currency may be included in the carrying amount of the related assets provided the carrying amount does not exceed the lower of replacement cost and the recoverable amount of the asset.	21-31 and 21-34	

Item	Description	IAS Ref.	Yes, no or N/A

Disclosure

293   Are the following disclosed with respect to the translation of the financial statements of foreign operations:
- The methods used?
- The net exchange difference for the period taken to shareholders' interests as a result of translating the financial statements of foreign (independent) operations?
- The net exchange difference for the period taken to income as a result of translating the financial statements of integrated operations?
- The procedure selected (closing or average rates) for translating the income statements of foreign entities?

IAS Ref.: 21-37

INFORMATION REFLECTING THE EFFECTS OF CHANGING PRICES

Note: Enterprises do not need to disclose the information required by IAS 15, Information Reflecting the Effects of Changing Prices, *in order for their financial statements to conform with International Accounting Standards.*

Where the information required by IAS 15 is disclosed, it should be presented using an accounting method reflecting the effects of changing prices and should be provided on a supplementary basis unless such information is presented in the primary financial statements.

IAS Ref.: 15-23 and 15-27

294   Are the following disclosed:
- The amount of the adjustment to or the adjusted amount of property, plant and equipment?
- The amount of the adjustment to or the adjusted amount of cost of sales?
- The adjustments relating to monetary items, the effect of borrowing or equity interests when such adjustments have been taken into account in determining income under the accounting method adopted?
- The overall effect on results of the above adjustments, as well as any other items reflecting the effects of changing prices that are reported under the accounting method adopted?

IAS Ref.: 15-24

Item	Description	IAS Ref.	Yes, no or N/A
295	When a current cost method is adopted, is the current cost of property, plant and equipment disclosed?	15-25	
296	When a current cost method is adopted, is the current cost of inventories disclosed?	15-25	
297	Are the methods adopted to compute the information required in 294–296 above described, including the nature of any indices used?	15-26	

FINANCIAL REPORTING IN HYPERINFLATIONARY ECONOMIES

Note: Hyperinflation is indicated by characteristics of the economic environment of a country, which include, but are not limited to, the following: 29-3

- *The general population prefers to keep its wealth in nonmonetary assets or in a relatively stable currency. Amounts of local currency held are immediately invested to maintain purchasing power.*
- *The general population regards monetary amounts not in terms of the local currency but in terms of a relatively stable foreign currency; prices may be quoted in that currency.*
- *Sales and purchases on credit take place at prices that compensate for the expected loss of purchasing power during the credit period, even if the period is short.*
- *Interest rates, wages and prices are linked to a price index.*
- *The cumulative inflation rate over three years approaches, or exceeds, 100%.*

Item	Description	IAS Ref.	Yes, no or N/A
298	Are the financial statements, whether they are based on a historical cost approach or a current cost approach, stated in terms of the measuring unit current at the balance sheet date?	29-38	
299	Are the corresponding figures for the previous period and any information in respect of earlier periods stated in terms of the measuring unit current at the balance sheet date?	29-38	

Item	Description	IAS Ref.	Yes, no or N/A
300	Is the gain or loss on the monetary position included in income and separately disclosed?	29-39	
301	Where the reporting currency is the currency of a hyperinflationary economy, is the statement of changes in financial position presented in terms of cash and cash equivalents?	29-40	
302	Are the following disclosed: • The fact that the financial statements and the corresponding figures for previous periods have been restated for the changes in the general purchasing power of the reporting currency and, as a result, are stated in terms of the measuring unit current at the balance sheet date? • Whether the financial statements are based on a historical cost approach or a current cost approach? • The identity and level of the price index at the balance sheet date and the movement in the index during the current and the previous reporting period?	29-41	
303	When an economy ceases to be hyperinflationary and the enterprise discontinues the preparation and presentation of its financial statements in accordance with IAS 29, does it treat the amounts expressed in the measuring unit current at the end of the previous reporting period as the basis for the carrying amounts in subsequent financial statements?	29-42	

SPECIMEN FINANCIAL STATEMENTS

PRESENTED IN CONFORMITY WITH INTERNATIONAL ACCOUNTING STANDARDS

The following specimen consolidated financial statements are of a fictitious company and have been prepared to be in conformity with International Accounting Standards (IAS) in effect at September 30, 1993. They are for illustrative purposes only, and show the disclosures and formats that might be expected for a group of this size. Other formats, accounting treatments and disclosures may be permissible.

The intention is to show a relatively simple set of financial statements and not to show all conceivable disclosures. For example, the financial statements do not include examples of prior period adjustments, changes in accounting policy, government grants, construction contracts, reporting in a hyperinflationary economy, or reporting information to reflect the effects of changing prices.

In addition, the statements include a statement of cash flows rather than a statement of changes in financial position. The revised IAS 7, *Cash Flow Statements*, is effective for periods beginning on or after January 1, 1994. Until that date, IAS 7, *Statement of Changes in Financial Position*, remains in effect.

IASC's Statement of Intent

The IASC has adopted a comprehensive Statement of Intent, "Comparability of Financial Statements," which will eliminate many of the choices of accounting treatments permitted under current IASs. An IASC project, the "Improvements Project," is underway to implement the Statement of Intent. In relation to the Improvements Project, exposure drafts of revised IASs have been issued on the following:

Research and Development Activities
Inventories
Capitalization of Borrowing Costs
Revenue Recognition
Construction Contracts
Property, Plant and Equipment
The Effects of Changes in Foreign Exchange Rates
Extraordinary Items, Fundamental Errors and Changes in Accounting Policies
Retirement Benefit Costs

The board of the IASC has considered the responses to many of these exposure drafts and, for certain of them, has agreed and announced changes that will be incorporated into the final standards.

A summary of the principal impacts of the Statement of Intent (as at the time of this writing) is included as an appendix to the chapter on International Accounting Standards. The Improvements Project is expected to be complete by the end of 1993.

This checklist does not incorporate the changes currently being proposed either by the Improvements Project, except insofar as revised standards have been issued by September 30, 1993, or in other areas, i.e., accounting for income taxes and financial instruments. However, where applicable, the accounting treatment chosen for the purposes of these specimen financial statements is the treatment recommended to be retained or to be designated as the benchmark treatment by the Improvements Project. An important exception is that land and buildings are included in the specimen financial statements at valuation, rather than the proposed benchmark treatment of historical cost. This has been done because valuation is an accepted accounting treatment for property, plant and equipment in many countries, and we wished to illustrate the treatment of the surplus.

XXX INTERNATIONAL S.A. CONSOLIDATED FINANCIAL STATEMENTS FOR THE YEAR ENDED DECEMBER 31, 1992

XXX INTERNATIONAL S.A.
CONSOLIDATED FINANCIAL STATEMENTS
FOR THE YEAR ENDED DECEMBER 31, 1992

AUDITORS' REPORT TO THE SHAREHOLDERS

We have audited the consolidated financial statements of XXX International S.A. set out on pages 5 to 21 for the year ended December 31, 1992 in accordance with International Standards on Auditing.

In our opinion, the financial statements fairly present the financial position of XXX International group at December 31, 1992 and the results of its operations and cash flows for the year then ended in accordance with International Accounting Standards.

Coopers & Lybrand S.A.
Geneva, Switzerland
February 26, 1993

XXX INTERNATIONAL S.A.
CONSOLIDATED INCOME STATEMENT
For the Year Ended December 31, 1992

(In thousands of Swiss Francs)	Notes	1992	1991
Sales		80,421	64,838
Cost of sales		(43,132)	(36,082)
GROSS MARGIN		37,289	28,756
Distribution		(2,154)	(1,814)
Selling and marketing		(7,076)	(5,740)
Research and development	10	(3,419)	(2,019)
General and administration		(14,272)	(12,504)
TOTAL OPERATING EXPENSES		(26,921)	(22,077)
OPERATING INCOME		10,368	6,679
Interest income		124	115
Income from investments			
—Associated companies		485	461
—Other		436	1,078
Interest expense		(3,422)	(3,398)
Foreign exchange gain (loss)		(124)	425
TOTAL NONOPERATING EXPENSE		(2,501)	(1,319)
INCOME BEFORE TAXATION		7,867	5,360
Taxation	2	(1,781)	(2,465)
INCOME BEFORE MINORITY INTERESTS AND EXTRAORDINARY ITEMS		6,086	2,895
Minority interests		(573)	(393)
INCOME BEFORE EXTRAORDINARY ITEMS		5,513	2,502
Extraordinary items	3	(344)	—
GROUP SHARE OF NET INCOME	18	5,169	2,502

The attached notes form an integral part of these consolidated financial statements.

XXX INTERNATIONAL S.A.
CONSOLIDATED BALANCE SHEET
As at December 31, 1992

(In thousands of Swiss Francs)	Notes	1992	1991
ASSETS			
CURRENT ASSETS			
Cash and short-term deposits		8,496	5,564
Accounts receivable	4	16,726	13,174
Marketable securities	5	3,738	3,489
Inventories	6	11,091	9,670
TOTAL CURRENT ASSETS		40,051	31,897
NONCURRENT ASSETS			
Property, plant and equipment	7	34,022	27,258
Investments	8	4,753	5,727
Intangible assets	9	2,045	1,840
Deferred development costs	10	1,084	1,473
Goodwill	11	1,254	1,055
TOTAL NONCURRENT ASSETS		43,158	37,353
TOTAL ASSETS		83,209	69,250

XXX INTERNATIONAL S.A.
CONSOLIDATED BALANCE SHEET (Continued)
As at December 31, 1992

(In thousands of Swiss Francs)	Notes	1992	1991
LIABILITIES			
CURRENT LIABILITIES			
Accounts payable	12	11,186	8,705
Taxation		1,926	1,863
Dividends payable		1,707	1,598
Current portion of long-term debt	13	4,521	4,392
TOTAL CURRENT LIABILITIES		19,340	16,558
LONG-TERM LIABILITIES			
Long-term debt	14	29,874	26,196
Pension obligations	16	686	704
Deferred taxation		2,599	2,548
TOTAL LONG-TERM LIABILITIES		33,159	29,448
TOTAL LIABILITIES		52,499	46,006
MINORITY INTERESTS		2,630	2,171
SHAREHOLDERS' EQUITY			
Share capital	17	7,422	6,390
Reserves		20,658	14,683
TOTAL SHAREHOLDERS' EQUITY	18	28,080	21,073
TOTAL LIABILITIES, MINORITY INTERESTS AND SHAREHOLDERS' EQUITY		83,209	69,250

The attached notes form an integral part of these consolidated financial statements.

XXX INTERNATIONAL S.A.
CONSOLIDATED CASH FLOW STATEMENT
For the Year ended December 31, 1992

(In·thousands of Swiss Francs)	Note	1992	1991
CASH FLOWS FROM OPERATING ACTIVITIES			
Cash receipts from customers		79,241	64,345
Cash paid to suppliers		(63,986)	(54,569)
Cash generated from operations		15,255	9,776
Interest paid		(3,546)	(2,973)
Income taxes paid		(1,631)	(1,076)
NET CASH FROM OPERATING ACTIVITIES		10,078	5,727
CASH FLOWS FROM INVESTING ACTIVITIES			
Acquisition of subsidiary	19	(5,338)	—
Purchase of plant, property and equipment		(2,484)	(3,399)
Proceeds from the sale of equipment		210	955
Proceeds from sale of investments		2,637	2,946
Acquisition of investments		(1,041)	(1,943)
Interest received		114	573
Dividends received		449	443
NET CASH USED IN INVESTING ACTIVITIES		(5,453)	(425)
CASH FLOWS FROM FINANCING ACTIVITIES			
Proceeds from the issuance of share capital		3,096	—
Proceeds from long-term debt		1,342	5,391
Payment of long-term debt		(4,619)	(7,463)
Dividends paid		(1,564)	(1,500)
NET CASH USED IN FINANCING ACTIVITIES		(1,745)	(3,572)
Effect of change in foreign currency rates on the cash balance at the beginning of the year		52	70
NET INCREASE IN CASH AND CASH EQUIVALENTS		2,932	1,800
CASH AND CASH EQUIVALENTS AT THE BEGINNING OF THE YEAR		5,564	3,764
CASH AND CASH EQUIVALENTS AT THE END OF THE YEAR		8,496	5,564

The attached notes form an integral part of these consolidated financial statements.

XXX INTERNATIONAL S.A.
NOTES TO THE CONSOLIDATED
FINANCIAL STATEMENTS

GENERAL

XXX International S.A. (the Company) is incorporated in Switzerland. The XXX International Group (the Group) is involved in the manufacture of household electrical goods, the manufacture of textiles for the clothing trade and the printing of tertiary education textbooks.

NOTE 1. ACCOUNTING POLICIES

The consolidated financial statements of the Group have been prepared in accordance with the accounting and reporting requirements of the International Accounting Standards issued by the International Accounting Standards Committee. The consolidated financial statements have been prepared using the historical cost convention, except that land and buildings are included at valuation. Significant accounting policies adopted by the Group are as follows:

1.1 Principles of consolidation
The consolidated financial statements include the financial statements of the parent company and its subsidiaries. The effects of all transactions between entities within the consolidated financial statements are eliminated in full. A subsidiary is an entity that is controlled by the Company, usually evidenced by ownership, directly or indirectly, of more than 50 percent of the voting share capital of the entity. Subsidiaries are accounted for using the purchase method.

Associated entities in which the Company has a significant but not a controlling interest are accounted for using the equity method. Significant interest is usually evidenced by the Company owning, directly or indirectly, between 20 percent and 50 percent of the voting share capital.

Investments held for the long term, other than subsidiaries and associates, are stated at cost, unless there has been an impairment in value below cost that is other than temporary. In that case the investment is written down to its realizable value and the decrease is charged to income.

Joint ventures in which the Group has an interest are included in the consolidated financial statements using the proportionate consolidation method.

1.2 Revenue recognition
Sales are recorded in the financial statements at the date goods are delivered to customers or services are performed.

1.3 Property, plant and equipment
All fixed assets other than land and buildings are included at cost. Cost includes all costs directly attributable to bringing the asset to working condition for its intended use. Financing costs that are attributable to the purchase or construction of a fixed asset are included in cost.

Land and buildings are stated at market value, based on annual valuations by external independent valuers. Increases in carrying value arising on revaluation are credited directly to a revaluation reserve within shareholders' equity. On the disposal of a previously revalued property, any amount relating to that asset remaining in the revaluation reserve is transferred directly to retained earnings.

Depreciation is recorded by a charge to income computed on a straight-line basis so as to write off the cost or valuation of the assets over their expected useful lives. The expected useful lives are as follows:

Buildings	50 years
Machinery and equipment	5–15 years
Fixtures	5–10 years

Land is not depreciated as it is deemed to have an infinite life.

1.4 Goodwill

At the date of acquisition, the excess of the purchase price of a subsidiary over the fair value of the net assets acquired is capitalized and amortized over the expected period of benefit, normally five years.

1.5 Intangible assets

Intangible assets are recorded at cost and are amortized on a straight-line basis over their expected useful lives. The expected useful lives of patents and trademarks varies from five to ten years.

1.6 Marketable securities

Marketable securities held for the short term are stated at the lower of cost or market value determined on an individual investment basis. Market value is determined using the selling price quoted on the Stock Market at the close of business on the balance sheet date.

1.7 Inventories

Inventories are stated at the lower of cost or net realizable value. Cost is calculated on a first-in first-out (FIFO) basis. Cost includes direct materials, direct labor and an appropriate proportion of variable and fixed overhead expenditure, the latter being allocated on the basis of normal operating capacity.

1.8 Research and development

Research and development costs are written off as incurred, except that development costs are capitalized and amortized over the period of expected future benefits where it is expected that the product under development will be profitable and will be produced. The period of amortization normally does not exceed five years.

1.9 Foreign currencies

Transactions denominated in foreign currencies are recorded in Swiss francs at the exchange rates in effect at the date of the transactions. Outstanding foreign currency monetary items at the balance sheet date are reported at the exchange rate in effect at that date. Differences arising on settlement of monetary items or on reporting short-term foreign currency monetary items at rates different from those at which they were recorded in the period are recognized in income for the period.

The assets and liabilities of foreign subsidiaries are translated at the exchange rate in effect at the balance sheet date, and the income statement is translated at an average exchange rate for the year. Differences arising from the translation of the financial statements of foreign subsidiaries are taken to a foreign currency translation reserve in shareholders' equity.

1.10 Taxation

Taxation on income is accounted for using the liability method. Under this method, the expected effects of differences in the timing of reporting items in income and reporting them for tax purposes are recorded as deferred taxation at the tax rates that are expected to apply when the timing differences reverse. The current rates have been used for this purpose. Deferred taxation is accrued for all timing differences, except that deferred tax benefits are carried forward only where there is a reasonable expectation of realization.

Taxes payable by the Group on distribution to the Company of the undistributed profits of subsidiaries and associates are accrued, except where there is no intention to distribute those profits.

1.11 Leased assets

Assets leased under agreements that transfer to the Group substantially all the risks and rewards incident to ownership (finance leases) are treated as if they had been purchased outright. At the inception of a finance lease agreement the asset is recorded in property, plant and equipment and a liability is recorded for the capital element of the leasing commitments. Lease rental payments are treated as comprising a capital element, which is applied to reduce the liability outstanding, and an interest element, which is charged to income.

Lease rental payments under lease agreements other than finance leases (operating leases) are charged to income over the period of the lease on a straight-line basis.

1.12 Pensions

All companies within the Group provide defined benefit pension plans for employees. The funds are valued once every three years by professionally qualified independent actuaries. The rates of contribution payable are determined by the actuaries. Pension costs are accounted for by charging the expected cost of providing pensions over the period during which the Group benefits from the employees' services. The effects of variations from regular cost are spread over the expected average remaining service lives of plan members.

NOTE 2. TAXATION

A reconciliation between the reported income tax expense and the theoretical amount that would arise using a maximum basic corporation tax rate follows:

(In thousands of Swiss Francs)	1992	1991
Income before taxation	7,867	5,360
Income tax calculated at a basic corporate tax rate of 40% (1991—40%)	3,147	2,144
Effect of lower tax rates in other countries	(1,241)	(74)
Effect of utilizing previously unrecognized tax losses	(108)	(96)
Effect of income not assessable to tax	(160)	(17)
Effect of expenses not deductible for tax purposes	143	508
Income tax charge for the year	1,781	2,465

At December 31, 1992, Group companies had tax losses amounting to Fr 175,000 (1991—Fr 445,000); the estimated related tax benefits of Fr 70,000 (1991—Fr 178,000) had not been accounted for. These tax losses may be carried forward by the companies in question indefinitely.

NOTE 3. EXTRAORDINARY ITEM

(In thousands of Swiss Francs)	1992	1991
Flood damage to facilities and inventory	494	—
Tax benefit	(36)	—
	458	—
Minority interest in extraordinary item	(114)	—
	344	—

On March 23, 1992, the Group's facilities and warehouse in Johnstown, Pennsylvania, USA were severely damaged in a flood caused by a reservoir dam bursting after heavy rain. The total damage, less estimated insurance recoveries, has been recorded as an extraordinary item.

NOTE 4. ACCOUNTS RECEIVABLE

(In thousands of Swiss Francs)	1992	1991
Accounts and notes receivable—trade	11,447	9,191
Receivable from associated companies	2,347	1,206
Receivable from directors	986	1,046
Other receivables and prepaid expenses	1,946	1,731
	16,726	13,174

NOTE 5. MARKETABLE SECURITIES

(In thousands of Swiss Francs)	1992	1991
Net book value	3,738	3,489
Market value	4,312	4,819

NOTE 6. INVENTORIES

(In thousands of Swiss Francs)	1992	1991
Raw materials	2,749	2,407
Work in progress	2,411	2,165
Finished goods	5,931	5,098
	11,091	9,670

NOTE 7. PROPERTY, PLANT AND EQUIPMENT

(In thousands of Swiss Francs)	Land & Buildings	Machinery & Equipm't.	Fixtures & Fittings	Total
1992				
Cost or valuation				
Cost at January 1, 1992		18,855	13,938	32,793
Valuation at January 1, 1992	5,862			5,862
Additions in the year	—	9,432	980	10,412
Disposals in the year	—	(886)	—	(886)
Revaluation in the year	131	—	—	131
Effect of foreign currency movement	—	—	738	738
Cost at December 31, 1992		27,401	15,656	43,057
Valuation at December 31, 1992	5,993			5,993
Depreciation				
Depreciation at January 1, 1992	—	5,640	5,757	11,397
Charge for the year	82	1,938	1,856	3,876
Depreciation on disposals	—	(463)	—	(463)
Revaluation in the year	(82)	—	—	(82)
Effect of foreign currency movement	—	—	300	300
Depreciation at December 31, 1992	—	7,115	7,913	15,028
Net book value at January 1, 1992	5,862	13,215	8,181	27,258
Net book value at December 31, 1992	5,993	20,286	7,743	34,022

(In thousands of Swiss Francs)	Land & Buildings	Machinery & Equipm't.	Fixtures & Fittings	Total
1991				
Cost or valuation				
Cost at January 1, 1991		18,804	11,669	30,473
Valuation at January 1, 1991	5,831			5,831
Additions in the year	—	1,964	1,435	3,399
Disposals in the year	—	(1,913)	(321)	(2,234)
Revaluation in the year	31	—	—	31
Effect of foreign currency movement	—	—	1,155	1,155
Cost at December 31, 1991		18,855	13,938	32,793
Valuation at December 31, 1991	5,862			5,862
Depreciation				
Depreciation at January 1, 1991	—	4,706	4,121	8,827
Charge for the year	75	1,814	1,544	3,433
Depreciation on disposals	—	(880)	(289)	(1,169)
Revaluation in the year	(75)	—	—	(75)
Effect of foreign currency movement	—	—	381	381
Depreciation at December 31, 1991	—	5,640	5,757	11,397
Net book value at January 1, 1991	5,831	14,098	7,548	27,477
Net book value at December 31, 1991	5,862	13,215	8,181	27,258

Land and buildings were revalued to market value on the basis of valuations carried out by external independent valuers as at December 31, 1992.

Included in machinery and equipment at December 31, 1992 are assets with a net book value of Fr 4,146,000 (1991—Fr 4,266,000) held under finance leases.

Borrowing costs amounting to Fr 64,000 (1991—Fr 27,000) have been capitalized during the year as part of the cost of construction and are included in additions above.

No potential liability to tax arises as a result of the revaluation of land and buildings.

At December 31, 1992, the Group had entered into commitments to purchase Fr 1,649,000 of fixed assets (1991—Fr 2,162,000).

NOTE 8. INVESTMENTS

(In thousands of Swiss Francs)	1992	1991
Associated companies		
Balance at January 1	1,952	1,816
Equity earnings	485	461
Dividends received	(350)	(325)
Associated companies at December 31	2,087	1,952
Other investments	2,666	3,775
Total investments	4,753	5,727

The market value of the other investments at December 31, 1992 was Fr 3,142,000 (1991—Fr 3,968,000).

NOTE 9. INTANGIBLE ASSETS

(In thousands of Swiss Francs)	1992	1991
Patents and trademarks		
Balance at January 1	1,840	2,146
Acquired during the year	639	—
Amortized during the year	(434)	(306)
Balance at December 31	2,045	1,840

NOTE 10. DEFERRED DEVELOPMENT COSTS

(In thousands of Swiss Francs)	1992	1991
Balance at January 1	1,473	1,876
Amortized during the year	(389)	(403)
Balance at December 31	1,084	1,473

In addition to the amortization charge, research and development expenses incurred during the year and not deferred amounted to Fr 3,030,000 (1991—Fr 1,616,000).

NOTE 11. GOODWILL

(In thousands of Swiss Francs)	1992	1991
Balance at January 1	1,055	1,396
Acquired during the year	686	—
Amortized during the year	(487)	(341)
Balance at December 31	1,254	1,055

NOTE 12. ACCOUNTS PAYABLE

(In thousands of Swiss Francs)	1992	1991
Accounts and notes payable—trade	9,472	6,983
Payable to associated companies	934	899
Payable to directors	456	467
Other payables and accrued expenses	324	356
	11,186	8,705

NOTE 13. LONG-TERM DEBT

(In thousands of Swiss Francs)	Interest Rate %	1992	1991
Payable after 5 years	8.4	4,011	1,921
Payable in 2–5 years	9.2	14,121	19,343
Payable in 1–2 years	10.3	11,742	4,932
		29,874	26,196
Current portion of long-term debt	10.4	4,521	4,392
Total long-term debt		34,395	30,588

Property, plant and equipment with a book value of Fr 28,500,000 (1991—Fr 25,600,000) has been pledged as security for Fr 24,388,000 (1991—Fr 18,687,000) of borrowings.

Included in borrowings is Fr 2,797,000 (1991—Fr 2,925,000) in respect of finance leases, of which Fr 649,000 (1991—Fr 694,000) is payable within one year (note 14). The average interest rate on finance leases is 12.7 percent.

NOTE 14. LEASE COMMITMENTS

A summary of commitments in relation to finance leases follows:

(In thousands of Swiss Francs)	1992	1991
Payable in 2–5 years	1,648	2,203
Payable in 1–2 years	1,212	830
Payable within 1 year	695	746
	3,555	3,779
Less future finance charges	(758)	(854)
Provided in the financial statements (note 13)	2,797	2,925

A summary of commitments in relation to noncancellable operating leases with terms of more than one year, but not provided for in the financial statements follows:

(In thousands of Swiss Francs)	1992	1991
Payable in 2–5 years	896	907
Payable in 1–2 years	386	260
Payable within 1 year	275	184
	1,557	1,351

NOTE 15. CONTINGENCIES

An action is pending against a subsidiary company in respect of an alleged incident of pollution. The maximum fine that can be imposed is Fr 5,000,000. The directors believe there is no substance to the allegation and do not expect the Group to suffer any loss. No provision has been made in these consolidated financial statements in respect of this matter.

NOTE 16. PENSION OBLIGATIONS

Approximately 60 percent of the Group's employees are covered by defined benefit pension plans.

The cost to the Group of these pension plans is assessed in accordance with the advice of independent qualified actuaries using an accrued benefit valuation method. The latest actuarial valuation of the plans was at June 30, 1992. The significant assumptions used in these valuations relate to return on fund investments and the rates of increase in salaries and pension benefits. The assumptions used varied according to the economic environment in the country of each plan. The assumed returns on investments ranged from 5 percent to 9.5 percent, and the assumed rates of increase in salaries and pension benefits ranged from 3 percent to 6 percent.

The amount of Fr 686,000 (1991—Fr 704,000) in long-term liabilities represents the excess of the accumulated cost of the pension plans over the amounts funded.

The value of vested benefits exceeds the total of the net realizable value of the pension plan assets and excess accumulated cost by Fr 3,285,000 (1991—Fr 3,560,000). This is being funded by amortizing the amount over the expected average remaining lives of the employees and will be fully amortized by 2003.

NOTE 17. SHARE CAPITAL

(In thousands of Swiss Francs, except nominal value and number of shares)	1992 Number	Fr	1991 Number	Fr
Issued and fully paid bearer shares of Fr 100 each				
At January 1	63,900	6,390	63,900	6,390
Issued during the year	10,320	1,032	—	—
At December 31	74,220	7,422	63,900	6,390

On March 1, 1992, 10,320 shares were issued for Fr 300 cash each.

At December 31, 1992, 10,000 options (1991—10,000) to purchase shares at Fr 400 each, exercisable before December 31, 1998, were outstanding.

NOTE 18. SHAREHOLDERS' EQUITY

(In thousands of Swiss Francs)	Share Capital	Share Premium	Reval'n Reserve	Foreign Currency Reserve	Retained Earnings	Total Equity
Balance at January 1, 1991	6,390	3,294	2,413	—	7,633	19,730
Net income for 1991					2,502	2,502
Dividends					(1,598)	(1,598)
Foreign currency translation adjustment				333		333
Revaluation of land and buildings			106			106
Balance at January 1, 1992	6,390	3,294	2,519	333	8,537	21,073
Net income for 1992					5,169	5,169
Dividends					(1,673)	(1,673)
Foreign currency translation adjustment				202		202
Revaluation of land and buildings			213			213
Issue of shares	1,032	2,064				3,096
Balance at December 31, 1992	7,422	5,358	2,732	535	12,033	28,080

The share premium, revaluation and foreign currency reserves cannot be distributed.

NOTE 19. GROUP STRUCTURE

On June 15, 1992, the Group acquired all of the voting shares of XXX (Africa) Ltd. for a total consideration of Fr 5,686,000 cash. At the date of acquisition, the assets of XXX (Africa) Ltd. included a bank balance of Fr 348,000; the net cash outflow for the acquisition was therefore Fr 5,338,000. The financial statements of XXX (Africa) Ltd. have been included in these consolidated financial statements using the purchase method. Goodwill on consolidation amounting to Fr 686,000 arose on the acquisition and is being amortized on a straight-line basis over the estimated period of benefit of five years.

A summary of the assets and liabilities of XXX (Africa) Ltd. at June 15, 1992, the date of acquisition, and at December 31, 1992, excluding goodwill, follows:

(In thousands of Swiss Francs)	December 31, 1992	June 15, 1992
Cash	543	348
Current assets (excluding cash)	4,159	3,661
Noncurrent assets	6,283	5,694
Intangible assets	528	639
Total assets	11,513	10,342
Current liabilities	(1,463)	(986)
Noncurrent liabilities	(4,686)	(4,356)
Total liabilities	(6,149)	(5,342)
Net assets	5,364	5,000

During the year, XXX (Africa) Ltd. contributed Fr 1,654,000 to the net income before tax of the Group.

A listing of significant subsidiaries, associates and joint ventures follows:

Name	Country of Incorporation	Percentage Ownership
Subsidiaries		
XXX (Africa) Ltd.	Nigeria	100%
XXX (Asia) Inc.	Japan	100%
XXX (US) Inc.	USA	75% (note 20)
XXX (UK) Ltd.	England	100%
Associates		
XXX (Europe) Gmbh	Germany	25%
Joint Ventures		
XXX Venture	France	33%

With respect to XXX Venture, the following have been included in the consolidated financial statements using the proportionate consolidation method:

(In thousands of Swiss Francs)	1992	1991
Current assets	3,291	3,044
Noncurrent assets	4,632	4,811
Current liabilities	(1,804)	(1,756)
Noncurrent liabilities	(1,046)	(1,216)
Income	6,576	6,182
Expenses	(4,118)	(3,997)

NOTE 20. POST BALANCE SHEET EVENT

On February 14, 1993, the remaining 25 percent of XXX (US) Inc. not already owned by the Group was acquired for Fr 4,050,000 cash.

NOTE 21. RELATED PARTY TRANSACTIONS

A summary of transactions during the year with related parties follows:

(In thousands of Swiss Francs)	1992	1991
Associated companies		
Sales	2,854	2,321
Purchases	2,696	2,204
Dividends received	350	325
Directors		
Remuneration for services as directors	1,843	1,625

NOTE 22. SEGMENTAL INFORMATION

Geographical segments

(In thousands of Swiss Francs)	Europe	Asia	USA	Africa	Elimin's	Consol'ed
1992						
Sales to customers outside the Group	30,431	18,118	22,441	9,431	—	80,421
Intersegment sales	4,321	1,621	2,239	960	(9,141)	—
Total sales	34,752	19,739	24,680	10,391	(9,141)	80,421
Segment result	3,193	1,800	3,167	1,727	(488)	9,399
Unallocated expenses						(1,532)
Consolidated income before tax						7,867
Segment assets	31,249	15,638	19,821	15,208	(1,337)	80,579
Unallocated assets						2,630
Total assets						83,209
1991						
Sales to customers outside the Group	28,644	16,004	20,190	—	—	64,838
Intersegment sales	4,431	1,594	2,626	—	(8,651)	—
Total sales	33,075	17,598	22,816	—	(8,651)	64,838
Segment result	3,501	1,632	2,567	—	(341)	7,359
Unallocated expenses						(1,999)
Consolidated income before tax						5,360
Segment assets	37,694	13,638	16,848	—	(943)	67,237
Unallocated assets						2,013
Total assets						69,250

Industry segments

(In thousands of Swiss Francs)	Electrical	Textiles	Printing	Elimin's	Consol'ed
1992					
Sales to customers outside the Group	40,614	21,446	18,361	—	80,421
Intersegment sales	2,146	944	316	(3,406)	—
Total sales	42,760	22,390	18,677	(3,406)	80,421
Segment result	4,795	1,642	3,127	(248)	9,316
Unallocated expenses					(1,449)
Consolidated income before tax					7,867
Segment assets	44,394	13,539	23,196	(461)	80,668
Unallocated assets					2,541
Total assets					83,209
1991					
Sales to customers outside the Group	33,492	20,227	11,119	—	64,838
Intersegment sales	1,513	863	201	(2,577)	—
Total sales	35,005	21,090	11,320	(2,577)	64,838
Segment result	4,114	1,532	1,125	(198)	6,573
Unallocated expenses					(1,213)
Consolidated income before tax					5,360
Segment assets	38,812	11,418	17,320	(294)	67,256
Unallocated assets					1,994
Total assets					69,250

Intersegment transactions are made on normal commercial terms.

GLOSSARY

Absorption costing: A method whereby the cost of inventories is determined by the inclusion of an appropriate share of both variable and fixed costs, the latter being allocated on the basis of normal operating capacity.

Accounting concepts: The basic assumptions that underlie the financial statements of business enterprises.

Accounting methods: See **accounting procedures**.

Accounting policies: The specific **accounting principles** followed by an entity.

Accounting principles: The rules that guide the measurement, classification and interpretation of economic information and communication of the results through the medium of financial statements.

Accounting procedures: The methods followed by an entity in applying **accounting principles**.

Accounting standards: Those **accounting principles** that have been given formal recognition by a standard-setting body.

Accounts payable: Monetary liabilities of an entity due to another entity, generally arising from the purchase of goods or performance of services.

Accounts receivable: Monetary assets of an entity due from another entity, generally based on the sale of goods or performance of services.

Accrual(s) concept: The recognition and recording in the accounting records of the effects of transactions and other events when they occur (and not as cash or its equivalent is received or paid) and their reporting in the financial statements of those accounting periods.

Acquisition accounting: See **purchase method**.

Additional paid in capital: Amounts paid by shareholders in excess of the minimum amount required for the shares to be fully paid. For all practical purposes, this equates to **share premium**.

Allowed alternative accounting treatment: An expression used in International Accounting Standards to denote an accounting treatment that is allowed, under those standards, as an alternative to the **benchmark accounting treatment**.

Amortization: The same as **depreciation**, but generally used in relation to intangible **capital assets**.

Annuity method: See **depreciation**.

Associated company: A company that is not a subsidiary of another company but in which that other company exercises significant influence. In many jurisdictions significant influence is presumed where the investing company holds 20 percent or more of the equity of the investee.

Average cost: An accounting method in which the cost of an item is determined by applying a weighted average of the cost of all similar items at a point in time or over a period.

Base stock: See **inventory**.

Benchmark accounting treatment: An expression used in International Accounting Standards (IASs) to denote one accounting treatment where more than one treatment is permitted by an IAS. Where a permitted accounting treatment other than the benchmark accounting treatment (an **allowed alternative accounting treatment**) is used in financial statements, entities are encouraged to publish a reconciliation with the benchmark accounting treatment. Also, there are situations where such a reconciliation is required.

Business combination: A transaction whereby one economic unit unites with or obtains control over another economic unit. (**Consolidated financial statements** are normally used for the combined entity's financial reporting.)

Capital asset: An asset, whether tangible or intangible, intended for long-term use and held as such.

Capital expenditure: An expenditure to acquire or add to a **capital asset**.

Capital stock: The ownership interest represented by shares (stock) of a company.

Closing (exchange) rate method: The same as the **current rate method** except that revenue and expenses are also translated at rates in effect at the balance sheet date.

Common shares (stock): A class of stock representing the residual equity in the company's assets and earnings. Also known as ordinary shares in some jurisdictions.

Completed contract method: A method of accounting for long-term contracts that recognizes gross profit only when completed goods have been finally delivered or services have been rendered in full (or substantially so).

Conservatism: The concept that, when uncertainty exists, estimates attempt to ensure that income is not overstated. Conservatism does not encompass the deliberate understatement of income. See also **prudence concept**.

Consolidated financial statements (accounts): Financial statements that present separate but related legal entities as a single economic entity.

Contingency: An existing condition that involves uncertainty as to possible gain or loss to an entity and that will be resolved when a future event occurs or fails to occur.

Contributed surplus: See **surplus**.

Creditors: A term used for **accounts payable** in some jurisdictions.

Current assets: Assets reasonably expected to be realized in cash or sold or consumed within the normal operating cycle of the business, generally one year.

Current cost accounting: A method of accounting in which data is expressed in terms of current rather than historical cost.

Current (exchange) rate method: A method of translating foreign currency where all assets and liabilities are translated at the foreign exchange rate in effect at the balance sheet date, and revenue and expense items are translated generally at a weighted-average rate in effect during the period.

Current liabilities: Liabilities generally payable within one year of the balance sheet date or whose liquidation is expected to require the use of current assets.

Current/noncurrent (exchange) rate method: A method of foreign currency translation where **current assets** and **liabilities** are translated at the foreign exchange rate in effect at the balance sheet date, and noncurrent assets and liabilities are translated at the rates in effect at the time of the related transactions. Revenue and expense items are generally translated at a weighted-average rate in effect during the period.

Debtors: A term used for **accounts receivable** in some jurisdictions.

Declining balance method: See **depreciation**.

Defeasance: Commonly used to describe the release of a debtor from a primary obligation. In a *legal* defeasance the creditor formally acknowledges the release of the debtor from the primary obligation. In an *in-substance* defeasance the debtor irrevocably places risk-free assets in trust (sufficient to meet the servicing requirements of the debt) and the possibility that the debtor will be required to make future payments with respect to the debt is remote.

Deferral (deferred) method: See **tax allocation**.

Defined benefit pension plan: A pension plan in which the amount of retirement benefits is determined in relation to a participant's earnings and/or years of service.

Defined contribution benefit plan: A pension plan in which benefits are computed by reference to the contributions paid into the fund, together with investment earnings thereon.

Depreciation: The measure of the wearing out, consumption or other reduction in the useful economic life of a fixed asset whether arising from use, passage of time or technical obsolescence. There are many methods of calculating depreciation, including:

- [ ] **Annuity method**—A depreciation method in which the periodic charge is computed such that the net carrying value of the asset at any point in time is its net present value as computed using the rate of return implicit in the decision to purchase the asset.

- [ ] **Declining balance method**—See **diminishing balance method**.

- [ ] **Diminishing balance method**—A depreciation method in which the periodic charge is computed as a constant fraction of the depreciated cost so that the depreciation base is written off by the estimated date of retirement.

- [ ] **Double declining balance method**—A depreciation method that is a variant of the **diminishing balance method** in which the constant fraction used is double the fraction that would be used to write off the depreciation base using the **straight-line method**.

- [ ] **Straight-line method**—A depreciation method in which the periodic charge is computed by dividing the depreciation base by the number of periods of service life.

- [ ] **Sum-of-the-years'-digits method**—A method of depreciation in which the depreciation base is allocated to the individual years on a reducing basis by multiplying it by a fraction in which the numerator is the number of years + 1 of estimated life remaining, and the denominator is the sum of the series of numbers in the total estimated life.

☐ **Unit(s)-of-production method**—A method of depreciation in which the periodic charge is that proportion of the depreciation base that the production during the period bears to the total estimated production to be obtained from the asset.

Diminishing balance method: See **depreciation**.

Directors' emoluments: Compensation paid in cash or in kind by a company to its directors for services as a director or in other capacities.

Direct method: An expression used in connection with cash flow statements to describe a method under which gross operating cash flows from receipts and payments are disclosed. (Compare **indirect method**.)

Double declining balance method: See **depreciation**.

Effective tax rate: The amount of income tax (including deferred tax) recognized as an expense by an entity, expressed as a percentage of its income before tax.

Equity method: A basis of accounting for equity investments in other entities whereby the investment is initially recorded at cost and the carrying value is adjusted thereafter to show the investor's pro rata share of the postacquisition earnings or losses, and other movements in shareholders' funds of the investee.

Factoring of receivables: The sale of receivables, usually at a discount, to provide the vendor with cash and/or to relieve the vendor of the risk of collecting the receivables.

FIFO (First-in first-out): See **inventory**.

Finance (financial) lease: A lease that transfers substantially all the risks and rewards incident to ownership of an asset to the lessee. Title may or may not eventually be transferred.

Financial period: The period of time for which financial statements are prepared. In the case of reporting to shareholders, this period is generally a year.

Fiscal period: Generally synonymous with **financial period**, but may be used in certain countries to describe the period subject to tax assessment.

Fixed assets: A term used for **capital assets** in some jurisdictions.

Fixed costs: Costs of production that remain relatively constant from reporting period to reporting period irrespective of variations, within normal operating limits, in the volume of production.

Foreign currency transactions: Transactions of the reporting entity denominated in a currency other than its reporting currency.

Franked investment income: An expression that usually denotes that the dividend that creates the income has had tax paid on it at the corporate level and that the recipient receives a credit for that tax paid.

GAAP (Generally accepted accounting principles): Those accounting principles that have become established in a particular jurisdiction by formal recognition by a standard-setting body or by authoritative support or precedent.

Going concern concept: The accounting concept that a business will continue in operation for the foreseeable future and that assets are therefore accounted for on the basis of continued use as distinct from market or liquidation value.

Going concern value: The carrying value of an asset or of net assets based on the **going concern concept**.

Goodwill: An intangible asset of a business when the business has value in excess of the sum of its net identifiable assets.

    □ **(Consolidated) goodwill**—The excess of the price paid by an acquirer for a company over the fair value of the acquiring company's interest in the identifiable net assets acquired.

    □ **Negative goodwill**—The excess of the fair value of the interest acquired in the identifiable net assets of a company over the price paid by the acquirer.

Group financial statements (accounts): See **consolidated financial statements (accounts)**.

Hedge (foreign currency): Action taken, whether by entering into a foreign currency contract or otherwise, with the objective of avoiding or minimizing possible untoward financial effects of movements in exchange rates.

Historical cost accounting: A method of accounting in which data is expressed in terms of the units of currency in which a transaction originally took place.

Holding company: A company that controls one or more other companies (**subsidiaries**).

Hypothecation: The pledging of an asset as collateral for a liability.

Imparity principle: A principle applied in certain European countries that requires recognition of unrealized losses but forbids recognition of unrealized profits. Analogous to the **prudence concept**.

Imputed interest: Interest calculated at a market-related rate, used where a reasonable amount of interest is not specifically stated, to determine the carrying value of an asset or a liability.

Independent foreign operation: See **self-sustaining foreign operation**.

Indirect method: An expression used in connection with cash flow statements to describe a method under which net operating cash flow is determined by adjusting net profit or loss for the effects of transactions of a noncash nature, any deferrals or accruals of past or future operating cash receipts or payments, and items of income or expense associated with investing or financing cash flows. (Compare **direct method**.)

Individual evaluation concept: The concept that assets and liabilities should be determined and valued independently, and revenues and expenses, and assets and liabilities should not be netted.

Individual Valuation Concept: See **individual evaluation concept**.

Instalment sale: A sale in which the price is to be settled by a series of payments over a period of time.

Intangible assets: Nonmonetary assets without physical substance, including, but not limited to, brand names, copyrights, franchises, intellectual property, licenses, mastheads, patents and trademarks.

Integrated foreign operation: A foreign operation that is financially or operationally interdependent with the reporting entity so that the exposure to exchange rate changes is similar to the exposure that would exist had the transactions and activities of the foreign operation been undertaken by the reporting entity.

Inventory: Items of personal property that are held for sale in the ordinary course of business (finished goods), are in the process of production for such sale (work in process/progress) or are to be currently consumed either directly or indirectly in the production of goods or services to be available for sale (raw materials and supplies). There are various methods of establishing inventory cost, including the following more common methods:

☐ **Base stock**—An accounting method under which a predetermined fixed amount of inventory is regarded as an unavoidable minimum and is stated at its cost when such inventory was first established. Inventory quantities in excess of the minimum are valued at a more current cost.

☐ **FIFO (First-in first-out)**—A method of establishing inventory cost in which cost is determined as though items of inventory are sold or consumed in order of their acquisition.

☐ **Latest purchase price method**—An accounting method whereby the carrying value of similar items is determined by applying the cost of the last item purchased.

☐ **LIFO (Last-in first-out)**—A method of establishing inventory cost in which cost is computed as though items most recently acquired are sold or consumed before those acquired earlier.

☐ **Retail method**—An accounting method (principally used by retailers) under which the inventory is first priced on the basis of the selling prices marked for the products, and a percentage reduction is made from the total selling price for the inventory (or major groupings of inventory) to approximate inventory cost.

☐ **Specific identification method**—An accounting method under which the cost of each item is ascertained separately.

Joint control: The contractually agreed sharing of control over an economic activity such that none of the venturers is in a position to unilaterally control the venture. This is a term usually used in connection with **joint ventures**.

Joint venture: A contractual arrangement whereby two or more parties undertake an economic activity that is subject to joint control. See **joint control**.

Latest purchase price method: See **inventory**.

Leverage: The relationship between the return earned with the use of borrowed funds and the cost of those funds.

Leveraged leases: A special type of financing lease arrangement that involves a long-term creditor as well as a lessor and lessee. The long-term creditor provides nonrecourse financing so that the lessor may acquire the leased asset. (The creditor may have recourse to the leased asset.) This arrangement provides the lessor with substantial "leverage" in the transaction. Typically, the lessor's net investment declines during the early years and rises, perhaps more than once, before its final elimination.

Liability method: See **tax allocation**.

LIFO (Last-in first-out): See **inventory**.

Listed companies: Companies whose **stock** (shares) or bonds have been accepted for trading by a recognized securities (stock) exchange.

Matching concept: The **accounting concept** that provides that expenses and revenues be correlated in order to determine net income for an accounting period.

Material (materiality): Describes information whose omission, nondisclosure or misstatement would mislead financial statement users when making evaluations or decisions.

Members: A term often used to describe the shareholders of a company.

Merger accounting: See **pooling of interests method**.

Minority interest: That part of the results of operations and of net assets of a **subsidiary** attributable to interests that are not owned, directly or indirectly through subsidiaries, by the **parent**.

Monetary item: Money, or claim to money, whose monetary value is fixed by contract or otherwise. This includes such items as **accounts receivable, accounts payable** and cash and bank balances.

Monetary/nonmonetary method: A method of translating foreign currency under which **monetary items** are translated at the current rate while nonmonetary items are translated at their historical exchange rates.

Negative goodwill: See **goodwill**.

Net realizable value: The estimated selling price in the ordinary course of business less costs of completion and less costs necessarily incurred in order to make the sale.

Operating lease: A lease other than a **finance lease**.

Par value: The nominal or face value of shares (stock).

Parent company: See **holding company**.

Pension plan curtailment: A significant reduction in, or elimination of, defined benefit accruals for present employees' future service.

Pension plan settlement: An irrevocable action that relieves the employer (or the plan) of primary responsibility for an obligation and eliminates significant risks related to the obligation and the assets used to effect the settlement.

Percentage of completion method: A method of accounting for contracts that recognizes gross profit in proportion to the degree of completion under a contract.

Pooling of interests method: A method of accounting for a **business combination** under which two entities merge and their net assets are carried in the combined entity's financial statements at the premerger book values. Income of the combined entity includes income of the combining entities for the entire financial period in which the combination took place.

Portfolio basis: A method of valuing securities where the value of all (or a group of) securities is assessed in the aggregate rather than individually.

Preference (preferred) stock (shares): A class of **capital stock** with special rights or restrictions as compared with other classes of stock of the same company. The preference generally attaches to the distribution of dividends at a fixed annual rate, with or without priority for return of capital on liquidation of the company.

Prior period (year) adjustment: Charges or credits that arise in the current period as a result of errors or omissions in the preparation of the financial statements of one or more prior periods.

Product financing arrangement: A transaction in which an entity sells and agrees to repurchase **inventory**, with the repurchase price equal to the original sale price plus carrying and financing costs.

Proper returns: UK terminology for financial information sent by branches to the head office of a company and considered by the auditors, who have not visited the branch, as adequate for their audit.

Proportional consolidation: See **proportionate consolidation**.

Proportionate consolidation: A method of accounting and reporting whereby a venturer's share of each of the assets, liabilities, income and expenses of a jointly controlled entity is combined on a line-by-line basis with similar items in the venturer's financial statements (or reported as separate line items in the venturer's financial statements).

Proprietary company: An expression used in certain countries to describe a private company.

Prudence concept: The concept that revenues and profits are not recognized until realized in the form of cash or of other assets the ultimate cash realization of which can be assessed with reasonable certainty, and provision is made for all known liabilities and losses whether the amount of these is known with certainty or not.

Public company: A company whose shares are listed on a stock exchange or otherwise available to the public investor.

Purchase method: A method of accounting for a **business combination** under which the net assets acquired are carried in the acquiring entity's **consolidated financial statements** at their cost to that entity. Income of the acquiring entity includes income of the acquired entity from the date of acquisition.

Real guarantees: An expression used in certain countries to define all guarantees except personal guarantees.

Realization concept: The accounting concept that revenue should generally be recognized when there has been an exchange transaction involving the transfer of goods and services.

Replacement value: The cost of replacing currently an asset with another asset that will render similar services.

Required accounting treatment: An expression used in International Accounting Standards (IASs) to denote the accounting treatment specified by an IAS where only one accounting treatment is permitted. (Compare **benchmark accounting treatment**.)

Retail pricing method: See **inventory**.

Retained earnings: See **surplus**.

Revenue: Proceeds from the sale of goods and services, gains from the sale or exchange of assets, interest and dividends earned on investments, and other realized increases in the owners' equity in a business, except as resulting from capital contributions and adjustments.

Revenue expenditure: An expenditure that is properly chargeable against the revenue of a business.

Self-sustaining foreign operation: A foreign operation that is financially and operationally independent of the reporting entity so that exposure to exchange rate changes is limited to the reporting entity's net investment in the foreign operation.

Share capital: See **capital stock**.

Share premium: See **additional paid in capital**.

Specific identification method: See **inventory**.

Standard costs: Predetermined product costs established on the basis of planned products or operations, planned cost and efficiency levels, and expected capacity utilization.

Statutory tax rate: The rate of tax imposed by the taxing authorities on income as computed for tax purposes.

Stock: In some countries, this word is used to describe **inventory**. In other countries, it is an abbreviation for **capital stock**.

Straight-line method: See **depreciation**.

Subsidiary: A company that is controlled by another company (**holding company**).

Substance over form: An accounting concept requiring that transactions affecting an entity be presented in financial statements in a manner that is in agreement with the actual underlying transaction rather than the legal form of the transaction.

Sum-of-the-years'-digits method: See **depreciation**.

Surplus: The excess of net assets over the stated value of the **capital stock** of an entity. There are three common types of surplus:

□ **Capital surplus**—Retained earnings appropriated for a specific purpose. In many jurisdictions this is known as a capital reserve.

□ **Contributed surplus**—Capital donations from shareholders and others and additional paid in capital.

□ **Earned surplus/retained earnings**—The cumulative amount of earnings retained by an entity.

Suspensive sale: See **instalment sale**.

Tax allocation: The process of apportioning income taxes among accounting periods when there are timing differences between accounting and taxable income in order to relate the provision for income taxes to accounting income in each period.

□ **Deferral (deferred) method**—A method of applying the tax allocation basis in which the amount by which the current tax provision differs from the amount of taxes currently payable is considered to represent the deferment to future periods of a benefit obtained or expenditure currently incurred. Adjustments are not made to accumulated amounts to reflect changes in tax rates.

□ **Liability method**—A method of applying the tax allocation basis in which the amount by which the current tax provision differs from the amount of taxes currently payable is considered to reflect the recognition in the current period of taxes expected to be recoverable or payable in a future period. Adjustments are made to accumulated amounts to reflect changes in tax rates.

Tax-effect accounting methods: See **tax allocation**.

Temporal method: A method of translating foreign currency under which cash, receivables and payables, and other assets and liabilities carried at current prices are translated at the foreign exchange rate in effect at the balance sheet date or a contractual rate, where applicable; assets and liabilities carried at historical prices are translated at the rates in effect at the time of the related transactions. Revenue and expense items are generally translated at a weighted-average rate in effect during the period.

Temporary differences: As defined in US SFAS No. 109, a difference between the tax basis of an asset or liability and its financial statement amount that will result in taxable or deductible amounts in future years when the reported amount of the asset or liability is recovered or settled, respectively. Some temporary differences cannot be identified with a particular asset or liability for financial reporting, but (a) result from events that have been recognized in the financial statements, and (b) will result in taxable or deductible amounts in future years based on provisions of the tax law. Events that do not have tax consequences do not give rise to temporary differences.

Treasury stock: (1) Shares that can be purchased directly from the issuer rather than on the open market. (2) Shares repurchased by the original issuer.

Troubled debt restructuring: A transaction whereby a creditor, for reasons related to the debtor's financial difficulties, grants a concession to the debtor that the creditor would not otherwise consider.

Turnover: The proceeds from the sale of goods and services falling within a company's ordinary activities.

Unit(s)-of-production method: See **depreciation**.

Value added tax: A tax levied at each stage in the production and distribution chain on the basis of the value that is added to goods passing through that stage.

Variable costs: Costs of production that vary directly, or nearly directly, with the volume of production.

Yellow Book: A publication issued by the United Kingdom's International Stock Exchange dealing with disclosure and other requirements for quoted companies.